ENCYCLOPEDIA

OF

SOUTHERN

CULTURE

CHARLES REAGAN WILSON
& WILLIAM FERRIS

Coeditors

ANN J. ABADIE
& MARY L. HART

Associate Editors

Sponsored by
The Center for the Study of Southern Culture
at the University of Mississippi

ENCYCLOPEDIA

OF

SOUTHERN

CULTURE

VOLUME 3

Literature—Recreation

☆ ☆ ☆ ☆ ☆ ☆ ☆ ☆ ☆ ☆ ☆ ☆ ☆ ☆ ☆ ☆

ANCHOR BOOKS

DOUBLEDAY

New York London Toronto Sydney Auckland

AN ANCHOR BOOK
PUBLISHED BY DOUBLEDAY
a division of Bantam Doubleday Dell Publishing Group, Inc.
666 Fifth Avenue, New York, New York 10103

ANCHOR BOOKS, DOUBLEDAY, and the portrayal of an anchor
are trademarks of Doubleday, a division of Bantam Doubleday
Dell Publishing Group, Inc.

Encyclopedia of Southern Culture was originally published in hardcover
in one volume by the University of North Carolina Press in 1989. The
Anchor Books edition is published by arrangement with the University
of North Carolina Press.

Both the initial research and the publication of this work were made possible in part through a grant from the Division of Research Programs of
the National Endowment for the Humanities, an independent federal
agency whose mission is to award grants to support education, scholarship, media programming, libraries, and museums, in order to bring the
results of cultural activities to a broad, general public.

Book design by Chris Welch

Library of Congress Cataloging-in-Publication Data

Encyclopedia of Southern culture / Charles Reagan Wilson & William
Ferris, coeditors; Ann J. Abadie & Mary L. Hart, associate editors.
—1st Anchor Books ed.
p.   cm.
"Originally published in hardcover in one volume by the University of
North Carolina Press in 1989"—T.p. verso.
Includes bibliographical references and index.
Contents: Vol. 1. Agriculture–Environment–v. 2.   Ethnic Life–Law–
v. 3.   Literature–Recreation–v. 4.   Religion–Women's Life.
1. Southern States–-Civilization—Encyclopedias.   2. Southern States—
Encyclopedias.   I. Wilson, Charles Reagan.   II. Ferris, William R.
F209.E53   1991   975'.003   90-973
                                                CIP

ISBN 0-385-41547-8

"Tell about the South. What's it like there.
What do they do there. Why do they live there.
Why do they live at all."

WILLIAM FAULKNER
Absalom, Absalom!

The *Encyclopedia of Southern Culture* was
produced through major grants from the Program
for Research Tools and Reference Works of the
National Endowment for the Humanities, the
Ford Foundation, the Atlantic-Richfield
Foundation, and the Mary Doyle Trust.

The publication of this volume
was made possible by the
Fred W. Morrison Fund of the
University of North Carolina Press.

CONTENTS

CONSULTANTS

AGRICULTURE
Thomas D. Clark
248 Tahoma Road
Lexington, Ky. 40503

ART AND ARCHITECTURE
Jessie Poesch
Department of Art
Tulane University
New Orleans, La. 70118

BLACK LIFE
Thomas C. Holt
Department of History
University of Chicago
Chicago, Ill. 60637

EDUCATION
Thomas G. Dyer
Associate Vice President for
Academic Affairs
University of Georgia
Old College
Athens, Ga. 30602

ENVIRONMENT
Martin V. Melosi
Department of History
University of Houston
Houston, Tex. 77004

ETHNIC LIFE
George E. Pozzetta
Department of History
University of Florida
Gainesville, Fla. 32611

FOLKLIFE
William Ferris

Center for the Study of
Southern Culture
University of Mississippi
University, Miss. 38677

GEOGRAPHY
Richard Pillsbury
Department of Geography
Georgia State University
Atlanta, Ga. 30303

HISTORY AND MANNERS
Charles Reagan Wilson
Center for the Study of
Southern Culture
University of Mississippi
University, Miss. 38677

INDUSTRY
James C. Cobb
Honors Program
P.O. Box 6233
University of Alabama
Tuscaloosa, Ala. 35487-6322

LANGUAGE
Michael Montgomery
Department of English
University of South Carolina
Columbia, S.C. 29208

LAW
Maxwell Bloomfield
Department of History
The Catholic University of
America
Washington, D.C. 20017

LITERATURE
M. Thomas Inge
Randolph-Macon College
Ashland, Va. 23005

MEDIA
Edward D. C. Campbell, Jr.
Virginia State Library
11th Street at Capitol Square
Richmond, Va. 23219

MUSIC
Bill C. Malone
Department of History
Tulane University
New Orleans, La. 70118

MYTHIC SOUTH
George B. Tindall
Department of History
University of North Carolina
Chapel Hill, N.C. 27599

POLITICS
Numan Bartley
Department of History
University of Georgia
Athens, Ga. 30602

RECREATION
John Shelton Reed
Department of Sociology
University of North Carolina
Chapel Hill, N.C. 27599

RELIGION
Samuel S. Hill

Department of Religion
University of Florida
Gainesville, Fla. 32611

SCIENCE AND MEDICINE
James O. Breeden
Department of History
Southern Methodist University
Dallas, Tex. 75275

SOCIAL CLASS
J. Wayne Flynt
Department of History
Auburn University
Auburn, Ala. 36830

URBANIZATION
Blaine A. Brownell
School of Social and Behavioral
Sciences
University of Alabama at
Birmingham
Birmingham, Ala. 35294

VIOLENCE
Raymond D. Gastil
48 E. 21st Street
New York, N.Y. 10010

WOMEN'S LIFE
Carol Ruth Berkin
Baruch College
City University of New York
17 Lexington Avenue
New York, N.Y. 10010

FOREWORD

Can you remember those southern elder men who "jes' set" on their favored chair or bench for hours, every day—and a year later they could tell you at about what time of day someone's dog had trotted by? And the counterpart elderly ladies, their hands deeply wrinkled from decades of quilting, canning, washing collective tons of clothing in black cast-iron pots, in which at other seasonal times pork fat was rendered into lard, or some of that lard into soap? These southern ancestors, black and white, have always struck me as the Foundation Timbers of our South, and I think that we who were reared and raised by them, and amongst them, are blessed that we were.

I consider this *Encyclopedia of Southern Culture* the answer to a deep need that we resuscitate and keep alive and fresh the memories of those who are now bones and dust, who during their eras and in their respective ways contributed toward the social accretion that has entered legend as "the southern way of life," which we continue today.

It is a culture resulting from the antebellum mixture of social extremes based on the chattel slavery that supported an aristocratic gentility; in between the slaves and planters a vast majority struggled for their own survival. Centuries of slavery were abolished by an indelible war whose legacies continue to haunt us. The southern memory is of generations of life, of the good and the bad, the humor and the suffering from the past. The southerner does not sentimentalize but only remembers.

Out of the historic cotton tillage sprang the involuntary field hollers, the shouts, and the moanin' low that have since produced such a cornucopia of music, played daily, on every continent, where I have been astounded at how much I heard of the evolved blues, jazz, and gospel—as well as bluegrass and country—all of them of direct southern origin.

Equally worldwide is southern literature. Writers took the oral traditions of the South—the political rhetoric, preaching, conversational wordplay, and lazy-day storytelling—and converted them into art. The latest addition to southern literature is this *Encyclopedia*, no small part of whose greatness, I think, is that it is compiled by many researchers who did not simply read books but who rubbed shoulders with those whom they interviewed and recorded and studied. They walked and talked with the sharecropper farmers, the cooks, the quiltmakers, the convicts, the merchants, the fishermen, and all the others who make these pages a volume of living memories.

The region and its people have undergone dramatic changes in the last decades, overcoming much, although not all, of the poverty of the past, and they are now sharing in the nation's prosperity. Old ways that divided the people have fallen away to be replaced by new dreams. The hard lessons from the past are not forgotten in this *Encyclopedia.* I testify that this *Encyclopedia of Southern Culture* mirrors the very best of what has lately come to be called "the new South." Never before have such volumes been produced by a team so committed to distilling and presenting our southern distinctiveness.

Alex Haley

ACKNOWLEDGMENTS

These volumes could never have been completed without the assistance of countless individuals. The coeditors and associate editors wish to thank our consultants and contributors for their planning, researching, and writing of articles. We should note that Raven McDavid helped to plan the Language section before his untimely death in 1984. Clarence Mohr's work on the early design of the *Encyclopedia* provided the basic organizational structure for the volumes. Many scholars reviewed articles, made suggestions for improvements, and verified factual material. Richard H. Brown, of the Newberry Library in Chicago, advised wisely on *Encyclopedia* matters, as with other projects of the Center for the Study of Southern Culture. Howard Lamar offered sage counsel on the *Encyclopedia* from its earliest planning stages. Research assistants Elizabeth Makowski and Sharon A. Sharp supervised the review and verification of entries, assisted by numerous teaching assistants and volunteers, and also served as staff writers. Editorial assistants Ann Sumner Holmes, Ginna Parsons, and Karen McDearman Cox supervised final production of copy and served as endless sources of good advice and varied skill. Lolly Pilkington read the entire manuscript with a skilled eye. Teaching assistants in the Department of History and the Southern Studies program spent much time in the library checking and rechecking information and reading galley proof. Personnel in the John Davis

Williams Library of the University of Mississippi often came to our rescue, and we are grateful to the many archivists and librarians across the nation who assisted us with obtaining illustrations. Special thanks are due the staff of the University of North Carolina Press, especially its director Matthew Hodgson, editor-in-chief Iris Tillman Hill, managing editor Sandra Eisdorfer, and Ron Maner, Pamela Upton, and Paula Wald.

The *Encyclopedia of Southern Culture* was produced with financial support from the National Endowment for the Humanities, the Ford Foundation, the Atlantic-Richfield Foundation, and the Mary Doyle Trust. The Graduate School and alumni and friends of the University of Mississippi donated required funds for a matching NEH grant in 1983, and the editors are grateful for their assistance. Donors include: The James Hand Foundation by Kathleen Hand Carter; Mrs. R. R. Morrison, Jr.; Mrs. Hester F. Faser; David L. May; James J. Brown, Jr.; Lynn Crosby Gammill; First National Bank of Vicksburg, Mississippi; The Goodman Charitable and Educational Trust, Hallie Goodman, Trustee; Dr. F. Watt Bishop; Robert Travis; Mrs. Dorothy Crosby; Christopher Keller, Jr.; Worth I. Dunn; Wiley Fairchild; Mrs. Eric Biedenharn; John S. Callon; Betty Carter; Shelby Flowers Ferris; Mary Hohenberg; Mr. & Mrs. John Kramer; Samuel McIlwain; and Prescott Sherman.

INTRODUCTION

The American South has long generated powerful images and complex emotions. In the years since World War II, the region has undergone dramatic changes in race relations, political institutions, and economic life. Those changes have led some observers to forecast the eventual end of a distinctive southern region. Other scholars and popular writers point to continuities with past attitudes and behavior. The *Encyclopedia of Southern Culture* appears during a period of major transition in the life of the South and is in part a reflection of these changes. It examines both the historical and the contemporary worlds of southern culture. The *Encyclopedia*'s editors have sought to assemble authoritative, concise, thoughtful, substantive, and interesting articles that will give scholars, students, and general readers a useful perspective on the South.

SOUTHERN CULTURE

The *Encyclopedia*'s definition of "the South" is a cultural one. The geographical focus is, to be sure, on the 11 states of the former Confederacy (Alabama, Arkansas, Florida, Georgia, Louisiana, Mississippi, North Carolina, South Carolina, Tennessee, Texas, and Virginia), but this tidy historical definition fails to confront the complexities of studying the region. Delaware, Kentucky, Maryland, and Missouri were slave states at the beginning of the Civil War, and many of their citizens then and after claimed

a southern identity. Social scientists today use statistical data covering the "census South," which includes Delaware, Maryland, West Virginia, Oklahoma, and the District of Columbia. The Gallup public opinion polling organization defines the South as the Confederate states plus Oklahoma and Kentucky.

Moreover, the realities of cultural areas require a broadened definition. Cultural areas have core zones, where distinctive traits are most concentrated, and margins, where the boundaries of the culture overlap with other cultural areas. The *Encyclopedia*'s articles explore the nature of both these core areas and margins in the South. The borders of the South have surely varied over time. In the colonial era Delaware was an agricultural slave state with a claim of being southern. Maryland was a southern state, sharing much with its neighbor, Virginia, in a Chesapeake subculture. Maryland did not join the Confederacy, but soldiers from the state fought in the Confederate armies and one finds Confederate monuments in Baltimore. St. Louis was a midwestern city and the gateway to the West, but southerners have also claimed it. The Mississippi River culture tied St. Louis to areas of the Lower South, and southerners have often been associated with it. John F. Kennedy once said that Washington, D.C., was known for its southern efficiency and northern charm. Carved from an area of Maryland as a concession to southerners, Washington was a slaveowning area and was once a center for slave auctions. Later, under Woodrow Wilson, a southern-born president, the nation's capital became a racially segregated bastion reflecting southern regional mores. Washington has also long been a center for southern black migration, an educational mecca for blacks, and a center for black musicians, artists, and writers. Most recently, geographical proximity to Appalachia has made Washington a center for the performance of such other expressions of southern culture as bluegrass music. Contemporary Washington, however, appears to be less and less "southern," and urban historians consequently omit it from the list of regional cities (and thus there is no separate entry on Washington in the *Encyclopedia.*

Contributors to the *Encyclopedia* at times transcend geography and history when examining questions of regional consciousness, symbolism, mythology, and sectional stereotyping. The "South" is found wherever southern culture is found, and that culture is located not only in the Deep South, the Upper South, and border cities, but also in "little Dixies" (the southern parts of Ohio, Indiana, Illinois, and parts of Missouri and Oklahoma), among black Mississippians who migrated to south Chicago, among white Appalachians and black Alabamians who migrated to Detroit, and among former Okies and Arkies who settled in and around Bakersfield, California. This diaspora of southern ethnic culture is also found in the works of expatriate southern artists and writers. Although Richard Wright and Tennessee Williams lived in Paris and New York, respectively, they continued to explore their southern roots in their writing.

The South exists as a state of mind both within and beyond its geographical boundaries. Recent studies of mythology suggest that the New York theater in the late 19th century and Hollywood in the 20th century have kept alive images, legends, and myths about the South in the national consciousness. One can view the American South and its culture as international property. The worlds of *Roots*, *Gone with the Wind*, blues, country music, rock and roll, William Faulkner, and Alice Walker are admired and closely studied throughout the world. The South has nurtured important myths, and their impact on other cultures is a vital aspect of the *Encyclopedia*'s perspective. In the end, then, the *Encyclopedia*'s definition of the South is a broad, inclusive one, based on culture.

These volumes focus specifically on exploring the culture of the South. In the 1950s anthropologists Alfred Kroeber and Clyde Kluckholn cataloged 164 definitions of culture, suggesting the problems then and now of a precise definition. To 19th-century intellectuals culture was the best of civilization's achievements. Matthew Arnold was perhaps the best-known advocate of this Victorian-era ideal, and H. L. Mencken—the South's nastiest and most entertaining critic in the early 20th century—was also a believer in it. Mencken argued in his essay "The Sahara of the Bozart" (1920) that the upper-class, aristocratic southerner of the early 19th century "liked to toy with ideas. He was hospitable and tolerant. He had the vague thing that we call culture." Mencken found the South of his era severely wanting, though, in this ideal of culture. He saw in the South "not a single picture gallery worth going into, or a single orchestra capable of playing the nine symphonies of Beethoven, or a single opera-house, or a single theater devoted to decent plays, or a single public monument (built since the war) that is worth looking at, or a single workshop devoted to the making of beautiful things." Mencken allowed that the region excelled "in the lower reaches of the gospel hymn, the phonograph and the chautauqua harangue."

The South of Mencken's day did trail the rest of the nation in the development of important cultural institutions; but today the South, the nation, and the world celebrate the "lower reaches" of southern culture. This judgment on the value of the sounds and words coming from the region reflects 20th-century understandings of culture. Anthropologists have taken the lead in exploring the theoretical aspects of cultures. Edward Burnett Tylor gave a classic definition of culture as "that complex whole which includes knowledge, belief, art, morals, law, customs, and any other capabilities and habits" acquired by the members of a society. For students of culture, the goal was to study and outline discrete cultural traits, using this definition to convey the picture of a culture. During the 20th century another major anthropological theory of culture emerged. Kroeber, Bronislaw Malinowski, and Ruth Benedict stressed the study of pattern, form, structure, and organization in a culture rather than the simple listing of observed traits. Patterns could include customs associated with food, labor, and manners as well as more complex social, political, and economic systems.

Recently culture has been viewed as an abstraction, consisting of the inherited models and ideas with which people approach their experiences. The theory of social structure, first developed by British anthropologist Alexander Reginald Radcliffe-Brown in the 1930s and 1940s, stressed that culture must include recognition of the persistence of social groups, social classes, and social roles. The structuralist theories of Claude Lévi-Strauss attempt to apply abstract mathematical formulae to society. Although social anthropologists avoid the term *culture*, they have insured that the study of culture not neglect social background.

The theoretical work of Clifford Geertz is especially significant in understanding the definition of culture developed for the *Encyclopedia of Southern Culture*. Geertz defines *culture* as "an historically transmitted pattern of meanings embodied in symbols, a system of inherited conceptions expressed in symbolic forms." Through culture, humans "communicate, perpetuate, and develop their knowledge about and attitudes toward life." This contemporary definition stresses mental culture, expressed through symbol systems, which gives human beings a framework for understanding one another, themselves, and the wider world. Culture patterns, including material, oral, mental, and social systems, are blueprints for organizing human interaction.

The *Encyclopedia of Southern Culture* is not intended as a contribution to the general study of culture theory, although awareness of theories of culture has been useful background in the conceptualization of the volumes and in the selection of topics. The volumes attempt to study within the southern context what 20th-century humanist T. S. Eliot said, in *Notes towards the Definition of Culture*, was culture—"all the characteristic activities and interests of a people." Articles in the volumes deal with regional cultural achievements in such areas as music, literature, art, and architecture. The broader goal of the volumes is to chart the cultural landscape of the South, addressing those aspects of southern life and thought that have sustained either the reality or the illusion of regional distinctiveness. The volumes detail specific cultural traits, suggest the cultural patterns that tie the region together, point out the internal diversity within the South, and explore with special attention the importance of social structure and symbolism. Above all, the volumes have been planned to carry out Eliot's belief that "culture is not merely the sum of several activities, but a *way of life.*"

Eliot's definition of culture, then, can be seen as a working definition for the *Encyclopedia of Southern Culture.* In order to foster interdisciplinary communication, the editors have included the full range of social indicators, trait groupings, literary concepts, and historical evidence commonly used by students of regionalism. The criteria for the all-important selection of topics, however, have been consistently to include the characteristic traits that give the South a distinctive culture.

A special concern of the *Encyclopedia* has been to identify distinctive regional characteristics. It addresses those aspects of southern life and thought—the individuals, places, ideas, rituals, symbols, myths, values, and experiences— which have sustained either the reality or the illusion of regional distinctiveness. The comparative method has been encouraged as a way to suggest contrasts with other American regions and with other societies. One lesson of earlier regional scholarship has been the need to look at the South in the widest possible context. The editors of the *Encyclopedia* have assumed that the distinctiveness of southern culture does not lie in any one trait but rather in the peculiar combination of regional cultural characteris-

tics. The fundamental uniqueness of southern culture thus emerges from the *Encyclopedia*'s composite portrait of the South. The editors asked contributors to consider individual traits that clearly are unique to the region. Although some topics may not be uniquely southern in themselves, contributors have been asked to explore particular regional aspects of those topics. Subjects that suggest the internal diversity of the region are also treated if they contribute to the overall picture of southern distinctiveness. The Cajuns of Louisiana, the Germans of Texas, and the Jews of Savannah, for example, contribute to the distinctive flavor of southern life. Their adaptations, and resistance, to southern cultural patterns suggest much about the region's distinctiveness.

The question of continuity and change in southern culture is another central concern of the *Encyclopedia.* Contributors have examined themes and topics in an evolutionary framework. Historians represent by far the largest group of contributors to the project. The volumes do not attempt to narrate the region's history in a systematic way, a task ably achieved in the *Encyclopedia of Southern History* (1979), but contributors from all disciplines have developed material within an appropriate time perspective. As Clifford Geertz has written, culture is "historically transmitted," a fact that is especially relevant for the study of the South, where the apogee of cultural distinctiveness may well have been in an earlier period. Because the *Encyclopedia* focuses on culture rather than history, historical topics were chosen because they are relevant to the origin, development, or decline of an aspect of southern culture. Given the historical shape of southern cultural development, one would expect less material on the colonial era (before there was a self-conscious "South") and increased concentration of material in the Civil War and postbellum eras (perhaps the high points of southern cultural distinctiveness). Nearly all articles include historical material, and each overview essay systematically traces the development of a major subject area. In addition, such selected historical entries as "Colonial Heritage," "Frontier Heritage," and "Civil War" are included with a cultural focus appropriate to the volumes.

STUDY OF SOUTHERN REGIONALISM

The *Encyclopedia of Southern Culture* reflects a broad intellectual interest in regionalism, the importance of which in the United States is far from unique when seen in a global context. The struggle to accommodate regional cultures within a larger nation is an experience common to many Western and Third World peoples. Despite the contemporary developments in transportation and communication that promise the emergence of a "global village," regionalism is an enduring reality of the modern world. The Basques in Spain, the Scots in Britain, the Kurds in the Middle East, and Armenians in the Soviet Union are only a few examples of groups that have recently reasserted their regional interests.

Although public emphasis on the United States as a cultural melting pot has sometimes obscured the nation's enduring regional heritage, the study of regionalism has long been a major field of scholarship involving leading authorities from many academic disciplines

both in the United States and abroad. The *Encyclopedia* is part of the broader field of American Studies, which has dramatically evolved in recent years from a focus on such regional types as the New England Yankees, the southern Cavaliers, and the western cowboys and Indians. Since the 1960s studies of black life, ethnic life, and women's life have significantly changed the definition of American culture. In the 1980s the study of American region, place, and community—whether it be a Brooklyn neighborhood or a county in rural Mississippi—is essential to understanding the nation. In the context of this American Studies tradition, the *Encyclopedia* focuses on the American South, a place that has influenced its people in complex and fascinating ways.

Significant bodies of research exist for all major regions of the United States, but by almost any standard the American South has received the most extensive scholarly attention. Since the 1930s virtually all aspects of southern life have come under increasingly rigorous, systematic intellectual scrutiny. The *Encyclopedia of Southern Culture* is a collaborative effort that combines intellectual perspectives that reflect the breadth of Southern Studies. Sociologists, historians, literary critics, folklorists, anthropologists, political scientists, psychologists, theologians, and other scholars have written on the region, and all of these fields are represented by contributors to the *Encyclopedia*. Journalists, lawyers, physicians, architects, and other professionals from outside the academy have also studied the South, and their contributions appear in these volumes as well.

Students of the South operate within a well-developed institutional framework. The proliferation of academic journals that focus on the South has mirrored expanding disciplinary boundaries in regional scholarship. The *Journal of Southern History*, the *Southern Review*, the *Southern Economic Journal*, *Social Forces*, the *Southern Folklore Quarterly*, the *Virginia Quarterly Review*, the *South Atlantic Quarterly*, and the *Southwestern Political Science Quarterly* are only a few of the titles that have specialized in publishing material on the region. The contemporary era has witnessed a dramatic expansion in the publication of books on the South. The University of North Carolina Press was the first southern university press to publish an extensive list of titles on the South, and by the early 1950s the press alone had produced some 200 studies. Works on the region are now published by university presses in every southern state and find a ready market with national publishers as well.

Research on the South has led to greater appreciation of the region's internal diversity, which is reflected in the study of smaller geographical areas or specialized themes. Such recent periodicals as the *Appalachian Journal*, *Mid-South Folklore*, and *South Atlantic Urban Studies* illustrate the narrowing geographical and topical focus of recent scholarship on the South. Overlapping interests and subject matter shared among regional scholars have exerted a steady pressure toward broadening disciplinary horizons. Meaningful cooperation among disciplines is complicated by differences of vocabulary and method, but students of the American South demonstrate a growing awareness that they are engaged in a common endeavor that can be furthered as much by cooperation as by specialization. Such periodicals as *Southern Quarterly*, *Southern Studies*, and *Per-*

spectives on the American South have established forums for interdisciplinary study.

In recent years regional scholarship has also influenced curriculum development in colleges and universities. Leading institutional centers for the study of the South include the Center for the Study of Southern Culture at the University of Mississippi, the Institute for Southern Studies at the University of South Carolina, the Institute for Southern Studies at Durham, N.C., and the Center for the Study of Southern History and Culture at the University of Alabama. Appalachian study centers are located at, among other places, the University of Kentucky, East Tennessee State University, Appalachian State University, Mars Hill College, and Berea College. The Institute for Texan Cultures is in San Antonio, and Baylor University launched a Texas Studies Center in 1987. The Center for Arkansas Studies is at the University of Arkansas at Little Rock, while the University of Southwestern Louisiana's Center for Louisiana Studies concentrates on Cajun and Creole folk culture. These developments are, again, part of a broader interest in regional studies programs at universities in other regions, including the Center for the Study of New England Culture at the University of Massachusetts at Amherst and the Great Plains Center at the University of Nebraska.

The *Encyclopedia of Southern Culture* grows out of the work of the University of Mississippi's Center for the Study of Southern Culture, which was established in 1977 to coordinate existing university resources and to develop multidisciplinary teaching, research, and outreach programs about the South. The center's mission is to strengthen the university's instructional program in the humanities, to promote scholarship on every aspect of southern culture, and to encourage public understanding of the South through publications, media productions, lectures, performances, and exhibitions. Center personnel administer a Southern Studies curriculum that includes both B.A. and M.A. degree programs; a Ford Foundation–funded, three-year (1986–89) project aimed at incorporating more fully the experiences of blacks and women into the teaching of Southern Studies; an annual United States Information Agency–sponsored project for international scholars interested in regional and ethnic cultures; such annual meetings as the Porter L. Fortune Chancellor's Symposium on Southern History, the Faulkner and Yoknapatawpha Conference, and the Barnard-Millington Symposium on Southern Science and Medicine; and a variety of periodicals, films, and media presentations. The center administers these programs in cooperation with the on-campus departments in the College of Liberal Arts, the Afro-American Studies program, and the Sarah Isom Center for Women's Studies. The University of Mississippi and its Center for the Study of Southern Culture provided the necessary institutional setting for coordinating the diverse needs of the *Encyclopedia*'s hundreds of participants.

Recognizing both the intellectual maturity of scholarship in the American South and the potential role of regional study in consolidating previously fragmented academic endeavors, the *Encyclopedia* planners conceived the idea of an interdisciplinary reference work to bring together and synthesize current knowledge about the South. Scholars studying the South have been served by

a number of reference works, but none of these has had the aims and perspective of the *Encyclopedia of Southern Culture*. The 13-volume series, *The South in the Building of the Nation* (1909–13), which attempted a comprehensive survey of the region's history, was the closest predecessor to this encyclopedia. Other major works include the 16-volume *Library of Southern Literature* (1908–13), Howard W. Odum's monumental *Southern Regions of the United States* (1936), W. T. Couch's edited *Culture in the South* (1936), and, more recently, the *Encyclopedia of Southern History* (1978), the *Encyclopedia of Religion in the South* (1984), and the *History of Southern Literature* (1986).

Like any major reference work, the *Encyclopedia* addresses the long-range needs and interests of a diverse reading audience. Before launching the project the editors consulted extensively with leading authorities in all areas of American Studies and Southern Studies and sought additional advice from directors of comparable projects. Planning for the original single-volume edition began in 1978 with the compilation of a working outline of subjects that had received frequent attention in major studies of regional culture. During the fall of 1979 some 270 U.S. and international scholars received copies of the preliminary topical list, together with background information about the project. Approximately 150 of these scholars, representing a variety of disciplines, responded to this mailing, commenting upon the potential value of the proposed volume and making suggestions concerning its organization and content.

In 1980 the Center for the Study of Southern Culture commissioned several scholars to prepare detailed lists of topics for major sections of the volume, and to write sample articles as well. The National Endowment for the Humanities supported the *Encyclopedia of Southern Culture* with a 1980–81 planning grant and grants covering 1981–83 and 1984–86. The Ford Foundation, the Atlantic-Richfield Foundation, and the Mary Doyle Trust also provided major funding. Full-time work on the *Encyclopedia* began in September 1981. The content of the volume was divided into 24 major subject areas, and the editors selected a senior consultant to assist in planning the topics and contributors for each section. During the fall and winter of 1981–82, the consultants formulated initial lists of topics and recommended appropriate contributors for entries. In general, the consultants were actively involved in the initial stages of planning and less involved in later editorial work. Project staff handled the paperwork for assignments. The editors sent each contributor a packet of information on the project, including the overall list of topics, so that contributors could see how their articles fit into the volume as a whole. Authors were encouraged to make suggestions for additional entries, and many of them did so. When contributors were unable to write for the volume, they often suggested other scholars, thus facilitating the reassignment of articles. The editors assumed the responsibility for editing articles for style, clarity, and tone appropriate for a reference book. They reviewed all entries for accuracy, and research assistants verified the factual and bibliographical veracity of each entry. The senior consultants, with their special expertise in each subject area, provided an additional check on the quality of the articles.

ORGANIZATION AND CONTENT OF THE ENCYCLOPEDIA

The *Encyclopedia of Southern Culture* is a synthesis of current scholarship and attempts to set new directions for further research. The *Encyclopedia*'s objectives are fourfold: (1) The volumes provide students and general readers with convenient access to basic facts and bibliographical data about southern cultural patterns and their historical development. (2) By bringing together lucid analyses of modern scholarship on southern culture from the humanities and the social sciences, the *Encyclopedia* is intended to facilitate communication across disciplinary lines and help stimulate new approaches to regional study. It attempts to integrate disparate intellectual efforts and represents an innovative organization and presentation of knowledge. (3) The volumes can serve as a curriculum component for multidisciplinary courses on the American South and provide a model for scholars wishing to assemble similar research tools in other regions. (4) Viewed in its totality, the *Encyclopedia* locates the specific components of regional culture within the framework of a larger organic whole. At this level, the volumes attempt to illuminate the nature and function of regionalism in American culture.

The editors considered an alphabetical arrangement of articles but concluded that organization of information into 24 major sections more accurately reflects the nature of the project and would provide a fresh perspective. Cross-references to related articles in other sections are essential guides to proper use of the *Encyclopedia*, enabling readers to consult articles written on a common topic from different perspectives. Sections often reflect an academic field (history, geography, literature), but at times the academic division has been rejected in favor of a section organized around a cultural theme (such as social class) that has become a central scholarly concern. In general, the sections are designed to reflect the amount and quality of scholarship in particular areas of regional study. Articles within each section are arranged in three divisions. The overview essay is written by the *Encyclopedia*'s consultant in that section and provides an interpretive summary of the field. That essay is followed by alphabetically arranged thematic articles and then by alphabetically arranged, brief topical-biographical sketches.

Although the editors and consultants conceived each section as a separate unit, sections are closely connected to one another through cross-references. The titles of major sections are brief, but the editors have grouped together related material under these simple rubrics. The Agriculture section thus includes rural-life articles, the Black Life section includes articles on race relations, Social Class includes material on social structure and occupational groups, and Industry includes information on commercial activity.

Several sections deserve special comment in regard to their organization and content. The Black Life section (Vol. 1) contains most, though not all, of the separate entries on southern black culture. The editors placed Richard Wright and Ralph Ellison in Literature (Vol. 3) to honor their roles as central figures in *southern* (as well as black) literature, and most blues musicians are similarly

found in Music (Vol. 3). But the list of biographies in Black Life is intended to stand on its own, including individuals representing music, literature, religion, sports, politics, and other areas of black achievement. The *Encyclopedia* claims for southern culture such individuals as Mary McLeod Bethune, Ida Wells-Barnett, Arna Bontemps, and James Weldon Johnson, who traditionally have been seen as part of black history but not southern culture. The separate Black Life section is intended to recognize the special nature of southern black culture—both black and southern. Black culture is central to understanding the region and the *Encyclopedia*'s attempt to explore this perspective in specific, detailed topics may be the most significant contribution of these volumes toward understanding the region. Although the terms *Afro-American* and *Euro-American* are sometimes used, *black* and *white* are more often used to refer to the two major interrelated cultures of the South. These terms seem the clearest, most inclusive, and most widely accepted terms of reference.

The Women's Life section (Vol. 4) has similar aims. Many thematic articles and biographies of women of achievement appear in this section, which is designed to stand on its own. Scholars in the last 20 years have explored southern women's cultural values and issues, and their work provides a distinctive perspective on the region. Gender, like race and social class, has set parameters for cultural life in the South. The section includes articles on family life, childhood, and the elderly, reflecting the major responsibilities and concerns of women. The inclusion of these topics in this section is not meant to suggest that family responsibilities were the sole concern of women or that men were uninvolved with family, children, and the elderly. The articles usually discuss both male and female activities within the family. Scholarship on family life has often focused on women's roles, and family matters traditionally have played a significant part in women's lives. Most of the Women's Life section is concentrated, however, on concerns beyond the family and household, reflecting the contemporary scholarship in this area.

The Education section (Vol. 1) presented especially difficult choices of inclusion, and again, a selective approach was adopted. The flagship state public university in each southern state is included, but beyond that, institutions have been selected that represent differing constituencies to suggest the diversity of educational activity in the region. Berea College, Commonwealth College, the University of the South, and Tuskegee Institute each reflect an important dimension of southern education. The inclusion of additional school entries would have departed from the *Encyclopedia*'s overall guidelines and made a four-volume reference work impossible.

The History and Manners section (Vol. 2) contains a mix of articles that focus on cultural and social dimensions of the South. Combining topics in history and manners reflects the editors' decision that in a reference work on cultural concerns, history entries should deal with broad sociocultural history. There are, thus, no separate, detailed entries on Civil War battles, but, instead, long thematic articles on the cultural meaning of battlefields, monuments, and wars. The article on Robert E. Lee discusses the facts of Lee's life but also the history of his image for southerners and Americans.

Overview essays in each section are interpretive pieces that synthesize modern scholarship on major aspects of southern culture. The consultants who have written them trace historical developments and relate their broad subjects to regional cultural concerns. Many specific topics are discussed within overview essays rather than through separate entries, so readers should consult the index in order to locate such material. As one might expect, major subject areas have developed at a different pace. In such fields as literature, music, religion, folklife, and political culture, a vast body of scholarship exists. In these areas, the *Encyclopedia* overview essays provide a starting point for those users of this reference work interested in the subject. Such other fields as law, art, science, and medicine have only recently emerged as separate fields of Southern Studies. In these areas, the overview essays should help define the fields and point toward areas for further research.

Most thematic, topical, and biographical entries fall clearly within one section, but some articles were appropriate for several sections. The Scopes trial, for example, could have been placed in Religion, Law, or Science and Medicine. Consultants in Black Life, Music, and Women's Life all suggested Bessie Smith as an entry in their categories. The article on cockfighting clearly related to the Recreation section but was placed in Violence to suggest how recreational activities reflect a culture of violence. The gospel music articles could have appeared in Religion, but the editors decided that Music was the most appropriate category for them.

Much consideration and consultation with authorities in relevant fields occurred before such decisions were made on topics that did not fit perfectly into any one section. Readers should rely on the index and cross-references between sections to lead them to desired entries.

Biographies focus on the cultural significance of key individuals. The volumes do not claim to be exhaustive in their biographical entries. Rather than attempt to include all prominent people in a subject area, the editors decided to treat representative figures in terms of their contributions to, or significance for, southern culture. In selecting individuals, the goal was to include biographies of those iconic individuals associated with a particular aspect of the region's culture. Consultants identified those major figures who have immediate relevance to the region. The editors and consultants also selected individuals who illuminate major themes and exemplify southern cultural styles. Persons in this category may have made special contributions to southern distinctiveness, to cultural achievements, or to the development of a characteristic aspect of southern life. The Music and Literature categories have been given somewhat fuller biographical attention than other subject areas, a decision that is warranted by southern achievements in those areas. In addition to the separate biographical entries, many individuals are discussed in such thematic articles as "Linguists" or "Historians," which outline contributions of key persons to certain fields. Readers should consult the index in each volume to locate biographical information on southerners who appear in that volume.

The *Encyclopedia* includes biographies of living persons as well as the deceased. It is especially concerned with regional cultural issues in the contemporary South, and the inclusion of living individuals was crucial to establishing continuities between past and present. Entries on Bill Moyers and Charles Kuralt, for example, help readers to understand that the journalistic traditions of the South have been extended into the television age.

Selecting approximately 250 individuals for inclusion in the *Encyclopedia of Southern Culture* was no easy task. The list of potential individuals was widely circulated, and the choices represent the informed judgment of our consultants and contributors, leading scholars in the field of Southern Studies. The selection of biographies was made in light of the *Encyclopedia*'s overall definition of culture. The goal was not to list every cultural trait or include every prominent individual in the South but to explore *characteristic* aspects of the region's life and culture and to show their interrelationships. The biographical entries are not simply descriptive, factual statements but are instead intimately related to the broader thematic and overview essays. Biographical entries were meant to suggest how a representative individual is part of a broader pattern, a way of life, in the American South.

Interdisciplinary study has become prominent in a number of scholarly areas, but in few is it as useful as in the study of region. The interrelatedness of such specific fields as politics, religion, economics, cultural achievement, and social organization becomes especially obvious when scholars study a region. Interdisciplinary study of the South is a means of exploring humanity in all its aspects. The intellectual specialization of the modern world often makes this study difficult, but the editors of the *Encyclopedia* hope these volumes will promote that goal. Scholars exploring various aspects of the South's life now compose a distinct field of interdisciplinary Southern Studies, and the *Encyclopedia* joins those scholars in common effort to extend the present bounds of knowledge about the South.

The Editors
Center for the Study of Southern Culture
University of Mississippi

EDITORS' NOTE

The *Encyclopedia* is divided into four volumes and 24 major subject areas, arranged in alphabetical order. A table of contents listing articles in each section is found at the beginning of the section. An overview essay is followed by a series of alphabetically arranged thematic essays and then brief, alphabetically arranged topical-biographical entries. Readers are urged to consult the index, as well as the tables of contents, in locating articles.

When appropriate, articles contain cross-references to related articles in other sections. Material is cross-referenced only to similar-length or shorter material. Thematic articles, for example, are cross-referenced to thematic articles or to short topical articles in other sections but not to longer overview essays. Topical-biographical entries are cross-referenced to topical-biographical articles in other sections but not to

longer overview or thematic essays. Each cross-reference to related material lists the section in small capital letters, followed by the article title. If the entry is a short topical-biographical article, the title is preceded by a slash. The following example is a cross-reference to, first, a thematic article and, then, a topical-biographical entry, both in the Folklife section:

See also FOLKLIFE: Storytelling; / Clower, Jerry

Every effort was made to update material before publication. However, changes in contributors' affiliations, in biographical data because of the death of an individual, and in the names of institutions, for example, could not be made after the book went to press.

LITERATURE

M. THOMAS INGE

Randolph-Macon College

CONSULTANT

☆ ☆ ☆ ☆ ☆ ☆ ☆ ☆ ☆ ☆

Overleaf: William Faulkner, c. 1930

LITERATURE

||||||||||||||||||||||||||||||||||||||||||||||||||

One could argue that literature in the American South began as early as 1608 when the explorer and adventurer Captain John Smith published his promotional pamphlet *A True Relation of Occurrences and Accidents in Virginia*, the first of a series of accounts, each of which became more embellished, to include finally the story of his rescue by Pocahontas. Or, to move ahead a hundred years, perhaps southern letters began with the secret diaries, character sketches, poems, and satiric prose of the true Renaissance gentleman in residence at Westover, William Byrd II. But because America as an independent nation did not exist until 1776 and neither Smith nor Byrd considered himself other than a British citizen, the most one can say is that they established the traditions of exaggeration, irony, wit, stylistic versatility, and experimentation with form that would characterize southern literature.

Despite general impressions to the contrary, the intellectual life of the colonists in what would become the southern states was rich and varied. In the political and cultural center of Williamsburg citizens attended the theater, gave concerts for each other, built well-designed houses with beautifully patterned gardens, collected selective but impressive libraries, wrote articulate and well-argued letters to friends at home and abroad, read classical authors in the original Greek and Latin, and engaged in political and religious debate. Colonial authors expressed themselves in poetry and prose, satire and invective, essays and pamphlets. Noteworthy published works of the period include the translation into heroic couplets of Ovid's *Metamorphoses* (1626) by George Sandys, Jamestown treasurer and director of industry and agriculture; a humorous prose account of colonial life interspersed with lively poetry, *A Character of the Province of Maryland* (1966), by indentured servant George Alsop; the engaging first history of Virginia, *The History and Present State of Virginia* (1705), written by a plantation owner and member of the House of Burgesses, Robert Beverley; *The Sot-Weed Factor* (1708), a verse satire by poet laureate of early Maryland, Ebenezer Cooke whose point of view and low-life subject matter were precursors of the southern humor tradition; the two very early novels written by the master of grammar school and professor at the College of William and Mary, Arthur Blackamore, *The Religious Triumverate* (1720) and *Luck at Last; or, The Happy Unfortunate* (1723); and the works of New Light Presbyterian minister and later president of Princeton University, Samuel Davies, who composed hymns, elegies, sermons, and poems, many of the last of which were collected in *Miscellaneous Poems, Chiefly on Divine Subjects* (1752).

During the revolutionary period lawyer, architect, educator, scientist, philosopher, governor of Virginia, secretary of state, vice president, and president of the United States, Thomas

Jefferson served as the intellectual center of a burst of rational and enlightened thought about the American political state, the foundations of society, and the nature of man. The creative energy of Jefferson and such colleagues as Richard Bland, Patrick Henry, James Madison, and John Taylor was invested in political treatises, pamphlets, oratory, and cogent essays rather than belles lettres. Although he wrote only one full-length book, *Notes on the State of Virginia* (1785), perhaps the most significant political and scientific work of its time, it was through his composition of the text of the Declaration of Independence (1776) that Jefferson had a lasting and profound impact on the subsequent history of the political, social, and cultural life of the South and the nation. It is, then, a literary document of the first order. Jefferson continues to arrest our attention as a man of great creative intellect through biographies, histories, plays, poems, and novels about his life and relationships.

Antebellum Era. Political and economic leadership in the South by the end of the 18th century had moved from Virginia to South Carolina, especially Charleston, when it became clear that raw cotton was to be that state's and the region's essential product and that slavery was therefore necessary to the future. For the first 50 years the southernmost outpost of the British empire in America, Charleston became a major commercial center and supported the development of a wealthy merchant and planter class, which in turn encouraged a lively cultural life including one of two newspapers published in the South, a library society, and bookstores. It was at one of these, Russell's Bookstore, that the members of the "Charleston School" gathered under the leadership of statesman and critic Hugh Swinton Legaré, editor and contributor to the *Southern Review* (1828–32). The group included among its membership romantic poet Paul Hamilton Hayne, editor of *Russell's* magazine (1857–60), and other lyrical sentimental poets of the pro-Confederacy school such as Henry Timrod, "Laureate of the Confederacy."

The most influential member of the group, and probably in his time the best-known southern writer, was William Gilmore Simms, editor during his career of 10 periodicals and author of over 80 volumes of history, poetry, criticism, biography, drama, essays, stories, and novels, including a series of nationally popular border romances about life on the frontier and historical romances about the American Revolution. He was one of the first to make a profession of writing. Simms's only serious rival as a writer in the South was Baltimore politician John Pendleton Kennedy, whose informal fictional sketches in *Swallow Barn* (1832) helped establish the plantation novel, which in its depiction of a mythic genteel past and an ideal social structure has found hundreds of imitators in American romance fiction.

Less-accomplished but talented fiction writers of the time, all of whom wrote historical romances heavily under the influence of Scott, Cooper, and Irving, and all Virginia born, were Nathaniel Beverley Tucker, William Alexander Caruthers, and John Esten Cooke. Two extremely popular southern sentimental novelists of the time were Augusta Jane Evans Wilson and Caroline Lee Hentz, both of whom succeeded where many men had failed—achieving financial independence as professional writers.

A southern-born slave, William

Wells Brown, wrote the first novel by an American black, *Clotel; or, The President's Daughter* (1853), based on the rumor that Thomas Jefferson had fathered a daughter with one of his slaves. In writing what was, in essence, a novel of social protest, Brown established the mainstream tradition for black fiction in this country. Another important work of black protest was the *Narrative of the Life of Frederick Douglass* (1845), the work of a former slave who was America's leading abolitionist organizer, orator, newspaper editor, and political figure. The first book published by a black in the South was *The Hope of Liberty* (1829), which contained poems decrying the slaves' condition, by George Moses Horton of North Carolina.

The only writer of this period who, with the passage of time, was to rise to a level of national and international prominence was Edgar Allan Poe, whose relationship to his southern heritage may indirectly be seen in his work. Although he was raised in Richmond, attended the University of Virginia, and edited the *Southern Literary Messenger* (1834–64) in Richmond from 1835 to 1837, he turned away from regional materials for the most part in his poetry, fiction, and criticism to devote himself to a form of literary expression that aspired to universality in style and structure. His poetry in which sound and sensuality superseded sense, his fiction in which meaning or message was secondary to emotional impact, and his criticism in which independently and objectively derived standards are used in the evaluation of artistic success, would help shape, first in Europe and then in this country, the modern literary sensibility. Creative writing throughout the world was never the same after Poe. So dazzling was the achievement of

Poe from the modern point of view that the work of numerous contemporary southern poets pales in comparison. This includes the sentimental, romantic, lyric poetry of Irish-born Richard Henry Wilde of Georgia, Thomas Holley Chivers also of Georgia, British-born Edward Coote Pinkney of Maryland, Philip Pendleton Cooke of Virginia, Theodore O'Hara of Kentucky, and James Matthewes Legaré of South Carolina.

Outside of Poe, the most influential writing produced by the antebellum South was the work of a group of humorists who had no literary pretensions and therefore were free of the prevailing influences of the literary marketplace. They were lawyers, doctors, editors, politicians, and professional men who set down for the amusement of newspaper readers stories and tales they heard as they traveled through the frontier territories of Georgia, Alabama, Mississippi, Tennessee, or Louisiana— what was then called the Old Southwest. The sketches and fictional pieces they wrote were realistic, bawdy, vulgar, and often brutal, but they were written in a language and style close to the southern idiom and the point of view of everyday people. No one was more surprised than they when their sketches were collected between hard covers and soon constituted an impressive bookshelf of what would prove to be classics of southern humor: Augustus Baldwin Longstreet's *Georgia Scenes* (1835); William Tappan Thompson's *Major Jones's Courtship* (1843); Johnson Jones Hooper's *Some Adventures of Captain Simon Suggs* (1845); Thomas Bangs Thorpe's edition of *The Big Bear of Arkansas* (1845), which included his famous title story originally published in an 1841 issue of the *Spirit of the Times*, where much of this humor first appeared; Henry Clay Lewis's *Odd Leaves from the Life of a Louisiana Swamp Doctor* (1850); Joseph Glover Baldwin's *The Flush Times of Alabama and Mississippi* (1853); and Charles Henry Smith's *Bill Arp, So Called* (1866). Related to this tradition in its uses of comic exaggeration and oral folklore was *A Narrative of the Life of David Crockett* (1834) in which the part Crockett played as an author is uncertain.

The most accomplished of the humorists of the Old Southwest was Tennessean George Washington Harris, creator of the irascible Sut Lovingood, the liveliest comic figure to emerge from American literature before Huckleberry Finn. His first sketches were contributed to the New York *Spirit of the Times* and to Tennessee newspapers in the 1840s; however, the Lovingood stories were not collected until after the Civil War as *Sut Lovingood, Yarns Spun by a "Nat'ral Born Durn'd Fool"* (1867). In masterful use of dialect, striking control of metaphor and imagery, and kinetic creation of explosive action, Harris was to have no match until Mark Twain and William Faulkner, both of whom read Harris with appreciation.

Through studying Harris and the other southern humorists, Samuel Clemens, or Mark Twain, learned his trade, and his first published sketches, such as "Jim Smiley and His Jumping Frog" (1865), belong to this school of humor. Born of southern parents in Missouri, and raised in the slaveholding community of Hannibal on the Mississippi River, employed as a steamboat pilot on the great river from St. Louis and Cairo down to New Orleans from 1857 to 1861, and enlisted briefly in the Confederate army before deserting to go with his brother to Nevada, Clemens and his formative experiences were more southern than western. His masterwork, *The Adventures of Huckleberry Finn* (1885), is the most incisive satire ever written of southern attitudes, customs, and mores, aside from its central importance as a pivotal work of American literature. In Clemens, frontier humor was brought to a high level of literary artistry and through Clemens was transmitted to the majority of subsequent practicing humorists. Modern southern writers who have maintained this tradition include Guy Owen of North Carolina; William Price Fox, Jr., and Mark Steadman, Jr., of South Carolina; Robert Y. Drake, Jr., of Tennessee; and Roy Blount, Jr., of Georgia.

Local Color Era. If frankness and realism were dominant characteristics of frontier humor, the movement that superseded it was devoted to delicacy and romanticism. The development of a number of large-circulation, well-paying magazines in New York after the Civil War and an intense interest in things regional encouraged the local color movement, which Bret Harte's California stories instigated. Peculiarities of speech, quaint local customs, distinctive modes of thought, and stories about human nature became the primary subject matter of this fictional movement, and because the South had an abundance of all these qualities in the popular American mind, southern authors flourished. Unlike the frontier humorists, these were conscious craftsmen producing a marketable commodity; thus the finished product says more about popular misconceptions of the South in many cases than it says about the reality, and nothing that might upset the sensibilities of a young maiden, to use William Dean Howells's criterion, was allowed to see print. Although once thought to be early realists, many of the local color writers described a quaint and curious world that may never have existed.

In any case, they came from all parts of the South to vie for space in the popular magazines and described in their fiction the worlds they inhabited—George Washington Cable, Kate Chopin, Grace King, and Ruth McEnery Stuart from Louisiana; Thomas Nelson Page and John Esten Cooke (in his postwar fiction) from Virginia; Richard Malcolm Johnston, Harry Stillwell Edwards, and Will N. Harben from Georgia; James Lane Allen from Kentucky; Sherwood Bonner from Mississippi; and Mary Noailles Murfree from Tennessee. The aesthetic sensibilities of such writers as Cable, Chopin, and Murfree allowed them to achieve a level of psychological sophistication in their characters and a stylistic skill unusual for their times.

Joel Chandler Harris's popularity was also fed by the same interests that fostered the local color writers, but his was a special achievement. Although the exterior settings and scenes for his stories of Uncle Remus were directly out of a romantic world of a Thomas Nelson Page, the stories themselves are remarkable renderings of Afro-American folktales, in which Brer Rabbit serves as an exemplum for black survival in an Anglo-American world. Harris greatly improved, then, on the legacy of happy darky stereotypes that Page and the Mississippi dialect poet Irwin Russell had left. One black writer who spoke for his own race in local color fiction was Charles Waddell Chesnutt, raised in North Carolina, but he had to begin his literary career by disguising his racial identity because of the prejudice that

only whites could understand and explain blacks.

The American reading audience seemed to glory in the tales of southern times "befo' de wah," but some southern writers and leaders began a movement to reject that heritage for a concept of a New South that would be industrialized, modernized, and adapted to the larger pattern of American economic and social development. George Washington Cable and Joel Chandler Harris were supporters of this movement, but the intellectual leaders were journalists Walter Hines Page and Henry W. Grady, and Booker T. Washington in the black community.

Their sentiments were shared by the best postwar poet in the South, Sidney Lanier of Georgia, whose poetry aimed for a musical and tonal beauty that stressed sound over content and whose literary criticism attempted to establish a basis for versification in the principles of music. Less-accomplished poets publishing at the end of the 19th century and the beginning of the 20th were John Bannister Tabb of Virginia; former slave Albery Allson Whitman, Madison Cawein, Cale Young Rice, and Olive Tilford Dargan, all of Kentucky; Lizette Woodworth Reese of Maryland; William Alexander Percy of Mississippi; and John Gould Fletcher of Arkansas, at first a member of the Imagist school of poets in London and later a member of the Fugitive poets, but overshadowed by more talented writers of both groups.

At the turn of the century, southern literature was dominated by several writers residing in Richmond, Va. Mary Johnston produced a series of popular historical romances set in Virginia, while her friend Ellen Glasgow, much more the insightful and talented artist, wrote a series of distinctive and well-crafted novels designed to constitute a social history of the state. Her critical realism was counterbalanced by the medieval romanticism and fantasy of James Branch Cabell, whose epic biography of Manuel set in Poictesme turns out to be, after all, an ironic, disguised commentary on the manners and mores of his real world. The following generation of writers in Richmond proved to be eminent journalists and historians—Douglas Southall Freeman, who finally left newspaper work after 34 years to complete his distinguished biography of Robert E. Lee; Clifford Dowdey, who had equal success in magazine editing, publishing historical novels, and writing Civil War histories; and Virginius Dabney, who paralleled a career in journalism with that of a liberal commentator on history, politics, and social change in the South.

Southern Literary Renaissance. In a November 1917 issue of the New York *Evening Mail* Baltimore journalist H. L. Mencken published his notorious essay, "The Sahara of the Bozart," in which he excoriated the South as being culturally backwards and "almost as sterile, artistically, intellectually, culturally, as the Sahara Desert." In his usual fashion, Mencken was, of course, exaggerating, but almost as if in response the next two decades witnessed an overwhelming production of literature by southern authors, called the "Southern Literary Renaissance." Some literary historians have not been happy with the term, given the quantity of writing in the South up to that time, but if the term is also used to mean a "flowering," then it is clearly appropriate.

Mencken's attack, of course, had nothing to do with initiating the Renaissance, which was the culmination of a number of historic and cultural forces at work in southern society. The region had experienced a military defeat on its own soil and the trying Reconstruction era, which brought about a period of self-analysis and reflection on the values it had fought to preserve and in some cases a reaffirmation of those values. Some white southerners assumed a burden of guilt with regard to the treatment of blacks, but nonetheless maintained a belief in white superiority. Resistance to cultural reconstruction intensified the traditional regional sense of identity and distinctiveness in which some took pleasure and from which others felt the need to escape. These tensions stirred the creative sensibilities of writers, who were instructed well by southern history in mortality and the inevitability of death—concerns that would bring their themes to a level of universal relevance.

These matters were treated in the grand and eloquent style of William Faulkner, the major writer to emerge from the Renaissance and the greatest American writer of the 20th century. Using local, family, and Mississippi history, Faulkner constructed a fictional world populated by southern figures of tragedy and comedy who acted out his major theme of the human heart in conflict with itself. His stylistic innovations under the influence of James Joyce, his mastery of external and internal landscape, the incredible range of characterization in his fiction, and the affirmative spirit that provides a philosophic base for his work—all these promise to make him a writer for the ages, a Shakespeare in southern homespun.

Major writers contemporary with Faulkner were Thomas Wolfe, who attempted a herculean transformation of his personal dislocation as a southerner into fiction of bardic proportions; Richard Wright, who achieved a disturbing, razor-sharp portrayal of what growing up black in the South and America meant and forced whites to pay attention; and Robert Penn Warren, whose fiction constitutes a lifelong philosophic discourse on the meaning of history, the nature of man, and the compromises necessary in building a workable political and social system. Though overshadowed by Faulkner's achievement, all three achieve distinctive voices in fiction.

Others worked in Faulkner's shadow but followed their own separate sensibilities with notable results, as evidenced by the stylistically perfect stories of Katherine Anne Porter, the keen sensitivity to adolescence in the fiction of Carson McCullers and James Agee, and the richly textured re-creations in the southern vernacular of myth and metaphor in Eudora Welty's stories and novels. Except for their lack of artistic discipline and willingness to publish too much too fast, Erskine Caldwell and Jesse Stuart might have entered this golden circle; as it is, they remain of interest because of the philosophically opposite variations they offer on some of the same material handled by Faulkner. The single writer who reached more readers than all these major writers put together and has probably done more to shape the larger public's attitude toward the South was Margaret Mitchell. With more enthusiasm than artistry and less skill than imagination, she wrote one novel, *Gone with the Wind* (1936), which remains an enigma but must be counted a significant event of the Renaissance.

A host of other fiction writers should be accounted for in any survey of the Renaissance, including Harriette Simpson Arnow, Hamilton Basso, Roark Bradford, Brainard Cheney, Alfred Leland Crabbe, Caroline Gordon, Dubose Heyward, Zora Neale Hurston, Andrew Lytle, William March, Julia Peterkin, Josephine Pinckney, Marjorie Kinnan Rawlings, Elizabeth Madox Roberts, Lyle Saxon, Evelyn Scott, Lillian Smith, James Still, T. S. Stribling, Jean Toomer, and Stark Young.

Although drama was never to be a major mode for southern writers, Paul Green began in the 1920s a 50-year career as the successful author of folk plays and historic symphonic dramas; Lawrence Stallings had a notable success in collaboration with Maxwell Anderson, *What Price Glory?* (1924); Lillian Hellman, beginning with the popular reception of *The Little Foxes* (1939), wrote a series of sensitive treatments of life in southern settings; and Tennessee Williams began in the 1940s a singularly distinctive career as the author of numerous plays that examined in depth and detail southern elements of life and character and gained for himself a reputation as one of America's three most accomplished playwrights (along with Eugene O'Neill and Arthur Miller).

A formidable body of poetry emerged during the Renaissance beginning with the publication in 1922 of the first issue of the *Fugitive*, a little magazine edited by a group of young faculty members and students at Vanderbilt University in Nashville. Many would mark the event as the official beginning of the Southern Literary Renaissance. Although they were for the moment in agreement that modern poetry must escape the conventionalism of the past, the major figures were to follow different patterns of development—John Crowe Ransom finding in irony and paradox the tension necessary to good poetry, Allen Tate turning to abstract methods as more suitable for treating the dislocations in modern society evident to the traditional sensibility, Robert Penn Warren preferring narrative forms deeply philosophical in their import, and Donald Davidson finding more compatible folk narratives incorporating history and the lives of influential southern figures. Merrill Moore, John Gould Fletcher, and, for a brief time, Laura Riding were associated with the Fugitive poets. A young Randall Jarrell would come to Vanderbilt in the early 1930s to study under Ransom, Davidson, and Warren and under their influence to begin writing poetry striking in its combination of the erudite with the ordinary and its contrast of desperate violence with the seemingly peaceful surface of daily life. Two black poetic voices of the period who used their southern experiences in ethnically sensitive verse were James Weldon Johnson and Arna Bontemps, the former best known for his political activities with the NAACP and the latter as the author of the lyrics for the musical *St. Louis Woman.*

After the *Fugitive* ceased publication in 1925, the four major forces—Ransom, Davidson, Tate, and Warren—began discussions about the state of the South in political and economic terms and found themselves in agreement that only by resisting modern progress and technology could the region maintain a hold on the virtues of its traditional agrarian past. Joining forces with eight other southern intellectuals, including writers Stark Young, John Gould Fletcher, Andrew Lytle, and John Donald Wade, they published the Agrarian manifesto *I'll Take My Stand* (1930), a major document in the debate between science and humanism in the 20th cen-

Reunion in 1956 of the Fugitive poets (left to right, front row) Allen Tate, Merrill Moore, John Crowe Ransom, Donald Davidson, and (back row) Robert Penn Warren

tury. The only other prose volume to generate more controversy during the Renaissance was W. J. Cash's effort to interpret *The Mind of the South* (1941), which has proven to be more valuable as a study of the mind of *a* southerner—Cash himself.

In the exciting intellectual milieu of the Fugitive and Agrarian movements, modern southern literary criticism had its birth. Ransom, Tate, and Warren had already been practicing criticism early on, but Ransom in particular began to encourage the development of a formalist approach called the New Criticism, which assessed a work of art on its own terms apart from its relation to the life of the artist or the times in which it was written. One of Ransom's best students at Vanderbilt, Cleanth Brooks, would develop the system more fully, incorporating it in two highly influential textbooks written in collaboration with Robert Penn Warren, *Understanding Poetry* (1938) and *Understanding Fiction* (1943). The adherents to this critical approach became more single-minded in its application than either Ransom or Brooks ever intended, as demonstrated by the fine biographical and historical criticism practiced by Brooks in his important studies of William Faulkner.

Ransom, Davidson, Tate, Warren, and Brooks also provided another service in establishing a role model for the modern man of letters as teacher, all serving throughout their literary careers as lecturers in American universities and becoming, in effect, some of the first writers in residence. A number of university teachers achieved national distinction as practicing critics, scholars, and historians of southern culture, including Edwin Mims and Richmond Croom Beatty at Vanderbilt; Jay B. Hubbell at Duke; Benjamin Brawley at Morehouse and Howard; Floyd Stovall at the University of Virginia; Randall Stewart at Brown and Vanderbilt; Lewis Leary at Duke and Columbia; Edd Winfield Parks at Georgia; Sterling A. Brown, Saunders Redding, and Arthur P. Davis at Howard; Richard Beale Davis at Tennessee; and C. Vann Woodward at Johns Hopkins and Yale University.

As if the first generation had not been sufficient to leave an indelible mark on American letters, a second generation of Renaissance writers flooded the bookstores with their works following World War II. Flannery O'Connor arrested the attention of everyone by producing stories and novels shocking in their use of perversely exaggerated southern characters but orthodox in the Catholicism that informs their meaning. William Styron moved away from the stylistic influence of Faulkner and his early novels to achieve a major mode of fiction based on history and personal experience. Truman Capote published stories of impeccable style, while developing what

he would call the "nonfiction novel," and his childhood friend Harper Lee wrote a single novel, *To Kill a Mockingbird* (1960), which remains a classic for its sensitive treatment of adolescence and racism in an Alabama town. Another one-novel writer, Ralph Ellison, captured history, folklore, music, and the political significance of the black man in America in *Invisible Man* (1952), which was as much concerned with the existential fate of modern man as with the black experience. Walker Percy's interests in Christian existentialism provided a foundation for his increasingly conservative novels, and John Barth brilliantly played with and reworked all the traditional forms and points of view developed in the entire history of fiction.

A beginning list of other significant practitioners of short fiction and the novel among the second generation Renaissance writers should include Doris Betts, Fred Chappell, Ellen Douglas, Shelby Foote, Jesse Hill Ford, Ernest J. Gaines, George Garrett, William Goyen, Shirley Ann Grau, Chester Himes, Madison Jones, John Oliver Killens, David Madden, Cormac McCarthy, Marion Montgomery, Reynolds Price, Mary Lee Settle, Elizabeth Spencer, Peter Taylor, Margaret Walker, John A. Williams, Calder Willingham, and Frank Yerby.

The leading poet to emerge in the postwar period was James Dickey, trained at Vanderbilt and devoted to the achievement of a careful balance between the formal and the emotional within an intricate poetic structure, and raising the ordinary experience to the level of epiphany. His novel *Deliverance* (1970) is a metaphoric study of man's potential for violence and salvation. Other poets to attract critical praise include A. R. Ammons, Wendell Berry,

John William Corrington, Julia Fields, Dabney Stuart, and Miller Williams.

A second generation of university teachers continued the earlier critical explorations of southern literature and scholarship; many of them were trained by members of the first generation: C. Hugh Holman at North Carolina; Arlin Turner at Louisiana State University and Duke; Richard Weaver at Chicago; Lewis Simpson at LSU; Ruel Foster at West Virginia; Thomas Daniel Young and Walter Sullivan at Vanderbilt; Floyd Watkins at Emory; Louis D. Rubin, Jr., at Hollins and North Carolina; and Louise Cowan at the University of Dallas. Southern journalists who established a tradition for crusading liberal journalism in the 1950s were Ralph McGill, Hodding Carter, Harry Ashmore, and Willie Morris, but in a class by himself was Tom Wolfe, a founder of the free-wheeling, personal, stylistically fluid school of New Journalism.

Contemporary Era. Some scholars argue that the Renaissance is over, that contemporary writers share too little in the sense of southern tradition and are swept up in faddish social causes and personal crises, but a third generation of considerable promise has emerged. Although they both came to fiction late in their lives, black novelists Robert Dean Pharr and Alex Haley attracted attention in the 1970s, Haley in particular for his re-creation of the history of his family in America, *Roots* (1976). Other writers producing fiction and poetry of note are Lisa Alther, Maya Angelou, Pat Conroy, Nikki Giovanni, Gail Godwin, Barry Hannah, Beverly Lowry, James Alan McPherson, Bobbie Ann Mason, Lee Smith, Anne Tyler, Alice Walker, and Sylvia Wilkinson. Many of them are black and female, perhaps a sign of racial and feminine liberation at work in the South.

Whatever the future may hold for literature in the South, the social changes and the cultural challenges at work in the rapidly changing cities of Atlanta, Charlotte, Birmingham, Nashville, and Richmond, as well as the suburbs and the countryside along interstate routes 95 and 85, create the kinds of intellectual conflict that often stir the imagination and stimulate creative writing. Whether in the form of fiction, poetry, or play; memoir, history, or journalism; docudrama, screenplay, or criticism, in all likelihood, the last distinctively southern writer, like the last southern gentleman, has not yet been seen.

See also BLACK LIFE: Literature, Black; / Bontemps, Arna; Chesnutt, Charles W.; Douglass, Frederick; Free Southern Theater; Gaines, Ernest J.; Haley, Alex; Hurston, Zora Neale; Johnson, James Weldon; Murray, Pauli; Toomer, Jean; Walker, Margaret; HISTORY AND MANNERS: / Byrd, William, II; Jefferson, Thomas; MEDIA articles; MYTHIC SOUTH: / Agrarians, Vanderbilt; Mitchell, Margaret; Yerby, Frank; RELIGION: Literature and Religion; SOCIAL CLASS: Lower Class, Literary; WOMEN'S LIFE: Writers; / Chesnut, Mary Boykin; Chopin, Kate; Peterkin, Julia Mood

M. Thomas Inge
Randolph-Macon College

Robert Bain, *Southern Writers: A Biographical Dictionary* (1979); Richmond Croom Beatty, Floyd C. Watkins, and Thomas Daniel Young, eds., *The Literature of the South* (1952; rev. ed., 1968); John M. Bradbury, *Renaissance in the South: A Critical History of the Literature, 1920–1960* (1963); Louise Cowan, *The Fugitive Group: A Literary History* (1959); Donald Davidson, *Southern Writers in the Modern World* (1958); Richard Beale Davis, *Intellectual Life in the Colonial*

South: 1565–1763 (1978); Richard Gray, *The Literature of Memory: Modern Writers of the American South* (1977); C. Hugh Holman, *Three Modes of Southern Fiction* (1966); Jay B. Hubbell, *The South in American Literature* (1954); Anne Goodwyn Jones, *Tomorrow Is Another Day: The Woman Writer in the South, 1859–1936* (1981); Richard H. King, *A Southern Renaissance: The Cultural Awakening of the American South, 1930–1955* (1980); Michael O'Brien, *The Idea of the American South, 1920–1941* (1979); Ladell Payne, *Black Novelists and the Southern Literary Tradition* (1981); Joseph V. Ridgely, *Nineteenth-Century Southern Literature* (1980); Louis D. Rubin, Jr., ed., *The American South: Portrait of a Culture* (1980), *The Wary Fugitives: Four Poets and the South* (1978), with Robert D. Jacobs, eds., *South: Modern Southern Literature in Its Cultural Setting* (1961), with others, *A History of Southern Literature* (1985); Lewis P. Simpson, *The Dispossessed Garden: Pastoral and History in Southern Fiction* (1975); Edmund Wilson, *Patriotic Gore: Studies in the Literature of the Civil War* (1962); Thomas Daniel Young, *The Past in the Present: A Thematic Study of Modern Southern Fiction* (1981). ✩

Agrarianism in Literature

||||||||||||||||||||||||||||||||||||||||||||||||||||||||||||||||

The ideas associated with agrarianism in this century may be stated as an interrelated set of beliefs:

1. The cultivation of the soil is an occupation singularly blessed by God that provides benefits from direct contact with physical nature. It is the mother of all the arts and instills in the cultivator such spiritual and social virtues as honor, courage, self-reliance, integrity, and hospitality.

2. The standard by which an economic system is judged is not the amount of prosperity it produces but the degree to which it encourages independence and morality. Because the farmer's basic needs of food and shelter are always met through a cooperative relationship with nature, only farming offers complete self-sufficiency regardless of the state of the national economy.

3. The life of the farmer is harmonious, orderly, and whole, and it counteracts the tendencies toward abstraction, fragmentation, and alienation that have come with modern urban existence. The farmer belongs to a specific family, place, and region; participates in a historic and religious tradition; and has, in other words, a sense of identity that is psychologically and culturally beneficial.

4. Since nature is the primary source of inspiration, all the arts, music, literature, and other forms of creativity are better fostered and sustained in an agrarian society. The mass-produced culture of the industrial society lacks the individuality, humanity, and simple beauty of folk culture.

5. The thriving cities created by industry, technology, and capitalism are destructive of independence and dignity and encourage crime and corruption. The agricultural community, on the other hand, which depends on friendly cooperation and neighborliness, provides a possible model for an ideal social order.

These ideas are the culmination of a philosophical development that is a part of the mainstream of Western civilization. In classical literature, Hesiod, Aristotle, Cicero, Vergil, and Horace are among those who reiterated the advantages of country life and husbandry over the other modes of existence and occupations. From the Middle Ages through the Renaissance and down to the 18th century, most major and minor writers praised the pastoral and rural life over city life and cursed the materialism and decadence fostered by the new spirits of commercialism and progress. When the European settlers arrived in North America, they brought with them these ideas as a part of their cultural heritage.

The land of the New Englanders was hard and stony and poorly suited to farming. The fertile soil and amenable climate of the South, however, naturally encouraged agriculture as the primary economic pursuit of the entire region. Among his contemporaries, Virginian Thomas Jefferson did more to advance experimentation and technique in agriculture than anyone else by introducing his own innovations and inventions and including agricultural science in the curriculum of the University of Virginia. Of greater importance to southern thought was his early formulation of the agrarian ideal in query 19 of his *Notes on the State of Virginia* (1785), where he states, "Those who labour in the earth are the chosen people of God, if he ever had a chosen people, whose breasts he has made his peculiar deposit for substantial and genuine virtue." Jefferson's concise statement of fewer than 400 words has inspired almost two centuries of literary, social, and political debate.

The place of agriculture in the wealth of the new nation was contested in the early party battle between the Federalist and Republican forces led respectively by Alexander Hamilton and Jefferson. The Federalists favored a centralized federal government, controlled by a propertied few, supported by commercial and industrial expansion. The Republicans, however, favored reliance on local government, under the leadership of a natural aristocracy of talent and virtue, with a primarily agrarian national economy based in independent farmers and landholders. The tensions of this debate were to reverberate down to and beyond the Civil War, which some have contended was basically a struggle between the two competing economies. While Jefferson's democratic theories largely prevailed in politics, Hamilton's industrial program prevailed in the economic sphere as America realized the extent of its natural resources and looked to capitalism to exploit them.

Southern literature offers a wide variety of novels, poems, and stories that deal in imaginative ways with the theories and realities of agrarianism. The virtues of agrarian life were celebrated in the 19th century in the works of John Esten Cooke, Joel Chandler Harris, Richard Malcolm Johnston, John Pendleton Kennedy, Sidney Lanier, Mary Noailles Murfree, Thomas Nelson Page, William Gilmore Simms, Henry Timrod, and Mark Twain. In 1930 agrarianism was the unifying force for a group of writers led by John Crowe Ransom, Donald Davidson, Allen Tate, and Robert Penn Warren of Vanderbilt University in Nashville, which resulted in the publication of a symposium *I'll Take My Stand: The South and the Agrarian Tradition*. To one degree or another, these ideas were to remain the subject matter of much of their later poetry, fiction, and criticism, especially in Davidson's work.

Along with the portraits of the husbandman as an honest champion of individualism, southern literature also contains obverse portraits of poor white farmers as lazy, shiftless, uncouth members of a mongrel race. William Byrd II of Westover initiated this brutish characterization with his colonial sketches of the idle lubberlanders observed in North Carolina during his survey of the boundary line between that state and Virginia. Reacting partly out of his upper-class sensitivities and partly out of the tradition that North Carolina was a refuge for criminals and malcontents, Byrd fathered a long-continuing series of descriptions of poor white degenerates, extending through 19th-century southern writing, the humor of the Old Southwest, and local color fiction, down to Erskine Caldwell's lustful and depraved sharecroppers. H. L. Mencken also had little sympathy for the romance of agrarianism and called the farmer "a tedious brand of ignoramus, a cheap rogue and hypocrite, the eternal Jack of the human pack."

In this century, the writers whose fiction and poetry are reflective of agrarian problems and principles include Ransom, Davidson, Tate, Warren, Ellen Glasgow, Caroline Gordon, Andrew Lytle, Margaret Mitchell, Flannery O'Connor, Elizabeth Madox Roberts, Mary Lee Settle, Jesse Stuart, Alice Walker, Eudora Welty, Thomas Wolfe, and Stark Young.

Agrarian themes are particularly important in William Faulkner's fictional saga of Yoknapatawpha County. The passing away of the wilderness in the face of industrialism and commercialism is the theme of his story "The Bear," and in the Snopes trilogy (*The Hamlet*, *The Town*, and *The Mansion*) Faulkner projected on a broad canvas the conflict between agrarianism and materialism, the principles of the first embodied in the defeated chivalry of the Sartoris family, and the valueless animalism of the second embodied in the successful Snopes breed. The independent, small-farm families, such as the McCallums and the McCaslins, are always favorably treated. Faulkner was concerned in much of his work with the transformation of the idyllic agrarian society into the modern urban industrial world. Popeye of *Sanctuary*, described as a mechanical creature with a face of stamped tin, grows hysterical at the sight of fields and trees, and thus stands as Faulkner's ultimate symbol of the machine and its effects on society.

Many southern writers continue to hold onto the humanism inherent in agrarianism, and some of its concerns have found a voice in the modern ecology, environmental, and back-to-the-land movements. However, as farming ceases to be a way of life in the South and elsewhere, the coherent philosophy it once represented will likely lose much of its impact or find a new mode of expression.

See also HISTORY AND MANNERS: / Byrd, William, II; Jefferson, Thomas; MYTHIC SOUTH: / Agrarians, Vanderbilt; Mencken's South

M. Thomas Inge
Randolph-Macon College

M. Thomas Inge, ed., *Agrarianism in American Literature* (1969); Leo Marx, *The Machine in the Garden: Technology and the Pastoral Ideal in America* (1964); Henry Bamford Parkes, *The American Experience* (1947); Twelve Southerners, *I'll Take My Stand: The South and the Agrarian Tradition* (1930). ☆

Appalachian Literature

The literature of Appalachia has coincided with distinct historical developments: the early exploration by

Indians, hunters, trappers, and adventurers; the pioneer period characterized by scattered settlement and an agrarian lifestyle (barely interrupted by the Civil War); and the exploitation of coal and wood during the turn of the century, spawning mass migration. Cratis Williams, in a classic dissertation on Appalachian literature, divided the literary-historical periods into three: (1) early exploration to 1880, (2) 1880–1930, (3) 1930–present. Called "pioneer," the first period included writers who sought a distinct James Fenimore Cooper-like flavor. Writers such as Mary Noailles Murfree, who wrote about real Appalachian characters and situations set in the Great Smoky Mountains, typify the second era. The last period began shortly after the Great Depression and saw the emergence of literary figures who carved a place in American letters for Appalachian themes and characters. In the mid-1980s this group is passing that torch to a younger set of regional writers such as Wilma Dykeman, Harry Caudill, Jim Wayne Miller, Lillie D. Chaffin, Earl Hamner, Jr., Jane Stuart, Loyal Jones, and Jack Weller.

Among the notable members of the post-1930 group were Jesse Stuart, with his more than 40 books covering biography, autobiography, novel, short story, poetry, essay, and journalism; Harriette Simpson Arnow, with her powerful novel *The Dollmaker* (1954); James Still, with his highly respected attention to art and craft in fiction, short story, and poetry in *River of Earth* (1940), *On Troublesome Creek* (1941), and *Hounds on the Mountain* (1937); and Thomas Wolfe, the famed author of *Look Homeward, Angel* (1929) and *The Hills Beyond* (1935).

The themes of Appalachian literature have followed historical developments closely. The early writing consisted mainly of diary or journal accounts of travel through the region when trappers and traders first began to form their impressions. Higgs and Manning in their 1975 anthology include works from John Lederer, who began to write about the region in 1669; John Fontaine, whose journal published in 1838 included accounts of his travels into the Blue Ridge and the Shenandoah Valley; Timothy Flint, whose *Biographical Memoir of Daniel Boone* (1833) was perhaps the most widely read biography of the early 19th century; James Kirke Paulding, whose *Letters from the South* (1816) demonstrated the captivating qualities of the Appalachian Mountains; and Anne Newport Royall, called America's first hitchhiker, who wrote of the unspoiled region in her *Sketches of History, Life, and Manners in the United States* (1826).

Immediately following this period a group of writers emerged who exploited the stereotypes and romantic notions associated with the region. Although the mountaineers were not specifically the object of their writing, they emerged from a larger pool of "southern characters" whose adventures, romances, brave feats, and foolish ways were chronicled in such works as those by Mark Twain, George Washington Harris, and David (Davy) Crockett. Tall tales, backwoods humor, and romanticism were major thematic elements of this literary era "in which men were more than a match for the wilderness that surrounded them."

The next period was dominated by native writers such as John Fox, Jr. (*Trail of the Lonesome Pine* [1931] and *The Little Shepherd of Kingdom Come* [1931]), Mary Noailles Murfree (*In the*

Tennessee Mountains [1884] and 25 other works, mostly fiction set in the southern mountain area), and Elizabeth Madox Roberts (*The Time of Man* [1926], *The Great Meadow* [1930], and hundreds of poems published in national magazines). Their works were largely romantic and were often written in dialect. Sentimentality and a neoromanticism merged with Appalachian stereotypes and motifs to set the tone until the 1930s. Feuding, the Civil War in Appalachia, moonshining, and historical romance became common topics.

The 1930s were characterized by native writers who developed local material into larger, more universal themes. This period was dominated by Jesse Stuart, James Still, Harriette Simpson Arnow, James Agee, and Thomas Wolfe. Their writing is highly conscious of custom and tradition as it forms the total consciousness of America. If Appalachia was exemplary of America's pioneer past, then their duty, as these writers saw it, was to find meaning in, and to come to grips with, the passing of the folkways that had so tightly bound the isolated Appalachia to that past. They would be compelled to announce the significance of that passing to the "modern world," which might not have otherwise paused to learn of it. Many of these writers simply ignored the stereotypes and transcended the local color stories by developing more universal themes.

The final period began in the 1950s. Younger, better-educated, and more socially conscious writers began to develop a literature examining the region through its social consciousness, political issues, historical significance, religious disposition, and economic impact. Most notable among these books are Harry Caudill's *Night Comes to the* *Cumberlands* (1962), *Watches of the Night* (1976), *Theirs Be the Power* (1983), and a half-dozen other documentary and fiction pieces; Jack Weller's *Yesterday's People* (1965), which is probably one of the most widely discussed books ever written on southern Appalachia; Ron Eller's scholarly study *Miners, Millhands, and Mountaineers: The Modernization of the Appalachian South, 1880–1930* (1981), which traces the history of the industrial movement in Appalachia and its impact upon this once-pristine region; John C. Campbell's *The Southern Highlander and His Homeland*, the classic 1921 study, which details the history and lifestyle of the southern Appalachians; Henry David Shapiro's *Appalachia on Our Mind: The Southern Mountains and Mountaineers in the American Consciousness, 1870–1920* (1978), which does much to help identify the role of the Appalachian people in the larger American culture; Horace Kephart's *Our Southern Highlanders* (1913), a social history of the Appalachian region; John Gaventa's *Power and Powerlessness: Quiescence and Rebellion in an Appalachian Valley* (1980), a work of Appalachian political theory and a history of the mine wars in the 1930s; and David E. Whisnant's *All That Is Native and Fine: The Politics of Culture in an American Region* (1983), a study of cultural intervention by outsiders in Appalachia.

Others who frequently write about the region include Fred Chappell (poetry and short stories), Jeff Daniel Marion (poetry), James B. Goode (poetry and essays), Lee Pennington (poetry, short stories, criticism, and drama), Billy Edd Wheeler (poetry, song lyrics, and music), Jean Ritchie (poetry, song lyrics, and music), George Scarbrough (poetry), John Rice Irwin (histories and documentaries), Loyal Jones (histories, essays, and documentaries), and Gurney Norman (novels, short stories, and poetry).

Several current periodicals have consistently published Appalachian literary criticism, poetry, short fiction, and topical essays. Among the notable ones are *Appalachian Journal: A Regional Studies Review*, *Appalachian Heritage: A Magazine of Southern Appalachian Life and Culture*, *Foxfire*, *Mountain Life and Work: The Magazine of the Appalachian South*, *Appalachian Notes*, and *The Plow: The Monthly Magazine for Mountain People*.

Substantial anthologies on the region are rare but a few good ones exist: Ambrose Manning and Robert J. Higgs's *Voices from the Hills*, Cecille Haddix's *Who Speaks for Appalachia?*, Joy Pennington's *Selected Kentucky Literature*, and Ruel Foster's *Appalachian Literature: Critical Essays*. There are also several good bibliographies. The most complete one is Charlotte T. Ross's *Bibliography of Southern Appalachia*. Others include Louise Boger's *The Southern Mountaineer in Literature* (1976), Robert Munn's *Appalachian Bibliography* (1968), and Appendices A-G "A Guide to Appalachian Studies" (Autumn 1977 issue of *Appalachian Journal*). A few shelf lists are also helpful: the fiction and poetry list of the Berea College Weatherford-Hammond Mountain Collection, the Council of Southern Mountains' *Bibliography of the Appalachian South*, *Appalachian Outlook* (a cumulative listing of periodical literature issued by the University of West Virginia Library), and the Appalachian Book and Record Shop's *Appalachian Literature and Music: A Comprehensive Catalogue* (which is arranged by 11 topics, is fully

indexed, and contains approximately 635 entries).

Appalachian literary history includes a variety of writing, which adds to the evolving body of American letters. A part of that literature unmistakably has kinship with the South. The rural agrarian mind-set, the mass in-migration from nearby southern states, the fierce independence as evidenced by the bloody union movements (which may parallel the ideas reflected in the Civil War), the emphasis upon folk tradition and culture, the history of oral tradition, and the inclination to use literature to express sociological or anthropological concerns are all characteristics that prove the link. But many other aspects of the literature make it a legitimate entity apart from the southern literary experience. A frequent theme in Appalachian literature, for example, has been the struggle by Appalachians to bridge the gulf between traditional Appalachian culture and contemporary America. Appalachian writing remains an independent body of letters struggling for a place in American, including southern, literature.

See also EDUCATION: / Campbell, John C.; ETHNIC LIFE: Mountain Culture; / Appalachians; FOLKLIFE: / "Hillbilly" Image; INDUSTRY: Industrialization in Appalachia; LANGUAGE: Mountain Language; MYTHIC SOUTH: Appalachian Culture; RELIGION: Appalachian Religion; SOCIAL CLASS: Appalachia, Exploitation of; WOMEN'S LIFE: Writers, Women

James B. Goode
University of Kentucky
Southeast Community College

George Brosi, ed., *Appalachian Literature and Music: A Comprehensive Catalogue* (1981); James B. Goode, *Temporary Finding*

Guide: Southeast Community College Oral History Project, 1978–1983 (1984); Cecille Haddix, ed., *Who Speaks for Appalachia?: Prose, Poetry, and Songs from the Mountain Heritage* (1975); Robert J. Higgs and Ambrose Manning, eds., *Voices from the Hills* (1975); Jim Wayne Miller, *Appalachian Journal* (Autumn 1977); Cratis Williams, "The Southern Mountaineer in Fact and Fiction" (Ph.D. dissertation, New York University, 1961). ☆

Autobiography

||||||||||||||||||||||||||||||||||||||||

Southern autobiographers exhibit a historical consciousness typical of southern literature. They value religious or moral interpretations of the world, are loyal to family, friends, and community, and unavoidably confront a heritage of slavery and racial struggle. Largely because of the irony and tragedy of southern history, the regional autobiographers are conscious of human imperfection, social injustice, and the existence of evil in the world. At the same time, they are storytellers who in a casual, literary way reveal the individual context of regional history and the distinctiveness of southern culture while preserving and continuing the dialogue between region and nation.

Until the 19th century, southern autobiography could not be distinguished from the established form of English spiritual autobiography. Southern autobiographers, including Thomas Jefferson, were prominent public officials who equated their professions with their identity and function in *American* history. As sectional conflict became more pronounced and serious, autobiography became more popular, and ordinary southerners more frequently wrote their autobiographies. Antebellum plantation mistresses silently recorded their life stories in their diaries, and escaped slaves wrote narratives detailing their journeys from South to North. Among antebellum diaries, *Mary Chesnut's Civil War* (edited by C. Vann Woodward, 1982) most elaborately details antebellum southern cultural life, landscape, social events, political controversy, and domestic relations. It is, as well, a moral critique by a southern aristocrat experiencing the social tumult and disruption of civil war. The diary exemplifies the cultural ambivalence of a South in crisis, a questioning of traditional social and moral behavior, of patriarchy and the slave system, and of the ever-apparent disparities between the myth of the leisured southern lady and the reality of her everyday life.

Chesnut's portrait of the antebellum South is enhanced by a reading of the hundreds of slave narratives that established the literary form for black autobiography in America. Most significant among them are the narratives of William Wells Brown (1847), Henry Bibb (1849), James W. C. Pennington (1849), Sojourner Truth (1850), Solomon Northup (1853), Samuel Ringgold Ward (1855), Booker T. Washington (1911), and the three-volume autobiography of Frederick Douglass (1845, 1855, 1881). The cultural foundation for the narratives was laid within the slave community, where the religion of the quarters provided a moral framework for criticizing the slave system. Each author condemns the institution of slavery for its inherent evil nature and its racism. At the same time, the narratives portray the heroic struggle of black families who battled forced separation, sale, and migration to maintain strong kinship networks. Committed to the betterment of the South and the advancement of their race, slave narrators present the evils of the slave system, not of its perpetrators. The slaves' unique heritage, their existence in bondage, their fusion of African and evangelical religion, and the strength of the slave community represent their vital contribution to southern autobiography.

More recent southern autobiographers are guided by a historical consciousness that fuses identity and community. They are acutely conscious of southern cultural distinctiveness, as created and maintained through individual lives. Five autobiographical masterworks exemplify the character of modern southern autobiography: Richard Wright's *Black Boy* (1945), William Alexander Percy's *Lanterns on the Levee* (1941), Katherine Du Pre Lumpkin's *The Making of a Southerner* (1946), Willie Morris's *North Toward Home* (1967), and Will Campbell's *Brother to a Dragonfly* (1977).

Richard Wright's autobiography condemns racism while describing the author's quest for human dignity and achievement as a writer. Family history and racial struggle provide the foundation for Wright's rebellious spirit, his distrust of authority, tradition, and the white world. Like antebellum slave narrators, Wright found it necessary to gain an education and then leave the South in order to escape danger and achieve his goals. He nevertheless retains a loyalty to the South and a sense of place that guide the development of his life. Nostalgically, he recalls the Mississippi landscape, the "yellow, dreaming waters of the Mississippi River and the verdant bluffs of Natchez," "the drenching hospitality in the pervading smell of sweet magnolias," and "the aura of lim-

itless freedom distilled from the rolling sweep of tall, green grass swaying and glinting in the summer sun." Wright left the South in order to understand it more clearly; and he wrote *Black Boy* so that others would join him in the struggle against racism.

William Alexander Percy and Katherine Du Pre Lumpkin, both of whom are descendants of slaveholders, wrestle with the assumptions behind racial inequality and sectional conflict, while placing their life histories within the context of southern history. Born in 1885 and 1897, respectively, each inherited some of the values and lifestyles that characterized the Old South. Both define their lives by describing a shared heritage: the settlement of the South, the importation of slaves, Reconstruction, the development and demise of the sharecropping system, the Depression, World War I, and the civil rights movement that emerged at the turn of the century. Percy's *Lanterns on the Levee* is the sensitive exposition of a southern aristocrat who feared the rule of the masses and was determined to confront the criticism of northern liberals in order to defend the cultural traditions of the Old South. Writing during a time when the nation viewed the South as poor, backward, and disease ridden, Percy describes an idyllic southern childhood, including his early exposure to religion, turtle soup, and crawfishing along the Mississippi River. Impressionistically, he outlines his life with Delta landscapes and history, friends and relations, cultural traditions, and his favorite stories. He discusses his confrontations with northern liberals when he attended Harvard, when he served in the army during World War I, and when northern journalists criticized as racist his decisions as chairman of the Greenville, Miss., Flood Relief Committee, after the disastrous flood of 1927. Thoughtfully and carefully, he rationalizes and attempts to justify white supremacy, manifesting a patience and tolerance for slow change that is absent from more recent southern autobiography.

Unlike Percy, Katherine Du Pre Lumpkin altered her racial attitudes as southern society changed and the incongruities of the old life, particularly between racism and Christian doctrine, became apparent to her. Her vivid descriptions of family and community portray southern culture in its most basic sense: a living record of voices and lives. Lumpkin struggles to overcome her bondage to slavery, transmitted to her through several generations of relatives and through acquaintances who taught her to accept the inequality between white and black. She represents well a changing South, and ultimately rejects racial inequality and discrimination, as well as "the entire peculiar set of ways which it allegedly justified."

Willie Morris's autobiography, *North Toward Home*, best illustrates how 20th-century southerners become acutely conscious of regional identity and southern ethnicity when they travel to the North. A Mississippi childhood shapes and informs the autobiography, as Morris describes his travels from Mississippi to Texas to New York. In New York he is stereotyped by northerners, black and white, who assume that he is backward, uneducated, unsophisticated, and racist. Thrust back upon himself and his past, he befriends other southerners up North: Richard Wright, Ralph Ellison, and William Styron. His conversations with them enable him to define his cultural identity and to formulate a clear definition of southern temperament, intellect, and imagination:

. . . easygoing conversation; the casual talk and the telling of stories, in the Southern verbal jam-session way; the sense of family and the past and people out of the past; the congenial social manner and mischievous laughter; the fondness of especial *detail* and the suspicion of more grandiose generalizations about human existence; the love of the American language in its accuracy and vividness and simplicity; the obsession with the sensual experience of America in all its extravagance and diversity; the love of animals and sports, of the outdoors and sour mash; the distrust in the face of provocation of certain manifestations of Eastern intellectualism . . . and a pointed tension just below the surface of things, usually controlled but always there.

Morris's autobiography provides evidence for the persistence of southern regional distinctiveness and the sense of place that defines southern lives.

Will Campbell's *Brother to a Dragonfly* exemplifies the interconnectedness a southerner perceives between self, family, morality, and community. Like Lillian Hellman's outstanding autobiography, *Pentimento* (1973), Campbell's autobiography views the author through a portrait of another. The lives of Will and Joe Campbell intertwine within the context of Mississippi social history. In the Campbell family, each brother's identity is assigned and unquestioned. Joe is the worker; Will is the preacher. Through tales of mischief, Will recalls their childhood: his nearly burning down an outhouse or fooling the WPA when they tested southern schoolchildren for hookworm. As youngsters, the brothers are intimate friends, but their lives diverge during adulthood after Will attends Yale and receives what Joe calls his "bachelor's of sophistication." When desegregation and civil rights become Will's mission during the 1950s, the brothers find themselves on opposite sides of racial issues. Joe increasingly adopts the role of the dragonfly—grasping for stability and security where there is none, becoming addicted to sedatives and amphetamines, and finally committing suicide. *Brother to a Dragonfly* describes two responses to the historical changes that affected 20th-century southern life: the Depression, World War II, integration, and the civil rights movement. Will and Joe Campbell's lives are "bound inextricably together . . . sometimes in a nearness approaching, surpassing illness. And sometimes so far apart that neither could hear the cry of the other."

Regardless of their race or social class, southern autobiographers define their lives within the shared context of southern history and culture. They present a realistic portrait of the South, while assessing and interpreting their relationship to the region, constructing a meaning through autobiography. One of the best-known recent autobiographies, Theodore Rosengarten's *All God's Dangers: The Life of Nate Shaw* (1974), was a landmark in using oral history to tell the life story of Alabama sharecropper Ned Cobb; it conveyed the experience of one who lived through the dramatic changes of the 20th-century South yet would not have written a traditional autobiography. Despite their individual diversity, the authors of autobiographies portray a shared re-

gional identity and cultural past, which have created the rich southern literary imagination. They indicate that South and North differ, in their landscapes, interaction patterns, traditions, and social conventions. Southern autobiographers differ from American autobiographers in general because of their historical consciousness. They stress the importance of family and community to identity and art, combining introspection, parable, and social critique to convey the cultural history of the South.

See also FOLKLIFE: / Cobb, Ned (Nate Shaw); MEDIA: / Morris, Willie; RELIGION: / Campbell, Will; WOMEN'S LIFE: / Chesnut, Mary Boykin

Ruth A. Banes
University of South Florida

Ruth A. Banes, in *Perspectives on the American South*, vol. 3, ed. James C. Cobb and Charles Reagan Wilson (1985); Cleanth Brooks, *Journal of Southern History* (February 1960); Will Campbell, *Brother to a Dragonfly* (1977); Harry Crews, *A Childhood: Biography of a Place* (1978); Frederick Douglass, *Life of an American Slave* (1845); Ellen Glasgow, *The Woman Within* (1954); Lillian Hellman, *Three* (1979); Zora Neale Hurston, *Dust Tracks on a Road* (1942); Katherine Du Pre Lumpkin, *The Making of a Southerner* (1946); Willie Morris, *North Toward Home* (1967); William Alexander Percy, *Lanterns on the Levee* (1941); John Shelton Reed, *One South: An Ethnic Approach to Regional Culture* (1982); Charles P. Roland, *Journal of Southern History* (February 1982); Lillian Smith, *Killers of the Dream* (1949); C. Vann Woodward, *The Burden of Southern History* (1960), ed., *Mary Chesnut's Civil War* (1981); Richard Wright, *Black Boy* (1937). ☆

Biography

||||||||||||||||||||||||||||

Almost 40 years ago, in his own study of Leonardo da Vinci, Sigmund Freud warned that biographers, for personal reasons, often choose heroes for their subjects. Out of their own "special affection," Freud wrote, "they then devote themselves to a work of idealization." Intolerant of anything in their subject's inner or outer life that smacks of human weakness or imperfection, biographers "then give us a cold, strange, ideal form instead of a man to whom we could feel distinctly related." Freud might have added that because the majority of biographers have been white men, so are the subjects of most biographies, South and North.

Two of the best examples of this kind of deification in southern biography are Thomas Jefferson and Robert E. Lee, both of whom have been the subjects of numerous biographies. The "Sage of Monticello" was truly an eloquent, erudite scholar and a brilliant statesman, but his chief biographers—James Parton, Douglas Southall Freeman, Merrill Peterson, and Dumas Malone—have glorified his accomplishments, minimized or denied his flaws, and canonized his name so that a demigod, not a man, emerges from the pages of their biographies. Not until 1974 and the appearance of Fawn Brodie's eye-opening psychobiography, *Thomas Jefferson: An Intimate History* (1974), did someone finally put flesh and bone on Jefferson. Brodie's Jefferson was ambivalent about love and power, slavery and revolution. Brodie's Jefferson was extremely virile and passionate and at the same time compulsively controlled. Most controversial of all, Brodie insisted that ru-

mors of Jefferson's longtime love affair with Sally Hemmings, one of his slaves, were indeed true. The vehemence with which Jefferson's white male biographers, particularly Peterson and Malone, have leaped to their subject's defense in this sensitive matter is evidence of a continued refusal to admit that Jefferson had even a particle of human frailty.

Jefferson's sanctified image has been matched only by that of Robert E. Lee. Of the two Virginians, Lee is the one who, for most southerners, evokes the lump in the throat, the tearful faraway gaze. This is partly because Lee's biographers have purposely created and perpetuated the Lee myth: the man of flawless character; the perfect son, husband, and father; the noble officer torn between love for Union and loyalty to Virginia; the gallant general and brilliant militarist defeated only by overwhelming odds. He exemplified all that was best in the Old South, in the vanquished Confederacy. For the white South, Lee was a saint.

Thomas Connelly, in *The Marble Man: Robert E. Lee and His Image in American Society* (1977), traces the fascinating history behind the creation of the Lee legend. During and immediately after the Civil War, Lee was only one of several celebrated Confederate military leaders. Others, like Thomas "Stonewall" Jackson, Joe Johnston, and Pierre T. Beauregard, were rivals for southern popularity. Lee even received criticism from his earliest biographers for his alleged mistakes at Gettysburg. But in the mid-1870s, shortly after Lee died, a group of Virginians led by General Jubal Early, one of Lee's corps commanders, took control of the Southern Historical Society and its influential papers. For personal reasons, their image of the Civil War centered upon Lee and the Virginia military theater. So they decided to raise Lee far above the other war heroes, silence any critics, and downplay or discredit the exploits of other Confederate generals. Connelly shows how every subsequent biography of Lee, including Douglas Southall Freeman's prizewinning four-volume work, has taken its cues from these far-from-disinterested Virginia men.

Connelly suggests that none of Lee's biographers tells much about the inner man or the drives that shaped his life. Like Freeman, they paint a superficial portrait of Lee, leaving out his humanity, giving readers a man more marble than flesh. The real Lee, the essential Lee, says Connelly, has been buried under the hero symbol. And though his own book is a history of Lee biographies, not a biography of Lee, Connelly's "Epilogue" raises the kind of questions about Lee—his troubled marriage, his ambivalence over slavery and secession, his morbidity and haunting sense of failure, his parochial vision of war—that should provide the meat for a new biography.

Jefferson was a statesman, Lee a military leader; politics and the military were traditional avenues to male power. Not surprisingly then, much of southern biography focuses on politicians and generals. Southerners, active in the American Revolution, dominated presidential politics for the first quarter of a century of the new nation and dominated federal politics until secession in 1861. So there has been no dearth of biographies about southern statesmen like George Washington, Jefferson, James Madison, James Monroe—all from Virginia—John C. Calhoun, and Andrew Jackson. Civil War leaders Jefferson Davis and Alexander Stephens have also had their biographers, although in the case of these two political foes, early biographies were acts of justification with the biographers carrying old fights into print. Southern fire-eaters like Robert Barnwell Rhett, William Lowndes Yancey, Edmund Ruffin, and James Henry Hammond have received less attention, although several new biographies have appeared, among them Drew Gilpin Faust's *James Henry Hammond and the Old South* (1982) and Betty L. Mitchell's *Edmund Ruffin: A Biography* (1981). And, of course, Robert E. Lee's comrades in arms—Longstreet, Jackson, Jeb Stuart, Beauregard, Johnston—have all been the subjects of essentially military biographies.

The usual subjects for southern biography have been white and male, and they have come, almost exclusively, from the upper classes. Those men not blessed with wealth and/or family position at birth, like Washington, Lee, and Hammond, had the good sense to marry wives who had been. But politics sometimes makes for strange bedfellows, so biographers have studied the lives of important rednecks like populist rebel Tom Watson, "Kingfish" Huey Long (who liked to masquerade as a redneck despite his respectable yeoman background), and rock-and-roll sensation Elvis Presley. C. Vann Woodward's *Tom Watson: Agrarian Rebel* (1938) and T. Harry Williams's Pulitzer Prize-winning *Huey Long* (1969) are fine examples of this kind of southern biography.

Whether biographers are discussing Jefferson's paradoxical feelings about slavery, Ruffin's unapologetic defense of the peculiar institution, or Watson's vicious race baiting, race itself has been a constant theme in southern biography. But distressingly few biographies have been written about blacks. Those that do exist have usually treated men working in one way or another toward black liberation and racial justice. Thus, in Stephen B. Oates's *The Fires of Jubilee: Nat Turner's Fierce Rebellion* (1935), readers witness the re-creation of the dramatic but short life of a black revolutionary, a slave convinced he is God's violent instrument for the salvation of his people. Benjamin Quarles and Nathan Huggins, biographers of runaway slave and abolitionist Frederick Douglass, reveal a man just as dedicated to black freedom but convinced, at first, that this freedom could be won through nonviolence. Booker T. Washington's biographers, Louis Harlan and Bernard Weisberger, demonstrated his commitment to racial self-improvement through accommodation to segregation. And finally, Oates's recent *Let the Trumpet Sound: The Life of Martin Luther King, Jr.* (1982) vividly connects the line of history that exists among these four black leaders. Like Turner, King was nurtured by his family and encouraged to feel he was somebody special, a Moses for his people. Like Washington, he was committed to improvement for his race, but unlike the great founder of Tuskegee, he was not satisfied with segregated "racial uplift" programs. With Douglass, he believed in peaceful means to conquer racism and thus embraced Gandhian techniques of nonviolent resistance in order to combat racial oppression and social injustice.

If few biographies exist on southern black men, there are fewer still on black women. Southern white women have fared better with the recent emphasis on women's history, but not much. Biographies of southern white women, like those of white men, usually deal with the concept of honor, because, as his-

torian Bertram Wyatt-Brown argues in *Southern Honor: Ethics and Behavior in the Old South* (1982), honor was the psychological and social linchpin of the antebellum South. For southern white men, honor required "both riches and a body of menials"; for white women, honor required sexual innocence and a childlike meekness. This "cult of true womanhood" touched women North and South, but southern men made a fetish out of extolling the purity and excellence of southern womanhood and, by extension, southern civilization. Biographers of southern women have shown how their subjects accept, reject, or modify this feminine domestic ideal.

Gerda Lerner's *The Grimké Sisters from South Carolina* (1970) recounts the lives of Sarah and Angelina Grimké, daughters of a South Carolina planter, who refused to accept meekly the South's peculiar institution of slavery and moved to the North to become the first salaried female abolitionists and the first American women to speak in public. These two women, who were the epitome of piety and purity—both were Quakers—violated the sacred cannons of southern honor to perform what they believed was God's own work.

Elizabeth Muhlenfeld's portrait of Mary Boykin Chesnut reveals a South Carolina woman much like the Grimké sisters in class background and wealth. She, too, hated slavery, calling it a "monstrous institution," not out of any sympathy for the slaves, but because of the plight of white women whose honor depended on ignoring evidence of miscegenation in their own families. Unlike the Grimké sisters, Chesnut never left the South, and she became an ardent Confederate. Yet she, too, spurned the southern feminine ideal. In antebellum days this educated, intelligent, but childless woman often felt like a useless ornament; in the postwar period, she took charge of the family plantation.

Nancy Milford's biography *Zelda* (1970), the tragic story of Zelda Sayre Fitzgerald, gives the reader a 20th-century twist on the 19th-century feminine ideal of southern white womanhood. Zelda Sayre, a Montgomery, Ala., belle who lived life in the fast lane, rejected the innocent passivity of the "true woman" to boldly embrace the modern "New Woman": the flapper who used her good looks and sexual allure to get what she wanted from men. But this new brand of femininity was equally perverse, even schizophrenic, and Zelda finally succumbed.

Hero worship—or heroine worship—may be a kind of secular religion in America, South and North. Individuals like Washington, Jefferson, and Lee have taken on an almost Christlike aura, and to suggest that such men, such symbols of sectional and national righteousness, had blemishes and complex motivations like other human beings frequently raises more than a few hackles. But to deify human beings, no matter how accomplished and worthy, sacrifices truth to illusion in biography. To limit southern biography to great white men would sacrifice the richness, variety, and wholeness of southern history. Fortunately the many fine, probing biographies of southerners, male and female, black and white, that have appeared in recent times promise to make Freud's warnings increasingly unnecessary by giving readers life-size, not larger-than-life, subjects to whom they can feel more than "distantly related."

See also BLACK LIFE: / Douglass, Frederick; King, Martin Luther, Jr.; Turner, Nat; Washington, Booker T.; HISTORY AND MANNERS: / Davis, Jefferson; Hammond, James Henry; Jackson, Stonewall; Jefferson, Thomas; Lee, Robert E.; Madison, James; Stuart, Jeb; MEDIA: / Freeman, Douglas Southall; MUSIC: / Presley, Elvis; POLITICS: / Calhoun, John C.; Jackson, Andrew; Long, Huey; Watson, Thomas; SCIENCE AND MEDICINE: / Ruffin, Edmund; WOMEN'S LIFE: / Chesnut, Mary Boykin

Betty L. Mitchell
Southeastern Massachusetts
University

Black Literature
||||||||||||||||||||||||||||||||||||||

See BLACK LIFE: Literature, Black

Civil War in Literature
||||||||||||||||||||||||||||||||||||||||||||||||||||||

One of the anomalies of the American literary imagination has been its inability—in spite of the vast amount of ink consumed in the effort—to derive a major poem, novel, or play from the central crisis in the national existence. This failure seems even more curious because one of the prominent characteristics of the southern literary mind, at least of the white literary mind, has been the compulsive remembrance of the Civil War. But the southern writer—and this would appear to be a primary reason for the want of a southern *War and Peace*—has been less concerned to reconstruct the actual time of the struggle than to recount the consequent loss of the antebellum southern culture and, in the response to this loss, the creation of a postbellum culture of survival.

Reaching its first full-fledged expression in *Marse Chan: A Tale of Old Virginia* (1884) by Thomas Nelson Page and its most profound and complex expression in *The Sound and the Fury* (1929) and *Absalom, Absalom!* (1936) by William Faulkner, the enactment of this drama has found a continuing, significant, if attenuated, expression in novels as recent as those of Walker Percy, especially *The Moviegoer* (1961) and *The Last Gentleman* (1966), and of William Styron, notably *Sophie's Choice* (1979).

Even the earliest southern writing about the Civil War, in the period from the firing on Fort Sumter to the final surrender, produced no treatment of the war comparable to Walt Whitman's *Drum-Taps* (1865) or Herman Melville's *Battle-Pieces and Aspects of the War* (1866). In contrast to these limited but distinctive representations of marching and fighting, the best southern poet of the time, Henry Timrod, wrote celebratory poems about the birth and mission of the Confederacy—"Ethnogenesis," "The Cotton Bowl," "Carolina," "A Cry to Arms"—and reached his highest poetic achievement with the exquisite classical "Ode," written to be sung at a memorial service in Charleston's Magnolia Cemetery for the dead of a lost war. On a clearly lesser level of literary achievement, the years of the Confederacy found their voice in "Maryland, My Maryland" by James Ryder Randall; "Music in Camp," "Burial of Latané," and "Lee to the Rear" by John R. Thompson, editor of the *Southern Literary Messenger* from 1847 to 1860; and "Little Giffen," a popular sentimental ballad about a Confederate soldier by Francis Orray Ticknor. In the immediate aftermath of the war Father Abram Joseph Ryan became the poetic spokesman of the Lost Cause in such banal yet influential effusions as "The Conquered Banner" and "The Sword of Robert Lee."

The most effective literature of the Confederacy remained largely unknown for a generation or longer in journals, diaries, and letters. Among the most valuable of the contemporary records are those by Sarah Morgan Dawson (1842–99), Kate Stone (1841–1907), and Mary Boykin Chesnut (1823–86). Published in 1913 under the title *A Confederate Girl's Diary*, Dawson's account of the war years as she witnessed them in Louisiana's capital city of Baton Rouge and in New Orleans is informed by a perceptive eye for detail and a lively intelligence; brought out in 1955 under the title *Brokenburn: The Journal of Kate Stone*, Stone's record of life on a northern Louisiana plantation and later, after the flight of her family from federal invaders, in the east Texas town of Tyler, is also marked by a penchant for realistic detail.

The Dawson and Stone works are surpassed in both literary and historical importance by the account of the Charleston aristocracy during the Confederate period by Mary Boykin Chesnut. First published in 1905 and again in 1949 as *A Diary from Dixie*, Chesnut's work took on a new significance when C. Vann Woodward, after careful study of the manuscripts, concluded that the diary was written not in the 1860s but between 1881 and 1884, its basis being a journal Chesnut had kept intermittently in the era of the Confederacy. Published in 1981 as *Mary Chesnut's Civil War*, Woodward's edition of the presumed diary shows that it is essentially an incipient novel. Yet while the motive to make her journal into a work of art reduces Chesnut's reliability as a factual witness, Woodward observes, it enhances her depiction of "the chaos and complexity of a society at war" and endows individual lives across the whole Confederate social spectrum with dramatic reality. A similar power to invest the age of the Civil War with graphic reality emanates from the extensive correspondence of the Jones family of Liberty County, Ga. As collected and edited by Robert Manson Myers in *The Children of Pride: A True Story of Georgia and the Civil War* (1972), the Jones family documents constitute the most remarkable epistolary record yet discovered of a southern family in the years immediately before, during, and after the Civil War. Possessing a literary quality conferred both by well-educated minds and by a deep feeling for the drama of life, the Jones letters belong on the shelf of the best southern writing.

In some cases the southern experience of the Civil War as recorded in memoirs by Confederate army officers also deserves a place on the literary shelf, for example, *Destruction and Reconstruction: Personal Experiences of the Late War* (1879) by Richard "Dick" Taylor, *War Reminiscences and Stuart Cavalry Campaigns* (1887) by John Singleton Mosby, and "Lee in Pennsylvania" (in *Annals of the War Written by Leading Participants*, 1879) by James Longstreet. Of greater significance, however, is "The History of a Campaign That Failed" (*Century Magazine*, 1885), a quasi-fictional memoir in which Mark Twain, a private in a hastily organized volunteer Confederate unit in Missouri, describes his enlistment, brief service, and desertion. By implication a profound questioning of the meaning of war as a social institution, "The History of a Campaign That Failed" is unique in southern writing about the Civil War.

Except insofar as *A Connecticut Yankee in King Arthur's Court* (1889) can be interpreted as a reflection on the Civil War, Mark Twain did not use the war as a subject for his stories and novels. In fact, although Sidney Lanier in his hastily composed *Tiger-Lilies* (1867) attempted to use his war experiences as the basis of a novel critical of war, southern postbellum fiction largely followed the romantic pattern established by John Esten Cooke in *Surry of Eagle's Nest* (1866) and *Mohun* (1869). Persisting well into the 20th century in numerous, now-forgotten popular novels, the romantic mode is illustrated in *The Cavalier* (1901) and *Kincaid's Battery* (1908) by George Washington Cable; by the early 20th century Cable had fallen away from the realism of his first Civil War novel, *Dr. Sevier* (1884), in which he had announced his sympathy with the antislavery motive and provoked the criticism that eventually drove him from the South. Cable's early realism was in a sense picked up by Ellen Glasgow in *The Battle-Ground* (1902), one of the novels that would eventually comprise a "social history" of Virginia, in which she hoped to rectify a failing of the southern literary imagination that Chesnut had felt but had lacked the literary sophistication to define, namely a "deficiency in blood and irony."

The rectifying irony in Glasgow's attitude toward the Confederacy pales in comparison with the ironic scope of the southern literary vision in the decade following World War I. At the end of the decade a southern woman writer, Evelyn Scott, published a large, panoramic novel, boldly experimental in technique, entitled *The Wave* (1929). Intended by Scott to be a "progression" toward her final design, the writing of "a comédie humaine of America," this novel, now unjustly neglected, may be the most ambitious attempt to embrace the Civil War in its totality. For most readers the image of the war is more convincingly presented in a still-famous novel that, in its mingling of southern piety and irony, is probably a better novel than serious literary critics have generally said, *Gone with the Wind* (1936) by Margaret Mitchell. From the standpoint of literary art the Civil War is more enduringly presented in Faulkner's only novel that focuses on the war years, *The Unvanquished* (1938). This work employs a family and community situation as a microcosm of the conflict, as do *The Forge* (1931) by T. S. Stribling, *None Shall Look Back* (1937) by Caroline Gordon, and *The Fathers* (1938) by Allen Tate. *Shiloh* (1952), by Shelby Foote, strikingly presents the war through a few selected participants in one battle. But Foote's achievement in *Shiloh* is minor compared with his success in his massive three-volume *The Civil War: A Narrative History* (1958, 1963, 1974). A masterpiece of the art of narrative, this work has been compared in its sustained narrative skill and power to the writings of Thucydides, Gibbon, Clarendon, and Henry Adams. Walker Percy has called it the "American Iliad." Foote's triumph in historical narrative underlines the fact that no southern writer has written a battlefield story possessing the classic quality of Stephen Crane's *The Red Badge of Courage* (1895). The southern novelist has been better at creating plot situations and characters that embody the long, haunted aftermath of the Civil War, as in Faulkner's *The Sound and the Fury* and *Absalom, Absalom!*

The direct use of the Civil War as setting and theme in southern poetry has never been more pronounced than it was in the time of Timrod and Ryan. One of the most noted poems of the 20th-century Southern Literary Renaissance, "Ode to the Confederate Dead" (the first version of this appeared in 1926), by Allen Tate, employs the dead soldiers of the South not primarily as defenders of a historical society but as symbols of a capacity for chivalric action that has been lost in the fragmented, narcissistic society of the present century. Critical of Tate for using the Confederate dead merely as symbolic, Donald Davidson composed "The Army of Tennessee," a poem in the conventional heroic manner, but he never published it. His finest Civil War poem, "Lee in the Mountains"—a long meditation by the defeated general projected through a modified stream-of-consciousness technique—is a part of the literature associated with the southern culture of survival.

See also BLACK LIFE: Literature, Black; HISTORY AND MANNERS: Civil War; MYTHIC SOUTH: / Mitchell, Margaret; WOMEN'S LIFE: / Chesnut, Mary Boykin

Lewis P. Simpson
Louisiana State University

Daniel Aaron, *The Unwritten War: American Writers and the Civil War* (1962); Robert A. Lively, *Fiction Fights the Civil War* (1957); Edmund Wilson, *Patriotic Gore: Studies in the Literature of the American Civil War* (1962). ☆

Folklore in Literature

||||||||||||||||||||||||||||||||||||||||||||||||||

With the exception of Native American lore, folklore, like language and literature, came to this country as part of the cultural baggage of the various waves of its settlers. In the South its sources were mainly British, African, and French, with important admixtures of Spanish and German, and touches of almost everything else.

From the beginning, new experiences and a new environment eroded this imported lore and reshaped it to new purposes. Erosion and adaptation may be rapid, but the emergence of a new folklore, like the development of a distinctive and significant literature, is always slow. It was slowed further in the United States by increasing literacy, mobility, urbanization, homogenization, and the influence of the mass media. Forces at work in the South, however, and not alone its geography and history, reduced the effect of such inhibiting factors while encouraging the evolution of a southern folklore and easing its incorporation into its literature. The result was to enhance the regional flavor of southern letters.

If the Puritans of New England were a people of the book, then southerners harkened enthusiastically to pentecostal tongues—and to the silvery words of their politicians at the hustings, the tall tales of their hunters and riverboatmen, the animal stories of their slaves, the brags, songs, and sayings that were part of the life of what came to be folk communities. Mark Twain charmed audiences all over the world because he knew from his memories of folklife that the way the tale is told is as important as the tale itself. Style, the manner in which things are said and done, was prized, whether on a bear hunt in the backwoods or at a Mardi Gras ball. In short, the living word and the performance, the marrow of folklore, were likewise the marrow of southern culture.

The most obvious feature distinguishing the South from the rest of the United States was its racial composition and the resulting historical developments provoked by profound sectional difference. Like others who crossed the Atlantic, Africans brought with them their myths and their music, their beliefs and their words. Folklore travels in the heart of humankind and therefore had the power to survive even the horrors of the middle passage and the merciless process of annihilation of African traditions that took place upon arrival. The archsurvivor, Brer Rabbit, was born in Africa.

People forget their victories and virtues but never their defeats and sins. Thus, southerners were hypersensitive to the past, for it included racial repression and the loss, on their own precious soil, of the bloodiest war in American history, followed by a decade of military occupation. Original sins and lost causes can be the cement of a culture and the germ of its folklore and literature.

As the North raced into the Industrial Age, the South seemed to stand still. Its folk traditions remained in place. Such southern writers as George Washington Cable, Joel Chandler Harris, Mary Noailles Murfree, and Charles Chesnutt—local colorists for whom folklore was a vital element—won national recognition. From the viewpoint of the Gilded Age, the postbellum South was backward. It valued old ways more than new dollars. The South's literary success may be attributed to its reluctance to deny its past. It refused to run away from its history, traditions, and reverence for form.

Folklore in literature is not folklore in the raw. Certainly a folktale told in its natural habitat is art of its own kind, but literary art is another kind of performance. The explorer John Lawson, who included folk materials in his descriptions of the interior of Carolina, was a sophisticated writer using what he found to render his account vivid or incorporating what he saw and heard because it was too good to pass up. The contributors of frontier sketches to the *Spirit of the Times*, a popular sportsman's journal in the antebellum period, were mostly lettered men—doctors, lawyers, college presidents, army officers—with a taste for the earthiness and oddities of folklore, and a talent, not untrained, for storytelling. Professional writers who employed folklore, such as William Gilmore Simms, bent it to an immediate purpose. Even such classic American writers as Edgar Allan Poe, Mark Twain, and William Faulkner were less concerned with folklore as such than with the ways it could serve their art.

John Lawson's *New Voyage to Carolina* (1709) exemplifies one of the earliest genres of southern literature, the travel account. He describes a thousand-mile journey from Charleston to the foothills of the Blue Ridge Mountains with a ready eye for the inhabitants' customs and lore, which he sets down with gusto and exploits with literary skill. Thus, he provides a lively description of Indian deer hunters who disguise themselves so perfectly with antlers and skins that they sometimes shoot each other. Lawson's method here is to record a curious hunting practice and then dramatize it with a folk story. Or, he brings a gritty account of starved and abused Indian dogs to a climax with a literary application of a folk remedy: "It is an infalliable Cure for Sore Eyes, even to see an *Indian's* Dog fat." Or, he illustrates the prodigious power of rattlesnakes by citing their ability "to charm Squirrels . . . in such a way that they run directly into their Mouths." Lawson also contributes to the emergence of indigenous southern legend as he moves from an authentic history of the Lost Colony and speculation about its fate to a local folktale: "I cannot forbear inserting here a pleasant story that passes for an uncontested Truth among the Inhabitants of this Place; which is, that the Ship, which brought the first colonies, does often appear among them, under sail, which they call Sir Walter Raleigh's Ship." Paul Green, whose plays drew upon southern lore and legend, would use this material for his historical drama *The Lost Colony* (1937).

Edgar Allan Poe and William Gilmore Simms, the major professional writers of the antebellum period, each used folklore in a different, though characteristic, way. Poe saw himself as an alienated poet, ideally the resident of a dreamland "Out of space—Out of time," and his settings and sources are usually consistent with this vision. "The Gold Bug" is a notable exception. His source is the folk motif of the buried treasure, particularized in the widespread legends of Captain Kidd. His locale is Sullivan's Island, which he knew well from his military service at Fort Moultrie on the South Carolina coast. His characters, if not southern folk types, are southern stereotypes—William Legrand, the withdrawn, decayed aristocrat, and Jupiter, the faithful, comic, superstitious black servant. Even his narrator is familiar, a rational man doubting the sanity of the friend whose summons he answers. (There is much here reminiscent of the timeless "The Fall of the House of Usher." Is this, too, within the context of southern folklore?) For the black servant, the gold bug that he and his master find is an object of superstitious dread, and Poe uses it for minstrel-show effects. "I'm berry sartain dat Massa Will bin bit somewhere about de head by dat goole-bug," Jupiter tells the narrator. The rational faculties of Legrand, an amateur scientist, have been superseded by his fancies—his mind, as the narrator comes to believe, "infected with some of the innumerable Southern superstitions about money buried." These "Southern superstitions" are validated by the recovery of the pirate treasure. Poe's concern is the balance between rational method, epitomized in Legrand's solution of a cryptogram, and the irrational, here represented by a romantic legend and the inexplicable force of superstition. In "The Gold Bug" folklore is associated with poetry and revery and is a way of knowing what surpasses rational methodologies and precedes their application.

In *The Yemassee* (1835), one of his romances of the southern frontier, William Gilmore Simms expands Lawson's account of the rattlesnake's fabulous powers into a flamboyant set piece. The heroine, a "peerless forest flower," goes into the wilderness to meet her lover, an English officer. Entranced by the beauties of nature, she is captivated "by a star-like shining glance—a subtle ray, that shot out from the circle of green leaves." She is dazzled by its "dreadful beauty" and then transfixed with terror when she realizes that what she sees is the "fascinating gleam" in the eyes of a rattlesnake. As the snake slithers toward her and coils to strike, it is shot through the head by the arrow of her lover's Indian ally. Simms, in a footnote, doubts the rattler's "power over persons" but claims to have heard of "numberless instances," a sufficient

number, in any case, "for the romancer." Not given to subtleties, the sexual implications of his serpent in Eden would have surely surprised him. Simms's end was melodrama, and a folk belief was his means.

In 1870, the year he died, Simms wrote a North Carolina mountain sketch for *Harper's*, "How Sharp Snaffles Got His Wife and His Capital." It is essentially a tall tale, told at a hunting camp by a backwoods trickster whose nickname, "Big Lie," indicates his qualities as a hunter, sharp operator, and storyteller. His performance, much appreciated by his backwoods peers and the gentleman hunters who comprise his audience, is presented within a descriptive frame by one of the latter. Such separation between the genteel observer who transcribes the tale and the folk artist who tells it may be a way of maintaining a distance of generation, caste, race, or political persuasion, but always a factor for the southern writer is the art of the performance itself. This was not entirely an aesthetic matter. In southern culture, the way a thing is done is significant. Simms himself, in this story, was reaching back to the frontier humor of the Old Southwest, with its folkloric situations, in order to recover his own literary capital, the northern readership he had lost during the sectional conflict; and he reached forward toward the emerging local color movement, likewise seamed with folklore.

In Mark Twain's *The Adventures of Huckleberry Finn* (1885) identifiable elements of folklore give this masterpiece its flavor as they serve complex purposes, and the folklife of the Mississippi Valley, broadly speaking, provides physical and moral texture. The role of the runaway slave, Jim, is evidence of this. Poe's Jupiter, with his superstitious gibberish about the gold bug, is little more than a comic stereotype. But Mark Twain's Jim, a comparable character at the outset, becomes in the end not simply a rounded character, a stereotype humanized, but the spiritual center of the book. To accomplish this transformation (as well as to move his plot, enhance verisimilitude, and add humorous touches), Mark Twain uses superstition.

Superstitions, by definition, are the supernatural beliefs that some disdain but others accept. At the beginning of the novel, Tom Sawyer and Huck to amuse themselves play upon Jim's belief in witches. Jim also believes in ghosts, weather signs, omens, and dreams. On the river with Huck, he becomes a free and living man, and when he puts his superstitions to work, they become effectual. This natural world has a place for the supernatural, and Jim's superstitions save his own life and Huck's and ultimately make possible Huck's spiritual salvation as well. In two other great books, *Adventures of Tom Sawyer* (1876) and *Life on the Mississippi* (1883), southern folklife also functions memorably. Seeking a cure for warts in a graveyard

Scene from The Reivers, *the 1969 film made from William Faulkner's novel*

at midnight, as the folk remedy requires, is the occasion that initiates the plot of *Tom Sawyer. Life on the Mississippi* contains the classic description of the folklife of raftsmen, including their songs and dances, brags and fights, beliefs and stories. It is a genre painting, both realistic and idealized.

Like Mark Twain, William Faulkner embodied within his southern particularity a moral depth and artistry that brought him the acclaim of the world. Faulkner's novella *The Bear* (1942) is a capstone to a series of earlier, major works that emerged from his response to the southern cultural experience. Its motif, a ceremonial hunt of a totemic animal, is universal, but the version he adopts derives from American Indian lore and, more immediately, from countless stories of bear hunts in backwoods oral tradition. Stories of this kind had already made their way into antebellum popular culture through the media of the Davy Crockett almanacs and the sporting journals. Thomas Bangs Thorpe's "The Big Bear of Arkansas" (1841), a case in point, is essentially a literary creation originating in southern hunting lore. So is *The Bear.*

The Bear, like *Huckleberry Finn*, is an initiation story in a pristine natural setting. Sam Fathers, "son of a negro slave and a Chickasaw chief," is teacher and surrogate parent of young Ike McCaslin, in an analogue to the relationship of Huck and Jim. His knowledge of woodcraft, which he imparts to Ike, has moral validity, like Jim's old beliefs. In the end Ike learns how to hunt Old Ben, the legendary bear, and how to "relinquish" his quarry and his heritage. Though it contains specific folk elements (e.g., the hunt motif), *The Bear* transcends them and emphasizes folklife, the totality of the culture, rather than its details. This transcendence and extension, even as they detach *The Bear* from its folkloric detail, bring folklore and literature into closer proximity and make their southernness universal.

Faulkner moved beyond folklore at a pivotal time for both folklore and southern tradition generally. There are southern-style ironies in this movement to a broader context: the irony of lost causes won and regrets for the loss of old ways assuaged. Ironically, southern literature has attained its greatest eminence at a time when the South becomes more and more like the rest of the country, and its folklore, a prime source of its distinction, withers under the increasing pressure of literacy. Ultimately, at its best, literature absorbs folklore, and in this way assures its survival.

See also FOLKLORE articles

Hennig Cohen
University of Pennsylvania

Gene Bluestein, *The Voice of the Folk: Folklore and American Literary Theory* (1972); Daniel Hoffman, *Form and Fable in American Fiction* (1965); Bruce A. Rosenberg, in *Interrelations of Literature*, ed. Jean-Pierre Barricelli and Joseph Gibaldi (1982); Constance Rourke, *American Humor: A Study of the National Character* (1931). ☆

Humor
||||||||||||||||

Southern humor, like much of the best southern writing in general, has been boisterous and physical, often grotesque, and generally realistic. On the whole, it has no doubt been better re-

ceived and more appreciated outside the region than in it. Mark Twain, a frontier writer in essence but joyfully proclaimed as southern these days, was recognized and lionized first by the Brahmins of Boston and the London literary establishment. And William Faulkner was certainly a puzzle to the people of Oxford in his time. Writing has never been a particularly admired occupation in the South, and its comic writers, as well as the most perceptive serious writers, have singled out aspects of southern culture that many southerners would sooner forget. This combination has produced what many southern readers would no doubt characterize as a literature of betrayal. But adversity can be beneficial to an artist, furnishing the stone of resistance against which his or her talent may be honed. A hostile climate is frequently the best one a writer could ask for—especially a comic writer.

Southern humor fits fairly well into the chronological framework of four periods usually applied to American humor generally: (1) 1830 to 1860, (2) 1860 to 1925, (3) 1925 to 1945, and (4) 1945 to the present.

1830 to 1860. This was the most energetic and inventive period for purely comic writing in the history of southern letters, if not the most respectable. It saw the establishment of the major comic stereotypes that would, it seems, serve southern humor more or less forever. The dominant figure was the frontiersman, and he is the literary ancestor of the redneck-hillbilly who is still around. In this period the black minstrel also appeared. Of the writers who can be classified as primarily comic (the southwestern yarnspinners), the best were Augustus Baldwin Longstreet (*Georgia Scenes*), William Tappan

Thompson (the Major Jones character), Thomas Bangs Thorpe (*The Big Bear of Arkansas*), Johnson J. Hooper (the Simon Suggs character), and George Washington Harris (the Sut Lovingood character). All these writers were regarded as subliterary (by themselves as well as by others), and most were published outside the South, many in Porter's *Spirit of the Times*—a New York periodical. Generally these writers carefully separated themselves from the disreputable characters of their sketches by using an "envelope" structure, in which a literate narrator introduced the illiterate character who told the story. Hooper and Harris stand a bit closer to their characters than discretion would seem to dictate—a fact that Hooper, at least, later regretted. But there was always a certain amount of ambivalence in the attitude of these writers toward their disreputable "Suts" and "Simons," and at times the characters undoubtedly function as alter egos for the proper men who undertook to describe their antics. In any event, Harris was an authentic comic genius—recognized in his own day by Edgar Allan Poe and imitated later by an appreciative William Faulkner.

1860 to 1925. Mark Twain, though more western than southern, was the foremost figure of this period. In his own day he was classified as a literary comedian and local colorist, very closely related to such writers as Artemus Ward and Bret Harte, and it took time for the genius of his combination of humor and local color to be recognized as serious literature—which it was. Of the pure literary comedians—"phunny phellows"—Bill Arp is probably the outstanding southern example, but for the most part these comic writers tended to be western and midwestern. After the

Civil War, the general taste of the region ran strongly to plantation memories of moonlight and magnolias, and the writer who could combine a reverence for the good old days with chaste and genial humor was absolutely assured of success. That was the formula developed to such good effect by Joel Chandler Harris in his Uncle Remus stories.

1920–1945. This was the golden age of southern writing, the time of the Southern Renaissance. The best southern writers began to combine serious literary purpose with profoundly comic elements. Southern humor—at least that written by southerners—would henceforth be a leaven in the hard brown bread of literature. William Faulkner and Erskine Caldwell were among the best practitioners of art, but an intrinsic comic element can be found in the work of nearly all southern writers of the first rank. There were many purely comic artists in the years between the wars, for this was also a golden age for American comedy—in magazines, in films, and on the radio. But the dominant influence on written humor was the *New Yorker* magazine, and although not many of its writers were New Yorkers, none of them were southern. In motion pictures and on the radio, southern characters did appear, but as often as not they were little more than parodies of existing southern types.

1945 to the Present. Flannery O'Connor, Eudora Welty, and Walker Percy are among the premier writers of the South in this period, and they are all writers with a highly developed comic talent. All of them are much more than comic, but comedy is, again, an intrinsic element in their writing. In popular works by comic southern writers, such as William Price Fox's *Southern Fried*, Guy Owen's *The Ballad of the Flim-*

Flam Man, and Mac Hyman's *No Time for Sergeants*, the humorous stereotypes continue to be what they had been before—poor whites (hillbilly, redneck, and rural) and blacks. On television, *The Real McCoys*, *The Andy Griffith Show*, and *The Beverly Hillbillies* have enjoyed considerable success.

It is something of a truism that the American South is a unique region in America. Visitors remark that it is more like a foreign country than any other area contained within the national boundaries. And while American writers are still producing plenty of comedy tied to ethnic minority groups, the South remains the only *region* that still has identifiable comic types associated with it—Texans and hillbillies are notable in this respect, and the "grits" jokes of Carter's presidency are proof that the rural South still has a strong identity. The South seems to be the only section of the country that outsiders still consider fair game for comic jibes—a fact noted by Roy Blount, Jr., in *Crackers*.

But the uniqueness of the region is giving way to the inexorable leveling process of the culture. And comedians like Jerry Clower, television programs like *Hee Haw*, and the moonshine-car-smashing films of Burt Reynolds constitute something like a self-parody of former southern comic types. Russell Baker, Terry Southern, Tom Wolfe, and Hunter S. Thompson are all southern by birth, but their writing, like the fiction of John Barth, Donald Barthelme, and Barry Hannah, transcends regional boundaries. The best comic writing is being done by southern writers who cannot be identified as southern in any superficial way. It would be premature, if not witless, to predict the demise of southern humor. But that it seems to be in a period of transition—like every other aspect of the culture—seems undeniable.

See also FOLKLIFE: Storytelling; / Clower, Jerry; HISTORY AND MANNERS: / Gardner, Dave; MEDIA: Comic Strips; / *Andy Griffith Show*; *Beverly Hillbillies*; Grizzard, Lewis; Reynolds, Burt

Mark Steadman
Clemson University

Jesse Bier, *The Rise and Fall of American Humor* (1968); Walter Blair, *Native American Humor* (1960); Sarah Blancher Cohen, ed., *Comic Relief: Humor in Contemporary American Literature* (1978); Wade Hall, *The Smiling Phoenix: Southern Humor from 1865 to 1914* (1965); M. Thomas Inge, *The Frontier Humorists: Critical Views* (1975); Raven I. McDavid, Jr., and Walter Blair, eds., *The Mirth of a Nation: America's Great Dialect Humor* (1983); Constance Rourke, *American Humor: A Study of National Character* (1931); Louis D. Rubin, Jr., *The Comic Imagination in American Literature* (1973). ☆

New Critics
||||||||||||||||||||||||||||||||

John Crowe Ransom long ago complained that no one had defined what the critic's responsibilities were. Criticism, he said in 1937, was in the hands of amateurs who had insufficient instruction to prepare them to perform the important function for which they were responsible. The 20th century, Ransom believed, had produced some of the most important poetry in the history of English literature, but it was difficult verse and no one made it available to the general reader. The poets and the philosophers should be culture's critics, but the modern poet's understanding of his craft was "intuitive rather than dialectical" and the philosopher's "theory is very general and his acquaintance with the particular work of art is not persistent and intimate." Only the college teachers of literature were left, and "they are learned but not critical men." They "spend a lifetime compiling the data of literature" and yet rarely "commit themselves" to a literary judgment. Criticism, Ransom concluded, must be precise and systematic; it must be "the collective and sustained effort of learned persons"; adequately trained persons in the universities should do it.

Almost as if on cue, the year following Ransom's challenge two of his former students, Cleanth Brooks and Robert Penn Warren, who had become university teachers of literature, published a new approach to the teaching and reading of poetry, one that they had been using in mimeograph form in their classes. It was *Understanding Poetry* (1938), which in the subsequent 20 years went through four editions and left a lasting impression on the way poetry is taught and read. Rather than disseminating facts of the authors' lives or historical and cultural information about the times in which they lived, it demonstrated that if a poem is to reveal its unique quality, it must be read purely as poetry and not as history, biography, philosophy, or anything else. Rather than dealing with the kind of questions that lead to vague, impressionistic interpretations of a poem—the kind included in most textbooks of the time—*Understanding Poetry* offered concrete, inductive analyses of some 200 poems, demonstrations of how poems should be read, and questions that stated explicitly and exactly the "approach" to

literature upon which the book was based. This approach is explained in a lengthy and detailed "Letter to the Teacher": "(1) Emphasis should be focused on the poem as poem; (2) Discussion of all poems should be specific, concrete and inductive; (3) A poem, if it is to be fully understood, must always be treated as an organic system of relationships and never thought to be included in one or more isolated lines or parts."

This book, followed by *Understanding Fiction*, also by Brooks and Warren (1943), and *Understanding Drama*, by Brooks and Robert B. Heilman (1945), surely contributed to the improved audiences for creative writers to which Ransom referred. The critical principles in these books came from the theoretical criticism of Ransom, as well as from that of his friends, associates, and former students. "Poetry," Ransom explained in *The World's Body* (1938), "is the kind of knowledge by which we must know that which we cannot know otherwise." Its intent is not to "idealize" the world, but to help its readers to "realize" it, to know its "common actuals," its "concrete particularities" (what he calls "the world's body"), which science, social science, and philosophy have attempted to reduce to abstract principles. The world that poetry reveals is not one of absolute innocence, one in which a reader should expect "to receive the fragrance of the roses on the world's first morning." The poetic world is a postscientific world, one that is revealed through both intellect and emotion. Only poetry can show the "body and solid substance of the world, that which has retired into the fullness of memory." With a combination, however, of image and idea, figure and statement, the poet can "construct the fullness of poetry, which is counterpart to the world's fullness."

In *The New Critics* (1941), the book that gave the movement under discussion its name, Ransom sought to identify the cognitive function of poetry by examining the way in which it differs from prose discourse. Allen Tate, like Ransom, was concerned with the unique nature of poetic discourse and the specific order of knowledge it contains. He agreed with Ransom that the poet attempts to reconstitute reality, not to make some comment about it. One of the first betrayers of literature, Tate said, was Matthew Arnold, who "extended the hand of fellowship to the scientist" and tried to make literature and religion synonymous. I. A. Richards followed Arnold's lead by suggesting that the significance of poetry resides in a "mere readiness for action." He could not find in poetic thought "action" itself. Readers of poetry are, therefore, merely passive recipients; they do not expect poetry to move them to significant action or reveal to them a fundamental truth.

In their attempt to restore literature to its rightful place in the center of human life, Ransom and Tate were joined by Cleanth Brooks and Robert Penn Warren. Soon after *The World's Body* (1938) appeared, Brooks published *Modern Poetry and the Tradition* (1939), in which he hoped to assist those readers—whose "conception of poetry is . . . primarily defined . . . by the achievements of the Romantic poets"—to appreciate the poetry of their own age. One must go back beyond the 18th century, Ransom and Brooks both insist, to find poets who do not attempt to oversimplify human experience by removing all discordant elements from it.

Although Warren is well known for the essays in which he introduced readers to important modern writers—Wil-

liam Faulkner, Peter Taylor, Katherine Anne Porter, Eudora Welty, John Crowe Ransom, and many others—he did write at least one basically theoretical essay. In "Pure and Impure Poetry" he argues that one finds in poetry many points of resistance: there is tension between the rhythm of the poem and the rhythm of speech; between the formality of the rhythm and the informality of the language; between the general and the abstract; between the beautiful and the ugly. This statement of tension among the various elements of a poem is very similar to Ransom's theory of the discord between its structure and texture. Both critics believed the poem is achieved through this tension.

The southerners who developed the New Criticism did so as a collective effort. Two earlier movements served as background for this collective literary endeavor. The Fugitives of the 1920s, including Ransom, were interested in a new poetry that would depart from traditional romantic, sentimental, southern verse. The Nashville Agrarians, including Ransom, Tate, Brooks, and

Robert Penn Warren, American man of letters, 1979

Warren, were social critics, concerned with social and economic ideas; their ideas appeared in the symposia *I'll Take My Stand* (1930) and *Who Owns America?* (1936). As an organized movement, Agrarianism was over by 1937, though, and New Criticism had already begun to assume central importance. The New Critics made a number of periodicals into organs for disseminating their views. Brooks and Warren edited *Southern Review* from 1935 to 1942, Ransom founded the *Kenyon Review* in 1940 and remained its editor for over two decades, and Tate made the venerable *Sewanee Review* into a quarterly for literary and critical studies reflecting his theories. In addition to their textbooks and quarterlies, the influence of the New Critics was also felt through teaching, as they shaped a generation of students at Vanderbilt, Louisiana State University, Kenyon College, the University of Minnesota, Bread Loaf, and Yale. One can chart the changing geography of New Criticism, as its leaders moved from Nashville to Baton Rouge to Gambier, Ohio, and finally to New Haven, Conn. The peak of the New Criticism was in the 1940s and 1950s, but its influence continues to be felt.

The effect of the New Critics upon the understanding of what a poem is and how it works has been profound. One of their most enduring achievements is to make available the material essential to exploring the cognitive function of literature. Surely every student who has had an introductory course in literature in this country since World War II has been affected by the concerns of Ransom, Tate, Brooks, and Warren, even in the unlikely event that he has never heard the name of any one of them.

Thomas Daniel Young
Vanderbilt University

Louise Cowan, *The Southern Critics* (1972); Richard Foster, *The New Romantics: A Reappraisal of the New Criticism* (1962); William J. Handy, *Kant and the Southern New Critics* (1963); Murray Krieger, *The New Apologists for Poetry* (1968); Robert Wooster Stallman, in *A Southern Vanguard*, ed. Allen Tate (1947); Walter Sutton, *Modern American Criticism* (1963); Thomas Daniel Young, ed., *The New Criticism and After* (1976). ☆

North in Literature

||||||||||||||||||||||||||||||||||||||||||||||||||||||

Flannery O'Connor's first published story, "The Geranium," opens with an old man, come up from the South to stay with his daughter in New York, looking "out the window fifteen feet away into another window framed by blackened red brick." He is waiting for the people across the way to put a potted geranium on the sill, even though "those people across the alley had no business with one. They set it out and let the hot sun bake it all day and they put it so near the ledge the wind could almost knock it over. They had no business with it, no business with it." In "Judgement Day," her final story and retelling of the matter of "The Geranium," O'Connor's displaced old southerner stares through a window looking "out a brick wall and down into an alley full of New York air, the kind fit for cats and garbage. A few snowflakes drifted past the window but they were too thin and scattered for his failing vision." "The Geranium" ends with a man across the alley telling the old southerner to mind his own business; "Judgement Day" ends with old Tanner grotesquely dead, his feet dangling over the apartment house stairwell "like those of a man in the stocks."

O'Connor's images of New York as a sterile desert and New York as a freezing prison almost too neatly epitomize the North as it figures in southern literature. Sometimes it is a wasteland awaiting apocalypse, even at times an infernal region of horror. In Alice Walker's *Meridian*, "The subway train rushed through the tunnel screeching and sending out sparks like a meteor. . . . Ninety-sixth street flashed by, then 125th, then there was a screaming halt, a jolt as the car resisted the sudden stop, and the doors slid back with a rubbery thump. The graffiti, streaked on the walls in glowing reds and yellows, did not brighten at all the dark damp cavern of the station." Sometimes the North as viewed by southerners is a region of freezing cold, lacking in human warmth and community. The hero of Robert Penn Warren's *A Place to Come To*, a southern-bred academic who spends most of his life in Chicago, a city he thinks of as a "benign and *fourmillante* hive of de-selfedness," toward the end of the novel goes walking along the shore of Lake Michigan, "watching the sparse flakes ride in over the darkening water, out of the infiniteness of the north," toying with the idea he is "some lost man with nothing before him but the snow-blind lake and nothing behind but the tundra, and only one obligation, or doom—that of survival."

The image of the North as a dark region of cold finds its classic expression in the closing words of William Faulkner's *Absalom, Absalom!*, when Shreve McCannon, the Canadian, asks Quentin Compson, the Mississippian who soon afterward kills himself in Cambridge, Mass.: " 'Why do you hate the South?' " Quentin's reply, "quickly, at once, im-

mediately," is: " 'I dont hate it, . . . I dont,' he said. *I dont hate it* he thought, panting in the cold air, the iron New England dark; *I dont. I dont! I dont hate it! I dont hate it!*" Faulkner's New England is a region of cold, iron, darkness; it is not a good place. And such is the case with the North as depicted in southern literature in general, particularly in southern literature of the 20th century.

Such was not always the case, however. As John Hope Franklin has pointed out, southerners who traveled to and wrote about the North in the early decades of the 19th century found the region "invariably interesting and frequently attractive and admirable." In 1836 John H. Hammond wrote from Philadelphia to his wife in South Carolina: "I never was in so delightful a city. Chestnut Street is worth all I ever saw before in the way of commercial elegance. You must see it." Two years earlier, William Carruthers, in the novel *The Kentuckian in New-York*, had advised: "Every southerner should visit New York. It would allay provincial prejudices, and calm his excitement against his northern countrymen. The people here are warm-hearted, generous, and enthusiastic, in a degree scarcely inferior to our own southerners." Even while Carruthers was testifying to the warmth and generosity of the "northerns," however, the southern penchant for looking favorably, even enviously, upon the North was weakening, and the land of the Yankees was increasingly viewed as a spawning ground of evil and corruption. A negative view of the North was prompted in part by the South's growing defensiveness with regard to the matter of slavery, its sense of being beleaguered in the expanding American union. It may also have been part of the South's emerging sense of itself as, in Lewis P. Simpson's words, "a special redemptive community fulfilling a divinely appointed role in the drama of history." Perhaps more importantly, the unfavorable view of the North taking shape in southern literature was congruent with criticisms of northern society being formulated by northerners themselves.

William R. Taylor's *Cavalier and Yankee: The Old South and American National Character* notes that early in the 19th century Americans of the North and the South began to worry about the direction their democracy seemed to be taking, "about the kind of aggressive, mercenary self-made man who was making his way in their society. . . . In the face of the threat posed by this new man, Americans—genteel and would-be genteel—began to develop pronounced longings for some form of aristocracy. . . . They sought, they would frankly have conceded, for something a little old-fashioned." The democratic-egalitarian, commercial-industrial North was not a region in which such a fantasy could take root, but the agrarian-hierarchical South did lend itself to such mythologizing. By the 1930s, Taylor points out, the "legendary Southern planter, despite reservations of one kind or another, began to seem almost perfectly suited to fill the need" for a hero who could be invested with admirably aristocratic virtues. Concomitantly, "the acquisitive man, the man on the make, became inseparably associated with the North." In elaborating the myth of Cavalier and Yankee, northern writers, such as Sarah Hale, James K. Paulding, and Harriet Beecher Stowe, were probably more influential than writers from the South.

The image of the North in southern literature is, then, to some extent, a curious legacy *from* the North. That image, at any rate, which has persisted since before the Civil War, unmodified except during those years when evangelists for the New South were wooing northern capital and good feeling, is not very different from the harshly critical portrait of the urban and industrial North to be found in northern writers. O'Connor's brick walls are not as frighteningly alienating as those confronting Melville's Bartleby; Faulkner's Cambridge is almost idyllic if compared to the muddy suburb of James's *The Bostonians*.

It is no surprise, then, that images of the North provided by black southerners such as Walker and Ellison and Wright, agree with those projected by white southerners. Blyden Jackson has argued that "all negro fiction tends to conceive of its physical world as a sharp dichotomy, with the ghetto as its central figure and its symbolic truth," but such a vision—of the North as a confining and dehumanizing prison—is not alien to the imagination of white southerners (at the beginning of *Sophie's Choice*, William Styron's narrator describes himself, "self-exiled to Flatbush," as "another lean and lonesome young Southerner wandering amid the Kingdom of the Jews"). Faulkner would have felt himself in sympathy with the words that begin Richard Wright's *American Hunger*, the account, published in 1977, of what happened to "black boy" after he had escaped from the South: "My first glimpse of the flat black stretches of Chicago seemed an unreal city whose mythical houses were built of slabs of black coal wreathed in palls of gray smoke." And Faulkner would have sympathized with the ending of his fellow southerner's account of his sojourn in the North. Sitting alone in his narrow room, "watching the sun sink slowly in the chilly May sky," he is nevertheless determined to "hurl words into this darkness and wait for an echo." Alone in the cold dark of the North, he is yet determined "to tell, to march, to fight, to create a sense of the hunger for the life that gnaws in us all, to keep alive in our hearts a sense of the inexpressibly human."

Robert White
York University
Ontario, Canada

John Hope Franklin, *A Southern Odyssey: Travelers in the Antebellum North* (1976); Jay B. Hubbell, *The South in American Literature, 1607–1900* (1954); Blyden Jackson, *The Waiting Years: Essays on American Negro Literature* (1976); Lewis P. Simpson, *The Man of Letters in New England and the South: Essays on the History of the Literary Vocation in America* (1973); Robert B. Stepto, *From Behind the Veil: A Study of Afro-American Narrative* (1979); William R. Taylor, *Cavalier and Yankee: The Old South and American National Character* (1961). ☆

Periodicals

|||||||||||||||||||||||||||||||

The southern periodicals of paramount cultural importance have been the literary magazines, the most impressive of which were the antebellum *Southern Review* [Charleston] (1828–32), the *Southern Literary Messenger* (1834–64), the *Southern Quarterly Review* (1842–57), and the *Magnolia* (1840–43). Twentieth-century titles of note include the *Sewanee Review* (1892–), the *Southern Review* [Baton Rouge] (1935–42,

n.s. 1965–), the *South Atlantic Quarterly* (1902–), and the *Virginia Quarterly Review* (1925–). The problems that beset the antebellum editor were given a definitive summary in two letters from William Gilmore Simms, printed January and February of 1841 in the *Magnolia*, which Simms, against his better judgment, would soon edit. Literary magazines were begun with "confident hope and bold assurance" but ended in "early abandonment" because two essentials were lacking in the South— contributors who possessed literary talent and subscribers who could pay when promised. The task of the 20th-century southern editor has been easier because he often has the support of a college or university as well as having contributors with literary talent.

Although most literary magazines in the 19th century floundered and failed, agricultural magazines such as the *American Farmer* (1819–97) and the *Southern Planter* (1841–1973) survived and even prospered modestly by reaching the planter class, from whom the literary magazines could never entice much-needed subscriptions. Religious magazines also outlived literary magazines; but their flowering was not until the 1850s, after southern churches had broken away from the North and were providing financial support for their own magazines. At least two political and economic magazines, *Niles' Weekly Register* (1811–49) and *De Bow's Review* (1847–61), persisted and apparently thrived for a reason Simms knew too well: the real passion of the southern male reader was for politics. It was, therefore, essential that historical and political articles have a prominent place in each issue of a literary magazine. A strictly belles-lettres magazine had no chance of survival in the South. The

Orion (1842–44) was founded by William Richards, a scholarly minister, and his artist brother, Thomas Addison Richards, with the intention of publishing southern literature and featuring etchings of southern scenes. Political articles were added too late. The *Orion* was the handsomest antebellum magazine, but it perished in less than two years.

Although the *South Carolina Weekly Museum* (1797–98) is credited as being the pioneer southern magazine, the first with tangible influence on the character of subsequent magazines was the *Southern Review*, edited in Charleston by William and Stephen Elliott and the scholarly lawyer Hugh Swinton Legaré. Legaré, with his impressive classical learning, his devotion to neoclassical tenets, his rational political conservatism, and his judicial fairness as critic, contributed notably to the self-image of southern editors. Southern magazines have been edited, usually briefly, by men of letters (Poe, Simms, Hayne, Tate); but most of the work has been done by professionals like Legaré, Daniel K. Whitaker, and John Reuben Thompson, all of whom had a strong ulterior motive of promoting a southern literature to rival the best efforts in the North.

These editors of antebellum southern literary magazines were consistently conservative in their political and social views and in their literary tastes. New ideas (such as transcendentalism, positivism, and unitarianism) and new literary movements (including Romanticism, and, later, naturalism) were regarded with suspicion. The editors were professedly traditional in their views of what should be said about literature. Henry Timrod, writing in *Russell's* in 1857, complained of the lingering influence of the Scottish rhetoricians.

Lord Kames was still the model for a literary critic in Charleston, and Hugh Blair was the author of what continued to be the most widely used rhetoric in the South. Until Timrod and Paul Hamilton Hayne started writing for *Russell's*, there was little interest in sympathetic or reproductive criticism, advocated for indigenous American works in the North as early as the 1830s and 1840s. Southern editors were apparently convinced that they were judicious in contrast to many northern editors, who were seen as unfair to southern writers and as advocates of northern writers. But by the 1850s sectional tensions had made it almost impossible for editors like Thompson of the *Southern Literary Messenger* and Paul Hamilton Hayne of *Russell's Magazine* to maintain any pretense of objectivity about northern literature and magazines.

There was an attempt to revive southern magazines immediately after the Civil War and to continue the traditions of maintaining critical standards against the intrusions of popular taste and of promoting a proper southern literature. Editors of the new magazines of the 1860s, *Southern Opinion*, *Southern Magazine*, and the *Land We Love*, tended to be "unreconstructed," idealizing the Old South and showing less sympathy toward new trends in literature than the antebellum editors had. New writers, including Sidney Lanier and Thomas Nelson Page, were introduced; but southern magazines still faced the old problem of few contributors and subscribers. There was a new problem as well: southern magazines lacked the resources to compete with a new type of periodical, the pictorial magazine, most successfully exemplified by *Harper's Weekly*. The best literary magazine before the 1890s was the

Southern Bivouac, (1882–87), which published some of the best work of Paul Hamilton Hayne.

The renaissance of southern magazines began in the 1890s with the *Sewanee Review* in 1892, published by the University of the South, and the *South Atlantic Quarterly*, started 10 years later in 1902 at Trinity College, now Duke University. The *Sewanee Review* continued the tradition of promoting southern literature without being provincial; the *South Atlantic Quarterly*, founded by historian John Spencer Bassett, began with an emphasis on social and political issues, earning a reputation for controversy, and gradually became more literary. By the time these two magazines were joined in 1925 by the *Virginia Quarterly Review* and in 1935 by a new *Southern Review*, the dream of the antebellum editors was being realized. The Southern Literary Renaissance sparked by the writings of William Faulkner, Robert Penn Warren, Katherine Anne Porter, John Crowe Ransom, Allen Tate, Thomas Wolfe, and others, was well under way.

Twentieth-century southern magazines had two important advantages over their predecessors—the flowering of southern literature and, in some cases, a dependable means of financial support, the southern college or university. Editors could at long last pay contributors and more nearly compete with northern magazines. Southern magazines could retain their southern identity but become truly national and even international. Modernism in literature and in literary criticism could be supported. The avant-garde, however, was not pushed. With few exceptions—the *Fugitive* (1922–25) in Nashville and the *Double Dealer* (1921–26) in New Orleans—the South did not develop the true home of the avant-garde, the little

magazines, and those that did appear were not experimental. Conservatism and traditionalism still prevailed. There were conservative social and political essays. The criticism of industrialization and of positivism in philosophy begun by George Fitzhugh in *De Bow's Review* in the 1850s and 1860s was renewed in the Agrarian essays of Donald Davidson, Allen Tate, John Crowe Ransom, and other contributors to the 1930 Agrarian manifesto *I'll Take My Stand*. Literary criticism and formalist analysis were practiced in the *Southern Review* in the 1930s under Robert Penn Warren and Cleanth Brooks, in southern critic John Crowe Ransom's *Kenyon Review*, a bastion of the New Criticism, and in the *Sewanee Review* under Allen Tate in the 1940s.

The day of the southern literary magazine had come. Some magazines were as influential as northern magazines. Circulation of the *Sewanee Review* and the *Southern Review* even exceeded 3,000. And yet a proper perspective on these literary magazines must be maintained. As far as a mass southern audience is concerned, the situation has not changed greatly. In 1860 *Southern Field and Fireside* (1859–65) could afford the luxury of hiring the discouraged John Reuben Thompson away from the *Southern Literary Messenger* for the handsome salary of $2,000 a year. Today's *Field and Fireside* equivalent, *Southern Living*, (1966–), is in the 1980s the most widely read southern magazine, with an estimated circulation of 2 million.

See also INDUSTRY: / *De Bow's Review*; MEDIA: Magazines; / *Southern Exposure*; *Southern Living*

Richard J. Calhoun
Clemson University

Richard J. Calhoun, *Southern Literary Journal* (Fall 1970); John C. Guilds, *Southern Literary Journal* (Spring 1972); Jay B. Hubbell, in *Culture in the South*, ed. W. T. Couch (1934), *The South in American Literature* (1954); Robert D. Jacobs, *Southern Literary Journal* (Fall 1969); Frank L. Mott, *A History of American Magazines*, 5 vols. (1930–68); John R. Welsh, *Southern Literary Journal* (April 1971). ☆

Popular Literature

IIIIIIIIIIIIIIIIIIIIIIIIIIIIIIIIIIIIIIIIIIIIIII

The romantic South has been a mainstay of popular fiction in the United States from the beginning of mass market publishing. John Pendleton Kennedy, the first major novelist to set fiction on southern plantations, achieved early popularity with *Swallow Barn, or A Sojourn in the Old Dominion* (1832) and *Horse-Shoe Robinson* (1835). These novels were patterned after the works of Sir Walter Scott and painted a picture of the Virginia gentry and romantic plantation life that would become typical in popular fiction during the next decades. Almost immediately, southern settings became the symbol for romance, aristocracy, gallant chivalry, grandeur, and a lifestyle of elegant leisure.

By the 1850s the "plantation romance" had become moderately successful. Eliza Ann Dupuy set her 1857 novel, *The Planter's Daughter: A Tale of Louisiana*, in Louisiana, and Mary J. Holmes, who published *Meadow Brook* that same year, wrote of plantation life in Kentucky. In general, these works portrayed the South as a region containing only plantations, genteel planters, delicate and beautiful women, and contented slaves.

None of the antebellum novelists portraying southern life and culture was, however, the equal of Emma Dorothy Eliza Nevitte (E.D.E.N.) Southworth. One of the most prolific and popular American novelists of all time, Southworth used plantation settings in her romantic novels. Among her many best-selling works were *Shannondale* (1850) and *Virginia and Magdalene* (1852). Like all of her books, Southworth's novels of the South were contemporary "domestic romances," a form that dominated American best-sellers until late in the century. Typically, Southworth's tales offered no truly distinctive southern themes, but they did contribute greatly to popular imagery of the plantation South. Southworth and her contemporaries filled their novels with palatial homes, endless social gaiety, princely and gallant aristocrats, and sentimental belles.

Harriet Beecher Stowe's *Uncle Tom's Cabin* (1852), essentially a domestic novel, not only caused a stir over the slavery issue, but also spawned numerous novels in imitation and elicited a healthy number of proslavery novels. In spite of Stowe's didactic, antislavery tone, *Uncle Tom's Cabin* tended to reinforce the image of romance and aristocracy associated with the South. In fact, the true villain of the novel, Simon Legree, was a northerner. Although Stowe's book was intended to condemn and vilify the institution of slavery, the work also contributed to the popular image of the South as a romantic region, an image that has dominated popular fiction since the antebellum era.

The Civil War and the end of the slave system did not weaken the impulse of popular authors to glorify the plantation South. Quite the contrary, the antebellum South took on new romance as a "lost civilization," and popular writers celebrated the Old South with nostalgia.

Joel Chandler Harris offered his *Uncle Remus* tales from 1888 through 1906. These "folktales" reflected a world of racial harmony on the South's plantations. Similarly, F. Hopkinson Smith's popular novelette of 1891, *Colonel Carter of Cartersville*, delineated a world of contented servants and genteel masters.

The works of Harris and Smith were typical and widely popular, but their impact was not nearly so great as that of Thomas Nelson Page. More than any other postbellum writer, Page codified the popular image of the Old South, rounding out the traditional stereotypes of the beautiful young belle, her chivalrous beau, and the faithful slave. Like almost all of his works, *In Ole Virginia, or Marse Chan, and Other Stories* (1887) was a collection of short stories, which centered on romance among the southern aristocracy. Narrated by elderly freedmen, the stories recalled the glory and tranquility of the perfect social order that, in Page's view, prevailed before the war. Most significantly, they depicted loyal and totally devoted slaves who believed that their own happiness was tied to that of their masters.

Later in his career Page became disillusioned with the state of race relations in the post–Civil War South. In *Red Rock: A Chronicle of Reconstruction* (1898) and *The Red Riders* (1924) Page developed more sinister characterizations of black people. Along with Thomas Dixon, Jr., who published *The Clansman: An American Drama* in 1905, Page blamed the South's difficulties, particularly racial and economic problems, on the freedmen and northern interventionists. Implicit in the Page and Dixon novels of the Reconstruction South was the glorification of the Old South as an idyllic Garden of Eden.

From about 1890 and continuing into the 1930s the historical novel was a dominant genre of popular fiction in the United States, and novels of the antebellum South assumed a central position. Most of the Old South best-sellers that emerged were of the "moonlight-and-magnolias" variety. Mary Johnston, who wrote more than 20 historical novels, penned significant portrayals of both the antebellum and postbellum South. Her *Miss Delicia Allen* (1933) was a classic story of aristocratic grace and romance on a Virginia plantation, and *The Long Roll* (1911) remains one of the best popular treatments of the impact of the Civil War. Stark Young's widely successful *So Red the Rose* (1934) explored life on a Mississippi plantation. Young continued the tradition developed by Page, and he seemed to argue that the Old South was a highly admirable society and that its demise after the Civil War was a crushing blow to civilization itself. Ellen Glasgow was not only popular, but talented as well. Her novel *The Battle-Ground* (1902) demonstrated that the South could be portrayed as a many-faceted society with flaws as well as strengths. Although Glasgow portrayed the southern elite in rather grand and romantic fashion, she also recognized the importance of the yeoman farmer and the poor white in the southern social structure.

By the mid-1930s popular writers, following Glasgow's lead, seemed to be on the verge of offering a more accurate and realistic treatment of the Old South. But a single event, the publication in 1936 of *Gone with the Wind*, brought popular fiction squarely back into the romantic and sentimental portrayal that had flourished for so long. Margaret Mitchell's incredibly successful novel relied on stock settings and stereotypes to mythologize the Old South more effectively and more popularly than any other book before or since. Moreover, the sections of *Gone with the Wind* that deal with the Reconstruction South clearly portray the antebellum era as a lost and glamorous period of aristocratic gentility and high romance.

Mitchell's immediate successor was Frank Yerby, a black writer whose short fiction exploring racial issues had won literary acclaim. Yerby turned to historical fiction in 1946 with the publication of *The Foxes of Harrow*. He eventually became one of the most popular novelists of all time. Although he worked within a "pot-boiler" formula, Yerby was always careful to research the historical background of his tales in meticulous detail. His works continued the romantic tradition established by Margaret Mitchell, but Yerby was also careful to include details of life in the slave quarters. Additionally, Yerby's portrayal of sexuality among the planter elite was more explicit than earlier writers'.

Yerby's popularity undoubtedly piqued the public's interest in romantic fiction set in the Old South. Kyle Onstott cashed in on the trend with *Mandingo* in 1957, the same year that Yerby issued *Fairoaks*. But the novels were quite different. Yerby's novel provided a wealth of accurate information related to slave life and culture, including a sensitive and painfully detailed passage on the slave trade. On the other hand, *Mandingo* can make no claim to historic accuracy. Onstott's novel and its several sequels are still in print, and total sales for the series are around 30 million copies.

The world of *Mandingo* is a miasmic wasteland of slavebreeding plantations, populated by vicious masters, their drunken wives, generously endowed "breeding studs," and eager and wanton "breeding wenches." *Mandingo* might be passed off as a prurient example of the worst tendencies in popular fiction were it not for its impact on the publishing industry. Onstott's success was so great that hundreds of imitations, mostly paperback originals, were published over the next quarter of a century. All of them relied on sensational portrayals of interracial sexuality, degenerate aristocrats, and black people who found it impossible to control their libidinous desires. The widespread popularity of the post-Onstott "plantation novel" attests to his importance in developing popular imagery of the Old South as a land of "lust in the dust."

Onstott's successors in this genre included Norman Daniels, the author of skillful paperback originals in several genres, who created the "Wyndward Plantation" series (1969 and after), and Raymond Giles, who wrote the "Sabrehill" saga (1970–75). Marie de Jourlet offered several novels in the "Windhaven" series beginning in 1978, and Richard Tresillian initiated his "Bondmaster" series in 1977, with each novel enjoying an initial print run of roughly 700,000 copies. Although Tresillian's series is set in the West Indies, the novels are clearly modeled on Onstott's work, and the books often use details and portrayals based on United States settings. Finally, Lonnie Coleman's hardback best-seller *Beulah Land* (1973) evolved into an influential series, which was eventually adapted as a controversial television miniseries. Coleman's history was somewhat more accurate than that of the other popular novelists, but his concentration on themes of miscegenation, degenerate gentry, and "women on the pedestal" clearly indicated his debt to Onstott's work.

Although the so-called poor white

generally has been neglected in popular fiction set in the South, the paperback reprinting of Erskine Caldwell's *Tobacco Road* (1947; hardcover edition 1932) spawned an impressive trend in "backwoods" novels that extended throughout the 1950s and maintained moderate success in the 1960s. *Tobacco Road* was a racy tale of poor sharecroppers and seemed to strike a responsive chord among readers who had tired of the "moonlight-and-magnolias" imagery. The paperback sales of the work far outstripped the publisher's expectations, and soon dozens of authors were rushing to cash in on the trend. Indeed, the paperback publishing revolution seemed to provide the perfect outlet for Caldwell's many imitators. In the words of one publisher, the "backwoods" novels centered on the "earthy humor, the primitive passions and quaint ways of Southern hill folk." These "folk" were libidinous, raucous, and illiterate, and the stories involved cockfighting, moonshining, prostitution, gambling, and general depravity.

Other notable "backwoods" authors included John Faulkner (William's brother), whose *Cabin Road* (1951) was reprinted at least six times, Jack Boone, who offered *Dossie Bell Is Dead* in 1951, and Charles Williams, who published a series of novels using variations on a single theme. Under titles such as *Hill Girl* (1951), *River Girl* (1951), and *Girl Out Back* (1958), Williams penned stories in which a dishonest and somewhat brutish "po' white" meets his match in a tough and ruthless backwoods siren with whom he falls in love. Williams was imitated by many, including Cord Wainer (pseudonym of Thomas B. Dewey) with *Mountain Girl* (1952), Allen O'Quinn with *Swamp Brat* (1953), and Jack Woodford and John B. Thompson with *Swamp Hoyden* (no date).

Cover from 1956 paperback edition of Erskine Caldwell's best-seller

Although dozens of additional authors might be mentioned, none was able to capture the spirit of the "backwoods" formula and play to the demands of the audience quite so well as Harry Whittington, who also wrote under the pseudonyms of Hallam Whitney and Whit Harrison. His works included *Backwoods Hussy* (1952), *Shack Road* (1953), *Cracker Girl* (1953), *Shanty Road* (1954), and *Backwoods Tramp* (1959). His "backwoods" tales were enormously popular and eventually gave the formula its name. Later in his career Whittington helped to complete the "Falconhurst Series" begun by Kyle Onstott, and he created the popular "Blackoaks" series of plantation novels which were published under his Ashley Carter pseudonym.

Even after the rise of Kyle Onstott

and the backwoods formula, both considered male genres, there remained a market for less violent and less racist versions of romantic fiction set in the antebellum South. This genre continued to maintain substantial popularity into the 1980s. Mainly targeted at women, historic romances in an Old South setting were very similar to the traditional historical romance set in *any* period. By the 1970s the form was referred to as the "bodice ripper" by critics. In these tales the principal focus was on the romantic involvement of the heroine and a rough but handsome hero, a macho figure who often nearly raped the heroine in their first sexual encounter, an act that only served to heighten her desire for him. The setting was essentially a mere backdrop for the romance, but the overall portrayal served to extend and popularize the "moonlight-and-magnolias" image of the Old South, albeit in somewhat unsavory fashion.

Many authors wrote popular novels of this sort, and recent representative titles include *Wild Honey* (1982) by Fern Michaels, Julia Grice's *Emerald Fire* (1978), and *Texas Temptress* (1985) by Jean Haught. Other novelists adapted the Old South setting to closely related genres in the general field of romantic fiction. For example, Jane Aiken Hodge's *Savannah Purchase* (1970) is little more than the traditional "gothic romance" set in the Old South. Even major figures in feminine romantic fiction, such as Kathleen Woodiwiss, could not resist the temptation to set their sentimental and always passionate tales in the antebellum South. Woodiwiss's romantic *Ashes in the Wind* (1979) is typical of the feminine fiction set in the Old South during the past decades. It recounts the tale of "an impudent, plantation bred beauty" with "reckless bravado" who falls in love with a "ramrod straight Yankee" who renders her "incapable of reason." Such paperback romances, coupled with occasional best-selling historical fiction such as John Jakes's *North and South* (1982), have helped to maintain the popular romantic image of the "lost civilization" of the antebellum South.

Popular fiction set in the South has provided a consistent and rather limited perspective on the region since the rise of mass fiction during the two decades prior to the Civil War. Geographically the region has been depicted either as one great plantation or as an impoverished wasteland of "hill folk" and backwoods hamlets. Only two levels of society have been portrayed, the elite planter class (including their slaves) and the extremely poor white class. In the former case novelists have either presented a highly idealized and romantic image or have depicted a depraved and sadistic society that glorifies violence and justifies racism. In portraying poor whites writers have contented themselves with simplistic images of illiterate and sexually active bumpkins. Black southerners have most often appeared in fiction set in the antebellum era and have been relegated to one of two categories—wanton, sex-starved slaves or contented, childlike slaves intent on making their masters happy. Popular fictional portrayals of the South, however inaccurate, have had an enormous impact upon public perceptions of the region and its people.

See also MEDIA: / *Mandingo*; MYTHIC SOUTH: Plantation Myth; / Mitchell, Margaret; "Moonlight-and-Magnolias" Myth; *Uncle Tom's Cabin* (book); Yerby, Frank

Christopher D. Geist
Bowling Green State University

Earl F. Bargainnier, *Journal of Popular Culture* (Fall 1976); Bill Crider, *Journal of Popular Culture* (Winter 1982); F. Garvin Davenport, Jr., *The Myth of Southern History: Historical Consciousness in Twentieth-Century Southern Literature* (1967); Robert B. Downs, *Books That Changed the South* (1977); Francis Pendleton Gaines, *The Southern Plantation: A Study in the Development and the Accuracy of a Tradition* (1925); Christopher D. Geist, *Southern Quarterly* (Spring 1980); Jack Temple Kirby, *Media-Made Dixie: The South in the American Imagination* (1978); James M. Mellard, *Journal of Popular Culture* (Summer 1971); C. Michael Smith, *Journal of Popular Culture* (Winter 1982); Alice K. Turner, *New York* (magazine) (13 February 1978). ☆

Publishing
|||||||||||||||||||||||||||||||

Although the migration of big business to the South and the decay of northern urban centers are undisputed, there have been no major book publication centers in the South, with the exception of university presses. In 1981, of the 1,200 publishers in the country issuing five or more titles annually, 83 were located in the South. Of the annual national production of 66,000 titles, southern presses issued 2,200 titles, one-fourth of which bore the imprints of university presses. The South, with over one-fourth of the nation's population, published only 3 percent of its book titles. Why did southern printshops and booksellers not develop into publishing houses prior to 1830, the period of greatest growth in the publishing industry? Why did the balance of activity in publishing shift from localized presses in the late 18th century to cen-

ters like New York and Philadelphia at the beginning of the 19th century rather than to Charleston or Richmond? The answers reside in the very nature of the region.

Historically, the establishment of those primal founts of heresy and rebellion, printing presses, was inhibited in the South by royal governors; geographically, the South had only limited access to distribution routes that would enable it to claim interior markets; demographically, the South never developed those large population centers necessary to support major publishing houses; culturally, the South remained dependent on the North and England for too long—moving to create its first publishing centers several decades after the northern publishing houses had established their fortunes by issuing cheap reprint editions of English works; and, traditionally, the southern ideal of cultural isolation created an insular society that, until tensions began to arise between the North and the South prior to the Civil War, felt no need for active regional publishing. By the 1850s when the southern press first called for a regional publishing center, New York and Philadelphia already dominated the American publishing industry, and whatever hopes the South might have had of creating a parallel publishing center in the wake of the regional sentiment that preceded the Civil War were dashed with those of the southern cause during that conflict.

For all this, southern university presses have recorded notable achievements in the 20th century. The titles published by these presses reflect a close identification with their region. The story of publishing in the South falls into five stages: (1) the establishment of the printing industry in the colonial

South, (2) the effort to establish a southern publishing center in the antebellum South, (3) the expansion of that industry during the Civil War, (4) the production of southern titles during Reconstruction, and (5) the formation of southern university presses in the 1920s and 1930s.

The desire to establish a press in the South preceded its establishment by close to half a century. The earliest southern printers combined the functions of printer and publisher in their shops. They served at the discretion of royal governors who, like their English monarch, perceived the printer to be promulgator of disobedience and heresy. Thus, in 1682, when William Nuthead attempted to establish the first southern press in Jamestown, the Virginia Council banned printing of any kind in the colony, and Nuthead moved his press to Maryland. Only in 1730, nearly a century after the establishment of the first press in New England, did the Virginia Assembly reconsider its act and, succumbing to a need for a public printer, lure William Parks to Williamsburg. Within succeeding decades presses were established in Charleston, S.C. (1731), New Bern, N.C. (1749), and Savannah, Ga. (1762), at the behest of colonial assemblies, which, like Virginia's, found the dangers of insurrection posed by the free printer to be less threatening than the need for someone to make clear the confused manuscript copies of the acts of the assembly.

More than one-half of all titles produced in the South during this period were legal (assembly proceedings, executive utterances, and statutes), whereas the titles of New England presses were 46 percent theological and only 17 percent legal. The figures have been misread to imply that southern colonial interests were legal rather than theological. In fact, the number of government publications issued in both regions was about the same. What the figures suggest is that the South never developed interests—beyond those of governmental procedure—that required active regional publication. Whatever regional controversies took place in the South, like the smallpox inoculation controversy of 1738–39 chronicled by Lewis Timothy's Charleston press, were amply treated in pamphlets. The population density of the New England area, its cultural diversity, its trumpeting of rights and launching of crusades—all these resulted in the kind of polemics that supported a functioning regional press; the scattered nature of the southern population, its cultural homogeneity (only 12,320 unnaturalized foreigners were counted in the South in 1820 in contrast to 41,335 in the rest of the nation), its insular nature, and its confidence in traditional values required no such outlet.

Until the end of the 18th century the book publisher in America was a tradesman, either a bookseller who printed editions for his own shop or a printer who sold the products of his press in a back room. By 1830 this structure had become outmoded. In the publishing centers of New York and Philadelphia, craft and trade functions were abandoned by the publisher who turned his attention to selecting books to be printed and marketed on the basis of popular appeal and potential profits. In the 1830s, for instance, the Philadelphia firm of Carey & Hart boldly purchased all the seats in a mail stage to ship Bulwer Lytton's *Rienzi* (1836) to New York, beating the New York firm of Harpers in their own market. In contrast, John Russell of Charleston chose William

Gilmore Simms's *Areytos* (1846) as his firm's first imprint, basing his decision not on the profit motive but on an idealistic desire to serve the literary needs of his region. Russell's firm (with a stock valued at $20,000) was essentially a bookstore, not a publishing house. In the North publishing had become a competitive business in and of itself—in the South it remained the avocation of printers and booksellers.

The American copyright act of 1790, which provided that the works of English authors could be reprinted in America without payment of royalties, had a great part in encouraging the growth of the northern publishing houses. New York became a trade center after the War of 1812 by developing a triangular trade that carried cotton from the South to England, manufactured goods from England to New York, and northern and foreign goods from New York to the cotton ports. The preference of the average American reader prior to 1840 for English authors was reflected in the publishing industry (only 30 percent of the titles published at this time were written by American authors), so that the publishing industry was largely an import industry. This fact not only contributed to the growth of the New York firms—ideally situated at the center of the American import system— but paradoxically created the very situation in which the early domination of the publishing trade by northern houses would appear least threatening to southern audiences. Literature imported into the South, whether channeled through northern or southern shops, reflected English values rather than the values of either region. Although some important titles were reprinted in the South during this period, the favorite publishers of southern readers were northern houses

that "puffed" and promoted their wares. Works published in the South, though technically comparable to their northern counterparts, were simply not promoted. A book published in the North would receive national distribution, but southern-issued books were rarely even read in neighboring states.

By 1840, when approximately half the books printed in the United States were written by American authors, the North with its Protestant work ethic and business acumen had acquired a virtual monopoly on book publishing. Not until the middle of that decade did southern authors, who perceived the increased interest in publishing among their northern counterparts, feel themselves uncomfortable with northern publishing houses; and not until the northern publishing houses began exporting to the South books and texts espousing northern rather than English ideals did the South feel sufficiently besieged by northern culture and propaganda to establish its own publishing houses.

As tensions increased between the North and the South prior to the Civil War, the South came to resent keenly its literary vassalage to the North. One writer complained of textbooks, which were prepared by northern men unfamiliar with the South, that devoted 2 pages to Connecticut onions and broomcorn and only 10 lines to Louisiana and sugar. Charges of moral laxity made by the abolitionists angered southerners who, because of the limited number of publishing houses established in their region, saw no means of promoting their side of the issue. Southern authors, like William Gilmore Simms, who sought a national audience found that the novels they published in the South sold far less than those that came out of the North. Although a substantial number of

Simms's titles were printed by southern presses, of the major works only *The Sword and the Distaff* (published in 1852 by Walker, Richards of Charleston) was of southern issue. By 1858 Simms, who had extensive experience with both northern and southern publishers, could remark that there was "not in all the Southern States a single publisher." Less prestigious writers found themselves in the dilemma of either subsidizing their own works in southern houses that lacked the capital of the northern operations or seeking publication in the North where southern writers were widely considered to be inferior.

Prior to the Civil War only three publishing houses of any consequence, Randolph & English and West & Johnston in Richmond and Sigismund H. Goetzel in Mobile, existed in the South. Richmond, New Orleans, and Charleston were the printing centers. The desire for reading matter did not cease with the Civil War, however, although blockades cut off northern book sources. Much that he produced during the war was ephemeral, but the southern publisher, his competition to the North removed, flourished.

Of the 105 book titles published in the Confederacy between 1861 and 1865, nearly one-third were published in Richmond and most of these were by West & Johnston. In the early days of the war southern publishing houses issued the essential field manuals and military handbooks, but by 1862 the South was forced, in a way that it had never been, to turn to itself for books and authors. West & Johnston, in searching for regional talent, unearthed Augusta Jane Evans [Wilson] whose novel *Macaria* (1864) outsold any other edition in the South. The Richmond firm

also issued the Confederacy's first original drama, James Dabney McCabe's *The Guerillas* (1863). In all, the Confederacy produced 49 works of fiction, 29 volumes of verse, 15 songsters, and 5 dramas among other miscellaneous publications.

Had Reconstruction been less agonizing, the Confederate presses might well have developed into a publishing center of some kind. But with the end of the war, the hopes of southern publishers were vanquished. The products of the few Reconstruction presses, most notably Clark & Hofeline of New Orleans, were devoted to embittered defenses of the South and to angry denunciations of the North. Among Clark & Hofeline's imprints were Randell Hunt's *Appeal in Behalf of Louisiana, to the Senate of the United States for the fulfillment of the constitutional guaranty to her of a republican form of government as a state in the union* (1874) and James Dugan's satirical depiction of postwar Louisiana, *Doctor Dispachemquic; A Story of the Great Southern Plague of 1878* (1878). But for all his bravado, the southern publisher working in the Reconstruction era found himself enduring a period of emotional and financial bankruptcy. When in 1922 the first state university press was established at the University of North Carolina, it was the only professionally staffed, continually publishing book publisher in all the states that once composed the Confederacy.

The university presses, which have flourished in the South during the 20th century, have filled a need for serious scholarly southern study that was, prior to their inception, both ignored and misunderstood by northern publishing houses. Most of these presses (Duke University Press, the University of

North Carolina Press, the University of Georgia Press, the University of South Carolina Press, the Louisiana State University Press, the Southern Methodist University Press, the University of Tennessee Press, and the University Presses of Florida) were established in the 1920s, 1930s, and 1940s—when their treatment of the social and economic ills of the region was often controversial. Others (the University Press of Mississippi, the University of Texas Press, and the University Press of Virginia) have been established only in the past few decades.

W. T. Couch, who became assistant director of the University of North Carolina Press in 1925 and its director in 1932, sought the kind of regional studies, books on the South written by southerners, that would shake the region out of its complacency. Under his direction the press produced a number of important regional studies, like Howard W. Odum's *Southern Regions of the United States* (1936) and Stella Gentry Sharpe's *Tobe* (1939), as well as critical studies of textile unions, mill villages, child labor, lynching, and race relations. Couch's aggressive attitude toward regional studies filled a vacuum left by northern houses and provided the South with a publishing center, which, as an organ of the region it served, offered a means of defining and molding a "New South" during the days of the New Deal. His leadership set the tone for other southern university presses.

The representation of the southern university presses among the nation's university presses is more indicative of the intellectual health of the region than are the figures relating to publishing as a whole. Of the 2,300 titles published by the nation's university presses in 1981, close to 500 were issued by southern university presses. Yet the impact of the university press on the South, especially in the 1920s and 1930s when a modern South was in its early stage of self-definition, has been out of proportion to its productivity. For the first time in their history, southerners read analyses of their region written by southerners and selected for publication by southerners. The impact was enormous.

The number of presses the South should have 100 years from now will depend on how the needs of the industry are met by the region. On 11 February 1982 Harcourt Brace Jovanovich, Inc., a major New York publishing house since 1919, announced its decision to move its operations from New York to centers in Florida and California. Although a single move of this kind does not suggest a trend, William Jovanovich's announcement did express a genuine dissatisfaction with New York as a publishing center, and in the future other major publishers may also head South.

See also EDUCATION: / Couch, W. T.

Carol Johnston
Clemson University

Book Forum, vol. 3 (Nov. 2, 1977); Richard Barksdale Harwell, *Confederate Belles-Lettres* (1941); Jay B. Hubbell, in *American Studies in Honor of William Kenneth Boyd*, ed. David Kelly Jackson (1940); Hellmut Lehmann-Haupt, *The Book in America: A History of the Making and Selling of Books in the United States* (1951); *Literary Market Place with Names and Numbers: The Directory of American Book Publishing* (1982); Madeleine B. Stern, *Imprints on History: Book Publishers and American Frontiers* (1956); John Tebbel, ed., *A History of Book Publishing in the United States*, 4 vols. (1972–81). ☆

Regionalism and Local Color

|||||||||||||||||||||||||||||||||||||||||||

Although the terms *regionalism* and *local color* are sometimes used interchangeably, regionalism generally has broader connotations. Whereas local color is often applied to a specific literary mode that flourished in the late 19th century, regionalism implies a recognition from the colonial period to the present of differences among specific areas of the country. Additionally, regionalism refers to an intellectual movement encompassing regional consciousness beginning in the 1930s.

Even though there is evidence of regional awareness in early southern writing—William Byrd's *History of the Dividing Line*, for example, points out southern characteristics—not until well into the 19th century did regional considerations begin to overshadow national ones. In the South the regional concern became more and more evident in essays and fiction exploring and often defending the southern way of life. John Pendleton Kennedy's fictional sketches in *Swallow Barn*, for example, examined southern plantation life at length.

The South played a major role in the local color movement that followed the Civil War. Although the beginning of the movement is usually dated from the first publication in the *Overland Monthly* in 1868 of Bret Harte's stories of California mining camps, a disproportionate number of contributors of local color stories to national magazines were southerners. The genesis of the local color movement was not surprising. The outcome of the Civil War signified the victory of nationalism over regional interests. With the increasing move toward urbanization and industrialization following the war and the concurrent diminishing of regional differences, it is not surprising that there was a developing nostalgia for remaining regional differences. Local color writing, which was regionally, and often rurally, based and usually took the form of short stories intended for mass consumption, met a need for stories about simpler times and faraway places.

Although local color writing encompassed a number of regions, including New England and the Midwest, southern local color had about it a special quality—the mystique of the Lost Cause. In many stories written about life in the antebellum South there was an idealization of the way things were before the war; the South was often pictured in these stories not as it actually had been but as it "might have been." Representative of this writing is the fiction of Thomas Nelson Page, whose tales of Virginia plantation life in such stories as "Marse Chan" pictured beautiful southern maidens, noble and brave slaveowners, and happy, contented slaves. Although not all southern local color writing depicted the South in such romanticized terms, the exotic and quaint characteristics of this region were dominant motifs.

Southern writers after the Civil War wrote about a variety of places and people, providing a sense of the diversity of the South. Sidney Lanier's poems ("The Marshes of Glynn," 1878, "Sunrise," 1887) offered images from the marshes of south Georgia; Richard Malcolm Johnston's *Georgia Sketches* (1864) and *Dukesboro Tales* (1871) presented stories of the "cracker"; Mississippian Irwin Russell's sketches and *Collected Poems* (1888) popularized the use of black dialect in literature; and Sherwood Bonner's *Dialect Tales* (1884) and her accounts of Tennessee mountain life dealt with the everyday life of plain folk.

Other writers achieved more national fame and literary success in portraying aspects of southern life. George Washington Cable immortalized the Creoles of south Louisiana in the pages of *Scribner's Monthly* and then in such books as *Old Creole Days* (1879) and *The Grandissimes* (1884); Mary Noailles Murfree spent her summers in the Cumberland Mountains of Tennessee and then wrote about the mountaineers, using pen names such as Charles Egbert Craddock and E. Emmett Dembry, in the *Atlantic Monthly* and in a book of stories, *In the Tennessee Mountains* (1884); James Lane Allen created initial literary images of Kentucky life and people with stories in *Harper's Magazine* (April 1885) and in such books as *Flute and Violin, and Other Kentucky Tales and Romances* (1891) and *Kentucky Cardinal* (1894); and Joel Chandler Harris used folklore in his *Uncle Remus: His Songs and Sayings* (1880), which created enduring portraits—some say stereotypes—of black southerners. Other local colorists included Kate Chopin, Ruth McEnery Stuart, Charles E. A. Gayarré, and Grace E. King (Louisiana); Margaret Junkin Preston and Mary Johnston (Virginia); John Fox, Jr. (Appalachia); and Lafcadio Hearn (New Orleans).

As a genre southern local color writing flourished through the 1890s, after which this genteel mode of writing lost popularity. At the turn of the century regional writing in the South was still evident, as in the Virginia-based novels of Ellen Glasgow, whose work attempted a more realistic depiction of the strength and weaknesses of the South. By the 1930s there was a resurgence of interest in regionalism, this time as an intellectual movement. Writers sought to treat each of the regions of the country as discrete geographical, cultural, and economic entities. Again the South played a major role in the regional movement. In fact, a cornerstone of the movement was the manifesto *I'll Take My Stand: The South and the Agrarian Tradition* by Twelve Southerners, published in 1930. The authors of this work, among them John Crowe Ransom, Donald Davidson, Allen Tate, and Robert Penn Warren, argued that the South, having held on to its agrarian culture longer than the rest of the country, could serve as a model for a society in which man rather than the machine was dominant. Citing the dehumanization brought about by industrialization and the assembly line, the authors posited that, although the South would not remain entirely agriculturally based, the southern way of life was more conducive to a full relationship between man and his surroundings.

Although the regional, agrarian philosophy set forth in *I'll Take My Stand* was to a great degree sociological in its thrust, as was much writing about regionalism at this time, there was in the South a corresponding literary movement, known as the Southern Literary Renaissance, which, although not always parallel to the regional movement in its philosophic principles, also emphasized the importance of regional setting and tradition to individuals' lives. Notable writers of this period who explored the importance of their southern heritage and environment included William Faulkner, Robert Penn Warren, and Thomas Wolfe. Although it may be argued, and rightly so, that their works are universal in their implications, each writer's work is firmly rooted in the southern region.

In the decades since the 1930s literature and the other arts that grew out of southern culture have flourished. Such writers as Flannery O'Connor, Carson McCullers, and, more recently, Eudora Welty and Walker Percy, have continued to place characters and action in the South. Although their work is regional, it is universal as well. Each writer, through the exploration of specific characters and places, seeks answers to the questions of life and death that concern all men and women. One can conclude of the work of these contemporary southern writers that all art must find its roots in a specific place or region. The best art is not *of* a region but *transcends* region.

In the last quarter of the 20th century, the South seems to have retained many regional distinctions. Although the region has not lived up to its position as the agrarian model so bravely postulated in *I'll Take My Stand*, it has not succumbed entirely to the homogeneous tendencies resulting from mass media and the shift in population toward the Sunbelt. The South continues to assert in its art its distinctive regional qualities.

See also MYTHIC SOUTH: Regionalism; / Agrarians, Vanderbilt; WOMEN'S LIFE: / Chopin, Kate

Anne E. Rowe
Florida State University

George Core, ed., *Regionalism and Beyond: Essays of Randal Stewart* (1968); Donald Davidson, *The Attack on Leviathan: Regionalism and Nationalism in the United States* (1938); Merrill Jensen, ed., *Regionalism in America* (1951); Claude M. Simpson, ed.,

The Local Colorists: American Short Stories, 1857–1900 (1960); Robert E. Spiller et al., eds., *Literary History of the United States* (1963). ☆

Sex Roles in Literature

The heritage of a strong class and caste system in the South narrows the range of roles for men and women in southern literature. Within that range the most prominent writers of the modern South—Ellen Glasgow, William Faulkner, Robert Penn Warren, and Eudora Welty—explore the depths of a variety of individual characters. In southern fiction, as in most American writing, a confused identity is often attributed to failure to deal with sexuality directly and responsibly, whereas healthy sexuality becomes the basis for self-awareness.

The southern white male appears in fiction most frequently as either the gentleman-father or his cavalier son. The prototype of the gentleman-father appears in John Pendleton Kennedy's *Swallow Barn* (1832). Frank Meriwether has dominion over all, white and black; his wife's control of daily plantation life frees him for leisure and contemplation. Meriwether's fictional descendants include the ineffectual Gerald O'Hara in Margaret Mitchell's *Gone with the Wind* (1936) and Battle Fairchild, continuing Meriwether's life into the 1920s in Welty's *Delta Wedding* (1946). Faulkner shows the deterioration of the southern aristocrat in alcoholic Mr. Compson in *The Sound and the Fury* (1929), portrays Sutpen ironically attempting to become a gentleman and found a dynasty in *Ab-*

salom, Absalom! (1936), and further mocks the tradition in Flem Snopes's journey to his mansion-mausoleum. Warren satirizes the figure of the southern gentleman in Bogan Murdock, with his bogus sense of honor, in *At Heaven's Gate* (1943) and even has Jed Tewksbury, a redneck-scholar in *A Place to Come To* (1977), jokingly refuse to become an "S. G."

The fictional cavalier frequently dies young; if not, he may become a gentleman-father, a rake (like Rhett Butler), or a true southern bachelor. Thomas Nelson Page's hero in "Marse Chan" (1885), the ideal cavalier, dies in the war. Faulkner's cavaliers, often confused about sexual roles, are likely to destroy themselves early, like young Bayard in *Sartoris* (1929) and Quentin Compson. In *All the King's Men* (1946) Warren details Jack Burden's rebellion against his aristocratic heritage in his long journey toward becoming a true gentleman. Will Barrett, Walker Percy's protagonist in *The Last Gentleman* (1966), is haunted by his past, particularly his gentleman-father's suicide. In *The Second Coming* (1980) Will finally frees himself from the past and achieves a sensitive relationship with a sexually free younger woman. Faulkner excels in his depictions of true southern bachelors, especially Ike McCaslin, whose obsession with the past destroys his marriage.

The prevailing roles in fiction for the southern white female are the lady-mother and the belle. Kennedy's Lucretia Meriwether, controlling domestic life in spite of her physical weakness, is followed by fictional lady-mothers like Ellen O'Hara and Ellen Fairchild. Augusta Jane Evans [Wilson] gives characters like Edna Earl in *St. Elmo* (1866) the education and opportunity to choose

nontraditional roles, but they usually marry gentleman-fathers. In *The Awakening* (1900) Kate Chopin focuses on the unfolding sexual identity of Edna Pontellier, who marries and bears children, then realizes she is unsuited for the role of "mother-woman" in her Creole society. Glasgow's protagonist in *Virginia* (1913) rigidly follows the pattern of her lady-mother's life but loses her husband to an unconventional New York actress. Faulkner's Granny Millard in *The Unvanquished* (1938) is strong, but she relies on the conventions of society to the point of destruction; Mrs. Compson is lady-mother evolved into controlling matriarch.

The life of a fictional belle is short; for she is most often portrayed as moving toward the goal of marrying a cavalier, as Kennedy's Bel Tracy does, and settling down as a lady-mother. The refusal to play the role of belle can have grave consequences, as seen in Faulkner's Drusilla Hawk and Caddy Compson. Katherine Anne Porter's Miranda, in "The Old Order" and other stories, must reject the legacy of the belle with her destructive sexuality before she can live as an independent woman. Glasgow's incisive portrait of Eva Birdsong in *The Sheltered Life* (1932) shows that marriage does not always offer the belle a new role; Scarlett O'Hara, rebelling at the prospect of becoming a lady-mother, finds new options in the chaos of the Reconstruction. However, in *The Moviegoer* (1961) Percy gives hope for stability in the comfortable role of the southern lady, while her cousin-husband Binx Bolling assumes the role of gentleman-father. The fictional South of the 1920s produces a variation on the role of belle with the flapper, most notably Temple Drake in *Sanctuary* (1931) and Sue Murdock in *At Heaven's Gate*, both of whom illustrate the dangers of irresponsible sexual freedom.

Although the fictional southern woman's sexuality may destroy her or imprison her in a prescribed role, it may also free her from tradition. Glasgow's lower-class rural protagonist in *Barren Ground* (1925) is saved from the entrapment of an illegitimate pregnancy by miscarrying. Faulkner's mythic Eula Varner Snopes is imprisoned by her sexuality, but Lena Grove in *Light in August* (1932) placidly bears her illegitimate child. In *The Reivers* (1962) Corrie rejects her life as a prostitute and is rewarded with an optimistic future with Boon Hogganbeck. Welty's Gloria in *Losing Battles* (1970) rejects the opportunity for freedom through education but gains a strong sexual identity in her relationship with Jack Renfro; and Laurel McKelva Hand in *The Optimist's Daughter* (1972) finds hope for an independent future in understanding her parents' marriage and her own. Doris Betts portrays, in *The River to Pickle Beach* (1972), the healthy sexuality and strong marriage of Bebe and Jack Sellars, contrasted with the destructive perversion of Mickey McCane. Betts also confronts the complexity of woman's struggle for independence through librarian Nancy Finch in *Heading West* (1981). Percy's Allison is freed from a conventional role in society by mental illness, which allows her to find a positive relationship with Will Barrett.

Demeaning roles for black men and women, especially as the child and the brute, haunt the pages of southern fiction from *Swallow Barn* through *Gone with the Wind* and after. Less demeaning but still lacking individuality and dignity are the tragic mulatto, male or female, and the faithful uncle or mammy. However, a few black char-

acters, mostly in recent fiction, are freed from these roles and given autonomy as human beings. In *Clotel* (1853) William Wells Brown traces the suffering of three generations of mulatto women under the domination of insensitive southern gentlemen who perceive them as the lowest of human beings—black and female. George Washington Cable focuses on the Creole society of Louisiana for his moving story of Honoré Grandissime, a free man of color, in *The Grandissimes* (1880). In *The House Behind the Cedars* (1900) Charles W. Chesnutt allows Rena Walden to question her role in society as a black woman who appears white; her brother John can live with dignity only by assuming the identity of a southern cavalier. Faulkner portrays mulatto characters, especially Joe Christmas and Charles Bon, as individuals in their quests for identity; likewise, Warren's Amantha Starr in *Band of Angels* (1955) and Margaret Walker's Vyry in *Jubilee* (1966) transcend the limitations of stereotyping.

The stereotype of the black uncle, such as the narrator of "Marse Chan," has occasionally been displaced by the role of the autonomous black male. In spite of the ending of *The Adventures of Huckleberry Finn* (1885) Mark Twain gives the character of Jim dignity and wisdom in his quest for identity as a free man. Tea Cake, in Zora Neale Hurston's *Their Eyes Were Watching God* (1937), is an independent man who is strong enough to think of Janie's happiness as well as his own. Faulkner gives Rider in "Pantaloon in Black" (1940) the sensitivity to be destroyed by the real human emotion of grief. Through the struggles of Bigger Thomas in *Native Son* (1940) Richard Wright emphasizes the significance of race and sex in attaining self-identity, even in defeat.

Black leaders Ned and Jimmy, although destroyed by the white society in Ernest J. Gaines's *The Autobiography of Miss Jane Pittman* (1971), are autonomous.

The fictional black mammy, often seen in contrast to the aloof white lady, may have originated in the local color fiction of Sherwood Bonner; Mitchell and others strengthened the stereotype. Occasional black women characters are more complex, like Twain's Roxy in *Pudd'nhead Wilson* (1894), strong and passionate, or like Faulkner's Dilsey, superior to the white Compsons in her patience, her love, her wisdom, her endurance. Rather than portraying Janie in *Their Eyes Were Watching God* as a tragic mulatto or turning her into a mammy, Hurston develops her as an independent woman with love for and commitment to a strong black man. Gaines's Miss Jane, old and wise, is in no sense a stereotyped mammy; in fact, like Janie, she is not even a biological mother. Rather, Gaines gives her identity as a strong, brave, loving, free black woman.

See also BLACK LIFE: Literary Portrayals of Blacks; Literature, Black; HISTORY AND MANNERS: Sexuality; / Gays; MYTHIC SOUTH: / Cavalier Myth; Good Old Boys and Girls; "Mammy"; WOMEN'S LIFE: Belles and Ladies

Martha E. Cook
Longwood College

Francis Pendleton Gaines, *The Southern Plantation: A Study in the Development and the Accuracy of a Tradition* (1924); Anne Goodwyn Jones, *Tomorrow Is Another Day: The Woman Writer in the South, 1859–1936* (1981); Richard H. King, *A Southern Renaissance: The Cultural Awakening of the American South, 1930–1955* (1980); Anne Firor Scott, *The Southern Lady: From Ped-* *estal to Politics, 1830–1930* (1970); William R. Taylor, *Cavalier and Yankee: The Old South and American National Character* (1961). ☆

Theater, Contemporary

The Barter Theater, one of the oldest professional regional theaters in the nation, was a unique product of the Depression-era economy. Founded in 1932 by Virginia-born actor Robert Porterfield and located in the Town-Hall Opera House of Abingdon, the company in its first season made a profit consisting of $4.30 plus three barrels of jams and jellies and assorted surplus foods, some of which were canned and stored and used to "pay" playwright royalties. Growing slowly but steadily, in 1945 it became the official state theater of Virginia.

The Barter Theater holds a distinctive place in the annals of regional theater, which has generally had a shaky history. At the turn of the century hundreds of legitimate professional theaters could be found throughout the United States, but in the decades before World War II the Barter was one of less than a dozen outside New York City.

Although the Little Theater movement of the 1920s, the Federal Theater Project (founded in 1935 as part of the Works Progress Administration), and the American National Theater and Academy (1935) had sought to counter the influences of motion pictures and the radio and had expressed a commitment to audiences throughout the country, the situation for regional theater remained bleak. Professional theater activity had once been supported even in remote locales, but outside of New York it had all but ceased by 1940.

Not surprisingly, the postwar modern regional theater movement first bore fruit away from the East Coast. A principal concern of those active in it was decentralization, so cities closer to Broadway, despite their artistic traditions, received less initial attention. Modern American regional theater *began* in the Southwest, however, largely because of one dynamic personality, Margo Jones.

In June of 1947 Jones, a native Texan, a teacher, and a director, opened Theater '47 (the date changed annually) in Dallas. Conscious of the need for innovation yet responsive to public taste, she helped develop new talents and popularize important playwrights such as William Inge and Tennessee Williams. Inge's *Farther Off From Heaven*, retitled *Dark at the Top of the Stairs*, was the theater's initial production. Both Williams's production of *Summer and Smoke* and Jerome Lawrence and Robert E. Lee's *Inherit the Wind* debuted in Dallas before moving to Broadway.

In the same year, 1947, another "southern belle with a will of iron," Nina Vance, established the Alley Theater of Houston. Recruiting local support through a postcard campaign (the cards bore two words: "Why Not!"), Vance fostered what has been called the most regional of regional theaters.

A fully professional company by the mid-1950s, the Alley was one of the first professional resident theaters to receive major financial support from the Ford Foundation. From its quarters in an abandoned fan factory (225 seats), the theater moved into Houston's spacious $3.5 million playhouse in 1968.

Among the Alley's most notable productions was Paul Zindel's Pulitzer Prize-winning *The Effect of Gamma Rays on Man-in-the-Moon Marigolds*, which premiered in 1965.

In 1955 a Richmond theater became the first in the nation to be located in a fine arts museum. With its stable physical setting (audience capacity of 500) and consistent community support, Virginia's Museum Theater was able to develop into a full equity company before the start of its 1972–73 season.

Two years later actor-producer George Touliatos began his work with an amateur group that performed in the basement of the King Cotton Hotel, and he went on to found The Front Street Theater of Memphis. By 1959 the company moved to a refurnished movie house. Front Street Theater performed a broad range of plays, from *Othello* to *Guys and Dolls*, until financial burdens forced it to close in the late 1960s. More recent Memphis productions have been developed by black playwright Levi Frazier.

A similarly significant if short-lived regional experiment, Repertory Theater of New Orleans, opened in the fall of 1966 under the direction of Stuart Vaughan. From the onset, the federally funded company faced strong competition from the very popular Le Petit Theater de Vieux Carré. Failing to establish itself as an integral part of the local scene, the theater closed its doors after the 1971–72 season.

Established in Jackson, Miss., in 1963, Free Southern Theater was an outgrowth of civil rights activism, especially that of the Student Nonviolent Coordinating Committee. Dedicated to presenting nonstereotypic views of southern blacks, the company had relocated in New Orleans by 1964, alternating tours of rural areas in the South with resident seasonal productions.

Actors Theater of Louisville, founded in 1964 by Richard Black, presented bills featuring the classics, but leavened its fare with bold, often controversial productions such as *End Game* and *Slow Dance on the Killing Ground.* Continuing the theater's tradition of responsiveness to new talent, *Crimes of the Heart* by Beth Henley (1979) and *Getting Out* by Marsha Norman (1979) made their pre-Broadway premieres on its stage.

In 1968 the $13 million Atlanta Memorial Cultural Center opened to house symphony, ballet, and also resident drama produced by Atlanta's Repertory Theater. Reorganized as the Alliance Theater in 1969, it supplemented offerings by that city's already active and innovative Pocket Theater.

Professional resident companies now exist throughout the South, but they are not the only sources of serious, quality drama. Adding to the diverse dramatic scene are community and educational theaters and university-affiliated companies, such as the illustrious Carolina Playmakers; festival theaters such as the High Point, N.C., and Anniston, Ala., Shakespeare festivals; and the Festival of Southern Theater at the University of Mississippi. Lighter fare is offered by ever-popular dinner theaters like Sebastiáns in Orlando, Fla., while annual outdoor dramas, staged in unique open air settings like that of the 2,900-seat Mountainside Theater in Cherokee, N.C., continue to attract regional and national interest.

See also BLACK LIFE: Theater, Black

Elizabeth M. Makowski
University of Mississippi

Robert Gard et al., *Theatre in America* (1968); Sandra Schmidt, *Southern Theatre* (1971–); *Tulane Drama Review* (Summer 1963); Joseph Wesley, *Regional Theatre* (1973). ☆

Theater, Early

||||||||||||||||||||||||||||||||||||||

A long period of vitality, from the colonial era to the Civil War, marked theater in the South. Virginia, the only colony other than Maryland not to pass legislation against the theater, was a center of American theatrical life during the colonial period. The first known play to be acted in America, *Ye Bare and Ye Cubb*, was performed at Cowle's Tavern, in Accomac County, in 1665, and in the next century the first theater was erected there, at Williamsburg.

Charleston, S.C., was, however, the South's theatrical center for 100 years. The first dramatic season opened in 1735 with Thomas Otway's *The Orphan* performed in the city's courtroom; in a prologue, the actors ridiculed the theatrical censorship of New England. The following year plays were staged at the city's new Dock Street Theater.

In 1790 two pioneers in the Georgia backcountry opened Augusta's first theater. Professional actresses from Baltimore, Ann Robinson and Susannah Wall, established themselves in a converted schoolroom, where they staged performances of *The Beaux Stratagem*, *Douglas*, and a variety of simplified 18th-century dramas. The final performance of the group coincided with George Washington's postelection trip to Augusta, with a banquet honoring the president held in the makeshift theater.

Touring companies provided audiences in the colonial South with the chance to see many of the best works of English drama. London's Lewis Hallam began his American tour in 1752 at Williamsburg with *The Merchant of Venice*. David Douglass's American Company visited Virginia theaters from 1758 to 1761. Douglass's 1773–74 season in Charleston, according to one chronicler, "the most brilliant" of colonial America, included 58 plays, 20 of which were musicals. Shakespeare, however, was the favorite dramatist, with *Richard III* and *Romeo and Juliet* his most popular works.

Postrevolution conditions helped to encourage the production of native dramatic writing in the South. From 1793 in Charleston, for example, there were strong resident companies, managers who encouraged native playwrights, newspaper critics, and the Federalist-Republican controversy, which often turned the stage into a political platform.

William Ioor (1780–1850), a country doctor living near Charleston and a fervent Jeffersonian, wrote his first play, *Independence* (1805), to praise the small farmer and country life. Although its setting was England, *Independence* dramatized Jefferson's agrarian philosophy. Ioor's *Battle of Eutaw Springs* (1807) commemorated the last Revolutionary War battle in South Carolina and indirectly condemned contemporary impressment by Great Britain. A prototype of the southern gentleman appeared as a humorous, hospitable farmer named Jonathan Slyboots.

John Blake White, also from Charleston, wrote plays advocating American social reform. His *Modern Honor*, presented in 1812, was the first antidueling play given in America. After 1825 novelist William Gilmore Simms continued the tradition of dramatic writing with *Michael Bonham, or the Fall of Bexar* (written 1844; produced 1852), favoring the annexation of Texas, and *Norman Maurice, or The Man of the People* (published 1851), a proslavery play set in Missouri.

In Virginia, dramatist Robert Munford (1737–83), a planter and a member of the House of Burgesses, wrote *The Candidates* (published in 1798), which satirized corruption in electioneering, and *The Patriots* (published in 1798), which ridiculed intolerant Tories and Whigs. George Washington Parke Custis (1781–1851) wrote several patriotic plays including *The Indian Prophecy* (1827) and *Pocohontas* (1836). The fascination with history, state pride, and an agrarian bias—themes that emerge in some of these early regional plays—would continue to be distinctive hallmarks of southern drama.

In the 19th century, architecture testified to the popularity both of serious drama and extravaganza. At the turn of that century even minor southern towns had their sometimes opulent theaters.

In Richmond, the Marshall Theater (1838), remodeled and named in honor of Chief Justice John Marshall in 1838, was said to rival, in its "pure classical character," with its burnished gold, crimson, and damask, the celebrated New Orleans Caldwell. Destroyed by fire in 1862, the theater was rebuilt in the midst of the Civil War by determined Richmonders.

The elegant North Broadway Opera House, which opened in 1887 in Lexington, Ky., made that already performance-conscious city even more theater oriented. With a seating capacity of 596, illumination provided by 250 gaslights, and a stage large enough to be adapted for the chariot race in the 1904 production of *Ben Hur*, the Opera House attracted touring companies and talents like Lillian Russell, the Barrymores (John, Ethel, and Lionel), Sarah Bernhardt, James O'Neill, and Helen Hayes.

Mobile's splendid Saenger Theater, built at a cost of $750,000 in 1927, was the capstone of a chain of playhouses located throughout the South. The Springer Opera House (1871), of Columbus, Ga., booking such notables as Mme. Modyeska, Irene Dunne, and Edwin Booth, continued as a legitimate theater well into the Depression.

Whether performing in opera houses or in rented halls, professional stock and touring companies, vaudeville acts, and minstrel shows enlivened the southern theater scene into the 20th century. Not until the second decade of the century, when live performances were forced to compete with "talkies" and with the radio at home, did the era of decentralized professional theater in the South, and in the nation at large, decline. It would not be revitalized until the modern regional theater movement of the late 1940s and early 1950s.

A new movement in drama did begin, though, at the University of North Carolina in the 20th century with the folk plays of the Carolina Playmakers and later the outdoor dramas of Paul Green. This close associate of the Playmakers started his career with folk plays like *In Abraham's Bosom* (1926), about a black educator in the New South, for which he received the Pulitzer Prize. Disenchanted with the commercial theater of New York, Green advocated taking drama to the people and exploiting regional material. Under the influence of Bertolt Brecht's epic theater, Green began his series of symphonic dramas

in 1937 with *The Lost Colony*, celebrating the 350th anniversary of Virginia Dare's birth. It was performed on the historical site, Roanoke Island, N.C., and has been repeated almost every summer since. By "symphonic" Green meant the blending of all the stage arts in one production, including spectacle, music, and acting.

Green's dramas, almost all produced in the South, commemorate historic events of the region. The first category deals with the early explorers' transmission of their culture to a new land. *The Lost Colony* was in this category as were *The Founders* (1957, featuring John Rolfe and Pocohontas of the Jamestown settlement, performed at Williamsburg) and *Cross and Sword* (1965, at St. Augustine, Fla.). The second category, the making of America, includes *The Common Glory*, Green's second most popular production. This play about Jefferson and the Revolution exemplifies the glory of democracy through Cephus Sicklemore, a propertyless but patriotic humorist; expresses Jefferson's philosophy of the individual's importance in forming the corporate personality; and presents the battle of Yorktown. It opened in 1947 at the Lake Matoaka Amphitheater, Williamsburg. Among Green's colleagues with productions in the South and elsewhere, Kermit Hunter dramatized Indian history in *Unto These Hills* (published in 1950 and performed at Cherokee, N.C.).

Significant links exist between early and modern drama in the South. The first native plays and outdoor dramas reflect the fascination with history, state pride, and the sense of place found in the region. These affirmative plays reveal also such distinctive southern qualities as an agrarian, antiurban bias and a liking for outdoor, spectacular entertainment. As a balance to urbane plays, epitomized by those of Tennessee Williams, which have also attained wide popularity in the South, the historical dramas have given expression to deep-seated feelings of the people.

See also BLACK LIFE: Theater, Black; REC-REATION: Traveling Shows

Charles S. Watson
University of Alabama

Rodney M. Baine, *Robert Munford: America's First Comic Dramatist* (1967); James H. Dormon, Jr., *Theater in the Ante-Bellum South, 1815–1861* (1967); Clarence Gohdes, *Literature and Theater of the States and Regions of the U.S.A.: An Historical Bibliography* (1967); Vincent S. Kenny, *Paul Green* (1971); Hugh S. Rankin, *The Theater in Colonial America* (1965); Charles S. Watson, *Antebellum Charleston Dramatists* (1976). ☆

Travel Writing
||||||||||||||||||||||||||||||||||||||||||||

Between 1948 and 1962 the University of Oklahoma Press published six bulky volumes devoted to description of and comment upon travel books about the South: E. Merton Coulter's bibliography of travels in the Confederate South and five other volumes, under the general editorship of Thomas D. Clark, dealing with books published between 1527 and 1955. All told, these six bibliographical volumes take into account 2,703 titles. Although they include many books that are perhaps only marginally travel accounts (memoirs, for example, written long after journeys undertaken, or accounts of military campaigns and ex-

periences), the editors are under no illusion that they have ferreted out all the travel books that explore or venture into the South. In the decades since 1955 many more travel books about the South have appeared.

Categorizing and evaluating this welter of writing is difficult. Even if one puts aside the obviously superficial and leaves out of the reckoning all those books that are more strictly "guides-to" than "reports-upon" (guidebooks to southern cities and regions began to circulate prior to the Civil War), and even if it were possible to assess the biases and prejudices all travelers to the South carry in their carpetbags, this most troublesome question would still remain: In "travel writing," is the "travel" of more importance than the "writing"? Does one read a travel book primarily as a more or less reliable *record* of things seen and persons encountered? Or does one read a travel book primarily for the *recording* of the traveler's experiences? Some travel books, of course, inform the historical sense while at the same time appealing to an aesthetic bent, but such books are exceptional. A literary critic can term Henry James's *The American Scene* (1904) "one of the great American documents," but a historian is apt to complain that James, in writing of Charleston, gives "the impression of having visited a state of mind rather than a city." And a historian might find vexing what other readers might find entertaining in the earliest English-language travel writing about the South—John Smith's "unusually vivid imagination."

Smith, whose *True Relation of . . . Virginia* was printed in 1609, was, in his active, roving life if not in his tendency to embroider fact with fiction, a typical early traveler. Of the more than

100 travel books by observers from the British Isles or by English colonials written between 1600 and 1750, 40 were by preachers and missionaries, 30 by government officials, 12 by merchants and fur traders, 10 by doctors and scientists, and others by ship captains, land speculators, and surveyors. Indians and natural history, and the unpleasantness and difficulty of travel, were major concerns of these writers. Perhaps most entertaining among these early writings are William Byrd's 1728 *History of the Dividing Line*, with its Virginian put-down of North Carolina and its inhabitants, and Ebenezer Cooke's *The Sot-Weed Factor* (1708), a virulent verse diatribe against Maryland and its settlers.

The second half of the 18th century in the South was a time of war, new nationhood, and expansion westward across the Appalachians, as well as a period in which slavery and the condition of blacks began to claim the attention of travelers. Most reliable among these reporters were those whose business and professional concerns had prompted their travels, men such as Thomas Jefferson, whose *Notes on the State of Virginia* appeared in 1785; William Bartram, whose *Travels through North Carolina* (1791) recounts his pioneering botanical expeditions; and Philip Vickers Fithian, whose journals deal with his employment as a tutor in the Tidewater and his work as a frontier missionary.

By the turn of the century the corps of travelers in the South had been swelled by numerous Europeans, who came to America sometimes on professional errands but more frequently as observers of the American experiment in democracy. They were drawn to the South by Washington's Mt. Vernon, a

mecca for travelers, but they also wished to investigate plantation society and to inquire about the growth and expansion of slavery. Increasingly, the South was viewed as a region distinct from the rest of the new United States, almost as another country. Access to this South was primarily by water—along the coastal shipping lanes and into the interior by way of the Ohio and Mississippi. Notable among travel accounts of the first decades of the 19th century are Thomas Ashe's *Travels in America* (1808), John Melish's *Travels through the United States of America* (1812), J. K. Paulding's *Letters from the South* (1817), and Timothy Flint's *Recollections of the Last Ten Years* (1826).

As the American nation lurched toward civil war in the middle decades of the century, more and more travelers visited the South; Thomas D. Clark observes that never again would there be so many "in so short a time." By the 1830s most travelers moved along segments of what had become an established "Grand Tour" in America: along the seaboard to Georgia, across Alabama to Mobile and New Orleans, then up the Mississippi and Ohio, with dips into the interiors of Tennessee and Kentucky. Many of the travelers were distinguished Europeans (Charles Dickens, Harriet Martineau, Charles Lyell, Fredrika Bremer, Alexis de Tocqueville, Frederick Maryatt), but the most important travel writing of the antebellum years (Tocqueville's *Democracy in America* is not really a travel book) was the work of a young New Englander, Frederick Law Olmsted, who published three books detailing his travels through the South, with *A Journey in the Seaboard Slave States* (1856) being perhaps the most readable. After the war, which occasioned a good bit of fortuitous travel, travelers from abroad tended to bypass the South in their eagerness to board transcontinental trains headed west, but Americans, particularly American journalists, flocked to the South to see and report on postwar conditions and Reconstruction efforts. In addition, "promotional" travel writing extolling the attractions of a "New South" began to appear. The booster literature may not have advanced southern prosperity, but books such as Whitelaw Reid's *After the War: A Southern Tour* (1866) may have furthered the efforts of Radical Republican legislators; later, James Pike's *The Prostrate State: South Carolina under Negro Government* (1874) and Edward King's *The Great South* (1875) undoubtedly helped into being a climate of opinion that welcomed the end of Reconstruction efforts. The last decades of the century were notable for several quirky individualistic classics of southern travel writing: Mark Twain's *Life on the Mississippi* (1883); Charles Dudley Warner's *On Horseback* (1888), about a trip into some of the more rugged sections of Appalachia; and Nathaniel Bishop's two books about his small-craft voyages along the seaboard and down the Mississippi—*Voyage of the Paper Canoe* (1878) and *Four Months in a Sneak-Box* (1879).

In the 20th century the South again figured in the "grand tour" of visitors from abroad, and after World War I the automobile and better highways made the region more accessible to visitors of all sorts, who came in search of health, for economic advantage, and out of curiosity about southern social conditions—with race relations the topic of most concern. Attempting to "get at the facts" about black-white relations was the motive for Ray Stannard Baker's

Following the Color Line (1908); Jay Saunders Redding's *No Day of Triumph* (1942) is about an auto trip undertaken to obtain insight into the lives of southern blacks; and the issue of race is ever present in Jonathan Daniels's *A Southerner Discovers the South* (1938), which Rupert B. Vance characterizes as "the definitive travel account of the South in the depression." Other striking books from the Great Depression era are Erskine Caldwell and Margaret Bourke-White's *You Have Seen Their Faces* (1937) and James Agee and Walker Evans's *Let Us Now Praise Famous Men* (1941), two books that wed prose and photography. Photographs began to be incorporated in southern travel books as early as the first decade of this century, being essential and integral parts of Clifton Johnson's explorations of southern rural life, *Highways and Byways of the South* (1904) and *Highways and Byways of the Mississippi Valley* (1906). Today, the camera—still, motion picture, video—is as ubiquitous an instrument of southern travel "writing" as the word processor.

Since World War II, when technological change and new wealth set in accelerated motion forces that would forever alter the old agrarian order, and since the Supreme Court's *Brown* v. *Board of Education* decision of 1954, which marked a drastic unsettling of the "color line" in the South, there has been no abatement of the fascination with, and concern about, the land below the Mason-Dixon line. Books continue to appear that undertake to explore and explain what Jonathan Daniels termed the South's "warm dark." Among all these books, among all this travel writing about the contemporary South, three in particular stand out: John Howard Griffin's *Black Like Me* (1961), about the southern encounters of a white man who chemically darkens his skin; Albert Murray's account of his tentative return to the land of his birth and youth, *South to a Very Old Place* (1971); and perhaps the finest of all the reports on voyages in the wake of Huck and Jim's archetypal trip down the Mississippi, the Britisher Jonathan Raban's *Old Glory* (1981).

See also ART AND ARCHITECTURE: Photography; HISTORY AND MANNERS: / Byrd, William, II; Jefferson, Thomas; Olmsted, Frederick Law; MEDIA: / Daniels, Jonathan

Robert White
York University

Thomas D. Clark, ed., *Travels in the Old South: A Bibliography*, 3 vols. (1956), *Travels in the New South: A Bibliography*, 2 vols. (1962); E. Merton Coulter, *Travels in the Confederate States: A Bibliography* (1948); Eugene Schwaab and Jacqueline Bull, eds., *Travels in the Old South, Selected from Periodicals of the Times* (1973). ☆

Women's Literature

See WOMEN'S LIFE articles

AGEE, JAMES

(1909–1955) Writer.

Born in Knoxville, Tenn., in 1909, James Agee was to remain a dedicated southerner until his death in New York City in 1955. His childhood in Knoxville and his adolescence at St. Andrew's School, later evoked in two of his novels, *A Death in the Family* (1957), which won the Pulitzer Prize in 1958,

and *The Morning Watch* (1950), shaped his sensibility and his imagination and provided him with crucial and contradictory experiences—that of happiness and bereavement (after his father's death), that of community and solitude (in the religious atmosphere of the school). Leaving the South to study at Exeter and Harvard, and later becoming the most gifted and versatile writer in the Henry Luce empire, Agee nevertheless liked to think of himself as a sort of hillbilly stranded in the sophisticated world of academia.

When asked by *Fortune* to write an article on sharecroppers, with photographer Walker Evans, he welcomed this opportunity of going back to his roots, "all the way home." This assignment also awakened his sympathy for, and sense of commitment to, the southern poor and led to his most striking work, *Let Us Now Praise Famous Men* (1941), which became a book on three tenant farmer families in the 1930s. It contains some of Agee's best writing: as a poet alive to the "cruel radiance of what is," as an ethnographer respectful of "the other," and as an impassioned humanist angry with injustice and pretense.

Wavering between his attraction to worldly intellectuals and his longing for a humbler, more authentic life in the South, he also vacillated between experimental and realistic writing. Intent on improving his art, he was no less concerned for people, and for the events that shook his times—the Depression, the rise of fascism, the war. As an artist he was extremely curious about all aesthetic forms: poetry (*Permit Me Voyage*, 1974), photography, journalism, and movie making. His passion for the cinema, born in his early childhood in Knoxville, drove him to become one of the most attentive and witty film critics

James Agee, Tennessee poet, novelist, and critic, 1930s

and a versatile screenwriter, who went to Hollywood and worked with such directors as Charles Laughton (*The Night of the Hunter*) and John Huston (*The African Queen*). As a journalist, he contributed many articles for *Time* and *Fortune*, and Paul Ashdown has collected the best of Agee's articles from those magazines in *James Agee: Selected Journalism* (1985).

Concerned to avoid involvement in any movement, whether literary or ideological, Agee stands as an isolated, original artist who voyaged far but who never forgot his dedication to his real homeland, the South.

Geneviève Fabre
University of Paris

Alfred Baxson, *A Way of Seeing: A Critical Study of James Agee* (1972); Laurence Bergreen, *James Agee* (1984); Mark R. Boty, *Tell Me Who I Am: James Agee's Search for Selfhood* (1981); Peter H. Ohlin, *Agee* (1966); Kenneth Seib, *James Agee: Promise and Fulfillment* (1968). ☆

BROOKS, CLEANTH
‖‖
(b. 1906) Critic.

The son of a Methodist minister, Cleanth Brooks was born in Murray, Ky., and grew up in the villages and small towns of that state and of west Tennessee in which his father served as pastor. After graduating from the McTyeire School in McKenzie, Tenn. (1920–24), he attended Vanderbilt University, from which he received a bachelor's degree in 1928. The following year he earned a master of arts degree from Tulane University and enrolled as a Rhodes Scholar in Exeter College, Oxford University, from which he earned a B.A. (Honors) in 1931 and a B.A. Litt. the following year.

After leaving Oxford he accepted a position in the English department of Louisiana State University. On 12 September 1934 he married Edith Ann Blanchard. The following year he and Robert Penn Warren, who had recently joined the faculty, and a small group of scholars and critics from the university founded the *Southern Review*, which before it ceased publication in 1942 was one of the most distinguished literary quarterlies ever published in America. Many of the writers later called the "New Critics" were regular contributors.

Brooks's reputation as one of the most respected modern American critics is based primarily on three books: *Modern Poetry and the Tradition* (1939), *The Well Wrought Urn: Studies in the Structure of Poetry* (1947), and *William Faulkner: The Yoknapatawpha Country* (1963). Some of the other books he has written are *Literary Criticism: A Short History*, with W. K. Wimsatt (1957); *The Hidden Gods: Studies in Hemingway, Faulkner, Yeats, Eliot, and Warren*

(1963); *American Literature: A Mirror, Lens, or Prism?* (1967); *A Shaping Joy: Studies in the Writer's Craft* (1971); and *William Faulkner: Toward Yoknapatawpha and Beyond* (1978).

In addition to the influential books of criticism he has written, Brooks coedited four textbooks that brought the principles of the New Criticism into the classroom and virtually revolutionized the way literature is taught and read: *An Approach to Literature*, with John T. Purser and Robert Penn Warren (1936, 1939, 1952, 1964, 1975); *Understanding Poetry*, with Robert Penn Warren (1938, 1950, 1956, 1960); *Understanding Fiction*, with Robert Penn Warren (1943, 1959); and *Understanding Drama*, with Robert B. Heilman (1945).

Thomas Daniel Young
Vanderbilt University

John Edward Hardy, in *Southern Renascence: The Literature of the Modern South*, ed. Louis D. Rubin, Jr., et al. (1953); Lewis P. Simpson, ed., *The Possibilities of Order: Cleanth Brooks and His Work* (1976); Thomas Daniel Young, *Tennessee Writers* (1981). ☆

CABLE, GEORGE WASHINGTON
||||||||||||||||||||||||||||||||||||||||||||
(1844–1925) Writer and critic.

During the local color era Cable wrote of Creole New Orleans, and he has been called the most important southern artist working in the late 19th century, as well as the first modern southern writer. He is praised both for his courageous essays on civil rights, such as *The Silent South* (1885) and *The Negro Question* (1890), and for his early fiction about New Orleans, especially *Old Creole Days*

(1879), *The Grandissimes* (1880), and *Madame Delphine* (1881). Cable was not a Creole himself, but he had deep roots in New Orleans. He was born and grew up there, and, after service as a Confederate soldier, he returned to live and work in the city until 1885, when he moved to Massachusetts.

Cable's study of the colonial history of Louisiana while writing sketches for the *Picayune* revealed "the decline of an aristocracy under the pressure of circumstances," as well as the "length and blackness" of the shadow in the southern garden. In his essay "My Politics" Cable tells how his reading of the *Code Noir* caused him such "sheer indignation" that he wrote the brutal story of Bras-Coupé, incorporated later as the foundation of *The Grandissimes*. Cable connected the decline of the Creoles to their self-destructive racial pride, and his best work, *The Grandissimes*, makes clear that such racial arrogance has direct application to broader problems of southern history, especially the black-white conflict after 1865. Like the best stories of *Old Creole Days*, *The Grandissimes* balances sympathy for and judgment of New Orleans and the South, but it is stronger because it "contained as plain a protest against the times in which it was written as against the earlier times in which its scenes were set."

Cable continued to write about New Orleans and Louisiana throughout his long career, most notably in *Dr. Sevier* (1884), *The Creoles of Louisiana* (1884), and the Acadian pastoral *Bonaventure* (1888). In all, he published 14 novels and collections of short fiction, with his last novel, *Lovers of Louisiana*, appearing in 1918, just seven years before his death. In his career after *The Grandissimes* Cable was unable to reconcile his love for the South with his abhorrence of slavery and racism. The result was a

George Washington Cable, late 19th-century critic of southern society

split in his career—the polemical essays embody the spirit of reform and the New South, while the romances, beginning with *The Cavalier* (1901), attempt to retrieve an idyllic past, devoid of the problems of racism.

See also ETHNIC LIFE:/Cajuns and Creoles; Creole

Thomas J. Richardson
University of Southern Mississippi

Cable's diary, cited in Newton Arvin, "Introduction" to *The Grandissimes* (1957); Shirley Ann Grau, "Foreword" to *Old Creole Days* (1961); Thomas J. Richardson, ed., *The Grandissimes: Centennial Essays* (1981); Louis D. Rubin, Jr., *George W. Cable: The Life and Times of a Southern Heretic* (1969); Merrill Skaggs, *The Folk of Southern Fiction* (1972); Arlin Turner, *George W. Cable: A Biography* (1956). ☆

CALDWELL, ERSKINE
||||||||||||||||||||||||||||||||||||||||||||||||||||
(1903–1987) Writer.

The son of an itinerant preacher, Erskine Caldwell was born in Coweta County, Ga., in 1903. After an edu-

cation that included four semesters at the University of Virginia, Caldwell began to write short fiction, taking a series of odd jobs to support himself until he arrived in New York in the spring of 1930. Shortly thereafter he began to publish the novels of southern life for which he is most famous. In *Tobacco Road* (1932), *God's Little Acre* (1933), and *Trouble in July* (1940), among others, Caldwell wrote with a strong sense of moral outrage at the grotesque dehumanization of the tenant farmer, who had been reduced to grinding poverty by the social and economic system.

Caldwell was sensitive as well to the effects of racial injustice and wrote of it powerfully both in his novels and in such notable collections of short fiction as *Kneel to the Rising Sun* (1935). His strong sense of social consciousness spilled over from his fiction into compelling documentaries. Some, such as *Some American People* (1935), were written alone; others, among them *You Have Seen Their Faces* (1937) and *Say! Is This the U.S.A.?* (1941), were collaborations with his second wife, the photographer Margaret Bourke-White.

Along with William Faulkner, Caldwell helped to establish a dominant southern literary stereotype of the Depression, creating characters who were amoral, shrewd, venal, and gullible, reflecting primarily the basic human impulses of lust and the urge for propagation, but who nonetheless displayed an almost mystical connection with the land. Caldwell's indictment of society, however, lacked Faulkner's nostalgic fondness for a redemptive if quixotic historical ideal. Mixing the southern traditions of comic exaggeration and an often sadistic violence, Caldwell evolved a gothic humor that emerged in what may arguably be regarded as comic masterpieces—*Journeyman* (1935) and *Georgia Boy* (1943). More subtle is the mixture of fact and exaggeration that informs the supposedly autobiographical *Call It Experience* (1951).

Throughout his career, Caldwell had to defend himself against charges of pornography that stemmed from his treatment of both sexuality and hysteria in southern revivalism and that led to the widespread banning of his books. Caldwell did not think of himself as exclusively a regional writer, insisting that "I'm not exactly a Southerner or I'm not a Floridian; I'm not a Georgian; I'm not anything you can name or pin down because I have lived everywhere and I like everywhere I've lived." Nonetheless, his work is unmistakably rooted in a sense of place. "I think regional writing is more important than trying to be universal," he acknowledged.

Caldwell has yet to achieve significant critical recognition, nor will his writing likely ever again enjoy the popularity that saw his work translated into 27 languages and made him one of the most widely read novelists in the world. In both his journalism and his fiction, however, the "cycloramic depiction of Southern life," as he called it, reveals a portrait that is at once historical and outside of history, an unflinching documentary and part of the ongoing development of southern myth. He died 12 April 1987.

See also MEDIA: / Caldwell, Erskine, and Film

Stanley Trachtenberg
Texas Christian University

James Korges, *Erskine Caldwell* (1969); Scott MacDonald, *Critical Essays on Erskine*

Caldwell (1981); Guy Owen, *Southern Literary Journal* (Fall 1979). ☆

CAPOTE, TRUMAN
||||||||||||||||||||||||||||||||||||||||||||||||||
(1924–1984) Writer.

Truman Capote, who was born Truman Streckfus Persons in New Orleans on 30 September 1924, the son of J. A. (Arch) Persons, later took the name of his stepfather. Capote early determined to be a writer and spent much of his childhood in the lonely pursuit of putting stories down on paper. Following the divorce of his parents, he made his home with relatives in Monroeville, Ala., but in the 1930s went to live with his mother in New York City and later in Connecticut, where he attended high school. Although his formal education ended there, he found a substitute in his reading. After his mother and his stepfather moved back into New York City in the 1940s, Capote took a job as an office boy at the *New Yorker*, the magazine that would eventually publish many of his stories and nonfiction pieces.

Truman Capote achieved overnight fame at the age of 23 with the publication of *Other Voices, Other Rooms* (1948), his first novel. He had already dazzled the New York literary world with his prizewinning stories. A gifted prose stylist—"a fanatic on rhythm and language," as he told one interviewer—he never quite fulfilled his great promise as a writer, though he published a second novel (*The Grass Harp*, 1951) that he later rewrote for the stage, as well as several volumes of short fiction and collections of essays, memoirs, and travel pieces. His early short stories were collected in *A Tree of Night and Other Stories* (1949) and *Breakfast at Tiffany's* (1958), whose centerpiece was the novella that gave the book its title.

Capote's tour de force was *In Cold Blood*, first published serially in the *New Yorker* in 1965 and then as a book; he described it as a new form—the nonfiction novel. A gripping account of the mass murder of a Kansas farm family, it follows the two young killers from the murder scene to their eventual execution five and one-half years later. *In Cold Blood* was enormously successful and was followed by an equally successful motion picture.

Though his roots were in the South, Truman Capote lived most of his life in New York City. A celebrity himself and a man who cherished the art of conversation, he cultivated the rich and famous of the world and was a frequent guest on network television talk shows. When he died in 1984 during a visit to California, he had still not published his much-talked-about novel *Answered Prayers*.

Charles East
Baton Rouge, Louisiana

James Dickey, *Paris Review* (Fall 1985); Lawrence Grobel, *Conversations with Capote* (1985); Kenneth T. Reed, *Truman Capote* (1981); "Truman Capote," *Writers at Work: The Paris Review Interviews*, ed. Malcolm Cowley (1958); "Truman Capote," *Current Biography Yearbook 1968.* ☆

CLEMENS, SAMUEL LANGHORNE ("Mark Twain")

(1835–1910) Writer.

Although Samuel Clemens initially tasted fame and employed his pen name in Nevada and California, he traced his "Mark Twain" pseudonym to his pilot days on the Mississippi River, and many features of his writings can also be attributed to that southern background. Clemens was born 30 November 1835 in the border state of Missouri and grew up in Hannibal, but his father was a Virginian and his mother was from a Kentucky family. Sam Clemens became a printer, working in New York, Pennsylvania, Ohio, Illinois, and Missouri before becoming a steamboat pilot. As a pilot posted at the river ports of St. Louis and New Orleans from 1857 until 1861, Clemens glided regularly through the Deep South sugarcane fields of Louisiana and Mississippi.

The South's watershed year of 1861 was momentous for Clemens, who accompanied his brother Orion to the Far West. Subsequently, Clemens moved east to Buffalo and then settled in the New England climate of Nook Farm in Hartford, Conn. His family, too, moved northward—to Fredonia, N.Y., and to Keokuk, Iowa. These shifts resulted in a hybridization, reflected in his literature, of the traditions and atmosphere of the South, the extravagance and energies of the West, the taboos and commerce of the East. But Louis D. Rubin, Jr., has argued persuasively that "the southern experience of Samuel L. Clemens is so thoroughly and deeply imaged in his life and work that one may scarcely read a chapter of any of his books without encountering it," and that in *A Connecticut Yankee* (1889) "the whole ambivalent love-hate relationship of Sam Clemens with the South is dramatized" to indicate "the South's similarity to feudal England."

Mark Twain objected to the South's pretensions. Remembering the grand, absurd village names of his youth, he chose "St. Petersburg" as the name for his fictional river town, trying to catch and satirize those grandiose dreams of splendor. After the Civil War, Twain would blame the historical novels of Sir Walter Scott for the "romantic juvenilities" and "inflated language and other windy humbuggeries" that still bedeviled the South. Returning to the river for a nostalgic visit in 1882, Clemens was aghast to learn that duels were still being fought by prominent citizens of New Orleans. However, as his steamboat drew into the Louisiana reaches of the Mississippi, he found himself admiring the "greenhouse" lawns and "dense rich foliage and huge, snow-ball blossoms" of the magnolia trees that, along with a "tropical swelter in the air," announced that he was "in the absolute South, now—no modifications, no compromises." On the streets of New Orleans, too, he "found the half-forgotten Southern intonations and elisions as pleasing to my ear as they had formerly been. A Southerner talks music."

This homeland had been a place of

Samuel Clemens (Mark Twain), one of the nation's best-known novelists, c. 1905

grief and disappointment for Twain. In Memphis he had knelt helpless and agonized while his brother Henry died from scalding burns suffered when the steamboat *Pennsylvania* blew up in 1858. Twain also knew firsthand the uncouth, ruffian character of river-town idlers; he portrayed their cruelties in a backward Arkansas town in *The Adventures of Huckleberry Finn.*

Like most southern authors of his generation, Twain felt obliged to explain why he had lived in a land that countenanced human slavery. "In my schoolboy days I had no aversion to slavery," he testified. "I was not aware that there was anything wrong about it. No one arraigned it in my hearing; the local papers said nothing against it; the local pulpit taught us that God approved it." Ultimately, Twain became a great American writer in part because his family *had* owned slaves, so that he felt a lifelong involvement in that system of bondage. His finest novel, *The Adventures of Huckleberry Finn* (1885), like Faulkner's *Absalom, Absalom!*, addresses the volatile racial issue that has periodically threatened the unity of a nation. Twain's entrée to the pages of the high-brow *Atlantic Monthly* was a poignant story inspired by a black woman cook he met at Quarry Farm near Elmira, New York. An angry essay of 1901, "The United States of Lyncherdom," castigated Missouri for joining the southern states in resorting to mob violence against accused blacks, though Twain conceded that "the people in the South are made like the people in the North—a vast majority of whom are right-hearted and compassionate."

Twain could also portray an idealized South. One commentator, Arthur Pettit, has observed that in *The Adventures of Tom Sawyer* (1876), Mark Twain transformed antebellum Hannibal "into a Golden Age of prelapsarian innocence and charm." The image of this dozing village rose before Twain's eyes again and again, although *The Tragedy of Pudd'nhead Wilson* (1894) discloses lurking secrets behind the "white-washed exteriors" of a similar town, Dawson's Landing. Twain's benign movie-reel depiction of the typical downtown district appeared in "Old Times on the Mississippi" (1875), a passage later subsumed in *Life on the Mississippi* (1883); the stir and bustle on Water Street when a black drayman called out "S-t-e-a-m-boat a-comin'!" and the boat came into sight on "the great Mississippi, the majestic, the magnificent Mississippi, rolling its mile-wide tide along, shining in the sun," vividly evoked this scene even for readers who had seen neither that river nor any states bordering it.

Always he acknowledged sincere admiration for amenities of life taken for granted in the South. He lauded its gastronomic delights in *A Tramp Abroad* (1880), listing and praising 20 southern dishes such as "fried chicken, Southern style," "black bass from the Mississippi," "hot corn-pone, with chitlings," "hot hoe-cake," hominy, butter beans, and apple puffs. His mental map of the Quarles farm where he spent his boyhood summers—the main log house, the smokehouse, the slave quarters, the orchard, the tobacco field, the schoolhouse—was re-created for his autobiographical recollections.

Although Twain had a broader and more venturesome approach to fiction than his contemporaries George Washington Cable, Joel Chandler Harris, and Thomas Nelson Page, he is equally indebted with them to the shaping forces of southern culture. His experiments in reproducing black dialect, such as "A True Story," compare favorably with the studied idiom in Harris's *Uncle Remus* (1880) and Page's "Marse Chan" (1884); Jim's patois and Huck's vernacular in *Huckleberry Finn* enriched the form of the American novel forever. In language and in delineation of character, setting, and society, his sketches, short stories, and novels have influenced writers as diverse as Thomas Wolfe, Erskine Caldwell, and William Faulkner. The beneficiary of a tradition of southern frontier humor, Mark Twain multiplied their notable achievements into the richer legacy he bequeathed to modern southern authors.

Alan Gribben
University of Texas at Austin

Justin Kaplan, *Mr. Clemens and Mark Twain* (1974); Lewis G. Leary, *Southern Excursions: Essays on Mark Twain and Others* (1971); Arthur G. Pettit, *Mark Twain and the South* (1974); Louis D. Rubin, Jr., *The Writer in the South* (1972); Thomas A. Tenney, *Mark Twain: A Reference Guide* (1977). ☆

DAVIDSON, DONALD
(1893–1968) Writer and critic.

Of the 12 writers who, in 1930, published *I'll Take My Stand: The South and the Agrarian Tradition*, Donald Grady Davidson remained the most firmly committed to "the cause of agrarianism versus industrialism." Not a farmer's but a schoolteacher's son, he was born on 18 August 1893, in the village of Campbellsville, Tenn., near the Alabama border, but spent most of his mature life in Nashville, studying at Vanderbilt University before World War I and returning there after the war to teach and to write, until his death on 25 April 1968. For a half century he worked as a cultivator in the field of letters, contributing to the Southern Literary Renaissance through his poetry, his criticism, and his active encouragement of talent. He was one of the founders of the *Fugitive* magazine, which in the early 1920s published poetry of such high quality that it quickly gained an international reputation, despite its regional character. As Davidson observed in the final issue of the *Fugitive* in 1925, "the strangest thing in contemporary poetry is that innovation and conservatism exist side by side"; his own poetry reflected his consciousness of the paradox that the traditional culture of the South was in the process of disappearing at the very moment when its highest artistic expression was being achieved.

Like most educated southerners of his generation (and like Thomas Jefferson before them), Davidson was as much a classicist as an agrarian, viewing Greek and Latin as fundamental to civilization, but looking skeptically "On a Replica of the Parthenon" built in a city park in Nashville, amid the noise and smoke of motors, and asking: "What do they seek, / Who build, but never read, their Greek?" He favored a native southern idealism, of the sort mirrored in such memorable poems as "Sanctuary" and "Hermitage," where he re-created imaginatively the pioneer family farm of his ancestors, and in "Meditation on Literary Fame," where he declared:

Happy the land where men hold
    dear
Myth which is truest memory,
Prophecy which is poetry.

Davidson was the heir not only of southern agrarianism and classicism,

but of southern puritanism (his father came from Blue Stocking Hollow, Tenn.), and he sometimes sounded like a Hebrew prophet in his denunciation of material progress (which he believed to be detrimental to a truly humane culture) and in his praise for the relative poverty and simplicity, even the backwardness, of the South as a region. The latter qualities allowed the oral tradition of storytelling and ballad singing to flourish, laying the basis for literary art to develop naturally (to him, it was no accident that Mississippi was one of the lowest states in the nation in per capita income and one of the richest in talented writers). For Davidson, a strong regional loyalty was essential to a writer's integrity, as he argued persuasively in his essay "Still Rebels, Still Yankees," and he admired those modern writers outside the South who kept a definite identification with their place, such as Robert Frost, William Butler Yeats, and

Donald Davidson, Vanderbilt Agrarian, late 1940s

Thomas Hardy. Davidson's own loyalty to the South may have limited his appeal and his reputation outside it, but the genuineness of his convictions was evident in everything he wrote and gave fervor and keenness to both his poetry and his prose. His style was intellectually rigorous and spare, and if his weakness was for didacticism, he was above all a teacher, and in his generation, a great one. A fine poet, an exacting critic, and an able editor, in addition to being an inspiring teacher, Davidson exerted a powerful influence in the creation of a rich modern literature for the South.

First to be mentioned among his many books are *Poems, 1922–1961* (1966); *Still Rebels, Still Yankees and Other Essays* (1957); and *Southern Writers in the Modern World* (1958).

William Pratt
Miami University (Ohio)

John Fair and Thomas Daniel Young, eds., *The Literary Correspondence of Donald Davidson and Allen Tate* (1974); Thomas Daniel Young and M. Thomas Inge, *Donald Davidson* (1971), *Donald Davidson: An Essay and a Bibliography* (1965). ☆

DICKEY, JAMES
|||||||||||||||||||||||||||||||||||||||||||||
(b. 1923) Writer.

A native of Atlanta, Ga., James Lafayette Dickey was born 2 February 1923. A football player in high school and college and an air force combat veteran of World War II, Dickey in his life and his art exhibits a physically aggressive quality matched by few significant poets. He received a bachelor's degree (1949) and a master of arts degree (1950) from Vanderbilt University, where he was in-

fluenced by Monroe K. Spears and was surrounded by the Fugitive-Agrarian literary tradition of Donald Davidson, John Crowe Ransom, and Allen Tate. He taught at Rice Institute in Houston and at the University of Florida, served in the Air Force again during the Korean War, and traveled afterward in Europe. Dickey broke out of academia in 1956 and into the world of advertising, where he was successful in both New York City and Atlanta.

By the end of the decade, however, Dickey grew weary of "selling [his] soul to the devil during the day and buying it back at night." Three national poetry prizes from 1958 to 1959 and a Guggenheim Fellowship in 1961 confirmed his decision to leave advertising and go again to Europe, basing himself in Positina, Italy, from 1962 to 1963. From 1960 to 1964 he published three books of poems: *Into the Stone*, *Drowning with Others*, and *Helmets*. When *Buckdancer's Choice* appeared in 1965, Dickey garnered the National Book Award and enormous public notice for being what *Life* magazine called "The Unlikeliest Poet." Dickey was appointed Consultant in Poetry for the Library of Congress,

James Dickey, South Carolina poet and novelist, 1980s

1966 to 1968, recognition of a firm national reputation.

By 1969 Dickey had published two books of criticism—*The Suspect in Poetry* and *Babel to Byzantium*—and moved to Columbia, S.C., to teach at the University of South Carolina. The 1970s saw the publication of Dickey's best-selling and increasingly well regarded novel, *Deliverance*; four books of poetry—*The Zodiac*; *Tucky the Hunter* (a children's book); *The Strength of Fields*; and *The Eye-Eaters, Blood, Victory, Madness, Buckhead,* and *Mercy*; four books of belles lettres—*Self-Interviews, Sorties, Jericho: The South Beheld,* and *God's Images*; two screenplays—*Deliverance* and *The Call of the Wild*; and several limited-edition shorter works.

Dickey's southernness is inescapable. He relies frequently on storytelling, often with a typically southern version of exuberance and broad humor, as in "Cherrylog Road" and "The Shark's Parlor." His sense of southern place is strong in poems like "Going Home" and "Hunting Civil War Relics at Nimblewill Creek" and in prose works like *Deliverance, Jericho,* and the work-in-progress, *Wilderness of Heaven,* with artist Hubert Shuptrine. Family is important, both immediate, as in "The Celebration," "The String," and "Messages," and ancestral, as in "The Escape" and "Dover: Believing in Kings." Racial issues arise rarely in Dickey's work, with "Slave Quarters" the conspicuous exception. Whatever guilt appears in Dickey's poems is most often attached to war, as in "The Firebombing," or to a mysterious, ghostly dread regarding one's sheer existence, as in "The Other," "The String," and perhaps *The Zodiac*. Religion appears as a curious amalgam of southern fundamentalism and animistic neoromanticism, as in "May Day Sermon," "Approaching Prayer," and "The Heaven of Animals."

More conventionally, Dickey embraces bluegrass music (he plays 6- and 12-string guitars quite well), espouses athletics as personal and community rituals of a peculiarly southern mystique, and keeps to the middle ground in southern politics and economics. Dickey's works show no deep longing for a return of the Old South; rather, he appears comfortable between city and country. Content in the New South suburbs, he calls Columbia "a mixture of university town, southern political capital, and military base." The natural scene is important, of course, "the way it balances Appalachia and the Atlantic," but the clichés of southern living are always modified in Dickey's works—and apparently in his life.

Robert W. Hill
Clemson University

Richard J. Calhoun, ed., *James Dickey: The Expansive Imagination* (1973); Jim Elledge, *James Dickey: A Bibliography* (1979); Stuart Wright, *James Dickey: A Descriptive Bibliography of First Printings of His Works* (1982). ☆

DIXON, THOMAS, JR.
(1864–1946) Writer.

Born in the rural North Carolina Piedmont a year before the Civil War ended, Thomas Dixon lived to see the atomic bombing of Hiroshima and the end of World War II. Between 1902 and 1939 he published 22 novels, as well as numerous plays, screenplays, books of sermons, and miscellaneous nonfiction. Educated at Wake Forest and Johns

Hopkins, Dixon was a lawyer, state legislator, preacher, novelist, playwright, actor, lecturer, real-estate speculator, and movie producer. Familiar to three presidents and such notables as John D. Rockefeller, he made and lost millions, ending up an invalid court clerk in Raleigh, N.C.

Paradoxically, Dixon is among the most dated and most contemporary of southern writers. In genre an early 19th-century romancer, thematically Dixon argued for three interrelated beliefs still current in southern life: the need for racial purity, the sanctity of the family centered on a traditional wife and mother, and the evil of socialism.

In the Klan trilogy—*The Leopard's Spots* (1902), *The Clansman* (1905), *The Traitor* (1907)—and in *The Sins of the Fathers* (1912), Dixon presents racial conflict as an epic struggle, with the future of civilization at stake. Although Dixon personally condemned slavery and Klan activities after Reconstruction ended, he argued that blacks must be denied political equality because that leads to social equality and miscegenation, thus to the destruction of both family and civilized society. Throughout his work, white southern women are the pillars of family and society, the repositories of all human idealism. *The Foolish Virgin* (1915) and *The Way of a Man* (1919) attack women's suffrage because women outside the home become corrupted; with the sacred vessels shattered, social morality is lost. In his trilogy on socialism—*The One Woman* (1903), *Comrades* (1909), *The Root of Evil* (1911)—he attacks populist socialism expressed in such works as Edward Bellamy's *Looking Backward*, arguing that it is impossible for all classes to be equal in a society. Dixon's last novel, *The Flaming Sword* (1939),

written just before he suffered a crippling cerebral hemorrhage, combines the threats of socialism and racial equality, presenting blacks as communist dupes attempting the overthrow of the United States. Through all his work runs an impassioned defense of conservative religious values.

Young Dixon's religious and political beliefs were melded in a crucible shaped by his region's military defeat and economic depression and by the fiercely independent, Scotch-Irish Presbyterian faith of the North Carolina highlands. As a student reading Darwin, Huxley, and Spencer, he suffered a brief period of religious doubt. But his faith rebounded stronger than ever, and Dixon sought the grandest pulpit he could find. He abandoned a successful Baptist ministry in New York for the larger nondenominational audience he could reach as a lecturer and, after the success of *The Leopard's Spots*, as a novelist and playwright. With the movie *Birth of a Nation* (based on *The Clansman*), Dixon believed he had found the ideal medium to educate the masses, to bring them to political and religious salvation. Although his work is seldom read today, both in his themes and as a political preacher seeking a national congregation through mass media, Thomas Dixon clearly foreshadowed the politicized television evangelists of the modern South.

See also MEDIA: / Dixon and Film

James Kinney
Virginia Commonwealth
University

Raymond A. Cook, *Fire from the Flint: The Amazing Careers of Thomas Dixon* (1968), *Thomas Dixon* (1974); F. Garvin Davenport, *Journal of Southern History* (August 1970). ☆

ELLISON, RALPH
|||||||||||||||||||||||||||||||||||||||||
(b. 1914) Writer.

Born on 1 March 1914, in Oklahoma City, Okla., Ralph Waldo Ellison grew up in the black communities of the city's East Side. His father, Lewis Alfred Ellison, died when Ralph was three, leaving his wife, Ida Millsap Ellison, with the arduous task of supporting Ralph and her younger son, Herbert, on the meager wages she earned as a service worker. Ellison left Oklahoma City when he was 19 and left the South when he was 22. Although he has lived practically all of his adult life in New York City, the lasting influence of his immersion in southern black folk life and culture is readily evident in the contents of his essays and in both the form and meaning of his fiction.

Between the two world wars, Oklahoma City was one of the South's strongholds for black blues and jazz. From his early childhood through his young adulthood, Ellison was absorbed with blues and jazz and knew several of the city's musicians. He balanced his strong affinity for blues and jazz with his interest and training in classical music. Music was his first love, but his mother provided him with an environment rich also in the other arts. Even as a child he was an avid reader of imaginative literature, and during his school years he excelled as a student, musician, and athlete.

When he graduated from Douglass High School in 1931, he could not afford to attend college. He worked at odd jobs during the next two years, and in 1933, with a music scholarship, he entered Tuskegee Institute in Alabama as a major in classical music. At Tuskegee he sustained his interest in blues and jazz and continued to read widely in various disciplines, especially literature. His chance reading of T. S. Eliot's *The Waste Land* during his sophomore year marked the beginning of his desire to become a professional writer rather than a professional musician.

In the summer of 1936 he went to New York City with the intent of saving enough money by the fall to complete his education at Tuskegee. Failing to do so, he remained in New York, where he studied music and sculpture and the craft of various literary artists. In New York he met Langston Hughes, Richard Wright, and other black writers who encouraged his ambition to become a writer. His job as a researcher for the New York Federal Writers' Project from 1938 to 1942 provided him with his first steady employment since coming to New York.

With experience as editor of *Negro Quarterly*, with a few short publications behind him, and with a Rosenwald Fellowship, in 1944 he concentrated on writing a novel. His first attempt was unsuccessful, and in 1945 he began work on another novel, *Invisible Man*. Except for time he devoted to his wife Fannie McConnell (he married in 1946), his life from 1945 to the publication of *Invisible Man* in 1952 was spent in polishing his novel, whose content and sophisticated artistry were derived primarily from Ellison's knowledge of music, southern black folklife, American culture, and literature.

Invisible Man was greeted with high critical acclaim. In 1953 it won the National Book Award and the Russwurm Award. By the mid-1960s it had been accepted as an American classic and Ellison as a first-rate American novelist.

In 1965 a poll of prominent authors, critics, and editors declared *Invisible Man* to be the most distinguished work of American fiction published since 1945. The publication of his collection of essays, *Shadow and Act* (1964), revealed that he also was an astute essayist and a perceptive critic of literature and music and of southern and American culture in general.

Since the 1960s he has been a favorite speaker on the lecture circuit, has taught at the University of Chicago, Rutgers, and other institutions, has received numerous honorary degrees and awards (including France's Chevalier de l'Ordre des Artes et Lettres and America's Medal of Freedom), and has been a favored subject among literary critics and literary and cultural historians in the United States and abroad. Since his retirement in 1980 from New York University after 10 years as a chaired professor in the humanities, Ellison has worked on his long-awaited second novel.

J. Lee Greene
University of North Carolina
at Chapel Hill

John Hersey, ed., *Ralph Ellison: A Collection of Critical Essays* (1974); R. S. Lillard, *American Book Collector* (November 1968); James A. McPherson, *Atlantic Monthly* (December 1970); Carol Polsgrove, *American Book Collector* (November–December 1969). ☆

FAULKNER, WILLIAM
(1897–1962) Writer.

William Cuthbert Faulkner was born on 25 September 1897, in New Albany, Miss. The great-grandson of William Clark Falkner, a southern novelist and Confederate officer, Faulkner was responsible for adding the *u* to his family name—just as he was responsible for transmogrifying his native South into a universal place of the imagination in brilliant novels and stories that have put him first among 20th-century American writers of prose fiction.

Faulkner came to maturity at a time when Mississippi and the South were changing. He grew up a part of post–Civil War southern culture, which was dominated by memories of the Old South and the war, and yet he experienced also the modernizing forces of the early 20th century in the region. He had romantic instincts, expressed in his early poetry and prose and in his enlistment in the Royal Canadian Air Force in 1918, hoping to be a gallant fighter pilot. He went back to Oxford, Miss., in that same year, though, and pursued work as a writer. Lawyer Phil Stone encouraged him, financially and intellectually, introducing him to the work of modernists such as T. S. Eliot.

Faulkner spent several months in New Orleans in 1925, becoming friends with Sherwood Anderson and other creative talents there, and in July of that year embarked on a walking tour through parts of Europe. With the exception of stints working as a screenwriter in California, he mostly lived thereafter in Mississippi. His first novel, *Soldiers' Pay*, appeared in 1926, followed by *Mosquitoes* in 1927.

All of Faulkner's major novels reflect his southern rootedness. Beginning with *Flags in the Dust* (published as *Sartoris* in 1929), he creates a mythical Mississippi county, Yoknapatawpha, in which his main characters and their families confront not only specifically southern subjects—such as a native Indian pop-

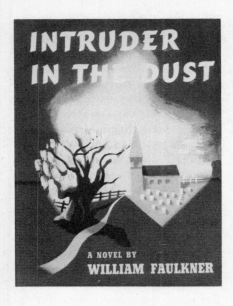

INTRUDER
IN THE DUST

A NOVEL BY
WILLIAM FAULKNER

Cover from William Faulkner's 1947 novel

ulation, the Civil War, plantation life, and race relations—but also themes that transcend a regional focus. *Absalom, Absalom!* (1936), perhaps Faulkner's greatest achievement, explicitly conjoins his southernness and his universality in the partnership of the southerner, Quentin Compson, and the Canadian, Shreve McCannon, Harvard roommates, whose exploration of the southern past provokes questions about the meaning of history itself.

In *The Sound and the Fury* (1929), his first great novel, Faulkner depicts several generations of a southern family, the Compsons, with a sophisticated handling of point of view and human voice that is equal to the greatest work of his European contemporaries. In *As I Lay Dying* (1930), *Light in August* (1932), *The Hamlet* (1940), and *Go Down, Moses* (1942), Faulkner portrays many different kinds and classes of southerners exemplified by the Bundrens, the Snopeses, and the McCaslins; he also conveys penetrating insights into southern Protestantism, miscegenation, and discrimination that again point beyond themselves—especially in the figure of Joe Christmas—to fundamental concerns about the nature of human identity and how it is shaped.

Other leading Faulkner novels include *Pylon* (1935), *The Unvanquished* (1938), *The Wild Palms* (1939), *A Fable* (1954), and his last major work, *The Reivers* (1962). *Sanctuary* (1931) was one of the few Faulkner novels to sell well, and he had abiding financial problems that led to his work in films and as a short story writer for popular magazines. His accomplished short fiction appears in *Collected Stories* (1950) and *Uncollected Stories* (1979). Despite his critical success, especially in Europe, all of Faulkner's novels were out of print when Malcolm Cowley's edited *Portable Faulkner* appeared in 1946 and led to a steadily rising appreciation, and sale, of his work.

In the latter part of his career Faulkner became increasingly aware that he had established his apocryphal county as a counterweight to the actual South, where he had spent most of his life. In *Requiem for a Nun* (1951), he juxtaposed the development of Yoknapatawpha and its town, Jefferson, with the history of Mississippi and its capital, Jackson. In this underrated experimental drama, as well as in his later Snopes novels *The Town* (1957) and *The Mansion* (1959), he directly addressed the issue of the South's changing culture and political structure in the context of world history and national events—as he did at the same time in numerous public letters, speeches, and interviews, especially after receiving the Nobel Prize in 1950. He died in Oxford, Miss., on 6 July 1962.

See also GEOGRAPHY: / Faulkner's Geography; MEDIA: / Faulkner and Film; MYTHIC SOUTH: / Yoknapatawpha County

Carl E. Rollyson, Jr.
Wayne State University

John E. Bassett, *William Faulkner: An Annotated Checklist of Criticism* (1972), *William Faulkner: An Annotated Checklist of Recent Criticism* (1983); Joseph Blotner, *William Faulkner: A Biography*, 2 vols. (1974); Louis Daniel Brodsky and Robert W. Hamblin, eds., *Faulkner: A Comprehensive Guide to the Brodsky Collection*, 2 vols. (1982–84); Cleanth Brooks, *William Faulkner: The Yoknapatawpha Country* (1963), *William Faulkner: Toward Yoknapatawpha and Beyond* (1978); Thomas L. McHaney, *William Faulkner: A Reference Guide* (1976); Michael Millgate, *The Achievement of William Faulkner* (1965). ☆

FOOTE, SHELBY
||||||||||||||||||||||||||||||||||||||||||||
(b. 1916) Writer.

Shelby Foote, author of six novels and a three-volume narrative history of the Civil War, was born 17 November 1916 and raised in Greenville, Miss. Among the early influences on his writing career was William Alexander Percy, an uncle of Foote's lifelong friend, novelist Walker Percy.

After attending the University of North Carolina, Foote returned to Greenville in 1939 and enlisted in the Mississippi National Guard. While waiting for his unit to be called to active duty, Foote wrote his first novel, *Tournament*, set in the fictional town of Bristol in the also fictional Jordan County. This Delta locale is the setting for four of Foote's six novels.

The publication of *Tournament* was delayed until 1949 by Foote's World War II service as an artillery captain in Europe. After the war, Foote settled in Greenville and resumed his writing career. In the four years following the publication of *Tournament*, he wrote and published four novels: *Follow Me Down* (1950), the story of a tenant farmer/evangelist who commits a murder; *Love in a Dry Season* (1951), which he considers his only comedy; *Shiloh* (1952), a fictional re-creation of the Civil War battle told through a series of first-person monologues; and *Jordan County* (1954), a collection of seven short works detailing the history of Foote's fictional county in reverse chronological order.

With five novels completed and a solid critical reputation established, Foote moved to Memphis in 1953. There he began work on *The Civil War: A Narrative* (3 vols.), an endeavor that required 20 years to complete. It contains more than 1,650,000 words and is an account of the events, sights, sounds, and feel of the Civil War. *Volume One: Fort Sumter to Perryville* was published in 1958, *Volume Two: Fredericksburg to Meridian* in 1963, and *Volume Three: Red River to Appomattox* in 1974. Historian T. Harry Williams described *The Civil War: A Narrative* as "one of the historical and literary achievements of our time."

After completing his Civil War history, Foote returned to writing novels. In 1978 he published *September, September*, the tale of the kidnapping of a black child in Memphis, where Foote continues to live.

David Dawson
Memphis, Tennessee

George Garrett, *Mississippi Quarterly* (Winter 1974–75); *Mississippi Quarterly* (special issue on Foote, Fall 1971); Louis D. Rubin,

Jr., *Prospects*, vol. 1 (1974); Helen White and Redding S. Sugg, *Shelby Foote* (1982). ☆

GLASGOW, ELLEN
||||||||||||||||||||||||||||||||||||||||||||||
(1873–1945) Writer.

Ellen Anderson Gholson Glasgow, born in Richmond, Va., on 22 April 1873, published her first novel, *The Descendant*, in 1897, when she was 24 years old. With this novel Glasgow began a literary career encompassing four and a half decades and comprising 20 novels, a collection of poems, one of stories, and a book of literary criticism. Her autobiography, *A Woman Within*, was published posthumously in 1954.

Born into an aristocratic Virginia family, the young Glasgow rebelled against the conventional modes of feminine conduct and thought approved by her caste. Educated at home and through her own energetic readings in philosophy, social and political theory, and European and British literature, she developed a mind with enough strength and resilience to confront the truths of human experience without the sheltering illusions carefully nurtured by the dying southern aristocratic order she saw about her.

Glasgow's strong intellect led her to a conscious channeling of her creative energies toward the making of a substantial body of fiction. The framework of these works was to be, as she stated in 1898, at age 25, "a series of sketches dealing with life in Virginia." As she matured artistically, this early half-formed intention realized itself in a series of novels that constitutes a social history of her native Virginia. The great organizing ideas of her fiction are the conflicts between tradition and change,

matter and spirit, the individual and society. The natural bent of her mind taught her that realism and irony were the best tools with which to fashion a new southern fiction to take the place of the sentimental stories of a glorified aristocratic past that dominated the regional fiction of her day. Through her poor white heroes and heroines, she introduced democratic values seldom found in the works of other southern writers outside Mark Twain. From the very beginning of her intellectual and creative life, she rejected Victorian definitions of femininity dominating the social attitudes of her day.

Glasgow produced seven novels of enduring literary merit. *The Deliverance* (1904), the best of her early novels, offers a naturalistic treatment of the class conflicts emerging after the Civil War. Its evocation of the Virginia landscape and tobacco farming invites comparison with Hardy's epics of the soil. In her women's trilogy—*Virginia* (1913), *Life and Gabriella* (1916), and *Barren Ground* (1925)—Glasgow assigns each of her Virginia heroines a fate deter-

Ellen Glasgow, Virginia author, 1922

mined by her response to the patriarchal code of feminine behavior that had formed her, a code that, as Glasgow shows so well in *Barren Ground*, always pitted women against their own biological natures. After *Barren Ground*, which marked her arrival at artistic maturity, Glasgow produced three sparkling comedies of manners—*The Romantic Comedians* (1926), *They Stooped to Folly* (1929), and *The Sheltered Life* (1932), the last the author's finest work. In these novels of urban Virginian life depicting the clash of generations, she again shows her women characters reacting to patriarchal stereotypes limiting their individuality and growth, while at the same time exposing either with comic or with satiric irony the limitations these views of women place on the male characters who hold them.

A popular writer, Glasgow was on the best-seller lists five times. In 1942 she received the Pulitzer Prize for her last published novel, *In This Our Life*, though by this time her powers had declined. Her artistic recognition had reached its height in 1931, when, as the acknowledged doyenne of southern letters, she presided over the Southern Writers Conference at the University of Virginia. For many years the victim of heart disease, she died in her sleep at home in Richmond on 21 November 1945.

Tonette Bond Inge
Randolph-Macon College

C. Hugh Holman, *Three Modes of Southern Fiction: Ellen Glasgow, William Faulkner, Thomas Wolfe* (1966); M. Thomas Inge, ed., *Ellen Glasgow: Centennial Essays* (1976); Julius Rowan Raper, *From the Sunken Garden: The Fiction of Ellen Glasgow, 1916–1945* (1980), *Without Shelter: The Early Career of Ellen Glasgow* (1971). ☆

GREEN, PAUL
(1894–1981) Playwright.

Paul Green was born 17 March 1894 on a farm in Harnett County, near Lillington, N.C. He worked side by side with the black tenants and hired hands, whom he regarded as part of his larger family. He dramatized this background in his poems, stories, novels, and plays.

In the early 1920s he wrote one-act folk dramas as a student at the University of North Carolina at Chapel Hill. *The No 'Count Boy*, first published in 1924 in *Theatre Arts Magazine*, gave Green his first recognition beyond the South. In 1925 *The No 'Count Boy* won the Belasco Cup competition in New York City. In *The Hawthorn Tree* (1943) Green elaborated on his imaginative concept of the "folk," referring to "the people whose manners, ethics, religious and philosophical ideals are more nearly derived from and controlled by the ways of the outside physical world . . . than by the ways and institutions of men in a specialized society." The success of *The No 'Count Boy* led to the publication of two collections of Paul Green's plays in 1925 and 1926. A longer version of one of these plays, *In Abraham's Bosom*, was awarded a Pulitzer Prize in May 1927. Other Broadway plays were *The Field God* and *The House of Connelly*, subtitled *A Drama of the Old South and the New*. These plays helped establish Paul Green's place among America's leading playwrights.

Instead of writing for what he termed the commercial theater of New York, however, he decided to produce his plays outdoors, amalgamating pageant, music, dance, and poetry into a theater he created and named "symphonic drama." Celebrating events and characters in history as well as nationalistic myths, Green defined symphonic drama in his 1948 "Author's Note" to *The Common Glory* as "that type of drama in which all elements of theatre art are used to sound together—one for all and all for one, a true democracy. The theatre of such a drama is sensitized and charged with a fierce potential of evocation and expressiveness for any moment." The most famous of these symphonic dramas is *The Lost Colony* (1937), the story of Sir Walter Raleigh's dream of settling America in the late 16th century. The play is produced each summer for thousands of visitors to North Carolina.

Paul Green recognized early the dramatic richness of his native South, championing always human rights and his thought that "the greatest sin society can commit is to cause a man to miss his own life."

Shelby Stephenson
Pembroke State University

Vincent Kenny, *Paul Green* (1971); Walter S. Lazenby, Jr., *Paul Green* (1970); William S. Powell, ed., *Dictionary of North Carolina Biography*, vol. 2 (1986). ☆

HARRIS, GEORGE WASHINGTON

||||||||||||||||||||||||||||||||||||||||||||||
(1814–1869) Writer.

Harris was born in Allegheny City, Pa., but his parents were probably North Carolinians. At five he was taken to Knoxville, Tenn., by his married half brother, Samuel Bell, who opened a metalworking shop. Harris received little formal education, was early apprenticed, and by his late teens had served as captain for a Tennessee River steamboat. In 1835 he married Mary Emiline Nance, tried large-scale farming in Blount County, Tenn., and lost his land, a slave, and even household goods. By 1843 he was back in Knoxville operating a metalworking and jewelry shop.

While living on his farm Harris had already begun to contribute to local newspapers, and during the next decade he practiced a variety of literary forms and published in the internationally circulated sporting magazine, the New York *Spirit of the Times*. During 1843 Harris published, under the pen name "Mr. Free," four formal letters describing rural customs, sports, and hunts. Presented from a gentlemanly perspective, the Tennessee backwoods is evoked in versions of pastoral. In 1845, in "The Knob Dance," Harris created a fictional account of a ritual frolic presented in the comic dialect of a narrator whose extravagance and sense of community are richly expressive of deep patterns of the folk culture. Action and language celebrate freedom, intensity, and the joys of the body.

In 1854, again in the *Spirit*, Harris expanded his comic depiction of southern backwoods life with the creation of his vital, intense, "nat'ral born durn'd fool," Sut Lovingood, a Tennessee youth who declares his brains are "mos' ove the time onhook'd," recounting his family background in a comic, grotesque fable of conflict with his father and flight from home. Throughout the 1850s Harris created a variety of adventures for his character, many revised and included in *Sut Lovingood's Yarns* in 1867.

Although Harris's achievement is complex, two areas stand out. Harris peoples his backwoods with self-assertive characters and develops Sut as an arresting seer. Sut's folk speech, metaphorically rich and presented in painstakingly detailed dialect, is an unsurpassed creative distillation of the American comic vernacular. Inseparable from this aesthetic achievement and embodied in it is a set of unique, uninhibited southern social and political ideas.

Harris's topics cluster around the prankster's search for excitement, the family and community, the reduction of authority figures—sheriffs, judges, preachers, and fathers—and the complexities of relations between the sexes. Some episodes convey the responses of the insular community to outsiders, such as blacks, Jews, Catholics, Mormons, and Yankees. Harris's first political targets were Tennesseans, but later he treated many national figures, including James Buchanan, John C. Frémont, Abraham Lincoln, and numerous abolitionists. Other targets were "strong minded women," philosophers, and utopian theorizers. His reductive satires express dramatically the narrowest fears and hatreds of his community.

Writers such as Mark Twain, William Faulkner, and Flannery O'Connor have praised Harris's characterization and language. Critics' responses have been from "Rabelaisian" to "repellent." Clearly, Harris's range extends from vituperative satire to the ambiguities of grotesque realism and, finally, to the celebratory mode of folk humor.

Milton Rickels
University of Southwestern Louisiana

George Washington Harris, *High Times and Hard Times*, ed. M. Thomas Inge (1967), *Sut Lovingood: Yarns Spun by a "Nat'ral Born Durn'd Fool"* (1867); Milton Rickels, *George Washington Harris* (1965). ☆

HARRIS, JOEL CHANDLER
(1848–1908) Writer.

Harris, the illegitimate son of Mary Harris and an Irish laborer, was born on 9 December 1848, near Eatonton, Ga. His death from nephritis came in Atlanta on 3 July 1908.

Harris's formal schooling was spotty, but he read widely in world, English, and American literature, with Goldsmith's *The Vicar of Wakefield* being his favorite book. His major training came at the hands of Joseph Addison Turner, who edited *The Countryman*, a weekly newspaper published at the middle Georgia plantation Turnwold. From 1862 to 1866 young Harris worked on the paper, read from Turner's library, and listened to the speech and tales of the plantation blacks. It was his beginning as a writer.

Harris worked for several other newspapers before joining the staff of the Atlanta *Constitution* in 1876 as associate editor. Here he began publishing his famous Uncle Remus stories, using the black dialect he had heard on the plantation. His fame soon spread nationally because of the Uncle Remus tales, and three major Remus books followed: *Uncle Remus: His Songs and His Sayings* (1880), *Nights with Uncle Remus* (1883), and *Uncle Remus and His Friends* (1892). Numerous other volumes of the tales were published both during his lifetime and posthumously.

Diverse in taste and talents, Harris also wrote six children's books, all set on a Georgia plantation, and several novelettes and novels—most importantly, *Sister Jane: Her Friends and Acquaintances* (1896), a novel that depicts antebellum Georgia, and *Gabriel Tolliver: A Story of Reconstruction* (1902), his major long work. Other ventures into long narrative include an autobiographical novel, *On the Plantation* (1892), the setting of which is Turnwold. Adept at the short story, Harris produced five collections, the main ones being *Mingo, and Other Sketches in Black and White* (1884) and *Free Joe and Other Georgia Sketches* (1887). And with his son Julian he established *Uncle Remus's Magazine* in 1907.

Although Harris disavowed regionalism in art ("My idea is that truth is more important than sectionalism, and that literature that can be labeled Northern, Southern, Western, or Eastern, is not worth labeling at all"), his writings are unsurpassed in reflecting the southern environment. His short stories are born of the Georgia soil, his novels echo the strains of the Civil War South, his editorials for the *Constitution* deal with southern social and political issues, and, of course, his famed Uncle Remus tales capture the diction and dialect of the plantation blacks while presenting genuine folk legends. Enlivened with gentle humor and irony, Harris's portraits of the Georgia Negro and his faithful handling of the folk tales constitute his major contributions to southern and American literature. His was a southern voice with a national range.

See also FOLKLIFE: / Brer Rabbit

David B. Kesterson
North Texas State University

R. Bruce Bickley, Jr., *Joel Chandler Harris* (1978), with Karen L. Bickley and Thomas H. English, *Joel Chandler Harris: A Reference Guide* (1978); Arthur Hobson Quinn, *American Fiction: An Historical and Critical Survey* (1936); Bernard Wolfe, *Commentary* (July 1949). ☆

HELLMAN, LILLIAN
(1905–1984) Writer.

Lillian Florence Hellman was born of Jewish heritage in New Orleans, La., on 20 June 1905, the only child of Julia Newhouse and Max Bernard Hellman. During childhood, she divided her time between New York, where her father's job took him when she was quite young, and New Orleans, attending schools in both cities. Between 1922 and 1924 she attended New York University but left before her senior year to work as a manuscript reader for publisher Horace Liveright. On 31 December 1925 she married Arthur Kober, a theatrical press agent, and spent the ensuing four years reading scripts for New York producers, writing book reviews for the New York *Herald Tribune*, and traveling. In the fall of 1930 she and Kober moved to Hollywood, where he worked as a script-writer for Paramount and she as a manuscript reader for Metro-Goldwyn-Mayer and where, in November 1930, she met Dashiell Hammett, a successful and popular writer. In March 1931 Hellman moved back to New York and shortly thereafter divorced Arthur Kober and began her 30-year relationship with Hammett.

After writing a few short stories and discovering that was not to be her literary mode, Hellman collaborated with critic Louis Kronenberger on a play, *Dear Queen*, which was completed in 1932 but never produced. In November 1934 *The Children's Hour* opened on Broadway and was both a hit and a sensation, at least partially because it introduced the topic of lesbianism to the American stage. Its success sent its author back to Hollywood, where she adapted *Dark Angel* from a novel by Guy Bolton and did a sanitized film version of *The Children's Hour* entitled *These Three*. For the next 30 years she continued to write for both the stage and screen, doing movie versions of Sidney Kingsley's *Dead End* (1937) and of Horton Foote's novel *The Chase* (1966), as well as of her own plays *The Little Foxes* (1941) and *The Searching Wind* (1944), in addition to a documentary, *North Star* (1943).

Her other plays included *Another Part of the Forest* (1946), *The Autumn Garden* (1951), and *Toys in the Attic* (1960). The last play and *Watch on the Rhine* (1941) each won a New York Drama Critics' Circle Award for best American play of the year. Hellman also adapted a number of works for the Broadway stage.

Having grown disillusioned with Broadway, Hellman turned in the 1960s from writing plays and began a series of autobiographical memoirs, which included *An Unfinished Woman* (1969), *Pentimento* (1973), and *Scoundrel Time* (1976), the last her account of the McCarthy years after World War II, her blacklisting in Hollywood, and her appearance before the House Un-American Activities Committee.

Although only four of Hellman's plays—*The Little Foxes*, *Another Part of the Forest*, *Autumn Garden*, and *Toys in the Attic*—have southern settings and southern characters (some based on her family), they are among her best writing. In a 1939 interview about *The Little Foxes*, probably her most enduring work, she indicated that she chose the South as a setting "because it fitted the period I wanted for dramatic purposes and because it is a part of the world whose atmosphere I personally am familiar with as a Southerner. I also wanted a certain naive or innocent quality in some of my characters which I

could find in the South but which would have been quite out of place in any other American setting." And late in her life, when she had lived in the Northeast for some 55 years, she admitted that she still considered herself a southerner, despite the fact that at age 11 she had moved North: "I came from a family of Southerners. It wasn't simply that I was brought up and down from the South. I came from a family, on both sides, who had been Southerners for a great many generations."

Jackson R. Bryer
University of Maryland

Mark W. Estrin, *Lillian Hellman: Plays, Films, Memoirs: A Reference Guide* (1980); Doris V. Falk, *Lillian Hellman* (1978); Katherine Lederer, *Lillian Hellman* (1979); Richard Moody, *Lillian Hellman: Playwright* (1972). ☆

HEYWARD, DuBOSE
(1885–1940) Writer.

Edwin DuBose Heyward, the son of aristocratic white parents, was among those who protested Mencken's indictment of the South as the "Sahara of the Bozart." Although Heyward deserves credit for calling attention to the folklore and legends of Low Country South Carolina and the mountains of North Carolina, his greatest achievement was his creation of black characters, especially the lame beggar Porgy. And though the name of their creator is often forgotten, his Porgy and Bess have taken their places among the legendary characters of the American imagination.

That achievement is the result of a series of fortunate collaborations. The germ of Heyward's novel *Porgy* (1925) was a newspaper article on a crippled beggar, but Heyward, who had spent a year working for a steamship company on a Charleston waterfront, had developed a keen ear for black speech and a sensitivity to the black community. The novel was a popular success, widely praised. His wife, Dorothy Hartzell Kuhns, a dramatist, recognized the dramatic potential of the novel, and the couple collaborated on the play *Porgy*, which opened in New York in 1927 to resounding acclaim. It was counted a part of the Harlem Renaissance and was certainly an important event for black performers, who had previously found limited opportunities for serious drama. The play was later the inspiration for George Gershwin's opera *Porgy and Bess* (1935). Heyward wrote the libretto and, assisted by Ira Gershwin, most of the lyrics. George Gershwin had insisted that the work be an opera, not a musical, which it would have become if Heyward had had his way. Since Heyward's death, most Americans know Porgy and Bess only through the opera.

Brass Ankle (1931), the only play Heyward wrote alone, is a study of miscegenation. It is the only Heyward play in which white characters dominate, but its success was limited. With his wife, he collaborated on *Mamba's Daughter* (1939). The play, written for Ethel Waters, who played Hagar, was the first serious Broadway play to make a star of a black woman. Heyward had plans to make into an opera *Star Spangled Version* (1939), his novel based on the effect of the New Deal on blacks in the Virgin Islands, but his early death prevented that.

In his novel *Peter Ashley* (1932), Heyward looked at his native Charleston through the eyes of history. Peter, a young aristocrat who has been educated in Oxford, knows that the course of the Confederacy is wrong, but his heart finally leads him to that side. In the 1920s Heyward made his commitment to the cause of southern art and its future by founding, with Hervey Allen and John Bennett, the Poetry Society of South Carolina. He lectured throughout the state and read his poems. His *Carolina Chansons: Legends of the Low Country*, with Allen, appeared in 1922. His other verse collections were *Skylines and Horizons* (1924) and *Jasbo Brown and Selected Poems* (1931). Important as these works were to the Southern Literary Renaissance, calling attention to the region and its folklore, they helped train Heyward for his more powerful explorations of black experience, especially of the black lovers Porgy and Bess.

Joseph M. Flora
University of North Carolina
at Chapel Hill

Hervey Allen, *DuBose Heyward: A Critical and Biographical Sketch* (1927); Frank Durham, *DuBose Heyward: The Man Who Wrote Porgy* (1954), *DuBose Heyward's Use of Folklore in His Negro Fiction* (1961). ☆

KENNEDY, JOHN PENDLETON

(1795–1870) Writer.

Descendant of a Tidewater Virginia clan, Kennedy was born in Baltimore, Md. He studied law with an uncle after receiving his formal education at a local academy and at Baltimore College. Following his admission to the bar in 1816, he practiced law rather aimlessly while writing essays and satirical pieces. In 1820 he began a political career as a member of the Maryland House of Delegates. Returning to creative writing, Kennedy published *Swallow Barn* (1832), a pioneer contribution to plantation literature that enjoyed moderate success. Capitalizing on a genre made popular by James Fenimore Cooper, Kennedy published his best work, *Horse-Shoe Robinson*, in 1835. An American historical romance, it was an early contribution to the legend of the southern role in the Revolution. Appearing in 1838, Kennedy's *Rob of the Bowl* was a tale of religious and political rivalries in 17th-century Maryland. His budding career as a romancer ended with his election to the U.S. House of Representatives in 1838. Kennedy subordinated his creative work to his political and business interests for the remainder of his life. His last major literary work was *Memoirs of the Life of William Wirt* (1849).

As Kennedy grew to manhood during the early years of the 19th century, he saw his native Baltimore change from village to thriving commercial town—its atmosphere becoming distinctly less southern. Such changes wrought their effect upon Kennedy. His ties to the South were strong, but his commitments to the border state he lived in led him to fear the rise of southern sectionalism and to embrace a nationalistic point of view.

Kennedy's place in southern letters rests on *Swallow Barn*, *Horse-Shoe Robinson*, and *Rob of the Bowl*. Of the three romances, *Swallow Barn* proved to be the most important in reflecting an image of a self-conscious South. Though the book cataloged all that seemed good in the plantation world, it also satirized the provinciality of a closed Virginia society. Despite his somewhat sympathetic depiction of slavery in *Swallow Barn*, Kennedy was convinced that the institution kept Virginia and the rest of the South from enjoying the benefits of commercial and industrial expansion. He portrayed Virginians after the Revolution living in a dream world that slavery and sectionalism would turn into a nightmare.

L. Moody Simms, Jr.
Illinois State University

Charles H. Bohner, *John Pendleton Kennedy: Gentleman from Baltimore* (1961); Jay B. Hubbell, *The South in American Literature, 1607–1900* (1954); Joseph V. Ridgely, *John Pendleton Kennedy* (1966). ☆

LONGSTREET, AUGUSTUS BALDWIN
(1790–1870) Writer.

Longstreet is remembered today for his collection of humorous stories, *Georgia Scenes* (1835). A native of Augusta, Ga., he earned a degree from Yale University in 1813, studied law in Litchfield, Conn., and returned to his home state. He later attained professional success as a lawyer, a superior court judge, a proprietor and editor of a newspaper (the *State Rights Sentinel*, which he used as a forum for his political views, especially for a defense of slavery and nullification), a Methodist minister, and president of four institutions of higher learning (Emory College in Georgia, Centenary College in Louisiana, the University of Mississippi, and the University of South Carolina).

His experiences as a lawyer and judge in Georgia furnished Longstreet with an opportunity to observe southerners of every social class, and he made use of these people as characters for *Georgia Scenes*. Ostensibly related by two refined narrators—Hall, a country gentleman, and Baldwin, an urbane judge—the 19 sketches are populated by crackers, dirt eaters, crafty horse traders, and other indigenous southern types. The clash of the narrators' values and highly literate writing styles with the values and vernacular speech of the rural people that Hall and Baldwin encounter is the basis for much of the humor of the volume.

Walter Blair called *Georgia Scenes* "the first and most influential book of Southwestern humor." Longstreet's themes and techniques foreshadowed those in the works of such antebellum humorists as Johnson Jones Hooper and George Washington Harris, who followed in this tradition, a tradition that attracted Mark Twain during his writing career. In his use of the South and its people to create a sense of place in fiction, Longstreet opened new territory later traveled by such local colorists of the postbellum period as Richard Malcolm Johnston and Thomas Nelson Page and by writers of the 20th century, from William Faulkner to Eudora Welty.

Georgia Scenes is also important as social history. In it Longstreet wished to depict representative "Characters, Incidents . . . in the First Half Century of the Republic" in his state because he realized that complex social and economic forces had already begun altering the mores and daily activities there. In the book, for example, the narrator Hall described in detail a no-holds-barred Georgia fight, a backwoods shooting match, and the brutal sport of gander pulling; the narrator Baldwin contrasted the attitudes and popular tastes of the time with those of his youth. For the most part, Longstreet projected an optimistic view of the narrowing of the gulf between wealthy planters and poor whites, but he recognized that both classes would lose something of their unique lifestyles in the process. Perhaps the most notable aspect of *Georgia Scenes* is Longstreet's generally objective portrayal of southern poor whites, a group frequently viewed with complete disdain by other antebellum writers.

Mark A. Keller
Middle Georgia College

Kimball King, *Augustus Baldwin Longstreet* (1984); James B. Meriwether, *Mississippi Quarterly* (Fall 1982); John Donald Wade, *Augustus Baldwin Longstreet: A Study in the Development of Culture in the South* (1924, new ed. 1969). ☆

LYTLE, ANDREW
(b. 1902) Writer.

Born in Murfreesboro, Tenn., Andrew Lytle graduated from Vanderbilt University, where he met the Fugitive poets and was a minor contributor to the *Fugitive* magazine. His essay "The Hind Tit" in *I'll Take My Stand* (1930) establishes the philosophical basis for Lytle's agrarianism: humankind must understand "nature's invincible and inscrutable ways" in order to prevent people from brutalizing either nature or one another. A defense of the yeoman farmer and a critique of industrialism, this essay reveals the milieu for much of Lytle's fiction, not the plantation economy of the Lower South but the disappearing folk culture of the upcountry farms of middle Tennessee. Lytle's first book, *Bedford Forrest and His Critter Company* (1931), is a biography of the Tennessee Civil War hero that examines strategic weaknesses within the Confederate high command, especially the inept leadership of General Braxton Bragg, and "the one great mistake" of Jefferson Davis: to rest the foundation of the Confederacy on cotton and not "the plain folk" like those who fought under Forrest. As a historian and writer of cultural essays, many of which were collected in *The Hero with the Private Parts* (1966), Lytle has continued to examine the South's legacy of defeat, but unlike many of his contemporaries he does not accept the legacy of guilt. Influenced by Spengler, Lytle associated the decline of southern tradition with the decline of the West, "the gradual fall from a belief in a divine order of the universe into a belief in history, that is man judging man as the final authority of meaning in life."

As a writer of dramatic, not didactic, fiction, Lytle has been careful to distinguish between the voice of the artist and that of the cultural critic. In *The Long Night* (1936), a boy's private need to avenge his father's murder is finally dissolved in the public violence of the Civil War. Through its examination of pride and the often violent code of the Scotch-Irish clan, this novel presents both the light and dark sides of southern tradition. *At the Moon's Inn* (1941), the story of Hernando de Soto's unsuccessful effort to conquer the wilderness of Spanish Florida, places Lytle's agrarian beliefs within the context of Western civilization, not just American history. *A Name for Evil* (1947) clearly reveals that a literal regeneration of the southern past is not possible.

Rejecting the outer world of political, social, and religious restraints, Lytle's alienated characters either turn inward toward the self or outward toward the only remaining institution, the isolated family, and this, Lytle says, "require(s) of the family more meaning than it can sustain." The result—as in the fiction

of Poe and Faulkner—is physical and spiritual incest, which leaves both family and community severely diminished but not entirely broken in Lytle's masterpiece, *The Velvet Horn* (1957). His most recent book, *A Wake for the Living* (1975), is a family and social memoir that celebrates traditional southern life and mores in the face of death.

Thomas M. Carlson
University of the South

M. E. Bradford, ed., *The Form Discovered: Essays on the Achievement of Andrew Lytle* (1973); Victor A. Kramer et al., *Andrew Lytle, Walker Percy, Peter Taylor* (1983); Stuart Wright, *Andrew Nelson Lytle: A Bibliography 1920–1982* (1982). ☆

McCULLERS, CARSON
(1917–1967) Writer.

Born and raised in Columbus, Ga., Carson McCullers published her first novel in 1940, following the most important decade in the history of southern letters. She extended the tradition of the Southern Literary Renaissance by employing the modern South as a symbolic setting in all of her major fiction. More importantly, her work uses the harsh symbolism of southern life to re-create the universal failures and anxieties of modern America.

In *The Heart Is a Lonely Hunter* (1940) her allegorical structure—the complex solar system of grotesque "lonely-hearts" in complementary orbits—is perfectly balanced by an intensely realistic documentation of the social conditions discovered in a southern mill city during the Depression. It remains her finest effort. *Reflections in a Golden Eye* (1941), her second novel, is an example of the modern Gothic; McCullers's tale of bizarre sexuality on a peacetime army base demonstrates considerable versatility and artistic daring. *The Ballad of the Sad Café* (1941, 1951) is a more traditional work in the Gothic mode. The distancing effect of the balladeer-narrator allows the bizarre characters and strange events to be unified in one of the most intriguing novellas in modern southern fiction.

After a long silence caused by physical and psychological problems during the war, McCullers re-created some of the literary and popular success of her first novel in *The Member of the Wedding* (1946). This smaller portrait of the mill city again probes social relationships and individual feelings through the symbolic use of the alienated adolescent. It is a narrower achievement, though one that was more accessible for a popular audience in the stage (1951) and screen (1952) versions that made the author famous and financially secure.

McCullers worked for over a decade on *Clock without Hands* (1961), her last novel. Unfortunately, her long and debilitating illness made the successful completion of the book impossible. The novel's weak characterization and stereotyped action cannot create a structure strong enough to make order of the complicated changes transforming the South in the days of integration.

Like many southern writers, Carson McCullers developed an ambivalent attitude toward her native land; in her northern expatriation she cut herself off from the southern roots of her vision, yet she never developed others to replace them. Her achievement was still a considerable contribution to the fiction of the Southern Literary Renaissance.

Joseph R. Millichap
Western Kentucky University

Virginia Spencer Carr and Joseph R. Millichap, in *American Women Writers: Bibliographical Essays* (1983); Virginia Spencer Carr, *The Lonely Hunter: A Biography of Carson McCullers* (1975). ☆

MENCKEN, H. L.
||||||||||||||||||||||||||||||||||||||||||
(1880–1956) Editor, essayist, and critic.

Henry Louis Mencken was a writer of enormous national influence who also played a leading role in southern intellectual life of the 1920s. A native of Baltimore, he became a contributor to the *Smart Set* and the *American Mercury*. As such, he was, Walter Lippmann wrote, "the most powerful personal influence on this whole generation of educated people." In particular, he conducted a crusade against American provincialism, puritanism, and prudery—all of which he believed he found, to a degree larger than elsewhere, in the states below the Potomac and Ohio. Mencken shocked southerners when he published a severe indictment of southern culture, "The Sahara of the Bozart," which first appeared in 1917 in the New York *Evening Mail* and was reprinted in his book, *Prejudices, Second Series* (1920). In his essay he charged that the South was "almost as sterile, artistically, intellectually, culturally, as the Sahara Desert." "In all that gargantuan paradise of the fourthrate," he contended, "there is not a single picture gallery worth going into, or a single orchestra capable of playing the nine symphonies of Beethoven, or a single opera-house, or a single theater devoted to decent plays." Most southern poetry and prose was drivel, he charged, and "when you come to critics, musical composers, painters, sculptors, architects and the like, you will have to give it up, for there is not even a bad one between the Potomac mud-flats and the Gulf." Nor, Mencken added, a historian, sociologist, philosopher, theologian, or scientist.

The essay, written in characteristic Menckenian hyperbole, suggested that the condition of the modern South was especially lamentable because the antebellum South, particularly Virginia, had been the seat of American civilization. Mencken attributed the decline of southern culture to the "poor whites" who, he charged, had seized control of the South after the Civil War. Particularly to blame were the preachers and the politicians. What the South needed, he maintained, was a return to influence of a remnant of the old aristocracy.

Mencken's "Sahara" and other essays on the "godawful South" attracted widespread attention in Dixie in the decade that followed. Traditional southerners denounced him as a "modern Attila," a "miserable and uninformed wretch," a "bitter, prejudiced and ignorant critic of a great people." But other southerners such as James Branch Cabell, Howard W. Odum, Gerald W. Johnson, Paul Green, Thomas Wolfe, and Wilbur J. Cash declared their agreement with the substance of the indictment.

The Southern Literary Renaissance followed Mencken's "Sahara," and literary historians have suggested that Mencken shocked young southern writers into an awareness of southern literary poverty and thus played a seminal role in the revival of southern letters. But as important as Mencken's effect on southern literature was his effect on the general intellectual climate of the "progressive" South. Menckenism became, as the 1920s progressed, a cultural force, a school of thought for iconoclastic southerners. Not all young southern-

ers accepted him: Donald Davidson, Allen Tate, and other southern Agrarians challenged him with particular vigor. In the mid-1930s Mencken lost interest in the South, as the South lost interest in him. Nevertheless, his impact on southern letters, even if indirect, was felt for many years.

See also MYTHIC SOUTH: / Mencken's South

Fred Hobson
University of Alabama

Carl Bode, *Mencken* (1969); Fred Hobson, *Serpent in Eden: H. L. Mencken and the South* (1974); William H. Nolte, *H. L. Mencken, Literary Critic* (1966). ☆

O'CONNOR, FLANNERY
(1925–1964) Writer.

Flannery O'Connor was born a Roman Catholic in Savannah, Ga., on 25 March 1925. She attended parochial school there until 1938, when her father's disseminated lupus was diagnosed and the family moved to Milledgeville, Ga., the home of the author's maternal grandparents. O'Connor attended high school in Milledgeville and went on to that town's Georgia State College for Women as a major in English and social science. Her father died in 1941. Upon her graduation from college in 1945 she received a Rinehart Fellowship to the Writers' Workshop of the University of Iowa. She received an M.F.A. from Iowa in 1947, a year after her first story had appeared in *Accent*. From Iowa she went to Yaddo, where she started her first novel, *Wise Blood*. She met Robert and Sally Fitzgerald while in New York and moved in with them in Ridgefield, Conn., in 1949.

In 1950 her own disseminated lupus was diagnosed, and she moved to her mother's farm, Andalusia, just outside Milledgeville. She finished *Wise Blood* there and published the book with Harcourt, Brace in 1952. Her collection of short stories, *A Good Man Is Hard to Find*, came out in 1955; her second novel, *The Violent Bear It Away*, in 1960. She died on 3 August 1964, a year before her last collection of stories, *Everything That Rises Must Converge*, appeared. Her other posthumous publications are *Mystery and Manners* (1969), *The Complete Stories* (1971), and *The Habit of Being: Letters of Flannery O'Connor* (1979).

O'Connor worked with the traditional themes and characters of the South. But because of her specifically religious view, she seemed to find new meaning in them as she focused on postlapsarian existence. Her grotesques usually reflect some spiritual shortcoming with their physical handicaps. Her southern children are as deeply into sin as her adults; her adults are as helpless in this life as her children. And the vanity of aristocratic backgrounds is a trap for the sinner. To her the land, traditionally a symbol of well-being in southern literature, is one more sign of the foolish accumulation of earthly stores that gets no one into heaven. The industrialization of the South that Faulkner symbolized so well with the car of *The Reivers* came to be just another sign of human vanity as Hazel Motes of *Wise Blood* established "The Church Without Christ" in a broken-down Essex, a vehicle that ends up in the kudzu of a Georgia pasture. O'Connor even discovered religious implications in polite southern conversation. Her rednecks and aristocrats alike point inadvertently to a godless world as they make casual statements such as "a good man is hard to find" or "the life you save may be your own."

Religion, of course, has long been a concern of southern writers; but probably no successful writer of the region has treated it as specifically and as thoroughly as O'Connor. Her considerable talent lay in rendering scenes with vivid accuracy, allowing them to reflect, almost invariably, the emptiness of existence in worlds—southern and otherwise—without Christ.

See also RELIGION: / O'Connor and Religion

G. W. Koon
Clemson University

Kathleen Feeley, *Flannery O'Connor* (1972); Sally Fitzgerald, ed., *The Habit of Being: Letters of Flannery O'Connor* (1979); Melvin J. Friedman and Lewis Lawson, eds., *The Added Dimension: The Art and Mind of Flannery O'Connor* (1966); Josephine Hendin, *The World of Flannery O'Connor* (1970); Miles Orvell, *Invisible Parade: The Fiction of Flannery O'Connor* (1973). ☆

PAGE, THOMAS NELSON
(1853–1922) Writer.

Thomas Nelson Page, author of short stories, novels, essays, and poetry, is best known for his role as literary spokesman for the glories of the Old South. Born in 1853 and only 12 years old when the Civil War ended, Page, writing in the plantation genre of John Pendleton Kennedy and others, created of the antebellum South a mythical, would-be land of noble gentlemen and ladies, of contented slaves, a society ordered by the laws of chivalry.

A descendant of the prominent but no longer wealthy Nelson and Page families, and a native of Virginia, Page attended Washington College and later studied at the University of Virginia for a legal career. Page married in 1886, and his wife died two years later. He practiced law in Richmond from 1876 until 1893, when he moved with his second wife, the former Florence Lathrop Field, to Washington. Although Page became active in the social life of the capital and later served six years as ambassador to Italy under Woodrow Wilson, he continued in his writing to depict Virginia and the passing of the old order there. His works, set for the most part in the South, comprised 18 volumes when they were published in a collected edition in 1912.

In Ole Virginia (1887) was Page's first collection of short stories treating the antebellum South. Other works dealt with later periods in southern history. For example, *Red Rock* (1898) was a sympathetic portrait of the South during Reconstruction, and *John Marvel, Assistant* (1909) depicted the New South of the early 20th century. Page was consistently a proponent of the southern way of life, and in such stories as "Marse Chan" in *In Ole Virginia* his finest sketches were realized. In this story, told by a faithful exslave, of a young southerner who died for the southern cause and who placed duty and honor above all personal gain, Page postulates a kind of heroism that seemed to be missing from modern life. Page's South, of course, was finer than any real place could ever be, but he satisfied the nostalgia of his readers for what might have been—a place where heroic men and women adhered to a code of perfect honor. Only in the 20th century would Ellen Glasgow and, later, the writers of the Southern Literary Renaissance dispel the romantic image of the Old South

so carefully fashioned by Thomas Nelson Page.

See also MYTHIC SOUTH: / "Moonlight-and-Magnolias" Myth

Anne E. Rowe
Florida State University

Theodore Gross, *Thomas Nelson Page* (1967); Kimball King, "Introduction" to Thomas Nelson Page, *In Ole Virginia or Marse Chan and Other Stories* (1969). ☆

PERCY, WALKER
(1916–1990) Writer.

Percy was a novelist and lay philosopher whose important and popular writings embody his vision of a sadly dualistic existence. Percy himself was raised first in Birmingham, Ala., and then, after his parents' deaths, in Greenville, Miss., by his father's cousin William Alexander Percy (author of *Lanterns on the Levee*). He took a bachelor of science degree in chemistry from the University of North Carolina at Chapel Hill and an M.D. from Columbia's College of Physicians and Surgeons in 1941. Working as a pathologist at Bellevue Hospital in New York, Percy contracted tuberculosis. While recuperating he began to read such existentialist writers as Dostoevsky, Camus, Sartre, Marcel, Heidegger, and Kierkegaard. Convinced by them of the inadequacy of scientific methods that "cannot utter a single word about an individual as individual," Percy determined to be a novelist. He did not practice medicine again.

Percy returned south, married Mary (or "Bunt") Townsend, whom he had met in Greenville, moved with his bride to Covington, La., and became a Roman

Catholic. For the next 15 years he published philosophical essays in scholarly quarterlies and learned to be a novelist. His first novel, *The Moviegoer*, was published in 1961 and won the National Book Award. His works include five other novels—*The Last Gentleman* (1966), *Love in the Ruins: The Adventures of a Bad Catholic at a Time Near the End of the World* (1971), *Lancelot* (1977), *The Second Coming* (1980), and *The Thanatos Syndrome* (1987)—a collection of essays, *The Message in the Bottle: How Queer Man Is, How Queer Language Is, and What One Has to Do with the Other* (1975), and a nonfiction volume entitled *Lost in the Cosmos: The Last Self-Help Book* (1983).

Percy's novels are distinctly southern because they are set almost exclusively in the South and because their protagonists are all southern men. The novels are clearly placed; streets and homes in New Orleans, antebellum homes along the River Road, a country club in Birmingham, a hotel in Asheville—all are clearly recognizable. But if Percy is southern in his sensuous apprehension of place, he is southern also in his concern with the ideal. The southern patrician outlook taught him by William Alexander Percy brought meaning to terms like "honor" and "gentlemen"; these are meanings whose limits Percy exposes but whose values he never abandons. Perhaps the wry satire of his novels owes more to a Roman Catholic sense of man's fallibility and an aristocratic southern sense of right (and hence of the absurdity of departures from the right) than to Percy's readings in absurdist literature. Mid-20th century problems such as the civil rights struggle and the Kennedy assassination are alluded to in Percy's fiction, but the central focus is always upon the dilemma of being at once alive *in* this world and alive *to* it. Percy's nonfiction is principally concerned with the ways in which language impedes or enhances the business of being alive to this world and the next. It is southern only in the remarkable particularity of some of the images Percy uses.

Panthea Reid Broughton
Louisiana State University

Panthea Reid Broughton, ed., *The Art of Walker Percy: Stratagems for Being* (1979); Robert Coles, *Walker Percy: An American Search* (1978); Martin Luschei, *Walker Percy: The Sovereign Wayfarer* (1972); *Southern Quarterly* (Walker Percy issue, Summer 1982); J. O. Tate, in *Perspectives on the American South*, vol. 3, ed. James C. Cobb and Charles Reagan Wilson (1985). ☆

POE, EDGAR ALLAN

(1809–1849) Writer.

The South's most renowned literary artist of the 19th century spent most of his productive years as a struggling jour-

Walker Percy, Louisiana novelist, 1983

nalist in large northern cities. Born on 19 January 1809, in Boston, Mass., Poe was the second child of David and Elizabeth Arnold Poe, both active theatrical performers on the East Coast of the United States. His father mysteriously disappeared in 1810, and after his mother's subsequent death, in December 1811, he became the foster son of John Allan, a prominent Richmond, Va., tobacco merchant who gave Poe many childhood advantages. In 1826 he attended the University of Virginia, leaving after only a few months to join the United States Army. His first volume of poems, entitled *Tamerlane and Other Poems*, was privately published in 1827; a second volume, *Al Aaraaf, Tamerlane, and Minor Poems*, appeared in 1829, shortly after he was honorably discharged from the army. Aided by his foster father, he entered West Point in 1830 as a cadet, but was soon discharged for failing to heed regulations. Beginning in 1829, influential writers and journalists like John Neal and John P. Kennedy began to support his efforts to attain literary prominence. *Poems*, a third volume of poetry, was published in 1831.

Thoroughly trained in the classics and in the rhetoric and aesthetics of the Scottish common-sense school of philosophers, Poe was, according to the critic Robert D. Jacobs, indeed a southerner by temperament and inclination. Many of his formative years were spent in the southern cities of Richmond and Baltimore, the latter being the home of his blood relatives. Choosing a literary career after the death of his foster father, Poe began to contribute critical reviews to the Richmond *Southern Literary Messenger* in 1835 and later became its editor for two years. He married Virginia Clemm, his cousin who was less than

14 years old, in 1836. Until his death in 1849, Poe worked tirelessly as an editor and a reviewer, composing at the same time poetry, fiction, reviews, and essays of the highest literary excellence. He contributed to several noted American periodicals and newspapers; and in October 1845 he edited and briefly owned his own magazine, *Broadway Journal*.

Poe published his only major long piece, *The Narrative of A. Gordon Pym*, in 1838 and a short story collection, *Tales of the Grotesque and Arabesque*, in 1839. His poem "The Raven," printed in the New York *Evening Mirror* on 29 January 1845, brought him considerable recognition. *Tales*, a second collection of short stories, and a third volume of poems, *The Raven and Other Poems*, appeared in 1845. After the death of his wife in January 1847, he continued to write and to pursue his ambition of owning his own magazine. In early October of 1849, while traveling to New York to marry Sarah Royster Shelton, a widowed former sweetheart, Poe stopped in Baltimore, where he was later found ill on a city street. He died in a Baltimore hospital on 7 October 1849. His unexpected death was noted by nearly every significant newspaper and magazine in the eastern United States.

A controversial figure, Poe has been the subject of much speculative analysis. Generally, his biographers conclude that his instability as a person was in part due to the pressure of being a journalist. Although periodically he experienced poverty and the ill effects of poor health, Poe managed to perfect a variety of literary forms. He absorbed the current wave of romantic thought, which in his day brought significant changes in literary theory and practice. His classical bent, along with his background in Scottish philosophy and aesthetics, contributed to his theory of unity of effect and to his ideas about the short poem. He and Nathaniel Hawthorne introduced the ambiguities of symbolism in their Gothic tales, and Poe is credited with defining the short story as a distinct literary form. His attempts to formulate an objective method for writing poetry had some impact upon the French Symbolist poets of the later decades of the 19th century. In the area of popular literature, he is said to have fathered the modern detective story and some forms of science fiction.

Poe believed his art—all art—should be evaluated by international, rather than national or regional, standards, but he was, nonetheless, frequently identified at the time with the South. He did not defend his region's politics or social customs, like other antebellum southern writers, but his lyricism was common to southern poets. Raised a Virginian, Poe sometimes posed as the southern gentleman, even if transcending regionalism in his work.

J. Lasley Dameron
Memphis State University

James A. Harrison, ed., *The Complete Works of Edgar Allan Poe* (1902); Robert D. Jacobs, *Poe: Journalist and Critic* (1969); Arthur H. Quinn, *Edgar Allan Poe: A Critical Biography* (1941). ☆

PORTER, KATHERINE ANNE

‖‖‖

(1890–1980) Writer.

Porter was born in Indian Creek, Tex., on 15 May 1890, the fourth of five children born to Harrison Boone and Mary Alice Porter. Her mother's death before she was two and her father's ineffectuality as a provider led to her being brought up in poverty by her severely puritanical grandmother. Porter was so deeply affected by these events—the deprivation, the social embarrassment of being perceived, she thought, as "poor white trash," her father's emotional unreliability, and her grandmother's relentless prohibitions on her behavior—that throughout her life she reacted against or simply denied this early unhappiness.

Porter early began to rely on a vivid imagination to create a life—and soon a past—more palatable to her than that she experienced. She fabricated so many stories about herself, and was so persuasive in doing so, that biographers endlessly recorded "facts" that had never been true. Porter's imagination also contributed significantly to the richness of her finest stories, in which (through protagonists who were personae for herself) she described her family as once aristocratic, living in a plantation home with still-loyal former slaves, longing for more prosperous days. In writing such stories as "Old Mortality" and "The Old Order," Porter was like other southern writers who found the imagined past much more congenial than the troubled present. In a recurring character such as Miranda, Porter conveyed her sense of herself as a child of the "lost (Civil) War" and explored the historical, familial matrix out of which she had emerged.

Although Porter's stories are sometimes set in the South and the pasts remembered are often linked to southern history, Porter's larger themes are not uniquely southern. She was concerned with the universal issue of how human beings create myths about themselves that keep them from recognizing and responding to one another's needs, with how, indeed, the immersion in myth can lead human beings, through blindness, to be accomplices in evil. The children in her stories gradually learn the falsehood of adult myths and in doing so find their own loneliness confirmed. Porter's personal ambivalence toward these matters—her oscillation between human involvements as crippling and isolation as a kind of death—suggests the remarkable candor of her stories, whose power often resides precisely in their delineation of human failures.

In later years, public recognition of Porter's achievements included honorary degrees, Guggenheim Fellowships, Fulbright and Ford Foundation grants, the O. Henry Memorial Award, and the Pulitzer Prize. Although her only novel, *Ship of Fools* (1962), was considered a failure because of its heavy-handed ironies, Porter's place in American fiction was already secure. In the subtlety, precision, and insight of her best work, she had proven herself a genius of the short story.

Porter's major works include *Flowering Judas and Other Stories* (1930), *Pale Horse, Pale Rider: Three Short Novels* (1939), *The Leaning Tower and Other Stories* (1944), *The Old Order: Stories of the South* (1944), *The Days Before* (1952), *A Defense of Circe* (1955), *Ship of Fools* (1962), *Holiday* (1962), *The Collected Stories of Katherine Anne Porter* (1965), and *The Collected Essays and Occasional Writings of Katherine Anne Porter* (1970).

Gail L. Mortimer
University of Texas at El Paso

Jane Krause DeMouy, *Katherine Anne Porter's Women: The Eye of Her Fiction* (1983); Joan Givner, *Katherine Anne Porter: A Life* (1982); Myron M. Liberman, *Katherine Anne Porter's Fiction* (1971); William L. Nance, *Katherine Anne Porter and the Art of Rejection* (1964). ☆

RANSOM, JOHN CROWE

(1888–1974) Writer and critic.

John Crowe Ransom was born 30 April 1888 in Pulaski, Tenn., the third of five children of Methodist minister John James Ransom and his wife Ella Crowe Ransom. John Crowe attended the Bowen preparatory school in Nashville, completing a rigorous program in classical languages, English, history, mathematics, and German. Entering Vanderbilt University at 15, he continued his classical studies. He was a Rhodes Scholar at University College, Oxford, from 1910 to 1912, reading widely in classics and philosophy. In 1914 Ransom accepted an instructorship in English at Vanderbilt, where he immediately began the method of teaching that, through texts written in the late 1930s and early 1940s by his former students Cleanth Brooks and Robert Penn Warren (the "New Critics"), was to dominate the teaching of literature in American colleges and universities for nearly 30 years: close analysis of individual texts with emphasis on the uses of language.

Except for army service during World War I, followed by a term at the University of Grenoble, Ransom remained in the English department at Vanderbilt until 1937 (teaching many summer sessions in other colleges and programs). His first volume of poetry, *Poems about God*, appeared in 1919.

In the fall of 1919 Ransom began meeting with the group that would, in 1922, begin to publish the *Fugitive*, a magazine whose name signified flight from "the high-caste Brahmins of the Old South" (according to Ransom's foreword). Ransom, an already-published poet and a respected teacher, was sought out for advice and judgment by such younger members of the group as Donald Davidson and Allen Tate (and later Warren, Andrew Lytle, Jesse Wills, and others). The *Fugitive*, which lasted 19 issues, from 1922 to 1925, and expired not for lack of funds but for want of an editor, published the bulk of Ransom's mature poetry, collected in the volumes *Grace after Meat* (1924) and *Chills and Fever* (1924). In 1927 *Two Gentlemen in Bonds* was published, containing some of Ransom's best poems: "Dead Boy," "Blue Girls," "Janet Waking," "Vision by Sweetwater," "Antique Harvesters," and "The Equilibrists."

In *God without Thunder* (1930) Ransom proposed that new rationalistic theologies were destructive of the religious sense, for they destroyed a person's respect for the mysterious universe and elevated "science," which analyzes and uses "nature" rather than fearing and loving it. Ransom's religious ideas were coordinate with his defense of the South in "Reconstructed but Unregenerate," his essay for *I'll Take My Stand* (1930), and other essays about the South in contemporary society, such as "The South Defends Its Heritage" and "The South—Old or New?" For the former Fugitives and others who published *I'll Take My Stand*, the respect and love for nature associated with farming, especially family subsistence farming, were intimately bound up with the best social values of the culture—filial piety, kindliness, good manners, respect for the past, contemplativeness, and appreciation not only of the natural world but of art.

The publicity focused upon *I'll Take My Stand* and a series of debates related to it made the agrarian position a focal point for discussion of broad cultural values of American society. In an essay for a 1936 collection, *Who Owns America?: A New Declaration of Independence* (edited by Herbert Agar and Allen Tate), Ransom retreated from the extreme agrarian position, acknowledging that the South must accept industrialization in order to preserve economic autonomy. By 1940 Ransom had called the agrarian ideal a "fantasy" in the *Kenyon Review*, thus making public and final his defection from the economic position he had defended a decade before. The espousal of humane values—including respect for the mysteries—was not recanted, but became the center of Ransom's poetic theory in *The World's Body* (1938), *The New Criticism* (1941), and later essays.

Ransom accepted a teaching position at Kenyon College in Gambier, Ohio, in 1937 and founded the *Kenyon Review*

John Crowe Ransom, Vanderbilt Agrarian, 1927

two years later. During Ransom's editorship of the *Kenyon Review* (1939–59), he published important works by such southern writers as Andrew Lytle, Randall Jarrell, Caroline Gordon, and Flannery O'Connor. Although Ransom had left the South and had abandoned the agrarian program, he remained a staunch spokesman for the aesthetic and ethical values formulated in the essays and poems of his Vanderbilt period. He died 2 July 1974, in Gambier, Ohio.

Suzanne Ferguson
Ohio State University

Louis D. Rubin, Jr., in *The New Criticism and After*, ed. Thomas Daniel Young (1976); John L. Stewart, *John Crowe Ransom* (1962); Thomas Daniel Young, *Gentleman in a Dustcoat: A Biography of John Crowe Ransom* (1976). ☆

SIMMS, WILLIAM GILMORE
(1806–1870) Writer.

Simms was born in Charleston, S.C., and lived much of his life in or near it, making frequent visits to northern publishing centers and to the Gulf Coast and the southern mountains. His extensive knowledge of southern regions influenced novels and tales set in the Low Country, such as *The Yemassee* (1835), *The Partisan* (1835), and *The Golden Christmas* (1852), which trace the development of the region from the colonial era through the Revolution and into the antebellum period. Simms also published border and mountain romances like *Richard Hurdis* (1838) and *Voltmeier* (1869), set in the antebellum backwoods South.

To a greater extent, perhaps, than any other 19th-century southern author, he gave a comprehensive picture of his region in its historical and cultural diversity—of the Low Country with its class hierarchy, its agrarian economy, its increasingly conservative politics, and its keen sectional self-consciousness; of the Gulf South, both civilized and violent, part plantation, part frontier; and of the Appalachian Mountain South in its pioneer phase. His writing exhibits qualities that mark southern literature from its beginnings: a sense of time and history, a love of southern landscape, a respect for southern social institutions, and a firm belief in class stratification and enlightened upper-class rule. In addition to fiction, poetry, drama, orations, and literary criticism, he wrote a history and a geography of South Carolina and biographies of Francis Marion, Captain John Smith, the Chevalier Bayard, and Nathanael Greene. At the beginning and near the end of his career, he edited several South Carolina newspapers, and in the 1840s and 1850s he served as editor of important southern journals, among them the *Magnolia*, the *Southern and Western*, and the proslavery *Southern Quarterly Review*, which gave voice to sectional issues.

The embodiment of southern letters, Simms was also an influential spokesman for what he saw as the region's social and political concerns. A unionist in the 1832 nullification controversy, in the 1840s he supported the intensely nationalistic Young America group, which pushed for American freedom from British literary models. Active in politics, he served in the South Carolina Legislature from 1844 to 1846, conferred with prominent planters like James Henry Hammond about southern agricultural policies, conducted a copious correspondence with fire-eating Beverley Tucker of Virginia about slavery and secession, and helped develop the proslavery argument. As his southern nationalism mounted in the 1840s and 1850s, he supported the annexation of Texas and advocated the creation of a southern empire in the Caribbean. When the Civil War broke out, he served as advisor to several southern politicians and made elaborate proposals for Confederate military defenses. During the war he wrote little of literary importance save the lively backwoods novel *Paddy McGann* (1863); after it, he ruined his health by the incessant writing and editing chores he took on to support his impoverished family. Energetic and often humorous, his work is important for its sweeping picture of the colonial and antebellum South in its regional diversity and also for its representation of continuing southern literary and intellectual issues.

Mary Ann Wimsatt
Southwest Texas State University

C. Hugh Holman, *The Roots of Southern Writing: Essays on the Literature of the American South* (1972); James E. Kibler, Jr., *The Poetry of William Gilmore Simms: An Introduction and Bibliography* (1978), with Keen Butterworth, *William Gilmore Simms: A Reference Guide* (1980); Mary C. Simms Oliphant et al., eds., *The Letters of William Gilmore Simms* (1952–56). ☆

STUART, JESSE
|||||||||||||||||||||||||||||||||||||||||
(1906–1984) Writer.

One of seven children, Stuart was born 8 August 1907 in a log cabin in W-Hollow near Greenup in the northeast corner of Kentucky. After attending Plum Grove school and completing high school in Greenup, Stuart graduated from Lincoln Memorial University (B.A., 1929) in Harrogate, Tenn., and did graduate work at Vanderbilt (1931–32) and George Peabody College in Nashville, Tenn. Stuart led a busy and productive life, writing nearly 50 books, serving as a teacher and administrator in local schools, and farming in his beloved W-Hollow. He died on 17 February 1984 and was buried in Plum Grove Cemetery near W-Hollow, his lifelong home.

Stuart spent over 50 years exploring his native locale and making good use of local characters and incidents. One of Appalachia's most prolific writers, Stuart portrayed southern mountain and hill people to a reading audience that was becoming interested in Appalachians as distinct cultural types. His W-Hollow stories, published in collections from *Head O' W-Hollow* (1936) and *Men of the Mountains* (1941) to *Thirty-Two Votes before Breakfast* (1974), depict elemental experiences of life—births, deaths, funerals, weddings, elections, marital and intergenerational relationships. His poetry, collected in several volumes from *Man with a Bull-Tongue Plow* (1934) to *Hold April* (1962), also celebrates the youth, men, and women of W-Hollow.

Many of Stuart's novels mirror a youth's (usually a narrator's) growing awareness of himself, an awareness shaped by the conflicting demands of a small nuclear family and the larger society that surrounds it. In *Trees of Heaven* (1940) young Tarvin Bushman sees the virtues of both the town and the hill way of life and is prepared at the end of the novel to try to merge the best qualities of the two. The young boy Sid, the outsider in the Tussie clan in *Taps for Private Tussie* (1943), gains knowledge of the Tussies and appreciation for "book-learning" and formal education. David Stoneking, in *Daughter of the Legend* (1965), has been part of the Melungeon culture and will presumably carry that culture beyond the setting of Sanctuary Mountain.

Stuart's own struggles in growing up and coming to a broader and deeper view of life are recorded in *Beyond Dark Hills* (1938). His efforts to educate youth are told in *The Thread that Runs So True* (1949) and *To Teach, To Love* (1970). His recuperation from a nearly fatal heart attack is described in *The Year of My Rebirth* (1956).

Stuart's last book, *The Kingdom Within* (1979), recounts an out-of-body experience in which Shan Powderjay, Stuart's fictional alter ego, attends his own funeral along with all of Stuart's "head children"—the fictional characters he created.

Donald H. Cunningham
Texas Tech University

J. R. LeMaster and Mary Washington Clarke, eds., *Jesse Stuart: Essays on His Work* (1977); H. Edward Richardson, *Jesse: The Biography of an American Writer—Jesse Hilton Stuart* (1984). ☆

STYRON, WILLIAM

(b. 1925) Writer.

Born and raised in Newport News, Va., William Styron received his preparatory education at Christchurch School, in rural Tidewater, and his college education in North Carolina, first at Davidson College and then at Duke. His earliest work was written at Duke under the tutelage of William Blackburn. After graduation in 1947 Styron left the South, and he has subsequently pursued his career in Europe and New York.

Styron's decision to live and to write outside the South has perhaps fueled critical disagreement over how closely his fiction should be linked to a regional context. With the publication of *Lie Down in Darkness* in 1951, some critics have noted a strong thematic, technical, and stylistic indebtedness to southern writers, especially William Faulkner and Robert Penn Warren. The dominant thrust of Styron criticism has been to weigh lightly these regional influences, concentrating instead on the universal dimensions of his themes and identifying broader contemporary ideas, from existentialism to the French *nouveau roman*.

Few who have read the entire corpus of Styron's work, however, would deny that important southern perspectives exist in his fiction. Much of the power of *Lie Down in Darkness* derives from the novel's highly evocative rendering of its suburban Tidewater country club setting, and Styron's strongly delineated characters are grotesque distortions of

William Styron, Virginia author, 1982

the conventional character stereotypes of southern gentleman, southern lady, and southern belle. Though Styron consciously moved his setting from Virginia to Europe in *Set This House on Fire* (1960), the novel's primary characters remain southerners, and they re-create the tragic narrative, sitting in a boat on the Ashley River a few miles from one of the South's oldest and most legendary cities. Styron returned triumphantly to his Virginia fictional terrain in *The Confessions of Nat Turner* (1967), a narrative of the infamous and bloody slave uprising, which enlists the Old Dominion's hallowed plantation tradition as part of a provocative and unflinching analysis of black rage. In Styron's most recent novel, *Sophie's Choice* (1979), the horrors of Auschwitz and of a fatally destructive relationship between a Polish concentration camp survivor and her brilliant but insane Jewish lover are filtered, much like the action of *Set This House on Fire*, through a point of view that is both intensely personal and southern.

William Styron does not share the historical perspective of an earlier generation of southern writers in which individual failure is inextricably linked to the failure of community or culture. It would be a mistake, however, to underestimate the importance of the South, and particularly of his native state, in his novels. Though he deftly inverts their romantic associations, the traditional staples of the southern novel— the plantation, the cavalier figure, and the idea of gentility—occupy an important place in Styron's fiction.

See also BLACK LIFE: / Turner, Nat

Ritchie D. Watson
Randolph-Macon College

Philip W. Leon, *William Styron: An Annotated Bibliography of Criticism* (1978); Robert K. Morris and Irving Malin, *The Achievement of William Styron* (1981); Marc L. Ratner, *William Styron* (1972). ☆

TATE, ALLEN
(1899–1979) Writer and critic.

The most cosmopolitan of major modern southern writers, [John Orley] Allen Tate was a prime exemplar of his own theory that the highest artistic achievements come from a combination of native and foreign influences. He was born on 10 November 1899, in Winchester, Ky., a town in the heart of the Bluegrass country. Family loyalty first led him away from home, for he followed his elder brothers to Vanderbilt University in Nashville and there encountered the writers who were to determine the course of his life. John Crowe Ransom and Donald Davidson were his teachers, Robert Penn Warren was a younger fellow student, and all became colleagues in the *Fugitive* magazine, which began appearing in 1922 while Tate was still an undergraduate.

By 1930 Tate had produced the centerpiece of modern southern poetry, the "Ode to the Confederate Dead," using techniques of imagery and deliberate fragmentation learned from foreign poetry to portray the experience of a native southerner who felt cut off from the traditional society he wished to memorialize. His theme in this masterful poem, as in the equally masterful literary essays he wrote and in his only novel, *The Fathers* (1938), was the decline, not simply of southern tradition but of the whole tradition of Western civilization, which he came to see as the result of the loss of religious faith. "Modern man suffering from unbelief," he wrote near

Allen Tate, Tennessee poet, early 1920s

the end of his illustrious career, was what all his writing was about.

Tate was by education and conviction a Renaissance man, a Classical Christian humanist, but by force of circumstance he became a modernist, trapped unwillingly in what he called "the squirrel cage of modern sensibility," a "provincialism of time" (more constrictive than the old provincialism of place) where solipsism, or uniquely personal intuition, was the sole alternative to scientific determinism, or positivism, as the measure of truth and value. His theory was that traditional society, where people were bound into community by ties of family, locale, and religion, had been replaced by industrial society, in which the only ties were economic and political; the southern writer's vantage point, living in a place where the agrarian community was still alive, if rapidly vanishing, made him an eyewitness to the change from traditional to industrial society, which in other places was already an accomplished fact.

Tate's definition of the Fugitive was "quite simply a Poet: the Wanderer, or even the Wandering Jew, the man who carries the secret wisdom about the world." He lived out this definition himself, as he went from Nashville to New York, where he became part of another group of writers, less regionally aligned, that included Hart Crane, Malcolm Cowley, and E. E. Cummings, then to Paris on a Guggenheim Fellowship, where he spent some time in the circle of Gertrude Stein, with Ernest Hemingway, Scott Fitzgerald, and Archibald MacLeish, then back to Southwestern College in Memphis, where he taught, to Princeton University, to the Library of Congress, as its first Consultant in Poetry, to the University of the South, where he edited the *Sewanee Review* for a few distinguished years, and finally to the University of Minnesota, where he became Regents Professor of English. His career had taken him far away from the South and earned him an international reputation and many honors, including the Bollingen Prize for Poetry and the presidency of the National Institute of Arts and Letters, but he had always remained a southerner as well as a Fugitive. At the end of his life he returned to Tennessee, where he died, in Nashville, on 9 February 1979.

Southerner, American, and internationalist in turn, Tate retained his regional identity all his life, nowhere more convincingly than in his late poem, "The Swimmers," where he recalled his Kentucky boyhood in an elegant series of *terza rima* stanzas that are a triumphant blend of the local and the universal. He wrote and edited many notable books; much of his best work can be found in *Collected Poems, 1919–1976* (1977); *Essays of Four Decades* (1968); and *Memories and Opinions, 1926–1974* (1975).

William Pratt
Miami University (Ohio)

Ferman Bishop, *Allen Tate* (1967); George Hemphill, *Allen Tate* (1964); Radcliffe Squires, ed., *Allen Tate and His Work: Critical Evaluations* (1972); Thomas Daniel Young and John Hindle, eds., *The Republic of Letters in America: The Correspondence of John Peale Bishop and Allen Tate* (1981). ☆

WALKER, ALICE
||||||||||||||||||||||||||||||||||||||||||
(b. 1944) Writer.

Alice Walker, author of The Color Purple, **1976**

Alice Walker's *The Color Purple* is saturated with the atmosphere of the South, the rural Georgia farmland of her childhood. Walker, who has written more than 10 books of poetry, fiction, biography, and essays, finds strength and inspiration in the land and the people: "You look at old photographs of Southern blacks and you see it—a fearlessness, a real determination and proof of a moral center that is absolutely bedrock to the land. I think there's hope in the South, not in the North," she says.

Alice Walker was born in 1944 in Eatonton, Ga., the youngest of eight children. Her parents were poor sharecroppers. As a child, she read what books she could get, kept notebooks, and listened to the stories her relatives told. She attended Spelman College in Atlanta and graduated from Sarah Lawrence College in Bronxville, N.Y., where her writing was discovered by her teacher Muriel Rukeyser, who admired the manuscript that Alice had slipped under her door. Rukeyser sent the poems to her own editor at Harcourt Brace, and this first collection of Walker's poetry, *Once*, was published in 1965. From 1966 through 1974 Walker lived in Georgia and Mississippi and devoted herself to voter registration, Project Head Start, and writing. She married Mel Leventhal, a Brooklyn attorney who shared her dedication to civil rights in his work on school desegregation cases. Their daughter Rebecca was born in 1970. After they left the South, Walker and Leventhal lived for a while in a Brooklyn brownstone, then separated. Alice Walker now lives in rural northern California, which she chose primarily for the silence that would allow her to "hear" her fictional characters.

Alice Walker is the literary heir of Zora Neale Hurston and Flannery O'Connor. Walker has visited O'Connor's home in Milledgeville, Ga., and Hurston's grave in Eatonville, Fla., to pay homage. Walker's novels *The Third Life of Grange Copeland* (1977), *Meridian* (1976), and *The Color Purple* (1982) and short stories *In Love and Trouble* (1973) and *You Can't Keep a Good Woman Down* (1980) capture and explore her experiences of the South. She draws on her memories and her family's tales of Georgia ancestors in creating the portraits of rural black women in *The Color Purple*. Their speech is pure dialect—colloquial, poetic, and moving. Walker's poems too are filled with the rich landscape and atmosphere of the South.

Consciousness of the South has always been central to Alice Walker. The flowers and fruits in her California garden recall her mother's garden back in Georgia, a place so important to Walker that it became the inspiration for her collection of essays entitled *In Search of Our Mother's Gardens: Womanist Prose* (1983). Her mother's creativity was a compelling example to Alice Walker as well as a constant source of beauty amid the poverty of rural Georgia.

Among her many accomplishments and honors, Alice Walker has been Fannie Hurst Professor of Literature at Brandeis University and a contributing editor to *Ms.* magazine. In her writing and teaching she continually stresses the importance of black women writers. She edited a Zora Neale Hurston reader and a biography of Langston Hughes for children. Her literary awards include the Rosenthal Award of the National Institute of Arts and Letters, the Lillian Smith Award for her second book of poems, *Revolutionary Petunias* (1972), and the American Book Award and the Pulitzer Prize for fiction for *The Color Purple.*

Elizabeth Gaffney
Baruch College
City University of New York

David Bradley, *New York Times Magazine* (January 1984); Robert Towers, *New York Review of Books* (12 August 1982); Alice Walker, Atlanta *Constitution* (19 April 1983). ☆

WARREN, ROBERT PENN
||||||||||||||||||||||||||||||||||||||||||||||||||||||||||||||||||
(b. 1905) Writer.

Described by Allen Tate as the most gifted person he had ever known, Robert Penn Warren has excelled in every area in which his literary interest has taken him. Pulitzer Prize-winning novelist and poet, literary critic, social historian, biographer, editor and essayist, creator of plays and short stories, insightful cowriter of pedagogical guides to understanding literature and rhetoric, Warren has created a large body of work that reflects the major themes and concerns of the southern writer.

Born in 1905 in Guthrie, Ky., Warren entered Vanderbilt University at 16 in 1921. By 1923 he was a member of the Nashville Fugitive group, and in 1930 he contributed to that group's Agrarian manifesto, *I'll Take My Stand.* During the interim he had graduated summa cum laude from Vanderbilt, earned a master of arts degree in English at the University of California at Berkeley, and spent two years as a Rhodes Scholar at Oxford.

Warren's first published book, *John Brown: The Making of a Martyr* (1929), reflected his early interest in history, especially the tragic social and historic events that produced the 20th-century South. During the 1930s he taught at both Vanderbilt and Louisiana State University, collaborated on *An Approach to Literature* (with Cleanth Brooks and John T. Purser), wrote *Thirty-six Poems,* helped found the *Southern Review,* collaborated again with Brooks on *Understanding Poetry,* and published his first novel, *Night Rider.*

Warren's early work typifies the range of his interest in poetry, fiction, and criticism. The intelligence he and Brooks brought to bear on textual analysis in *Understanding Poetry* and its sequels shows through precept and example the major tenets of the New Criticism that had such a formative influence on American letters during the middle of this century.

The 1940s saw Warren move from Louisiana State University to the University of Minnesota and publish more poetry, criticism, novels, and short fiction. The most critically acclaimed of these was the Pulitzer Prize-winning *All the King's Men* (1946), a novel that is almost a case study in characteristic southern literary concerns. Based on the career of Huey P. Long, it considers such themes as man and change in history, the difficulty of self-knowledge, human responsibility, free will, problems of ends justifying means, and the southern social condition. It also demonstrates the southerner's characteristic concern with time and its meaning, his fascination with the power of rhetoric, and his propensity toward violence. His other major fiction includes *At Heaven's Gate* (1943), *World Enough and Time* (1950), *Band of Angels* (1955), *The Cave* (1959), *Wilderness* (1961), *Flood* (1964), *Meet Me in the Green Glen* (1971), and *A Place to Come To* (1977).

In 1950 Warren accepted a professorship at Yale, where he served until retirement. He became the only person ever to receive a Pulitzer Prize for both fiction and poetry when he received the award again in 1957 for *Promises: Poems 1954–1956*. In this and his subsequent poetry Warren treats personally the same themes of original sin, self-knowledge, love, and human possibilities he presents more objectively in his fiction. His meditations on history— *Brother to Dragons* (1953), *The Legacy of the Civil War* (1961), and *Jefferson Davis Gets His Citizenship Back* (1980)—deal with the same philosophical concerns.

Warren's creative energies have continued to sustain him. He has also continued to garner honors—a National Book Award, two Guggenheim awards, a MacArthur Foundation Fellowship, the Bollinger Prize for poetry, the Na-

tional Medal for Literature, and even, for *Now and Then* (1978), a third Pulitzer Prize. In 1986 he was named the nation's first poet laureate.

Ladell Payne
Randolph-Macon College

Leonard Casper, *Robert Penn Warren: The Dark and Bloody Ground* (1960); Neil Nakadate, *Robert Penn Warren: A Reference Guide* (1977), *Robert Penn Warren: Critical Perspectives* (1981); Marshall Walker, *Robert Penn Warren: A Vision Earned* (1979). ☆

WELTY, EUDORA

(b. 1909) Writer.

Born in Jackson, Miss., Eudora Welty attended Mississippi State College for Women and graduated from the University of Wisconsin. After attending Columbia University School of Business, Welty moved back to her home in Jackson, worked for the Works Progress Administration as a junior publicity agent, and began seriously to pursue a career as a writer. She has continued to live in Jackson and has received both the Pulitzer Prize and the American Book Award for fiction.

Welty has never belonged to a southern school of writers such as the Agrarians. Her fiction seldom deals with southern history, but the southern milieu informs her writing, perhaps most obviously in her depiction of family life. Welty's earliest stories tend to focus upon individuals unable to overcome a crippling isolation, and her subsequent fiction deals with complex family relationships. Only child Laurel McKelva Hand in *The Optimist's Daughter* (1972) learns to know herself by coming to understand the web of love and separateness that was her parents' marriage. On a larger scale, the extended southern families in *Delta Wedding* (1946) and *Losing Battles* (1970), whether they consist of prosperous Delta gentry or impoverished hill folk, know both the triumphs and the tragedies of their individual members. Though Welty does not portray family in the simplistic fashion that southern romances have made a cliché, she does share the South's preeminent concern with family life.

The oft-discussed southern sense of place also characterizes Welty's fiction, as she herself has noted. Southern writers, Welty has written, feel "passionately about Place. Not simply in the historical or philosophical connotation of the word, but in the sensory thing, the experienced world of sight and sound and smell, in its earth and water and sky and in its seasons." And certainly the "experienced world of sight and sound and smell" establishes a credible backdrop for all of Welty's stories, even those that rely upon fantasy or dream such as *The Robber Bridegroom* (1942) and *The Wide Net* (1943).

Eudora Welty, 1977

But place in Welty's fiction also serves as an emblem of values or of their absence. The isolation of Tom Harris in "The Hitch-Hikers," Phoenix Jackson's harmony with nature and with man in "A Worn Path," the willful ignorance that typifies Morgana, Miss., in *The Golden Apples* (1949), the destructive incursions of modern society into this same community—all are inextricably tied to Welty's various uses of setting. The literary sense of place is mirrored in Welty's collection of Depression-era photographs, *One Time, One Place* (1971).

Throughout her stories, which were brought together and published in 1980 as *The Collected Stories of Eudora Welty*, Welty displays an acute ear for southern speech and storytelling. Tall-tale narration is seen in *The Ponder Heart* (1954). But nowhere is speech more vividly rendered than in *Losing Battles* (1970). This novel about a family reunion consists almost wholly of stories told by family members. The Vaughns and Beechams and Renfros retell old stories, they add new stories that will be retold at future reunions, and everyone participates in the telling—Percy with his "thready" voice, Etoyle who "embroiders," Aunt Beck with her "mourning dove's" voice, everyone. The sound of these voices draws the reader into *Losing Battles* and makes him part of the family reunion. The oral tradition of the South seems to live in the written word.

Finally, Welty's concern with time, with the overwhelming importance of the past, with human mortality is a concern that has always been central to great writers, with southerners notably among them. Welty has written, "We are mortal: this is time's deepest meaning in the novel as it is to us alive. Fiction shows us the past as well as the present moment in mortal light; it is an art served by the indelibility of our memory, and one empowered by a sharp and prophetic awareness of what is ephemeral. It is by the ephemeral that our feeling is so strongly aroused for what endures, or strives to endure." Such an awareness of mortality and of its implications for their lives proves crucial to Welty's protagonists—to Audubon in "A Still Moment," to Virgie Rainey in *The Golden Apples*, to Jack Renfro in *Losing Battles*. Indeed, it is a sense of human transience that permits Laurel McKelva Hand to realize more fully than any of Welty's other characters that life is "nothing but the continuity of its love."

In *One Writer's Beginnings* (1984) Welty explores, in three autobiographical essays, the experiences of her early life in Mississippi. In describing how she became a writer, she reveals the same sense of family, place, and time that informs all of her fiction. The book deals only briefly with the plots and characters in Welty's fiction, but it tells much about the concepts and values that make that fiction so profoundly significant and that make Eudora Welty one of the 20th century's most important writers.

Warren Akin IV
and Robert J. Linn
Floyd Junior College

Suzanne Marrs
State University of New York
at Oswego

Michael Kreyling, *Eudora Welty's Achievement of Order* (1980); Peggy Whitman Prenshaw, ed., *Conversations with Eudora Welty* (1984), *Eudora Welty: Critical Essays* (1979); Ruth M. Vande Kieft, *Eudora Welty*

(1962); Robert Penn Warren, *Kenyon Review* (Spring 1944). ☆

WILLIAMS, TENNESSEE
(1911–1983) Dramatist.

Tennessee [Thomas Lanier] Williams was born in Columbus, Miss., in 1911. His mother was the daughter of an Episcopal minister. His father, from Tennessee, had among his ancestors Sidney Lanier and Tennessee's first governor and first senator. A traveling salesman, he was home very little; and his wife and children, Williams and his older sister Rose, lived with his wife's parents. In about 1919 Williams's father moved his family to St. Louis, thus taking his children out of a traditional southern environment to a big-city life, in which at least part of the time they lived in apartments in relatively poor neighborhoods.

The nostalgia for a southern past reflected in plays such as his first two successes, *The Glass Menagerie* (1945) and *A Streetcar Named Desire* (1947), is in part clearly a product of Williams's bitter dislike of the new environment and his fond memories, perhaps exaggerated, of the old. Williams himself is reflected in Tom Wingfield in *Menagerie*, who, like Williams, became a wanderer because of his unhappiness with his home environment, and in Blanche DuBois in *Streetcar*, who, like Williams, bitterly misses her gracious past and finds the modern world alien and forbidding. *Streetcar* and a later play, *Cat on a Hot Tin Roof* (1955), won the Pulitzer Prize. After *The Night of the Iguana* (1962) his plays failed to be popular successes, but he continued to write and be produced. All his major plays are set in the South and concern southerners, except *Iguana* (Mexico) and the expressionistic *Camino Real* (1953; set in Central America).

His southerners represent a wide variety: most importantly, Tom's mother Amanda in *Menagerie*, a genteel southerner displaced in St. Louis; Blanche and her sister Stella, fallen aristocrats in lower-class New Orleans; Stella's husband Stanley Kowalski and his friends, born to the neighborhood; an upper-class New Orleans family in *Suddenly Last Summer* (1956); transplanted Sicilians in a Gulf Coast town in *The Rose Tattoo* (1951); middle-class small-town southerners and Latin American "invaders" in the early 20th century in *Summer and Smoke* (1948); a corrupt southern politician in *Sweet Bird of Youth* (1959); and poor white southerners risen to money and power in *Cat on a Hot Tin Roof*. Oddly, however, his plays include almost no blacks and none prominently.

The most important dramatist to come out of the South, Williams provided innumerable insights into southern life and character, conveying authenticity to southerner and non-southerner alike. Like Chekhov, his dramatic master, Williams's best plays go beyond the world of their origin to achieve portraits of human nature and human situations that are of universal interest and validity.

Despite a nervous collapse, alcoholism, drug dependence, and scant critical acclaim, Williams continued to write in his Key West, Fla., home until his death, at 71, in a New York hotel room. Ironically, and against his stated wishes, he was buried in Calvary Cemetery, in the city he claimed to despise. "He came into the theater bringing his poetry," dramatist Arthur Miller said in his final tribute, "his hardened edge of

romantic adoration of the lost and the beautiful."

Jacob Adler
Purdue University

Esther Jackson, *The Broken World of Tennessee Williams* (1965); Jac Tharpe, ed., *Tennessee Williams: A Tribute* (1977); Nancy Tischler, *Tennessee Williams: Rebellious Puritan* (1961). ☆

WOLFE, THOMAS
(1900–1938) Writer.

His parentage and the time and place of Thomas Wolfe's birth created the cultural tug and pull underlying most of his writing. His father's Pennsylvania roots and his mother's close ties to the southern highlands were the first of many opposing forces that shaped Wolfe and were to be the subject matter of his plays and novels.

Born in a place (Asheville, N.C.) still suffering from the ravages of the Civil War and Reconstruction, Wolfe not only sensed the brighter prospects of the North but felt the clash of power and ideas that kept largely pro-Union western North Carolina and pro-Confederacy eastern North Carolina from solving scores of problems facing the state. "The Men of Old Catawba" explores some of the cultural differences dividing his native state.

Much of western North Carolina remained poverty stricken long after other areas of the state had begun to recover from the war. Yet amidst the poverty still evident in Asheville were signs of fabulous wealth, such as the building of the Biltmore House. Thousands of tourists crowding into such expensive quarters as Grove Park Inn began to vie with of migration, religious beliefs, political notions, and educational values linked to Asheville's southern highlands heritage, which was largely Scotch-Irish with an admixture of German, English, African, and Indian stock.

The time and place of Wolfe's collegiate education also helped to shape him and to provide materials for his plays and novels. When Wolfe attended the University of North Carolina, champions of the ideas and goals of the New South held important posts and were working to solve the economic, educational, and health problems of the state and region. Progressive teaching was in the air, but Wolfe still clung to many of the agrarian values of his maternal forebears, a position made clear in his sympathetic portrayal of Nebraska Crane in *You Can't Go Home Again*.

Thomas Wolfe and his mother at her boarding house, My Old Kentucky Home, Asheville, North Carolina, 1937

one another for choice lots in Asheville and surrounding towns. A boom in building seemed to point the way out of poverty and toward power for Ashevillians and their mountain neighbors. Wolfe's mother lodged many of the tourists in her boarding house, My Old Kentucky Home, and bought, swapped, and sold lots with such zeal and success that she became one of Asheville's wealthiest women. Asheville was thus aswirl with diverse groups of people and ideas when Wolfe was growing up there.

Beginning with *Welcome to Our City*, a play Wolfe wrote while at Harvard (1920–23), and continuing with *Look Homeward, Angel* (1929) and parts of *You Can't Go Home Again* (1940), Wolfe chronicled Asheville's hectic rush toward becoming a tourist mecca, and he reached back in *The Mountains* (1970), *The Hills Beyond* (1941), and *The Web and the Rock* (1939) to trace the patterns

Still another shaping experience at Chapel Hill was his study of Hegelian philosophy under Horace Williams, who reinforced Wolfe's tendency to see opposite positions. As the late C. Hugh Holman showed many years ago, this philosophic training informs the picture Wolfe painted of the South and North and provides vital clues to understanding Wolfe and his surrogate protagonists, Eugene Gant and George Webber.

His graduate studies at Harvard, his subsequent teaching and writing career in New York City, and his European travels led Wolfe to see the provincialism of his youth, but at the same time the golden visions of the North inspired by his father's stories were growing tarnished. Wolfe's tumultuous affair with wealthy stage designer Aline Bernstein began in 1925 but ended in 1930 with his increasing resentment of her involvement in the sophisticated New York literary and theatrical scene. During the years following the 1929 stock market crash, Wolfe saw both human suffering and the heroic will to endure and thus turned from his Joycean dream of winning love, fortune, and fame to work toward achieving a dream of America he had had in France.

He would celebrate America, become her bard, speak as her prophet, embrace both the South and the North, and assume the mantle of Whitman. But Wolfe came to this bardic role with some limitations: he had not lost the mountaineer's penchant for deflating the social claims of plantation aristocrats, he excessively despised the money-grubbing proclivities of Snopesian people escaping from hard times, he too eagerly defined and described his world in Hegelian terms, and he had not overcome racial prejudice. Still, his achievement as a writer was enormous: one of his contemporaries, William Faulkner, ranked Wolfe as one of the nation's greatest writers.

John L. Idol, Jr.
Clemson University

David Donald, *Look Homeward: A Life of Thomas Wolfe* (1987); Leslie A. Field, comp., *Thomas Wolfe: Three Decades of Criticism* (1968); C. Hugh Holman, in *South: Modern Southern Literature in Its Cultural Setting*, ed. Louis D. Rubin, Jr., and Robert Jacobs (1961); Louis D. Rubin, Jr., *Thomas Wolfe: The Weather of His Youth* (1955); Floyd C. Watkins, *Thomas Wolfe's Characters: Portraits from Life* (1957). ☆

WRIGHT, RICHARD

(1908–1960) Writer.

Born near Natchez, Miss., on 4 September 1908, Richard Wright, like the famous protagonist of his first novel, was a native son. The child of a sharecropper who deserted the family in 1914, young Richard moved with his mother during his early years from one to another of the extended family's homes in Arkansas and Jackson, Miss., living in Memphis after he completed the ninth grade. Poverty and the fear and hate typifying post-Reconstruction racial relations in the Lower South, more than the sustaining power of black culture or education in segregated schools, prepared him to be an author. If he omitted from his autobiographical record his experience with middle-class values in his mother's family, or the effect of the motions and rituals of the black world, there was psychological truth in his record of nativity as written in *Black Boy* (1945). He was surely a product of the older South and of the great black migration to the cities; his distinction lay in his refusal to be simply a product.

In "The Ethics of Living Jim Crow," published in a WPA writer's anthology, *American Stuff* (1937), which first appeared in the year he moved from Chicago to New York City, Wright revealed the dynamics of his life's work as an author. Caste, he says, prescribed his public behavior; but though he knew its requirements, he would not accede. Terror could not induce him to adopt the pretense that he knew his place. Conflict was unavoidable and its only resolution was violence.

Uncle Tom's Children (1938, and expanded 1940), the collection of novellas with which Wright won his first literary success, indicates by an irony of its title the goal southern whites had for southern blacks. The stories are united by the theme of collective response to racist terror, as the children of Uncle Tom refuse to accept the popular stereotype.

Lawd Today was the first example of Richard Wright's extension of southern learning to life in the migrant black communities of the North, but this apprentice novel was not published until 1963. *Native Son* (1940) first carried his insights to a large and appreciative audience. A Guggenheim Fellowship to complete the novel, its selection by the Book-of-the-Month Club, and its arrival within weeks at the top of the best-seller list attested to the appearance of a major American author. In the compelling character of Bigger Thomas, Wright creates a complex symbol of a rising awareness that no risk is too great in order to become master of one's own life. Through creating sympathy for Bigger's violent actions, Wright carries the tradition of protest to new lengths.

His insider's view of Jim Crow earned Wright acclaim for his use of literary naturalism. His projection of violence and rebellion against social conditions led to his emergence as a major literary voice of black America.

Wright's next book, *12 Million Black*

Richard Wright, Mississippi-born writer who became an expatriate in France, c. 1940

Voices (1941), presents a folk history extending from slavery's middle passage through the development of an Afro-American culture in the South and the hope of a black nation as a result of migration north. On the other hand, *Black Boy*, an ostensible autobiography representing the birth of the artist, necessarily suppresses the importance of group experience in order to focus on the power of the individual sensibility. Wright forged his identity among his people on southern ground but sought room to write by passage into modern life, symbolized by northern cities. This strategy becomes even clearer in the second part of the autobiography, published as *American Hunger* in 1977.

In time Wright found that Jim Crow knew no regional boundaries. Chicago and then New York constrained him as much as had Mississippi. So in 1946 he moved with his wife, Ellen Poplar, whom he had married in 1941, and their daughter to Paris. Suggestions have been made that the self-imposed exile, which was to last until Wright's death in 1960, sapped his creativity. To be sure, distance prevented intimate knowledge of contemporary changes in his native region and the black migrant communities; yet he created two novels concerning American racial relations and politics even after his exile. *The Outsider*, presenting an existentialist antihero living in Chicago and New York, appeared in 1953, and *The Long Dream*, a comprehensive reimagining of coming-of-age in Mississippi, appeared in 1958. Other fiction from the exile years includes *Savage Holiday* (1954), an experiment in raceless fiction, and the collection of stories, old and new, posthumously published as *Eight Men* (1961). This record of production hardly suggests flagging creativity.

Even more important to Wright's career, however, was the energy he found in exile to undertake four studies on a global scale. *Black Power* (1954) relates observations on his travels in the Gold Coast shortly before it became the nation of Ghana; *The Color Curtain* (1956) reports on the anticolonial positions developed at the conference in Bandung; *Pagan Spain* (1957) records a trip into a culture Wright viewed as a survival of premodern Europe; and *White Man Listen!* (1957) collects essays on race in America and the European colonies.

Despite the apparent departure from the experience of the American South in these later works, continuity exists between the original treatments of Jim Crow and the commentary on historical change in Africa and Asia. The prevailing subject remains race relations between whites and blacks, but beyond that is the more profound connection Wright saw in the special history of "colored" peoples. To be black in America, he believed, was to be marched forcibly into the pain of the modern world that even powerful white society could not fully comprehend. As a representative black American Wright already had lived the historical experience that awaited the Third World. By the power of literary imagination, Wright with matchless skill drew forth the significance of his southern education for world citizenship.

John M. Reilly
State University of New York
at Albany

Charles T. Davis and Michel Fabre, *Richard Wright: A Primary Bibliography* (1982); Michel Fabre, *The Unfinished Quest of Richard Wright* (1973); John M. Reilly, in *Black American Writers: Bibliographical Essays*, ed. M. Thomas Inge and Maurice Duke (1978). ☆

YOUNG, STARK
(1881–1963) Writer and critic.

Born in Como, Miss., 11 October 1881, Stark Young, a versatile figure in the Southern Literary Renaissance, devoted his life entirely to the arts and achieved widespread recognition for his contributions as teacher, poet, playwright, director, drama critic, fiction writer, essayist, translator, and painter. His parents were both descended from distinguished families who emigrated from the British Isles in the 17th and early 18th centuries.

Young's feelings and attitudes were powerfully influenced by the southern ways of living in Como and Oxford, Miss., to which his father moved after his second marriage. Young attended elementary school in Como and received his baccalaureate from the University of Mississippi. In 1902 he was awarded the master of arts degree from Columbia University. He taught English at the University of Mississippi, the University of Texas, and Amherst College, and began publishing poetry, plays, and aesthetic criticism.

After moving to New York in 1921, Young entered a period of intense activity in the theater. He became drama critic for the *New Republic* and a member of its editorial board as well as that of *Theatre Arts*. Soon he was recognized as the leading New York critic. He associated himself with the Provincetown Players and the Theatre Guild. His own plays, *The Colonnade* (1924) and *The Saint* (1925), both dealing with southern themes and reflecting Young's southern values, were produced with success. As early as 1923 he began to assemble from his drama criticism several volumes treating virtually every aspect of the theater: *The Flower in Drama* (1923), *Glamour* (1925), *Theatre Practice* (1926), and *The Theater* (1927).

While still involved in drama criticism, Young turned to fiction. He published *Heaven Trees* (1926), *The Torches Flare* (1928), and *River House* (1929). In 1930 he wrote the concluding essay, "Not in Defense, but in Memoriam," for *I'll Take My Stand*, supporting the manifesto of the Nashville Agrarians. In all of these works, as in others like *The Three Fountains* (1924), *Encaustics* (1926), *The Street of the Islands* (1930), and *Feliciana* (1935), Young's object was to identify those elements of life in the Old South that should be preserved in subsequent generations. His final novel, *So Red the Rose* (1934), was the most complete and powerful statement of his position. Although critical of the urban, industrial, highly competitive life in the North, Young had no desire to resurrect the southern civilization that had perished in the Civil War. Consistently, he defended the traditional values of the individual, the family, and the community, values that ultimately derived from classical humanism and the art of Western society.

By 1940 Young believed that the New York theater had declined notably from the promise and achievements of the 1920s and early 1930s. When changes at the *New Republic* rendered his position there less congenial, he began to think of retirement; and in 1947, after writing more than a thousand essays during the previous 40 years, he resigned. In 1959 he suffered a stroke from which he never fully recovered. He died 6 January 1963.

John Pilkington
University of Mississippi

Thomas L. Connelly, *Tennessee Historical Quarterly* (March 1963); John Pilkington, *Stark Young* (1985), ed., *Stark Young, A Life in the Arts: Letters 1900–1962* (1975). ☆

MEDIA

EDWARD D. C. CAMPBELL, JR.

Virginia State Library

CONSULTANT

☆ ☆ ☆ ☆ ☆ ☆ ☆ ☆ ☆ ☆

Overleaf: Tennessee Ernie Ford as an announcer for WOPI radio, Bristol, Tennessee, 1939

MEDIA

||||||||||||||||||||||||||||

IN the late 1920s radio listeners in the South, and even nationwide, could tune in to KWKH in Shreveport and hear the exuberant W. K. Henderson sign on with "Hello, world, doggone you!" Each day, "talkin' to you," Henderson cajoled, attacked, and generally stirred up emotions. His program was in exaggerated form the embodiment of the mass media: communication to inform, to entertain, to influence, and to make money. He was also distinctly southern. Broadcasting from "Lou-ee-siana," he was representative of a print and broadcast media that traditionally had had regional characteristics.

By the mid-19th century the South had begun to stamp its identity on the region's early forms of media. *Southern Field and Fireside*, the *Southern Literary Messenger*, *Magnolia*, and the *Southern Planter* by title alone denoted periodicals attuned to a sectional readership. Little changed with the post-Civil War magazines; *Southern Opinion*, *The Land We Love*, *Southern Bivouac*, and especially *Confederate Veteran* left little doubt that a large part of the South was staunchly unchanged and a land apart.

After Reconstruction the other print media—newspapers—helped bolster change and initiate a "New South." Francis Dawson's Charleston *News and Courier* in the 1880s pitted itself against the politics of "Pitchfork Ben" Tillman; Henry W. Grady of the Atlanta *Constitution* and Henry Watterson of the Louisville *Courier-Journal* stressed the

region's need for new industry, refined agricultural techniques, and general social and economic progress. In many respects, southern print media were part of a national, and not just a southern, progressive trend. They reflected national patterns in growth as well. Taking newspapers as an example, by 1890 the number of weeklies had tripled nationally in just two decades. Correspondingly, in the South there were over 1,800 weeklies in 1890; just 20 years before, barely 500 existed.

But despite following broad trends in growth, business practices, journalistic techniques, and even slanting editorials in support of "progress," print media nonetheless remained very much a regional product. Local issues continued to dominate the news—in the South that often meant fashioning overblown claims of economic success and racial harmony.

By the first decades of the 1900s the region's magazines and journals reflected a healthy renewal. The new growth began with the University of the South's *Sewanee Review* in 1892. Although it first stressed southern literature, the later *South Atlantic Quarterly* printed essays on social and political topics. The *Virginia Quarterly Review* in 1925 and a new *Southern Review* in 1935 joined the renaissance of southern periodicals. Often affiliated with universities, the publications not only reflected the newest literature and most penetrating thinking of their region but with their academic associations and interests also spoke to a national audience on far broader issues of criticism, art, and social philosophy. Like the newspapers, however, they were still southern in outlook. Amidst examples of the New Criticism, there were, for instance, essays by John Crowe Ransom, Donald Davidson, and other so-called Agrarians warning against the headlong rush to modernization at the expense of the South's character.

But while the Charlotte *Observer* or Nashville's short-lived, innovative *Fugitive* magazine fulfilled media's functions to inform and influence, they had a relatively small audience. A new, burgeoning southern broadcast industry— whose primary functions were to entertain and to make money—garnered a far more enthusiastic following and, more important, a far broader one.

Within the first quarter of 1922, 11 radio stations received broadcast licenses, including WWL in New Orleans and Atlanta's WSB. During the 1930s growth slowed greatly, and the South could claim less than 12 percent of the country's radio listeners. Not until the late 1940s did the number of stations significantly expand.

The critical need for programming, though, created an outlet for the region's talent. The resulting impetus to showcase local country music performers led to a distinct southern radio format, Nashville's WSM being the most famous of numerous examples. In November 1925 the station began broadcasting the "WSM Barn Dance"; a year later the enormously popular show was renamed the "Grand Ole Opry," the regional counterpart to the "Grand Opera" network programs.

Spurred on by the popularity of turn-of-the-century nostalgic southern writers, theatrical and musical representa-tions of the region's antebellum history, and even the attraction of the South to artists and lithographers, the infant film industry in the early 1900s turned to the region as a proven and easily recognizable topic for commercial motion pictures. The productions by their very number and success did as much to form southerners' views of themselves as they did to form the impressions of non-southerners.

To be sure, some productions were directed by native southerners—D. W. Griffith or King Vidor for instance—but primarily the complimentary media image of the South so prevalent between 1900 and 1945 was a product of outside forces. Some films, such as *Cabin in the Cotton* (1932) or *In This Our Life* (1942), were not by any means positive media views of the South's poor or privileged. But the vast majority, and there were hundreds of films on the Civil War alone, presented a genial, pleasurable land in musicals such as *Dixiana* (1930), light dramas such as *Virginia* (1941), and even comedies like *Steamboat 'Round the Bend* (1935).

Stereotypes of the region and its pace of life were widespread and popular in other media, too. For example, the nation's newspaper comic pages presented delighted readers with a range of humorous, likable characters. Most successful were William Morgan De Beck's 1934 creation *Barney Google and Snuffy Smith*; Al Capp's *Li'l Abner*, first introduced the same year; and Walt Kelly's *Pogo*, syndicated in 1948.

After 1945 the South continued to be a source of media material. Different times, though, influenced the media to develop a different product and view. In the motion picture industry demands for new story lines, more contemporary attitudes, and even more excitement influenced Hollywood, for instance, to increase greatly its film adaptations of the works of William Faulkner, Tennessee Williams, Robert Penn Warren, Ellen Glasgow, Carson McCullers, Erskine Caldwell, and Lillian Hellman. The South was hardly the same; from a film image represented by, say, *Jezebel* in 1938, the South by the 1960s was instead best symbolized in film by *Cat on a Hot Tin Roof* (1958).

Besides the popular, national media, the media within the region after World War II also reexamined old assumptions. Newspapers in particular once again scrutinized the South. Newspapermen such as George Fort Milton of the Chattanooga *News*, Jonathan Daniels of the Raleigh *News and Observer*, and Mark Ethridge of the Macon *Telegraph and News* and later the Louisville *Courier-Journal* all represented the increasingly liberal attitude among the region's editorial writers. Virginius Dabney of the Richmond *Times-Dispatch* attacked a range of regional ills: religious fundamentalism, the poll tax, and segregation. The Atlanta *Constitution*'s Ralph McGill labeled the separate-but-equal doctrine "undemocratic" and won a Pulitzer Prize in 1959 for a series on racial terrorists.

The preoccupation with matters southern was not so nearly duplicated in the region's post-1945 magazines, however. The number of magazines edited and printed in the South continued to grow, but new probing publications such as *Southern Exposure* became fewer; even the South's periodicals of primarily a regional orientation declined. Magazines such as *Southern Living*, with a 1.9 million circulation, or *Southern Interiors* were outdone by, for example, *Boys' Life*, with 1.5 million

subscribers, and *Mother Earth News* with 1 million readers.

The newest southern broadcast industry, television, reflected the same trends since 1945: sustained growth in southern outlets matched by declining attention paid the region itself. Television, like radio 25 years earlier, grew slowly at first and then steadily. Richmond's WTVR secured the South's first license in 1948, but it was not until 1953 that each southern state could claim a station. As with radio, initially the local stations filled airtime with local talent and religious programming. But by 1980 the southern television industry included 350 stations, 32 percent of the national total; by then, many of the stations were no longer particularly southern, but were parts of broadcast groups, such as LIN Broadcasting headquartered in Cincinnati with stations in Tennessee and Virginia. Atlanta's Cable News Network and WTBS, like their smaller counterparts, were not even intended to reflect a regional reference point.

However, if the South's commercial stations had forsaken regional themes, the commercial networks did not. Network television, like film, sustained an interest in portraying the South. From *The Andy Griffith Show* to *The Beverly Hillbillies* and *Carter Country*, to *The Waltons* and the *Dukes of Hazzard*, the region's rural scene has still proved popular and profitable. More serious programming—*Roots* or *The Autobiography of Miss Jane Pittman*—has proved probing material can succeed as well.

Programming reflective of the stations' locale, therefore, has increasingly become the preserve of the South's noncommercial, educational television stations. For instance, SCETV in Columbia, S.C., the University of North

Carolina's educational station, and both Alabama's and Kentucky's statewide ETV systems have produced popular and news programs on Afro-American history, state politics, and adaptations of regional literature.

Southern media—in the form of newspapers, magazines, journals, and more recently radio and television—has evolved from a means of communication often logically enmeshed in regional concerns and interests to institutions intent on presenting the South's diversity and sometimes exposing its admitted shortcomings.

See also BLACK LIFE: Film Images, Black; Press, Black; INDUSTRY: / Grady, Henry W.; LITERATURE: Agrarianism in Literature; New Critics; Periodicals; / Davidson, Donald; Ransom, John Crowe; MUSIC: / Grand Ole Opry; MYTHIC SOUTH: / Agrarians, Vanderbilt

> Edward D. C. Campbell, Jr.
> Virginia State Library

Erik Barnouw, *Tube of Plenty: The Evolution of American Television* (1975); *Broadcasting-Cablecasting Yearbook: 1985* (1985); Edward D. C. Campbell, Jr., *The Celluloid South: Hollywood and the Southern Myth* (1981); Thomas D. Clark, *The Southern Country Editor* (1948); Thomas J. Cripps, *Slow Fade to Black: The Negro in American Film, 1900–1942* (1977); Warren French, ed., *The South and Film* (1981); William C. Havard, *Virginia Quarterly Review* (Winter 1983); M. Thomas Inge, ed., *Handbook of American Popular Culture* (1978–81); Jack Temple Kirby, *Media-Made Dixie: The South in the American Imagination* (1978); J. Fred MacDonald, *Blacks and White TV: Afro-Americans in Television since 1948* (1983), *Don't Touch That Dial: Radio Programming in American Life, 1920–1960* (1979); Horace Newcomb, *Appalachian Journal* (Autumn–Winter 1979–1980); Sam G. Riley, *Magazines of the American South* (1986); Peter A. Soderbergh, *Mississippi Quarterly* (Winter 1965–1966); Morton Sosna, *In Search of the Silent South: Southern Liberals and the Race Issue* (1977); *Southern Exposure* (Winter 1975); George B. Tindall, *The Emergence of the New South, 1913–1945* (1967). ☆

Actors and Actresses

||||||||||||||||||||||||||||||||||||||||||||||||||||||

Actors are trained to depict fictitious characters who have no relation to the actor's personal life. There is no reason, therefore, why any capable actor cannot play a southerner on the stage or in a movie, or why a southern actor cannot assume the roles of non-southern characters. Indeed, many of the most famous southern characters in movies have been played by actors born outside the South. Clark Gable (Rhett Butler) was born in Cadiz, Ohio, and Vivien Leigh (Scarlett O'Hara and Blanche DuBois) was a British citizen born in India. Bette Davis, remembered for several southern roles, most notably in *Jezebel* (1938) and *The Little Foxes* (1941), was born in Massachusetts. Gregory Peck, from La Jolla, Calif., played the model southern liberal in *To Kill a Mockingbird* (1963); and Broderick Crawford, from Philadelphia, played the demagogue Willie Stark in *All the King's Men* (1949). And, of course, actors born and reared in the South have often made their reputations in roles that had nothing to do with their southern background.

The South has, in any event, produced some of the best actors to grace the silver screen. From bit players to important stars, actors from the South have become an integral part of the American myth of Hollywood. Perhaps one facet of southern life that has influenced youth in the region toward acting is the southern penchant for storytelling. Most southerners, however, have had to leave the state of their birth in order to pursue their careers, and only a few, such as Burt Reynolds, have consistantly returned to the South to make movies.

No list with limited space can catalog all southern actors, but what follows is a sketch of some actors who were born in the South, with an emphasis on their southern roles, if any. As with many entertainers, the dates and places of birth are often questionable, as records are sometimes contradictory, but care has been taken to use data from reliable sources. The actors are here arranged geographically.

Virginia. Bill Robinson (born in Richmond in 1878, died in 1949) made his fame as Bojangles, the tap dancer with Shirley Temple. In both *The Little Colonel* (1935) and *The Littlest Rebel* (1935) he played the faithful family servant and accompanied Temple in some of her best-remembered dance routines. In *So Red the Rose* (1935) Randolph Scott (Orange County, 1903) played Duncan Bedford, son of the Old South during the Civil War. He also carried his southern demeanor into numerous westerns, such as *The Texans* (1938) and *Fort Worth* (1951). Joseph Cotton (Petersburg, 1905) played the good Texan in *Duel in the Sun* (1946) as well as the family physician in *Hush . . . Hush, Sweet Charlotte* (1964). Margaret Sullavan (Norfolk, 1911–60) was Valette Bedford, the young belle of the southern household in *So Red the Rose.* Sister and brother Shirley MacLaine (Richmond, 1934) and Warren Beatty (Richmond, 1937) heard family stories of the South from their father. She played the daughter in a southern family full of conflict in *Hot Spell* (1958), and he achieved fame as Clyde Barrow racing across Texas and Oklahoma with Bonnie Parker in *Bonnie and Clyde* (1967). Other Virginia actors and examples of their films with southern settings include Richard Arlen, Lynn Bari (*Man from Texas*), James Bell (*Streets of Laredo*), Jack Holt (*The Littlest Rebel*), Mae Murray (*To Have and to Hold*), John Payne (*El Paso*), and George C. Scott.

North Carolina. Sidney Blackmer (Salisbury, 1896–1973) had small roles in *The Little Colonel* and *Duel in the Sun*, and then played an aging author living in a southern town in *The View from Pompey's Head* (1955). Ava Gardner (Smithfield, 1922) sang her way through the part of Julie Laverne in *Show Boat* (1951) and also sang in *Lone Star* (1952), a historical drama set in the early days of Texas. Kathryn Grayson (Winston-Salem, 1923) was also both singer and actress. She sang in *The Toast of New Orleans* (1950) and *Show Boat* (1951). In *The Vanishing Virginian* (1942) she had played Rebecca Yancey of Virginia in a sentimental account of the Old South. Andy Griffith (Mount Airy, 1926) created the role of Will Stockdale, the hayseed who enjoys the army in *No Time for Sergeants* (1958). He also played Lonesome Rhodes, a country boy in Arkansas who gains fame and power, in *A Face in the Crowd* (1957).

South Carolina. This state has produced few who followed the actor's trade. Nina Mae McKinney (Lancaster, 1913–67) was selected by King Vidor to play Chick, the female temptress, in *Hallelujah* (1929), his all-black musical.

Georgia. Charles Coburn (Savannah, 1877–1961) had the title role in *Colonel Effingham's Raid* (1945), in which he played a retired Confederate officer who sets life straight in a Georgia town. Generally known for his suave, sophisticated roles, Melvyn Douglas (Macon, 1901–81) had a different role in *Hud* (1963), in which he played the head of a tough modern Texas family. He returned to his more accustomed roles in *Hotel* (1967) where, as the cultured owner of a hotel in New Orleans, he tried to preserve the hotel's aging charm. Joanne Woodward (Thomasville, 1930) achieved fame playing a Georgia woman with three personalities in *The Three Faces of Eve* (1957). She went on to depict Faulkner women in *The Long Hot Summer* (1958) and *The Sound and the Fury* (1959). Burt Reynolds (Waycross, 1936) is the prototype of the southern "good old boy," a persona he created as Gator McKlusky in *White Lightning* (1973) and *Gator* (1976) and as the Bandit in *Smokey and the Bandit* (1977). In his more serious roles Reynolds can project another side of southern character, as he did in *Deliverance* (1972). Other Georgia actors have included Claude Akins (*The Defiant Ones* and *Inherit the Wind*), May Allison, Edward Andrews, Oliver Hardy (*The Fighting Kentuckian*), Miriam Hopkins, Louise Huff, Stacy Keach (*The Heart Is a Lonely Hunter*), Lee Tracy, and Jane Withers.

Florida. Prissy in *Gone with the Wind* (1939) was played by Thelma "Butterfly" McQueen (Tampa, 1911). She also had a role in *Cabin in the Sky* (1943). Even though Sidney Poitier was born in Miami almost by accident (his Bahamian parents were there on business), he later moved there and grew up in that southern city. In *The Defiant Ones* (1958) he played Noah Cullen chained to Tony Curtis on a southern chain gang. In *In the Heat of the Night* (1967) he

was Virgil Tibbs, a Philadelphia detective visiting his mother in a small southern town; and he had the lead role in *Porgy and Bess* (1959), George Gershwin's musical set in Charlestown, S.C. Faye Dunaway (Bascom, 1941) was the Texas country girl Bonnie Parker, looking for a way out of her small hometown in *Bonnie and Clyde*. She also played a member of a gang kidnapping an old man in Miami in *The Happening* (1967). Other Floridia actors include Elizabeth Ashley, Judy Canova (*Louisiana Hayride, Carolina Cannonball*), Pat Boone (*Mardi Gras*), Wanda Hendrix, Frances Langford (*Mississippi Gambler, Dixie Jamboree*), Lincoln Perry (Stepin' Fetchit), and Ben Vereen (*Roots*).

Alabama. Ben Cameron, the Little Colonel, perhaps one of the best examples of mythical southerners from *Birth of a Nation* (1915), was played by Henry B. Walthall (Shelby County, 1878–1936). The film had been directed by the most southern of directors, D. W. Griffith, from Kentucky, who had begun his career as an actor. Walthall had acted in *In Old Kentucky* (1909) and later was to play southern roles in a remake of *Tol'able David* (1930) and in *Cabin in the Cotton* (1932). Other actors from Alabama include Mary Anderson, Tallulah Bankhead, Gertrude Michael (*Flamingo Road*), and Gail Patrick (*Mississippi*).

Tennessee. Of all southern actresses, perhaps Elizabeth Patterson (Savannah, 1874–1966) played the most roles with southern connections. In addition to numerous minor roles as a southern woman, she played the grandmother in *The Vanishing Virginian*, the lady who stands up against a lynch mob in *Intruder in the Dust* (1949), and the prim old wife in *Tobacco Road* (1941). George Hamilton (Memphis, 1939) played the son in a Texas family in *Home from the Hill* (1960) and Hank Williams in the movie biography of the country singer, *Your Cheating Heart* (1965). Other Tennessee actors include singer Dolly Parton and Marjorie Weaver (*Kentucky Moonshine*).

Kentucky. Patricia Neal (Packard, 1926) has played contrasting southern roles. In *Bright Leaf* (1950) she was a rich girl, but in *Hud* she was the hard-bitten housekeeper for the Bannon men. Warren Oates (Depoy, 1928) made his reputation playing tough characters in numerous westerns. In *In the Heat of the Night* he depicted the local deputy in the Mississippi town visited by Virgil Tibbs. Other Kentucky actors include William Conrad (*Lone Star*), Irene Dunn (*Show Boat*), Henry Hull (*El Paso*), Arthur Lake, Victor Mature, and Una Merkel (*Comin' Round the Mountain* and *The Kentuckian*).

Mississippi. Dana Andrews (Collins, 1909) had two important southern roles in the same year. He was Dr. Tim in John Ford's version of Erskine Caldwell's novel *Tobacco Road*, and he was also featured in Jean Renoir's film set in Georgia, *Swamp Water* (1941). Elvis Presley (Tupelo, 1935–77) began his movie career with several southern films—*Love Me Tender* (1956), *Loving You* (1957), and *King Creole* (1958). His persona was usually some variation of the poor boy singer who overcomes obstacles to make good and win the girl. Other Mississippi actors include Roscoe Ates, James Earl Jones (*The Great White Hope*), Larry Semon, and Stella Stevens.

Louisiana. Dorothy Lamour (New Orleans, 1914), best remembered for her "Road" films with Bob Hope and Bing Crosby, made a film with Crosby called *Dixie* (1943). In it she played the girlfriend of Dan Emmett, the author of the song "Dixie." Jeffrey Hunter (New Orleans, 1926–69) played in many westerns, some of which were set in Texas, such as *Three Young Texans* (1954) and *The Man from Galveston* (1964). In the Walt Disney version of *The Great Train Robbery* (1956) he had the role of the Confederate conductor who leads the chase to recover the stolen train. Other Louisiana actors include Mary Alden (*Birth of a Nation*), Louis Armstrong (*New Orleans*—playing himself), Ben Turpin (*Uncle Tom without the Cabin*), Kitty Carlisle, and Paul Burke.

Texas. In *Flamingo Road* (1949) Joan Crawford (San Antonio, 1908–77) had the role of a carnival girl who retired to a crude southern town. In this role she was courted, then given up, by another Texan, Zachary Scott (Austin, 1914–65), who also starred in another Renoir film set in the rural South, *The Southerner* (1945). Audie Murphy played himself as war hero in *To Hell and Back* (1955) and Billy the Kid in *The Kid from Texas* (1950). Biography also was well suited to Sissy Spacek (Quitman, 1949). In *Coal Miner's Daughter* (1980) she portrayed singer Loretta Lynn, who is from Butcher Holler, Ky. Other Texans in the movies include John Arledge (*Gone with the Wind*), Gene Autry (*Texans Never Cry*), Joe Don Baker (*Walking Tall*), Florence Bates (*San Antonio*), John Boles (*The Littlest Rebel*), Carol Burnett, Vikki Carr, Bebe Daniels (*Dixiana*), Linda Darnell, Sandy Duncan, Shelly Duvall (*Nashville*), Dale Evans (*The Yellow Rose of Texas*), Corinne Griffith, Hope Hampton, Ann Harding, Martha Hyer, Carolyn Jones (*King Creole*), Evelyn Keyes (*Gone with the Wind*), Guy Kibbee, Bessie Love, George McFarland (Spanky in *The Little Rascals*), Fess Parker (*Davy Crockett*), Valerie Perrine (*The Last American*

Hero), Paula Prentiss, Debbie Reynolds, Ann Sheridan, and Rip Torn (*Sweet Bird of Youth*).

Robert A. Armour
Virginia Commonwealth University

Ephraim Katz, *The Film Encyclopedia* (1979); *The New York Times Film Review, 1913–1968* (1970); David Thomson, *A Biographical Dictionary of the Cinema* (1975); *The World Almanac and Book of Facts, 1987* (1986). ☆

Civil Rights and Media

Both print journalism and electronic journalism nurtured dramatic images of the South during the civil rights movement, and both changed as a result of it. The early years of the movement in the South from 1954 to 1965 came at a time of tremendous technological advancement in the media. The rise of national network news reporting in the United States coincided with the first years of the civil rights movement. The relationship between the two is complex because television news developed into a national media partly through its experiences in the South during the civil rights struggle, and civil rights organizers and activists learned to use the emerging electronic press as a means of advancing their agenda.

A national press, and especially a visually oriented media, made the sweeping changes in the South not only possible but imperative by propelling the civil rights struggle into the homes of Americans across the country and even into the White House. At the same time, journalists themselves recognize that the civil rights movement helped to shape the operation of television and radio network journalism for the future. Such veteran reporters and photographers of the civil rights story as John Chancellor, Harry Reasoner, Dan Rather, Chuck Quinn, Herbert Kaplow, Robert Schakne, Jack Nelson, Haynes Johnson, and David Halberstam are among today's best-known journalists.

One of the earliest uses of media in civil rights was a documentary produced by Howard University School of Law professor Charles Houston. In 1930 Houston traveled to South Carolina to record for the National Association for the Advancement of Colored People the disparity between black schools and white schools. He used a 16mm camera to produce *Examples of Educational Discrimination among Negroes in South Carolina*, a documentary film showing graphically the reality of racial discrimination among school children.

The 1955 trial in Mississippi of two white men, Roy Bryant and J. W. Milam, accused of murdering 14-year-old Emmett Till from Chicago, became one of the first media events of the modern civil rights movement. Both the white and black national press arrived in Money, Miss., to report on the trial. The Emmett Till case provides an example of the patterns of media coverage that would continue for most of the civil rights era. Local law enforcement officials developed a seige mentality once the national press became involved. They quickly moved from a vigorous prosecution of the two accused of killing Till to a refusal to even acknowledge that it was Till's body that was found. The local press became defenders of the prevailing southern white attitudes in racial conflicts.

The members of the press themselves were segregated. White journalists from around the country and from the state were seated near the front of the courtroom, while black journalists were seated in the back of the room at a card table. Besides *Jet* magazine, reporters and correspondents came from *Ebony* magazine, the Chicago *Defender*, the Pittsburgh *Courier*, the Baltimore *Afro-American*, the *Amsterdam News*, and the National Negro Press Association. Seated with them were Till's mother and a black member of Congress. *Jet* magazine's publication of the mutilated face of the corpse signaled one of the most important roles the media played in reporting the civil rights story. The *Jet* photograph was responsible for outrage across the nation and a mobilization of the black community.

Throughout the years of the civil rights movement, reporters and photographers from both the electronic media and the print media shaped the image of the South in the nation and the world. White community leaders tried to use the news media to gain support among white Americans for "our way of life," while black leaders used the media to show the inhuman and un-American treatment of blacks in the South. Community leaders became concerned about the future of economic development in the South as the violence and racial strife were broadcast across the country.

Civil rights leaders such as the Reverend Martin Luther King, Jr., soon realized the impact that the presence of the national media could have on the success or failure of a project. Civil rights strategists began to plan events that would attract the attention of the national press, especially television crews. When the media arrived, the chances of success for the movement improved. The national media became the ally of civil rights leaders in presenting their case to an American public.

The presence of the national press did not guarantee success, though. The Albany, Ga., campaign (November 1961–August 1962) by King is one example of a civil rights protest that failed even with the presence of the national press. The Albany campaign saw mass arrests, including that of King, but the deft handling of the situation by local white leaders, including Sheriff Laurie Pritchett and other local white leaders prevented the campaign from winning its civil rights goals.

Few civil rights protests were as well contained by white leaders as those at Albany. Southern white intransigence at King's next campaign, in Birmingham during April and May of 1963, resulted in televison and newspaper accounts of police dogs attacking demonstrators and firehoses spraying black children. Police commissioner Theophilus Eugene "Bull" Connor emerged from the ugly violence as a major symbol of racial conflict. The emotional responses these scenes evoked shook the nation and forced Birmingham leaders to deal with civil rights leaders. In March 1965 the American Broadcasting Company interrupted its regularly scheduled programming to broadcast the graphic images of people being trampled by police horses at the Edmund Pettus Bridge in Selma, Ala. Those scenes of "bloody Sunday" brought thousands of people to Alabama to make the march to Montgomery from Selma. President Lyndon B. Johnson announced the introduction of voting rights legislation within days of the broadcast of the scenes from Selma.

Technology had made possible live addresses from the White House and

Congress, and Presidents Dwight Eisenhower, John F. Kennedy, and Johnson used this means to communicate national government expectations to southern leaders. Perhaps the most ironic use of the live televised address was the appeal by President Kennedy for a peaceful solution to the threat of violence at the University of Mississippi on the Sunday that James Meredith arrived on campus. Kennedy's words to the state were echoing through televison sets across the nation as rifle fire and tear gas bursts were resounding on the campus.

The president's power to command media attention was once used to circumvent a civil rights activist's access to the national media. President Johnson envisioned the 1964 Democratic Convention as a harmonious meeting to confirm his leadership of the party and nominate him for the presidency. Mississippian Fannie Lou Hamer's testimony before the Credentials Committee was carried live by the television networks, and her story of the beatings she suffered in Mississippi was so dramatic that it threatened to disrupt the convention. This so angered President Johnson that he ordered his aide to announce an immediate presidential press conference. Johnson's strategy kept Hamer off the air temporarily, but her testimony was given extensive coverage during the evening news.

Southerners who became journalists in the civil rights era were frequently from rural backgrounds where segregation was not challenged. Often their experiences in reporting changed their beliefs about race relations in the South. Many of these reporters came to recognize that the southern system of segregation was morally and legally wrong. Other southern white journalists and white-owned newspapers as well as broadcast stations continued to uphold racial segregation.

Black and white journalists often were in physical danger. White journalists in some cases were especially vunerable because they were visible outsiders in the midst of predominently black activists or protesters; segregationists accused the journalists of provoking racial troubles. Throughout the civil rights struggle, journalists and photographers were targets for segregationist violence. Several were beaten, including National Broadcasting Company reporter Richard Valeriani. One journalist, French reporter Paul Guihard, was killed during the riot on the University of Mississippi campus in 1962.

In 1987 the Public Broadcasting System aired the six-part series, *Eyes on the Prize*, produced by Blackside Productions. The series told the story of the civil rights movement in the South through news and television footage and with interviews with civil rights participants and reporters. This compilation of photographs and film footage proved that media coverage of the civil rights movement has left an enduring visual and aural image of a crucial period in southern history. The University of Mississippi sponsored a 1987 symposium on civil rights and the media and has recorded videotaped oral history interviews with journalists who covered the story.

See also BLACK LIFE: Freedom Movement, Black; LAW: Civil Rights Movement

Marie Antoon
University of Mississippi

Jack Bass and Jack Nelson, The Orangeburg Massacre (1970; rev. ed., 1984); Clayborne

Carson, *In Struggle: SNCC and the Black Awakening of the 1960s* (1981); *Covering the South: A National Symposium on the Media and the Civil Rights Movement* (videotapes, Center for the Study of Southern Culture, University of Mississippi, 1987); David J. Garrow, *Protest at Selma: Martin Luther King, Jr., and the Voting Rights Act of 1965* (1979); Howell Raines, *My Soul Is Rested: The Story of the Civil Rights Movement in the Deep South—Told by the Men and Women Who Made It Happen* (1977); Juan Williams, *Eyes on the Prize: America's Civil Rights Years, 1954–1965* (1987). ☆

Comic Strips
||||||||||||||||||||||||||||||||||

For almost 40 years, except for an occasional appearance or incidental use as background, the South did not feature in the American comic strip. In 1934, however, two cartoonists turned to southern materials and produced characters that were to influence the way the larger population has viewed southerners.

A young artist from Connecticut named Alfred Gerald Caplin, or Al Capp, first discovered the charm of the South while ghosting some comic-strip sequences about hillbilly characters for Ham Fisher's *Joe Palooka* in 1933. On 20 August 1934 the world saw the debut of his own creation, *Li'l Abner*, which eventually would reach approximately 60 million readers in 900 American newspapers and 100 foreign papers in 28 countries.

The central character, Abner Yokum, was a large, handsome, and hopelessly naive young man who, along with his parents, Mammy and Pappy Yokum, his girlfriend, and later wife, Daisy Mae,

and the other residents of Dogpatch, represented for Capp a kind of innocence that he described in this way: "This innocence of theirs is indestructible so that while they possess all the homely virtues in which we profess to believe, they seem ingenuous because the world around them is irritated by them, cheats them, kicks them around. They are trusting, kind, loyal, generous and patriotic."

Although originally set somewhere in the mountains of Kentucky, Dogpatch soon took on a fantasy identity of its own, which had a good deal in common with the Lubberland described by William Byrd II in his 18th-century histories of the dividing line between Virginia and North Carolina. Dogpatch corresponded to the actual South in only a few ways: in its emphasis on kinship and the family unit, an acceptance of the individual and the grotesque, a reliance on violence when the social order is disrupted, and a depleted agrarian economy that annually brings starvation when the turnip crop is destroyed by insects. Southern religion, race, literature, and culture were never allowed in Dogpatch, where the satire was directed at the national scene rather than the local and at man's inhumanity to man rather than at regional mores. However, like the humorists of the Old Southwest, Capp relied heavily for his humor on dialect, exaggeration, the grotesque, and lively narrative action. There are many similarities, for example, between the riots instigated by Sut Lovingood in the yarns of George Washington Harris and Marryin' Sam's five-dollar wedding special.

In the same year that Capp began *Li'l Abner*, another major southern character appeared in an already widely popular strip about the sporting life. William

Morgan De Beck, or Billy De Beck, of Chicago, had begun *Barney Google* on 17 June 1919. Barney and his racehorse, Spark Plug, took the nation by storm and generated millions of dollars worth of merchandise, a popular song, and three stage musicals that toured the country. In 1934 Barney became the manager for a wrestler named Sully, and to escape some trouble they headed into the Kentucky hills and met a bootlegger named Snuffy Smith and his wife Loweezy. Snuffy and his mountaineer friends stole the spotlight and slowly dominated the strip until, after De Beck's death in 1942, his assistant, Fred Lasswell, took the strip entirely into the fictional Appalachian community.

This was no incidental excursion into an exotic environment on the part of De Beck but the result of a personal fascination with the life and culture of the mountaineer. De Beck read deeply in the literature of Appalachia and in particular was intrigued by the Tennessee writers George Washington Harris and Mary Noailles Murfree and by the Ozark folklore collections of Vance Randolph. He traveled into the mountains of Virginia and Kentucky, talked with the natives, and made numerous sketches of people and places. Under his hand, the comic strip reflected a brilliant use of Appalachian language, folklore, customs, motifs, themes, and stories inspired by his reading and experience.

The Snuffy Smith drawn over the last 40 years by Fred Lasswell has obscured the work of De Beck. Both Lasswell's Snuffy and Capp's Li'l Abner have been charged with encouraging Americans to consider southern mountaineers as backward, lazy, dumb, and unable to cope with the modern world. Neither has presented a very flattering portrait (though neither made a claim to realism or accuracy), but De Beck's original Snuffy may be considered a legitimate addition to modern art and literature about Appalachia, free of the charge of defamation.

Two strips inspired by the success of *Li'l Abner* were *Ozark Ike* in 1945 and *Long Sam* in 1954. Basically a sports strip, Ray Gotto's *Ozark Ike* brought an ignorant and inept baseball player and his blonde girlfriend Diana out of the hills and onto the bush-league playing fields. Though the art was distinctive, the continuity was weak, and the strip was only a moderate success. *Long Sam*, created by Al Capp, written by his brother Elliott Caplin, and drawn by Bob Lubbers, involved a beautiful hillbilly girl whose mama never allowed her to see a man. Although the art was striking, the plot device wore thin and it became a routine strip. For both these strips, the use of southern backgrounds was merely incidental and served only to maintain the Capp stereotypes.

In 1943 a former Disney animator from Connecticut, Walt Kelly, created a comic-book series about a black boy named Bumbazine and his pet alligator Albert in the Okefenokee swamp. This was the genesis of his 1946 strip *Pogo*. Kelly had studied Georgia dialect while working for the army's language section during the war, and, although there is no certain evidence, he must have encountered the Uncle Remus tales of Joel Chandler Harris. Like the stories of Uncle Remus, *Pogo* was an animal fable, told in dialect, about the techniques of survival in a largely hostile world. The innocent Pogo Possum, the vain Albert Alligator, the cynical Porky Porcupine, and other denizens of the swamp acted out morality plays in the style of the drama of the absurd with multilayered social, political, and philosophic meanings. The southern setting and pseudodialect, however, were merely a means to achieve Kelly's larger artistic concerns in one of the most brilliant comic strips of our time. As a teller of moral fables in an original idiom, Kelly belongs in the company of Mark Twain and William Faulkner.

One might make a case for Jeff MacNelly's 1978 *Shoe* as a southern comic strip, but the birds that populate its world are representative of broad types of human behavior, and there is little in it of a distinctive southern flavor. As an adopted Virginian, however, MacNelly has absorbed much of his southern environment in his fine sense of the grotesque and appreciation for hyperbole.

Entirely southern in content is *Kudzu* by Doug Marlette, a native of Greensboro, N.C. Introduced in 1981 while Marlette was working for the Charlotte *Observer*, *Kudzu* details the life and hard times of an adolescent of the same name, beset by an itch to write like Thomas Wolfe; beleaguered by his dominating mother, his redneck Uncle Dub, an ineffective preacher named Will B. Dunn, and a sarcastic parrot named Doris; befriended by Maurice, a black who aspires to be a great blues singer without undergoing any hardships; and hopelessly in love with Veranda, an indifferent southern belle who finds it difficult to choose between baton twirling and cheerleading as a career. Set in Bypass, N.C. (based partly on Laurel, Miss., Sanford, Fla., and other towns where Marlette lived), the widely popular *Kudzu* is the first genuinely southern comic strip by a southern artist that gently but incisively satirizes the culture and mystique of the South.

See also ENVIRONMENT: / Kudzu; ETHNIC LIFE: Mountain Culture; FOLKLIFE: / Brer Rabbit; "Hillbilly" Image; HISTORY AND MANNERS: / Byrd, William, II; LANGUAGE: / Randolph, Vance; LITERATURE: / Harris, George Washington; Harris, Joel Chandler; Wolfe, Thomas; MYTHIC SOUTH: Appalachian Culture

M. Thomas Inge
Randolph-Macon College

Al Capp, *The World of Li'l Abner* (1953); Maurice Horn, *The World Encyclopedia of Comics* (1976); M. Thomas Inge, *Appalachian Journal* (Winter 1977); Jerry Robinson, *The Comic: An Illustrated History of Comic Strip Art* (1974). ☆

Film, Blaxploitation

The term *blaxploitation film* is a euphemism for a genre of tightly budgeted, poorly scripted and acted, and highly stereotypical films starring black performers and more often than not treating subjects related to black life and culture. The films were a commercial response to the heightened sense of black awareness spawned by the civil rights and black power movements of the 1960s and 1970s. In still another sense they were a handy, short-term, and specifically targeted solution to a general decline in moviegoing, and the films' themes and characters were designed to attract inner-city audiences back to theaters.

Many of the films in question were set in northern urban ghettos and centered on the exploits of various pimps, prostitutes, hustlers, drug dealers, hit men, super spades, crime fighters, and buffoons. A representative sampling would include *Superfly*, *Shaft*, *Coffy*, *Cleopatra Jones*, *The Mack*, *Trick Baby*, *Hit Man*, *Foxy Brown*, *Willie Dynamite*,

Sweet Sweetback's Badass Song, Truck Turner, Legend of Nigger Charley, Black Belt Jones, and *Trouble Man.* Other films—not of the blaxploitation genre—that appeared during the period and won critical acclaim include *Sounder, Claudine, A Warm December, Save the Children, Uptown Saturday Night, Five on the Black Hand Side,* and *Lady Sings the Blues.*

When the South was the setting for films of the blaxploitation genre, it was often in a rural locale where racial passions were stirred and a very complex social and political situation was reduced to gross stereotypes. Southern blacks were more important as consumers than as subjects in blaxploitation films, but some films did represent a new view of the antebellum South. Films such as *Slaves* (1969), *The Quadroon* (1971), *Mandingo* (1975) and its sequel *Drum* (1976), and *Passion Plantation* (1978) had as central characters blacks who were angry foes of a brutal slave system. Dino De Laurentis, executive producer of *Mandingo,* argued that his movie, for example, meant to go "beyond the sentimentalized South of other films" and show "the true brutalizing nature of slavery." Even these films, however, used sensationalized advertising and exploited nudity, multiracial sex, and violence, undermining pretentions to present a serious new view of history.

Although highly successful financially, the blaxploitation films were the objects of intense criticism. Blacks did not reap financial benefits from most of the films because the directors, producers, and distributors were predominantly white. Black performers, who were generally starving for parts, were presented with weak scripts that required them to play one-dimensional characters. Blacks did not serve as writers, technicians, or directors or have other important behind-the-scenes roles.

The films were also thought to present a one-sided image of black life, one in which certain negative lifestyles and practices were presented to the exclusion of more favorable images and diversity. Blaxploitation films were also troubling because they tended to transmit undesirable values to adolescents and young adults. Crass materialism, drug use, inhumane male/female relationships, social degradation, violence, and a general glorification of nonproductive lifestyles were major concerns of critics. The movies were said to undermine the work ethic because many of the characters were dropouts from the regular economy, choosing instead to live by their wits. The level of violence in the movies was also singled out for special concern. The impression given was that black lives were very expendable and violence was a legitimate means of resolving disputes. The violence against women, the degraded and dependent image of women, and the glorification of casual and irresponsible sex were particularly intense and enduring concerns of black feminists.

See also BLACK LIFE: Film Images, Black

Earl Picard
Atlanta University

Francis W. Alexander, *Black Scholar* (May 1976); Donald Bogle, *Toms, Coons, Mulattoes, Mammies, and Bucks: An Interpretive History of Blacks in American Film* (1973); Thomas J. Cripps, *Black Film as Genre* (1978); Daniel Leab, *From Sambo to Superspade: The Black Experience in Motion Pictures* (1976); Richard A. Maynard, ed., *The*

Black Man on Film: Racial Stereotyping (1974); Webster L. Wallace, "Attitudes of Black College Freshmen Students toward Contemporary 'Controversial' Films" (Ph. D. dissertation, Georgia State University, 1975); Renee Ward, *Black Scholar* (May 1976). ☆

Film, Contemporary

IIIIIIIIIIIIIIIIIIIIIIIIIIIIIIIIIIIIIIIIIIIIIIIIIIIIII

Following a spate of Old South plantation romances and similar Civil War epics in the late 1930s (films such as *So Red the Rose* and *Gone with the Wind*), Hollywood motion pictures about the South changed to more contemporary, realistic treatments in the years following World War II.

Among the first such motion pictures were several drawn from best-selling novels, specifically Robert Penn Warren's *All the King's Men* and William Faulkner's *Intruder in the Dust.* Like the novels, the film adaptations dealt with topics of concern not only in the South but throughout the nation in the 1940s: the rise of a dictatorial political boss in Robert Rossen's 1949 film version of *All the King's Men* and race relations in the MGM film *Intruder in the Dust*, directed by Clarence Brown (also 1949). The Faulkner adaptation—filmed on location in Oxford, Miss., Faulkner's hometown—explored the reaction of a southern town to a black falsely accused of murdering a white.

Race relations played a part in several Faulkner adaptations (*The Sound and the Fury*, Martin Ritt, 1959, and *Sanctuary*, Tony Richardson, 1961), but the film adaptation of Harper Lee's best-selling novel, *To Kill a Mocking-bird* (Robert Mulligan, 1963), provided one of the more dramatic presentations of the conflict within a small southern town, as did the later *In the Heat of the Night* (Norman Jewison, 1967). The film of Carson McCullers's *Member of the Wedding* (Fred Zinneman, 1952) gave full expression to the personal relationships between white families and their black servants.

Political themes were the focus of *All the King's Men* and *A Lion Is in the Streets* (Raoul Walsh, 1953), both of which dealt with fictional characters based on Louisiana's political "Kingfish," Huey Long. Perhaps the most impressive political film about the South in recent years has been Robert Altman's epic-length *Nashville* (1975). *Nashville* brought together strands of patriotism in the South with country music, mysterious political candidates, and political assassination to give a chillingly prophetic view of contemporary trends in the South and nation. (*Nashville*'s prediction of a southern political "unknown" becoming president anticipated the candidacy of Georgia's Jimmy Carter in 1976.)

Robert Altman's *Thieves Like Us* (1974) was an interesting nostalgic sociological study of Mississippi during the Depression era of the 1930s. Filmed on location in Mississippi (Jackson, Parchman penitentiary, Canton, and other locales), it carefully created a portrait of young people casually drawn into a life of crime in filmic parallel to Bonnie and Clyde. Another nostalgic picture of an era—the 1950s—was seen in the Max Baer film *Ode to Billy Joe* (1976), which was an original screenplay based on the popular song by Mississippi singer Bobbie Gentry. That film explores sexual confusion—that of Billy Joe McCallister in recognizing his budding homosexuality—in the less sophisticated and more sexually repressive 1950s.

These post–World War II films dealt with realistic topics such as politics, race relations, and explicit sexual matters; they also achieved realism by being filmed on location in southern small towns to render an accurate physical environment. Oxford, Miss., has been used for several films (*Intruder in the Dust* and *Home from the Hill*); Louisiana for Faulkner's *The Long Hot Summer*; north Mississippi for *Ode to Billy Joe*; Selma, Ala., for *The Heart Is a Lonely Hunter*; and Nashville for the film of the same name. In the 1980s, Texas provided locales for films like *Tender Mercies*; *Paris, Texas*; *Places in the Heart*; and Horton Foote's *1918*, while Tennessee became the backdrop for 1984's *The River*.

Jere Real
Lynchburg College

Edward D. C. Campbell, Jr., *The Celluloid South: Hollywood and the Southern Myth* (1981); Fred Chappell, *Southern Humanities Review* (Fall 1978); Jack Temple Kirby, *Media-Made Dixie: The South in the American Imagination* (1978). ☆

Film, Decadent South

|||||||||||||||||||||||||||||||||||||||||||||||||||||

Drawing heavily upon the work of southern Gothic writers such as Tennessee Williams, Carson McCullers, Truman Capote, and William Faulkner, a genre of films dealing with the South as a region of decadence and depravity emerged in the years following World War II. In these films, the South was often portrayed as dark, exotic, morbidly gloomy, violent, and both sexually repressed—generally because of religion—and sexually obsessed.

Like the literary works that often spawned these motion pictures, such films contained elements of Gothic romanticism found in the psychological insights of Freud and Jung. Once, in attempting to define and explain the southern Gothic, Tennessee Williams termed it a literary style that sought to capture "an intuition, of an underlying dreadfulness in modern experience," thus frequently making use of violent and grotesque external symbols.

A Gothic sensibility is easily discerned in such works of William Faulkner as *As I Lay Dying, Sanctuary, The Sound and the Fury, Light in August,* and, notably, in his famous short story "A Rose for Emily." Similarly, it is found in such Williams plays as *A Streetcar Named Desire* (which deals with madness and rape), *Sweet Bird of Youth* (rape and castration), *Cat on a Hot Tin Roof* (homosexuality and nymphomania), and *Suddenly Last Summer* (adultery, madness, homosexuality, Oedipal love between mother and son, and, ultimately, cannibalism).

All the above-cited Williams plays were adapted for films by Hollywood in the 1950s and 1960s, as were several of the William Faulkner titles. Additionally, some of Faulkner's short stories were filmed as decadent plantation melodrama—most notably *The Long Hot Summer* (directed by Martin Ritt, 1958)—as was Williams's play set in an abandoned plantation house in the Mississippi Delta, *The Seven Descents of Myrtle*, filmed as *The Last of the Mobile Hot Shots* (1969).

While Tennessee Williams's *A Street-*

car Named Desire (filmed in 1951 by Elia Kazan) offered Vivien Leigh as Blanche DuBois, a kind of fallen Scarlett O'Hara, in gentle but devastating conflict with the brutish Stanley Kowalski (Marlon Brando), that film's decadent air resulted primarily from its New Orleans French Quarter setting rather than from the inherent plot devices or characterization. Yet, its ominous brooding quality of impending madness and possible violence was a forerunner of more explicitly developed decadent themes in such films of Williams as *Suddenly Last Summer* (directed by Joseph Mankiewicz, 1959) and in his only script written exclusively for film, the 1956 Elia Kazan film *Baby Doll*.

In *Suddenly Last Summer*, Katharine Hepburn is Violet Venable, a wealthy New Orleans matron who plots the forced lobotomy of her niece, Catherine Holly (Elizabeth Taylor), simply to save the reputation of her poet-son, Sebastian Venable, a homosexual with ravenous sexual appetites; Sebastian eventually is devoured alive by a band of boys in a Spanish village.

As Williams had used the grotesque

Carroll Baker in the title role in Tennessee William's **Baby Doll** *(1956)*

to sensational and morbid effect in *Suddenly Last Summer*, so he did it again in his film *Baby Doll*, set in the Mississippi Delta, with a similarly grotesque situation used to comic effect. There Silva Vaccarro, the owner of a cotton gin burned to the ground by Archie Lee Meehan, resolves to get vengeance by seducing Archie Lee's child bride, Baby Doll, before Archie Lee can ever consummate his marriage to her. As played by Eli Wallach, Carroll Baker, and Karl Malden, the film approached the comic grotesquerie of Faulkner's funeral scene in *Sanctuary*.

A similar mood is found in film versions of Carson McCullers's novels: first in *Member of the Wedding* (1957, Fred Zinneman); most flamboyantly in the John Huston film *Reflections in a Golden Eye* (1967); and in *The Heart Is a Lonely Hunter* (filmed in 1968 by Thomas Ryan), in which a young girl desperately tries to establish contact with a deaf-mute jeweler. *Reflections* brought the repressed sexuality theme of much southern Gothic fiction to the setting of a Georgia army post where a closeted homosexual captain pursued an unyielding and disinterested young soldier, while the soldier, taught by fundamentalist religion to view sex as sinful, is fulfilled by riding nude on horseback. The film also offered Julie Harris as a frustrated army wife who resorts to self-mutilation prior to going mad.

Most decadent South films portrayed the region as a land of much-violated sexual taboos and eccentric behavior by impoverished aristocrats. Many were adaptations of outstanding southern writers, but a few other Hollywood productions played on the same elements manipulated less effectively by lesser talents. A typical example is Otto Preminger's 1967 film, *Hurry Sundown* (with Michael Caine and Jane Fonda as unconvincing southerners), which merged some of the Gothic elements with a civil rights sociology.

See also HISTORY AND MANNERS: Sexuality; LITERATURE: Sex Roles in Literature; / Capote, Truman; Faulkner, William; McCullers, Carson; Williams, Tennessee

Jere Real
Lynchburg College

Edward D. C. Campbell, Jr., *The Celluloid South: Hollywood and the Southern Myth* (1981); Warren French, ed., *The South and Film* (1981); Jack Temple Kirby, *Media-Made Dixie: The South in the American Imagination* (1978). ☆

Film, Documentary
||||||||||||||||||||||||||||||||||||||||||||||||||||

The South has made a unique contribution to the documentary film. It has been both the subject and setting of artistically significant documentary films and more recently the home and support of documentary filmmakers and filmmaking units who have advanced the art of the documentary form and used film to record and preserve important aspects of southern culture.

Among the classic southern documentaries is Pare Lorentz's *The River* (1937), one of the best-known American documentaries set primarily in the South. Produced by the U.S. Farm Security Administration, this film considered the effects of deforestation and soil erosion on the Mississippi River and its tributaries. After depicting a tragic history of misuse and abuse, the documentary concludes optimistically by promoting the Tennessee Valley Authority as a model of river and flood control and an effective means of generating power and stimulating positive social change. The film was also an artistic success, combining powerful images of devastation with Virgil Thomson's intense musical score and Thomas Chalmers's somewhat didactic, if poetic, free-verse commentary. *The River* engendered interest in an important regional problem and suggested some possible solutions at the same time that it advanced the art of the American social documentary.

Another documentary classic set in the South is Robert Flaherty's *Louisiana Story* (1948). With major financial backing from the Standard Oil Company, Flaherty produced a poetic, semidocumentary story about oil exploration in southern Louisiana from the point of view of a native Cajun boy and his family. The film suggested that traditional aspects of southern culture could coexist with modern technology and the exploitation of natural energy resources. The pastoral beauty of Richard Leacock's photography and the serenity of Virgil Thomson's score help to smooth over and reshelve, cinematically, the many problems and contradictions inherent in technological changes that have affected traditional southern values and lifestyles.

In 1952 George Stoney produced an important documentary film about black midwives in Georgia titled *All My Babies*. This film focuses on the high infant mortality rate in the South at that time and suggests that careful preparation both physically (in terms of cleanliness) and psychologically (in terms of developing positive attitudes toward prenatal and postnatal care) could improve the situation. Stoney combines starkly realistic and direct images of midwifery and actual childbirth with spiritual music and a soft but effective narration by one of the midwives. The simplicity and directness of this film make it a classic exploration of southern social and public health problems.

The tradition of southern social documentary form has been continued more recently by several southern filmmakers who explore serious social problems within contemporary southern society. Elizabeth Barrett's *Coal Mining Woman* (1978) was made by Appalshop films, which began in 1969 as a community film workshop in Kentucky and developed into a vital center for the cinematic preservation of Appalachian folk culture. Barrett's *Coal Mining Woman* examines some of the physical and emotional hazards in the working conditions of women coal miners and the attempts of women to achieve a better working environment. Exploring a similar problem from a broader perspective, Barbara Kopple's *Harlan County, Kentucky* (1976) has achieved international acclaim and stimulated world interest in the plight of coal miners and coal-mining unions in Kentucky. Koppels' film rebuilds a powerfully dramatic confrontation between unionized and nonunionized working groups. Another important, if somewhat more notorious, social problem in the South is scrutinized by James Reston, Jr., and the University of North Carolina Television's *Ku Klux Klan* (1982). This public television documentary film provides a chilling behind-the-scenes look at a group devoted to extremist politics and the perpetuation of racial prejudice in the South. The specific events investigated by Reston are those that led to the

shooting deaths of several members of the Communist Worker's party in Greensboro, N.C. Bill Vanderkloot's *Iron Horse* (1982) focuses upon the subtle but pervasive problem of southern intolerance toward the free expression of ideas and artistic impulses, especially during the 1950s. Vanderkloot deploys a unique blend of documentary footage, interviews, and re-creations and reconstructions of historical events to depict the violent response of students at the University of Georgia to an abstract sculpture of a horse constructed on campus by sculptor Abbot Pattison.

Not all documentaries about the South have centered on social problems, however. Many recent documentary films have introduced audiences to the unique personalities of men and women who live and work south of the Mason-Dixon line. In 1978 and 1979 Ross McElwee, a native of North Carolina and an MIT-trained documentary filmmaker who is currently an artist in residence at Harvard University, created two cinema verité portraits of native southerners. *Charleen* is an intense, revealing film about Charleen Swansea, a "poetry-in-the-schools" teacher in Charlotte, N.C. The daughter of a false-teeth manufacturer and friend and correspondent of great poets like Ezra Pound and e. e. cummings, Charleen engages her students, audiences, and friends with her impassioned appreciation of life and art. McElwee's film is an unrelenting, penetrating, yet compassionate exploration of the public and private life of a vivacious, intelligent southern woman. His next film, *Space Coast*, assesses the impact of the decline of the space program at Cape Canaveral, Fla., upon the private lives of several admittedly bizarre residents of a typical southern community. These real-life "characters" include a woman newspaper reporter who has covered over 1,600 consecutive space launches and still struggles for new clichés to describe these events, a Bible-toting motorcycle gang leader who lost his job as a maintenance man at the space center, and an abusive owner of a small construction company who doubles as the host of a children's television program while building low-cost housing for the retirees who have replaced the departing engineers. There is something pathetic about these people, despite McElwee's best efforts to treat them as sympathetic but tragic figures caught in the middle of profound social, economic, and cultural changes.

Another probing examination of personalities in a Florida town is Errol Morris's *Vernon Florida* (1980). Morris's film is less an investigation of the social contexts and cultural changes that affect personalities and daily lives than it is a questioning of what it means to be human in an absurd world. Morris focuses on the personal obsessions of a preacher who earnestly delivers a sermon on the meaning of the word "therefore" in Paul's Epistles, a turkey hunter who talks about his "big game" with all the dramatic angst of an existentialist facing death, and a small-town policeman who sits and waits for something, anything, to happen, like one of the characters in Samual Beckett's *Waiting for Godot*. Like McElwee's *Space Coast*, Morris's *Vernon Florida* hovers between an appreciation of unusual southern characters and an unflattering depiction of bizarre behavior and skewed personalities that borders on the satirical.

Southern documentary does not, however, exclusively focus on southern eccentrics. *Lila* (1980), by Fran Furst-Terranella and Cheryl Gosa, is a gentle portrait of Atlanta's Lila Bonner-Miller, a great-grandmother, a doctor and psychiatrist, an artist, and a community leader at the age of 80. *Lila* almost reverently documents the life of a woman who insists that she's "not gonna talk about senility, because I'm not gonna fool with it." *Lila* is not quite a didactic treatise against stereotypical representations of the elderly, but the film does insist that, although Dr. Bonner-Miller may be "extraordinary," older people can, and do, lead rich, productive existences.

Some southern documentaries assume the form of cinematic essays on aspects of southern culture. Marjie Short's *Kudzu* (1976) is a humorous essay about the uses and abuses of a prolific southern plant. Kudzu, Short explains through various interviews, was imported from Japan in the 1930s as a means of combating soil erosion in the South. This documentary, which Short made while at Boston University, won an Academy Award; it effectively blends contrasting opinions and information about the ubiquitous plant in an amusing and enlightening way, although emphasizing the former. Usually sympathetic to her interviewees, Short sometimes seems to approach her subject from the outside and evokes humor at both the behest and the expense of her southern subjects.

This point of sympathy versus ridicule and "inside" versus "outside" perspectives on the South separates native from nonnative documentary filmmakers and filmmaking units. Stan Woodward's *It's Grits* (1981) is quite similar to *Kudzu* in form and subject matter but it also typifies the native southerner's somewhat more understanding treatment of southern culture, customs, and personalities. Although *It's Grits* is a humorous essay about a popular ethnic food, it rarely elicits amusement at the expense of southerners, although it sometimes enthusiastically exposes the naïveté of northerners, sufficiently gullible to be persuaded that tobacco plants are "grits bushes." Even the most unsophisticated or idiosyncratic southern personalities, such as a woman who eats grits with "coon and possum" and a man who freezes "gritsicles," are treated with warmth and respect rather than derision.

Tom Davenport's *Thoughts on Fox Hunting* (1979) explores and questions the place of traditional English fox hunting in a Virginia context. In part the film is structured around Lord Peter Beckford's 1781 classic book of the same title. Davenport uses subjective camera techniques and skillful editing to involve the spectator in the fox's point of view and to intensify the inherently dramatic action of the chase. Working in cooperation with the Curriculum in Folklore at the University of North Carolina, Davenport also created a richly sympathetic portrait of a master North Carolina tale-teller, John E. "Frail" Joines, in *Being a Joines* (1982). This film studies the changes that have swept the life of one rural North Carolina family and powerfully documents important aspects of southern folk culture.

Uniquely southern literary and musical arts and artists have been preserved on film by many southern filmmakers and filmmaking units. Ross Spears's James Agee Film Project produced a feature-length documentary entitled *Agee* (1980) about the life and literary work of James Agee, a well-known poet, film critic, and author. This lyrical film combines contemporary interviews with dramatic reconstructions of events in Agee's life that had a significant impact on his creative expression. William Ferris, Les Blank, and Bryan Elsom have all explored southern blues and jazz music with sensitivity and deep understanding. Ferris's film *Give My Poor Heart Ease* (1973) focuses on a Mississippi Delta bluesman who sings in a barbershop about the loss of his woman and his money. Filmmakers Les Blank and Bryan Elsom go beyond recording performances for posterity and future study. They use cinematic techniques that capture the spirit and sense of the music and the sensibility of musicians through camera placement, shot selection, and editing rhythms. Their films paint inner portraits of artists and their working methods, as in Elsom's *A Night in Tunisia: A Musical Portrait of Dizzy Gillespie* (1980), which combines an instructional film about jazz with an intense, affectionate, and evocative portrait of a major jazz artist. Elsom's careful lighting and compositions are as aesthetically eloquent as Gillespie's music. The film won the Best Film award at the London Film Festival in 1981.

Les Blank is a prolific documentarian whose films, many of which explore traditional southern and southwestern music and culture, have achieved international recognition. *The Blues Accordin' to Lightnin' Hopkins* casually, yet acutely, searches through the social milieu from which blues music emerged and documents an ethnic lifestyle and social context as it penetrates beneath the surface of the blues and the personality of a unique artist, Lightnin' Hopkins. Blank's films, amicable, warm, deeply felt, and insightful, have examined a number of ethnic and traditional subjects, most notably music and cultural rituals celebrated in the Mardi Gras in *Always for Pleasure*, Cajun life in *Spend It All*, and Cajun food and zydeco music in *Dry Wood and Hot Pepper*.

Within the context of a rich and active film culture that documents traditional southern passions, problems, and personalities, some southern filmmakers have produced films that extend the normal limits of the documentary itself as an art form. Bryan Elsom's *Alabama Departure* (1979) is an experimental documentary and a poetic journey through southern Alabama, in which images gliding through an abandoned resort town covered with Spanish moss are blended with an almost magical combination of natural and artifical sounds. Like *Alabama Departure*, Jan Millsapps's *Folly Beach Journal* (1981) experiments with the conventional boundaries of the documentary. A cinematic journal of the filmmaker's self-reflections through her episodic encounters with the environment of a South Carolina beach, the film compiles live action and animation into a visual autobiographical record that is also a compelling depiction of the fluid, cyclical rhythms of the site where ocean and land meet.

See also ENVIRONMENT: / Kudzu; HISTORY AND MANNERS: / Grits; LITERATURE: / Agee, James; MUSIC: / Hopkins, Lightnin'; SOCIAL CLASS: / Coal Mining; VIOLENCE: Harlan County, Ky.; / Ku Klux Klan

> Gorham Kindem
> Laurie Schulze
> University of North Carolina
> at Chapel Hill

Linda Dubler, *American Film* (April 1986); Lewis Jacobs, *The Documentary Tradition* (1971); Gorham Kindem, *Southern Quarterly* (Spring–Summer 1981). ☆

Film, "Hick Flick"

IIIIIIIIIIIIIIIIIIIIIIIIIIIIIIIIIIIIIIIIIIIIIIIII

The forces of the law and its relationship—sometimes favorable, sometimes malign—with working-class white southerners constitute one of the basic elements in what has been termed in recent years the "hick flick." This film genre has been extremely popular throughout the South, creating its initial "cult" audience through limited drive-in theater showings, later moving into more widespread commercial theater distribution, and eventually achieving mass commercial and entertainment appeal and major "star" actors' appearances.

The precedent for such formula films might be the 1958 Arthur Ripley film, *Thunder Road*, in which a youthful Robert Mitchum foiled the constant attempts of law enforcement officials to stop his illegal moonshine whiskey operations. That film, like so many that followed and expanded on its basic conflict, was notable for its high-speed automobile chase sequences, now a staple of the genre. Indeed, the popular *Dukes of Hazzard* television series utilized many salient aspects of the "hick flick" as the basis for its rural situation comedy.

In the motion pictures, however, the conflicts involving the southern working-class white hero (and sometimes heroine, though the genre largely is devoted to both the adventurous and sexual exploits of a macho male hero) have taken both comic and serious directions. In the comic version the southern lawman (often a small-town police chief or a county sheriff) becomes an exaggerated buffoon who is regularly outwitted by the working-class protagonist, who is involved in illegal, but generally victimless, activities. In a sense, the comic southern law figure may be seen as the modern equivalent of the *miles gloriosus* (the braggart soldier) of Roman comedy. This kind of comic law figure was seen in the series of Burt Reynolds films that began with the highly successful *Smokey and the Bandit* and was carried through several sequels with Jackie Gleason as Sheriff Buford T. Justice. As in *Thunder Road*, the "illegality" was the transport of alcoholic beverages, but in the *Smokey* films the beverage was a particular brand of beer. These films—together with Reynolds's earlier *Gator* films—are marked by a glib southern hero who combines his rebellious attitude and contempt for organized authority, especially that of the local lawman, with a kind of Robin Hood–Don Juan adventurism.

In a more serious vein, the law achieves an authoritarian upper hand, either by misuse of legal authority (in such films as *Mason County Line*, *Jackson County Jail*, and in the 1984 film *Tank*) or through simple force of a sadistic will. This same sadistic law enforcement figure appears in a related type of film where the working-class hero actually is imprisoned—the Paul Newman film *Cool Hand Luke*, the Burt Reynolds film *The Longest Yard*, or the more recent John Schneider film, *Eddie Macon's Run*. In each case, the protagonist is accused of only a minor crime and, while in jail, continues his conflict with a sadistic prison system and administrative law figure. (A more dramatic version of this theme is developed in the true-story film adaptation *Brubaker*, which featured Robert Redford as a well-meaning warden trying to clear up the corruption of an Arkansas prison system.) Occasionally, the serious "hick flick" combines the defiant aspects of the working-class hero with those of an honest lawman trying to overcome massive corruption in the society of which he is a small part; that kind of confrontation marked the various *Walking Tall* films.

Both serious and comic, the basic appeal of the genre lies in the depiction of an average man overcoming, outmaneuvering, or facing down an opponent who represents unfair, authoritarian power—even that of the legal system itself. The "hick flick" provides an interesting parallel with "blaxploitation films," which focus on underworld black heroes and their conflict with southern white society.

See also LAW: Police Forces; MYTHIC SOUTH: / Rednecks

Jere Real
Lynchburg College

Edward D. C. Campbell, Jr., *The Celluloid South: Hollywood and the Southern Myth* (1981); Jack Temple Kirby, *Media-Made Dixie: The South in the American Imagination* (1978). ☆

Film, Musical

|||||||||||||||||||||||||||||||||||||||

The South emerged as a setting for song-and-dance films partly because of the enormous Broadway success of the stage adaptation of Edna Ferber's novel *Show Boat* in 1928, with Jerome Kern and Oscar Hammerstein II's memorable score, just as talking pictures were beginning to revolutionize the industry. Universal rushed a "part-talking" version starring Laura LaPlante into production for 1929 release. It has disappeared, with most of its generally unsatisfactory hybrids; but it launched a vogue for the riverboat musical films, which included Buddy Rogers's *River of Romance* (1929) and Bing Crosby's *Mississippi* (1935), two versions of the same fable, as well as Crosby's *Rhythm on the River* (1940) and *Dixie* (1943), and a spectacular remake of *Show Boat* itself with Helen Morgan, Paul Robeson, and other members of the original Broadway cast (1936). After World War II a third *Show Boat* (1951) was followed by Elvis Presley's *Frankie and Johnny* (1966), but these failed to match the success of the earlier films.

Two other southern musical subgenres that were established in the late 1920s also appear to have run their course. An early start was made toward establishing a tradition of all-black musicals, emphasizing talented black song-and-dance performers. The happy life of the slaves on the old plantation was exploited in early two-reel short subjects like *Slave Days* (1929) and *Night in Dixie* (c. 1930), while the feature-length *Hearts in Dixie* (1929) made the New South look like the Old. All-black casts were subsequently featured in *The Green Pastures* (1936), which, although set in Heaven, featured the Hall Johnson choir's rendition of spirituals in a Dixie-like setting, and *Cabin in the Sky* (1943), which provided the best filmed record of Ethel Waters's remarkable voice. (On the other hand, the only filmed Bessie Smith performance was her rendition of "St. Louis Blues" for a 20-minute program filler.)

Romantic New Orleans was also quickly appropriated as a setting for screen musicals. Casting about for a follow-up to Bebe Daniels's enormously successful *Rio Rita* (1929), RKO hit upon the idea of commissioning the screen's first original musical score for *Dixiana* (1930), which also boasted the talents of black tap dancer Bill "Bojangles" Robinson. Since then most major musical stars have graced extravaganzas set in the Crescent City: Mae West's *Belle of the Nineties* (1934), Bing Crosby's *Birth of the Blues* and Marlene Dietrich's *The Flame of New Orleans* (both 1941), Bob Hope's *Louisiana Purchase* (1942), Mario Lanza's *The Toast of New Orleans* (1950), and Pat Boone's *Mardi Gras* (1958). The great black jazz singer Billie Holiday had her only major screen role in *New Orleans* (1947); but this series seems to have ended with the film that made best use of the setting, Elvis Presley's *King Creole* (1958).

During the 1930s the southern musical also became a special preserve of popular child entertainers. Bill "Bojangles" Robinson enjoyed the best of his scandalously few film opportunities dancing with Shirley Temple in *The Little Colonel* (1935) and *The Littlest Rebel* (1935); Miss Temple's archrival at 20th Century Fox, Jane Withers, made *Can This Be Dixie?* in 1936; and their male rival at Universal, Bobby Breen, made *Rainbow on the River* (1936) and *Way Down South* (1939). These were succeeded by such "hillbilly" musicals as Bob Burns's *Mountain Music* (1937) and *The Arkansas Traveler* (1938), the Weaver Brothers and Elviry's misleadingly titled *Grand Ole Opry* (1940), and Judy Canova's long series for Republic from *Sis Hopkins* (1941) to *Lay that Rifle Down* (1955). *The Singing Brakeman* (1929) was a short film featuring country singer Jimmie Rodgers. An elaborate grotesquerie related to this subgenre was an adaptation of the stage play *Li'l Abner* (1959), with live actors prancing around as Al Capp's comic-strip characters.

The 1930s was also the decade of

biographical films, and the South's beloved Stephen Foster came in for his share with *Harmony Lane* (1935), starring Don Ameche, who also had portrayed Alexander Graham Bell and other notables, and *Swanee River* (1939), Al Jolson's last attempt to recover his earlier film popularity. Foster's music was also featured in *My Old Kentucky Home* (1938), another vehicle for the popular black Hall Johnson choir.

The Old South has not fared well in musical films. Walt Disney's attempt to reinvigorate the plantation myth in *Song of the South* (1946), though popular with the public, was criticized by blacks and ridiculed by reviewers. Although the South produced in Elvis Presley the most durable star for modest musicals since Bing Crosby, only a few of Elvis's films (besides the aforementioned *Frankie and Johnny* and *King Creole*) were set in the South. His first film, *Love Me Tender* (1956), was set in Texas after the Civil War, but only *Loving You* (1957), *Wild in the Country* (1961), and *Kissin' Cousins* (1964) were set in the rural southern regions where Presley had grown up. After these films he was packed off to Hawaii, Acapulco, Las Vegas, the Seattle World's Fair, and other fantasylands far from Mississippi.

The enormously popular *Reader's Digest*, seeking new fields to conquer, made a spectacular entry into film production in 1973–74 with musical versions of Mark Twain's *Tom Sawyer* and *Huckleberry Finn*, both with southern settings. Although *Tom Sawyer* was well received and did well at the box office, *Huckleberry Finn* was a disaster with both reviewers and the public. The magazine has not continued its project of revamping American classics, and other producers have shied away from such ventures.

Especially in view of the continuing

James Baskett and Bobby Driscoll as Uncle Remus and Johnny in Walt Disney's Song of the South *(1946)*

success of the television program *Hee Haw* and Opryland's popularity as a tourist attraction, the best prospects for future musical South films appears to be films employing country music stars. Except for *Coal Miner's Daughter* (1980), based on the life of singer Loretta Lynn, such films have been few and not particularly successful. Robert Altman's *Nashville* (1975) was viciously critical of the city and its music industry and was shunned by established troupers for the Grand Ole Opry. Willie Nelson made something of a hit with *Honeysuckle Rose* (1981, retitled *On the Road Again* for television), but his *Barbarosa* (1982) quickly disappeared. *The Best Little Whorehouse in Texas* (1982) showcased Dolly Parton as well as Burt Reynolds. Kenny Rogers's only production, *Six Pack* (1982), was popular in small towns and at drive-ins, and he appears to offer the only current possibility for restoring the Bing Crosby/Elvis Presley tradition of small-scale, tuneful films. With few musical extravaganzas being produced at all, the days of the riverboat romances seem over.

See also BLACK LIFE: Film Images, Black; MUSIC: / Foster, Stephen; Presley, Elvis; Smith, Bessie; RECREATION: / Showboats; URBANIZATION: / New Orleans

Warren French
Indiana University

Andrew Bergman, *We're in the Money: Depression America and Its Films* (1971); Edward D. C. Campbell, Jr., *The Celluloid South: Hollywood and the Southern Myth* (1981); Thomas J. Cripps, *Slow Fade to Black: The Negro in American Film, 1900–1942* (1977); Jane Feuer, *The Hollywood Musical* (1982); John Russell Taylor and Arthur Jackson, *The Hollywood Musical* (1971). ☆

Film, Plantation
||||||||||||||||||||||||||||||||||||||||||||

From just off screen a small, wooden model of a Mississippi steamboat was pushed across what was obviously just a tub of water. To the back of the tub was attached a simple drawing of vast cotton fields and a porticoed mansion. Though technically crude, that 1903 silent film adaptation of *Uncle Tom's Cabin* first presented on film what quickly became the cinematic mythology of a grand Old South.

In the first years after 1865 a general interest in descriptive, regional color developed, focusing on dialect and folktales, descriptions of the antebellum social scene, and characterizations of the planter class. It was not long before southern writers such as Thomas Nelson Page and George Cary Eggleston were regular contributors to such leading northeastern periodicals as *Atlantic Monthly*, *Lippincott's*, and *Scribner's Magazine*.

Matters southern were not just for periodicals, though. Sometimes lavish, sometimes simple, presentations of plantation stereotypes—large homes, prim belles, imposing colonels, and contented slaves—were standard fare for stage productions as, for example, with the popular Lew Johnson's Plantation Minstrels. Artwork such as Eastman Johnson's, nostalgic prints by Currier & Ives, songs by Stephen Foster—all contributed further to a mystique of plantation culture.

The earliest silent films were therefore quick to adopt what had become an established, familiar setting. As the early, predominantly urban motion picture theaters attracted ticket buyers eager for excitement, the romantic plantation image was perfect for the new medium: in very brief films the stories furnished escape with by-then instantly recognizable characters and settings.

Silent film productions such as *The Planter's Wife* (1909), *In Slavery Days* (1913), or *Colonel Carter of Cartersville* (1915) presented a gentle, pastoral South dominated by wealth and tended by large numbers of slaves. One reviewer, after seeing *The Confederate Spy* (1910), commented that such films were important, because "in that way a better understanding of the Southern people can be disseminated." So dominant did the image become that even *Uncle Tom's Cabin* was reworked so as to change completely its liberal slant. Southerner Harry Pollard, directing *Uncle Tom's Cabin* for Universal Studios in 1927, remarked that the story actually provided a chance to comment on "the gallantry, charm, hospitality, and gentility of the antebellum days."

No one, however, created a stronger

statement of that than D. W. Griffith, also a southerner (ironically, few from the region directed or produced tales of the plantation). Griffith regarded *Birth of a Nation* (1915) as an accurate portrayal of the South. Taking his story from Thomas Dixon, Jr.'s novel *The Clansman*, Griffith indeed found the attractive plantation lifestyle so prevalent that the home of his fictionalized well-to-do South Carolina family was described as "a more representative reproduction than any that has yet appeared on the screen of the typical dwelling place."

The commercial viability of sound films after 1927, the onset of the Depression with its accompanying heightened need for entertaining motion pictures, and even the attraction of a predominantly agrarian South as counterpoint to a devastated industrial economy all made the plantation theme more attractive, exaggerated, and profitable during the 1930s. An initial wave of tentative sound shorts—*Dixie Days* (1928) and *Slave Days* (1929), for example—followed by the feature-length *Hearts in Dixie* (1929) centered the story around singing and dancing blacks. But once the general formula was proven popular in sound productions, a steady stream of musicals, comedies, and dramas emerged with the planter's family as focus and the slave as foil or comic relief.

RKO's *Dixiana* (1930) included the first original music commissioned for a film. Bill "Bojangles" Robinson danced through *The Littlest Rebel* (1935) with Shirley Temple. *Can This Be Dixie?* (1936) and *Way Down South* (1939) also featured child stars. Paramount Pictures paired W. C. Fields and Bing Crosby in *Mississippi* in 1935; the same year the studio released *So Red the Rose*. The latter served as an example of the extremes to which the film industry had

taken the plantation story line. Posters drew audiences to "see the Old South ride again," while press releases claimed that star Margaret Sullavan personally made the Confederate flag used in the picture.

David O. Selznick's *Gone with the Wind* (1939), however, was the capstone to Hollywood's fictionalization of the South in the 1930s. Having purchased the film rights to Margaret Mitchell's 1936 bestseller for $50,000, Selznick devoted himself to making his film even better than Warner Brothers' *Jezebel*. Rushed into production in 1938 to upstage Selznick International's projected epic, *Jezebel* had been almost an inventory of familiar antebellum clichés. In response, Selznick meticulously fashioned his image of the plantation life style; impressed critics and audiences alike proclaimed the atmosphere "faithful."

The coming of World War II quickly brought changes to Hollywood. The films produced in such profusion before

Bette Davis in Jezebel *(1938)*

were now strongly discouraged by the Office of War Information's Motion Picture Section. Fighting a war for the free world and democracy, the government could hardly condone repeated celebrations of the plantation. The change was soon obvious, as in the 1943 musical *Dixie*, in which characterizations of the slaves and scenes of plantation life were essentially omitted in favor of southern urban settings.

By the late 1940s even more pressure was brought to bear. Various court decisions and Truman's integration of the armed services, in addition to the first federal laws aimed at ending discrimination, all signaled Hollywood that the Old South stories would have to adapt to the times. Change was soon evident. By 1947, in *The Foxes of Harrow*, a slave kills her child and herself rather than submit to further life on the plantation; in *The Mississippi Gambler* (1953) and *The Gambler from Natchez* (1954) images of slavery were few. And by 1957, in both *Raintree County* and especially *Band of Angels*, the antebellum South's mythical lifestyle and system of labor were objects of considerable reinterpretation if not derision.

By the late 1960s television was accelerating the decline of the traditional Hollywood studio system, as well as drawing people away from the old downtown theaters. Freed from the usual commercial constraints, a number of filmmakers found in the theme of the plantation, especially slavery, an appropriate framework for analyzing contemporary society. Racial violence, the debate over civil rights, and black separatist movements all contributed to productions such as *Slaves* (1969), *The Quadroon* (1971), *Mandingo* (1975) and its sequel *Drum* (1976), as well as *Passion Plantation* (1978). All reversed previous formulas by making the slave the central figure.

But as the political climate cooled so too did the productions. Just as *Gone with the Wind* and *Slaves* reflected their respective periods, recent films such as *Roots* (1977, 1979) have pointed to a more balanced assessment of the plantation in film, seen from the perspective of both the mansion and the slave quarters.

See also MUSIC: / Foster, Stephen; MYTHIC SOUTH: Plantation Myth; / *Uncle Tom's Cabin*

Edward D. C. Campbell, Jr.
Virginia State Library

Edward D. C. Campbell, Jr., *The Celluloid South: Hollywood and the Southern Myth* (1981); Thomas J. Cripps, *Slow Fade to Black: The Negro in American Film, 1900–1942* (1977); Jack Temple Kirby, *Media-Made Dixie: The South in the American Imagination* (1978); Peter A. Soderbergh, *Mississippi Quarterly* (Winter 1965–66). ☆

Film, Southern
IIIIIIIIIIIIIIIIIIIIIIIIIIIIIIIIIIIIIII

Although two of the most popular and historically important American films—director-producer D. W. Griffith's *Birth of a Nation* (1915) and producer David O. Selznick's *Gone with the Wind* (1939)—are archetypal southern classics, the "southern" as a distinctive film genre has not flourished as did the "western." To be sure, most of the techniques that accounted for the success of *Birth of a Nation* (as a suspense film, not an ideological drama) became the basic conventions of horse operas. The "southern" itself, though, evolved through markedly different stages, reaching its greatest popularity in the 1930s, the 1950s, and the late 1970s.

Before the spectacular success of his epic feature, Griffith, a native Kentuckian, set in the South a number of the several hundred one-reel narratives he ground out for Biograph between 1908 and 1914 (*In Old Kentucky, The House with Closed Shutters*). His first film that extended nickelodeon features to two reels was finally released in two parts as *His Trust* and *His Trust Fulfilled* (1911), the story of an exslave's devotion to the daughter of his master, who was killed in the war. After the introduction of feature films around 1915, however, Griffith returned to a southern setting only for *A Romance of Happy Valley* (1919), his most nearly autobiographical film about growing up in rural Kentucky, but one that exercised little influence on future films.

Indeed, from the 1920s only Buster Keaton's unique *The General* (1926), a Civil War farce about a stolen locomotive, has established itself as a southern classic. The South, however, attracted the critical eyes of filmmakers during the first years of talking pictures before the Hays Office production code (1934) drastically changed the tone of American film fare. *I Am a Fugitive from a Chain Gang* (1932), *The Story of Temple Drake* (1933, from William Faulkner's *Sanctuary*), and *Wild Boys of the Road* (1933) were bitter attacks on decadent racial and prison policies and on the wealthy families that controlled the South.

The advent of the Motion Picture Producers Code precluded such offerings and saw them replaced by sentimental tales that developed a myth of old Dixie,

like Shirley Temple's *The Little Colonel* (1935) and *The Littlest Rebel* (1935), W. C. Fields's *Mississippi* (1935), and Will Rogers's posthumous *Steamboat 'Round the Bend* and *In Old Kentucky* (1935). This trend culminated in the grandest of several film versions of *Show Boat* (1936), one of the greatest examples of the musical South film.

A more somber tone colored those films dealing with the threat of rebellion hanging over the antebellum South, including *So Red the Rose* (1935, from Stark Young's novel) and *Jezebel* (1938), both of which foreshadowed *Gone with the Wind*, only recently voted the all-time favorite of American filmgoers. Cecil B. DeMille attempted to continue the epic tradition with *Reap the Wild Wind* (1942), but shortages of color film and a pronounced interest in current events during World War II shortened the life of a promising genre.

The Old South occasionally reappeared in films like *The Foxes of Harrow* (1947) and *Band of Angels* (1957), a watered-down version of Robert Penn Warren's tale of miscegenation, but these traditional deglamorizing films failed to distract audiences from searching new looks at the modern South. A frightening antilynching film, *They Won't Forget*, aroused so much controversy in 1937 that filmmakers did not go so far in portraying cynical southern politicians again before World War II, but the film versions of Lillian Hellman's play *The Little Foxes* and Erskine Caldwell's novel *Tobacco Road* (both 1941) left distinctly unfavorable impressions of the region.

From such beginnings would emerge after the war the largest coherent body of films so far made about the South, the "southern Gothics," based often upon the writings of William Faulkner and Tennessee Williams or derived from them. Efforts were made at the end of the war to present more endearing pictures of the South in Jean Renoir's *The Southerner* (1945) and Walt Disney's *Song of the South* (1946), a mixture of animation and live action based on Joel Chandler Harris's Uncle Remus stories, but audiences found Renoir's tribute "arty," and critics found Disney's popular musical saccharine.

The South especially took a beating in 1949 with the film versions of Robert Penn Warren's *All the King's Men* and Faulkner's *Intruder in the Dust*, which appeared along with Elia Kazan's overt attack on racism in *Pinky*. The new trend was really given impetus by the film versions of Tennessee Williams's successful plays *The Glass Menagerie* (1950) and *A Streetcar Named Desire* (1951), which whetted the appetite for more of Williams's shockers—*The Rose Tattoo* (1954), *Baby Doll* (1956), *The Fugitive Kind* (1960), and *Suddenly Last Summer* (1959), which still stands unchallenged as the climactic revelation of aristocratic decadence. However, botched versions of Faulkner's *The Sound and the Fury* (1959), *The Long Hot Summer* (1958), and *Sanctuary* (1961) proved no match for these, and the Gothic genre trailed off into titillating horror shows like *Hush . . . Hush, Sweet Charlotte* (1964).

Excellent films treating racial problems more realistically than in earlier years began to appear—*The Intruder* (1962), *To Kill a Mockingbird* (1963), *Nothing But a Man* (1964), *In the Heat of the Night* (1967), and *Sounder* (1972)—but they established no formula. More important from the viewpoint of establishing a genre have been *Deliverance* (1972, from James Dickey's novel) and the *Walking Tall* series,

which began in 1973 and portrayed the South as a still violent frontier prone to vigilante action. The 1970s also saw a brief flourishing of films like *Mandingo* (1975) and *Passion Plantation* (1978), which turned the plantation legend upside down by celebrating the uprisings of defiant blacks against decadent masters. Attacks on continuing labor problems in the modern South, like *Harlan County, Kentucky* (1976) and *Norma Rae* (1979), were more positively received.

The best possibilities for the development of a continuing popular southern genre, however, seem likely to be in the use of country music materials. Although Robert Altman's *Nashville* (1975) was shunned by the Grand Ole Opry's faithful, films like *Coal Miner's Daughter* (1980), the story of singer Loretta Lynn; Willie Nelson's *Honeysuckle Rose* (1982); and especially Burt Reynolds's *Smokey and the Bandit* films (1977, 1980), which employ the same kind of rural characters and humor as television programs like *Hee Haw* and the *Dukes of Hazzard*, have proved particularly popular with Sunbelt drive-in crowds.

Warren French
Indiana University

Edward D. C. Campbell, Jr., *The Celluloid South: Hollywood and the Southern Myth* (1981); Fred Chappell, *Southern Humanities Review* (Fall 1978); Warren French, ed., *The South and Film* (1981); Jack Temple Kirby, *Media-Made Dixie: The South in the American Imagination* (1978); Andrew Sarris, *The American Cinema: Directors and Directions, 1929–1968* (1968); Peter A. Soderbergh, *Mississippi Quarterly* (Winter 1965–66). ☆

Film Images

||||||||||||||||||||||||||||||||

Hollywood has presented the South as a corrupted Eden, dwelling first on an idyllic image and later on a harsher ("realistic") vision. Throughout, the treatment of the South centers upon the tension between a mythic ideal and a severely flawed reality. Perhaps because the industry knew it was dealing with a national myth, the most important film representations of the South have been adaptations of literary works.

The idyllic South image was fully represented by two early masters of the silent cinema, D. W. Griffith and Buster Keaton. Their artistry and the fullness of their vision assured the South of complex representation in American cinema.

With *Birth of a Nation* (1915) Griffith introduced the epic feature film using innumerable technical and narrative innovations. Himself a Kentuckian, Griffith presented the South as an elegant, idealistic, humane civilization ruined by the ravages of the Civil War and the intrusive politics of its aftermath. Justifiably charged with perpetuating racist stereotypes, the film can with equal fairness be read as an earnest idealist's view of a lost social harmony. The unprecedented scope of Griffith's spectacle established the tradition of the southern epic. It implied that this historic territory required a large canvas and a flamboyant style to cover its tumultuous events and the sweeping emotions of its characters, a tradition amply sustained by *Gone with the Wind* (1939) and *Raintree County* (1957).

Buster Keaton's representation of the South was rooted in the comic artist's pathos more than in spectacle. He opens *Our Hospitality* (1923), his second feature, with a noncomic presentation of hero Willie McKay's slow train trip home to the Shenandoah Valley, where he has inherited both a family estate and a family feud with the Canfields. Keaton lovingly re-creates the period detail, atmosphere, and especially the courtly code of conduct that restrains even the most violent of passions in the South. In *The General* (1926) Keaton played Johnnie Gray, the quintessential southern soldier, in a comic version of the famous railway robbery by James J. Andrews at Big Shanty, Ga., in 1862 (recounted in William Pittenger's book *Daring and Suffering: A History of the Great Railroad Adventure*, 1863). Although Keaton had to do his filming in Cottage Grove, Ore., because Tennessee patriots objected to a comedy being made about that heroic escapade, the result was a stirring demonstration of the modest hero's integration of both his patriotic and romantic duties, with an incidental line of solid, inventive comedy.

Keaton's *Steamboat Bill Jr.* (1928) concludes what is, in effect, if not in intention, an Old South trilogy. Here he plays an eastern college boy who joins his father on a Mississippi riverboat, emblematically named *The Stonewall Jackson*. Through pluck and romance he ends the feud between his traditionalist father and a new-style industrialist. In all three films the humorous pathos and the romantic interest gloss a common concern with ending violent social divisions. The first deals with the tension between personal ambition and the social code in the prewar South, the second with the same conflict during the war, and the third with the need for postwar reconciliations. The trilogy covers the traumatic history of the South and its reconciliation of opposing forces, first within itself, then with the North, and finally with the emerging new economic and social structure. Through all adversity, Keaton embodies the doomed but undaunted spirit of the South: even when he tries to protect himself under a broken dam—with an umbrella!

Keaton's kind of modest social history by analogue proved more fertile ground for subsequent filmmakers than the epic vision (and expense) of Griffith. During the 1930s the bleak life of southern sharecroppers provided the most dramatic image of the whole country's suffering during the Depression. The familiar rural tragedies—erosion, flood, drought, dust storms, and disintegrating relationships—expressed a sense of man as victim of both social and natural disasters. In this regard, Michael Curtiz's *Cabin in the Cotton* (1932) was an important film despite its saccharine ending, a fantasy of implausible reconciliation between the classes. The classics in this vein are King Vidor's *Our Daily Bread* (1934), John Ford's *The Grapes of Wrath* (1940), and Ford's follow-up, *Tobacco Road* (1941), with the latter turning Erskine Caldwell's novel into a populist critique of the sharecropper's life, alternating passages of fine, lyrical observation with broadened comedy. Whereas Caldwell blamed the South's antiquated social system for the people's poverty and their inescapable debt to the banks, the film blamed the banks for the new farming system. That is, the film seemed to endorse the tenant-farming system that the novel attacked! A more clear-headed and moving portrayal of the tenant farmer's hardship can be found in Jean Renoir's *The Southerner* (1945). As the producer of *Cabin in the Cotton, The Grapes of Wrath*, and *Tobacco Road*, Darryl F. Zanuck must be acknowl-

edged as an important impetus toward social realism in Hollywood.

Social realism as a genre was sadly susceptible to sensationalism, as in *White Bondage* (1937) and *John Meade's Woman* (1937), where social critique gave way to a hackneyed image of corrupt villains. Unfortunately, this cynicism dominated post–World War II Hollywood visions of the South. Anthony Mann's *God's Little Acre* (1958) broadened even further the comedy and the bawdry of *Tobacco Road*. Another minor tradition details the region's corrupt power structure. Examples include the Huey Long surrogate of *All the King's Men* (1949); the corrupt citizen-bosses in Tony Richardson's *Sanctuary* (1961), a violation of Faulkner's *The Sound and the Fury* (arguably the most unjust classic adaptation ever filmed), Vincent Minnelli's *Home from the Hill* (1960); and two Tennessee Williams adaptations, *The Fugitive Kind* (1960) and *Sweet Bird of Youth* (1962).

The device of concentrating evil in a single villain turns to caricature and cliché in the recent tradition of the redneck sheriff, which Rod Steiger began innocently enough in Norman Jewison's *In the Heat of the Night* (1967) but which was ballooned and repeated in countless television commercials and in the *Smokey and the Bandit* film series. Other films have blamed southern corruption upon an entire community. In contrast to these many B films stand a few thoughtful, responsible works, most notably Clarence Brown's *Intruder in the Dust* (1949), *Inherit the Wind* (1960), and *To Kill a Mockingbird* (1963). Here the tradition of a tight, enclosed community in the South provides a critique of prejudice, the mob mind, and reactionary conservatism.

Even the seamiest social realism

draws upon the idyllic vision, however. Implicit in every lynching scene set in the South is the audience's memory of the nobility in the Griffith and Keaton visions. The mythic and the realistic treatments converge in the most successful film ever made about the South, *Gone with the Wind*. The spectacle and the sweep of this epic seem antithetical to the grainy, close focus of *The Grapes of Wrath*, which appeared within a few months, but both are documents of periods of economic depression. Both show survivors of financial ruin and social upheaval longing to return to a lost agrarian simplicity. Tom Joad's resolution—"Can't nobody lick us. We'll go on forever, Pa. We're the people."—is memorable though it pales beside the indomitable Scarlett O'Hara's unsentimental resolve: "As God is my witness . . . I'll never be hungry again."

Scarlett (Vivien Leigh) again makes the South stand for the whole nation. She continues and deepens her girlish revolt against stifling traditions to become a strong and practical, though ever-selfish, character. When Rhett Butler (Clark Gable) returns to the past gentility of Charleston, Scarlett prefers to recover her roots in the soil of Tara. But it fails to nourish her in the new times. She vomits the turnip begrudgingly yielded by the scorched red earth. Under the pathetic illusion that she can somehow recover her lost past, she throws herself into the new industrialization. The adaptability that fulfilled the hero in the Keaton trilogy dooms the heroine to a soul-destroying progress in this more modern South.

As America sees itself in both the mythic and the realistic depictions of the South, something of an unarticulated guilt often emerges through these chronicles of lost innocence. At its source,

Griffith and Keaton aimed to re-create the past in the documentary style of Matthew Brady and the history texts, as if recovering the bygone images could erase the intervening loss. The more modern reflex is to expose the seaminess of the present. Martin Ritt's *Sounder* (1972), for example, a return to 1930s social realism, offsets his more conventional exploitation of the southern-boss myth in *The Long Hot Summer* (1958).

Guilt is most explicit in the films that present the South in terms of steamy sexuality. In some instances there is a political implication. When Temple Drake is raped in *Sanctuary*, the South is violated. The coarsening of Scarlett O'Hara is the South's coarsening under pressure, so too the rape and maddening of Blanche DuBois in *A Streetcar Named Desire* (1951). Indeed, most of the Tennessee Williams adaptations can be read as a psychodrama about the South, with solitary suppression and forced sexual conformity the traumas of a culture torn between futilely trying to sustain its character and the temptation to sell itself to the new order.

In John Huston's innovative adaptation of Carson McCullers's *Reflections in a Golden Eye* (1967), the shallow sensibility of northern order is undermined by southern deviance in all its kinky and glorious vitality. In the prints as originally released (but later withdrawn and replaced by more conventional ones), Huston drained the image of all color but a pale, glowing amber until the murder at the end brought a full burst of technicolor. The effect was the viewer's tremulous involvement in the characters' withdrawal from reality into their own private natures, private eroticism, private harmonies and heats, until the repressive public world imposed an illusion of order.

In all these films, the public history replays and amplifies private tensions. Even in Walt Disney's *Song of the South* (1946) there is a strain between the fantasy animation of the Uncle Remus stories and the traumatic world in which the live-action character (James Baskett) operates as guide, pal, and sentimental surrogate for a fatherless boy (Bobby Driscoll). In Hollywood's persistent vision the South represents both a lost, ideal past and a corrupt, hypocritical, and repressive present. The cool, perfect mansions and their reeking ruins, the brightest and the most brutish, stand balanced together. The two visions are inseparable and contiguous: when Bette Davis plays a southern belle (*Hush . . . Hush Sweet Charlotte* 1964), cleared of 37 years of guilt for a murder she did not commit, there is a belated justice for her antebellum *Jezebel* (1938). Vivien Leigh's Blanche DuBois draws upon the same actress's Scarlett, as she cowers behind whimsical, longing illusions to escape the vicious reality that shattered her beautiful dream of the South.

As anthropologist Claude Lévi-Strauss suggests, a myth functions to provide a logical model, overcoming a contradiction not by explaining anything, but by displacing mythic difficulties with those it raises itself. When America sees itself in Hollywood's South, the flawed present harkens back to another Eden, fragile and spent. Hollywood's South stands as one of the nation's key cultural myths.

See also MYTHIC SOUTH articles

Maurice Yacowar
Brock University

Edward D. C. Campbell, Jr., *The Celluloid South: Hollywood and the Southern Myth*

(1981); Fred Chappell, *Southern Humanities Review* (Fall 1978); Jack Temple Kirby, *Media-Made Dixie: The South in the American Imagination* (1978); Peter A. Soderbergh, *Mississippi Quarterly* (Winter 1965–66). ☆

Film Production

Moviemaking in the South dates back to the 19th century when travelogs and early precursors to the newsreel such as *U.S. Cavalry Supplies Unloading at Tampa, Florida* and *Transport Ships at Port Tampa* (both 1898) were shot as part of the coverage of the Spanish-American War.

But despite the emergence of New South Sunbelt politics and the important continuing role southerners play in American cultural life, the region still suffers from antebellum stereotypes dating back more than a century. Thus, one should make a distinction between film and television productions actually made in the South and films made about the South. In the often-mythic southern film genre, much as in the western, the movie industry for decades artificially romanticized the South or portrayed the dark side of race relations by falsely picturing a world of sentimentality and salaciousness unrepresentative of Dixie as a whole.

A local production base (which existed during the silent era and once again is being reestablished throughout the South) may well result in a more realistic, pro-southern image than that of a Hollywood art director creating "Tara" on a California backlot. Indeed, the stereotypical "moonlight-and-magnolias" screen image of the South is an unfortunate by-product of the consolidation of American motion picture production in greater Los Angeles.

During the pioneering years of the industry hundreds of films were shot in authentic locales by movie companies operating semipermanently in a number of southern states. Even after Hollywood's opulent rise during World War I to its position as the world's preeminent movie mecca, many films and television episodes continued to be shot on location regionally. These precedents have today helped spur a burgeoning local media industry of increasing importance and sophistication.

Pointing to the development of the South as a major "Third Coast" film and video center, regional production in the mid-1980s has an economic impact estimated at up to $3 billion annually. Even conservative motion picture and television statistical projections expect the South to maintain its impressive media industry growth through the rest of the decade. This is particularly true when taking into account not only highly touted feature-film releases and broadcast television programs, but also television commercials, business training and public relations films, documentaries, and other specialized productions.

Early moviemakers such as D. W. Griffith were first attracted to the South by its warm climate, scenic beauty, relative proximity to New York, historic setting, and civic hospitality. These positive lures have been augmented over the years by other developments that further encourage expanded utilization of southern settings:

1. Cheaper production costs (averaging 10 to 40 percent below California) because of right-to-work wage-union conditions;

2. Locally experienced crews, extras, and support personnel for needs ranging from laboratories to catering services;

3. Ready availability of nearly a dozen large new studio soundstages ranging from the $30 million Las Colinas Dallas Communications Complex (*Streamers*, *Silkwood*) in Texas to the $17 million, 32-acre Wilmington Center in North Carolina (*Year of the Dragon*, Stephen King's *Cat's Eye*);

4. Aggressive marketing by state and city film and television commissions providing valuable assistance from red-tape cutting clearances to location-scouting services;

5. Successful track records and positive cooperation from many independent producers working in the South;

6. Increasing availability of local financing;

7. The demise of the old studio system; and

8. The conveniences afforded by rented, mobile technology.

Historically, the most serious regional challenge to the dominance of "West Coast Filmland" occurred in Florida, which for a brief period from 1908 to 1917 seemed destined to become *the* major producing center in the country. As late as 1914 so many movie troupes were attracted to the north Florida city of Jacksonville that the metropolis was widely heralded as "The World's Winter Film Capital." The end of the motion picture Patents Trust and defeat of a Jacksonville mayor popular with industry figures contributed to the exodus to California. But Florida never entirely severed its film and television connections (*Flipper* and *Miami Vice* are examples) and today vies with Texas as the number-three production site in the United States after California and New York.

Texas is particularly well situated to take advantage of the continuing need for entertainment and information programming. Between 1923 and 1980 more than 140 feature films, made-for-television movies, and television series pilots were shot on location in Texas; nearly as many major projects (108) with gross budgets in excess of $375 million were completed in the four years 1981 through 1984. Among the more notable recent releases are multi-Oscar winner *Terms of Endearment*, Tri-Star Pictures' *Places in the Heart* starring Sally Field, and Wim Wenders's *Paris, Texas*, which received the prestigious Golden Palm Award at the 1984 Cannes Film Festival.

Other southern states and cities also have long filmic histories and are now emerging from their cameo role in the industry. Louisiana, for example, hosted several dozen studio ventures during the silent years. These ranged from the prolific Selig Company, famous for its animal menagerie, and the National Film Corporation, maker of the earliest *Tarzan* releases, to less reputable stock promotions pushed by shady motion picture salesmen. Since the end of World War II, Louisiana has experienced a renaissance with more than 100 productions shot at in-state locations, including *Easy Rider*, *Sounder*, and *The Autobiography of Miss Jane Pittman*.

Because of its position as the South's leading motion picture equipment distribution center and major supplier of theater equipment and supplies along the East Coast, North Carolina already has a sizable investment in the film industry. Asheville's mountains and famed Biltmore estate (used most prominently for the Academy Award-winning *Being There*) have attracted a number of film companies over the years. Although the North Carolina Film Office has been particularly active since its formation in 1980, many observers credit Shelby, N.C., businessman-actor Earl Owensby with spurring banking interest in locally based productions. Specializing since the early 1970s in low-budget, profitable, regional "backwoods" and exploitational screen stories typified by *Chain Gang* and *Tales of the Third Dimension*, Owensby's Shelby studio now encompasses six soundstages. He plans to expand in Myrtle Beach, S.C., during the mid-1980s by opening a new $200 million studio project complete with theme park, airport, and 10 soundstages employing 1,200 people.

Georgia's film office, created under then-Governor Jimmy Carter, also actively boosts its cinematic possibilities by working closely with major Hollywood personalities such as Burt Reynolds in making pictures like *The Longest Yard* and *Sharkey's Machine*. Alabama, Kentucky, Mississippi, South Carolina, and most other states now have similar governmental departments advertising to promote film and television production. These agencies also generally offer a videotape or slide location library, publish directories of technicians and additional guides, catalog climatological information, host conferences, and provide other useful services. Current developments can be followed by reading trade press coverage in *Back Stage*, *Daily Variety Florida Golden Pages*, *Hollywood Reporter*, *Millimeter*, *On Location*, and *Shooting Commercials*, as well as official state publications such as *Film Texas*.

Richard Alan Nelson
University of Houston

George Adcock, *The South Magazine* (November–December 1977); Paul W. Beutel, "Development of the Feature Film Industry in Texas, 1955–1965" (M.A. thesis, University of Texas at Austin, 1979); James R. Buchanan, *Texas Business Review* (January 1972); Warren French, ed., *The South and Film* (1981); Gene Gautier, *Woman's Home Companion* (November 1928–March 1929); Gulf State Research Institute, *Development of the Motion Picture Industry in Louisiana* (May 1971); Kalton C. Lahue, ed., *Motion Picture Pioneer: The Selig Polyscope Company* (1973); Todd E. Lindley, "Major Developments in the American Cinema 1908–1913 as Reflected by the Film Industry in New Orleans" (M.A. thesis, University of New Orleans, 1973); Richard Alan Nelson, *Florida and the American Motion Picture Industry, 1898–1980*, 2 vols. (1983); Don Umphrey, "The Economic Impact of the 1980 Film/Tape Industry in Texas" (Texas Film Commission, January 1982); *U.S. News & World Report* (19 November 1984). ☆

Journalists, Modern South

As the American liberal creed spread to the South in the 20th century, its converts included a small but influential number of southern newspapermen, who, beginning in the 1930s, helped to revive the idea of a New South of economic, educational, and racial progress. A decidedly Yankee notion, progress had not historically won much applause in Dixie, but during the disastrous Great Depression even southerners recognized that change might mean escape from poverty and starvation. In such recognition dwelt at least the half-hearted acceptance of another long-standing Yankee notion: the South as a problem to be solved. To this end, the journalists of the Modern South focused a critical yet affectionate eye on their native region. From the gloomy 1930s to the tumultuous 1960s and beyond, their central message was that the South, if not too firmly pressed by neo-abolitionists, might finally emerge from its colonial status to rejoin the Union.

Modern South journalists brought to their work an abiding attachment to most southern traditions, but what set them apart was their avowal that "ancestor whooping" had become a hindrance. The author of that sprightly phrase, Jonathan Daniels of the Raleigh *News and Observer*, forthrightly established the stance of the new breed of southern journalists in the World War II and *Brown* v. *Board of Education* era when he noted that even if "one Reb can beat ten Yankees, it is irrelevant." Above all, these men (among others, Virginius Dabney in Richmond, W. J. Cash in Charlotte, Mark Ethridge in Louisville, John Temple Graves in Birmingham, Hodding Carter in Greenville, Miss., Ralph McGill in Atlanta, and Harry Ashmore in Little Rock) thought themselves realists. No longer could they accept the moonlight-and-magnolias mythology of southern life. At the same time they disdained to consort too closely with what they called "liberals" (i.e., northerners) or with neo-Gradyite chamber of commerce boosters. Rather, they wrote balanced commentaries that noted southern flaws but cautioned about the difficulties attending their correction. Daniels, Dabney, and their successors counseled a middle-path road to progress via civility, reasonable compromise, and gradual reform.

Liberal newspapermen of the Modern South set forth an agenda for gradual change on the eve of World War II. Although they wrote a good deal about poverty and the South's dismal educational record, their version of the mind of the Modern South was, as ever, preoccupied with race. Lynchings and poll taxes must go. Lest they be convicted, however, of preaching Yankee doctrine (which, of course, they were), progressive journalists at first advocated state rather than federal solutions to such evils; moreover, they emphasized that it was in the interest of whites to help lift up blacks, because no human resource could be wasted in the struggle to rid the South of poverty and ignorance. In league with other southern liberals, the leading journalists of the late 1930s undertook an editorial campaign for racial moderation.

Ironically, however, the War Against Aryan Supremacy interrupted the nascent southern effort at racial reform. Chaos and disorder abroad were paralleled by a kind of disorder at home that blasted the hopes of Virginius Dabney and others to effect gradual, peaceful change in the southern racial ethos. Down home the war brought enormous social disruption in the form of firm black insistence, seconded by the ever-present northern "agitators" (i.e., liberals), not only that lynching be ended but that Jim Crow segregation be dismantled. When Mark Ethridge of the Louisville *Courier-Journal* assured southern whites that segregation would not be undone by the war-born Committee on Fair Employment Practices, northern liberals railed at the hypocrisy of their distant cousins in the South.

Southern liberals such as Dabney and John Temple Graves, so optimistic in 1940, by 1943 wondered aloud whether northerners understood that racial discrimination could never be ended forcibly. Only by "gradual evolutionary development," necessarily suspended for the duration of the war against Hitler and the Japanese, would the South ever consent to anything like equal opportunity for blacks. Irked at agitators, Graves spoke for southern liberals: "The friendship of the white liberal Southerner is the Negro's basic hope there."

This kind of not-so-hidden warning spoke more to the concerns of southern liberals than to the hopes of black people. Its intended audience, however, was moving rapidly beyond earshot. The war years worked a profound change among many blacks in the North and South, among northern white liberals, and in turn among southern white liberals, who were thrown off balance by the assertiveness of the "New Negro." Heretofore relatively quiet, these blacks and their white allies used the war (almost traitorously, in the view of southern liberals) to present their own program of reform, the blueprint for which bespoke neither moderation nor gradualism nor acceptance of leadership by southern liberals. From the mid-1940s to the late 1960s, therefore, journalistic proponents of a Modern South found themselves not so much leading a reform movement as tagging along in hopes of making such a movement palatable to moderates in Dixie. Harry Ashmore later described their task as "trying to preserve order at an incipient riot."

Recognizing that the war had loosed forces of radical change, and, more to the point, recognizing the obvious thrust of a series of Supreme Court decisions in the 1940s and early 1950s against Jim Crow education, journalists such as Virginius Dabney, Jonathan Daniels, and Hodding Carter adopted for a brief time what might be called the doctrine of "separate-but-this-time-truly-equal." This attempt to introduce fair treatment for blacks within the parameters of segregation was a classic example of the progressive road to a Modern South: good-hearted, fair-minded, but unenlightened southerners must be ever so gently coaxed to do right, both because it was right and because the courts were going to force the issue anyway. The *Brown* v. *Board of Education* decision in 1954 asserted a principle ("Separate educational facilities are inherently unequal") that, when implemented by federal district judges, undercut the ameliorative strategy of southern liberals. The phrase "with all deliberate speed" turned out to be not a gentle breeze of gradualism but a false calm before the storm.

These liberal journalists loved the South and believed in reason and in law and order. Although they feared that the courts might force too rapid a pace in the black's stride toward freedom, they did their best to convince readers that law must triumph over emotion, that black and white could live (i.e., go to school) together in harmony, and that the South would be the better for the change, however disagreeable and confusing things might be in the short run. Progressive editors after *Brown* v. *Board of Education* appealed to moderates in the South, who, precisely because they loved their native region, must obey the new law of the land. Frequently the McGills and the Ashmores were disappointed, of course, because on more than one occasion from *Brown* v. *Board of Education* to Selma (1965) the "re-

spectable people" in the South stayed home and allowed what Ashmore called "the thin-lipped men" literally to dynamite the path to racial progress.

The path to the Modern South, therefore, was considerably more wrenching than that envisioned in the optimistic scenarios of the earliest liberal journalists. In the first place, none of them had predicted the role assumed by southern blacks in the civil rights revolution after World War II. Nor did they particularly applaud it at first; they were accustomed to leading, not following, and were thus dismayed and offended by the activism of the New Negro. In time most of the liberal newspapermen overcame the paternalism they shared with so many white southerners (and not a few white northerners) and accepted the assertiveness and admired the courage of southern blacks who struck on their own for a New South.

More difficult to accept was the failure of their beloved South to live up to its own best traditions except under the outside pressure of Yankee law and guns. By the late 1950s it was clear that the South, if left alone, might *not* do right. Ralph McGill angrily charged in 1964 that the "practicing moderates contributed largely to the undoing of a fine, honorable word. . . . There is nowhere on record a single constructive plan or action proposed by so-called moderates."

The years after the *Brown* decision left liberal editors profoundly shaken, though by no means utterly destroyed. If leadership had passed from them in significant measure, important work remained to be done. Without their editorials condemning violence, the acceptance of the law among their constituents, the decent folk of Dixie, might have been even more belated than it was. Ralph McGill in Atlanta, Hodding Carter in Greenville, Harry Ashmore in Little Rock, and many others expressed a Modern South conviction that to love the South was to insist that its people examine their society and change its worst aspects. The cumulative effect of several decades of such conviction and criticism by insiders who so clearly wanted the best for and from their region at least established the context within which "massive resistance" might ultimately be overcome. A new kind of racial accommodation did seem to exist in many parts of the South by the 1970s. Perhaps Ashmore's famous "epitaph for Dixie"—the title of his 1958 book—was only a bit premature.

The role of journalists in achieving that accommodation and in writing that epitaph by modernizing the southern consciousness required them both to display their southernness and partially to overcome it. Twentieth-century southern journalists, for instance, have surely lived by SPT—Southern People's Time. "More time" from the mouths of reactionaries meant "never," but southern liberals expressed the more common connotation: "Very slowly, we will reach our destination, and you Yankees make a mistake to try to hurry us, because life's not like that down here."

In striking fashion southern journalists have carried the burden of an ancient love-hate relationship with Yankeedom; southernness is symbiotically entwined with Yankeeness. The very idea of a New South (the Modern is the Newest South—there may be others to come) is an attempt to Yankeeize the South, to achieve the American creed of racial equal opportunity, to become prosperous, to triumph over adversity. But southerners, forward-looking editors no exception, have preferred to approach these goals gingerly, without prodding from Yankee missionaries, improvers, and South-baiters. For it is bad enough to become abolitionists and businessmen; outside pressure in that direction is insufferable. Put another way, the southern search for respectability in the modern world has necessitated Yankee imitation. This has been since the 1930s a very painful process psychologically, involving as it has the partial adoption of the ways of the archenemy.

For all their modernity, southern progressive journalists have been Lost Causers of a (mild) sort, too. Paternalistic, defensive, past-haunted in spite of themselves (as Hodding Carter once noted), they have been enthralled by the southern consciousness and its traditionalism. As liberals, they distanced themselves just enough from the southern way of life to see its weaknesses, its excesses, in some cases, indeed, its horrors. As natives who remained steadfastly loyal to their region while imploring it to join the modern world, liberal editors in the last half-century collectively delivered a running commentary on the demise of the Lost Cause and on its replacement by the Modern South. By the 1970s and 1980s southerners had become prominent in the national news media (Dan Rather, Hodding Carter III, Bill Moyers, Charles Kuralt, and Tom Wicker come to mind), and the subjects of their reporting and commentary were no longer primarily southern. Irony of ironies, when the South in the late 20th century became chic, southern journalists were no longer thought of particularly as southerners. The Modern South had arrived. In the 1980s journalists who had cogently commented on the latter stages of its journey were asking, along with their academic cousins, whether this Newest South meant no more South.

See also MYTHIC SOUTH: / Cash, W. J.

Gary L. Williams
Rollins College

Harry Ashmore, *An Epitaph for Dixie* (1958), *Hearts and Minds: The Anatomy of Racism from Roosevelt to Reagan* (1982); Hodding Carter, *Southern Legacy* (1950); Virginius Dabney, *Atlantic Monthly* (January 1943); Jonathan Daniels, *A Southerner Discovers the South* (1938); Charles W. Eagles, *Jonathan Daniels and Race Relations: The Evolution of a Southern Liberal* (1982); John T. Kneebone, *Southern Liberal Journalists and the Issue of Race, 1920–1944* (1985); Morton Sosna, *In Search of the Silent South: Southern Liberals and the Race Issue* (1977). ☆

Journalists, New South

IIIIIIIIIIIIIIIIIIIIIIIIIIIIIIIIIIIIIIIIIIIIIIIIIIIIIIII

The idea of a New South, born after the Confederate defeat, was rhetorically transformed by journalists into a palpable reality during the 1880s. All histories of the New South movement list newspaper editors as prime movers, and chief among them were Henry W. Grady of the Atlanta *Constitution*, Francis W. Dawson of the Charleston *News and Courier*, Henry Watterson of the Louisville *Courier-Journal*, Richard Hathaway Edmonds of the *Manufacturers' Record* in Baltimore, and Daniel Augustus Tompkins who, as an industrialist, bought three newspapers, including the Charlotte *Observer*, to proclaim his gospel of work. These men argued for industrialization, enlightened agricultural practices, racial har-

mony, and national reconciliation, and if their vision of progress exceeded social and economic reality, they closed the gap by proclaiming a triumphant South. Their names, rather than those of politicians, attracted national attention and drew invitations to speak on behalf of the region, and, in the cases of Grady and Dawson, they were dominant influences in state politics.

The importance of the journalists can be accounted for in two ways. First, the persistence of relative economic privation and a sense of second-class citizenship within the nation created a demand in the South for publicists who could transform the region's promise into claims of actual accomplishment. Though rightly charged with fabricating myths of southern success, abundance, and racial goodwill, the images they fashioned were enduring and served to balance the region's deeper sense of frustration and failure. Second, New South journalists were part of a larger trend toward preeminence of both the news and newspapers in national life. Between 1870 and 1900 the number of daily newspapers in the United States quadrupled, from 489 to 1,967, and the number of copies increased six times, from 2.6 million to 15 million. The number of weekly papers tripled in the same period, rising from 4,000 to more than 12,000 by the end of the century. Proportionately, the South experienced the same growth. At war's end 182 weeklies were available, three years later the number swelled to 499, and within 20 years 1,827 weeklies were serving a largely rural audience.

Accompanying the explosion in readership came the ascendance of news over editorial opinion, especially in the dailies. The reporter upstaged the editor because telegraphy had dissociated

Henry Watterson, editor of the Louisville Courier-Journal, c. 1910

communication from transportation, thereby enabling news to be, in fact, new. No longer was the newspaper simply an editorial digest, concocted by editors for partisan ends. Moreover, new printing technologies made for rapid dissemination of the news, and large evening editions began to appear in urban areas. Southern journalism, however, was not in lockstep with national trends. For one thing, the southern experience with democracy and literacy was different from that of the rest of the nation; it came late and, in part, by force. Responding to the New South, southern editors found themselves in a position not unlike that experienced by northern journalists 50 years earlier. The "penny press" that sprang up to serve Jacksonian democracy encouraged an editorial style called "personal journalism." Editors were also owners, and they used their position—indeed they believed it their duty—to shape public opinion. Such became the calling of New South editors, most of whom obtained a small amount of capital, usually from a northern investor, acquired con-

trolling interest in a struggling newspaper, and then built circulation by determined advocacy.

Francis W. Dawson's career was typical of the pattern. At the age of 20 he changed his name from Austin John Reeks and left his native England to fight for the Confederacy. At war's end he moved to Charleston, where, with aid from friends, he acquired the Charleston *News* for $6,000 in cash and the Charleston *Courier* for $7,100. Dawson showed an independent streak by opposing the Straightout movement, which was designed to restore white supremacy, and later by showing occasional irreverence for the state's military and political hero, Wade Hampton. Still, the *News and Courier* became the dominant voice in the Palmetto State. When "Pitchfork Ben" Tillman sought power after 1885, he did so by attacking Dawson, not the elected leadership. Dawson did not shy away from editorial controversy and in that respect was more like Horace Greeley before the war than like Joseph Pulitzer, who was famed for ushering in the "new journalism" of the 1880s. Dawson believed that an editor must "write for or against something; for or against an idea; for or against a party," but as his son later put it, he also knew "that a newspaper while assuming the leadership of public opinion could not and must not fight against the unanimous will of the community which it represented."

Thus, no matter how crusading the editor or how personal the journalism, newspapers in the South were constrained to reflect the sentiment of the dominant whites in their respective communities. Failing to be representative or even arousing personal antagonism could mean the start of a rival newspaper, as when Patrick Walsh of the Augusta *Chronicle* had to fight off the upstart *Gazette* in 1887; and rival newspapers, no matter how faltering, threatened circulation and profits. The leading New South editors not only represented their metropolitan constituencies, they also influenced their country cousins. Even before the 1880s these weeklies had set up a chorus for industrialization and railroads, but increasingly they took their cues, if not their lines, from Grady, Dawson, Watterson, and Edmonds. When Dawson and Grady came to their untimely deaths in 1889, it occasioned great mourning and public grief throughout the rural South.

New South journalists offered their readers more than promises of prosperity. They provided respectable connections with a national community of opinion leaders. The rise of the fourth estate in the last half of the 19th century spawned a group of journalists who spurned traditional party allegiance, in part out of a felt need to maintain the independence of their class. In so doing, they fashioned a national fraternity that housed Liberal Republicans and New South Democrats. They united on civil service reform, free trade, and a view that only the "best men" should rule (by which they meant not black, not immigrant, not subscribing to an "ism," and not politicians pandering to these groups). The most famous journalists of the day belonged to the fraternity, including E. L. Godkin, Carl Schurz, George William Curtis, Samuel Bowles III, and Charles Dana, the man who pinned the label Mugwump on this group when they bolted the Republican party in 1884. Through these men, New South editors talked to the nation in ways the region's political leaders could not.

Finally, New South editors were good

journalists. The larger dailies assembled excellent staffs, kept up with advances in technology, and produced newspapers that were aesthetically pleasing for the day and interesting to read. Henry Grady advanced the art of interviewing to the point that imitators made it a staple of reportorial practice. His invitation to address the New England Society of New York on the subject of the New South was the direct outgrowth of his interviews and reports on the Charleston earthquake of 1886. Adolph Ochs of the Chattanooga *Times* proved that good management could turn a profit and later applied the same principles in rescuing the *New York Times* from ruin (he would not be the last southerner to make his mark on that distinguished newspaper). And, as with all good newspapers, the New South journals mirrored their times. Not that out-groups such as blacks or opposition political movements received fair play, but they did get covered, even though the coverage itself was biased and often vicious. The net result has been that critical readings of these journals provide an excellent introduction to the multidimensional New South.

See also INDUSTRY: / Grady, Henry W.; MYTHIC SOUTH: New South Myth

E. Culpepper Clark
University of Alabama
at Birmingham

E. Culpepper Clark, *Francis Warrington Dawson and the Politics of Restoration: South Carolina, 1874–1889* (1980); Thomas D. Clark, *The Southern Country Editor* (1948); Edwin Emery and Michael Emery, *The Press and America: An Interpretive History of the Mass Media* (5th ed., 1984); Paul M. Gaston, *The New South Creed: A Study in Southern Mythmaking* (1970); Raymond B. Nixon,

Henry W. Grady: Spokesman of the New South (1943); Joseph F. Wall, *Henry Watterson: Reconstructed Rebel* (1956); C. Vann Woodward, *Origins of the New South, 1877–1913* (1951). ☆

Magazines

||||||||||||||||||||||||||

The new Sunbelt prosperity in recent decades has been mirrored by substantial growth in southern magazine publishing. The 1982 *Ayer Directory of Publications* lists 1,486 nonnewspaper periodicals published in the 11 states that made up the Confederacy, plus Kentucky.

Since World War II the number of southern periodicals has more than doubled, and the growth rate of magazines in this region has outstripped that of the nation as a whole. Texas, with 342 nonnewspaper periodicals, ranks first in the South, followed by Virginia (259), Florida (212), Tennessee (150), Georgia (130), North Carolina (111), Kentucky (80), South Carolina (68), Alabama (62), Louisiana (55), Mississippi (29), and Arkansas (26).

Only four southern periodicals have circulations of 1 million or above: *Upper Room*, a religious periodical printed in 40 languages, 2.1 million; *Southern Living*, the South's premier regional magazine, 1.9 million; *Boys' Life*, a nationally distributed youth magazine, 1.5 million; and *Mother Earth News*, an energy-ecology magazine, 1 million. Six more have circulations in excess of 500,000, and an additional 41 have circulations of at least 100,000.

Of these 51 high-circulation periodicals, 7 are devoted to outdoor/sports/

wildlife interests, 6 are airline inflight magazines, 5 are agricultural periodicals, 5 are motor club/motoring periodicals, 5 are religious in focus, 5 are youth magazines, 5 are rural electric periodicals, 4 are house and garden/decorating/antiques magazines, 3 are published for persons in the military, 2 are regional magazines aimed at a general audience, and 4 are classified here as miscellaneous. Of an additional 32 southern periodicals in the 50,000–100,000 circulation category, the largest group, 8, are regional and city magazines and the next largest category, 7, are outdoor/sports/wildlife magazines.

Something of southern culture can be deduced from these figures. To be successful in the South, a magazine needs focus. Few homegrown general-interest magazines have been taken to the South's bosom; in fact, the South historically has been known as a magazine graveyard. Most of the region's larger magazines are aimed at a specialized audience of persons having a strong interest in outdoor recreation, agriculture, homes, and antiques—each a deeply engrained part of the southern mystique. The South, for example, has long been regarded as the heart of the Bible Belt. Southerners also regard themselves as "closer to the soil" than the average American; agriculture, though losing ground to urban development, is still a vital southern industry. Finally, the southerner has not completely lost his feelings for the "old home place," even in today's increasingly mobile southern culture.

Most of the remaining 1,403 periodicals are relatively small but range widely in circulation and serve a bewildering array of interests, from *Cats Magazine*, circulation 81,000, a pet-lover's periodical in Port Orange, Fla.;

to Dallas's *Black Tennis Magazine* (5,000); to Houston's *Ultra Magazine* (75,000) for the society-minded; to Chattanooga's *Glider Rider* (13,200) for hang-glider enthusiasts; to *Chase Magazine* (3,200), a Lexington, Ky., offering for fox hunters; to *American Atheist* (15,800) in Austin, Tex.

The South's growing technological base is reflected in the *Journal of Petroleum Technology* (40,000) in Dallas, and its more traditional industries can be seen in Memphis's *Cotton Farming* (42,679) and *Cotton Grower* (39,829) and in *America's Textiles* (30,881) in Greenville, S.C.

The South's interest in the past has its reflection in a number of successful magazines of recent vintage: *Antique Monthly* in Tuscaloosa, founded in 1967, with a 1980 circulation of 87,000, and two Kermit, Tex., magazines—*American Collector* (1969; 152,000) and *Antiques USA* (1980; 110,000).

Southern preoccupation with sports has made possible Waco's *Texas Football* (1960; 205,000), San Antonio's *Skeet Shooting Review* (1946; 18,500); Houston's *Horseman* (1956; 125,265); the Woodbridge, Va., *Running Times* (1977; 51,000); and Miami's *Florida Sportsman* (1969; 81,200).

Leading outdoors/conservation magazines are *Southern Outdoors* (1953; 177,054) in Montgomery, Ala.; Raleigh's *Wildlife in North Carolina* (1947; 47,000); Houston's *Texas Outdoor Guide Magazine* (1968; 102,000); *Outdoor America* (1922; 48,500) from Arlington, Va.; and Richmond's *Virginia Wildlife* (1937; 113,000).

Some scholars say the South's first magazine was *North Carolina Magazine; or, The Universal Intelligencer* (1764–65?); others classify this periodical as a newspaper and cite *South Carolina Weekly Museum* (1797–98) in Charleston as the first true magazine south of Baltimore.

Many of the best-remembered titles from the South's magazine past were literary magazines that functioned as mouthpieces for southern high culture. Prominent among these were the *Southern Literary Messenger*, edited in Richmond from 1835 to 1837 by Edgar Allan Poe, and the *Southern Review* (1828–32) in Charleston, edited by the Stephen Elliotts, father and son. Today's southern literary magazines are university-based. Notable among them are the venerable *Sewanee Review* at the University of the South, *Carolina Quarterly* at the University of North Carolina, *Shenandoah* at Washington and Lee, and the *Southern Review* at Louisiana State University.

Publishing just after the Civil War was difficult because of materials shortages and the population's impoverishment. Some leaders in this period were *De Bow's Commercial Review of the South and West* (1848–80) in New Orleans, *Scott's Monthly* (1865–69) in Atlanta, and *Southern Bivouac, A Monthly Literary and Historical Magazine* (1882–87) in Louisville. The only southern magazines to reach 100,000 circulation by 1885 were Atlanta's *Sunny South* (1875–1907) and Louisville's *Home and Farm* (1876–1918). A later favorite of the South was *Uncle Remus's Magazine* in Atlanta (1907–13), edited by Joel Chandler Harris; its circulation had reached 200,000 by Harris's death. The *Progressive Farmer* first appeared in 1886 but did not achieve its great influence until the early 20th century.

In the 1960s and 1970s the biggest growth category in southern magazine publishing was city and regional magazines, which contained articles on a wide range of topics, focused on geography. Many have been born and many have died since 1960. The 1960s mainly saw the creation of city magazines, and in the 1970s southern publishers turned to founding new regional magazines that covered an area larger than a city—part of a state, an entire state, parts of several states, or even the South in general.

Prominent city magazines include *New Orleans*, *D* in Dallas, *Houston City Magazine*, *Houston Monthly*, *Atlanta*, and *Memphis Magazine*; regionals include the undoubted leader, *Southern Living*, plus *Texas Monthly*, *Brown's Guide to Georgia*, *Country Magazine*, *Shenandoah Valley Magazine*, *Tar Heel: The Magazine of North Carolina*, and *Sandlapper*.

Even more recently, a number of southern magazines that specialize both by geography and by topic are meeting success. Examples are *Southern Accents*, an Atlanta house and garden magazine featuring ultra-exclusive southern homes; *Houston Home and Garden*; *Texas Homes Magazine*; and Arkansas's *Southern* magazine, which began in 1986 and focuses on the region's cultural distinctiveness. In the South, a region of relatively small cities, the key to substantial circulations appears to be a practical and well-thought-out focus or specialization.

See also AGRICULTURE: / *Progressive Farmer*; INDUSTRY: / *De Bow's Review*; LITERATURE: Periodicals

Sam G. Riley
Virginia Polytechnic Institute

Ben Moon, *Journalism Quarterly* (Winter 1970); Frank Luther Mott, *History of American Magazines*, 5 vols. (1938–68); Theodore Peterson, *Magazines in the Twentieth Century* (1972); Lyon Richardson, *A History of Early American Magazines, 1741–1789* (1931); Sam G. Riley, *Index to Southern Periodicals* (1986), *Journalism Quarterly* (Autumn 1982), *Magazines of the American South* (1986); John Tebbel, *The American Magazine: A Compact History* (1969); Roland E. Wolseley, *The Changing Magazine: Trends in Readership and Management* (1973). ☆

Newspapers

||||||||||||||||||||||||||||||||||

In appearance, depth of coverage, and content, southern papers differ little from newspapers in the rest of the nation. Their strengths are essentially the same, as are their several shortcomings. This lack of marked regional distinctiveness is possibly a result of the changes industrialization brought to the region.

Today's South—defined here as the 11 states of the Confederacy plus Kentucky—is home to 28 percent (483) of the nation's dailies and 23 percent (1,778) of all weeklies in the United States. In like proportion, 24 percent of the 100 top-circulation papers in America are located in southern cities. Largest of these are the Miami *Herald* (483,095), the Houston *Chronicle* (384,305), the Houston *Post* (348,571), the New Orleans *Times-Picayune/States-Item* (275,376), and the Dallas *Times Herald* (245,325).

Size, of course, is no measure of quality. The Pulitzer Prize, given for reporting, editorial writing, and public service, is one of the best measures of journalistic performance. The southern paper that shines brightest is the Louisville *Courier-Journal*, with six Pulitzer awards; the *Courier-Journal* was also the first southern paper to win a Pulitzer (1918). Other standout papers are the Atlanta *Constitution*, with four Pulitzers in the three categories; the Miami *Herald* and the *Miami News*, with three each; and the Montgomery (Ala.) *Advertiser*, the Norfolk *Virginian-Pilot*, the *Arkansas Gazette* in Little Rock, the St. Petersburg *Times*, and the Gainesville (Fla.) *Sun*, with two each. Gene Miller of the Miami *Herald* is the only writer on a southern paper to have won two Pulitzers, and Hazel Brannon Smith of the Lexington (Miss.) *Advertiser* was the only southern woman to receive a Pulitzer (1964) until 1980, when Bette Swenson Orsini of the St. Petersburg *Times* was corecipient of the prize for national reporting. In the early years Pulitzers often went to southern papers for courageous stands against lynching, the Ku Klux Klan, and other manifestations of prejudice. Recent prizes have less frequently involved stories on racial issues.

Most lists of "best newspapers" include only the large metropolitan dailies. This article will mention some of the newspaper leaders in each southern state in three categories: metro dailies, smaller dailies, and weeklies.

The best of Alabama's metropolitan papers is the Birmingham *News*, known as a "writer's paper," and possibly the strongest link in the Newhouse chain. Outstanding smaller dailies are the Decatur *Daily* and the Anniston *Star*; a standout among weeklies is the Monroe *Journal*.

Of Arkansas city newspapers, the *Arkansas Gazette* is the clear choice. The Pine Bluff *Commercial* is a fine smaller daily with an outstanding editorial writer, Paul Greenberg; and the North Little Rock *Times* is consistently the best weekly.

The Miami *Herald* with its large editorial staff is Florida's best daily, followed by the St. Petersburg *Times* and the Orlando *Sentinel*. Among smaller dailies, Lakeland's *Ledger*, Fort Myers's *News-Press*, and Cocoa's *Today* stand out. Better weeklies are the Melbourne *Times*, *Gadsden County Times* (Quincy), and Titusville *Star Advocate*.

Atlanta's *Constitution* and *Journal*, followed by Macon's *News* and *Telegraph* are the leading Georgia metros; the Griffin *News* is well known in the smaller daily category; and among weeklies, the Dawsonville *County Advertiser and News* and the Swainsboro *Forest-Blade* are of fine quality. The Augusta *Chronicle*, established in 1785, is the South's oldest surviving paper.

Clearly, the Louisville *Courier-Journal* is Kentucky's finest metro; most respected among smaller dailies is the Paducah *Sun*. An extraordinary weekly is the crusading *Mountain Eagle* ("It Screams!") of Whitesburg.

Though its reputation has slipped in recent years, the New Orleans *Times-Picayune/States-Item* is Louisiana's premier daily. Gannett's Shreveport *Times* and the independent Baton Rouge *Advocate* are quality small dailies, and the innovative *Greater Plaquemines Post* is a frequent award winner among weeklies.

Jackson's *Clarion-Ledger* is Mississippi's best daily. Smaller dailies of note are the Greenwood *Commonwealth* and Biloxi-Gulfport *Daily Herald*. Quality weeklies include the Tylertown *Times*, *Lawrence County Press* (Monticello), and Kosciusko *Star-Herald*.

North Carolina choices in each category are the Charlotte *Observer*, the

Morganton *News Herald*, and the Smithfield *Herald*; South Carolina's are the Greenville *News*, the Myrtle Beach *Sun-News*, and the Hilton Head Island *Island Packet*; Tennessee's are the Memphis *Commercial Appeal*, the Jackson *Sun*, and the Clinton *Courier-News*.

Texas's best metros are in Dallas, where the Times-Mirror group's *Times Herald* and Belo Corporation's *News* provide an example of competition breeding excellence. Good smaller dailies are the Corpus Christi *Caller* and the Lufkin *News*, and quality weeklies are the Marble Falls *Highlander* and Fort Stockton *Pioneer*.

Virginia selections are the Richmond *Times-Dispatch*, the only statewide metro; the Fredericksburg *Free Lance-Star*; and the *Coalfield Progress* in Norton.

Today's South has no southern "newspaper of record" in the sense that the Richmond *Enquirer* filled that role in the Old South of the early 1800s when it was edited by the elegant and influential Thomas Ritchie.

Most of the South's earliest newspapers employed the designation "Gazette" in their mastheads, as in the earliest, the *South Carolina Gazette* (Charleston, founded in 1732). Gazettes appeared as the first newspapers in the following states: Virginia (Williamsburg, 1736), North Carolina (New Bern, 1751), Georgia (Savannah, 1763), Florida (*East-Florida Gazette*, St. Augustine, 1783), Kentucky (Lexington, 1787), Tennessee (the *Knoxville Gazette*, 1791), Mississippi (Natchez, 1799), and Arkansas (Port of Arkansas, 1819). Alabama's first paper was the *Mobile Centinel* (1811) and Texas's was the *Texas Republican* (Nacogdoches, 1819). Louisiana's first was published in French—the *Moniteur de la Louisiane* (New Orleans, 1794).

In the revolutionary era some of the earliest southern newspapers, such as the *South Carolina Gazette*, one of the papers in Benjamin Franklin's "chain," were staunchly behind the patriot cause. Others steered a less certain course. The *Georgia Gazette* became the *Royal Georgia Gazette* during the British occupation of Savannah, and the *South-Carolina and American General Gazette* of Charleston, originally a patriot organ, became the *Royal Gazette* when founder Robert Wells turned it over to son John. A second *Virginia Gazette*, this one in Norfolk, was removed to a British ship in 1775 and was published briefly from that unsteady location.

The nine dailies of New Orleans in the 1840s, most especially the *Picayune*, *Delta*, *Crescent*, *Tropic*, and *Bee*, enjoyed a period of prominence during the Mexican War. Outstanding among the special correspondents they dispatched to cover the action were George W. Kendall, cofounder of the *Picayune*, and James "Mustang" Freaner of the *Delta*.

During the Civil War southern papers suffered severe shortages of newsprint, ink, and labor, and they were subject to stiffer military censorship than their northern counterparts. When Associated Press copy was cut off, the Press Association of the Confederate States of America, or P.A., was founded to provide wire copy, operating during 1863 and 1864. The Memphis *Appeal* abandoned its physical plant just before the capture of that city in 1862 and set up on a flatcar. The "Moving Appeal" continued to publish in four states.

Important postwar journalists were Henry W. Grady of the Atlanta *Constitution* and Henry Watterson of the Louisville *Courier-Journal*, both leading spokesmen for the "New South."

The coming of chain ownership to the

South began in earnest in the 1920s with E. W. Scripps's son Robert, who purchased or founded in that decade the Norfolk *Post*, Birmingham *Post*, Ft. Worth *Press*, Knoxville *News*, El Paso *Post*, Memphis *News-Scimitar*, and Knoxville *Sentinel*. Since that time the independent newspaper owners of the South have seized the tax advantages offered by chain purchase with an avidity that has matched publishers in other parts of the nation.

Certainly, southern journalism has seen its share of colorful individuals: "Parson" William Brownlow, the picturesque mountaineer who edited and published the Knoxville *Whig*, last of the Union holdouts in the Civil War period; Cassius M. Clay of Kentucky, founder of the antislavery *True American* in Lexington, who armed his paper's offices with rifles and a cannon; Opie Read of the *Arkansas Traveler* in Little Rock, which built a large circulation based on Reed's humorous sketches of rural life; and W. B. Townsend, who founded Georgia's *Dahlonega Nugget* in 1892 and composed his stories while setting them in type. The Atlanta *Journal* alone can boast having employed humorist Don Marquis; Erskine Caldwell, chronicler of red-clay poverty; Margaret Mitchell, author of *Gone with the Wind*; and Grantland Rice, the first American newspaperman to gain fame writing about sports.

Of the 205 foreign-language newspapers currently published in the United States, only 12 are located in the largely homogenized South; all 12 are in Florida and Texas. Eight are Spanish-language papers, the best known of which are probably Miami's daily *Diario Las Americas* and the Dallas weekly *El Sol De Texas*. The Miami *Herald*'s all-Spanish edition, *El Miami Herald*, has also been a successful response to the tremendous influx of Hispanics that has altered that city's cultural makeup. The remaining four are two Czech weeklies in Granger and West, Tex.; an Italian weekly in Tampa, Fla.; and a Swedish weekly in Austin, Tex.

The South makes a stronger showing in black newspapers. Of the 210 being published nationwide, 86 (41 percent) are in the South. The greatest number are Florida (18), Texas (16), and Georgia (13). Atlanta has five black papers; Dallas, Houston, and Fort Worth have four each; and Miami three. Of the 86, the sole daily is the *Atlanta Daily World*. Largest of the weeklies are Houston's *Forward Times* and Little Rock's *Southern Mediator*. Few southern whites are aware of these papers, which is evidence of the persistence of two cultures in the South despite the great strides that have been made toward racial harmony. The first American Indian newspaper, the *Cherokee Phoenix*, was published in New Echota, Ga., from 1828 to 1834.

Because an area's newspapers generally reflect the population they serve, a paper's failings tend to be those of its readers. Particular problems for southern papers are shortsightedness, a reluctance to look farther than one's own borders; triteness, most especially in the community correspondents' columns of small-town weeklies; and a failure to lead in redressing social ills.

The latter problem is mainly a failure of the editorial page, where far too many southern papers resort to bland "canned copy" rather than producing incisive opinions written locally. In so doing, these papers serve as lapdogs to vested interests rather than as watchdogs for their readers. How many of today's southern editors and columnists will enjoy the reputation for courage earned by yesterday's Douglas Southall Freeman and Virginius Dabney of Virginia, Nell Battle Lewis of North Carolina, Henry Watterson of Kentucky, John Temple Graves of Alabama, Hodding Carter of Mississippi, or Julian Harris and Henry W. Grady of Georgia?

See also BLACK LIFE: Press, Black; INDUSTRY: / Grady, Henry W.; LITERATURE: / Caldwell, Erskine; MYTHIC SOUTH: / Mitchell, Margaret

Sam G. Riley
Virginia Polytechnic Institute

John D. Allen, in *Culture in the South*, ed. W. T. Couch (1934); Thomas D. Clark and Albert D. Kirwan, *The South since Appomattox: A Century of Regional Change* (1967); Robert Spencer Cotterill, *The Old South: The Geographic, Economic, Social, Political, and Cultural Expansion, Institutions, and Nationalism of the Ante-Bellum South* (1936); Edwin Emery and Michael Emery, *The Press and America: An Interpretive History of the Mass Media* (1978); Frank Luther Mott, *American Journalism: A History, 1690–1960* (1962); Francis Butler Simkins, *The South, Old and New: A History, 1820–1947* (1947). ☆

Newspapers, Country

||||||||||||||||||||||||||||||||||||||||||||||||

The Civil War all but decimated southern country newspapers. Only 182 weeklies, nearly all of them short-staffed and many published with substitute paper and inks on worn-out equipment, survived after Appomattox. Yet the southern country press reemerged to serve its region as a unifying element and a catalyst for change. To an extent seldom found elsewhere in the world, country newspapers in the postwar American South reflected an intimacy with their readers and a profound identification with the region's culture. A Henry Watterson of the Louisville *Courier-Journal* or a Henry W. Grady of the Atlanta *Constitution* commanded—and deserved—national attention; but it was in the town halls and country courthouses that the real New South took shape and the soul of southern journalism grew.

The community press generally existed to report local items that would appear in no other newspaper and to recognize and encourage local progress. Post–Civil War southern country papers, however, were additionally characterized by the problems that a one-party political system and a one-crop agricultural economy posed. Most debilitating of all was the difficulty of publishing a balanced community newspaper in a multiracial environment where old prejudices died hard. Many southern editors simply ignored news of the black community. As late as 1960 a leading black spokesman declared, "If you read the white press, Negroes are never born, never finish school, never marry, never have children, and never win any honors." Papers that did report on the black community were apt to segregate such news well inside the paper under such headings as "News of Colored." Often a thin line replaced the heading; news of the black community appeared below the line. No other label was necessary.

Southern black leaders attempted, with only limited success, to develop newspapers of their own. The first, *L'Union*, published half in French and half in English, appeared in New Orleans in 1862; the *Colored American* of Augusta, Ga., began in 1865. Both represented attempts to explain to blacks their new constitutional rights.

The white press, meanwhile, grew rapidly; 20 years after the end of the Civil War, southern newspapers had increased tenfold, to 1,827. Most were modest-sized county seat weeklies, their thin economic base bolstered by income from legal advertising and county job printing contracts. The editors extolled the virtues of the small family farm and of shopping with hometown merchants, while simultaneously promoting their communities as sites for urgently needed industrial development. Attention in the news columns focused overwhelmingly on local matters. "If it doesn't happen here, as far as my paper is concerned, it doesn't happen at all," a North Carolina editor said, and many of his fellow southern editors would have agreed with him.

The editorial columns of southern country newspapers reflected, and often gave direction to, the conservatism of their audiences. But the region also produced an astonishing number of spirited editors who have spoken out, often explosively, against the prevailing climate of opinion. The South's first commercial printers, John Buckner and William Nuthead, for example, were shut down by royal authorities soon after they set up shop in Gloucester County, Va., in 1682; they were chastised for presuming to publish without an official license. Nuthead resurfaced three years later in St. Mary's, Md., where, under a different jurisdiction, he established the South's first ongoing commercial press.

After licensing and other forms of prior restraint began to disappear, crusading southern editors often faced another, and potentially even more sinister, kind of repression—the hard disapproval of their fellow citizens. In Lexington, Ky., for example, when Cassius M. Clay launched an abolitionist newspaper, the *True American*, he and his small staff endured hatred from throughout the community. Undaunted, Clay lined the outside door with sheet iron, then "purchased two brass four-pounder cannon at Cincinnati and placed them, loaded with shot and nails, on a table breast high; had folding doors secured with a chain, which could open upon the move and give play to my cannon. I furnished my office with Mexican lances, and a limited number of guns. There were six or eight persons who stood ready to defend me. If defeated, they were to escape by a trap-door in the roof; and I had placed a keg of powder, with a match, which I could set off and blow up the office and all my invaders; and this I should most certainly have done." Proslavery forces gave Clay a wide berth for several weeks, but then, when the nervy publisher was recovering at his home from typhoid fever, they broke into his newspaper office, neatly packed up his type cases and his press, and shipped everything to Cincinnati.

The literature of southern journalism is filled with colorful, sometimes shocking, stories of country editors who risked life and property by attacking racism in all its manifestations. Several of these individuals—Hodding Carter and Hazel Brannon Smith of Mississippi, among other southern country editors—received Pulitzer Prizes for courage and excellence in editorial writing. P. D. East established the *Petal Paper* (1953) in Petal, Miss., and made it into an institution of small-town racial liberalism. His memoir *The Magnolia Jungle* (1960) chronicled his conflicts. Editors and reporters thrived on politics and parlayed their early journalistic experience on southern country newspapers into positions of national prominence. Turner Catledge began his newspaper career on the Neshoba, Miss., *Democrat* and ended it as the distinguished editor of the *New York Times*, where the chief political columnist was Arthur Krock, formerly of Glasgow, Ky., who became the only journalist ever to be honored with four Pulitzer Prizes. Some southern editors made news as well as reported it; more than a few were elected to legislative seats, and several country editors—W. D. Jelks of Alabama, James J. Vardaman of Mississippi, Keen Johnson of Kentucky, James Stephen Hogg of Texas, and Robert Taylor of Tennessee among them—were elected governors. Also, network television news teams and national newspaper and newsmagazine staff rosters currently contain the names of many correspondents who earned their spurs covering political rallies in the South.

In addition to political matters, the southern country editor typically devotes a great deal of space to local history. While many community editors everywhere feel a strong sense of tradition, southern country editors often write about local pioneers in tones approaching reverence. As one result, regional historians—and the South has had superb ones—can find in the files of the country press an uncommonly rich vein of authoritative source material, nostalgic though it may be.

Historically, though, sentimentalism has not characterized other aspects of country newspapers' operations, and modern equipment has been eagerly embraced. Since the Civil War, when the loss of slave help signaled an end to cheap labor, southern editors have been national leaders in developing improved production facilities and in adopting labor-saving methods and equipment.

Southern weeklies were trailblazers in the adoption of offset lithography, which ushered in a dramatic new era in printing technology; and in 1939 the Opelousas, La., *Daily World* attracted wide attention by becoming the first daily newspaper to publish exclusively by this process. Since that time nearly all the country's community papers and most of the metropolitan dailies have adopted the offset system.

Editorial and advertising staffs remain overwhelmingly white, despite a number of vigorous efforts to hire, retain, and promote minority employees. Studies indicate that some 2,700 black newspapers have been founded in the United States, 70 percent of them in the South. Relatively few have lasted more than a year. Many southern publishers strive to meet the American Society of Newspaper Editors' goal of developing in their newsrooms by the year 2000 the same racial percentages as in the society as a whole but face such problems as a shortage of trained minority applicants.

See also BLACK LIFE: Press, Black; INDUSTRY: / Grady, Henry W.

Ronald Truman Farrar
University of Kentucky

Thomas D. Clark, *The Southern Country Editor* (1948); Cassius M. Clay, *The Life of Cassius Marcellus Clay* (1886); William C. Havard, *Virginia Quarterly Review* (Winter 1983); Douglas C. McMurtrie, *History of Printing in the United States: The Story of the Introduction of the Press and of Its History and Influence during the Pioneer Period in Each State of the Union*, vol. 2 (1936); Frank Luther Mott, *American Journalism: A History, 1690–1960* (1962); William Howard Taft, *American Journalism History: An Outline* (1968). ✩

Radio Industry

|||||||||||||||||||||||||||||||||||||||

Radio communication designed for reception by the general public is known as broadcasting. The origins of southern broadcasting are indistinct. Clearly, southerners engaged in wireless telegraphy and telephony before the advent of formal broadcasting. As early as 1892 Nathan B. Stubblefield, a melon farmer, transmitted speech successfully from a small shack near his farmhouse in Murray, Ky., but he hardly intended to reach the general public. Nevertheless, a historical marker on the outskirts of Murray announces to all that the site is "The Birthplace of Radio."

Beginning in 1912, federal regulation required every wireless transmitter operator to secure a license from the Department of Commerce's Radio Service Section. The Radio Act of 1912 made amateur operators aware that a significant number of them were scattered across the country. Under the law, "call letters" were assigned to each licensee, and a list of the radio stations so licensed was published. Radio clubs sprang into existence for the exchange of information, and the contact between them tended to reinforce the enthusiasm of their members. From such organizations came many of the early broadcasters of the 1920s.

The first licenses issued in the South under the specific classification of broadcasting were granted in February 1922 to two utility companies, one in Alabama and the second in Arkansas. Montgomery Light & Water Power Company of Montgomery, Ala., received the call letters WGH, and the Pine Bluff Company, a division of Arkansas Light and Power, was given WOK. As with many early stations, though, the realities of broadcasting quickly overcame the glowing visions of the initial moments on the air. The result was that both soon vanished from the roster of operational stations.

Within a month the pace had quickened. During March 1922 nine more southern stations were licensed, including two destined to be mainstays among the region's broadcasters—WWL in New Orleans, licensed to Loyola University, and WSB, operated by the Atlanta *Journal*. But the southern states were slower to develop substantial radio facilities than the nation as a whole. Indeed, a continuing complaint of Dixie politicians during the middle 1920s was the supposed discrimination being suffered by a South saddled with inadequate radio service.

The 1928 Annual Report of the Federal Radio Commission, created by Congress in 1927 to bring some order out of the chaos of broadcasting's first decade, revealed that the 11 former Confederate states (excluding the border states of Missouri, Kentucky, and Maryland) could boast only 77 operating stations, slightly more than the state of Illinois alone and just 11.6 percent of the nation's total. Further, per capita incomes that trailed badly behind national figures prevented the number of "radio families" in the South from approaching the totals for the United States as a whole. While the South's share of American families was 28.9 percent in 1930, its percentage of radio families was a scant 11.9 percent. Northern radio families at the same time exceeded 76 percent.

Despite the relatively slow overall development, some individual broadcasters made their impact felt. One of the most flamboyant and controversial was William Kennon Henderson, whose unvarying formula—"Hello, world, doggone you! This is KWKH in Shreveport, Lou-EE-siana, and it's W. K. Henderson talkin' to you"—introduced him to a daily radio audience that stretched across the bulk of the United States. He continually exceeded his authorized power and usurped frequencies not assigned him. A New Orleans newspaper referred to Henderson as the "Bolshevik of radio," but admitted that "nearly every home in the South where there's a radio set has listened to him."

In 1929 Henderson embarked upon his most famous crusade; he declared war on the nation's retail chain stores. He castigated them on the air as "dirty, low down, daylight burglars" and as "damnable thieves from Wall Street." Moreover, Henderson established a nationwide organization, ostensibly to assist him in the chain-store struggle. Naming it the "Merchant Minute Men," he bragged that it numbered 35,000 independent merchants in 4,000 towns throughout the country by 1931. The deepening depression, however, mired Henderson in debt, and increasing pressure from creditors forced him to acquiesce in the sale of the station to new owners in 1933.

From its earliest days southern broadcasting developed a close association with country music. With the coming of radio, southern folksingers found an important new outlet for their talents. Probably the first station to feature country music was WSB in Atlanta. Within a few months after going on the air in 1922, WSB was presenting several folk performers including the Reverend Andrew Jenkins, a blind gospel singer, and Fiddlin' John Carson. With WSB leading the way, radio stations all over the South and the Midwest, as well,

began offering country musicians and singers.

No discussion of southern country music and its relation to radio would be complete without recognizing the impact of Nashville's Grand Ole Opry. The vehicle by which it gained attention was WSM, a station owned by the National Life and Accident Insurance Company. In November 1925, just a month after WSM first went on the air, it broadcast a program initially known as the WSM Barn Dance. A year later the country music show acquired the new name of Grand Ole Opry (to contrast it with the Grand Opera concerts being broadcast by the networks). Agents of National Life often took advantage of the connection by introducing themselves to potential clients as being from the Grand Ole Opry Insurance Company. By World War II the program had become the most important country music show on the air, especially after 1939, when the National Broadcasting Company began carrying a 30-minute segment on the network every Saturday night.

Stations such as Memphis's WDIA and Nashville's WLAC were key institutions in the spread of black music in the 1940s and 1950s. WDIA popularized the blues of the Mississippi Delta and Beale Street. WLAC was typical of other stations in broadcasting news and popular music during the days but switching to blues, gospel, and rhythm and blues at night. The station's 50,000-watt signal reached 20 states, and its format made celebrities of disc jockeys such as William T. "Hoss" Allen and John R. (Richbourg).

The immediate postwar years saw a broadcasting explosion. In October 1945 there were some 900 commercial AM stations in the United States, but soon that situation was dramatically changed. By June 1948 over 2,000 AM broadcasters were on the air, plus something new—about 1,000 FM licensees and 109 television stations, the latter representing the wave of the future. Translated into community terms, the number of towns and cities with stations grew from 566 on V-J Day to 1,063 in early 1947. The growth was greatest in the smaller hamlets, which lacked radio facilities before the war. In Louisiana, for example, there were just 13 operating stations in 7 cities in 1941, but 10 years later there were 45 stations and local service had finally come to the rural areas of the state.

Although the best-known programs deserted radio for the new medium of television, radio was still regarded as a successful business opportunity. The number of AM and FM licensees continued to grow to the point that virtually every American town of respectable size now has its own station or stations. As for the larger cities, to cite just three southern examples, Atlanta today has a choice of 12 AM and 10 FM stations; Houston has 11 AM and 15 FM; and New Orleans 11 AM and 12 FM stations.

Outstanding among stations based in the larger metropolitan areas are those broadcasting on clear channel frequencies with 50,000 watts of power, making them regional or even interregional rather than just local operations. Among this group are such longtime southern broadcasting leaders as WSB (Atlanta), WHAS (Louisville), WWL (New Orleans), WOAI (San Antonio), WSM (Nashville), and WRVA (Richmond). All date from the 1920s and thus can cite over a half century of broadcast experience.

See also MUSIC: / Grand Ole Opry

C. Joseph Pusateri
University of San Diego

John H. De Witt, Jr., *Tennessee Historical Quarterly* (Summer 1971); C. Joseph Pusateri, *Enterprise in Radio: WWL and the Business of Broadcasting in America* (1980); Reginald Stuart, *New York Times* (12 July 1982); Barnwell R. Turnipseed, "The Development of Broadcasting in Georgia" (M.A. thesis, University of Georgia, 1950); Wesley H. Wallace, "The Development of Broadcasting in North Carolina, 1922–1948" (Ph.D. dissertation, Duke University, 1962). ☆

Television Industry

New York's television station WNBT inaugurated the first commercial telecasts on 1 July 1941. But it was not until 22 April 1948 that Richmond's WTVR began broadcasting; it has ever since billed itself as "the South's first television station." That fall stations opened in Atlanta, Fort Worth, Louisville, Memphis, and New Orleans. The next year, 1949, Miami and Charlotte stations went on the air. Not until 1953, after a temporary Federal Communications Commission (FCC) moratorium on new licenses, were stations sanctioned in Mobile, Charleston, Jackson, and Little Rock.

Those first licenses awarded between 1948 and 1953 permitted at least one station in each of 12 southern states. The region's television broadcast industry since then has sustained considerable growth relative to its population and market share. For example, during the late 1940s the FCC granted licenses to only 16 southern stations, but during the 1950s it licensed 145, followed by 97 in the 1960s (many were for PBS or state education system channels), and another 92 since 1970.

Thus, by 1980 the region had approximately 350 stations, or 32 percent of the nation's total. That year Texas led all southern states with 72 stations, followed by Florida with 45. Arkansas had the least, 14, with Mississippi's 18 next. During the initial development of the southern television broadcasting industry, stations were overwhelmingly affiliated with one of the three major commercial networks. However, by the early 1960s many more of the region's new stations chose to be independent commercial enterprises or were intended as nonprofit educational broadcast facilities. As of 1980 network-affiliated stations accounted for 58 percent of the South's total, and independent and nonprofit channels for 42 percent.

Many of the region's commercial stations were originally closely held organizations, perhaps the most famous being KTBC in Austin, Tex., owned by Lady Bird Johnson. KTBC-TV received one of the first licenses awarded in 1952 after the FCC's four-year freeze. More importantly, it was the only VHF channel assigned to the market, providing the station with a monopoly against UHF competition. It illustrated a station's potential impact upon its viewing area.

Upon occasion the stations, particularly those locally owned, could offend elements of their white viewing audience simply by offering network programming. In 1952 Georgia's Governor Herman Talmadge spoke for many when he attacked network television for racially integrated programming, which he believed would lead to a "complete abolition of segregation customs." Later when the networks in 1957 announced a censorship of racially objectionable words such as "massa" and "old black Joe" from the songs of Stephen Foster, some southern white viewers reacted with considerable anger.

A decade later it was local programming that came under attack for perpetuating just what the networks had been accused of ending. For instance, liberal public protest in 1969 prevented a license renewal for WLBT in Jackson, Miss. Then owned by the Lamar Life Insurance Company, the station fought charges that it utilized its air time to promote segregation and in general denied use of its airwaves to blacks and civil rights proponents. A U.S. federal court found WLBT in violation of its license obligation to serve the Jackson community, 40 percent of which was black. It was the first time a television license was lost on substantive grounds.

In a similar but far broader action, the FCC in 1975 denied the renewal of eight licenses held by the Alabama Educational Television Commission, a state agency. The federal government determined that the eight stations were racially discriminatory in overall programming and were guilty of "pervasive neglect" of the state's black population. A considerable improvement in the stations' operations led eventually to a restoration of broadcast rights.

As was true of the industry as a whole, however, stations increasingly began to serve a broader community and at the same time to represent a wider ownership. KWTX Broadcasting Co., for example, by 1980 included stations in Waco and Bryan, Tex., as well as affiliates in Louisiana and Oklahoma. Many of the corporations are not even southern: the LIN Broadcasting Company, headquartered in New York, and the Scripps-Howard Broadcasting Company in Cincinnati manage stations in Florida, Tennessee, Texas, and Virginia as well as Illinois, Ohio, and Oklahoma.

In recent years southern television has demonstrated considerable business acumen and innovative promise. The Turner Broadcasting System's Atlanta-based "superstation" WTBS and Cable News Network (CNN) are but the most familiar examples of regional production for a national audience. Numerous other local stations have begun to contribute original programming; Miami PBS station WPBT in 1982 produced *A House Divided: Denmark Vesey's Rebellion*, one of many productions originating from public televison stations in particular. Especially well known in the ETV industry is the Southern Educational Communications Association (SECA), both a production center and regional network. Based in Columbia, it is usually referred to as "the South Carolina Network." Among its productions have been William F. Buckley's *Firing Line* and *Lowell Thomas Remembers* as well as a series of regional theater and dramatized short stories. SECA serves 87 public television stations in 16 states with both instructional and general programming.

Edward D. C. Campbell, Jr.
Virginia State Library

Erik Barnouw, *Tube of Plenty: The Evolution of American Television* (1975); *Broadcasting-Cable Yearbook: 1980* (1980); Les Brown, *Encyclopedia of Television* (1982), *The New York Times Encyclopedia of Television* (1977); J. Fred MacDonald, *Blacks and White TV: Afro-Americans in Television since 1948* (1983); *Southern Exposure* (Winter 1975). ☆

Television Movies
||||||||||||||||||||||||||||||||||||||||||||||

Over eight nights in January 1977 approximately 130 million Americans watched all or part of the television miniseries *Roots*. The eighth segment of *Roots* averaged 51 percent of the possible television audience and 71 percent of the actual audience, a record at that time. *Roots* broke the previous record set by the first broadcast of the 1939 classic *Gone with the Wind* in November 1976, which attracted 47 percent and 65 percent shares of the respective audiences. These figures not only document the immense popularity of media depictions of Dixie, but also demonstrate the complications inherent in differentiating among media forms.

Neither *Gone with the Wind* nor *Roots* is, strictly speaking, a television movie. *Gone with the Wind*, of course, was created as a theatrical film, and its drawing power in 1976 can be attributed precisely to its earlier exclusion from the smaller screen. *Roots* was originally planned as an eight-week miniseries; ironically enough, Fred Silverman's decision to present it on eight consecutive nights was motivated by his fear of a flop. By stricter definition, television movies are dramatizations using video technology intended entirely for home viewing at a single sitting. In any case, television "movies" concerned with the South, like other media depictions of the region, use the symbols provided by its history to dramatize the contradictions of larger American myths. Although the television movie has a relatively short history—the first three were made in 1964—over the past two decades the form has grown to be a staple of television programming. Each of the three major networks makes dozens each year, while educational networks, cable television companies, and independent producers provide even more. In general, the television movie was developed in response to changes in the feature-film industry. The breakup of the big studios and the fragmentation of the mass audience meant that Hollywood was producing fewer pictures suitable for televising. To satisfy their omnivorous appetite for film, the networks soon were making their own movies. NBC began its *World Premieres* in 1966, ABC launched its *Movie of the Week* in 1968, and CBS followed suit with its *Friday Night Movies* in 1971. Essentially, the television movies are the "B" pictures of the contemporary era. Like the traditional program fillers of the past, they are low-budget, topical, melodramatic, genre pieces.

The predominant television image of the South depicts rural innocence, whether at home in Mayberry or expatriated to Beverly Hills. These mindless series portraits reflect the "hick flicks" of the past that presented Will Rogers, Bob Burns, Lum and Abner, and others at home and abroad. The present-day "gasoline operas" starring good old boys like Burt Reynolds inspired the antics of the *Dukes of Hazzard* characters. Television movies presented minor variations in dozens of yokel epics and open-road sagas. Most of these efforts are immediately forgettable except in terms of confirming the American predilection for innocence triumphant and pretension-leveling comedy, which can be traced back as far as the 19th-century stage and the humor of the Old Southwest.

A more serious version of rural innocence was the phenomenon of the Waltons. "Serious" television writer

Earl Hamner, Jr., re-created his memories of Appalachian family life during the 1930s for a Christmas movie, *The Homecoming*, which proved a surprisingly strong draw in 1971. It inspired a very successful series, *The Waltons* (1972–81), and several other special movies, such as *A Wedding on Walton's Mountain* (1982). Production values were excellent, striking a fine balance of realism and sentiment. The social importance of *The Waltons* existed in its affirmation of simple, agrarian, and familial values in fictional form during a decade when America veered sharply away from them in reality.

The plantation South, probably because of production costs, was less often seen on television. This situation changed in the 1970s when the ongoing American reconsideration of its racial myths elicited several important works. The first was the adaptation in 1974 of black author Ernest J. Gaines's harshly realistic novel, *The Autobiography of Miss Jane Pittman*. Cicely Tyson projected the personality of a slave girl who lived long enough to participate in the civil rights demonstrations with such power that many viewers thought her a historical figure. Indeed, New York Governor Hugh Carey listed Jane Pittman in a speech honoring actual black heroes and heroines. Cicely Tyson also re-created Harriet Tubman, the black emancipationist, in *A Woman Called Moses* (1978), from a script by black writer Lonnie Elder III. Some of the scenes in this television movie, including one in which the young slave woman is harnessed to pull a farm wagon, are among the most powerful and moving depictions in any art form of the American national sin of slavery.

The most important, if not the most artistically successful, of television's plantation images exists in *Roots*. For all of its limitations, the made-for-television miniseries must rank with *Uncle Tom's Cabin*, *Birth of a Nation*, and *Gone with the Wind* as popular dramatizations of America's complex racial myths. In fact, *Roots* might be viewed as a contemporary *Uncle Tom's Cabin*, a work that simply upends the stereotypes of *Birth of a Nation* and *Gone with the Wind*. In Dixon's or Mitchell's novels blacks are either docile or demented; in Alex Haley's novelized family memoir, whites are either evil or weak, or both. Such stereotyping does not make for subtle art, but it does create exciting entertainment. *Roots* was all of that on television, mixing the traditional sensationalism of floggings and miscegenation with a cathartic wallow in collective guilt.

Roots spawned sequels, of course, and as they became better they suffered in popularity. *Roots: The Next Generations* (1979) proved much stronger if less popular television, and *Palmerstown, U.S.A.* (1980), an irregular series based on Haley's youth in Henning, Tenn., lasted just a season. These later works demonstrate some interesting connections with *The Waltons* and other family fare. Perhaps *Roots*'s ultimate success was in its combination of a nightmare past with the dream of the nuclear family reunited in the future.

Since *Roots*, television movies about the South have covered all the genres. The plantation South has appeared once more in *Freedom Road* (1979), a reprise of *Roots* characterized by Muhammad Ali's inept acting, and *Beulah Land* (1980), a *Gone with the Wind* ripoff presenting the moonlight-and-magnolias mythology intact. The Civil War received extensive treatment from both northern and southern viewpoints in *The Blue and the Gray* (1982). The docudrama, an important variant of contemporary television movies, was represented well in *King* (1978), a thoughtful biography of the martyred civil rights leader ably portrayed by Paul Winfield. The country music film, a big screen subgenre in recent years, had small-screen exposure in *Stand by Your Man* (1982), the story of oftenmarried country star Tammy Wynette.

A woman who does stand by her man, Gertie Nevels, is at the center of *The Dollmaker* (1984), perhaps the finest television movie about a southern character ever made. Jane Fonda played a beleaguered mountain woman transplanted to Detroit by the migrations to the defense plants of World War II. The television version proved a literate adaptation of Harriett Arnow's neglected classic novel.

The Dollmaker represents the literary adaptations that, like their sources, remain the most complete and complex visions of the South. Some were done by the commercial networks, such as ABC's recent remake of *A Streetcar Named Desire* (1983), which presented Ann-Margret grappling with the grand role of Blanche DuBois. Cable networks like HBO, as well as PBS, have also remade Tennessee Williams's plays; Showtime presented a memorable *Cat on a Hot Tin Roof* in 1984 with Jessica Lange and Tommie Lee Jones. PBS underwrote the *American Short Story* (1977–80), with fine short versions of works by William Faulkner, Richard Wright, Mark Twain, Katherine Anne Porter, Flannery O'Connor, and Ernest J. Gaines.

None of these literate works captured the audience ratings of *Roots* or *Gone with the Wind* or the *Dukes of Hazzard*, precisely because they pictured the lights and shadows of southern life. Through the southern genre's simplified stereotypes, television movies both reflect and reinforce the generic patterns found in other popular media; therefore, television movies not only form an important piece in the mosaic of the southern experience, but also finally tell us a good deal about the national use of the symbols provided by southern history.

See also MYTHIC SOUTH articles

Joseph R. Millichap
Western Kentucky University

Tim Brooks and Earle Marsh, *The Complete Directory to Prime Time Network TV Shows, 1946–Present* (1979); Jack Temple Kirby, *Media-Made Dixie: The South in the American Imagination* (1978); Marsha McGee, *Journal of American Culture* (No. 3, 1983); Horace Newcomb, *Appalachian Journal* (Autumn–Winter 1979–80); Eric Peter Verschuure, *Journal of Popular Culture* (Winter 1982). ☆

Television Series
||||||||||||||||||||||||||||||||||||||||||||||||

With the exception of the "Old West," no region of the United States has been subjected to such frequent treatment on network series television as has the South. Networks occasionally featured southern themes and settings in separate episodes of dramatic anthology series throughout the 1950s, but the earliest southern presence in series television was in the country music/variety format. ABC's *Hayloft Hoedown* (1948) was short-lived, but its energetic assortment of country music, square dancing, and rural comedy hinted at things to come. As with other series such as *Kobb's Korner* (a 1948–49 CBS entry ostensibly set in Shufflebottom's General Store, U.S.A.) and the popular *Midwestern Hayride* (syndicated 1947–67, NBC/ABC, 1951–59), *Hayloft Hoedown* was not directly linked to the South. Nevertheless, performers and audience alike understood that the humor, music (including yodeling), dress (overalls and flannel shirts were ubiquitous), and general demeanor of the artists were somehow linked to life and culture south of the Ohio River. *Midwestern Hayride* regulars included "The County Briar Hoppers" and the "Pine Mountain Boys," groups whose names were clearly intended to evoke the rural South. Although not nearly so fast paced nor so finely produced, these early series contained all the elements that would make the more self-consciously southern *Hee Haw* a success in the 1970s.

The Real McCoys (ABC 1957–62, CBS 1962–63) was the first major fictional television series featuring southerners. This situation comedy with dramatic overtones was set on a small California ranch, but the central characters were a family of West Virginians who had migrated west in search of a better life. The McCoy family consisted of Amos, his grandson and his wife, Luke and Kate, and Luke's younger brother and sister, Little Luke and Hassie. This extended, nearly impoverished, but always resilient farm family relied heavily upon its southern heritage to weather hard times. Themes of pride, religious values, determination, willingness to work hard, and, perhaps most of all, the preeminence of the family dominated episodes, and this portrayal set the tone for many series to follow.

The Real McCoys was quite successful, once having risen to fifth place in the year-end Nielsen ratings, and probably influenced CBS to try in 1960 *The Andy Griffith Show*, the success of which is often credited with the rise of the southern/rural situation comedy as a dominant form of television in the 1960s.

Both series had demonstrated that situation comedies in southern settings (or at least those featuring southern characters) could draw respectable audiences. The series *were* more popular in the South and in rural areas in general, but their national and urban appeal was strong enough to entice advertisers. In 1962 James T. Aubrey, president of CBS, sensed a trend, and he played a key role in the introduction of *The Beverly Hillbillies* (1962–71), which was instantly and overwhelmingly popular.

By 1965 CBS offered three additional situation comedies set in the South: *Petticoat Junction*, *Green Acres*, and *Gomer Pyle, U.S.M.C.* In 1968 Andy Griffith left his series and it became *Mayberry, R.F.D. Hee Haw*, a country music/variety show, found a place in the CBS schedule the following year. Such successes at CBS inspired ABC to offer southern series. The network included the animated *Calvin and the Colonel* in the 1961–62 schedule and in 1965–66 offered *Tammy*, a situation comedy set in a Louisiana bayou, and *The Long Hot Summer*, a dramatic series based on William Faulkner's short novel, *The Hamlet*, but none of these ventures had lasting impact.

By 1970 advertisers had begun the demographic study of television audiences, and, although the CBS series were still successful, the network decided to eliminate the southern programs from its 1971–72 schedule. These shows drew too heavily on rural, southern, and small-town portions of the populace to satisfy Madison Avenue. Nevertheless, all the CBS comedies remained popular in syndication into the 1980s, and their impact on the image of the South and of southerners has been enormous. Moreover, *Hee Haw*'s producers simply refused to allow the show to die. The series continued in first-run production for syndication, and, as of the 1983–84 season, seemed as healthy as ever in scores of local markets throughout the nation. NBC later attempted to resurrect the country music format with *The Nashville Palace*, but the 1981 series was a dismal failure.

After a one-year hiatus the South rose again in network prime-time programming, and once again CBS led the way. After surprisingly high ratings were achieved by *The Homecoming*, a 1971 Christmas special, in 1972 the network decided to develop a series around the Depression-era struggles of the Walton family from the Blue Ridge Mountains of Jefferson County, Va. Although *The Waltons* had a rocky beginning, the series built a loyal following and was one of the more positive portrayals of the South in series television. The tradition of *The Waltons* was extended by *Palmerstown, U.S.A.* in 1980, which depicted race relations in Henning, Tenn., in the 1930s and 1940s. Launched as a seven-episode miniseries in the spring, *Palmerstown, U.S.A.* was successful enough to be returned as a regular series the next season. Alex Haley, the author of *Roots*, and Norman Lear were the series's creators.

Other series of the 1970s and early 1980s were often less than positive in their portrayals of the South and its people. *The Texas Wheelers* began its brief ABC run in 1974. The Wheelers were poor, rural Texans (a lazy, scheming, and cantankerous widower and his four children), and the series exploited the "poor white trash" stereotype. In 1977 ABC launched *Carter Country*, a situation comedy set in a tiny village in rural Georgia. Also in 1977, NBC offered *The Kallikaks*, the story of a poor Appalachian family that moved to California to run a service station. The *Dukes of Hazzard* (CBS) and *The Misadventures of Sheriff Lobo* (NBC) appeared in 1979. The former was a mixture of comedy, adventure, hot cars, and "good old boy" escapades, while the latter featured the antics of a slightly corrupt law officer. These series portrayed the South as a raucous, backward, and largely rural region populated by stereotypical redneck white people and dishonest public officials.

Recent series have portrayed the New South, including *Dallas*, the saga of the oil-rich Ewing family, and *Flamingo Road*, a racy nighttime soap opera set in Florida. Only *Dallas*, which began its CBS run in 1978, has enjoyed lengthy popularity. *Flamingo Road* ran on NBC from 1980 to 1982 and was set in a "small Southern town" run by Sheriff Titus Semple, a small-time political boss. Both series featured the unsavory antics of wealthy southerners, but in some respects the characterizations and plots were not distinctively southern. With minor alterations these dramatizations, especially *Dallas*, might easily be set in other regions. Nevertheless, popular images of the South as a land of corruption and avarice among the well-to-do were undoubtedly affirmed.

Matt Houston opened on ABC in 1982. The program, which features a Texan who solves crimes while in California, simply provided an attractive backdrop for run-of-the-mill detective yarns. Early in 1983 CBS launched *The Mississippi* as a midyear replacement. The series concerned Ben Walker, a lawyer who traveled the river in search of adventure. Along the way he defended a series of desperate clients who could not afford to pay for legal services. In many instances the stories centered on distinctly southern themes and issues, including sensitive episodes on racism and bigotry in the region.

The fall of 1983 brought five new series, none overly successful. CBS offered *Cutter to Houston*, which was the story of three doctors working in comparatively primitive conditions in Cutter, Tex., a small town of "rednecks and cowgirls." NBC's *The Yellow Rose* was set on a sprawling ranch in west Texas and was as much a contemporary western as a southern series. *Boone*, on NBC, told the story of a 1950s Tennessee youth who wanted to become a Grand Ole Opry star—his family wanted him to sing in the church choir. Two continuing dramas were set on southern military bases—*For Love and Honor* on NBC and *Emerald Point N.A.S.* on CBS. Both extended the popular association of the South with military life.

With a few exceptions, television series have depicted the South as a backward, somewhat uncivilized, largely rural, simple, and rather monolithic region. Geographic variations seemingly do not exist in television's Dixieland— Hooterville (*Petticoat Junction* and *Green Acres*), Mayberry (*The Andy Griffith Show* and *Mayberry, R.F.D.*), Frenchman's Bend (*The Long Hot Summer*), and even Walton's Mountain (*The Waltons*) are curiously similar. *Hee Haw*'s "Cornfield County" setting exploits every conventional stereotype of the rural, small-town South, from the ubiquitous general store to the ramshackle cabins of the small farmer. Fictional Hazzard County, the setting of the enormously successful *Dukes of Hazzard* series, is a land of swamps (complete with alligators!), fertile valleys, pine barrens, and mountains; in short, the fictional county's geography is that of the South as a whole.

Moreover, the geographically indiscriminate television South is populated by characters who are often far easier to deal with in terms of stereotypes than as individuals. Several clusters of characters are easily identified. First are the young, buxom country belles who, as often as not, romp through the countryside in cut-off jeans and panty hose, including Daisy of the *Dukes of Hazzard*, Elly May of *The Beverly Hillbillies*, and the three daughters of *Petticoat Junction*'s lead character. Pathetically inept bumpkins who frequently are unable to function competently in their occupational roles comprise a second group. A few examples include the title character in *Gomer Pyle, U.S.M.C.*, Deputy Barney Fife of *The Andy Griffith Show*, Jethro of *The Beverly Hillbillies*, Sheriff Roscoe P. Coltrane of the *Dukes of Hazzard*, and, from the same series, the naive Deputy Enos Straight, a character who was spun off in the short-lived *Enos* series.

Experienced, somewhat timeworn, but always witty bearers of southern folk wisdom form another major group of characters, with Jed Clampett of *The Beverly Hillbillies* being one of the finest examples. Three others worthy of mention, all dressed in the familiar bib overalls so often associated with this stereotype, are Grandpa Amos of *The Real McCoys*, Grandpa Zeb Walton, and the *Dukes of Hazzard*'s Uncle Jesse. The unscrupulous and corrupt southern "boss" stereotype is best represented by Jefferson Davis Hogg of the *Dukes of Hazzard* and *The Long Hot Summer*'s Will Varner. Even J. R. Ewing of *Dallas* can be forced into this mold. Shiftless, "no account" southerners, video versions of "poor white trash," appear in such creations as Zack Wheeler of *The Texas Wheelers* and Uncle Joe Carson of *Petticoat Junction*. Expectedly, "good old boys" abound in the television series South, with Bo and Luke Duke, who careen through Hazzard County in their hot car, "General Lee," providing the purest examples.

Although these stereotypes are the most common, nearly all of the stereotypes traditionally associated with the South have been portrayed in television series. The only major exception has been the traditional negative black stereotypes, which rarely appear on network television. Indeed, the opposite has sometimes been the case, as in *Carter Country*. This series featured policeman Curtis Baker, a talented black man from the North, who worked for a "lovable redneck sheriff." Baker was surrounded by bumbling white southerners, from the overweight major to Deputy Harley Puckett, good old boy *par excellence*.

The closest network television has come to presenting negative stereotypes of southern blacks in a regular, continuing series format was probably the 1961–62 animated series, *Calvin and the Colonel*. However, ABC was fairly cautious, for the civil rights movement was gaining momentum. The series was clearly derived from the *Amos 'n' Andy* series, which had been presented nearly a decade earlier, but *Calvin and the Colonel* featured the antics of a community of animals from the Deep South.

Although this tactic served to quiet potential critics, there really was little question that the series was centered on black stereotypes: the voices of the colonel, a devious fox, and Calvin, a dimwitted bear, were supplied by Freeman Gosden and Charles Correll, the white actors who had performed *Amos 'n' Andy* on radio. Later series, primarily *Palmerstown* and *The Waltons*, also relied to a certain degree on black stereotypical characters in minor roles. However, these series regularly featured both black and white characters who were *not* stereotypes but who represented fully developed and individualized southerners.

Overall, television's portrayal of the South is a mixed bag of negative and positive images. Often seen as a region where family and community ties are strong and vital, a recurring theme nevertheless suggests that many southerners in positions of power take advantage of those virtues. Although some southerners are characterized as wise and witty, more are depicted as crude and insensitive bumpkins. Except for the comic-book violence of the *Dukes of Hazzard* and similar series, the image of the South as a violent region has not played a significant part in television's portrayal. Yet few series have grappled with the region's many difficulties in such important areas as race relations and economic structures, preferring instead to highlight superficial conflicts in their stories. An entire segment of the southern population, the middle class, is rarely treated in the television South. Instead, writers and producers offer stereotypical images of the very wealthy (*Dallas*) and the rural poor (*The Waltons* and *The Texas Wheelers*). While there have been some attempts to deal with the South and southern topics in dramatic series, the most common type of television series to portray the South has been the situation comedy. The television South has been a land of fantasy, redneck humor, adventure, and family drama, and as such has played an important role in the formation of popular images and attitudes toward the South, both within the region and in the nation at large.

Southfork Ranch, home of the television series **Dallas**

See also BLACK LIFE: / Haley, Alex; MYTHIC SOUTH articles

Christopher D. Geist
Bowling Green State University

Roy Blount, Jr., *TV Guide* (2 February 1980); Tim Brooks and Earle Marsh, *The Complete Directory to Prime Time Network TV Shows, 1946–Present* (1979); Larry J. Gianakos, *Television Drama Series Programming: A Comprehensive Chronicle, 1947–80*, 3 vols. (1978); Jack Temple Kirby, *Media-Made Dixie: The South in the American Imagination* (1978); Marsha McGee, *Journal of American Culture* (No. 3, 1983); Horace Newcomb, *Appalachian Journal* (Autumn–Winter, 1979–80); Eric Peter Verschuure, *Journal of Popular Culture* (Winter, 1982). ☆

ALTMAN, ROBERT

(b. 1925) Film director.

The South represents a cross section of American attitudes and lifestyles in the films of Robert Altman. His southerners embody some of the best and worst traits of the American public. They are typically proud, resilient, and forceful, but they are also prone to racial and regional biases, to stubbornness and greed. Complacency appears to be the dominant trait of the southerner. In this quality the southerner most resembles the majority of the population of the United States—a population that, according to Altman, implicitly accepts corrupt political and economic institutions as natural parts of the American way of life. The South is depicted as a locus of conservatism in the United States. Altman seems to argue that the tendency to ignore or reject platforms for social change often results in the denial of individual freedom. This perspective is clearly suggested in Altman's films with southern characters or settings, such as the early films *M*A*S*H** (1969) and *Brewster McCloud* (1970), and is more fully developed in the later films *Thieves Like Us* (1974), *Nashville* (1975), and *Health* (1980).

In *M*A*S*H**, Captain Duke Forrest (Tom Skerritt) voices a set of racial prejudices that unfortunately have always been a part of the American national character. In *Brewster McCloud*, Houston is the perfect setting for a satiric attack on the dreams, ambitions, and foibles of middle America in general and the South in particular. *Thieves Like Us* is the director's first serious investigation of life in the South itself. The film depicts a claustrophobic and actively hostile environment for three convicts on the run, and from this landscape Altman draws some bleak generalizations about southern culture. The complacent acceptance of violence in *Nashville* also provides a striking index of the decadence of society within this large southern city. The songs in the film repeatedly describe a potentially strong and uncompromising American who has capitulated to superior and corrupt forces, basing that surrender on terms that enhance his material surroundings. *Health* is a similar, perhaps more cynical, essay on political institutions that have run out of control.

In these films Altman, who is a midwesterner born in Kansas City, Mo., uses settings, characters, and interactions based in the urban and rural South to present a composite picture of America—his sobering vision of complacency and hypocrisy in American life. He indicates the possibly deadly effects of racism, unrestrained regional ethnocentrism, and apathy toward reform. He argues that these corrupt social, political, and economic forces may lead to the loss of freedom in this country, unless they are first recognized as abusive conditions and then corrected.

Gerard Plecki
Chicago, Illinois

Gerard Plecki, in *The South and Film*, ed. Warren French (1981). ☆

THE ANDY GRIFFITH SHOW

IIIIIIIIIIIIIIIIIIIIIIIIIIIIIIIIIIIIIIIIIIIIIIIIIIII

The Andy Griffith Show, first televised by CBS on 3 October 1960, was one of the most enduring and influential of the television series set in the South. The series, which was inspired in part by the earlier success of *The Real McCoys* (ABC 1957–62, CBS 1962–63), starred Griffith as Sheriff Andy Taylor of Mayberry, a fictional North Carolina hamlet. Taylor, a widower raising his young son Opie (Ronny Howard), lived with Bee Taylor (Frances Bavier), his aunt. Other characters populating Mayberry over the years included Deputy Barney Fife (Don Knotts in a role that earned him five Emmy Awards), gas station attendants Gomer and Goober Pyle (Jim Nabors and George Lindsey), town drunk Otis Campbell (Hal Smith), barber Floyd Lawson (Howard McNear), and two of Andy's sweethearts, drugstore clerk Ellie Walker (Elinor Donahue) and the woman he eventually married, teacher Helen Crump (Anita Corsaut). These recurring supporting characters, along with several others, helped add a remarkable air of verisimilitude to the series, and viewers came to know and understand their distinctively individualized personalities far better than they

did those of most series characters of the era.

Mayberry, and by extension the small-town, rural South it represented, was a bucolic haven in which nothing ever happened. Most of the individual episodes centered on the difficulties and misunderstandings that arose among the friends and neighbors in the community. Andy used his considerable charm and homespun wisdom to settle these disputes and to return Mayberry to a state of peacefulness and order at the conclusion of each tale. Occasional outsiders, including relatively few criminals, considering Andy Taylor's occupation, would disrupt the everyday rhythms of Mayberry until Andy's timely intercession. Other stories revolved around Andy's domestic life; he constantly worked to build Opie's character and to reassure Aunt Bee of her value to both the community and the Taylor household. Many episodes involved Andy's tact in dealing with Barney's ec-

Andy Griffith and Frances Bavier as Andy Taylor and Aunt Bee in **The Andy Griffith Show**

centricities. Deputy Fife was so incompetent that Andy allowed him only a single bullet, which he had to carry in his pocket rather than in his gun. In numerous episodes Andy's major aim was to prevent Barney from getting into serious trouble and to keep the sensitive Fife from discovering just how gullible and inept he was. Andy Taylor was the quintessential and ever-present wise southerner (later manifestations included Grandpa Zeb in *The Waltons* and Jock Ewing in *Dallas*), and Barney Fife was the stereotypical "hickish" buffoon (Sheriff Rosco P. Coltrane of the *Dukes of Hazzard* continued the type), two character models that have become so common in television's Southland as to be almost obligatory.

In addition to delineating lasting themes and stereotypes, *The Andy Griffith Show* had an even more significant role in Dixie's television history. The series was an instant and enduring success in the ratings. In its initial season A. C. Nielsen listed the show fourth in overall popularity and first among situation comedies; by its final season (1967–68) the series was number one in the overall ratings. It never dipped below seventh place during its entire run. Inevitably such success in television spawns imitations and spin-offs. Soon CBS entered its "rural comedy" (most of these programs were, in fact, *southern* comedies) era, and the airwaves became cluttered with series of such varied quality as *The Beverly Hillbillies*, *Green Acres*, *Petticoat Junction*, and *Gomer Pyle, U.S.M.C.*, in which Jim Nabors reprised his Mayberry creation. When Andy Griffith left his series in 1968, new lead characters moved to town, and *Mayberry, R.F.D.* continued successfully until 1971 when, in search of younger and more urban audiences,

CBS dropped all its southern-oriented series.

In 1986 NBC aired *Return to Mayberry*, a nostalgic television movie that reunited most of the original cast of *The Andy Griffith Show*, with the notable exceptions of Frances Bavier, who was ill, and Howard McNear, who died in 1969. In the story Andy returned to Mayberry after 18 years in Ohio; Andy and Barney both ran for sheriff, with Andy getting the position; Barney and his longtime sweetheart, Thelma Lou, reunited and married; and Opie and his wife had their first child and planned a job-related move from Mayberry. The characters' slow-paced, laid-back lives had changed, but warmth and humor still pervaded the fictional southern town.

Christopher D. Geist
Bowling Green State University

Tim Brooks and Earle Marsh, *The Complete Directory to Prime Time Network TV Shows, 1946–Present* (1979); Richard Kelly, *The Andy Griffith Show* (1981). ☆

APPALSHOP
||||||||||||||||||||||||||||||||

Appalshop is a rural arts and education center in Whitesburg, Letcher County, Ky. Founded in 1969 in one of the poorest and most rural areas in the nation, Appalshop produces and distributes creative materials relating to southern mountain culture.

Appalshop began as the Community Film Workshop of Appalachia, training poor and minority youth in film and television production. Artists at the workshop soon formed a nonprofit media center, and since then Appalshop's purposes have been to document Appalachian life, produce educational materials, nurture indigenous culture, destroy stereotypes of Appalachians, encourage community discussion, and relate the region and its people to other people and places.

Appalshop sponsors numerous specific programs. Roadside Theater develops and presents original theatrical work. It began in 1974 as an itinerant troupe trying to perform in a way appropriate to the region's theatrical heritage, which was found less in traditional separate theater than in church worship, storytelling sessions, and musical performances. In 1986 the ensemble performers gave 126 shows in 50 communities, over half of which were rural. Roadside Theater sponsored arts programs in schools and colleges, appeared nationally through the National Performance Network and regional tours, and performed at a Scandinavian festival.

June Appal Recordings features traditional and contemporary mountain music. The record label distributes over 40 albums in bluegrass, gospel, folk, blues, and old-time music. Appalshop schedules 112 hours a week of programming on WMMT-FM, its noncommercial radio station, develops and distributes other regionally oriented work, and provides free training for local volunteers. WMMT began operations in 1985.

Appalshop's television unit is Headwaters, which annually produces seven half-hour programs. The Kentucky Educational network broadcasts these productions, as do public stations in Virginia, West Virginia, and Tennessee. Mountain Photography is another division of Appalshop. It assembles, exhibits, and publishes books, including Wendy Ewald, ed., *Portraits and Dreams* (1985) and Loyal Jones, *Appalachia: A Self-Portrait*.

Appalshop films are among the best-known documentaries of southern life. They deal with political, economic, social, and cultural topics. Recent films include *Buffalo Creek Revisited* (Mimi Pickering, director, 1984), *Sunny Side of Life* (Scott Faulkner, Anthony Stone, and Jack Wright, directors, 1985), *Strangers and Kin: A History of the Hillbilly Image* (Herb E. Smith, director, 1984), and *Coal Mining Women* (Elizabeth Barret, director, 1982). Other Appalshop films have dealt with chairmaker Chester Cornett (*Hand Carved*, Herb E. Smith, director, 1981), home medical remedies (*Nature's Way*, John Lang and Elizabeth Barrett, directors, 1973), the Old Regular Baptist Church (*In the Good Old Fashioned Way*, Herb E. Smith, director, 1973), dulcimers (*Sourwood Mountain Dulcimers*, Gene DuBey, director, 1976), and strip mining (*Strip Mining: Energy, Environment and Economics*, Frances Morton and Gene DuBey, directors, 1979).

Charles Reagan Wilson
University of Mississippi

Leslie Bennetts, *New York Times* (1 December 1984); Jack Fincher, *Smithsonian* (December 1981); Sharon Hatfield, *Southern Changes* (June–July 1984); Kathleen Hulser, *Independent* (October 1983). ☆

ATLANTA *CONSTITUTION*

The Atlanta *Constitution* was first published by Carey W. Styles in July 1868 as a response to Reconstruction radicalism. Styles subsequently sold the paper to William A. Hemphill, and in 1876 reporter and then city editor of the Atlanta *Intelligencer* Evan Park Howell purchased a half interest in the enterprise, thus beginning a long-term family involvement. *Herald* correspondent Henry W. Grady and Joel Chandler Harris soon joined Howell's staff, and the *Constitution* began to build its national reputation.

Part owner and managing editor after 1880, Grady successfully employed correspondents, new technology, and innovative journalistic techniques such as the interview to increase weekly circulation from 10,000 to 140,000, making the *Constitution* the most widely circulated paper of its kind in America. Convinced that the region was "heartily sick of sectionalism" and in desperate need of northern capital to support industrialization, Grady championed his New South creed in the pages of the *Constitution* and from speakers' platforms in Boston and New York.

Clark Howell succeeded Grady and became editor-in-chief in 1897. Under his management the newspaper supported civic improvement, engaged in a caustic political debate with the rival Atlanta *Journal*, frequently gave way to sensationalism, and won its first Pulitzer Prize for investigative reporting in 1931.

On questions of race Howell, like Grady, supported the separate-but-equal myth—a conciliatory stance not altered until liberal journalist Ralph McGill assumed editorship in 1938. Awarded the Pulitzer in 1959 for "long, courageous, and effective editorial leadership," McGill opposed racial terrorism, Klan activities, and, ultimately, segregation, placing the *Constitution* in the vanguard of New South journalism.

Merged with the Atlanta *Journal* since 1950, the *Constitution* continues to be a separate daily. It is owned by Cox enterprises and has a Sunday circulation exceeding 540,000.

See also INDUSTRY: / Grady, Henry W.; LITERATURE: / Harris, Joel Chandler; URBANIZATION: / Atlanta

Elizabeth M. Makowski
University of Mississippi

Wallace B. Eberhard, *Journalism Quarterly* (Spring 1983); Sidney Kobre, *Development of American Journalism* (1969); *Newspaper Directory* (1985); Raymond Nixon, *Henry W. Grady: Spokesman of the New South* (1943). ☆

THE BEVERLY HILLBILLIES

Universally despised by critics and totally neglected in Emmy Award considerations, *The Beverly Hillbillies* nevertheless stands as one of the most popular television series to feature southerners and to represent to the general public lifestyles that are supposedly southern. The Columbia Broadcasting System series premiered in September 1962 and according to A. C. Nielsen was the highest-rated series by the end of the 1962–63 season, with an estimated audience of about 60 million. The series maintained its popularity for several years and was rated no lower than 12 through the 1968–69 season.

Jed Clampett, the family's patriarch, discovered oil while hunting on his impoverished Ozark farmstead, became fabulously wealthy, and, to use the words of the series's hit theme song, "moved to Beverly—Hills, that is—swimming pools and movie stars." He was accompanied into this strange and materialistic new world by his cantankerous but lovable mother-in-law, Granny Daisy Moses, and his naive daughter and bumbling nephew, Elly

May Clampett and Jethro Bodine. These characterizations were performed, in order, by Buddy Ebsen, Irene Ryan, Donna Douglas, and Max Baer, Jr. Other characters included the Clampetts' slightly dishonest California banker, Milburn Drysdale (Raymond Bailey); Jane Hathaway (Nancy Kulp), who was Drysdale's love-starved, wallflower secretary; and a wacky assortment of Ozark visitors and Beverly Hills socialites. Lester Flatt and Earl Scruggs, who wrote and performed the theme, sometimes appeared as themselves.

As might be expected, the plots revolved around the Clampetts' inability to cope with their new surroundings. Audiences laughed at Jethro's attempts to understand "courting" in Beverly Hills, or at Elly May's adjustment to modern fashion—she believed a brassiere to be a "double-barreled sling shot." Granny thought the billiard table was a "fancy eatin' table" and Jed thought "golfs" were animals to be clubbed to death with an elaborate collection of woods, irons, and a putter. The Clampetts continued to eat squirrel and opossum, practiced folk medicine, and always dressed in worn homespun. Many episodes depicted Drysdale's attempts to take advantage of the Clampetts and to use their fortune for his own benefit. Inevitably, the innocence and basic goodness of the Clampetts triumph over Beverly Hills characters who value money and material possessions more than honesty and integrity. And, throughout all their trials and tribulations, the Clampett clan exhibits a strong sense of family loyalty, a trait almost universally associated with the portrayal of southerners in television series.

Although ratings had slipped by 1970, the series was still a respectable success when it was cancelled after the 1970–71 season. Network officials had determined that the audience was too heavily rural to attract major advertisers. *The Beverly Hillbillies* remains significant for several reasons other than its phenomenal ratings successes. First, although "corny" (the series was often sponsored by Kellogg's), the series was totally without violence in an era when television fare was severely criticized as overly violent. The series also led to an impressive array of spinoffs and imitations, including *Green Acres* and *Petticoat Junction*, causing the decade of the 1960s to be labeled the heyday of southern sitcoms. It also led indirectly to a host of other comedy series based on outlandish situations, not all of which included southerners. Finally, its emphasis on the stereotype of the backward, poor southern hillbilly did much to fix the image in popular consciousness. The series remains widely available and popular in local syndication and on cable systems through the 1980s.

See also FOLKLIFE: / "Hillbilly" Image

Christopher D. Geist
Bowling Green State University

Tim Brooks and Earle Marsh, *The Complete Directory to Prime Time Network TV Shows, 1946–Present* (1979); Arthur Hough, *Understanding Television: Essays on Television as a Social and Cultural Force*, ed. Richard P. Adler (1981); Alex McNeil, *Total Television: A Comprehensive Guide to Programming from 1948 to the Present* (1980); Horace Newcomb, *TV: The Most Popular Art* (1974). ☆

BIRTH OF A NATION
IIIIIIIIIIIIIIIIIIIIIIIIIIIIIIIIIIIIIIIIIIIIIIIIIII

D. W. Griffith's film *Birth of a Nation* (Epoch, 1915) celebrates the Ku Klux Klan. This organization, according to the film's subtitles, saved the South from the anarchy of black rule by reuniting former wartime enemies "in defense of their Aryan birthright." Griffith based his film on two novels by the Reverend Thomas Dixon, Jr., *The Leopard's Spots* (1902) and *The Clansman* (1905).

One of the most controversial and profitable films ever made, the movie set many precedents. It was the first film to cost over $100,000 and exact a $2 admission, the first to have a full-scale premiere, and the first to be shown at the White House. President Woodrow Wilson reportedly declared, "It's like writing history with lightning. My only regret is that it is all so terribly true."

Originally called *The Clansman* when it opened in Los Angeles 8 February 1915, it was retitled *Birth of a Nation* just prior to its Broadway showing in March. Fully exploiting the motion picture as a propaganda vehicle, Griffith used every device he had developed in his years at Biograph studio—long shot, closeup, flashback, montage—to create excitement and tension. Provocative subtitles heightened his messages, and southern audiences acclaimed the film enthusiastically; horsemen in Klan costumes often rode through towns prior to the film's showing to promote box-office receipts. In cities like New York, Chicago, and Boston, however, the film was greeted with pickets, demonstrations, and lawsuits.

For a time, Newark and Atlantic City, N.J., banned the film, as did St. Louis, Mo., and the states of Kansas, West Virginia, and Ohio. (In the 1950s Atlanta banned the film, fearing that the violence of some scenes might provoke audience emulation.) As a result of the widespread interest in *Birth of a Nation*, newspapers began to review new films regularly, and motion picture advertising began to appear in the press. This film helped make moviegoing a middle-class activity, and its success led to the erection of ornate movie palaces in fashionable districts.

The two-part film centered on two families, the Camerons of South Carolina and the Stonemans of Pennsylvania, who are eventually joined in marriage. An idyllic, gracious, carefree antebellum South, based on the labor of happy slaves, is shattered by bloody battles and the devastation and defeat of the Confederacy. With the assassination of Lincoln, the South appears to be doomed to black control. Part two concerns the Reconstruction period and focuses on the Little Colonel, Ben Cameron (Henry B. Walthall), who is in love with Elsie Stoneman (Lillian Gish), daughter of a Negrophile congressman and his black mistress. One of the key scenes shows the Little Colonel's sister (Mae Marsh) hurling herself off a cliff, terrified by the black renegade Gus's lustful pursuit. "For her who had learned the stern lesson of honor we should not grieve that she found sweeter the opal gates of death," reads the subtitle.

Two kinds of blacks appear in the film: the sober, industrious slaves inspired by Uncle Tom who stay on as loyal servants after the war and the freedmen, portrayed as arrogant, lecherous, and bestial. Instead of working in the cotton fields, the former slaves make a mockery of legislative government, spend time carousing in saloons, lust after white women, and demand "equal rights, equal politics, equal marriage." The rise of the Ku Klux Klan led by the Little Colonel promises to restore the social order, disenfranchise the blacks, protect southern womanhood, and reunite the nation.

The film is said to have inspired the revival of the Klan in November 1915 and to have promoted the passage of the prohibition amendment. Generally regarded as a masterpiece and the greatest American silent film, *Birth of a Nation* has never, because of its overt racism, received unequivocal praise.

See also LITERATURE: / Dixon, Thomas, Jr.; VIOLENCE: / Ku Klux Klan

Joan L. Silverman
New York University

Roy E. Aitken, *The Birth of a Nation Story* (1965); Fred Silva, ed., *Focus on The Birth of a Nation* (1971); Edward Wagenknecht and Anthony Slide, *The Films of D. W. Griffith* (1975). ☆

CALDWELL, ERSKINE, AND FILM

The works of Erskine Caldwell have achieved enormous popularity. *Tobacco Road* has sold well over 3.5 million copies; *God's Little Acre* has reached sales considerably over 8 million, more than even *Gone with the Wind*. It is no surprise, then, that Hollywood has taken note of the enormously popular stories of Caldwell's rural and poverty-stricken South.

Films of the contemporary South produced during the same period as the novels were predominantly in a lighter vein, such as *Carolina* (1934) or *Virginia* (1941). Warner Brothers's exposé *I Am a Fugitive from a Chain Gang*

(1932) and *Cabin in the Cotton* (1932), from Harry Kroll's novel of class conflict, were exceptions, but Caldwell presented the film industry with more than just a stock exception to the usual. Called a southern "hovelist" by some, Caldwell mercilessly struck at the controversial, powerful, titillating, and depressing aspects of a steamy and backward South. Despite huge book sales, the writer's themes required careful handling by Hollywood.

Not until 1941, nine years after its publication, did a studio take a chance on filming *Tobacco Road*. Though based on Jack Kirkland's extremely successful theater version of the novel and with a cast that included Dana Andrews, Ward Bond, and Gene Tierney, the story was vastly changed from a shocking novel to an almost farcical film for 20th Century Fox. In order to capture Caldwell's tale accurately, director John Ford and scriptwriter Nunnally Johnson would have faced enormous censorship problems in the early 1940s, and hence they developed instead a story line of rustic humor and glamorized southern poor folk, all enhanced by slick studio techniques.

Another attempt to adapt Caldwell's work to the screen was not made until 1958. Surely, many reasoned, the times were better for more forthright productions. By the 1950s, Hollywood had purchased the screen rights to works by William Faulkner, Tennessee Williams, Robert Penn Warren, and Lillian Hellman. *God's Little Acre* was released by Security Pictures/United Artists and featured Robert Ryan as Ty Ty Walden. Although this adaptation captured the realism that *Tobacco Road* missed, critics believed that it still lacked the sociological significance that Caldwell's novels provided.

In 1961 Warner Brothers touted

Claudelle Inglish as, at last, authentically depicting Caldwell's settings, characters, and native region. Taken from the writer's 1958 story, the movie featured Diane McBain as the daughter of a tenant farmer (Arthur Kennedy) and the object of a rich man's (Claude Akins) affections. A critic for *Time* summarized the story succinctly as merely another exploration of the "Deep (read shallow) South."

For all the success and impact of Caldwell's considerable literary effort, Hollywood appeared each time unable to translate the novels to the screen as anything more than rural humor or salacious drama.

See also LITERATURE: / Caldwell, Erskine

Edward D. C. Campbell, Jr.
Virginia State Library

Erskine Caldwell, *Call It Experience* (1951); Edward D. C. Campbell, Jr., *The Celluloid South: Hollywood and the Southern Myth* (1981); James D. Devlin, *Erskine Caldwell* (1984); Warren French, ed., *The South and Film* (1981). ☆

CARTER, HODDING

(1907–1972) Newspaper editor.

William Hodding Carter, as editor of the Greenville, Miss., *Delta Democrat-Times* from 1938 until a short time before his death in 1972, was a major advocate of racial tolerance and an ardent opponent of the system of state-supported racial segregation in the South, particularly in his own state of Mississippi. His battle against racism and other forms of intolerance was a consistent theme in the editorial writing of his own newspaper, in his magazine articles, and in his novel, *The Winds of Fear* (1944).

In that novel, a young journalist, Alan Mabry, tried to bring racial tolerance to the troubled town of Carvell City, a town caught "in this tragic predicament of race." But, as Carter wrote, the racial hatred in his novel "could have happened in almost any of the small towns of the South," and "it might also be happening today in any other section of the country." At the conclusion of *The Winds of Fear*, Alan Mabry sums up his own resistance to racial hatred: "At least, he had confronted the Thing, and the Thing had been for the moment beaten. If you stood against the Thing, then people would eventually listen."

Hodding Carter's writing career was a clear example of one man's stand against the "Thing" of racial bigotry, an attitude shaped in him in childhood. As *Time* magazine once reported, Carter lived with two childhood memories: first, seeing as a six-year-old a gang of white boys chasing a black, and, later, coming across the slain black victim of a lynching.

A Louisianian by birth, he was educated at Bowdoin College in Maine (B.A., 1927) and studied journalism at Columbia University (B.A. Litt., 1928). Carter joined the staff of the New Orleans *Item-Tribune* in 1929 and later became night manager for the United Press in New Orleans. He next served with the Associated Press in Jackson, Miss., as bureau manager, but was dismissed in early 1932 for "insubordination." Carter had married Betty Brunhilde Werlein in October 1931, and they moved to Carter's hometown of Hammond, La., where they launched the *Daily Courier* newspaper.

During the 1932–35 period, one of Carter's chief targets was Louisiana political boss and U.S. Senator Huey Long. After Long's assassination in

1935, Carter moved to Greenville, Miss., where he first established the *Delta Star* newspaper, later merged it with a competitive paper, and became publisher-editor of the *Delta Democrat-Times*.

During World War II, Carter served in the Army Bureau of Public Relations, later helped begin the Middle East editions of *Yank* and *Stars and Stripes*, and also served in intelligence activities.

Returning to Mississippi at age 38, Carter then took up the antibigotry editorial stance that resulted in a 1946 Pulitzer Prize for editorials against racial intolerance. The award specifically cited his pleas for fairness for returning nisei veterans of World War II. In that editorial he had urged his readers to "shoot the works in a fight for tolerance" and suggested that bigotry was always possible, even in a democracy, when "an active minority can have its way against an apathetic majority." Carter remained active as editor until just a few years before his death, when his son, Hodding Carter III, assumed the editorship. Hodding Carter III became widely known in the late 1970s as the State Department spokesman for the administration of President Jimmy Carter.

Hodding Carter's writing includes articles for *American Magazine*, *The New Republic*, *The Nation*, *The Saturday Evening Post*, and the *New York Times Magazine*; among his books are *First Person Rural* (1963); *Where Main Street Meets the River* (1953); *The Winds of Fear* (1944); *Southern Legacy* (1950); *The Angry Scar* (1959); and one volume of verse.

Jere Real
Lynchburg, Virginia

John T. Kneebone, *Southern Liberal Journalists and the Issue of Race, 1920–1944* (1985); Donald Paneth, *The Encyclopedia of American Journalism* (1983); James E. Robinson, "Hodding Carter: Southern Liberal, 1907–1972" (M.A. thesis, Mississippi State University, 1974). ☆

THE COLOR PURPLE

In December 1985 Warner Brothers released the movie version of the novel *The Color Purple* by Georgia native Alice Walker. Produced with a $14 million budget and directed by Steven Spielberg, the film grossed almost $29 million during the first month of its release. Its popularity made it one of the most influential visual portrayals of southern black life.

The novel, for which the author won a Pulitzer Prize and an American Book Award, portrays impoverished southern blacks. Its setting is an imaginary rural Georgia town during the first four decades of the 20th century. The focus is the abuse, struggle, and self-discovery of Celie, a black woman whose letters to God and to and from her sister Nettie comprise the narrative. The strength of relationships between women and the oppression of black women are central themes.

Although the movie brought increased attention to controversial elements in the novel, its own treatment of the story stimulated additional dispute. Critics claimed, for example, that the movie was simplistic and romanticized, distorting the intense and somber tone of Walker's novel. Advertisements for the movie said, "It's about life. It's about love. It's about us. . . . Share the joy." Spielberg's neglect of the novel's lesbian theme caused further complaint, even though the explicitness of the relationship between Celie and blues singer Shug Avery had been partly responsible for criticism of the novel.

Most public controversy, however, focused upon Spielberg's depiction of black men. Many blacks were outraged by the portrayal of black men as violent, abusive, and cowardly. The picketers who marched outside a Los Angeles theater where the movie was premiering were only one group of many (including the National Association for the Advancement of Colored People and the Coalition Against Black Exploitation) that publicly expressed objections. A commonly held view was that the considerations of commercial moviemaking had taken precedence over the sensitive presentation of racial issues in the novel.

On the other hand, supporters heralded the movie as an important milestone for blacks in the film industry. In her contract with the filmmakers, Walker had required that no less than half the cast and crew be women, blacks, or other "Third World" people. Celie's husband, Mr. ———, was played by black actor Danny Glover, who had received acclaim for his work in several other recent movies. The four main women characters were played by Whoopie Goldberg (Celie), Akosua Busia (Nettie), Margaret Avery (Shug), and Oprah Winfrey (Sofia). Goldberg, whose role in the movie marked her screen debut, had initially wanted the part of Sofia, Celie's spirited stepdaughter-in-law. Winfrey was born in Koscuisko, Miss., and is the only one of the four who is actually a native of the South. She, along with Goldberg and Avery, was nominated for an Academy Award, but neither they nor any of the other eight *Color Purple* nominees won.

Contemporary black composer Quincy Jones was one of the film's coproducers and, along with several other songwriters, composed the musical score, which included blues, jazz, African, and gospel music. The score ignited further controversy as parts were said to be suspiciously similar to music written by Frenchman Georges Delerue for a British film, *Our Mother's House*, made almost 20 years earlier.

Despite the controversy surrounding its production and adaptation of Walker's novel, *The Color Purple* was a successful movie. Filmed in North Carolina, Africa, and Hollywood, it received widespread publicity. The product pleased even the story's author, who described it as "a beautiful child of the book."

See also LITERATURE: / Walker, Alice

Jessica Foy
Cooperstown Graduate Programs
Cooperstown, New York

Lisa Belkin, *New York Times* (26 January 1986); Susan Dworkin, *Ms.* (December 1985); Mona Gable, *Wall Street Journal* (19 December 1985); Nan Robertson, *New York Times* (13 February 1986); E. R. Shipp, *New York Times* (27 January 1986); Marie Saxon Silverman, *Variety* (12 March 1986). ☆

CREWS, HARRY
||||||||||||||||||||||||||||||||||||
(b. 1935) Writer.

A son of tenant farmers, Harry Edward Crews was born 6 June 1935 in Bacon County, Ga. Between his life on the subsistence farm and his full professorship in the University of Florida English Department that had denied him admission as a graduate student, he served in the

Marine Corps; attended the University of Florida (B.A., 1960; M.S.Ed., 1962); knocked around the country for 18 months on a motorcycle; taught in a junior high school and a junior college; wrote five-minute daily inspirational stories of achievement for Nelson Boswell, a Florida radio commentator; and passed through the academic ranks at Florida. In 1972 Crews received the Arts and Letters Award from the American Academy and Institute of Arts and Letters.

Harry Crews claims to have written his first novel, a detective story, when he was 13. His first published story, "The Unattached Smile," appeared in 1963; his most recent work, a novel entitled *All We Need of Hell*, was published in 1987. In the intervening years he produced 11 books—8 novels, an autobiography, and 2 collections of essays and stories. Many of his stories first appeared in national magazines, notably *Esquire* and *Playboy*, and he is an example of the prominent place southern writers have long had in those magazines. His stories are rooted in the intersection of biography and history; the biography is poor white, the history is southern. His characters are engaged in a futile struggle to balance the achievement ethic and marketing ethos of modern society against traditional cultural values.

Each of his novels, from *The Gospel Singer* (1968) through *All We Need of Hell*, has received mixed reviews. Critics and reviewers seem unable to agree on either the content or significance of Crews's books. Most, however, react strongly to them. He is in the southern Gothic tradition, and each of his novels has been identified by various critics as his best. Crews's comments on his own work suggest that he regards *Naked in Garden Hills* (1969), *The Gypsy's Curse* (1974), and *A Childhood: The Biography of a Place* (1978) as among his best.

A Childhood is a superb ethnography of a rural subsistence community from the perspective of Crews's people. It details the first five years of his life and traces the consequences of the transition from subsistence farming to a one-crop agricultural and industrial economy. The autobiography shows that Crews's fiction follows the survivors of that culture, whose hermetic seal was broken by the intrusion of the outside world or, more commonly, the outmigration of its inhabitants. *A Childhood* and *A Feast of Snakes* (1976), two of his most widely acclaimed works, may be the best examples of the literary and analytic talents of Harry Crews.

His works illuminate both an internal struggle—heart versus mind—and an eternal struggle—man versus society and culture. His characters, often "freaks," come to appear less unusual as their struggles with each other, place, time, and culture create the story. Crews's work provides important insights into the Americanization of the South and the southernization of America.

Harry Crews's other books are *This Thing Don't Lead to Heaven* (1970), *Karate Is a Thing of the Spirit* (1971), *Car* (1972), *The Hawk Is Dying* (1973), *Blood and Grits* (1979), and *Florida Frenzy* (1982).

Larry W. DeBord
University of Mississippi

Larry W. DeBord and Gary L. Long, *Southern Quarterly* (Spring 1982); David K. Jeffrey and Donald R. Noble, *Southern Quarterly* (Winter 1981); Gary L. Long and

Larry W. DeBord, *Texas Review* (Fall–Winter 1983). ☆

CURTIZ, MICHAEL
|||||||||||||||||||||||||||||||||||||||||||||
(1888–1962) Film director.

Ironically, this director, who ranks with D. W. Griffith and King Vidor in shaping the celluloid image of the South, was neither born nor raised in America, let alone in the South. Born in Budapest in 1888, Michael Curtiz (née Mihaly Kertesz) was one of the film world's most prolific and versatile directors. The peripatetic Hungarian directed more than three dozen films in seven European countries before Warner Brothers brought him to Hollywood in 1926, where he completed well over 100 more films of extraordinary variety. While working within the Warners' studio system, he gained a reputation as a harsh taskmaster on the set, often barking out orders in his celebrated fractured English. Among the many westerns, swashbucklers, social dramas, musical comedies, and romantic adventures directed by the colorful Curtiz were several that dealt with expressly southern themes.

The first to appear was *Cabin in the Cotton* (1932), a melodrama featuring Bette Davis and Richard Barthelmess in the midst of bitter struggles between sharecroppers and landowners in the cotton-growing South. Lynchings and child marriages were among the topics of Curtiz's 1937 *Mountain Justice*, which told the story of a young nurse (Josephine Hutchinson) who helped a doctor set up a clinic in the Tennessee mountains, much to the outrage of her Bible-thumping father. Three years later, Curtiz directed a "southern-western" entitled *Virginia City*, which

starred Miriam Hopkins as a Confederate spy seeking to transfer $5 million of Nevada gold to CSA coffers. She was helped by fellow Confederate spy Randolph Scott, but hindered (and inevitably romanced) by dashing Yankee Errol Flynn.

Curtiz continued to explore southern themes following World War II with *Flamingo Road* (1949), which traced the fortunes of a tough young woman (Joan Crawford) from her job as a carnival dancer through her romance with a deputy sheriff (Zachary Scott) to her eventual marriage to a prominent southern politician. *Bright Leaf* followed two years later, focusing on the rise and fall of a vengeful North Carolina tobacco magnate (Gary Cooper) at the turn of the century. As a publicity tactic, Warner Brothers held the film's world premiere in Raleigh, N.C.

Curtiz left Warner Brothers during the 1950s to direct for other American film companies, but the resulting films were generally inferior to his cinematic output of the 1930s and 1940s. Among these films was *The Proud Rebel* (1958), about the efforts of a Confederate veteran (Alan Ladd) to help his young son who had been struck dumb on seeing his mother killed by Sherman's troops. The same year saw the creation of *King Creole*, an adaptation of Harold Robbins's *A Stone for Danny Fisher*. Set in New Orleans, the film centered on a young Bourbon Street nightclub performer (Elvis Presley) and his conflicts with his father and a gangster. The seaminess of the novel was toned down considerably for this early Presley vehicle. Two years later, Curtiz directed a remake of *The Adventures of Huckleberry Finn*, starring Eddie Hodges in a wholesome portrayal of the title character and boxing champion Archie

Moore in a remarkable performance as Jim. Curtiz's last film was *The Comancheros* (1961), a strictly standard western featuring John Wayne battling renegades in Texas. Curtiz died in 1962.

Martin F. Norden
University of Massachusetts
at Amherst

Kingsley Canham, *The Hollywood Professionals* (1973); Martin F. Norden, *Southern Quarterly* (Spring–Summer 1981). ☆

DABNEY, VIRGINIUS
||||||||||||||||||||||||||||||||||||||||||||||||||||||
(b. 1901) Journalist and author.

Born and raised in Charlottesville, Va., Virginius Dabney completed a bachelor's and a master's degree and graduated Phi Beta Kappa from the University of Virginia, where his father was a professor of history. After graduation Dabney began his journalism career in 1922 as a reporter for the Richmond *News-Leader*. Six years later he became an editor for the Richmond *Times-Dispatch* and in 1936 assumed the position of editor-in-chief. Dabney edited the Richmond *Times-Dispatch* between 1936 and 1969, winning the Pulitzer Prize in 1948 and other awards for his editorials. In *Liberalism in the South* (1932), Dabney chronicled a southern liberal tradition that embraced Thomas Jefferson as its leader and defended civil liberties and intellectual freedom. Through the 1930s Dabney's editorials expanded upon these values, defending the right of labor to organize, aid to distressed sharecroppers, elimination of the poll tax, and legislation to prevent lynchings.

His *Below the Potomac* (1942) reported optimistically on the state of the region but also evidenced his early recognition of potentially powerful challenges to racial segregation. Like most white southern liberals, Dabney believed that racial justice could be achieved without abandoning segregation. Black protest against Jim Crow during World War II disturbed him, and he warned the nation of an impending racial crisis. His editorial proposal to abolish segregation on public transportation in Richmond (1943) and his part in the founding of the Southern Regional Council (1944) reflected these fears, and he tried but failed to defuse black militance through demonstrations of white goodwill. His conviction that growing pressure on an unwilling South for racial reform portended disaster contributed to his postwar shift toward conservatism.

When the U.S. Supreme Court outlawed school segregation in 1954, Dabney acknowledged that the South must comply with the decision and endorsed local option as the best means to slow the change. Advocates of massive resistance to desegregation, however, insisted upon total white solidarity, and Dabney reluctantly acquiesced. After the courts rejected Virginia's massive resistance, Dabney returned to his persistent editorial theme of gradualism in reform as preferable to protest and conflict. By the time of his retirement, few recalled his onetime reputation as a leading southern liberal. Since retirement Dabney has written several popular books on Virginia's history. These works display a mix of decency and defensiveness characteristic of southern liberalism before the civil rights movement. Dabney's career reflects the prominent role journalists played in 20th-century southern liberalism and also reveals how swiftly southern race relations have changed since World War II.

See also SOCIAL CLASS: / Southern Regional Council

John T. Kneebone
Virginia State Library

Virginius Dabney, *Across the Years: Memories of a Virginian* (1978); John T. Kneebone, *Southern Liberal Journalists and the Issue of Race, 1920–1944* (1985); Morton Sosna, *In Search of the Silent South: Southern Liberals and the Race Issue* (1977). ☆

DANIELS, JONATHAN

(1902–1981) Journalist and author.

Jonathan Worth Daniels was born 26 April 1902, the son of Josephus Daniels, owner and editor of the Raleigh (N.C.) *News and Observer*. He grew up in Raleigh and in Washington, where his father served as secretary of the navy. After receiving B.A. and M.A. degrees in English from the University of North Carolina, he studied law briefly at Columbia University before entering journalism. He wrote for the Louisville (Ky.) *Times*, the *News and Observer*, and *Fortune* magazine in the 1920s, and in 1933 became the editor of the Raleigh daily. During World War II he served as an administrative assistant to the president; he resumed the editorship of the family paper after his father's death in 1948 and relinquished it only in the late 1960s.

From an early age Daniels dissented from southern cultural norms regarding religion, sex, liquor, gambling, and race. His 1921 college yearbook described him as "very impressionable to anything that smacks of innovation just so it threatens some old, traditional customs; therefore, he is of that coterie styled as the left wing of Carolina thinkers." In 1930, for example, his novel *Clash of Angels* satirized conventional religious dogma. The editor earned a reputation in the 1930s as a southern liberal because of his ardent support for the New Deal, his defense of organized labor, and his proposals for equal treatment of blacks. W. J. Cash even described Daniels in 1941 as "sometimes waxing almost too uncritical in his eagerness to champion the underdog." After World War II, Daniels allied with the state's two leading liberal politicians, Frank P. Graham and Kerr W. Scott. More important, he endorsed the *Brown* v. *Board of Education* decision and led the opposition in North Carolina to massive resistance to school desegregation.

Daniels expressed his liberal views on the *News and Observer*'s editorial page and in dozens of essays and more

Jonathan Daniels, editor of the Raleigh News and Observer, *c. 1950*

than a score of books. His popular *A Southerner Discovers the South* (1938) explored the changes occurring in race relations, agriculture, and industry and recounted stories about southerners in the Depression. Three years later *Tar Heels* provided a more detailed portrait of his native state. His understanding of southern history influenced much of Daniels's work. In 1938, for instance, he saw the South's faults but claimed that the Civil War had only "served as an alibi—a magnificent alibi—for them all"; instead of excuses Daniels wanted change. In the tumultuous 1950s Daniels saw parallels with Reconstruction and acknowledged that in neither period was any side faultless. His constant attention to southern themes revealed Daniels's affection for his region at the same time he implored it to change. The Charlotte *Observer* hailed Daniels as "a graceful writer and tart social critic" and "a force for progress in North Carolina" and the South.

See also EDUCATION: / Graham, Frank P.; LAW: / *Brown* v. *Board of Education*

Charles W. Eagles
University of Mississippi

Charlotte *Observer* (10 November 1981); Jonathan Worth Daniels Papers, Southern Historical Collection, University of North Carolina; Charles W. Eagles, *Jonathan Daniels and Race Relations: The Evolution of a Southern Liberal* (1982). ☆

DAVIS, BETTE
‖‖‖‖‖‖‖‖‖‖‖‖‖‖‖‖‖‖‖‖‖‖‖‖‖‖‖‖‖‖‖‖‖‖
(b. 1908) Actress.

Born in Lowell, Mass., in 1908, Bette (Ruth Elizabeth) Davis made her stage debut in 1928, but fame came from her long film career, which began in 1931. Bette Davis has played a variety of roles—the good sister, the supportive wife, the career woman, and the courageous martyr. Nevertheless, she gained notoriety for a specific type of character, "the bitch," which was introduced in her first portrayal of a southern woman. Madge Norwood, the blond, rich seductress of a bewildered sharecropper, evoked both sensuality and aloofness in *Cabin in the Cotton* (1932). Although Bette Davis went on to play unpleasant women who were not southerners, some of her most notable characters were belles whose behavior tended both to symbolize and to indict southern culture.

Davis's characterizations were always more or less femmes fatales. A repertoire of mannerisms—darting eyes that signify duplicity, gestures verging on the hyperkinetic, and a strutting, confident walk—convey both toughness and vulnerability. These gestures helped to define the film image of the high-strung southern belle. Davis's bad women sought liberation from social and cultural definitions of women's roles, but their transgressions were always contained within those very definitions—hence, the power and pathos of many of her performances. They encouraged audiences to scrutinize not only the sinning woman but the culture that judged her. Davis's wicked southern women of the late 1930s and early 1940s anticipated the degenerate belles of post–World War II motion pictures.

In *Jezebel* (1938) Julie Marsden's defiance of the rules of behavior imposed by antebellum New Orleans society was connected with the decadence of that society. The plague that permitted Julie to sacrifice herself to achieve redemption also pointed to the South's failure to confront its own backwardness. Regina Giddens and her brothers, in *The Little Foxes* (1941), represented the capitalist New South—greedy exploiters who cared little for their community and upstarts who lacked the charm and sensibilities of the Old South. Yet Regina's viciousness derived, in part, from impotent rejection of the stultifying systems, old or new, which permitted no outlet for the satisfaction of her desires. Desire impelled Stanley Timberlake in the adaptation of Ellen Glasgow's *In This Our Life* (1942) to destroy one man and nearly destroy another—a black prelaw student who was accused of the hit-and-run murder that she committed. Selfish and unrepentent to her death, Stanley represented the unchecked darker side of a contemporary South split between the declining genteel traditions, which are associated with progressive reformism, and the advancing forces of avarice.

Davis's Maggie in *The Great Lie* (1941) was a mature, stable southern woman who represented simplicity and traditional values. When Maggie prevails over a selfish, urban northerner in a love triangle, the country of Maryland's landed gentry and loyal retainers is the victor in a dramatic opposition frequently employed in American media. And there is Charlotte in *Hush . . . Hush, Sweet Charlotte* (1964), a mixture of southern Gothic and horror film. Maligned by the community for a murder she did not commit, the repellant, childlike recluse is, in a narrative reversal, victimized by her charming Yankee cousin.

Ida Jeter
St. Mary's College
Moraga, California

Bette Davis, *The Lonely Life: An Autobiography* (1962); Whitney Stine with Bette Davis, *Mother Goddam* (1975). ☆

DIXON, THOMAS, JR., AND FILM

Thomas Dixon Jr.'s Klan novels became the literary source for *Birth of a Nation* (1915), one of the most historically important and financially successful movies in the early American film industry. The film, one of the first feature-length motion pictures, is remembered for its technical innovations, its romantic depiction of the South, and its racial views.

D. W. Griffith and his company purchased the rights from Dixon to make a film based on *The Clansman* for a large percentage of the profits from the movie. Griffith, the most prominent filmmaker of his day and himself a southerner, was willing to pay dearly for the rights because the topic of a southerner returning home after the Civil War to a changed society appealed to him and provided him with a vehicle for telling the southern version of the war and Reconstruction.

The plot of the film remained basically that of *The Clansman*, with significant additions drawn from Dixon's stage plays of *The Clansman* and *The Leopard's Spots*. Griffith did, however, make important shifts in tone: he made the novel's racism less inflammatory, all but eliminated Dixon's view of a commercialized South, and deemphasized the novel's detailed history of the Ku Klux Klan.

Dixon claimed that up to the time of the New York screening of the film it had retained the title of the novel, but he became so carried away with the film's drama during this screening he cried out that it should be given the grander title, *Birth of a Nation*. The story is doubted by later scholars but has become part of the myth surrounding the film.

Dixon's success with *Birth of a Nation* led him to other film projects. He established the Dixon Studios, and from 1916 to 1923 he produced five additional films, including one entitled *The Fall of a Nation* (1916), which expressed fear that America's early pacifism during World War I would lead to its destruction. The other films were based on Dixon's writings and promoted his social and economic theories, but none brought the financial success or critical acclaim of the first film with which he was associated.

See also LITERATURE: / Dixon, Thomas, Jr.; VIOLENCE: / Ku Klux Klan

Robert A. Armour
Virginia Commonwealth University

Robert M. Henderson, *D. W. Griffith: His Life and Work* (1972); Russell Merritt, *Cinema Journal* (1972). ☆

DUKES OF HAZZARD

The mass media's fascination with southern idiosyncrasies has contributed to television's celebration of the South's alleged differences from the rest of the nation. Whereas television's main characters, both fictional and real, have traditionally been intelligent, well educated, successful, affluent, and middle class, this is not so if the characters are southerners. The highly rated *Dukes of Hazzard* provided a 1980s view of a southern extended family (Uncle Jesse and cousins Bo, Luke, and Daisy Duke) in weekly episodes in which they fought for "truth, justice and wild driving." Perhaps the real star of the show was the boys' souped-up Dodge Charger, appropriately named "General Lee." This car served as the show's tribute to southern stock car racing and was regularly wrecked several times during each show. Most critics bombed the *Dukes*, but viewers, particularly in the South, loved it and kept it in the top 10 in the Nielsen ratings for several seasons.

Plots on *Dukes* revolved around the Duke clan and their run-ins with the Hazzard mayor, Boss J. D. Hogg, and his sidekick, Sheriff Roscoe P. Coltrane, or various outsiders who came into town and stirred up trouble in Hazzard County. As has often been the media stereotype, southern politicians and law enforcement officers were caricatured as zany, ignorant incompetents. The good old Duke boys were handsome; Uncle Jesse was wise and unflappable; and cousin Daisy was usually portrayed as a scantily clad, ultra-feminine tomboy. The show's theme song, sung by the outlaw country singer Waylon Jennings, set the stage for the action. Bo and Luke Duke were just good old boys who never meant any harm, but they had been in trouble with the law since they were born. This stereotype of rowdy boys and corrupt politicians and law enforcers has regularly been applied to southerners by the media.

The stereotypes included in *Dukes of Hazzard* fostered the viewers' image of the South as a wild and crazy place where most people were basically simple and good, but a few were merely simple. Middle-class morality and cleanliness were linked to southern rural poverty and good times in themes rich with the adolescent fantasy of outwitting the law. The portrayal of the South as a frontierland populated by independent souls in charge of their own destinies undoubtedly led to some of the show's popularity among southerners. This theme of individual rights also reflected American ideals and drew a large following from the rest of the nation as well. In some ways the South was portrayed as a land of opportunity. According to *Dukes*, if you have enough gumption and a good heart, all your dreams can come true. *Dukes* considered the South to be a land of freedom, escape, laughter, traditional moral values, and simple people. Good and evil were easily defined, and the good guys always won.

Marsha McGee
Northeast Louisiana University

David Johnston, *TV Guide* (12 July 1980); Horace Newcomb, ed., *Television, the Critical View* (1979). ☆

DUNAWAY, FAYE
(b. 1941) Actress.

Faye Dunaway was born 14 January 1941, in Bascom, Fla., the daughter of a career army officer. She distinguished herself as a member of the University of Florida's student acting company, and after further training, she joined the new Lincoln Center Repertory Company in New York in 1962. After a succession of roles on and off Broadway, her performance in *Hogan's Goat* led to her film debut in *The Happening* (1967). She quickly established herself as a major star only a few months later with her performance as the ill-fated Bonnie Par-

ker in Arthur Penn's *Bonnie and Clyde*, one of the films that marked the turn from western to southern settings in popular adventure dramas.

Although this performance earned her an Academy Award nomination, she has not since been typecast in southern roles. Rather, selecting her relatively infrequent performances with great care, she has played demanding roles in films with varied international settings. She was nominated for a second Academy Award for her performance in Roman Polanski's *Chinatown* (1974), and she was at last honored as best actress for her portrayal of a tough television executive in *Network* (1976).

See also VIOLENCE: / "Bonnie and Clyde"

Warren French
Indiana University

Amy Gross, *Vogue* (March 1979); Jack Hamilton, *Look* (13 December 1966); Charles Moritz, ed., *Current Biography* (1973). ☆

FAULKNER, WILLIAM, AND FILM

William Faulkner wrote screenplays for most of his adult life. Although he considered fiction his primary interest and achievement and often denigrated his screenwriting and many studio practices, he indicated admiration for such films as *Citizen Kane*, *The Magnificent Ambersons*, and *High Noon* and satisfaction with his own work for directors Howard Hawks and Jean Renoir. His friendship and collaboration with Hawks led to the films *Today We Live* (1933, Faulkner's first screen credit, from his story "Turn About"), *The Road* to Glory (1936), *To Have and Have Not* (1944), *The Big Sleep* (1946), and *Land of the Pharaohs* (1955, Faulkner's last screen credit). Faulkner contributed significantly to these films and also wrote for Hawks some scenes for *Air Force* (1943) and several unproduced scripts, including *War Birds* (1933), *Sutter's Gold* (1934), *Dreadful Hollow* (1943), and *Battle Cry* (1943). For Renoir he wrote much of *The Southerner* (1945).

Faulkner went to Hollywood in 1932, perhaps with the intention of writing a vehicle for Tallulah Bankhead, which may have been *The College Widow*. He worked at MGM for one year, although much of his work was done at his home in Oxford, Miss., and mailed to the studio. Early scripts were often closely related to the themes of his fiction. His first treatment, *Manservant* (1932), was an adaptation of his story "Love"; *The College Widow* (1932) was often reminiscent of *Sanctuary*; *Turn About*, released as *Today We Live*, included some interesting twists on *The Sound and the Fury*; *War Birds* concerned the wartime experiences of John and Bayard Sartoris and was a significant link between *Flags in the Dust* and *The Unvanquished*; and the *Mythical Latin-American Kingdom Story* (1933) reflected an active interest in the Conrad of *Nostromo*. Like most of the scripts he produced at this time, the treatments *Absolution* (1932) and *Flying the Mail* (1932) were centrally concerned with aviation and possibly reflected his disappointment at not having flown in combat during World War I. Of all these, only *Turn About* was filmed and released. His work on the film *Lazy River* (1934) was not used.

Faulkner later worked at 20th-Century Fox, receiving screen credit on *The Road to Glory* and *Slave Ship* (1937)

and doing uncredited work on *Banjo on My Knee* (1936), *Four Men and a Prayer* (1936), *Submarine Patrol* (1938), and *Drums along the Mohawk* (1939). Other work at this time included material for *Gunga Din* (RKO, 1939) and *Dance Hall* (Fox, 1941). (The dates given refer to the release date of each produced film; Faulkner was at Fox from 1935 to 1937.) Of this group, only *The Road to Glory* and an unpublished screenplay for *Drums along the Mohawk* can be considered significant work.

Faulkner was at Warner Brothers on a ruinous seven-year contract that began in 1942, but he did no work for them after 1945. He worked on many unproduced films during this period or provided interesting scripts that were not used on produced films. The best unproduced scripts were *The De Gaulle Story* (1942), *Country Lawyer* (1943), and *Fog over London* (1944). The best screenplays that were rejected were for the produced films *Mildred Pierce* (1945) and *Stallion Road* (1947). He made recognizable contributions to the produced films *Deep Valley* (1947) and *The Adventures of Don Juan* (1945) and also worked on such films as *Northern Pursuit* (1943), *God Is My Co-Pilot* (1945), and *Escape in the Desert* (1945). A 1943 story conference on *Who?*, a film about the unknown soldier, gave him the basic idea for his novel *A Fable*. During this period he wrote several independent scripts of special interest: *Dreadful Hollow* (c. 1943, for Hawks, about vampires), *Revolt in the Earth* (1942, loosely adapted from *Absalom, Absalom!*), and *Barn Burning* (1945, from his story of the same name). His best work from this period includes the shooting script for *To Have and Have Not*, the first draft of *The Big Sleep* (coauthored with Leigh Brackett), contributions to *The South-*

erner (which have not yet been precisely identified; Renoir and Faulkner each claimed to have written the script), and *Dreadful Hollow.*

After his term at Warner Brothers, Faulkner wrote several teleplays, including an adaptation of his novella *Old Man* (1953); CBS produced his teleplays *The Brooch* (1953), *Shall Not Perish* (1954), and *The Graduation Dress* (1960). He performed minor revisions on the script for MGM's film *Intruder in the Dust* (1949, directed by Clarence Brown and shot in Oxford) and went to Egypt with Hawks to work on *Land of the Pharaohs.*

Of the many Faulkner novels adapted for the screen by others by far the worst is *The Sound and the Fury* (1959, directed by Martin Ritt). Others include *The Story of Temple Drake* (1933, from *Sanctuary,* directed by Stephen Roberts; a relatively scandalous film that contributed to the demand for a production code); *Intruder in the Dust,* generally regarded as a classic; *The Tarnished Angels* (1957, from *Pylon,* stylishly directed by Douglas Sirk); *The Long Hot Summer* (1958, from *The Hamlet,* directed by Martin Ritt); *Sanctuary* (1961, from *Sanctuary* and *Requiem for a Nun,* directed by Tony Richardson); and *The Reivers* (1969, directed by Mark Rydell). A recent adaptation is Faulkner's story "Tomorrow" in a fine film distinguished by an excellent script by Horton Foote (*Tomorrow,* 1971, directed by Joseph Anthony). Faulkner short stories were filmed in the 1980s as *A Rose for Emily, Two Soldiers, The Bear,* and *Barn Burning.*

The South was a significant presence in Faulkner's film writing. Southern characters or locations are important aspects of *The College Widow, Absolution,*

War Birds (alternate title, *A Ghost Story*), *Louisiana Lou* (*Lazy River*), *Banjo on My Knee, Revolt in the Earth, Deep Valley, Country Lawyer* (one of his best), *Battle Cry,* and of course *The Southerner.*

See also LITERATURE: / Faulkner, William

Bruce F. Kawin
University of Colorado
at Boulder

Regina L. Fadiman, *Faulkner's Intruder in the Dust: Novel into Film* (1977); Evans Harrington and Ann J. Abadie, eds., *Faulkner, Modernism, and Film: Faulkner and Yoknapatawpha, 1978* (1979); Bruce F. Kawin, *Faulkner and Film* (1977), *Faulkner's MGM Screenplays* (1982), with Tino Balio, eds., *To Have and Have Not* (1980); George Sidney, "Faulkner in Hollywood: A Study of His Career as a Scenarist" (Ph.D. dissertation, University of New Mexico, 1959). ☆

FOOTE, HORTON
(b. 1916) Writer.

Horton Foote, playwright and award-winning television and motion picture writer, was born in Wharton, Tex., and began his career as an actor. From 1933 to 1935 he studied at the Pasadena Playhouse Theatre and from 1937 to 1939 at an acting school in New York City. He appeared in several Broadway plays in the late 1930s and early 1940s and from 1942 to 1945 managed a production company in Washington, D.C., where he also taught playwriting.

Foote's first play to be produced professionally was *Texas Town,* which opened at the Provincetown Playhouse in New York in 1942. A number of his plays were produced on Broadway, among them *Only the Heart* (1944), *The*

Chase (1952), *The Trip to Bountiful* (1953), and *The Traveling Lady* (1954). Much of Foote's best work has been done in television, a medium that he entered when he wrote a teleplay for *The Kraft Television Theatre* in 1947. His work was frequently seen on *Playhouse 90*, *DuPont Show of the Week*, and other important dramatic series during the so-called Golden Age of Television in the 1950s. His adaptation of Harper Lee's *To Kill a Mockingbird* (1962) earned him an Academy Award for best screenplay based on material from another source.

Foote's other film credits include *Baby, the Rain Must Fall* (1965); *Tender Mercies* (1983), for which Robert Duvall received an Academy Award for best actor; *The Trip to Bountiful* (1985), for which Geraldine Page received an Academy Award for best actress; and *1918* (1985), which starred the writer's daughter, Hallie Foote. He has also done adaptations of stories by southern writers such as Flannery O'Connor (*The Displaced Person*) and William Faulkner (*Old Man, Barn Burning, Tomorrow*).

Most of Horton Foote's plays and films have been set in the fictional town of Harrison, Tex. Foote's strength, as more than one writer has noted, has been his ear for the speech of his part of the country.

Charles East
Baton Rouge, Louisiana

Samuel G. Freedman, *New York Times Magazine* (9 February 1986); Joseph R. Millichap, in *American Screenwriters: Dictionary of Literary Biography*, vol. 26, ed. Robert E. Morsberger, Stephen O. Lesser, and Randall Clark (1984); *Who's Who in the Theatre: A Biographical Record of the Contemporary Stage*, vol. 1: Biographies (1981). ☆

FORD, JOHN
||||||||||||||||||||||||||||||||
(1895–1973) Film director.

One of America's most famous filmmakers, John Ford was also one of the foremost interpreters of its land and legends. Born Sean O'Feeney to Irish immigrant parents in Cape Elizabeth, Me., he followed his brother Francis to Hollywood, where he directed his first movie in 1917. From that time his name became almost synonymous with the western genre; in fact, the look of the West was, for most moviegoers, established by Ford's many films using Monument Valley in Utah as a backdrop. Interspersed among his numerous westerns, however, is a large body of films devoted to the South and its lifestyles. Approximately 11 works, including films like *Steamboat 'Round the Bend* (1935), *Tobacco Road* (1941), *The Sun Shines Bright* (1954), and *The Horse Soldiers* (1959), focus on the region's distinctive people and places.

Because he did not have a personal familiarity with the South to draw on, Ford often turned to the widespread myths and stereotypes of popular literature, which account for both the strengths and weaknesses of his films. Three works, for instance, were based on the local color writings of Irvin S. Cobb, and they carry over some of the racial stereotypes and cultural beliefs of that source. Because his was essentially a South of the imagination, though, Ford placed far less weight on the distinctive look of the region than was the case in his westerns. Instead, he grounded these films in character, especially focusing on figures who live in the backwash of the Civil War. Inhabiting a fallen world—or one in the midst of that fall—these characters are called upon to impart order to their community, to hold fast to a set of values when all ideals seem called into question. Consequently, a human landscape dominates these films and substitutes for the more iconic geography of his westerns.

Ford's primary interest was always the nature of the human community, and its capacity to endure through the strength of its individual members formed the abiding theme of his films. This communal motif links his famous westerns—*Stagecoach*, *My Darling Clementine*, *The Searchers*—to films as diverse as the Welsh coal-mining saga, *How Green Was My Valley*; the dust-bowl tale, *The Grapes of Wrath*; and his comedy about the South Seas, *Donovan's Reef*. In his southern films he fashioned a mythos that speaks clearly to a traditional concern with the individual and his community that has always marked southern culture.

J. P. Telotte
Georgia Institute of Technology

Peter Bogdanovich, *John Ford* (1978); Tag Gallagher, *John Ford: The Man and His Films* (1986); Andrew Sinclair, *John Ford* (1979). ☆

FREEMAN, DOUGLAS SOUTHALL
‖‖
(1886–1953) Editor and biographer.

By virtue of his authorship of seven magisterial volumes, Douglas Southall Freeman achieved national fame in the 1940s as the preeminent authority on Confederate military history. He was already a notable figure in his native Virginia as editor of the Richmond *News Leader* (1915–49), a radio newscaster, and a frequent public orator. Though his career broadened in his later life, Freeman steadfastly refused to leave Richmond. As professor of journalism at Columbia University from 1934 to 1941, he fulfilled his teaching obligations there one day each week and commuted overnight from Richmond to New York by Pullman.

Both Freeman's devotion to Virginia and his discipline that allowed him several simultaneous careers followed naturally from the example of his father, a veteran of Lee's army and a strong advocate of order, industry, and perseverance. At 17 Douglas accompanied his father to a Confederate reunion and determined to record for posterity the heroism of his elder's army. After graduation from Richmond College he equipped himself with a doctorate in history from Johns Hopkins University with that specific goal in mind. He also wanted a public career, and only in 1915, the year he assumed the newspaper editorship, did he begin to work on *R. E. Lee*. Twenty years later the four-volume biography received a Pulitzer Prize, but only after Freeman finally assigned himself a weekly stint of 14 hours to ensure its completion. His strict regimen (he allowed himself 17 minutes, precisely, to drive to work) was only possible, Freeman often remarked, because he had a remarkably cooperative wife, Inez Goddin Freeman.

The quality Freeman most admired in his cavalcade of heroes was fortitude, which Lee exemplified almost perfectly in Freeman's view. The commander's subordinates, as *Lee's Lieutenants* (1942–44) would demonstrate, mustered impressive fortitude along with some very human frailties. Freeman considered the three volumes of the *Lieutenants* his best work, and critics have generally agreed.

To embark on an attempted definitive

biography of George Washington when Freeman was 58 and still a busy public figure was an ambitious undertaking, but he lived to complete six volumes (1948–54) and to cover all but six years of his subject's life. After his assistants wrote the final volume, the completed work earned Freeman a posthumous second Pulitzer Prize in biography. Not as popular as the Confederate books, *George Washington*, the final tribute from a puritan son to his symbolic ancestors, nevertheless strengthened Freeman's position as one of the foremost American biographers of his time.

John L. Gignilliat
Agnes Scott College

John L. Gignilliat, in *Twentieth Century American Historians: Dictionary of Literary Biography*, vol. 17, ed. Robert E. Morsberger, Stephen O. Lesser, and Randall Clark (1984); Dumas Malone, in *George Washington*, vol. 6, by Douglas Southall Freeman (1954); T. Harry Williams, *Journal of Southern History* (February 1955). ☆

GOLDEN, HARRY
||||||||||||||||||||||||||||||||||||||||||||
(1902–1981) Editor, publisher, author.

Born Harry Goldhirsch and raised on the Lower East Side of New York, Harry Golden moved to Charlotte, N.C., to work as a salesman and a reporter during the Depression. In 1941 he founded *The Carolina Israelite*, a one-man newspaper published until 1968 with a national circulation at its peak of 40,000. A collection of his pieces was published in 1958 under the title *Only in America*, which became a national best-seller and was followed by 19 other books. "I got away with my ideas in the South," he said, "because no Southerner takes me—a Jew, a Yankee, and a radical—

seriously. They mostly think of a Jew as a substitute Negro, anyway."

A roly-poly American original, he sat in his Kennedy rocker with his feet barely touching the floor, like a Jewish Buddha with a cigar. The office walls were crowded with books and dozens of autographed pictures of famous acquaintances who subscribed to the paper, such as Carl Sandburg, Harry Truman, William Faulkner, John F. Kennedy, Bertrand Russell, Ernest Hemingway, and Adlai Stevenson. In the corner stood his celebrated cracker barrel where he threw finished articles for the paper, which went to press when the barrel was full.

His numerous "Golden plans" infuriated segregationists and delighted southern intellectuals, not because they were absurd but because they were rooted sufficiently in southern myth to work perfectly well should anyone be astute enough to try them. When the South became embroiled in school desegregation and "massive resistance," he proposed the "Vertical Integration Plan," which stated that:

> The white and Negro stand at the same grocery and supermarket counters; deposit money at the same bank teller's window; pay phone and light bills to the same clerk; walk through the same dime and department stores and stand at the same drugstore counters. It is only when the Negro "sets" that the fur begins to fly.
>
> . . . Instead of all those complicated proposals, all the next session needs to do is pass one small amendment which would provide *only* desks in all the public schools of our state—*no seats*. The desks should be those standing-up jobs, like the old-fashioned bookkeep-

ing desk. Since no one in the South pays the slightest attention to a vertical Negro, this will completely solve our problem . . . in fact this may be a blessing in disguise. They are not learning to read sitting down anyway; maybe standing up will help.

His "White Baby Plan" sprang from his mind when he read of two black schoolteachers who wanted to see a revival of Olivier's *Hamlet* in a segregated movie theater and borrowed the white children of two friends to take in with them. They were sold tickets without hesitation; prompting Golden to suggest:

. . . People can pool their children at a central point in each neighborhood, and every time a Negro wants to go to the movies all she need do is pick up a white child— and go.

Eventually the Negro community can set up a factory and manufacture white babies made of plastic, and when they want to go to the opera or to a concert, all they need do is carry that plastic doll in their arms. The dolls, of course, should all have blond curls and blue eyes.

Golden punched the paunches of a lot of southern politicians who were taking themselves too seriously and stirring up fears of the black. He had no peer when it came to poking holes in southern segregation and pointing up the South's hypocrisy by manipulating its mores. He proposed a way to solve the problems of busing school children and of prayer in schools in one grand step, by permitting "prayers on the bus instead of the classroom."

With national fame came the revelation that in 1929 he had been sentenced to four years in prison for mail fraud resulting from the misdeeds of a brokerage firm he ran. He had pleaded guilty and had served 18 months, after which he was paroled. After imprisonment Golden had returned to his Irish Catholic wife, the former Genevieve Gallagher, and his four sons, changed his name, and moved to North Carolina to start a new life. In December 1973 President Richard M. Nixon gave Golden a full pardon.

He was often the target of threats of violence, yet his humor seemed to be his armor, leading eventually to his full acceptance by the southern establishment that honored him with degrees and awards. When his home was burned down in 1958, the Charlotte police and the FBI helped him decipher the charred list of *Carolina Israelite* subscribers.

Two years before he died on 2 October 1981, he summed up his life by saying he was "a newspaper man, an American, a Jew, a Democrat and a Zionist, in that order." The Raleigh *News and Observer* added on his death that "he was also a highly literate prophet and satirist whose views and commentary made a beneficial difference in the affairs of the South and the nation."

Eli Evans
Revson Foundation

Eli Evans, *The Provincials: A Personal History of Jews in the South* (1974); *New York Times* (3 October 1981). ☆

GONE WITH THE WIND
||||||||||||||||||||||||||||||||||||||||||||||||||||||||||||

Gone with the Wind is the preeminent example of the Civil War and Reconstruction novel. Written by the Atlantan Margaret Mitchell between about 1926 and 1930, it was published in 1936, won the Pulitzer Prize, and has enjoyed unmatched popularity for a novel, becoming part of national and regional folk culture.

The novel tells the story of the rise and fall of the planter class through the fictional histories of southern families. Against this background of chaos and disintegration, Mitchell narrates the history of one woman's survival. Scarlett O'Hara, a giddy belle before the conflict, overcomes the deprivations of war and reconstruction to achieve the wealth and power of a New South entrepreneur. Finally, Mitchell interweaves these themes with the more personal one of unrequited love: Scarlett's for the dreamy aristocrat Ashley Wilkes, and Rhett Butler's for Scarlett.

Especially after David Selznick's romanticized film version of 1939, the novel has been taken as the quintessential representation of the moonlight-and-magnolias plantation romance. It does deal with the romantic themes, particularly as represented in southern literature of the late 19th century. It introduces old-school aristocrats and young gallants, stereotypical belles and great ladies; it celebrates faithful slaves and loyal blacks; it condemns worthless field hands and troublemaking freedmen; and political reconstruction is presented as unrelieved violence, corruption, and profligacy.

Yet the novel breaks significantly with the conventional romance and includes major motifs of modernist fiction and 20th-century culture. It debunks and demythologizes: Mitchell represents the planter class as a wildly mixed lot mostly of arrivistes and self-made men who inhabit a crude frontier. The

Clark Gable and Vivien Leigh as Rhett Butler and Scarlett O'Hara in **Gone with the Wind** *(1939)*

novel also manifests insistent tendencies toward realism: it depicts the horrors of war, the shallowness of wartime propaganda and southern ideology, the prevalence of poor white culture, the greed of wartime profiteers, and the exploitation of postwar southern capitalism. Mitchell's social system rests on a ruthlessly Spencerian struggle for survival in which violence and immorality triumph over grace and decency. Characterization is founded on even more modern psychological values. Thus, conflict in the novel stems less from the Yankees than from Scarlett's ambivalence toward her mother, Rhett's hatred of his father, a broader Oedipal conflict between younger southerners and their ancestors, and a split personality or social schizophrenia pervading the South.

Finally, in sharpest contrast to the traditional romance but in harmony with modernistic values, the novel deals with themes of rebellion, alienation, and irresolution. The narrative is open ended; no happy conclusions cap the novel's bitter struggles. In such ways, Mitchell adapts the "gentle Confederate novel" to the realism and pessimism of post–World War I culture. By this same measure, *Gone with the Wind* fits appropriately into the Southern Literary Renaissance in this period and the effort of southern writers and intellectuals to deal with the conflict between their past and the modernist future.

See also MYTHIC SOUTH: / Mitchell, Margaret; "Moonlight-and-Magnolias" Myth

Darden Asbury Pyron
Florida International University

Richard B. Harwell, *Gone with the Wind as Book and Film* (1983); Darden Asbury Pyron, *Recasting: Gone with the Wind in American Culture* (1983). ☆

GRIFFITH, D. W.

(1875–1948) Film director.

David Wark Griffith was probably the man most responsible for expanding into films the depictions of a mythic, romantic Old South common in fiction. His movie, *Birth of a Nation*, (1915), told the story of the Civil War and Reconstruction from the point of view of the defeated South.

Griffith was born in Crestwood, Ky., on 22 January 1875. His father, a colonel in the Confederate army, entertained his children with stories of his exploits in battle; and a cousin added to family folklore with tales of the organization of the Ku Klux Klan. During these family times, the youthful Griffith developed his love of the South. He left Kentucky to begin a career as an actor and playwright; but when that career never bloomed, he reluctantly accepted jobs acting in a new but slightly disreputable medium—motion pictures. He became intrigued by the potential of movies, and by 1908 he was directing films for the American Biograph Company in New York. During the next five years he directed over 400 short films at Biograph and became recognized as the major filmmaker of his time. Often he turned to his native South for plots and settings for his films, 11 of which were set during the Civil War.

In 1912 Griffith joined the Epoch Producing Company and began making a major full-length motion picture. Using Thomas Dixon, Jr.'s emotional novel *The Clansman* as his main source, Griffith produced a film that he believed would tell the truth about the Civil War and the years following it. The story describes two families, one northern and one southern. The young men on both sides go off to fight, but after the war one of the southern men—Little Colonel—returns to his ruined home to find the society he had known in chaos. The narrative portrays the Reconstruction era as a violent period, ending only with the restoration of white rule. Griffith's view of the South in this film is a mixture of his romanticism and realism. He had a romantic view of the Old South's social structure, based on the family and an agrarian way of life, yet his desire to tell the truth and his interest in the photographic qualities of his medium led him to portray battle scenes and other historical vignettes, such as the surrender at Appomattox, with fidelity to history. The war itself was not glorified in Griffith's films, and his most powerful images of it are of soldiers lying dead on the battlefield. The charge of Confederate troops at northern trenches is an emotional moment (James Agee called this "the most beautiful shot I have seen in any movie"), but the bravery of that moment was tempered by the sure defeat soon to follow.

Birth of a Nation caused considerable controversy because of its racial views, but it was to become the most successful movie of its time. Griffith later made two more films with southern settings, *A Romance of Happy Valley* (1919, now lost) and *The White Rose* (1923); neither had the vitality of his earlier southern films. He died in Hollywood in 1948.

See also LITERATURE: / Dixon, Thomas, Jr.

Robert A. Armour
Virginia Commonwealth University

Robert M. Henderson, *D. W. Griffith: His Life and Work* (1972); Russell Merritt, *Cinema Journal* (1972). ☆

GRIZZARD, LEWIS

(b. 1946) Newspaper columnist and humorist.

Born 20 October 1946 in Fort Benning, Ga., Lewis Grizzard grew up in the small Georgia town of Moreland. He and his mother moved there in 1946 after she divorced his father, who was a professional soldier. Grizzard graduated from the University of Georgia and worked as a sportswriter in Athens and Atlanta, Ga., and in Chicago. He returned to Atlanta as a columnist for the Atlanta *Constitution* in 1978. His column is now syndicated to more than 200 newspapers with 9 million readers.

The South has a long tradition of newspaper columnists who have recorded the region's folkways and social manners. These columnists have drawn on and contributed to southern traditions of humor and storytelling. Grizzard is among the most successful and insightful contemporary observers of the changing South. From the New South bastion of Atlanta, Grizzard embodies the traditional southern white male's confrontation with modern America.

Grizzard grew up as a small-town boy, and he often writes of his childhood home and of friends such as Weyman C. Wanamaker ("a great American"), Curtis "Fruit Jar" Hainey (the town drunk), and Hog Phillpot, Cordie Mae Poovey, and Kathy Sue Loudermilk. He tells stories of real-life characters, ordinary people whose stories may be offbeat, nostalgic, sentimental, poignant, or tragic. Called the Faulkner of the common man, Grizzard champions his social class of origin—the plain (often poor) whites. Living in the capital of the new southern upper-middle class, he also is an astute observer of southern Yuppies. He has chronicled, and sometimes protested, the appearance in Atlanta of "hanging fern" restaurants and singles bars, BMWs replacing pickup trucks, and the drinking of wine coolers instead of beer.

Grizzard's significant contribution is his assertion of southern distinctiveness and tradition in the face of a changing South. He defends southern traditions in an age when the small towns of his youth have been enveloped by modern cities such as Atlanta. In his books he tries "to keep the South alive and rekindle it." He writes about country music, trains, pickup trucks, country stores, barbecue, long-necked bottles of beer, fishing, revivals, Sunday schools, saying grace before meals, snuff, pool halls, Vienna sausages, RC Cola, moon pies, juke joints, honky tonks, front porches, dogs, and stock car and dirt track racing. He is a die-hard University of Georgia football fan, often lambasting rival Georgia Tech. He is defined by his sex—a champion of male rights in an age of women's liberation—and his age—a baby boomer who looks back fondly to growing up as part of the Elvis generation.

Lewis Grizzard's books include *Kathy Sue Loudermilk, I Love You* (1979), *Won't You Come Home, Billy Bob Bailey?* (1980), *Don't Sit under the Grits Tree with Anyone Else but Me* (1981), *They Tore Out My Heart and Stomped that Sucker Flat* (1982), *If Love Were Oil, I'd Be about a Quart Low* (1983), *Elvis Is Dead, and I Don't Feel so Good Myself* (1984), *Shoot Low, Boys— They're Ridin' Shetland Ponies* (1985), and *My Daddy Was a Pistol and I'm a Son of a Gun* (1986).

Charles Reagan Wilson
University of Mississippi

David C. Foster, *Atlanta* (October 1986); David Treadwell, Los Angeles *Times* (19 June 1986). ☆

JOHNSON, GERALD
||||||||||||||||||||||||||||||||||||||||||||||||||||||||
(1890–1980) Journalist, biographer, and historian.

Perhaps best known for his contributions to the *New Republic* over a quarter century, Gerald White Johnson was a leader in the southern critical awakening of the 1920s. Born in Riverton, N.C., and reared in the town of Thomasville in the Carolina Piedmont, Johnson followed other members of his family to Wake Forest College and then into journalism. After serving in World War I, he became an editorial writer for the Greensboro, N.C., *Daily News* and

a spokesman for a new, liberal South. In 1922 he caught the eye of notorious South-watcher H. L. Mencken, and Mencken helped him publish in the iconoclastic southern little magazine *The Reviewer* of Richmond and in Mencken's own *American Mercury*. By the mid-1920s Johnson was firmly established as the leading interpreter of the contemporary South. His articles in the *American Mercury* and other magazines described a benighted South of Ku Klux Klansmen, religious fundamentalists, and cotton mill barons and workers. His attitude toward benighted southerners, however, was never so harsh as that of his mentor, Mencken. Partly because of his own southern heritage and Baptist upbringing, he was able to bring an understanding, even a sympathy, to his subject that Mencken rarely displayed.

In 1926 Johnson joined Mencken in Baltimore as an editorial writer and columnist for the Sunpapers, and from that point on his interests were not exclusively southern. He became a serious student of American history, a biographer of Andrew Jackson and numerous other figures, and in the 1930s a fervent supporter of Franklin D. Roosevelt and the New Deal. After he left the Sunpapers in the 1940s, he gained renown as a columnist and commentator, remaining a liberal Democrat until his death. In his later years, he did not forget the South entirely. Some of his most moving essays, appearing largely in the *Virginia Quarterly Review*, were tributes to liberal southerners he had known. But his most important role in southern history was the one he had played in the 1920s as the most perceptive of analysts for national magazines in search of the southern story.

See also LITERATURE: / Mencken, H. L.;
MYTHIC SOUTH: / Mencken's South

Fred Hobson
University of Alabama

Fred Hobson, *South-Watching: Selected Essays of Gerald W. Johnson* (1983); Gerald W. Johnson, *America-Watching: Perspectives in the Course of an Incredible Century* (1976). ☆

KAZAN, ELIA

(b. 1909) Film director.

One of America's most important stage and screen directors and latterly a novelist, Elia Kazan has often used the South as the setting for his vision of the individual identity suppressed or impeded by social pressures.

In *Pinky* (1949) Kazan made one of Hollywood's first approaches to the problems of racial prejudice, but his use of starlet Jeanne Crain as the black female lead never quite succeeded. A more credible mammy-granddaughter bridge was established in *Wild River* (1960), between Jo Van Fleet and Lee Remick. Here Kazan played out the individual-versus-society conflict on two contrary fronts, one between a diehard landholder (Van Fleet) and the Tennessee Valley Authority, the other between the progressive outsider (Montgomery Clift) and the reactionary rural community. The liberated screen of the 1960s enabled Kazan graphically to depict the crust of dead and numbing traditions through which the individual spirit had to break. The moral torpor of the citizenry appeared through either fly-buzzing sleepiness or vigilante violence.

Kazan can take some credit for the matured American cinema through two film adaptations he made with Tennes-

see Williams—*A Streetcar Named Desire* (1951) and *Baby Doll* (1956). *A Streetcar Named Desire* was the first true adult film in America, though to please the censors it required considerable change. Kazan had no foreknowledge or control of about a dozen small cuts in wording. The ambiguously happy ending in the film, which suggests that Stanley Kowalski will be punished by Stella's desertion for his rape of Blanche DuBois, was a compromise to allow the film to keep even the oblique representations of the rape.

In *Baby Doll* a pathetic dreamer is overcome by a pragmatic realist. Kazan shot this film on location at Benoit, Miss., using many townsfolk as extras, most notably some local blacks as a kind of silent chorus, chortling at the whites' pretensions and frustrations. On this occasion in 1956 Kazan expressed his love for the South and its people: "I'm terribly moved by their problems and their attempts to meet them. Under an onionskin-thin surface is a titanic violence: That is drama. I don't think Northern people, especially Northern intellectuals, know much about it. I didn't until I went to the South and lived there."

Maurice Yacowar
Brock University

Michel Ciment, *Kazan on Kazan* (1973); Toby Cole and Helen Krich Chinoy, eds., *Directors on Directing* (1964); Jim Kitses, *Cinema* (Winter 1972–73). ☆

KILPATRICK, JAMES J.

(b. 1920) Journalist.

James Jackson Kilpatrick, Jr., born in 1920 in Oklahoma City, Okla., is a nationally syndicated newspaper columnist of conservative political outlook who defines his own political affiliation as "Whig." He first achieved national attention in the late 1950s and early 1960s when, as editor of the Richmond *News Leader*, he became one of the leading journalistic advocates of resistance to the U.S. Supreme Court's 1954 *Brown* v. *Board of Education* ruling, which outlawed segregation in the public schools of the South.

A 1941 graduate of the University of Missouri School of Journalism, Kilpatrick joined the staff of the Richmond *News Leader* and between 1941 and 1949 served in virtually every "beat" of a daily newspaper before becoming chief editorial writer for the paper in 1949. In 1951 at age 31 he succeeded Douglas Southall Freeman as editor.

As editor, following the 1954 decision, he argued for "gradualism" in the integration of the races in the South. His 1962 book, *The Southern Case for School Segregation*, summarizes many of his editorial views: "In the South, the acceptance of racial separation begins in the cradle. What rational man imagines this concept can be shattered overnight?" He criticized those who sought integration in the South as "men in high places whose hypocrisy is exceeded only by their ignorance, men whose trade it is to damn the bigotry of the South by day and to sleep in lily-white Westchester County by night."

Kilpatrick in his books and editorials used traditional constitutional arguments and the states' rights principles so effectively that his opponents credited him with stimulating the "massive resistance" legislative measures that were attempted first by Virginia and later by other southern legislatures.

"Patience, the South would ask of its adversaries," Kilpatrick said as he regularly espoused evolutionary change in the 1960s. "If there is ever to be in the South any significant degree of desegregation in public institutions, let alone any significant degree of integration in society as a whole, it can come effectively in one way only: slowly, cautiously, voluntarily, 'some time in the future.' "

Ultimately, Kilpatrick saw change as inevitable. Although he felt that the South would maintain "essential separation of the races for years to come," Kilpatrick also predicted that "doors that have been closed will open one by one. And a South that once would have regarded these innovations with horror will view them at first with surprise, then with regret, for a time with distaste, and at last with indifference."

A syndicated columnist, Kilpatrick became known to wider audiences through television appearances on the "Point-Counterpoint" feature of the CBS program *60 Minutes*. In addition to his earlier books, *The Sovereign States* (1957) and *The Smut Peddlers* (1960), his recent writing includes *The Foxes' Union* (1977); with Eugene McCarthy, *A Political Bestiary* (1978); with William Bake, *The American South: Four Seasons of the Land* (1980); *The American South: Towns and Cities* (1982); and *The Writer's Art* (1984).

See also LAW: *Brown* v. *Board of Education*

Jere Real
Lynchburg, Virginia

Neil A. Graver, *Wits and Sages* (1984); William C. Havard, *Virginia Quarterly Review* (Winter 1983); Charles Moritz, ed., *Current Biography* (1981); *Time* (30 November 1970). ☆

KING, HENRY

|||||||||||||||||||||||||||||||||||||||

(1892–1982) Film director.

Henry King was born near Christiansburg, Va., 24 June 1892. When a teenager, he left the family farm to become a song-and-dance man with a blackface theatrical troupe. Further acting experience on the road led him eventually into films, playing supporting roles with the then-popular Baby Marie Osborne. Like many of his contemporaries, King gravitated to directing as an alternative to acting and found he liked the work. Even he could not recall the number of quickly made films, mostly westerns, for which he served as actor-director before 1920. His big break came in 1921 when he was assigned to direct young matinee idol Richard Barthelmess in *Tol'able David*, a sentimental tale of King's native southern mountains. The Russian director-theorist Pudovkin praised the film for its naturalness, and it remains in circulation today as an outstanding example of silent-film artistry.

Thereafter, as a contract director for Fox Films (subsequently 20th Century Fox), King directed more than 60 films, including some of the studio's major productions of the 1930s and 1940s like *Alexander's Ragtime Band* and *In Old Chicago*. He rarely had a chance to work on stories about the South, but, after D. W. Griffith abandoned rural subject matter in the 1920s, King became the screen's most sympathetic interpreter of such materials. He was assigned such films as the first *State Fair* (1933, starring Will Rogers), *Carolina* (1934), a remake of Griffith's *Way Down East* (1935), *Ramona* (1936), and *Maryland* (1940), on the infrequent occasions that Fox scheduled such productions. He continued working until 1962, when Darryl F. Zanuck, with whom King had collaborated closely, lost control of the studio.

Although he was not highly regarded by film critics, he was twice nominated for Academy Awards—for *The Song of Bernadette* (1943) and *Wilson* (1944). His day came at last when, beginning on 30 June 1978, New York's Museum of Modern Art celebrated his 90th birthday by honoring him with a seven-week retrospective of his films. He died in his San Fernando Valley home on 29 June 1982.

Warren French
Indiana University

New York Times (30 June 1978). ☆

KURALT, CHARLES

||||||||||||||||||||||||||||||||||||||||||||||||||

(b. 1934) Television and radio correspondent.

Charles Bishop Kuralt grew up in Wilmington, N.C., absorbing and observing southern traits. One of his heroes during childhood was Edward R. Murrow, who once read Kuralt's winning entry in the American Legion's "Voice of Democracy" contest over CBS radio. Kuralt pursued his interest in journalism at the University of North Carolina, where he earned a B.A. degree in 1955. He was a reporter and columnist for the Charlotte *News* from 1955 to 1957, and his work won the Ernie Pyle Memorial Award in 1956. He joined CBS news as a writer in 1957 and became a correspondent in 1959. At CBS Kuralt has served as correspondent in Latin America, as West Coast bureau manager, and as anchor. In 1972 he became the host of a CBS radio show called *Dateline America*.

Kuralt's popular series *On the Road*,

consisting of stories of his travels throughout America in a van, began in 1967 and appears frequently on the *CBS Evening News*. He offers poignant slices of American life through his musings on his travels and interviews with people he encounters, usually on back roads and often in rural settings. *On the Road* won Emmy Awards in 1969, 1978, and 1981. His unique, folksy, conversational style is key to Kuralt's popularity. In 1979 he took the same style to his job as anchor for the critically successful CBS program *Sunday Morning*. For a short time beginning in 1980 he was also the host of the *CBS Morning News*. Kuralt's first weekly CBS series premiered in the summer of 1983, but it was not renewed. He has been the host of many CBS television specials.

Kuralt is the author of several books that elaborate on his travels in America, including *Southerners: A Portrait of a People* (1986), which explores the southern heritage and traditions in photographs and Kuralt's characteristically personal narration. He draws on his own experiences and North Carolina background frequently in the text. As in all of his work, Kuralt demonstrates the warmth and good humor that prompted *Newsweek* in 1983 to call him "our favorite visiting uncle."

Karen M. McDearman
University of Mississippi

Charles Kuralt, *Dateline America* (1979), *On the Road with Charles Kuralt* (1985), *To the Top of the World: The Adventures and Misadventures of the Plaisted Polar Expedition, March 28–May 4, 1967* (1968), with Loonis McGlohan, *North Carolina Is My Home* (1986); *Newsweek* (4 July 1983); William Howard Taft, *Encyclopedia of Twentieth-Century Journalists* (1986). ☆

LEIGH, VIVIEN
(1913–1967) Actress.

Vivien Leigh is known to generations of southerners as Scarlett O'Hara in the movie version of Margaret Mitchell's epic of the Old South, *Gone with the Wind*, and as Blanche DuBois in the movie version of Tennessee Williams's play *A Streetcar Named Desire*. That Leigh, British by birth and upbringing, could have not only convincingly played, but in large part created, these beloved and familiar southern characters is a tribute to her remarkable acting ability.

Born 5 November 1913 in Darjeeling, India, to British parents, Vivian Mary Hartley spent her childhood in Europe. Beginning at age seven, she was educated at convent boarding schools, where she indulged an already passionate interest in plays and the theater. In February 1932 she enrolled in the Royal Academy of Dramatic Art in London, but upon her marriage in December to Herbert Leigh Holman she reluctantly gave up her studies.

Leigh's professional career began with the British film *Things Are Looking Up* (1934). Her first agent suggested she adopt a stage name and Leigh (her husband's middle name) was agreed upon.

Vivien Leigh as Blanche DuBois in A Streetcar Named Desire *(1951)*

The producer of her first successful play on the London stage, *The Mask of Virtue* (1935), was responsible for altering the spelling of her first name, because he thought "Vivien" more feminine. Under contract to Alexander Korda, Leigh made several films and performed in several plays before setting her sights on the role of Scarlett O'Hara in *Gone with the Wind*, which was to be made by David O. Selznick in the United States. Reportedly, Selznick and the film's director, George Cukor, almost immediately decided to give Leigh the part upon meeting her. Selznick was concerned about the American public's reaction to his casting an Englishwoman for the part and tried to diffuse negative feelings by referring to Leigh as "the daughter of a French father and Irish mother," emphasizing the parentage that she shared with the character of Scarlett. The British press doubted her ability to disguise her accent and play the part of a fiery southern belle. Certainly, the American public's relatively easy acceptance of Leigh in the role stemmed in part from the traditional association of the southern states with Great Britain. Furthermore, Leigh's performance was so intense and believable that many people agreed with Selznick and Cukor that she was, indeed, the one Scarlett. Her portrayal won her the first of two Academy Awards.

After obtaining a divorce settlement in which she relinquished custody of her daughter, Leigh married Laurence Olivier in October 1940. They made a wartime picture together—*That Mrs. Hamilton* (1941)—and played opposite each other on the stage in Great Britain and the United States many times from 1937 through 1957. Her 1949 portrayal of Blanche DuBois in Tennessee Williams's *A Streetcar Named Desire* on the London stage was directed by Olivier and led to her role in the American screen version of the play. Leigh reportedly became obsessed with the character of Blanche in much the same way as she had with that of Scarlett O'Hara, and attempted to understand her in depth. Indeed, her portrayal of the tragic southern figure of fallen aristocracy, whose fading beauty and vain attempts to regain a life of gentility lead her to madness, was intense on both the stage and the screen. The film, which opened in September 1951, was produced and directed by Elia Kazan and won Leigh her second Academy Award for Best Actress.

Always subject to violent mood swings, Leigh was diagnosed as manic-depressive and schizophrenic in her later years. In addition, she had suffered from tuberculosis since 1945. She made several more films and plays after *Streetcar*, including another Tennessee Williams adaptation, but her work became erratic as she became increasingly ill. She died on 8 July 1967.

Karen M. McDearman
University of Mississippi

Felix Barker, *The Oliviers: A Biography* (1953); Anne Edwards, *Vivien Leigh: A Biography* (1977). ☆

LOUISVILLE COURIER-JOURNAL

Kentucky's leading antebellum newspapers reflected the quandary of the border state. Supportive of union, G. D. Prentice's Louisville *Journal* experienced steadily declining circulation as the sectional crisis took its toll, while the secessionist *Courier* was forced by federal troops to close its offices in 1861.

After the war, *Courier* editor Walter N. Haldeman resumed publication and in 1868 bought the failing *Journal* as well as Louisville's third major paper, the *Democrat*. The consolidation produced the Louisville *Courier-Journal*, and the young journalist Henry Watterson (1840–1921) became the editor. Watterson's flamboyant personality and powerful editorial style extended the paper's influence far outside its region.

Cultivating the physical image of a Kentucky colonel, Watterson was a Confederate veteran who admired Lincoln and advocated the Greeley Liberal Republican ticket; an opponent of carpetbag rule, he was acknowledged by Booker T. Washington as a "liberal concerning the Negro, or any underdeveloped" group. At 28 he had already worked as a music critic for the *New York Times*, a reporter for the Washington *Daily States*, and, after the war, had resuscitated the Nashville *Banner*. By 1880 his editorial leadership had boosted combined circulation of the *Courier-Journal* to 50,000, making it the largest paper west of the Alleghenies.

While never emerging as a "fighting liberal," Watterson, like Henry W. Grady, did much to bridge the postwar gulf between North and South. From his offices just four blocks south of the Mason-Dixon line, he sounded many of the same notes as Grady, proclaiming his version of the New South—"The New Departure." His political enthusiasm set him apart, however. He was unabashed in his support of the 1876 Democratic party nominee, Samuel J. Tilden, "the ideal statesman," he

crossed party lines with ease, and was so vehemently—and unpopularly—opposed to the Democratic free-silver platform in the 1890s that the paper lost half of its circulation in a year.

In 1917 Watterson's prowar editorials made the *Courier-Journal* the first southern paper to win a Pulitzer Prize. In the same year the newspaper and its evening edition, the Louisville *Times*, were sold to Judge Robert Worth Bingham, and in protest over Bingham's support of the League of Nations, Watterson resigned. More conservative and less distinctly a personality newspaper under Bingham's ownership, the *Courier-Journal* continued to increase its readership—73,000 by the 1920s—and to sustain the quality of writing that would result in the award of five more Pulitzers for reporting, public service, and editorials.

Bingham died in 1937 and was succeeded by his son Barry, who shared editorial and publishing responsibilities, as well as a record of government service, with Mississippi native Mark Ethridge. Universally regarded, according to a Chicago *Sun* tribute, "as one of the most forceful, intelligent and progressive newspaper men in America," Ethridge quickly emerged as an archetypical New South editor. Both he and Bingham were sensitive to the responsibilities incumbent upon even the most benign media monopoly and for a time featured syndicated columnists so ideologically disparate that the paper was charged with confusing freedom of the press with columnar chaos.

Retaining its reputation for incisive reporting and high cultural content, the *Courier-Journal* has a current daily circulation of over 175,000 and a Sunday circulation of over 330,000. It is edited and published by Barry Bingham, Jr.

The Bingham family, however, sold its interest in the paper in 1986.

See also URBANIZATION: / Louisville

Elizabeth M. Makowski
University of Mississippi

Sidney Kobre, *Development of American Journalism* (1969); Frank Luther Mott, *American Journalism: A History, 1690–1960* (1962) Kenneth Stewart and John Tebbel, *Makers of Modern Journalism* (1952); Joseph F. Wall, *Henry Watterson: Reconstructed Rebel* (1956). ☆

McGILL, RALPH

(1898–1969) Newspaper editor and publisher.

Ralph McGill (left), editor of the Atlanta Constitution, *1939*

As associate editor, editor, and publisher of the Atlanta *Constitution* from 1938 to his death in 1969, Ralph McGill campaigned for equal civil rights for blacks. While writing of politics, religion, economics, poetry, poker, bees, the press, farming, war, sports, cooking, and foreign affairs, this Pulitzer Prize winner became recognized for his commentary on southern society.

McGill was a peculiar social reformer, a reluctant crusader with common sense and a good sense of humor. Showing a deep concern for the "troubles of others," he took on many causes. He enjoyed the give and take of political debate and chided persons who avoided controversial subjects. This restless rebel disliked seeing defenseless people exploited, whether Jew, black, or artist.

Unless a school or synagogue had been bombed or a black person harmed, McGill generally approached social issues "something like a teacher," coaxing and prodding listeners more than berating them, often leaving his audience choices to make. McGill explained that one cannot "get too far ahead of the audience"; otherwise "you find yourself" communicating "to just a small group." So as not to stampede his readers, McGill often softened his persuasion with the claim that he was not arguing "pro or con" but "to create some understanding." But when the deed deserved stronger criticism, McGill was ready: "Not all the perfumes of Araby will wash clean the political hands of Mississippi's Governor Ross Barnett."

Although a Democrat, McGill saw himself politically "just left of center" and "highly idealistic about life." Because of "human limitations," however, he felt that social progress "moves like an inch worm." His moderate and realistic stance on race relations angered racists and segregationists and frustrated some liberals. McGill admitted "there is schizophrenia" in "running with the hare and dropping back . . . to see how the hounds are making out," but "there also is Americanism and good politics as well."

From McGill's moral strength and communicative compromise evolved "a primer of Southern thinking" that he taught friend and foe. He argued that the "old customs" controlling race relations could be resolved permanently only "within the Southern pattern." One more federal law was not the answer; southerners had "to do what is right."

Searching for solutions to racial problems that were both fair and feasible, McGill adapted his arguments and goals to changing conditions between 1940 and 1969. From 1940 to 1950 he "held up and cried aloud" the South's "record of shame" in discriminating against blacks in courts, education, employment, voting, government, housing, religion, and social services. During the 1940s McGill worked for "separate *and equal*" opportunities for blacks and whites. Beginning in 1949 he tried to prepare citizens for the Supreme Court's ultimate ruling against segregation in public schools, a decision for which the region's leaders had no mechanism with which to work. By 1953 McGill declared that "segregation by law no longer fits today's world." From 1954 to 1969 he escalated his criticism of racial evils and his prescriptions for home remedies. "Weary of excuses and evasions," McGill pronounced that "segregation is dead." No longer could a citizen's "rights be compromised." To educate readers and to save the South's public schools, McGill explained that the region could not afford dual school systems. He analyzed historical causes of racial attitudes, including old sectional loyalties, slavery, the Civil War, agrarianism, migration to cities, and the economy. In a highly personable, lucid,

and potent style, McGill corrected false negative images assigned to blacks, analyzed other myths of the Solid South, and wrote on such favorite regional topics as the "unconstitutionality of the Constitution," states' rights politics, and racially mixed marriages.

Cal M. Logue
University of Georgia

D. C. Kinsella, "Southern Apologists" (Ph.D. dissertation, University of St. Louis, 1971); Ralph McGill, *The South and the Southerner* (1959). ☆

MANDINGO
||||||||||||||||||||||||||||||

Mandingo, a novel written by Kyle Onstott (1887–1966) and originally published by Denlinger's, a small Virginia publishing house, significantly recast the portrayal of the antebellum South in American popular fiction. The widely popular 1957 work, which one reviewer called "a slimy mess," eschewed the moonlight-and-magnolias vision of the Old South in favor of an image liberally spiced with violence, racism, and miscegenation. The plot centered on the Maxwells, Warren and his son Hammond, and their interactions with slaves and neighbors. The Maxwell estate, the fictional Falconhurst Plantation, was, to quote from the book, "the most unusual plantation in Alabama." The unique nature of Falconhurst derived from its cash crop: instead of cotton or some other staple, slave breeding provided the Maxwells with a marketable commodity.

The *Mandingo* story line, which became the standard for plantation fiction ever since, had Hammond Maxwell court and marry Blanche Woodford, a stereotype of the belle on the pedestal.

Although Blanche was attractive, Hammond continued to lust after young slave women. Rejected by Hammond, Blanche sought sexual gratification with Mede, the pure Mandingo breeding stud whose only responsibilities on the plantation were impregnating slave women and wrestling for the amusement of his owners. When Hammond discovered the liaison between Blanche and Mede, he sadistically murdered both of them. In the world of Falconhurst Plantation it was acceptable for white men to share sexuality with black women, but it remained a sin of the gravest sort for a black man to so much as look at a white woman with desire in his eyes.

Wildly inaccurate from a historical perspective, *Mandingo* nevertheless remains one of the most popular plantation novels of all time. It is still in print (Fawcett paperback), was made into a film in 1975, spawned scores of imitations, and, at last count, had inspired eight sequels. Collectively known as the "Falconhurst Series," *Mandingo* and its

sequels sold at least 30 million copies through 1980. Onstott's son once said that *Mandingo* had no significance and that it was "like eating peanuts." Because of the book's overwhelming influence upon popular fiction, however, the mass understanding (or, rather, the mass misunderstanding) of the nature of the antebellum South and of the American slave system has been greatly shaped by Onstott's vision of the Old South as a miasmic wasteland of vast plantations on which both masters and slaves engaged in orgiastic sex and sadistic violence.

See also MYTHIC SOUTH: / "Moonlight-and-Magnolias" Myth

Christopher D. Geist
Bowling Green State University

Earl F. Bargainnier, *Journal of Popular Culture* (Fall 1976); Marsha Marks, *Studies in Popular Culture* (Winter 1977); *Time* (13 May 1957); *Washington Post* (21 May 1975). ☆

Perry King (center, left) as Hammond and Ken Norton (center, right) as Mede in Mandingo *(1975)*

MEMPHIS *COMMERICAL APPEAL*

To maintain the presence of a Democratic newspaper in Memphis, Colonel Henry Van Pelt took over the defunct *Western World and Memphis Banner of the Constitution* in 1840. In 1841 he changed the paper's name to the *Weekly Appeal*, and the first issue appeared on 21 April. With hopes of appealing to "the sober second thought of the people," a phrase adopted as the newspaper's motto, Van Pelt used the paper to promote the Democratic principles of states' rights and a strict interpretation of the Constitution. In 1847 the paper began daily publication, except on Mondays, and published weekly and tri-weekly editions as well.

As dissension between the North and South increased during the 1850s, the *Appeal* became a strong advocate of southern nationalism. Editors John R. McClanahan, Leonidas Trousdale, and Benjamin F. Dill believed that the Democratic party and southern unity were the South's only hopes for maintaining its rights within the Union. Their stance, in a city with few slaves and many northern commercial ties, was bold. Not until late in 1860, though, did the paper become an exponent of secession, and then it determined to be a voice for the South throughout the war. Fleeing Memphis just hours before occupation by federal troops, Dill and McClanahan (Trousdale left the paper in 1860) settled and published the *Appeal* first in Grenada, Miss., then in Jackson; Atlanta, Ga.; Montgomery, Ala.; and Columbus, Ga. In Columbus, at the war's end, Union soldiers finally captured Dill and destroyed some of the equipment of what one officer called "this defiant rebel sheet." With Dill as sole editor, the *Appeal* reappeared in Memphis on 5 November 1865. Dill's death two months later marked the beginning of a short period of instability; but in 1868 John McLeod Keating began a 21-year term as editor. Under his direction, the paper became an advocate of the New South movement, promoting sanitation reform, agricultural diversification, manufacturing, and political rights (but not social equality) for blacks.

When William Armistead Collier bought the newspaper in 1889, Keating became editor of the newly established Memphis *Daily Commercial*. In 1890 Collier purchased the *Avalanche*, a rival newspaper in the city. By 1893, however, the *Appeal-Avalanche* had fallen

victim to financial misfortune. The Commercial Publishing Company bought the paper in 1894 and issued the first edition of the *Commercial Appeal* on 1 July 1894.

Charles Patrick Joseph Mooney edited the paper from 1908 to 1926. Although it gave no support to the cause of racial equality, the *Appeal* won a Pulitzer Prize in 1923 for its coverage and condemnation of Ku Klux Klan activities. J. P. Alley's cartoon "Hambone," featuring a little black man, became a popular feature and appeared regularly until it was discontinued following the assassination of Martin Luther King, Jr., in 1968. One of Mooney's primary local concerns centered upon the Memphis political machine of Edward Hull Crump. "Boss" Crump's control of local politics began with his 1909 election as mayor and continued later through his position as a Shelby County trustee. While the *Appeal* did not favor the state prohibition law, Crump would not even enforce it. Mooney and others used this failure to force Crump's resignation as mayor in 1916, but the principle of one-man rule had been and remained the editor's chief concern.

Before his death, Mooney encouraged the establishment of an evening paper. The first *Evening Appeal* was published on 1 December 1926 but, in June 1933, was absorbed into the morning paper. The *Commercial Appeal* came under chain ownership when the Scripps-Howard news organization, the current owner, acquired it in 1936. Today, the *Appeal* publishes only morning and Sunday editions and no longer officially allies itself with any political party. Its circulation is over 227,500 daily and in excess of 292,000 on Sundays.

Jessica Foy
Cooperstown Graduate Programs
Cooperstown, New York

Thomas Harrison Baker, *The Memphis Commercial Appeal: The History of a Southern Newspaper* (1971); Neil B. Cope, "A History of the Memphis *Commercial Appeal*" (Ph.D. dissertation, University of Missouri, 1969); *The 1986 IMS/AYER Directory of Publications* (1986). ☆

MORRIS, WILLIE

(b. 1934) Writer.

Willie Morris, Mississippi-born journalist, editor, essayist, and novelist, continues the long-standing tradition of the southern man of letters as explainer of the South to the rest of the nation, to itself, and to himself. Seeing the South as "the nation writ large," he has probed the complexities of the region and of the country.

When he was six months old, Morris's family moved from Jackson, where he was born in 1934, to Yazoo City, Miss., which, Morris says, "Gave me much of whatever sensibility I now possess." At 17, told by his father "to get the hell out of Mississippi," he entered the University of Texas. As editor of the *Daily Texan*, he battled both the oil and gas interests of Texas and the university's board of regents before graduating as a Rhodes Scholar. After earning the B.A. and M.A. degrees at New College, Oxford University, he returned to Austin in 1960 to edit the liberal *Texas Observer*.

Hired as an editor at *Harper's Magazine* in 1963, Morris became editor-in-chief in 1967. He made *Harper's* probably the most significant magazine in America during a time of fundamental change. In 1965, on the 100th anniversary of Appomattox, his special supplement, *The South Today*, sought to "illuminate for non-Southerners the in-teraction of North and South, and make it more clear that the assignation of regional guilt or failure is each day becoming a more subtle and complex question" and to provoke for southerners an "awareness of the moral nuances of their own society."

After resigning from *Harper's* in 1971, he settled in Bridgehampton, Long Island. In 1980, perhaps drawn by that "chord of homecoming" that he sensed to be "one of the very threads of my existence as a Southern American of the Twentieth Century," Morris became writer in residence at the University of Mississippi, where he remains.

In all his works, Morris reveals himself "still a son of that bedeviled and mystifying and exasperating region, and sen[sing] in the experience of it something of immense value and significance to the Great Republic." That sense, reconciling in Willie Morris's writings "the old warring impulse of one's sensibility to be both Southern and American," brought Dan Wakefield to write, "In the deepest sense we all live in Yazoo. Mr. Morris' triumph is that he has made us understand that."

William Moss
Clemson University

Willie Morris, *North Toward Home* (1967), *Terrains of the Heart and Other Essays on Home* (1981), *Yazoo: Integration in a Deep-Southern Town* (1971); Dan Wakefield, *New York Times Book Review* (16 May 1971). ☆

MOYERS, BILL

(b. 1934) Journalist.

Billy Don Moyers was born 5 June 1934 to a poor farm family in Hugo, Okla., which is in Oklahoma's "Little Dixie" area located in the southeastern corner of the state. His family moved within a few months to Marshall, Tex., where Moyers grew up. A good student active in school affairs, Moyers worked at a local grocery store and became a reporter for the Marshall *News Messenger* while still in high school. Moyers attended North Texas State University and earned his B.A. in journalism from the University of Texas at Austin in 1956. He studied ecclesiastical history at the University of Edinburgh the following year and gained a B.D. degree in 1959 from the Southwestern Baptist Theological Seminary in Ft. Worth, Tex. He became an ordained Baptist minister.

While still an undergraduate, Moyers was involved in Lyndon B. Johnson's 1954 reelection campaign. Johnson later hired Moyers as a personal assistant, and by 1960 he was coordinating Johnson's vice-presidential campaign. Moyers was associate director (1961–62) and then deputy director (1963) of the Peace Corps, special assistant (1963–67) to President Johnson and his press secretary (1965–67), and publisher of *Newsday* (1967–70).

From the early 1970s Moyers has been one of the nation's most respected broadcast journalists, specializing in public affairs programs. He was editor-in-chief of the Public Broadcast System's *Bill Moyers Journal* (1971–76, 1978–81), editor of and chief correspondent for *CBS Reports* (1976–78), and senior analyst for CBS news programming (1981–86). He has produced such innovative series as the 17-part *Creativity with Bill Moyers* and the 21-hour *A Walk through the Twentieth Century*. Moyers is the author of *Listening to America: A Traveler Rediscovers His Country* (1971).

Bill Moyers has extended the long tradition of southern journalism into broadcast media. In his work he explores foreign policy and national political issues, but he has continued to explore the character of his native region as well. He has sought out for interviews such diverse southerners as James Dickey, Maya Angelou, Robert Penn Warren, Jimmy Carter, and Myles Horton. He returned to his hometown of Marshall to study changing race relations for a television show in 1983. *Newsweek* (4 July 1983) has described him as "the journalist as moralist" and a "Texas Populist," and both apt descriptions seem to have origins in his southern background.

Charles Reagan Wilson
University of Mississippi

Katherine Bouton, *Saturday Review* (February 1982); *Current Biography* (1976); *Harper's* (October 1965); *Newsday* (4 June 1974). ☆

NASHVILLE TENNESSEAN

Founded in 1812 as the Nashville *Whig*, today's *Tennessean* is the result of 15 consolidations over the years. Throughout most of that time, and particularly in the 20th century, it has been a strong editorial voice in its region.

One of the early ancestors, the Nashville *Union*, was organized as home political organ of Andrew Jackson. For a year after the Civil War another ancestor paper was partially owned by Henry Watterson, who left Nashville to take over the Louisville *Journal*.

The modern history of the newspaper began on 12 May 1907 when Colonel Luke Lea, a colorful politician, organized a new paper, the Nashville *Ten-*

nessean. Grantland Rice was his first sports editor. Within a few years Lea's new paper absorbed a leading competitor, the *Union and American.*

Morning, evening, and Sunday editions were published by Colonel Lea until March 1933, when, as a result of the Depression, the papers were placed under a federal receiver, Lit J. Pardue, an attorney and former newsman. Under Pardue's guidance the papers grew, and in 1937 Silliman Evans, Sr., a Texan, bought the *Tennessean* papers at public auction. Evans revitalized the *Tennessean* and remained its chief executive until his death in 1955. His son, Silliman, Jr., was publisher until his death in 1961, and then the leadership passed to his younger brother, Amon Carter Evans. In 1979 the Evans family sold the *Tennessean* to the Gannett Company of Rochester, N.Y.

John Seigenthaler has edited the *Tennessean* since 1962 and is also president and publisher. In 1982 he assumed an additional role as first editorial director of *USA Today*, the nation's first national, daily, general-interest newspaper.

Some of the brightest names in American journalism have been associated with the *Tennessean.* Those who have worked for the paper over the past 40 years include David Halberstam, Tom Wicker, Will Grimsley, Ed Clark, Wallace Westfeldt, Patrick Anderson, Creed Black, Jesse Hill Ford, Fred Graham, Bill Kovach, Elizabeth Spencer, James Squires, Wendell Rawls, Jr., Reginald Stuart, and U.S. Senator Albert Gore, Jr.

See also URBANIZATION: / Nashville

John Siegenthaler
Nashville, Tennessee

Robert E. Corlew, *Tennessee: A Short History* (2d. ed., 1981); *The 1986 IMS/AYER Directory of Publications* (1986). ☆

NEW ORLEANS TIMES-PICAYUNE

On 27 January 1837 the first issue of the New Orleans *Picayune* appeared. A morning daily, its name was taken from a local coin worth about six and a quarter cents and reflected its "penny press" format. The founders were Francis Asbury Lumsden of North Carolina and George Wilkins Kendall of New Hampshire.

Lumsden served as the senior editor, and Kendall was the roving reporter who won fame as a Mexican War correspondent. The *Picayune* had its own pony express carrying eastern newspapers to its shop between 1837 and 1839 and bringing news from Mexico and Texas during the Mexican War. By 1839 Alva Morris Holbrook, who had bought into the paper, became its business manager.

In the last half of the 19th century the *Picayune*'s chief rivals were the *Times*, founded in 1863 by Union supporters, and the *Democrat*, begun in 1875 as an organ of the Redeemers. These two were merged into the *Times-Democrat* in 1881. In 1914 that paper, in turn, was absorbed by the *Picayune* to create the *Times-Picayune.*

The last of the original proprietors, A. M. Holbrook, died in 1876, and his widow, Eliza Poitevent, a poet and journalist whose pen name was Pearl Rivers, took over the paper's supervision. Eliza Holbrook later married the *Picayune*'s business manager and part owner, George Nicholson. She was instrumental in presenting society news, a young people's page, and a strong literary section. She also featured women reporters such as the nationally famous lovelorn columnist Dorothy Dix (Elizabeth Gilmer). The Nicholsons both died in 1896.

In 1933 the *Times-Picayune* purchased the *Daily States*, an afternoon paper that used the facilities of the *Times-Picayune* plant but kept its own identity and staff. The *States* was merged in 1958 with the New Orleans *Item*. The *States-Item* continues to put out a separate afternoon paper but shares the Sunday edition with the *Times-Picayune*. The *Times-Picayune* moved into its present plant at 3800 Howard Avenue in 1968 and is under local management, although Samuel I. Newhouse of New York acquired the majority of the paper's stock in 1962. Throughout its existence, the *Times-Picayune* has adhered to a moderately conservative approach to political and social issues.

See also URBANIZATION: / New Orleans

Joy Jackson
Southeastern Louisiana University

Thomas Ewing Dabney, *One Hundred Great Years: The Story of the Times-Picayune* (1944); *Louisiana: A Guide to the State* (rev. ed., 1971). ☆

PAGE, WALTER HINES
||||||||||||||||||||||||||||||||||||||||||||||||||||||
(1855–1918) Social reformer,
diplomat, and journalist.

Walter Hines Page made cultural improvement of the South his greatest single concern. His birth and upbringing in an antisecessionist North Carolina farmer-businessman's family during the Civil War era exposed him to the effects of both the physical ruin of the Confederate defeat and what he came to regard as the flight from reality in fealty to the Lost Cause. Page's earliest interests and ambitions were literary, and when, after graduate study, teaching, and newspaper work in the North, he returned to Raleigh in 1883 to found a newspaper, *The State Chronicle*, he wanted most to make North Carolina and the South hospitable to the highest forms of art, scholarship, and literature. Although Page became a New South advocate after the manner of Henry W. Grady, he placed his greatest reliance on educational improvement, which he advocated and promoted for the rest of his life. Within two years Page wearied of his native state's backwardness and provinciality and reentered big-city northern journalism, which remained his profession until his ambassadorship to Great Britain during the last five years of his life.

Page did not live in the South after 1885, but his home region was seldom far from his thoughts. Starting with his "Mummy letters" to *The State Chronicle* in 1885, he loosed a stream of criticism and exhortation at southerners, hammering at the basic themes of disenthrallment from the past, hard work in field and factory, and, most important, good schools for all people at all levels. Page usually traveled below the Potomac several times a year and spoke and wrote frequently on southern subjects. His most effective piece of cultural reform advocacy was "The Forgotten Man," originally a speech in Greensboro in 1897, later published in his book *The Rebuilding of Old Commonwealths* (1902). Page also wrote a pseudonymous novel, *The Southerner* (1909), in which he again preached the need to overcome ignorance, sloth, and nostalgia.

Perhaps his two greatest services to southern culture were indirect. One started as participation in the educational and philanthropic crusades, which led to the establishment of the Southern Education Board and General Education Board, on both of which he served. The other was sponsorship as a magazine editor and book publisher of such diverse black and white southern writers as Booker T. Washington, Charles W. Chesnutt, Mary Johnston, Ellen Glasgow, and Thomas Dixon, Jr. Through his myriad activities Page left a strong though not always welcomed mark on the growth of southern culture in the late 19th and early 20th centuries.

See also BLACK LIFE: / Chesnutt, Charles W.; Washington, Booker T.; EDUCATION: / General Education Board; LITERATURE: / Dixon, Thomas, Jr.; Glasgow, Ellen

John Milton Cooper, Jr.
University of Wisconsin
at Madison

John Milton Cooper, Jr., *Walter Hines Page: The Southerner as American, 1855–1918* (1977). ☆

RENOIR, JEAN
||||||||||||||||||||||||||||||||||||||||||
(1894–1979) Film director.

Forced from his homeland by the war, French director Jean Renoir came to America in 1941 to continue his filmmaking career. Because of his international reputation, he found ready employment in Hollywood, although the American system of front-office supervision and control sharply contrasted with the creative freedom he enjoyed in France. He countered the problems of a strange land and a new system, how-

ever, by shooting several films on location and by grounding them in a strong sense of the culture. Two of these early projects dealt with the South, a region with which he had no familiarity.

His first film, *Swamp Water* (1941), contrasts the natural world of the Okefenokee swamp—vast, unpredictable, and dangerous—with the human community surrounding it. Despite its dangers, the world of nature is shown to be a place of refuge and even a source of life. The wrongfully accused murderer Keefer finds sanctuary from local "justice" in the swamp and over the years even develops an immunity to its poisonous cottonmouths. After finding Keefer, young Ben Ragan becomes his partner, selling the skins from the old man's trapping. From this partnership, Ben gains an economic independence from his family, finds love with Keefer's daughter Julie, and eventually clears the old man's name. The encounter with this dangerous world thus brings these people a new life and leads to a rejuvenation of their society.

The Southerner (1945) was filmed shortly after Renoir obtained American citizenship. Adapted from George Sessions Perry's novel *Hold Autumn in Your Hand*, the film attempted to capture the rhythms and flavor of life as a southern tenant farmer; adding to this portrait's texture, Renoir consulted William Faulkner on the region's dialects. The resulting "chronicle . . . of soil, seasons and weather," as James Agee described it, stirred much controversy throughout the South. The subject of a Ku Klux Klan–backed boycott, *The Southerner* was ultimately banned in Tennessee because of its supposed exaggerations of the plight of the South's poor.

Hardly indicting the region's poverty, *The Southerner* develops the relationship between the individual, nature, and society explored in *Swamp Water* to disclose a nobility in the human spirit. Tenant farmer Sam Tucker and his family endure storms, disease, hostile neighbors, and a flood in trying to win subsistence from land that had long lain fallow. Although his crop is washed away, Tucker emerges stronger and more resolved to succeed, while his family, too, finds its bonds strengthened. It is this strength of spirit, springing from the encounter with a foreboding but not malevolent nature, that Renoir's film lauds. Like the Agrarians in this respect, Renoir found in the southerner's closeness to the land a significant value, seeing in that contact the potential for fulfilling and even ennobling human nature.

See also MYTHIC SOUTH: / Agrarians, Vanderbilt

J. P. Telotte
Georgia Institute of Technology

Leo Braudy, *Jean Renoir: The World of His Films* (1972); Raymond Durgnat, *Jean Renoir* (1974). ☆

REYNOLDS, BURT
‖‖‖‖‖‖‖‖‖‖‖‖‖‖‖‖‖‖‖‖‖‖‖‖‖‖‖‖‖‖‖‖‖‖‖‖‖
(b. 1936) Actor.

Compared to Clark Gable by American and European reviewers of his 1973 movie *White Lightning*, Burt Reynolds adds a strong dash of informal virility to the gentility of a late 20th-century Rhett Butler. Born 11 February 1936 in Waycross, Ga., with strong strains of both Italian and Cherokee in his lineage, he grew up there and in Florida. Attending Florida State University gave him as much of a chance to play football as to act, but when injuries ended his

gridiron career, he began spending time in both Florida and New York to get whatever stage or television work he could find. Signing with an agent in 1958 started his film career, though his largely uninspiring movies did little to advance his ambitions. But appearances in the early 1970s on late-night talk shows such as Johnny Carson's *Tonight* first gained him national attention as an interesting, amiable person.

After establishing a solid reputation as a decent actor who either got trapped in unsatisfactory vehicles or appeared in decent television shows that were subsequently canceled (*Hawk,* 1967; *Dan August,* 1970), Reynolds became a major entertainment figure in 1972. In that year two important media events occurred: *Deliverance* was released, and Reynolds became the first male nude centerfold when he appeared in *Cosmopolitan* magazine at editor Helen Gurley Brown's request. His role in the movie, adapted from James Dickey's best-selling novel, portrayed Atlanta

Burt Reynolds as "Bandit" in Smokey and the Bandit *(1978)*

businessman Lewis as a tough, resourceful, intelligent man pushed to the limits by vicious circumstances. Along with the film image of the strong, attractive southerner on the abortive camping trip came the magazine photograph of an amused sex symbol, wearing a grin and little else. Through numerous films that he has made since then, the image has been consistent: a real "hunk" (the term was first used consistently in describing him), irresistible to ladies and well able to handle himself with other men.

A southern Robin Hood with sex appeal, operating just beyond the law in a car culture whose inhabitants go to drive-in movies, Reynolds can also put on a three-piece suit, Guccis, and a Rolex to deal effectively with big-time crime bosses. The image of the lovable rogue engaged in picaresque journeys across the American landscape (*Smokey and the Bandit* I, 1977, and II, 1980, *Cannonball Run* I, 1981, and II, 1984) is reinforced by those other roles that present him as a natural athlete (*The Longest Yard*, 1975, *Semi-Tough*, 1977, *Stroker Ace*, 1983), or a tough, competent cop/detective (*Hustle*, 1976, *Rough Cut*, 1980, *City Heat*, 1984), or a comedian unafraid to expose his shortcomings or foibles to the world's laughter (*The End*, 1978, *Paternity*, 1985, *Best Friends*, 1983). Reynolds successfully mixes these modes while returning consistently to the southern hero. A revealing clue to Reynolds's identity as a southerner is the sequence in the movie *Best Friends* in which his mother-in-law fixes him a huge bowl of grits as befits a good southern boy. Although he hates grits, he accepts graciously. His persona in popular culture radiates this polite, genteel, good-natured southern charm, as do the public-spirited actions

he makes through his contributions to theater in Florida.

See also LITERATURE: / Dickey, James

Peter Valenti
Fayetteville State University

B. Cohen, *New York Times Magazine* (29 March 1981); Richardt J. Hurwood, *Burt Reynolds* (1979); Nancy Streebeck, *The Films of Burt Reynolds* (1982). ☆

RICHMOND TIMES-DISPATCH

The Richmond *Times-Dispatch*, with the largest and widest circulation in Virginia, dates its origins from 1850, when its parent paper, the Richmond *Dispatch*, was founded by James A. Cowardin. At the end of a decade it boasted a circulation of 18,000. The *Dispatch* early announced that it was "devoted to the news and eschewing political affiliates." By contrast, the Richmond *Times*, founded in 1886 and purchased soon thereafter by Joseph Bryan, did not hesitate to take strong stands on controversial issues, such as corrupt elections and the free-silver issue of the 1890s.

Joseph Bryan bought the *Dispatch* in 1903 and combined it with the *Times* to constitute the *Times-Dispatch*. Members of the Bryan family have been associated with the paper as publishers off and on ever since. John Stewart Bryan, son of Joseph Bryan, was publisher from 1940, when the paper merged with the Richmond *News Leader*, until his death in 1944. He was succeeded by his son, D. Tennant Bryan, publisher from 1944 to 1977. Tennant Bryan is also chairman of the board of Media General, the recently formed chain that includes both Richmond papers as well as other papers and television stations. His son, John Stewart Bryan III, took over as publisher of the two papers in 1977.

Most editors of the *Dispatch* and the *Times-Dispatch* served only a few years. Joseph Bryan was editor of the *Times* from its acquisition in 1889 until its merger with the *Dispatch*, and then of the *Times-Dispatch* until his death in 1908. The longest tenure in the editorship was that of Virginius Dabney, who served from 1936 until his retirement in 1969. He was awarded the Pulitzer Prize for editorial writing in 1948.

The *Times-Dispatch* led the South in the 1930s in advocating a federal anti-lynching law and was the first newspaper in the region to urge a significant breach in the segregation front when in 1943 it proposed abolition of segregation on streetcars and buses. It backed Franklin D. Roosevelt the four times he ran for president, but with "diminishing enthusiasm," as the editor stated. Although often supportive of Senator Harry F. Byrd and his political machine, it was sometimes highly critical. The *Times-Dispatch* claimed, with good reason, to be "Virginia's State Newspaper," and its influence was, and is, considerable. In recent years it has been more conservative than in the period 1936 to 1954.

See also URBANIZATION: / Richmond

Virginius Dabney
Richmond, Virginia

Silas Bent, *Newspaper Crusaders: A Neglected Story* (1939); Lester J. Cappon, *Virginia Newspapers, 1821–1935* (1936); Virginius Dabney, *Across the Years: Memo-*

ries of a Virginian (1978), *Richmond: The Story of a City* (1976). ☆

RITT, MARTIN
(b. 1920) Film director.

Martin Ritt's only connection with the South before he began making the first of his eight films about the region was his brief attendance at Elon College in North Carolina on a football scholarship in the 1930s. Born in New York on 2 March 1920, Ritt began his acting career in New York in the late 1930s with the Group Theater and directed plays while in the army during World War II. Returning to New York after the war, he worked as an actor and director on stage and also on television until he was blacklisted from that medium in 1951. Ritt directed the first of his 23 films, *Edge of the City*, in 1957 and soon followed it with *The Long Hot Summer* (1958), his first southern movie, loosely adapted from William Faulkner's *The Hamlet*. His other films set entirely or partially in the South are *The Sound and the Fury* (1959), *Sounder* (1972), *Conrack* (1974), *Casey's Shadow* (1978), *Norma Rae* (1979), *Back Roads* (1981), and *Cross Creek* (1983). Except for *The Sound and the Fury*, made on a Hollywood back lot, all were filmed on location in Alabama, Florida, Georgia, and Louisiana.

The most frequent themes in these films involve the relationships among family members; the effects of outsiders on close-knit communities; the isolation of the community, family, or individual; and the place of blacks in the South. (Ritt offers a West Texas variation on many of these themes in his 1963 film *Hud.*) The most successful of Ritt's films, both artistically and commercially is *Sounder*, a loving portrait of a family of black sharecroppers during the Depression. It was widely praised by contemporaries as easily the best recent movie about blacks and perhaps the best such film ever, though some viewers, both black and white, saw it as patronizing and dishonest. Ritt's most entertaining look at the South is *The Long Hot Summer*, a travesty of its source but a lively, funny, sexy portrayal of a larger-than-life southern family. In his most typical film, *Conrack*, a white liberal arrives in a poor black community, tries to right all its wrongs, and leaves defeated but a better man for the experience. Ritt seems unaware that the blacks the hero has tried to help may be even worse off since their hopes have been raised only to be quashed.

Although some view *Norma Rae* and *Back Roads* as strident and unbelievable, Ritt's movies are generally well acted and are never boring, but they always present an outsider's frequently condescending view of the South. He seems drawn too much to the backward, melodramatic, and sentimental aspects of the region. Almost no signs of progress are evident in Ritt's South. The main virtue of his films is their delineation of the effects of social and economic forces on the family.

Michael Adams
Louisiana State University

Michael Adams, *Southern Quarterly* (Spring–Summer 1981); Bruce Cook, *American Film* (April 1980); Sheila Whitaker, *The Films of Martin Ritt* (1972). ☆

ROOTS
||||||||||||||||||||

Roots, a landmark event in the history of television and in the media portrayal of the South, was based on Alex Haley's 1976 best-selling book of "faction" (Haley's word for his blend of fiction and history). Haley recounted his family's descent from Kunta Kinte, an African stolen into slavery in the 1760s. The 12-hour, ABC teleplay was presented on consecutive evenings, 23–30 January 1977.

Roots dramatized the social history of slavery and its impact on both master and slave as seen through the eyes of four generations of Haley ancestors. Never before had a mass audience been treated to such a realistic—and controversial—representation of slavery. Kinte, kidnapped from an Africa too idyllic in portrayal, endured the debilitating passage on a slave ship only to be faced with additional cruelty while adjusting to enslavement on a Virginia plantation. He was viciously whipped until he renounced his African name in favor of "Toby," and, after he made an abortive escape attempt, his foot was severed by poor-white slave catchers. Over the generations, Kinte's progeny faced rape, beatings, family separations, insensitive masters, and numerous instances of degradation and racist brutality. Even after emancipation Haley's ancestors were tormented by sadistic Klansmen and the vagaries of the sharecropping system. Yet in the face of all this, their sense of familial continuity and pride endured and ultimately triumphed.

The success of the "miniseries" was enormous. ABC programming director Fred Silverman had scheduled the series over consecutive evenings for fear of low ratings, but he need not have worried. A. C. Nielsen estimated that about 130 million Americans saw some portion of *Roots*. Astonishingly, the audience for the final episode was nearly half the population of the United States.

Each program ranked in the top 13 most-viewed programs of all time, with the 30 January episode ironically unseating the 1976 telecast of *Gone with the Wind* for first place. Thus, *Roots*'s neoabolitionist version of southern history symbolically and literally replaced the romantic and apologetic moonlight-and-magnolias imagery, which undoubtedly reached its zenith in *Gone with the Wind*. There is considerable disagreement over the cause of the unprecedented interest in *Roots*. Coming in the wake of the nation's bicentennial celebrations, *Roots* may have touched a responsive chord in an audience predisposed to an interest in history. Haley's emphasis on tracing his family's origins, and his successful, though painstaking, efforts to uncover a personal heritage clouded by generations of enslavement demonstrated that genealogy was a fruitful and rewarding pursuit; countless thousands of Americans, urged on by *Roots*, began seeking their own family histories. Finally, as several television critics noted, *Roots* was a very gripping drama that synthesized several popular television formulas; the presentation, with its similarities to television soap opera particularly evident, was simply very fine television entertainment.

It is more difficult to assess the cultural meaning of the *Roots* phenomenon. Some, particularly black intellectuals, charged that *Roots* merely provided a rather painless means to expiate white guilt tied to generations of racism without confronting the audience with the complex of issues that continues to bedevil race relations in this country. Others criticized *Roots* as a corrective that went too far, a version of the past in which white characters were stereotyped even as earlier media presentations had stereotyped black characters and had

trivialized the situations they faced. Although the audience was certainly treated to vivid and brutal scenes depicting slavery as a dehumanizing institution (*Time* magazine referred to *Roots* as "middle-of-the-road *Mandingo*"), many critics argued that slavery was even worse than the teleplay suggested. For example, slave quarters were depicted as rather more substantial and comfortable than most slaves would have known; then, too, the life of the field hand—the most common of American slaves—was almost totally missing from the presentations.

Still other observers worried that *Roots* had the uncanny impact of strengthening traditional stereotypes of black people, especially those that suggested a tendency toward resignation to misfortune and mistreatment. One black scholar, Robert Chrisman, noted that the final message of *Roots* seemed to suggest that survival by any means is the ultimate goal of life. The episodes certainly demonstrated the manner in which the slaves adopted masks in certain situations (some referred to this as "Tomming"), and it may indeed have been possible for viewers to misinterpret this intentional posturing as personal weakness rather than as attempts to "put one over on the master."

The success of *Roots* led naturally to a sequel. Although Haley's book rapidly skimmed over the post-1880 years, he agreed to cooperate with executive producer David L. Wolper and producer Stan Margulies—both of whom worked on the original project—to develop *Roots: The Next Generations*. This 12-hour continuation, telecast 18–25 February 1979, was not as successful as the original but nevertheless fostered considerable viewer interest. *Roots II* remained the story of one family, but it was a bit more conscious of connecting the Haley history to social and cultural issues. Both miniseries were repeated on network television, were widely viewed in syndicated rerun and as part of college and public school courses, and were distributed in scores of other nations. Together these telecasts represent one of the most important forces in shaping popular images of the American South in media history.

See also BLACK LIFE: / Haley, Alex; MYTHIC SOUTH: "Moonlight-and-Magnolias" Myth

Christopher D. Geist
Bowling Green State University

Horace Newcomb, ed., *Television: The Critical View* (1979); Frank Rich, *Time* (19 February 1979); Howard F. Stein, *Journal of Popular Culture* (Summer 1977); *Time* (14 February 1977); David L. Wolper and Quincy Troupe, *The Inside Story of T.V.'s Roots* (1978). ☆

SCOTT, ZACHARY
||||||||||||||||||||||||||||||||||||||||||||||||
(1914–1965) Actor.

Film actor Zachary Thomas Scott, Jr., was born 24 February 1914 in Austin, Tex., the son of a prominent surgeon. He dropped out of the University of Texas after his first year to begin an acting career in provincial British theaters. Returning to complete college, he became a mainstay of the University of Texas's theatrical program before moving on to national stock companies and Broadway. His screen career began most auspiciously when he was put under contract by Warner Brothers to play the lead in the film version of Eric Ambler's popular novel of intrigue, *A Mask for Dimitrios* (1944), featuring the then popular villainous team of Peter Lorre and Sidney Greenstreet.

His greatest opportunity came the following year, however, when the distinguished French director, Jean Renoir, working in exile in Hollywood, chose Scott to replace Joel McCrea in the leading role of *The Southerner*, an adaptation of George Sessions Perry's novel *Hold Autumn in Your Hand*. Even the hypercritical James Agee admired Scott's performance in this tribute to the South. With his next film, *Mildred Pierce* (1945), however, Scott returned to the suavely villainous roles in which he was thereafter typecast. His only subsequent role of importance in a Hollywood film about the South was in another sensational Joan Crawford vehicle, the film version of Robert Wilder's novel *Flamingo Road* (1949). Hoping to escape typecasting, Scott for his next-to-last film went to Mexico to star in Luis Buñuel's *The Young One* (*La Joven*, 1960), the last of 19 surrealistic melodramas that the master made in that country beginning in 1947.

The film has, however, never been distributed in the United States. Scott retired from the screen in 1962, a few years before his death from a malignant brain tumor, in his hometown of Austin on 3 October 1965. The new Austin Civic Playhouse was shortly afterward named in his memory.

Warren French
Indiana University

Hart Wegner, in *The South and Film*, ed. Warren French (1981). ☆

SOUTHERN EXPOSURE
||||||||||||||||||||||||||||||||||||||||||||||||||||||||||

Southern Exposure is the bimonthly journal of the Institute for Southern Studies, Durham, N.C. A nonprofit educational and research organization, the Institute for Southern Studies was founded in 1970 by journalist Howard Romaine and by Sue Thrasher, then policy studies fellow in Washington, D.C.

With a board of directors headed by legislator and civil rights activist Julian Bond, and a young, biracial staff, many of whom had been actively involved in the freedom movement of the previous decade, the institute launched a variety of projects aimed at preserving and advancing progressive traditions in the South. Acting as a clearinghouse as well as a research center, it helped community organizers formulate policy, conducted seminars and planning sessions, and developed materials for classroom use.

In 1973, partly to assist the institute financially and partly to create a wide audience for its work, director Bob Hall suggested publishing a magazine, and *Southern Exposure* was born. Named after a 1946 muckraking book by Stetson Kennedy, *Southern Exposure* offered an alternative, liberal framework for understanding social and political phenomena in the South. Its first issue, focusing on militarism in the South, included an exposé by a former Lockheed employee, state-by-state statistics on defense spending, essays, book reviews, and a listing of regional antimilitary groups.

Retaining this single-focus format, subsequent issues were organized around topics such as agribusiness and energy cartels; sit-ins and Sunbelt prosperity; histories of the Ku Klux Klan; health care; and organized labor. Concerned that the journal remain a forum for the exchange of ideas from varying perspectives, the editors encouraged submissions from journalists and activists, as well as scholars, and strove for a mix of writing styles. In its 10-year

history, *Southern Exposure* has featured investigative reporting by Neal Peirce and Kirkpatrick Sale, interviews by Robert Sherrill, short fiction by Alice Walker, and profiles of congressmen and corporate heads along with the recollections of miners, migrant workers, and prison inmates.

Although primarily concerned with questions of social progress, politics, and the economy, *Southern Exposure* frequently examines the distinctive regional culture. Special issues have celebrated southern literature, black music and art, and folklife. Poetry, graphics, oral history, and feature articles assessing the impact of rapid change on southern traditions appear regularly.

Published six times a year with a circulation of nearly 8,000, *Southern Exposure* now has seven departments including the syndicated *Facing South*—a column that appears in over 80 newspapers, magazines, and newsletters. The journal continues to encourage alternative action and to challenge stereotyped notions by chronicling the richness and diversity of the South.

Elizabeth M. Makowski
University of Mississippi

Katherine Gruber, ed., *Encyclopedia of Associations* (1986); *Southern Exposure*, vols. 1–14. ☆

SOUTHERN LIVING

Established in 1966 as an offshoot of *Progressive Farmer* magazine, *Southern Living* got off to a somewhat uncertain start: one early article was a guide to choosing a daughter's first brassiere. Since then, however, it has flourished as "the acknowledged 'Lifestyle Bible' for the able-to-buy segment of (the southern) market"—that is, the burgeoning southern middle class. By 1980 paid circulation was approaching 2 million, which placed *Southern Living* in every fourth or fifth middle-class household in the South. It was among the top 15 of all U.S. magazines in advertising revenues, a remarkable performance for a magazine published in Birmingham, circulated almost entirely in the South, and priced higher outside the region.

Southern Living's "South," for subscription and promotion purposes, includes 17 states and the District of Columbia, but 1980 circulation exceeded 3 percent of the white population only in a smaller region bounded by Louisiana, Arkansas, Tennessee, and Virginia. Although Texas and Florida supplied the largest numbers of readers, the heart of the magazine's readership, per capita, was found in a band extending from Mississippi east and north to North Carolina.

Most of the magazine's staff and its contents are organized into four departments: travel and entertainment, food, gardening and landscaping, house design and decoration. Many of its features are not conspicuously "southern," but regional emphases are clearly evident, especially in the travel section and in some advertising. Articles often begin with phrases like "A traditional part of Southern hospitality . . ." or "In the South, we have always . . ."—useful information for those readers (and there must be many) who are first-generation southerners, nouveau riche, or both. *Southern Living* is also the only house-and-garden magazine to name an all-star football team, and no other publishes as many recipes for game or as many advertisements for bourbon whiskey.

Never is heard a discouraging word in *Southern Living*, and its relentlessly upbeat treatment of southern life has undoubtedly contributed to its success among readers unaccustomed to seeing their region praised in glossy magazines. In only one area has the magazine even implied a criticism of the southern status quo: it has consistently supported programs of downtown revitalization and historic preservation, despite the overtones of "planning" and government interference. Characteristically, the magazine presents such programs as a matter of preserving traditional amenities and fostering business; it also conducts its campaign not in the abstract but by pointing to successful examples in specific southern towns. A new department called "In the Community" has given this concern officially recognized and continuing standing in the magazine.

Reflections of the South's changing culture and social structure do make their way into several regular editorial columns. "Southerners," for example, presents profiles of accomplished or otherwise praiseworthy individuals from a variety of fields: craftspeople, scholars, community leaders, and "do-gooders" in the best and broadest sense. "Books about the South" each month reviews (favorably) the products of commercial, university, and vanity presses—and provides a real service by reviewing many books that would otherwise pass unnoticed. A more recent addition is the "Southern Journal," a page or two of prose or poetry, usually nostalgic, by southern writers, often distinguished.

Like other "shelter" magazines, *Southern Living* seldom advocates or even implies advocacy of anything other than gracious living. It accurately portrays public life in the South as increasingly biracial; with equal accuracy, it shows at-home entertaining as still lily-white. In this and much else, it reflects its readers' sensibilities and seldom attempts to shape them, except by an occasional nudge (it suggested once, for instance, that evergreen azaleas may have been overused in southern landscaping). Its readers naturally find the magazine's idealized portrayal of their lives agreeable and often flattering; others may find it a valuable resource for understanding the South's new urban and suburban middle class. In 1985 ownership of the magazine passed to Time Inc., which purchased Southern Progress Corporation from some 200 descendants of its founders for a reported $480 million.

See also AGRICULTURE: / *Progressive Farmer*

John Shelton Reed
University of North Carolina
at Chapel Hill

John Shelton Reed, *One South*: *An Ethnic Approach to Regional Culture* (1982); Stephen A. Smith, *Myth, Media, and the Southern Mind* (1985); Allen Tullos, *Southern Changes* (July 1979). ☆

TURNER, TED
||||||||||||||||||||||||||||||||||||||
(b. 1939) Businessman.

Robert Edward Turner III is chairman of the board of Turner Broadcasting System, president of the Atlanta Braves, chairman of the board of the Atlanta Hawks, and a major figure in contemporary southern culture. In January 1970, at the age of 31, Turner bought WTCG, a failing UHF television station in Atlanta; in December 1976 WTCG

became the nation's first satellite superstation; and in August 1979 the call letters were changed to WTBS to reflect the station's role as the financial flagship of Turner Broadcasting System. Turner owns 87 percent of the stock of TBS, a holding company comprising Superstation WTBS, Cable News Network (1980), CNN Headline News (1982), and Cable Music Channel (1984), as well as the Atlanta Braves (1976) and Atlanta Hawks (1977) professional sports teams.

Although Ted Turner's acquisitive entrepreneurial activity might suggest to some that he is a modern disciple of Henry W. Grady, others would suggest that he is more akin to Rhett Butler. Variously described as "brash," "outspoken," and "controversial," Turner has been dubbed "The Mouth of the South"—a title intended to describe his personal style as much as his media empire. His flamboyance is often highlighted and his notoriety increased by incidents such as his accompanying Jimmy Carter as an "official guest" aboard Air Force One and in the Pres-

Ted Turner, media entrepreneur, 1980s

idential Box to watch the Georgia Bulldogs in the Sugar Bowl, and his winning the America's Cup in his yacht, *Courageous*, with a skipper's skill that would have proven valuable in running Union blockades. Media industry analyst Paul Kagan noted that Turner's "style is to go for the next brass ring," and when he announced his 1985 plan for a takeover of Columbia Broadcasting System, an analyst with J. C. Bradford confessed, "he's known for doing things that can't be accomplished." Even Scarlett would be impressed.

Turner's major contribution to shaping southern culture, however, is in his role as the 20th-century storytelling equivalent of Joel Chandler Harris's Uncle Remus. WTBS currently reaches over 31 million homes, and its programming innovations have freed southern storytellers from the bondage of the national media gatekeepers in the studios of New York and Los Angeles. Often dismissed as merely "old movies, reruns, and sports," the TBS cable fare has a deeper meaning. The "Portrait of America" series offers southerners a chance to tell about their own states, as well as the rest of the nation, from a different perspective that is not shackled by old stereotypes; the "Nice People" segments present the good deeds of unsung heroes among the common folk; and even the old movies and reruns serve to offer visions and reinforce traditional values from earlier times. Documentary programming has examined the dangers of nuclear war and such problems as world population, food supply, and youth unemployment, and Turner recently financed a $6 million Jacques Cousteau special on the Amazon, because, as he said, "Someone has to keep Cousteau going."

Whether watching features on the Muscle Shoals recording industry and southern rock bands, the "muscle shows" of Georgia Championship Wrestling (which pit good against evil), stories about historic restoration and neighborhood preservation in southern cities, scenes of southern good old boys on the stock car circuit, or flashbacks on the records of Hank Aaron and Hank Williams, viewers are also listening to the stories of Ted Turner. In the modern media environment of the South, satellite dishes have replaced tire gardens in southern yards, and color televisions have helped to compensate for the absence of front porches on the doublewide mobile homes. Ted Turner's role as a modern storyteller must be seen as a major contribution to the creation, maintenance, and transmission of the public images of contemporary southern culture.

See also INDUSTRY: / Grady, Henry W.; LITERATURE: / Harris, Joel Chandler

Stephen A. Smith
University of Arkansas

Daniel F. Cuff, *New York Times* (5 April 1985); Sandra Salmans, *New York Times* (15 August 1983). ☆

UNCLE TOM'S CABIN

The most frequently performed stage play in America from 1853 to the late 1920s, *Uncle Tom's Cabin* was an obvious choice for early filmmakers. At least nine separate screen versions appeared between 1903 and 1927. The numerous feature films, short subjects, and cartoons utilizing its characters and themes finally began to fade out in the mid-1960s. The last known "Tom" film, a German-language color production, was issued in 1965.

The earliest films owed more to the Tom shows than they did to the original novel. Sigmund Lubin's May 1903 version preceded by three months Edwin S. Porter's widely admired film for Edison. Lubin promised potential customers that his film would appeal even to those "who opposed the emancipation of the slaves."

Porter used a single camera for his one-reel, 12-minute film. Fourteen scenes performed in front of painted backdrops were announced by a series of titles that replaced the theater curtain. Whites in blackface played the leading black parts, as they were to do until 1914 when a 72-year-old black actor (Sam Lucas) first played Uncle Tom on the screen. Not content merely to photograph a Tom show from a seat in the orchestra, Porter used double exposure for the angels who came to take Little Eva and Uncle Tom to heaven; added a paddle-wheel steamboat race complete with thunder, lightning, and an explosion; and concluded with various tableaux showing Lincoln the Emancipator and General Lee's surrender.

The appeal of the Tom shows and the films that followed cannot be attributed to their abolitionist sentiments but rather to their stirring melodramatic scenes featuring stock characters who had become part of the national folklore: patient, humble Uncle Tom, the epitome of Christian submission and forbearance; angelic Little Eva, the personification of virtue and innocence; the mischievous, irrepressible Topsy; and the archvillain, the heartless, cruel Simon Legree.

Porter's 1903 film was followed in 1910 by two competing versions. The Vitagraph *Uncle Tom's Cabin* was released in three reels, each shown separately. Both Imp and Kalem issued Tom films in 1913 followed by the World Film version the next year. In a 1918, five-reel version for Paramount, the actress Marguerite Clark played both Topsy and Eva.

In 1927 a 10-reel superproduction was released by Universal. Expected by its sponsors to be the definitive version and "the answer to *Birth of a Nation*," it was directed by Harry Pollard, who himself had played Uncle Tom in blackface for Imp in 1913. James B. Lowe, a black actor, played Uncle Tom but was overshadowed by the histrionics of George Siegmann in the role of Simon Legree. Most of the action concerned the romance of the "nearly white" slaves Eliza and George Harris. The film cost $2 million; took almost two years to make, in the course of which 16,000 separate scenes were photographed on location; and used 5,000 actors as well as 10,000 magnolias. According to *Motion Picture World* (November 1927), "The picture is so constructed that features objectionable South of the Ohio may be eliminated without emasculating the production." This film was reissued in 1958 with a new sound track and Raymond Massey as narrator. Advertisements urged 1958 audiences to "Hate Simon Legree, Pity Uncle Tom, Love Little Eva and Laugh at Topsy."

Some by-products of the Uncle Tom industry include *Uncle Tom's Cabin* (remakes in 1913, 1914), *Death of Simon Legree* (1915), *Uncle Tom's Caboose* (1920), *Little Eva Ascends* (1922), *Uncle Tom's Uncle* (1926), *Topsy and Eva* (1927), and *Uncle Tom's Cabana* (1947). Shirley Temple played three scenes as Little Eva in *Dimples* (1936),

Jane Withers the same year sang "Uncle Tom's Cabin Is a Cabaret Now" in *Can This Be Dixie?*, and Judy Garland played Topsy in *Everybody Sing* (1938). Betty Grable and June Haver played twin Topsys in *The Dolly Sisters* (1945), and Abbott and Costello portrayed Eva and Legree in *Naughty Nineties*, also in 1945. In 1956 *The King and I*, a musical remake of the play *Anna and the King of Siam*, featured a ballet called "The Small House of Uncle Thomas."

See also MYTHIC SOUTH: / *Uncle Tom's Cabin*

Joan L. Silverman
New York University

Thomas F. Gossett, *Uncle Tom's Cabin and American Culture* (1985); Lewis Jacobs, *The Rise of the American Film: A Critical History* (1939); Edward Wagenknecht, *The Movies in the Age of Innocence* (1962). ☆

VIDOR, KING
|||||||||||||||||||||||||||||||||||
(1895–1982) Film director.

Descended from Hungarian immigrants, King Wallis Vidor was born in Galveston, Tex., in 1895. As a teenager he worked as an assistant projectionist and used a handmade camera to complete a number of short films. One film, depicting a hurricane that struck Galveston, was shown throughout Texas. With this background, Vidor traveled to Hollywood, where he worked as an extra and a writer before making several independent shorts and then setting up his own small studio, Vidor Village. After moving to MGM Studios, Vidor established a reputation for his ability to handle large projects and his concern with social issues. Following his great success with silent features such as *The Big Parade* (1925) and *The Crowd* (1928), Vidor made the transition to sound films with such successful explorations of poverty and the Depression as *Street Scene* (1931) and *Our Daily Bread* (1934). In his later career he increasingly turned to epic productions that largely lacked the intense social consciousness of the earlier films.

Viewed in the context of his large canon, relatively few of Vidor's films deal with the South. Those that do, however, are among his best and heavily emphasize the geography of the region. His early feature *The Jack Knife Man* (1920) uses the Mississippi River as its backdrop; *Wild Oranges* (1924), based on the Joseph Hergesheimer novel, focuses on the coastal islands and swamps of Georgia; *Hallelujah* (1929), shot on location in the Memphis area, uses an all-black cast to describe rural southern culture; and *So Red the Rose* (1935), a predecessor to *Gone with the Wind*, depicts plantation life during the Civil War. What these and his other southern films demonstrate is Vidor's special concern with nature and its power, a concern that finds particular emphasis in the recurrent images of rivers and swamps in his films.

This emphasis on environment points up a major theme running throughout Vidor's work. His films generally lack real villains, simply because he usually depicts life itself, represented in nature, the land, or human circumstances, as man's greatest challenge. At the same time, Vidor has asserted that "the whole universe springs from the individual." Consequently, his films typically focus on a tension between man and his environment. In both his more personal films, like *Street Scene*, and his epic works, like *War and Peace* (1956), a sense of the individual's struggle with the world he inhabits and of his ability to win a personal victory over it clearly emerges.

J. P. Telotte
Georgia Institute of Technology

John Baxter, *King Vidor* (1976); King Vidor, *A Tree Is a Tree* (1952). ☆

THE WALTONS
||||||||||||||||||||||||||||||||||||||||

The Waltons, television's long-running series (1972–81) about a close-knit Virginia mountain family during the Depression, gave viewers a romantically idealized picture of the rural South. This poor but proud three-generation family regularly brought a nostalgic rush to viewers who remembered the Depression and gave many other Americans an ideal family for which to wish and strive. Grandma and Grandpa Walton, the Walton parents, and their seven children reaffirmed weekly the moral uplift of cooperative family effort, intergenerational contact, and the basic values of simple, honest living long associated with the predominant media view of the traditional rural South. Each Walton was the noble southerner personified.

Although *The Waltons* was based on the family life of screenwriter Earl Hamner, Jr., many critics argued that the unfailingly wholesome atmosphere found in the Walton home seldom exists in the real world and that the program stereotyped the southern mountaineer's life. However, *The Waltons* included plots based on common human experiences, examined problems that do not have easy solutions, and explored the value of stability in a rapidly changing society. The show also equated poverty with an elevated moral sense, idealized rural living, and proposed eventual solutions to every family problem that arose. Nowhere in sight were complex issues such as social isolation, divorce, alcoholism, troubled children, lonely elders, or other crises that plague many American families. When crises did emerge among *The Waltons*, positive solutions were written into the script.

The technical excellence and the careful attention to detail by Lorimar Productions, the company responsible for *The Waltons*, along with fine performances by the actors, helped to garner the series numerous awards. The show emerged at a confused time in American social history. Vietnam, drugs, women's liberation, civil rights, divorce, and other elements of rapid social changes left Americans longing for stability and a safe haven at home. The Walton family came from a mythological South to give the nation an idealized security.

The Waltons was one of those rare programs rated highly by young and old alike and has been the only long-running dramatic series presenting a serious, positive portrayal of southerners and life in the South. Although stereotyped, its characters were always portrayed as people whose values, lifestyle, and ideals the rest of the nation would do well to emulate. It presented an idealized, positive view of the American and southern past, and many viewers watched faithfully because they were left with the feeling that it just might still be possible for all to be right with the world.

Marsha McGee
Northeast Louisiana University

New York Times Magazine (18 November 1973); *Saturday Evening Post* (November 1973). ☆

WDIA
||||||||||||||

In the fall of 1948 WDIA in Memphis, Tenn., became the first radio station in the South to adopt an all-black programming format. The station was owned by two white businessmen, but the man most responsible for the format change at WDIA was Nat D. Williams, a local black high school history teacher. Williams was brought into the station to do his own show on an experimental basis; it proved to be an overnight sensation. He was the first black radio announcer in the South to play the popular rhythm-and-blues records of the day over the airways. His show was so successful that within six months of its debut WDIA had changed its format from a classical music station to one appealing solely to black listeners and advertisers.

In addition to initiating an entirely new music format, Williams launched a wide variety of programming innovations at WDIA and recruited other talented blacks onto the airways. His first recruits were fellow high school teachers A. C. Williams and Maurice Hulbert. Both men went on to have long and distinguished careers in black radio. His most famous recruit was a youthful B. B. King, who used the exposure on WDIA to initiate his career as the country's premiere urban blues artist. In addition to these black males, Nat D. Williams also recruited the South's first black female announcers to WDIA's airways; two of the best known were Willa Monroe and Starr McKinney, both of

whom did programs oriented toward black women.

Gospel music, religious programs, and black news and public affairs shows were also prominent on WDIA. The most acclaimed public affairs program was called "Brown America Speaks"; it was also created and hosted by Nat D. Williams. The program addressed race issues from a black perspective and won an award for excellence from the prestigious Ohio State Institute for Education in radio in 1949. With the success of WDIA, other radio stations around the country also began to adopt black-oriented formats, and black radio became a fixture in commercial broadcasting nationwide. WDIA still programs for a black audience in Memphis, making it the oldest black-oriented radio station in the country.

See also MUSIC: / Beale Street; URBANIZATION: / Memphis

Bill Barlow
Howard University

Margaret McKee and Fred Chisenhall, *Beale Black and Blue: Life and Music on Black America's Main Street* (1981); Charles Sawyer, *The Arrival of B. B. King: The Authorized Biography* (1980). ☆

WILLIAMS, TENNESSEE, AND FILM
||||||||||||||||||||||||||||||||||||||||||||||||||||||||

One of America's greatest dramatists, Tennessee Williams helped American film grow up. The idea of an adult category of film began with the landmark adaptation of Williams's *A Streetcar Named Desire* (1951). The film replaced Jessica Tandy with Vivien Leigh as Blanche DuBois, but otherwise the original Broadway company (Marlon Brando, Karl Malden, Kim Stanley, director Elia Kazan) brought the classic production to the screen. The film was one of the first to use an all-jazz score and brought method acting to the mass audience. Williams and Kazan again collaborated (and ran athwart the censors) on *Baby Doll* (1956), a spirited but now innocuous black comedy against which Cardinal Spellman, without having seen the film, inveighed from the pulpit of St. Patrick's Cathedral.

In addition to the *Streetcar* transfer, two other Williams adaptations rank as great films—John Huston's hearty and humorous *The Night of the Iguana* (1964) and Joseph Losey's sumptuous and sublime parable, *BOOM* (1968). In both cases Williams's material evoked strong, personal responses from brilliant directors.

Otherwise, the Williams film canon reads like an absurd chronicle of bowdlerization. Incredible happy endings were imposed upon the films *The Glass Menagerie* (1950), *The Rose Tattoo* (1955), and *Sweet Bird of Youth* (1962), and Williams's florid characterizations were softened, simplified, and made sentimental. Often the directors tended to literalize Williams's extremely poetic tones, especially in *The Rose Tattoo* (1955), *Cat on a Hot Tin Roof* (1958), The Fugitive Kind (1960), and—in Williams's own questioning view—*Suddenly Last Summer* (1959). Happier balances were achieved in *Summer and Smoke* (1961) and *The Roman Spring of Mrs. Stone* (1961). In *Period of Adjustment* (1962) Williams's social vision was trivialized into situation comedy, heedless of its metaphors.

Two minor films are of unusual interest. Sidney Lumet's *Last of the Mobile Hotshots* (1969) is based upon Williams's much underrated play *Kingdom of Earth*. Lumet shifted the focus from the survival of religious instincts to the topic of racism in the decaying South. As the dying heir of the Old South traditions, James Coburn plays a curious variation upon Blanche DuBois. Similarly, Sidney Pollack's *This Property Is Condemned* (1966) starts with a Williams one-act play but develops into a kind of analysis of the Williams canon. The three women in the family represent the three faces of Blanche DuBois: girl-child, glamorous tease, and aging hypocrite. The film develops several other characteristic Williams themes: the heroine's flight into fantasy from the brutish male world, the poetry of the "ghost garden" (i.e., "bone orchard," cemetery), the heroine's full-throated but thwarted desire to "breathe" deep and free, and the passion for life that one wandering spirit can pass on to another. The doomed dreamer, Alva (Natalie Wood), is won and betrayed by the stable, practical company man, Owen Legate (Robert Redford).

In the horde of American films about the South, the Williams works stand out for their magnificent poetry and their charged, psychological realism. Williams presents the southern experience as the nation's neurosis, a culturewide tension between the lusty and poetic energy (an id form) and the cold, suppressive community (an ego form). Williams often brings an outsider, whether a virile Sicilian or a footloose poet/dreamer into a suffocating community, to rouse the lynch mob's dread of freedom and healthy release. In this quintessential vision of Americana, both the dreamer's expansive fantasy and the community's vicious realism exemplify Williams's obsession with man's retreat to fantasy or to mendacity.

Williams's most significant contribution may be his vision of the nation's psychopathology played out in the political-passionate history of the South. Quite understandably, in Jean-Luc Godard's film *La Chinoise* (1967), a young revolutionary writes Williams's name on a blackboard list of heroes who have advanced world freedom and equality. As reservations are raised, some of the names are erased. But Williams remains uncompromised.

See also LITERATURE: / Williams, Tennessee

Maurice Yacowar
Brock University

Foster Hirsch, *Cinema* (Spring 1973); Gene D. Phillips, *The Films of Tennessee Williams* (1980); Maurice Yacowar, *Tennessee Williams and Film* (1977). ☆

WLAC

Founded in 1926, Nashville radio station WLAC is one of the top-ranked AM stations in its home city and among the best known in the South. Billboard Broadcasting Corporation is its owner, having purchased it from the Life and Casualty Insurance Company in 1978. The station serves a population of about 486,000 and is on the air 24 hours every day. A network affiliate of the Columbia Broadcasting System (CBS), WLAC-AM today broadcasts primarily all-talk programming.

From the mid-1940s through the early 1970s, however, WLAC was known widely for its rhythm-and-blues programming. It became known as "Blues Radio" as its nighttime disc jockeys almost exclusively played black music—

blues, rhythm and blues, and soul. While the station's 50,000 watts of power brought listeners from most parts of the country, the majority of the audience listened from the South. Many were blacks, and the disc jockeys catered to their preferences, at the same time influencing the musical tastes of the region, the nation, and both white and black artists whose music—rock and roll—would eventually dominate the popular music world.

In the mid-1940s Gene Nobles began playing black music when requested by students at Tennessee State and Fisk universities. Randy Wood, who owned an appliance store in Gallatin, Tenn., then decided to try selling by radio the records he had hoped in vain to sell to his store customers. On 17 February 1947 Nobles advertised records by Eddy Arnold, Nat King Cole, Johnny Mercer, and Ella Mae Morse, and Randy's Record Mart soon became the largest mail-order record store in the world. WLAC flourished, luring advertisers as well as listeners.

The station's most popular feature during this era was disc jockey John Richbourg and his 1:00 to 3:00 A.M. blues show. He became known as "John R." and the "granddaddy of soul." Because he promoted their music and often was the first to play their records or to prerelease a record to test the market, he became a favorite of the black artists. If he liked a record that was not immediately popular, he played it persistently until it became a hit. Such was the case with Otis Redding's "These Arms of Mine," an example of Richbourg's assertion that he and his WLAC colleagues did not just play hits—"We *made* hits." Richbourg broadcast his last show on WLAC on 1 August 1973 and died in 1986.

Of WLAC's blues disc jockeys, Bill "Hoss" Allen was the only one still with the station after rock and roll pushed rhythm and blues out of the programming. He broadcast a late-night, black gospel show in the mid-1980s, when the station had turned otherwise to an all-talk format.

Remembered for its music, its disc jockeys, and its advertisements for sponsors such as Red Top Baby Chicks ("50 percent guaranteed to be alive at the time of delivery"), White Rose Petroleum Jelly, and Royal Crown Hair Dressing, the blues era at WLAC entertained a generation of listeners who probably numbered between 8 and 12 million at its peak. Although programs like "Garden Gate," featuring "The Old Dirt Dobber" Tom Williams, and a talk show conducted by Nashville media personality Ruth Ann Leach have been very successful, WLAC made its biggest impact during the years when the catch phrase "This is John R. comin' at ya from way down in Dixie" could regularly be heard.

Jessica Foy
Cooperstown Graduate Programs
Cooperstown, New York

Walter Carter, *The Tennessee Showcase* (29 November 1981, 20 December 1981); Ron Courtney, *Goldmine* (February 1984); Nelson George, *Billboard* (19 April 1986); Gerry Wood, *Billboard* (18 June 1983); *The Working Press of the Nation*, vol. 3 (1985). ☆

WOODWARD, JOANNE
(b. 1930) Actress.

Joanne Woodward, known for her Academy Award–winning performance in *The Three Faces of Eve* and for other strong performances in movies and films for television, was born 27 February 1930 in Thomasville, Ga., and grew up in Greenville, S.C. She attended Louisiana State University for two years in the late 1940s, returned to Greenville, where she was active in the Little Theatre, and did summer stock for a season before going to New York to study at the Neighborhood Playhouse Dramatic School with Sanford Meisner.

Her first television appearance was in *Penny*, a teleplay produced by Robert Montgomery, and this led to roles in television plays on *Studio One, Kraft Television Theatre, U.S. Steel Hour*, and *Omnibus*. These early appearances attracted the attention of Hollywood, and in 1954 Woodward signed a contract with 20th Century Fox that permitted her to divide her time between films and television. In 1953 she had understudied the two lead roles during the Broadway run of William Inge's *Picnic*, and three years later she made her Broadway debut in the short-lived play *The Lovers*.

The Three Faces of Eve (1957) was

Joanne Woodward as Quentin Compson in **The Sound and the Fury** *(1959)*

not her first film, but it was the film that brought her stardom. She was subsequently cast in films adapted from the works of Tennessee Williams (*The Fugitive Kind*, 1960, in which she co-starred with Marlon Brando) and William Faulkner (*The Long Hot Summer*, 1958, and *The Sound and the Fury*, 1959).

Woodward received her second Academy Award nomination for *Rachel, Rachel* (1968) and her third for *Summer Wishes, Winter Dreams* (1973). She won a New York Film Critics Circle Award for *Rachel, Rachel*, which was directed by her husband, actor Paul Newman. In addition to her film awards Joanne Woodward has twice received Emmys. She received the award for outstanding lead actress in a television drama or comedy special for her performance in *See How She Runs* in 1979, and in 1985 for her moving portrayal of a victim of Alzheimer's disease in *Do You Remember Love?*

Charles East
Baton Rouge, Louisiana

Current Biography (1958); Monica M. O'Donnell, ed., *Contemporary Theatre, Film, and Television*, vol. 1 (1984). ☆

WSM
||||||||||||

See MUSIC: Grand Ole Opry

YOUNG, P. B.
|||||||||||||||||||||||||||||||||

(1884–1962) Newspaper editor and publisher.

Born on 27 July 1884 in Littleton, N.C., Young received his early education at Reedy Creek Academy and at age 15 went to work as an office boy for a local white newspaper. He enrolled at St. Augustine's College in Raleigh, where he later taught printing and supervised publications from 1903 to 1906.

Young married Eleanor Louise White in 1906, and they soon moved to Littleton, where Young became a foreman at his father's printing shop. In 1907 Young took a new position in Norfolk as a plant foreman for the *Lodge Journal and Guide*, the mouthpiece of a fraternal order; in 1910 he borrowed $3,050 from a local bank and purchased the paper, which became the Norfolk *Journal and Guide*.

Within weeks of its founding, the *Journal and Guide* evolved from a four-page fraternal tabloid of 500 circulation into an eight-page, 40-column weekly. It never missed an issue, and by 1930 Young claimed a circulation of approximately 30,000, a payroll of $50,000, and 45 employees. The *Guide* was the largest and best-edited black weekly in the South.

Although Young never graduated from college, he influenced black education in the South through his membership on various educational boards. From 1930 to 1940 he was a board member of the Anna T. Jeanes Foundation; he also served on the boards of Hampton Institute, Hampton, Va. (1940–44) and St. Paul's Polytechnic Institute, Lawrenceville, Va. (1933–54). Young was first elected as a Howard University trustee in 1933. In 1936 he was elected chairman of the executive committee of this board, and in 1943 he became the school's first black chairman of the board.

Young's concerns extended beyond the boundaries of education. He used his position as chairman of the Norfolk Committee on Negro Affairs, as well as stories in his *Journal and Guide* on dilapidated housing as the incubator of crime and poverty, to pressure city officials to organize a crime conference in 1937. Norfolk soon organized a Housing Authority, with Young as chairman of the Negro Advisory Committee (NAC).

Young founded the Norfolk chapter of the National Association for the Advancement of Colored People (NAACP) in 1917, and during the 1930s he hammered away in defense of the Scottsboro boys. His editorials in defense of William Harper, a convicted black rapist in Virginia, generated a new trial and an acquittal. He vigorously opposed lynching, and his editorials on the deterioration of black schools in Prince George and Surry counties generated a state investigation that resulted in improved schools for blacks. He also worked to equalize teachers' salaries in Virginia.

After Japan attacked Pearl Harbor in December 1941, Young promptly announced his support of President Roosevelt's war initiatives. Throughout the war the *Journal and Guide* often carried front-page articles headlining stories of black heroism, with editorials on the exclusionary policies of the armed forces as well as employment inequities within the defense industry. Young quickly endorsed the Pittsburgh *Courier*'s February 1942 call for a "Double V" campaign—to fight discrimination at home and to promote victory over the enemy abroad. On the other hand, Young opposed A. Philip Randolph's proposed march on Washington by 100,000 blacks to protest discrimination in the defense industry. "What will they think in Berlin?" he asked. Randolph's proposal and increased racial tension prompted Young to organize a meeting of influential southern blacks in Durham, N.C., on 20 October 1942 to outline "what the Negro wants." The conference established Young as the titular head of black leadership in the South. Meanwhile, the *Journal and Guide*'s circulation climbed to 80,000, and its employees numbered approximately 75.

Young remained a firm supporter of the New Deal. His change from a conservative Republican to militant independent during the 1920s and to a moderate Democrat in the 1930s epitomized black politics in the New South. But after the war Young saw that his strategy of conciliation and compromise and his "gentlemen, go slow" approach to race relations were inconsistent with the NAACP's militant crusade against segregation. After the Supreme Court, in *Brown* v. *Board of Education*, declared segregated public schools unconstitutional, he continued to vacillate between the positions of a Bookerite conservative and a liberal statesman. He believed that southerners would "gracefully and calmly" accept desegregation and predicted that "segregated public schools will eventually disappear." He characterized the *Brown* decision as a turning point in stopping the westward march of communism.

P. B. Young died in Norfolk on 9 October 1962.

See also BLACK LIFE: National Association for the Advancement of Colored People; LAW: / Scottsboro Case

Henry Lewis Suggs
Clemson University

Henry Lewis Suggs, *The Black Press in the South* (1984). ☆

MUSIC

BILL C. MALONE

Tulane University

CONSULTANT

☆ ☆ ☆ ☆ ☆ ☆ ☆ ☆ ☆ ☆ ☆

Overleaf: Squatter's son with a new guitar, Shenandoah Valley, Virginia, 1935

MUSIC

||||||||||||||||||||||||||

For at least a century and a half the South has fired the imagination of musicians and songwriters. As a land of romance and enchantment, and as the home of exotic people—both black and white— the South has inspired a seemingly unending body of songs that speak longingly of old Virginia or the hills of Caroline, while also singing the praises of the region's towns, counties, hills, rivers, bayous, plains, and people. As a source of songs and musical images, the South has spawned a veritable industry of songwriters, from Stephen Foster, Will Hays, and Dan Emmett in the 19th century, to Johnny Mercer, Hoagy Carmichael, Allen Toussaint, Tom T. Hall, Dolly Parton, and Hank Williams, Jr., in our own time. Visions of lonesome pines, lazy rivers, snow-white cotton fields, smoky mountains, and hanging moss have forever ignited the creativity of America's poets and lyricists, while also fulfilling the fantasies of an audience that prefers to believe there is a land where time moves slowly, where life is lived simply and elementally, and whose inhabitants hold clearly-defined values and dearly love to make music.

Southerners *have* made music, and many of them have performed it with distinction, thereby contributing immeasurably to the making and enrichment of American music as a whole. Singers, songwriters, musicians, merchandisers (promoters and record producers), folklorists, and others whose lives in some way intersect with music have proliferated in the South. Some performers, of course—like Mary Martin, Kate Smith, and Ann Miller—have carried little of the South in their styles. Nevertheless, like classical pianist Van Cliburn or opera singer Leontyne Price, many have become internationally famous. The success enjoyed by such musicians has been immensely satisfying to the regional pride of southerners, but these entertainers project little regional identity. On the other hand, such singers as Jimmie Rodgers, Bessie Smith, Mahalia Jackson, Elvis Presley, Hank Williams, Ray Charles, and Charlie Daniels have exhibited southernness in their dialects and lifestyles. And their music has, for the most part, embodied styles of performance that were indigenous to or deeply rooted in the South. A few performers, such as Charlie Daniels and Hank Williams, Jr., have been self-consciously southern in their aggressive "nationalism" or "regionalism." Consequently, many of the dominant American music styles of the 20th century—from country to jazz—have been southern in origin.

The folk South has given the nation much of its music. There are many southern forms of music, from blues to Cajun and Tex-Mex, and each has its own special features. Nevertheless, they share an interrelatedness that reflects the pluralism of the culture. The folk South has been basically biracial; that is, its basic components have been Afro-American and Anglo-American, cultures that in turn were never "pure" but were instead composites of Old World elements. Blacks and whites have shared music with each other since the colonial era. A "common folk pool" of songs and instruments, strongly audible in the 19th century but still exhibiting strength in our own time, reminds one of the mutual interchange that has long occurred among southerners of all racial and ethnic backgrounds.

Although many scholars have argued convincingly that the African admixture has made southern music distinctive and appealing (syncopation, improvisation, blue notes), other groups have contributed much of importance to the shaping of regional music forms. Pockets of "ethnic" music have existed all over the South (Czech, German, Polish, Tex-Mex, Cajun). The Germans made important contributions to music at the folk, popular, and high-art levels through shape-note hymnody in the Shenandoah Valley; folk dances such as "Herr Schmidt," the schottishe, and polka; accordion popularity in Louisiana and south Texas; music publishing houses; music societies; and roles as teachers and classical musicians. Cajuns created a distinctive melange of country, pop, and blues music in southwest Louisiana and exported it to southeast Texas and the Mississippi-Alabama Gulf Coast. French-speaking black people in Louisiana, in turn, created their own exciting fusion, a popular style known as zydeco (a mixture of rhythm and blues and Cajun, with "French" lyrics). Since the 1920s elements of the Cajun style have made their way, via commercial exposure, into the national pop-culture mainstream.

Folk culture was never isolated from the world at large. Music has moved back and forth across the thin and imaginary line that separates folk and popular culture. The folk, in fact, borrowed much from both high-art and popular sources. Some rural dances were of middle- or upper-class origins—the square dance came from the cotillion; the black cakewalk was a burlesque of formal white dancing; the Virginia Reel was a variation of the upper-class dance called the Sir Roger de Coverley. Many fiddle tunes that have become hallowed in the folk-rural tradition, such as "Under the Double Eagle" and "Red Wing," came from marches or pop tunes, and many other "folk" songs came from "popular" composers. The blackface minstrel shows of the mid and late 19th century repeatedly introduced items—such as the five-string banjo, instrumental and vocal styles, songs, dances, comedy—that were preserved in southern rural culture. Some songs collected from black informants in the late 19th century actually began their lives on the minstrel stage. Furthermore, the chautauqua tents, medicine shows, tent-rep shows, vaudeville, and the popular music industry all introduced styles and songs that became part of the southern folk process.

Many songs that rural southerners cherished and preserved started out on Tin Pan Alley and were published on sheet music designed for urban, middle-class consumers. Songs such as "The Letter Edged in Black," "Little Rosewood Casket," "I'll Be All Smiles Tonight," "The Blind Child," and "Wildwood Flower" celebrated the values of family, home, church, and traditional human relationships, or bemoaned their disintegration, and these songs found a welcome reception among rural and small-town southerners. Their descendants still preserve the songs in bluegrass and old-time country music.

Southern music was originally perceived by outsiders as "black" music,

Child with phonograph, Transylvania, Louisiana, 1939

and the imagery surrounding the music often projected plantation scenes with happy or doleful "darkeys." The presumption that blacks were musical was made very early in American history. Captains of slave ships, slave traders, plantation masters and overseers, travelers, and others who came in contact with slaves often commented on black musicality, as did Thomas Jefferson in his *Notes on the State of Virginia* (1784). Blackface minstrelsy profited greatly from public perceptions concerning black music, but considerable doubt exists about how much of the minstrel repertoire really came from black or southern sources (the minstrel men, who were mostly northern-born entertainers, borrowed from all kinds of sources, pop and folk, and from cultures outside the South). Whatever the source, minstrel material moved back into the South and permanently influenced the music made there.

Authentic black musicians eventually profited from an association with minstrelsy. Such black groups as the Georgia Minstrels began flourishing after the Civil War. As late as the 1920s many black entertainers still called themselves "minstrels." Both blessings and burdens obviously accompanied the minstrel association. Blacks obtained an entree into the world of show business, but they also carried with them some of the degrading aspects of minstrelsy—the wearing of cork and the depiction of blacks as comic characters (practices that carried over into the "coon song" era).

Black musicians made their first real breakthrough into the realm of American popular culture in the late 19th century, a process that flowed through two important channels—high-art cultivation and sponsorship, and the "underground" movement of black musicians into new geographical regions. The American fine-arts establishment discovered black music in the guise of the famous "spirituals." These songs appeared in print in scattered sources before the 1860's, but their real introduction to the northern literati came through the groundbreaking collection, *Slave Songs from the Southern United States* (compiled by three missionaries to the freedmen and published in 1867). Nevertheless, the songs remained known to only a few people until the 1870s when a small choir of black students from Fisk University in Nashville popularized the spirituals in the North and, eventually, Europe. By the turn of the century such songs as "Go Down, Moses" and "Swing Low, Sweet Chariot" were being performed on the concert stage and in symphonic arrangements. In content and style the spirituals represented a major slice of black folk culture, but they did not tell the whole story of black musical life or even of black religious expression.

Meanwhile, black musicians were insinuating themselves into the popular consciousness of American life, well apart from the activities of the high-art establishment (but certainly not apart from the influence of commercial white culture). Emancipation saw the migration of black musicians from the country to town, from town to town, to other parts of the South, and ultimately to cities all over the North. Southerners, of course, heard black musicians everywhere—on street corners, on work gangs, at public gatherings, and in religious settings. But black musicians who hoped to make money at their trade, or to attain some kind of independence moved into the honky-tonks, saloons, brothels, juke joints, medicine shows, minstrelsy, or black vaudeville. Often, as in the brothels of New Orleans or in the clubs of St. Louis, the audiences were white or mixed. In areas of high black population density, such as the Mississippi Delta, or in institutions where a white presence was rare—such as the black church—musicians were free to be as expressive as they desired. Presumably, a higher percentage of African traits were preserved in such environments than in regions where blacks and whites mingled freely. Most black musicians, however—whether religious or secular—tended to have different repertories, and even performing styles, for white and black audiences.

Black musicians demonstrated a mastery of any instrument with which they came in contact. Pianists, though, made the first big musical impact on American life. Barrelhouse pianists roamed through the Southwest and up the rivers, laying the basis for a variety of modern styles such as "fast western" and "boogie woogie." Piano players proliferated in the "sporting houses" of New Orleans, Kansas City, St. Louis, Sedalia, and other cities, playing a mixture of pop, ragtime, and blues. Some of them,

including Ferdinand "Jelly Roll" Morton, became famous.

Black piano styles influenced most musicians who heard them, and they gradually began to make their way into mainstream American music, particularly after World War I when the nation became jazz crazy. Jazz, though, was preceded by ragtime, another piano-based musical phenomenon that took the country by storm at the end of the 19th century. Itinerant piano players, mostly black, created the style out of folk forms. Scott Joplin, who was one of them, put many of these "rags" down on paper and tried to convert them into classical forms. His "Maple Leaf Rag" became a national hit, and by 1900 ragtime was the popular rage. White songwriters and musicians, such as Irving Berlin in "Alexander's Ragtime Band," appropriated the name, if not always the true style, of ragtime. Songwriters, both white and black, who wrote for Broadway or Tin Pan Alley, combined the ragtime style with lyrics about "Negro life." The results were the "coon songs"—songs that perpetuated myths and stereotypes of black people (the myth of a childlike but musical people).

By the beginning of the 1920s black musical styles had made major inroads into American cultural life at both the "serious" and "popular" levels. Blues music was also achieving considerable popularity, largely through the work of W. C. Handy and songs like "St. Louis Blues." Mainstream white performers often did ragtime, jazz, or blues numbers, or songs that were influenced by them. White audiences, then, had considerable exposure to "black" forms, although many people heard such music only through "slumming" (visits to black juke joints or to other places of "unrespectable," "naughty," entertainment).

B. B. King with band, c. 1955, photograph on a wall at Club Paradise, Memphis, Tenn.

Americans associated black music with images of exotic southern life on plantations and in juke joints. Sheet music often reinforced the romance with illustrations of alleged southern scenes, and in the popular mind, black music and southern music were synonymous.

When the full-scale commercialization of southern music came in the 1920s, most Americans already had strong preconceptions about the South and its music. Southern musical styles could not help but be colored by such images, and the musicians and their commercial promoters responded to these southern-spiced images. Commercialization was made possible by major innovations in media dissemination in the United States. Radio and phonograph recording, above all, made possible the maturation and dissemination of southern-born musical styles. The media exploitation of grass-roots music had both positive and negative consequences. Media coverage pro-

moted the standardization and homogenization of styles and weakened local or regional traits. On the other hand, it also presented such styles to a larger audience, encouraged professionalization, and promoted the cross-fertilization of musical styles. Musicians learned from each other, and they became more acutely conscious of audience tastes. Some styles died or remained only locally rooted; others achieved new life, and developed healthy and strong variations.

The 1920s saw the "discovery" and commercialization of a wide variety of "ethnic" music forms, as well as most of the grass-roots genres of the South: jazz, blues, gospel (black and white), Cajun, German, Czech, Tex-Mex, and hillbilly. The first significant southern band to be recorded was done so more or less by accident. The Dixieland Jazz Band, a group of white boys from New Orleans, was playing in clubs in Chicago when they made their first recordings in 1917. They made the nation jazz conscious, while also popularizing the word jazz. Not until 1923 did the first all-black jazz band, that of King Oliver, also playing in Chicago, make its first recordings. By the middle of the 1920s jazz had burgeoned, both in the United States and Europe, and was attracting aficionadoes and musicians elsewhere. The musical form moved away quickly from its folk and southern roots, but southerners continued to play invaluable roles in its development. The first star, for example, was the New Orleans–born trumpeter Louis Armstrong.

Blues also won great popularity during the 1920s, partly through its alliance with jazz. W. C. Handy had earlier contributed greatly to the form's popularity, but radio and recording did most to make Americans conscious of this exciting style. The first blues singers to become highly visible in American popular culture were black women who sang generally to the accompaniment of jazz bands. These classic blues singers, led principally by the "Empress of the Blues," Bessie Smith, were performers who usually had considerable experience in black vaudeville or on medicine shows. In 1926, however, with the recording of the Texas-born Blind Lemon Jefferson, a guitarist with a supple, wailing vocal style, American entertainment received its first strong infusion of rural black music. This has generally been described as the "country blues"—a predominantly masculine style, usually accompanied by guitars or other string instruments, with rural-folk inflections.

The wide variety of black folk styles that became commercialized in the 1920s came to be subsumed under the rubric of *race music*. Not all performers were blues singers. Some were "song-

sters," that is, entertainers who performed many different styles and songs. But they and the jug bands, string bands, pianists, and gospel singers were advertised in the same record catalogues. And of course most of them shared musical traits because styles flowed freely from entertainer to entertainer. Gospel musicians, for example, might assert their estrangement from the world, but "worldly" musical riffs and phrases constantly intruded into their songs and performances, just as musical ideas born in the church have always affected the performances made by secular black musicians.

Given the reputation for musicianship that white country entertainers enjoy today, white folk music was discovered remarkably late. When hillbilly music was first recorded in the 1920s, only 20 years or so had elapsed since the first faint glimmers of recognition of "mountain music" or "Anglo-American balladry" occurred. White folk music really went unrecognized until the 20th century. Only an occasional traveler, missionary, or local colorist made reference to frolics, country dances, singing schools, or camp meetings. One receives little understanding from these accounts of how the music was performed or what was performed (even though the social context of such performances is sometimes well described).

The discovery of white folk music came in the years before World War I. The perception that such music was a resource worthy of preservation came in the context of the rapid industrialization of the nation, the "new immigration, the rise of cities, and other related factors that seemed to bode ill for the continued existence of rural, peasant-derived culture. Folklorists and other interested people sought to preserve folk music be-

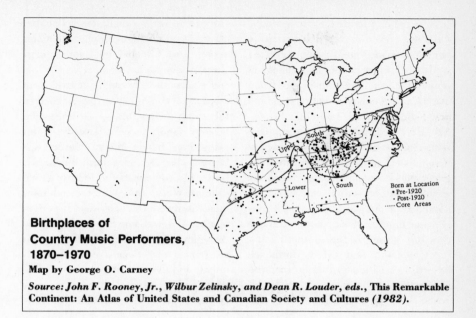

**Birthplaces of
Country Music Performers,
1870–1970**
Map by George O. Carney

Source: John F. Rooney, Jr., Wilbur Zelinsky, and Dean R. Louder, eds., **This Remarkable
Continent: An Atlas of United States and Canadian Society and Cultures** *(1982).*

fore it succumbed to modern forces.
They viewed such music as a static and
pure phenomenon, and the product of a
racially homogeneous, i.e., Anglo-
Saxon, culture. Some high-art musicians and composers eagerly utilized
folk music for artistic purposes, presenting arrangements of it in concerts
and recitals and arguing, as did John
Powell of Virginia, that it might make
the basis of a national music.

Two famous collectors, John A.
Lomax and Cecil Sharp, did most to
demonstrate the wealth of folk music
that still existed in the United States.
Lomax's *Cowboy Songs and Other Frontier Ballads* (1910) profited from the
popular and romantic perception of cowboys as white knights or Anglo-Saxon
heroes—even though cowboy culture
was racially and ethnically eclectic, and
the songs themselves came from diverse
sources. Cowboy songs soon made their
way into the larger society, through the
high-art concerts of such musicians as

Oscar Fox and David Guion, the
phonograph recordings of singers like
Bentley Ball and Carl Sprague, and performances of a multitude of radio and
movie cowboys.

Cecil Sharp was primarily a student
of folk dance in his native England.
Largely through the influence of Olive
Dame Campbell, a settlement schoolteacher in the Kentucky hills, Sharp
traveled through much of southern Appalachia between 1916 and 1918, with
his assistant Maud Karpeles, collecting
ballads and folksongs. Sharp's expedition came after the preoccupation of
local color writers and journalists with
the southern mountains. Writers of fiction created images of mountaineers in
the 19th century that flowed into American popular culture. These images of a
"strange and peculiar people" living in
a land where "time stood still," a people
who preserved "Elizabethan folkways,"
influenced the attitudes that surrounded
the music. The music was perceived as

the product of a dying culture—a body of ballads and folksongs that needed to be collected with great urgency.

Although most people had visions of a static culture, Sharp discovered that singing was common to both young and old in the mountain areas that he visited. He noted that many of the oldest British folksongs still endured in variant forms. Sharp made great contributions to folk music scholarship, but his work nevertheless had serious omissions. He ignored religious songs and instrumental dance tunes, although both traditions were very strong in the southern hills. The scholarship and song performance (by serious recitalists) that he inspired long reflected Sharp's critical judgments. When the first "hillbilly" records were made in the 1920s, the reactions

made to them by scholars, collectors, critics, and the recording men themselves were affected by prior perceptions of mountain folk music.

Radio stations began using live, local talent almost as soon as they opened in the South in the 1920s—string bands, fiddlers, family gospel groups, yodelers, "Hawaiian" bands. Many of the acts appeared on an irregular, unplanned basis, but some stations, led by WBAP in Fort Worth in 1923, created barn dance formats—regular, weekly performances of downhome entertainment. By the middle of the decade phonograph companies also began recording such talent, and the resulting "industry" was described by several terms, the most common of which was hillbilly. The hillbilly music of the 1920s and 1930s re-

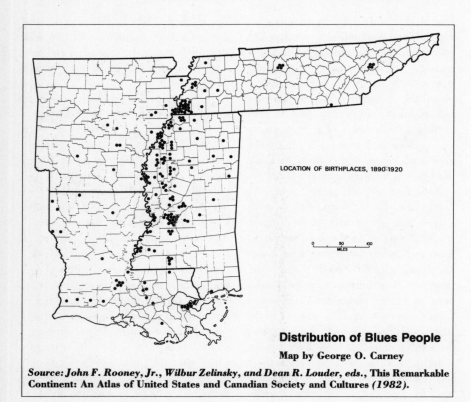

LOCATION OF BIRTHPLACES, 1890-1920

0   50   100
MILES

Distribution of Blues People

Map by George O. Carney

Source: *John F. Rooney, Jr., Wilbur Zelinsky, and Dean R. Louder, eds.,* **This Remarkable Continent: An Atlas of United States and Canadian Society and Cultures** *(1982).*

veals a white folk culture far different from that described by Cecil Sharp or by the romantic Anglo-Saxonists. Neither the culture nor the music were ethnically or racially homogeneous, nor were they static. Most crucially, both the music and the culture from which it derived were strongly shaped by commercialization and technology. The music was simultaneously conservative, eclectic, and absorptive; it came from many sources.

All southern forms underwent extensive change and experienced some degree of national expansion during the 1930s and 1940s. Expanded radio coverage introduced southern musicians to audiences in every corner of the United States and in Canada. American business allied itself with grass-roots music, and the resulting advertising was mutually beneficial to both music and commerce. Radio programming also prompted the burgeoning of personal appearances, and promoters and booking agents moved to exploit the developing interest. Hollywood played a major role in making musicians visible to the outside world. Musicians of all types—from Louis Armstrong to Roy Acuff—occasionally appeared in short features or sometimes played roles in full-length films. Singing cowboys, of course—led originally by Gene Autry in 1934—constituted a distinct genre of filmmaking up to the early 1950s. Because of this exposure, Autry may very well have been the best-known southern-born musician in the world.

The heightened commercialization of these decades, along with the consequent competition among musicians, encouraged major stylistic innovations that have ever since been part of the nation's music. Performances in nightclubs, bars, and honky-tonks—all of

Guitar on the wall of a house in Tutwiler, Mississippi, 1968

which proliferated after the repeal of prohibition in 1933—required louder and more percussive sounds. Drums and string basses became common in all kinds of bands, and electric instruments began to make their way into musical organizations by the middle of the 1930s. Pioneering musicians such as steel guitarist Bob Dunn experimented with amplifiers and homemade electric pickups, but by the end of the decade guitar manufacturers were merchandising their own lines of electrified instruments. Fledgling musicians everywhere were introduced to electric guitars through the performances of such great southern performers as Dunn, Charlie Christian, and Aaron "T-Bone" Walker.

World War II and the years immediately following it saw the nationalization of southern music. The migrations made by civilians and servicemen during those years—to the cities, to the North, and around the world—did much to transport southern-born styles to other areas while also bringing southerners in direct contact with other forms of music. Black migration to the North and to the West Coast had begun much earlier but was particularly strong during the World War II era. Migration encouraged a new consciousness among young black people, and life in the American ghettoes inspired musical experimentation. Although both black gospel music and blues had southern rural roots, they achieved new vitality in the segregated neighborhoods of the cities. Georgia-born Tom Dorsey and Louisiana native Mahalia Jackson, for example, contributed greatly to the emergence of modern black gospel music through their work in the churches of Chicago and other cities of the North. Other black migrants in such urban areas as Chicago, Detroit, Los Angeles, and Harlem were far less spiritual than Mahalia, but no less influential and innovative. They created the aggressive, electrified version of blues known as rhythm and blues, as well as its many offshoots, such as rock and roll, soul, and the Motown Sound.

A multitude of small record labels which catered to the grass-roots music styles of the South appeared after the war, in and outside the region. Meanwhile, the big record labels found increasing commercial success with such southern musicians as Hank Williams, Eddy Arnold, Louis Jordan, and Elvis Presley. Although most earlier recordings of southern talent had taken place in such cities as New York, Chicago, or Los Angeles, or in makeshift "studios" hastily assembled by traveling record men in southern towns, postwar recording tended increasingly to be in such southern cities as Dallas, Houston, New Orleans, Memphis, Macon, Muscle

Jerry Lee Lewis, rockabilly and country singer, 1970s

Shoals, and Nashville. Nashville became one of the three or four leading music centers in the nation, first on the strength of the talent affiliated with the Grand Ole Opry and later through the recording of all kinds of music. Memphis did not rival Nashville as a music center, but it was the birthplace of a musical revolution that swept across the world. In 1954 Sam Phillips recorded Elvis Presley for his Sun label and saw that exciting singer become the vanguard of what would soon be known as rock and roll. Elvis, Carl Perkins, Jerry Lee Lewis, Roy Orbison, and other Sun label "rockabillies" joined with such musicians as Buddy Holly and the Everly Brothers to popularize a fusion of hillbilly and rhythm and blues that was redolent of the working-class South and its musical eclecticism.

Since the 1950s southern-born music styles have flowered commercially and have made themselves known around the world. None, however, have remained "pure," and each has spawned a variety of offshoots or substylings that run the gamut from the "traditional" to the "progressive." The Cajun and *musica Tejana* (Tex-Mex) styles have moved somewhat out of their ethnic enclaves—away from southwest Louisiana and the barrios of south Texas—to win wider national hearings. Folk festival performances and exposure on the nationally-syndicated television show *Austin City Limits* have permitted such entertainers as the Balfa Brothers, Clifton Chenier, and Flaco Jiménez to attract converts from all regions of the nation. Although these styles have interrelated with other musical forms that lie around them and have both influenced and been influenced by them— the accordion's centrality in Cajun, German, and Mexican *conjunto* bands is illustrative—they nevertheless maintain the imprint of the cultures that gave them birth.

Other southern-born styles have been less successful in maintaining regional identity. Indeed, the promise of national acceptance and prosperity has inspired deliberate efforts by musicians and promoters alike to create products with broad appeal and limited sociocultural identification. The goal is the homogenized mainstream, and vehicles are the crossover record, the top-40 record format, and the television special. Many people in country music (the term that has been used since the early 1950s to describe the hillbilly field), have campaigned for the use of the word *American* to designate their music (seemingly oblivious to the existence of many American styles of music). Only one musical genre, southern gospel, consciously gives itself a southern label, an effort to distinguish its music from the melange of modern pop religious sounds known as *Christian contemporary*. The gospel quartets clearly have been influenced by

The Soul Stirrers, southern gospel group, c. 1950

other forms of music, but they nevertheless still convey the flavor of singing conventions and old-time evangelism. The Christian contemporary musicians, on the other hand, exude the sounds and ambience of pop radio, an ambience that has no regional identification.

Country music has prospered as an industry and has won a respect that scarcely seemed possible back in its hillbilly and honky-tonk days. But no field of music has been more torn by debates concerning loss of identity. Nashville is still the commercial capital of country music, but the city periodically encounters some competition from places such as Austin, Tex., where healthy artistic alternatives are presented. Much of the music now bearing the "country" label has little relationship to southern, rural, or working-class life, but instead is aimed at middle-class urban listeners who presumably have little regional or class identification. Nevertheless, tradition-based sounds and styles still endure—as seen in the growing popularity of the acoustic-oriented bluegrass field, in the proliferation of festivals devoted to homespun or old-time music, and in the commercial success enjoyed by such young "traditionalists" as Ricky Skaggs, Reba McEntire, George Strait, Randy Travis, and Dwight Yoakum.

What, then, is the state of southern music in the late 1980s? Southern-born musicians of all varieties still thrive, and they still continue to make major contributions to the nation's cultural life. Their music, however, reflects increasingly the national experience and the powerful communications revolution that has come to dominate our existence and shape our choices. Some musicians, such as Hank Williams, Jr., and Charlie Daniels, are aggressive southern nationalists, and songs like "Dixie on My Mind" and "The South's Gonna Do It Again" sometimes spice their repertories. The South, of course, has never ceased to have exotic appeal for Americans. It still fuels the imaginations of songwriters, and at times the region assumes such a central focus in American life that our popular culture and popular music are dramatically affected.

One such occasion came in the early 1980s during the administration of President Jimmy Carter. This southern president brought country musicians into the White House and otherwise gave patronage and exposure to entertainers from the South. Considerable media attention was devoted to a group of young entertainers whose music was described as "southern rock"—the Allman Brothers, the Marshall Tucker Band, the Charlie Daniels Band, Lynyrd Skynyrd, Wet Willie, Sea Level, ZZ Top. They were often aggressively southern in attitude and rhetoric, sometimes to the point of jingoism, and a few of them— like Charlie Daniels—projected postures of machismo and hedonism that are generally associated with southern masculinity. Except for the moments when Daniels picked up his fiddle and played a lively hoedown, the music of the southern rock bands seemed little different from that played by rock musicians around the world. Rather than indicating a renewed infusion of originality into the nation's musical mainstream, the success enjoyed by the southern rockers instead demonstrated the all-pervasive influence of the media and the primacy of youth in contemporary popular culture.

Southern music, then, is now American music. Southerners have exported their musical treasures to the world and have in turn absorbed much that the larger world has to offer. The resulting syntheses continue to provide enjoyment and enrichment. Southern styles may not be as distinctive as many people would like, and observers might with good reason bemoan their dilution and disappearance, but one can scarcely ignore the fact that the folk cultures that produced them are undergoing similar dissolution. Happily, much of the best of the older traditions—such as old-time fiddling, clog dancing, and sacred harp singing—are being preserved and revitalized by interested groups, and increasing numbers of young people are being won over to the old-time arts. Within the realm of commercial music young musicians like the blues guitarist Stevie Ray Vaughan and honky-tonk country singer Dwight Yoakum prove it is still possible to create new, exciting, and commercially successful sounds by building on the time-tested musical formulas of the past. Finally, regardless of the directions its musicians may take in the years to come, the South will not soon lose its romantic aura nor its capacity to evoke mythmaking and popular imagery. The South will sing, and it will be sung about.

See also BLACK LIFE: Music, Black; GEOGRAPHY: Migration Patterns; HISTORY AND MANNERS: World War II; INDUSTRY: / Music Industry; MEDIA: Film, Musical; MYTHIC SOUTH: / Carter Era; RECREATION: Traveling Shows; WOMEN'S LIFE: Blues-singing Women

Bill C. Malone
Tulane University

Roger D. Abrahams and George Foss, *Anglo-American Folksong Style* (1968); Bob Artis, *Bluegrass: From the Lonesome Wail of a Mountain Love Song to the Hammering Drive of the Scruggs-Style Banjo, The Story of an American Musical Tradition* (1975); Earl Bargainneer, *Mississippi Quarterly* (Fall 1977); Carl Belz, *The Story of Rock* (1969); Lois S. Blackwell, *The Wings of the Dove: The Story of Gospel Music in America* (1978); Rudi Blesh, *Shining Trumpets: A History of Jazz* (1958), with Harriet Janis, *They All Played Ragtime* (1966); John Broven, *Walking to New Orleans: The Story of New Orleans Rhythm and Blues* (1974); Harry O. Brunn, *The Story of the Original Dixieland Jazz Band* (1960); Robert Cantwell, *Bluegrass Breakdown: The Making of the Old Southern Sound* (1984); Samuel Charters, *The Bluesmen: The Story and the Music of the Men Who Made the Blues* (1967), *The Country Blues* (1959); Ronald Davis, *A History of Opera in the American West* (1965); Bill Ellis, *Journal of American Folklore* (April–June 1978); Dena J. Epstein, *Sinful Tunes and Spirituals: Black Folk Music to the Civil War* (1977); Harry Eskew, "Shape-Note Hymnody in the Shenandoah Valley, 1816–1860" (Ph.D. dissertation, Tulane University, 1966); David Evans, *Big Road Blues: Tradition and Creativity in the Folk Blues* (1981); William Ferris, *Blues from the Delta* (1978); Linnell Gentry, *A History and Encyclopedia of Country, Western, and Gospel Music* (1961); Archie Green, *Only a Miner: Studies in Recorded Coal-Mining Songs* (1972); Douglas B. Green, *Country Roots: The Origins of Country Music* (1976); John Greenway, *American Folksongs of Protest* (1953); Peter Guralnick, *Lost Highway: Journeys and Arrivals of American Musicians* (1979), *Sweet Soul Music: Rhythm and Blues and the Southern Dream of Freedom* (1986); Tony Heilbut, *The Gospel Sound: Good News and Bad Times* (1971); George Pullen Jackson, *White Spirituals in the Southern Uplands* (1933); Henry Kmen, *Music in New Orleans: The Formative Years, 1791–1841* (1966); Ottis J. Knippers, *Who's Who among Southern Singers and Composers* (1937); Alan Lomax, *Folk Songs of North America* (1960); Bill C. Malone, *Country Music, U.S.A.: A Fifty-Year History* (1968; rev. ed., 1985), *Southern Music—American Music* (1979), with Judith McCullough, eds., *Stars of Country Music: Uncle Dave Macon to Johnny Rodriguez* (1975); Alan P. Merriam and Robert J. Branford, *A Bibliography of Jazz* (1954); Jim Miller, ed., *The Rolling Stone Illustrated History of Rock 'n' Roll* (1976); Hans Nathan, *Dan Emmett and the Rise of Early Negro Minstrelsy* (1962); Paul Oliver, *Blues Fell This Morning: The Meaning of the Blues* (1960), *Savannah Syncopators: African Retentions in the Blues* (1970), *The Story of the Blues* (1969); Américo Paredes, *A Texas-Mexican Cancionero: Folksongs of the Lower Border* (1975); Jan Reid, *The Improbable Rise of Redneck Rock* (1974); Jim Rooney, *Bossmen: Bill Monroe and Muddy Waters* (1971); Neil V. Rosenberg, *Bluegrass: A History* (1985); Tony Russell, *Blacks, Whites, and Blues* (1970); William J. Schafer and Johannes Riedel, *The Art of Ragtime: Form and Meaning of an Original Black American Art* (1973); Arnold Shaw, *Honkers and Shouters: The Golden Years of Rhythm and Blues* (1978); O. G. Sonneck, *Early Concert-Life in America* (1907); Eileen Southern, *The Music of Black Americans: A History* (1971; 2d ed., 1983); Nicholas Spitzer, in *Long Journey Home: Folklife in the South*, ed. Allen Tullos (1977); Marshall Stearns, *The Story of Jazz* (1956); Frank Tirro, *Jazz: A History* (1977); Jeff Todd Titon, *Early Downhome Blues: A Musical and Cultural Analysis* (1977); Robert C. Toll, *Blacking Up: The Minstrel Show in Nineteenth-Century America* (1974); Nick Tosches, *Country: The Biggest Music in America* (1977); Charles R. Townsend, *San Antonio Rose: The Life and Music of Bob Wills* (1976); Barry Ulanov, *A History of Jazz in America* (1955); D. K. Wilgus, *Anglo-American Folksong Scholarship since 1898* (1959); Mark R. Winchell, *Southern Quarterly* (Spring 1984); Charles K. Wolfe, *Grand Ole Opry: The Early Years, 1925–1935* (1975), *Kentucky Country: Folk and Country Music of Kentucky* (1982); *Tennessee Strings: The Story of Country Music in Tennessee* (1977). ☆

Bluegrass

||||||||||||||||||||||||||||

Bluegrass is a form of country music that grew out of the music of the Grand Ole Opry star Bill Monroe and his Blue Grass Boys during the late 1940s and early 1950s. Bluegrass is frequently associated with southern Appalachia, but the members of Monroe's most influential band were from outside that region (Monroe came from western Kentucky, Lester Flatt from central Tennessee, Chubby Wise from north Florida, and Earl Scruggs from the North Carolina Piedmont) and the music in its definitive form was first heard in Nashville. It did have its strongest early popularity in Appalachia, where such groups as the Stanley Brothers and their Clinch Mountain Boys and Lester Flatt, Earl Scruggs, and the Foggy Mountain Boys, performing at WCYB in Bristol on the Tennessee-Virginia border, emulated Monroe's music and developed his sound into a style. It also gained popularity among Appalachian migrants in

Michigan, Indiana, Ohio, Pennsylvania, Maryland, the District of Columbia, and Delaware. The music was popular throughout the South and found receptive listeners among country music fans in every corner of North America—particularly in more isolated rural areas.

Like most country music of the postwar era, bluegrass was principally aimed at and consumed by blue-collar workers, farm families, and other working-class people of rural origins. Like most forms of country music, it had roots in the dance, home entertainment, itinerant theater, and religious-musical traditions of the rural South, particularly the highland regions. Hence, it was most familiar to listeners in that part of the country, although it appealed to many non-Southerners because of its novelty and because its ingredients were part of a common Anglo-American folk heritage. Bluegrass's popularity is now confined to a relatively small number of avid fans.

A number of musical traits combine to make bluegrass a distinctive type of country music. A typical bluegrass band consists of from four to seven individuals—more often men than women—who sing and accompany themselves with acoustic (rather than electric) string instruments. In comparison with other kinds of country music singing, bluegrass is pitched quite high (particularly for men), often reaching tones an octave above middle C. Many bluegrass vocals involve more than one voice. With duets the second part (tenor) is sung above the melody; trios include a part below the melody (baritone), and in religious quartets a bass part is added. Basically these are harmony parts, but there is a tendency—particularly in duets—toward vocal polyphony. In trios the tenor and baritone parts are sometimes arranged so that the melody is the lowest or highest part. Most bluegrass music is in duple meter; tempos are generally faster than in other kinds of country music. Rhythm is characterized by a stress on the offbeat.

Much attention is paid by musicians and fans alike to the unamplified instruments used in bluegrass. These include two used mainly for rhythm—guitar and string bass—and several others—mandolin, banjo, and fiddle—that play melody ("lead") and provide rhythm and background for vocalists. Lead instrumentalists take solo breaks between verses of songs and provide harmonic and rhythmic background, often in antiphonal relationship to the vocal. Instrumental pieces feature alternating solos, as in many forms of jazz. Certain individuals have initiated basic bluegrass instrumental techniques—notably Earl Scruggs for the banjo and Bill Monroe for the mandolin. Considerable value is placed upon the ownership and use of the proper instruments. Old mandolins, banjos, and guitars of the make and vintage associated with the leading musicians fetch handsome prices, and reproductions of these instruments, both homemade and commercially manufactured, have proliferated. Many publications on bluegrass deal with instruments and instrumental techniques.

The classic bluegrass repertoire resembles that of older (1925–55) country music. A significant number of traditional folksongs and tunes are regularly performed, but recent, newly composed music predominates. Secular songs deal with such topics as memories of the old home and family, love affairs, and the problems of urban life. The religious repertoire reflects a wide range of sources, from old spirituals to newly composed gospel songs, and such songs are performed by virtually every bluegrass band. Forming an important component of bluegrass, instrumentals both demonstrate the virtuosity expected of musicians and symbolize the music's ties to fiddle-dominated dance music of the past.

Through their identification of instrumental styles with earlier traditions, as in their often militant defense of non-electrified instruments, bluegrass fans stress the essentially conservative form of their music, even though it differs significantly in many aspects from earlier styles. In the late 1940s, when it was a vital new sound, bluegrass was perceived within the country music trade as "backwoods," or old-fashioned, mainly because, despite its musical innovations, the instrumentation, vocal style, and song content were regional, traditional, and familiar. But as with any commercial form, changes and innovations have been essential for bluegrass performers wishing to establish individuality and gain a market; bluegrass fans have debated the propriety of any changes in the music of their favorite bands. Now bluegrass musicians attempt to retain their traditionalist fans while downplaying the bluegrass label for fear it may stereotype them and thereby frighten away others who are potential consumers of their music. The fans, not the professional musicians, named the music, and they are most concerned about maintaining its purity.

Throughout the history of bluegrass, phonograph recordings have provided income and publicity, as well as sources of style and repertoire. In the 1940s most bluegrass groups played on radio and made their living by touring rural communities in the Southeast. The most influential bands were those of Monroe, Flatt and Scruggs, and the Stanley

Brothers. By the early 1950s a number of other groups had been organized, including those of Reno and Smiley, Mac Wiseman, and Jim and Jesse. Many of the musicians who started bluegrass bands at this time had, like Flatt and Scruggs, worked in Bill Monroe's band. Today his role as a teacher and perpetuator of this music is reflected in his title, "the father of bluegrass."

During the 1950s bluegrass performers appeared increasingly on local television shows, on "package" shows with other country music performers touring larger centers, and in urban "hillbilly" bars, which catered to rural immigrants. Among the new groups that emerged as influences in the mid-1950s were the Osborne Brothers and Jimmy Martin.

At the beginning of the 1960s the urban folksong revival opened college concert halls, coffee houses, and folk festivals throughout the nation to bluegrass. For the first time new groups were dependent less upon regular radio or television exposure and more on records and concerts to build their careers. The most important new groups in this era were the Country Gentlemen and the Dillards—located in Washington, D.C., and Los Angeles, respectively. Flatt and Scruggs were, by the 1960s, nationally known, partly because of their exposure via the folk boom, but particularly because of their role in the highly successful television series *The Beverly Hillbillies*, for which they provided theme music and made yearly cameo appearances.

During the 1960s a revival of Bill Monroe's career, then in eclipse, led to his first bluegrass festival, organized near Roanoke, Va., by promoter Carlton Haney in 1965. In the next five years the idea of the bluegrass festival as an annual weekend event slowly spread; a

landmark was Monroe's own festival at his country music park in Bean Blossom, Ind., first held in 1967. By the end of the decade few of the pioneering groups, other than Monroe's, were intact. Jim and Jesse, the Osborne Brothers, and the Dillards had "gone electric." Both Flatt and Scruggs and Reno and Smiley had split, Carter Stanley had died, and John Duffey, cofounder of the Country Gentlemen, had retired from that group. In spite of these changes, the bluegrass festival idea had caught on, and by 1971, when Bill Monroe was elected to the Country Music Hall of Fame, the music was better established than ever before, with hundreds of festivals each year, the largest of which attracted audiences in the tens of thousands.

During the 1970s bluegrass music developed in a number of directions across a spectrum ranging from the "traditional" approach of the bands hewing closely to the sound and repertoire of the 1945–55 period to that of "newgrass" groups using rock repertoire and arranging techniques while retaining bluegrass instrumentation and performance styles. By the mid-1970s bluegrass was festival oriented, further outside the country music orbit in some ways, but because of its success in the festival milieu, more highly respected within the country music business. Monroe continued to be an important figure, as did Ralph Stanley and Lester Flatt; Jim and Jesse and the Osborne Brothers returned to the fold; and John Duffey teamed up with other Washington-area musicians to form the influential Seldom Scene. A host of younger musicians were active, including the Louisville-based Newgrass Revival, which mixed country rock with bluegrass in a way that created some

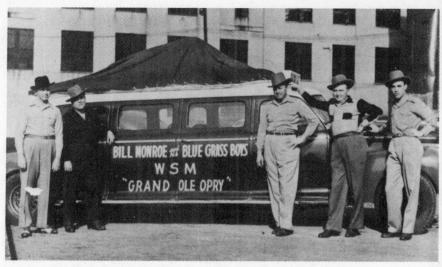

Bill Monroe and the Bluegrass Boys, the classic bluegrass group, c. 1950

controversy among fans, and J. D. Crowe and the New South, which worked toward a country-bluegrass synthesis. At the beginning of the 1980s these and other bands shared the marketplace with individual performers like Earl Scruggs, Ricky Scaggs, and David Grisman who divided their musical time between bluegrass and other forms.

As the festival movement grew, a bluegrass "establishment" appeared. Specialized record companies— County, Rebel, Rounder, and Sugar Hill are the best-known labels—were established, and regional clubs, often called "area committees," appeared. A few national and many local magazines were initiated, several gaining extensive readerships. The oldest and largest is *Bluegrass Unlimited*, published in northern Virginia, close by the Washington, D.C., area, which is reckoned by most to be the center of bluegrass music activities in the United States today. There are now instrumental instruction books and recorded instruction courses for this once aural-oral style. Spread by festivals and certain types of media exposure (particularly television and movie soundtracks) bluegrass is performed throughout the United States and Canada, though its greatest popularity is in the Southeast. There is interest in the music outside North America, particularly in Japan and Western Europe, where U.S. bands tour regularly and some local bands perform. Although a number of musicians make their living from the music, it is increasingly maintained and perpetuated by amateur and semiprofessional musicians. Today, bluegrass is encountered at fiddle conventions and contests and at other traditional musical gatherings throughout the South. Once a specialized musical style performed only by a few, it has become a standard form of southern musical expression, one, by virtue of its popularity outside the region, that is more accessible and understandable to outsiders than were earlier indigenous forms.

Neil V. Rosenberg
Memorial University
St. Johns, Newfoundland

Thomas Adler, *Folklore Forum*, 7 (1974); Bob Artis, *Bluegrass: From the Lonesome Wail of a Mountain Love Song to the Hammering Drive of the Scruggs-Style Banjo, The Story of an American Musical Tradition* (1975); Fred Bartenstein, *Journal of Country Music* (Fall, 1973); Robert Cantwell, *Bluegrass Breakdown: The Making of the Old Southern Sound* (1984); George O. Carney, *Journal of Geography* (1974); Neil V. Rosenberg, *Bluegrass: A History* (1985), *Journal of American Folklore* (April–June 1967); L. Mayne Smith, *Journal of American Folklore* (July–September 1965). ☆

Blues

||||||||||||||||

In the 1890s several new musical forms arose in the black communities of the southern and border states. Among the most important of these forms were ragtime, jazz, and blues. The generation that created this new music had been born in the years immediately following the Civil War, the first generation of blacks that did not directly experience slavery. As this generation reached maturity in the 1890s, there arose within it a restlessness to try out new ideas and new courses of action. New economic, social, and political institutions were created to provide a network of mutual support within the black community in the face of a hardening of discriminatory patterns of race relations and Jim Crow legislation. Pentecostal denominations with a more emotional style of worship arose to meet the spiritual needs of many who were trying to improve their lot in life and cope with problems of urban migration, industrialism, and unemployment.

These social changes were reflected in new developments in the arts at all levels—formal, popular, and folk—and in none of the arts was the ferment as intense as in music. In border states like Missouri, Kansas, and Kentucky, where blacks had greater opportunities to obtain formal training in music and were exposed to a variety of popular and even classical music forms, they created ragtime. At this same time the first stirrings of jazz were heard in southern cities along the Atlantic and Gulf coasts, particularly in New Orleans. Blues, on the other hand, was created in the rural areas and small towns of the Deep South, particularly in the areas of large plantations, such as the Mississippi Delta, and in industries that required heavy manual labor, such as mining, logging, levee and railroad construction, and freight loading. Those who sought work as sharecroppers and harvesters on the plantations and in the other industries were hoping to escape the drudgery and hopelessness of life on tiny plots of worn-out farmland and earn some cash for their labor. With little education or property, and no political power in a completely segregated society, they often encountered intolerable working conditions and moved frequently from one plantation or job to another.

Out of this dissatisfaction arose the blues, a music that reflected not only the social isolation and lack of formal training of its creators but also their ability to make do with the most basic of resources and to survive under the most adverse, oppressive circumstances. Blues drew from Western formal music in only the most superficial ways and instead was comprised almost entirely of resources and elements taken from the existing black folk music tradition. Unlike ragtime and jazz, blues has never been fully accepted by mainstream America as a distinct major musical form. Instead it has tended to be viewed as a rather simple and limited, though at times charming and powerfully expressive, type of music, suitable mainly as raw material for jazz, rock and roll, or some other more complex popular music. In the history of these other types of music blues is viewed as one of the "roots."

Blues introduced a number of new elements into American musical consciousness. The most novel in its initial impact, and now one of the most pervasive elements in American popular music, is the "blue note." Blue notes generally occur at the third and seventh degrees of the scale, though sometimes at other points as well, and can be either flatted notes, neutral pitches, waverings, or sliding tones occurring in the range between the major and minor of these points on the scale. Another primary musical characteristic is the role of the accompanying instrument as a second voice. The musical accompaniment in blues is not simply a rhythmic and harmonic background to the singing. It constantly interacts with, punctuates, and answers the vocal line. Finally, blues introduced a new realism combined with greater individualism into American popular song. During the 1890s most popular songs were either humorous, sentimental, or tragic, dramatizing unusual or exotic situations. The "coon songs" that depicted black life generally portrayed either nostalgic scenes of the old plantation, romantic love, or absurd humor. Blues, on the other hand, dealt with everyday life and met its subjects head-on in an open-ended celebration of life's ups and downs. Although blues focused on relationships between men and

women, it did not avoid commenting on such subjects as working conditions, migration, current events, natural disasters, sickness and death, crime and punishment, alcohol and drugs, sorcery, and racial discrimination. As a secular music, blues generally avoided making religious statements, although it could ridicule preachers and discuss the temptations and powers of the devil, and as a highly individualistic statement it seldom mentioned family and organized community life other than the immediate context of the dance or party where the music was performed. Blues developed an extraordinary compactness of form and startling poetic imagery in order to make its points on such a broad range of subjects.

The basic vocal material for early folk blues came from hollers that were sung by workers in the fields and in other occupations requiring manual labor. Hollers were sung solo in freely embellished descending lines employing blue notes and a great variety of vocal timbres. The words tended to be traditional commonplace phrases on the man-woman relationship or the work situation, with successive lines linked to one another through loose thematic associations and contrasts. Hollers appeared to be a direct reflection of the singer's state of mind and feelings poured out in a stream of consciousness. This type of singing had existed long before the 1890s. It was noted by observers during the slavery period and has clear parallels in some singing traditions in Africa and other Afro-American cultures; but it was in the American South that these free, almost formless, vocal expressions were set to instrumental accompaniment and given a musical structure, an expanded range of subject matter, and a new social context.

The accompaniment was most often played on instruments that had been rarely used in older forms of black folk music—the piano, the harmonica, and especially the guitar. For the guitar unorthodox tunings were often used to obtain drone effects. The technique of bending strings helped to achieve blue notes, and sometimes the player would slide a knife, bottleneck, or other hard object along the strings to produce a whining tone, a technique adapted from African stringed instruments. At times the performer established a simple rhythmic pattern behind the singing and then answered the vocal lines with short repeated melodic/rhythmic figures on the guitar. Blues of this sort are basically instrumentally accompanied hollers, and they allow much of the vocal freedom of the older type of song to be preserved. A few rural blues singers still compose and perform blues in this manner. Other performers, however, saw the need for greater structure in their blues and began to fit the vocal lines taken from hollers to existing harmonic patterns. Usually these patterns accommodated stanzas of 8, 12, or 16 measures, but the blues singers left space at the ends of their lines for the instrument to answer the vocal.

The pattern that proved to be predominant by the early 20th century contained three lines of four measures each. The second line repeated the first, and the third line was different but rhymed with the first two. The lines began respectively with harmonies in the tonic, subdominant, and dominant chords but always resolved to the tonic. This now-familiar 12-bar AAB pattern derived from 3-line patterns found in such folk ragtime tunes as "Bully of the Town"

and blues ballads like "Stagolee" and "Boll Weevil." Blues singers slowed the tempos of these tunes and left room at the ends of the lines for their instrumental response.

As the blues spread in the early 20th century, local and regional performance traditions developed in different parts of the South. At the local level, performers would share a repertoire of traditional verses and melodic and instrumental phrases, recombining these endlessly and often adding further musical and lyrical elements of their own creation to form blues that sounded original yet familiar at the same time. Within broader geographic regions the performers generally shared an overall musical stylistic approach and sometimes variants of certain songs in their repertoires. For instance, in the Mississippi Valley and adjacent areas the folk blues was the most intense rhythmically and emotionally, more modal and less harmonic in conception, often structured upon short repeated melodic/rhythmic phrases, and tending to extract the maximum expression from each note. Variants of tunes like "Catfish Blues" and "Rolling and Tumbling" are familiar to many blues singers throughout this region.

In Texas the guitarists often set up a constant thumping rhythm in the bass, while treble figures were played in a rather free rhythmic style in response to vocal lines that tended more to float over the constant bass rhythm. From Texas guitarists like Aaron "T-Bone" Walker came the contemporary style of lead guitar playing, in which the guitar lines often seem to float over a steady rhythm supplied by the other instruments in the band. In Virginia and the Carolinas, as well as some parts of Georgia and Florida, another style developed featuring lighter, bouncier rhythms, virtuoso playing, a harmonic rather than modal conception, and a pervasive influence of ragtime music on the blues. In whatever region the early folk blues was performed, the contexts were usually the same. Generally this music was played at house parties; roadhouses called juke joints; outdoor picnics for dancing; and for tips from onlookers on sidewalks, railroad stations, store porches, and wherever else a crowd might gather.

In the first decade of the 20th century professional singers in traveling shows began to incorporate blues into their stage repertoires as they worked in the towns and cities of the southern states. W. C. Handy, at that time the leader of a band sponsored by a black fraternal organization in Clarksdale, Miss., encountered folk blues and was so impressed by the music's appeal to both black and white audiences that he began to arrange these tunes for his own group of trained musicians. His success led him to Memphis, and there he published his first blues in sheet music form in 1912. Other blues was published that same year, and soon a flood of new blues compositions appeared from southern songwriters, both black and white, drawing on the resources of folk blues. The songwriters considered folk blues raw material to be extensively reworked and exploited.

At first the general public perceived blues as a novel type of ragtime tune with the unusual features of blue notes and three-line stanzas. The professional singers were generally women accompanied by a pianist or a small jazz combo. They performed in both the North and South in urban cabarets and vaudeville theaters and sometimes in traveling shows that visited the smaller southern towns. This professionalized type of blues first appeared on phonograph records by black singers like Ma Rainey, Bessie Smith, Clara Smith, and Ida Cox, beginning in 1920. By 1926 the record companies began to record folk blues artists, mostly male singers playing their own guitar accompaniments, like Blind Lemon Jefferson from Texas, Charley Patton and Tommy Johnson from Mississippi, and Peg Leg Howell and Blind Willie McTell from Georgia. By the end of the 1920s the companies were also recording many boogie-woogie and barrelhouse pianists such as Pinetop Smith and Roosevelt Sykes.

String bands, brass bands, and vocal quartets had incorporated blues into their repertoires by the first decade of the 20th century, but by the late 1920s there had arisen new types of ensembles created mainly to perform blues. Perhaps the closest to folk blues were the jug bands, which generally consisted of a guitar and harmonica supplemented by other novelty or homemade instruments such as a jug, kazoo, washboard, or one-stringed bass. Jug bands were recorded in Louisville, Cincinnati, Memphis, Birmingham, and Dallas, and similar kinds of "skiffle" bands existed in many other cities and towns in the South and North.

The combination of a full chorded rhythmic piano and guitar playing melodic lead lines also became popular at this time. The chief exponents of this style of blues were pianist Leroy Carr and guitarist Francis "Scrapper" Blackwell, who were based in Indianapolis. Pianist Georgia Tom (Thomas A. Dorsey) and guitarist Tampa Red (Hudson Whitaker) also made many popular recordings at this time, often performing "hokum" blues that contained humorous verses and double entendre refrains. Various combinations of stringed instruments as well as jug bands also performed hokum blues. By the mid-1930s blues bands not uncommonly consisted of a string section made up of blues musicians and a horn-and-rhythm section made up of artists with a jazz background. One of the most popular of such groups, the Harlem Hamfats, featured trumpet, clarinet, piano, guitar, second guitar or mandolin, string bass, and drums.

The continuing influence of jazz and the rise to prominence of the electric guitar served to reshape the sound of the blues in the years following World War II. Small "jump" bands of jazz-influenced musicians became popular in the late 1940s and 1950s, often performing a mixture of blues and sentimental popular songs. Folk blues guitarists in the rural South converted to the new electric guitar, and a new type of blues combo appeared consisting usually of one or two electric guitars, bass, piano or electric organ, drums, and sometimes an amplified harmonica. This type of blues reached its peak of development in Chicago in the 1950s with the bands of artists such as Muddy Waters (McKinley Morganfield) and Howlin' Wolf (Chester Burnett), both originally from Mississippi.

A synthesis of the hard down-home style of blues and the sophisticated jump blues was achieved by Aaron "T-Bone" Walker from Texas and B. B. King, a Mississippian who had moved to Memphis. Both men had strong roots in the folk blues tradition and had learned to play electric lead guitar fronting a large band of trained musicians. Their vocals were delivered in an impassioned shouting style showing the influence of gospel singing. This type of

Howlin' Wolf, bluesman, 1970s

blues, developed by Walker in the 1940s and brought to its peak of development by King in the 1950s, remains the most popular blues style.

While blues has had a history of its own, it has also had a profound influence upon other types of popular music in the 20th century. When popular blues began to be published in 1912 and performed by trained musicians, it was perceived as a new type of ragtime tune with a novel three-line verse form and the exotic element of blue notes. The use of blue notes not only helped to loosen up the formalism of ragtime but also soon paved the way for improvisatory jazz performance. The bulk of the repertoire of the early jazz bands consisted of blues tunes and ragtime tunes incorporating blue notes. The blues form has continued to be a staple for jazz compositions, and whenever jazz has seemed to become overly sophisticated, one usually hears calls for a return to the blues.

In the years before World War I, southern Anglo-American folk musicians began performing blues learned from black musicians. By the 1920s "hillbilly" artists from all parts of the

South were recording the blues. Beginning in 1927 the Mississippi singer and guitarist Jimmie Rodgers popularized a distinct type of blues by combining folk blues learned from black artists with a yodeling refrain derived from both black field hollers and German/Swiss yodeling that had been popularized on the vaudeville stage. Over the years blues has given to varieties of country music, such as western swing and honky-tonk, not only the blues form but the qualities of improvisation and greater realism as well.

In the 1950s blues-influenced country music combined with black rhythm and blues to produce a new form of music that came to be known as rock and roll. The blues form and blues instrumental techniques were very prominent in most rock-and-roll styles through the 1960s and have continued to be important factors in this music's development up to the present. Blues gave rock and roll not only an important verse form but also its basic instrumentation and instrumental technique as well as a frankness in dealing with themes of love and sex that proved attractive to an adolescent audience.

Finally, blues could even be said to have influenced gospel music. Thomas A. Dorsey, generally considered the "father of gospel music," was a former blues pianist and songwriter. By the early 1930s he was composing gospel songs using blue notes and showing a greater individualism and worldliness in the themes. While gospel has seldom utilized the blues verse form, it has shown blues influence through its use of blues tonality and emphasis on the individual.

Most Americans today are probably more familiar with blues-influenced music than they are with blues itself.

Nevertheless, blues is still a thriving form of music, existing in a variety of styles. In the South there are still excellent solo performers of folk blues, while small combos featuring electric lead guitar perform regularly in black communities in the region as well as in northern and West Coast cities. Blues can be heard today in forms close to the earliest folk blues, showing that it is still in touch with its roots, and within modern jazz and rock and roll, showing the enormous impact it has had over the last century.

See also BLACK LIFE: Music, Black; / Johnson, Robert; WOMEN'S LIFE: Blues-singing Women

David Evans
Memphis State University

Bruce Bastin, *Crying for the Carolines* (1971), *Red River Blues: The Blues Tradition in the Southeast* (1986); Samuel Charters, *The Bluesmen: The Story and the Music of the Men Who Made the Blues* (1967); David Evans, *Big Road Blues: Tradition and Creativity in the Folk Blues* (1982), *Tommy Johnson* (1971); John Fahey, *Charley Patton* (1970); William Ferris, *Blues from the Delta* (1978); Paul Oliver, *Conversation with the Blues* (1965), *The Meaning of the Blues* (1963), *The Story of the Blues* (1969); Harry Oster, *Living Country Blues* (1969); Robert Palmer, *Deep Blues* (1981); Jeff Todd Titon, *Early Downhome Blues: A Musical and Cultural Analysis* (1977). ☆

Cajun Music

||||||||||||||||||||||||||||||||||

Cajun music blends elements of American Indian, Scotch-Irish, Spanish,

German, Anglo-American, and Afro-Caribbean musics with a rich stock of western French folk traditions. The music traces back to the Acadians, the French colonists who began settling at Port Royal, Acadia, in 1604. The Acadians were eventually deported from their homeland in 1755 by local British authorities after years of political and religious tension. In 1765, after 10 years of wandering, many Acadians began to arrive in Louisiana, determined to re-create their society. Within a generation these exiles had so firmly reestablished themselves as a people that they became the dominant culture in south Louisiana, absorbing other ethnic groups around them. Most of the French Creoles (descendants of earlier French settlers), Spanish, Germans, and Anglo-Americans in the region eventually adopted the traditions and language of this new society, thus creating the south Louisiana mainstream. The Acadians, in turn, borrowed many traits from these other cultures, and this cross-cultural exchange produced a new Louisiana-based community—the Cajuns.

The Acadians' contact with these various cultures contributed to the development of new musical styles and repertoire. From Indians, they learned wailing styles and new dance rhythms; from blacks, they learned the blues, percussion techniques, and improvisational singing; from Anglo-Americans, they learned new fiddle tunes to accompany Virginia reels, square dances, and hoedowns. The Spanish contributed the guitar and even a few tunes. Refugees and their slaves who arrived from Santo Domingo at the turn of the 19th century brought with them a syncopated West Indian beat. Jewish-German immigrants began importing diatonic accordions (invented in Vienna in 1828) toward the end of the 19th century when Acadians and black Creoles began to show an interest in the instruments. They blended these elements to create a new music just as they were synthesizing the same cultures to create Cajun society.

The turn of the 20th century was a formative period in the development of Louisiana French music. Some of its most influential musicians were the black Creoles who brought a strong, rural blues element into Cajun music. Simultaneously, blacks influenced the parallel development of zydeco music, later refined by Clifton Chenier. Although fiddlers such as Dennis McGee and Sady Courville still composed tunes, the accordion was rapidly becoming the mainstay of traditional dance bands. Limited in the number of notes and keys it could play in, it simplified Cajun music; songs that could not be played on the accordion faded from the active repertoire. Meanwhile, fiddlers were often relegated to playing a duet accompaniment or a simple percussive second line below the accordion's melodic lead.

By the mid-1930s, Cajuns were reluctantly, though inevitably, becoming Americanized. Their French language was banned from schools throughout south Louisiana as America, caught in the melting pot ideology, tried to homogenize its diverse ethnic and cultural elements. In south Louisiana, speaking French was not only against the rules, it became increasingly unpopular as Cajuns attempted to escape the stigma attached to their culture. New highways and improved transportation opened this previously isolated area to the rest of the country, and the Cajuns began to imitate their Anglo-American neighbors in earnest.

The social and cultural changes of the 1930s and 1940s were clearly reflected in the music recorded in this period. The slick programming on radio (and later on television) inadvertently forced the comparatively unpolished traditional sounds underground. The accordion faded from the scene, partly because the old-style music had lost popularity and partly because the instruments were unavailable from Germany during the war. As western swing and bluegrass sounds from Texas and Tennessee swept the country, string bands that imitated the music of Bob Wills and the Texas Playboys and copied Bill Monroe's "high lonesome sound" sprouted across south Louisiana. Freed from the limitations imposed by the accordion, string bands readily absorbed various outside influences. Dancers across south Louisiana were shocked in the mid-1930s to hear music that came not only from the bandstand, but also from the opposite end of the dance hall through speakers powered by a Model-T behind the building. The electric steel guitar was added to the standard instrumentation and drums replaced the triangle as Cajuns continued to experiment with new sounds borrowed from their Anglo-American neighbors. As amplification made it unnecessary for fiddlers to bear down with the bow to be audible, they developed a lighter, lilting touch, moving away from the soulful styles of earlier days.

By the late 1940s, the music recorded by commercial producers signaled an unmistakable tendency toward Americanization. Yet an undercurrent of traditional music persisted. It resurfaced with the music of Iry Lejune, who accompanied the Oklahoma Tornadoes in 1948 to record "La Valse du Pont d'Amour" in the turn of the century Louisiana style and in French. The recording was an unexpected success, presaging a revival of the earlier style, and Iry Lejune became a pivotal figure in a Cajun music revival. Dance halls providing traditional music flourished, and musicians such as Lawrence Walker, Austin Pitre, and Nathan Abshire brought their accordions out of the closet and once again performed old-style Cajun music, while local companies began recording them. Cajun music, though bearing the marks of Americanization, was making a dramatic comeback, just as interest in the culture and language quickened before the 1955 bicentennial celebration of the Acadian exile.

Alan Lomax, a member of the Newport Folk Festival Foundation who had become interested in Louisiana French folk music during a field trip with his father in the 1930s, encouraged the documentation and preservation of Cajun music. In the late 1950s, Harry Oster began recording a spectrum of Cajun music ranging from unaccompanied ballads to contemporary dance tunes. His collection, which stressed the evolution of the music, attracted the attention of local activists, such as Paul Tate and Revon Reed. The work of Oster and Lomax was noticed by the Newport Foundation, which sent fieldworkers Ralph Rinzler and Mike Seeger to south Louisiana. Cajun dance bands had played at the National Folk Festival as early as 1935, but little echo of these performances reached Louisiana. Rinzler and Seeger, seeking the unadorned roots of Cajun music, chose Gladius Thibodeaux, Louis "Vinesse" Lejune, and Dewey Balfa to represent Louisiana at the 1964 Newport Folk Festival. Their "gutsy," unamplified folk music made the Louisiana cultural establishment uneasy, for such "unrefined" sounds embarrassed the upwardly mobile Cajuns who considered the music chosen for the Newport festival crude— "nothing but chanky-chank."

The instincts of the Newport festival organizers proved well-founded, as huge crowds gave the old-time music standing ovations. Dewey Balfa was so moved that he returned to Louisiana determined to bring the message home. He began working on a small scale among his friends and family in Mamou, Basile, and Eunice. The Newport Folk Foundation, under the guidance of Lomax, provided money and fieldworkers to the new Louisiana Folk Foundation "to water the roots." With financial support and outside approval, local activists became involved in preserving the music, language, and culture. Traditional music contests and concerts were organized at events such as the Abbeville Dairy Festival, the Opelousas Yambilee, and the Crowley Rice Festival.

In 1968 the state of Louisiana officially recognized the Cajun cultural revival, which had been brewing under the leadership of the music community and political leaders, such as Dudley LeBlanc and Roy Theriot. In that year, it created the Council for the Development of French in Louisiana (CODO-FIL), which, under the chairmanship of James Domengeaux, began its efforts on political, psychological, and educational fronts to erase the stigma Louisianans had long attached to the French language and culture. The creation of French classes in elementary schools dramatically reversed the policy that had formerly barred the language from the schoolgrounds.

Domengeaux's efforts were not limited to the classroom. Influenced by

Rinzler and Balfa, CODOFIL organized a first Tribute to Cajun Music festival in 1974 with a concert designed to present a historical overview of Cajun music from its origins to modern styles. The echo had finally come home. Dewey Balfa's message of cultural self-esteem was enthusiastically received by an audience of over 12,000.

Because of its success, the festival became an annual celebration of Cajun music and culture, not only providing exposure for the musicians but presenting them as culture heroes. Young performers were attracted to the revalidated Cajun music scene, while local French government officials, realizing the impact of the grass-roots, began to stress the native Louisiana French culture. Balfa's dogged pursuit of cultural recognition carried him farther than he had ever expected. In 1977 he received a Folk Artist in the Schools grant from the National Endowment for the Arts to bring his message into elementary school classrooms. Young Cajuns, discovering local models besides country and rock stars, began to perform the music of their heritage. Yet they did not reject modern sounds totally. Performers such as Michael Doucet and Beausoleil are gradually making their presence known in Cajun music, replacing older musicians on the regular weekend dance hall circuit and representing traditional Cajun music at local and national festivals.

See also ETHNIC LIFE: Cajuns and Creoles

Barry Jean Ancelet
University of Southwestern Louisiana

Barry Jean Ancelet, *The Makers of Cajun Music / Musiciens Cadiens et Créoles* (1984); Glenn R. Conrad, ed., *The Cajuns: Essays* on *Their History and Culture* (3d ed., 1983); *J'etais au bal: Music from French Louisiana* (Swallow 6020); *Louisiana Cajun Music* (Old-Timey Records, 108, 109, 110, 111, 114, 124, and 125); *Louisiana French Cajun Music from the Southwest Prairies* (Rounder Records, 6001 and 6002); Lauren Post, *Cajun Sketches from the Prairies of Southwest Louisiana* (2d ed., 1974); Irene Therese Whitfield, *Louisiana French Folk Song* (1969). ☆

Classical Music and Opera

IIIIIIIIIIIIIIIIIIIIIIIIIIIIIIIIIIIIIIIIIIIIIIIIIIIIIIIIIIIIIIII

By the 18th century it had become a mark of social distinction for members of the seaboard gentry to demonstrate an appreciation of good music and even play an instrument themselves. Jefferson enjoyed the violin and collected a fine music library, consisting of pieces by Corelli, Bach, Handel, and Haydn, whereas William Byrd's library at Westover included examples of English and Italian opera. Williamsburg emerged as the music center of Virginia, after Peter Pelham began giving recitals there in 1752. Amateur concerts were also held weekly in the drawing room of the Governor's Palace.

Musical life in Charleston became even more sophisticated. The first known concert in that city was presented in April 1732 when John Salter, a local church organist, offered a program in the council chamber. The first ballad opera given in America, *Flora, or, Hob in the Well*, was staged at the courtroom in Charleston three years later. In 1762 the St. Cecilia Society, the oldest musical society in the United States, was founded by 120 Carolina gentlemen who supported a paid orchestra and a yearly series of concerts. Foreign artists were occasionally imported; Maria Storer, perhaps the finest singer to perform in colonial America, was heard in February 1774. The St. Cecilia Society remained in existence until 1912, although the orchestra was eventually reduced to a quintet.

The Moravian settlements of the colonial South, most notably Salem, N.C., held musical festivals, built organs, and were noted for the quality of their choral singing. Other German and French immigrants brought with them a love of serious music and often scores of musical instruments. By the 19th century New Orleans had eclipsed Charleston as a music center, especially in the production of French and Italian opera. By the Civil War violinist Ole Bull and pianist Louis Moreau Gottschalk had played concerts all through the South, while soprano Jenny Lind had been heard in Richmond, Charleston, New Orleans, Natchez, and Memphis.

The first opera known to have been presented in New Orleans was André Grétry's *Sylvain*, given on 22 May 1796, at the St. Peter Street Theater, although there is reason to think earlier productions had been staged there. Later works by Boieldieu, Mehul, Dalayrac, and Monsigny (all stalwarts in Paris) were heard at the St. Peter Street Theater. Throughout the 19th century New Orleans had at least one resident opera company. The Théâtre d'Orléans was built in 1809, rapidly becoming the city's cultural center. The theater burned in 1813, but was quickly rebuilt. Artists were recruited each season from the Paris Opera House, making the staging of works by Rossini, Spontini, Mozart, Gluck, Cherubini, and other European masters possible. Meyerbeer's *Les Huguenots* and Donizetti's

Lucia di Lammermoor (sung in French) were but two of the many operas to receive American premieres at the Théâtre d'Orléans.

In 1835 Meyerbeer's *Robert le Diable* was staged for the first time in the United States at James Caldwell's Anglo-American Theater on Camp Street in New Orleans. The following season an Italian troupe presented the American premiere of Bellini's *Il Pirata* at the St. Charles Theater. After 1859 the French Opera House became the city's major lyric theater. Soprano Adelina Patti was engaged for a series of performances during the theater's second season, whereas Massenet's *Herodiade*, Lalo's *Le Roi d'Ys*, and Saint-Säens's *Samson and Delilah* all received their initial American staging there after the Civil War. The well-rehearsed and lavishly mounted productions featured ballet adeptly prepared in the French tradition. Closed during the Civil War, the French Opera House reopened to become "the lyric temple of the South." Not until the close of the century, as New Orleans evolved from a Latin city to a predominantly Anglo-American one, did the theater fall on hard times. The French Opera House burned in 1919, following years of neglect and financial decline.

Although French conductor Antoine

Memphis's Grand Opera House, early 1900s

Jullien had led concerts in New Orleans before the Civil War, Patrick S. Gilmore rejuvenated a taste for "monster concerts" in 1864, when he assembled a chorus of 5,000 and a band of 500 to perform in Lafayette Square to celebrate Louisiana's return to the Union, a jubilee complete with fife-and-drum corps, church bells, and cannons. Resident orchestras of professional stature were not to return to the South, however, until the 20th century. By 1890, 6 of the 34 symphony orchestras of the United States classified as major orchestras were located in the South. Of those the Dallas Symphony was the first to achieve that status. An orchestra for Dallas had been conceived in 1900 when Hans Kreissig, a German musician stranded in the city, gathered together what local talent he could and organized the Dallas Symphony Club. Five years later a more formal attempt to establish a symphony was made by Walter Fried, who had studied conducting in Germany. The modern Dallas Symphony was launched in 1945 with the appointment of Antal Dorati as conductor. Dorati broadened the standard romantic repertoire to include unusual selections by Schumann and Mendelssohn and introduced both classical and modern compositions, not always to the pleasure of conservative Dallas audiences. When Dorati accepted an offer from the Minneapolis Symphony in 1949, he was replaced by Walter Hendl, formerly associate conductor of the New York Philharmonic. Since 1958 the Dallas Symphony has met with varying success under the leadership of Paul Kletzki, Georg Solti, Donald Johannos, Anshel Brusilow, and Eduardo Mata.

The Houston Symphony, begun in 1913 under Julian Paul Blitz, reached major status after Efrem Kurtz was made director in 1948. Later a succession of superlative conductors—including Sir Thomas Beecham, Leopold Stokowski, Sir John Barbirolli, and Andre Previn—honed the Houston Symphony into the finest orchestra in the South. On tour under Barbirolli in 1964, the symphony performed at Philharmonic Hall in New York City, winning a prolonged ovation. Two years later the orchestra moved into the resplendent Jesse H. Jones Hall for the Performing Arts; it is currently under the direction of Michael Palmer.

Other major symphony orchestras in the South include the Atlanta Symphony under Robert Shaw, the New Orleans Symphony under Maxim Shostakovich, the North Carolina Symphony under the direction of Gerhardt Zimmerman, and the San Antonio Symphony under the direction of Lawrence Smith. In addition, 10 of the nation's 18 regional orchestras are located in the South. Every southern city of importance has received international concert artists on tour: Paderewski, Caruso, Iturbi, Gigli, Rubinstein, Heifetz. Pianist Van Cliburn from Kilgore, Tex., who won the International Tchaikovsky Competition in Moscow in 1958, and soprano Leontyne Price from Laurel, Miss., have each achieved world recognition on the concert stage and through recordings.

During the 1920s the Chicago Civic Opera and later the San Carlo Opera toured the larger southern cities, and New York's Metropolitan Opera Company makes annual visits to Atlanta and Dallas. Resident opera returned to New Orleans in 1943, soon evolving into the New Orleans Opera House Association under the direction of Walter Herbert. Unusual French works have occasionally been revived by the New Orleans Opera, and Verdi's *Attila* was staged by the company in 1969 for the first time

in this country since 1850. By 1980 the South supported 14 professional opera companies, 3 of them of major importance.

The Greater Miami Opera Association was begun in 1941 on a limited budget under the management of Arturo Di Filippi. The first opera staged by the Florida company was *I Pagliacci*, with Di Filippi himself singing the role of Canio. Under Robert Herman the company expanded its budget, employing singers like Eileen Farrell, Franco Corelli, Joan Sutherland, and Luciano Pavarotti in his American debut. The Houston Grand Opera was formed in 1956, with Richard Strauss's *Salome* its initial work. A mounting of *Die Walküre* in 1959 gave the South a rare look at Wagner's *Ring* cycle, whereas Massenet's *Don Quichotte* in 1969 and Rossini's *La Donna del Lago* in 1981 were both operas rarely presented anywhere in the United States. The company also revived Scott Joplin's long-forgotten ragtime opera *Treemonisha* and Gershwin's *Porgy and Bess*, productions that were eventually taken to Broadway and the West Coast.

The Dallas Opera, founded in 1957 by Lawrence V. Kelly, has enjoyed solid financial backing and unusual artistic leadership. Soprano Maria Callas launched the company with a series of performances that included a gala concert, Verdi's *La Traviata*, Cherubini's *Medea*, and Donizetti's *Lucia di Lammermoor*. Nicola Rescigno was named musical director, while Italian stage director Franco Zeffirelli did his first work in America with the Dallas company. Alexis Minotis was imported from the Greek national theater to mount the internationally acclaimed production of *Medea*, which eventually traveled to Covent Garden, La Scala, and Epidaurus. Jean Rosenthal and later Tharon Musser came from Broadway to supervise the company's lighting. Joan Sutherland, Montserrat Caballé, Jon Vickers, Teresa Berganza, Gwyneth Jones, Placido Domingo, Helga Dernesch, and the legendary Italian soprano Magda Olivero all made their American debuts with the Dallas Opera, while the company has staged the American premieres of Handel's *Alcina* and Vivaldi's *Orlando Furioso*.

Charleston reemerged as a music center when Gian Carlo Menotti brought the Spoleto Festival to the New World in May 1977. Since then summer offerings in Charleston have ranged from Tchaikovsky's *The Queen of Spades* (with Olivero as the old Countess) to Haydn's *Creation* to Barber's *Vanessa* to Shostakovich's *Lady Macbeth of the Mtsensk District*. Other southern opera companies include the Charlotte Opera Association, Civic Opera of the Palm Beaches, the Fort Worth Opera, Opera Memphis, and Opera/South in Jackson, Miss.

The South has inspired a variety of serious compositions. Bohemian-born Anton Philip Heinrich immigrated to the United States in 1805, publishing his *The Dawning of Music in Kentucky* 15 years later. Early in the 20th century Henry F. Gilbert wrote *Dance in Place Congo* and a *Negro Rhapsody* based on black folk melodies. George Gershwin spent several months in South Carolina gathering material for his opera *Porgy and Bess*, and Ferde Grofé, Gershwin's orchestrator on *Rhapsody in Blue*, himself wrote *Mississippi Suite* in 1925.

John Powell, a native of Richmond, Va., who studied in Vienna, used Afro-American themes in his *Negro Rhapsody* (1918) and Anglo-American folk tunes in his overture *In Old Virginia* (1921). William Grant Still, born on a plantation near Woodville, Miss., developed into a major spokesman for blacks in serious music. His *Afro-American Symphony* was initially performed by the Rochester Philharmonic in 1931, although opera remained the composer's great love. *A Southern Interlude* and especially *A Bayou Legend*, both dating from the 1940s, have solidified Still's reputation among opera enthusiasts. Carlisle Floyd, a native of Latta, S.C., established himself as an American opera composer of the first order with *Susannah* in 1955 and has continued to write prolifically in that field. *Wuthering Heights* was commissioned by the Santa Fe Opera in 1958, whereas *The Passion of Jonathan Wade*, set in North Carolina during the Civil War, received its premiere four years later at the New York City Opera under a Ford Foundation grant. *Willie Stark*, based on Robert Penn Warren's novel *All the King's Men*, was first staged by Harold Prince in 1981 for the Houston Grand Opera, in a production that combined elements of the operatic and Broadway theater.

Of composers working in a modern idiom, Georgia-born Wallingford Riegger stands at the forefront. Riegger produced a number of dance scores for Martha Graham, then concentrated more on orchestral forms. His *Fourth Symphony* (1959) was performed by the Boston Symphony Orchestra and judged by national critics to have both head and heart appeal. Other southern art composers include William Levi Dawson from Alabama, Lamar Stringfield from North Carolina, and Don Gillis from Texas.

See also RECREATION: Traveling Shows; / Spoleto Festival; St. Cecilia Ball

Ronald L. Davis
Southern Methodist University

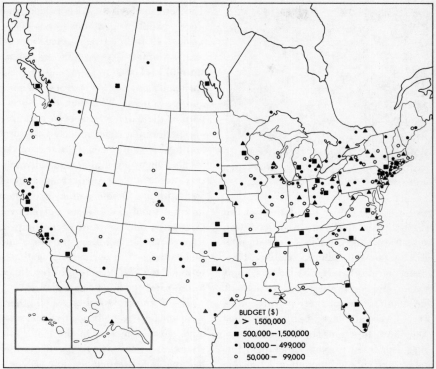

North American Symphony Orchestras
Map by George O. Carney
Source: *John F. Rooney, Jr., Wilbur Zelinsky, and Dean R. Louder, eds.*, **This Remarkable Continent: An Atlas of United States and Canadian Society and Cultures** *(1982)*.

Ronald L. Davis, *A History of Music in American Life*, 3 vols., (1980–82); Quaintance Eaton, *Opera Caravan* (1957); Robert Bartlett Haas, ed., *William Grant Still and the Fusion of Cultures in American Music* (1972); Henry A. Kmen, *Music in New Orleans: The Formative Years, 1791–1841* (1966); Hubert Roussel, *The Houston Symphony Orchestra, 1913–1971* (1972); Albert Stoutamire, *Music of the Old South: Colony to Confederacy* (1972). ☆

Country Music

‖‖‖‖‖‖‖‖‖‖‖‖‖‖‖‖‖‖‖‖‖‖‖‖‖‖‖‖‖‖‖‖‖

Although country music is a powerful cultural presence in the United States and an international export of growing magnitude, it is difficult to define. It has been a creation and organic reflection of southern working-class culture, changing as that society has changed, but it has been simultaneously a dynamic element of American popular culture. In the 60 years or so since Texas fiddler Eck Robertson made the first documented phonograph recording by a white rural entertainer, the music has become a massive industry with an appeal that cuts across social, generational, and geographic lines.

Country music had its origins in the folk culture of the South—a diverse culture that drew upon the interrelating resources of Europe and Africa. It was British at its core but eclectic in its bor-

The Gully Jumpers, early country music string band, 1920s

rowing. Long before the decade of the 1920s, when the radio and recording industries made their first exploitations of southern folk talent, fiddlers, banjoists, string bands, balladeers, and gospel singers proliferated throughout the South. Most of their performances were given at house parties or other community functions such as house raisings, fish fries, or corn shuckings, but many were able to function on a broader basis, and in a quasi-professional manner, at fiddle contests or in medicine or vaudeville shows. Musicians drew upon their inherited folk resources for songs and performing styles, but they also picked up any compatible material that was adaptable to their styles and that fit their community aesthetic standards from black entertainers or from the vast panoply of 19th-century popular music. The establishment of radio stations in the South after 1920 (including WSB in Atlanta, WSM in Nashville, WBAP in Fort Worth) and the recording of rural performers after 1922 encouraged further professionalization as well as the development of an "industry."

The early entertainers were rural, for the most part, but not exclusively agricultural. Country music has always been a working-class music (although not self-consciously so until the 1960s).

The performers of the early period, who were usually part-time musicians, worked as railroad men, coal miners, textile workers, carpenters, wagoners, sawmill workers, cowboys, and even occasionally as country lawyers, doctors, and preachers. Whatever their occupation, their dialects, speech patterns, and performing styles reflected the rural South. Given the social context of the 1920s, when the rural and socially conservative South seemed greatly out of step with a dynamic nation, and when its rural inhabitants seemed given over to strange oddities and eccentricities, such as snake handling, tenantry, and nightriding, it is not surprising that a term such as *hillbilly* should be affixed to the rural music of the region.

The commercialization of southern rural music had both positive and negative consequences. On one hand, folk styles and folksongs received a wider hearing and, presumably, longer leases on life than they otherwise would have had; on the other hand, folk styles were homogenized and diluted, and traditional songs were gradually replaced with newly composed ones. But too much has been made of this change. Folk styles were never pure; folksongs were drawn from a multitude of sources; and folk musicians were never reluctant to accept or seek some kind of reward for their talents.

The string bands of country music's first decade, including such colorful examples of self-parody as the Skillet Lickers, the Fruit Jar Drinkers, the Possum Hunters, and Dr. Smith's Champion Hoss Hair Pullers, as well as the more conventionally named groups such as the North Carolina Ramblers and the East Texas Serenaders, played hoedown tunes and British dance tunes, but they were also receptive to current popular dance tunes and especially to ragtime, which remained a national passion in the World War I period. Songs originally designed for the parlor piano, such as "Chicken Reel," "Redwing," or "Over the Waves," or for marching bands, such as "Under the Double Eagle," made their way into the repertoires of string-band musicians and have become permanently ensconced in the country music repertoire. Singers also ranged far and wide for their songs.

A large percentage of the early hillbilly songs came from 19th-century popular music, the "parlor songs," which had originally been written by professional composers and disseminated on lavishly illustrated sheet music among the nation's urban middle class. Such songs as "The Letter Edged in Black," "Little Rosewood Casket," "Little Old Log Cabin in the Lane," "Listen to the Mockingbird," and "Molly Darling" found a home among rural southerners long after ceasing to be fashionable with their original audience. Many of these sentimental favorites are still performed regularly by bluegrass and old-time country entertainers.

Country entertainers, therefore, were torn between tradition and modernity. They were loyal to their own communities but were eager to build a wider audience. Neither they nor their promoters (radio and recording men, booking agents, advertisers) were quite sure whether the most feasible promotional method would involve a rustic or an urbane approach. Country performers might have preferred conventional suits or even formal attire, but they were encouraged to clothe themselves in rustic or cowboy costumes. The conflict between rusticity and urbanity has been a factor in country music development, in sound as well as in image.

Although string bands and homespun acts predominated on early hillbilly recordings and on radio shows, the star system soon asserted itself and individual talents rose to the top. Vernon Dalhart (born Marion T. Slaughter in Jefferson, Tex.) contributed to the music's commercial acceptance by recording, in 1924, such national popular songs as "The Prisoner's Song" and "Wreck of the Old 97." Uncle Dave Macon, a comedian, singer, and five-string banjoist from Tennessee, was one of the first stars of the Grand Ole Opry and a repository of 19th-century folk and popular songs. Although there were a host of pioneer performers, the most seminal, the ones whose impacts are still felt in the music today, were the Carter Family, from Virginia, and Jimmie Rodgers, from Mississippi, both of whom were first recorded in early August 1927 in Bristol, Tenn. No group better embodied the mood and style of the family parlor and country church than the Carters; their three-part harmony, Maybelle's unique guitar style, and their large collection of vintage songs (such as "Wildwood Flower" and "Will the Circle Be Unbroken") still influence country singers today. In Jimmie Rodgers, the former railroad brakeman from Meridian, Miss., the music found its first superstar. Rodgers personified the rambling man, an image in sharp juxtaposition to that which the Carter Family projected. His "blue yodel," his appealing personal style and tragic early death, plus his eclectic repertoire of blues, hobo, train, rounder, and love songs, made him, posthumously, the "father of country music."

Country music not only survived the Great Depression but also solidified its position in American popular culture and greatly broadened its market. The

1930s were the heyday of live radio programming, and cowboy singers, duets, string bands, yodelers, and balladeers could be heard everywhere, even in New York City. Radio barn dances—Saturday-night variety shows with a rural or folk flavor—prevailed in many cities, but none was more important than WSL's National Barn Dance (Chicago) or WSM's Grand Ole Opry in Nashville. The Grand Ole Opry, which first went on the air in 1925, really affirmed its status as a national institution when it gained network affiliation on NBC in 1939. The 50,000-watt, clear-channel stations, such as WSM and KWKH in Shreveport, La., played crucial roles in circulating country music, but no stations had a more profound impact in the national dissemination of country and gospel music than the Mexican-border stations—popularly called X-stations because of their call letters (XERF, XEG, and the like). Their powerful transmission, sometimes surpassing 100,000 watts, blanketed North America with rural music (from the Carter Family to the Stamps Quartet), evangelism, and incessant advertising, which have become part of our national folklore. Radio exposure led to broadened public appearances and the emergence of booking agents and the complex framework of music business promotion.

As the professionalism and commercialization of country music proceeded, the nature of the music also changed. Traditional songs continued to appear with great frequency in the repertoires of such groups as the Blue Sky Boys and Mainer's Mountaineers. Nevertheless, newly composed songs gradually edged the older ones aside, and fledgling performers increasingly sought to find a commercial formula as successful as that of Jimmie Rodgers. Stylistically,

the southeastern hoedown-oriented string bands and the "brother duets" (acts such as the Monroe Brothers who usually featured mandolin and guitar accompaniment) relied heavily on old-time songs and ballads and remained conservative in performance and material. On the other hand, musicians from the southwestern part of the South (Texas, Louisiana, and Oklahoma) were more innovative, producing dynamic styles that would revolutionize country music. Very few observers recognized distinctions within country music before World War II, and performers with widely varying styles and repertoires often appeared together on radio shows or on radio barn dances. Whether cowboy singer, mandolin-and-guitar duet, or hot string band, they all conveyed a homespun or down-home feeling, and hillbilly was the rubric that covered them all. Nevertheless, a modern perspective suggests the great differences among them. In 1934 Gene Autry, a radio hillbilly singer from Texas, went to Hollywood, where he became the first great singing cowboy in film. The romance of the cowboy would have been appealing to country singers in any case, but Autry's Saturday afternoon horse operas, his syndicated Melody Ranch radio show, and his very popular recordings magnified the appeal while providing country musicians with an identity much more respectable than that of the hillbilly. The romantic movie-cowboy songs declined significantly after World War II, but singers wearing cowboy costumes endured long after that.

More strongly reflective of evolving southwestern culture than the movie cowboy songs was western swing, the jazz-influenced strong-band music popularized by Milton Brown and his

Musical Brownies, the Light Crust Doughboys, and Bob Wills and the Texas Playboys. The western swing bands were eclectic in repertories and were receptive to new stylistic ideas, including the use of drums, horns, and electrified instruments. Developing alongside western swing, and drawing its inspiration even more directly from the bars and dance halls of the Southwest, was honky-tonk music. Country music's entrance into white roadhouses, which were called generically "honky-tonks," divested the music of much of its pastoral innocence and tone. The result was a realistic musical sound that documented the movement of country people into an urban industrial environment.

World War II was both the major catalyst for change in country music and the chief agent in its nationalization. The country music industry itself languished under wartime restraints: shellac rationing (which reduced the number of records released), the military drafting of musicians, and the scarcity of gas and tires (which limited personal appearances). On the other hand, jukeboxes became ubiquitous accoutrements in bars, cafés, and penny arcades, and country records began appearing on them in cities like Detroit, Chicago, and Los Angeles (in part, a reflection of the movement of southerners to northern and western industrial centers). The Grand Ole Opry gained its reputation as a mecca for country fans during the 1940s, and Tennessean Roy Acuff, who joined the show in 1938, became the unquestioned king of country music during those years, taking his roadshows to all parts of the United States and holding down the most important time slots on the Saturday night Opry. His versions of "Wabash Cannon Ball" and "The Great Speckled Bird" made both his name and that of the Opry famous throughout America. Above all, in the wartime crucible of economic and demographic change and heightened migration, the mood, style, and appeal of country music were destined to change significantly.

Country music's first great commercial boom came in the years immediately following the war, continuing to about 1955. Postwar prosperity and the ending of wartime restraints generated an unprecedented demand for amusement. Record labels proliferated; new barn dances, such as the Louisiana Hayride, competed with the Grand Ole Opry, and thousands of jukeboxes reverberated with the songs of such country entertainers as Eddy Arnold, Kitty Wells, Lefty Frizzell, and Hank Williams. By the time Williams died on 1 January 1953, pop singers were "covering" his songs, and country music was winning commercial acceptance and respectability that had earlier been scarcely dreamed of. Just a few short years later, country music's "permanent plateau of prosperity" had been shattered by the revolution wrought by Elvis Presley and the rockabillies. All forms of traditional country music suffered temporarily as promoters and recording men began their urgent searches for young and vigorous stylists who could re-create what Elvis had done and who could hold that youthful audience that now dominated American music. One consequence of this quest was the creation of a pop style of country music, known generally as "country pop" or "the Nashville Sound." This form of music was considered to be a compromise that would appeal to both old-time country fans and the newly sought pop audience. By using vocal choruses and a sedate form of instrumentation (vibes, violins, piano, a muted bass), country-pop singers would avoid the extremes of both rockabilly and hillbilly.

Commercially, country music's development since the late 1950s has been one of the great success stories of American popular culture. Country performers now enjoy patronage around the world, and country concerts are regularly presented in the White House and on the Mall of the Smithsonian Institution. Country music's spectacular ascent and expansion have been accompanied by self-doubts and contradictions, and by anguished debates among performers and fans concerning the music's alleged dilution or loss of identity. Many adherents fear that the music may lose its soul as it gains the world. Although the quest for crossover records remains a powerful passion in modern country music, revivals of older country forms have periodically taken place since the rock-and-roll era. Honky-tonk music lives in the performances of men like George Jones, Merle Haggard, Moe Bandy, and the father of the style, Ernest Tubb. Bill Monroe and his fellow bluegrass practitioners have preserved the acoustic style of instrumentation and the "high lonesome" style of singing; bluegrass festivals are held somewhere almost every weekend from May until November. Doc Watson, Grandpa Jones, and Wilma Lee Cooper periodically revive the older country songs, even dipping occasionally into the songbag of ancient British material.

One of the most remarkable manifestations of interest in older songs and styles has come through the performances of youthful entertainers, or through older musicians who have catered to youth. Emmylou Harris, who was raised in Virginia, came to "hard country" through the influence of her friend and mentor, the country-rock singer Gram Parsons. Her fresh, uncluttered style of singing and her choice of material are considerably more traditional than most of the women singers who grew up in the country music world. Willie Nelson, a veteran honky-tonk singer from Texas and one of country music's greatest writers, has probably done most to bridge the gap between the rock-oriented youth audience and country music. He has done so by being receptive to their music and their heroes and by affecting a lifestyle and mode of dress (beard, earring, jogging shoes) that put them at ease. In the process, he has introduced his young fans to the best of older country and gospel songs. The 1980s has seen the emergence of young performers such as Ricky Scaggs, Dwight Yoakum, Randy Travis, Steve Earle, and George Strait, who consciously revive and update traditional forms of country music.

Country music, then, endures in many manifestations. Yet it remains as resistant to definition as it did over 60 years ago when it was first assuming an organized commercial identity. It has become a phenomenon with worldwide appeal, but it maintains its southern identification. Nashville remains its financial hub, the center of a multimillion-dollar music business. Country singers still come from southern working-class backgrounds in surprising numbers, and both they and the lyrics of their songs convey the ambivalent impulses that have always lain at the center of country music and southern culture: puritanism and hedonism, a reverence for home and a fascination with rambling, the sense of being uniquely different and at the same time more American than anyone else. Country songs convey a down-home approach to life and an elemental view of love, home, and patriotism that are absent from other forms of American music. In an age of computerized complexity, country music owes its appeal to the yearning for simplicity and rootedness that permeates modern American society.

See also INDUSTRY: / Music Industry; MEDIA: Film, Musical; WOMEN'S LIFE: Blues-singing Women

Bill C. Malone
Tulane University

Douglas B. Green, *Country Roots: The Origins of Country Music* (1976); Chet Hagan, *Country Music Legends in the Hall of Fame* (1982); Bill C. Malone, *Country Music, U.S.A.: A Fifty-year History* (1968; rev. ed., 1985), *Southern Music—American Music* (1979), with Judith McCullough, eds., *Stars of Country Music: Uncle Dave Macon to Johnny Rodriguez* (1975); Melvin Shestack, *The Country Music Encyclopedia* (1974); Ivan Tribe, *Mountaineer Jamboree: Country Music in West Virginia* (1984); Charles K. Wolfe, *Kentucky Country: Folk and Country Music of Kentucky* (1982), *Tennessee Strings: The Story of Country Music in Tennessee* (1977). ☆

Dance, Development of

||||||||||||||||||||||||||||||||||||||||||||||||||

Ethnic dance traditions and the latest dances dictated by changing fashions in European high culture were not common in the dispersed settlements of the South. Into the mid-20th century the South's reluctance to adopt popular dance trends and the security afforded it by folk traditions dictated regional dance expressions. No historical studies, however, offer a broad perspective on the development of dance in this region. Folklore studies of dance remain geographically specific and do not deal with issues of time.

Three European nations provided the greatest influence on the development of dance in the Anglo-American South. From the West Indies, Spain penetrated what is now Florida. Spanish court dances such as the *chacona* and *gibao* as well as peasant dances have been described in Mexico and the West Indies. England first settled the Chesapeake and, after 1713, extended its claim to what would become the 13 American colonies and also parts of the West Indies. France occupied the natural harbor of New Orleans and explored the Mississippi River, north and west. The court and folk traditions of England and France thus entered American life. Among black slaves rich dance traditions from Africa via the slaves in the West Indies flourished, bringing to America such dances as the Chica and the Juba.

The predominantly Anglican society of the early and mid-18th-century South did not find the amusement of theatrical and fashionable dancing a social disruption like the Calvinists of the Northeast did. Itinerant dancing masters and musicians, like William Dering, Francis Christian, George Brownell, Peter Pelham, and Charles and Mrs. Stagg, connected the upper and middle classes of townships and plantations in a network of teaching circuits. These teachers brought a western European classical aesthetic, technique, and repertoire of essentially baroque court dances—minuet, rigaudon, allemande, gavotte, and others. As the Northeast diversified and expanded its population, these itinerants moved north to cities like Baltimore, Philadelphia, and Boston. Dancing masters filled a social need for the accomplishments of polite company—conducting oneself gracefully at the many military tributes and encampment celebrations, birthnight balls, and festivities for visiting dignitaries. Urban musical societies and clubs, like the St. Cecilia Society of Charleston, S.C. (1762), sanctioned the private performances of music and dance.

Those persons whose daily lives in the South did not allow free time to pursue refinements of high culture retained their traditional dances, which they performed on a seasonal basis and which supported community cohesion. Thus, sailors' competitive jigs, African slaves' tribal dances, and faded variations of

17th-century dances from western Europe (for example, the pavan, allemande, corrante, sarabande, galliard, passapied, and minuet) mixed loosely with less intensely performed popular dances like those English country dances modeled on John Playford's *The English Dancing Master* (1651–1726) and, after 1720, informal French contra dances.

The black slaves' dances served as a mechanism for keeping alive many African traditions, particularly those associated with funerals and with festive occasions. Popular dances with distinct African roots included the Buck, the Ring Dance, and the Cakewalk. Although whites frequently described blacks' dances as wild and offensive, slave owners touted their slaves' dancing abilities, had slaves dance as entertainment for guests, and sponsored

Women dancing, Birmingham, Alabama, 1928

dancing contests among slaves from various plantations. In New Orleans many unique black dance traditions developed. Slaves meeting at the city-approved assembly site known as Congo Square enjoyed such popular dances as the Babouille and the Cata, and voodoo traditions from the West Indies also influenced the developing black dance forms in New Orleans.

Economic opportunities presented by the South's climate, fertile land, and raw materials motivated steady trade and settlement. Three centuries of diverse settlement made for a heterogeneous population. However, with the exception of towns like Charleston and New Orleans, whose greater density and economic diversity made them a stage for the display of cultural differences in status and roles, homogeneous communities in which daily life was narrowly focused on agricultural subsistence characterized inland life.

The commitment to an agrarian way of life slowed the development of commerce, manufacturing, and transportation in the South until well into the 20th century. This meant that traditions and styles in physical expression in the South, as in other areas of culture, were generally insular. For example, the conventions of 18th-century public life—dramatized courtesy, elaborate rules of deportment, and formal conduct of events—dominated regional dance. The Northeast and Northwest supported lyceums and established public education in the early 19th century, but the cause of public education was not strongly pursued in the South. Public schools and educational programs typically promoted dance activities. Specifically, physical education programs used dance and helped contribute to the widespread acceptability and appreci-

ation of dance as a useful function of everyday life, something that was lacking in the South except for a few private academies. Furthermore, the emphasis even in private academies was on traditional, 18th-century rationalizations of dance and not on new ideas from physical educators and dancing masters of high fashion. Without a mass communications network afforded by public education and good transportation, the cultural life of the South did not support modern dance.

The growth of southern towns in the late 18th century and of cities in the mid-19th century intensified the contrast between ethnic, social, and theatrical dances and made the nonverbal language of gestures and attitudes in these styles an important aspect of communication. In a city like New Orleans, for example, French, German, Spanish, and English cultures not only met but vied. Dancing cemented participants' and observers' ethnic and national ties. Cajuns, Creoles, mulattoes, and quadroons—representing the infusion of immigrants into the American South—identified performer and observer with dances. Competition and cooperation developed between theaters and opera houses as well as between those individuals involved in the Mardi Gras and other seasonal festivities.

Theatrical tours helped to knit the South together and give it connections to the mass audience and the fashionable dance activities in the rest of the United States. Theatrical managers brought well-known European and American performers of pantomime, the romantic ballet, and other dance forms into all areas of the South. Charleston, S.C., haven for expatriate Frenchmen and emigrants from the West Indies, had been a theatrical center as far back as the 1790s. French dancer and choreographer Alexandre Placide (c. 1750–1812), a multitalented performer whose pantomime productions were the most popular theatrical dance genre of their day, sent southern touring companies north to Richmond. The Louisiana Purchase of 1803 drew theatrical dancers, itinerant dancing masters, and popular and fashionable dance culture west with the settlers. The Ohio and Mississippi rivers provided easy travel, and their shore towns had entertainment-starved audiences. Samuel Drake (1769–1854), James H. Caldwell (1793–1863), Noah Ludlow (1795–1886), and Solomon Smith (1801–1869) were the most famous theatrical managers to exploit the southern frontier.

Dancers like the black American William Henry Lane, "Master Juba" (1825–52), minstrel artists like the blackface Thomas Dartmont Rice, who apparently invented the character of Jim Crow in 1828, and later road companies (1843–1908) that used the minstrel theme romanticized the South to audiences all over the country. Depicting contented, artless slaves, minstrel shows usually only parodied black dance traditions and thus shaped long-held views of black dance as shuffling, rhythmic, and comical. Minstrel shows were popular nationwide during the 1800s. River showboats that presented theatrical dancers, music, and dramatic entertainments were popular from 1836 to 1925.

In the early 20th century the Appalachian and Ozark mountain regions and other protected pockets of culture in the American South remained free from the currents of modern commercial and economic development. These areas attracted disciples in the new scholarly disciplines of folklore and anthropology who felt that early American cultural patterns, including those of music and dance, might still survive in the South untouched by modern times. An early noteworthy researcher in this new fieldwork was British musicologist Cecil Sharp, founder of the English Folk Dance Society, who, in 1916–17, believed he had found vestiges of 17th-century dance in rural Kentucky and Tennessee.

The history of dance in the American South offers folklorists and cultural historians a unique challenge. In contrast to 20th-century national trends the South's historical insularity in ethnic culture, high culture, and folk traditions and styles of performance has contributed to regional distinctiveness in ways yet to be fully explored.

See also BLACK LIFE: Dance, Black

Gretchen Schneider
Arlington, Virginia

Norman Arthur Benson, "The Itinerant Dancing and Music Masters of Eighteenth-Century America" (Ph.D. dissertation, University of Minnesota, 1963); John W. Blassingame, *The Slave Community: Plantation Life in the Antebellum South* (1972); Thomas A. Burns and Doris Mack, *Southern Folklore Quarterly* (September–December 1978); Jane Carson, *Colonial Virginians at Play* (1965); Lynne F. Emery, *Black Dance in the United States from 1619 to 1970* (1972); Henry A. Kmen, *Music in New Orleans: The Formative Years, 1791–1841* (1966); Douglas McDermott, *Theatre Survey* (May 1978); Nancy Lee Chalfa Ruyter, *Reformers and Visionaries: The Americanization of the Art of Dance* (1979); Marshall Stearns and Jean Stearns, *Jazz Dance: The Story of American Vernacular Dance* (1968). ☆

Entertainers, Popular

|||||||||||||||||||||||||||||||||||||||||||||||||

The general public has its own images of southernness: on one hand are images of a graciousness, gentility, politeness, or pride thought to be characteristic of the antebellum elite; on the other hand are images of crudeness, rowdiness, orneriness, or oafishness associated with backwoods rural folk. While some southern-born entertainers strive to capture and project a southern persona, incorporating characteristics often thought of as southern, others work to distance themselves from any regional identification. Entertainers therefore may be from the South but not representative of the South. An overview of entertainers in a variety of categories provides insight on the impact of southernness on performers' careers and popularity.

Various television actors and actresses have been cast in roles that present caricatures of southern personality: for example, Jim Nabors (Alabama) as Gomer Pyle, the goodhearted, inept, hayseed marine; Andy Griffith (North Carolina) and Don Knotts (West Virginia) as Sheriff Andy Taylor and Deputy Barney Fife, folksy small-town law officers; and Polly Holliday (Alabama) as Flo, a spunky diner waitress whose favorite rejoinder is "Kiss my grits!" Tennessee Ernie Ford often portrayed on his own program and in guest roles a gullible, likable, southern hillbilly, though his southern persona has been broader. Ford also conveys a folksy wisdom and is associated with such southern traditions as gospel music, for which he has won a Grammy Award, and good, down-home cooking, an ideal he has promoted through commercials.

Other performers convey their south-ernness not through characterization but through accents, their personalities, and comments about their roots. For example, Dinah Shore (Tennessee), singer and performer on television, radio, and the stage, conveys vivaciousness coupled with southern graciousness, warmth, and poise, and her soft southern accent is still very evident. Several southern singers who have hosted their own television shows are also good examples, among them Glen Campbell (Arkansas), Mac Davis (Texas), and Bobby Goldsboro (Florida). Devotees of *Star Trek* (created by Texan Gene Roddenberry) no doubt noted DeForest Kelley's (Georgia) southern accent in his role as Dr. McCoy. Charles Kuralt's (North Carolina) *On the Road* vignettes of life in small towns and out-of-the-way places in the United States usually focused on family-centered, slow-paced lifestyles of "common people" and thus celebrated many values associated with the South.

In the early years of television black performers faced tremendous obstacles, and inroads by southern black performers have been recent. Southern television station owners and managers openly objected to appearances of black performers on such variety programs as the *Ed Sullivan Show* and the *Milton Berle Show*, and edited out segments with black performers before airing some shows locally. Early television appearances by black actors and actresses were limited to such roles as the maid played by Butterfly McQueen (Florida), in a variety of programs. In 1956 Nat "King" Cole (born in Alabama but raised in Illinois) hosted his own television show, the first nationwide network program with a black host; but the show lasted only one year because of lack of sponsorship.

Significant changes followed the broad national television coverage of the civil rights movement in the 1960s. Even then, few black entertainers who openly confronted racial issues were accepted as television performers. Two groundbreakers from the South were Moms (Jackie) Mabley (North Carolina) and Nipsey Russell (Georgia). Known almost solely to black audiences for many years, Moms Mabley stands as the grandmother of all black comediennes. She started performing in the black vaudeville circuit, but Mabley did not become widely known until the 1960s, when her record albums became successful and she appeared frequently as a guest or guest host on late-night television talk shows. Nipsey Russell also pioneered the open handling of racial issues, primarily in his nightclub routines. Russell, like Mabley, made appearances on and occasionally hosted late-night talk shows in the 1960s and 1970s, and in the 1970s he became the first black master of ceremonies on nationally televised programs when he cohosted the *Les Crane Show* and *The Wide World of Comedy*. Though inroads have been made, opportunities for black performers on television remain limited and exploration of their southern experience is rare.

In contrast, white "hillbilly" and good old boy/good old girl images have proved popular and easy to handle. The stars of *Hee Haw*, Roy Clark (Virginia), Buck Owens (Texas), and Minnie Pearl (Tennessee), for example, have portrayed stereotyped rural southerners. Minnie Pearl's career, especially, has centered on the distinctive southern hillbilly style of music, costume, and humor. With a price tag dangling from her hat, Minnie salutes audiences with an exaggerated "Howdy," tells down-home yarns, and counsels young women on how to catch and keep a man.

Some southerners are best known for a combination of southern and western traits reflected in their roles. Fess Parker (Texas), for instance, gained popularity by portraying Walt Disney's version of Davy Crockett and later a resourceful, independent, honest, soft-spoken Daniel Boone. Affable cowboy or western figures have also been played by such actors as Ben Murphy (Arkansas), Andrew Prine (Florida), and Steve Forrest (Texas). Forrest, however, as a recently added character on the immensely popular TV series *Dallas*, contends with the quintessential southern bad guy, the avaricious, power-hungry Texas oil baron J. R. Ewing, played to the hilt by Larry Hagman (Texas).

Known primarily as emcee of the Miss America pageants, Bert Parks (Georgia) has been associated with the promotion of traditional American values. Two former Miss Americas, Mary Ann Mobley (Mississippi) and Phyllis George (Texas), whom many people still think of as classic southern beauties, have translated their pageant successes into varied roles on television. Many actresses famous for their physical beauty are not, however, typically identified by their southern roots. Among them are models-turned-actresses Cybill Shepherd (Tennessee), Lauren Hutton (South Carolina), and Farrah Fawcett (Texas). Fawcett was one of three southern women starring in the highly popular show *Charlie's Angels*, which had no regional theme. Kate Jackson (Alabama) and Jaclyn Smith (Texas) also played in the series.

Other television performers not generally seen as southern are William

Conrad (Kentucky); Morgan Fairchild, Linda Day George, and John Hillerman (Texas); Gil Gerard (Arkansas); Earl Holliman (Louisiana); Stacy Keach and Jane Withers (Georgia); Patrick O'Neal (Florida); Gerald McRaney (Mississippi); MacKenzie Phillips (Virginia); and Wayne Rogers (Alabama). *Sesame Street* and Muppet fans probably are not aware that puppeteer and director Jim Henson hails from Greenville, Miss.

Former professional athletes Fran Tarkenton (Virginia), Bill Russell (Louisiana), and Don Meredith (Texas) are now familiar sportscasters and commentators. Other southern-born sportscasters include Keith Jackson (Georgia) and Howard Cosell (North Carolina), known for an acerbic style not usually associated with the South. Meadowlark Lemon (North Carolina) has entertained crowds not only as a key trick-shot basketball player for the Harlem Globetrotters but also as a performer on television and in movies. Likewise, Mohammed Ali (Kentucky) moved from the boxing ring to a variety of entertainment roles.

Newscasters Dan Rather and Bob Schieffer (Texas) are but two southerners currently prominent on network broadcasts, as are game-show hosts Peter Marshall (West Virginia) and Wink Martindale (Tennessee). Comedians Steve Martin (Texas), Soupy Sales (North Carolina), and Foster Brooks (Kentucky) and comediennes Carol Burnett (Texas) and Pat Carroll (Louisiana) are not usually pictured as southern performers. Fannie Flagg's (Alabama) southern accent is still apparent and is incorporated in her work.

A number of well-known southern movie actors and actresses have played both distinctively southern parts and a range of other roles. A few of these performers and their notable films with southern roles are the following: Ned Beatty (Kentucky) in *Nashville*, Robby Benson (Texas) in *Ode to Billy Joe*, Betty Lynn Buckley (Texas) in *Tender Mercies*, Gary Busey (Texas) in *The Bear*, Ossie Davis (Georgia) in *Gone Are the Days*, Diane Ladd (Mississippi) in *Alice Doesn't Live Here Anymore*, Sondra Locke (Tennessee) in *The Heart is a Lonely Hunter*, Randy Quaid (Texas) in *The Last Detail*, Burt Reynolds (Georgia) in *Smokey and the Bandit*, Beah Richards (Mississippi) in *Hurry, Sundown*, Sissy Spacek (Texas) in *Coal Miner's Daughter* and *The River*, Rip Torn (Texas) in *Cross Creek*, and Joanne Woodward (Georgia) in *The Sound and the Fury* and *The Long Hot Summer*.

Some southern performers have become associated with southern parts, such as Joe Don Baker (Texas) in *Walking Tall*, Bo Hopkins (South Carolina) in *White Lightning*, and Tommy Lee Jones (Texas) in *Coal Miner's Daughter*. In contrast there are southern actors and actresses very seldom associated with southernness, such as Powers Booth, Shelley Duvall, Valerie Perrine, Paula Prentiss, and Dennis Quaid (Texas); Jim Brown (Georgia); Faye Dunaway (Florida); Louise Fletcher and Dean Jones (Alabama); George Hamilton (Tennessee); and Shirley MacLaine and George C. Scott (Virginia). Of course, some southern-born actors and actresses have not actually grown up in the South. James Earl Jones, for example, was born in Tate County, Miss., but grew up on a farm near Jackson, Mich. A critically acclaimed actor of stage, movies, and television, Jones has maintained ties with his state of birth through such projects as narration of a media presentation on Mississippi for the New Orleans World's Fair and of a film *Painting in the South*.

The southern roots of a number of famous stage performers might surprise audiences. Actress, singer, author, and former United Nations representative Pearl Bailey was born in Newport News, Va., but moved to Philadelphia in her teens. Texans Cyd Charisse, Kathryn Crosby, Mary Martin, Ann Miller, David Purdham, and Debbie Reynolds and South Carolinian Bettye Ackerman have all enthralled audiences. Sultry Eartha Kitt has roots in South Carolina but grew up in New York City.

Musical trends have been strongly influenced by talented southern performers, who have pioneered a wide variety of musical forms. Because musical forms are so varied and markets exist for many types of musical expression, reflections of southern experiences and perspectives have been more forcefully and directly expressed by singers, songwriters, and musicians than by performers in most other realms of popular entertainment.

Jazz is southern in origins, and the South has continued throughout the 20th century to produce great jazz musicians. Louisiana and surrounding areas produced the largest number of early southern performers: Louis Armstrong, King Oliver, Jelly Roll Morton, and Kid Ory were among the giants from Louisiana. Nearby Texas produced keyboard soloist Teddy Wilson and Ornette Coleman; and Mississippi was the birthplace of Lester Young and Mose Allison. But the eastern South produced Fletcher Henderson (Georgia), the "First Lady of Jazz" Mary Lou Williams (Georgia), John Coltrane (North Carolina), and Dizzy Gillespie (South Carolina).

The blues grew from work songs, spirituals, hymns, and field shouts of blacks in the South. A roll call of blues masters abounds with southerners, and the following is only a brief listing: Eddie Boyd, James Cotton, Arthur "Big Boy" Crudup, John Lee Hooker, Robert Johnson, B. B. King, Muddy Waters, and Howlin' Wolf (Mississippi); Albert Collins, Lightnin' Hopkins, and Blind Lemon Jefferson (Texas); Clarence "Gatemouth" Brown and Leadbelly (Huddie Ledbetter) (Louisiana); W. C. Handy (Alabama); the Reverend Gary Davis (South Carolina); "Sleepy" John Estes, Alberta Hunter, and Bessie Smith (Tennessee); Ida Cox, Jesse "Lone Cat" Fuller, and Sonny Terry (Georgia); and Helen Humes (Kentucky). Many of the most popular white blues performers have also been from the South, including Janis Joplin (Texas), Johnny Winter (Mississippi), and Stevie Ray Vaughan (Texas). Some performers combine elements of blues with those of other genres, and one prime example is Ray Charles (Georgia), singer, composer, and pianist, who has combined gospel, blues, country, big-band jazz, rhythm, pop, and rock sounds.

Many of soul's top performers have southern roots, including such masters as "Soul Brother Number One," James Brown (Georgia); "Lady Soul," Aretha Franklin (born in Tennessee, raised in Michigan); and "High Priestess of Soul," Nina Simone (North Carolina). Other leading soul, soul-pop, and soul-folk performers include the Bar-Kays and the Box Tops (Tennessee); Archie Bell and the Drells, and Joe Tex (Texas); Brook Benton (South Carolina); Jerry Butler and Betty Everett (Mississippi); Al Green (Arkansas); Millie Jackson and Otis Redding (Georgia); Wilson Pickett (Alabama); and Bill Withers (West Virginia). Several soul performers also influenced disco trends, most notably, Isaac Hayes (Tennessee), Thelma

Houston (Mississippi), and Johnnie Taylor (Arkansas).

Nationally popular rhythm-and-blues performers from the South have included Johnny Ace, and Booker T. and the MGs (Tennessee); Jesse Belvin (Arkansas); Gary "U.S." Bonds (Florida); Ruth Brown (Virginia); Peabo Bryson (South Carolina); The Crusaders, and Barry White (Texas); Roy Hamilton, and Gladys Knight and the Pips (Georgia); Clarence "Frogman" Henry, Ernie K-Doe, The Meters, and The Neville Brothers (Louisiana); David Ruffin (Mississippi); and Eddie Kendricks and Percy Sledge (Alabama).

Southern rock-and-roll greats abound, and some are legendary: Fats Domino (Louisiana), Buddy Holly (Texas), Jerry Lee Lewis (Louisiana), Elvis Presley (Mississippi), and Little Richard (Georgia). Others, too, have gained a wide following, such as Jayne County (Georgia), Bo Diddley (Mississippi), the Dixie Cups (Louisiana), Inez and Charlie Foxx (North Carolina), Jimmy Gilmer and the Fireballs (Texas), Ronnie Hawkins (Arkansas), Brenda Lee (Georgia), Sam the Sham and the Pharaohs (Texas), and Gene Vincent (Virginia).

Founded in 1968 in Macon, Ga., the Allman Brothers Band garnered a large following and set the style for subsequent southern rock groups through their skillful blend of blues, rhythm, country, gospel, and rock. Their style has been described as one that "reflected emergence of the 'New South.'" Other popular groups followed in their footsteps; for example, the Atlanta Rhythm Section, Big Star, Blackfoot, K.C. and the Sunshine Band, the Marshall Tucker Band, Molly Hatchet, .38 Special, Wet Willie, and ZZ Top. Two rock bands that have most conspicu-

ously conveyed a regional identification are the Charlie Daniels Band, with such hits as "The South's Gonna Do It Again" and "Devil Went Down to Georgia," and Lynyrd Skynyrd, with "Sweet Home Alabama." A cocky, rowdy, southern pride has been associated with both groups.

The group Alabama has been one of the nation's most popular country-rock groups during the 1980s. Other famous southern country-rock and country-pop groups and individual performers include the Amazing Rhythm Aces, Rita Coolidge, and Ray Stevens (Tennessee); the Everly Brothers, Crystal Gayle, and Tom T. Hall (Kentucky); Freddy Fender, The Bobby Fuller Four, Johnny Horton, Kris Kristofferson, Barbara Mandrell, Roger Miller, Michael Murphey, Jeannie C. Riley, and Kenny Rogers (Texas); Bobbie Gentry (Mississippi); Emmylou Harris (Alabama); The Outlaws, and Johnny Tillotson (Florida); and Joe South (Georgia).

No discussion of southern performers would be complete without mention of the many outstanding country-and-western artists. A few of these performers are Roy Acuff, the "King of Country Music" (Tennessee); Waylon Jennings, Willie Nelson, and Tanya Tucker (Texas); and Conway Twitty and Tammy Wynette (Mississippi). Loretta Lynn (Kentucky) and Dolly Parton (Tennessee) are particularly famous for their songs about strong, independent, resourceful women, in contrast to the faithful, ever-suffering, role-bound women so often portrayed in country music. Lynn and Parton are excellent examples of performers who convey pride in their rural southern roots both through their music and through interviews.

Perhaps the most aggressively southern performer today in style is Hank Williams, Jr. Songs such as "Dixie on My Mind" and "If Heaven Ain't a Lot Like Dixie, Then I Don't Want to Go" convey a militant regionalism, one that reflects, at times, a traditional southern defensiveness, but, at other times, a self-conscious, good-natured toying with a regional identity. In contrast, though, are various performers who have nurtured a southern image, but a genteel, low-key one, such as Chet Atkins, the "Country Gentleman" (Tennessee), Eddy Arnold, the "Tennessee Plowboy" (Tennessee), and Sonny James, the "Southern Gentleman" (Alabama).

Pop musicians and singers associated generally with mainstream sounds tend not to reflect regional identities. A number of popular entertainers particularly well known during the 1940s and 1950s hail from the South, including Polly Bergen, Pat Boone, and Judy Canova (Florida), Rosemary Clooney (Kentucky), and Kate Smith (Virginia). Other pop entertainers, many of whom have combined such sounds as folk, funk, and rock, include the Classics IV (Georgia), The Commodores (Alabama), the Mike Curb Congregation (Georgia), Tyrone Davis (Mississippi), Jackie De-Shannon (Kentucky), the Royal Guardsmen (Florida), Bobby Hebb (Tennessee), Randy Newman (Louisiana), Paul and Paula (Texas), Lionel Ritchie (Alabama), B. J. Thomas (Texas), and Mason Williams (Texas). Big-band leaders Harry James and Fletcher Henderson, both from Georgia, have also played major roles in the popular music trends in America.

Southern folk, folk-pop, and folk-rock artists include, among others, Leo Kottke (Georgia), Phil Ochs (Texas), Odetta Holmes (Alabama), and Loudon Wainwright III (North Carolina), all of whom reflect unique aspects of their southern heritage. Other performers such as gospel greats the Dixie Hummingbirds (South Carolina), Cajun fiddler Doug Kershaw (Louisiana), zydeco master Clifton Chenier (Louisiana), and "harmelody" pioneer Ornette Coleman (Texas) project distinctive southern rhythms through their music, giving glimpses of the wide variety of sounds represented in the South.

An overview of southern performers and the southern persona in popular entertainment shows that in some entertainment realms—particularly television—southernness is encouraged only when a caricature of southerners or southern life serves a need within a program geared to mass appeal. Popular music allows for much greater expression of regional identity. Although stereotyped southerners still abound in movies, in recent decades there have been not only a greater variety of roles but also more multifaceted ones portraying southerners and southernness. This trend may not herald any southern renaissance, though; in most popular media the pressures of homogenization and the emphasis on mass appeal tend to mitigate against nurturance of uniquely southern traits, characterizations, and outlooks.

See also: MEDIA articles

Sharon A. Sharp
University of Mississippi

Mike Kaplan, ed., *Variety—International Showbusiness Reference* (1981); W. Augustus Low and Virgil A. Clift, eds., *Encyclopedia of Black America* (1981); Monica O'Donnell, ed., *Contemporary Theatre, Film, and Television*, vol. I (1984); Jon Pareles, ed., *The Rolling Stone Encyclopedia of Rock 'n' Roll*

(1983); Harry A. Ploski and James Williams, eds., *The Negro Almanac: The Afro-American* (1983); Charlemae Rollins, *Famous Negro Entertainers* (1967); Melvin Shestack, *The Country Music Encyclopedia* (1974); Mabel M. Smyth, ed., *The Black American Reference Book* (1976). ☆

Festivals, Folk Music

||||||||||||||||||||||||||||||||||||||||||||||||||||||||

Music festivals have been part of southern cultural experience at least since the fiddlers' contests of the mid-18th century. Prior to 1900, however, most communally shared music was sung and played informally at family reunions, corn shuckings and barn raisings, on court and election days, at house dances, revivals and all-day singings at churches, rent parties, school commencements, county fairs, and on a variety of other occasions that brought families, neighbors, and communities together. Festivals modeled partly on these early forms continue in local benefits and fund-raisers (for volunteer fire companies, rescue squads, and the like) in which food and musical performances are the main attractions.

The hundreds of music festivals currently in evidence mirror both the South's cultural diversity and the complex patterns of cultural development and change the region has undergone. Fiddlers' contests, now in their third century, multiplied especially after the mid-1920s, stimulated by both Henry Ford's national promotional efforts and the growth of commercial country music (and especially its radio barn dances). Camp meetings and sacred harp singings still take place annually at Benton,

Ky., Tifton, Ga., Etowa, N.C., and elsewhere. Commercial gospel music of the variety that emanated from the mass revivals of Dwight L. Moody (1837–99) and Billy Sunday (1863–1935), their many successors and local imitators, and the mainly southern-based black and white gospel music industry that grew in their wake (e.g., companies owned by James D. Vaughan and R. E. Winsett in Tennessee) is performed and celebrated weekly either by local congregations, at commemorative anniversary celebrations for gospel quartets, in commercial "all night singings," at state and regional gospel singing conventions (e.g., the Albert E. Brumley sing at Springdale, Ark., and the West Virginia state convention at Nebo). Old-time music festivals such as those at Union Grove, N.C., Galax, Va., and Asheville, N.C., have drawn thousands of visitors annually for many decades. Other older forms, including blues and jazz, are celebrated in festivals such as the Delta Blues Festival in Greenville, Miss., the New Orleans Jazz and Heritage Festival, and jazz festivals at Hampton, Va., and Mobile, Ala.

Festivals styled on older social forms and presenting traditional musical idioms to local audiences exist side by side with those that present more recent idioms in festivals that feature more contemporary music and whose audiences assemble from both near and far. Deriving some of their stimulus from the efforts of educational and cultural missionaries who established industrial, settlement, and folk schools among lowland blacks and upland whites at the turn of the century, these more contemporary festivals proliferated after the mid-1920s, and they received further encouragement from supporters such as Allen Eaton and New Deal agencies.

In the post–World War II period increasing leisure and tourism expanded the market for public cultural presentations, as did the so-called folk revival of the late 1950s and 1960s, some of whose major figures (e.g., the Seegers) had learned about southern music partly by attending earlier festivals. Recently, music festivals have been spurred by the post-1965 growth of federal and state funding for cultural activities (and especially by the advent of state, regional, and federal folklife programs). Further impetus has derived from renewed cultural awareness and pride among minority cultural groups (e.g., the Cajun festival at Abbeville, La., and related observances among Cherokee and Lumbee Indians in North Carolina).

In recent years bluegrass festivals have probably multiplied more rapidly than any other type of music festival in the South. The first one was at Luray, Va., in 1962; scores of them are now held every year, organized by major bluegrass performers (e.g., Mac Wiseman and Carter Stanley), bluegrass promoters such as Carlton Haney (Camp Springs, N.C.), and a variety of local individuals and institutions. Commercial country music is the focus for many other recent festivals, which range from one-time local events headlined by a Nashville star performer, to annual "memorial" festivals (for Hank Williams at Mt. Olive, Ala.; Jimmie Rodgers at Meridian, Miss.; W. C. Handy at Florence, Ala.; and the Carter Family at Hiltons, Va.), to weekly performances at seasonal country music parks (e.g., Hiawassee, Ga.). Entrepreneurial development and promotional efforts—frequently with a dual link to tourism and local agriculture (rice, cotton, sugarcane, peaches, and pecans in the lowlands; apples and tobacco in the uplands)—have produced many music and cultural festivals.

The public "folklife festival," in which music is frequently the most prominent feature, is another important recent form. Drawing distant inspiration from such events as Bascom Lamar Lunsford's Mountain Dance and Folk Festival (Asheville, N.C., 1928), the White Top Folk Festival (White Top, Va., 1931), and the National Folk Festival (1934), but patterned more specifically upon the Smithsonian Institution's Festival of American Folklife (1967), folklife festivals (e.g., the North Carolina Folklife Festival and the Blue Ridge Folklife Festival at Ferrum College [Va.]) tend to emphasize precommercial musical idioms.

In their many forms, folk music festivals in the South bespeak both a deep attachment to local and regional tradition, and a creative and integrative sensitivity to cultural change. In a few cases they also reveal a need to invent (for self, local community, or audience) "traditions" whose authenticity is open to question: festivals at Grandfather Mountain and Red Springs, N.C., and Virginia Beach, Va., present a largely fictitious version of Scottish highland music, and the dulcimer festivals at Birmingham, Ala., and Mountain View, Ark., celebrate a romanticized feature of Appalachian music and culture. Music festivals remain, however, one of the most vital contexts in which southerners celebrate their cultural past and interpret their present cultural identity to others.

See also RECREATION: Festivals

David E. Whisnant
University of Maryland,
Baltimore County

Robert Cantwell, *Bluegrass Breakdown: The Making of the Old Southern Sound* (1984); Archie Green, *John Edwards Memorial Foundation Quarterly* (Spring 1975); Eric Hobsbawm and Terence Ranger, eds., *The Invention of Tradition* (1983); Bill C. Malone, *Southern Music—American Music* (1979); David E. Whisnant, *All That Is Native and Fine: The Politics of Culture in an American Region* (1983), *Folk Festival Issues: Report From a Seminar* (1979); Joe Wilson and Lee Udall, *Folk Festivals: A Handbook of Organization and Management* (1982). ☆

Gospel Music, Black

||||||||||||||||||||||||||||||||||||||||||||||||||

Despite its immense popularity, widespread appeal, and influence on American popular music, Afro-American gospel music is a comparably recent music phenomenon. Rooted in the religious songs of the late 19th century urban revival, in shape-note songs, spirituals, blues, and ragtime, gospel emerged early in the 20th century.

The term *gospel music* suggests many things to different people. In its most general application, the word simply refers to any religious music, regardless of the music's age or origin. Congregational songs, ring shouts, quartets, sacred harp choirs, sanctified groups, and even some work songs would all qualify. Less broadly, the term *gospel* refers to an innovative, popular style of music combining secular forms, particularly ragtime and blues, with religious texts.

Composed, modern black gospel music became an important style during the 1930s. Thomas A. Dorsey is generally regarded as its "father," although it could be argued that C. A. Tindley

should wear that mantle. Tindley was actively composing during the first decade of the 20th century, but his songs did not gain widespread popularity among blacks until the 1920s and 1930s. Dorsey himself was inspired by Tindley's reworkings of older revival songs, blues, and spirituals. Dorsey's own songs, however, made up the first wave of modern gospel music during the Depression.

Thomas A. Dorsey began his career as a blues and gospel singer. He enjoyed an immensely successful stint as a professional blues musician during the 1920s. By the early 1930s he had turned his attention entirely to religious music. During the 1930s and 1940s Dorsey worked with two influential figures, Mahalia Jackson and Sallie Martin. In addition he toured the country as a performer and lecturer and wrote some 500 gospel songs including "There Will Be Peace in the Valley" and "Precious Lord, Take My Hand."

Reverend Herbert W. Brewster, another important composer from this period, was pastor of the East Trigg Baptist Church in Memphis, Tenn. A contemporary of Dorsey, Brewster composed scores of gospel songs beginning in the early 1930s. Many of his compositions were written specifically for his choir of the Brewster Singers, but two of his songs, "Move on up a Little Higher" and "Surely, God Is Able," gained wider popularity.

The music and language of these early gospel songwriters helped to promote an interest in their compositions. Although the compositions of Dorsey and others are formally notated and printed, they almost always undergo a transformation during performance. One of the strong appeals of this music, in fact, is that it encourages participation and improvisation on the part of an audience that feels comfortable with the use of primary chords, standardized chord progression, metaphorical language, and frequent biblical illusions.

By the mid-1930s, the appeal of gospel music within black culture was quite evident, and it was soon embraced by commercial record companies wishing to capitalize on its popularity. Radio stations and the major radio networks featured its music on their live broadcasts. These attempts at mass marketing quickly led to a sense of professionalism among the performers. By the onset of World War II a small but growing cadre of people made their living singing, writing, or promoting black gospel music.

In the decade following 1945 the popularity of groups such as the Spirit of Memphis, Alex Bradford, the Soul Stirrers, Queen C. Anderson, Sallie Martin, and the Famous Blue Jay Singers grew. Dozens of professional and semiprofessional groups appeared on programs throughout the country and recorded for an expanding network of local and regional companies. This interest is well illustrated by Mahalia Jackson's recording of "Move on up a Little Higher" and the Ward Singers's version of "Surely, God Is Able," which both sold a million copies in 1950.

Interest in black gospel music gripped the country and every city and small town in the South staged gospel music programs in churches and auditoriums. New artists such as the Dixie Hummingbirds and Shirley Caesar emerged, initially as second line acts, then as headliners. Soloists such as Ira Tucker of the Dixie Hummingbirds and Claude Jeter of the Swan Silvertones became well known among devotees. Lavish gospel programs were staged by Joe

Bostic in New York City and Erskine Fausch of New Orleans. With widespread appeal, groups could afford extravagant costumes and could travel in comfort. Local nonprofessional black gospel groups emulated the dress and singing styles of more popular musicians and even adopted their names. Nearly a half dozen local or semiprofessional groups exploited the "Soul Sisters" name, for instance.

This increasing popularity and professionalism ultimately turned some of the more conservative church members away from contemporary gospel music. By the mid to late 1950s there was something of a blacklash against "secularization," most clearly manifested in the opulent manner in which some singers lived.

Black gospel music has changed greatly since the middle 1950s. It has become more sophisticated, particularly in terms of marketing and musical diversity. Popular singers such as William Gaither and Andrae Crouch have had formal musical training and education, which have led to more complicated arrangements.

These changes are part of a natural musical and cultural evolution. Black gospel music changed as the demands of popular culture increased and as Afro-Americans strove toward middle-class status. Black gospel music remains, however, essentially conservative, and its principal mission remains constant—to lift the spirits of its participants and to help them express their religion.

See also BLACK LIFE: Music, Black

Kip Lornell
Ferrum College

Horace Clarence Boyer, *Black Perspectives in Music* (Spring 1979); Harry Eskew and Paul Oliver, in *The New Grove Dictionary of Music and Musicians*, vol. 5, ed. Stanley Sadie (1980); David Evans, *Jazz Forschung/Jazz Research* (1976); Tony Heilbut, *The Gospel Sound: Good News and Bad Times* (1971); Eileen Southern, *The Music of Black Americans: A History* (1971; 2d ed., 1983). ☆

Gospel Music, White

||||||||||||||||||||||||||||||||||||||||||||||||||

For most people, the term *white gospel music* connotes a type of music characterized not so much by style as by content. Although the sound of different types of white southern gospel can range from that of a sedate vocal quartet to an amplified country band, or from a singing convention assembly of 300 voices to the simple brother duet harmony framed by mandolin and guitar, the message of the music is usually a direct and often optimistic reflection of a working-class Protestant ethos. Since white gospel music emerged as a recognized form in the 1870s and 1880s, it has tended to graft this message onto a rich variety of vernacular musics, both folk and pop; this has given white gospel an ambiguous and confusing stylistic identity. To many southerners, though, white gospel is associated with vocal quartets or family groups, singing in three- or four-part harmony, accompanied by a piano, guitar, or other stringed instruments. Also, for many of them, gospel is not a formal church music to be used in regular Sunday services, but a brand of Christian entertainment to be enjoyed at special church

singings, at concerts, on television and radio, and on records.

The roots of gospel music lie in pre–Civil War southern hymnody traditions such as camp-meeting songs, sacred harp singings, and revival music, but the real beginnings of modern southern gospel can be traced to two events occurring in the 1870s—the emergence of the Ruebush-Kieffer publishing business in the Shenandoah Valley of Virginia and the publication and popularity of a series of books of "general hymns" by two northern-based song leaders, Ira D. Sankey and Phillip P. Bliss. Aldine S. Kieffer, the main force behind the Shenandoah Valley tradition, was a Confederate veteran who happened to be the grandson of Joseph Funk, whose 1851 song book *Harmonia Sacra* (or "Hominy Soaker," as it was fondly called in the South) was published in a format using seven shapes for different notes—as opposed to the four shapes in the sacred harp tradition. After the war, as the older four-shape systems lost favor, Kieffer began his company in 1866 with an old friend, Ephraim Ruebush, whom he helped free from a Union prison camp, and began a 50-year campaign to popularize the seven-shape note system. He did this by founding the South's first Normal Singing School at New Market, Va., in 1874; by starting a periodical called *The Musical Million*, to help develop singing conventions and spread news of backwoods singing schools, in 1870; by training and sending across the South singing-school teachers; and by publishing a series of songbooks, such as *The Christian Harp* (1877), a collection of lively, "singable" songs designed for "special singing" rather than for use in regular church services. Not only did the seven-shape notation system of the Reubush-Kieffer

Company take root in the South, but the company provided a training ground for hundreds of later writers and singers; and the company itself, with its multi-faceted operation, became a model for dozens of other gospel publishing companies in the South from 1875 to 1955.

The type of song that filled these new books had its prototype in Sankey's and Bliss's 1875 collection *Gospel Hymns and Sacred Tunes*, published in New York and Cincinnati. Although the term *gospel musick* had been used in print as far back as 1644 in London, the intense popularity of the Sankey-Bliss collection, as well as its use by the popular evangelist Dwight L. Moody from 1875 to 1899, was the real source of the term *gospel music* in American culture. The songs in this collection and in others that followed in the 1880s and 1890s derived from the rise of Sunday school songs in the 1850s, songs that were deliberately designed for younger singers; they were more rhythmical than the older hymns, more sentimental, more optimistic, and often patterned on popular secular songs. Though popular nationwide, the new gospel hymns were especially successful in the South, where many of them even entered folk tradition: "Bringing in the Sheaves," "What a Friend We Have in Jesus," "Sweeping through the Gates," and "Let the Lower Lights Be Burning." The rise of southern shape-note publishers in the late 19th century provided outlets for hundreds of amateur songwriters to follow in the gospel song tradition. By the turn of the century graduates of the Ruebush-Kieffer Company had started publishing companies in Georgia (A. J. Showalter, J. B. Vaughan), Texas (Trio Music, Showalter-Patton), Arkansas (Eureka Music Company), and Tennessee (E. T. Hildebrand).

The most successful and influential of these publishers, though, was to be a Giles County, Tenn., native named James D. Vaughan (1864–1941). Early in life Vaughan studied with Ruebush-Kieffer graduate E. T. Hildebrand and later worked with B. C. Unseld, who had been the first teacher in the Rue-bush-Kieffer normal schools. Vaughan became a singing-school teacher and composer and by 1903 had settled in Lawrenceburg, Tenn., where he began publishing songbooks using the seven-shape system. By 1909 he was selling 30,000 books a year; by 1912, 85,000 books a year. One or two new books were published each year, often in paperback form and often containing as much as 75 percent new material and 25 percent old standards or favorites. Some rural churches used Vaughan's books in regular services, but most of the books were used in county or statewide singing conventions and specialty singing.

Vaughan's business sense, talent, and personality allowed him to build his company into the South's largest and to establish his own singing schools at Lawrenceburg, making it the citadel of modern gospel music. He also, however, used a number of important innovations to publicize his work. Like Ruebush-Kieffer, he started a magazine, *Vaughan's Family Visitor* (1912–present), to announce singing schools, news, and songbooks; in 1922 he began his own record company, Vaughan Records, to help popularize new songs and saw it become the South's first home-based record company. He bought his own radio station, WOAN, and encouraged his singers to perform on other commercial stations. Most important of all, though, he used quartets made up of his singing teachers to tour the South, giving free concerts of Vaughan's music.

The Vaughan quartets were a spectacular success wherever they went, and soon the company had 16 different quartets on the payroll; some of these quartets became popular in their own right and soon eclipsed the company they were representing. By the late 1920s groups like the McDonald Quartet, from southern Missouri, were able to travel independently and make a living with their music. The classic southern gospel quartet—four men and a piano—comes from Vaughan's innovations.

The Vaughan Company continued to publish until 1964, but its alumni set up important rival companies that were even more innovative and aggressive. One of Vaughan's editors, V. O. Stamps, joined forces with J. R. Baxter, Jr., to form the Stamps-Baxter Music and Printing Company in 1926. Using as their theme song, "Give the World a Smile Each Day," Stamps-Baxter sought out the best of the new, younger songwriters; helped get their quartets record contracts with major labels like RCA Victor, Columbia, and Brunswick; and used radio shows to sell their songbooks. With its effective base of operations in Dallas, the company soon shared the dominance of the market with Vaughan; they made an important move toward taking gospel music out of the church and into the realm of pure entertainment when they staged an "all-night sing" in the Cotton Bowl in 1940—thus creating a format that would characterize southern gospel for years.

During the 1930s—when the paperback gospel songbook publishers were at their height—Vaughan claimed cumulative sales of over 5 million books, and some 40 to 50 independent publishers issued such books. In addition to Vaughan and Stamps-Baxter, leaders included Hartford (Arkansas), R. E. Winsett (Tennessee), J. M. Henson (Atlanta), and the Stamps Quartet Company (Texas, formed by Frank Stamps, V. O.'s brother). During this decade, too, independent singing groups arose, and, although not formally associated with the companies, they used their songs for their repertoires. The most successful of these was the Texas family known as The Chuck Wagon Gang, who recorded and broadcasted widely, featuring such tunes as "After the Sunrise," "Jesus Hold My Hand," and "A Beautiful Life."

By the end of World War II the balance of power had shifted away from the song-publishing companies to the quartets and gospel groups; major country radio shows like the Grand Ole Opry had gospel groups as regular members, and in 1946 the Homeland Harmony Quartet of Atlanta saw its "Gospel Boogie" ("Everybody's Gonna Have a Wonderful Time Up There") become a nationwide pop hit. In the late 1940s Georgian Wally Fowler left his country band, formed the Oak Ridge Quartet, and began promoting package tours of new gospel stars, often renting an auditorium for a commercialized version of the "all-night sings." A nationwide fad for pop-gospel music in the early 1950s attracted huge audiences for young groups like the Blackwood Brothers, the Statesmen, the Jordanaires, and the Happy Goodman Family. Country artists like the Bailes Brothers, James and Martha Carson, Molly O'Day, and the Louvin Brothers made gospel a major part of their repertoire, while the newly emerging bluegrass bands often borrowed gospel repertoire and quartet singing styles.

By the end of the 1950s the quartet style no longer dominated southern gospel. Family groups such as the Speer Family and the Rambos injected country and even pop music into their performances, and groups like the Inspirations and the Kingsmen sometimes used five or six singers and a battery of backup instruments. The 1970s saw the rise of smooth, sophisticated "praise music" by singers like Dallas Holm and "contemporary Christian music" by singers like Amy Grant and Texan Cynthia Clawson, who had more in common with Broadway music and even rock than southern gospel. The southern gospel style was by the mid-1970s being referred to as "traditional gospel" and, although no longer on the cutting edge of American religious music, was still the most popular form of nonprofessional music across the South, still heard in homes, in churches, and at gatherings from Virginia to Texas.

Charles K. Wolfe
Middle Tennessee State University

Clarice Baxter and Vide Polk, *Gospel Song Writers Biography* (1971); Lois S. Blackwell, *The Wings of the Dove: The Story of Gospel Music in America* (1978); Jesse Burt and Duane Allen, *The History of Gospel Music* (1971); Ottis J. Knippers, *Who's Who among Southern Singers and Composers* (1937); Charles K. Wolfe, *American Music* (Spring 1983), in *Folk Music and Modern Sound*, ed. William Ferris and Mary L. Hart (1982). ☆

Honky-Tonk Music

||||||||||||||||||||||||||||||||||||||||||||||

Honky-tonk, also called "hard country" or "beer-drinking music," projects the mood and ambience of its birthplace, the beer joint. Born in the 1930s, honky-tonk became virtually *the* sound of mainstream country music from the late 1940s to about 1955, when rock and roll forced changes in all forms of American popular music. Since then it has endured as a vigorous subgenre of country music, with such important musicians as Ray Price, George Jones, and Moe Bandy making crucial contributions to its development.

Although conditions that contributed to its development prevailed throughout the South and on the West Coast, honky-tonk music experienced its most significant development in the states of Texas, Louisiana, and Oklahoma. There, in the oil-boom atmosphere of the mid-1930s, the combined forces of prohibition repeal and increased professionalization in the still-new hillbilly music field led to the movement of musicians into the taverns and beer joints where their music was welcomed. When country music entered the honky-tonks, its performing styles and thematic content changed significantly. Musicians sought a beat that could be felt even if it could not be heard above the din and merriment of weekend revelers, and they effected instrumental changes that would enhance and diversify their sounds; hence the adoption of electric instruments. Above all, much of the tone of country music changed in this atmosphere of wine, women, and song, where potential danger lurked behind the gay facade and where "honky-tonk angels" lured their men. No force has proved more important in diminishing the pastoral impulse of country music, nor in documenting the transition made by rural southerners to urban industrial culture.

If the 1930s were important as years of nourishment, the war years were absolutely indispensable in both the maturation and popularization of honky-tonk music. As never before in southern history, people fled agriculture and made their way by the thousands to the towns and industrial centers of the South, as well as to cities in the Midwest and on the West Coast. While civilians changed their locales and occupations, their military sons and daughters moved to training camps both in and out of the South and to combat theaters around the world. For a people in transition, who were urban in residence, yet rural in style and outlook, the adjustment was often fraught with frustration and pain. Adjustments were made in diverse ways and with varying degrees of success, but many men sought to reaffirm their identities in a sympathetic setting—over a bottle of beer in a honky tonk. Servicemen fought the loneliness of enforced separation from loved ones and friends, while their civilian relatives sought relief from the pressures of work and family responsibilities. The music of the honky-tonks, whether performed by live bands or jukeboxes, reflected increasingly the preoccupations of socially and geographically displaced people. Never before had a form of music so effectively mirrored the concerns of the southern working class.

Rustic sounds still thrived in country music during the 1940s; the decade, after all, marked the heyday of Roy Acuff as well as the beginning of the acoustic-based bluegrass style. But sounds introduced and nourished in the honky-tonks of Texas predominated, and names like Bob Wills, Ted Daffan, Cliff Bruner, Moon Mullican, Al Dexter, and Ernest Tubb dominated the jukeboxes. Many of their songs described the world of the honky-tonk itself, detailing the pleasures to be found

"Down at the Roadside Inn," or confessing the sorrows that might come from overindulgence ("Driving Nails in My Coffin," "Headin' Down the Wrong Highway"). Al Dexter's "Pistol Packin' Mama," the giant country hit of 1943 and a "crossover" of the first magnitude, grew out of its singer-composer's experiences in the oil-town-honky-tonk atmosphere of east Texas in the 1930s. More often, though, the songs concentrated on matters that had little or nothing to do with the honky-tonk. Instead, they commented on the private concerns of listeners. Voicing the cry-in-your-beer side of honky-tonk, almost to the point of suicidal impulse, were such songs as Rex Griffin's "The Last Letter," Ted Daffan's "Born to Lose," and Floyd Tillman's "It Makes No Difference Now," which poured forth from a thousand jukeboxes and were carried around the world by lonely, homesick southern servicemen. When Ernest Tubb moved to the Grand Ole Opry in 1943, his Texas-born, beer-joint-shaped style gained a national forum. As he won disciples, his style influenced the music of country entertainers from West Virginia to California.

In the prosperous years that followed World War II, as country music enjoyed its first great period of national expansion, the Texas sounds and styles continued to attract the patronage of country fans everywhere. The honky-tonk style never exercised a complete monopoly during the period, but, for all practical purposes, it had become the all-pervasive sound of mainstream country music. The typical band was small and featured a fiddle, a steel guitar, a "take-off" guitar (one that could take lead, solo passages), a rhythm guitar whose chords were played in closed, percussive fashion, a string bass, and often a piano. The musicians were capable of performing the hot instrumental licks pioneered by the western swing bands of the 1930s, but instrumentation, while crucial and distinctive, was generally subordinated to the needs of a vocalist. A new generation of honky-tonk singers had emerged, men like Hank Thompson, Webb Pierce, and Lefty Frizzell, who were among the most distinctive stylists that the country music field has seen. Surpassing them all, however, was the young singer from Alabama, Hank Williams, whose career marked the greatest commercial flowering of the honky-tonk style.

When Williams died in 1953, few could have anticipated that very soon the honky-tonk style would be driven from recordings and that country music as a whole would be in shambles. As the rock-and-roll wave inundated American music, traditional country music was driven underground to small record labels and back to the bars as promoters and recording men began their frantic search for young, vigorous performers who could imitate Elvis Presley. The rock-and-roll invasion proved temporary, but it left in its wake a continuing consciousness of the youth market and a decision by the Nashville music industry to produce a middle-of-the-road product that would be appealing to both country and pop audiences. Honky-tonk music, of course, did not die, but it could not remain dominant in such a social context. In an industry obsessed with "crossovers," the hard honky-tonk sound was unwelcome and even embarrassing. Furthermore, the temptation among performers to cross over to the more lucrative and respectable country-pop field was irresistible.

Honky-tonk music remains a vigorous subgenre of country music, but few entertainers are consistently faithful to it. In the late 1950s and early 1960s Ray Price, with his band the Cherokee Cowboys, made crucial contributions to the modern honky-tonk sound, featuring duet harmonies on vocal choruses and a thoroughly electrified sound built around a pedal steel guitar, a heavily bowed fiddle, and walking electric bass patterns. But after popularizing the sound among a host of disciples, Price abandoned the style for the country-pop field he had earlier resisted. George Jones, the Texas singer whose supple style resembled the moaning, bent notes of the pedal steel guitar (first introduced on Webb Pierce records), remains faithful to the honky-tonk sound, but his producers often smother him under a barrage of string instruments and vocal choruses. Buck Owens, who claims both Texas and California, became country music's leading vocalist in the early 1960s with an exciting sound that reflected both the honky-tonks of California and the energy of rockabilly music. He too has since abandoned the style.

At the beginning of the 1980s only Moe Bandy (born in Meridian, Miss., and reared in San Antonio, Tex.) seemed able to prosper in the honky-tonk genre. His clean, crisp articulation of lyrics dealing with those staples of honky-tonk music—drinking, cheating, and heartbreak—are complemented perfectly by a fiddle, pedal steel guitar, and walking bass. The mid-1980s witnessed a revival of honky-tonk music with young entertainers such as Randy Travis and George Strait.

Of all country styles honky-tonk has most closely reflected southern working-class culture and has best marked the evolution of the southern folk from rural to urban industrial life. Although intimately associated with the urban adjustment of southern plain folk, honky-tonk music has been ignored by folklorists because it is not pastoral and because it does not protest. It is dismissed by many, perhaps, because it is too real. Honky-tonk instrumentation both attracts and repels: to many, the whine of the pedal steel guitar and bounce of the shuffle beat evoke elemental impulses and emotions. Honky-tonk music conjures up distasteful, seedy images. The lyrics and instrumentation of honky-tonk music evoke emotional pain, isolation, and human weakness that everyone has shared. The songs can be so full of trite self-pity that they drown listeners in their sentimentality. But at its best, honky-tonk music speaks to loneliness and the need for human empathy felt by each person.

See also HISTORY AND MANNERS: World War II; RECREATION: Roadhouses

Bill C. Malone
Tulane University

Bill C. Malone, *Country Music, U.S.A.: A Fifty-year History* (1968; rev. ed., 1985), with Judith McCullough, eds., *Stars of Country Music: Uncle Dave Macon to Johnny Rodriguez* (1975). ☆

Jazz
||||||||||||

"Jazz started in New Orleans," Ferdinand La Menthe "Jelly Roll" Morton pronounced confidently to Alan Lomax in 1938. Morton's magisterial oral autobiography-history resounds with invaluable insights into the story of jazz, New Orleans in the 1890s, and southern life and culture. But like many great insights, this is a *mythic* truth.

Jazz was an agglomeration of black and white folk musics, a rich synthesis that occurred in southern, southwestern, midwestern, and eastern urban centers in the last decade of the 19th century. Jazz began in New Orleans as well—but ragtime and blues musicians wandered the Gulf Coast, the Mississippi Delta, the redlight districts of Washington, Baltimore, Kansas City, New York City, and St. Louis. Early black folk music became widely identified as southern in its associations with vaudeville, theater, circuses, as part of a vast cultural myth of the Old South plantation days, building on Stephen Foster's songs, on the spirituals of the Fisk Jubilee Singers, and on the traditions of blackface minstrelsy.

New Orleans, the most cosmopolitan and urbane center in the South before and after the Civil War, provided a hospitable climate for local and itinerant musicians and had a long tradition of musical culture, high and low. In the second half of the 19th century New Orleans mixed a vivid combination of musics—brass band marches, parlor music, Creole and Cajun folksongs, Caribbean musics, church music—and produced a style known as "ragtime," after the spicy, syncopated piano music of the Mississippi River Valley. By about 1915, this new music was often called "jass" or "jazz." Other musical centers flourished at the same time: Memphis, with its bawdy Beale Street district featuring W. C. Handy's dance orchestra; Kansas City, with legions of ragtime writers and publishers; St. Louis, a repository for even more intense ragtime playing, composing, and publishing.

Jazz drew on local scenes and traditions, indigenous southern sensibilities and languages. Handy captured blues songs from the Delta, with resonant lines like "I'm going where the Southern cross the Dog," a near-mystical reference to a Mississippi railroad junction of the Southern and the Yazoo-Delta lines ("Yellow Dog Blues"). Or Jelly Roll Morton could sing, "Michigan water tastes like sherry wine, Mississippi water tastes like turpentine" ("Michigan Water Blues"). Local customs and scenes were paid homage by southern musicians, as Morton hailed the Lake Pontchartrain resort area in "Milenberg Joys" or Louis Armstrong recalled a Basin Street brothel in "Mahogany Hall Stomp."

Jazz in the South was created and exported by blacks and whites, by musicians of every ethnic background—Irish, Italian, French-Spanish-Creole, Jamaican, German, Greek, Protestant, Catholic, and Jewish. This diversity of backgrounds guaranteed variety within the music. Place-name blues celebrated the region: "Atlanta Blues," "Vicksburg Blues," "Memphis Blues," "New Orleans Blues." Other kinds of jazz registered local color: "Beale Street Blues," "South Rampart Street Parade," "Bogalusa Strut," "Chattanooga Stomp," "Ole Miss," "Chef Menteur Joys." Jazz drew from church music—"Sing On," "When the Saints Come Marching In," "Down by the Riverside"—and from popular exotica—"Big Chief Battle-Ax," "Hindustan," "Lena from Palesteena," "The Sheik of Araby," "Chinatown." The music consciously echoed opera, military bands, call-and-response church singing, ethnic dance music, country blues singing, genteel parlor songs, light classics, and Tin Pan Alley productions.

Southern music absorbed cosmopol-

itan influences easily and converged with a wide world of vaudeville and minstrel shows, road companies of musicals and operettas, and the long-established French Opera in New Orleans's *Vieux Carré*. The most local and original of New Orleans traditions, Mardi Gras, adopted as its musical theme "If Ever I Cease to Love," a ditty from a New York musical. And another "jazz standard" was created from a New York publisher's arrangement of a novelty march by Yale student Porter Steele—"High Society."

The turn of the century witnessed an explosion of popular music creation and dissemination. Phonograph records, piano rolls, and sheet music made possible a nationwide popular musical culture on a large scale. Scott Joplin's "Maple Leaf Rag" (1899) probably sold a million copies in sheet music form, published first in Sedalia, Mo. Local publishers and artists sprang up everywhere, with important centers in southern and midwestern cities: St. Louis, New Orleans, Kansas City, Indianapolis, and Chicago. Southern music was exported on a grand scale, and local fairs and exhibitions held in Atlanta and New Orleans, the Chicago Columbian Exposition of 1893, and the St. Louis World's Fair of 1904 brought Americans into direct contact with the new southern music.

In New Orleans instrumental music was in constant demand for parties, formal dances, in neighborhood dance halls, cabarets, and social clubs. Popular social dances like the waltz, mazurka, schottische, quadrilles, and reels along with black vernacular dances created a need for a wide range of highly rhythmic accompaniment. By the 1890s strongly syncopated dance music of the sort echoed in piano ragtime was pro-

Jazz perfomer Bunk Johnson (left) and folk-blues musician Leadbelly (right), late 1940s

vided by various instrumental combinations. In the regulated redlight district (sardonically nicknamed "Storyville" after the alderman who proposed its legislation), ragtime and blues piano players worked in bordellos. In the rest of the city, bandsmen played for dances and parties.

Charles "Buddy" Bolden, a black cornetist, was the best-known leader of a rough-and-ready early jazz band of the 1890s. "Papa" Jack Laine, a white drummer-entrepreneur, organized many dance and marching bands around 1900. John Robichaux formed a long-lived "society" orchestra that read popular music scores. Freddie Keppard, another cornet virtuoso, led a group called That Creole Band on extensive vaudeville tours from New Orleans after 1910. But the New Orleans band that created a nationwide (ultimately worldwide) consciousness for a new popular music was the Original Dixieland Jazz Band—five white New Orleanians from Jack Laine's stable who went to Chicago, New York, then London, making in 1917 and 1918 the first New Orleans jazz records and achieving a monumental success in vaudeville and cabaret appearances.

The repertoire of the Original Dixieland Jazz Band was that of New Orleans jazz as it had developed for some

20 years: "Tiger Rag," "Livery Stable Blues," "Clarinet Marmalade," "Ostrich Walk," "Bluin' the Blues," and others became jazz staples and were drawn from the shared traditions of black and white musicians. The Original Dixieland Jazz Band Americanized jazz and jazzified America. Imitations of their music were heard everywhere, and "jazz" passed from the argot of the *demimonde* (where it meant either sexual intercourse or sexual fluids) into the vocabulary of middle America as the name of this new physical, sensual music. The Original Dixieland Jazz Band was followed by a continuous out-migration of southern musicians to Chicago, New York, the West Coast, and Europe. What had been a provincial oddity, a local delicacy like hog's maw, grits, or pralines, a purely regional music, became a significant force in world culture.

A "second generation" of musicians who grew up in the earliest days of New Orleans jazz disseminated it as a complex and sophisticated musical form, a form based on individual improvisational styles blended into an intuitive whole: Jelly Roll Morton (piano-composer); Joseph "King" Oliver (cornet), who took young Louis Armstrong to Chicago in 1922; Sidney Bechet (clarinet, soprano sax), who took jazz genius to Europe in 1919 with the Southern Syncopated Orchestra; Johnny Dodds (clarinet); Edward "Kid" Ory (trombone); Warren "Baby" Dodds (drums). The New Orleans Rhythm Kings, Clarence Williams's bands, and many other New Orleans bands recorded and brought live jazz to the speakeasies of 1920s America.

The impact of the new jazz recordings was catalytic. Jazz was absorbed and imitated by society dance bands everywhere by 1920, with great financial success realized by white bandleaders like Art Hickman, Paul Specht, and Paul Whiteman. "Jazz" to most Americans of the mid-1920s was simply synonymous with "pop music" of any description, and novelist F. Scott Fitzgerald could create the idea of a "Jazz Age." Jazz was identified with youth, excess, exuberance, sin, and license, with gin mills and crime, with some of the old redlight-district stigma.

In the 1920s and 1930s jazz was established in Chicago and New York, with luminaries like Fletcher Henderson (from Birmingham), Edward "Duke" Ellington (from Washington, D.C.), Jack Teagarden (from Texas), and others rising to the top of the jazz world. Jazz also flourished in the South, especially in so-called "territory" bands that succeeded regionally. Top-flight big bands created their own versions of jazz (now known more frequently as "swing") in Kansas City (Bennie Moten, Harlan Leonard, Walter Page), Missouri (Charlie Creath, Jesse Stone, the Missourians), Memphis (Jimmie Lunceford), Texas (Don Albert, Alphonso Trent), and New Orleans (Sam Morgan, Fate Marable, Armand J. Piron). Some of these groups made the national scene: Bennie Moten's band became the great Count Basie orchestra of the 1930s; the Missourians became Cab Calloway's band; and Jimmie Lunceford created one of the most innovative bands of the era.

Other southern jazz stars became nationally known: blues singers like Gertrude "Ma" Rainey, Bessie Smith, and Ethel Waters rose from backgrounds in minstrelsy and vaudeville to great fame. Jazz virtuosi like Louis Armstrong, Jimmie Noone, Sidney Bechet, and others established exalted standards for playing. Itinerant blues pianists like Pinetop Smith, Jimmy Yancey, Eurreal "Little Brother" Montgomery, Crippled Clarence Lofton, Albert Ammons, Meade Lux Lewis, and Pete Johnson popularized a form of Deep South keyboard style most commonly called "barrelhouse" or "boogie-woogie" piano, which enjoyed a wild vogue in the late 1930s. A rough, powerful form of piano blues, the music was familiar in turpentine camps and rural juke joints a generation before it reached the nation's radios and phonographs.

The South supplied vernacular dances to America after jazz became a national phenomenon in 1918. The brisk one-step "animal dances" of 1910—the Grizzly Bear, Bunny Hug, Turkey Trot, Cubanola Glide—were superseded by the Charleston, the Black Bottom, Varsity Drag, tangos, the Lindy Hop, Suzie-Q, and dozens of variants based on old black social dance patterns. Formalized versions of such dances could be seen at big dance halls, in revues like the famous Cotton Club extravaganzas in Harlem, and in vaudeville routines by such stars as Bill "Bojangles" Robinson, Florence Mills, Snakehips Tucker, and John Bubbles. Jazz was music for dancing, and long before aficionados made it intellectually respectable, America voted with its feet for the new music.

By the 1930s radio had joined with the phonograph to popularize jazz. Radio promotion helped establish bands like those of Duke Ellington and Benny Goodman, while jazz-oriented dance bands like the Coon-Sanders Orchestra, the Casa Loma Orchestra, Paul Whiteman's band, and others brought jazz into the nation's parlors nearly every day over network radio. What started as a provincial cultural phenomenon in one generation became the best-known trademark of America, a symbol for the nation's youthful vitality and melting-pot variety. In Europe, jazz was studied, imitated, and admired to the point of worship by young students and musicians.

The movements of modern jazz after the 1930s have been nationwide, with important centers of activity on the East and West coasts. The South, however, has continued to contribute major jazz artists, such as pianist-composer Thelonious Monk, the Adderly brothers, Nat and Julian ("Cannonball"), and young trumpet virtuoso Wynton Marsalis. Jazz of every variety flourishes in southern cities, from "revivalist" centers like New Orleans's French Quarter, Memphis's Beale Street area, and St. Louis's Gaslight Square to cabarets and concert-hall performances in every major city. Since the 1950s, jazz has moved from the center of popular musical culture to become a kind of "alternative culture" of great vigor and variety.

Jazz was woven into the fabric of southern life. An urban synthesis of rural musics, it reflected the development of the modern South after the turn of the century. Created by black musicians from a multiethnic culture, jazz unified the nation's sensibility. Jazz radically altered its listeners through its feelings about freedom, equality, imagination, joy, and physical vitality.

See also BLACK LIFE: Music, Black; RECREATION: Mardi Gras; WOMEN'S LIFE: Blues-singing Women

William J. Schafer
Berea College

Joachim Ernst Berendt, *The Jazz Book: From Ragtime to Fusion and Beyond* (1982); Rudi Blesh, *Shining Trumpets: A History of Jazz* (1976); Leonard G. Feather, *The Book of Jazz: From Then till Now* (1965); Mark C. Gridley, *Jazz Styles: History and Analysis* (1985); Rex Harris, *The Story of Jazz* (1960); Nat Hentoff, *Jazz Is* (1976); Gunther Schuller, *The History of Jazz* (1968); Marshall Stearns, *The Story of Jazz* (1956); Frank Tirro, *Jazz: A History* (1977); Barry Ulanov, *A History of Jazz in America* (1972); Otto Werner, *The Origin and Development of Jazz* (1984). ☆

Minstrelsy
||||||||||||||||||||||||||||

It is something of a historical paradox that the popular desire for an autonomous cultural tradition in the South—one separating it from the perceived imperfections of the industrial North and of European civilization—should induce the region's white citizenry to turn to the enslaved Afro-Americans for their music, dance, and humor. Blackface minstrelsy is the clearest antebellum example of this contradictory cultural pattern. In the 1820s individual white thespians began doing imitations of Afro-American song and dance in urban theaters. Their performances presented clownlike images of black slaves, portraying them as superstitious, happy-go-lucky "dancing darkies." The actors blackened their faces with burnt cork to accent these caricatures. The most renowned of the early blackface performers were George Washington Dixon, who created a sensation with his "Zip Coon" character, and Thomas D. Rice, who popularized the song and dance, "Jump Jim Crow." Rice copied his famous act from an elderly, crippled, Afro-American stable hand—and even borrowed his suit of ragged clothing for the initial stage performance. His comic rendition of "Jump Jim Crow" was an overwhelming success, catapulting him into a much-heralded tour of the major entertainment halls in the United States and then England. By the 1840s blackface minstrelsy in the South had evolved into a stylized entertainment formula based on the music, dance, and comedy of Afro-Americans and featuring an entire troupe of actors for the show.

From its inception, minstrelsy's characterization of black people was stereotyped. Plantation slaves were depicted as contented, comical, and childlike, while urban house servants were portrayed as dandies and dummies who aped white mannerisms and longed to be white themselves. Most of the popular figures in antebellum minstrel entertainment were from the South and had some knowledge of Afro-American folklore prior to putting on burnt cork. The best known among these performers were Dixon, Rice, Dan Emmett, E. P. Christy, and Stephen Foster. Although its performers reinforced the prevailing racism of the era, both in the South and the North, southern minstrelsy presented a more complex and even varied caricature of African slaves to the American public than had been attempted in previous decades. And even though the characters were terribly distorted, one important effect of the antebellum minstrel tradition was to help force the issues of slavery and emancipation to the forefront of the nation's political agenda. Moreover, the song and dance performed by the white minstrels laid the groundwork for a better appreciation of authentic Afro-American music and humor by white Americans. This trend became more evident in the postbellum era.

After the Civil War black entertainers joined the ranks of minstrelsy, and by the 1870s they dominated the minstrel scene. The more popular and profitable of these troupes, however, were still owned and operated by such white entrepreneurs as Charles Callender, owner of the famous Georgia Minstrels, and W. A. Mahara, owner of the popular Mahara's Minstrels. This select group of white owners and managers, and those who followed in their footsteps, insisted that the material and the format of the shows remain faithful to the content and formulas of early blackface minstrelsy. They required the black entertainers they hired to reproduce the outdated routines of the antebellum minstrel tradition. In essence, they functioned as guardians of the old-culture order, and their collective endeavors resulted in the perpetuation of demeaning racial stereotypes in American show business well into the 20th century. Talented black entertainers who joined the white-owned minstrel troupes often found themselves between the hammer and the anvil with respect to their cultural identity and their artistic integrity. The white entrepreneurs dominated the business; they determined who could work in the most prestigious companies and offered limited fame and fortune in exchange for the Afro-American performers' compliance with the blackface minstrel legacy. Although there was some latitude in negotiating these arrangements, even the most popular—and, therefore, potentially the most powerful—of the black performers in these shows sacrificed their artistic independence in return for stardom and financial gain.

The careers of minstrelsy's most acclaimed Afro-American performers— James Bland, Billy Kersands, and Bert

Williams—offer a clear, if disheartening, illustration of the dilemmas of black minstrel entertainers. Bland, known as the "Negro Stephen Foster," was an accomplished musician and composer who wrote over 700 songs in his lifetime, among them "Oh Dem Golden Slippers" and "Carry Me Back to Old Virginny." Although his material included some authentic black folklore, it was overshadowed by a permeating nostalgia for the Old South and slavery. The characters in his songs and his stage performances were replicas of the antebellum minstrel stereotypes—contented plantation slaves, faithful servants, and comic urban dandies being the most prominent. Only during an extended tour of Europe was he able to perform without the customary blackface makeup and routines.

Likewise, Billy Kersands, the most popular Afro-American minstrel entertainer of the postbellum period, based his comedy routines on demeaning racial caricatures of his own people. He portrayed black males as dull-witted and gullible, while burlesquing black woman as matronly and unattractive. To his credit, Kersands also made good use of authentic Afro-American folk humor, and he was an excellent dancer who pioneered the use of soft-shoe dancing routines on the minstrel stage. These aspects of his performances may have offset his more self-abasing comedy routines and help to explain his widespread popularity among black people in the South. Billy Kersands's successor to the throne of minstrel comedy was Bert Williams, the last major Afro-American entertainer to perform in blackface. His career began in the 1890s and peaked in the 1910–20 period when he became the first Afro-American to perform with the Ziegfeld Follies. He was a brilliant humorist, but he was also locked into the role of a hapless, antebellum darky, in spite of criticism from his own race. This situation led fellow comic W. C. Fields to comment that "Bert Williams is the funniest man I ever saw, and the saddest man I ever knew."

With the advent of the 20th century, minstrelsy in the South went into a slow but steady decline. Some of the more popular troupes like F. S. Wolcott's Rabbit Foot Minstrels, based in Port Gibson, Miss., and the black-owned Silas Green's Minstrels from New Orleans, La., continued to perform for segregated southern audiences, bolstered by an influx of talented female blues singers such as Ma Rainey and Bessie Smith. But the heyday of southern minstrelsy was over, and it was eventually replaced by other forms of entertainment like vaudeville and motion pictures. The minstrel tradition left behind a conflicting legacy: it was the training ground for many gifted Afro-American entertainers who would not have had the opportunity to develop their talents otherwise, but it was also the spawning ground for many degrading racial stereotypes that found their way into the popular culture of 20th-century America.

See also BLACK LIFE: Dance, Black; Music, Black; / Jim Crow; Silas Green Show

Bill Barlow
Howard University

Gary D. Engle, ed., *This Grotesque Essence: Plays from the American Minstrel Stage* (1978); Hans Nathan, *Dan Emmett and the Rise of Early Negro Minstrelsy* (1962); Ike Simond, *Old Slack's Reminiscence and Pocket History of the Colored Profession from 1865 to 1891* (1974); Robert C. Toll, *Black-*

ing Up: The Minstrel Show in Nineteenth-Century America (1974). ☆

Música Tejana

||||||||||||||||||||||||||||||||||||

Música Tejana, or "Tex-Mex music" as it is sometimes called, is the music of the Texas-Mexicans or *Tejanos*. Inhabiting the same geographic area of south Texas, the *Tejanos* have successively been citizens of a Spanish colony, independent Mexico, the Republic of Texas, the Confederate states, and the United States of America. The development of *música Tejana* is interwoven with the history of the *Tejanos* from the 1700s to the present.

In a cultural sense, from the 1700s until the early 1900s, the *Tejanos* were basically a Mexican provincial people, living in an isolated frontier area of the southern United States. In the past 50 years there has been a steady migration of *Tejanos* from the farms and *ranchos* of south Texas to the urban industrial centers in Texas and throughout the United States. *Tejanos* have incorporated aspects of Anglo-American culture, but overall they have resisted becoming a colonized and absorbed people. They have developed a unique regional Texas-Mexican culture, which is one of the most distinctive subcultures in the South and one that is reflected in the *Tejanos'* own musical styles. Over the course of two centuries *música Tejana* has resulted from a blending of early Spanish and Mexican music; French-European styles filtered through Mexico; Latin-Caribbean music; and now Mexican and American popular music. *Música Tejana* is thus an espe-

cially revealing indicator of the subregion of south Texas and the role of music in reflecting broader ethnic patterns within the South.

Little is known about the beginnings of *música Tejana*. Paintings and diaries depict *fandangos*, or dances, held in San Antonio and south Texas through the 1800s, but they give little descriptive information about the sound of the music other than to call it "Spanish" or "Mexican." Violins and *pitos* (wind instruments of various types) usually provided the melody with a guitar for harmonic accompaniment. Sometimes a rustic drum called a *tambora ranchera* was used to accentuate the rhythm.

By the mid to late 1800s, *Tejano* musicians were playing the Spanish and Mexican dance music less and were adopting a new European style that was trickling in from central Mexico. In the 1860s Maximilian, backed by his French army, ruled in Mexico. In his court in Mexico City and in garrisons throughout the country, the European salon music and dances of the time, such as the polka, waltz, mazurka, and schottische, were popular. These styles were enthusiastically embraced in south Texas by the *Tejanos*.

The *Tejanos'* musical culture was also influenced by the Germans who began immigrating to the central Texas area in the 1840s. These German-Texans also favored the European salon music and dances. At times they would hire local *Tejano* musicians to play for their own celebrations.

By the late 1800s the informal *Tejano* bands of violins, *pitos*, and guitars were almost exclusively playing European salon music genres for the local dances. Taking root in this frontier area, far from its European and central Mexican source, this music was being thoroughly adapted to the *Tejano* aesthetic. With French and German styles layered over the base of Spanish and Mexican music, the modern development of *música Tejana* began.

Between 1900 and the 1930s three important *Tejano* styles began to distinguish themselves. The tradition of the *guitarreros*, or singing guitarists, was the first style to become solidified and commercially popular. Using the waltz and polka rhythms with a simple guitar accompaniment, the *guitarreros* imparted stories, news, information, and morals in their songs. They sang primarily in the cantinas and at local male gatherings where listening to and discussing the songs were often combined with drinking and rowdy behavior. Dance music, on the other hand, was always instrumental (until the 1940s). Because of the feeling that words were superfluous to dancing, and partially to separate it from the cantina context, *Tejano* instrumental dance music was kept separate from the *guitarreros'* vocal style.

From the informal ensembles of musicians of the late 1800s, two styles of instrumental dance music emerged as the *Tejanos* entered the 20th century. A new German instrument, the diatonic button accordion, which was perfectly suited to playing the polkas and waltzes, was gaining great popularity among rural *Tejanos* engaged in agricultural labor. Shopkeepers and skilled *Tejanos* working in the small towns however, were hiring small bands of musicians called *orquestas típicas*. The style of these bands was similar to the earlier violin, *pito*, and guitar dance ensembles, but they had become more organized and sophisticated over time.

From the 1920s to the 1940s, lured by the economic promises of the urban American way of life, many *Tejanos* moved to the cities of south Texas—San Antonio, Corpus Christi, Brownsville, and Laredo. The rural agricultural workers had few skills to advance themselves in their new environment and became employed in low-paying, working-class jobs. The shopkeepers and skilled *Tejanos* from the towns moved into more upwardly mobile, middle-class positions in business and trades. In the cities, the difference between the aspirations and cultural values of the working-class *Tejanos*, on the one hand, and the emerging middle-class *Tejanos*, on the other, became more evident and pronounced. The working class, who suffered from discrimination and received few economic benefits from contact with Anglo-American culture, sought refuge within their own traditional culture. The middle class, encouraged by economic gains, however, saw the adoption of some American culture and values as a passport to greater opportunity and a release from Anglo-American prejudice. Working-class musical groups, or *conjuntos*, developed one distinctive musical tradition, and the middle-class bands, renamed *orquestas Tejanas*, developed another.

By the 1940s and 1950s these two dance music styles were intrinsically tied with the identities of these different segments of the *Tejano* community. Over the basic foundation of the traditional *Tejano* music of 1900, the conservatism and resistance to acculturation of the *conjuntos* and the incorporation of Anglo-American stylistic traits in the *orquestas Tejanas* created two unique Texas-Mexican styles.

Música Norteña, meaning "music of the North" (from the point of view of Mexico), played by *conjuntos*, is synonymous with the sound of the German diatonic button accordion. The instrument may have been brought and popularized by the Germans and Bohemians settling in central Texas or by the Germans working in the mining and brewing industries in northern Mexico. Newspaper accounts nonetheless show that by 1898 *Tejanos* in rural areas of the south Texas *chaparral* were playing their Texas-Mexican polkas, waltzes, and schottisches on a one-row, one-key button accordion.

Norteña accordion music began as a solo tradition. The accordion gradually replaced the violins and *pitos* as the preferred instrument for dance music in the rural areas, but because it was played in the rural areas of the *ranchos* for the laboring people, the button accordion became associated early on with working-class *Tejanos*. As more of these *Tejanos* moved from the *ranchos* to the cities, the instrument was heard in the houses and cantinas of the *barrios* (*Tejano* neighborhoods). By the 1930s the popularity of the *Norteña* style was such that accordionists, paired with guitarists or *bajo sexto* (a 12-string bass guitar, originally from central Mexico) players, began recording their own ranch-style *Tejano* polkas. Following the lead of the *guitarreros* by making "ethnic records" for American companies, the developing *conjuntos* were commercializing their style and bringing the nostalgia for the *rancho* to the city.

Although accordion dance music had been popular for some 30 years in rural areas, two men, Santiago Jiménez from San Antonio and Narciso Martínez, from the lower Rio Grande Valley, were responsible for pioneering the *Norteña* style on recording and radio broadcasts in the 1930s. Because of their popularity and exposure on recordings, their individual accordion styles became models for a generation of musicians. Jiménez had a smooth, fluid style of playing the polkas and waltzes he composed, and he emphasized the bass notes and chords of his instrument. Expanding his *conjunto*, he utilized a guitarist for harmonic accompaniment and added a *tololoche*, or upright bass, for a stronger bass line. Martínez meanwhile had a faster, more ornamented style than Jiménez and emphasized the treble buttons of his accordion. Rarely using the bass notes or chords of his instrument, Martínez delegated the harmonic accompaniment and bass line completely to his accompanying guitarist. Both musicians used the newer two-row, two-key model of accordion.

In the 1940s, taking over the singing tradition of the *guitarreros*, these pioneer accordionists began to add song lyrics with duet harmonies to their previously instrumental dance music. The typical lyrics of lost love, often framed in a rural setting, seemed to reflect the working-class *Tejanos'* ties with the past on the *rancho* and their resistance to adopting urban American culture.

By the 1950s *música Norteña* was crystallizing into a mature style as a second generation of accordionists came to popularity in the working-class cantinas, clubs, and dance halls. Tony de la Rosa, from Kingsville, Tex., became an extremely popular performer in that decade. He used amplification for the four instruments that by this time had become standard in the *conjuntos*—accordion, *bajo sexto*, bass, and drums.

De la Rosa's *conjunto* was also one of the first of a score of groups to perform on what became known as the migrant trail. Areas like Fresno, Calif., and Chicago, Ill., accumulated large communities of transplanted *Tejanos* who paid well to have *conjuntos* from Texas play for their weekend dances.

From the late 1950s to the 1980s the four-member amplified *conjunto* has changed little. *Música Norteña* has continued its conservative stance toward Anglo-American culture by reflecting and reinforcing the identity and values of the working-class *Tejano* public. Despite his recent flirtations with Anglo-American styles, Flaco Jiménez, son of the pioneer accordionist Santiago Jiménez, and his *Norteña* style best exemplify the *conjuntos* of the past 20 years. Like his father, Flaco has been a commercially successful and influential performer within the *Tejano* community.

In the late 1800s *orquestas típicas* (small, genteel orchestras of violins, flutes, clarinets, mandolins, and guitars) formed in south Texas from the earlier informal *Tejano* ensembles. Their audience was primarily a middle-class one, made up of small-town shop owners and skilled employees descended from those tenacious *Tejanos* who had held their land in the face of the Anglo-American economic advance. With more continuous income from their clientele, these bands playing *música Tejana* became better trained and more professional than ever before. When these small-town *Tejano* patrons moved to the cities in the 20th century, the *orquestas* followed.

Orquestas Tejanas developed in an urban environment among those *Tejanos* seeking to balance their traditional culture and the trappings of middle-class American culture. Striving to play in a smoother, more orchestrated style, blending *Tejano*, Latin, and American music, the *orquestas Tejanas* took over in the cities where the *orquestas típicas* had left off. Paralleling the rise of the *conjuntos*, by the 1930s and 1940s the *orquestas Tejanas* were solidifying their style on recordings and were a necessity for the dances of the more upwardly mobile segment of *Tejano* society.

Beto Ville, a saxophone player from south Texas, is recognized as the father of the *orquesta Tejana* style. Patterning his *orquesta* after American dance bands, like that of Glenn Miller, he used a full horn section, trained musicians, and written musical arrangements. Thus, the flutes and violins of the *orquestas típicas* were replaced by trumpets, saxophones, and trombones. The new *orquestas Tejanas*' choice of repertoire was American foxtrots and swing music and Latin-Caribbean dances popularized in the United States by the orchestras of musicians such as Desi Arnaz and Xavier Cugat. But never straying too far from their ties to *Tejano* culture, they also played highly arranged versions of the same *Tejano* polkas and waltzes played by the *conjuntos*.

In the 1950s the *orquesta Tejana* style crystallized into a well-developed form adding sound reinforcement, complex vocal arrangements, and some new instruments—the electric guitar, the electric bass, and the electric organ. By the 1960s and 1970s two groups, "Little Joe y la Pamilia" and "Sunny Ozuna and the Sunliners," were at the top of popularity. A new generation of *orquestas Tejanas* was playing for a younger, well-educated, more affluent *Tejano* audience. The groups still played American and Latin dance music, but foxtrots were replaced by rock and soul music and earlier Latin dances like the Mambo and Rumba were replaced by New York-Cuban Salsa music. But refusing to lose touch completely with their Texas-Mexican traditions, the newer bands continued to play polkas as the core of the *orquesta Tejana* style.

The tradition of singing troubadours, with a long history in Spain and Mexico, has also shaped *música Tejana*. The *guitarreros* in Texas represented a continuation of that tradition. By the late 1800s and early 1900s many professional *guitarreros* sang in the plazas and cantinas of south Texas towns. Their repertoire consisted of romantic, lyrical songs spawned by the popularity of the operatic style in Mexico and local ballads called *corridos*, which developed from the transplanted Spanish romance ballad tradition. When singing topical *corridos* of local or national events, the *guitarreros* were often the only source of news for the local population.

La Plaza del Zacate, or "Haymarket Square," in San Antonio was a favorite gathering place for many of these singers through the 1930s. In the 1920s American recording companies such as Vocalion, RCA, Okeh, Bluebird, and Decca came to San Antonio. Setting up makeshift studios in hotels, they made "ethnic records" of local groups to sell to the growing *Tejano* market. The *guitarreros* that performed in Haymarket Square were some of the first to be commercially recorded. Duets such as Pedro

Lydia Mendoza, Tejana singer, from the Les Blank film Chulas Fronteras *(1976)*

Rocha and Lupe Martínez, Juan Gaytán and Timoteo Cantú, and "*Los Hermanos Chavarria*" (the Chavarria Brothers) were well known in the plazas as well as on recordings by the early 1930s. Although the *guitarrero* style was mostly a male tradition, one of the most famous of these singers was a young girl with a beautiful quavering voice—Lydia Mendoza, "*La Alondra de la Frontera*" (The Lark of the Borderlands). She began recording at an early age with her musical family but later enjoyed a solo career with her famed recordings of songs such as "*Mal Hombre*" (Bad Man) and "*Pero Ay Que Triste*" (But Oh How Sad).

The commercial heyday of the *guitarreros* was short-lived, however. The same factors of urbanization that prompted the recording companies to see a commercial value in the style ultimately wrought irrevocable changes in the singing tradition. English- and Spanish-language radio and other mass media were taking over the *guitarreros'* role as the major source of news and information. Also, by the 1940s in the urban environment attitudes about the separate functions of the singing and dance-music traditions had become blurred. The working-class *conjuntos* in the cities gravitated toward performing in the cantinas that had been the domain of the *guitarreros*. In the more permissive urban atmosphere the *conjuntos* could add romantic song lyrics and duet harmonies to their polkas and waltzes without alienating their audience. The *guitarreros* then slowly faded from commercial popularity as their function had been usurped by the media and the dance-music tradition.

Although singing guitarists, or *mariachis* as they are now called, are prevalent today in Texas, their repertoire and style are part of a more general Mexican musical tradition made popular by Mexican movies and records of the past 40 years. Few of the old-style *guitarreros* remain.

Today within the *Tejano* community, one can find an audience for almost any style of *Tejano*, Mexican, or Anglo-American music. Country-and-western music sung in Spanish, *Tejano* rock and jazz, *música tropical* from the Caribbean, *mariachi* music, and the veteran *Tejano* styles can all be heard on radio stations and in dance halls throughout south Texas. Nonetheless, *Tejano* working-class and middle-class economic positions, perspectives, and identities have changed little in the past 25 years, and *música Norteña* and the *orquestas Tejanas* continue to appeal to the largest segments of the *Tejano* community.

See also ETHNIC LIFE: / Mexicans

Dan W. Dickey
Austin, Texas

Kay Council, "Exploratory Documentation of Texas *Norteño-Conjunto* Music" (M.A. thesis, University of Texas at Austin, 1978), *Texas Observer* (25 March 1977); Dan Dickey, *The Kennedy "Corridos": A Study of the Ballads of a Mexican American Hero* (1978), *Texas Observer* (16 July 1976); Américo Paredes, *A Texas-Mexican Cancionero: Folksongs of the Lower Border* (1976), *With His Pistol in His Hand: A Border Ballad and Its Hero* (1958); Manuel Peña, in *And Other Neighborly Names: Social Process and Cultural Image in Texas Folklore*, ed. Richard Bauman and Roger D. Abrahams (1981), *The Texas-Mexican Conjunto: History of a Working Class Music* (1985); Chris Strachwitz, *Texas-Mexican Border Music* (1974). ☆

Protest
||||||||||||||||||||

Despite the South's reputation as a conservative region, both protest activities and protest music have flourished at various times in its history. Indeed, southerners have played vital roles in the shaping of the protest genre in this century.

Protest has never been absent from American music. America's revolution against the British was waged in song as well as on the battlefield, and antebellum reformers fought slavery and alcohol in scores of militant songs. In the years surrounding World War I the famous Industrial Workers of the World (IWW) made music an integral part of their struggle with capitalism, and their *Little Red Songbook* continues to be a source of anthems for anyone concerned with labor rights or social justice.

Protest music as a distinct genre, though, developed in the 1930s in the context of the Great Depression and was linked directly to southern workers' struggles for economic dignity. Long presumed to be docile and fatalistic, the southern folk made themselves known in a number of dramatic ways during that period—through their presence in relief offices and hobo jungles, through their migrations (as in the case of the Okies), and, above all, in the wave of strikes that made such names as Gastonia and Marion, N.C., and Harlan County, Ky., well known throughout the United States. The traditional southern habit of ballad making was put to the service of topical songs, which commented on a wide range of social grievances. Such songs even appeared in the repertories of professional country and blues performers, as exemplified by

Frank Welling and John McGhee's "The Marion Massacre" (about the shooting of unarmed strikers in North Carolina), the Monroe Brothers' "The Forgotten Soldier Boy" (about the Bonus Marchers of 1932), and Billie Holiday's "Strange Fruit" (about lynching). Even cowboy singer Gene Autry recorded a song of tribute for a radical labor leader—"The Death of Mother Jones."

Most socially conscious songs, however, emerged from areas of worker discontent that dotted the southern landscape. There, "conservative" southern workers often came in contact with ideologically radical labor organizers and political activists, many of whom came from the North, who further fueled the impulse toward song making. In the Mississippi River Delta area of Arkansas, a black sharecropper and preacher named John Handcox supplied songs like "Raggedy" and "There Are Mean Things Happening in This Land" for his fellow farmers and members of the Southern Tenant Farmers' Union who had organized to protect themselves from landlords. At least one of his songs, "Roll the Union On," moved into the possession of union members in other parts of the country.

In Gastonia, N.C., a young mother and millworker named Ella May Wiggins emerged as a spokesperson for the striking cotton-mill workers who walked out of their plants in protest against low pay and the dehumanizing "stretch out" system (a requirement that workers operate additional machines at the same pay). The Gastonia strike attained national notoriety when the Communist-dominated National Textile Workers Union appeared with its policy of "dual unionism," which challenged both the conservative American Federation of Labor and the local power structure.

Wiggins's songs lifted the morale of the workers and presented their case to a larger public. They also gave her the reputation of "labor agitator," and when she was shot to death on 14 September 1929, while riding in the back of a truck with other strikers, many people felt that she had been singled out for execution. She became a martyr in the American labor community, and her songs were printed in such liberal and radical journals as the *Nation* and *New Masses* and were sung at northern labor rallies by such activists as Margaret Larkin.

Strikes in the coal-mining district of Harlan and Bell counties, Ky., inspired a similar wave of topical ballad making. One of the most famous labor songs in American history, "Which Side Are You On?," appeared when Florence Reece, the wife of a Harlan County organizer, voiced her anger at the brutality of the company-paid deputy sheriffs. The most famous trio of balladeers, though, to come out of the Kentucky coalfields was Aunt Molly Jackson and her brother and half-sister, Jim Garland and Sara Ogan. Before they were blacklisted and forced to leave Kentucky, each of them turned out a steady stream of songs that graphically portrayed the grim lives of coal miners while also championing their rights. These included Aunt Molly's "Dreadful Memories" and "I Am a Union Woman," Garland's "I Don't Want Your Millions Mister" and "Ballad of Harry Simms" (about a young Communist organizer who was killed by company "gun thugs"), and Ogan's "I Hate the Capitalist System."

These and other songs like them moved north to become the nucleus of an incipient urban folk music movement. They were taken by the northern radicals who recognized their organizing potential, and of course, by such southern singers as Aunt Molly Jackson, Jim Garland, and Woodrow Wilson "Woody" Guthrie. Until he moved in 1940 to New York, where he became part of the labor/radical community, Guthrie had been identified as a hillbilly singer with a storehouse of traditional songs and a guitar style roughly copied after that of Maybelle Carter. The Okemah, Okla., native, though, had been a champion of his fellow Okie migrants ever since he began singing over KFVD in Los Angeles in 1937. With such songs as "Talking Dust Bowl Blues," "Dust Bowl Refugee," and "Do-Re-Mi," Guthrie established his reputation as a champion of the poor and dispossessed. In New York he was welcomed as "the new Joe Hill" and very quickly became the center of a coterie of musicians, which included such fellow expatriate southerners as Aunt Molly Jackson, Brownie McGhee, Sonny Terry, Josh White, Sis Cunningham, Lee Hays, and Huddie "Leadbelly" Ledbetter. He also inspired a host of disciples within his northern audiences, including most notably Cisco Houston, Jack Elliott, and Pete Seeger, who preserved Guthrie's commitment to the use of the folksong as a weapon in the struggle for social justice.

The protest-song movement of the 1930s and 1940s was confined to a narrow segment of Americans—labor activists, radical intellectuals, and some college students. That of the late 1950s and early 1960s, on the other hand, was of a much broader scope and was in fact introduced to virtually every American home through the media of national television and stereophonic sound reproduction. Again, southerners played direct and vital roles in the development of a body of protest material. Although modern protest song making was clearly

linked to the traditions and singers of the 1930s, especially through the continued presence of such activists as Pete Seeger, the phenomenon gained most of its inspiration from the civil rights movement. In the aftermath of the Montgomery Bus Boycott in 1956 black people began resurrecting older religious songs to provide moral strength and spiritual sustenance in their marches and demonstrations, and, in the time-tested folk fashion, they attached new words to old folk and religious melodies. Such songs as "Oh Freedom" and "We Shall Not Be Moved" filled the air in places like Selma and Birmingham where black people battled against the entrenched forces of segregation and racial bigotry.

The most famous and stirring song of the civil rights movement, "We Shall Overcome," came from a still-surviving center of 1930s radicalism, the Highlander Folk School in Grundy County, Tenn. Apparently based on a gospel song written by Charles Tindley in 1901, "I'll Overcome Some Day," the song was taken to the folk school by black workers who had sung fragments of it during a 1946 strike. Zilphia Horton, wife of the school's director, Myles Horton, added some verses to it and taught them to the other students. White folk singer Guy Carawan introduced the song to the civil rights movement when he sang it during sit-in workshops at Nashville in 1960. During the first half of the decade students sponsored by the Student Nonviolent Coordinating Committee (SNCC), such as Bernice Reagon and Julius Lester, took the song to every section of the South. By the time President Lyndon B. Johnson quoted the phrase in a speech endorsing the 1964 Civil Rights Act, "We Shall Overcome" had become known, in at least fragmentary form, to most Americans. Indeed, the whole grass-roots phase of protest singing was superseded by the absorption of such songs by American popular culture. Civil rights songs, antiwar songs, and ballads protesting against a wide range of social evils became vital ingredients of a major urban folk music revival that swept the United States in the early 1960s. Southern singers continued to play distinctive roles, but usually on phonograph recordings, in coffee houses and college folk music clubs, in auditorium concerts, or on radio and television broadcasts. Sis Cunningham, an Arkansas-born veteran of 1930s labor struggles, provided a forum for new songwriters with her journal, *Broadside*. Another Arkansas singer and radical, and an alumnus of both the Almanac Singers and Weavers, Lee Hays, functioned as an elder statesman for the new protest musicians. In conservative Dallas, a most unlikely milieu for radical music, singer-writer Lu Mitchell lent encouragement to singers of all kinds and acted as a kind of mentor-patron for the small folk music community there. Among the singers who were active throughout the nation were such southern-born musicians as Odetta Felious (Alabama), Hedy West (Georgia), Carolyn Hester (Texas), Tom Paxton (Oklahoma), and Phil Ochs (Texas). Of course, a very large contingent of singers and musicians received their introduction to music through their participation in the urban folk revival. Among the more important who went on to successful careers in other forms of music were Gram Parsons, from Georgia, and Michael Murphey and Janis Joplin, both from Texas.

Protest music faded perceptibly during the 1970s as national polarization subsided in the aftermath of the Viet-

nam War. Adult Americans exhibited a growing conservative impulse, and younger people were won increasingly to the more aggressive, electronic sounds of rock music. Nevertheless, some singers and writers have remained faithful to the cause of human rights and social justice and have never wavered in their utilization of music for such purposes. Guy and Candie Carawan and Jane Sapp still promote local folk music resources at the Highlander Education and Research Center in Tennessee; Si and Kathy Kahn sing and write songs as part of their work as community organizers in the north Georgia mountains; Art and Margo Rosenbaum, working in the same area of Georgia, have documented the lives of poor black and white people through sketches, photographs, and traditional songs. In 1966 Anne Romaine and Bernice Reagon, fine singers in their own right, organized the Southern Folk Festival Tour, which provided wider exposure for native folk singers. In the annual tours that followed, audiences saw and heard such powerful singers as Hazel Dickens from West Virginia. Strongly reminiscent of such earlier singers as Aunt Molly Jackson, Dickens sang older material and her own compositions, which dealt with contemporary problems of poverty and social and sexual inequality.

Protest music appears occasionally in the repertories of professional musicians, and listeners to country music in the late 1960s and early 1970s discovered that protest does not always have an explicit ideological reference. A spate of country songs during those years defended the Vietnam War, protested against protesters and counterculture lifestyles, attacked welfare programs, and identified with establishment values, while others criticized small-town hypocrisy, documented worker alienation and exploitation, commented on environmental waste and pollution, and indicted the mistreatment of Indians and migratory workers.

See also BLACK LIFE: / "We Shall Overcome"; ETHNIC LIFE: / Okies; SOCIAL CLASS: / Highlander Folk School; Southern Tenant Farmers' Union; VIOLENCE: Harlan County, Kentucky; WOMEN'S LIFE: / Jackson, Aunt Molly; Reece, Florence

Bill C. Malone
Tulane University

R. Serge Denisoff, *Great Day Coming: Folk Music and the American Left* (1971), *Journal of American Folklore* (January–March 1969); Lawrence Gellert, *Negro Songs of Protest*, Rounder 4004; Archie Green, *Only a Miner: Studies in Recorded Coal-Mining Songs* (1972), *Sing Out* (July 1966), *Textile Labor* (April 1961); John Greenway, *American Folksongs of Protest* (1953); John W. Hevener, *Which Side Are You On?: The Harlan County Coal Miners, 1931–39* (1979). ☆

Ragtime
|||||||||||||||||||||||||

In the generation following the Civil War, various elements of southern folk music, especially black-evolved styles from the Mississippi Valley, coalesced to form a piano music known by the 1890s as "ragtime." Marked by an idiomatic syncopation in the treble (right-hand) part against a steady, marchlike bass (left-hand) part, the piano rag developed as a highly formalized music in 2/4 time, built of three or more contrasting strains.

In its origins ragtime drew from blackface minstrel sources, string-band music, sentimental parlor music, brass-band music, and many other heterogenous sources. Called "jig-piano" or "ragged time" by early practitioners, it was transformed at the turn of the century by black composers in the Missouri-Kansas region into a serious, carefully notated musical genre. Among the principal pioneers of piano ragtime were Thomas Turpin (c. 1873–1922), James Scott (1886–1938), Artie Matthews (1888–1958) and, most centrally, Scott Joplin (1868–1917) and his protegés—Arthur Marshall (1881–1968) and Scott Hayden (1882–1915).

In 1897 the first score entitled a "rag" appeared in print—white bandleader-arranger William H. Krell's "Mississippi Rag." Within weeks this was followed by Thomas Turpin's "Harlem Rag." Scott Joplin entered the scene in 1899 with "Original Rags" and "Maple Leaf Rag," the single composition that most epitomized and defined the genre for the public. Other popular artists like Benjamin Harney (1873–1938), Hubert "Eubie" Blake (1883–1983), and James P. Johnson (1894–1954) worked on the East Coast with songs, blues, and other musical materials related to ragtime. Between 1895 and 1905 ragtime spread across the United States via itinerant pianists, mechanical player-piano rolls, gramophone records, published sheet-music scores, and adaptations of the music to bands, orchestras, and every other musical medium. The two decades between 1895 and 1915 can justifiably be called the "ragtime age."

Ragtime became the basis for the whole modern popular music industry. Its infusion of fresh Afro-American musical styles and practices turned the nation from European models and provided a basic matrix of syncopated, contrapuntally voiced, rhythmically sophisticated music from which followed jazz, and rock and roll. It was identified in the public mind with black southern culture, especially through widely popular ragtime songs, which continued the old minstrelsy imagery of the idyllic South of carefree easy living on magnolia-scented plantations. Ragtime also transformed popular social dancing, especially in the years after 1910. One early ragtime song, written by Roberts and Jefferson in 1900, summarized (and satirized) the wild enthusiasm for the new music:

I got a ragtime dog and a ragtime cat
A ragtime piano in my ragtime flat;
Wear ragtime clothes, from hat to shoes,
I read a paper called the "Ragtime News."
Got ragtime habits and I talk that way,
I sleep in ragtime and I rag all day;
Got ragtime troubles with my ragtime wife,
I'm certainly living a ragtime life.

The impact must have seemed revolutionary to a generation hitherto unexposed to popular musical fads disseminated by mass media.

The "classic" piano rag developed by Turpin, Scott, Joplin, and others evolved into a simple but effective form: a bisectional construction connecting strains of 16 bars, typically, in an arrangement or sequence of (for example) AA BB A // CC DD. The first section of the rag (AA BB A) always featured a return of the first strain of a cyclical manner. The second section (CC DD) featured two (or more) strains in varied sequences. There are two primary variations in the form: (1) a *linear* construction (e.g., AA BB A // CC DD) or (2) a *rounded* construction, which returns to

material from the rag's first section, the A or B strains (e.g., AA BB A // CC DD A or AA BB A // CC A DD). The multirhythmic nature of the "classic" piano rag (so-called by Scott Joplin and his publisher John Stilwell Stark [1841–1927] of Sedalia, Mo.) challenged composers to use a broad variety of compositional creativity.

In the mid-1890s Ben Harney dazzled New York City with ragtime songs like "You've Been a Good Old Wagon" (1895) and "Mr. Johnson, Turn Me Loose" (1896), replete with forceful syncopations, exuberant melody, and racy colloquial lyrics. At the same time, the cakewalk was popularized via vaudeville and minstrelsy. The cakewalk was a stylized "walk-around" dance performed to syncopated march music, livelier and more extroverted than the fast two-step popular since the mid-1880s. Frederick "Kerry" Mills composed "At a Georgia Camp Meeting" (1896) and "Whistlin' Rufus" (1899); Sadie Koninsky had one popular hit in "Eli Green's Cakewalk" (1896); J. Bodewalt Lampe published "Creole Belles" (1899); and ragtimer Charles L. Johnson of Kansas City wrote "Doc Brown's Cakewalk" (1899).

From popular songs and dances ragtime evolved also to purely instrumental music—a highly idiomatic and "pianistic" form invented by the itinerant Mississippi Valley entertainers. Composers like Turpin, Joplin, and Scott served their apprenticeships as pianists in saloons, bordellos, or small theaters with traveling minstrel shows, or aboard riverboats. Their music was lively, loud, and percussive, designed to make a piano sound like a band, to carry over the sounds of high conviviality. It was derived from familiar folk styles and practices, echoing banjo and guitar music, hoedown dance rhythms, and the sentimental strains of popular song.

Traces of the folk origins in *pastiche* construction of early piano rags occur in Joplin's "Original Rags" (1899) and Seymour and Roberts's "St. Louis Tickle" (1904). Joplin's title indicates that he has composed a *set* of original themes (little "rags") that are then assembled in a linear suitelike form of one highly inventive strain after the other. The Seymour and Roberts rag commemorated the St. Louis World's Fair and the "ticklers" (pianists) who lined the "pike" or midway, and it included a very old river-culture folk tune, which Jelly Roll Morton later played and sang as "Buddy Bolden's Blues." The piano-rag form allowed for maximum inventiveness *and* borrowing from the folk culture.

After 1899 the nationwide popularity of Joplin's "Maple Leaf Rag" opened a lucrative market for piano rags, piano rolls, and ragtime "professors" as entertainers. Joplin created dozens of unique, carefully crafted rags—"The Easy Winners" (1901), "The Chrysanthemum" (1904), "The Ragtime Dance" (1906), and "Magnetic Rag" (1914). James Scott, from Neosho, Kan., entered the scene with works like "Sunburst Rag" (1909) and "Climax Rag" (1914). The impact of this new force was so great that a young white composer growing up in New Jersey, Joseph Lamb (1887–1960), could become a major composer in the wake of Joplin and Scott, studying the Stark scores and beginning his own publication in 1908 with "Sensation Rag" and producing a series of deeply felt, black-inspired rags like "Excelsior Rag" (1909), "American Beauty Rag" (1913), "The Ragtime Nightingale" (1915), and "Bohemia Rag" (1919). In a curious postlude to the ragtime era, Lamb would be rediscovered and resume his composing career in the late 1950s, after a 40-year hiatus.

John S. Stark was the disseminator of classic ragtime, printing Joplin, Scott, Lamb, Matthews, Marshall, and other ragtime giants. When he saw the magnitude of his ragtime publishing success, Stark became a champion of "high-class" or "quality" ragtime, which he and Joplin differentiated from popular songs, improvisational folk rags, or ephemeral mass-produced ditties. Stark insisted that rags should be played carefully, at moderate tempos, as written. Stark and Joplin viewed ragtime as a genuine Afro-American art form, and Stark was for his day a remarkably tolerant and fair-minded collaborator with the black composers he sponsored. His large, handsome piano scores are aesthetic prizes of the epoch.

While ragtime became a genuinely national music, composed and published in towns and cities all across the United States, it also achieved international fame, becoming for Europe an indication of America's lively genius. Its roots in the Mississippi Valley remained firm, and Ferdinand "Jelly Roll" Morton (1885–1941) from New Orleans recalled the large numbers of itinerant pianists and composers from New Orleans through Memphis and St. Louis on up to Chicago in the years around 1900. As the music was published and distributed, other "schools" of nonnotated ragtime flourished, with an important East Coast or "stride" piano group including James P. Johnson, Eubie Blake, Charles Luckeyth Roberts (1887–1968), and later Thomas "Fats" Waller (1904–43). Ragtime artists like Joe Jordan (1882–1971), New Orleans's Tony Jackson (1876–1921), and many others made Chicago a base.

Ragtime was not a wholly southern phenomenon, but its taproots were in the Deep South and Southwest, and it reflected an authentic musical culture of the Mississippi Valley and environs. It was a powerful influence on a new instrumental music, later called "jass" or "jazz," which grew in the region in the years around 1900. Early jazz musicians uniformly referred to their music as "ragtime," though it was largely an improvised, unnotated form of syncopated dance music.

The impact of ragtime on America—and world—culture is hard to overstate. The imaginative brilliance, emotional depth, and sheer *joie de vivre* of the music shaped all subsequent popular music. It introduced the black musical imagination and sensibility to a receptive general audience and established high standards for popular composition. When commercial songwriters and arrangers in New York City, in the area dubbed "Tin Pan Alley," took up the thrust of ragtime, around 1910, they were simply passing on a dense, complex, and culturally significant body of musical information and practices. George and Ira Gershwin in 1918 memorialized the ragtime era with "The Real American Folk Song (Is a Rag)." The music that had begun as nobody's music had become everybody's music.

Although the ragtime era seemed dead and gone by 1920, swept away during World War I by the advent of jazz and the new one-step and fox-trot dances, its basic themes and patterns profoundly influenced American music. The lyrics added to Joplin's "Maple Leaf Rag" promised that it would "shake de earth's foundation," and indeed it did.

William J. Schafer
Berea College

Edward A. Berlin, *Ragtime: A Musical and Cultural History* (1980); Rudi Blesh and Harriet Janis, *They All Played Ragtime* (1966); David A. Jasen and Trebor Jay Tichenor, *Rags and Ragtime: A Musical History* (1978); William J. Schafer and Johannes Riedel, *The Art of Ragtime: Form and Meaning of an Original Black American Art* (1973); Terry Waldo, *This Is Ragtime* (1976). ☆

Rock, Southern

||||||||||||||||||||||||||||||||||||||||

Southern rock was a self-consciously regional subgenre of rock music that emerged in the early 1970s and reached its commercial and creative peak near mid-decade. It represented the fusion of black and white musical styles and was particularly derivative of black rhythm and blues. It was concert oriented rather than dance oriented, flourishing on FM rather than AM radio, and was best suited to the extended album format (33 rpm) rather than single recordings (45 rpm). Much southern rock evoked explicit images of southern culture and emphasized such traditional themes as masculine aggression, the superiority of rural life, and unbridled individualism. It was highly amplified and electrified—the standard southern rock ensemble featured twin electric lead guitars and dual drum sets as well as various electric keyboards and electric bass. Though it appealed most strongly to white southern working-class teenagers, southern rock also generated a huge and intensely loyal following among white college students.

In the late 1960s, as rock replaced rock and roll as the dominant mode of American popular music and as emphasis shifted from dance to concerts, most southern musicians followed in the wake of such innovative artists as the Beatles, Bob Dylan, and the Rolling Stones. Regional distinctions were all but erased in the rush to emulate the rock heroes and heroines as generational allegiance superseded other forms of affiliation and identification. Many southerners, the overwhelming majority Texans, played minor roles in the crystallization of rock culture—Janis Joplin, Steve Miller, Shawn Phillips, Johnny Winter, Doug Sahm. All of them left the South to pursue careers in San Francisco and Los Angeles. Only Johnny Rivers of Baton Rouge, La., achieved a degree of commercial success to rival the Beatles. Rivers, who began his career as a rockabilly stylist in the manner of Elvis Presley, was one of the nation's most popular recording artists from 1964 to 1967 while retaining a measure of his southern identity.

The only important recordings issued from the South in the 1960s came from Atlanta, Memphis, and Muscle Shoals, Ala. In Atlanta, producer and publisher Bill Lowery oversaw a small but talented corps of artists, which included Billy Joe Royal, Ray Stevens, Jerry Reed, Joe South, and Tommy Roe. Few of the hits produced under Lowery's aegis displayed a distinctive regional sound. From Memphis came the most consistently successful and memorable southern recordings of the 1960s. Stax Records was home to the seminal Memphis studio band, Booker T and the MGs (a biracial group), as well as such pioneer "soul" singers as Sam and Dave, Wilson Pickett, Joe Tex, Carla Thomas, and Otis Redding. The Stax sound, a modification and extension of urban blues, offered no synthesis of southern forms, though it was undeniably south-

ern in style. In the late 1960s former Muscle Shoals sidemen Chips Moman and Dan Penn formed AGP studios and began producing hit recordings by Elvis Presley ("Suspicious Minds") and a local group, the Box Tops. The Box Tops, led by vocalist Alex Chilton, recorded numerous hits in a blues-oriented rock style: "The Letter," "Cry Like a Baby," "Soul Deep," "Sweet Cream Ladies." They were the immediate precursors of the first definitive southern rock group, the Allman Brothers Band. In Muscle Shoals, Fame Records claimed at least two major soul artists—Percy Sledge and Aretha Franklin. Among the highly esteemed Muscle Shoals studio musicians of the late 1960s was the brilliant guitarist, Duane Allman (born in Nashville and reared in Tennessee and Florida).

In 1969 Duane Allman and his brother Gregg, a vocalist and keyboard player, formed the original Allman Brothers Band, which also included guitarist Dicky Betts, bassist Berry Oakley, and drummers Butch Trucks and Jaimoe Johnson. The Allmans were among the first acts to sign with the fledgling Capricorn Records, a Macon, Ga., company established in 1969 by Otis Redding's former manager, Phil Walden. The Allmans soon spearheaded a southern rock movement that centered around Walden and his Capricorn label. Their first and second Capricorn albums, *Live at Fillmore East* (1971) and *Eat a Peach* (1972), established the Allmans as the preeminent southern rock band. They produced a rich body of work informed by both rhythm-and-blues and country music. Unfortunately, the death of both Duane Allman and Berry Oakley in motorcycle accidents in 1971 and 1972, respectively, robbed the group of much of its creative momentum. By 1975 the

Allman Brothers Band had ceased to exist in any meaningful sense.

Literally hundreds of groups had arisen in the wake of the Allman Brothers, many of them gaining affiliation with the Capricorn label. Among the most successful southern rock bands were Grinderswitch, the Outlaws, Cowboy, Wet Willie, Molly Hatchet, .38 Special, the Atlanta Rhythm Section, the Amazing Rhythm Aces, Lynyrd Skynyrd, the Marshall Tucker Band, and the Charlie Daniels Band. Of these, only the last four achieved any semblance of the Allmans' commercial and artistic attainments.

The Amazing Rhythm Aces, a Memphis band, employed a light, quasi-pop sound exemplified by their 1976 hit, "Third Rate Romance." The song was a success on both the country and pop record charts.

Lynyrd Skynyrd, from Florida, performed in a hard-rock style strikingly similar to the Allman Brothers. They openly celebrated their southern origins in songs like "Sweet Home Alabama" (1974) and on numerous albums released on the Atlanta-based Sounds of the South label (a subsidiary of the Music Corporation of America). Their most important albums were *Lynyrd Skynyrd* (1973), *Second Helping* (1974), and *One More For the Road* (1975). Like the Allmans, Lynyrd Skynyrd suffered from a tragic accident, an airplane crash that claimed the lives of bandleader and vocalist Ronnie Van Zandt, vocalist Cassie Gaines, and guitarist Steve Gaines in 1977.

The Marshall Tucker Band, from Spartanburg, S.C., created probably the most original and eclectic sound of the southern rockers. They drew from such diverse sources as modern jazz and western swing and regularly featured such uncommon rock instruments as the flute and the saxophone. Led by Toy Caldwell, who often played pedal steel guitar, the Marshall Tucker Band has remained closer to country music than blues. Among the group's most notable efforts were such Capricorn albums as *A New Life* (1974), *Searchin' for a Rainbow* (1975), and *Long Hard Ride* (1976). Despite the death of bassist Tommy Caldwell in 1978, the group has continued to perform and record in the 1980s.

The Nashville-based Charlie Daniels Band has been the one southern rock ensemble to be identified primarily with country music. The band has also been the most commercially successful southern rock act. Largely as a result of the group's popularity, southern rock's most enduring influence exists in the country realm. Such artists as Hank Williams, Jr., the Bellamy Brothers, and Alabama have sustained and extended the southern rock legacy into the 1980s.

Stephen R. Tucker
Tulane University

Michael Bane, *White Boy Singin' the Blues: The Black Roots of White Rock* (1982); Steve Cummings, *Southern Exposure* (Spring–Summer 1974); Courtney Haden, *Southern Exposure* (Summer–Fall 1977); Jim Miller, ed., *The Rolling Stone Illustrated History of Rock 'n' Roll* (1980); Norm N. Nite, ed., *Rock On, Volume II: The Illustrated Encyclopedia of Rock 'n' Roll* (1978). ☆

Rock and Roll

Rock and roll is the generic term used to describe the dominant strain of American popular music from 1955 to 1965. In general, rock and roll was teenage-oriented dance music that synthesized elements of black and white folk and popular music styles, specifically and most conspicuously, rhythm and blues and country (or "hillbilly") music. The term *rock and roll* was first popularized by northern disc jockey Alan Freed in the early 1950s, but its widest use came after 1955 when Bill Haley and the Comets released "Rock Around the Clock," the first legitimate rock-and-roll recording to rise to the top of the national pop music charts. Michigan-born Haley (b. 1925) was an anomaly: a rock-and-roll artist from outside the South, though his music was rooted firmly in southern-derived idioms. Haley was soon superseded as the dominant figure in rock and roll by Elvis Presley, born in Tupelo, Miss., and reared in Memphis, Tenn. All of the subsequent rock-and-roll innovators, with the arguable exception of Chuck Berry (born, San Jose, Calif., 1926), were native southerners: Carl Perkins (born, Bermis, Tenn., 1932); Jerry Lee Lewis (born, Ferriday, La., 1935); Buddy Holly (born, Lubbock, Tex., 1936); Fats Domino (born, New Orleans, 1928); Little Richard (born, Macon, Ga., 1932).

From 1955 to 1958 rock and roll remained largely a southern phenomenon. The two principal regional recording centers were Memphis and New Orleans, each of which produced a distinctive idiom of its own.

Memphis, long a cultural crossroads where various southern musical traditions flourished, especially Mississippi Delta blues and hillbilly music, produced a dynamic hybrid known as rockabilly. Rockabilly was firmly rooted in country music but drew heavily from black sources, most notably gospel and rhythm and blues. It was characterized by small ensembles (often a trio), stringed instrumentation, and a persistent yet light beat layered over frenzied vocalizing and an echo produced in the recording studio. The classic rockabilly sound, engineered by Sam Phillips and performed by Elvis Presley (vocal and acoustic rhythm guitar), Scotty Moore (electric lead guitar), and Bill Black (acoustic upright bass) was first recorded at Phillips' Sun Records studio in Memphis in July 1954. Sun soon attracted dozens of aspiring young musicians from across the South who performed in a style similar to Presley's. Important Sun artists after Presley were Carl Perkins, Jerry Lee Lewis, Johnny Cash, Billy Riley, Sonny Burgess, Roy Orbison, Charlie Rich, and Conway Twitty. A definitive rockabilly group from Memphis, which recorded for the New York-based Coral label, was the Rock 'n' Roll Trio (Johnny Burnette, Dorsey Burnette, and Paul Burlison).

After 1955 the basic Memphis rockabilly sound underwent a gradual modification. Elvis Presley moved toward a mainstream rock-and-roll sound after signing with RCA Victor in November 1955. Jerry Lee Lewis introduced his own boogie-woogie-based piano style into rockabilly with his first Sun releases in 1955. Beginning in 1957 Buddy Holly created an original pop-influenced variant of rockabilly, exemplified by such recordings as "That'll Be the Day" (1957), "Peggy Sue" (1957), and "Rave On" (1958). In Louisiana, Dale Hawkins recorded in a strong blues-influenced style, which gained its greatest expression in the hit recording "Suzie Q" (1957). Numerous influential rockabilly artists lived and recorded in Los Angeles after 1955, including Gene Vincent (originally from Virginia), whose best-known song was "Be Bop a Lula" (1956); Wanda Jackson (originally from Oklahoma), the most talented female rockabilly performer; Eddie Cochran, next to Carl Perkins, the finest rockabilly songwriter, who recorded such definitive items as "Summertime Blues" (1958) and "Something Else" (1959); and Ricky Nelson (born in New Jersey), who sold more rockabilly recordings than anyone other than Presley. Nelson and the Nashville-based Everly Brothers followed Presley and Holly in moving rockabilly in the direction of pop music by removing much of the rawness and dynamism from the idiom. The Everly Brothers were especially significant for introducing the traditional hillbilly duet style into rock and roll. Their best recordings, such as "Wake Up Little Susie" (1957) and "Bye, Bye Love" (1957), retained much of the potency of early rockabilly. A few mainstream country performers also recorded in a rockabilly mode, most notably Marty Robbins and Johnny Horton.

The New Orleans sound, which formed the second major component of southern rock and roll, was infused with the blues. It was characterized by small ensembles (usually five or six pieces) whose central instrument was the piano. Accompaniment usually consisted of saxophones, drums, electric bass, and horns. It was noted for a heavy, rolling beat and Caribbean-derived polyrhythms. New Orleans vocalists, most of whom were black, sang with the thick inflections indigenous to the city. Most of the songs identified with New Orleans rock and roll were exuberant, joyous, and urgent, yet less frenzied than those from rockabilly music. Lyrics were seldom teen oriented.

Though no record label of comparable importance to Sun existed in New Orleans—most of the city's recordings were released by West Coast companies such as Imperial and Specialty—virtually every recording made in the city came from the studio of engineer and producer Cosimo Matassa. Matassa and Dave Bartholomew, a musician, writer, and producer, were key figures in the evolution of a distinctive New Orleans rock-and-roll style.

The quintessential New Orleans rock-and-roll performer was Fats Domino, a musical heir of the great rhythm-and-blues pianist Professor Longhair (Henry Roeland Byrd). Domino was a popular rhythm-and-blues recording artist in the early 1950s, and he made his entry onto the national pop charts in 1955 with "Ain't That a Shame." In the 1955–60 period, Domino produced a remarkable series of hit recordings, including "Blueberry Hill" (1956) and "I'm Walkin' " (1957).

Other important contributors to the New Orleans sound included Lloyd Price, Smiley Lewis, Huey Smith, Clarence "Frogman" Henry, Frankie Ford, Bobby Charles, and Jimmy Clanton. Clanton, a white performer, accomplished the closest approximation of the New Orleans style to a mainstream rock-and-roll sound with recordings like "Just a Dream" (1958). The only non-Louisiana artist to play a significant role in the popularization of the New Orleans style was Little Richard (Penniman) of Macon, Ga. Little Richard became one of the most dynamic and controversial rock-and-roll performers of the 1950s with such hits as "Tutti Frutti" (1955) and "Rip It Up" (1956).

By the early 1960s rockabilly music had largely been subsumed by the rock-and-roll mainstream. The New Orleans sound remained a vital and distinctive regional rock-and-roll form, though it too declined in popularity and experienced a certain degree of accommodation with the mainstream approach. Both Memphis and New Orleans ceased to be important recording centers. Most southern musicians left to work in Los Angeles, New York, or Nashville where, if successful, they tended to produce recordings of minimal regional identity. Southern rock and roll, which, in the forms of rockabilly and New Orleans music, had exerted a formative influence on the creation of a national rock-and-roll style, now merely existed as one element within the broad form as evinced by such representative recordings of the period as Johnny Tillotson's "Poetry in Motion" (1960), Johnny Burnette's "You're Sixteen" (1960), and Elvis Presley's "Return to Sender" (1962).

After 1963 American rock and roll began to succumb to the so-called British Invasion, spearheaded by the Beatles, who were soon followed by such groups as the Rolling Stones, the Animals, and Gerry and the Pacemakers. Ironically, the British invaders were themselves extremely indebted to the southern-derived forms of early rock and roll and thus revived much of the southern character and identity of the music. The most successful American rock-and-roll recording artist of the mid-1960s was Johnny Rivers, a native of Baton Rouge, La. (born 1940), who had begun his musical career as a rockabilly stylist. Rivers's music combined many varied styles, from urban folk music to rockabilly, but retained its essential southern character.

By 1966 the Beatles and Bob Dylan (another musician devoted to southern musical forms) led the way toward "rock," as contrasted to rock and roll.

Rock had a general, national (and even international) identity. It was a form oriented more toward concerts than dance and was linguistically and thematically sophisticated and complex. Only in the early 1970s, with the emergence of the Allman Brothers Band and the attendant success of Capricorn Records of Macon, Ga., did a specific, self-conscious, and identifiable southern rock style evolve.

See also URBANIZATION: / Memphis; New Orleans

Stephen R. Tucker
Tulane University

Jason Berry, Jonathan Forse, and Tad Jones, *Up From the Cradle of Jazz: New Orleans Music since World War II* (1987); John Broven, *Rhythm and Blues in New Orleans* (1978); Colin Escott and Martin Hawkins, *Sun Records: The Brief History of the Legendary Record Label* (1980); Charlie Gillett, *The Sound of the City: The Rise of Rock and Roll* (1970); Jim Miller, ed., *The Rolling Stone Illustrated History of Rock 'n' Roll* (1980); Robert Palmer, *A Tale of Two Cities: Memphis Rock and New Orleans Roll* (1979). ☆

Sacred Harp

|||||||||||||||||||||||||||||||

On most weekends somewhere in the Deep South, one can find a gathering of amateurs singing from *The Sacred Harp*, a tunebook first published in Georgia (but printed in Philadelphia) in 1844. *The Sacred Harp*, one of many tunebooks of the 19th-century South, is the most popular of several that survived, the others being Joseph Funk's *Genuine Church Music* (Harrisonburg, Va.,

1832; now entitled *New Harmonia Sacra*); William Walker's *Southern Harmony* (Spartanburg, S.C., printed in New Haven, Ct., 1835, with later editions in Philadelphia), used in an annual singing in Benton, Ky.; Walker's *Christian Harmony* (Spartanburg, S.C.; printed in Philadelphia, 1866), used in Alabama, western North Carolina, and Mississippi; and W. H. and M. L. Swan's *New Harp of Columbia* (Knoxville, Tenn., 1848), used in eastern Tennessee. In contrast to the limited geographical spread of these other tunebooks, *The Sacred Harp* is used in regularly scheduled singings in Georgia, the Florida Panhandle, Alabama, Tennessee, Mississippi, and Texas.

The Sacred Harp is a product of the American singing-school movement, which flourished in New England in the late 18th century and spread to the rural South and Midwest in the early 19th century. As is typical of other tunebooks of its kind, *The Sacred Harp* is oblong in shape and contains an opening summary of the rudiments of music for use in singing schools, followed by an anthology of harmonized music.

The invention of shape notes around 1800 facilitated the learning of music reading and proved so popular in the South and Midwest that practically every singing-school book, including *The Sacred Harp*, used the four-shape notation of William Little and William Smith's *The Easy Instructor* (Philadelphia, 1802), which became standard in the pre–Civil War period. The major scale was notated as shown in Figure 1. In sacred harp singing it has become standard practice to sing through a song first using the fa-sol-la solmization syllables before singing the words; hence the designation "fasola" singing.

The music in *The Sacred Harp* and

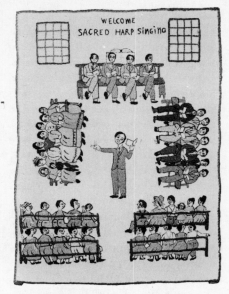

Ethel Mohamed stitchery depicting sacred harp singing, photographed in 1977

Figure 1.

fa sol la fa sol la mi fa
1   2   3   4   5   6   7   8

other shape-note tunebooks, although primarily intended for singing-school use, is predominantly set to religious texts, primarily those of 18th-century English hymn writers, especially those of Isaac Watts (1674–1748). The texts were compiled from the collections of Watts and of numerous other words-only hymnals known in the early 19th-century South, such as South Carolinian Staunton S. Burdett's *Baptist Harmony* (1834) and Georgian Jesse Mercer's *The Cluster* (5th ed., 1835).

The texts found in *The Sacred Harp* are strongly Calvinistic in theology with their emphasis on the sovereignty of God and the depravity of mankind. They are also otherworldly, with much emphasis on the vanity of this world and a longing for death and the afterlife, as in Charles Wesley's "Animation" (SH-103).

And let this feeble body fail
And let it faint or die;
My soul shall quit this mournful vale,
And soar to worlds on high.

Broadly speaking, the music in *The Sacred Harp* may roughly be divided into three categories:

1. Psalm or hymn tunes, ranging from those of metrical psalmody and of 18th-century American hymnody to folk hymnody of the early 19th century and even later 19th- and 20th-century tunes essentially in the same earlier styles.
2. Fuging tunes—tunes in which all voices move together in the opening phrases followed by a second section in which the voices enter separately in imitation and then move together once again to approach the final cadence. The second section was normally repeated, making a compact ABB form.
3. Longer pieces—normally designated odes or anthems. These pieces, often with prose texts such as scripture, are multi-sectional and are generally regarded as the most challenging to the singers.

The music of *The Sacred Harp* is printed in open-score format in three (later four) voice parts with the melody in the tenor. In practice, the treble and tenor parts are doubled by men and women, creating a richer, fuller sound.

The type of music most commonly associated with *The Sacred Harp* is folk hymnody in which melodies, and sometimes texts as well, first appeared in oral tradition. These folk hymns are related melodically to Anglo-American secular folksong and are characterized by such traits as the use of gapped scales and the modes. The frontier camp meetings from the early 1800s added simplified folk hymns, termed "revival spirituals" by George Pullen Jackson, to the corpus of folk hymnody, with repeated phrases and often the addition of a refrain. To "On Jordan's Stormy Banks I Stand" (SH-128) was added the following refrain:

I am bound for the promised land,
I am bound for the promised land,
O who will come and go with me?
I am bound for the promised land.

The Sacred Harp was compiled by two Georgia Baptist singing school teachers, Benjamin Franklin White (1800–1879) and Elisha J. King (c. 1821–44). Little is known of King, listed as the composer of more songs in the first edition of *The Sacred Harp* than any other person, for he died in the same year it was published. In contrast, much is known of White, who lived for more than three decades after its publication and was greatly influential in its acceptance. A native of South Carolina, White moved to Harris County, Ga., around 1840. He served as mayor of Hamilton, as clerk of the inferior county court, and as a major in the militia before the Civil War. In addition to composing, compiling, and teaching in singing schools, White in 1847 founded and led for more than two decades the Southern Musical Convention, an important organization in promoting sacred harp singing.

During White's lifetime, *The Sacred Harp* was revised and enlarged under the auspices of the Southern Musical Convention in 1850, 1859, and 1869, increasing the original 263 pages of 1844, respectively to 366, 429, and 477 pages. With the 1859 and especially the 1869 editions, the fuging tunes received a more prominent place. Indeed, so prominent are fuging tunes in this tradition that they constitute a large portion of the favorites in current sacred harp singings. Another change was the increasing number of tunes in four voice parts rather than three, even though White himself composed in three parts only.

Without attempting to treat all editions of *The Sacred Harp*, which are described in detail by Buell E. Cobb, mention will be made of those that remain in current or recent use:

1. The Cooper revisions, made under the supervision of W. M. Cooper of Dothan, Ala., in 1902 with subsequent editions in 1907, 1919, 1927, 1950, and 1960. The Cooper revision is used in southern Alabama, northern Florida, southern Mississippi, and eastern Texas.
2. The James revision, called the *Original Sacred Harp*, revised by a committee of 23 with Joe S. James of Douglasville, Ga., as chairman and published in 1911. This revision was used for singings in central and south Georgia through 1975, when these singers changed over to the Denson revision.
3. The J. L. White revisions, the fifth edition of *The Sacred Harp*, brought out in 1909 in Atlanta by the son of B. F. White. It was rejected for its concessions to modernity, but White brought out another revision in 1911 omitting objectionable aspects of his earlier edition. Although used at one time in several states, the White book today is restricted to north Georgia.
4. The Denson revision, published by the Sacred Harp Publishing Company in 1936, with later editions in 1960,

1967, and 1971. Although appearing later than the editions of Cooper and White, the Denson revisions are more traditional. In 1933 Thomas Denson organized the Sacred Harp Publishing Company and purchased all legal rights to *The Sacred Harp* from the James family. The Denson revision is by far the edition of *The Sacred Harp* most widely used today.

A sacred harp singing is an informal gathering that emphasizes fellowship and group singing. A typical day's singing begins about mid-morning. Singers are seated facing each other in a square grouped by the four voice parts: tenor (melody), bass, treble, and alto. Each person who wishes to do so leads one or two songs (a turn at leading is called a "lesson" after traditional singing-school terminology). The song is first vocalized by the shape-note syllables and then sung to its words. At the close of the morning the singers adjourn for the traditional dinner on the grounds, a feast of home-cooked food set out on tables for all to enjoy. After lunch the singing continues, normally through at least the middle of the afternoon. When the time comes to close, the final song is often *Parting Hand* (SH-62) by Jeremiah Ingalls.

Sacred harp singing reflects traditional southern culture in terms of its music, its religious outlook, and its sense of community. The sacred harp tradition has preserved styles of music prominent in the pre–Civil War South through the institution of the singing school and many of the rural churches. In addition to the corpus of music from early America, sacred harp singing reflects a traditional southern manner of performance. For example, the tone color of sacred harp singing with its bite and edge contrasts with the sweeter styles of singing found outside the South.

Although sacred harp singings are not church services, they commonly take place in churches. The religious outlook of sacred harp singing is reflected in the piety that is manifested at these gatherings. For example, singings normally open and close with prayer and personal testimonies are often given. Southern religion is also exemplified in the sacred harp singers' use of the parlimentary procedures found in the democratic church business meeting of the rural congregations. The music is from the singing-school tradition, yet it includes the music of Baptists, Methodists, and others in the Upland South before the Civil War. Although these mainline denominations in large measure moved away from the sacred harp tradition, an increasing number of hymn tunes from its pages have appeared in their recent hymnals. The theological perspective of the main denomination to support sacred harp singing—the Primitive Baptists—is expressed in many of the texts of the songs, with their stern Calvinism, their willingness to face death, and their emphasis on the hereafter.

Especially strong in sacred harp singing is the southern sense of community with its focus on the family. The annual reunions of sacred harp singers can be likened to the annual southern family reunions. Furthermore, certain families such as the Densons have played crucial roles in preserving sacred harp singing. These singings are a time for remembering. Some gatherings are memorial singings named after a prominent sacred harp singer. An important feature of many sacred harp singings is the memorial lesson(s), in which the recently deceased are remembered in word and in song. All in all, the conservative values that sacred harp singing embraces and preserves are representative of traditional southern culture.

Harry Eskew
New Orleans Baptist
Theological Seminary

Buell E. Cobb, Jr., *The Sacred Harp: A Tradition and Its Music* (1978); Charles Linwood Ellington, "The Sacred Harp Tradition: Its Origin and Evolution" (Ph.D. dissertation, Florida State University, 1969); Harry Eskew, in *New Grove Dictionary of Music and Musicians*, ed. Stanley Sadie, vol. 17 (1980); Dorothy D. Horn, *Sing to Me of Heaven: A Study of Folk and Early American Materials in Three Old Harp Books* (1970); George Pullen Jackson, *The Story of the Sacred Harp, 1844–1944* (1944), *White and Negro Spirituals: Their Life Span and Kinship* (1943), *White Spirituals in the Southern Uplands* (1933). ☆

Spirituals

||||||||||||||||||||||||

Spirituals are Afro-American sacred folksongs, sometimes also called anthems, hymns, spiritual songs, jubilees, or gospel songs. Distinctions between these terms have not been precise, different terms being used in different communities at different times. The term *spiritual song* was widely used in English and American hymnals and tunebooks during and after the 18th century, but *spiritual* was not found in print before the Civil War. Descriptions of the songs that came to be known by that name appeared at least 20 years earlier, and Afro-American religious singing recognized as distinct from white psalms and hymns was described as early as 1819.

The musical elements that distinguished Afro-American songs from European folksong were described by travelers and traders in Africa in the early 17th century. The elements that appeared exotic and unfamiliar to these Europeans included strong rhythms—accompanied by bodily movement, stamping, hand-clapping, and other percussive devices to accent rhythm—gapped scales, general group participation, improvised texts (frequently derisive or satiric in nature), and the call-and-response form in which leader and responding chorus overlapped. To the European observers the music seemed wholly strange, although later analysts would find elements common to European music. The performance style of African music was one of its unique aspects, one that has survived in many forms of Afro-American music.

In Africa song played a prominent

Gospel music singer, Centreville, Miss., 1972

role in religion, public ceremonies, and work, in which song was used to regulate the pace. Though scholars do not agree about whether harmony was present, the simultaneous sounding of more than one pitch was common. Vocal embellishments were widely used, and a strong, rasping voice quality was admired. These musical elements continued among the Africans transported to the New World and were reported by numerous witnesses of slave singing throughout the West Indies and the North American mainland during the mid-17th century. Songs to accompany dancing were most frequently reported, with work songs a close second. Not much is yet known about the transmission of African religions to North America, so the relation of the spirituals to African religious song is still largely a matter of conjecture.

The conversion of Africans to Christianity, considered a prerequisite to the development of the spiritual, proceeded slowly. In the 17th century individual slaves were often converted by the families with whom they lived on low country plantations; although in the southern colonies some planters opposed the baptism of their slaves in the belief that baptism might disrupt the master-slave relationship. Where planters permitted religious instruction, the Africans responded with enthusiasm; but the few missionaries sent from England were kept too busy ministering to the widely separated white population to permit much attention to the blacks or the Indians. By the mid-18th century a few Presbyterian ministers, led by Samuel Davies of Hanover, Va., made special efforts to convert blacks within their neighborhoods, using Isaac Watts' hymnbooks shipped from England. The style of singing European hymns may have been influenced by African musical patterns, but scholars have no concrete information about the singing of African songs during this period.

Toward the end of the 18th century Methodist itinerants, such as Bishop Francis Avery, assisted by the black exhorter Harry Hosier, began to hold meetings lasting several days. Large crowds overflowed the meeting rooms, and blacks and whites attended these meetings together. On the frontier, where the population was very widely scattered and organized churches were few, the camp meeting developed, beginning with the Cane Ridge, Ky., meeting in August 1801. Black worshipers attended this meeting, and they participated in white camp meetings throughout the antebellum period. As blacks and whites worshiped and sang together in an atmosphere highly charged with emotion mutual influences were inescapable. The call-and-response style of singing was ideally suited to this kind of participatory service, where vast numbers of people required musical responses they could learn on the spot. The practice of "lining out," in which a leader sang or read two lines of a hymn to the congregation who then repeated them, was widely used in churches with illiterate members or with too few books to go around. The camp meeting provided an introduction for both groups to the sound and style of each other's singing.

The first documented reports of distinctive black religious singing date from the early 19th century, somewhat earlier than the first organized missions to plantation slaves. Spirituals were not transcribed in musical notation until the Civil War, and, when they were, conventional musical notation was inadequate to convey the distinctive features of the music as it was performed. Whatever degree of acculturation may have existed, certain elements in the music could not be represented in a notation developed for European music. The more sensitive transcribers explicitly stated that their transcriptions could not capture all they heard—notes outside the scale system—"blue" notes, swoops, glissandos, growls, rhythmic complexities, and the overlapping of leader and chorus in the call-and-response style.

In the South during the antebellum period spirituals were sung widely and were discussed in letters, diaries, and the periodical press, but they were largely unknown in the North. When wartime conditions brought plantation slaves into contact with northern whites, the songs became known to a wider public. Individual songs were published as sheet music or in magazine articles, and a comprehensive collection was published in 1867, *Slave Songs of the United States*, edited by William Francis Allen, Charles Pickard Ware, and Lucy McKim Garrison. Although the transcriptions had to omit many of the characteristic and distinctive features of the music because of the notational system, the collection was an attempt to preserve songs that otherwise might have been lost. The collection set a pattern for transcribing the songs in conventional musical notation (despite its shortcomings) that was followed in more influential collections of songs as sung by the Fisk Jubilee Singers, the Hampton Singers, and other touring groups from predominantly black schools in the South. The college groups had been trained in European music and were conscious of their mission to herald the emerging black population. After northern and European audiences heard spirituals, their popularity was firmly established. Songs were modified in their arrangement for concert performance, although the extent of this modification has not been determined.

As the spirituals grew more popular, elaborate arrangements that departed still more widely from the folk originals were made, for both solo singers and for choirs. Beginning in 1892 a theory was developed that spirituals were based on European folk hymns and other forms of white popular music, a theory based solely on the examination of the published transcriptions. The elements of improvisation and the performance style were not considered. Only with the advent of sound recording has it been possible to study the performance itself. Current performances cannot fully replicate antebellum ones, but they can capture much of the excitement described by 19th-century listeners. Ethnomusicologists may be able to reconstruct the music as it was performed in earlier eras by utilizing field recordings and contemporary descriptions.

See also BLACK LIFE: African Influences; Creolization; Religion, Black; Slave Culture; EDUCATION: / Fisk University

Dena J. Epstein
University of Chicago

Afro-American Spirituals, Work Songs, and Ballads, Library of Congress Recording AAFSL3; James H. Cone, *The Spirituals and the Blues: An Interpretation* (1972); Dena J. Epstein, *Sinful Tunes and Spirituals: Black Folk Music to the Civil War* (1977); Miles Mark Fisher, *Negro Slave Songs in the United States* (1953); George Pullen Jackson, *Spiritual Folk Songs of Early America* (1964), *White Spirituals in the Southern Uplands* (1933); Lawrence W. Levine, *Black*

Culture and Black Consciousness: Afro-American Folk Thought from Slavery to Freedom (1977); A. E. Perkins, *Journal of American Folklore* (July–September 1922). ☆

Square Dancing and Clogging

||||||||||||||||||||||||||||||||||||||||||||||||||||

Square dance in the South has traditionally provided a means to exercise the virtually universal human tendency to move to the accompaniment of music. It is best to think of *square dance* as a generic term for a variety of related dance forms, styles, and occasions. In the popular imagination, traditional square dancing is often associated with the South; in its assorted revivalistic forms the square dance has become a national phenomenon.

Cecil Sharp, the English collector and scholar of folk music and dance, helped bring the square dance to national—and even international—attention after encountering it in Kentucky. In 1918 Sharp wrote, "In the course of our travels in the Southern Appalachian Mountains in search of traditional songs and ballads, we often heard of a dance, called the Running Set, but as our informants had invariably led us to believe that it was a rough, uncouth dance, remarkable only as an exhibition of agility and physical endurance, we had made no special effort to see it." When Sharp and his colleague Maud Karpeles finally did encounter the dance at the Pine Mountain Settlement School in eastern Kentucky, they were captivated by it, and Sharp felt certain that they had found a relic of English dance traditions older than any on record. Actually, they had "discovered" a dance that, although rooted in English and French dance forms, is generally thought to be a 19th-century American development—the southern square dance.

Dancing to the chanted instructions of a caller—one of the major identifying features of square dancing—emerged about the time of the War of 1812. The other common square-dance features—the couple as the basic unit, danced interactions between couples in a bounded group, the group arranged in a simple geometric formation—may be found in any number of British and French antecedent dance forms, folk, popular, and elite. The calling distinguishes the dance.

In the South, couples generally arrange themselves in squares consisting of four male-female couples or in circles made up of as many couples as can be accommodated. Less frequently the dance may take the form of two parallel lines, one for men, one for women, with couples facing each other. The caller may dance, or he or she may stand nearby.

Traditionally the music is provided by a fiddle, fiddle and banjo, or by any of the typical string-band ensemble forms. The fiddle repertoire in the South is, in fact, dominated by square-dance tunes. Although no distributional studies of the square dance in the South exist, the dance-tune repertoire has been played by fiddlers all through the region. It seems reasonable to conclude from this that square dancing may be, or might formerly have been, found wherever there has been an active dance-tune tradition—virtually everywhere in the South.

Square dancing has traditionally been a part of the community life in the South. Moreover, it has often provided one of the major settings for community interaction. Until the World War II era people commonly danced in the homes of their neighbors, particularly in farming areas. Such events were essentially parties for the neighbors, and all were invited. Other community events have also been occasions for dancing. These include communal work activities (corn shuckings and log rollings), picnics and barbecues, holiday observances, and other festivals. A rise in commercially motivated dances in local armories and other halls has, in many instances, kept people dancing despite the declining significance of some of the older community social events. The dance associations themselves seem to encourage friendly interactions between community members, young and old, male and female, and the dancing itself seems to involve the enactment, at some deep level, of community norms and expectations, such as the notion of the couple as a basic social unit.

Each dance typically involves a number of formulaic movements in response to the caller's instructions. Many dance calls, such as "Ocean Wave" and "Cage the Bird," are known widely across the South; others may be limited to subregions. Dance movements will sometimes vary in their execution (in response to the formulaic calls) according to local and regional preferences.

Square dancing is also traditionally a part of southern Afro-American culture, despite its dominant association with Anglo-Americans. Slave narratives describe square dancing among slaves, and recent interviews with black musicians and dancers suggest that square dancing was often a feature of rural life in southern black communities through perhaps the 1930s.

A number of 20th-century revivalistic

movements have added to the complexity of the square dance in the South. These range from dance schools and festivals under the sponsorship of southern Appalachian cultural and educational institutions to the efforts of various national square-dance organizations. The latter have tended to emphasize new dance styles based on traditional dances but showing the touch of the choreographer. Typically identified as western dancing, this is generally bound up in a large network of local clubs, whose members dress in stylized cowboy-cowgirl garb and dance to records rather than to live music. A number of publications and supply houses, regional and national, cater to revivalist dancers. As a result of the various dance revivals, many communities in the South typically have a range of square-dance activities, from regionally traditional forms done perhaps weekly at a VFW or sportsman's club, and done occasionally at festivals, to square-dance groups practicing precision dance forms derived from regional models, to clubs that are part of the western square-dance movement. There may well be more people dancing in the South today than ever before.

Clog dancing is a group dance, synthesizing the older square dance and the solo "buck and wing" or "buck dance." Buck dancers traditionally danced on bare earth, front porches, or parlor floors, their arms hanging loose at their sides and their feet close to the floor. The origin of the term *buck and wing* is unclear, but it was used in Lancashire, England, in the early part of this century to describe dancing in wooden shoes. Buck dancing likely has roots in the folk dances of Scotch, Irish, and English immigrants to the Appalachian Mountains, but black dancing patterns also influ-

enced its development through minstrel performers and traveling medicine shows. Ceremonial Indian dances, with their toe-heel, toe-heel movement, also were a likely influence on white mountain buck dancing.

Clog dancing probably originated in the mountains of western North Carolina in the 1920s or 1930s, associated with the Asheville Mountain Dance and Folk Festival. A landmark was a 1939 performance in Washington, D.C., by the Soco Gap Dancers for President Franklin Roosevelt and British King George VI. This was apparently the first time cloggers used costumes, and publicity from the performance helped popularize clogging in the 1940s. Taps were added and costumes became more prominent as the folk dance became increasingly oriented toward public performance. James Kesterson, of Henderson County, N.C., introduced precision clogging in the late 1950s, and his popular Blue Ridge Mountain Dancers won the Asheville Festival five times in the 1960s.

Precision clogging groups like Kesterson's dance to patterned footwork in unison in set routines. They frequently emphasize colorful costumes and choreography, using both old-time mountain music and popular tunes. The other main type of clogging is freestyle, or traditional. Here the dancers follow time to the music, but each performer has spontaneous footwork, improvising steps as the team moves about the floor. Freestyle clogging is especially associated with older mountain folk culture, but clogging in general remains a not-uncommon practice in mountain areas of the South.

Burt Feintuch
Western Kentucky University

S. Foster Damon, *The History of Square Dancing* (1957); Lynne F. Emery, *Black Dance in the United States from 1619 to 1970* (1972); Burt Feintuch, *Journal of the Folklore Institute* (January–April 1981); Cecil J. Sharp and Maud Karpeles, *The Country Dance Book, Part V* (1918, 1946). ☆

Tex-Mex
|||||||||||||||||||||

See *Música Tejana*

Western Swing
||||||||||||||||||||||||||||||||||||||

Like so many other forms of American music, western swing is a cultural product of the South. The founders of the music borrowed from other southern styles—ragtime, New Orleans jazz, folk, frontier fiddle music, pop, Tex-Mex, and country and classic blues. In one stage of development, they borrowed heavily from big-band swing. Despite its eclecticism, western swing has remained one of the most distinctive genres in southern musical history. Western swing brought a new vitality and sophistication to the country music of the South.

All three periods in the development of western swing were inextricably interwoven with the career of Bob Wills. The first of these eras was the formative period in Texas; second, the years of experimentation and maturity in Oklahoma; and finally, the years of national recognition and musical influence.

James Robert Wills was born into a family of fiddle players near Kosse in east Texas. He eventually combined folk fiddle music with the blues, jazz, and ragtime from the "black belt" of east Texas. This was the nucleus from which western swing grew. When he was 10, Bob Wills played his first dance as a fiddler at a ranch in west Texas. For the rest of his career he played dance music. The most obvious characteristic of western swing is that the music "swings," or is danceable.

The early fiddle bands often had only a fiddle and an accompanying guitar or mandolin. When Bob Wills moved to Fort Worth in 1929, he started the Wills Fiddle Band featuring only his fiddle and Herman Arnspiger's guitar. In 1929 Wills and Arnspiger recorded on the Brunswick label what may have been the first western swing ever put on record, "Wills Breakdown" and "Gulf Coast Blues." Wills soon added Milton Brown as vocalist and his brother Durwood Brown on guitar. The Wills Fiddle Band became the Light Crust Doughboys in 1930 and eventually played on the Texas Quality Network, originating at WBAP in Fort Worth and broadcasting on the network in Waco, Houston, and Oklahoma City. The Wills group was, if not the first, among the first to play western swing and to perform it on radio.

Between 1929 and 1933 Bob Wills revolutionized popular music in Texas. His success and fame spread throughout the state and inspired the formation of numerous fiddle bands that played his type of swinging dance music. The first and most successful in terms of first-rate western swing was Wills's protégé, Milton Brown, who came into the Wills Fiddle Band with little or no musical experience. He learned quickly from Wills and left the Light Crust Doughboys in 1932 to form a group called

Milton Brown and His Musical Brownies. Outside of Wills himself, Brown was the most important figure in the formative years of western swing. The Wills-Brown style could soon be heard in many western-swing bands, in the Light Crust Doughboys, W. Lee O'Daniel's Hillbilly Boys, Cliff Bruner's Texas Wanderers, the True Wranglers, Bill Boyd and His Cowboy Ramblers, The Hi-Flyers, Jimmy Revard and His Oklahoma Playboys, Adolph Hofner and His Texans, Bob Dunn's Vagabonds, Roy Newman and His Boys, the Sons of the Pioneers, the Prairie Ramblers with Patsy Montana, and Shelly Lee Alley and the Alley Cats, to name a few of the better-known recorded groups.

By the time Bob Wills moved the Playboys from Waco, Tex., to Oklahoma in 1934, the formative years of western swing were over. East and west Texas gave birth to his music; Fort Worth was its nursery; and it reached full maturity in Tulsa, Okla., between 1934 and 1942. There the music moved out of its southwestern provincialism to a much broader audience. Wills's experimental spirit led him to take the music far beyond its fiddle-band origins. Shortly after he arrived in Oklahoma, he added enough horns to give him a second front line made up of trumpet, saxophone, and trombone. The reeds and brass played more modern, uptown music and therefore appealed to a broader audience. Wills added drums and began to lay down a solid jazz beat heretofore unheard of in the fiddle-band tradition. In short, he was moving further from his rural roots to jazz, blues, race music, and popular music. Wisely, he kept his front line of fiddles and added more guitars, both amplified and acoustic. By 1938 he could play anything from folk and breakdown fiddle music to a George

Gershwin composition and give them a swinging rhythm and solid beat. The recordings from his first session in 1935, for Vocalion (later Columbia), outsold every other artist in the Vocalion catalog.

In April 1940, with an orchestra of 18 members, Wills recorded the song that took the nation by musical storm and introduced western swing to hundreds of thousands of people who otherwise would never have heard it. The song itself revealed much of the evolution and history of western swing. It was originally a breakdown fiddle selection recorded with Wills's heavy 2/4 jazz beat and was called "San Antonio Rose." In 1940 he recorded it with his horn band without the use of any fiddles. It was recorded in the big-band style of the period and was entitled "New San Antonio Rose." Wills sold 3 million recordings of it, and Bing Crosby brought it to a new audience when his recording sold over 1.5 million discs. Crosby had his second gold record, and Bob Wills was soon in Hollywood making movies. His hollering and "Ah haas" and western swing were assured of a place in Americana and the history of American music.

During World War II and in the postwar years, western swing underwent its final stage of development. From the early 1940s to the early 1950s, the music enjoyed its most successful years. As a style, it was so popular that western-swing bands performed in movies, over radio, and on the earliest television shows. At that time the term *western swing* was first used, although historians cannot pinpoint its first usage. Before World War II the bands that performed in the style were labeled everything from "hot dance," "hillbilly," "hot string," "country dance," and "old time" to "novelty hot dance." The musical establishment simply did not know what to call this new hybrid sound, and recording companies listed Wills, the Light Crust Doughboys, and others in "race catalogs" with black artists. Wayne Johnson, who played in the saxophone section of the recording of "New San Antonio Rose," explained in an interview how the terms *western* and *swing* were brought together in the 1930s to describe the Bob Wills style. "That was the swing era, and people were swing dancing. . . . In the Bob Wills band, we did exactly the same thing with a western flavor. We were still playing the same kind of beat, the same kind of arrangements and everything else," but Johnson added, "Bob also had the western flavor, because of the fiddles, the steel guitars, the costumes."

Some authorities believe the term was first used in reference to Spade Cooley and his band on the West Coast. Cooley grew up in Oklahoma and was a fan of Bob Wills and His Texas Playboys. When Cooley organized his band in California in the 1940s, the Wills sound was obvious, but Cooley's band played from written arrangements and produced a clean, rehearsed sound, a sound that was distinctive and very popular. Spade Cooley appeared in films and made many successful recordings. His ability as a musician, bandleader, and showman helped gain new audiences and national acceptance for western swing.

In the postwar years many other musical groups got on the western-swing bandwagon. Bob Wills's brother, Johnnie Lee, formed Johnnie Lee Wills and the Boys and was successful from the war years to 1958. Leon McAuliffe organized the Cimmaron Boys, one of the most popular of all western-swing bands. Luther J. Wills, another of Bob Wills's brothers, had minor success with an excellent band called the Rhythm Busters. In the early 1950s Bob Wills's youngest brother formed Billy Jack Wills and His Western Swing Band in northern California; the band leaned toward rhythm and blues and anticipated the rockabilly style. On the West Coast, Tex Williams performed in a western-swing style and recorded big-selling novelty songs. Hank Penny spread western swing from Alabama to Nashville. Pee Wee King was successful both as a bandleader and as the composer of "Tennessee Waltz." Bob Wills's great singer, Tommy Duncan, left the Texas Playboys in 1948 and hired some of the best musicians in the field for his Western All Stars.

World War II was a watershed in the history of American music. The age of the big bands began to close about the time the war ended. Television soon cut into the audiences that had kept the dance floors hot before and during the war. Dance audiences, though quite large until the late 1940s, began to dwindle and no longer supported the big bands. Western-swing groups, such as Wills's Texas Playboys, took fewer musicians on the road. Stringed instruments dominated western swing as never before. Styles did not change; they continued to play dance music, to produce jazz and swing. Fiddles in particular became more important after the war. There were generally more of them in the bands, and they were used to a greater extent, particularly as an ensemble. The "take off fiddlers" still took jazz choruses. The guitarists, especially in the Cooley, McAuliffe, and Bob Wills bands, continued to use their guitars like traditional jazz or swing instruments. They took choruses and improvised as jazzmen do with trumpets and clarinets. When the western-swing bands no longer had enough reeds and brass to provide the sound of the big-swing bands, they relied on guitars to simulate it. They often combined guitars, steel guitars, and amplified mandolins into a string ensemble to simulate a big-band horn section.

After 1950 television and new entertainment habits shifted popular tastes away from western-swing bands. Young people of that affluent decade, who for the first time dominated record buying and determined the direction of much of American entertainment, began to dance to different drummers. Western swing went into a decline and might well have ended like the big bands in the early 1950s had it not been for the unyielding popularity of Bob Wills and the use of so many stringed instruments by Wills and other western-swing bands. Wills and others in his field influenced rockabillies like Bill Haley, Buddy Holly, and Elvis Presley. The influence of western swing on country music was even greater and continues to this day.

When Bob Wills's health forced him to retire in the mid-1960s, an era ended. Three groups discovered western swing in the 1970s and have kept its sound and history alive. Country-and-western performers claim it as part of their music, and Merle Haggard, Alvin Crow, Red Steagall, Asleep at the Wheel, Waylon Jennings, Willie Nelson, and Ray Price either play it in a pure form or draw from its repertoire. Some rock artists such as Commander Cody, Charlie Daniels, and others perform in the swing style. Finally, many jazz artists performing on strings are continuing what western swing did years ago.

See also GEOGRAPHY: Southwest

Charles R. Townsend
West Texas State University

Bill C. Malone, *Country Music, U.S.A.: A Fifty-year History* (1968), *Southern Music— American Music* (1979); John Morthland, liner notes, *Okeh Western Swing*, Epic EG 37324; Tony Russell, *Blacks, Whites, and Blues* (1970); Chris Strachwitz and Bob Pinson, *Western Swing*, Old Timey T 105; Charles R. Townsend, Brochure notes to *For the Last Time*, United Artists UA-LA216–J2, "Homecoming: Reflections on Bob Wills and His Texas Playboys, 1915–1973," *San Antonio Rose: The Life and Music of Bob Wills* (1976). ☆

Zydeco

||||||||||||||||||

Zydeco is a fast, syncopated dance music of Louisiana's black Creole population. Played in urban and rural dance halls from St. Martinville and Lafayette to Houston's black French Fifth Ward, it has evolved in Louisiana over the last 150 years, influenced by Cajun, Afro-American, and Afro-Caribbean cultures. Some zydeco musicians may prefer a more Cajun sound, while other musicians, especially in urban settings, mix blues and soul into the music, reflecting the increasing impact of Afro-American mainstream culture. But nearly all zydeco groups maintain a rhythmic complexity in their music that harkens to their Afro-Caribbean inheritance, an inheritance also found in the early spasm bands of New Orleans jazz and the great "second-line" rhythm-and-blues pianists like Huey "Piano" Smith, Professor Longhair, and Fats Domino.

Zydeco reflects the multicultural and multiracial background of the Creole population on the French Gulf Coast from southern Louisiana into southeast Texas. In French Louisiana' and the French Caribbean, the term *Creole* originally referred both to descendants of the French and Spanish colonists from the Old World and to African slaves born in the New World. This original meaning of *Creole*, which refers to the planter class as well as to people from New Orleans and southeastern Louisiana, still persists. The other meaning of *Creole* (the one used here) developed later. It refers to the French-speaking people whose mixed ancestry may include black slaves from the Caribbean and American South, *gens libres de couleur* (free people of color), and Spanish, French, and German planters and merchants, local Indian tribes, Anglo-Americans, and Cajuns.

Many persons in southwestern French Louisiana who identify themselves as Creole or *noir* have some parentage from the Cajuns or Acadians—the peasant farming, fishing, and trapping people who entered the area over a 30-year period (1760s to 1800), following their expulsion from what is now called Nova Scotia. The cultural ties between Creoles and Cajuns are more significant than the genetic ties: the two cultures share, in part, essential features of life, including religion, festivals, foods, language, and music.

The largest numbers of black and *mulâtre* ("mulatto") French-speaking people came to Louisiana either as slaves for French planters in the second half of the 18th century or as *gens libres de couleur* both before and after the Haitian revolution of 1791–1803. In general, to be of "mixed" blood or *mulâtre* carried greater social status. The shift in the

use of the term *Creole* may have come from its use by such persons of "mixed" blood claiming their European ancestry, and from an attempt to distinguish the descendants of French culture from the English-speaking *Américains* (Americans), who acquired the territory in 1803.

The word *zydeco* is thought to be a creolized form of the French *les haricots* (snapbeans). Zydeco music is said to take its name from a dance tune in both the Cajun and Creole traditions called *Les Haricots Sont Pas Salés* (The Snapbeans Are Not Salted). The spelling of zydeco used here is one found on posters advertising dances and promoting bands in south Louisiana and southeast Texas. Alternate spellings are *zodico, zordico,* and *zologo*. All of these are English spellings used to represent the Creole pronunciation. A closer phonetic spelling would be *zarico* (stress on the last syllable), which preserves the French *a* and *r*.

Zydeco refers not only to the fast, syncopated dance numbers in a Creole band's repertoire, but also to the dance event itself. Old-time musician Bébé Carriére of the Louisiana prairie town of Lawtell says that in the old days word of a dance would be left at the general store or someone would ride around the countryside on horseback yelling, *"Zydeco au soir . . . chez Carrière!"* (Zydeco tonight at the Carrière's place!) Similarly, in urban Houston, the lyrics of *Bon Ton Roulet* by Clarence Garlow describe people going "way out in the country to the zydeco."

Because of the cultural interchange between Cajuns and Creoles in southwest Louisiana, there has been a tendency to overlook the differences between Cajun music and zydeco. Cajun music places more emphasis on developing the melodic line, while zydeco melodies are played much faster and consist of Acadian or Afro-American blues tunes placed in an Afro-Caribbean rhythmic framework. The rhythms are highly syncopated, with accents often shifting to various beats.

Whether the original Cajun tune is a one-step—a "la-la"—or a two-step dance, it can be transformed into a zydeco by the Creole musician, with faster tempo, melodic simplification, and increased syncopation. The rhythm may also change when a Cajun two-step—which accents the first and third beats—is played with the accents on the second and fourth beats. The melody, although simplified to a repeated figure, remains unrecognizable.

Even genres from outside the Afro-Caribbean and Acadian cultural sources, such as Afro-American blues and the Central European polka and mazurka, may be performed in a zydeco style. This is also true of the waltz, which the Creoles probably inherited from the Cajun and other traditions.

The repertoire and style of individual zydeco musicians may be either more Cajun, more Afro-American, or more Afro-Caribbean. For example, Creole musicians such as Fremont Fontenot of Basile and the Carrière brothers of Lawtell often play in a Cajun style because of their strong European cultural affiliations (though these performers do play zydeco and blues). On the other hand, the Lawtell Playboys of Frilot Cove and Sampy and the Bad Habits of Carencro show more Afro-Caribbean and Afro-American inclinations (though they also play waltzes and enjoy "French music"). As young accordionist Clinton Broussard says, "Zydeco bands, they all plays the same tunes, but everybody got their own style to do it."

Although West Indian influences on Louisiana culture can be traced in language, foods, folk beliefs, and in music, a musical form called zydeco or sounding like zydeco did not exist in the French West Indies. This suggests the importance of contact between Cajuns and black Creoles in generating a music form unique to Louisiana.

One item that does survive more directly from the Afro-French West Indian inheritance (although in modified form) is the dance *Calinda*. A dance called *Calinda, Kolenda, Kolinda*, and other names is mentioned in travelers' accounts as appearing in the French West Indies—Martinique, Guadeloupe, and Santo Domingo—as well as Trinidad from the late 18th century onward. Recent anthropological studies also note the presence of the dance in contemporary French West Indies in the contexts of *vodoun* (voodoo) worship and social dancing, Mardi Gras, and *Rara* festivities. The *kalinda* may involve such diverse activities as mock stick fighting and erotic courtship gestures.

Slaves gathering in New Orleans's Congo Square in the early 19th century were said to have danced the West Indian style *Calinda*. In rural French Louisiana, *Calinda* was transformed by Cajuns into a two-step and by Creoles into a zydeco. It has become part of the dance band repertoire, and hints of eroticism or extraordinary behavior have been submerged in the lyrics, which refer to dancing the old dances in a way that will make old women mad. Thus, *Calinda* becomes the name of a young woman enticed by her beau to dance too close while her mother is not looking. That *Calinda* may still have Afro-Caribbean influences is indicated by its heavily syncopated beat and by accordionist Delton Broussard's comment that "back toward New Iberia (in the area with more French West Indies influence), they want *Calinda* to dance wild to. You get to Lake Charles, and they want that French waltz." Removed from its West Indies source, *Calinda* is now a part of most Cajun and zydeco bands' repertoires.

At dances in the Creole community today, zydeco musicians usually choose fewer waltzes and more blues and fast two-steps than do Cajun musicians. While Cajun bands make wide use of the violin (an Acadian inheritance), they rarely play the vest *frottoir* (a metal rubbing board worn as a vest and played with spoons, can openers, or thimbles). Played by old-time and rural zydeco groups, the vest *frottoir* has its antecedents in Africa and the Caribbean as a scraped animal jaw, notched stick, and later, a washboard. The current model, made in Louisiana by tinsmiths, became popular in the 1930s when sheet metal was introduced to the area for roofing and barn siding. Also popular is the Cajun *bas trang* or *'tite fer* (triangle).

The accordion, used in both zydeco and Cajun music, was probably introduced to the area by German immigrants in the 1870s. The traditional model, and the one made by a number of local accordion makers, is the *une rang*ée (one row) diatonic push-pull instrument. It is used by Cajuns and most rural and old-time zydeco musicians. Urban performers have also experimented with the two- and three-row button accordion, and the chromatic piano accordion.

Cajun music and zydeco are meant for dancing. Indeed, the choice of dance halls and preferred musical style often mark the boundaries of Cajun and Creole communities. Performance of both of these types of Louisiana French music in a club setting is usually highly amplified for dancing, the lyrics are difficult to hear above the music or noise of the club. In general, lyrics to the dance tunes are not as elaborate as those of the home singing traditions. They are often fragmentary and tend to convey a "feeling" rather than a story.

While Cajun music has been influenced by country and western music in style and instrumentation (the steel guitar), zydeco has been affected more by rhythm and blues and soul music. Urban bands, such as Sampy and the Bad Habits and Mike and the Soul Accordion Band, have dropped the *frottoir* and violin, switching to two- and three-row accordions and sometimes adding a lead guitar. Though these bands play relatively slower zydeco numbers at a dance, the continued impact of the Creole and Cajun repertoire in urban areas is retained, as both bands still play waltzes and highly syncopated numbers.

Afro-American traditions have long existed side by side with the Afro-Caribbean and Cajun traditions in south Louisiana's Creole community. But since World War II they have become heavily integrated with Creole traditions and lifestyles. These changes in zydeco music reflect the acculturation of the Creole population into English-speaking Afro-American culture.

Creole culture remains strongest in the countryside, and here the dance hall is an essential social institution. Men and women come to dances well-dressed in sport coats and ties, pantsuits, carefully set hair, and jewelry. At a rural dance hall like the Ardoins' *Club Morris* in Duralde, entire families, from children to grandparents, come to dance. Zydeco is also performed at church dances, barbecue picnics, occasional *fais-do-do* (house dances), and in a variety of urban clubs that alternate bookings with discjockey and soul bands.

The new popularity of such bands as Terrence Semiens and the Mallet Playboys, Buckwheat *Ils Sont Partis Band*, and Fernest Arceneaux and Thunder reflect this change. On the other hand, more traditional groups such as Delton Broussard and the Lawtell Playboys, the Lawrence Ardoin Band, and John Delafose and the Eunice Playboys perform in a more French-influenced style. The new broader range of zydeco styles as projected in films, television programs, records, radio and at the newly formed (1983) Zydeco Festival in Opelousas suggests that Creole music is increasingly a symbol for cultural emergence of the Afro-French people of rural and urban south Louisiana.

Nicholas R. Spitzer
Smithsonian Institution

Amédée Ardoin, *The First Black Zydeco Recording Artist*, Louisiana Cajun Music, vol. 6, ed. Chris Strachwitz with liner notes by Michael Doucet, 1981, Old Timey LP 124; Clifton Chenier, *Louisiana Blues and Zydeco*, record, 1965, ed. with notes by Chris Strachwitz, Arhoolie LP F 1024; Nicholas R. Spitzer, "Zydeco and Mardi Gras: Creole Identity and Performance Genres in Rural French Louisiana," (Ph.D. dissertation, University of Texas at Austin, 1986), *Zydeco: Creole Music and Culture in Rural Louisiana*, film, Center for Gulf South History and Culture, Abita Springs, La., 1984; *Zodico: Louisiana Creole Music*, record, 1978, ed. and booklet Nicholas R. Spitzer, Rounder Records 6009; *Zydeco*, record, 1967, ed. with liner notes by Chris Strachwitz, Arhoolie LP F 1009. ☆

ACUFF, ROY
||||||||||||||||||||||||||||||
(b. 1903) Country music singer.

Roy Acuff was the dominant country singer of the World War II years and the first living person to be elected to the Country Music Hall of Fame in 1962.

Generally described as "the king of country music," a title first given to him by baseball player Dizzy Dean, Roy Claxton Acuff was born in Maynardville, Tenn., on 15 September 1903. Acuff was a star athlete at Central High School in Knoxville (winning 12 athletic letters), but after suffering a heatstroke in 1929 during a Florida fishing trip, he abandoned a promising baseball career and began perfecting his skills as a fiddler and singer. He joined a medicine show in 1932 as a musician and comedian, and in the following year he began performing with a string band, the Tennessee Crackerjacks, on WROL in

Roy Acuff, the "King of Country Music," 1930s

Knoxville. From 1934 to 1938 Acuff and his band played, at various times, on both WROL and WNOX in Knoxville and were part of the cast of the Mid-Day Merry Go Round at the latter station. In 1936 Acuff recorded for the Okeh label one of his most famous songs, "The Great Speckled Bird." The performance of this song during an audition at the Grand Ole Opry on 19 February 1938 probably did most to win him a permanent position on that famous show.

Acuff's rise to fame in country music paralleled that of the Grand Ole Opry in American entertainment. He was the first host of the show after it attained network status on NBC in 1939. During the war such Acuff songs as "The Great Speckled Bird," "Wabash Cannon Ball," and "Precious Jewel" appeared on jukeboxes all over the nation, and Acuff and his band—now called the Smoky Mountain Boys—drew larger crowds than any other act in country music. Polls indicated that Acuff enjoyed great popularity among American military personnel, and he even outpolled pop vocalist Frank Sinatra in a two-week contest sponsored by the Armed Forces Network. Acuff's earnest, emotional singing style and his preference for religious, sentimental, and old-time songs seemed to make him a fitting symbol of bedrock American values. According to legend, a Japanese banzai charge on Okinawa hurled these taunts at Americans: "To hell with Roosevelt; to hell with Babe Ruth; to hell with Roy Acuff!"

Although his record sales declined significantly after World War II, and his style became increasingly anachronistic amidst the wave of rock, pop, and swing sounds that inundated country music, Acuff maintained a high public visibility. He enjoyed considerable economic affluence as the coowner, along with Fred Rose, of Acuff-Rose Publishing Company, and he ran strongly, though unsuccessfully, as the Republican candidate for governor of Tennessee in 1948. He continued to appear each Saturday night at the Grand Ole Opry, established a souvenir and gift shop at Opryland, remained active in Tennessee Republican politics, and often acted as a spokesman for country music. When the Nitty Gritty Dirt Band made Acuff a central focus of their best-selling album, *Will the Circle Be Unbroken*, in 1972, the young country-rock musicians demonstrated just how far the Smoky Mountain Boys' name and influence had extended into American popular culture.

Bill C. Malone
Tulane University

Elizabeth Schlappi, *Roy Acuff* (1978). ☆

ALL-DAY SINGINGS

All-day singing has long been one of the most cherished social institutions of the rural South. The term has been applied to a wide range of musical affairs and even has its counterpart in the all-night singings of modern gospel quartet music, but it is most closely associated with the shape-note singing convention.

Singing conventions are events that feature the performance of shape-note music, of both the four-shape and seven-shape varieties. The four-shape conventions have always been the more conservative in that they adhere to the use of one songbook, usually the venerable *Sacred Harp*, first published by Benjamin F. White in 1844, and they tend to resist newer songs and innovative styles of performing them (they instead preserve the Fasola style of singing). In short, the four-shape people try to remain faithful to the music and, in some respects, the way of life of their ancestors. The seven-shape conventions, which are by far the most numerous of these events, were originally marked by their acceptance of the do-re-mi system of singing, and they have generally been receptive to innovations in songs and singing style. The singers at such conventions sing not from one book but from a wide variety of paperback shape-note hymnals generally published twice a year by such companies as Vaughan, Winsett, and Stamps-Baxter. The song repertoire therefore includes both the older, familiar religious material and the newest songs "hot off the press." Although everyone in attendance is encouraged to sing, performances are also made by soloists, duets and trios, and often by visiting professional quartets. People clearly attend these conventions not merely to sing but also to be entertained.

Whatever the style of singing, the singing conventions meet regularly throughout the rural and small-town South, often on a monthly basis in the case of the seven-shape singers, but much more infrequently in the case of the Fasola people. Singers gather at a church or at the county courthouse, renew old acquaintances, sing for several hours under the guidance of experienced song leaders, and then sit down at long tables for a sumptuous feast of fried chicken, ham, potato salad, assorted pastries, and other delectables brought by the guests and participants. The practice of combining food and religious music long ago gave rise to the term "all-day singing with

dinner on the grounds," which describes one of the most common events in the rural South.

Bill C. Malone
Tulane University

Alan Lomax, *Commentary on All Day Singing from "The Sacred Harp,"* Prestige Records 25007. ☆

ARMSTRONG, LOUIS
(1900–1971) Jazz musician and entertainer.

Born 4 July 1900 in New Orleans, Daniel Louis "Satchmo" Armstrong achieved acclaim as a jazz emissary to the world. Duke Ellington once called him "the epitome of jazz."

As a child Armstrong played music on the streets of New Orleans and received musical training in the public schools and at the Coloured Waif's Home (1913–14). He heard and was influenced by such early jazz performers

Louis Armstrong, premier jazz musician, c. 1931

as Charles "Buddy" Bolden, William "Bunk" Johnson, and Joseph "King" Oliver, who became his mentor. Armstrong performed briefly in a New Orleans nightclub at age 15 but did not become a full-time professional until he was 17. He joined Edward "Kid" Ory's band in 1918 and thereafter played with other jazz greats and led his own groups, especially the Hot Five and the Hot Seven, in the 1920s. His recording debut was with Oliver in 1923. Recordings made him a celebrity, and he toured widely in the 1930s, including a trip to Europe in 1932. He acquired his nickname "Satchmo" in England from the editor of a music magazine. Armstrong made a historic recording with Jimmie Rodgers, the father of country music, on 16 July 1930. Rodgers sang his "Blue Yodel No. 9" with accompaniment by Armstrong on the trumpet, and his wife, Lillian Hardin Armstrong, on piano.

Armstrong was a popular international figure by the 1940s and thereafter performed around the world; played at major jazz festivals; recorded frequently; performed in Broadway musicals, on radio, and later on television; and appeared in 60 films (including *Cabin in the Sky*, 1943; *New Orleans*, 1947; *High Society*, 1956; *Satchmo the Great*, 1956; *Jazz, the Intimate Art*, 1968; and *Hello, Dolly*, 1969). He died in New York City on 6 July 1971.

Armstrong's powerful trumpet and soulful, gravelly singing voice, as well as his infectious smile and effusive good humor, helped to establish the image of the archetypical jazzman. "Satchmo" communicated to everyone the irrepressible message that jazz was "good-time" music. His nickname, as well as his use of street vernacular for expressions of endearment and cordiality, reflected the communal New Orleans roots of the music.

The jazz personality that Armstrong helped create grew out of the southern urban underclass found most clearly in New Orleans. Armstrong's demeanor was as a loose-mannered, self-assertive (i.e., "bad"), somewhat "hip" good-time person whose music was a refuge from the external world. The jazz personality that emerged with Armstrong from the southern urban world included a bold and flirtatious manner, a zany sense of humor, a familiarity bordering on impertinence in interpersonal contact, a flashy, fancy code of dress, and an open and adventurous attitude toward life. Certainly, all jazz people have not fit this personality mold, but Armstrong— the most influential role model available to early jazz performers—did much to implant that abiding notion in the public mind.

Armstrong's jazz personality reflected certain aspects of the black culture in the South. He found his niche through music entertainment, a common pattern among blacks in southern urban areas. He drew on the vernacular tradition of black street and saloon life. His loose manner reflected an easygoing tolerance essential to the southern black underclass and fit squarely into the laid-back folk tradition. The hip mentality infusing the jazz personality is also a form of pride, validating the jazzman's self-assertiveness ("badness") in musical activities.

Curtis D. Jerde
W. R. Hogan Jazz Archive
Tulane University

Louis Armstrong, *Swing That Music* (1936), *Satchmo* (1954); Robert Goffin, *Horn of Plenty: The Story of Louis Armstrong*

(1947); Max Jones and John Chilton, *Louis: The Louis Armstrong Story, 1900–1971* (1971). ☆

AUTRY, GENE

(b. 1907) Country and western singer.

Though he became known throughout the world as a symbol of the West, Gene Autry's music remained firmly rooted in the southern soil from which it came. Orvon Gene Autry was born on a ranch near Tioga, Tex., on 29 September 1907 and moved to a ranch near Achille, Okla., as a youth. He was interested in a career in entertainment from an early age and even joined a medicine show in his teens; but it was as a guitar-strumming blue yodeler—under the influence of the enormously popular Jimmie Rodgers—that Autry achieved his first success as an entertainer in the late 1920s.

Although he continued to perform blue yodels as late as his 15th film (*The Old Corral*, 1936), he abandoned slavish imitation of Rodgers to adopt a gentler country sound, best exemplified by his first major record success, *That Silver Haired Daddy of Mine* (1931). A pure cowboy period followed, with popular records like *The Last Roundup* and *Tumbling Tumbleweeds* in the early 1930s, followed by standards like *Mexicali Rose*, *South of the Border*, and *There's a Gold Mine in the Sky* among many others. By the late 1930s his recordings were predominantly country love songs and had settled into an immediately recognizable style: swelling violins and muted trumpet for mainstream appeal, yet with a trademark steel guitar and Autry's straightforward, homespun, laconic voice most prominent. Like all great country singers, he possessed the ability to convey honesty, sincerity, and lack of affectation in his delivery; he sang as though he were speaking with each listener on a one-to-one basis. His recording career reached its apex in the late 1940s, with the multimillion-selling children's records *Here Comes Santa Claus* and *Rudolph the Red-Nosed Reindeer*.

The first singer-actor to popularize the singing cowboy in film, Autry fostered a new musical and film genre of worldwide popularity in a film career that included some 93 films and 91 television programs. He was a country songwriter of consequence; a record seller seldom matched in recording history, with major hits spanning years (1930–51) and styles; an enormously successful businessman and owner of the California Angels baseball club; and a cultural icon who brought an image of the West and western music to the world.

Of primary significance, however, was Gene Autry's adherence to an unabashedly sincere country singing style throughout his career. His stature as a major entertainer in the 1930s and 1940s gave country music a badly needed dignity and respectability, and though he is not often given credit for such a pioneering role, it was largely Autry and the singing cowboys who followed in his footsteps who made millions aware of the sincerity and emotion inherent in the music of the hills and ranges.

Douglas B. Green
Nashville, Tennessee

Gene Autry, with Mickey Herskowitz, *Back in the Saddle Again* (1978); Douglas B. Green, *Journal of Country Music* (May 1978); Bill C. Malone, *Country Music,*

U.S.A.: A Fifty-year History (1968, rev. ed., 1985). ☆

BALFA, DEWEY

||||||||||||||||||||||||||||||||||||||

(b. 1927) Cajun folk musician.

Dewey Balfa is one of the nation's most widely respected folk musicians and Cajun cultural activists. His calm, homespun eloquence and sincerity have made him a spokesman for traditional cultures in general, but most of his battles to save his Cajun French culture are fought with a fiddle in south Louisiana, his home.

Balfa's musical heritage is a family affair. "My father, grandfather, great-grandfather, they all played the fiddle, and, you see, through my music, I feel they are all still alive." Balfa's father, Charles, was a sharecropper on Bayou Grand Louis in rural Evangeline Parish near Mamou. He instilled a love of life and music in his children, and Dewey and his four brothers grew up making music for their own entertainment. Born 20 March 1927, Dewey Balfa began playing the fiddle when he was about 13. Dewey had many models to follow, some outside the family, some even outside the culture. "You know, I was influenced by J. B. Fusilier, Leo Soileau, Harry Choates, and I think Bob Wills and the Texas Playboys had a little effect on my fiddling."

Dewey and his brothers soon were playing together for family gatherings and house dances. In the 1940s, when dance halls were at the height of their popularity, the Balfa Brothers band stayed busy, sometimes playing eight dances a week. String bands dominated Cajun music in the 1940s. The traditional music of Balfa's French Louisiana became increasingly Americanized as it was influenced by western swing, bluegrass, and country music. In the years following World War II, musicians such as Iry Lejeune, Nathan Abshire, Alphé Bergeron, and Lawrence Walker dusted off their long-abandoned accordions to perform again and to record traditional Louisiana Cajun French music. Many people were convinced after that of the need for deliberate efforts to encourage the maintenance of the music's traditional form.

In 1964 Balfa played as a last-minute replacement on guitar at the Newport Folk Festival, and after that, national and local interest was focused on traditional south Louisiana music. Balfa was involved in Louisiana contests sponsored by the Newport Folk Festival to discover talented musicians, and in 1967 the Balfa Brothers band performed at the Newport Folk Festival. South Louisiana itself was soon providing greater encouragement to its traditional artists such as Balfa. As a result of the overwhelming response to Lafayette's 1974 "Tribute to Cajun Music," the music festival has become an annual outdoor event. Dewey Balfa saw the festival all along as a way to attract young musicians to Cajun music. Two of Balfa's brothers died in a 1978 automobile accident, but Dewey Balfa and other family members continue to perform and to carry the spirit of the Balfa Brothers.

Barry Jean Ancelet
University of Southwestern Louisiana

Barry Jean Ancelet, *Louisiana Life* (September–October 1981), *The Makers of Cajun Music / Musiciens Cadiens et Créoles* (1984); John Broven, *South to Louisiana: The Music of the Cajun Bayous* (1983). ☆

BANJO
||||||||||||||||||

The five-string banjo is a distinctive feature of the indigenous rural music of the South; it is generally not indigenous to rural music elsewhere. But while the banjo has been commonly associated with rural white southern culture, urban and black influences have significantly shaped its history.

The banjo originated in black culture, proto-banjos having been brought by slaves from Africa. Until recently, legend honored Joel Sweeney as the inventor of the five-string banjo. This Virginian, around 1830, allegedly improved the slave instrument by adding a short, high-pitched fifth (or thumb) string to its original four. However, reliable illustrations show that some slave banjos in the Americas had short thumb strings well before Sweeney was born.

Until the 1830s the banjo was strictly a black instrument. The first whites to play it became, like Sweeney, minstrel performers, and it became an essential element in the minstrel show, which was born in the urban North in 1843 and became the most popular entertainment form of the century. Minstrel banjo playing, a down-stroking style undoubtedly reflecting preexisting black performance, also became the early style of white rural performers, who called it "frailing" or "clawhammer." By the 1870s the banjo was being played widely by southern rural whites, who probably learned from both black musicians and minstrel players who toured the South with minstrel shows, circuses, and medicine shows. Blacks continued to play the banjo, and until recently musical exchange between white and black players was active; now, however, only a few blacks play.

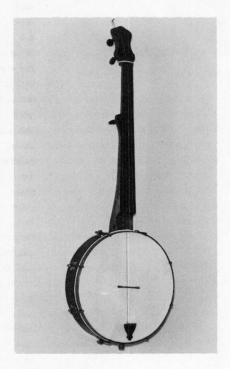

An 1850s fretless banjo

The first major group of styles, frailing, continues to be used in the South and, through the impetus of Pete Seeger and other figures in the folksong revival of the 1960s and 1970s, has also spread elsewhere. The second major group of styles, finger-picking, entered rural tradition around the turn of the century, apparently in imitation of "classical" banjo, which developed in the 1870s and 1880s as the successor to the minstrel style on the stage and in urban areas. The early, two-finger styles are still used, but in the 1940s Earl Scruggs and other southerners transformed them into the more driving, syncopated, three-finger style known as bluegrass banjo, the most widely heard style at present, as bluegrass gains popularity in rural and urban areas far from the South.

Despite the spread of revivalist "old-time" players and bluegrass, the five-string banjo remains a symbol of the rural South.

Robert B. Winans
Wayne State University

Dena J. Epstein, *Ethnomusicology* (September 1975); Scott Odell, in *New Grove Dictionary of Music and Musicians*, vol. 2, ed. Stanley Sadie (1980); Robert B. Winans, *Folklore and Folklife in Virginia* (1979), *Journal of American Folklore* (October–December 1976). ☆

BEACH MUSIC

A treasure of popular culture in the Carolinas, beach music is not historically indigenous to Carolina beaches, where it now finds its greatest popularity, and does not traditionally celebrate beach culture. The origins of beach music lie in both the blues of the mid-20th-century South and the harmonious rhythm and blues of urban black street-corner singing groups like the Clovers, who enjoyed national success in the 1950s. Visitors to the Carolinas often find familiar oldies sanctified as classic "beach music."

The development of beach music as a cultural phenomenon began in the post–World War II era, as whites were attracted to the previously taboo music and dance of blacks. With the expansion of modern roadways and the mass availability of automobiles, this music became accessible in city concert halls and in the developing beach towns.

Beach music prospered in the late 1950s and early 1960s, but submerged somewhat in the Vietnam era, as both musically and thematically it had become traditional and therefore suspect in the social and political climate of the time. Amid the frenzy of hard rock and the earnestness of "message music," rhythm and blues was by no means hip, cool, or relevant for many young people. In this period *beach music* emerged as a cover term for an eclectic assortment of rhythm-and-blues songs. Some people claim the term always existed, but many insist that it did not appear until around 1970 or later. Though the temptation is to credit the Drifters' "Under the Boardwalk" from 1964 with popularizing the term, beach music more likely arose from a nostalgic looking back toward happier tunes in the past, symbolized by the music that permeated them.

With the advent of disco music in the late 1970s, beach music revitalized and prospered. The return of "touch dancing" at this time contributed to the popularity of the "shag," beach music's dance ritual. Essentially a sophisticated, more refined cousin of the jitterbug (and not related to the shag of the Northeast in the 1940s), the shag became the focal point of beach music. The shag was decreed the state dance by the South Carolina Legislature in 1985, and beach music has become a cultural icon in the Carolinas. Purists seek to preserve it in its earliest, most intricate forms, and a circuit of dance competitions has developed with support from a growing number of teaching professionals.

With the resurgence of beach music in the late 1970s and early 1980s, the beach music scene became self-conscious and lyrically self-glorifying, celebrating itself and the beer-drinking, love-making side of beach culture in regional, independently produced songs such as the Embers' 1979 "I Love Beach Music." Performers now are mostly white, reside principally in the Carolinas, and stress the horns in their rhythm sections.

The resurgence of beach music reached its peak in the early part of the 1980s with two Beach Music Awards shows filmed in 1982 and 1983 in Myrtle Beach, S.C., a capital for the music. A Society of Stranders (from "The Grand Strand," the popular name for the northeast South Carolina coastal area) meets each year in North Myrtle Beach and brings thousands of beach music fans together for several days of festivities. Some predicted that it would "go national," but this has not occurred. Beach music's true value lies in the regional bonding it inspires in the Carolinas.

Stephen J. Nagle
University of South Carolina,
Coastal Campus

Orin Anderson, *Sandlapper* (June 1981); Bill King, Atlanta *Constitution* (6 June 1981); Steven Levy, *Rolling Stone* (30 September 1982); Stephen J. Nagle, *On The Beach* (Summer 1983). ☆

BEALE STREET
||||||||||||||||||||||||||||||||||||

Beale Street, one of the most celebrated streets in the South, was the black main street of Memphis and of the surrounding rural region, comparable in its heyday to Auburn Avenue in Atlanta and Maxwell Street in Chicago. Beginning at the Mississippi riverfront and extending eastward a mile and a half, the street was lined with commercial buildings, churches, theaters, parks, elegant mansions, everyday dwellings, and apartment houses.

The diversity of its built environment showed that Beale was a mosaic of southern cultures. For more than a century, indigenous white and black southerners, Italian Americans, Greek Americans, Chinese Americans, and Jews lived or worked on Beale.

Unlike its northern counterparts, Beale Street never became a black ghetto. But it was Beale's black culture that gave the street its fame, and the street stood as testimony to the decision of black people to strive to achieve the American Dream in their American homeland, the South, rather than to move North. From the 1830s, when the street was laid out, to the Civil War, black people were present on Beale Street, either as slaves living in quarters behind their masters' homes or as free blacks, some of whom owned Beale Street property. After emancipation, thousands of freed slaves left the declining farms and small towns of the rural South and came to Memphis and to Beale Street in particular, seeking to fulfill the promises of freedom. Alongside white-owned establishments, they founded banks, insurance companies, retail shops, newspapers, schools, churches, fraternal institutions, nightclubs, and political and civil rights organizations. From the 1880s to the 1920s Beale was one of the South's most prosperous black communities. On weekends, thousands of blacks from Memphis and the surrounding countryside came to Beale for shopping and entertainment, crowding the sidewalks so thickly "you had to walk in the street to pass by."

As the urban center of black nightlife for north Mississippi, east Arkansas, and west Tennessee, Beale attracted hundreds of musicians and became one of the nation's most influential centers of Afro-American music. Variety was its hallmark—vaudeville orchestras, marching bands, ragtime, jug bands, blues, jazz, big bands, and rhythm and blues. A meeting place for urban and rural styles, Beale served as a school where young talent was nurtured and it produced musicians who shaped the course of American music. In 1909 W. C. Handy was the first person to pen the blues, a form of music he had first heard in the Mississippi Delta town of Clarksdale, thus enabling it to be played around the world.

Since the 1920s Beale Street has produced a succession of outstanding jazz musicians, such as Jimmy Lunceford, a principal creator of the big-band sound. In the 1940s and 1950s Beale Street musicians like B. B. King and Bobby "Blue" Bland blended traditional blues with jazz arrangements to help produce the new form of music known as rhythm and blues. In the 1950s young white musicians from the region like Elvis Presley were attracted to the music, dance, and dress styles of Beale Street and merged these with their country music traditions to shape a new type of music, rockabilly, and to lay the foundations for rock and roll.

But if Beale Street was a cultural sanctuary, it was a precarious one. Segregation denied blacks effective access to political and economic power beyond their own community, and they were therefore unable to protect their Beale Street haven when hard times came. After World War II, downtown Memphis, like other American inner cities, began to change radically in character; the two most dramatic responses, the civil rights movement and urban renewal, transformed Beale. While the civil rights movement achieved integration of Memphis's public facilities, it ironically damaged Beale by enabling blacks to do business throughout the city. The assassination of Martin Luther King, Jr., near Beale and the turbulent aftermath accelerated the street's decline. Urban renewal then cleared most of the old buildings in its supportive community.

In the late 1970s and 1980s, however, Beale Street like other historic areas in the South has received new recognition as a cultural resource; and governmental, nonprofit, and private organizations have substantially revitalized the street. The resultant preservation of original landmarks together with the establishment of new nightclubs, restaurants, retail stores, and an interpretive center has produced a significant blend of old and new, and the future development of the street will no doubt continue to reflect major trends of urban southern culture.

See also URBANIZATION: / Memphis

George McDaniel
Center for Southern Folklore

Margaret McKee and Fred Chisenhall, *Beale Black and Blue: Life and Music on Black America's Main Street* (1981). ☆

BECHET, SIDNEY
||||||||||||||||||||||||||||||||||||||||||||||||||
(1897–1959). Jazz musician and composer.

Like Jelly Roll Morton, Sidney Joseph Bechet, who was born 14 May 1897 in New Orleans, was a black Creole, a member of the group that played a pivotal part in the genesis of jazz. He grew up in the rich musical environment of

New Orleans, taught himself clarinet, and later studied sporadically with George Bacquet, "Big Eye" Louis Nelson, and Lorenzo Tio, Jr. By about 1910, he was performing with established New Orleans bands such as Bunk Johnson's. In 1914 he began to tour, settling in Chicago in 1917.

He performed in Europe from 1919 to 1921. He was among the first jazzmen to be critically praised; in 1919 the Swiss conductor Ernest Ansermet called him "an artist of genius." Also in 1919 Bechet began playing the soprano saxophone, and made it his primary instrument the rest of his life. In the mid-1920s, he recorded with Clarence Williams and Louis Armstrong and worked briefly with Duke Ellington. From 1925 to 1928 he toured Germany, France, and the Soviet Union. He returned to the United States with Noble Sissle's band and performed intermittently with it through 1938. During the revival of traditional jazz beginning about 1939, he was praised as one of the master jazz pioneers, and his career rebounded. From 1951 he lived in France, where he became a celebrity as the dominant figure in traditional jazz. He composed both short works (*Petite Fleur*) and longer works (*Nouvelles Orléans*) and appeared in a number of films.

Bechet was one of many jazz pioneers who moved from New Orleans to Chicago during the 1910s and 1920s, and, making records there, spread jazz from its southern beginnings to the nation and beyond. Like Armstrong, Bechet's melodic voice was so strong and original that he came to dominate his ensembles; both musicians helped transform early jazz from an ensemble music to a soloist's art. Bechet made the soprano saxophone into a jazz instrument and set the standard by which all subsequent players have been measured. He developed a strong, individual jazz voice, distinctive for its rhythmic freedom, flowing expressiveness, rich tone, and wide vibrato. He greatly influenced Duke Ellington's saxophonist Jimmy Hodges, who, in turn, perpetuated Bechet's legacy. Bechet was also notable for the longevity of his musical career, which spanned nearly 60 years, and for maintaining his beautiful style almost until his death in Paris, 14 May 1959.

John Edward Hasse
Smithsonian Institution

Sidney Bechet, *Treat it Gentle* (1960); Hans J. Mauerer, *A Discography of Sidney Bechet* (1969); Raymond Mouly, *Sidney Bechet: Notre Ami* (1959); Martin Williams, *Jazz Masters of New Orleans* (1967). ☆

BLACKWOOD BROTHERS
Gospel music singers.

Perhaps the most popular group in southern gospel music history, the Blackwood Brothers parlayed their rural Mississippi sharecropping background into a million-dollar entertainment empire. For many fans in both the South and the Midwest, the Blackwoods defined the singing quartet style that is the backbone of classic southern gospel music and engineered many of the musical and promotional innovations that permitted gospel singers to professionalize their music. They were among the first to issue their own phonograph records, to break from the songbook publishers that had dominated gospel music for the first four decades of the century, to begin their own radio transcription service, to consciously seek out and adapt new or original songs, to travel by air, and to adapt harmonies and accompaniment appealing to a nationwide popular audience.

The original quartet was formed in 1934 at Ackerman, Miss., by three brothers, Roy, Doyle, and James, sons of a Delta sharecropper and his wife who sang casually in church; the fourth member was Roy's young son, R. W. By 1937 the group found itself broadcasting on radio at Jackson, Miss., doing not only gospel but pop and country tunes, and after April 1939 they performed on a 50,000-watt station, KWKH, recently opened in Shreveport, La. Here they began an affiliation with the songbook publisher V. O. Stamps, who provided them with a car, contracts, a stipend, and a piano player, thus casting them into the format of "four men and a piano" that had become characteristic of earlier gospel quartets. In 1940 Stamps sent them to Shenandoah, Iowa, where they began a decade's stay at KMA that saw them develop their unique style and build a huge following in the Midwest.

At Shenandoah the quartet began to experiment with modern harmonies

The Blackwood Brothers, gospel music quintet, 1950s

(built on sixth and ninth chords), developing their precise enunciation and diction and borrowing verve, dynamics, and solo breaks from pop and black gospel music. In 1946 they began to make records, first on the White Church label and then on their own Blackwood label, recording some 49 singles between 1946 and 1951. A move back to Memphis in August 1950 put them in the center of the then-burgeoning gospel movement, where both black and white groups vied for air time and for places at "all-night sings." With their broadcasting base at WMPS, the Blackwoods—now with only two of the original four still singing—became one of the first postwar gospel groups to sign with a major label when they began recording for RCA Victor on 4 January 1952. Hit records and a win on the nationally broadcast *Arthur Godfrey Talent Scouts* show in 1954 followed, but barely two weeks after the Godfrey show two members of the group, R. W. and bass singer Bill Lyles, were killed in a plane crash.

Within a month the Blackwoods had recovered and regrouped and were back on the concert circuit; another Blackwood, Cecil, the brother of R. W., stepped in, as did bass singer J. D. Sumner, who was to play an important role in the group's sound throughout the 1950s. A string of national television appearances and successful record albums followed in the mid-1950s, and the group's promotional activities reached new heights through their founding of the National Quartet Convention in 1957 and of a new all-gospel record company, Skylite, in 1960 as well as through the purchase of several of the old gospel songbook companies, which had fallen on hard times. From 1967 to 1977 the group won numerous Grammy awards and as late as the mid-

1970s still featured James Blackwood, his son Jimmy, and his nephew Cecil.

The Blackwood Brothers discography is voluminous. In addition to hundreds of singles, it includes at least 58 long-playing albums on RCA Victor from 1956 to 1973 and at least 42 albums on the Skylite label from 1961 to 1981; probably 20 albums exist on various other labels. Songs the Blackwoods have been most associated with include "Have You Talked to the Man Upstairs" (their first RCA hit and the winning song on the Godfrey show), "Swing Down Chariot," "My Journey to the Sky," "Paradise Island," "In Times Like These," "Looking for a City," and "The Old Country Church."

Charles K. Wolfe
Middle Tennessee State
University

James Blackwood, with Don Martin, *The James Blackwood Story* (1975); Kree Jack Racine, *Above All: The Fascinating and True Story of the Lives and Careers of the Famous Blackwood Brothers Quartet* (1967). ☆

BOLDEN, BUDDY
(1877–1931) Jazz musician.

The story of Charles "Buddy" Bolden is part of the earliest history of New Orleans jazz. Bolden was an accomplished cornetist and one of the first musicians to mix ragtime and blues into a sound that would later be called "jazz." He was born in New Orleans on 6 September 1877. His father, a drayman, died of pneumonia when Bolden was six years old. His mother worked to support the family, and Bolden and his sister did not have to work as children. No other members of the Bolden family were interested in music; Bolden learned from religious and various types of street music heard in New Orleans in the late 19th century. His natural musical ability showed itself when he began to play the cornet at age 17.

Bolden played in small string bands for dances and parties and in parades in New Orleans between 1895 and 1900. He achieved citywide fame around 1900 as the leader of his own band. Until 1906 Bolden continued to improvise his music, attracting a considerable following of admirers and being dubbed the "King" of New Orleans jazz. He and his band played in parks and at picnics, in city music halls, lawn parties, and bars. Sometimes they traveled outside New Orleans, playing at train stops along the way. Bolden was immersed in his music, enjoyed drinking, and was said to have hypnotic powers over women.

In the spring of 1906 Bolden began to have severe headaches and reportedly suffered from delusions. He attacked his mother in a fit and was taken into police custody. Once released, Bolden continued to play, but friends said he became increasingly depressed and easily angered. His erratic behavior led to another arrest in September 1906. His condition deteriorated quickly after his release, and in June 1907 Bolden was committed to the Insane Asylum of Louisiana where he spent the last 24 years of his life. The official cause of his insanity was listed as alcoholism.

Bolden achieved his status as the legendary ancestor of jazz after his death. Jazz fans repeat fictional stories such as the one in which Bolden supposedly blew his cornet so hard that the tuning slide flew out and landed 20 feet away. Most of the stories suggest the remarkable power of Bolden's playing. Even the New Orleans *Times-Picayune* in 1940 reported that Bolden "played with such volume that it is said he could often be heard while playing across the river in Gretna." "King" Bolden's increasing notoriety as a musician is underscored by the tragic nature of his short but inspired career.

Karen M. McDearman
University of Mississippi

Ole Brask, *Jazz People* (1976); Donald M. Marquis, *In Search of Buddy Bolden: First Man of Jazz* (1978). ☆

BROWN, JAMES
|||||||||||||||||||||||||||||||||||||||||
(b. 1933) Soul music singer.

"Soul Brother No. 1," "The Godfather of Soul," and "Mr. Dynamite" are all names credited to the only black rhythm-and-blues artist of the 1950s to successfully bridge the gap to soul artist in the 1960s and funk artist in the 1970s. Maintaining his popularity through 30 years, James Brown single-handedly anticipated and shaped 1970s funk and, to a slightly lesser degree, disco music. The repercussions of his aesthetic conceptualizations are heard everywhere on black radio in the 1980s. His influence can be detected in European new wave music, West African Afro-beat, and West Indian reggae.

Brown was born 3 May 1933 near Augusta, Ga., in abject poverty. Twenty-one years later he formed the first version of his Famous Flames. Initially the Flames sang gospel music only. They soon adapted their highly emotional repertoire to secular subjects and started working regularly in and around Macon, Ga. A demo tape of the secularized gospel song "Please, Please, Please" was sent to King Records in Cincinnati (at the time one of the leading independent record labels specializing in black music), and in February 1956 James Brown and the Famous Flames recut the song and attained their first top-10 rhythm-and-blues hit. It would be four years before Brown would cross over to the pop charts and nine years before "Papa's Got a Brand New Bag (Part I)" would go top 10 on the pop charts.

In that nine-year period Brown developed his legendary show-stopping revue with supporting singers, comedians, and dancers. His bands rehearsed meticulously, achieving a professionalism virtually unknown in rhythm and blues or rock and roll, while Brown exuded nonstop energy replete with dancing, splits, knee drops, microphone acrobatics, and his fabled simulated collapse. The whole package was captured on vinyl in *Live at the Apollo*, a 1962 album, which, although a hardcore rhythm-and-blues album, reached the number-two spot on *Billboard*'s album charts and stayed on the charts for a total of 66 weeks.

James Brown, soul singer, 1960s

Brown began with a style based on gospel intensity and interaction. His early records consist largely of call and response between himself and the Famous Flames. The Flames would echo, shadow, double, and respond to Brown's every nuance. The instrumentalists on these early records largely played a 12/8 triplet feel over a pronounced back beat. By 1959 Brown, originally a drummer, started to change his style, opting for increasingly complex out-front, crack rhythmic arrangements usually consisting of extended one-chord vamps featuring repetitive "groove" vocal figures, choked rhythm guitar, staccato horn bursts, and broken two- and three-note bass patterns. In both styles Brown's singing was marked by a complete lack of inhibition, extensively utilizing gospel devices such as falsetto cries, grunts, hoarse screams, and gasps.

Brown has completely controlled his career. He has written lyrics, produced records, and made all executive decisions, eventually managing himself and forming his own record production company. He also put himself in the vanguard of the black consciousness movement through records such as "Say It Loud, I'm Black and I'm Proud." As a classic example of the rags-to-riches American dream, Brown's importance as a symbol to black youth cannot be overestimated. Forty million-selling records and over one hundred chart entries later, James Brown remains "The Hardest Working Man in Show Business."

Robert Bowman
Memphis, Tennessee

Tony Cummings, in *The Soul Book*, ed. Ian Hoare (1975); Gerri Hirshey, *Nowhere To*

Run: The Story of Soul Music (1984); Robert Palmer, in *The Rolling Stone Illustrated History of Rock 'n' Roll*, ed. Jim Miller (1980). ☆

BRUMLEY, ALBERT
|||||||||||||||||||||||||||||||||||||||||||||||||||||
(1905–1977) Gospel music songwriter.

Albert E. Brumley was one of the premier composers of gospel songs and was intimately associated with the rise and expansion of the southern gospel quartet business. Many songs from his repertoire still command the allegiance of musicians in both the gospel and country fields (and particularly in bluegrass music, where his songs are frequently played).

Brumley was born near Spiro, LeFlore County, Okla., on 29 October 1905 into a tenant-farm family that provided inspiration for many of his most popular songs. He began writing songs shortly after attending his first singing school in 1922 at the Rock Island community in eastern Oklahoma, but none were published until 1927 when "I Can Hear Them Singing Over There" appeared in *Gates of Glory*, a convention songbook issued by the Hartford Music Company of Hartford, Ark. Brumley was intimately associated with the Hartford Company from 1926 to 1937, first as a student in its Musical Institute, and then as a traveling teacher in many of its shape-note singing schools, as a bass singer in some of the Hartford Quartets, and as a staff writer. Above all, Brumley profited from the guidance and counsel of Eugene M. Bartlett, the owner of the Hartford Company and the writer of such songs as "Victory in Jesus," "Everybody Will Be Happy over There," and "Take an Old Cold Tater and Wait."

In January 1932 Brumley's most famous song, "I'll Fly Away," was published by the Hartford Company in one if its many paperback songbooks, *Wonderful Message*. Reminiscent of 19th-century camp-meeting songs with its catchy rhythm and repeated chorus, "I'll Fly Away" has since been recorded over 500 times in virtually every field of music and has become one of the standards of white gospel music. Brumley eventually composed over 600 songs, first for the Hartford Company up to 1937, then for the Stamps-Baxter Company from 1937 to 1945, and finally for the Stamps Quartet Publishing Company after 1945. Such songs as "Jesus Hold My Hand," "I'll Meet You in the Morning," "I Found a Hiding Place," "Camping in Canaan's Land" (co-written with Eugene M. Bartlett), and "If We Never Meet Again" won a wide circulation in homes and churches all over the South through the performances of the quartets. Radio was a prime medium through which his songs were popularized, and Brumley wrote a very popular song, "Turn Your Radio On," which paid tribute to that powerful commercial force while advising listeners to "get in touch with God" by tuning in "the Master's radio."

Although Brumley said that he never consciously wrote a country song, several of his songs (in addition to the purely gospel numbers mentioned previously) have become standards in the country and bluegrass fields. These include "By the Side of the Road," "Dreaming of a Little Cabin," "Did You Ever Go Sailin'," "Nobody Answered Me," and "Rank Strangers to Me." These sentimental and nostalgic songs, which juxtapose memories of a cherished but decaying rural past with visions of a reconciliation with loved ones

in heaven, have struck sensitive chords among many southerners who have been conscious of their region's disquieting transition from ruralism and agriculture to urban industrialism. Indeed, all Brumley's songs, both religious and secular, spoke directly to people who often felt discouraged in a world of disappointment and bewildering change. Consequently, his songs were particularly cherished during the Depression when people needed the comfort and assurance of a personal, caring Savior.

Brumley wrote few songs after World War II, but he remained in the music business as the owner of the Hartford Company and Albert Brumley and Sons, and was the promoter of two music festivals, the Sunup to Sundown Sing in Springdale, Ark., and the Hill and Hollow Folk Festival in Powell, Mo. Before his death on 15 November 1977, Brumley was named to the Gospel Music Hall of Fame and the Nashville Song Writers Hall of Fame. He is buried near Powell, Mo., where he had resided since 1931.

Bill C. Malone
Tulane University

Clarence Baxter and Vide Polk, *Gospel Song Writers Biography* (1971); Ottis J. Knippers, *Who's Who among Southern Singers and Composers* (1937); *Music City News* (July 1965). ☆

BYRD, HENRY (PROFESSOR LONGHAIR)

(1918–1980) Rhythm-and-blues musician.

Professor Longhair was a pioneer of the post–World War II New Orleans rhythm-and-blues idiom. Although he made the transition to rock and roll with modest commercial results, his artistic influence on popular music in the Crescent City was immense. Pianist-composer Allen Toussaint dubbed him "the Bach of Rock."

Born in Bogalusa, La., a rural sawmill town, Henry Roeland Byrd moved to New Orleans as a child. He grew up near Rampart Street, then a musical strip connecting black central-city wards to the downtown neighborhoods. His early exposure to music came in church, which he attended with his mother; she played guitar and piano. For the most part, though, Byrd was self-taught, inspired by blues pianists like Kid "Stormy" Weather, Champion Jack Dupree, and Isidore "Tuts" Washington.

As a teenager Byrd acquired his sense of rhythm by tap dancing. In time, he took the drum-infused movements of his feet and translated them to piano, adding layers of melody to intricate rhythm patterns. Chief among them was

Professor Longhair, New Orleans rhythm-and-blues musician, 1978

boogie-woogie. Another important influence was Sullivan Rock, an obscure honky-tonk pianist about whom little is known.

Byrd—or Fess as fans called him—played with a sizzling left hand, and to this percussive flavor he added "a mixture of mambo, rhumba, and calypso." This fusion resonates in "Go to the Mardi Gras," an anthem that is now a classic and is played on hundreds of jukeboxes during Carnival.

His stage name came in 1947 at the Caldonia Inn. The white proprietor announced, "We'll call you Professor Longhair and the Four Hairs Combo." In the early 1950s, recording with Atlantic Records, he cut the memorable "Tipitina." By the late 1960s he had sunk into obscurity, but the following decade saw a gallant comeback. In 1977 friends opened Tipitina's, a club that served as Byrd's home base in New Orleans.

Byrd's albums include *New Orleans Piano*, *Mardi Gras in New Orleans*, *The Last Mardi Gras*, and *Crawfish Fiesta*, which was being shipped to record stores when he died on 30 January 1980. The jazz funeral in his honor was one of the largest and most exciting in recent memory. An excellent video documentary, *Piano Players Seldom Play Together*, features Toussaint, Tuts Washington, and Professor Longhair, and includes moving scenes at Byrd's funeral.

Jason Berry
New Orleans, Louisiana

Jason Berry, Jonathan Forse, and Tad Jones, *Up from the Cradle of Jazz: New Orleans Music since World War II* (1987); John Broven, *Rhythm and Blues in New Orleans* (1978); Jeff Hannusch, *I Hear You Knockin'*

(1985); Robert Palmer, *A Tale of Two Cities: Memphis Rock and New Orleans Roll* (1979) ☆

CARTER FAMILY
||||||||||||||||||||||||||||||||||||||||||
Country entertainers.

The Carter Family was one of country music's most influential groups and a valuable link to the music's folk origins. The family was composed of Alvin Pleasant (A. P.) Carter who was born in Scott County, Va., in 1891, his wife Sara Dougherty Carter who was born in Wise County, Va., in 1898; and A. P.'s sister-in-law Maybelle Addington Carter, who was born at Nickelsville, Va., in 1909. After their marriage on 18 June 1915, A. P. and Sara began singing for friends and relatives who gathered at their home at Maces Spring in the Clinch Mountains of Virginia. After Maybelle married A. P.'s brother Ezra in 1926, she joined the duo, bringing an exceptional talent for the autoharp, banjo, and guitar.

The trio made their first records for the famous talent scout Ralph Peer and the Victor Company in Bristol, Tenn., on 1 and 2 August 1927. Recording at the same session where Jimmie Rodgers made his debut, the Carter Family introduced a style of performing that remained recognizable and appealing for many years, and they began circulating a body of songs that still endures in the repertoire of modern country musicians. From 1927 to 1943 the Carters popularized their large catalog of gospel, sentimental, and traditional songs at personal appearances, on live radio broadcasts, on transcriptions, and on recordings made until 1941 for the Victor, American Record, Decca, and Columbia companies. Most country and folk music fans still know such Carter Family songs as "Wildwood Flower," "Keep on the Sunny Side," "Worried Man Blues," "I'm Thinking Tonight of My Blue Eyes," and "Will the Circle Be Unbroken."

Vocally, the Carter Family featured Sara's strong soprano lead, Maybelle's alto harmony, and A. P.'s baritone. Instrumentally, the family's distinctive sound was centered around Maybelle's much-copied guitar style, which was supported usually by rhythm chords produced by Sara on the autoharp. Although she sometimes played other styles, Maybelle generally used a thumb-brush technique in which the thumb picked the melody on the bass strings while the fingers provided rhythm with a downward stroke of the treble strings. This style was immensely appealing to other guitarists, and her version of "Wildwood Flower" was the model used by most fledgling guitarists when they did their first solo guitar piece.

Although their records circulated widely, the Carter Family was best known to millions of Americans through their performances over the Mexican border station XERA from 1938 to 1941. During these years the Carter children also began performing, and after 1943, when the original trio officially disbanded, new versions of "the Carter Family" began to emerge. Maybelle began performing with her daughters Helen, June, and Anita (as Mother Maybelle and the Carter Sisters), and by 1950 the group had begun a Grand Ole Opry career that would last for 17 years. The Carter Family became more dramatically linked to mainstream country music in 1968 when June Carter married Johnny Cash. Mother Maybelle and her daughters were regular members of

Cash's road show until 1973. Neither A. P. nor Sara remained active in music after 1943 (and in fact had separated in 1933), but they did join with their children, Joe and Janette, to make records in 1952 and 1956 for the Acme label.

The Carter Family won renewed respect and recognition during the urban folk revival of the early 1960s from a legion of new fans who knew them only through their old records and radio transcriptions. Maybelle, however, became an active participant in the folk scene, and she and Sara in 1967 made one album for Columbia called *An Historic Reunion*. A. P. died in 1960, and Maybelle and Sara died within two and a half months of each other in late 1979. The country music industry paid tribute to the trio in 1970 by naming them to the Hall of Fame.

Bill C. Malone
Tulane University

Bill C. Malone, *Country Music, U.S.A.: A Fifty-year History* (1968; rev. ed., 1985); Irwin Stambler and Grellin Landon, *The Encyclopedia of Folk, Country, and Western Music* (2d ed., 1983); Charles K. Wolfe, *Tennessee Strings: The Story of Country Music in Tennessee* (1977). ☆

CHARLES, RAY
||||||||||||||||||||||||||||||||||||||||
(b. 1930). Rhythm-and-blues musician.

Charles's recording career has spanned close to 40 years, yet his fame and influence lie with a series of recordings made for Atlantic and ABC-Paramount from 1955 to 1962. These recordings exhibited unprecedented versatility as Charles recorded jazz, blues, gospel, show tunes, and finally country and western music. His significance rests primarily on his fusing of gospel with pop and blues styles and, secondarily, his liberation of country and western as white-only music.

Born 23 September 1930 in Albany, Ga., as Ray Charles Robinson, he and his family moved to Greenville, Fla., where, at the age of six, he developed glaucoma and became blind. His father died when Charles was young, and when his mother passed away in 1945, Charles turned to music full time to provide a living for himself.

Wanting to get away from Florida, he moved to Seattle, Wash., in 1947. There, he dropped his surname to avoid confusion with the boxer Sugar Ray Robinson. In 1948 he made his first records for Bob Geddins's Swingtime label. These first recordings were done with a trio made up of Charles's piano plus guitar and bass. They imitated the recordings of performers such as Nat "King" Cole and Charles Brown. After he made several top-10 rhythm-and-blues hits in this style in 1951 and 1952, Atlantic Records bought his contract.

The recordings for Atlantic gradually exhibited less polish and more blues and gospel influence. In late 1953 Charles arranged and played piano on New Orleans guitarist Guitar Slim's monumental "The Things That I Used To Do." Slim's impassioned gospel-influenced vocal must have set Charles's mind whirring, as his very next sessions were cut in New Orleans without session musicians, and they exhibited a marked gospel feel.

In 1955 in Atlanta Charles hit his stride. Recording at a local radio station, he cut "I Got a Woman." Featuring horns and a churchy piano rather than the "tasteful" jazz guitar heard on the majority of his earlier cuttings and featuring an unrestrained vocal track replete with falsetto shrieks, the record became a number-two rhythm-and-blues hit. Several similar gospel-pop records followed, some written by Charles, many others adapted from extant gospel songs. The Pilgrim Traveler's "I've Got a New Home" became "Lonely Avenue"; Clara Ward's "This Little Light of Mine" became "This Little Girl of Mine"; and the Caravan's "What Kind of a Man Is This, Nobody But You Lord" became simply "Nobody But You."

Charles had effectively created a whole new phase of black pop music, which laid the basis for the unrestrained soul vocalists of the 1960s. This period of his recording career culminated in the 1959 recording of his self-penned "What I Say." The record opens with a blues gospel electric piano hammering out a Latinish rhythm and builds through a series of fragmentary choruses to extended call and response between Charles and his three-piece female backup vocalists, the Raelets. The record sounds like the re-creation of a revival meeting and, at the time, was seen by many as blasphemy. Although consequently banned on several radio stations, it nonetheless became a number-six pop hit and opened a huge white audience for Charles. In the meantime he recorded a number of jazz sessions with vibist Milt Jackson in addition to a number of blues and standards sessions.

"What I Say" prompted ABC-Paramount Records to entice him away from Atlantic. For the first few years at ABC Charles recorded material similar to his Atlantic output, although gradually the Ralph Burns Orchestra increasingly made its presence felt. Hoagy Carmichael's "Georgia" was his biggest hit in this period.

The year 1962 saw the release of a revolutionary album entitled *Modern Sounds in Country and Western Music*, with several ensuing hit singles including "I Can't Stop Loving You" and "You Don't Know Me." At the time, the idea of a black jazz/blues/soul artist recording white country music was extremely daring. Nevertheless, the album went on to sell 3 million copies and further established Charles with a middle-of-the-road white audience.

Since then, Charles's output has been steady but less original. His recordings are generally a heavily orchestrated pastiche of contemporary pop hits, nostalgic sentimental tunes, Broadway standards, and the odd blues. In 1968 he formed his label, Tangerine Records, which was distributed by ABC-Paramount, and in 1973 he formed the independent Crossover Records (an apt name), whose products were later distributed by Atlantic.

Robert Bowman
Memphis, Tennessee

Ray Charles, with David Ritz, *Brother Ray: Ray Charles' Own Story* (1978); Tony Cummings, in *The Soul Book*, ed. Ian Hoare (1975); Gerri Hershey, *Nowhere To Run: The Story of Soul Music* (1984). ☆

CHENIER, CLIFTON
||||||||||||||||||||||||||||||||||||||||||||||||||||||
(1925–1988) Zydeco musician.

Born 25 June 1925 near Opelousas in Saint Landry Parish, La., Clifton Chenier is the nation's premier zydeco performer. His father, Joseph, played the accordion, and he took his sons, Clifton and Cleveland, to local parties where he performed. The two boys themselves started playing at a young age—Clifton the accordion his father gave him, and Cleveland his mother's rub board. In the early 1940s they performed with Clarence Garlow's group in clubs around Lake Charles, La., and in 1947 Clifton left home and joined his brother in Lake Charles. The two worked at the oil refineries in Port Arthur, Tex., and formed the Hot Sizzling Band that played along the Texas-Louisiana Gulf Coast in the late 1940s and early 1950s.

J. R. Fulbright, a talent scout for Elko Records in California, met Chenier in 1954 and made the first recording of his music. During the middle and late 1950s Chenier recorded for the Imperial, Specialty, Chess, Argo, Checker, and Zynn labels, and he and his band toured not only in the Southwest but on the West Coast and in Chicago.

Known mostly as a rhythm-and-blues artist in the early 1960s, Chenier returned to his south Louisiana roots after signing with Chris Strachwitz's Arhoolie Records in 1964 and recording zydeco music on such albums as *Louisiana Blues and Zydeco*, *Bon Ton Roulet*, *King of the Bayous*, and *Bogalusa Boogie*. He recorded the classic zydeco song "Oh! Lucille" in 1966 for Crazy Cajun Records in Pasadena, Tex. In the late 1960s Chenier toured widely, including appearances at the Berkeley Blues Festival (1966), the Newport Folk Festival (1969), and in Europe (1967–69). In the 1970s his name became synonymous with the best in zydeco, and he remained a popular performer in rhythm and blues clubs as well.

Known as the "Black King of the South" and the "King of Zydeco," Chenier performs wearing a crown and leading his sometimes-raucous group, the Louisiana Hot Band. Poor health from a kidney infection plagued him in 1979, but he returned to better health in the early 1980s. He continued to play east Texas–southern Louisiana clubs and performed nationally as well until his death in 1988. Les Blank's *Dry Wood and Hot Peppers* (Flower Films, 1973) captured Chenier in performance and in his off-stage lifestyle.

Charles Reagan Wilson
University of Mississippi

Barry Jean Ancelet, *The Makers of Cajun Music / Musiciens Cadiens et Créoles* (1984); John Broven, *South to Louisiana: The Music of the Cajun Bayous* (1983); Sheldon Harris, *Blues Who's Who: A Biographical Dictionary of Blues Singers* (1979). ☆

CLINE, PATSY
(1932–1963) Country singer.

Patsy Cline, born Virginia Patterson Hensley on 8 September 1932, was one of the first country-and-western entertainers to become successful on both the country and popular music charts. Her first big success was winning the *Arthur Godfrey Talent Scouts* contest in January 1957 with her hit song, "Walkin' After Midnight." Over the next six years, Cline became the highest-ranked female singer with the Grand Ole Opry and achieved such popular success that Bill C. Malone has called her "the first woman to dethrone Kitty Wells from her position as 'queen of country music.' "

Virginia Hensley grew up in Winchester, Va., where she displayed a talent for music early in life. She played the piano and cultivated an intense interest in country music, dedicating herself to becoming a serious singer when she was a young teenager. Bill Peer, a

Patsy Cline, country music star, 1957

Programmed Album in 1962. She was elected to the Country Music Hall of Fame in 1973.

Cline's career was cut short tragically in March of 1963 with her death in a plane crash. She remains a popular country music figure and her records have continued to be released and sold worldwide. She was a prominent character in Loretta Lynn's autobiography, *Coal Miner's Daughter*, the successful screen version of which premiered in 1980. Patsy Cline's own life was portrayed in *Sweet Dreams* (1985), starring Jessica Lange as the legendary vocalist.

Karen M. McDearman
University of Mississippi

Bill C. Malone, *Country Music, U.S.A.: A Fifty-year History* (1968, rev. ed., 1985); Ellis Nassour, *Patsy Cline* (1981). ☆

disc jockey and musician with ties in Nashville, has been credited with giving Patsy Cline her first professional break as well as her first stage name in 1952. In the spring of 1953 Patsy Hensley married Gerald Cline, a contractor she met during one of her performances. Though they divorced in January 1957 and she married Charlie Dick in September of the same year, Cline kept the name under which she had her first commercial success.

Cline's music was characteristic of the traditional style in country music, and also part of the "Nashville Sound," a calculated attempt by the country music industry to attract new listeners from the pop market while retaining the older ones. Innovations included replacing fiddles and steel guitars with background voices and smooth instrumentation. Among Cline's biggest hits were "I Fall to Pieces" (1960), "Crazy" (1961), and "She's Got You" (1961). She received numerous awards, including *Billboard* magazine's Favorite Female Artist and *Cash Box*'s Most

DANIELS, CHARLIE

(b. 1936) Country-rock singer.

Charlie Daniels, a native of Wilmington, N.C., became one of the leading exponents of southern rock music in the 1970s. In 1967, after more than a decade as an obscure veteran of the southern club circuit, Daniels began working as a studio-session musician in Nashville. His most notable session work occurred in the period from 1969 to 1971, when he backed rock star Bob Dylan on a series of albums.

In 1971 Daniels formed his own band and a year later experienced substantial record sales with a satirical single release, "Uneasy Rider." The song and the album on which it appeared helped identify Daniels to rock audiences, though he continued to live and record in Nashville. Daniels was a versatile performer who most often played either guitar or fiddle. His dynamic work on the fiddle reinforced his identification as a country artist. From 1973 to 1977 Daniels gained little recognition as a recording artist, due undoubtedly to his marginal position between rock and country. In 1975 he reemerged as a successful recording artist, with a best-selling album, *Fire on the Mountain*, and a hit single, "The South's Gonna Do It Again." By the mid-1970s country rock had become a potent commercial subgenre within country music, and Daniels had established himself as an exemplar of the sound. In addition, "The South's Gonna Do It Again" became a veritable anthem of the southern rock movement. Daniels was perhaps the preeminent musical spokesman of the region.

In 1979 Daniels released *Million Mile Reflections*, an album that rapidly gained platinum status (over 1 million units sold) and also yielded one of the most popular single recordings of the decade, "The Devil Went Down to Georgia." A quintessential Daniels number, it reflected the southern folk tradition in both content and style but tapped the contemporary rock idiom for most of its rhythmic impetus. Other albums include *Night Rider* (1975), *High Lonesome* (1976), and *Saddle Tramp* (1976).

Daniels often generated controversy both for his outspoken political views— he was one of the few Nashville artists to openly oppose the Vietnam War and campaigned ardently for Jimmy Carter in 1976 and 1980—and for his spirited defense of country music against such critics as jazz musician Stan Kenton. Perhaps Daniels's most impressive contribution to southern music has been the Volunteer Jams, a popular series of concerts held annually in Murfreesboro,

Tenn. Few individuals have symbolized the South in popular culture as directly and indelibly as Charlie Daniels.

Stephen R. Tucker
Tulane University

Bob Allen, *Country Music* (April 1980); Russell Shaw, *Country Music* (March 1977). ☆

"DIXIE"

The word *Dixie* has been a part of the American vocabulary ever since it appeared in the song "Dixie's Land." The song, though closely associated with the history of the South, is not of southern origin. Both tune and text were written by Ohio native Daniel D. Emmett in 1859, shortly before the outbreak of the Civil War. The song immediately attained popularity, first in the North, then as a "battle hymn" in the secessionist Confederate states. The word *Dixie* even became a synonym for the South.

What was compelling about the tune was its blend of incisiveness and exhilaration, giving force to such sentences as "Den I wish I was in Dixie, Hooray! Hooray! In Dixie Land, I'll took my stand, To lib an die in Dixie." The song was commissioned by the Bryant's Minstrel Troupe, a highly successful company, and was performed for the first time in New York on Broadway on 4 April 1859 under the title "Plantation Song and Dance, / Dixie's Land / Introducing the whole Troupe in the Festival Dance." The scene involved voices (solo and group alternating), with instrumental accompaniment, and steps and gestures in imitation of black plantation dances. It was pure entertainment, amply supported by the comedy style of all six stanzas. The protagonist was a black, who, following a minstrel tradition, expressed his yearning for the never-never-land of the southern plantation, a view with special appeal to a white audience.

After the theatrical event came a swift transformation of "Dixie's Land." With the accents and tempo of a quickstep, it became a fierce military statement. Confederate soldiers used new words such as "Southrons, hear your country call you," but sections of the original were retained.

The origin of the word "Dixie" has not yet been clarified; there is no evidence of its existence as a name on southern plantations. Yet it was known to entertainers, for a playbill of 1850 listed a play (probably blackface) "The United States Mail and Dixie [a postboy] in Difficulty." Continuing a trend of early black minstrel music, the tune of "Dixie's Land" includes elements of British folksong: an Irish hornpipe pattern at the beginning and traces of Scotch tunes in the second part.

Hans Nathan
Arlington Heights, Massachusetts

Hans Nathan, *Dan Emmett and the Rise of Early Negro Minstrelsy* (1962; 2d ed., 1977); John A. Simpson, *Southern Folklore Quarterly* (1981). ☆

DIXIE HUMMINGBIRDS
||||||||||||||||||||||||||||||||||||||||||||||||||||
Gospel music group.

The Dixie Hummingbirds, a gospel "quartet," most of whose members were from South Carolina, began their long recording career in the late 1930s with the selection "When the Gates Swing Open" (Decca 7645). Ira Tucker, their famous lead singer, joined the group in 1940, soon followed by Willie Bobo, their well-known bass singer. The Birds, as they came to be known, consisted by 1945 of James Walker, Ira Tucker, William Bobo, Beachey Thompson, and James Davis, the original leader. Guitarist Howard Carroll, joined the quartet in the early 1950s. All the various male groups were usually referred to as "quartets," even though most of them consisted of five or six members.

The recording of black quartets singing spirituals and gospel songs began with the Dinwiddie Colored Quartet's 1902 Victor recording of "Down on the Old Camp Ground"; so the quartet genre had a considerable history before the Dixie Hummingbirds appeared.

The performing style, the musical structure, and the vocal literature of the quartets changed in the 1930s, and the Birds arrived toward the end of the transitional period, so that they, together

The Dixie Hummingbirds, gospel music quartet, c. 1950

with the Blind Boys of Mississippi, the Soul Stirrers of Tyler, Tex., the Blue Jays of Alabama, the Pilgrim Travelers, and the Spirit of Memphis became the first of the more modern gospel quartets.

If one excludes the Golden Gate Quartet, a very popular transitional group, the Birds were the only gospel quartet to achieve a measure of success with white listeners. They have always been regarded by black audiences as among the foremost of the quartets. Their first interracial success came during 1942 at Café Society Downtown in New York City, where they received a standing ovation. Their second such success came in 1966 at the Newport Folk Festival. Finally, a million or more young white listeners became acquainted with them in 1973 when they were included on Paul Simon's "Loves Me Like a Rock" in his successful album *There Goes Rhymin' Simon*.

Tony Heilbut devotes an entire chapter of his book *The Gospel Sound: Good News and Bad Times* (1971) to the Birds, and his study remains the best (and almost only) source of information on the group. Heilbut mentions "Trouble in My Way," "Let's Go out to the Program," and "In the Morning" as perhaps their best recorded performances. To that trio might be added the "Devil Can't Harm a Praying Man," which is on the album *A Christian Testimonial* (Peacock PLP 100).

Those interested in the music and early history and development of the gospel quartet will find the following discs informative: *An Introduction to Gospel Song* (Folkways RF 5), *Brighten the Corner Where You Are* (New World Records NW 224), *Birmingham Quartet Anthology* (Clanka Lanka CL 144,001/ 002; the American distributor is Douglas Seroff, Box 506, Rt. 3, Goodletts-

ville, Tenn.), and *Jubilee to Gospel* (John Edwards Memorial Foundation JEMF 108).

William H. Tallmadge
Berea College

Barbara Baker, "Black Gospel Music Styles—1942–75" (Ph.D. dissertation, University of Maryland, 1978). ☆

DOMINO, FATS

(b. 1928) Rock and rhythm-and-blues musician.

Antoine "Fats" Domino is to his home city, New Orleans, what Elvis Presley and B. B. King are to Memphis, and what Roy Acuff is to Nashville—the personification of musical values closely associated with that city. His popular recordings for Lew Chubb's Imperial label—many of which were produced with Dave Bartholomew and engineered by Cosimo Matassa—represent a distillation of the New Orleans sound; piano virtuosity featuring right-hand triplets and a dominant bass line; heavy second-line rhythms from either Domino's left hand or the shuffle of a drummer; and harsh but powerful horn riffs, often featuring tenor saxophone solos from Herb Hardesty or Lee Allen. Domino's mellow, agreeable vocals find a comfortable home within this instrumental context. Taken together, these elements define the sound of New Orleans during the 1950s.

Born in New Orleans on 26 February 1928, Domino inherited the musical sensibility that shaped his music. His father was an accomplished violinist. His older brother-in-law, Harrison Verrett, had played guitar and banjo with Dixieland jazz ensembles led by Kid

Ory and Papa Celestin. Verrett tutored young Domino and later served as his advisor and as a member of his band. In New Orleans Domino was surrounded by master pianists like Henry Byrd ("Professor Longhair"), Cousin Joe, Walter "Fats" Pichon, and Leon T. Gross ("Archibald"). He assimilated these local influences, as well as the influences of non–New Orleans pianists like Meade Lux Lewis, Albert Ammons, and Pete Johnson. To his piano, Domino added a gentle and easy vocal style, complete with exotic Creole accent, that stood in contrast to the rawer, darker voices of the gutbucket country blues singers of the Deep South.

Domino has had more commercial success than any other New Orleans musician, and his biggest hits came from 1950 to 1963, when he recorded on the Imperial record label. Twenty of Domino's records have sold over a million copies (the number keeps growing as his records continue to sell), among them such classics as "The Fat Man" (his first record), "Ain't It a Shame," "I'm in Love Again," "Blueberry Hill," "Blue Monday," "I'm Walkin'," and "Walking to New Orleans." White audiences enthusiastically bought his records, and white artists such as Pat Boone, Ricky Nelson, Elvis Presley, and the Beatles either covered his hits or imitated his sound.

Domino made successful transitions from rhythm and blues to rock and roll and now does occasional Las Vegas lounge acts. He continues to play throughout the world to audiences who appreciate his music for its contemporary appeal rather than for its nostalgic value. In 1986 Domino became 1 of only 10 charter inductees into the Rock and Roll Hall of Fame, an institution established by members of the recording industry to honor achievement in that field. That same year he was also featured in a nationally televised special entitled *Fats Domino and Friends.*

Jay Orr
Country Music Foundation
Nashville, Tennessee

John Broven, *Rhythm and Blues in New Orleans* (1978); Peter Guralnick, in *The Rolling Stone Illustrated History of Rock 'n' Roll*, ed. Jim Miller (1980); Robert Palmer, *A Tale of Two Cities: Memphis Rock and New Orleans Roll* (1979). ☆

DORSEY, THOMAS

(b. 1899) Blues and gospel musician and composer.

An important figure in both blues and gospel music, Thomas Andrew Dorsey was born in Villa Rica, Ga., on 1 July 1899. His father was a Baptist minister and moved the family to Atlanta, Ga., in 1904. During the years just prior to World War I Dorsey sang and played piano for private parties and at clubs throughout Atlanta. After briefly attending Morehouse College, he moved north and settled in Chicago, Ill., by 1916.

The period between 1916 and 1932 was marked by a deep professional involvement with popular music, especially the blues. He worked with several Chicago-based vaudeville acts and during the mid-1920s toured with a band that worked the TOBA (known colloquially as Tough on Black Artists) circuit across the South and urban North. He and Tampa Red (Hudson Whittaker) formed an extremely popular duo, with Dorsey playing piano, Tampa Red performing on guitar, and both men singing a mixture of blues and risqué numbers.

Thomas Dorsey, gospel music songwriter and performer, 1975

This partnership remained strong for about four years, during which Dorsey also recorded with the Famous Hokum Boys, the Black Hill Billies, and the Hokum Jug Band.

Although much of his early life was spent as a popular entertainer and blues pianist, singer, and composer, Thomas Dorsey always retained an avid interest in and respect for gospel music. In 1932 he decided to give up popular music entirely and devote his talent to sacred music. He met with some resistance initially, both from those who associated Dorsey with "the devil's music" and by the promoters and musicians who prospered because of his popularity.

Thomas Dorsey persisted in his gospel music career, however, and the period between 1932 and 1950 is marked by his influence. He worked extensively with Mahalia Jackson and also helped Roberta Martin and Sallie Martin early in their careers. Dorsey's promo-

tion of these and other singers helped to move black gospel music into the realm of popular music after World War II.

Dorsey is perhaps best known as a gospel song composer. An early publication, "Precious Lord, Take My Hand," is one of the most popular gospel songs ever written. Over his lengthy career, Dorsey has composed approximately 500 songs, including "When the Last Mile Is Finished," "Wings over Jordan," "If You See My Savior," and "There Will Be Peace in the Valley."

Kip Lornell
Ferrum College

Arna Bontemps, *Common Ground* (Autumn 1942); Sheldon Harris, *Blues Who's Who: A Biographical Dictionary of Blues Singers* (1979); *Living Blues* (March 1975); Paul Oliver, in *New Grove Dictionary of Music and Musicians*, vol. 5, ed. Stanley Sadie (1980). ☆

DULCIMER

The plucked dulcimer, often called the Appalachian dulcimer, is a southern mountain folk instrument. Its sound is soft and restrained, with a gentle charm and a slight touch of melancholy. Its diatonic scale and heavy drones make it sound like a gentler version of bagpipes. The most common shapes are the "teardrop" and the "figure-eight," but other shapes are sometimes made. Dulcimers usually have three or four strings (although they may have as many as eight) running over a fretboard. The diatonic scale of the fretboard makes the dulcimer an ideal instrument to accompany songs in the various modes. Mountain people have used them for generations to accompany the tragic English and Scots ballads as well as to play sprightly instrumental pieces.

The dulcimer is a lap instrument, played with the tuning pegs to the left (for right-handed musicians). In the traditional style the melody is played on the string nearest the player while the other strings drone. The earliest dulcimers had frets under the first string only. The left hand stops the strings, often with the aid of a "noter" (a small cylinder of very hard wood), while the right hand strums the strings with a quill or plectrum or plucks the strings as though playing a banjo or guitar.

Although the dulcimer first appeared in its American form in the Appalachian South, it is structurally related to the German *scheitholt*, the Swedish *hummel*, and the Norwegian *langeleik*. It may have been introduced to the Appalachians by Pennsylvania Germans.

The folk music revival of the 1960s brought the dulcimer to the attention of the urban audience, especially through the playing of two artists from the southern highlands, Jean Ritchie of Kentucky and Frank Proffitt of North Carolina. A new demand for the instrument created markets for traditional mountain craftspeople and sparked interest in the craft of dulcimer making by disaffected young urbanites. A number of southern craftspeople, such as A. W. Jeffreys of Virginia, Homer Ledford of Kentucky, Jean Schilling of Tennessee, Lynn McSpadden of Arkansas, and Stanley Hicks, Edsel Martin, and Edd Presnell of North Carolina, earned national reputations for their artistry as dulcimer makers.

Charles Joyner
University of South Carolina,
Coastal Campus

R. Gerald Alvey, *Dulcimer Maker: The Craft of Homer Ledford* (1984); Charles Faulkner Bryan, *Tennessee Folklore Society Bulletin* (March 1952, December 1954); Gene DuBey, *Sourwood Mountain Dulcimers* (Appalshop film, 1976); Charles Joyner, *Southern Folklore Quarterly* (December 1975); Jean Ritchie, *The Dulcimer Book* (1963); Charles Seeger, *Journal of American Folklore* (January–March 1958); L. Allen Smith, *A Catalogue of Pre-Revival Appalachian Dulcimers* (1983). ☆

ENGEL, LEHMAN

(1910–1982) Composer and conductor.

Time magazine called Lehman Engel "one of the nation's busiest and most versatile men-about-music." He was a composer, conductor, author, and teacher. *A Streetcar Named Desire*, *The Consul*, *Murder in the Cathedral*, and *Li'l Abner* are a few of the many, diverse Broadway shows with which he was associated as a composer or pit conductor. His efforts brought widespread recognition, including two Antoinette Perry ("Tony") awards: one in 1950 for conducting the Menotti opera *The Consul* and one in 1953 for conducting Gilbert and Sullivan operettas and *Wonderful Town*.

Born to Jewish parents in Jackson, Miss., Engel played the piano "by ear" until age 10, when his parents were able to afford piano lessons for him. He wrote that his first piano teacher was an "aristocratic southern lady" whose lessons, like those of his subsequent teachers, he quickly outgrew. He completed his first composition, *The Scotch Highlander*, shortly after he began taking piano lessons, and musical composition for the theater became one of his primary interests. A Jackson movie house, the Majestic Theater, with its small orchestra accompanying the silent movies, impressed the young boy greatly and provided some of his most memorable early experiences.

Although not an extremely talented pianist, Engel entered the Cincinnati Conservatory of Music upon graduation from high school. When he discovered that he had been eligible for a partial scholarship for piano lessons but was the only student not on scholarship, he became angry that his parents had spent so much money unnecessarily and transferred immediately to the Cincinnati College of Music. Two years later he turned down a faculty position at Cincinnati and moved to New York. With a graduate scholarship to the Julliard School, Engel took courses in composition from Rubin Goldmark and studied privately with Roger Sessions.

In New York, Engel worked diligently to make contacts and established his career. He persisted for several months in an attempt to meet Martha Graham, who encouraged him to write compositions for her dance company and for other concert dancers as well. *Within the Gates* provided his first Broadway credit. When he heard the music already written for the play, he expressed his dislike to director Melvyn Douglas, offering to write a new version by the next morning. Even though the play itself was unsuccessful, Engel's music was praised.

A group of madrigal singers was organized by the Federal Music Project, a subsidiary of the Works Progress Administration (WPA), and Engel was the group's conductor from 1935 to 1939. He composed music for the Federal Theater Project and the WPA Children's Theater before he began working with Orson Welles and John Houseman at their Mercury Theater. During World War II he joined the U.S. Navy, conducted a military orchestra at the Great Lakes Naval Training Station, and later served as chief composer of the navy's film division in Washington, D.C. His other pursuits included founding (with Aaron Copland, Marc Blitzstein, and Virgil Thompson) the Arrow Music Press, Inc., to publish the work of American composers; conducting more than 60 recordings for major record companies such as Columbia, Decca, and RCA Victor; composing four operas and music for radio, film, and television; writing books about musical theater; and teaching workshops in musical lyrics.

Nicknamed by some the "Poor Man's Lenny Bernstein," Engel became one of the most respected and sought-after musicians on Broadway. He never returned to the South to live but did return to Jackson to conduct the premiere performances of two of his operas. Engel died of cancer in 1982, but his life's accomplishments and honors had been many. With regard to the demands of writing music for the theater, Engel had often spoken of Mozart: "That genius had to write on order. He had no time for the muse to belt him." It seems that the same had been true for Engel himself.

Jessica Foy
Cooperstown Graduate Programs
Cooperstown, New York

Josh Barbanel, *New York Times* (30 August 1982); Lehman Engel, *This Bright Day: An Autobiography* (1974); Walter Rigdon, ed., *The Biographical Encyclopedia and Who's Who of the American Theatre* (1966); Nicolas Slonimsky, *Baker's Biographical Dictionary of Musicians*, (7th ed., 1984); *Time* (8 December 1958). ☆

FIDDLE AND FIDDLERS' CONVENTIONS

||||||||||||||||||||||||||||||||||||||||||||||||||||||||||

The fiddle is a four-string, bowed instrument—most often a violin, though resourceful musicians have fashioned facsimiles from cigar boxes and tin cans—upon which are played a variety of folk melodies, primarily for dancing. Some people argue that the fiddle has one string more than the violin—the one used to hang it on the wall. Because of its portability, its common use as dance accompaniment, and its folk heritage extending back to the 18th century in the British Isles and western Europe, the fiddle quickly assumed a role as the primary folk musical instrument of settlers in the New World. In the 19th and early 20th centuries southern fiddlers exhibited subregional variation according to such characteristics as bowing patterns, bowing method, fiddle placement, tunings, repertoire, tune titles, tune texts, tune structure, and instrumental accompaniment. The predominant tune forms in southern fiddling are variously referred to as reels, breakdowns, or hoedowns and are played in double meter to accompany dancing. Southern fiddlers also perform rags, waltzes, blues, and hornpipes, though these forms are less common.

In the second half of the 20th century improved travel conditions, the radio, the phonograph, and the proliferation of fiddle contests whose judges adhere to rigid aesthetic standards have blunted the more pronounced regional distinctions that once characterized southern fiddling. However, the broad stylistic designations of Appalachian or Blue Ridge (further subdivided into Galax, North Georgia, and others), Deep South (including the unique Mississippi fiddle

Fiddler, Tutwiler, Mississippi, 1967

bands, which show an apparent black influence), Ozark, Cajun, and Southwestern (sometimes referred to as "contest" style fiddling for its emphasis on ornate improvisation and precise execution) still have relevance.

Fiddlers' conventions, at which the central event is usually a competition or "contest," have become a primary performance outlet for contemporary fiddlers. As early as 1736, in Hanover County, Va., southern fiddlers competed against one another for prizes and prestige. The most famous contests were held in Atlanta; Union Grove, N.C., and Knoxville. In the early part of this century Henry Ford sponsored a series of competitions to determine a national champion through his automobile dealerships. Ford felt that fiddlers and fiddle music embodied the moral, conservative values he wanted his contests to inspire in those who attended them. Today, every fiddler in the South lives within easy distance of several of the numerous conventions sponsored by communities, civic groups, state agencies, local businesses, and regional and local fiddlers' associations.

Jay Orr
Country Music Foundation
Nashville, Tennessee

Linda C. Burman-Hall, "Southern American Folk Fiddling: Context and Style" (Ph.D. dissertation, Princeton University, 1973); Alan Jabbour, *American Fiddle Tunes from the Archive of Folk Song* [record and accompanying booklet] (1971); Earl V. Spielman, "Traditional North American Fiddling" (Ph.D. dissertation, University of Wisconsin at Madison, 1975). ☆

FISK JUBILEE SINGERS

The Fisk Jubilee Singers originally consisted of a black American group of eight singers and a pianist, all students at Fisk University in Nashville, Tenn. This double quartet together with musical director, George L. White; their chaperon, Miss Well; the pianist, and two other students to help with the packing and moving, set off on a tour in 1871 to raise money for their university. By 1880, when the university ended official sponsorship of the group, it had toured the northern United States, England, and Europe and had sung at the White House and for Queen Victoria. From the singing of this organization the world at large first became aware of a body of black music called "spirituals" (they were called "slave songs" in those days).

The term *jubilee* has a number of different meanings. It has been used to designate those black spirituals whose texts refer to freedom—freedom in death from the hardships of life followed by the attainment of heavenly bliss and freedom from slavery. The term has also been used to specify those spirituals having a joyous character, and it has been used to refer to the entire body of black spirituals. It has also been used in reference to special celebrations or annual events such as the Pinkster Jubilee, a celebration of Pentecost Sunday in certain areas of New York, Pennsylvania, and Maryland during the colonial period. It was at Columbus, Ohio, after the singers had been on the road for several weeks, White thought that the name "Jubilee Singers" would be a good one for the group. He had recalled the Old Testament "year of jubilee," a year provided by ancient Hebrew law when slaves were emancipated, and thinking of the students at the university, most of whom had been former slaves, he felt that their year of jubilee had come— "this little band of singers was a witness to it, an outgrowth of it."

Two years after the success of the Fisk choir the Hampton Institute also sent a choir on tour; they were followed by groups from Tuskegee and Utica institutes, but it was the name of the Fisk Jubilee Singers that remained in the public's memory.

See also EDUCATION: / Fisk University

William H. Tallmadge
Berea College

Alain Locke, *The Negro and His Music* (1936); J. B. T. Marsh, *The Story of the Jubilee Singers; with Their Songs* (1877); G. D. Pike, *The Jubilee Singers, and Their Campaign for Twenty Thousand Dollars* (1873); Thomas Rutling, *Tom: An Autobiography* (1907); William H. Tallmadge, brochure notes to *Jubilee to Gospel: A Selection of Commercially Recorded Black Religious Music, 1921–1953*, John Edwards Memorial Foundation, JEMF 108. ☆

FOSTER, STEPHEN

(1826–1864) Composer and songwriter.

Born in Lawrenceville, Penn., and raised in comfortable circumstances in a suburb of Pittsburgh, Stephen Collins Foster began composing for the black-face minstrel theater, where "Oh! Susanna," "Nelly Bly," and "Camptown Races" were popularized by the troupe of E. P. Christy. His ambition, however, was to be a composer of sentimental parlor songs on themes of romantic love and nostalgic yearning. Among his songs of this type are "Old Dog Tray," "Jeanie with the Light Brown Hair," and "Beautiful Dreamer." Although some of his songs achieved commercial success, Foster failed to capitalize on his successes and died in poverty.

In his minstrel songs Foster made no attempt to present realistically the song and speech of southern plantation slaves. In "Oh! Susanna," for example, the dialect, the deadpan irony, the references to southern places and foods, are merely conventions of the minstrel stage. The melody is no more Afro-American than it is English or Irish; the rhythm is that of the European polka. From about 1850 Foster began to modify the conventions of minstrelsy in the direction of middle-class sentimentality. Songs like "Old Folks at Home" and "Old Black Joe" attribute more delicate and varied sentiments to the stage black than had previously been the stereotype. In a few songs, like "My Old Kentucky Home," he omitted the dialect. Many of these less typical minstrel songs were popularized in dramatizations of *Uncle Tom's Cabin*. Indeed, Foster's notebooks reveal that "My Old Kentucky Home" was originally written as "Poor Uncle Tom, Good Night." Ironically, Foster's songs are, with the exception of Dan Emmett's "Dixie's Land," the best-known representatives of minstrelsy today.

Since the late 19th century Foster's songs have been widely accepted as genuine American folksongs. Although Foster never lived in the South, popular myth has associated him with the region. Florida and Kentucky have adopted "Old Folks at Home" and "My Old Kentucky Home," respectively, as official state songs. Bardstown, Ky., and White Springs, Fla., boast shrines to Foster's memory and music, the latter, on the Suwanee River, serves as home of the state's folklife program. Though black critic Alain Locke has observed that "Foster's ballads did more to crystallize the romance of the plantation tradition than all the Southern colonels and novelists put together," adaptations of Foster songs by Ray Charles and Taj Mahal have been sincere portrayals of Afro-American culture and experience. Sung in widely varying arrangements, often with bowdlerized texts, Stephen Foster's songs continue to form part of the musical experience of nearly every American.

David Warren Steel
University of Mississippi

William W. Austin, *"Susanna," "Jeanie," and "The Old Folks at Home"* (1975); John T. Howard, *Stephen Foster: America's Troubador* (1953; rev. ed., 1962); Richard Jackson, ed., *The Stephen Foster Song Book* (1974). ☆

FOUNTAIN, PETE

(b. 1930) Jazz musician.

Peter Dewey Fountain was born 3 July 1930 in New Orleans, La. His father was a drummer and violinist who played in local jazz bands in Biloxi, Miss., when Pete was young. Fountain's own musical interest began early, and he played the clarinet in the school band. While still very young, Fountain played with the Junior Dixieland Band, Phil Zito's International Dixieland Express, and the Basin Street Six.

Already an accomplished musician at 16, Fountain replaced Irving Fazola at the Opera House Burlesque Theater. At 19, Fountain joined the Dukes of Dixieland band in Chicago in 1949 and played with them until 1954. Fountain was a member of Lawrence Welk's orchestra from 1957 through 1960. In 1960 he opened his own club, The French Quarter, on Bourbon Street in New Orleans. He played at the club frequently, in addition to appearing on such television programs as the *Ed Sullivan Show*, *Kraft Music Hall*, and specials with Bob Hope and Bing Crosby. He has been an occasional guest on Johnny Carson's program, *The Tonight Show*, where he plays with Doc Severinsen's orchestra. Through television, he has become a prime symbol for Americans of contemporary New Orleans jazz.

In the early 1980s Fountain relocated his club, now called Pete's Place, to the New Orleans Riverside Hilton. He makes frequent appearances at the annual New Orleans Jazz and Heritage Festival. He has recorded nearly 50 records on the Coral label, including *South Rampart Street Parade*, *New Orleans at Midnight*, *Plenty of Pete*, and *Both Sides Now*.

Karen M. McDearman
University of Mississippi

Pete Fountain with Bill Neely, *A Closer Walk: The Pete Fountain Story* (1972); How-

ard Mandel, *Down Beat* (January 1985); Nicolas Slonimsky, *Baker's Biographical Dictionary of Musicians* (7th ed., 1984). ☆

GILLESPIE, DIZZY
‖‖‖‖‖‖‖‖‖‖‖‖‖‖‖‖‖‖‖‖‖‖‖‖‖‖‖‖‖‖‖‖‖‖‖‖‖‖‖
(b. 1917) Jazz musician.

John Birks "Dizzy" Gillespie was born 21 October 1917 in Cheraw, S.C. Gillespie showed his musical talent at an early age, and he began to play the trumpet when he was 15. He attended Laurinburg Institute in North Carolina, and when he was 18 Gillespie went to Philadelphia, where he joined a local jazz band. He played with the Cab Calloway and Earl Hines bands, and in 1944, when Hines's lead singer, Billy Eckstine, formed his own band, Gillespie joined the group.

Gillespie, along with his friend Charlie "Bird" Parker who also played with the Eckstine band, was an innovator of the jazz style known as bebop (or bop) beginning in the late 1940s. Bebop introduced revolutionary changes in the traditional rhythmic and harmonic jazz patterns. Gillespie and Parker made a few recordings after leaving Eckstine's band, but had difficulty finding club owners willing to let them play the new style. Club patrons preferred the blues and older style tunes that were danceable. Gillespie still plays in a style directly related to bebop, which eventually came to be heralded as a remarkable original development of jazz.

Gillespie was given the nickname "Dizzy" because of his playing style, which incorporates wild gesturing and grimacing. He is a trumpet virtuoso and has been credited for extending the upper ranges of the instrument and improvising long passages at speed. A brilliant showman, Gillespie has entertained thousands with his stage antics and superior instrumentals. His creativity is demonstrated in albums such as *In the Beginning* and *Oscar Peterson and Dizzy Gillespie*.

Karen M. McDearman
University of Mississippi

Ole Brask, *Jazz People* (1976); Ira Gitler, *Jazz Masters of the Forties* (1974); Marshall Stearns, *The Story of Jazz* (1956). ☆

GOTTSCHALK, LOUIS
||||||||||||||||||||||||||||||||||||||||||||||||||
(1829–1869) Classical music composer.

The most renowned American composer of the early 19th century, Gottschalk blended the European romantic tradition with black rhythms and Creole melodies he had experienced as a child in New Orleans. Gottschalk's works possess an individual charm and a spontaneity and verve that draw listeners inside the music. The son of a wealthy English Jew and a titled French Creole, the musician grew up in cultured surroundings and was recognized by age four as a prodigy. Seven years later, his teacher declared the boy must be sent to Paris to study further. In 1842 Gottschalk sailed for France, and a great aunt introduced him to Parisian society.

Having heard French and Italian opera in New Orleans, the youth preferred operatic transcriptions for piano over the German classics. In France he studied both piano and composition. During the revolutionary turmoil of 1848 he was forced to flee Paris, and during that absence he wrote the two piano pieces for which he is best remembered, *La Bamboula* and *La Savanne*. Both were drawn from folk music he had known as a child, and Parisian listeners were enchanted by their rhythmic virtuosity and exotic themes.

In 1849 the composer made his debut as a professional pianist in Salle Pleyel. While in France he performed for Hugo, Chopin, Bizet, and Berlioz, all of whom praised his work. He continued writing and enjoyed special success with *Le Bananier* and *Le Banjo*. He toured Switzerland and Spain, then in 1853 decided to return to the United States. His first New York concert, given in Niblo's Garden, was a triumph he repeated all over the United States. His flamboyant style met sharp criticism, although audiences were attracted by his personality and European reputation.

As Gottschalk became more the entertainer, his compositions grew increasingly sentimental; *The Dying Poet* and *The Last Hope* stand among the more saccharine. He spent six years giving concerts in the West Indies and writing orchestral works like his *Grand Tarantelle* and *A Night in the Tropics*. He returned to the United States, making the most of the fiction that surrounded his life, performing concerts in the thick of the Civil War, and touring the gold fields of California and Nevada. He also staged "monster concerts" in Latin America, but he grew despondent. In Rio de Janeiro he collapsed during a concert and died shortly afterwards. His body was eventually removed to Greenwood Cemetery, Brooklyn.

Ronald L. Davis
Southern Methodist University

Ronald L. Davis, *A History of Music in American Life: The Formative Years* (1982); John G. Doyle, *Louis Moreau Gottschalk, 1829–1869: A Bibliographical Study and Catalog of His Works* (1983); Louis Moreau Gottschalk, *Notes of a Pianist* (1964); Vernon Loggins, *Where the Word Ends: The Life of Louis Moreau Gottschalk* (1958). ☆

GRAND OLE OPRY
‖‖‖

The Grand Ole Opry is America's longest-running radio program. It began in 1925, soon after Nashville station WSM first began broadcasts as the voice of the National Life and Accident Insurance Company. This Nashville-based firm was then expanding rapidly, moving beyond its initial base of sickness and accident policies into the more profitable life insurance field. Along with classical ensembles and pop dance bands, country musicians like Dr. Humphrey Bate's Augmented Orchestra supplied early WSM programming and helped attract prospective policyholders.

The father of the Opry was WSM program director George D. Hay, who came to the station in November 1925, a few weeks after Bate's group arrived. Earlier, Hay had helped announce Chicago's WLS Barn Dance, a program that inspired country radio jamborees nationwide. By the year's end he had organized WSM talent into a regular Saturday-night show known simply as "the barn dance." Early performers included Hawaiian groups, minstrel acts, and military bands, but old-time string bands like Bate's soon prevailed.

Using strategies typical of the genre, Hay shaped the Opry into a folksy but highly commercial production that appealed to a broad-based audience of rural and small-town listeners scattered throughout the nation. He gave string bands names such as "Possum Hunters" or "Fruit Jar Drinkers" and urged them to wear countrified costumes. As master of ceremonies, Hay himself became the Solemn Old Judge, a stage persona with deep roots in American vaudeville and minstrelsy. In short, he made the Opry a variety show with a rural southern accent.

About 1927 Hay named the program the Grand Ole Opry in an impromptu parody of the National Broadcasting Company's *Music Appreciation Hour*, a classical program carried by WSM each Saturday just before the barn-dance show. "For the past hour," he announced, "we have been listening to music taken largely from the Grand Opera, but from now on we will present the Grand Ole Opry." Hay then introduced harmonica player DeFord Bailey, a black man whose musical portrait of a speeding locomotive symbolized the Opry's homespun realism, reminiscent of an authentic rural barn dance or husking bee.

Fan letters, commercial sponsors, and rising insurance income convinced National Life to continue the Opry despite opposition from proper Nashvillians, who saw it as a threat to the city's genteel reputation. As WSM's power climbed from 1,000 watts in 1925 to 50,000 in 1932, the program's radio audience expanded dramatically, and the Opry's position became secure. WSM's clear-channel signal, broadcast through a new, superbly engineered tower built in 1932, blanketed most of the nation, and the show steadily gained supporters in almost every state. By 1936 the Opry generated as much as 80 percent of the station's weekly mail. Southerners were the mainstay of the Opry audience, and WSM naturally played up southern themes in Opry costumes, band names, radio dialogue, and publicity. But the program's national audience increased pressures toward variety: within a decade, cowboys, western swing bands, and honky-tonk singers surpassed old-time string bands as the dominant acts in the Opry roster.

The Opry's listenership widened further after 1939, when the R. J. Reynolds Tobacco Company, makers of Prince Albert smoking tobacco, began sponsoring a half hour of the show on a 26-station NBC network. By 1952 this web had expanded to a coast-to-coast chain of 176 stations boasting a weekly audience of 10 million. Although WSM originated many other country or pop programs for network broadcast, the *Prince Albert Show* was by far the most visible and the longest running, lasting until 1961. Network airtime was especially important in sustaining the Opry through the late 1950s, a period in which most other radio barn dances withered in the face of competition from network television and the conversion of country radio stations to rock programming.

Along with the program's network connections, aggressive promotion, stylistic diversification, and the cultivation of a star system, television also helped

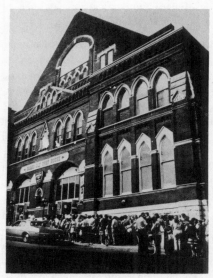

Ryman Auditorium, Nashville, early home of the Grand Ole Opry

the Opry thrive. Since the mid-1950s Opry performers have appeared on numerous network TV specials, as well as on syndicated programs produced by WSM or by independent firms. In 1978 the Public Broadcasting System aired portions of the Opry itself for the first time, and in 1985 the Nashville Network began carrying a live, half-hour segment to cable-television viewers across the nation.

Early in the Opry's evolution, a live audience became vital to the broadcast, and a popular stage show developed around the radio program. To gain ever greater seating space, the show moved from WSM's studios (located in the National Life Building in downtown Nashville) to a succession of local halls before settling in the Ryman Auditorium in 1943. The Ryman, which was originally called the Gospel Tabernacle, was built in 1892 with funds raised by riverboat captain Thomas G. Ryman. After a 31-year run there, the Opry shifted to the magnificent new Opry House at Nashville's Opryland theme park, opened in the early 1970s by NLT Corporation, successor to National Life. The Opryland USA complex now embraces a large hotel and serves as headquarters for the Nashville Network; the Music Country Network, a radio web linked by satellite; and the *General Jackson*, a Cumberland River showboat. Since 1983 these enterprises (including WSM radio but not WSM-TV, now owned by Gillett Broadcasting) have been operated by the Oklahoma Publishing Company, of Oklahoma City. Even in these elegant surroundings, however, the Opry has remained refreshingly informal, belying the planning each show requires. Announcers reading commercials, artists waiting to be introduced, and stagehands moving props all create a complex and entertaining spectacle.

In addition to drawing millions of tourists, the Opry has nurtured Nashville's music industry. About 1934 WSM organized its Artists Service, which booked Opry stars into schoolhouses and theaters, at first mostly in the Southeast. Before long, independent promoters were working with Opry officials to broaden the range of Opry tours throughout the United States and abroad. After World War II, as the Opry began to recruit country music's leading stars, national recording companies began to center their country recording operations in Nashville. Independent recording studios built by WSM engineers or musicians helped produce hits that further established Nashville's reputation as Music City, U.S.A., a name coined by WSM announcer David Cobb about 1950. Capitalizing on the Opry's popularity, Nashville-based music publishers furnished song material for stage shows and recording sessions and helped promote Opry artists' careers.

For more than 60 years the Grand Ole Opry has survived not only changes in media and corporate ownership but also transformations in sounds, styles, and repertoires, reflecting the adaptation of a rural-based music to an increasingly urban society. Today, the Opry is a showcase for almost every type of country music, including honky-tonk, bluegrass, old-time, cowboy, Cajun, and country-pop, all of which continue to enjoy widespread popular favor. As art and as enterprise, the Opry remains country music's most enduring institution and one of the most significant in the history of American popular entertainment.

John W. Rumble
Country Music Foundation

Jack Hurst, *Grand Ole Opry* (1975); John W. Rumble, notes to *Radio Barn Dances*, Franklin Mint Record Society, CW 095/096; Charles K. Wolfe, *The Grand Ole Opry: The Early Years, 1925–35* (1975). ☆

HANDY, W. C.

(1873–1958) Blues composer and performer.

In 1909 W. C. Handy's band was engaged by E. H. Crump's forces to deliver the black vote to their man. In his campaign for mayor of Memphis, Crump promised to clean up the city, particularly Beale Street. Though hired by Crump to promote his campaign, Handy wrote a piece called *The Memphis Blues*, which mocked this idea:

> Mister Crump won't 'low no easy riders here.
> Mister Crump won't 'low no easy riders here.
> I don't care what Mister Crump don't 'low.
> I'm gwine bar'l-house anyhow—
> Mister Crump can go an' catch hisself some air!

This was the first time the blues came out of the backwoods and the cotton fields, off the levees, work camps, and lonesome roads to land on main street. Called "Mister Crump" at the time, the piece was an immediate hit, launched W. C. Handy as a local celebrity, and helped elect Crump mayor of Memphis.

Born William Christopher Handy in Florence, Ala., eight years after the Civil War, Handy said he received no musical talent from his parents, nor did he have any encouragement from them when he showed promise in music. In fact, his father, a Methodist minister, hinted that he would rather see him dead than pursue a career in music. But his teacher knew music and taught his pupils to sing. By the age of 10, young Handy could "catalogue almost any sound that came to [his] ears, using the *sol-fa* system."

Handy's inspiration for the blues grew out of his personal experiences and the life around him. But his conscious decision to make the blues his forte was formed in Clarksdale, Miss. One night while playing a dance, he was asked to play some of his native music. He tried to comply. The request then came for a local group to be permitted to play. Three rather ragged young black men began to play, as he recalled in his autobiography, "one of those over-and-over strains that seemed to have no very clear beginning and . . . no ending at all. The strumming attained a disturbing monotony, but on-and-on it went, a kind of stuff that has long been associated with cane rows and levee camps."

Before long, "A rain of silver dollars began to fall around the outlandish, stomping feet. The dancers went wild." After it was over Handy strained his neck and saw "there before the boys lay more money than my nine musicians were being paid for the entire engagement. Then I saw the beauty of primitive music." Seeing that folks would pay money for this unpolished music, Handy concluded "there was no virtue in being blind when you had good eyes."

Handy was cheated out of his profits on the "Memphis Blues" when he published it in 1912. However, he lived long enough to have the copyright revert to him 28 years later. In 1914 Handy wrote the "St. Louis Blues," which became a national anthem and established Handy in the forefront of American composers. He proudly wore the title "Father of the Blues." In 1931 Memphis honored W. C. Handy by naming a park

for him, and in 1949 he was named among the 10 outstanding older men in the world.

Handy died of natural causes in 1958. Today the Handy Awards are presented in his honor each year at the Orpheum Theater on Beale Street in Memphis by the Blues Foundation to recognize the nation's outstanding blues musicians.

See also POLITICS: / Crump, E. H.

Leander C. Jones
Western Michigan University

W. C. Handy, ed., *A Treasury of the Blues* (1926), *Father of the Blues: An Autobiography*, ed. Arna Bontemps (1941). ☆

HAYS, WILL
|||||||||||||||||||||||||||||||||
(1837–1907) Songwriter.

Will Hays was one of America's most popular songwriters in the 19th century. Many of his songs still endure today.

William Shakespeare Hays was born in Louisville, Ky., in 1837. Although most of the details of his early life remain undocumented, he is known to have been the captain of the *Grey Eagle*, a Mississippi River steamboat, and was an authority on the lore and life of this nation's great interior river system. He was the river editor of the Louisville *Democrat* at the age of 19 and was later a columnist for many years on the Louisville *Courier-Journal* and the Cincinnati *Enquirer*. He served briefly during the Civil War as a war correspondent in the South. He was also a poet of popular, sentimental verse, and the writer of over 500 songs.

His first successful song was "The Drummer Boy of Shiloh" (1862), which was popular in both the North and South. Before his death in 1907, Hays achieved a popularity as a songwriter that was unsurpassed. Like most popular songwriters of the mid-19th century, Hays was much influenced by the repertoire and style of blackface minstrelsy, and he wrote both lighthearted and pathetic lyrics, some of which were couched in black dialect. His chief forte lay in the composition of nostalgic laments or tender love songs that breathed Victorian morality and imagery. Some of his popular compositions include "We Parted by the River Side" (1866), "I'll Remember You, Love, in My Prayers" (1869), "Mollie Darling" (1871), "Nobody's Darling on Earth" (1870), and "The Little Old Cabin in the Lane" (1871). He also wrote a poem, "The Faithful Engineer," on which the popular gospel song "Life's Railway to Heaven" was based.

Although music critics and historians have paid little attention to Hays and have never ranked him in the same class with Stephen Foster, in some ways his songs have been more popular than those of the great Pennsylvania composer. Hays never profited from high-art patronage as Foster did (Foster's songs, for example, were warmly endorsed by the Czech composer Anton Dvořák), and his compositions were never anthologized in the songbooks distributed among America's schoolchildren. Nevertheless, Hays's songs endured among the folk and have been collected often "in the field" by folklorists. His "Little Old Cabin in the Lane" inspired the creation of other well-known songs such as "Little Old Sod Shanty," "Little Joe the Wrangler," and "Little Red Caboose behind the Train." Hays's songs also received renewed life, and demonstrated their down-home appeal, in the commercial country music field where they were often performed. "Little Old Cabin" (recorded as "Little Old Log Cabin in the Lane") was one side of Fiddlin' John Carson's historic recording of 1923, the disc that marked the beginning of the country music industry. As late as 1948 the commercial power of Hays's songs was demonstrated when superstar Eddy Arnold recorded a best-selling version of "Mollie Darling" (spelled "Molly" on the label). As is true of much older musical material, Hays's songs have found much acceptance today among bluegrass musicians.

Bill C. Malone
Tulane University

Bill C. Malone, *Southern Music—American Music* (1979). ☆

HOOKER, JOHN LEE
(b. 1917) Blues singer.

"The King of the Boogie" began life near the city that spawned so many seminal blues musicians, Clarksdale, Miss. Born 1 of 11 children in a sharecropping family, he followed a familiar pattern of early exposure to both sacred and secular music, experimentation with homemade instruments, and migration first to Memphis and then further north. Arriving in Detroit during 1943, he recorded his first impressions in a song that would become among his most famous, "Boogie Chillen'." "I was walking down Hastings Street / I saw a little place called Henry's Swing Club / Decided I'd stop in there that night / And I got down . . ." Other well-known Hooker compositions include "Boom Boom" and "House Rent Boogie."

John Lee Hooker, bluesman, 1985

An extremely individual stylist, Hooker speaks with a slight speech impediment that brings a jarring intensity to his vocal phrasing when he sings. He combines this with a guitar technique that is paradoxically repetitive and yet utterly unpredictable. His radically syncopated playing, not constrained by the tyranny of bar lines, complements his own sense of meter. "Word by word, lyric by lyric music—that's from the book: that ain't the way I feel. If I feel some way, I'm gonna let it come out. . . . It might rhyme and it might not. I don't care."

At the height of its popularity among post–World War II black audiences Hooker's work contained another paradox, that of a southern phenomenon flourishing unabated and unmodified in the North. Where other rural southern musicians yielded to the standardizing, homogenizing forces of the commercial music business, Hooker continued to improvise material freely and pursue a rhythmic and metrical style so unique

as to make him difficult to accompany or imitate. Hooker steadfastly maintained the idiosyncrasies of a unique regional and individual stylist, and his success is a testament to the deeply affecting power of this most personal approach.

William A. Cochrane
University of Mississippi

Sheldon Harris, *Blues Who's Who: A Biographical Dictionary of Blues Singers* (1979); Robert Neff and Anthony Connor, *Blues* (1975); Paul Oliver, *Blues Off the Record* (1984); Jim O'Neil and Amy O'Neil, *Living Blues* (Autumn 1979). ☆

HOPKINS, LIGHTNIN'

(1912–1982) Blues singer.

Born 15 March 1912 in Centerville, Leon County, Tex., Sam "Lightnin' " Hopkins learned to play a homemade cigar-box instrument when he was eight, picked up a little about playing the guitar later from his brother Joel, sang in the church choir as a youth, and absorbed musical materials from fellow farm workers and in nearby bars. He was a hobo and traveled through Texas in the 1920s doing farm work and playing for small pay in clubs and bars and at dances and parties. He moved to Houston in the 1930s but was unable to find steady work as a musician and soon moved back near Centerville.

In the mid-1940s Hopkins was living in rural east Texas, surviving as a farm laborer and playing music in his free time. He went back to Houston and became a fixture in the blues scene on Dowling Street. A California talent scout arranged a recording session for Hopkins and Wilson Smith, his piano accompanist, in Los Angeles, and in 1946 Hopkins made his first recordings for Aladdin Records. In promoting the release, an Aladdin executive came up with the names of Lightin' Hopkins and Thunder Smith. Hopkins returned to Houston after spending some time in California. He recorded across the nation during the late 1940s and early 1950s, but he performed mostly at clubs around Houston.

Folklorist Mack McCormick met Hopkins in 1959 and promoted him on the folk music circuit of the early 1960s. In 1960 alone, Hopkins played a hootenanny at the Alley Theater in Houston, performed at the California Blues Festival in Berkeley, and debuted at Carnegie Hall on a bill with Bob Dylan and Joan Baez. Television shows were soon being made about him, and many of them appeared on the Public Broadcasting System. Throughout the 1960s and 1970s Hopkins continued recording, and record companies released many of his earlier titles. He recorded in this period on, among others, the Bluesville, Arhoolie, Prestige, and Verve labels, and he appeared throughout the 1960s and the 1970s at major folk festivals, on college campuses, and in clubs. The 1972 film *Sounder* used songs by Hopkins, and Les Blank's documentary film, *The Blues Accordin' to Lightnin' Hopkins*, appeared in 1968. Hopkins died in February 1982 in Houston.

Charles Reagan Wilson
University of Mississippi

Samuel Charters, *The Country Blues* (1959); Sheldon Harris, *Blues Who's Who: A Biographical Dictionary of Blues Singers* (1979); Irwin Stambler and Grellin Landon, *The Encyclopedia of Folk, Country and Western Music* (2d ed., 1983). ☆

HURT, MISSISSIPPI JOHN

(1893–1966) Blues singer.

Born in Teoc, Miss., Hurt was a self-taught guitarist who performed for many years in Avalon, Miss. He made his first recording in 1928. His most noted recorded selections, including "Candy Man," "Avalon Blues," "Spike Driver Blues," and "Stagger Lee Blues," were produced by the Okeh Recording Company. He appeared in public performance very little between 1929 and the early 1960s, but he gained popularity in 1963 through his appearance at the Newport Folk Festival. In 1963 he recorded the album presenting *Mississippi John Hurt: Folk Songs and Blues* for Piedmont Records. This album served as an incentive for the recording of "Worried Blues" in 1964. He toured extensively throughout the United States until his death 2 November 1966 in Grenada, Miss. Two of his most noted concert appearances were at Carnegie Hall and Town Hall. He became one of the most beloved of Mississippi Delta bluesmen, with an almost lyrical musical style.

Lemuel Berry, Jr.
Alabama State University

Samuel Charters, *The Bluesmen: The Story and the Music of the Men Who Made the Blues* (1967); Richard K. Spottswood, *Blues Unlimited* (August 1963). ☆

JACKSON, MAHALIA

(1911–1972) Gospel singer.

Born in New Orleans 26 October 1911, Mahalia Jackson grew up in the Baptist church, but she was heavily influenced by the music of Holiness congregations and such blues singers as Bessie Smith and Ma Rainey. She moved to Chicago in 1927, joined the choir of Greater Salem Baptist Church, and then in 1928 became a member of the Johnson Gospel Singers, composed of three Johnson brothers—Robert, Prince, and Wilbur—and Louise Lemon, who together were one of the first professional gospel singing groups. The group toured the midwestern states, and their concerts featured religious plays written by the director, Robert Johnson, and starring Johnson and Mahalia in the leading roles. Jackson met Thomas A. Dorsey in the mid-1930s and began a 14-year association with him, first as one of the singers he accompanied and later as the performer of his songs. Through his connection, she secured a recording contract with Decca Records in 1937 and cut four sides for the label, none of which attracted much attention.

Jackson's reputation as a soloist with the National Baptist Convention gained her a wide following, and with her 1947 recording of W. Herbert Brewster's "Move on up a Little Higher" she was catapulted into the limelight as a gospel star and was named the queen of gospel singers by 1950. She had her own radio program in Chicago, appeared on the Ed Sullivan and Dinah Shore television shows, and began a series of concert tours of Europe in 1952. She was invited to perform at one of the inaugural parties for President John F. Kennedy, and she sang at the March on Washington in 1963 and at the funeral of Martin Luther King, Jr. She appeared in several films, including *Imitation of Life* (1959) and *The Best Man* (1964). Jackson was offered huge sums to appear in nightclubs or to switch to a secular repertoire, but she rejected such offers. She did, however, record Duke Ellington's "Come

Mahalia Jackson, gospel singer, as portrayed on a paper fan produced by the Dilion Funeral Homes and Burial Association, Leland, Vicksburg, Greenville, Indianola, and Cleveland, Mississippi, 1968

Sunday" with his orchestra in 1958. Her dark, deep, and powerful contralto inspired many singers, including Aretha Franklin, Linda Hopkins, and Brother Joe May. Her best-known recordings include "Just Over the Hill," "In the Upper Room," and "He's Got the Whole World in His Hands."

Horace Clarence Boyer
University of Massachusetts,
Amherst

Horace Clarence Boyer, "The Gospel Song: An Historical and Analytical Study (M.A. thesis, Eastman School of Music, University of Rochester, 1964); Laurraine Goreau, *Just Mahalia, Baby* (1975); Tony Heilbut, *The Gospel Sound: Good News and Bad Times* (1971); Mahalia Jackson and Evan Wylie, *Movin' On Up* (1966); William H. Tallmadge, *Ethnomusicology* (May 1961). ☆

JEFFERSON, BLIND LEMON

(1897–1929) Blues singer.

Blind Lemon Jefferson was the South's most renowned country blues oracle in the 1920s. He was born blind into a poor sharecropping family on a farm about 50 miles east of Dallas, in 1897. Like other blind bluesmen, such as Blind Blake, Blind Willie McTell, and Gary Davis, he turned to music at an early age because it was the only way he could make a living. Early in his career, Jefferson became a popular bluesman in the east Texas farming communities around his birthplace. Then he took to the road; throughout the 1920s he made frequent trips outside of Texas to Oklahoma, the Mississippi Delta, Georgia, Virginia, and eventually Chicago, where he recorded for Paramount Records. In the late 1920s, Jefferson recorded over 90 songs. He proved to be the most commercially viable of all the rural blues musicians who made records during this period. His high-pitched voice and eclectic guitar style were especially popular among blacks in the South.

The blues repertoire that he recorded in Chicago reflected the range of themes prevalent in the black oral tradition in the South at the turn of the century. They included travel, work, sexual relationships, poverty, and prison life. His sympathies were always with the downtrodden. The blues he recorded was a mixture of traditional numbers such as "See See Rider" or "Boll Weevil Blues" and his own compositions like "Matchbox Blues"—which ultimately became one of his best-known signature pieces. Taken all together, Jefferson's blues lyrics reconstruct a first-hand account of Afro-American life in the South

during the early 1900s. They are humorous and painful, ripe with sexual metaphor and fantasy, skeptical about love, and strikingly blunt in their portrayal of the society from the perspective of those at the bottom.

Blind Lemon Jefferson was in Chicago for a recording session in December 1929 when he was found dead in a snowdrift. Apparently he lost his way after playing at a house party late one night and froze to death. His body was taken back to Texas for burial. Although he died young, he left an impressive blues legacy through the recordings he made in his lifetime. He is still known and respected as one of the greatest rural bluesmen of his era.

Bill Barlow
Howard University

Blind Lemon Jefferson, Milestone Records, M-47022; Samuel Charters, *The Bluesmen: The Story and the Music of the Men Who Made the Blues* (1967); Bob Groom, *Blind Lemon Jefferson* (1970); Sheldon Harris, *Blues Who's Who: A Biographical Dictionary of Blues Singers* (1979). ☆

JIMÉNEZ, FLACO

(b. 1939) *Conjunto* musician.

The Jiménez family has established a musical dynasty in the field of *música Norteña*, a south Texas contribution to music in the South. It began with Patricio Jiménez, who worked in San Antonio's Brackenridge quarry and learned the button accordion from local German-Texans in the early 1900s. His son, Santiago Jiménez, pioneered the Texas *Norteña* accordion style in San Antonio by performing on radio broadcasts and recordings beginning in the early 1930s. Since the 1950s Santiago's son, Leonardo "Flaco" (Skinny) Jiménez, now the third generation of the musical family, has developed *música Norteña* to heights of artistic virtuosity and gained international renown.

Flaco Jiménez grew up in an environment enriched by his grandfather's musical status in the community and his father's professional music career. Between the 1940s and early 1950s Santiago and his *conjunto* (group), Los Valedores, played most Saturday nights at the Gaucho nightclub in "el Westside" of San Antonio. On occasion Flaco accompanied his father to the club and sometimes, when Don Santiago took a break to drink a beer, he would let Flaco play a tune or two on the accordion with the band.

Flaco's professional career started in 1955 when, at the age of 16, he began playing with an established *conjunto*, Mike Garza y los Caminantes. By the late 1950s Flaco had formed his own group and was traveling to play at dances in Dallas and other Texas towns and cities.

In the early 1960s Flaco also began recording as his father had done 30 years before. The records were produced by new local San Antonio record companies that specialized in *Norteña* music. Some of his first hit songs such as "Hasta la Vista" (Until I See You), "Los Amores del Flaco" (The Loves of the Skinny One), and "Virgencita de mi Vida" (Little Virgin of my Life) were recorded in these years. In the same years, Flaco, like many other *conjunto* musicians, began to travel and carried *Norteña* music along what was referred to as "the migrant trail." Flaco and his *conjunto* traveled to Fresno, Calif., Chicago, and through the Midwest as well as in Texas, following the trail of Texas migrant farm workers.

Although a recognized artist on the accordion among Mexican Americans throughout the United States, until the early 1970s Flaco remained unknown to the larger American public. This situation changed, however, when he became friends with rock and blues innovators who were interested in *Norteña* music, such as Doug Sahm of San Antonio and Ry Cooder of California. Both musicians recorded on national record labels and helped open the door to Flaco's recognition in Anglo-American society. He has since recorded with these artists and has made several national television appearances. In the past few years, Flaco has also toured Europe and now regularly plays concerts at universities and music halls all over the country. In 1981 he recorded the soundtrack for the movie, *The Border*, with fellow musician Ry Cooder.

Flaco's brother is a well-known accordionist in San Antonio, and his teenage son David has recently made his first recordings, extending the Jiménez tradition into the fourth generation.

Dan W. Dickey
Austin, Texas

Manuel Peña, *The Texas-Mexican Conjunto: History of a Working Class Music* (1985). ☆

JOHNSON, BUNK

(1879–1949) Jazz musician.

One of the earliest black jazz cornetists, Willie Geary "Bunk" Johnson, who was born in New Orleans, began to study on that instrument at the age of eight and in 1894 joined his first band, the Adam Olivier Orchestra. From 1896 to 1898 he may have played second cornet with Buddy Bolden's band, the first in New Orleans renowned for improvising in a "hot" syncopated style. From 1900 to 1910 he toured in minstrel and circus bands and in ocean-liner orchestras. Returning to New Orleans in the 1910s, Johnson became locally famous as lead cornetist with the Eagle Band, a parade and dance band re-formed from the earlier Bolden band, and with the formal society orchestra of John Robichaux. Johnson resumed touring in the 1920s, but his career rapidly declined with the onset of the Depression. In 1931 he moved to New Iberia, where he worked as a WPA public-school music teacher, a sugarcane field hand, and a Tabasco pepper factory worker. By 1934 dental problems forced him to quit playing altogether, and his career seemed at an end.

In 1938, however, he was rediscovered by jazz critics William Russell and Frederic Ramsey, Jr., who had been directed to him by Louis Armstrong as a source for their book, *Jazzmen* (1939). This renewed attention spurred Johnson to resume playing, and in 1942 he made his first recordings in New Orleans with George Lewis and Jim Robinson. These records generated widespread enthusiasm among jazz critics and listeners, made Johnson a cult figure, and spawned a full-scale revival of "classic" New Orleans jazz, as distinct from later Dixieland styles. As the spearhead of this revival, Johnson's performances and recordings increased during his last years, including appearances in San Francisco with Mutt Carey and Kid Ory (1943) and in New York with Sidney Bechet (1945).

While Johnson's revival revealed much about the schooled proficiency of early black jazz instrumentalists, it also obscured his own contribution to early jazz. Faulty memory and self-aggrandizement have compromised many statements in his recorded interviews, and stylistic accretions in his belated recordings make them an undependable reflection of his early cornet style. One of the oldest of the technically skilled black brassmen in New Orleans, Johnson was a primary participant in the shaping of jazz, whereby vocal devices of rural blues and gospel songs were adapted to the forms, techniques, and rhythms of instrumental band music.

John Joyce
Tulane University

M. Berger, in *Frontiers of Jazz*, ed. Ralph De Toledano (1947); William Russell and S. W. Smith, in *Jazzmen*, ed. Frederic Ramsey, Jr., and Charles E. Smith (1939); Martin Williams, *Jazz Masters of New Orleans* (1967). ☆

JONES, GEORGE

(b. 1931) Country music singer.

A native of Saratoga, Tex., George Glenn Jones was born 12 September 1931. His childhood, spent in the area of east Texas known as the Big Thicket, was marked by poverty and abuse. When he was 10, his family moved to Kountze, Tex.; a year later they moved to Beaumont. His father, George Washington Jones, bought him a Gene Autry guitar, and he was soon singing on the streets with a tin cup. Never a serious student, he quit school in the seventh grade and had begun a honky-tonk career by age 16; he entered his first of four marriages at 18.

Upon completing two years of service in the Marine Corps, he returned to Beaumont in November 1953. Less than two months later, he recorded his first single, "No Money in This Deal," and began his 20-year association with Harold W. "Pappy" Daily, his producer and informal manager-advisor. In 1955 George Jones became a country disc jockey on KTRM, Beaumont, and appeared on the Louisiana Hayride; his first hit, "Why Baby Why," entered the charts in 1956, and he was off to Nashville, where he joined the Grand Ole Opry.

George Jones started his transition from an imitator of his idols Roy Acuff, Lefty Frizzell, and Hank Williams to an original vocal stylist whose unique talent would be compared with performers as diverse as Frank Sinatra and Aretha Franklin. Performers such as Waylon Jennings, Tom Petty, and Elvis Costello identify Jones as an important source of influence and inspiration. For many critics, fans, and performers he has become the standard against which "country" is measured. George Jones has produced number-one country songs in each of the past four decades; over 60 of his singles have achieved top-10 status on the country charts.

The authenticity with which Jones sings of heartbreak and headache was validated by news reports of his personal problems, that seemed to intensify in the period between 1975, when he was divorced from his third wife, country star Tammy Wynette, and March 1983, when he married Nancy Sepulveda and moved to Colmesneil, Tex. He struggled with alcohol, drug, and legal problems that threatened his life but not his popularity. In fact, he reached his largest audience at the time his personal life was most disorganized; his 1980 album

I Am What I Am with Billy Sherrill, his producer since 1972, won both Country Music Association and Grammy recognition. His first video, *Who's Gonna Fill Their Shoes*, won recognition as the country video of 1986.

George Jones's catalog of hits ranges from manic—"White Lightnin' "—to depressive—"The Window Up Above," "The Grand Tour," and "He Stopped Loving Her Today." His songs, performance, and life connect with the large number of southerners separated from traditional communities by migration and modernization. This group provides for him the most loyal fan-following in all of country music.

Larry W. DeBord
University of Mississippi

Bob Allen, *George Jones: The Saga of An American Singer* (1984); Dolly Carlisle, *Ragged But Right: The Life and Times of George Jones* (1984). ☆

JOPLIN, SCOTT
(1868–1917) Ragtime composer.

At the peak of his fame (1900–1905), Scott Joplin was billed in vaudeville as "King of Ragtime." His fame rested on the publication in 1899 of "Maple Leaf Rag," a brilliant piano solo in a new popular style called "ragtime." Joplin was a skilled itinerant musician born in 1868 near Texarkana, Tex. He studied piano and composition in Sedalia, Mo., at George R. Smith College (1896) to expand his musical horizons. Playing in saloons and bordellos from Texas to St. Louis, Joplin teamed with other black ragtime composers such as Otis Saunders and Louis Chauvin, helping them notate and sell their compositions. A farsighted publisher, John S. Stark of Sedalia, aided Joplin in his first steps to ragtime, and both men were enriched by this composer-publisher collaboration. Stark expanded his small venture into a fountainhead of "classic" piano ragtime, and Joplin wrote dozens of brilliant rags in the wake of "Maple Leaf Rag."

Joplin experimented with popular songs in a sentimental parlor vein in the mid-1890s, but his ability to compose and notate piano rags led him to ambitious works: "Original Rags" (1899), "The Easy Winners" (1901), "Elite Syncopations" (1902), "The Entertainer" (1902), "Pine Apple Rag" (1908), "Scott Joplin's New Rag" (1912), and some two dozen other published rags. Driven by a desire to make ragtime a respectable musical form, he and Stark admonished sheet-music buyers "DO NOT PLAY FAST," "IT IS NEVER RIGHT TO PLAY RAGTIME FAST," "DO NOT FAKE" (i.e., improvise). Joplin experimented with ragtime in a ballet, "The Ragtime Dance" (1900, published 1906), and a ragtime opera, *A Guest of Honor* (1903), now lost. He tried syncopated waltzes ("Bethena," 1905, and "Pleasant Moments," 1909) and a habañera ("Solace," 1909) and enlarged ragtime's vocabulary in advanced rags like "Euphonic Sounds" (1909) and "Magnetic Rag" (1914).

After traveling from Sedalia to St. Louis, thence to New York City and on vaudeville circuits, Joplin settled in Harlem. He never matched the fame and fortune of "Maple Leaf Rag," though his works were lauded for their consistent gentle genius. From about 1905 Joplin became consumed with ideas for "elevating" ragtime, via symphonic or operatic forms. He wrote an ambitious and unique folk-oriented opera, *Treemonisha*, performed only in rehearsal in 1915. Failure to achieve support for *Treemonisha* may have contributed to Joplin's collapse. He died 1 April 1917, in New York.

Joplin's peers in ragtime composition were Thomas M. Turpin, Charles H. Hunter, Charles L. Johnson, James Scott, and Artie Matthews. His collaborators included Louis Chauvin, Scott Hayden, and Arthur Marshall. He assisted the careers of S. Brunson "Brun" Campbell and Joseph F. Lamb and scores of other ragtime players who did not leave compositions. Joplin's version of ragtime derived from the playing of Mississippi Valley itinerant composers and from rich late 19th-century folk reservoirs. His contribution to Afro-American music lay in his skill as a composer: he created fluid, lyrical themes, organized them into the coherent multipart form of the piano rag, and forged an individualized, easily recognizable style. His works are marked by a delicacy and grace achieved by few of his contemporaries. Within the form of the piano rag as a serious composition (or "classic," the term he and Stark favored), Joplin fused the vigor of banjo tunes, the swing of country dances, and the limpidity of song. His mark on American popular music is deep and indelible, and interest in his work revived in the 1970s. *Treemonisha* was performed in Atlanta in 1972, and Joplin's compositions were chosen for the soundtrack of the popular 1973 motion picture *The Sting*.

William J. Schafer
Berea College

Rudi Blesh and Harriet Janis, *They All Played Ragtime* (1966); James Haskins and

Kathleen Benson, *Scott Joplin* (1978); Vera Brodsky Lawrence, ed., *The Collected Works of Scott Joplin* (1971); William J. Schafer and Johannes Riedel, *The Art of Ragtime: Form and Meaning of an Original Black American Art* (1973). ☆

KING, B. B.
|||||||||||||||||||||||||||||||
(b. 1925) Blues singer.

Riley "B. B." King was born on a plantation between Itta Bena and Indianola, Miss. One of five children, he often sang in local churches as a young child. When his parents separated, King moved with his mother to Kilmichael, Miss., where he sang in a school spiritual quartet from 1929 to 1934. After his mother's death, he returned to Indianola and continued to develop his music while working as a farmhand.

In 1946 King hitched a ride to Memphis and for 10 months lived with noted bluesman Bubba White, his mother's cousin. He returned to the Delta briefly at the end of 1947 and in early 1948 harvested a cotton crop. Later that year he returned to Memphis, this time for good, and worked amateur shows at the W. C. Handy Theater/Palace Theater. He frequently performed with Bobby Bland, Johnny Ace, and Earl Forrest in a group called "the Beale Streeters" and appeared regularly on his own "Pepticon Boy" show on WDIA radio in Memphis. His nickname, the "Beale Street Blues Boy," was shortened to "Blues Boy," then to "B. B." In 1950 his "Three O'Clock Blues" climbed to the top of the rhythm-and-blues charts and stayed there for four months. Its success launched his musical career, and he gave up his disc jockey job to go on the road with his own group, scarcely two

B. B. King, 1960s, photograph on a wall at Club Paradise, Memphis, Tennessee

years after he had made his last cotton crop in the Delta.

For nearly 20 years he performed some 300 one-night stands a year in black night spots known as the "Chitterlin' Circuit." Once a year he played week-long engagements in large urban black theaters such as the Howard in Washington, the Regal in Chicago, and the Apollo in New York.

In the early 1960s King's career was in a slump, with blacks finding his music uncomfortably close to their "down-home" roots and folk enthusiasts considering him too commercialized. King's return to fame came when the Rolling Stones, Paul Butterfield's Blues Band, and other British and American groups acknowledged him as their idol. After his first European tour in 1968 he was finally recognized by American critics, and since that time his career has steadily grown, with frequent television and film appearances.

King's guitar style is influenced by

blues guitarists Lonnie Johnson and T-Bone Walker and by jazz guitarists Django Reinhardt and Charlie Christian. He has always played with an electric guitar, which he nicknamed "Lucille." His delicate "bent" notes and powerful vocals echo the blues style of the Mississippi Delta where King first learned his music.

From his early years in rural Mississippi to his international acclaim, B. B. King's blues career is a rare success story. He has issued over 700 recordings and continues to produce and perform at a pace younger musicians would find exhausting. His achievements as a blues performer, composer, and spokesman were recognized in 1977 when Yale President Kingman Brewster awarded him an honorary doctorate of music with the accolade, "In your rendition of the blues you have always taken us beyond entertainment to the deeper message of suffering and endurance that gave rise to the form."

In "Why I Sing the Blues," King explains the meaning of his music:

When I first got the blues, they
    brought me over on a ship,
Man was standing over me, and a
    lot more with a whip,
Now everybody want to know why
    I sing the blues,
Well I've been around a long time,
    I've really paid my dues.

William Ferris
University of Mississippi

Sheldon Harris, *Blues Who's Who: A Biographical Dictionary of Blues Singers* (1979); Paul Oliver, *The Story of the Blues* (1969); Charles Sawyer, *The Arrival of B.B. King: The Authorized Biography* (1980). ☆

LEDBETTER, HUDDIE (LEADBELLY)

(1885–1949) Blues singer.

A singer and composer, Ledbetter was born 21 January 1885, two miles from Mooringsport, La., in the Caddo Lake area near the Texas border, where his parents, Wess Ledbetter and Sallie (Pugh) Ledbetter, owned 65 acres of farmland. Wess Ledbetter's parents in Mississippi had both been slain by the Ku Klux Klan. Huddie Ledbetter's maternal grandmother was a Cherokee, a fact he often mentioned.

Huddie Ledbetter was first exposed to music by his mother, who led her church choir. Two "songster" uncles, Bob and Terrell Ledbetter, encouraged him to become a musician. Huddie Ledbetter was soon known as the best guitar picker and songster in his part of Louisiana. At 16 he started visiting Fannin Street, the red-light district of nearby Shreveport. Here he heard accomplished blues musicians and learned their style and verses. He recalls these early experiences in his song "Fannin Street." Bud Coleman and Jim Fagin were two musicians with whom he worked closely.

Ledbetter soon moved away from Mooringsport. He married a girl named Lethe, and they worked together during summers on farms near New Boston, Tex., in the blackland counties east of Dallas. In the winter they moved to Dallas, where he played his guitar and sang in the red-light district. There he met the Texas bluesman Blind Lemon Jefferson and learned many songs from him.

He received the nickname "Lead Belly" (or "Leadbelly") because his voice was a powerful bass. A handsome, strongly built young man, he had early learned that he was attractive to women.

In Marshall, Tex., he attacked a woman who rejected his advances, was sentenced to a year on a chain gang, and escaped from prison three days later. In late 1917 Leadbelly became involved in another fracas over a woman. He was convicted on two counts, murder and assault to murder, on 24 May 1918. Once more he escaped from his cell, but on 7 June 1918, under the alias of Walter Boyd, he entered Shaw State Prison Farm, sentenced to 30 years at hard labor. For the third time he escaped. He was soon recaptured, and in 1920 he was transferred to the Central State Farm near Houston. He worked on labor gangs for 12 to 14 hours a day cutting logs and hoeing cotton, and through his strength and endurance he became the lead man on the fastest work gang.

Leadbelly was also known for his skill as a musician and was asked to sing when visitors came to the prison. When the governor of Texas, Pat M. Neff, came to visit, Leadbelly sang a plea for mercy to him:

(If I) had you, Governor Neff, like
   you got me,
I'd wake up in the mornin', and I'd
   set you free.

The governor was impressed with the man and his song, and on 15 January 1925 he pardoned Leadbelly, who had then served about six and a half years. After working for a Buick agency in Houston, Leadbelly returned to his home near Mooringsport in 1926. While he worked for the Gulf Refining Company, he continued to develop as a blues singer. In 1930 he was accosted by a group of men who wanted whiskey. Leadbelly wounded five of them with his knife and was sentenced to 10 years at hard labor for assault with intent to murder.

On 28 February 1930 he entered Angola Penitentiary in Louisiana and became the lead man on prison gangs, as he had in Texas. He composed another plea for mercy to Governor O. K. Allen of Louisiana. It was recorded (along with a song that was to become even more famous, "Irene, Good Night") by folklorists John and Alan Lomax in 1934. The Lomaxes played the record for the governor in his office and obtained a reprieve for Leadbelly on 7 August 1934.

The next month Leadbelly joined John Lomax in a journey that helped make both men famous. Lomax recorded folksongs in southern prisons, and Leadbelly accompanied him, telling of his own experiences and singing to encourage the inmates to record for Lomax. Lomax's tapes of Leadbelly's songs were eventually deposited in the Library of Congress. After 6,000 miles of travel, performances, and recording, they arrived in New York City. Leadbelly was given a resounding reception by the New York intellectual and literary scene, that embraced him as the "bad nigger."

Leadbelly's repertoire included traditional folk and children's songs, blues, and topical numbers, all of which are an important part of American folklore. His best-known songs include "Boll Weevil," "Rock Island Line," "Old Cottonfields at Home," "Take This Hammer," "Pick a Bale of Cotton," and "Midnight Special." Few other blues musicians have been so studied and appreciated. He died of myotrophic lateral sclerosis on 6 December 1949 at Bellevue Hospital in New York.

William Ferris
University of Mississippi

Richard M. Garvin and Edmond G. Addeo, *The Midnight Special: The Legend of Lead-*

belly (1971); John A. Lomax and Alan Lomax, *The Leadbelly Legend* (1965), *Negro Folk Songs as Sung by Lead Belly* (1936), Recordings of interviews and music made with Leadbelly, listed in Recording Division of the Library of Congress; Frederick Ramsey, *Last Sessions* (record), Folkways, FA-2941 and FA-2942. ✩

LEWIS, JERRY LEE
||||||||||||||||||||||||||||||||||||||||||||||
(b. 1935) Rock and country singer.

Jerry Lee Lewis of Ferriday, La., one of the most charismatic and controversial musicians of his generation, has long exemplified many of the most profound tensions in southern history.

Born on 29 September 1935 into an extremely talented yet volatile family—two of his cousins are television evangelist Jimmy Swaggart and country musician Mickey Gilley—Lewis's earliest and most indelible influences came from Pentecostal religion. As a child he was also attracted to secular sources, such as a black Ferriday juke joint called Haney's Big House. Lewis has cited Al Jolson, Jimmie Rodgers, Gene Autry, and Hank Williams as vocal influences, but his highly personalized boogie-woogie piano style reflects indigenous black folk sources from his immediate region.

By adolescence Lewis was a skilled entertainer, performing at numerous political rallies, religious services, talent contests, and nightclubs, and on radio in Natchez, Miss. In 1956 he began recording for Sun Records in Memphis and achieved national popularity and notoriety as perhaps the wildest of all rock-and-roll performers. To many observers, Lewis was a public menace, but from 1956 to 1958 he had numerous hit recordings, including "Whole Lotta Shakin' Goin' On" and "Great Balls of Fire," and made several appearances on

national television and in movies. Lewis generated copious public criticism in 1958 after marrying his 13-year-old second cousin, Myra Brown. Although he defended his marriage as customary in his native South, Lewis's recording career declined precipitously. Forced to tour incessantly (primarily in the South) for over a decade, he subsequently deepened his already vast repertoire and enhanced his reputation as an unrivaled live performer.

In 1968 Lewis staged a remarkable comeback in the country field, and more than a score of country hits ensued. Despite his success as a country artist, Lewis has continued to perform predominantly in the rockabilly style that had brought him his initial success. He has remained a successful recording artist well into the 1980s despite an uncanny series of financial, physical, and emotional crises.

By the late 1970s Jerry Lee Lewis was widely hailed by both popular journalists and scholars as one of the most creative and important figures in American popular culture. His peculiar resonance as a southern cultural symbol was matched only by Elvis Presley. No one has demonstrated a more thorough command of the South's musical heritage, from minstrelsy and blues to hymns and hillbilly music. His career has operated as a paradigm of the southern experience, dramatizing many of the region's fundamental tensions.

Stephen R. Tucker
Tulane University

Myra Lewis with Murray Silver, *Great Balls of Fire: The Uncensored Story of Jerry Lee Lewis* (1982); Robert Palmer, *Jerry Lee Lewis Rocks!* (1981); Nick Tosches, *Hellfire: The Jerry Lee Lewis Story* (1982). ✩

LITTLE RICHARD
|||||||||||||||||||||||||||||||||||||||||||||||

See Penniman, Richard

LOMAX, JOHN A.
|||||||||||||||||||||||||||||||||||||||||||||
(1867–1948) Folksong collector.

Born in Goodman, Miss., on 23 September 1867, John Avery Lomax was one of five sons of James Avery Lomax, a farmer, and Susan Frances (Cooper) Lomax both natives of Georgia. Although they always worked their own land, Lomax described his family as belonging to the "upper crust of the po' white trash." In 1869 they moved to a farm on the Bosque River near Meridian, Tex. From his country childhood Lomax acquired a love for and appreciation of the rural folklore he later captured on record. He absorbed the popular hymns he heard at the Methodist camp meetings his family attended.

In 1895, at 28, he entered the University of Texas, where he took courses with feverish enthusiasm and received his B.A. degree in two years. From 1897 to 1903, Lomax served the university simultaneously as registrar, secretary to the president, and steward of men's dormitories, for $75 a month. Subsequently, he became instructor and then associate professor of English at Texas Agricultural and Mechanical College (1903–10). Meanwhile, he doggedly pursued graduate studies despite financial constraints. He received the M.A. in literature in 1906 from the University of Texas and an M.A. in English from Harvard the following year.

Since childhood, Lomax had been writing down the cowboy songs he heard. His English professors at Texas had scorned such frontier literature as unworthy, but at Harvard, Barrett Wendell and George Lyman Kittredge strongly encouraged Lomax to continue his collecting. After his return to Texas, Lomax secured three successive fellowships that enabled him to travel through the cattle country with a notebook and a primitive recording machine. Around campfires and in saloon back rooms he persuaded cowboys to sing their songs. Among his findings were the well-known "Git Along Little Dogies" and "Home on the Range," the latter sung to him in San Antonio by a black saloonkeeper who had been a trail cook. The result was Lomax's first published collection, *Cowboy Songs and Other Frontier Ballads* (1910), which he dedicated to Theodore Roosevelt, a firm supporter of his efforts. The book is a landmark in the study of American folklore.

Later in 1932, with a contract from the Macmillan Company for a book of American folksongs and with support from the Library of Congress and the American Council of Learned Societies, he set out on the first of a series of collecting trips that were to occupy the rest of his life. He concentrated on recording songs of the southern black—blues, spirituals, and work chants. Often accompanied by his son, Alan, he visited remote rural black communities, lumber camps, and penitentiaries, where blacks were isolated and where singing softened the pain of prison life. The quality and number of the songs he recorded for the Library of Congress Archive of American Folk Song—more than 10,000 in all—reflect Lomax's unusual skill as a fieldworker. In the Arkansas Penitentiary he came upon two important songs, "Rock Island Line" and "John Henry," the rhythmic ballad of a "steel drivin' man."

Lomax's two collections, *American Ballads and Folk Songs* (1934) and *Our Singing Country* (1941), opened an entirely new area of American folk music to the public and were largely responsible for the folksong movement that developed in New York City and spread throughout the country. One of Lomax's discoveries was an influential figure in that movement: Huddie Ledbetter, nicknamed "Leadbelly" because of his deep bass voice. Lomax and his son found Leadbelly in a Louisiana penitentiary in 1933, arranged for his freedom, brought him to Greenwich Village in New York, and published *Negro Folk Songs as Sung by Lead Belly* (1936).

Lomax died on 26 January 1948 at the age of 80 of a cerebral hemorrhage while visiting in Greenville, Miss., and was buried in Austin, Tex.

William Ferris
University of Mississippi

John A. Lomax, *Adventures of a Ballad Hunter* (1947), *Cowboy Songs* (1922), Recordings at the University of Texas, Harvard University, and the Archives of American Folk Song at the Library of Congress, "The Ballad Hunter: John A. Lomax" (record), AAFS L53; D. K. Wilgus, *Anglo-American Folksong Scholarship since 1898* (1959). ☆

LUNSFORD, BASCOM LAMAR

(1882–1973) Music collector, performer, and promoter.

Born on South Turkey Creek in Buncombe County, N.C., and trained as a lawyer, Lunsford worked in a variety of occupations (college teacher, lawyer, newspaperman, seller of fruit trees and war bonds), but achieved local and national renown as a collector, performer, promoter, and interpreter of the old-time music and dance of western North Carolina. During the late 1920s, when mountain music and culture were being stereotyped and exploited for commercial (mainly media and tourism) purposes, Lunsford—who called himself "the squire of South Turkey Creek"— championed their dignity and worth.

In 1928 Lunsford began his Mountain Dance and Folk Festival in Asheville, first as a segment of the Chamber of Commerce-sponsored and booster-oriented Rhododendron Festival, but later as an independent event. During the next half century the festival became a major showcase for traditional Appalachian music and dance. It developed its own traditions, opening each year the first weekend in August, "along about sundown," with the fiddle tune "Grey Eagle." Some of its outstanding performers were banjo players Aunt Samantha Bumgarner and George Pegram, harmonica player Walter "Red" Parham, and the Soco Gap clog team led by Sam Queen.

Lunsford has been criticized for his somewhat idiosyncratic selectivity in presenting mountain music. During his lifetime, for example, no blacks ever performed at the festival, despite the existence of a substantial black population in the area. Nevertheless, as fellow festival promoter Sarah Gertrude Knott observed, Lunsford succeeded better than virtually all of his peers at "finding a way between the old and the new," uncovering and nurturing the oldest levels of tradition; presenting and interpreting traditional music and dance in a dignified manner; respecting the tastes, styles, and choices of the performers themselves; and honoring traditional values and idioms while remaining sensitive to the dynamic quality of tradition.

As a performer and collector, Luns-

ford recorded both for commercial phonograph companies (Okeh, Brunswick,
Columbia, Folkways) and for folklore archives at Columbia University and the
Library of Congress. Some of his personal papers and memorabilia are on
deposit at Mars Hill College in North
Carolina.

David E. Whisnant
University of Maryland,
Baltimore County

Bill Finger, *Southern Exposure* (Spring
1974); Loyal Jones, *Minstrel of the Appalachians: The Story of Bascom Lamar Lunsford* (1984); Harold H. Martin, *Saturday
Evening Post* (22 May 1948); David E. Whisnant, *Appalachian Journal* (Autumn–Winter
1979–80). ☆

MEXICAN BORDER STATIONS

Popularly known as X-stations because
of their call letters, the Mexican border
radio stations in the 1930s and afterwards were powerful disseminators of
music and other forms of popular culture
throughout North America. Their programming techniques and advertising
practices became part of the nation's
folklore, and they did much to make the
world at large conscious of southern
rural folkways.

With transmitters located on the Mexican side of the border and operating
with wattage generally far in excess of
that permitted in the United States,
X-station broadcasts could be heard
clearly in this country and Canada. The
era of border radio began in 1932 when
John R. Brinkley, "the goat-gland doctor" who promoted a cure for male sexual impotence, established XERA (later

XERA), with offices in Del Rio, Tex.,
and its transmitter in Villa Acuna, Mexico. XER claimed power of 500,000
watts, and Brinkley advertised his medical ideas and Del Rio hospital on it
and also leased time to other American businessmen who sold patent medicines and other products. Additional
stations, such as XEPN, XEAW, XENT,
and XEG, soon followed, with each of
them pursuing a pattern of radio programming similar to that pioneered by
Brinkley.

Late-night listeners were introduced
to an unforgettable torrent of Americana
on the border radio shows. Long-winded
announcers incessantly promoted such
products as baby chicks, songbooks,
records, photographs, prayer cloths,
Resurrection plants, Bibles, "genuine
simulated" diamonds, laxatives, hair
dyes, and other forms of patent medicines (such as Crazy Water Crystals),
and "autographed pictures of Jesus
Christ." Listeners were constantly so-
licited for money, asked to send in box-
tops and labels, and told to get their
orders in the mail immediately for once-
in-a-lifetime offers that were due to go
off the air forever at midnight.

Border radio advertising was accompanied also by strong doses of southern
popular culture: fundamentalist religion, populist politics, and grassroots
music of various kinds. Country musicians such as the Carter Family, the
Pickard Family, the Callahan Brothers,
and the Herrington Trio, cowboy singers
like cowboy Slim Rinehart, Jesse Rodgers, and the Utah Cowboy (J. R. Hall),
and gospel singers such as the Chuck
Wagon Gang and the Stamps Quartet
performed on the border stations either
in live broadcasts or on transcriptions.
They sold their sponsors' products,
hawked their own records and picture-
songbooks, and disseminated their par-

ticular versions of southern music to audiences in the most remote corners of North America. The radio stations still broadcast their southern-influenced programs.

Bill C. Malone
Tulane University

Gerald Carson, *The Roguish World of Dr. Brinkley* (1960); Bill C. Malone, *Country Music, U.S.A.: A Fifty-year History* (1968; rev. ed., 1985). ☆

MONROE, BILL

(b. 1911) Bluegrass musician.

William Smith "Bill" Monroe was born on 13 September 1911 on a farm near the small town of Rosine, Ohio County, in western Kentucky. The youngest of eight children, Monroe had extremely poor sight. He was a shy lad for whom his family's musical traditions afforded comfort and identity. His mother died when he was 10, his father when he was 16. He lived for several years with his Uncle Pen (Pendleton Vandiver), a fiddler who strongly influenced his music and who was later immortalized in song by Monroe. He also learned much from a black guitarist and fiddler, Arnold Shultz, with whom he played at dances. In 1929 he joined two older brothers at industrial jobs near Chicago. In 1932 the three became part of an exhibition square-dance team at the National Barn Dance on Chicago radio station WLS. In 1934 Bill and his brother Charlie became professional "hillbilly" radio singers. By 1938 their duets had become popular throughout the Southeast through their radio broadcasts in Iowa and the Carolinas, their personal ap-

pearances, and their Victor Bluebird recordings (1936–38).

In 1938 the brothers parted, and Bill formed his own group, the Blue Grass Boys. In October 1939 he joined the cast of the Grand Ole Opry on WSM, and he has been in Nashville ever since. His recordings for Victor (1940–41), Columbia (1945–49) and Decca/MCA (since 1950) have sold consistently over long periods; many are still in print. His compositions include instrumentals, religious songs, and secular songs on a variety of topics.

During the 1940s Monroe, who plays mandolin and sings in a distinctive high tenor voice, developed an innovative ensemble-band style based on the instrumental and vocal styles of earlier southeastern fiddle-band music. His band's sound, which included the five-string banjo of Earl Scruggs, was copied by a number of groups during the late 1940s. By the mid-1950s it was considered a style and had acquired the name "bluegrass"—taken from his band's name. In the late 1960s Monroe was the central figure in the emergence of bluegrass festivals. Monroe's reputation came not just from his musical ability and his skill as a composer but also from his role as a bandleader and teacher. In his early years he was as an older brother to his band members; he has become later in life a patriarch.

His contributions to country music were recognized in 1971 when he was elected to the Country Music Hall of Fame in Nashville. His national prominence was underscored in July 1982, when he was among the first recipients of the Annual National Heritage Fellowship Awards made by the Folk Arts Program of the National Endowment for the Arts. His award described him as "one of the few living American musicians who can justly claim to have created an entirely new musical style."

Neil V. Rosenberg
Memorial University
St. Johns, Newfoundland

Ralph Rinzler, in *Stars of Country Music: Uncle Dave Macon to Johnny Rodriguez*, ed. Bill C. Malone and Judith McCullough (1975); Jim Rooney, *Bossmen: Bill Monroe and Muddy Waters* (1971); Neil V. Rosenberg, *Bill Monroe and His Blue Grass Boys: An Illustrated Discography* (1974), *Bluegrass: A History* (1985). ☆

MORGANFIELD, McKINLEY (MUDDY WATERS)

(1915–1983) Blues singer.

Muddy Waters, bluesman, 1960s

Muddy Waters was born in Rolling Fork, Miss., and at an early age taught himself to perform on both the guitar and the harmonica. His skills as a young bluesman were widely advertised in north Mississippi and the Memphis, Tenn., area. During the early 1940s he recorded blues selections for folklorists Alan Lomax and John Work. Shortly after his recording session he joined the Silas Green Tent Show. Through his employment with Silas Green, he formed a professional association with William Lee Conley (Big Bill Broonzy). He made his first professional recording in 1946. Two of the musicians with whom he recorded include Andrew Luandrew (Sunnyland Slim) and Leroy Foster. Morganfield formed his own band, which performed in Chicago for several years and included such noted Chicago bluesmen as Willie Dixon, Otis Spann, Pat Hare, James Cotton, and Little Walter Jacobs. From 1942 to his death he recorded extensively. Among his most celebrated recorded selections are

"Caledonia," "Hoochie Koochie Man," "Rolling Stone," "Baby Please Don't Go," and "Mannish Boy." He also toured throughout the United States and in several foreign countries. His foreign tours included appearances in England, Australia, New Zealand, Germany, and France. His peers nicknamed him "Godfather of the Blues."

Muddy Waters bought his first electric guitar in 1944, and he became especially significant in introducing electrified instruments to the blues. It helped make the blues into ensemble music, and the electric blues was a major influence on rock and roll. Waters was a leader in the transformation of Delta blues from southern folk music into a nationally and internationally popular music.

Lemuel Berry, Jr.
Alabama State University

Living Blues (Autumn 1983, March–April 1985); Robert Palmer, *Deep Blues* (1981); James Rooney, *Bossmen: Bill Monroe and Muddy Waters* (1971). ☆

MORTON, JELLY ROLL (FERDINAND LE MENTHE)

||||||||||||||||||||||||||||||||||||||||||||||||||||||||||||||||||

(1885–1941) Jazz musician.

Self-proclaimed inventor of jazz, Ferdinand Le Menthe was among the earliest and most prominent of New Orleans jazzmen. Better known on the streets and among the world's musical fraternity as Jelly Roll Morton, he was born in 1885 on the Gulf Coast near New Orleans. His African-Mediterranean-Caribbean ancestry placed him among that city's Creoles of Color, and he drew from their musical traditions. Morton's family moved to New Orleans while the young Ferdinand was quite small, and he grew to manhood there within a community that enjoyed frequent contacts with Mexico and the Caribbean. The young Morton learned on his own to play various musical instruments and was playing on street corners in a band by age eight. He studied piano at age 10, learning from the resident pianist of the local French opera. Much of the European form and attitude long prevalent in jazz has its source in this kind of training received by Creole musicians such as Morton. By age 15 he was regarded as one of New Orleans's leading ragtime-blues pianists.

Morton grew up on the margin of the New Orleans marketplace, struggling to survive within the urban underclass. The street-and-saloon environment fostered the proliferation of flesh parlors and honky-tonk dance-halls where musicians of color often worked. Prevented from performing in formal musical circles, the city's schooled black musicians turned out of necessity to the honky-tonks, cabarets, and sporting houses in places like Storyville.

The honky-tonk culture of the urban underclass in the early 20th century

Jelly Roll Morton, jazz musician, early 1920s

formed a national network, which permitted artists like Morton to take their music to other cities. Between 1910 and 1925 Jelly Roll Morton performed in St. Louis, Los Angeles, San Francisco, Chicago, and New York, in addition to New Orleans. He toured with vaudeville shows operating out of Memphis and later Georgia. In the 1917 to 1923 period he performed mainly on the West Coast. In these and subsequent years Morton composed and recorded a host of songs on the piano, including such jazz classics as "The Pearls," "The Chant," "The Fingerbreaker," "New Orleans Joys," and "Buddy Bolden's Blues."

By the early 1920s Morton's interest, along with that of the rest of the nation, had shifted to jazz bands. He moved to Chicago where he recorded and performed frequently. There he organized and produced the Red Hot Peppers, a seven-piece classic jazz ensemble for which he composed and orchestrated such immortal jazz pieces as "Jungle Blues," "London Blues," "Hello Central, Give Me Doctor Jazz," "Sidewalk Blues," and "Georgia Swing." He moved to New York City in 1928, performing there in nightclubs and ballrooms, recording, working with musical revues, and touring out of town. In 1938 Alan Lomax extensively recorded Morton for the Library of Congress Archive of American Folksong.

See also BLACK LIFE: / Storyville

> Curtis D. Jerde
> W. R. Hogan Jazz Archive
> Tulane University

Alan Lomax, *Mister Jelly Roll* (1950); Martin Williams, *Jelly Roll Morton* (1963). ☆

MUDDY WATERS

See Morganfield, McKinley

NELSON, WILLIE

(b. 1933) Country music singer.

Willie Hugh Nelson was born in Fort Worth, Tex., on 30 April 1933 and was reared in the little central Texas town of Abbott, where he was exposed to a wide variety of musical influences. He grew up singing gospel songs in the Baptist church but also played in honky-tonks all over the state. Before he was a teenager, he began playing guitar in the German-Czech polka bands in the "Bohemian" communities of central Texas; he listened to the country music of Bob Wills, Lefty Frizzell, and Floyd Tillman, but he was also an avid fan of jazz and vintage pop music. All of these forms clearly influence the music he plays today.

Despite his skills as a guitarist and unorthodox singer (with his blues inflections and off-the-beat phrasing), Nelson's ticket to Nashville came through his songwriting. In 1960 he moved to Nashville, where he became part of an important coterie of writers that included Hank Cochran, Harlan Howard, and Roger Miller. Nelson made a major contribution to country music's post-rock-and-roll revival with such songs as "Funny How Time Slips Away," "Hello, Walls," "Night Life," and "Crazy," all of which were successfully recorded by other singers.

Recording for RCA Victor in the mid-1960s, Nelson became widely admired by his colleagues as a "singer's singer," but he did not achieve the stardom that he sought. In 1972 he relocated in Austin, Tex., where he became part of an already-thriving music scene that was strongly oriented toward youth who had grown up listening to rock and urban folk music. Nelson made a calculated attempt to appeal to this audience by changing his physical image: he let his hair grow long, grew a beard, began wearing a headband, an earring, jeans, and jogging shoes (a striking contrast to the well-groomed, middle-class appearance he had affected during his Nashville years). He also publicized himself with his huge annual "picnics," first held in Dripping Springs, Tex., in 1972 and 1973, and later staged in a variety of Texas communities, usually on the Fourth of July. These festivals were intended to bridge the gap between youth and adults, while bringing together varied lifestyles and musical forms. The picnics, however, soon lost their appeal to older people or to traditional country fans and instead became havens for uninhibited youth and for musicians who seemed most comfortable with a country-rock perspective.

After winning the youth audience, Nelson then captured the adult market. In 1975 he recorded a best-selling album called *The Red Headed Stranger*, and one song from the album, Fred Rose's "Blue Eyes Crying in the Rain," became the number-one country song of the year (it is ironic that the first superhit recorded by this master songwriter was a song written by someone else). Nelson's ascent to superstardom and his building of a large and diverse audience were accomplished without significant departures from his traditional style. Indeed, his repertoire became even more traditional as he reached back to the performance of older gospel, country, and pop songs. No one in American music performed a more eclectic sampling of songs. He also preserved his unorthodox style of singing and sang over a rather spare and uncluttered scheme of instrumentation, which was dominated by his own inventive, single-string style of guitar playing.

While Nelson has won a large array of country music awards since the mid-

Willie Nelson, outlaw country music singer, 1980s

1970s, including the Country Music Association's Entertainer of the Year award in 1979, his appeal has extended far beyond the country music world. Nelson has received favorable reviews for his role in several movies, such as *The Electric Horseman*; he has been feted constantly by the American media; and he has entertained often at political events, including the Democratic National Convention in 1980, during the Carter presidency. Few country singers have enjoyed such broad exposure.

Bill C. Malone
Tulane University

Jan Reid, *The Improbable Rise of Redneck Rock* (1974); Al Reinert, *New York Times Magazine* (26 March 1978); Lola Scobey, *Willie Nelson* (1982). ☆

OLIVER, KING
(1885–1938) Jazz musician.

Joseph "King" Oliver was born in or near New Orleans and became an early black jazz cornetist and bandleader. By 1900 he played cornet in a youthful parade band. From 1905 to 1915 Oliver became a prominent figure in various brass and dance bands and with small groups in bars and cafés. He soon gained the title "King" in competition with other leading local cornetists. In 1918 he joined a New Orleans band playing in Chicago and by 1920 was leading his own group there. He toured with this band in California in 1921 and, returning to Chicago the next year, enlarged it as King Oliver's Creole Jazz Band. This handpicked ensemble boasted some of New Orleans's best black instrumentalists, including Johnny and "Baby" Dodds (clarinet and drums, respectively) and Oliver's brilliant young protégé, Louis Armstrong (second cornet). The Creole Band's beautifully drilled performances at Chicago's Lincoln Gardens and its tour through the Midwest created a sensation among northern musicians, and in 1923 it made the most extensive series of recordings (some three dozen) of any early jazz band.

When several members, including Armstrong, left the band in late 1924, Oliver formed a new, larger dance orchestra with saxophones, called the Dixie Syncopators. This sporadically successful orchestra, with changing personnel, played in Chicago from 1925 to 1927 and at New York's Savoy Ballroom in 1927. Between 1926 and 1928 the orchestra made a number of recordings of uneven quality, though a few were popular hits. By 1930 Oliver's career as a soloist ended. From 1930 to 1936 he led a succession of small orchestras across the country, though a severe dental condition prevented him from playing. After 1936 he lived in Savannah with an ailing heart and spent his last year there running a fruit stand and working as a janitor in a pool hall. He died 8 April 1938.

One of the foremost first-generation New Orleans jazz cornetists, Oliver was a central figure in the transfer of ragtime and of the black blues and gospel song from nearby rural areas to the New Orleans urban band tradition. The recordings of his Creole Jazz Band are the best and most extensive documentation of how vocal blues and instrumental ragtime were fused by emerging jazz bands into a new music of distinctively black southern origins.

John Joyce
Tulane University

Frederic Ramsey, Jr., in *Jazzmen*, ed. Frederic Ramsey, Jr., and Charles E. Smith (1939); Martin Williams, *King Oliver* (1960); Lawrence Gushee, in *Jazz Panorama*, ed. Martin Williams (1962). ☆

PARSONS, GRAM

(1946–1973) Rock singer.

Born 5 November 1946 in Winterhaven, Fla., Gram Parsons was one of the most influential popular musicians of his generation. A devoted follower of Elvis Presley as a teenager, Parsons performed with rock-and-roll bands from 1959 until 1963, when he joined an urban folk music group, the Shilos.

After briefly attending Harvard in 1965, he joined the International Submarine Band and began drawing upon his southern background in an early attempt to synthesize country and rock. Beginning in the mid-1960s, Parsons devoted himself to what he called "cosmic American music"—essentially a dynamic combination of southern-derived styles with a solid country core.

The International Submarine Band dissolved in 1967, just prior to the release of *Safe at Home*, arguably the first complete country-rock album. In 1968 Parsons joined the popular folk-rock group the Byrds, and, in tandem with longtime member Chris Hillman, led the band in the direction of country music. The Byrds' *Sweetheart of the Rodeo*, released in 1969, was a landmark in the evolution of country rock. It also featured one of Parsons's finest compositions, "Hickory Wind," an evocative tribute to his southern childhood.

Both Parsons and Hillman went on to organize what became the definitive country-rock band, the Flying Burrito Brothers. As a Burrito, Parsons began to deepen his vision of the South, which had first emerged with "Hickory Wind." In his songs as well as his lifestyle, Parsons often portrayed himself as a southern country boy set adrift in the contemporary urban maelstrom. His finest song, "Sin City" (1969), was the classic statement of this theme.

After leaving the Burritos in 1970, Parsons produced little significant work until the release of his first solo album, *GP*, in 1973. The album featured Emmylou Harris on vocals and confirmed his mastery of the country-rock idiom. Throughout the album, the South was portrayed as an almost mythical land of stability and steadfastness.

On 19 September 1973 Gram Parsons died in Joshua Tree, Calif. An autopsy was inconclusive as to the cause of death. Several posthumous works, including *Grievous Angel* (1974), *Sleepless Nights* (1976), and *Gram Parsons and the Fallen Angels—Live 1973* (1982), attest to his exceptional gifts as a singer and songwriter. Much of his work continues to inform contemporary popular music, especially in the country field. The principal carrier of his legacy in the 1980s is his former partner, Emmylou Harris.

> Stephen R. Tucker
> Tulane University

Richard Cusick, *Goldmine* (September 1982); Sid Griffin, *Nashville Gazette* (April–June 1980); Judson Klinger and Greg Mitchell, *Crawdaddy* (October 1976). ☆

PEER, RALPH
||||||||||||||||||||||||||||||||
(1892–1960) Music publisher and talent scout.

Although he was born in Kansas City, Mo. (22 May 1892), and although he

never expressed a great fondness for southern folk music, Ralph Sylvester Peer became the single most important entrepreneur for country and blues recordings. He discovered, or was instrumental in the careers of, dozens of southern artists, both black and white, including Louis Armstrong, the Memphis Jug Band, Jimmie Rodgers, the Carter Family, Mamie Smith, the Georgia Yellow Hammers, Fiddlin' John Carson, Ernest Stoneman, Grayson and Whitter (with their initial recording of the murder ballad "Tom Dooley"), the Reverend J. M. Gates (one of the first black preachers to record extensively), the Reverend Andrew Jenkins (a prolific "event song" composer of items like "The Death of Floyd Collins"), and Gene Autry (who began as an imitator of Jimmie Rodgers). He initiated the practice of bringing recording crews into the South to document black and white folk music; he created the idea of having "blues" and "hillbilly" numerical series on commercial phonograph records; he was one of the first to publish and copyright country and blues songs; and he became in the 1930s and 1940s an innovative and trend-setting publisher of international reputation.

Peer's father was a Columbia Record Company phonograph dealer in Independence, Mo., and by the time he was 20, Ralph Peer was working full time in the retail record business. By 1920 he was in New York working for the Okeh Record Company (actually the General Phonograph Corporation), then one of the smaller of the record companies and one looking for ways to get an edge on their bigger competitors. They found one when, on 10 August 1920, Peer recorded black Cincinnati vaudeville performer Mamie Smith singing "Crazy Blues," a composition by a

Georgia native named Perry Bradford. The record sold 7,500 copies a week after its release and became the first in a long line of commercial recordings of blues by black artists. Three years later, in June 1923, Peer stumbled into a similar discovery for white folk music; on a field trip to Atlanta he recorded a mill-hand and radio personality named Fiddlin' John Carson. Peer thought Carson's singing was "pluperfect awful" but agreed to release his rendition of "The Little Old Log Cabin in the Lane," an 1871 pop song by Will Hays. It duplicated the success of "Crazy Blues," and soon Peer had initiated an "old-time music" record series on Okeh to parallel its blues series.

From 1923 to 1932 Peer made dozens of trips into southern cities such as Dallas, El Paso, Nashville, Memphis, Atlanta, New Orleans, Charlotte, Bristol, and others seeking out and recording on the spot hundreds of blues, gospel, jazz, country, Cajun, and Tex-Mex performers. On one such trip, to the Virginia-Tennessee border town of Bristol in August 1927, he discovered two acts that were to become cornerstones for commercial country music—the Carter Family and "blue yodeler" Jimmie Rodgers.

Dominating all of this, though, was Peer's unusual interest in both black and white music, and his perception of ways in which the two could mutually influence each other. He theorized that both genres were just emerging from their vernacular regional base into the national limelight. He encouraged acts like the Allen Brothers, the Carolina Tar Heels, and Jimmie Rodgers to incorporate blues into their music, and felt that this was one of the reasons that Rodgers enjoyed a wider national appeal than did the Carters.

In 1925 Peer left the Okeh Company and went to work for the Victor Company, trading his huge Okeh salary for more modest gains but an additional incentive: the right to control the copyrights on the new song materials recorded by his artists. Peer began to look for artists who could create original material that he could copyright for them and place in his newly formed Southern Music Publishing Company (1928); such artists would get payment not only for records but for song performance rights as well. The increased emphasis on new material encouraged many blues and part-time country singers to become professionals and prompted the music as a whole to become more commercialized. And throughout the 1930s and 1940s he continued to build a publishing empire (which exists today as one of the country's largest, the Peer-Southern organization) and to excel even at casual hobbies, such as horticulture, for which he received a gold medal for his important work. Though in later years he expressed disdain for the country and blues artists he developed ("I've tried so hard to forget them," he told a reporter), and though some of his artists felt that he had exploited them, Peer laid the foundation for the commercialization of American vernacular music and thrust the rich southern folk music tradition into the mainstream of American popular music.

See also INDUSTRY: / Music Industry

Charles K. Wolfe
Middle Tennessee State University

Nolan Porterfield, *Journal of Country Music* (December 1978); Charles K. Wolfe, in *The Illustrated History of Country Music*, ed. Patrick Carr (1979). ☆

PENNIMAN, RICHARD (LITTLE RICHARD)

|||||||||||||||||||||||||||||||||||||||||||||||||

(b. 1933) Rock-and-roll singer.

Born into a large black family in Macon, Ga., on 5 December 1933, Penniman adopted his nickname, Little Richard, about age eight when he began singing at church and school functions. In his early teens Little Richard was performing on the road all across the South. He sang in minstrel shows, attracting audiences and selling snake oil. He sang the blues in bands following migrant workers as far afield as Lake Okeechobee in Florida, and he journeyed into cities to find gay clubs, where he played Princess Lavonne in the first of his several transvestite acts. Before he was 20 he had recorded, with little profit, for RCA twice and for Peacock Records once. These songs were conventional jump blues that made him sound like a melancholy Dinah Washington.

Success came in New Orleans in September 1955 when he joined Robert "Bumps" Blackwell on Specialty Records and made "Tutti Frutti," one of the first and most important rock records. "Tutti Frutti" was a sublimated version of a bawdy song he had performed in sideshows for years but had never considered recordable. He and Blackwell then followed with a series of influential rock-and-roll hits. "Miss Ann" was about loving a white woman and included a 500-year-old rhyming folk riddle from the English oral tradition. "Long Tall Sally," backed with "Slippin' and Slidin'," narrated the antics of standard black folk figures such as John and Aunt Mary, along with more contemporary ones like Sally, who was "built for speed." "Keep a-Knockin'" and "Good Golly Miss Molly" emerged from the randy lore of prostitutes, circuses,

and after-hours clubs and was reshaped as pop and teen lore—as when he purred to Molly, "when you rock 'n' roll, can't hear your mother call."

By 1957, however, Little Richard was called away from rock and roll, entered Bible school, and began preaching. Since then he has made several attempts to return to the world of rock and roll that he helped create, and his performance as a rock-and-roll singer in the 1986 movie *Down and Out in Beverly Hills* brought good reviews and new attention. Nevertheless, he has not regained the power he had in the mid-1950s to mine the underground lore of the American South and fix it in an iconic style for the international youth culture.

W. T. Lhamon, Jr.
Florida State University

W. T. Lhamon, Jr., *Studies in Popular Culture* (1985); Charles White, *The Life and Times of Little Richard: The Quasar of Rock* (1984); Langdon Winner, in *The Rolling Stone Illustrated History of Rock 'n' Roll*, ed. Jim Miller (1976). ☆

POWELL, JOHN

|||||||||||||||||||||||||||||||||||||||||||

(1882–1963) Musician and composer.

Powell was born in Richmond, Va., where his father, a schoolteacher, and his mother, an amateur musician, provided his primary musical education at home. He then studied music with his sister and piano and harmony with F. C. Hahr, a one-time student of Liszt. After receiving his B.A. from the University of Virginia in 1901, he studied piano with Theodor Leschetizky in Vienna (1902–7). There he also was a student of composition with Carl Navratil

(1904–7). Powell made his debut as a pianist in Berlin in 1907. After four years of giving concerts in Europe, he returned to the United States, touring the country as a pianist and playing some of his own works. He continued to perform for many years in leading cities of Europe and America.

Powell composed many orchestral works, arrangements of folksongs, and choral settings; he also wrote three piano sonatas, one violin concerto, two piano concertos, and an opera, *Judith and Holofernes*. His other works include *Rhapsodie Negre* (piano and orchestra), 1918; *Sonata Virginianesque* (violin and piano), 1919; *In Old Virginia* (overture), 1921; *At the Fair* (suite for piano, also for orchestra), 1925; *Natchez on the Hill* (three country dances for orchestra), 1932; *A Set of Three* (orchestra), 1935; and *Symphony in A* (orchestra), 1947.

One of Powell's most important achievements lies in the area of ethnomusicology. A methodical collector of the South's rural songs, he was the founder of the Virginia State Choral Festival and the moving spirit behind the annual White Top Mountain Folk Music Festival. A member of the National Institute of Arts and Letters, Powell was honored by his native state when Governor John S. Battle designated 5 November 1951 as John Powell Day. Powell died in Charlottesville, Va., in 1963.

For the most part, southerners have contented themselves with inherited music, folksongs, and contemporary tunes. Apart from John Powell of Virginia, southern composers have remained virtually unknown except to other musicians. During the first half of the 20th century, however, Powell received national recognition and acclaim not only as a virtuoso performer of the classical repertoire at home and abroad but also as a composer of distinctively American music. Although Powell utilized Afro-American elements in his *Rhapsodie Negre* and *Sonata Virginianesque*, his abiding concern was with the cultivation of Anglo-American folk music, of which there existed a rich heritage in the South. His Virginian antecedents and environment had given him a profound sense of intimacy with the founders of the American nation.

Powell felt strongly about the value of those Anglo-Saxon cultural and ethical forces that he believed had motivated the molders of the American past; he wished to preserve them for future generations and insure the persistence of those Anglo-Saxon ideals that he regarded as characteristically American. By the early 1920s patient research and study had convinced Powell that American folk music derived from Anglo-Saxon sources was of fundamental importance to the cultural life of the United States and to the development of a truly national school of American music.

L. Moody Simms, Jr.
Illinois State University

Daniel Gregory Mason, *Music in My Time, and Other Reminiscences* (1983); L. Moody Simms, Jr., *Journal of Popular Culture* (Winter 1973). ☆

PRESERVATION HALL

This New Orleans institution celebrates the emergence of jazz as a popular musical innovation in the South. Philadelphians Allan and Sandra Jaffe founded the hall in the early 1960s at the suggestion of (and in property owned by) artist Larry Borenstein. Endeavoring to revitalize the roots of jazz, it has supported a resurgence of interest and activity in classic New Orleans jazz.

At its outset Preservation Hall provided a stage for fine old black jazz musicians who were unemployed. It also resuscitated a nearly extinct institution of musical life in the Crescent City—the community hall. Figures of the New Orleans revival such as George Lewis, Jim Robinson, and Alvin Alcorn took up musical residence there. Repeatedly throughout the past quarter of a century, classic jazz musicians of the city looked to Preservation Hall to renew the old idiom.

Like Perseverance Hall and San Jacinto Hall before it, Preservation Hall serves a total community. It addresses social and economic problems as well as cultural needs of the city's jazz people. The preservationist impulse itself accounts for the fundamental contribution of Preservation Hall. In an effort to preserve jazz, the Jaffes and their associates have recycled it, establishing for a new era the classic jazz aesthetic. The hall has in fact reinvented and revitalized its community for the future by reaching decisively into the past.

Preservation Hall has succeeded by combining imported, updated marketing techniques with an abiding appreciation for local, traditional lifeways. Its success rests in large part upon the generous life support it has provided to old jazz greats. Preservation Hall emerged as part of a national folk revival in the 1950s and 1960s, and its activities have sought from the beginning to underscore the primal claim to jazz of black Americans.

Curtis D. Jerde
W. R. Hogan Jazz Archive
Tulane University

Jason Berry, Jonathan Forse, and Tad Jones, *Up from the Cradle of Jazz: New Orleans Music since World War II* (1987); Al Rose and Edmond Souchon, *New Orleans Jazz: A Family Album* (1967; rev. ed., 1978). ☆

PRESLEY, ELVIS

(1935–1977) Rock-and-roll singer.

Presley is probably the most famous southerner of the 20th century. Born in Tupelo, Miss., and reared in Memphis in near poverty, he became an international celebrity and one of the wealthiest entertainers in history.

In 1954 Presley made his first recordings for Sam Phillips's Memphis-based Sun Records in a style that drew from diverse sources—gospel (black and white), blues (rural and urban), and country. In effect, he and his band forged a dynamic new musical synthesis, which later became known as "rockabilly." In 1955, after joining the Louisiana Hayride, a popular country

Elvis Presley, the "King of Rock and Roll," age 22, 1957

show broadcast from Shreveport, Presley toured extensively throughout the South and acquired a vast and fervent following. National recognition came in 1956 with the success of his first RCA Victor release, "Heartbreak Hotel," a series of network television appearances, and a movie, *Love Me Tender.* He was often the subject of controversy, both for his frantic performances and his conspicuous adoption of black-derived material and musical styles.

From 1956 to 1966, including his celebrated stint in the army (1958–60), Presley dominated popular music. After a brief decline in popularity during the mid-1960s, he began a sustained comeback in 1968 and 1969 with an acclaimed television special and a return to live performances for the first time since 1961.

In the 1970s Presley again became a major figure in American popular culture. As the decade progressed, he often returned to the southern-rooted material and styles of his youth. Songs like "Amazing Grace" (1971), "Promised Land" (1973), and especially "American Trilogy" (1972) dramatized and reiterated Presley's affinity for the South.

His death in 1977 and the subsequent outpouring of public interest in his life and music served to expose the many tensions and contradictions in southern culture, which he had so vividly symbolized. He was insolent yet courteous; narcissistic yet humble; pious (reflecting the Pentecostalism of his childhood) yet often hedonistic, especially in his final years; extremely wealthy yet ever conscious of his poor origins; his diet, accent, name, and most of all, his music, remained indelibly southern. His Memphis home, Graceland (open to the public since 1982), one of the most popular tourist attractions in the South, is an enduring reminder of the quintessentially southern character of Elvis Presley.

Stephen R. Tucker
Tulane University

Greil Marcus, *Mystery Train: Images of America in Rock 'n' Roll Music* (rev. ed., 1982); Dave Marsh, *Elvis* (1982); Jac Tharpe, ed., *Elvis: Images and Fancies* (1979). ☆

PRICE, LEONTYNE
(b. 1927) Grand opera and concert singer.

Leontyne Price was born in Laurel, Miss., where she grew up playing the piano and singing in the church choir. She graduated from Oak Park High School in 1944 and Wilberforce College in Ohio four years later. She then attended Juilliard School of Music on a scholarship, with financial aid from the Alexander F. Chisholm family of Laurel. Virgil Thomson selected her to sing the role of Saint Cecilia in a revival of his *Four Saints in Three Acts* on Broadway and at the 1952 International Arts Festival in Paris. After an audition with Ira Gershwin she won the female lead in an important revival of *Porgy and Bess* opposite William Warfield, playing to packed houses from June 1952 until June 1954 on Broadway and a world tour. Composer Samuel Barber asked her in 1953 to sing the premiere of his *Hermit Songs* at the Library of Congress, and in 1954 she gave a Town Hall recital to enthusiastic reviews.

The NBC Opera Theater's production of *Tosca* in January 1955 marked her professional debut in grand opera, although her first performance in a major opera house came two years later in San Francisco, as Madame Lidoine in Poulenc's *Dialogues of the Carmelites*. In succeeding seasons she returned to San Francisco to interpret the title role of Verdi's *Aïda*, Donna Elvira in *Don Giovanni*, Leonora in *Il Trovatore*, the lead in the American premiere of Carl Orff's *The Wise Maiden*, Cio-Cio-San in *Madame Butterfly*, Amelia in *Un Ballo in Maschera*, Leonora in *La Forza del Destino*, Giorgetta in *Il Tabarro*, and the title role of Richard Strauss's *Ariadne auf Naxos*. With the Lyric Opera of Chicago she first sang Massenet's *Thaïs*, one of her few failures, and the role of Liù in Puccini's *Turandot*. She also appeared in Handel's *Julius Caesar* and Monteverdi's *Coronation of Poppea* in concert form with the American Opera Society.

Her Metropolitan Opera debut came on 27 January 1961, as Leonora in Verdi's *Il Trovatore*. In October of that year she became the first black to open a Metropolitan Opera season, appearing as Minnie in Puccini's *La Fanciulla del West*. She later sang Tatyana in *Eugene Onegin*, Pamina in *The Magic Flute*, and Fiordiligi in *Così Fan Tutte* at the Metropolitan, opening the new house at Lincoln Center in Samuel Barber's *Antony and Cleopatra*. She has performed with the Vienna State Opera, at the Royal Opera House in London, the Paris Opera, La Scala, the Verona Arena, the Berlin Opera, the Hamburg Opera, and Teatro Colon. In 1961 she sang recitals at the World's Fair in Brussels and she has given concerts throughout the world. She has recorded extensively, including American popular songs and black spirituals. Leontyne Price often returns to Laurel, Miss., and gave one of the first nonsegregated recitals there. She re-

tired after a final performance on 3 January 1985.

Ronald L. Davis
Southern Methodist University

Sir Rudolf Bing, *5000 Nights at the Opera* (1972); Arthur J. Bloomfield, *50 Years of the San Francisco Opera* (1972); Hugh Lee Lyon, *Leontyne Price: Highlights of a Prima Donna* (1973). ☆

PRIDE, CHARLEY

(b. 1938) Country singer.

A little over a decade after Jackie Robinson broke the color barrier in baseball, Charley Pride accomplished a similar feat in country music. Born in Sledge, Miss., in the depths of the Great Depression to a family of poor cotton laborers, Pride has not only opened new avenues of acceptance to minorities but has set high standards of excellence in the field of country music.

While many blacks in the Mississippi Delta were drawn to the blues, Pride was interested more in country music, especially the songs of Hank Williams. At night he would listen to country music radio programs, memorizing the words of their songs. The only member of his family with any musical inclination, Pride scraped up enough money when he was 14 to buy his first guitar, which he learned to play by listening to different picking styles. (Pride received only $3 per 100 pounds of cotton he picked with his 10 brothers and sisters.) When Pride left Mississippi three years later, he departed not to pursue a career in music but to try for athletic success through baseball.

Pride's luck with baseball was short-lived. After stints with the Memphis

Red Sox and Birmingham Black Barons, teams in the Negro American League, and two years in the army in the late 1950s, Pride eventually made it to the minor leagues, playing in 1960 for a team in Helena, Mont. Pride often sang between innings; the response he received from the venture encouraged him to sing more. Through his landlady in Helena, he found his first musical break, singing in a local country bar. Still hungry to play major league baseball, Pride earned a tryout in 1961 from the California Angels. Unable to make the team, he returned to Helena, where he then worked for a refining plant and sang in area nightclubs. The nightclub performances led to an invitation from Red Sovine in 1963 to do a recording audition in Nashville. Pride auditioned in Nashville for Chet Atkins the following year and signed with RCA Victor after the session.

Since 1965, when he recorded his first hit single, "Snakes Crawl at Night," he has accumulated numerous gold records and country music awards. His first album, *Country Charley Pride* (1966), garnered the 1967 Most Promising Male

Artist Award from the Country Song Roundup. (Fearing the album would not sell well in the racially torn South, RCA released *Country Charley Pride* without Pride's picture on the cover.) In 1971 and 1972 he was named Male Vocalist of the Year by the Country Music Association. During the same period he released six albums that became gold and received three Grammy Awards, the first for Best Sacred Performance ("Did You Think to Pray"), the second for Best Gospel Performance ("Let Me Live"), and a third for Best Country Vocal, Male (*Charley Pride Sings Heart Songs*). *Billboard* gave its Trendsetter Award to Pride in 1970. In 1976 he received *Photoplay*'s Gold Medal Award, and in 1980 *Cash Box* named him its Top Male Country Artist of the Decade.

Pride's gold albums include *Country Charley Pride* (1966), *The Country Way* (1968), *Just Plain Charley* (1970), *Charley Pride 10th Album* (1970), *Charley Pride Sings Heart Songs* (1971), *Did You Think to Pray* (1971), and *The Best of Charley Pride, Vol. 2* (1972). Other top albums recorded by Pride are *Charley* (1975), *I'm Just Me* (1977), *You're My Jamaica* (1979), and *There's a Little Bit of Hank in Me* (1980). Over the past three decades he has released gold and top-10 singles such as "I Know One" (1967), "Does My Ring Hurt Your Finger" (1967), "Let Me Live" (1971), "Did You Think to Pray" (1971), "Amazing Love" (1973), "We Could" (1974), "I Got a Lot of Hank in Me" (1980), "Roll on Mississippi" (1981), and "Never Been So Loved" (1981).

Elizabeth McGehee
Salem College

Charley Pride, country music star, 1980s

Melvin Shestack, *The Country Music Encyclopedia* (1974); Irwin Stambler and Grellin Landon, *The Encyclopedia of Folk, Country and Western Music* (1969; 2d ed., 1983); *Who's Who among Americans* (1982); *Who's Who among Black Americans* (1975). ☆

REDDING, OTIS
||||||||||||||||||||||||||||||||||||||||||
(1941–1967) Soul singer.

Otis Redding epitomized the sound of soul music in the South in the 1960s. The "Big O," as he came to be known, was born in 1941 in Dawson, Ga., and was raised in nearby Macon, one of six children of a Baptist minister. Singing in church throughout his youth, Redding became increasingly fascinated by the rhythm-and-blues and rock-and-roll sounds to be heard on Macon radio, especially those of local luminary Little Richard, the Georgia Peach.

By 1956 Redding was playing locally with Johnny Jenkins and the Pinetoppers; by 1957 he was managed by Phil Walden (later of Allman Brothers and Capricorn Records fame); by 1958 he was married; and by 1960 he had cut his first single, "Shout Bamalama" for Bethlehem Records. The single revealed an exciting singer who had yet to grow beyond Little Richard imitation.

Deciding to try his luck elsewhere, Redding moved to California. He spent six months washing cars and recording two more singles, one for Finer Arts, the other for Alshire, both of which flopped. Back in Macon, Redding hooked up with guitarist Jenkins once again. The latter attracted the attention of Atlantic Records through a local hit entitled "Love Twist." Atlantic arranged for Jenkins to record at the still largely unknown Stax Studio in Memphis in 1962, and Redding was able to record "These Arms of Mine" and "Hey, Hey

Baby" at the end of the session. Jenkins's material remains unissued; Redding's recording became his first single and launched a career that was to end on 10 December 1967 when his plane, en route from Cleveland, Ohio, to Madison, Wis., plunged into Lake Minona. All the original members of his band, the Bar Kays, died in the crash with Redding save Ben Cauley and James Alexander. His funeral, held nine days later in Macon, was attended by 6,000 fans and a who's who of soul musicians and singers. He was survived by his wife Zelma and their three children.

Between 1962 and 1967 Redding recorded prolifically. He was able to adapt to almost any material, recording songs as diverse as Bing Crosby's "Try a Little Tenderness" and the Rolling Stones' "Satisfaction," as well as a host of originals that are now standards such as "Respect" and "I've Been Loving You Too Long." In contrast with many of the soul singers of the period, Redding was equally at home with ballads and up-tempo dance numbers. Many of the original compositions were co-written with Steve Cropper, the guitarist for the Stax house band Booker T. and the MG's. Cropper also produced Redding's records and, on most of these, the MG's coupled with the Bar Kays' horns provided the backup. Cropper was white, as were half of the Stax session musicians. This relatively rare musical integration was a large factor in making southern soul from Memphis and Muscle Shoals, Ala., so distinctive in the 1960s.

Redding's single style was immediately recognizable. His voice had a "catch" to it, and he was a master of timbral and dynamic variation and of rhythmic subtlety. In contrast to most soul performers, Redding never employed backup vocalists on his record-ings. A typical record such as "Try a Little Tenderness" continually adds in-struments as it progresses, with every-one gradually playing louder while the rate of activity increases, Redding's voice becomes strained, the plane of sound gradually shifts upward, the amount of call and responses increases, and, finally, the tension is released through a syncopated drum break over which Redding is so emotionally charged that he is reduced to singing vocables.

Live, Redding was the classic soul performer. He was always in action, continually sweating, discarding super-fluous clothes as the performance went on. He generally used Booker T. and the MG's or the Bar Kays as a backup band, but, as with the material, the type or quality of band did not really affect him.

He toured extensively from 1964 to 1967, achieving 17 hits on the rhythm-and-blues charts in the process (seven more Otis Redding records hit after his death). He had formed his own label, Jotis, recording Billy Young, Loretta Williams, and Arthur Conley, and he had also developed his own publishing company, Redwal Music. Redding was successful in Europe and was just start-ing to break through to the American white audience at the time of his death. Six months prior to that he had had a widely successful performance at the Monterey Pop Festival, and the song he was working on at the time of his death, "(Sittin on) The Dock of the Bay," iron-ically became his first number-one hit. It reflected a somewhat softer sound and, perhaps, indicated a new direc-tion.

Robert Bowman
Memphis, Tennessee

Clive Anderson, in *The Soul Book*, ed. Ian Hoare (1975); Gerri Hirshey, *Nowhere to Run: The Story of Soul Music* (1984); Jane Schiesel, *The Otis Redding Story* (1973). ☆

REVIVAL SONGS

The poetry and music of revivalism have been a major influence in American popular culture, especially in the South. In the first camp meetings around 1800, preachers found the psalms and hymns of congregational worship inadequate: traditional hymns did not sufficiently emphasize the individual's quest for sal-vation through specific stages (convic-tion, conversion, assurance) recognized by revival preachers; moreover, hymn-books were of little use in largely illit-erate gatherings, often held at night. In response to the camp-meeting environ-ment, Americans created two major forms of popular religious song during the period from 1810 to 1860.

"Camp-meeting songs," or "spiritual songs," were strophic poems, often in narrative form, stressing the stages of conversion and often referring to various groups at camp meetings: preachers, ex-horters, mourners, backsliders, and young converts, as in the following stanza from George Atkin's "Holy Manna":

Is there here a trembling jailer,
Seeking grace, and fill'd with fears?
Is there here a weeping Mary,
Pouring forth a flood of tears?
Brethren, join your cries to help them;
Sisters, let your prayers abound;
Pray, O pray that holy manna
May be scatter'd all around.

Written in a great variety of poetic meters, these songs were often set to secular tunes, including those of folksongs, traditional dances, military marches, and popular theater airs.

"Revival spiritual songs," or "choruses," consisted of couplets or quatrains, often taken from British evangelical hymnody, alternating with refrains:

On Jordan's stormy banks I stand,
And cast a wishful eye,
To Canaan's fair and happy land,
Where my possessions lie. [Samuel
  Stennant]
CHORUS: I am bound for the prom-
       ised land,
       I'm bound for the promised
       land,
       Oh, who will come and go
       with me?
       I am bound for the prom-
       ised land.

Often elements of the revival chorus appear between the lines of the original hymn:

I know that my redeemer lives,
    Glory, hallelujah.
What comfort that sweet sentence gives,
[Samuel Medley]
    Glory, hallelujah,
CHORUS: Shout on, pray on, we're get-
    ting ground,
       Glory, hallelujah,
       The dead's alive, and the lost
       is found.
       Glory, hallelujah.

Revival spiritual songs, with their call-and-response patterns, met the need for a flexible format in which new songs could be created and learned immediately by a large gathering.

Camp-meeting songsters, books containing revival poetry, were first published around 1810. The first southern collection of music for camp-meeting songs was Ananias Davisson's *Supplement to the Kentucky Harmony* (Harrisonburg, Va., 1820). Davisson's book, designed for "his Methodist friends," contained many camp-meeting songs and a few revival choruses. During the 1840s the music of many more revival spiritual songs was printed in southern tunebooks, including B. F. White and E. J. King's *The Sacred Harp* (1844) and William Houser's *The Hesperian Harp* (1848). After the Civil War, the black spiritual emerged, essentially the same as the revival spiritual, despite differences in the date and circumstances of its notation. Indeed, the prevalence of call-and-response forms in Afro-American music and the presence of blacks at early camp meetings suggest that mutual influences may have played a role in the spiritual song traditions of both races.

The revival movements of the late 19th century favored a new style of music based on urban models, especially the sentimental parlor song. "Gospel hymns" like "Sweet By and By" (S. F. Bennett and J. P. Webster) and "Leaning on the Everlasting Arms" (E. A. Hoffman and A. J. Showalter) have reached beyond the revival context. Many have entered the Sunday worship of southern denominations, where they are considered "old standard" hymns, to the virtual exclusion of the camp-meeting genres that preceded them. Late 19th-century gospel hymns were also the model for the flourishing repertoire of shape-note gospel convention and quartet music.

David Warren Steel
University of Mississippi

Dickson D. Bruce, Jr., *And They All Sang Hallelujah: Plain-Folk Camp-Meeting Religion, 1800–1845* (1974); George Pullen Jackson, *White Spirituals in the Southern Uplands* (1933); Ellen Jane Lorenz, *Glory, Hallelujah! The Story of the Camp-meeting Spiritual* (1978). ☆

RODGERS, JIMMIE
||||||||||||||||||||||||||||||||||||||||||
(1897–1933) Country singer.

Generally acknowledged as "The Father of Country Music," James Charles "Jimmie" Rodgers, who was born 8 September 1897 in Meridian, Miss., was a major influence on the emerging "hillbilly" recording industry almost from the time of his first records in 1927. Although Rodgers initially conceived of himself in broader terms, singing Tin Pan Alley hits and popular standards, his intrinsic musical talent was deeply rooted in the rural southern environment out of which he came, as seen in the titles of many of his songs: "My Carolina Sunshine Girl," "My Little Old Home

Jimmie Rodgers, the "Father of Country Music," 1929

Down in New Orleans," "Dear Old Sunny South by the Sea," "Mississippi River Blues," "Peach Pickin' Time Down in Georgia," "Memphis Yodel," "In the Hills of Tennessee," the original "Blue Yodel" ("T for Texas"), and others.

In adapting the black country blues of his native South to the nascent patterns of commercial hillbilly music of the day, Rodgers created a unique new form—the famous "blue yodel"—which led the way to further innovations in style and subject matter and exerted a lasting influence on country music as both art form and industry. Through the force of his magnetic personality and showmanship, Rodgers almost single-handedly established the role of the singing star, influencing such later performers as Gene Autry, Hank Williams, Ernest Tubb, George Jones, and Willie Nelson.

The son of a track foreman for the Mobile & Ohio Railroad, Rodgers in his twenties worked as a brakeman for many railroads in the South and West. Stricken by tuberculosis in 1924, he left the rails soon after to pursue his childhood dream of becoming a professional entertainer. After several years of hard knocks and failure, he gained an audition with Ralph Peer, an independent producer who had set up a temporary recording studio in Bristol, Tenn., for the Victor Talking Machine Company (later RCA Victor). There, on 4 August 1927, Rodgers made his first recordings. Within a year he reached national popularity and received billing as "The Singing Brakeman" and "America's Blue Yodeler." In 1929 he built a home in the resort town of Kerrville, Tex., and moved there in an effort to restore his failing health. The onset of the Depression and increasing illness further slowed the progress of his career, but throughout the early 1930s he continued to record and perform with touring stage shows. By the time of his death in New York City at 35 in May 1933, he had recorded 110 titles, representing a diverse repertoire that included almost every type of song now identified with country music: love ballads, honky-tonk tunes, railroad and hobo songs, cowboy songs, novelty numbers, and the series of 13 blue yodels. In November 1961 Rodgers became the first performer elected to Nashville's Country Music Hall of Fame, immortalized as "the man who started it all."

Nolan Porterfield
Cape Girardeau, Missouri

Bill C. Malone, *Country Music, U.S.A.: A Fifty-year History* (1968); Nolan Porterfield, *Jimmie Rodgers: The Life and Times of America's Blue Yodeler* (1979); Mrs. Jimmie Rodgers, *My Husband, Jimmie Rodgers* (1975). ☆

SCRUGGS, EARL

(b. 1924) Bluegrass musician.

Earl Eugene Scruggs was born on 6 January 1924, in Cleveland County, N.C., on a farm near the small community of Flint Hill. He was the youngest of five children. His father, who played the banjo, died when Scruggs was four; his mother, brothers, and sisters all played music. By the time he was six he was playing string band music with his brothers. Scruggs learned fiddle and guitar but specialized in the five-string banjo. Before he was a teenager he had developed a distinctive three-finger picking style based on that of older men in his neighborhood. In his teens Scruggs played locally with professional

bands, but World War II put a temporary end to this; he worked in a textile mill until 1945. In December 1945 he became a member of Bill Monroe's Blue Grass Boys on WSM's Grand Ole Opry. In personal appearances and recordings with Monroe, Scruggs created a sensation with his banjo playing, and he quickly became one of the most emulated instrumentalists in country music.

In 1948 Scruggs left Monroe and teamed up with his partner in the Blue Grass Boys, guitarist-singer Lester Flatt, to form the Foggy Mountain Boys. In 1953, after modest beginnings on small radio stations, their broadcast career was given a considerable boost by the sponsorship of a flour manufacturer, Martha White Mills. In 1955 they joined the cast of the Grand Ole Opry, where they became one of its most popular and widely traveled acts. During the late 1950s they were responsible for popularizing "bluegrass" with folk music audiences outside the South. Their greatest exposure came through their association in 1962 with the popular CBS television series *The Beverly Hillbillies*, for which they recorded the theme and incidental music. Many of their Mercury (1948–50) and Columbia (1951–69) recordings are still available. A key figure in the success of Flatt and Scruggs was Earl's wife, Louise Certain Scruggs, who acted as the band's booking agent and publicist, a role she still performs for her husband.

In 1969 Scruggs and Flatt separated. Earl began performing with sons Gary and Randy, and by 1972 they had organized as the Earl Scruggs Revue. With his banjo amplified, Earl fronted a band that featured country-rock repertoire and sound. The Revue (which eventually included another son, Steve) toured successfully throughout the

1970s, playing to younger, more urban audiences than those for which he and Flatt had performed. They recorded 16 albums for Columbia. By 1980 Scruggs was working as a single act, recording and appearing with various musicians, including the Dillards, Tom T. Hall, and Ricky Skaggs.

In 1971 Scruggs was closely involved with the conception and production of the award-winning album *Will the Circle Be Unbroken* (United Artists UAS 9801), which brought together members of the California rock group the Nitty Gritty Dirt Band with pioneer Nashville musicians. In this and other activities he has shown an interest in bridging the social and musical gaps between the rural South of his youth and the urbanized world of his sons.

Neil V. Rosenberg
Memorial University
St. Johns, Newfoundland

Neil V. Rosenberg, *Bluegrass: A History* (1985), in *Stars of Country Music*, ed. Bill C. Malone and Judith McCullough (1975); Earl Scruggs, *Earl Scruggs and the 5-String Banjo* (1968). ☆

SHAPE-NOTE SINGING SCHOOLS

The singing school was early America's most important musical institution. It offered a brief course in musical sight reading and choral singing, was taught by a singing master according to traditional methods, and used tunebooks that were printed manuals containing instructions, exercises, and sacred choral music. Singing schools arose from British antecedents around 1700 as part of an effort to reform congregational sing-

ing in colonial churches. In New England the movement grew quickly and culminated in the first school of American composers and in the publication of hundreds of sacred tunebooks (1770–1810). Singing schools existed in the South as early as 1710, when they are mentioned in the diary of William Byrd II of Virginia. The movement spread during the 18th century as a pious diversion among affluent planters along the Atlantic Seaboard. After the Revolutionary War, itinerant Yankee singing masters established singing schools in the inland and rural South. Both Andrew Law (1749–1821) of Connecticut and Lucius Chapin (1760–1842) of Massachusetts were teaching in Virginia by the 1780s; in 1794 Chapin moved to Kentucky, where he taught for 40 years. Singing schools offered young southerners a rare chance to socialize. Even today, many older southerners associate singing schools with their courting days.

The spread of singing schools through the South was aided by the invention of shape or patent notes. This system, first published by William Little and William Smith in *The Easy Instructor* (Philadelphia, 1801), used four distinctive note heads to indicate the four syllables denoting tones of a musical scale (*fa, sol, la* and *mi*) then employed in vocal instruction, making unnecessary the pupil's need to learn and memorize key signatures. Denounced by critics as uncouth, the simplified notation caught on in the South and West, where it became standard for sacred-music publication. In 1816 Ananias Davisson (1780–1857) and Joseph Funk (1777–1862), both of Rockingham County, Va., became the first southern singing masters to compile and publish their own tunebooks. By 1860 more than 30 sacred tunebooks, all in shape notes, had been compiled by southerners, although many of these were printed outside the South at Cincinnati or Philadelphia. One of the most popular of these was *The Southern Harmony*, by William Walker of Spartanburg, S.C.: 600,000 copies were sold between 1835 and the beginning of the Civil War. *The Sacred Harp* (1844), by Georgia singing masters B. F. White and E. J. King, is still in print and is the basis of a flourishing musical tradition in six southern states.

Southern singing masters continued to teach the music of their Yankee predecessors but also introduced "folk hymns," melodies from oral tradition which they harmonized in a native idiom and set to sacred words. Many, including tunes for "Amazing Grace" and "How Firm a Foundation," have remained popular and have become symbols of rural southern religion. Camp-meeting and revival songs with new refrains also formed part of the southern tunebook repertoire, especially after 1840. Southern singing masters established organizations such as the Southern Musical Association (1845) and the Chattahoochie Musical Association (1852, still active). These and other state and local conventions provided a forum where established teachers met to sing together, to examine and certify new teachers, and to demonstrate the accomplishments of their classes.

After the Civil War, singing schools and shape notes became increasingly identified with the South, while declining in popularity in other regions. Most teachers switched from the four-shape system to a seven-shape system to keep pace with new teaching methods. Leading singing masters established "normal schools" for the training of teachers. Periodicals such as *The Musical Million* (Dayton, Va., 1870–1915) helped to link teachers in many areas of the South. Small, cheap collections of music published every year began to supplant the large tunebooks with their fixed repertoire. Although folk hymns and revival songs continued to be published, gospel hymns derived from urban models entered the southern tradition.

In the 20th century singing schools have declined over most of the region, but have survived in a few areas. They seldom last more than two weeks of evening classes, and may be as brief as one week. Pupils pay at least a token fee, but few teachers, if any, attempt to make a living as singing masters. Contemporary singing schools fall into three categories: (1) "Tunebook" schools are associated with surviving 19th-century books such as *The Sacred Harp* or *The Christian Harmony*. These schools preserve much of the 18th-century American repertoire and performance practice. (2) Denominational schools are sponsored by churches, especially by those (Primitive Baptist, Church of Christ) that prohibit instrumental music in their worship. These schools use denominational hymnals, and, like their 18th-century predecessors, attempt to train skilled sight-readers for congregational singing. (3) Shape-note gospel singing schools are associated with the "little-book" seven-shape gospel repertoire. These schools, often sponsored by local singing conventions or by publishing companies, have declined since mid-century as community "sings" have been replaced by quartet performances. All three types of singing schools are regarded by their adherents as important means of transmitting musical knowledge, skills, and traditions to future generations.

David Warren Steel
University of Mississippi

Buell E. Cobb, Jr., *The Sacred Harp: A Tradition and Its Music* (1978); Harry Eskew, "Shape-Note Hymnody in the Shenandoah Valley, 1816–1860" (Ph.D. dissertation, Tulane University, 1966); George Pullen Jackson, *White Spirituals in the Southern Uplands* (1933). ☆

SMITH, BESSIE
||||||||||||||||||||||||||||||||||||||||||||
(1894–1937) Blues singer.

When Bessie Smith made her first recordings, in 1923, she carved for herself a permanent niche in blues and jazz history. By that time, her magnificent voice, captured by the relatively primitive acoustical equipment of the day, was already well known and greatly admired throughout the South.

Born in Chattanooga, Tenn., 15 April 1894, Smith had her first show-business experience when she was about eight: accompanied by her brother Andrew with his guitar, she danced and sang for small change on a Ninth Street corner. Another brother, Clarence, in 1912 arranged for her to join a traveling troupe led by Moses Stokes. With this company, which also included Gertrude "Ma" Rainey, Bessie Smith launched her professional career.

Within a year Bessie Smith had left the Stokes troupe and started to build a faithful following among southern theater audiences, especially in Atlanta, where she became a regular attraction at the "81" Theater. In the 1920s, she rose to the pinnacle of her profession and became the highest-paid black entertainer of her day. So great was her popularity that her appearances caused serious traffic jams around theaters from Detroit to New Orleans. During eight years as an exclusive Columbia Records artist, she made 156 sides, some of which saved that company from bankruptcy, and all of which, over a half century later, are still in catalogs throughout the world.

Promotional hype dubbed her "Empress of the Blues," and the title remains unchallenged, but Bessie Smith was not restricted to that idiom. She was, along with Louis Armstrong, the consummate jazz singer, and her majestic delivery became a major inspiration to such successful and diverse singers as Billie Holiday, Mahalia Jackson, and Janis Joplin.

A victim of the Great Depression, new musical trends, and a changing entertainment scene, Bessie Smith saw her career plummet in the early 1930s, but it was on the upswing as the decade went into its last lap. Sadly, the great singer was not to enjoy the comeback that seemed inevitable in 1937, nor would she ever know the enormous impact of her artistry on American music. On 26 September 1937, as she traveled from Memphis for an appearance in Clarksdale, Miss., a car accident took her life. Her tragic death inspired contemporary playwright Edward Albee's drama, *The Death of Bessie Smith*.

Chris Albertson
New York, New York

Chris Albertson, *Bessie* (1972). ☆

STILL, WILLIAM GRANT
|||||||||||||||||||||||||||||||||||||||||||||||||||||||||||||
(1895–1978) Musician and composer.

Known as the "dean of Afro-American composers," Still spent more than 50 years composing, conducting, and playing music that reflected a fusion of his spiritual and musical imagination, his diverse ethnic ancestry, and 20th-century American culture.

His mother came from black, Spanish, Indian, and Irish stock and his father from black, Indian, and Scotch stock. Still was born on 11 May 1895, on a Woodville, Miss., plantation near the Mississippi River. He lived there only nine months before his father, a teacher and bandleader, died, and his mother moved the family to Little Rock, Ark., where she began teaching. When Still was nine, his mother married a postal clerk who entered Still's life with a Victrola and opera records. The voice of Still's maternal grandmother filled their home with spirituals. He later wrote, "I knew neither wealth nor poverty, for I lived in a comfortable middle class home."

Still left home to study at Wilberforce University. His mother wanted him to be a physician, but Still had already taught himself to play the violin and wanted to be a musician. He left Wilberforce for the navy during World War I, eventually returning, against his mother's wishes, to study music at Oberlin College. He worked as a young musician with W. C. Handy in Memphis and New York, played the oboe in Eubie Blake's band, and orchestrated for Paul Whiteman and Artie Shaw. In the 1920s he studied composition with George W. Chadwick at the New England Conservatory and in New York with the French ultramodernist Edgar Varèse, who led Still into a dissonant, melodic, and traditional style, reflecting his black heritage. "I made an effort to elevate the folk idiom into symphonic form," Still said. Two Guggenheim Fellowships allowed him to concentrate on composition in the 1930s.

As a black man, Still achieved many "firsts." He wrote the theme for the 1939 New York World's Fair. He conducted WOR's all-white radio orchestra in New York. In 1931, when composer Howard Hanson conducted Still's *Afro-American Symphony* in Rochester, Still became the first black to have written a symphony performed by a major orchestra. In 1936 he was the first black to conduct a major orchestra, the Los Angeles Philharmonic, and two decades later, leading the New Orleans Symphony, he became the first black to conduct a major orchestra in the Deep South.

During the 1940s, when he wrote "And They Lynched Him on a Tree" and "In Memoriam: The Colored Soldiers Who Died for Democracy," his works sounded a social conscience theme. For violin and piano, he wrote Peruvian and Mexican ballads. His operas, with the libretto often written by his wife Verna Arvey, told of Haiti, Spanish colonial America, Africa, and roadside, gas-station life in America. Poet Langston Hughes wrote the libretto for Still's *Troubled Island*. Still lived in Los Angeles, and Hollywood benefited from his presence. He arranged for Columbia and Warner Brothers and wrote the scores for the *Perry Mason* and *Gunsmoke* television series and for the films *Lost Horizons* and *Pennies from Heaven*.

In addition to the Guggenheim Fellowships, Still received honorary degrees and many awards. In 1974 Still's *A Bayou Legend* opera premiered in Jackson, Miss., and then Governor Bill Waller named Still a "distinguished Mississippian." Though not a churchgoer, on every composition he wrote, "With humble thanks to God, the Source of inspiration." At age 83, on 3 December 1978, Still died in Los Angeles from a heart ailment.

Berkley Hudson
Providence, Rhode Island

Robert Bartlett Haas, ed., *William Grant Still and the Fusion of Cultures in American Music* (1972); *The Black Perspective in Music* (May 1975). ☆

STRING BAND TRADITION

Primarily a mid-19th and 20th century phenomenon, string bands have been, and continue to be, one of the South's major folk musical ensemble forms. They derive from both Anglo- and Afro-American musical cultures, although they are more frequently associated with whites than with blacks. String bands consist of a number of musicians, generally from three to six, most of whom play acoustic stringed instruments. The fiddle, present in the South from the earliest days of colonization, and the banjo, an instrument that developed in the 19th century from African roots, are typically the core instruments, usually joined by at least one guitar, an instrument that grew in popularity during the early years of this century. Although these are the major instruments, it is not at all uncommon to find others, including the mandolin, string bass, and piano. If there are vocalists—and there usually are—they are inevitably also instrumentalists.

A string band usually has in its repertoire a large number of tunes for square dancing, songs generally representative of the broad corpus of southern folksong, and recent country hit songs. The music is infectious, with fiddles speeding through the melody, propelled by a banjo played in an old-time "rapping" or "knocking" style and a guitar or two accentuating the beat with chords and connecting runs. Instrumental styles tend to be regionally defined. Singing is generally solo, although more modern harmonic vocal techniques are used increasingly.

String bands dominated the first decade of country music recordings, indicating the music's deep-seated ties to and familiarity within local communities. Groups had such colorful names as the Skillet Lickers, Dr. Smith's Champion Hoss Hair Pullers, Fisher Hendley and his Aristocratic Pigs, and Seven Foot Dilly and His Dill Pickles. By the mid- and late 1930s, though, the form had become less profitable for the record companies. Bands continued to be part of their communities, playing for such occasions as dances, picnics, and house parties. Their influence continues, providing a substantial foundation for string-based musical styles such as bluegrass and western swing. Many of the old "hillbilly" records from the 1920s and 1930s have been reissued and are available from specialty record dealers.

In recent years young musicians in the United States and abroad have taken up the string-band styles. Ironically, this string-band revival has been slow to come to the South, but its force is being felt increasingly. And the "old" bands, many of which never went away, continue to play.

Burt Feintuch
Western Kentucky University

Bill C. Malone, *Country Music, U.S.A.: A Fifty-year History* (1968), *Southern Music—American Music* (1979); Charles K. Wolfe, *Tennessee Strings: The Story of Country Music in Tennessee* (1977). ☆

SUN RECORDS

Johnny Cash, Jerry Lee Lewis, Roy Orbison, Carl Perkins, and Elvis Presley are among many musicians who first recorded their music at Sun Records. The most successful went on to record for larger companies, such as RCA and Columbia, but it was their early songs on the Sun label that launched their careers and reshaped southern and American popular music.

Sam Phillips was the founder of the Sun Record Company. Born in 1923 in Florence, Ala., he heard black gospel music and blues throughout his childhood. He became a disc jockey at radio station WLAY in Muscle Shoals and then worked in Decatur, Ala., at WLAC in Nashville, and at WREC in Memphis. In 1955 he cofounded the nation's first successful all-female radio station, WHER in Memphis. While he was still in Muscle Shoals, though, he took a correspondence course that led to his certification in radio engineering. This skill, together with his interest in black music, prompted him to open the Memphis Recording Service so that black southern blues artists would have a place to record their music. The studio was in a converted radiator shop on Union Avenue.

Phillips initially stayed in business by recording weddings, funerals, and speeches. When he recorded musicians' performances, he often leased the recordings to Jules and Saul Bihari, who sold them on their Modern and RPM labels, or to Leonard Chess, who owned the Chess label. During this time, Phillips made the first recordings of B. B. King, Howlin' Wolf, and other black singers who later became famous. He also recorded "Rocket 88," a highly successful song that has been called the first rock-and-roll hit. By 1952, however, legal disputes and competition from larger recording companies that lured his talented musicians away frustrated Phillips and convinced him to start his own label.

Early in 1952 the Memphis Recording Service became the Sun Record Company. It released its first record on 1 March 1952 but did not produce a hit

until a year later when Rufus Thomas recorded "Bear Cat." The company's second hit was "Just Walkin' in the Rain" sung by the Prisonaires, a group of black inmates at the state penitentiary. During the label's first years, Phillips primarily recorded black artists, but he sought to record black music performed by white singers, who would make the music acceptable to a wider audience. Ultimately, Sun's combination of white country music sung with a black rhythm-and-blues feel broadened the scope of American music and brought Sun Records the sound for which it became famous.

This "rockabilly" music was made most popular by Elvis Presley, whose first recordings were two Ink Spots numbers in 1953. Not pleased with the result, Phillips had Presley work with guitarist Scott Moore and bassist Bill Black and, in 1954, released Presley's first professional record, which contained the songs "That's All Right (Mama)" and "Blue Moon of Kentucky." It was immediately successful, and Presley recorded eight more songs for Sun before Phillips sold Presley's contract to RCA in 1955 for $35,000 plus $5,000 more for back royalties owed to the singer. The sum was an unprecedented amount in the business and provided Sun the financial stability to work with and record other white southern musicians, like Johnny Cash, Jerry Lee Lewis, Roy Orbison, and Carl Perkins.

With a spontaneous feel, an echo effect, and a simple, crisp, aggressive sound, Sun's recordings established several of its unknown artists as stars. Early in 1956 Carl Perkins's "Blue Suede Shoes" became a tremendous success, making the company solvent for the first time. Cash's first hit was "I Walk the Line" in the fall of 1956, and

Sun produced Roy Orbison's early recordings during the same year. Then, during 1957 and 1958, Jerry Lee Lewis proved profitable to Sun with his hits "Whole Lotta Shakin' Going On," "Great Balls of Fire," and "Breathless." Sun's subsidiary, the Phillips International label, produced major hits by Carl Mann and Charlie Rich.

In the early 1960s production was much less active and Sun's recordings appealed more to a local audience than to a national one. Cash, Perkins, and Orbison had all moved to larger recording companies, and Lewis left in 1962. Phillips retired in 1968 and, in the following year, sold a controlling interest in Sun to Shelby S. Singleton of Nashville. The sale brought the formation of the Sun International Corporation, headquartered in Nashville, and the transfer of the nearly 3,000 master tapes and the original record catalogs by Sun artists (excluding Presley, whose materials had previously been transferred to RCA).

The landmark Sun era had ended, but not before rejuvenating American popular music. Under the direction of Sam Phillips, Sun's artists established the rockabilly sound and the roots of rock and roll. Phillips and his company made this possible by nurturing the talents of southern artists; by marketing their music through 43 independent record distributors and an overseas distribution affiliate in London; and, most importantly, by concentrating on and developing a southern musical tradition.

Jessica Foy
Cooperstown Graduate Programs
Cooperstown, New York

Colin Escott and Martin Hawkins, *Catalyst: The Sun Records Story* (1975); Peter Gur-alnick, *Feel Like Going Home: Portraits in Blues and Rock 'n' Roll* (1971), *Lost Highway: Journeys and Arrivals of American Musicians* (1979); Brock Helander, *The Rock Who's Who* (1982); Robert Palmer, *Memphis* (December 1978); Barbara Sims, *John Edwards Memorial Foundation Quarterly* (Autumn 1976); *Variety* (25 June 1969). ☆

SWEENEY, JOEL WALKER

(c. 1810–1860) Musician.

Until recently, "Joe" Sweeney enjoyed legendary status as the "inventor" of the five-string banjo. As a boy, Sweeney learned to play the banjo from slaves on his father's farm, where he was born near present-day Appomattox, Va. According to the legend, he improved their African-derived instrument by fashioning a wooden hoop to replace the original gourd body, and, more importantly, by adding (around 1831) a short, high-pitched fifth (or thumb) string to the original four. The long-held claim that he thus invented the five-string banjo is supported by little documentary evidence, and recent informed opinion challenges it, primarily on the basis of illustrations clearly showing that some slave banjos had short thumb strings well before Sweeney was born. Slave banjos were undoubtedly quite variable in form, so Sweeney's real claim to fame is that he so popularized the particular form he grew up with that it became the standard. He was certainly the first documented white banjo player.

In the 1830s he traveled widely in the South performing, in blackface, the music of his black mentors; and he became a mentor himself, apparently teaching a number of the early, influential minstrel banjo players. In the

1840s he became a national celebrity, performing first with circuses and then with minstrel shows in northern cities; between 1843 and 1845 he toured and performed in England, reputedly including a performance for Queen Victoria. His brother, Sam, also an accomplished banjo player, was Jeb Stuart's personal minstrel during the Civil War. Joel Sweeney played a critical role in making the banjo an important and permanent part of southern music, especially in initiating and encouraging its widespread use by whites.

Robert B. Winans
Wayne State University

Gene Bluestein, *Western Folklore* (Winter 1964); Burke Davis, *The Iron Worker* (Autumn 1969); Scott Odell, in *New Grove Dictionary of Music and Musicians*, vol. 2, ed. Stanley Sadie (1980); Arthur Woodward, *Los Angeles County Museum Quarterly* (Spring 1949). ☆

TUBB, ERNEST
||||||||||||||||||||||||||||||||||||||||||||||
(1914–1984) Country singer.

Ernest Tubb was a major personality in country music from the early 1940s to his death on 6 September 1984. He was a much admired and imitated vocal stylist, a pioneer in the popularization of the electric guitar, a patron of young talent, and one of the leading architects of the popular honky-tonk style of country music.

Tubb was born on 9 February 1914 in the tiny community of Crisp, Tex., about 40 miles south of Dallas. Like many young fledgling musicians of his era, Tubb fell in love with the music of Jimmie Rodgers, and for many years he affected a singing-and-yodeling style

that was quite similar to that of the Mississippi Blue Yodeler. He never met his hero, but in 1936 Carrie Rodgers, Jimmie's widow, became Tubb's champion. She loaned him one of Rodgers's guitars, helped him obtain bookings in south Texas, and persuaded the Victor Company to sign Tubb to a contract. The Victor affiliation resulted in eight recordings but brought Tubb little money or fame.

Success did not really come to Tubb until the early 1940s. In 1940 he made the first of his recordings with Decca (an association that lasted until 1975); he began performing on KGKO in Fort Worth and touring for Universal Mills as the Texas Troubadour; and in 1941 he recorded the enduringly popular "Walking the Floor over You." On the strength of the song's popularity, Tubb was invited to join the cast of the Grand Ole Opry, becoming a permanent member of the show in January 1943. Tubb's move to Nashville was symbolic and representative of the growing influence of "western" styles in country music. He was one of the first musicians to bring an electric guitar to the stage of the Grand Ole Opry, an innovation that had already been heard on his records and in his Texas personal appearances. Tubb was a leading record seller and popular concert attraction in country music until the mid-1950s (when rock and roll and country-pop music emerged); and long after that period he continued to be one of the most active in-person performers in country music, averaging close to 300 personal appearances a year until the late 1970s.

Because of his evident commercial viability, Tubb was able to exert great influence in the country music field. He played a prime role in persuading his industry to replace the word "hillbilly" with "country"; he was one of the first country singers to make records with other established performers (such as the Andrews Sisters, Red Foley, and Loretta Lynn); he and his band of musicians, the Texas Troubadours, made crucial contributions to the development of the honky-tonk style of performance; and he provided encouragement and support to many younger entertainers such as Hank Williams, Johnny Cash, Loretta Lynn, Jack Greene, Willie Nelson, and Cal Smith. Tubb's admission to the Country Music Hall of Fame in 1965 was warmly endorsed.

Bill C. Malone
Tulane University

Ronnie Floyd Pugh, *Journal of Country Music* (December 1978, 1981), "The Texas Troubadours: Selected Aspects of the Career of Ernest Tubb" (M.A. thesis, Stephen F. Austin State University, 1978). ☆

VAUGHAN, JAMES D.
(1864–1941) Gospel music promoter.

James D. Vaughan played a major role in the popularization of gospel music in America during the first half of the 20th century. His promotion company, the James D. Vaughan Company, was founded in 1912 in the middle Tennessee community of Lawrenceburg and remained in operation until 1964.

Vaughan's enterprise began as a singing school and then was expanded to include sales of records, songbooks, and magazines. His first songbook, *Gospel Chimes*, was published under his own name in 1900. His company eventually published 105 songbooks, which enjoyed successful nationwide sales. Vaughan was a creative businessman

who sent male vocal quartets to churches around the country to promote his music and books. He started one of the first commercial radio stations in Tennessee, WOAN, to play his music and plug his songbooks. In 1922 one of the Vaughan quartets made a recording of their music, and, although it was not made in the South, the record was one of the first specifically designed for a southern audience.

A devout member of the Church of the Nazarene, Vaughan was influential in the development and spread of gospel music from the 1920s through the 1960s. Vaughan helped preserve the shape-note singing tradition, and his gospel music helped lay the foundation for American country music. The gospel songbooks that Vaughan distributed had a profound impact on southern cultural life. Singing schools and conventions and gospel singing at church-related functions were immensely popular through the 1960s and involved thousands of southerners. Vaughan's books were affordably priced and each sold an average of 117,000 copies.

Karen M. McDearman
University of Mississippi

J. L. Fleming, "James D. Vaughan: Music Publisher, Lawrenceburg, Tennessee, 1912–1964" (Ph.D. dissertation, Union Theological Seminary, 1971); Bill C. Malone, *Southern Music—American Music* (1979); Charles K. Wolfe, *Tennessee Strings: The Story of Country Music in Tennessee* (1977). ☆

WATSON, DOC
(b. 1923) Folk musician.

Arthel "Doc" Watson is a unique song stylist, an influential guitarist, and the repository of a vast range of American music originating in the South. Born 2 March 1923 in Deep Gap, N.C., Watson has been blind from birth. He grew up in a farm family oriented toward religion and music. His father was a song leader in the Baptist church, and the Watson family read the Bible and sang hymns most evenings. Watson learned traditional folksongs from his grandparents and his father, and the first instrument he played was the harmonica. He remembers at age six hearing a cousin play the banjo, and a brother-in-law gave him one several years after that.

Throughout Watson's youth, his father guided his musical education. Doc Watson's father gave him a harmonica each Christmas for years when he was a child, helped his young son learn the banjo, and then in 1934 made him a better banjo of hickory, maple, and catskin. His father gave him money to buy his first guitar after the young boy learned to play the Carter Family's "When the Roses Bloom in Dixie." From his father's wind-up gramophone and the radio, Doc Watson remembers hearing songs by the Carter Family, the Skillet Lickers, Mississippi John Hurt, and Barbecue Bob. He still performs and records the songs he listened to growing up. In addition to his early education in traditional music, commercial country, and the blues, he learned jazz, big-band, popular songs, and classical music while attending the North Carolina School for the Blind in Raleigh.

Doc Watson's first stage performance was at age 17 during a fiddlers' convention in Boone, N.C., where he played the "Mule Skinner's Blues." In 1941 he became a member of a group singing for local radio stations, and a woman in a local station gave him his nickname in this period. She suggested calling him "Doc" because "Arthel" was too formal.

Watson worked for nine years in the 1950s playing mostly electric guitar with Jack Williams and the Country Gentlemen, a five-piece dance band, and he continued playing traditional music at home with friends and family. Folklorist Ralph Rinzler came from the Smithsonian Institution in 1960 to record a friend of Watson's, Clarence Ashley, and after Rinzler heard Watson, he encouraged him to seek a solo identity nationally. The Folkways album *Old Time Music at Clarence Ashley's* became Watson's first recording, and he was soon popular on the folk club and college campus circuit. Watson began recording for Vanguard Records in 1964, and the following year his 15-year-old son Merle began recording and touring with his father.

Doc Watson is an influential exponent of guitar flat picking, which involves use of a simple flat pick rather than a thumb pick or finger picking. He is also an engaging storyteller, who explains the background to the songs he performs. Above all, his cultural significance is as an eclectic synthesizer of southern music. Watson absorbed the music of his time and place as a mid-20th-century rural southerner. He performs Jimmie Rodgers ("Miss the Mississippi and You"), the Delmore Brothers ("Blues Stay Away from Me"), Gaither Carleton fiddle tunes, A. P. Carter ("Keep on the Sunny Side"), Mississippi John Hurt ("Spikedriver Blues"), Barbecue Bob ("You Don't Know My Mind Blues"), Bob Wills ("Hang Your Head in Shame"), and Carl Perkins ("Blue Suede Shoes"). In concert he can draw from Ira Gershwin and Bob Dylan if requested. He has recorded over 30 albums.

Watson's son Merle traveled, performed, and recorded with his father and earned praise for his bottleneck slide guitar playing. He died in a tractor accident in 1986. Doc Watson still lives with his wife Rosa Lee a few miles from his birthplace in North Carolina.

Charles Reagan Wilson
University of Mississippi

Irwin Stambler and Grellin Landon, *The Encyclopedia of Folk, Country, and Western Music* (2d ed., 1983). ☆

WHITE TOP FOLK FESTIVAL

Held from 1931 to 1939 on White Top Mountain in southwest Virginia, this festival drew its participants from a tri-state (Tennessee, Virginia, North Carolina) area. It was organized and produced by composer, writer, collector, and clubwoman Annabel Morris Buchanan in collaboration with composer-pianist John Powell, and Abingdon, Va., attorney John A. Blakemore. Folktale collector Richard Chase, composer Lamar Springfield, and white spirituals scholar George Pullen Jackson also played prominent roles.

Featuring such traditional performers as chantey singer Sailor Dad Hunt, ballad singers Horton Barker and Texas Gladden, dulcimer player Sam Russell, clog dancer Harve Sheets, banjo player Jack Reedy, fiddler Jess Johnson, and numerous members of the Wohlford, Blevins, and Cruise families, the festival drew hundreds of performers, thousands of spectators (more than 10,000 when Eleanor Roosevelt made a state visit in 1933), and many nationally known academic folklorists, art critics, composers, and classical musicians. In its later years the festival also included the morris-and-sword dances, Punch 'n' Judy shows, and theatrical presentations (by the Barter Theater) favored by Richard Chase. Each annual event was covered extensively by the local, regional, and national press.

Potential performers were rigorously screened and frequently coached to conform to an image of traditional culture in the southern mountains as the precious vestiges of an ancient English (Anglo-Saxon) cultural heritage, needing protection from the corrupting influences of modernity, and valuable as both raw material for art-music composers and a potential basis for a distinctive American "national culture." John Powell also used the festival to promote the nativist cultural theories upon which he had earlier based his work with the white-supremacist Anglo-Saxon club of America (which he had founded in 1922 and used as a lobbying group for Virginia's antimiscegenation Racial Integrity Law of 1924). Local black musicians were prohibited from performing at the festival.

The festival anticipated hundreds of folk festivals that now exist throughout the South celebrating the region's diverse musical heritage.

David E. Whisnant
University of Maryland,
Baltimore County

John A. Blakemore Papers and Annabel Morris Buchanan Papers, Southern Historical Collection, University of North Carolina, Chapel Hill; John Powell Papers, Alderman Library, University of Virginia,

Charlottesville; David E. Whisnant, *All That Is Native and Fine: The Politics of Culture in an American Region* (1983). ☆

WILLIAMS, HANK

|||||||||||||||||||||||||||||||||||||||

(1923–1953) Country singer.

Widely acclaimed as country music's greatest singer and composer, Hiram Hank Williams was born on 17 October 1923 at Olive Hill, near Georgiana, Ala., the son of a sawmill and railroad worker. He was introduced to music in the Baptist church, where he was faithfully taken by his mother, and, according to popular legend, learned both songs and guitar chords from a black street singer in Georgiana, Rufus Payne ("Teetot").

Williams's evolution as a professional performer and composer began at the age of 14 when he won a talent show in a Montgomery theater singing "WPA Blues." He obtained his first radio job in the same year, 1937, at WSFA in Montgomery. When World War II— that crucible that integrated country music's disparate regional styles and ultimately nationalized it—came, Williams worked in the Mobile shipyards and sang regularly in the honky-tonks of south Alabama. By the time the war ended Williams had compiled eight hard years of performing experience and had built a style that reflected the composite musical influences of his youth: gospel, blues, and old-time country. Professionally, he acknowledged a debt to the Texas honky-tonk singer Ernest Tubb and to the Tennessee mountain singer Roy Acuff, whose styles Williams fused in a way that reflected a similar synthesis in the larger country field during the war and immediate postwar years.

Williams's ascendance to fame began shortly after the war when he became associated with Fred Rose, the famous Nashville songwriter and publisher. Rose encouraged Williams's natural songwriting abilities and published his songs; he helped him obtain recording contracts with Sterling and MGM Records; he persuaded Molly O'Day, one of the greatest singers of the time, to record some of Williams's compositions; and he helped him get a position on KWKH's Louisiana Hayride in Shreveport. The Hayride, which was then second only to the Grand Ole Opry as a successful country radio show, was the vehicle that launched Williams on the road to performing fame.

Hank Williams's national ascendancy came in 1949 when he recorded an old pop tune, "Lovesick Blues," which featured the yodeling he had learned from another Alabama singer, Rex Griffin. Williams soon moved to the Grand Ole Opry, where he became the most popular country singer since Jimmie Rodgers. In the brief span from

Hank Williams, country music star, c. 1950

1949 to 1953 Williams dominated the country charts with songs that are still considered classics of country music: "I'm So Lonesome I Could Cry," "Cold Cold Heart," "Your Cheating Heart," "Honky Tonk Blues," "Jambalaya," and many others. With his band, the Drifting Cowboys, Williams played a major role in making country music a national phenomenon. With a remarkably expressive voice that moved with equal facility from the strident yodeling of "Long Gone Lonesome Blues" to the gentle lyricism of "I Just Told Mama Goodbye," Williams communicated with his listeners in a fashion that has only rarely been equaled by other country singers. The word *sincerity* has no doubt been overused in describing the styles of country musicians, but in the case of Williams it means simply that he as a singer convincingly articulated in song a feeling that he and his listeners shared.

As a songwriter—not as a singer—Williams played a most important role in breaking down the fragile barriers between country and pop music. Williams's singing was quintessentially rural, and his own records never "crossed over" into the lucrative pop market. His songs, though, moved into the larger sphere of American popular music and from there, perhaps, into the permanent consciousness of the American people. Like no earlier country writer's works, Hank's songs appeared with great frequency in the repertoires of such pop musicians as Tony Bennett, Frankie Laine, and Mitch Miller. For good or ill, this popularization in pop music continues.

Commercial and professional success did not bring peace of mind to the Alabama country boy. A chronic back ailment, a troubled marriage, and a subsequent divorce and remarriage accentuated a penchant for alcohol that he had acquired when only a small boy. After being fired by the Grand Ole Opry for drunkenness and erratic behavior, he returned to the scene of his first triumphs—the Louisiana Hayride. He died of a heart attack on 1 January 1953, but his legacy lives on in his songs and in the scores of singers, including his immensely talented son, Hank, Jr., who still bear his influence.

Bill C. Malone
Tulane University

Bill C. Malone, *Country Music, U.S.A.: A Fifty-year History* (1968); Roger M. Williams, *Sing a Sad Song: The Life of Hank Williams* (1981). ☆

WILLS, BOB
|||||||||||||||||||||||||||||||
(1905–1975) Western-swing musician.

James Robert Wills was born near the town of Kosse in the black belt of east Texas on 6 March 1905. From his family he learned to play fiddle music, which had been part of frontier cultural life from the East Coast to west Texas. From the blacks in the black belt he learned blues and jazz. At age 10, Wills played his first dance at a ranch in west Texas; by then he had begun to add blues and jazz idioms to traditional fiddle music. This combination was eventually called "western swing" and became one of the most distinctive sounds in all of American music. There is probably no better example of cultural cross fertilization than Bob Wills's music, which brought together two strains of culture in the American South, one white, one black.

Wills performed his music at country

ranch dances in west Texas years before introducing it to the general public on radio stations in Fort Worth. In the early 1930s he organized the Light Crust Doughboys, broadcast over the Texas Quality Network, and soon revolutionized music in Texas. His greatest success was with his Texas Playboys in Tulsa, Okla., between 1934 and 1942. During those years he added brass, reeds, and drums, developing a band that by 1940 numbered 18 members. His recordings sold in the hundreds of thousands and his "San Antonio Rose" in the millions.

After the war he gave up most of the brass and reeds in his band and used more fiddles, guitars, steel guitars, and mandolins. This emphasis on strings helped Wills maintain his popularity even after the passage of the age of the big bands. Because of his use of stringed instruments, Wills influenced two musical forces of the South that have dominated American music to the present— rock and roll and country and western. Western swing left a marked impression on early rockabillies such as Bill Haley and the Comets, Buddy Holly and the Crickets, and Elvis Presley. But Wills's greatest influence was on country and western. The Country Music Association gave him its highest honor in 1968, naming Wills to the Country Music Hall of Fame.

What was it that made Wills's music appeal to the American people for more than 50 years? His music and style had many good qualities, but one quality stood out above all others—his music made people happy. At his dances, during his radio broadcasts, and through his recordings, Bob Wills helped the American people find times of happiness and escape during the Depression and World War II. This was the secret

to his success and one of his most direct contributions to humanity.

When Wills died in 1975, he left a rich cultural heritage. His compositions like "Faded Love," "Maiden's Prayer," and "San Antonio Rose" are part of the repertoire of American country and pop artists. He also helped bridge the gap between the black and white musical cultures when he began combining them as a boy. Out of that cultural mix came Bob Wills's richest legacy, the happy, swinging rhythms called "western swing."

Charles R. Townsend
West Texas State University

Ruth Sheldon, *Hubbin' It: The Life of Bob Wills* (1938); Al Stricklin with Jon McConal, *My Years with Bob Wills* (1976); Charles R. Townsend, *San Antonio Rose: The Life and Music of Bob Wills* (1976). ☆

YOUNG, LESTER
(1909–1959) Jazz musician.

Lester Willis "Pres" Young was an Afro-American tenor saxophonist whose influential style was viewed as revolutionary when first recorded during the late 1930s. He was a primary influence in the development of modern jazz.

Born in Woodville, Miss., Young was the oldest of three children raised in the vicinity of New Orleans. His parents divorced in 1910, and his father remarried and took his children with him to Minneapolis by 1920. Willis "Billy" Handy Young, Lester's father, was a talented musician who taught his children various instruments and later toured the South with his family in a band that played carnivals. Lester studied violin, trumpet, and drums but turned seriously to the saxophone by age 13. Young left the family band in 1927. He played in the next few years with Art Bronson's Bostonians, Eli Rice's Cotton Pickers, Walter Page's Blue Devils, Eugene Schuck's Orchestra, and Eddie Barefield at the West Club in Minneapolis.

In the fall of 1933 Young moved to Kansas City, where he played with numerous musicians, including Fletcher Henderson's orchestra and its star saxophonist, Coleman Hawkins. Early in 1934, Young joined William "Count" Basie, beginning an association that was to lead eventually to national recognition. During the mid to late 1930s Young was prominently featured on recordings and broadcasts with the Basie band. Although Young gained mixed reviews from critics, younger musicians were wildly enthusiastic. Important recordings included "Lester Leaps In" (1939) and many accompanying Billie Holiday.

Young left the Basie band in December 1940 to start his own group, which performed in New York in early 1941. He was involved with his own bands after that in Los Angeles and New York, before freelancing and then rejoining Basie in late 1943. During this second period with Basie, Young garnered the attention of the general public. In 1944 he won first place in the *Down Beat* poll for best tenor saxophonist. He won many awards thereafter and became popular with a new generation of musicians, among them John Coltrane, Sonny Rol-

lins, and Stan Getz. In 1956 Young was voted "Greatest Tenor Saxophonist Ever" in a list of prominent jazz musicians.

Young's style changed after 1940. His tone was heavier and his vibrato wider. He was more clearly emotional, using wails, honks, and blue notes in his solos. He was inducted into the army in 1944, beginning a nightmarish experience that included time spent at a detention barracks in Georgia. After the war he toured with his own small groups. He continued to develop and modify his style and was generally successful except when his drinking, which was habitual by the early 1950s, weakened him physically. He died in New York in 1959.

Young is a leading example of many great jazz performers who were born and reared in the South but gained fame outside the region. His impact on jazz was profound. His melodic gift and logical phrasing influenced musicians on many instruments, and his personal formulas turned up in countless jazz compositions and improvisations.

Lewis Porter
Rutgers University

Nat Hentoff, in *The Jazz Makers*, ed. Nat Shapiro and Nat Hentoff (1975); J. G. Jensen, *A Discography of Lester Young* (1968); J. M. McDonough, *Lester Young* (1980); Lewis Porter, *The Black Perspective in Music* (Spring 1981), *Lester Young* (1985). ☆

MYTHIC SOUTH

GEORGE B. TINDALL

University of North Carolina at Chapel Hill

CONSULTANT

Souvenir of the South

☆ ☆ ☆ ☆ ☆ ☆ ☆ ☆ ☆ ☆ ☆

Overleaf: A 1906 postcard depicting the cotton boll, a symbol of the South

MYTHIC SOUTH
||||||||||||||||||||||||||||||||||||||||||||||||||||||

Has the South always been mainly a region of the mind, as many have said, something that exists because people think it exists? Or has it been mainly a region defined by material characteristics of geography, climate, and resources—together with traits it has acquired in the course of its history?

Most would probably say it has been both. Historian U. B. Phillips, for instance, moved from one to the other in two classic definitions of the South. In "The Central Theme of Southern History" (1928), he described the unifying principle of the South as an idea, "a common resolve indomitably maintained" that the South should be and remain "a white man's country." In *Life and Labor in the Old South* (1929), on the other hand, he wrote: "Let us begin by discussing the weather, for that has been the chief agency in making the South distinctive." Geography and climate led in turn to staple crops, the plantation system, chattel slavery, racial problems, sectional conflict, and ultimately the Confederacy. Any serious effort to know the character of a people must confront its mythology, and Phillips's interpretations both belong in some respects to that realm, however matter of fact both may at first appear.

The term *mythology*, of course, conveys variant meanings. While myths are rooted in the religious impulse, they have become in the modern world increasingly secular in character. Some years ago anthropologist Raphael Patai offered a definition: "Myth . . . is a traditional religious charter, which operates by validating laws, customs, rites, institutions and beliefs, or explaining socio-cultural situations and natural phenomena, and taking the form of stories, believed to be true, about divine beings and heroes." Later, in his book *Myth and Modern Man* (1972), Patai reaffirmed the definition but deleted the word *religious*. Upon further reflection, he said, he would emphasize more the role of myth in shaping social life: "As I see it, myth not only validates or authorizes customs, rites, institutions, beliefs, and so forth, but frequently is directly responsible for creating them." Thus, the modern world has invented a great variety of myths of both past and future, ranging from Marxist and Nazi myths to myths of planetary escape, with or without theological overtones.

To place the more down-to-earth idea of the South in the realm of social myth is to place it firmly in the region of the mind, where close relatives are such concepts as ideology, symbol, image, and stereotype—the last in the sense that Walter Lippmann gave in his *Public Opinion* (1922), where stereotypes come to mean "pictures in our heads" that have more to do with preconceptions than with reality.

The distinguishing characteristic of social myths is that they develop more or less abstract ideas in concrete and dramatic terms. In the words of Henry Nash Smith, they "fuse concept and emotion into an image." Secular myths, like religious myths, remain true to their origin in a root word meaning "tale."

Historical Myths. The classic myths of the South can be summed up briefly in the oft-quoted statement of Jonathan Daniels: "We Southerners are a mythological people, created half out of dream and half out of slander, who live in a still legendary land." He was referring to the contrary images of the South that grew up in the 19th-century sectional conflict: the plantation idyll versus the abolitionist critique, the "Sunny South" versus the "Benighted South," or to cite the cultural events that have most vividly fixed them in the popular mind, *Uncle Tom's Cabin* versus *Birth of a Nation* and, more recently, *Gone with the Wind* versus *Roots*.

Major myths have given structure to the chronological development of the South. Southern myths have frequently been analyzed as discrete entities, but together their stories tell the story of the South. The myth of a southern garden paradise, a new Eden, provided the initial image of the region for many colonial southerners and northerners. It was a myth rooted in the perception of a bountiful environment. By the late 1700s the democratic, egalitarian South of Thomas Jefferson had become the norm, according to William E. Dodd. Dodd's theme has been reflected in the writing of other historians, largely in depicting a region subjected to economic colonialism by an imperial Northeast. The Jeffersonian image of agrarian democracy has been a favorite recourse of southern liberals.

By the 1830s, though, the myth of the Old South was becoming a dominant literary and cultural construct for northerners and southerners alike, as William R. Taylor has shown. The Old

South evokes images of kindly old marster with his mint julep, happy darkies singing in the fields, coquettish belles wooed by slender gallants. It is a romanticized moonlight-and-magnolias world, which yields all too easily to caricature and ridicule. Francis Pendleton Gaines noted, though, that "the plantation romance remains our chief social idyl of the past; of an Arcadian scheme of existence, less material, less hurried, less prosaically equalitarian, less futile, richer in picturesqueness, festivity, in realized pleasure that recked not of hope or fear or unrejoicing labor."

The myth of the Lost Cause focused on the Civil War experience of southerners. It told of noble, virtuous Christian warriors, the highest product of the Old South, defending the southern homeland from rapacious Yankees. Defeat was inevitable because of superior northern resources, but southerners defended their honor and in the process achieved spiritual victories. The Reconstruction era gave birth to a mythic view of southern whites facing the internal and external challenges to their maintenance of an orderly civilization. Exploitive northern carpetbaggers, traitorous southern scalawags, ignorant blacks, and brave but desperate ex-Confederates were the chief characters in this tale of good and evil.

Redemption of the South by the Bourbons brought peace to the region, in the mythic narrative, and promoted the emergence of a New South. Newspaper editors were the prime mythmakers, creating a New South creed that Paul M. Gaston has discussed at some length. New South advocates of the late 19th century promised to make the South as "rich, triumphant, and morally innocent" as the rest of the nation. They looked forward to a region absorbed into the national abundance of progress and equality.

The late 19th century, though, gave birth to a different myth as well—Populism. Despite talk of a New South, the region's people remained predominantly poor farmers, and the Populist myth made them southern heroes. Populist agrarian leaders were defenders of the poor, out to right the wrongs of industrial-commercial exploitation.

In the clever decade of the 1920s a myth of the Benighted South took shape. An older neoabolitionist myth of the Savage South was reinforced by a variety of images in that decade and after: the Scopes Trial, the Ku Klux Klan, lynchings, chain gangs, the Fundamentalist movement, hookworm and pellagra, the Scottsboro trials, labor violence. The response to the civil rights movement in the 1950s and 1960s gave new life to the Benighted South myth.

The Agrarianism of the Nashville Agrarians spoke, like the Populists, in a mythic rhetoric about the virtues of living on the land, although they seemed unclear whether God's chosen people had been southern planters or small farmers. Their manifesto, *I'll Take My Stand*, by Twelve Southerners, appeared by fortuitous circumstance in 1930 when industrial capitalism seemed on the verge of collapse. The ideal of traditional virtues such as, in Donald Davidson's words, "family, bloodkinship, clanship, folkways, custom, community" took on the texture of myth in their image of the agrarian South.

Another image from the Great Depression era was the Problem South, a concept emerging from the writings of sociological regionalists such as Howard W. Odum and Rupert B. Vance at the University of North Carolina. They told of a region with indisputable shortcomings but with potentialities that needed constructive attention and the application of regional social planning.

Contemporary Southern Mythology. "The myth-making faculty is still active in contemporary America," Max Lerner wrote in *America as a Civilization* (1957). During the 1970s and 1980s a new myth of the South emerged, an ambivalent mixture of extremes, combining elements of the Sunny South and the Benighted South with some ingredients of its own. The new "mytho-poets" began to sight on the southern horizons an extended "Sunbelt," stretching from coast to coast, its economy battening on agribusiness, defense, technology, oil, real estate, tourism, and leisure. The geographical definition of the Sunbelt remains uncertain, but it has come more and more often to be synonymous with the South.

Something about the Sunbelt image has a seductive appeal to southerners, so long consigned to the role of underdogs, although the Sunbelt seems to have been, like other myths, less the invention of southerners than of Yankees. The Sunbelt image surfaced first in a book by Kevin P. Phillips, *The Emerging Republican Majority* (1969), but lay dormant until revived by Kirkpatrick Sale in *Power Shift: The Rise of the Southern Rim and Its Challenge to the Eastern Establishment* (1979). Sale's book focused on the Southeast as a likely growth area for investment. The Sunbelt idea, however, is one myth that is subject to a statistical test. One cannot buy into the Sunbelt myth so long as only two southern states (Virginia and Florida) reach the national average per capita income, as the Department of Commerce reported for 1984.

Complexity and Contradictions. The complexity and contradictions of southern mythology, one can argue, make the mythology of the American West seem fairly simple by comparison. Fred Hobson, in his *Tell about the South: The Southern Rage to Explain* (1983), made up a suggestive list of myths with some overlapping, simply by compiling selected titles of books and articles published since 1945: "*The Emerging South, The Changing South,* 'The Disappearing . . . South,' 'The Vanishing South,' *The Enduring South,* 'The Distinctive South,' 'The American South,' 'The World South,' 'The Provincial South,' *The Democratic South,* 'The Embarrassing New South,' 'The South as a Counterculture,' *The Romantic South, The Uncertain South, The Militant South,* 'The Benighted South,' 'The Poetic South,' 'The Backward South,' 'The Progressive South,' *The Lazy South,* 'The Turbulent South,' 'The Squalid South,' 'The Solid South,' 'The Divided South,' 'The Devilish South,' 'The Visceral South,' and 'The Massive, Concrete South.' "

These neglected, among other things, the Jeffersonian yeoman, the Jacksonian frontiersman, chivalrous South-rons, New South boosters, insurgent Populists, the Fighting South, the Liberal South, the Anglo-Saxon (or Scotch-Irish?) South, the Vanderbilt Agrarians, the Chapel Hill Regionalists, the Bible Belt, and a gallery of patricians, rednecks, village nabobs, good old boys, and in general the surfeit of southern fried chic cooked up to celebrate the emergence of Jimmy Carter, the only president to date who was born and bred in the brier patch of the Deep South.

This catalog neither acknowledges nor sorts out the variety of southern black and female stereotypes that have either captivated or shocked the American sensibility. Studies of literature and popular culture, chiefly moving pictures and music, have only begun that process. Nor does the catalog deal with that newer version of the old religious myths that reserved the South for a high destiny—the Integrated South, purged by suffering and prepared to redeem the nation from bias and injustice.

Southern myths have been fostered in a variety of cultural forms. In the antebellum era, writers such as William Gilmore Simms and John Pendleton Kennedy helped create the plantation legend of the Old South as well as creating the tradition of popular literature fostering mythology. In the late 19th century, northern periodicals printed nostalgic articles and stories by southerners about the prewar era, and northerners seemed as taken with them as southerners were. Since the turn of the 20th century, American popular music has been a carrier of southern mythology. Tin Pan Alley's tunes, Broadway shows, country music, and even rock music have told of Dixie's virtues. Film and television are the most recent sources to create and spread mythic news of the South, drawing on previous symbolism. Throughout southern history, political speeches and religious sermons have spread regional mythology in the South's oral culture.

Mythology, which seemed more than two decades ago a new frontier of southern history, has since been penetrated by a number of scholars. Literary critics have provided perhaps the largest body of scholarship on southern mythology, focusing on the region's writers. Intellectual historians have studied political, economic, religious, military, and journalistic aspects of various myths. There remain many areas that have been little explored and others scarcely touched. Myths continue to appear in modern areas of southern cultural achievement. Popular culture increasingly produces America's celebrities and heroes, and those who come from the South take on aspects of earlier southern mythology. Sports produced Paul "Bear" Bryant, one of the nation's most successful college football coaches and a folksy agrarian hero out of earlier regional tradition. Elvis Presley drew on the region's rich heritage of black and white music and himself became a new symbol (for good or bad) of the modern South.

See also BLACK LIFE: Film Images, Black; Literary Portrayals of Blacks; LITERATURE: Agrarianism in Literature; Popular Literature; MEDIA articles; SOCIAL CLASS: Lower Class, Literary; WOMEN'S LIFE: Belles and Ladies

George B. Tindall
University of North Carolina
at Chapel Hill

David Bertelson, *The Lazy South* (1967); Carl Bridenbaugh, *Myths and Realities: Societies of the Colonial South* (1963); Edward D. C. Campbell, *The Celluloid South: Hollywood and the Southern Myth* (1981); W. J. Cash, *The Mind of the South* (1941); F. Garvin Davenport, Jr., *The Myth of Southern History: Historical Consciousness in Twentieth-Century Southern Literature* (1970); Michael Davis, *The Image of Lincoln in the South* (1972); Carl N. Degler, *The Other South: Southern Dissenters in the Nineteenth Century* (1974); Clement Eaton, *The Mind of the Old South* (1964); Howard R. Floan, *The South in Northern Eyes, 1831 to 1861* (1958); J. Wayne Flynt, *Dixie's Forgotten People: The South's Poor Whites* (1979); John Hope Franklin, *The Militant South* (1956); George Fredrickson, *The Black Image in the White Mind: The Debate on Afro-American Character and Destiny, 1817–1914* (1971); Francis Pendleton Gaines, *The Southern Plantation: A Study in the Development and Accuracy of a Tradition* (1924); Paul M. Gaston, *The New South Creed: A Study in Southern Mythmaking* (1970); Patrick Gerster and Nicholas Cords, eds., *Myth and Southern History*, 2 vols. (1974); Dewey W. Grantham, *The Democratic South* (1963); Fred Hobson, *Tell about the South: The Southern Rage to Explain* (1983); Winthrop D. Jordan, *White over Black: American Attitudes toward the Negro, 1550–1812* (1968); Alexander Karanikas, *Tillers of a Myth: Southern Agrarians as Social and Literary Critics* (1966); Jack Temple Kirby, *Media-Made Dixie: The South in the American Imagination* (1978); Lawrence W. Levine, *Black Culture and Black Consciousness: Afro-American Folk Thought from Slavery to Freedom* (1977); Bernard Mayo, *Myths and Men: Patrick Henry, George Washington, and Thomas Jefferson* (1963); Forrest McDonald and Grady McWhiney, *History Today* (July 1980); Shields McIlwaine, *The Southern Poor-White: From Lubberland to Tobacco Road* (1939); Gary B. Nash, *William and Mary Quarterly* (April 1972); Michael O'Brien, *The Idea of the American South, 1920–1941* (1979); Rollin G. Osterweis, *Myth of the Lost Cause, 1865–1900* (1973), *Romanticism and Nationalism in the Old South* (1949); Raphael Patai, *Myth and Modern Man* (1972); Merrill Peterson, *The Jefferson Image in the American Mind* (1960); David Potter, *The South and the Sectional Conflict* (1968); John Shelton Reed, *The Enduring South: Subcultural Persistence in Mass Society* (1971), *One South: An Ethnic Approach to Regional Culture* (1982); Louis D. Rubin, Jr., *Writers of the Modern South: The Faraway Country* (1963); Anne Firor Scott, *The Southern Lady: From Pedestal to Politics, 1830–1930* (1970); Charles G. Sellers, Jr., *The Southerner as American* (1960); Lewis P. Simpson, *The Dispossessed Garden: Pastoral and History in Southern Literature* (1975); David L. Smiley, *South Atlantic Quarterly* (Summer 1972); Kenneth M. Stampp, *Era of Reconstruction, 1865–1877*

(1965), *Journal of Southern History* (August 1971); William R. Taylor, *Cavalier and Yankee: The Old South and American National Character* (1957); George B. Tindall, *The Ethnic Southerners* (1976); Frank E. Vandiver, ed., *The Idea of the South: Pursuit of a Central Theme* (1964); John William Ward, *Andrew Jackson: Symbol for an Age* (1962); C. Vann Woodward, *The Strange Career of Jim Crow* (1955; rev. ed., 1966); Charles Reagan Wilson, *Baptized in Blood: The Religion of the Lost Cause, 1865–1920* (1980); Howard Zinn, *Southern Mystique* (1964). ☆

Appalachian Culture

|||||||||||||||||||||||||||||||||||||||||||||||||||||

From the 18th century, "culture" was a process by which the natural was turned into the "cultivated." Beginning in the mid-19th century, however, the unspecified polarities of "natural" and "cultivated," or the "primitive-modern" of common parlance, were elaborated into a variety of schemes that talked of "stages" of development and assumed the inevitability of a people's progress from lower to higher stages. An essential ambiguity toward the primitive persisted, however, throughout the 19th century. A "low" stage of cultural development was frequently valued more highly than any "higher" stage, as maintaining the virtues of the "noble savage" or, in the American context, of "our pioneer ancestors" against the sham sophistication and corrupt usages of modern life. The rise of systematic social science at the turn of the century gave new value to any "low" stage of development, as preserving, like a mammoth in ice, essential evidence for the understanding of social development as a process.

In the context of such a definition of culture, Appalachian culture was called "low" on the scale of development. Appalachia has been routinely defined as "the frontier" and later the "persisting frontier," where primitive patterns of culture prevailed. Both inside and outside Appalachia, moreover, the undeveloped character of Appalachian culture seemed a spur to development, whether through indigenous effort (including emigration from the region) or intervention by outsiders.

The identification of Appalachia as a distinct region of the nation and the mountaineers as a discrete population during the 1880s and 1890s occurred at the same time that social theory generally was beginning to view culture less as a stage in a universal process of development than as a particular set of beliefs or behavior. It associated culture with the places in which social groups lived. Initially, this took the form of explaining culture either as a response to a particular environment or as the product of environmental conditions in the sense that the environment was either conducive or not conducive to "normal" patterns of development from low to high levels of culture. Early in the 20th century, however, the association through explanation tended to drop out of most discussions of Appalachian culture, which now became the culture of place rather than the culture of people. Appalachia as a distinct region of the nation was now a real place, so most discussions of Appalachian culture in the 20th century began with the assumption that there must be *an* Appalachian culture that—whatever its origins—was as distinct as the region is distinct. Against this vision only John

C. Campbell protested (in *The Southern Highlander and His Homeland* [1921]), saying that Appalachian culture was merely a version of rural American culture—no more and no less.

In this context the great campaigns of the early 20th century began to identify the elements of Appalachian culture and then to teach them to the Appalachian people, if they were "desirable" beliefs or behavior, or to replace them with "more desirable" beliefs or behavior. Those engaged in this campaign were usually more familiar with the literature on Appalachia than with the southern mountains and mountaineers themselves, and they frequently misread the beliefs and behavior current in Appalachia. As frequently, they sought to teach the mountaineers patterns of belief and behavior that were essentially alien to them.

Ironically, from the 1890s efforts were made to teach the mountain people their "own" folklore, their "own" folk dance, including the Sword and Morris dances, which they had supposedly forgotten long before their emigration from England and Scotland but which were considered their native tradition nonetheless. As David E. Whisnant has recently shown, a variety of indigenous patterns of culture, like banjo playing and the celebration of "old" Christmas, whether inherited or locally created, were systematically suppressed as being inappropriate to a modern folk culture in Appalachia.

The emergence of cultural pluralism as a conviction in social theory during the 1920s and of cultural relativism as its analogue in anthropological theory changed little. Although these concepts reinforced the legitimation (achieved earlier by the words and work of home missionaries and social workers) of Ap-

palachia as a discrete region with a distinct culture, this culture continued to be viewed as "low," "primitive," "folk"—undeveloped in one way or another and hence unsuited for dealing with the modern world. This view persisted at least through the 1960s, appearing as a continuing theme in the literature on Appalachia and in the construction of social programs like the War on Poverty, which sought to modernize the mountaineer. Efforts were made to create a "viable" folk culture in the region. Many mountain people left the region in search of employment in the industrial centers of the Midwest, while others remained at home—to assimilate to mainstream American culture.

The view of Appalachian culture as low or undeveloped was dominant during the past 150 years and has colored all earlier general discussions of Appalachian culture. As a result, scholars have yet to establish the nature of Appalachian culture in the past, or even whether there *was* an identifiable Appalachian culture distinct from American culture. Nonetheless, the efforts of a new generation of scholars may yet overcome the biases of earlier accounts and by close and careful reading of the evidence develop an accurate picture of life in the past and present.

Henry D. Shapiro
University of Cincinnati

Allen Batteau, ed., *Appalachia and America: Autonomy and Regional Dependence* (1983); William W. Philliber and Clyde McCoy, eds., *The Invisible Minority: Urban Appalachians* (1981); Henry D. Shapiro, *Appalachia on Our Mind: The Southern Mountains and Mountaineers in the American Consciousness, 1870–1920* (1978); David E. Whisnant, *All That Is Native and Fine: The*

Politics of Culture in an American Region (1983). ☆

Benighted South

||||||||||||||||||||||||||||||||||||||||

If the 19th-century South was viewed by romantics, North as well as South, as the primal garden, Eden before the Fall, the 20th-century South—at least to many image makers—has often been something quite different. To be sure, the Benighted or Savage South had its origins in the 19th century: William Lloyd Garrison had referred to it as the "great Sodom" and Frederick Law Olmsted, Harriet Beecher Stowe, and other northern writers had written harshly of it. But in the early 20th century—more particularly in the decade of the 1920s—the idea that the South was savage or barbarian took hold even more strongly than before. The new image of the Benighted South was a result partly of actual events in the South during the 1920s and partly of the writings of social critics and novelists who focused attention on the dark side of the contemporary South. The writers did not, as traditional southerners often charged, invent the negative southern image: the events did that. The Scopes evolution trial in Dayton, Tenn., in July 1925; the anti-Catholicism shown during Al Smith's presidential campaign in 1928; textile strikes and violence in Gastonia and Marion, N.C., and in Elizabethton, Tenn., in 1929; the rise of the modern Ku Klux Klan and numerous lynchings, outbreaks of nightriding, and other manifestations of racial injustice—these events drew the attention of national journalists such as H. L.

Mencken and Oswald Garrison Villard; of prominent magazines such as the *Nation*, the *New Republic*, and the *Century*; and of social scientists such as Frank Tannenbaum of Columbia University, who wrote the aptly entitled *Darker Phases of the South* (1924). The Yankee crusade against the romantic southern image was carried out on several fronts: Tannenbaum concentrating on social ills; Villard and W. E. B. Du Bois, the black editor of the *Crisis*, focusing on racial matters; and Mencken in general command, attacking intellectual and cultural sterility. Mencken's essay, "The Sahara of the Bozart" (1920), was the most trenchant—and readable—indictment of the South, contributing more than any other work to the popular image of the Benighted South.

But the outsiders were hardly alone in portraying the South of the early 20th century as uncivilized, unsanitary, and violent. A native group of journalists and literary figures was perhaps even more effective in this role, presumably because they, as southerners, knew whereof they spoke. North Carolina newspapermen Gerald W. Johnson and W. J. Cash sent essay after essay to their mentor, Mencken, at the *American Mercury*, and the subjects of their essays were southern racism, religious barbarism, and intellectual sterility. Southern editors took their stands against racism and religious bigotry and won Pulitzers for their courage. As George B. Tindall has written, a "fifth column of native Menckens and Tannenbaums" found "an almost ridiculously simple formula for fame": they revealed "the grotesqueries of the benighted South."

Southern novelists were perhaps even bolder, or at least more graphic. Beginning in the early 1920s, writers such as T. S. Stribling of Tennessee and Clement Wood of Alabama, and slightly later Erskine Caldwell of Georgia, portrayed Dixie as a land of poverty, sloth, ignorance, and racial injustice. Stribling's Tennessee hillbillies and corrupt folk of northern Alabama were depicted in *Birthright* (1922), *Teeftallow* (1926), *Bright Metal* (1928), and his late trilogy, *The Forge* (1931), the Pulitzer Prize-winning *The Store* (1932), and *The Unfinished Cathedral* (1934). Caldwell became famous for his pictures of depraved poor whites in *Tobacco Road* (1932) and *God's Little Acre* (1933). And on their heels came greater, less exclusively regional writers, whose portrait of the South, for all its artistry, was judged by reviewers to be no more flattering. In *Look Homeward, Angel* (1929) Thomas Wolfe—in the words of one reviewer—"spat upon" the South. Wolfe's fictional town of Altamont—based closely on his hometown of Asheville, N.C.—he described as a "barren spiritual wilderness," which maintained a "hostile and murderous intrenchment against all new life." If Wolfe's South was intellectually barren and culturally sterile, that of William Faulkner was downright frightening. Between 1929 and 1936 the young Mississippian burst forth with a series of novels portraying a South of decaying gentry, idiocy, religious fanaticism, murder, rape, and suicide. *The Sound and the Fury* (1929) depicted the decline and fall of the Compson family, antebellum aristocrats who could not cope with the new order. *As I Lay Dying* (1930), Faulkner's tragicomic story of the attempt of a dirt-poor Mississippi family to bury their wife and mother, seemed to reinforce the worst image of southern degradation brought out by the journalists of the 1920s. *Sanctuary* (1931) was even more depraved—and, because it was sold to

Hollywood, even more influential in creating the image of a savage South. *Light in August* (1932) presented a gallery of southern grotesques and eccentrics. *Absalom, Absalom!* (1936), perhaps Faulkner's greatest novel, pictured a dark and violent antebellum South. And Faulkner's conniving poor whites, the Snopeses, were yet to come in *The Hamlet* (1940), *The Town* (1957), and *The Mansion* (1959).

By the mid-1930s the depiction of the South in contemporary fiction had become so sordid that even that earlier iconoclast, Gerald W. Johnson, was moved to call this latest Dixie-in-print "The Horrible South." Faulkner, Stribling, Caldwell, and Wolfe were "real equerries of Raw-Head-and-Bloody-Bones . . . the merchants of death, hell, and the grave . . . the horror-mongers-in-chief." *Sanctuary*, Johnson insisted, "put me under the weather for thirty-six hours." Yet, as Johnson maintained, the new picture of the South was a necessary corrective to the romantic picture of the Old, an antidote to Thomas Nelson Page. The South of 1930 was not so bad as its writers suggested—but the South of 1830 had never been so good.

The image of the Benighted South remained firmly entrenched in the national mythology throughout the 1930s. The Scottsboro case of the early thirties and President Roosevelt's pronouncement in 1938 that the South was "the Nation's No. 1 economic problem" insured that. Events of the next two decades did little to modify the image, and those of the 1960s brought the South the same widespread negative attention it had attracted in the 1920s and 1930s. Now Oxford and Selma and Birmingham were in the news, not Dayton and Gastonia and Scottsboro, but the result was the same: Yankee reporters again flocked South and reported that Dixie remained benighted, savage, somehow out of touch with modern civilization.

Only with the end of the civil rights movement—and the rise of the Sunbelt of the 1970s—did the image of a Benighted South begin to fade. In truth, perhaps the coming of interstate highways and widespread air-conditioning had as much to do with the new positive image of Dixie as the departure of lynching and the decline of racial segregation. In any case, as the South entered the last two decades of the 20th century, it was bolder and more confident than before, possessing shining new cities, a new base of wealth dependent on oil, aerospace, real estate, and leisure, and a working knowledge of the power of public relations. The image of the Benighted South it had consigned, in large part, to its past.

Fred Hobson
University of Alabama

Fred Hobson, *Virginia Quarterly Review* (Summer 1985); Gerald W. Johnson, *Virginia Quarterly Review* (January 1935); H. L. Mencken, *Prejudices, Second Series* (1920); George B. Tindall, *Virginia Quarterly Review* (Spring 1964). ☆

Community

|||||||||||||||||||||||||||||

For contemporary southerners the small-town community assumes mythic qualities. Images of community in southern history include plantations in the countryside, a separate black sense of community embodied in the slave

quarters, mill villages in the Carolina Piedmont, brush arbor camp meetings, crossroads country stores, the courthouse square, and neighborhoods in cities. The term *community* evokes feelings of warmth and sociability, yet it also summons memories of the violent compulsion of orthodoxy—the lynch mob was a symbol of the white community's consensus on racial mores in the age of segregation.

Pioneering anthropologists and sociologists used the "community approach" in studying small-town southern life in the 1930s. The Institute for Research in Social Science at the University of North Carolina at Chapel Hill, founded by Howard W. Odum in 1924, supported research on southern communities for the next two decades. Most southern community studies from the 1930s and 1940s were concerned with the internal structures and dynamics of community. While studies were done of mill towns, the classic community research of the 1930s dealt with race and class. John Dollard's *Caste and Class in a Southern Town* (1937) was an attempt to understand "the emotional structure" of Indianola, Miss. Dollard set out to study the personality of southern blacks through their life histories and saw a need to study the community in order to understand individuals living there. He called Indianola "Southern town," suggesting the influence of Robert S. Lynd and Helen M. Lynd's *Middletown* (1929). Other community studies in the South at this time include Allison Davis, Burleigh Gardner, and Mary Gardner's *Deep South: A Social Anthropological Study of Caste and Class* (1937), Hortense Powdermaker's *After Freedom: A Cultural Study of the Deep South* (1939), and Allison Davis and John Dollard's *Children of Bondage: The Personality of*

Negro Youth in the Urban South (1940). These studies analyzed social classes and racial groups and argued that southern towns and cities formed not one community but several.

Southern community studies of the 1940s and 1950s continued to be strongly influenced by social science. John Gillin (of the University of North Carolina at Chapel Hill) and his students analyzed five representative communities, publishing three of the studies (Morton Rubin, *Plantation County*, 1951; Hylan Lewis, *Blackways of Kent*, 1955; and John Kenneth Morland, *Millways of Kent*, 1958). Researchers used observation, questionnaires, interviews, statistical information, and even Rorschach tests to describe the way of life in each community and to place it in a broader theoretical framework designed by Gillin. Solon T. Kimball and Marion Pearsall's *The Talledega Story: A Study of Community Process* (1954) employed "event analysis," a new technique of southern community research, which explored how the people of Talledega carried out a local study of health needs. Pearsall's *Little Smoky Ridge: The Natural History of a Southern Appalachian Neighborhood* (1959) related a small mountain community to its physical setting, internal dynamics, and surrounding countryside. John Kenneth Morland's 1967 essay "Anthropology and the Study of Culture, Society, and Community in the South" suggested the need for community research dealing with southern values, sociocultural transmission, and educational development, none of which had been the central concerns of these earlier studies.

Recent studies view southern communities as historical processes rather than static institutions. To understand any community, one must observe and analyze its development over time. Although historians have produced numerous studies of colonial New England communities, surprisingly few studies exist of southern colonial communities. Darrett B. Rutman and Anita H. Rutman's *A Place in Time: Middlesex County, Virginia, 1650–1750* (1984) is a model work. Orville Vernon Burton's *In My House Are Many Mansions: Family and Community in Edgefield, South Carolina* (1985) and Randolph B. Campbell's *A Southern Community in Crisis: Harrison County, Texas, 1850–1880* (1983) bridge the antebellum and postbellum eras. Gail W. O'Brien's *The Legal Fraternity and the Making of a New South Community, 1848–1882* (1986) is a careful case study of how an elite group imposed its values on one southern community. Historians have not been alone in studying southern communities over time. Sociologist Elizabeth R. Bethel, in *Promiseland: A Century of Life in a Negro Community* (1981), and folklorist William Lynwood Montell, in *The Saga of Coe Ridge: A Study in Oral History* (1970), study black communities over time. The "community studies" approach today uses interdisciplinary methods and theories to explore southern culture from the grass roots in a way pioneered by the French *Annales* historians.

Modern southern literature preserves the image of small-town community life. Literary critics have linked the declining sense of community to the 20th-century Southern Literary Renaissance. Louis D. Rubin, Jr., wrote that the southern community of the late 19th and early 20th centuries "had been self-sufficient, an entity in itself, with a mostly homogenous population, relatively orderly and fixed in its daily patterns." Southern writers at that time were a part of their communities. They lived spiritually satisfying lives but did not produce great art. White writers of the post–World War I South, members of the generation that witnessed the breakup of cohesive community life, were unable to find "spiritual sustenance and order within community life itself" and became literal or symbolic exiles. Their great art was anchored in the creation of community images— Faulkner's Yoknapatawpha County, Wolfe's Altamont, N.C., and Welty's Morgana, Miss.

The southern sense of community has expressed itself in three important institutions. The courthouse square is perhaps the most potent, distinctive symbol of southern community. It is a center of business, political, and economic life drawing together people from both the small town and surrounding rural areas. The courthouse building and a tall Confederate monument (likely dating from between 1890 and 1920 and facing North) towered over the typical square. Around the square, government offices, jails, and banks were symbols of power. There were lawyers' offices, physicians' offices, hardware stores, department stores, furniture stores, drug stores, hotels, cafés, and by the 20th century, perhaps a funeral home and a dentist's office. The blacksmith was a fixture, succeeded in the 20th century by the gas station. There was often a farmers' market near the courthouse, with fresh vegetables and fruits displayed. John Dollard noted in the 1930s that the movie theater was a major community gathering spot.

Some community institutions around the courthouse square appealed primarily to women, others to men. The beauty parlor was a gathering place for women rich and poor. Eudora Welty's "Petrified Man" captures the conversations of the small-town beauty shop as women exchanged news and gossip. Here, young girls were initiated into the roles expected of women.

The barber shop and the pool hall were equivalent male institutions. The pace in the barber shop, like the beauty parlor, was typically slow, and the shop filled not only with those getting their hair cut but with others simply talking or listening. The pool hall was a rougher place, with aggressive talk. In it young adolescents exchanged opinions on sex, drinking, and gambling, and sometimes the exchange became violent. Playwright Mart Crowley grew up listening to such stories in his father's pool hall, "Crowley's Smoke House," in Vicksburg, Miss. In *Intruder in the Dust* Faulkner portrayed the barber shop and the pool hall as community institutions where one found expression of consensus and orthodoxy. The lynch mob might plot its action and gather up the young men hanging out in those places.

Another typically southern part of community life was the county, an important political and administrative institution. Amateur and professional historians have long used county history to define local history, and the modern "new social history" uses census, tax, court, and voting records to reconstruct life at the county level and relate it to broader regional patterns. As historian Robert C. McMath, Jr., notes, southerners thought of the government and the county as the same. "The seat of the county court also became a center of trade and, to a lesser extent, of organized social life."

Counties are made up of smaller communities or rural neighborhoods, which are often groups of extended kin living within territorial boundaries centered around a country store or church. These small hamlets include a tavern, a church, a store, a mill, a few houses, and, before the days of consolidation, perhaps a school. Post–Civil War share-croppers and tenants often moved within the bounds of these subcommunities within counties. While county government brought all citizens together for social, economic, and political reasons, pronounced differences existed between townspeople and those living in the nearby rural countryside. Townspeople saw themselves as more sophisticated than country people, often looked down on them, in fact, but depended on them economically.

The church was a third focus for the southern community. Colonial Anglican churches aspired to achieve community but had failed to do so by the mid-1700s. The rise of the evangelical sects in the 1700s established dissenting communities emphasizing personal religious experience, the symbolic ritual of baptism, and church discipline, and separating the chosen from the larger society. Southern evangelical Protestantism is a religion of individual religious experience, but conversion is the entrance to communal church life. Dominant evangelical churches in the South were intensely involved in caring for members of their religious communities. Historian Donald Mathews describes the southern church of the early 19th century as "a redemptive community."

The church building itself does not tower over the southern landscape the way the courthouse has, but the pervasiveness of small churches suggests that religious communities are organized by sect, race, and social class. Neighborhoods were commonly located around church buildings, representing what historian Orville Vernon Burton calls "communities within the larger community." Churches established community values and a rigorous moral code in frontierlike rural areas. The church was also a major focus for women's community concerns. Limited in their public roles in other areas of southern life, women were active in church organizations and groups, and those involvements often led to more extensive community involvement.

Blacks developed their own community in the South. The slave quarters, the Black Belt, the Delta plantation, the Carolina Low Country, and Tuskegee represent images of distinctly black southern communities. Even for migrants out of the region, the South and its local black communities remain "down home." As Robert B. Stepto notes, these places represent "the exhilarating prospect of community, protection, progress, learning, and a religious life while often birthing and even nurturing (usually unintentionally) a sense of enclosure that may reach claustrophobic proportions." Black folk culture has been a prime means for preservation of a distinctive sense of black community. In blues music and in tales of black folk heroes, individual characters symbolize the black community.

The relationship of blacks to *the* overall southern community remains unclear. Blacks had their own sub-communities, but there was also a larger community that had to be dealt with. Until very recently, this community was clearly dominated by whites. Whites controlled the power, set the agenda, and created the myths. James McBride Dabbs noted that blacks "were never a true part of this community," yet "the community was there, in some ways they belonged to it, household servants rather intimately." The South's elaborate rules of interracial etiquette, manners, and customs were designed to facilitate the functioning of communities inhabited by two races. The folk culture of blacks and whites, especially in small towns and rural areas, was a major expression of a shared sense of southern community, beyond ideology. Folktales, folksongs, and folk art all represented the preservation and transmission of a regionally distinct culture.

The civil rights movement was an effort to integrate the southern community. The movement integrated specific public schools and restaurants and developed a broader definition of the community of people who called themselves southerners. A central idea for Martin Luther King, Jr., was the "beloved community," and the title of his last book, *Where Do We Go from Here? Chaos or Community?*, indicated his concern for achieving a sense of community in both the region and the nation.

The civil rights movement occurred in the South in the context of specific communities—Montgomery, Selma, Albany, Birmingham, Memphis, and countless others. Scholars who have begun to explore the origin and development of the movement within specific communities include William H. Chafe, *Civilities and Civil Rights: Greensboro, North Carolina, and the Black Struggle for Freedom* (1980), Aldon D. Morris, *The Origins of the Civil Rights Movement: Black Communities Organizing for Change* (1984), and Robert J. Norrell, *Reaping the Whirlwind: The Civil Rights Movement in Tuskegee* (1985).

A final symbol of community in the contemporary South is the city neighborhood. The 1950s and 1960s were years of urban renewal, which often destroyed older structures and displaced people from their homes. Wealthy white suburbs grew on the edges of southern cities until the 1970s and 1980s, when a new trend developed. The energy crisis of the early 1970s, federal government Community Development Block Grants, and interest in historical preservation led affluent white southerners to look again to urban neighborhoods as residential areas. Ansley Park and Inman Park in Atlanta, Oakwood in Raleigh, Trinity Park in Durham, and the Oakleigh District in Mobile are but a few of the older urban neighborhoods that have been revived as places to live. Sometimes these areas become havens for southern yuppies at the expense of working-class people traditionally living there, but not always. In explaining the trend, Philip Morris of *Southern Living* stressed "the sense of place and community that most residents of reviving districts comment upon. They like the diversity of ages, of interests, of architecture, of viewpoint, that come together as an urban place." This interest in urban neighborhoods represents an attempt by southerners to preserve the regional ideal of community, a small-town southern ideal surviving in the context of big-city living.

Charles Reagan Wilson
University of Mississippi

Orville Vernon Burton and Robert C. McMath, Jr., eds., *Toward a New South?: Studies in Post–Civil War Southern Communities* (1982); James McBride Dabbs, *The Southern Heritage* (1958); Jean E. Friedman, *The Enclosed Garden: Women and Community in the Evangelical South, 1830–1900* (1985); Rhys Isaac, *The Transformation of Virginia, 1740–1790* (1982); John Brinckerhoff Jackson, *The Southern Landscape Tradition in Texas* (1980); Norman K. Johnson, *Southern Living* (January 1980); Lawrence W. Levine, *Black Culture and*

Black Consciousness: Afro-American Folk Thought from Slavery to Freedom (1977); Donald Mathews, *The Religion of the Old South* (1977); John Kenneth Morland, in *Perspectives on the American South: Agenda for Research*, ed. Edgar T. Thompson (1967); Philip Morris, *Southern Living* (November 1976); Louis D. Rubin, Jr., *Writers of the Modern South: The Faraway Country* (1967); Stephen A. Smith, *Myth, Media, and the Southern Mind* (1985); Robert B. Stepto, *From Behind the Veil: A Study of Afro-American Narrative* (1979). ☆

Family
|||||||||||||||||||||

Social historian Carl N. Degler identifies part of the South's unique appeal as being "in the human warmth and security of its commitment to family and kin," and he speaks with fascination of "the South—where roots, place, family, and tradition are the essence of identity." Degler says, "It is probable, though the evidence is skimpy, that in the southern English colonies and Southern states, kinship ties beyond the immediate family were more important than in the northern areas. Certainly that has been the traditional view. . . . And to this day Southerners acknowledge a more far-flung and more active kin network beyond the family of origin than people in other regions of the United States. . . . Unfortunately, though, the origins and development of this well-recognized propensity in the South for kin connections has been neither systematically delineated nor adequately explained." Both historical information and social science data about southern families are limited, yet powerful images of the southern family persist in the region's literature, music, and art.

Popular images of the southern family include small-town southerners sitting on a front porch at twilight, swapping stories; Sunday dinner around the table, where the best southern cooking is often served; black maids waiting on the white family and sometimes becoming, in effect, family members; long visits from maiden aunts and distant cousins; genealogists seeking their roots and sometimes engaging in ancestor worship; the reality of bitter family feuds as a counterpoint to sentimental family scenes; and family rituals such as births, weddings, and funerals, each an occasion for homecomings and celebrations of kin. Many movie and television portrayals have incorporated and exaggerated these images, stressing above all clannishness as a southern family trait. Traditionally, images of the region's families have dealt primarily with middle- or upper-class whites, very little with black families, and almost never with the families of any other ethnic or religious groups in the region. Although subgroups and particular families carry their own family-based folklore, myths about the power of the family group in the South rest largely on the experiences of white residents of rural areas or small towns.

Many myths about southern families are rooted in what Richard H. King has termed the "Southern family romance," the vision of the South as long being one huge plantation family ruled by powerful white patriarchs who protected both the gracious white women and the childlike, contented black slaves who were their charges. In this view family position governed social life, and family background was the criterion for judging social worth. This vision dominated the so-called local color literature popular from the late 1860s through the early 1900s, and many of its elements persisted in movies such as *Gone with the Wind.* Only recently have historians shed much light on actual family relations in the antebellum era. For instance, scholars once argued that slavery destroyed the black family, but historians recently have shown that the extended kinship system and the "fictive family," one composed of a wide network of community members who take care of each other, have been an institutional source of black cultural survival since before the antebellum era. The images that characterize the southern family romance have died hard, however, even in the face of historical and sociological findings on family relationships.

In the late 1930s and the 1940s social scientists began to examine the unique nature and power of the family in the social networks of the South. Sociologist and historian Margaret J. Hagood found in her late-1930s interviews with tenant farm wives in Georgia, Alabama, and the Carolinas that family-centered activities dominated their lives. "In the decades after the Civil War the family was the core of southern society; within its bounds everything worth while took place," commented social historian Francis Butler Simkins in 1947. Sociologist Rupert B. Vance wrote in 1948 that southern social life was centered in the home and that family solidarity was stressed so much that a clannishness prevailed. Many subsequent generalizations about the family in the South rested on two notions: (1) that extended kin networks predominate throughout the region and (2) that expectations for contact, mutual support, and affection between family members are high.

During the late 1940s sociologists Ernest Burgess and Harvey Locke provided support for these generalizations through their investigations of *familism,* a term denoting strong identification with one's family group and distrust of outsiders; emphasis on family goals, common property, and mutual support; and a desire to perpetuate the family group and its expectations. Early studies described Ozark and Appalachian highlanders as being highly familistic— as representing one end of a spectrum, with other rural residents generally being somewhat less familistic, and urban residents being considerably less so. As a consequence of being a predominantly rural region for much of its history, the South has been assumed by many to be on the higher-to-middle end of this continuum.

Other researchers have supported the general view of the familistic South. Sociologist Bernard Farber described the South and New England as having an "American-biblical kinship system," which functions in a highly stratified society to meld descent groups, limit the range of potential marriage mates, and solidify one's place in the social structure. Other scholars point to the region's population density, large numbers of kin residing within a given area, and existence of lineages over a long period of time as keys to the family's importance in southern culture. Sociologist John Shelton Reed notes that "the love it or leave it" notion applies even at the level of the family and that southerners identify loyalty to one's family as a characteristically southern trait.

Folklorists have gathered much information on the family's importance in preserving, shaping, and transmitting both the oral and material lore of the region through folk art, music, crafts, and stories. Over time southern families have probably differed not so much in the importance they place on the preservation of family records, mementos, and stories as in their resources for doing so. Wealthy whites, for instance, in the late 1800s and early 1900s often commissioned formal paintings or photographic family portraits; poorer white residents relied more on traveling photographers who worked in the field. Photographs of black and other minority families of the same and earlier eras are rare, as are genealogical records. Other sources of family lore abound, however, such as quilts, toys, and work implements passed down through generations. Southerners have also kept family tales alive through a rich oral heritage.

Some of the most powerful explorations of the nature of the family within the South have been by the region's writers. The local colorists had painted a broad, idealized, highly unrealistic vision of southern families and the South as a plantation family, and the writers of the Southern Literary Renaissance struggled to escape from that vision and formulate new understandings. For example, William Faulkner explored the tension between loyalty to family and allegiance to humanity; Tennessee Williams depicted the twisted personalities and relationships often shaped in families; and Eudora Welty examined the stabilizing but sometimes stultifying nature of family bonds. The compelling visions of these and other writers provide realistic, probing images of the ties that bind families.

Evidence of families as tradition bearers in the South persists in countless forms, yet in recent years southern families have experienced much the same rates of change as families throughout the rest of the nation, with growing numbers of divorces, single-parent families, and two-income couples seeking childcare. Also, the region is no longer predominantly rural, residents are very mobile, and most adults maintain frequent contacts only within the nuclear family and with parents and siblings. The impact of changing lifestyles and family forms on frequency of contact, perceived importance of family bonds, and emphasis on one's ancestry has yet to be seen; thus far scholars have not examined the impact of such changes as much as have writers such as Peter Taylor and country singers such as Loretta Lynn. Although the power of family bonds in the South may be changing, many southerners and non-southerners would agree with anthropologist Carole Hill that "the distinctiveness of the South may not be in empirical differences from other regions, but in its unique belief system." In countless ways the family still lies at the center of that system.

Sharon A. Sharp
University of Mississippi

Bert N. Adams, *Kinship in an Urban Setting* (1968); Carlene F. Bryant, *We're All Kin: A Cultural Study of a Mountain Neighborhood* (1981); Ernest W. Burgess and Harvey J. Locke, *The Family: From Institution to Companionship* (1945); Carl N. Degler, *Place over Time: The Continuity of Southern Distinctiveness* (1977), *At Odds: Women and the Family in America from the Revolution to the Present* (1980); Bernard Farber, *Kinship and Class: A Midwestern Study* (1971); Walter J. Fraser, Jr., R. Frank Saunders, Jr., and Jon L. Wakelyn, eds., *The Web of Southern Social Relations: Women, Family, and Education* (1985); Herbert G. Gutman, *The Black Family in Slavery and Freedom, 1750–1925* (1976); Margaret J. Hagood, *Mothers of the South: Portraiture of the White*

Tenant Farm Woman (1939); Peter L. Heller, Gustavo M. Quesada, David L. Harvey, and Lyle G. Warner, in *The Family in Rural Society*, ed. Raymond T. Coward and William M. Smith, Jr. (1981); Carole E. Hill, *Current Anthropology* (June 1977); Richard H. King, *A Southern Renaissance: The Cultural Awakening of the American South, 1930–1955* (1980); Sherry Konter, *Vanishing Georgia* (1982); John Shelton Reed, *One South: An Ethnic Approach to Regional Culture* (1982), *Southerners: The Social Psychology of Sectionalism* (1983), with Daniel J. Singal, eds., *Regionalism and the South: Selected Papers of Rupert Vance* (1982); Louis D. Rubin, Jr., *Writers of the Modern South: The Faraway Country* (1963); Merrill M. Skaggs, *The Folk of Southern Fiction* (1972). ☆

Fatherhood

||||||||||||||||||||||||||||||

Historically, sharp divisions between males and females characterized family responsibilities in the South. The man was regarded as the unchallenged patriarch, the strong, respected provider, the mainstay of southern society. The traditional image of the chivalrous southerner, as opposed to the greedy Yankee, was centered in the southern father's devotion to family, tradition, and race; all these restrained the "natural man" that supposedly emerged in the Yankee. At the same time the South has often been celebrated as a region that stressed the so-called masculine traits; a region demarcated by violence, hard-nosed football, stock car racing, a proclivity toward the military, and hawkish attitudes about war and foreign affairs. Yet, in the literature and sometimes in actuality, it is often a Scarlett

O'Hara or her mother who ends up running the plantation and the mill.

The patriarchal nature of the southern family has been attributed to slavery. Dependent upon slaves as producers of income, the family head, the southern father, had to maintain control of the peculiar institution, and attempts by family members to assert themselves against the head were thought to threaten slavery itself. As pro-slavery theorists justified the institution of slavery with every branch of knowledge, from the Bible to science, the rationale for the authority of the father in the household became increasingly the received wisdom of all southerners. Family, church, and community all reinforced patriarchy. Male dominance persisted in the political, cultural, religious, and economic spheres of the South.

Cotton ruled as King, not Queen, in the South. In the early 20th century, powerful U.S. Senator Ben Tillman used a South Carolina law allowing him to deed his grandchildren to himself, thus thwarting their mother's claim to custody. Except for a brief period during Reconstruction, not until after World War II was divorce legalized in South Carolina. Before child labor laws, southern children commonly worked in the textile mill for a family wage, which was paid directly to the father. In the South the father was the family head and considerable legal authority fortified his power.

Bertram Wyatt-Brown has shown that southerners venerated their male ancestors. Naming patterns in the South signified the importance of patriarchy. The tendency to name children after male family elders remains strong in the South where phone books today still show many juniors and thirds after a name. Although individualistic impulses were in some ways influential, duty to family and one's forebears was paramount. The southerner's respect for history and tradition was reinforced by his obedience to his forefathers.

The legendary southern father was much like the myth of the southern gentleman: well-educated and genteel, with a firm and commanding personality, which demanded deference from all family members and from nonaristocratic whites. Thus, the myth of southern fatherhood has a distinct class bias. Eugene D. Genovese's brilliant work showing that slaves had room for cultural autonomy and arguing the patriarchal nature of slavery suggests that the hegemony of the planter class prevented lower-class whites and slaves from being patriarchs themselves. Other scholars, disagreeing, have demonstrated that the planters' status did not prevent less affluent white or slave males from reigning in their own families. The patriarchal values pervaded all levels of the society and culture.

Popular literature, however, has characterized the lower-class white family as a disorderly one led by irresponsible, lazy, drunken fathers. Thus, ironically, in the South, which supposedly counterpoints the North's emphasis on lucre, fatherly success was associated with financial success.

The father in the black family was generally believed to be absent or nonexistent. Studies of urban areas in the North have shown that racism in the occupational structure of modern society has made it difficult for Afro-American men to get jobs in cities. Careful scrutiny of census and other demographic records shows that this is just as true of southern cities and even small towns and villages. Whereas towns and cities offered both protection and domestic jobs for black women, black men there were excluded from jobs other than those associated with farming. Hence, when sociologists studied black families in the cities they found males absent. In the rural South, however, where most blacks lived after slavery, landowning and tenant families were almost always headed by black men. White landowners were not willing to rent to female household heads unless they had nearly grown children to help in the fields. Thus, in the sparsely settled rural areas, not the cities where interviews and records were more easily available, the scholar found the black patriarch ruling his family very much as did his white counterpart.

Scholars have some records suggesting how planter class fathers treated their children. Fathers had intense but ambivalent feelings about their children. They lavished affection on them during infancy but were torn between their love for their children and their desire to see the children—especially the males—become independent. They might be terribly affectionate with the children one day and then completely unavailable the next. One fatherly technique was to alternate providing and withdrawing intimacy in order to teach discipline and right behavior; this technique internalized guilt and shame in the children.

Parents were seen as exemplars. The children were expected to emulate their parents and other worthy relatives as much as possible, to respect adults and to follow their basic moral precepts. Although fathers sought to teach their children independence, they also wanted the children to learn that they were not so much individuals as extensions of their parents. Their every move, therefore, was not only an indication of their own goodness, but just as importantly a reflection of parental worthiness.

One of the most important aspects of behavior that southern fathers could teach their children was aggressiveness. Even young girls were encouraged to be aggressive. But, of course, boys, and particularly the eldest boy, were the focus of this assertiveness training. Many southern fathers thought children should be given freedom to explore their surroundings, thus gaining the confidence needed to assert themselves fully. Sometimes, however, fathers went too far and merely spoiled their children. This mistake could end tragically, with the sons of prominent men often leading short and dissolute lives.

A variety of father images have appeared in southern literature and music, suggesting other dimensions to the role of the father in regional life. Sometimes fathers, like mothers, are sentimentalized, as in the Jimmie Rodgers country songs of the 1930s, "Daddy and Home" and "That Silver Haired Daddy of Mine." This attitude reflected the long Victorian influence in the South. Beverly Lowry's novel, *Daddy's Girl* (1981), offers a humorous contemporary look at one of the most important southern family relationships—father and daughter, an excessively loving, manipulative, and demanding relationship. The nurturing father is an equally strong image and shows the father passing down folk skills and wisdom to sons and daughters.

Fathers have also been portrayed in harsh terms. Religion has contributed a powerful father image: the father as the Calvinist God's patriarch on earth, the person ruling the southern household and the plantation with an iron fist. The father, to Joe Christmas in William Faulkner's *Light in August*, is a stern figure, always judging, ready to mete out justice to wayward children. The poverty of the postbellum and modern eras and the humiliation for blacks in the racial caste system have also shaped cultural attitudes toward fatherhood. One country song says father was "a farmer but all he ever raised was us." The sharecropping father is seen as frustrated, unable to provide a good life for his family. Richard Wright's harsh portrait of his father in *Black Boy* is an extreme version, although Alex Haley's *Roots* gives images of warm, loving, and strong black fathers.

The sociological study of fatherhood is relatively new, and as yet there is little reliable information on regional differences in attitudes toward fathering, degree of involvement of fathers in childcare, or parental authority patterns. In married-couple families with children present, southern fathers have already experienced marked changes in their sole responsibility as breadwinners during the last several decades because over half of their wives work outside the home. In the South, as elsewhere in the nation, the number of divorced fathers who have either sole or joint custody of their children is rising. Increasingly, fathers are emphasizing their nurturant roles, though social class differences, among others, still shape views about fathers as the authority figure in families.

Literary critic Richard H. King argues that the intellectuals and writers of the Southern Literary Renaissance in the 20th century were attempting symbolically to define their relationship with the region's "fathers." He notes the portraits of the "heroic generation" of ex-Confederates, the pictures of "stern, untroubled, and resolute" fathers that hung in southern parlors. Ironic sons and strong fathers have been predominant images in modern southern literature. Allen Tate explored this theme in his one novel, entitled *The Fathers.* Jack Burden in Robert Penn Warren's *All the King's Men* searches for an understanding of his—and through him, the region's—past by defining a complex relationship to his "father," both real and figuratively (in Willie Stark). William Faulkner seemed fascinated with the "father," portraying ruthless, sometimes cruel patriarchs such as Thomas Sutpen, Carothers McCaslin, and the older Sartoris. These powerful figures succeed, yet eventually, through self-centered pride, are brought to earth. Sutpen's downfall, in particular, comes from his failure to acknowledge his son because the son has black blood; issues of race are tied with fatherhood, as in other areas of southern life.

See also BLACK LIFE: Family, Black; FOLKLORE: Family Folklore; VIOLENCE: Honor

Orville Vernon Burton
University of Illinois

Orville Vernon Burton, *In My Father's House Are Many Mansions: Family and Community in Edgefield, South Carolina* (1985); Jane Turner Censer, *North Carolina Planters and Their Children, 1800–1860* (1984); Richard H. King, *A Southern Renaissance: The Cultural Awakening of the American South, 1930–1955* (1980); Daniel Blake Smith, *Inside the Great House: Planter Family Life in Eighteenth-Century Chesapeake Society* (1980); Bertram Wyatt-Brown, *Southern Honor: Ethics and Behavior in the Old South* (1982). ☆

Fighting South

IIIIIIIIIIIIIIIIIIIIIIIIIIIIIIIIIIIIIII

Few dimensions of southern cultural distinctiveness have provoked more comment than the supposed proclivity of Dixie's citizenry toward personal and societal violence. Prior to the Civil War, numerous European and northern travelers reported from the slave states that the southern people enjoyed soldiering and resolved interpersonal disputes with violence to an unusual degree. Twentieth-century scholars have substantiated this impression, meticulously delineating antebellum southern enthusiasm for wars, the national military establishment, private military academies, filibustering, dueling, and a wide array of other activities indicative of a peculiarly martial/violent regional temperament. The South's martial reputation survived Civil War defeat, won endorsement in the Lost Cause legend, and gained new vitality in the 20th century. It has been a popular concept that southerners have monopolized the army's officer corps, provided disproportionate support for America's role in both world wars and in Vietnam, perpetuated martial instincts with military titles and military preparatory schools, and enshrined violence (high homicide rates, the Ku Klux Klan) within their social mores.

Some recent commentators would relegate unique southern militarism to the realm of myth. The North, it has been discovered, also fostered a plethora of antebellum military academies and volunteer militia companies. Emphasis has been placed upon violence as an American problem rather than as a regional trait. Still, the South's fighting fame persists, encouraged by a tendency of

The Alamo, a shrine of the fighting South, San Antonio, Texas

southerners themselves to claim a special military heritage.

If myth, southern militarism has certainly been an operative fiction with considerable impact upon the region's historical experience. Pre–Civil War antislavery capitalized upon perceptions of an aggressive, violent "Slave Power." A mistaken faith that southerners—by virtue of their military traditions—would prove superior to northerners on the battlefield explains much of the risk-taking intrinsic to secession. In the Civil War northern stereotypes of southern warrior propensities retarded the progress of Union army campaigns. Recent evidence of the myth's substantive impact is more elusive, but when President Jimmy Carter in 1980 attributed his commitment to strategic arms limitation to a recognition that his native region had traditionally venerated "the nobility of courage on the battlefield," thus inducing southerners to lead "the rolls of volunteers and also . . . the rolls of casualties" in America's wars, he gave testimony to a lingering influence of perceptions of southern militarism upon the nation's history.

See also EDUCATION: Military Schools; HISTORY AND MANNERS: Military Bases; Military Tradition

> Robert E. May
> Purdue University

Michael C. C. Adams, *Our Masters the Rebels: A Speculation on Union Military Failure in the East, 1861–1865* (1978); F. N. Boney, *Midwest Quarterly* (Winter 1980); Robert E. May, *Historian* (February 1978). ✩

Garden Myth

||||||||||||||||||||||||||||||||

Although it is a regional variant of the generalized image of America as "the garden of the world," the pastoral image of the South may best be understood in contrast to that of New England. This contrast originated in the attitudes of the settlers of Massachusetts and Virginia toward the archetypal pastoral dominions of Western culture: the Hebraic Garden of Eden and the Hellenic domain of Arcadia. During their long history in the Western literary imagination these concepts have been interwoven. Eden and Arcadia have been symbols of the replacement of the cosmic (the nonconscious or organic) state of human existence with the consciousness of time and history. Simultaneously they have been symbols of an illusory recovery, through pastoral vision and artifice, of the prehistoric state of harmony among God (or gods), man, and nature.

The Edenic and Arcadian images have also served as metaphors of the poetic consciousness. The poetic consciousness has conceived of itself as a garden that has been invaded by history and dispossessed, as Emerson said, of its "original relation to the universe." For the first and last time the New World settlement, in particular the English settlement along the Atlantic Seaboard, seemed to make possible the inclusion of the pastoral vision in the historical consciousness. This golden prospect of the recovery of the archetypal garden was wholly illogical, since the pastoral vision had arisen in response to the differentiation of history. But in defiance of logic the tension between the fiction of the possible recovery of the garden and the reality of history has been, at least until very recently, at the center of the American literary mind.

In the course of New England settlement, notably in Massachusetts, the prospect of a pastoral restoration was associated primarily with the biblical image of Eden. Under the terms of their covenant with God, the Puritan migrants envisioned making their new home a "pleasure garden of the Lord God of Hosts." Transformed from a "garden of the covenant," a homeland of the Puritan elect, into the homeland of a post-revolutionary line of secular literary spirits (running from Emerson through Robert Lowell), New England remained a coherent symbol of an Edenic and/or Arcadian intervention in history. But in the South the pastoral vision developed differently. Although Edenic and Arcadian images of Virginia emerged in the writings of John Smith in the early 17th century, and these no doubt bear a relation to the vivid pastoral images in Robert Beverley's *History and Present State of Virginia* a century later, they did not constitute a continuous, closely structured vision of the South as the scene of pastoral redemption. The fundamental reason lies in the emphasis on the secular in the planting of the southern colony. In Virginia, as Perry Miller pointed out, historical expediency dictated the propagation of tobacco rather than the propagation of the faith. Increasingly tied to a chattel slave-labor system by the development of a world marketplace economy, tobacco cultivation provided the model for the South's use of land and slaves in the subsequent production of sugarcane and cotton. Although owning slaves was by no means universal among southerners who owned land, slavery, becoming the South's "peculiar institution," frustrated the desire of the literary mind to project the South as a pastoral homeland.

In the mythic rendition of the plantation as a garden, the slave master might be portrayed as a man of letters with his Virgil or Horace in hand while he supervised his slaves, but in truth the gardener was his illiterate African chattel. This knowledge haunted the quest in the South for the image of the pastoral as an intervening force in history. Its disturbing influence may be seen in Thomas Jefferson's turning from his one explicit denunciation of slavery in the *Notes on the State of Virginia* (1785) to a vision of the American yeoman on his freehold as the representative American; in John Pendleton Kennedy's equivocal treatment of slavery in *Swallow Barn* (1832); and in William Gilmore Simms's account of the relationship between Porgy and his slave Tom in *Woodcraft* (1852). Unwittingly, Simms dramatized the insight of Hegel into the master-slave connection. Although he believes he lives in the superiority of his own will, Hegel suggested, the master in actuality has no will and no existence save in the consciousness of his slave. The slave, moreover, knows this. In this symbiotic situation in the South all men of letters, being connected with the figure of the slave master through their involvement in the defense of slavery, were psychically dependent on the unlettered slave.

The repressed tension between the quest for pastoral redemption and historical reality did not become overt in the southern literary expression until the distance between the South of slavery and the South of freed slaves and freed masters (a society still more complex than the antebellum southern society) allowed for the ironic insights of William Faulkner, John Crowe Ransom, Allen Tate, Robert Penn Warren, Eudora Welty, William Styron, Walker Percy, and other white southern writers. Together with a small but significant number of southern black writers— among them Charles W. Chesnutt, Jean Toomer, Richard Wright, Ralph Ellison, and Ernest Gaines—20th-century southern writers have realized the literary possibilities of the drama of the dispossession of the pastoral ethos by the ethos of history. Making this drama their subject, they have made the alienated literary imagination, the dispossessed garden, yield the rich flowering known as the Southern Renaissance.

See also LITERATURE: Agrarianism in Literature

Lewis P. Simpson
Louisiana State University

David Brion Davis, *The Problem of Slavery in the Age of Revolution, 1780–1823* (1975); Leo Marx, *The Machine in the Garden: Technology and the Pastoral Ideal* (1964); Lewis P. Simpson, *The Brazen Face of History: Studies in the Literary Consciousness in America* (1980), *The Dispossessed Garden: Pastoral and History in Southern Literature* (1975); Henry Nash Smith, *Virgin Land: The American West as a Symbol and Myth* (1950). ☆

History, Central Themes

The earliest explanation of southern distinctiveness began with the climate. In 1778, when the South Carolina Assembly was debating the ratification of the Articles of Confederation, William Henry Drayton saw the union of the states as a threat to the plantation economy. "From the nature of the climate, soil and produce of the several states," he said, "a northern and a southern interest naturally and unavoidably arise." Meteorological conditions encouraged certain activities among the inhabitants, Drayton declared, and they in turn made possible a particular lifestyle that became characteristically southern.

One hundred and fifty years later U. B. Phillips agreed. "Let us begin by discussing the weather," he said, in a widely quoted statement, "for that has been the chief agency in making the South distinctive." To Phillips, as to Drayton, climate encouraged sectional interests by settlers in the American states.

From tobacco and rice to indigo and cotton and sugarcane, weather and soil imposed an agriculture of semitropical staple crops that yielded quick profits. The large returns induced planters to create ever larger estates, which led to a labor shortage. The availability of land and the lack of people willing to work for someone else together produced the plantation with its system of coerced labor. "The house that Jack built," as Phillips described it, grew inexorably from a determinative weather pattern.

Other interpreters echoed Phillips's views. Clarence Cason defined the South as that part of North America where the Fahrenheit thermometer reached 90 degrees in the shade at least 100 afternoons a year. The oppressive heat compelled cooks to concoct gastronomic delights to tempt sluggish appetites, thus giving rise to the food-and-condiment school of southern analysts. Other students suggested that the humid heat purified and strengthened a Nordic racial strain to engender a superior type of humanity, sometimes called cavalier.

The environmentalists thus explained the central theme of the South by the plantation and its products, themselves the result of climate and soil conditions. Staple crops, servile laborers, and lordly masters in theory emulated Old World manorial rulers—this was the South of Phillips and his followers.

The climate-determined South was largely mythic, however, and it appeared so self-serving—an excuse for such glaring inequities in the status quo—that it has been under constant attack. The idea was also difficult to defend in a region that extended through 15 degrees of north latitude, and from sea level to the forested heights of Appalachia, from humid woodlands to semiarid plains.

Even as critics questioned the climate theme, other students pursued the possibility that the South might be identified on the basis of behavior patterns. Charles S. Sydnor pointed the way to new paths of investigation, arguing that southern historians must define their subject before proceeding further. The plantation environment of rural farmlands and sparse population provided examples of the social patterns he used to define the region. W. J. Cash agreed, portraying the southern mind as "what happened when the tradition of aristocracy met and married with the tradition of the backwoods." John Hope Franklin identified the South as a violent land still under frontier conditions, with blood feuds, the dueling code, and a strong military tradition.

Earl E. Thorpe perceived a male sheikdom of erotic libertinism in a haremlike world of subjugated and complaisant women. Slavery was, in his view, as much a sexual institution as an economic or a social one. Other students, however, stressed the gynecocracy—the matriarchy—of the isolated estate, in the families of both masters and slaves. That same isolation and underpopulation convinced David Bertelson that the staple-crop society lacked social unity and showed little evidence of community activities, even those as important as road and bridge building. The lazy South was his version of the central theme.

The geographer Wilbur Zelinski discussed what he called "settlement characteristics" as a way of identifying the South. In house types and urban morphology, including a lack of spatial pattern to farm buildings and a high incidence of abandoned buildings, he found a "constellation of traits" that were coterminous with the South and represented regional characteristics.

Other students of southern society have at one time or another defined their subject in terms of such phenomena as fireworks at Christmas and a quiet Fourth of July, mockingbirds, xenophobia, a chivalric respect for the ladies, a slovenly and dialectical speech pattern, and shoeless, clay-eating poverty. Pellagra, malaria, and hookworm have also provided thematic interpretations.

Subsequent investigators saw significance in the region's religious expression. Known colloquially as the Bible Belt, the Southeast comprised the largest block of Protestant Christian evangelicals to be found anywhere, and at times that faith impelled people to attack the alluring temptations of flesh and mind. Publicity surrounding the 1925 trial of John T. Scopes in Dayton, Tenn., for teaching evolution dramatized the religious attitudes of southerners and made these beliefs an easy explanation for regional distinctiveness.

One-party politics and a preference for a confederated league of semiindependent member states ("states' rights") gave rise to another theme that took its cue from political platforms and voting patterns. Many political observers in more recent times have discussed the Sunbelt South and its implications for government policies.

The presence of black Americans, of course, has been a major guidepost to a definition of southern distinctiveness. The negative side of the region's racial and social relationships—slavery, segregation, violence, and disfranchisement—has provided interpretive themes. An exception came from historian-folklorist Charles Joyner, who wrote that "the transformation of African culture into Afro-American culture has been one of the major themes of American history, with innumerable implications for every aspect of American life."

Twentieth-century efforts by the national government to eradicate racial practices spurred irreconcilable white historians into pursuing still another central theme. The South, they declared, came into existence only under attack from outsiders. Egocentric sectionalism, or the hundred-year effort to reconstruct the South along northern dimensions, required otherwise divided southerners to unite in defense of their interests.

More recent analysts, such as C. Vann Woodward, have found the central theme of southern history to be southern history itself. Prosperity, optimism, and unvarying triumph, said to be the content of the national past, did not describe the aberrant record of southern history. That, went the argument, made the South, and southerners, different. Other students, such as George B. Tindall, sought the essence of the southern character in a preference for myth, the unreal, and the romantic, because reality was too unpleasant.

No single attribute or collection of conditions has succeeded in explaining satisfactorily the continuing awareness of a separate South. It may indeed be necessary to conclude that aside from the idea or belief, the South has no definite existence. That does not detract from its reality or its impact, for ideas are powerful forces in human affairs. The search for the American South is a chapter in the intellectual history of the country, and the idea of the South is one of the most significant facts in making the present what it is.

See also HISTORY AND MANNERS articles

David L. Smiley
Wake Forest University

David Bertelson, *The Lazy South* (1967); W. J. Cash, *The Mind of the South* (1941); Clarence Cason, *90° in the Shade* (1935); Robert S. Cotterill, *The Old South: The Geographic, Economic, Social, Political and Cultural Expansion, Institutions, and Nationalism of the Ante-bellum South* (1936); W. T. Couch, ed., *Culture in the South* (1934); Carl N. Degler, *The Other South: Southern Dissenters in the Nineteenth Century* (1974); John Hope Franklin, *The Militant South* (1956); Charles Joyner, *Down by the Riverside: A South Carolina Slave Community* (1984); Michael O'Brien, *The Idea of the American South, 1920–1941* (1979); U. B. Phillips, *American Historical Review* (October 1928); David Potter, *The South and the Sectional Conflict* (1968); Charles S. Sydnor, *Journal of Southern History* (February 1940); William R. Taylor, *Cavalier and Yankee: The Old South and American National Character* (1957); Earl E. Thorpe, *Eros and Freedom in Southern Life and Thought* (1967); Frank E. Vandiver, ed., *The Idea of the South: Pursuit of a Central Theme* (1964); C. Vann Woodward, *The Burden of Southern History* (1961); Wilbur Zelinsky, *Social Forces* (December 1951). ☆

Motherhood

||||||||||||||||||||||||||||||

Street slang and graffiti that commonly refer to one's mother in northern cities are less frequently found in the South, even in its urban areas. Call a southern boy a "son-of-a-bitch" and he might break both your legs. Not because you have insulted *him*; you have done far, far worse: you have insulted his *mother*. And to insult any southern mother is to insult Virtue, Piety, Honor, and the South.

Images and popular stereotypes of "southern mothers" have differed along regional, economic, class, and racial lines. Ideals of southern motherhood differ among ethnic and economic subcultures, yet two particular stereotypes of southern motherhood abound in the popular literature and movies—the black mammy and the upper-class white lady, both portrayed to perfection in *Gone with the Wind*.

Although a remarkable group of gifted scholars has written on southern white women, at present less is known about the white southern mother than about the Afro-American mother in the South. This is at least partly because reality is confused with an image central to the development of the southern white identity. Although David Potter argued that women have not participated in the formation of the national character of the United States, William R. Taylor claims that the South adopted essentially feminine characteristics because the region failed in the masculine world of the marketplace. Most recent studies demonstrate that the South did not fail in the chase after wealth but simply took a different and perhaps more lucrative path. After the Civil War, however, both adherents of the Old South legend and advocates of the industrial New South acquiesced in a sentimental portrayal of the plantation South, which held the southern lady at center stage to justify the existing social order.

In its worst forms the idealization of

the southern mother, and hence, the southern white woman, was used to justify the barbarism of lynching black men. Winthrop D. Jordan has shown how sexual fantasies of Europeans, especially the English, were projected onto Africans and combined with slavery to foster an intense racism. After slavery ended, protection of southern womanhood became a battle cry for the repression of southern blacks. Many whites portrayed the Afro-American as a destroyer of social order, and they saw the white family, the basis of social stability, as the most obvious point of defense against imagined or real attacks. According to this myth, white women symbolized the family and needed protection from rape or from intermarriage with black men. Thus, such fears expressed both sexual and social concerns.

W. J. Cash called the idolatry of southern white women "downright gyneolatry. . . . Hardly a sermon . . . did not begin and end with tributes in her honor, hardly a brave speech . . . did not open and close with the clashing of shields and the flourishing of swords for her glory. At the last, I verily believe, the ranks of the Confederacy went rolling into battle in the misty conviction that it was wholly for her that they fought."

Despite the romantic plantation literature, the aristocratic southern white wife was not the only figure idealized. All successful southern men owed their accomplishments to their mothers; whatever heights they attained were attributed to their mother's love, teachings, sacrifices, and examples. Two southern leaders identified with the common man were Andrew Jackson of the antebellum South and Ben Tillman of the late 19th-century period of agrarian unrest. Both

men's fathers died before the sons were born and both leaders were reared by their mothers—women celebrated for teaching correct patriarchal values to their famous sons. President Jackson praised his mother: "She was as gentle as a dove and as brave as a lioness. . . . The memory of my mother and her teachings were after all the only capital I had to start life with." U.S. Senator Tillman explained that his mother taught "habits of thrift and industry; to be ambitious; to despise shams, hypocrisy, and untruthfulness; to bear trouble and sorrow with resolution." As their nicknames, "Old Hickory" and "Pitchfork Ben," imply, both Jackson and Tillman were celebrated for the so-called masculine traits one might expect from leaders in a patriarchal society.

Historically, the southern woman was the guardian of the family. She had children with remarkable frequency, rarely disclosing the pain and suffering that accompanied almost constant childbearing. Usually she celebrated her childbearing role. When she was not confined to bed in pregnancy or childbirth, environmental, social, and economic conditions dictated her day-to-day routines: gardening, canning, preserving, cooking; spinning, weaving, sewing, knitting; washing, ironing, cleaning; nursing and caring for husband, children, friends, and animals.

Despite the differences between the North and the South, the role of the mother in the 19th century was very similar in both sections. She was the primary rearer of children and the inculcator of domestic moral values. According to the prevailing view, the southern woman was the moral superior of her husband, so upon her fell the burden of making a decent and moral home, providing a good example for her young children and a refuge for the family patriarch from the turmoil of the workplace or the realm of politics.

Because few public schools were available, the southern white matriarch played a substantial role in educating her children. The early education of most southerners therefore depended upon the knowledge of their mothers and the degree to which they took this role seriously. Some southerners were extremely well taught, but others lacked the most rudimentary book learning. Most mothers taught their girls to sew, weave, and care for younger children, while fathers taught their boys to handle responsibility.

As the upholder of key moral values, the woman was also expected to teach the children piety. She did this primarily by example. Although men were active in southern churches, the mother typically was the more constant churchgoer and usually inducted her children into the social order by taking them to church and by reading them the Bible.

Doris Ulmann photograph of a mother and her infant somewhere in the South, c. 1933

With religious values so closely allied to family solidarity, the woman's role in introducing the children to religious faith in the South was seen as an effective way for her to strengthen family ties. As keeper of the family's religious flame, the woman made sure her home was a refuge from the meanness of everyday life.

One of the reasons women increasingly took on teaching positions in the North in the 1840s and later in the South was that the female teacher was widely regarded as a sort of classroom surrogate mother who eased the transition of the young child from the home to the community and furthermore prepared the child to take his or her place in the rapidly emerging industrial society. Women assumed an important role in the classroom in the South even though industrial changes occurred very slowly there. Once public schools took hold in the South, the female teacher rapidly became almost universal in elementary schools, carrying out her maternal function of imparting the right values to the young.

The role of southern mother, nonetheless, sometimes conflicted with the southern ideal of womanhood. Whereas the mother was expected to be a preeminent moral guardian and a tower of strength, as well as efficient, protective, and self-reliant, the ideal woman was often seen as gentle, submissive, flighty, independent, and seemingly unfit to rear children. Certainly, southern women, like northern women, struggled under such contradictions and limitations. If there was a resolution to this dilemma for southern women, it emerged with age, the flighty behavior of the southern belle, desirable in young adulthood, changing suitably with the bearing of the first child.

As novelist Gail Godwin recently pointed out, the roles of wife and mother have traditionally given identity to the southern woman. Godwin's fictional composite southern lady responds to the question of identity: "Who am I? I am the wife of a wonderful husband and the mother of four adorable children, that's who I am." Modern writers have been much more unkind about the image and its impact on the South. Among others, Flannery O'Connor, Lillian Smith, and William Faulkner portray the damage done to women and to the South as they tried to live with the requirements of perfectionism that symbolized white southern motherhood. Women struggled to reconcile the expectations and realities of the modern world and the legend of southern motherhood. And southern white men have been accused by many pop psychologists of exhibiting a "madonna-whore" attitude toward women: the southern mother was worshiped and put upon a pedestal, while other women, those of lower economic status, the daughters of white tenants and textile workers, Afro-American or Indian women, were fair game for the South's young bloods.

The sentimentality of the Victorian era helped shape the image of southern white motherhood and has been preserved in modern regional popular culture. Early country singer Jimmie Rodgers sang "Mother, Queen of My Heart" and Hank Williams later wrote and recorded "Message to My Mother," one of a number of poignant country tunes dedicated to mourned dead mothers. Dolly Parton's "Coat of Many Colors" is a tale of the triumph of a mother's love over poverty. Southern popular culture, black and white, conveys images of endlessly toiling, long-suffering mothers. "Mama Tried" is Merle Haggard's tribute to a mother whose good influence was unable to keep her boy from trouble. "I'm the Only Hell My Mama Ever Raised" similarly is Johnny Paycheck's lament of a boy hell-bent for trouble who rejected his mother for questionable friends and fast cars.

The image of the southern black mother has taken a different path altogether. Although most black women worked in the fields and not in the planter's house, the most popular image of the black woman has been the mammy. The black mammy, like the southern lady, was also born in the white mind, a creation of slavery: "the black mammy, that creature of impeccable virtue, administrative skill, power and nurturing ability, who yet inexplicably remained in bondage." Suckling a white baby at one breast and a black child at the other, mammy was simple, religious, strong, practical, and tough enough to knock about male slaves caught with a finger in the pie or scores of home-sacking Yankee "blue-bellies" and poor white trash scalawags. Unlike the mythical southern aristocratic mother, mammies were not ladylike; whereas white women were viewed as unladylike if they worked, black women were considered lazy and impudent if they resisted working long hours at hard labor. The black mammy sweated over boiling cauldrons, toiled with wash, scrubbed the kitchen, and minded the children. The black mother had to take care of herself and she had to teach her children to survive their inferior place in society. Mammy's religious strength was elevated to sainthood by William Faulkner's character Dilsey.

Whereas white mothers were stereotypically submissive to their patriarchal husbands, the strength of the black mother led to the myth of the black matriarchy. The myth that black women were the dominant force within their families and that fathers were often absent originated with well-intentioned reformers and goes back at least to abolitionist literature. Early depictions of slave mothers pointed to the horrors of breaking up the family by selling children and spouses, the arbitrary beatings of slaves by whites, and the sexual exploitation of slave women by white men. Until the 1970s scholars and the public generally accepted the notion of the "weak," meaning fatherless, black home, and this in turn reinforced and influenced white society's attitudes toward black people in general. The concept of black matriarchy dominated scholarly literature and became a political issue in the wake of the controversial 1965 study by Daniel Moynihan, who held that the contemporary black matriarchal family had its principal origins in slavery. In the mid-1980s concerns about the black family gained new attention because of the increase from 29.3 percent in 1970 to 47.2 percent in 1982 in the percentage of black single-parent, female-headed families. Concern has focused particularly on the high percentage of those families who live below the poverty level. For example, in six southern states in 1980 over 60 percent of all the single-parent, female-headed families were black.

Many recent studies have corrected the grosser misconceptions about black family life, including that of the matriarchy. Herbert G. Gutman in particular has proved the Afro-American commitment to the family as an institution, in both slavery and freedom. He and other historians have confirmed for Afro-Americans what is normally assumed for other groups: the two-parent nuclear family was the normal means for organizing primary experience (sex relations, child rearing, and descent). As a result, scholars increasingly concentrate on other questions such as illegitimacy, attitudes toward working wives, influence of religion, and the division of authority in the family. Nevertheless, black leaders are also calling for more attention to the needs of poor, single-parent black families and to means for enhancing the stability of black families.

A certain irony in the study of the black matriarchy suggests, however, a symbiotic relationship between racism and sexism. For over 60 years scholars, mostly male, pointed to the black family and called it matriarchal and therefore deficient. With the civil rights movement young northern white women who came South began to see heroines in strong black women such as Rosa Parks and Fannie Lou Hamer. When the feminist movement needed heroines, it turned to the scholarly literature on the black matriarchy for role models. *Ms.* magazine devoted an issue to black women as historical heroines for modern women, at the same time that mostly white male scholars have been arguing that there was no black matriarchy.

One of the paradoxes within the historical scholarship of the last decade has concerned the place of black and white women within American families. As scholars have "rehabilitated" the male role in the black family, feminist scholars have shown the power of the wife within white middle- and working-class families. Historians are just beginning to understand the images and the roles of black and white mothers in the American South.

See also BLACK LIFE: Family, Black; Race Relations; HISTORY AND MANNERS: Sexuality

Orville Vernon Burton
University of Illinois

Maxine Alexander, ed., *Speaking for Ourselves: Women of the South* (1984); Irving H. Bartlett and Glenn Cambor, *Women's Studies*, vol. 2 (1974); Orville Vernon Burton, *In My Father's House Are Many Mansions: Family and Community in Edgefield, South Carolina* (1985); Walter J. Fraser, Jr., R. Frank Saunders, Jr., and Jon L. Wakelyn, eds., *The Web of Southern Social Relations: Women, Family, and Education* (1985); Herbert G. Gutman, *The Black Family in Slavery and Freedom, 1750–1925*; U.S. Department of Commerce, Bureau of the Census, *Current Population Reports*, Series P-20, no. 380 (1983), *General Social and Economic Characteristics, 1980* (by state) (1981). ☆

New South Myth

||||||||||||||||||||||||||||||||||||||||||||

Beaten and frustrated, the postbellum South furnished fertile soil for the growth of myth, for grafting the imagined upon the real to produce a hybrid that itself became a force in history. Hardly had Union armies sealed the fate of the Old South in 1865 before some men began to speak of a New South. By the early 1870s optimists were taking hope from defeat, envisioning a society that would be less sumptuous but more substantial than the antebellum plantation order to which they paid homage but which, they believed, had been shown wanting in the ordeal of war.

The advocates of a New South be-lieved that economic regeneration was the region's most pressing need. To solicit the northern capital necessary to effect that regeneration, they encouraged reconciliation between the old enemies. They promised to treat the black man fairly in his sphere, thereby seeking to soothe any northern consciences troubled by the abandonment of Reconstruction and to promote a harmony between the races that would foster the social stability so highly prized by potential northern investors. Racial accommodation and sectional reconciliation would do much to guarantee the *sine qua non* of the New South program, the development of an industrial economy that would restore prosperity and prominence to the region.

During the 1880s, largely because of the untiring labors of publicists such as Henry W. Grady of the Atlanta *Constitution* and Richard H. Edmonds of the Baltimore *Manufacturers' Record*, the New South idea became increasingly popular. To such molders of opinion, the proponents of the industrial ethos were broad-minded and progressive; its opponents, their numbers ever diminishing, narrow and reactionary. In Grady's celebrated "New South" address before an appreciative audience in New York in 1886, he proclaimed that southerners, having been converted to the Yankee way, were rejecting the ideal of leisure, replacing politics with business as their chief endeavor, and sharing liberally with the black man the region's mounting prosperity. Three years later, Edmonds wrote that the South's vast resources were already insuring the recovery of the position the region had held in 1860 as the richest section of the country. For Edmonds, Grady, and others of like mind, the ideal had been transformed into the actual.

By 1890 the myth of the New South as a land that was rich, just, and triumphant was perceived as reality by many southerners.

To a great degree the ascendancy of the myth was the result of wishful thinking. In point of fact, at the end of the century, the southern black man existed in circumstances little better than those of slavery; the prosperity vaunted by the New South spokesmen was largely illusory; the industrialization that had occurred—and it was never so prevalent as claimed—was often controlled by northerners. Still the stepchild of the nation, the South was hardly triumphant, rich, or just.

Nevertheless, the New South myth survived not only the challenge of statistics but also the attacks mounted by the desperate agrarians who embraced Populism in the 1890s. With Populism dying, the intellectual temper of the next 30 years, like that of the 1880s, was characterized by a romantic, optimistic faith in progress. By the 1920s the business boosters were excelling their ideological forebears in touting the advance of southern industrialization.

That advance was indeed rapid. As numerous industries underwent significant expansion during the 1920s, the number of manufacturing workers in the South rose by almost 10 percent while the rest of the nation suffered a decline of that same proportion. Yet if the boosterism of the dollar decade had a sounder basis in reality than did the boomerism of the 1880s, there was ballyhoo in generous measure all the way from the Mason-Dixon line to Florida's Gold Coast. The second-generation New South enthusiasts portrayed the region as a land basking in the rays of prosperity, even though the profits of southern industry often wound up outside the region and southern workers labored longer and earned less than did those in the North.

The clouds of the Great Depression eclipsed the myth, but only for a brief time. By the end of the 1930s, lifted by hopes of recovery and by southern indignation over the region's being labeled the nation's primary economic problem, the booster spirit was again ascendant. Moreover, the agrarian myth, which had earlier served as a counterpoise to the New South myth, lost much of its vitality as a force in man's affairs as many of its adherents either abandoned farming as a commercial enterprise or, succumbing to hard times and New Deal policies, left the land altogether.

World War II ushered in a degree of industrialization long dreamed of by southern promoters. Between 1939 and 1972 the number of factories grew by more than 160 percent and the number of workers in them by more than 200 percent. Prosperity accompanied the expansion of industry as per capita income in the South increased by 500 percent between 1955 and 1975—a rate 200 percent higher than that of the nation as a whole. The New South myth grew ever more compelling as the region's economic advance became ever more real. Yet just as important to strengthening the myth were the labors of the region's industrial promoters, who rivaled the boomers of the 1880s and the boosters of the 1920s in the quest for material progress. Intent upon maintaining what was called an excellent business climate, chambers of commerce, development boards, and newspapers often urged local and state governments to offer industrialists a variety of inducements such as public financing of plant construction, "startup" programs for new industries, tax reductions or exemptions, and courses in "union busting" at public universities to keep labor cheap, docile, and unorganized. Some promoters also encouraged the token integration of the races to help create a proper image elsewhere, which was but a minor variation on a major theme of the New South movement of a century before.

So striking was the region's economic advance and so successful was the selling of the South that by the late 1960s, pundits began referring to the latest New South as part of the Sunbelt, that region spanning the southern portion of the nation and growing rapidly in population, prosperity, and power. Underdogs for so long, southerners sometimes took what they considered well-deserved delight in the discomfiture of residents of the Frostbelt, who lamented the relocation of factories in the South. As had occurred a hundred years earlier, many southerners saw their region as just, triumphant, and rich—just in its treatment of the black man, triumphant in its economic struggle with the North, and rich in material goods.

The myth failed to reflect reality adequately. Despite changes in the law, blacks found that they were often still the victims of segregation and inequality. Despite the hyperbole accompanying the Sunbelt phenomenon, the belief that the South would soon reduce the North to beggary betrayed an ignorance of the facts. Despite increasing prosperity, the South was hardly rich; as of 1981, average annual per capita income in the region lagged behind that of the rest of the country by almost $2,000.

For all the hope that the New South myth has inspired—no mean achievement in itself—it has countenanced complacency toward social ills, resignation to the abuse of the natural en-

vironment, and the rise of a mass culture that diminished the personalism in human relations long cherished in the southern folk culture. Unless the New South myth can be more tightly harnessed in order to serve the general welfare, the idea could remain a negative influence.

See also HISTORY AND MANNERS: World War II; INDUSTRY articles; LITERATURE: Agrarianism in Literature; URBANIZATION: Urban Boosterism; Urban Growth; Urban Leadership

Wayne Mixon
Mercer University

James C. Cobb, *The Selling of the South: The Southern Crusade for Industrial Development, 1936–1980* (1982); Paul M. Gaston, *The New South Creed: A Study in Southern Mythmaking* (1970); Richard B. McKenzie, *Tax Review* (September 1982); George B. Tindall, *The Emergence of the New South, 1913–1945* (1967), *The Ethnic Southerners* (1976), *Houston Review* (Spring 1979). ☆

Northern Mythmaking

The southern cultural landscape is surely as diverse as the human, geographical, or economic landscapes that comprise it. Just as surely, southerners remain, as journalist Jonathan Daniels said, "a mythological people . . . who live in a still legendary land." Southern mythology, in turn, is the product of many cultural forces, both interregional and national in character.

The South has had sufficient materials, and certainly the imagination, to shape a fictitious past that its people could regard as true. But regions to the north of the Mason-Dixon line also had an important hand in these legendary creations. Perhaps because of the long-standing desire to discover a central theme for the southern experience, historians have not cultivated enough of a national perspective on the role the Yankee has played in both the original creation and the tenacious upholding of the South's legendary past. Studies of southern myths have too often failed to explore how regional myths attracted a national audience.

As historian Henry Steele Commager has emphasized, "the most familiar of Southern symbols came from the North: Harriet Beecher Stowe of New England gave us Uncle Tom and Little Eva and Topsy and Eliza, while it was Stephen Foster of Pittsburgh who sentimentalized the Old South, and even 'Dixie' had northern origins." Connecticut Yankee Stowe based her impressions of the South on extremely limited firsthand experience and, penning *Uncle Tom's Cabin* (1852) in Brunswick, Maine, gave national narrative strength and attention—to say nothing of credibility—to a kaleidoscope of mythical images and stereotypes, which a good many people even today assume are historically accurate portraits of the South and southerners before the war. She devised the faithful darky (Sambo) image of blacks; graphically portrayed a villainous version of the plantation overseer who uniquely symbolized the acquiescence of the North to southern myth by being of Yankee origins, from Vermont; and indirectly gave vitality to the related ideals of cavalier and southern belle.

To the same effect, Stephen Foster composed "Susanna" (1847) and "Old Folks at Home" (1851) prior to a one-month excursion into the South in 1852, after which he published "Massa's in de Cold, Cold Ground" (1852), "My Old Kentucky Home" (1852), and "Old Black Joe" (1860). These songs not only appealed to the emotions, but their lyrics voiced a strong sense of nostalgia for the old plantation. Immensely popular over the years, Foster's songs fed the American romantic imagination with a sentimentalized view of what life in the South allegedly was like before the Civil War, although most of them were composed in Allegheny County, Pa. Undeniably, Foster's plantation songs have had a legend-creating impact on the American popular mind, conveniently offering succeeding generations easily voiced and recyclable visions of an idealized life in the sunny South.

Three years after the appearance of Harriet Beecher Stowe's faithful old Tom, suffering Eliza, and sadistic Simon Legree, and in the midst of Stephen Foster's mythic musical production, another northerner came forward to offer additional weight to the developing myth of southern antebellum luxury. In 1855 David Christy of Ohio published his book *Cotton Is King*, and in the process he touched off a great deal of discussion both in America and Europe as to the industrial world's dependence upon the raw cotton of the South. The effect of this book was to obscure the realities of the South's diversified economy and create the impression that Dixie was an empire of plantations and slaveholders.

Even considering the influence of Harriet Beecher Stowe, Stephen Foster, and David Christy, perhaps nothing more emotionally captured the flavor of the southern image than the song "Dixie." Symbolic of the southern way of life, it was written in New York City by an Ohioan, Daniel Emmett, in 1859. Though used as a marching tune by both Union and Confederate forces during the Civil War, it soon became the unofficial national anthem of the South and has remained one of the most important sentimental expressions of southern regionalism ever since. By the time Jefferson Davis and Alexander Hamilton Stephens assumed the leadership of the Confederate States of America, the Emmett-inspired romance had already begun to work its magic. Clement Eaton has described the scene in this fashion: "On February 18, 1861, they were inaugurated in the state capitol at Montgomery, and at the ceremonies a band played the new song 'Dixie,' with its pervading nostalgia. Like the candles, coffins, patent medicines, tall silk hats, plows—indeed, most manufactured articles used in the South—the song that was destined to become the unofficial anthem of the Confederacy was also an import from the Yankee." Even with regard to their regional mythology, apparently, southerners had cause to regard themselves as a colony of the North.

The efforts of northerners to romanticize the South artistically are of course not limited to Stowe, Foster, Christy, and Emmett. Francis Pendleton Gaines has argued that northern drama and northern minstrelsy, to say nothing of northern artistic images of the South such as Eastman Johnson's *My Old Kentucky Home* (1859) and Winslow Homer's *Sunday Morning in Virginia* (c. 1870), gave special consideration to mythical plantation materials. The case can also be made, as William R. Taylor has done, that it was the literary energy of the North as well as the South—the work of James K. Paulding of New York, for example—that seeded the fictional

plantation in literature. And not to be forgotten are the numerous sentimental lithographs of Nathaniel Currier at Roxbury, Mass., and James Merrit Ives of New York City, who offered a national audience unblemished images of Americana, both North and South. Collectively, northern works of art from Stowe and Foster to Currier and Ives did much to create an image of southern history the verisimilitude of which was seldom examined by its avid consumers—an image at times at odds with fact, but of critical importance nonetheless to the development of a regional mythology.

But the questions remain: Why did the North find myths of the South so very comfortable and comforting? What caused this fusion of southern and northern sentiment? How was it that so many northerners became so distinctly of the southern persuasion? The South and the North became copartners in the creation of a regional pseudopast for a multitude of reasons: a latent "love of feudalism" and "romantic hunger" (democratic pretense to the contrary notwithstanding); "status anxiety" or "hankering after aristocracy" on the part of northerners being displaced in either the social or political power structures of 19th-century America; a pristine nostalgia for agrarianism while in the throes of national industrialization and urbanization; a need to hide and sustain an emergent national consensus regarding the place of race in American life. For some (Herman Melville and Mark Twain, for example), the mannered South served as an imaginative alternative to the frayed culture of America during the crass inelegance and inarticulateness of the Gilded Age.

Southern mythology has a clearly national as well as regional character. Northern writers such as Henry James and F. Scott Fitzgerald accorded the legends literary respect; disseminators of American values in popular school textbooks—such as the staunch New Englander David Saville Muzzey— adopted the southern mythical perspective in gushing sentimentally about the demise of the great plantation. It may well have been a northern army officer who first coined the term New South, as an expression of only slightly hidden regret for a southern civilization now "gone" and a cause now "lost." The northern regard for the South as "The Enchanted Country," in short, is long-standing. Many of the myths of the South were cultivated by those—North and South—who never owned a slave or planted an acre of cotton. The nation's genuine fondness for both the South and its mythology remains alive in Philadelphia (whether Mississippi or Pennsylvania), and in both Minneapolis and Montgomery. Southern mythology bears, of course, an indelible southern birthmark, but it also stands as testimony to the durable value of seeing the "southerner as American."

See also LITERATURE: North in Literature; MUSIC: / "Dixie"; Foster, Stephen

Patrick Gerster and
Nicholas Cords
Lakewood Community College
White Bear Lake, Minnesota

Howard R. Floan, *The South in Northern Eyes, 1831–1861* (1958); Francis Pendleton Gaines, *The Southern Plantation: A Study in the Development and Accuracy of a Tradition* (1924); Patrick Gerster and Nicholas Cords, eds., *Myth and Southern History* (1974), *Journal of Southern History* (November 1977); William R. Taylor, *Cavalier and Yankee: The Old South and American National Character* (1957); George B. Tindall,

in *The Idea of the South: Pursuit of a Central Theme*, ed. Frank E. Vandiver (1964). ☆

Plantation Myth

||||||||||||||||||||||||||||||||||||||

The plantation myth is a body of tales, legends, and folklore that defines the antebellum plantation and that is frequently extended to explain the social order of the entire South from Jamestown to Fort Sumter. It emphasizes the precapitalistic and essentially feudal characteristics of the plantation, with specific links to an English Cavalier tradition. It makes, for example, the early colonial South a refuge during the Puritan Revolution for royalist and Anglican gentry. In this context the plantation develops primarily as a social or cultural institution rather than an economic one. Money, then, economic self-interest, and capitalistic gain are secondary to a primitive, premodern desire for honor, distinction, and deference. Individuals function less as autonomous figures than as parts of a living social organism extending through time and space.

In the plantation myth, relationships are ordered along hierarchical lines, and the patriarchal family is the central defining device and metaphor. The well-born father/plantation master and his sons dominate the structure; beneath them are their women, wives and daughters, then children, and finally white dependents and black slaves. The slave order is similarly hierarchical and familial, if with some skewing in the gender roles: house servants rate higher than field-workers, craftsmen higher than unskilled workers, and the fair higher than the dark.

The actors in this social drama perform prescribed roles. Manners, behavior, and deportment lie at the heart of the system. Performance and appearance form its supreme good. The gentleman and the lady represent only the most popular and outstanding of the various roles or forms dictated by the system.

This legendary order centers on the Tidewater of Virginia and South Carolina. These areas constitute the two "mountains of conceit" of the old regional adage (with North Carolina as the "valley of humility"). The system, however, possesses notable outposts in various other localities around the region such as the Mississippi Delta, the Bluegrass counties of Kentucky, central Tennessee around Nashville, and the Piedmont of Georgia—the triangle northwest of Macon and Augusta. Insofar as plantation mythology might affect the entire region, most southern communities would have had a local version or model represented by a particular family or families. In this system, lesser slaveholding families of less prestigious origins defer to the greater, all slaveholders dominate whites without slaves, whites and males prevail over blacks and women, the country rules the cities, and aristocratic values overshadow commercial and business interests.

The plantation legend has four major sources. The first is the pre–Civil War southern impulse to differentiate itself ideologically from the North. A comparable northern attitude exaggerated southern peculiarity. The novels of John Pendleton Kennedy, the poetry of William Grayson, and the sociology of William Fitzhugh illustrate the southern impulse; Harriet Beecher Stowe's *Uncle Tom's Cabin* exemplifies the northern attitude.

The second source of the plantation legend lies in the post–Civil War period and in the southern need to romanticize its past as a means of comprehending its defeat and its radically altered situation after Appomattox. The former Confederates explained their defeat by creating a legendary chivalric past. Summarized in a plantation order, prewar society was too noble, good, and bright to have survived the onslaughts of industrial, middle-class capitalism from the North. In this way, the war itself developed as the capstone of the plantation legend. It became the ultimate knightly adventure: the Quixotic Quest, the Lost Cause, all the more precious because it was foredoomed to failure. The Old South thereby became a place out of time, its inhabitants as immortal as the Olympians. The plantation South became mythology.

The romances of John Esten Cooke and Thomas Nelson Page mirror the nostalgia of the ideal. Even they, however, fail to measure the full power of the mythology as a regional belief system up through the Southern Literary Renaissance. Indeed, that cultural revival stems in considerable measure from the efforts of a new generation to define its own identity in contrast to the heroes of the mythic past. Thus, the myth might be seen to receive its fullest expression as southerners of the 1920s and 1930s tried to exorcise the plantation ghosts, notably in William Faulkner's *Absalom, Absalom!*, in W. J. Cash's *The Mind of the South*, and in realistic and debunking aspects of Margaret Mitchell's *Gone with the Wind*, all of which appeared in a cluster between 1936 and 1941. This defeat-generated mythologizing existed between 1880 and World War II.

Although less chronologically confined, the third source of the plantation myth arose and thrived in the same period. It was a northern phenomenon, and its sources varied. Rooted partially in guilt and ambivalence about the war, especially its racial implications, Yankee celebration of the plantation myth derived a powerful dynamic from a bourgeois impulse to fantasize an alternative to its egalitarian, commercial, materialistic social order. By this means, the plantation legend functioned as a domestic version of the historical novels of Sir Walter Scott that were so popular on both sides of the Atlantic in the early 19th century. The southerners in Henry Adams's works, *Democracy* and *The Education of Henry Adams*, and in Owen Wister's *The Virginian* stand for the northern idealization of the old southerner. The enormous northern popularity of Page's work and the still larger national audiences of the mythologized *Birth of a Nation*, of Margaret Mitchell's book *Gone with the Wind*, and of the film made from the latter represent the same, continuing influences.

Historical reality offers the final source of the plantation myth and its vitality: the existence of some essential, material sources or roots of the mythological belief. This remains its most debated and even polemical aspect. In modern society the very concept of mythology is laden with negative values; "a truth that cannot be proven," the traditional definition of myth, stands in low repute in a modern, scientific world. The linking of a distinctive regional culture with mythology, then, has the effect of discrediting the notion of an essentially pre-modern order represented in the Plantation South. Pernicious, self-serving uses of plantation mythology (by southerners and northerners alike) have further discredited the concept. Nevertheless, scholars still argue the basic validity and accuracy of the social system suggested in the popular mythology.

Two general lines of thought have emerged among those committed to material accuracy behind plantation mythology. One group, led by Eugene D. Genovese, advances the material reality of a feudal system in the South that arose out of regional peculiarities of demography and economics, such as settlement patterns, mortality and morbidity rates, religious institutions, slavery, and debt and credit structures. Without dismissing these elements, a second group maintains that a value system came first and shaped the material reality toward the form of a feudal order. Bertram Wyatt-Brown leads this line of thought. By analyzing its material bases, both groups illuminate the sources of the plantation myth's persistence and vitality over time, and suggest reasons why even modern southerners perceive their lives and manners in peculiar ways.

See also AGRICULTURE: Plantations; LITERATURE: Popular Literature; / Page, Thomas Nelson; SOCIAL CLASS: Aristocracy

Darden A. Pyron
Florida International University

W. J. Cash, *The Mind of the South* (1941); Francis Pendleton Gaines, *The Southern Plantation: A Study in the Development and Accuracy of a Tradition* (1925); Paul M. Gaston, *The New South Creed: A Study in Southern Mythmaking* (1970); Eugene D. Genovese, *The World the Slaveholders Made: Two Essays in Interpretation* (1969), *Roll, Jordan, Roll: The World the Slaves Made* (1974); Raimondo Luraghi, *The Plantation South* (1975); Darden A. Pyron, *Recasting "Gone with the Wind" in American Culture* (1983); William R. Taylor, *Cavalier and Yankee: The Old South and American National Character* (1957); Frank E. Vandiver, ed., *The Idea of the South: Pursuit of a Central Theme* (1964); C. Vann Woodward, *The*

Burden of Southern History (1968); Bertram Wyatt-Brown, *Southern Honor: Ethics and Behavior in the Old South* (1982). ☆

Racial Attitudes

||||||||||||||||||||||||||||||||||||||||||||

Although it is impossible to measure racial attitudes directly, they may be gauged from written and oral expressions, gestures, and institutional arrangements. Attitudes may be analyzed as discrete entities. As one authority has suggested, the term *attitude* "suggests thoughts and feelings (as opposed to actions) directed toward some specific object (as opposed to generalized faiths and beliefs)." The term also "suggests a wide range in consciousness, intensity, and saliency in the response to the object."

Racial attitudes in the South have primarily involved whites and blacks. Attitudes toward American Indians and toward Asians have been less consistent and less pervasive. In general, both whites and blacks have held less pejorative attitudes toward these groups than toward each other. Nonetheless, both large groups have tended to see Indians and Asians as separate groups with distinguishing characteristics of their own. Blacks have had to deal with the fact that whites usually have less pejorative attitudes toward other non-white groups. Members of these smaller groups, of course, have their own attitudes toward other people whom they perceive as being racially different.

Among both blacks and whites, racial attitudes have hinged on a bipolar system of racial classification. Whites especially have defined all persons with perceptibly African ancestry as "colored," "Negro," or "black." Gradations of intermixed African and European ancestry, based largely on complexion, have carried some meaning. Both groups, while accepting the bipolar system, have accorded some measure of preference to lighter-skinned members of the "Negro" category. The phenomenon of "passing" testifies to the strength rather than the weakness of the bipolar system.

White attitudes toward blacks in America have never been peculiar to the South. Their expression and institutional implementation have indeed been more salient in areas where slavery persisted after the revolutionary era, but the underlying attitudes have always been remarkably similar throughout the country. Pejorative attitudes toward blacks were evident from the period of early settlement in all the English colonies. Regional distinctions within the southern colonies were fully as important as differences between the nascent North and South.

The origins of white racial attitudes may be found in the interaction of two powerful forces: certain important attributes of English culture, and the need for bound labor in land-rich colonies, which needed to export in order to survive. More generally, these origins lay in powerful urges for domination. The content of the attitudes was powerfully molded by the social and psychological insecurities engendered by the Anglo-European migration across the Atlantic into a land that worked to undermine traditional social controls.

Some scholars have held that these attitudes emerged inevitably as the ideology of an oppressive master class. Others have maintained that they were built into English cultural traditions

Stereotypical tobacco advertisement, date unknown

that themselves formed a part of an ancient western European heritage. A third group has viewed these two possibilities as simultaneous forces that interacted with each other to produce racial attitudes that have been remarkable in the history of world cultural contacts for their virulence, consistency, pervasiveness, and persistence through time.

Few scholars dispute these characteristics. From their earliest contacts with West Africans, both in Africa and America, the English regarded them as heathen, uncivilized, brutelike, and oversexed. They also placed great emphasis on physiognomic differences, on hair, facial characteristics, and especially on complexion. In that age, the concept of innateness of human characteristics was itself inchoate, but there was a persistent tendency to ascribe inherency to the black's physiognomy and cultural attributes.

The actual persistence of the Negro's "black" color was matched by the persistence on the part of whites in trying to explain it, in hoping that it might be changed by the American environment, and in using it as a social marker of

degraded status. The sexual charge in white attitudes also persisted, showing itself in fears of the sexually potent and aggressive male and in ambivalence toward the black female's sexuality. The sexual fears of white males were evident throughout several hundred years of violent retribution against black males and in the yawning gap between expressed ideals and actual practice concerning contact between white men and black women.

Racial *stereotypes* may be defined as the bundles of belief carried by the energy of attitudes. Common American stereotypes about blacks are at least two or three hundred years old. There is evidence in the 17th and 18th centuries of virtually all the imputations that can be found today. The reason, or energizing component, underlying the stereotypes varies. Expressions of these beliefs have appeared in such disparate media as jokes; informal and formal speech; symbols—human, bestial, and otherwise; locker-room walls; the Congressional Record; and somber scientific treatises. Any given stereotype may have little, much, or no basis in fact. Such stereotypes and their primary animating energies include the well-hung male and the hot and easy female (sexual aggression), shiftlessness (imposed social role), dark fingernail moons in light-skinned individuals (inherency, the taint of ancestry or "blood"), affinity with apes (sexuality, historical happenstance, and supposed physiognomic attributes), peculiar musicality (cultural reality). The very common imputation of mental inferiority has been heatedly debated for more than two centuries.

The reaction of blacks to this barrage has shown great variability and ambivalence. For many years blacks could not openly or safely express their attitudes.

Undoubtedly many blacks acquiesced to or embraced the value whites placed upon a light complexion and straight hair. Some black men welcomed and absorbed the imputation of special sexual potency. While rejecting the charge of mental inferiority as a slur and a fabrication, a great many black children were placed in such positions of inferiority that they could not help but develop a self-negating posture about their own abilities.

Blacks have long displayed and probably actually held a wide and inconsistent range of attitudes toward whites. Black attitudes are especially difficult to assess because American society has discouraged their open expression to whites and even to other blacks, as well as self-acknowledgment. These attitudes are probably more variable and complicated than those of whites toward blacks. In general, black attitudes have not had the shaping and sustaining support that white attitudes have had; they have not been molded into ideologies in defense of existing institutions such as slavery and segregation. As the controlling group, whites have formalized and institutionalized their attitudes through literature, scientific dogma, laws, institutions, the economy, and enforced interracial etiquette. Blacks have in some measure been forced to react to these formulations.

Out of necessity, blacks have been more realistic and more discerning about individual differences among whites, and thus less inclined to think stereotypically. The instinct for sheer survival in American culture has placed a premium on quick and perceptive analysis of white characteristics and behavior. Unable to afford the luxury of misassessment, blacks have been less prone to generalize and ascribe inher-

ency in white people. Sheer rage has animated some blacks, but often this force has been effectively checked by communal values that reject dysfunctional vengefulness. Obviously the imputation of dangerous aggressiveness to whites has a solid basis in fact. Less well known is the black perception of sheer stupidity on the part of whites, a view that for blacks often has a strong moral dimension.

Since 1960 there has been more change in racial attitudes than at any previous time. Some of this change is more apparent than real, for it has involved only the level of formal expression, not underlying attitudes. Thus, it is no longer polite (in the broadest, most potent sense of the term) to institutionalize pejorative attitudes in an obvious way or to express them in more public forums, such as the news media, advertising, political discourse, and directly to members of the other race. How much these changes are affecting actual attitudes is open to question. Certainly there has been some effect, especially among younger people. Yet there is much evidence to show that these attitudes have in some measure merely gone underground. Their presence is still revealed in private conversations, snide allusions, small-group confrontations, and such written media as hate mail and toilet stall doors.

The South has shared in these attitudes and in recent changes. What has distinguished the South has been the more open expression than elsewhere of broadly shared attitudes, through the institutions of prolonged slavery and segregation, and the open frankness of literate and oral expression. In recent years many blacks have voiced a preference for this openness because it permits blacks at least to know where they stand. On the other hand, many southern blacks have hated the institutional and economic results of these attitudes, as well as the implicit and actual violence that they have encouraged. Changing black views on this matter can be partially gauged by the tread of feet northward and now to a lesser extent back "home."

Thus, racial attitudes in the South have been peculiar not for their existence or their content but for their virulence, saliency, pervasiveness, and the predisposition of white people to overt action and of black people to fear, accommodation, resistance, and retaliation. In the South, open expression and implementation of white racial attitudes have been encouraged by the frequent contact between large numbers of blacks and whites over a long period of time. One can still find traces of these racial attitudes in Maine, but they have played a far more important role in the society and culture of Mississippi. And because they have been so long and deeply embedded in southern culture especially, the chances are that they will persist for a very long time. Certainly it is clear that the South has suffered in this respect from tendencies that have long existed in American society as a whole. In this respect, the South seems like the entire nation— only more so.

See also BLACK LIFE: Race Relations; HISTORY AND MANNERS: Manners; Sexuality

Winthrop D. Jordan
University of Mississippi

Gordon W. Allport, *The Nature of Prejudice* (1958); Angus Campbell, *White Attitudes toward Black People* (1971); John Dollard, *Caste and Class in a Southern Town* (1937);

George M. Fredrickson, *The Black Image in the White Mind: The Debate on Afro-American Character and Destiny, 1817–1914* (1971), *White Supremacy: A Comparative Study in American and South African History* (1981); Reginald Horsman, *Race and Manifest Destiny: The Origins of American Racial Anglo-Saxonism* (1981); Winthrop D. Jordan, *White over Black: American Attitudes toward the Negro, 1550–1812* (1969); Hortense Powdermaker, *After Freedom: A Cultural Study in the Deep South* (1939). ☆

Reconstruction Myth

When historians christened the civil rights struggle of the 1960s "the Second Reconstruction," it came as no surprise to anyone. Ever since Rutherford B. Hayes pulled the last federal troops from the southern states in 1877, the specter of renewed national intervention on behalf of racial equality had been the fundamental myth of southern political culture. The events of the Reconstruction period (usually seen as 1865–77), dramatic enough in their own right, took on demonic proportions in the imaginations of southern white conservatives who saw control by the "white supremacy Democrats" as the only road to salvation for their society. It took these "Redeemers" another quarter century to codify and institutionalize segregation and disfranchisement following the defeat of the Populist party—whose political revolt, according to Democratic campaign rhetoric, threatened to return the South to "the evils of Reconstruction." For yet another seven decades every proposal to alter the southern caste system or one-party rule prompted conservative Democrats to parade the great Reconstruction myth before their constituents or on the floor of Congress.

The Republican effort to reconstruct southern society and politics in the 1860s was, to be sure, a radical innovation in the American political tradition. The abolition of slavery during the Civil War was a revolutionary alteration of the southern economic system. In order to preserve a meaningful freedom for the former slaves, the Republican party favored a postwar policy of civil equality for blacks coupled with the establishment of a Freedmen's Bureau that would supervise the establishment of a free labor system in the South. In the political realm, Republicans found it necessary to enfranchise the freedmen after the war in order to prevent the former Confederates from dominating the new civil governments through the Democratic party. The votes of the freedmen, together with the support of a minority of southern whites, gave the Republicans an electoral majority in each state for at least a few years. This brief phase of Republican control in the South, together with the passage of egalitarian federal laws and constitutional amendments, was what conservative whites meant by the term *Reconstruction.*

Reconstruction's mythic cast of characters included the "carpetbaggers," whom southern whites portrayed as greedy interlopers exploiting the South; the "scalawags," who were traitorous native southern whites collaborating with the Yankees; the freedmen, who were sometimes seen as violent and depraved in the myth but mostly seemed ignorant and lost; and the former Confederates, who were the heroes of the story, all honorable, decent people with the South's best interests in mind.

Southern Democrats were willing to use any means necessary to end Republican control of their states, including political violence. Initially through secret organizations such as the Ku Klux Klan and later more openly, as with Wade Hampton's "Red Shirts" in South Carolina, the Democrats resorted to beatings, assassinations, and armed bands of horsemen at the polls to "redeem" the South from "Negro rule." They justified these extreme methods on the grounds that Reconstruction threatened the fundamental stability of their society: economic control by "the better sort," the social elevation of all whites, and the protection of white women from sexual aggression by blacks were at stake.

During the next two decades violence was occasionally used to discourage black political efforts, but the use of large-scale electoral corruption— against both black and white opponents—was a much more common Democratic tactic. Electoral corruption and violence escalated during the 1890s, when the People's party bolted the Democratic party. White conservatives justified both violence and corruption as necessary to prevent a return to black officeholding and Republican rule. By the turn of the century a growing number of northerners (even within the Republican party) had come to agree with the southern view. Ignoring the Fourteenth and Fifteenth Amendments— the "Reconstruction amendments"— the Supreme Court refused to overturn disfranchisement and accepted segregation as constitutional under the separate-but-equal formula.

During the Progressive era the southern view of Reconstruction became enshrined in the popular culture of the nation. Thomas Dixon's *The Clansman*

(1905) was a fictional embodiment of the Reconstruction myth, and William A. Dunning's *Reconstruction, Political and Economic, 1865–1877* (1907) was the best example of a series of historical monographs portraying white suffering in the era. In 1915 Woodrow Wilson held an enthusiastic showing of D. W. Griffith's new film, *Birth of a Nation*, at the White House. The president applauded its cinematic tribute to the great Reconstruction myth, complete with the stereotypical rescue of a white damsel from the hands of a black rapist by the heroic Ku Klux Klan. Two decades later *Gone with the Wind* provided a celluloid update of the myth that survives into the age of the VCR.

Whenever the Congress considered a federal antilynching bill in the years between the two world wars, southern Democrats warned of a return to Reconstruction. The same refrain greeted certain New Deal programs, Franklin D. Roosevelt's Fair Employment Practices Commission, and Harry Truman's desegregation of the armed forces. As the Supreme Court began to strike down the white primary, segregated institutions of higher education, and restrictive covenants in the late 1940s, southern conservatives grew concerned that the justices might actually decide to interpret the Reconstruction amendments literally. In *Brown* v. *Board of Education*, which decided the school desegregation cases in 1954, the Court looked seriously at the intent of the framers of the Fourteenth Amendment—ignoring the myth, for once, in favor of serious historical analysis—but concluded that the issue was irrelevant to its unanimous opinion outlawing segregation. In their denunciation of the *Brown* decision, the Citizens' Councils of the Deep South resuscitated the white-supremacy views of

the 19th century and warned of the perils of a new Reconstruction.

The myth was not just the shibboleth of the far right. When John F. Kennedy published his *Profiles in Courage* in 1956, he pictured the first Reconstruction as a tragic mistake. Even after he gained the presidency, Kennedy held to the southern view and initially resisted federal intervention on the side of civil rights because he did not want to ignore what he regarded as the lessons of history concerning federal intervention in the South. Displaying an intellectual curiosity rare among chief executives, however, Kennedy actually invited historian David Donald to the White House to lead an after-dinner discussion of what modern historians were saying about the Reconstruction era. Whether this discussion had any impact on the president's thinking is undocumented, but he proceeded to put the federal government behind the enforcement of civil rights in the South to a degree unprecedented since the 1870s.

For white southerners who had grown up believing in the Reconstruction myth, the prospect was terrifying and infuriating. To refer to federal intervention as a Second Reconstruction was, in their eyes, to condemn such an idea out of hand. They characterized northern whites who came south as Freedom Riders, voter registration workers, or demonstrators on picket lines as latter-day abolitionists or carpetbaggers. Southern whites who criticized segregation, disfranchisement, or the jailing of civil rights workers were scalawags. A rejuvenated Ku Klux Klan engaged in savage beatings, bombings, and assassination, only to be acquitted by all-white juries.

The Second Reconstruction was, however, far more successful than the first. This time federal intervention included systematic enforcement of civil rights legislation by the U.S. Justice Department, the Health, Education, and Welfare Department, and the courts. This time southern blacks used civil disobedience, manipulated the national media, won the support of northern public opinion, obtained effective legal representation through public-interest law firms, and created their own heroes in mythic proportions.

By 1970, when a series of political leaders below the Mason-Dixon line were proclaiming a "New South" that turned its back on racial prejudice, a great change had taken place in the region's political culture. Racial prejudice was still alive and well, of course, but for the most part public discussion of the race question was couched in euphemisms and code words of the sort familiar outside of Dixie. No longer could white politicians expect to be taken seriously if they yelled about the evils of Reconstruction. The Second Reconstruction had arrived—and white southerners had learned to live with it. Some, including historians of that first experiment in racial equality, even came to relish being called scalawags.

See also HISTORY AND MANNERS: Reconstruction; MEDIA: / *Birth of a Nation*; VIOLENCE: / Ku Klux Klan

Peyton McCrary
University of South Alabama

Claude G. Bowers, *The Tragic Era: The Revolution after Lincoln* (1929); Carl M. Brauer, *John F. Kennedy and the Second Reconstruction* (1977); John Hope Franklin, *Reconstruction after the Civil War* (1961); Paul M. Gaston, *The New South Creed: A Study in Southern Mythmaking* (1970); William Gillette, *Retreat from Reconstruction, 1869–* 1879 (1979); V. O. Key, Jr., *Southern Politics in State and Nation* (1949); James M. McPherson, *Ordeal by Fire: The Civil War and Reconstruction* (1982); Robert J. Norrell, *Reaping the Whirlwind: The Civil Rights Movement in Tuskegee* (1985); Kenneth M. Stampp, *Era of Reconstruction, 1865–1877* (1965); C. Vann Woodward, *The Burden of Southern History* (1961; rev. ed., 1968). ☆

Regionalism

||||||||||||||||||||||||||||||||

The concept of regionalism is a recent adaptation of the cultural theory of romantic nationalism and the lineal descendant of the idea of sectionalism. In the 18th century a *section* meant what today would be called an interest group and was only incidentally geographical in reference, when interests happened to be locally coherent. Romanticism, which became influential in the early 19th century, helped to promote a new and systematic theory of language, race, and geography that transformed the meaning of the word *sectionalism*. Romanticism held that there was an organic relationship between land and people, climate and social custom, which created national groups that, evolving historically, were recognizable by (and manifested themselves in) distinctive and persistent patterns of language, ideology, and religion, from which the individual took his identity. In the southeastern portion of the United States, the doctrine of states' rights became romanticized, whereby the state became a nation in miniature and hence potentially and morally entitled to self-determination. At the same time, the notion of national distinctiveness helped to fashion a conception of southern identity, which many thought should be embodied in political independence. Analytically, nationalism and sectionalism were not distinct, but sectionalism was generally held to be the political expression, energetic and watchful, of southern interests within a perpetuating federal union.

The failure of the Confederacy left the romantic theory of southern nationalism without an integrated political expression, a state, and cast into disfavor the sectional impulse, which was held responsible for the Civil War. Hence developed the transmuted romantic doctrine of *regionalism*, a word first used in the late 19th century. It referred to a depoliticized version of the theory of cultural distinctiveness, whereby portions of the Union retain their special character. This regionalist vision was first developed in literature. Local color writers, who flourished between the 1870s and 1890s, specialized in capturing through the narrative use of dialect and folk stories the pervading spirit of such places as New Orleans (George W. Cable), the Tennessee mountains (Mary N. Murfree), the Virginia Tidewater (Thomas Nelson Page), and Georgia (Joel Chandler Harris). These were students of a depoliticized folk, notably restricted now in scope to small and unintimidating areas. Through their writings a national periodical readership learned about the curious and harmless ways of other and different Americans.

The development of an unpolitical doctrine of regionalism in the United States may be explained by the history and structure of the American union itself. Because of federalism the notion of an American nation-state was slow to develop and a tradition of centralized government did not precede significant modernization. Although the regionalisms of Brittany and Catalonia arose, as did southern regionalism, as a mythic response to the strains of modernization, they were more prone than the South to demands for political autonomy because they had existed as entities before modernization and annexation by the larger nation-state. Southern regionalism had less clarity, being divided between states and variously defined regions within the South, and having been instigated entirely within the framework of the American union.

In the 20th century regionalism became a topic for sociological analysis, especially in the writings of Howard W. Odum and Rupert B. Vance, both of the University of North Carolina. They attempted to develop a sociology for a southern folk, in which the poverty of its colonial economy might be defined and remedied by voluntary action posing no threat to the stability of the nation. Odum was insistent that regionalism was a healthy recognition of diversity, not in conflict with national interests, whereas sectionalism was egocentric and disruptive: this distinction was challenged as spurious, most notably by the poet and social critic Donald Davidson. Odum hoped that regionalism might be advanced by groups of planning experts, with no stake in politics, whose diagnoses might be implemented. With no southern government, however, it was unclear how Odum's plans might be carried out. The strengthening of both the federal government and states by the New Deal undercut this strategy of regional social planning.

Since Odum, regionalism has ceased to be an ambitious political and social theory sympathetic to social change and has become instead implicitly conservative and atomistic. Largely opposed to urbanization and industrialization and to their encouragement of conformity in social customs, regionalism is often concerned now with promoting preindustrial values and habits somewhat in the spirit of William Morris. Regionalism itself, however, has paradoxically arisen because of that same modernization, and thus can be seen as a mythic system of ideological accommodation by which the material advantages of industrialization can still be enjoyed, while preindustrial values are celebrated and, occasionally, invented.

See also EDUCATION: / Odum, Howard W.; Vance, Rupert B.

Michael O'Brien
University of Arkansas

Michael O'Brien, *The Idea of the American South, 1920–1941* (1979); Howard W. Odum, *Southern Regions of the United States* (1936); John Shelton Reed, *One South: An Ethnic Approach to Regional Culture* (1982); Henry D. Shapiro, *Appalachia on Our Mind: The Southern Mountains and Mountaineers in the American Consciousness, 1870–1920* (1978); Anthony D. Smith, *Theories of Nationalism* (1971). ☆

Religion and Mythology

Religion, broadly defined, rests at the heart of southern culture and what it means to be a southerner. Even critics of the region, convinced that the South can be dismissed as the proverbial "buckle on the Bible belt," would concede as much. Unleashing diatribes against the South as was his fashion, H. L. Mencken abrasively declared the South of the 1920s to be "a cesspool of Baptists, a miasma of Methodism, snake charmers . . . and syphilitic evangelists." Southerners, as James McBride Dabbs has said in a more positive vein, are those Americans most "haunted by God." The central theme of southern culture, Samuel S. Hill has added, is religion, at least in the sense that to be southern is most often to see oneself as having "a radical dependence upon God." Protestantism is to the South what Islamism is to Iran or Judaism to Israel. Currently, evangelical Protestantism accounts for 90 percent of the religious loyalty of the region. Public opinion polls disclose that nine out of every ten southerners declare themselves Protestant, with nearly four out of every five of these being Baptist, Methodist, or Presbyterian. Thus, most observers of southern culture—sooner or later, and better sooner than later—come to terms with the region's religiosity.

The relationship of southern religion to southern mythology, although not at all patently clear, is nonetheless significant. Religion in almost every society, the South being no exception, stands in service to the process of social integration. The earliest meaning of the word religion is "to bind together." In this sense religion is a bonding agent of culture—it shapes community. Religion makes the business of relating to one's fellows easier by binding all to a common purpose. The sociologist Emile Durkheim said as much in his *Elementary Forms of the Religious Life* (1912). Religion, Durkheim argued, is the most basic of human symbolic systems, the key to culture, the "primal act." Religion renders a cosmology, thereby summarizing the deepest collective experiences of the cultural group. Religion, in this sense, is thick with meaning as it both shapes and expresses cultural ideology.

Myth functions in much the same fashion as religion and is nearly inseparable from it. It is at base a narrative, a "tale of the tribe"—the traditional stories a culture tells itself about itself. In edited, abbreviated form it simultaneously expresses, establishes, and enhances meaning for the cultural group. Myth conveys a culture's collective consciousness. Its function is to provide a society cultural paradigms that codify and structure the group's sense of reality, image of itself, and ultimately collective behavior. The collective dimension of myth serves as bearer of cultural meaning. Myths, psychologically, assure the mind and reaffirm the ancient collective way. In narrative form they act as mechanisms crucial to the dissemination and transmission of tradition and culture. Mythic tales are received and understood with a "religious" seriousness, for they offer an explanation of a culture. Both myth and religion, then, structure community and culture by providing an inner meaning for the group. They both are social facts, not collective fantasies. They offer cultural pictures, which establish group identity by linking past experience, current circumstances, and future expectations.

Southern culture in its formative stages was structured by a blending of religion and myth. The first southerners explored and settled the region in accordance with the religious and mythological premises of their age. Whether articulated in verse, fiction, and sermons, or borne at unconscious levels, myth pictured the region as a new Garden of Eden. Georgia, for example, was early declared to be "that promis'd Canaan." And as early as Robert Beverley's *The History and Present State of Virginia*, published in London in 1705, one witnesses, according to Lewis P. Simpson, "the origin of the plantation in the literary imagination as the fruition of the errand into paradise." Europeans planting themselves in the southern reaches of the New World filtered their experience through an imagination structured by religiously inspired and mythically designed attitudes about the South, and later generations of southerners would see their experience as but an extension of these attitudes. Thus, by the antebellum era there lay a religious substructure to southern culture.

Slavery, as the centerpiece of the South's antebellum pastoral world, not surprisingly took on the character of a religious institution. Southern culture and its peculiar institution became situated, ideologically and imaginatively, within a sacred and cosmic frame of reference at the hands of writers like William Gilmore Simms. Simms, from his plantation, Woodlands, offered the argument that because the black was totally unprepared for freedom, it was only appropriate that white southerners, under a holy contract with God, serve as stewards and "moral conservators" of the African. Early in the southern experience it was believed that European culture was planted in New World soil out of Divine purpose, and later southern generations developed racial myths based on the biblical myth of Ham. The "author" of the southern way of life, it was said, was God. Slavery, grounded in the Bible, was an extension of His law. Stories that explained the southern cultural experience were thus derived from religion and structured by mythology. Such cultural tales framed the white southerner's beliefs and values within a sacred history and functioned as myth. It was predictable that southerners would come to see themselves as being a "people" in the classical and biblical sense of the word.

By the time of the Civil War the South interpreted its historical experience in light of a transcendent religious-mythological reality. "We have pulled a temple down," exclaimed the men in Charleston, S.C., as they seceded from the union in December of 1860. The War for Southern Independence carried with it the aura of holy war. A Confederate myth born of the war years stoked the South's social imagination with stories of high purpose, high heroism, and high drama. A Crusade of the Planters bent on the region's salvation stirred the soul of the South as only religious energies could.

As the South emerged from the ashes of Shiloh, Vicksburg, and Chattanooga and discovered its cause to be "lost," it nonetheless carried with it the sense, as Charles Reagan Wilson has aptly suggested, that the region had been "baptized in blood." The myth of the Lost Cause, like earlier southern myths, resonated with religious imagery. Rituals celebrating the Lost Cause exploited the southern talent for ceremonial style. Through the introduction of social rituals such as Confederate Memorial Day and Confederate reunions, the southern past of both religion and myth was reunited with its tragic present. Southern mythology was institutionalized as a civil religion. Protestant churches and their clergy celebrated the Lost Cause, declaring that while the chosen people had lost their holy war, they had been purified and anointed for a yet greater purpose. Heroes such as Robert E. Lee were compared to Moses.

A new set of prophets arose in the South to voice new southern visions. For some, the promised land was destined to be one of racial harmony, economic fulfillment, and political parity with the North—a New South. For others, the Ku Klux Klan, replete with its religious symbolism and religious rituals, offered visions of a recycled South wherein an indomitable commitment to white supremacy would once again prevail. For still others, conservative Democrats—the Redeemers—seemed to represent a higher order of political virtue and to uphold antebellum codes of white rule, pay proper homage to the Lost Cause, and endorse the fiscal policies of the New South. Religion and myth once again came together in reciprocal fashion to structure a new cultural order in a reconstructed South.

Aristotle's *Poetics* long ago defined myth in a general sense as an old story, a traditional tale, but offered the further observation that myth, in essence, is not simply the story told but the plot within it. Herein, perhaps, lies the best clue to the convergence of southern myth and southern religion. Both share a common infrastructure—a patterned plot of paradise, paradise lost, and paradise regained. The Christian myth relates the story of a human destiny born to Edenic perfection, lost to an earthly salvation by the fall, and capable of being born again to a paradise regained. The South, in relation to its historical experience, long has felt itself a participant in much the same pattern of existence.

As initially conceived, the South was an Edenic paradise, its plantation paradise was lost via the Civil War, and the South since has entertained visions of a paradise regained. Southern blacks, as southerners too, also have seen their mythic history tied to a religious, Christian paradigm—a paradise symbolized by their ancestral African heritage. The plantation South was their "time on the cross" and paradise lost. Their recent experience, inspired by Martin Luther King, Jr.'s dream of having seen the Promised Land, was a paradise regained. Jonathan Daniels characterized southerners—both white and black—as "a mythological people . . . who live in a still legendary land" and are Bible centered. The Bible, with its tales of paradise and human destiny, is the South's ultimate text in both a religious and mythical sense.

Patrick Gerster
Lakewood Community College
White Bear Lake, Minnesota

James McBride Dabbs, *Haunted by God: The Cultural and Religious Experience of the South* (1972); Samuel S. Hill, *Southern Churches in Crisis* (1966); John Shelton Reed, *The Enduring South: Subcultural Persistence in Mass Society* (1972); Lewis P. Simpson, *The Dispossessed Garden: Pastoral and History in Southern Literature* (1975); Charles Reagan Wilson, *Baptized in Blood: The Religion of the Lost Cause, 1865–1920* (1980). ☆

Romanticism
||||||||||||||||||||||||||||||||||||

Southern self-consciousness emerged in the wake of the Romantic movement, which provided many of the ideological underpinnings for political and cultural nationalism in the Western world. Underlying this growing sense of distinctiveness were the growth of plantation slavery based on cotton, attacks upon this regional commitment to slavery, and the passing of the revolutionary generation of southern leaders committed to

Enlightenment ideas and ideals. Thus, the influence of romanticism upon the South coincided with and encouraged the historical development of a separatist mentality in the region.

Romanticism is itself a term applied to certain intellectual and artistic developments in Europe and America between approximately 1790 and 1830. It implies, however, a variety of aesthetic and epistemological positions, theories of society and history, and political visions. This has led Arthur O. Lovejoy, one of the most influential students of romanticism, to suggest that it would be more accurate to speak of "romanticisms" than to suggest a unified phenomenon. The term *romantic* is also associated with certain types and styles of thought, feeling, and behavior. It connotes, for instance, emotionality, passion, high spirits, self-dramatization, and the exotic. More pejoratively, romanticism is often associated with nostalgia, sentimentality, and overidealization.

Certain figures, events, and preoccupations taken to be "southern" have lent themselves to romantic renderings or were themselves by-products of the romantic sensibility. One thinks here of dashing cavaliers and lovely belles, of florid orators and fire-eating politicians, of heroic Hotspurs and melancholic Hamlets, and above all of the plantation legend and lost causes. The romantic perspective has also fastened upon images of the dark, haunted ruins of war-devastated plantations and celebrated the blasted hopes and melancholy despair of a proud but defeated people. On another level, the folk tradition of black and white music, the powerful emotional charge of Protestant revivalism, and the colorful but dangerous tradition of neopopulist demagoguery have also lent themselves to romantic depictions. Still, no matter how exuberant and boisterous the surface manifestations, southern romanticism has been most strongly attracted to nostalgia, loss, and, at a rarified level, to an obsession with time and history. More generally, if romanticism can be defined as the psychology of the extravagant, self-dramatizing, but ultimately futile gesture, then southern culture, whether taken in its "high" or "popular" incarnations, has been incorrigibly romantic.

Southern writers and intellectuals were initially suspicious of this romantic dimension of the southern experience. From their antiromantic point of view, regional romanticism was a smoke screen for inadequacies and deficiencies. As William R. Taylor's *Cavalier and Yankee* makes clear, antebellum southerners were not averse to questioning as well as celebrating the South's romantic impulses. In the 20th century W. J. Cash is perhaps the best known debunker of popular romanticism in the region. By romantic, Cash meant a lack of intellectual complexity and emotional sophistication, expressed in violence, rhetorical excess, and barely submerged feelings of sin and guilt. Cash's hope was that the South's romantic tendencies could be replaced by a realistic and critical habit of mind. Besides Cash, Lillian Smith also analyzed and condemned the southern tendency to mythologize the region's past. Finally, the work of William Faulkner can be seen as a reflection of and an attempt to cope with the tradition of the "family romance."

Romanticism can also be examined as an influence on the formal intellectual and literary life of the South. Where New England Transcendentalism was a romanticism of nature and the self, southern romantic thought focused on tradition and society. Indeed, where Cash saw the antebellum South as an intellectual wilderness, recent historians have detected a coherent intellectual elite in the South, well-schooled in the intellectual trends of the times, particularly in the counterenlightenment and antiliberal social thought.

As it emerged in the 1840s and 1850s romantic social theory rejected the contract theory of society and politics and objected to the utilitarian, materialistic tenor of daily life and of the emerging industrial order. Under the influence of figures such as Herder in Germany and Carlyle and Scott in Britain, southern intellectuals projected an image of the region as historically unique and organic. The South increasingly seemed to resemble the feudal, hierarchical society of medieval Europe more than it did the atomized society of industrial England or the industrializing North in America. At the center of this social and cultural vision stood the plantation system based on chattel slavery. Ideal social relations were based on the model of the family. Change, when it came, should be gradual and not sudden; in all cases it should be guided by an intellectual and political elite.

Though this romantic vision of an organic order never won out over modernizing tendencies and was dealt a serious blow by the abolition of slavery, it found expression later in the romantic fiction of the late 19th century and remained a subterranean impulse among southern intellectuals into this century. Indeed, with the reemergence of concern with regional identity in the 1930s, certain standard motifs of romantic social thought were voiced by groups such as the Vanderbilt Agrarians and took a populist coloring in the work of the regionalists at Chapel Hill. Some historians have even claimed that this was the consequence of direct influence from antebellum romantic social thought.

There is great irony in the resurgence of romantic social theory—at least in its conservative form—in the 1930s. The men who announced its essential themes were literary men whose critical preferences stood at cross-purposes with mainstream romantic poetry and aesthetics. Allen Tate, John Crowe Ransom, and Cleanth Brooks firmly rejected the view that a poem was an "overflow of emotion" or that it was best understood as the personal expression of the poet. Indeed, these "New Critics" rejected most romantic poetry as intellectually shallow and preferred the more structurally and conceptually complex verse of the metaphysical poets of the 17th century. On the other hand, New Critical aesthetics betrayed certain affinities with Coleridge's emphasis upon the deliberate nature of poetic composition and the importance of internal tensions to the organically constructed literary work. One might say that the aesthetics of New Criticism, with its emphasis upon tradition, hierarchy, structure, and organic form, more closely resembled conservative romantic social thought than it did mainstream romantic aesthetics.

Twentieth-century southern fiction also kept alive several aspects of romantic literature, apparent in the work of Edgar Allan Poe, and carried them over into literary modernism. Here one would have to mention the centrality of an alienated, self-conscious protagonist, a proclivity for the grotesque and the surreal, and an exploration of the recesses of the psyche through a kind of psychological gothicism. Besides the obvious example of Faulkner in *The Sound and the Fury* and *Absalom, Ab-*

salom!, there is the work of Tennessee Williams, Carson McCullers, and Flannery O'Connor and, more recently, Cormac McCarthy, Ishmael Reed, and Barry Hannah. Such writers taken together have continued a tradition of extravagance. Even in the work of novelist Walker Percy, as unromantic and unextravagant a writer as is imaginable, the darker strains of southern romanticism occasionally emerge and stand in tension with Percy's ironic vision and philosophical concerns.

Finally, many of the romantic tendencies in the popular culture and mythology of the South endure in the form of defiant gestures against political centralization, support for white supremacy, belief in the cult of Dixie and the Confederate flag, and the lasting popularity of *Gone with the Wind*. The South still remains a kind of exotic cultural "other" for the rest of America, though California is bidding to take its place. Still, these romantic and extravagant characteristics of the South have become a cultural tic or reflex, trotted out on special occasions or in emergencies, but rarely interfering for long with the South's effort to become modern.

See also ART AND ARCHITECTURE: Gothic Revival; HISTORY AND MANNERS: Modernism; Victorianism; LITERATURE: Agrarianism in Literature; New Critics; Popular Literature; Regionalism and Local Color; WOMEN'S LIFE: Belles and Ladies

Richard H. King
University of Nottingham

W. J. Cash, *The Mind of the South* (1941); Drew Faust, *A Sacred Circle: The Dilemma of the Intellectual in the Old South, 1840–1860* (1977); Richard H. King, *A Southern Renaissance: The Cultural Awakening of the American South, 1930–1955* (1980); Arthur

O. Lovejoy, *Essays in the History of Ideas* (1948); Michael O'Brien, *The Idea of the American South, 1920–1941* (1979); Rollin G. Osterweis, *Romanticism and Nationalism in the Old South* (1949); William R. Taylor, *Cavalier and Yankee: The Old South and American National Character* (1957); Twelve Southerners, *I'll Take My Stand: The South and the Agrarian Tradition* (1930). ☆

Stereotypes

||||||||||||||||||||||||||||||

A stereotype is, in the end, a composite of accurate generalization and dubious belief. The term stereotype—introduced to the social sciences by Walter Lippmann's book *Public Opinion* (1922)—refers to those "pictures in our heads" drawn from the proverbial "kernel of truth." Stereotypes are mental overstatements of difference, preconceived beliefs about classes of people, images that are sustained precisely because they contain an image of truth. Stereotypes are, in this sense, mental portraits drawn from a modicum of fact, exaggerated and simplified.

Findings regarding the so-called Contact Hypothesis—alleging that the greater the frequency of interaction between groups the lower the level of prejudice and stereotype—suggest the difficulty of abolishing southern or other stereotypes. Although the findings appear mixed, increased exposure or contact actually works, in some cases, to increase stereotyping. Those with an intermediate degree of interregional experience seem most likely to generalize about regional differences. In short, moderate amounts of both direct exposure and education solidify rather than weaken the impulse to stereotype. Regional stereotypes are likely to continue, along with the quest to understand the exact nature of the regional differences—North and South—that pattern these thoughts.

The South is often viewed as a land populated by a succession of predictable stock characters—formerly a land of happy darkies with watermelon or banjo, sadistic overseers, coquettish belles, chivalrous cavaliers, vengeful Klansmen, and more recently a land of rambunctious good old boys, demagogic politicians, corrupt sheriffs, country and western good old girls, nubile cheerleaders, football All Americans with three names, neurotic vixens with affinities for the demon rum, Bible-thumping preachers haunted by God, sugary Miss America candidates of unquestioned patriotism, toothless grizzled "po' white trash," and military "lifers" of considerable spit but little polish.

This stereotyped South is a country on the mental map of the national imagination, its citizenry a distillation of both fact and fiction. To many students of southern culture, the South has sustained its measure of regional distinctiveness because of a long-held and abiding set of cultural values that southerners believe clearly separate them

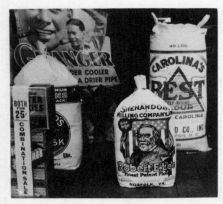

Grocery store window, Mebane, N.C., 1939

from American culture at large. The South, in this sense, has done much to create and perpetuate its regional stereotypes owing to their usefulness in helping to shape a self-image and a regional consciousness. For northerners the South is seen largely through a kaleidoscope of regional stereotypes and images. To them the South serves as both America at its extreme and as "Uncle Sam's other province."

George B. Tindall suggests that the temptation is to deal mentally with the South in accordance with the generally held categories of a Sunny South versus a Benighted South. Heavily edited cartoons of social reality portray on the one hand an ornamental, utopian, mythic South of gallant cavaliers and beauteous belles (or more recently, a Sunbelt South of the nouveau riche) and on the other a semisavage South of abject poverty feeding moral degeneracy. America's and the world's view of the South seldom transcended these hardened stereotypes. One's mental vision of the South seems either given to the romantic glow of late antebellum plantation splendor (or modernized versions thereof) or the counterimage of what W. J. Cash once saw fit to call the "romantics of the appalling." One must mentally arbitrate between and among the list of supposed southern traits that flow from such stereotyped belief. Southerners, as the story is told, are, at once, conservative, radical, tradition loving, courteous, loyal to family ties, conventional, generous, lazy, faithful, very religious, ignorant, stubborn, excessively nationalistic, jovial, honest, witty, kind, superstitious, naive, revengeful, stolid, and flamboyant. Indeed, the South and southerners have been many things to many people.

The notion of the Sunny South dates from earliest southern history and south-

ern consciousness. The pre-South, or if one prefers, the South of the colonial era, tried to fashion a Sunny South stereotype for public consumption. The discovery and exploration of the New World climaxed a European tradition of grand historical visions of a golden age, of paradise, and of a pure and sacred Eden, and such a view held particularly for the South. For Europeans, America was a mythical land from the beginning, but the South especially was thought destined to be paradise regained. The southern reaches of the fresh, green country of the New World seemed a confirmation of utopian promises. Early settlers in Roanoke Island on the Outer Banks of present-day North Carolina claimed to find "the soil richer, the trees taller, the ground firmer and the topsoil deeper." In 1716 Lieutenant Governor Alexander Spotswood of Virginia argued that the Blue Ridge Mountains shone with the sun's perpetual splendor. The Sunny South inspired the imagination with what Sir Robert Montgomery in 1717 called "natural Sweetness and Beauties." For later generations the South of course became, as W. J. Cash phrased it, "a sort of stage piece out of the eighteenth century, wherein gesturing gentlemen moved soft-spokenly against a background of rose gardens and dueling grounds, through always gallant deeds, and lovely ladies, in farthingales, never for a moment lost that exquisite remoteness which has been the dream of all men and the possession of none." The plantation South of the proverbial moonlight-and-magnolias myth enjoyed, and still enjoys, a career in song and story and was celebrated in various media, from the novel to the musical ballad to the motion picture.

The sectional stereotype of most recent vintage, yet very much in the Sunny South tradition, is the congenial view of the Southland as the Sunbelt. Building upon established mental and narrative conventions, the vision of the region is now said to be one of corporate profits, retirement havens, and salubrious climate. The new, bright image of the Sunbelt South, as with most social stereotypes, is partly based on fact. Although the image of the Sunbelt is a mental caricature of the southern situation, the features it exaggerates are indeed real ones. The South is, as many have reported, closing the economic gap between itself and the non-South. In 1930 the South's income was only 60 percent of the national average, but by 1980 the region had closed the gap to 90 percent plus. Yet, as A. J. Cooper, the black mayor of Pritchard, Ala., aptly put the matter in 1978: "There is a lot of shade in the Sunbelt." The South still has a higher proportion of poor than the rest of the nation. The Sunbelt image is at best a case of "sloppy regionalizing" (its patterns of supposed affluence better fit the West than the South). At worst, it is yet another case of mental shorthand at work—stereotyping on a grand scale, with an impact on public policy.

Scenarios of "another South," populated by rednecks, hillbillies, the prototypical itinerant suspenders-snapping Bible-toting preachers, political demagogues, Klansmen, and degenerate aristocrats, have also been part of the nation's mental image of Dixie. Long ago William Byrd II wrote in the colonial era of the region's "indolent wretches" in his *History of the Dividing Line*, while Augustus Baldwin Longstreet offered a fictional composite of the "bad southerner" in Ransy Sniffle, as did Johnson Hooper with Simon Suggs. Erskine Caldwell's portrait of the mindless, inarticulate, degenerate southern

"yahoo," with chewing-tobacco stains on his beard stubble, contributed to the view of the Sunny South as a region cursed by the ravages of pellagra and hookworm, a land of Baptist barbarians and vigilantes, which South-baiter H. L. Mencken dismissed as a grotesque, a country populated by the peculiar American species, *Homo Boobiens*. This South, of so-called hog-wallow politics and abnormal neuroticism, found additional portrayals in the southern gothic drama of Tennessee Williams (*The Glass Menagerie*, 1945), media advertising (Mountain Dew ads), and television shows and movies (*Dukes of Hazzard, Easy Rider*, and *Deliverance*).

Southern stereotypes—ranging from images of a pro-slavery South, the pro-secession South, the agrarian South, the states' rights South, the Confederate South, to the conservative South, the one-party South, the fighting South, the lazy South, the Klanish South, the civil rights South—all offer, in their way, a vision of a monolithic South that is out of keeping with the region's intricate complexity. As a result, southerners seldom have been understood much beyond these sharply etched categories.

See also BLACK LIFE: Film Images, Black; Literary Portrayals of Blacks; MEDIA articles

Patrick Gerster
Lakewood Community College
White Bear Lake, Minnesota

Walter Lippmann, *Public Opinion* (1922); John Shelton Reed, *The Enduring South: Subcultural Persistence in Mass Society* (1974), *One South: An Ethnic Approach to Regional Culture* (1982); Harry Triandis and Vasso Vasiliou, *Journal of Personality and Social Psychology* (November 1967); Frank E. Vandiver, ed., *The Idea of the South: Pursuit of a Central Theme* (1964); Robin

M. Williams, *Strangers Next Door: Ethnic Relations in American Communities* (1964). ☆

AGRARIANS, VANDERBILT
||||||||||||||||||||||||||||||||||||||||||||||||||||||||||||

The Vanderbilt (or Nashville) Agrarians were in a sense an extension of the literary circle that came to be known as the Fugitives in the early 1920s. By mid-decade the *Fugitive* magazine of poetry and criticism (1922–25) had ceased publication, and the Fugitives began to disperse. Two of its principal participants, John Crowe Ransom and Donald Davidson, remained on the Vanderbilt faculty and stayed in close touch with other members of the Fugitives, especially Allen Tate and Robert Penn Warren. These four were in large part responsible for planning and seeing into print the "southern book" they and others on the Vanderbilt campus talked about sporadically in the late 1920s.

The book was *I'll Take My Stand: The South and the Agrarian Tradition* (1930), by Twelve Southerners, the basic statement of the social, economic, political, and cultural position of the Agrarians, often referred to as a "Southern Manifesto." Just as the name "Fugitives" was applied to the magazine that launched a major literary movement, so the designation "Agrarians" labeled participants in what many perceived to be a translation of the Fugitive spirit into a related social movement.

The Fugitives had largely ignored politics in their concern with literature, and, according to Donald Davidson, they shifted their focus to social problems because of the Scopes Trial in Dayton, Tenn., in July 1925. The trial involved a contrived violation of a Tennessee statute prohibiting the teaching of evolution in public schools. It was conducted in a circus atmosphere under a powerful spotlight of national publicity designed, in the view of the incipient Agrarians, to ridicule the local culture and humiliate the plain folk of Tennessee. Not until the late 1920s did the conversations and exchanges of letters that followed result in the development of an eclectic manuscript containing contributions by such persons as historian Frank Owsley, psychologist Lyle Lanier, political scientist H. C. Nixon, biographer John Donald Wade, and novelists Robert Penn Warren, Stark Young, and Andrew Lytle. Ransom drafted, and the others subscribed to, a short introductory "Statement of Principles," in which the authors declared themselves southerners, "well acquainted with one another and of similar tastes . . . and perhaps only at this moment aware of themselves as a single group of men."

I'll Take My Stand is a defense of a traditional culture with an agricultural economic base threatened by a modern urban-industrial society. Allen Tate was later to refer to a more universal dimension of the book—a defense of religious humanism. The Agrarians eventually admitted that they were stronger on the critical side than they were in articulating positive values and developing practical ways of realizing their goals. The continuing appeal of the Agrarian manifesto is its critique of the centralized state and the modern mass society produced by an expanding industrial order that reduces man to a functional cog in a production machine, ruthlessly exploits nature, and makes a cash agreement the only binding one. The Agrarians are increasingly recognized as farsighted, even prophetic, observers rather than the reactionary, impractical supporters of the southern romantic moonlight-and-magnolias myth that many of the early critics accused them of being.

As a movement, Agrarianism made little or no headway, although some effort was made to expand the public's awareness of its main doctrines. In the early 1930s Ransom in particular debated prominent critics of the Agrarians before surprisingly large audiences in several cities. He also devoted himself to the pursuit of economic study with a view to producing a treatise on agrarian economics, but the project never went beyond a draft stage. For several years various members of the group were actively engaged in social and political criticism, much of which appeared in the *American Review*. Their last major group publication was *Who Owns America?* (1936), jointly edited by Herbert Agar and Allen Tate. In this book, essays by a substantial majority of the Agrarians were published with contributions from various English Distributists, whose leading advocates were Hilaire Belloc and G. K. Chesterton—Catholic traditionalists and prominent literary figures in England. Shortly thereafter, Ransom left Vanderbilt, and he and the other Agrarians turned entirely to their literary and academic preoccupations, although a number of them continued to engage in social commentary and political activism on an individual basis. Davidson never ceased to hope for further collective efforts to implement an Agrarian program.

See also LITERATURE: / Davidson, Donald; Lytle, Andrew; Ransom, John Crowe; Tate, Allen; Warren, Robert Penn; Young, Stark

William C. Havard
Vanderbilt University

William C. Havard and Walter Sullivan, eds., *A Band of Prophets: The Nashville Agrarians after Fifty Years* (1982); Thomas Daniel Young, *Waking Their Neighbors Up: The Nashville Agrarians Rediscovered* (1982). ☆

ANGLO-SAXON SOUTH
||||||||||||||||||||||||||||||||||||||||||||||||||||||||

The term *Anglo-Saxon* has been more a self-congratulatory and exhortatory banner than a precise definition. Its greatest vogue was after the Mexican War and again from the 1890s through the 1920s. Nationally, it was associated with territorial expansion and ethnic comparison, buttressed by Darwinian racial theorizing and hostility toward southern and eastern European immigration. In the South it came to represent white supremacy and the solidarity of northern European stocks. Although the term initially was used to distinguish the Englishman from the Celt or the Latin, the Huguenots were easily embraced as southern Anglo-Saxons, as were the Scots and the Scotch-Irish countrymen of Andrew Jackson and John C. Calhoun. In her epic of southern suffering and pride, Margaret Mitchell derived her quintessential heroine, Scarlett O'Hara, from well-assimilated Irish seed, without arousing purist complaint.

The pre–Civil War manifest Anglo-Saxon destiny was to absorb and assimilate other lands and peoples, but by the end of the century it had become an exclusionist philosophy. European and American theorists gave it a racial base. Teutonist professors such as Herbert Baxter Adams, the southern labor reformer Alexander McKelway, and others traced American democracy back to early Germany. Georgia's Methodist Bishop Warren A. Candler lauded

Anglo-Saxon expansion as God's chosen religious instrument. For naturalist writer Jack London, nature made the choice. The Anglophile North Carolina–born editor and diplomat Walter Hines Page believed that the Anglo-American race held the key to world progress.

The pessimistic side of Anglo-Saxon theorizing was represented by the patrician New England exclusionist Henry Cabot Lodge, who feared that the high birthrate of the new immigrants portended the decay and submergence of the old stock. Southern senators such as Alabama's Tom Heflin picked up the exclusionist refrain.

Although racial theorizing was the particular province of the Northeast, it was easy for southerners to clothe white supremacy in the popular Anglo-Saxon metaphor. Tribunes of white racialism led by South Carolina Senator Ben Tillman called upon Saxon yeomen to enforce black subordination. As the new immigration poured into the rest of the nation, it was popular to picture the South as the remaining bastion of Anglo-Saxon purity.

World War I divided the northern Europeans, and postwar restrictionism diminished the immigrant flow. The vogue of Anglo-Saxonism declined, leaving only the promise of the reborn Ku Klux Klan to protect Anglo-Saxon civilization from submergence by alien people, while the textile mills were lured south by promises of pure Anglo-Saxon labor that would not join unions or strike.

David Chalmers
University of Florida

Thomas F. Gossett, *Race: The History of an Idea in America* (1963); Martin E. Marty, *Righteous Empire: The Protestant Experience in America* (1970). ☆

APPALACHIAN MYTH

For the local writers and home missionaries who "discovered" Appalachia during the 1870s, the "otherness" of the region was axiomatic, and it gave shape to their activities. It yielded travel sketches and short stories that identified Appalachia as an exotic "little corner" of the nation, cut off from the more pleasing aspects of modern American life. It yielded home missionary work designed to integrate the mountaineers into the mainstream of American (Protestant) civilization.

Largely as a result of the literary exploitation of Appalachia by local color writers and the publicity generated to support home missionary work in the region, by the mid-1880s the image of Appalachia as a strange land inhabited by a peculiar people had become so well established in the American consciousness as to require both elaboration and explanation. Of what exactly did the otherness of Appalachia consist? Why was a region close to the centers of American population a strange land and its white, native-born, Protestant population of Anglo-Saxon descent a peculiar people? The answers to these questions, framed in a variety of ways and with a variety of possible implications to be drawn from them, comprised the myth of Appalachia, which contained the following assumptions: (1) the mountainous portions of six or more southern states formed a coherent topographic region; (2) the mountain people formed a homogeneous population; (3) social and economic conditions were the same throughout the mountain region; (4) the culture of the mountaineers—both their beliefs and their behaviors—was consistent throughout the region.

Which of these was the cause of the others was much debated from the mid-1880s, as were the supposedly real characteristics of the region's topography, population, society, economy, and culture. Also of concern, of course, was the matter of how Americans should feel about the existence of this strange land and peculiar people, and what they should do about it. The myth of Appalachia functioned to normalize and make acceptable Appalachian otherness, even if it did not convince everyone of the wisdom of the situation.

Those who saw Appalachian otherness as a threat to the achievement of national unity, or who identified one or another of the characteristics of mountain life and landscape as undesirable, viewed Appalachian otherness as a problem in need of explanation and the characteristics of mountain life as a fact needing modification. At the same time, however, many argued (beginning about 1895) that Appalachian otherness was legitimate in a nation characterized by regionalism and pluralism, but they wished nonetheless to understand the origin of this otherness. Many were also skeptical about one or another aspect of mountain life. Thus, although the myth of Appalachia has made Appalachian otherness seem normal for Americans, it has not impeded efforts by outsiders to modify some aspects of mountain life. Indeed, since the 1880s it has focused continuing attention on the area and has facilitated the planning (and legitimation) of a variety of schemes for "improving" conditions in the mountains.

The myth of Appalachia emerged as a way of explaining the image of Appalachia as a strange land inhabited by a peculiar people, but the myth itself generated additional images. The most prominent of these have been (in approximate historical sequence): (1) Appalachia is the opposite of America; (2) the mountain economy is primitive; (3) the mountaineers are a survival of America's pioneer population; (4) the mountaineers cannot leave the mountains without becoming deracinated; (5) the mountaineers are a hyper-rural population; (6) the mountaineers are a folk and their culture a folk culture; (7) the mountain economy is based on self-sufficiency in agriculture and manufacturing; (8) Appalachia serves as a model against which American civilization may be evaluated (in a wide variety of ways); (9) Appalachia is a pocket of poverty; (10) Appalachia has been victimized by outside (American) interests; (11) Appalachia has been (is) a colony of America; (12) the mountaineers when leaving the region retain their culture and thus become aliens in a strange land and among a peculiar people. The last three are currently dominant, although most of the others persist in one way or another in contemporary thought and action.

See also ENVIRONMENT: / Appalachian Mountains; ETHNIC LIFE: / Appalachians

Henry D. Shapiro
University of Cincinnati

Harry M. Caudill, *Night Comes to the Cumberlands: A Biography of a Depressed Area* (1962); Ronald D. Eller, *Appalachian Journal* (Autumn–Winter 1983–84), *Miners, Millhands, and Mountaineers: The Modernization of the Appalachian South, 1880–1930* (1981); John Gaventa, *Power and Powerlessness: Quiescence and Rebellion in an Appalachian Valley* (1980); Helen M. Lewis et al., *Colonialism in Modern America* (1978); Henry D. Shapiro, *Appalachia on Our Mind: The Southern Mountains and Mountaineers in the American Consciousness,*

1870–1920 (1978), *Appalachian Journal* (Winter 1983); David E. Whisnant, *All That Is Native and Fine: The Politics of Culture in an American Region* (1981), *Modernizing the Mountaineer: People, Power and Planning in Appalachia* (1981). ☆

CARTER ERA
||||||||||||||||||||||||||||||||||||||

The 1976 presidential campaign and subsequent election of Jimmy Carter signaled a major change in the South's image. The negative 1960s image of the South as the place of civil rights conflict gave way to the more favorable image of a land of charming eccentricities, a pleasant lifestyle, traditional small-town American values, and a booming Sunbelt economy.

When the 1976 campaign began, Carter was a hopeless long shot, but after he put together a string of primary victories, including capture of the black vote, the national media began to take notice. Carter's southern background became the key element in the national attention focused on the Georgian. Carter was soon being portrayed as a southern version of a Frank Capra film hero, talking about a government "as good and decent as the American people themselves." In the aftermath of Vietnam and Watergate, the nation seemed naturally to choose its presidential candidate from a region that knew the moral complexities of life and yet asserted simple Baptist moralisms and religiosity as a way of dealing with them. Carter played up his southern ties, telling cheering southern audiences, "Come January we are going to have a President in the White House who doesn't speak with an accent."

The Democratic party convention, held in New York City's Madison Square Garden in August of 1976, was a symbolic triumph not only for Carter but for the South as well. In the bicentennial year of the nation's independence, 111 years after the end of the Civil War, another stage of sectional reconciliation occurred, with a national political institution turning over its leadership to a son of the Deep South. The emotional high point was the last day of the meeting, when Martin Luther "Daddy" King led the convention in the singing of "We Shall Overcome."

After the convention, the national media devoted even more attention to understanding this new South that had produced Carter. *Saturday Review* published a symposium on the "South as the New America" in its 4 September 1976 issue; *U.S. News & World Report* did a feature on the "New South" on 2 August 1976; and *Time* magazine provided an in-depth look at the region through the "South Today" special section of its 27 September 1976 issue, which had articles not only on politics but on "The Good Life," "Those Good Old Boys," "Segregation Remembered," "Home-Grown Elegance" (food), football, stock-car racing, honky-tonk music, and an essay, "The South Tomorrow," by historian C. Vann Woodward.

Southern writers, particularly humorists, were kept busy chronicling and interpreting the Carters and the South to the nation. Larry L. King wrote "We Ain't Trash No More" for *Esquire* (November 1976). Roy Blount, Jr., emerged as one of the preeminent southern interpreters of the Carters. Watching Carter's nomination in New York City, Blount had said he felt "like a man who goes from being half eat up with hookworms to catching nice speckled trout with them." Labeling himself a "Crackro-American" writer, he published a series of magazine articles, later collected as *Crackers* (1982), which dealt with country music, opossums, southern women, good old boys, and other topics essential to understanding the region.

The mythology of the Carter era combined various existing images of the South. Interest in the Carter family as a collection of southern eccentrics was particularly pronounced. Wife Rosalyn seemed to be the "iron magnolia," sweet and gentle on the surface but tough underneath; Miss Lillian, the candidate's mother, was a feisty grande dame; sister Ruth Carter Stapleton was a faith-healing evangelist. And, finally, brother Billy was the beer-guzzling good old boy. Writers struggled to determine how "southern" Jimmy himself was. A peanut farmer, a nuclear engineer in the navy, a born-again Baptist, a businessman—Carter embodied paradoxical images of the Old and New South.

Plains, Ga., emerged as a new symbolic center of the southern experience. It appeared in news stories as a typically southern, yet also American, community. Its train depot, café, service stations, pool halls, and its barber shops and beauty parlors could have been midwestern, yet the presence of a seemingly high percentage of stereotypical southerners, as well as the ever-present racial and evangelical religious aspects, set Plains off as a clearly southern landscape. The peaceful quality of life in the rural and small-town South was much praised by observers, many of whom also lauded the bustling cities of the region.

Carter's inauguration day, 20 January 1977, evoked images of Jeffersonian simplicity, as the new president walked to the ceremonies. His inaugural address was a sermon, notable for its explicit use of civil religious "God language," seeing the nation under divine judgment. There were southern touches, such as the presence of James Dickey, the unofficial poet laureate of the administration, who wrote a poem entitled "The Strength of Fields," which he read at the preinaugural gala. "Everybody wants to be a Southerner now," he was quoted as saying. In addition to the seven inaugural balls, the world's largest square dance was staged. Peanut souvenirs were everywhere in the nation's capital. *Newsweek* magazine described "the dawning of a Dixiefied new era." Soon southern writers were being feted in the White House, and musicians such as the Allman Brothers, Charlie Daniels, and Willie Nelson performed there. *Carter Country*, a network television situation comedy featuring an inept white sheriff, a hip black deputy, and assorted small-town Deep South characters (it was set in Georgia), premiered in 1977.

As time passed, though, Carter and his administration were less frequently portrayed by the national media simply in southern terms. On a trip to the South in the summer of 1977, Carter noted that he was pleased to see fewer stories in the national media about his being a southerner. "Now I, like you, am an American," he said. In the 1980 campaign, the South, like the rest of the nation, deserted Carter. Nonetheless, the earlier Carter campaign and presidency helped to focus national attention on the South and led to changes in perception about the region and its people.

See also POLITICS: / Carter, Jimmy; WOMEN'S LIFE: Carter, Lillian; Carter, Rosalyn

Charles Reagan Wilson
University of Mississippi

Robert M. Pierce, in *Perspectives on the American South*, vol. 2, ed. Merle Black and John Shelton Reed (1984); Stephen A. Smith, *Media, Myth, and the Southern Mind* (1985). ☆

CASH, W. J.
|||||||||||||||||||||||||||||||||

(1900–1941) Journalist.

Wilbur Joseph Cash was a Piedmont southerner, born in Gaffney, S.C., in 1900, a graduate of Wake Forest College, a journalist for the Charlotte *News*, who died by his own hand in Mexico City in 1941. His influence rests upon a single work, *The Mind of the South*, published in 1941, an attempt to analyze the relationship between social consciousness and culture in the region. As a prose stylist, Cash was a talented rhetorician, much influenced by H. L. Mencken's slashing, witty, and barbed journalism, but developing his own version, narrower in range of reference and accomplishment, conversational, sentimental, humorous, candid, emotional, and possessed of great impetus of narrative; it is a style, like that of Thomas Wolfe, best relished in youth.

Cash is the leading proponent of the thesis of southern cultural unity, which he argues was fashioned by climate, physical conditions, frontier violence, clannishness, and Calvinist Protestantism, all of which conspired to create a romantic hedonism, a *zeitgeist* of antiintellectualism and prejudice most brutally expressed in racism, which Cash called the "savage ideal." Having evolved before the Civil War, this unity connects the Old and New South. For Cash the South's industrial transformation had failed to create the class consciousness and intellectual flexibility appropriate to such a society, thus the sensibility of the savage ideal had

remained the master of southern history. Cash himself was a liberal in racial matters by the standards of his time, that is, he had adjusted his views to deprecate the enemies of blacks, but not yet altered his own opinions to sympathize with black culture and personality. Cash's interpretation has proved most appealing to southern liberals who feel pessimistic about and trapped in southern provincial culture and find an explanation for their fetters in Cash's embittered portrait; his raciness of diction and exposition is the aesthetic counterpoint to, and the vindication of, their unease with southern society.

Michael O'Brien
University of Arkansas

Richard H. King, *A Southern Renaissance: The Cultural Awakening of the American South, 1930–1955* (1980); Joseph L. Morrison, *W. J. Cash: Southern Prophet* (1967); Michael O'Brien, *Journal of Southern History* (August 1978); C. Vann Woodward, *American Counterpoint: Slavery and Racism in the North-South Dialogue* (1971). ☆

CAVALIER MYTH
|||||||||||||||||||||||||||||||||||||||||||

The Cavalier myth generally functioned as a prominent aspect of the larger mythic worlds of the plantation and the Lost Cause. According to the myth, the southern Cavalier began his career as a planter or the son of a planter and reached his maturity as a Confederate soldier, generally, but not necessarily, an officer. The Cavalier myth evoked elements of English squirarchy, feudalism, and aristocracy. The Cavalier was courtly, wealthy yet nonmaterialistic, brave, honorable, and gentle. His martial aspects dominated during the war when his conduct was most frequently described as knightly—meaning courageous, devoted to the cause, pure, and still tender. Every Confederate soldier behaved like a Chevalier Bayard without fear and without reproach; he did all that man could do until he was finally overwhelmed. General Robert E. Lee stood as the primary example of the Confederate Cavalier.

The Cavalier began to emerge as a mythic character in plantation novels such as William Alexander Carruthers's *The Cavaliers of Virginia* (1834); he became stock in the plantation domestic novels and polemic writing of the immediate prewar decades; and this ideal reached a stereotypical apex in reminiscences and novels in the first half century after the Civil War, including such works as Thomas Nelson Page's "Marse Chan" (1887) and Thomas Dixon, Jr.'s *The Clansman* (1905). By the 1930s the Cavalier myth was becoming fragmented, as indicated by the Rhett Butler–Ashley Wilkes split in Margaret Mitchell's *Gone with the Wind* (1936).

The Cavalier supplied the glamour of wealth, caste, and lineage that Americans envied. He also stood as an antipode to the restless, materialistic society of the North. After the Civil War, he continued to function in these ways as a national ideal, but in the South he had special meaning as the standard bearer of chivalry's last stand and as the apotheosis of manly virtue. The Cavalier myth served both as an inspiration for those who wanted to push on into the New South and as a consolation for those who embraced the Old South as an unattainable Golden Age. With the coming of the civil rights movement, industrialism, and literary realism to the South, the romantic Cavalier ideal as part of the southern plantation setting no longer

seemed a usable ideal, although elements of the cluster of Cavalier traits still lingered. The Cavalier type, however, is still a major ideal in modern romances.

See also HISTORY AND MANNERS: / Lee, Robert E.

Susan S. Durant
University of Kentucky

Francis Pendleton Gaines, *The Southern Plantation: A Study in the Development and the Accuracy of a Tradition* (1925); Jack Temple Kirby, *Media-Made Dixie: The South in the American Imagination* (1978); William R. Taylor, *Cavalier and Yankee: The Old South and American National Character* (1957). ☆

CELTIC SOUTH

The idea of the Celtic origins of the southern white population is one of the major, but controversial, theories explaining the early development of southern culture. The ethnic polarization of the American colonies, with the English dominating New England and the Celts (Scottish, Irish, Scotch-Irish, Welsh, Cornish) dominating the South, was one factor making the Old South distinctive. By 1790, when the first U.S. census was taken, ethnic sectionalization was firmly established. In New England well over three-quarters of the people were of English origins, and English ways were firmly planted in the region. The Middle Atlantic states had a mixture of peoples, but the further south and west from Philadelphia, the more Celtic the population. In the Upper South, Celts and Englishmen each constituted about two-fifths of the population; in the Carolinas, more than half the people were Celtic, and Celts outnumbered Englishmen two to one. Celts dominated the interior from Pennsylvania southward, ranging in various areas from three-fourths to nearly a hundred percent of the population.

The significance of this distribution lay in its effects on migration patterns during the next six or seven decades. When New Englanders moved westward, most went along the Mohawk River across New York, then fanned out around the Great Lakes. The Celts filled the Ohio Valley and the trans-Appalachian South. In between were Germans and stragglers from the other two major ethnic groups. By the end of the antebellum period, the South's white population was three-quarters or more Celtic, New England and the upper Middle West were three-quarters or more English, and the border areas were mixed. The other major influence on southern culture, which also dated from the early colonial period, was the African heritage.

The Celts who settled in the South brought with them their non-English ways—including a pastoral economy based upon open-range herding, a leisurely lifestyle and a distaste for hard work, rural values that stressed wasteful hospitality and outdoor sports, the reckless indulgence in food and drink, a touchy and romantic sense of honor, and a strong tendency toward lawlessness and the settlement of disagreements by violent means—and they readily imposed these traditions upon their neighbors. Only a few settlers in the antebellum South, such as determined Yankees and isolated Germans as well as the enslaved Africans, managed to avoid acculturation into the prevailing Celtic cultural patterns.

Forrest McDonald
University of Alabama

Grady McWhiney
Texas Christian University

Rowland Berthloff, *Journal of Southern History* (November 1986); Forrest McDonald and Ellen Shapiro McDonald, *William and Mary Quarterly* (April 1980); Forrest McDonald and Grady McWhiney, *American Historical Review* (December 1980), *History Today* (July 1980), *Journal of Southern History* (May 1975, May 1985), *Names* (1982). ☆

"CRACKERS"
|||||||||||||||||||||||||||||||||||||||

Americans have long stereotyped poor white southerners with a variety of contemptuous terms including *honky*, *redneck*, *peckerwood*, *linthead*, *hoosier*, *shit kicker*, and *cracker*. The word *crackers* is among the oldest epithets used to describe white southerners, especially those from south Georgia and north Florida. The term extends back at least to the mid-1700s, when it was used in Scotland as a colloquialism for boaster. In Samuel Johnson's famous dictionary of 1755, a *cracker* was defined as a "noisy, boasting fellow."

By the 1760s the word was commonly used by coastal residents as an ethnic pejorative to designate Scotch-Irish frontiersmen in the South. These backcountry folk tended to be herdsmen who depended on an abundance of land for grazing livestock. With diminishing open rangeland in the early 19th century, some of these plain folk moved westward across the Appalachians to the frontier, but others headed into the piney woods of Georgia and Florida, an area that became the Cracker "home-land."

Travelers in this area in the 19th century wrote of the Crackers as poor white farmers, often dismissing them for "cracking," or pounding, corn for food. On the other hand, local histories and other accounts show the existence of a prosperous middle class, whose members typically owned a slave or two, grew corn and other commodities, and grazed cattle and hogs. From this perspective, most of these piney woods folk were not poor "corn crackers" but respectable "whip crackers," who used a long whip with a tip called a "cracker."

After the Civil War, the debt-ridden states of Georgia and Florida sold off much of the public land that Crackers had used for grazing livestock. Their economic lot worsened in the late 19th century, and landless Crackers went to mill towns for work or became sharecroppers or marginal farmers. By the turn of the 20th century the term *cracker* was a pejorative for a poor millworker or rural sharecropper. Some plain folk in south Georgia and north Florida managed, however, to continue a cattle-herding economy until after World War II.

Cracker is also a racial epithet used by black Americans as a contemptuous term for a southern white. In the early 1800s southern slaves and free blacks used the word *buckras*, which is from an African word, to refer to whites. By the 1850s, though, *cracker* was becoming the preferred term. After the Civil War, racial tension rose in the piney woods, as whites blamed freed slaves for their deteriorating economic situation. Mob violence against blacks occasionally occurred there, and the black population declined. Migrant southern blacks took their contempt for "crackers" with them to northern cities in the 20th century,

and today the term is often used in ghettoes in referring to all prejudiced whites.

In the 1970s *crackers* became a term of ethnic pride for some southern whites. The election of a south Georgian, Jimmy Carter, to the presidency in 1976 led to media stories about Cracker Chic, and humorist Roy Blount, Jr., used *Crackers* as the title of his book about southerners and the Carter era.

Charles Reagan Wilson
University of Mississippi

Raven I. McDavid, Jr., and Virginia McDavid, *Names* (September 1973); John S. Otto, in *Perspectives on the American South*, vol. 4, ed. James C. Cobb and Charles Reagan Wilson (1987). ☆

FITZHUGH, GEORGE
(1808–1881) Slavery advocate.

Fitzhugh, from Port Royal, Va., was the descendant of an old southern family that had fallen on hard times. He practiced law and struggled as a small planter but made a reputation with two books, *Sociology for the South* (1854) and *Cannibals All!* (1857), which alarmed northerners like Abraham Lincoln and roused southerners to take new and higher ground in defense of slavery.

Fitzhugh insisted that all labor, not merely black, had to be enslaved and that the world must become all slave or all free. He defined "slavery" broadly to include all systems of servile labor. These views had become commonplace in the South by the 1850s. His originality lay in the insight that slavery could only survive and prevail if the capitalist world market were destroyed. He understood that organic social relations and attendant values could not survive in a world dominated by capitalist competition and bourgeois individualism.

His call for war against the modern world, expressed in a harsh polemical style, made him a solitary figure. Numerous others agreed that free labor spelled class war and invited anarchy. They also agreed that slavery overcame the "social question" by establishing a master class that combined interest with sentiment to offer the masses security. But, having no confidence in his utopian vision of a reversal of history, they generally tried, however illogically, to convince the European and northern bourgeoisie to restore some form of slavery in a corporatist order.

Fitzhugh opposed secession until the last minute, arguing that a slaveholding Confederacy could not survive until the advanced capitalist countries had themselves converted. After the war, which once begun he loyally and enthusiastically supported, Fitzhugh sank into obscurity, becoming increasingly negrophobic and idiosyncratic. To all intents and purposes, he died at Appomattox.

Eugene D. Genovese
University of Rochester

Eugene D. Genovese, *The World the Slaveholders Made: Two Essays in Interpretation* (1969); Harvey Wish, *George Fitzhugh: Propagandist of the Old South* (1943). ☆

GOOD OLD BOYS AND GIRLS

The terms *good old boy* and *good old girl* are of southern origin. The terms describe social types, persons with particular social characteristics that make them identifiable to others. Although there are similar social types in other regions of the United States, the southern label may make them more obvious in the South.

The good old boy and girl have been pictured most frequently in popular literature. Perhaps the first reference to the social type was in William Byrd's *Histories of the Dividing Line Betwixt Virginia and North Carolina* (1728). W. J. Cash discussed the type in *The Mind of the South* (1941), but the first writer to use the term itself was Tom Wolfe in an essay on stock car racing hero Junior Johnson (*Esquire*, October 1967). William Price Fox, in *Southern Fried* (1962), presented several portraits of the type, including the legendary Georgia politician, Eugene Talmadge. Willie Morris's *Good Old Boy: A Delta Boyhood* (1971) was autobiographical, and Paul Hemphill in *The Good Old Boys* (1974) wrote lovingly of them, mainly because his father was one. Florence King's *Southern Ladies and Gentlemen* (1975) sees the good old boy as mean and nasty. Sharon McKern's *Redneck Mothers, Good Old Girls and Other Southern Belles* (1979) was one of the first literary applications of the concept to women. In *Crackers* (1980), Roy Blount, Jr., suggests that " 'good old boy' means pretty much the same as 'mensch.' "

The good old boy frequently appears in such country music songs as "Bar Room Buddies," "If You've Got the Money, I've Got the Time," and "Dang Me," and the term itself was used in Ansley Fleetwood's "Just Good Ol' Boys" (1979). Sometimes the term is used synonymously with "cowboy" in country music. Burt Reynolds embodied the good old boy in a series of movies in the 1970s.

The good old boy is described as blue collar, an outdoorsman, a patriot, something of a populist, basically conservative—a "man's man." He is also somewhat self-centered and scheming, particularly toward out-groups. Yet to his in-group he is an affable comrade and a man of integrity. Billy Carter, the brother of President Jimmy Carter and himself the essence of the type, has defined the good old boy as someone who rides around in a pickup truck, drinking beer and putting his empties in a sack. A redneck, by contrast, rides around in a pickup, drinking and tossing his empties out the window. The "redneck" as a concept describes a more menacing figure.

The good old girl has not been studied as systematically as the good old boy. She has traits of bluffness, camaraderie, and loyalty, which make her more comfortable with men than women. She is usually not seen as a sex object and, in fact, is somewhat asexual in social interaction. She is likely to possess the same affability and integrity as the good old boy and the same ability to manipulate people.

Ingram Parmley
Francis Marion College

Ingram Parmley, in *Perspectives on the American South*, vol. 1, ed. Merle Black and John Shelton Reed (1981); Edgar T. Thompson, *South Atlantic Quarterly* (Autumn 1984). ☆

HOSPITALITY

Hospitality is an intensely real aspect of southern culture, but it has often been misrepresented, as in the oft-told tale of the planter who waylaid travelers and took them at rifle point to visit his home. Other stories, some of them in otherwise accurate historical works, depict south-ern doors as swinging open to all comers, whatever their rank or degree.

Hospitality in the South was far more restricted than such tales would imply. In the 18th and early 19th centuries some of the most murderous outlaws in American history infested the South, and under such circumstances a householder would have been a fool to welcome some disreputable stranger into his home. Moreover, whatever else the South may have been, it was never a social democracy. The planter whose social aspirations led him to construct a mansion, or even a second story atop his dogtrot cabin, did not extend warm greetings to poor farmers or laborers who barely scratched out a living.

A commercial element also affected hospitality in the Old South. Travelers' accounts make clear that when they sought shelter in private homes travelers were expected to pay for their bed and their food. Frederick Law Olmsted nearly always paid 75 cents or a dollar as he made his way through the rural South, and many others had the same experience.

Southerners normally welcomed neighbors and relatives with open arms, and a stranger might also be joyously greeted if he bore letters of introduction from friends or relatives. Once received, the guest met few limitations; much of the substance of some planters, and some yeomen for that matter, was expended on visitors who often stayed too long. One finds few complaints in the records, however, and more than a little boasting.

The poverty that followed the Civil War curtailed hospitality, but "spending the day" with friends and kin persisted, and widowed or unmarried members of a family often lived by "visiting" their children, nieces, nephews, brothers, and sisters. The southerner is indeed hospitable to this day, loving nothing more than to entertain family and friends with the best food and drink he can afford. The automobile and the telephone make visiting far simpler than in early times; normally only guests who have traveled great distances stay overnight, and the length of such visits is limited by the construction of the modern home. But if the circumstances of southern hospitality have changed, the spirit remains the same.

Joe Gray Taylor
McNeese State University

Joe Gray Taylor, *Eating, Drinking, and Visiting in the South* (1982). ☆

LOST CAUSE MYTH
||||||||||||||||||||||||||||||||||||||||||||||||||||||

The phrase "the Lost Cause," popularized as the title of Edward A. Pollard's 1866 history of the Confederacy, became a common designation for the southern role in the Civil War. Most southerners felt it properly evoked the heroism and nobility of the Confederate

Confederate battle flags draping the Mississippi capitol, 1930s

armies, but beyond that the term did not symbolize any particular interpretation of the war. Although southerners may not have admitted it, the phrase nevertheless accurately reflected their ambivalence about the outcome of the war. "Lost" acknowledged the defeat of the Confederacy; "Cause" suggested the South had fought less for independence than for philosophical principles that might yet triumph.

The phrase "the Lost Cause" also became identified with the movement within the South to enshrine the memory of the Civil War. As early as a year after Appomattox, Confederate memorial associations were formed to care for the graves of the war dead. A few of the societies placed monuments in the cemeteries they constructed, and all celebrated Confederate Memorial Day every spring. The Southern Historical Society, founded in New Orleans in 1869 but later headquartered in Richmond, sought to preserve a true, i.e., southern, history of the war. In the 1880s this memorialization of the cause gradually became a celebration of the war, which continued into the first decades of the 20th century. During these years, the South dedicated monuments to the wartime leaders Lee and Davis, and many communities placed statues of Confederate soldiers on courthouse lawns or town squares. In 1889 several veterans' groups organized the United Confederate Veterans (UCV), which soon had camps throughout the region. In 1894 the United Daughters of the Confederacy was formed, and two years later a somewhat successful United Sons of the Confederacy appeared. With both veterans and descendants organized, the UCV reunions and monument unveilings attracted huge crowds for public celebrations of the Confederacy.

Historians offer various interpretations of the meaning and significance of the celebration of the war, but two approaches prevail. One stressed the political functions of the idea of the Lost Cause: providing support for states' rights, white supremacy, and the Democratic party. Some adherents of this approach treat the glorification of the Lost Cause as only a diversion from the real issues—another trick by which the Democratic establishment maintained its power. Others consider the Lost Cause notion a widely accepted social myth with a less explicit political role. The second approach emphasizes the cultural functions of the idea—helping southerners assimilate defeat and unifying southern society. Some of the historians who take this view argue that the Lost Cause myth became a civil religion and rendered southerners a people set apart by a special sense of mission. Others, pointing to similar activities in the North, suggest that the celebration of the war owed much to the social tensions of the 1880s and 1890s and did not serve so central a role in forming a southern identity. Most students of the idea of the Lost Cause, however, would agree that its development bestowed cultural authority on Confederate symbols that southerners in the 20th century continued to invoke in defense of various causes from intervention abroad to segregation at home.

See also HISTORY AND MANNERS: / Southern Historical Society; United Confederate Veterans

Gaines M. Foster
Louisiana State University

Susan S. Durant, "The Gently Furled Banner: The Development of the Myth of the Lost Cause, 1865–1900" (Ph.D. dissertation, University of North Carolina at Chapel Hill, 1972); Gaines M. Foster, *Ghosts of the Confederacy: Defeat, the Lost Cause, and the Emergence of the New South, 1865–1913* (1987); Rollin G. Osterweis, *The Myth of the Lost Cause, 1865–1900* (1973); Charles Reagan Wilson, *Baptized in Blood: The Religion of the Lost Cause, 1865–1920* (1980). ☆

"MAMMY"

The "mammy" character is a stereotype derived from history and popular culture. She is a black, middle-aged woman who has a strong, loud voice and wears an apron and a kerchief on her head. Her ample body and open, honest expression reveal that she is maternal and reliable. She is the southern archetype of the earth mother. Donald Bogle, who has classified the dominant images of blacks in film, said that the mammy

Mrs. Wilson's Nurse and Fat Baby, *photographer unknown, late 19th century*

figure is a "desexed, overweight, dowdy, *dark* black woman." Mammy is Aunt Jemima, an icon that recurs often enough to be easily recognized.

The mammy character recurs in fiction. She is William Faulkner's Dilsey in *The Sound and the Fury*, Carson McCullers's Berenice in *The Member of the Wedding*, Fanny Hurst's Delilah in *Imitation of Life*, and Margaret Mitchell's Mammy in *Gone with the Wind*. Actresses who play her in films have become icons of the mammy figure. Ethel Waters, Louise Beavers, and Hattie McDaniel are familiar "mammies" who have even become folk heroines.

Mammy as a character is the quintessence of strength, constancy, and integrity. She is not only capable, generous, and kind but also very religious, long-suffering, and sometimes scolding. A Christian oracle of wisdom, she passes her knowledge on to white characters whose lives are thereby enriched. She is the all-loving, loyal mainstay to a white family, giving all of herself to the family in this life and asking for nothing in return but heavenly reward.

Mammy is a dominant antebellum black image, personifying the spirit of endurance during the hard times of slavery. Under slavery, white families relied on black slaves to raise their children, nurse their sick, and cook and clean for them. The mammy character is historically derived from the house slave who was the personal servant of the white plantation owners. It was not unusual for the personal slaves of the master and mistress to sleep in the same bedroom with them to be on call should their service be needed during the night. Although they were better fed and dressed than the field slaves, the house slaves were treated as nonpersons. After emancipation, black women were still treated as mammy figures. The mammy image passed from southern plantations to day workers and domestic maids, and thus from the South to the North.

Victoria O'Donnell
North Texas State University

Donald Bogle, *Toms, Coons, Mulattoes, Mammies, and Bucks: An Interpretive History of Blacks in American Films* (1973); Carol Hymowitz and Michaele Weissman, *A History of Women in America* (1978); Victoria O'Donnell, in *The South and Film*, ed. Warren French (1981). ☆

MENCKEN'S SOUTH

H. L. Mencken of Baltimore was known in the 1920s as the archenemy of the American South, but in fact Mencken's view of the South was more complex than most of his detractors realized. He was best known for his diatribes against Dixie in "The Sahara of the Bozart" (1920) and other essays; the South, he claimed in the "Sahara," was a cultural and intellectual desert, a land run by poor whites, a colossal paradise of the fourth-rate. But if H. L. Mencken was the graphic realist in cataloging the numerous flaws of southern life in the early 20th century, he was also the most romantic of writers when he envisioned an earlier South. In many of the same essays in which he damned those states below the Potomac and Ohio, he also contended that, up until the Civil War, the South had been the American seat of civilization, a cultivated land "with men of delicate fancy, urbane instinct and aristocratic manner—in brief, superior men." In the antebellum South "some attention was given to the art of living. . . . A certain noble spaciousness was in the ancient southern scheme of things."

What Mencken had in mind when he spoke of an earlier cultivated South was, largely, Virginia of the 18th and early 19th centuries—and even in Virginia the spirit of free inquiry that Mencken prized had begun to decline long before the beginning of the Civil War. But, by his reasoning, the war itself was responsible for the complete "drying up" of southern civilization. After Appomattox, he contended, the aristocrats vanished—died, fled North, or lived out their days in obscurity—and the worthless, depraved poor whites seized control and dominated every aspect of southern life. Fanatical preachers, corrupt politicians, and nostalgic poetasters made the South the laughingstock of the nation. Such was H. L. Mencken's view of southern history, a view which, although not quite historically accurate, was widely circulated in the 1920s and 1930s. The antebellum South, in truth, was never so civilized—nor the postbellum South so barbaric—as the South of H. L. Mencken's imagination.

See also LITERATURE: / Mencken, H. L.

Fred Hobson
University of Alabama

Fred Hobson, *Serpent in Eden: H. L. Mencken and the South* (1974); H. L. Mencken, *Prejudices, Second Series* (1920), *Virginia Quarterly Review* (January 1935). ☆

MITCHELL, MARGARET
(1900–1949) Writer.

Born 8 November 1900 in Atlanta, Margaret Mitchell was as proud of her long-established Atlanta family as she was of *Gone with the Wind*. She wrote in 1941: "I know of few other Atlanta people who can claim that their families have been associated as long and intimately, and sometimes prominently, with the birth and growth and history of this city."

Mitchell was educated in Atlanta schools and at Smith College. After her mother died in the flu epidemic of 1919, Mitchell returned from Smith to Atlanta to keep house for her father and her brother. She made her debut in 1920 and in 1922 married Berrien Kinnard Upshaw. The marriage lasted barely three months.

In December 1922 Mitchell found a job on the staff of the Atlanta *Journal Sunday Magazine*. On the *Journal* she worked with such writers as Erskine Caldwell and Frances Newman. On 4 July 1925 she married John Robert Marsh, public relations officer of the Georgia Power Company, and in 1926 resigned her job because of ill health. She tried writing short stories but found no market for them, and they were eventually destroyed. Discouraged, she turned to the composition of a long novel for her own amusement during an extended recuperation.

Most of *Gone with the Wind* was completed by 1929. It was still incomplete, however, when in April of 1935 she somewhat quixotically allowed Harold Latham (on a scouting trip for the Macmillan Company) to see the manuscript. Macmillan's almost immediate acceptance was followed by months of checking for historical accuracy, filling gaps in the story, and rewriting. The book was a best-seller the day it was published, 30 June 1936, and dominated its author's life thereafter.

For the next 13 years Mitchell nursed an aging father and later an invalid husband, enthusiastically did war work, and maintained a massive amount of correspondence relating to *Gone with the Wind*. She wrote no more fiction and emerged from private life only occasionally, most notably for the premiere of the film *Gone with the Wind* on 15 December 1939 in Atlanta.

Accident-prone throughout her life, she met her death in an accident on 11 August 1949. Crossing Peachtree Street with her husband, she was struck by a speeding taxicab. She died five days later and was buried in Atlanta's Oakland Cemetery.

See also MEDIA: / *Gone with the Wind*

Richard B. Harwell
Athens, Georgia

Anne Edwards, *The Road to Tara: The Life of Margaret Mitchell* (1983); Finis Farr, *Margaret Mitchell of Atlanta: The Author of Gone with the Wind* (1965); Richard Harwell, ed., *Margaret Mitchell's "Gone with the Wind" Letters, 1936–1949* (1976); a collection of over 50,000 items of Miss Mitchell's correspondence, reviews of *Gone with the Wind*, magazine and newspaper articles, pictures, and other memorabilia is in the Manuscript Department of the University of Georgia Libraries, Athens. ☆

"MOONLIGHT-AND-MAGNOLIAS" MYTH

As a phrase, "moonlight and magnolias" has two distinct but related meanings. It is most commonly used as a derogatory epithet for the more excessive manifestations of sentimental cavalier-belle-plantation fiction. In this sense, it is a term of derision, as shown in Margaret Mitchell's defense of *Gone with the Wind*: "I've always been slightly amused by the New York critics who referred to GWTW as a 'moonlight and magnolia romance.' My God, they never read the gentle Confederate novel of the Nineties, or they would know better." Mitchell's statement also implicitly indicates the other less pejorative meaning of the phrase—the myth of an antebellum Golden Age, a myth created in the postbellum world of the 1880s and 1890s and a part of the larger myths of the plantation and the Lost Cause.

The conscious and recognized leader in creating this myth was Thomas Nelson Page, but he had a host of colleagues and imitators who can be found in the 17-volume *Library of Southern Literature* (1907), edited by Edwin Anderson Alderman and Joel Chandler Harris. Page's *In Ole Virginia* (1887) and *Red Rock* (1898) exhibit all the myth's elements. He fixed the past in time and held on to it. The antebellum South became the romantic "before the war," an Eden, a dream of chivalry; the Civil War became that period of heroism, when the Cause was lost but the South was not beaten on the battlefield; and Reconstruction was the vengeful rape by the vulgar North of the beautiful South. Though this idealized view was simplistic, its popularity with late 19th-century southerners was understandable, for in their economic and political privation they could at least remember, in Page's words, the time when "even the moonlight was richer and mellower." In both its glamour and pathos the myth also appealed to non-southerners and spread a nostalgic image of antebellum southern life across the nation. The anecdote of Union General Higginson's weeping over Page's "Marse Chan," a story apostrophizing the cavalier and belle through the words of an ex-slave has often been noted, and rightly so, for it is a symbol of the myth's effect.

The myth has become in the contemporary era an object of parody and an advertising gimmick. By keeping all the plantation paraphernalia, but adding three new elements, it has been transformed in novels and films into a new antebellum myth of sex, sadism, and miscegenation. The present pejorative meaning derives as much from this transformation as from weaknesses inherent in the original myth and says much about changes in the way both southerners and non-southerners have looked at the antebellum South for the past 100 years.

See also LITERATURE: / Page, Thomas Nelson

Earl F. Bargainnier
Wesleyan College

Earl F. Bargainnier, *Louisiana Studies* (Spring 1976), in *Icons of America*, ed. Ray B. Browne and Marshall Fishwick (1978), *Southern Quarterly* (Winter 1984). ☆

NATIONALISM, SOUTHERN

Like the American nationalism of which it was an offshoot, southern nationalism attempted to define clearly the circumstances in which 19th-century southerners found themselves. The coming of peace in 1815 allowed all Americans to turn inward and examine those characteristics and institutions that set them apart from other nations. Like Americans in general, southerners were intimately involved in all phases of this quest for nationality: campaigns for economic development, encouragement of a native literature, calls for improved

education, state constitutional revisions to broaden the franchise, religious revivals, and territorial expansion.

Giving each of these movements a peculiarly southern twist was a growing sense that in some fundamental way the southern states possessed shared interests that conflicted with those of the nation at large. As this perception grew and spread, increasing numbers of southerners began to agitate for a separate southern nation, which would possess all the cultural and political attributes they as Americans had long desired, but which also would protect that most vital of all southern interests, slavery. By 1860, though only a minority of southerners favored secession, the efforts of southern nationalists had won such an influential following that a southern nation took form.

The unsuccessful career of the short-lived Confederacy has persuaded many historians that southern nationalism never existed. Evidence to support that argument appears abundant. The Constitution of the Confederate States and that of the United States were virtual duplicates. The rival presidents and their governments moved along strikingly similar paths to strikingly similar policies on conscription, finance, and even battlefield strategy. After a brief and moderate Reconstruction, the South resumed full partnership in the Union. Confederate history does indeed show what southern nationalism was not. But it also convincingly shows what it was: an effort to be more fully and more purely American than other Americans, to subscribe more honorably, as southerners saw it, to the meaning of the Constitution.

By 1860 enough southerners perceived that the only way to live up to the definition of America they had been so instrumental in providing was to rebel, as their grandfathers had rebelled. "There is a habit of speaking derisively of going to war for an idea— an abstraction—something which you cannot see," wrote a southern editor in 1861. "This is precisely the point on which we would go to war. An idea is exactly the thing that we would fight for." Southern nationalism was—and is—above all else a state of mind.

John McCardell
Middlebury College

Avery O. Craven, *The Growth of Southern Nationalism, 1848–1861* (1953); John McCardell, *The Idea of a Southern Nation: Southern Nationalists and Southern Nationalism, 1830–1860* (1979); David Potter, *The South and the Sectional Conflict* (1968). ☆

PLACE, SENSE OF

"One place comprehended can make us understand other places better," wrote Eudora Welty in "Place in Fiction." The term *sense of place* as used in the South implies an organic society. Until recently southern whites frequently used *place* to indicate the status of blacks. James McBride Dabbs noted in 1957 that southern whites spent much time "keeping the Negro in his place" and foolishly considered themselves "happy because the Negro had a place." But racial "place" was only one aspect of a traditional southern attachment to the region—one had a place in a local community, among a broad kin network, and in history.

Attachment to a place gives an abiding identity because places associated with family, community, and history have depth. Philosopher Yi-Fu Tuan points out that a sense of place in any human society comes from the intersection of space and time. Southerners developed an acute sense of place as a result of their dramatic and traumatic history and their rural isolation on the land for generations. As Welty noted, "*feelings* are bound up with place," and the film title *Places in the Heart* captured the emotional quality that places evoke. *Home* is a potent word for southerners, and the *homeplace* evokes reverence.

The evidence for a deep-seated southern sense of place is extensive. The first settlers in the region, Native Americans, saw the lands of the Southeast as sacred ground, with all happenings in their specific places related to the rest of the cosmos. Native Americans named prominent physical landmarks and plants and animals in their local areas; their place names survive as evocative descriptions of the landscape.

From Mark Twain's Mississippi River to William Faulkner's Yoknapatawpha County, southern writers have created memorable literary landscapes of place. The lyrics of blues singers starkly evoke the Mississippi Delta, and country musicians sing a lyrical version of states' rights with titles such as "My Home's in Alabama," "Mississippi You're on My Mind," "Tennessee Mountain Home," and "Can't Wash the Sands of Texas from My Shoes." Folk artists draw from the long memory of people living in isolated rural areas for generations. They learn from older generations and convey the texture of life in a particular southern place through painting, carving, sewing, and other crafts.

Sociologists use the term *localism* to describe the sense of place in the South. The analysis of public opinion poll results shows that contemporary southern blacks and whites value their states more than non-southern Americans, and they more often emulate local family and neighbors. John Shelton Reed has concluded that "southerners seem more likely than other Americans to think of their region, their states, and their local communities possessively as *theirs*, and as distinct from and preferable to other regions, states, and localities."

Contemporary public policymakers have become aware of the threat economic development poses to preservation of the traditional southern sense of place. In the 1974 Commission on the Future of the South, a group of prominent regional leaders suggested to the Southern Growth Policies Board that an important goal of the modern South should be "to preserve and enhance, in meeting the issues of growth and change, the human sense of place and community that is a vital element of the unique quality of Southern life."

Charles Reagan Wilson
University of Mississippi

William Ferris, *Local Color: A Sense of Place in Folk Art* (1982); Lucinda H. MacKethan, *The Dream of Arcady: Place and Time in Southern Literature* (1980); John Shelton Reed, *The Enduring South: Subcultural Persistence in Mass Society* (1972); Stephen A. Smith, *Myth, Media, and the Southern Mind* (1985); Eudora Welty, *The Eye of the Story: Selected Essays and Reviews* (1978). ☆

POOR WHITES
||||||||||||||||||||||||||||||||||||||

Both outsiders and native southerners helped create and perpetuate myths about the South's poor whites, some of which had a strong basis in fact. An-

tebellum English and northern travelers described a white South consisting of plantation grandees at the top and wretchedly deprived poor farmers at the bottom. (Both groups, although in fact large, were outnumbered by small yeoman farmers.) The school of antebellum writers known as southwestern humorists were themselves from the upper classes, but the people they described were shrewd, somewhat bizarre, clay eaters who practiced emotional religion and engaged in violent eye gougings. The notion of the two-tiered society later served well the needs of abolitionists who blamed slavery for southern poverty; the comic stereotype of the southwestern humorists, although accurate in many respects, furnished the basis for one of the most enduring myths within American popular culture.

In the late 19th century new layers were added. A region struggling to maintain the values of its agrarian past while at the same time striving for material progress found the poor white useful. New South polemicists noted the breakup of the plantation and the rise of small farms, and they applauded the advent of small-farmer independence and democracy; actually, tens of thousands of whites were descending into tenancy. New South promoters also celebrated the textile mill, which in reality replaced one kind of deprivation with another. When other regions criticized the South for its racial violence or its inclination to elect demagogic politicians, southern apologists absolved themselves and generally blamed poor whites, who unfortunately were often prone to vote for racist demagogues.

In Appalachia a strange and peculiar people challenged America's Gilded Age notions of progress and homogeneity, and missionaries both secular and religious tried to convert the hillbilly primitives from their moonshine, religion, feuds, and culture. Later generations of Americans characterized them as backward hillbillies who were inclined toward incest, fundamentalist religion, laziness, and irresponsibility.

Those who sympathized with poor whites created their own set of myths. In James Agee's classic book, *Let Us Now Praise Famous Men*, the author eulogized poor whites caught in a cosmic dead end. In the novels of Erskine Caldwell the myth of "poor white trash" found its most popular expression. An idealistic generation in the 1960s and 1970s glorified Appalachian poor whites as the finest surviving example of primitive American innocence (a poor but self-contained life lived close to the land in relative isolation, with clean water and air and wonderfully imaginative folk crafts, lore, and music). Each of these descriptions of poor whites contained factual information upon which broad and sometimes unfair or inaccurate generalizations could be built.

Many Americans blame the South's problems on the Jeeter Lesters (of *Tobacco Road*), degenerates and racists, shiftless wanderers, wife-beaters, drunks, and ne'er-do-wells. They believe that such people also furnish the Ernest Angleys, Jerry Falwells, and Marjoe Gortners of American religion. According to the conflicting images of American popular culture, the southern poor white can be the shrewdly innocent Jed Clampett of *The Beverly Hillbillies* or a Pentecostal haunted by incestuous lust, the sodomite of James Dickey's *Deliverance*, or the tough, poor-boy-made-good Paul "Bear" Bryant, who wrestled bears in Fordyce, Ark., because he could make more by fighting the beasts than by chopping cotton. Poor

white music furnished many additional themes—the religious, fatalistic poor white or the "second-hand satin ladies" and "honky tonk angels." So far as myth is concerned, the poor white has been a man or woman for all seasons.

J. Wayne Flynt
Auburn University

Sylvia J. Cook, *From Tobacco Road to Route 66: The Southern Poor White in Fiction* (1976); J. Wayne Flynt, *Dixie's Forgotten People: The South's Poor Whites* (1979); Shields McIlwaine, *The Southern Poor-White: From Lubberland to Tobacco Road* (1939); Henry D. Shapiro, *Appalachia on Our Mind: The Southern Mountains and Mountaineers in the American Consciousness, 1870–1920* (1978); Merrill M. Skaggs, *The Folk of Southern Fiction* (1972). ☆

REB, JOHNNY

The Confederate soldier's image in regional culture is his cumulative representation in southern novels, poetry, illustration, and statuary, as well as in photography and historiography. Because the manner of this representation suggests popular beliefs about the Civil War and the Confederate experience, Johnny Reb's image is an important factor in southern history and the myths surrounding it.

This image has been eulogistic, reflecting southerners' sentimental attachment to the Confederate soldier. During the war years, patriotic speeches, editorials, and sermons idealized Johnny Reb as defender of morality and American liberty. Poetry by William Gilmore Simms, Paul Hayne, Henry Timrod, and others added romantic elements such as knightly valor to the image. The trials of war and defeat dimmed this early idealism, but developments after Appomattox contributed new elements of eulogy to the soldier's reputation. The elaborate rituals of Confederate Memorial Day, begun in 1866 to venerate the war dead, continued to sanctify the common soldier. Starting in the 1880s, veterans' reminiscences extended the warm glow of nostalgia to the war, and in these writings as well as in the grandiloquent oratory of veterans' reunions, Johnny Reb was exalted for his bravery, endurance, and devotion to duty. Furthermore, southerners' historical writings, begun soon after the war to chronicle—and justify—the Confederate struggle, depicted the fight as a valiant but doomed effort against overwhelming northern resources. This historiography of the Lost Cause ennobled Johnny Reb, particularly when it recounted his victories under Robert E. Lee against numerically superior enemies. "Overpowered by numbers" became a popular means of explaining defeat while maintaining the Confederate soldier's battlefield prowess.

Pictorial representation was an important element of the image. Two notable contributors were William L. Sheppard and Allen C. Redwood, talented illustrators whose drawings of Confederates appeared abundantly after the war in *Scribner's*, *Century*, and other northern periodicals. Their work for *Century* magazine's *Battles and Leaders of the Civil War* (1887) was widely circulated. Memorial statuary provided further visual imagery. Monuments to the Confederate dead were erected on courthouse squares throughout the South, especially during 1880 to 1910, and featured sculpted likenesses of Johnny Reb that endowed him with a perpetual youth. Effusive monument inscriptions underscored his constancy and courage.

One of the surest signs of sectional reconciliation after the 1880s was the increasing similarity of Johnny Reb's image to Billy Yank's, as eulogists hailed both soldiers for their American idealism and pluck. In this century, though, the viewpoints of some southerners tended to undercut Johnny Reb's nationalism and shaped his image as the opponent of progress in modern America. In the 1920s and 1930s the Fugitive poets of Vanderbilt—notably Allen Tate and Donald Davidson—used the Confederate fighting man as a symbol of their protest against contemporary culture, with its cities, cars, and consumer goods that threatened the traditional southern lifestyle. A generation later, segregationists expropriated the Confederate battle flag as their symbol of adherence to "traditional" southern ways. To an extent, each of these developments influenced Johnny Reb's image by characterizing him as a diehard defender of outdated values.

The Confederate soldier's image has consequently aged, as his relevance to modern southerners has waned. By and large, however, the eulogistic tradition remains strong, and Johnny Reb will probably remain a regional folk hero for southerners as well as an enduring reminder of what helps set them apart from the rest of the country.

See also HISTORY AND MANNERS: / Confederate Veteran; United Confederate Veterans

Stephen Davis
Atlanta, Georgia

Stephen Davis, "Johnny Reb in Perspective: The Confederate Soldier's Image in the

Southern Arts" (Ph.D. dissertation, Emory University, 1979); Susan S. Durant, "The Gently Furled Banner: The Development of the Myth of the Lost Cause, 1865–1900" (Ph.D. dissertation, University of North Carolina at Chapel Hill, 1972); Rollin G. Osterweis, *The Myth of the Lost Cause, 1865–1900* (1973); Charles Reagan Wilson, *Baptized in Blood: The Religion of the Lost Cause, 1865–1920* (1980). ☆

REDNECKS

In modern usage the term *redneck*, which did not come into common usage until the 1930s, is usually a negative expression describing a benighted white southerner. The redneck is any white southerner in the lower or working class, and his image looms large when the media focus on the South in transition. Various critics, whether southern blacks and liberals or northerners, gang up on the redneck and mercilessly dissect him. He is undereducated; he talks funny in a bewildering variety of southern accents, which feature double negatives, jumbled verb tenses, slurred and obsolete words, and all manner of crimes against standard, television English. He is too physical in his approach to life; he sets too high a premium on athletic prowess, and he gets into too many fights. He comes on too strong with women, and he may even scratch when he itches, wherever he or it might be. He eats too much coarse or greasy food like corn bread, grits, fried chicken, chicken-fried steak, and all manner of pork—everything from chops to a wide variety of barbecue. He even likes vegetables like collard greens and turnip greens and string beans cooked with his beloved pork, and worst of all, he seems to infringe on the black mo-

nopoly on "soul food." He tends to drink too much whiskey, and he spends too much time in tacky beer halls that play only country music and always on "high." He is noisy but inarticulate. He does not ski and has never seen a psychiatrist. He sometimes smells bad, especially after an eight-hour shift or a hunting trip. He occasionally still repairs his car in the front yard, and he might even leave the engine hanging from a branch of a chinaberry tree for a while. His presence may well depress the local real estate market. He is reactionary but sometimes radical and thus politically unreliable. His women (not ladies) reflect many of the same traits, and, besides, they chew gum vigorously and wear plastic hair curlers in public. And his children act as if they are just as good as anybody else.

Rednecks are known to have peculiar names. Males of the species go by such designations as "Bubba," "Slick," "Ace," "Rusty," Melvin, Leroy, Alvin, T. J., and L. W.; and sometimes grown men, even people in positions of great authority, run around calling themselves Bobby or Billy or Jimmy and insisting that everyone else do the same. Females answer to such names as Billy Jean, Lou Ann, Loretta, Ginny, Sue Ellen, Lawanda Kay, Peggy Joe, LaBelle, Mavis, Flo, Rose, and sometimes in the welter of Jodies, Bobbies, Billies, and Johnnies it is hard to tell whether the names are masculine or feminine. But whatever the name or the sex, you can be sure of one thing: the redneck is, above all else, an incorrigible racist.

The modern critique of the redneck emphasizes style more than substance, but it has some validity. The redneck is a rather plain, direct fellow, and he certainly will fight, especially when pushed. This fighting spirit often embarrasses the nation in normal times, but in wartime it is welcomed, and rednecks are among the first to enlist. The last, major charge against the redneck is certainly true; he is and always has been a racist at heart. But who is not and who was not? The southern redneck fits into the general harsh history of the human race, but given the extreme ethnic mix of his historical environment, he has earned no special distinction as a racist. His record is about par for the rugged course. The redneck's main problem is that he has always been open and candid in his conviction that blacks were inferior to whites. Yet at the same time over the centuries he has blended his culture and his blood with blacks, and in many day-to-day, practical ways he understands blacks perhaps better than his white detractors do. In a rough, earthy kind of way he may be less of a racist than those whites who denounce him so harshly.

In a literal sense the redneck was the average man in the South from the very beginning when white colonists settled along the Virginia and Carolina and finally the Georgia coasts. More commonly known then as "yeoman farmers," they peopled the southern half of the North American continent, moving relentlessly west toward the Pacific Ocean. They and their large families labored on the kind of fertile, cheap new land their European ancestors had not seen for over a thousand years. Under a blazing sun the exposed parts of their bodies tanned and hardened.

A wrinkled, reddened neck was no embarrassment to these proud, independent farmers who were the backbone of a fluid southern society, which allowed some of them to rise into the ranks of the planters. The average antebellum redneck owned his own land and occasionally a few slaves. He read and wrote functionally, voted without restrictions, bore his own arms, worshiped his own God, and generally enjoyed the life, liberty, and pursuit of happiness guaranteed to all free Americans.

Southern rednecks were not people to trifle with. When the Civil War erupted in 1861, they became the backbone of the Confederate armed forces, and they came within an ace of shattering the Union as their forefathers had shattered the British Empire in North America. Indeed, Lee's redneck infantry in Virginia developed into one of the most efficient killing machines of the 19th century.

Finally, the rednecks lost their war but not their pride. They returned to the land they knew so well, the good earth that had nurtured the southern folk for over two centuries. Over the years hard times in agriculture drove many down into some form of sharecropping, and then expanding industries lured many away from the soil. Today not many southern whites actually farm, and the term "redneck," when not used as a crude put-down, vaguely refers to lower- and working-class southern whites. Even so, it designates an important element of contemporary America's population, the most British group by blood and at the same time the group that has lived most closely with American blacks, another sturdy folk whose roots run deep in the soil of the South.

F. N. Boney
University of Georgia

F. N. Boney, *Georgia Review* (Fall 1971), *Southerners All* (1984); Larry L. King, *Of Outlaws, Con Men, Whores, Politicians, and Other Artists* (1980); John Shelton Reed, *Southern Folk, Plain and Fancy: Native White Social Types* (1986). ☆

SAMBO
||||||||||||||||||||

Sambo was a stereotyped character created by whites to denigrate blacks. The stereotype attacked black men by making them the objects of laughter. The Sambo character was probably the most tenacious stereotype of black people in both southern and American culture until the late 20th century.

The name *Sambo* is Hispanic in origin, deriving from a 16th-century word *zambo*, which meant a bowlegged person resembling a monkey. By the 19th century the name had come to refer to a person of mixed ancestry, and the word had derogatory connotations. Descended from court jesters of medieval Europe, the Sambo figure was found in the British colonies of North America from the early 1600s. By the end of the 19th century, according to Joseph Boskin, Sambo's "humorous innocence, reflected in a never-failing grin, was projected everywhere, his natural buffoonery celebrated in every conceivable way."

The Sambo image included such specific types as the Uncle Tom, Coon, Mulatto, Mammy, and Buck. It appeared in oral lore through jokes and stories. It was in newspapers, magazines, travel brochures, diaries and journals, novels, short stories, dime novels, and children's bedtime stories. Joel Chandler Harris's Uncle Remus stories reinforced the stereotype. Graphic expressions of Sambo were, if anything, even more prevalent. Prominent illustrators made Sambo drawings to accompany the text of novels. The figure showed up in sheet music cartoons, calendars, postcards, postage stamps, stereoscopic slides, playing cards, and comic strips; it appeared on billboards and posters and was often featured in popular Currier and Ives prints found in late 19th-century middle-class American homes. Businessmen used Sambo to sell household goods such as soaps, polishes, coffee, jellies, and colas. A national restaurant chain picked Sambo for its name and after World War II used the image for its logo. Sambo appeared in performance routines during minstrel shows, circuses, theatrical shows, and on radio shows, nickelodeon reels, and television programs. Stepin' Fetchit made Sambo the perpetual chauffeur in the movies. Sambo was concretely embodied in the material culture in items such as salt and pepper shakers, place mats, shoehorns, pillows, children's banks, dolls, and whiskey pourers. The ceramic Sambo was found on tables inside homes and as an iron jockey on front lawns.

Scholars even used the Sambo image in textbooks and classrooms as an accurate image of the black personality. Historians in the mid-20th century have explored the Sambo stereotype more critically, focusing on its relationship to the slave period. Stanley Elkins's *Slavery: A Problem in American Institutional and Intellectual Life* (1959) concluded that slavery was a total institution, like a concentration camp, which created a childish, dependent black personality, but John Blassingame's *The Slave Community: Plantation Life in the Antebellum South* (1972) better reflects current consensus, insisting that Sambo was an assumed identity—one of several slave personality types—taken on and used to manipulate whites for survival. Through Sambo's protective foil, blacks were "laughing to keep from crying."

The Sambo stereotype has been severely attacked since the 1950s. James Baldwin declared Sambo dead in *Notes of a Native Son* (1955). Civil rights protests and the threat of violence behind demands for black power made the Sambo image unbelievable. By the 1970s the nation's electronic and print media projected new cultural images of blacks that challenged the older stereotype. The end of Sambo represented the death of a white attempt to define black personality and culture.

Charles Reagan Wilson
University of Mississippi

Joseph Boskin, *Sambo: The Rise and Demise of an American Jester* (1986); Daniel J. Leab, *From Sambo to Superspade: The Black Experience in Motion Pictures* (1975). ☆

UNCLE TOM'S CABIN

Harriet Beecher Stowe set out to portray slavery as an institution, rather than the South as either a geographical or a cultural entity, in *Uncle Tom's Cabin*. The novel was begun in response to the Fugitive Slave Law of 1850. It was addressed to a national, not a regional, audience to whom Stowe made the argument that it was the educated, well-to-do, Christian gentlemen of the country, the hypocritical readers, in fact, who, through an indifference or cynicism that inhibited active opposition to slavery, were actually responsible for its continuation in American society and for the moral offense inherent in it.

The picture of the South that emerges in the novel is developed through three households, presented as types: the Shelbys of Kentucky, middle-class, kind, but subject to the pressures of a capitalist economy of which slavery is a part; the St. Clares of New Orleans, aristocratic, loving, but ineffectual as guardians of their enslaved servants be-

cause a debilitating skepticism undermines both Christian belief and political action; the Legree plantation, low-class, brutal, an example of how bad slavery can become. The Shelbys get very little space after the opening of the novel in which Mr. Shelby's sale of Uncle Tom and of Eliza's son, Harry, to pay some large debts initiates the two main plots. Shelby's predicament, being forced to sell against his own wishes and the strong feelings of his wife, shows the southern slaveholder caught in the grip of economic circumstance that is in no way unique to the South; indeed, Stowe frequently likens American exploitation of slaves to European exploitation of industrial workers. The Legree sequences at the end of the novel, although sensational and meant to provoke outrage at the institution of slavery, are not presented as typical either of it or of southern life. Not only is Legree himself a Yankee, but he also lives virtually beyond the pale of southern society, a day's journey up the Red River to a place described as wild and debauched. The suggestion is that Legree's wild domain is to the west of civilization, a horrible outpost on the Arkansas frontier.

Stowe sets her principle drama of southern life in the St. Clare household. Here, for example, is the kitchen, a place of playful leisure for the servants where the mystery of the cook's ways fosters an easy tolerance and affectionate community not to be found in the scrubbed and strictly managed kitchen of New England. The emotional atmosphere of the kitchen echoes the unruly abundance of southern land. Similarly, the décor of the bedroom belonging to little Eva, the novel's proselytizing child heroine, enhances her deathbed sermon on the gospel of love by suggesting a place of almost heavenly perfection:

"The windows were hung with curtains of rose-colored and white muslin. The floor was spread with matting which had been ordered in Paris . . . having round it a border of rosebuds and leaves. . . . Over the head of the bed was an alabaster bracket, on which a beautiful sculptured angel stood, with drooping wings, holding out a crown of myrtle-leaves." A mosquito net made of "light curtains of rose-colored gauze" hung over the bed. The gardens around this summer "villa" by Lake Pontchartrain are also idealized by the fond, and perhaps envious, gardener/novelist from New England. (One must not forget that Stowe invested in a southern plantation after the Civil War and made her winter home in Mandarin, Fla., for many years. Her letters to northern relatives dwell on the floral paradise at her back door.)

The South as portrayed in the St. Clare household, and often contrasted to the northern society of the hero's cousin from Vermont, is a humane culture—disorderly, tender-hearted, distressed about slavery. To be sure, the family does include two destructive types: Augustine St. Clare's arrogant and despotic brother, who raises a son like himself, and Marie St. Clare, the self-indulgent hypochondriac whose pampered childhood led to unmitigated hard-heartedness. Despite the presence of these hateful characters in its midst, the St. Clare family is a loving home for slaves and owners alike. Its greatest weakness, and by implication that of the southern culture it represents, is its vulnerability to abrupt transformations— from the rosy bower of the angelic child Eva and the kind paternalism of her father to the debauchery of the Legree establishment, a transformation brought about by the sudden accidental death of St. Clare. In sum, Stowe sees the South

of 1850 as beautiful, elegant, and weak, unable to sustain its gentlemanly ideal, which she values and praises, against the unscrupulous practices of the slave trade or the barbarity represented by the maddened and desperate Legree. In *Uncle Tom's Cabin*, the South is a garden of innocence and delight threatened by the snake of human cruelty; it is a lovely dream hovering on the verge of a nightmare.

See also MEDIA: / *Uncle Tom's Cabin*

Alice C. Crozier
Rutgers University

Alice C. Crozier, *Novels of Harriet Beecher Stowe* (1969); Thomas F. Gossett, *Uncle Tom's Cabin and American Culture* (1985); Moira D. Reynolds, *Uncle Tom's Cabin and Mid-Nineteenth Century United States: Pen and Conscience* (1985). ☆

WATERMELON

Watermelon is among the best examples of the mythic significance of food in southern culture. The eating of southern watermelon is one of the most symbolic rituals of southerners. To be sure, watermelon is not a unique possession of the American South. Watermelon seeds have been discovered in Egyptian tombs from thousands of years ago, and Mediterranean peoples have cultivated it for centuries. Northern Americans eat watermelon, although their climate enables them to raise only small-fruited and midget varieties.

An annual called *Citrullus lanatus*, southern watermelon is a member of the gourd family. It grows during the South's warm, humid summers, requiring a 120-day growing season. Southern watermelons are called "rampant-

Watermelon vendors, Warren County, Mississippi, 1975

growing varieties," and they have regionally meaningful names such as the Dixie Queen, Dixielee, Stone Mountain, Charleston Gray, Alabama Giant, Florida Giant, Louisiana Queen, Carolina Cross, and Africa 8. Africans introduced watermelon to Europe and later North America, and Indians in Florida were cultivating it by the mid-17th century. Thomas Jefferson grew watermelons at Monticello, but they were found more often among the crops of yeoman farmers than planters. Garden patches that fed many an impoverished southerner in the postbellum South often included watermelons. They were a low-cost treat even during the Depression, and some southerners still call the watermelon a Depression ham.

Watermelon has been especially associated in the United States with rural southern blacks. It became a prop identified with the stereotypical Sambo—the childlike, docile, laughing black boy was seen grinning and eating watermelon. This derogatory image was pervasive in popular literature and art, and watermelon-eating scenes later became stock features of films and newsreels. Watermelon has been, nonetheless, a cultural symbol used also in less negative ways as well by southerners and others. Folklore has long told of the proper ways to plant watermelon (by poking a hole in the ground and planting the seed by hand), and the ability to tell a ripe watermelon by thumping it was a legendary rural skill. Literature tells of the simple joys of eating watermelon. Tom Sawyer and Huck Finn (in Mark Twain's *Tom Sawyer, Detective: As Told by Huck Finn*) "snuck off" from Aunt Sally one night and "talked and smoked and stuffed watermelon as much as two hours."

The Skillet Lickers chose a traditional southern folk tune, "Watermelon on the Vine," for one of the earliest recordings of southern country music, and Tom T. Hall celebrated the melon in the more recent "Old Dogs, Children, and Watermelon Wine." The lyrics to the blues song "Watermelon Man" identified the succulent melon with sexual potency, and a 1970 Melvin Van Peebles film about the experiences of a white man who wakes up one morning with a black skin was also called *Watermelon Man*. The watermelon has been used as an advertising symbol, especially on roadsides to direct motorists to stands selling the delicacy. Miles Carpenter, of Waverly, Va., began carving wooden watermelon slices and painting them with enamel decades ago, and today he is recognized as an accomplished folk artist.

In the contemporary South the watermelon remains a part of the summer diet. Cookbooks have recipes not only for the traditional chilled melon, melon balls, pickled watermelon rind, and spiked melon, but also for watermelon and cassis ice, spiced watermelon pie, and watermelon muffins. But the importance of watermelon to southerners transcends its use as food. When popular periodicals discuss symbols of the region, they usually include watermelon (*Southern Magazine*, June 1987; *Texas Monthly*, January 1977). Summer recreation includes festivals, and watermelon is the central feature of festivals at Luling, Tex.; Hampton County, S.C.; Chiefland, Chipley, Lakeland, and Monticello, Fla.; Grand Bay, Ala.; Raleigh, N.C.; and Mize and Water Valley, Miss. The U.S. Watermelon Seed-Spitting Contest is held during the National Watermelon Association's annual convention in Moreven, Ga., the first week of March. Hope, Ark., may be the watermelon capital of the South. The town advertises itself with a logo that has a picture of a watermelon and the claim that Hope offers "a slice of the good life." Hope farmers regularly raise 100–150 pound watermelons.

Southerners would likely still agree with a passage in Mark Twain's *Pudd'n-head Wilson*: "The true southern watermelon is a boon apart and not to be mentioned with commoner things. It is chief of this world's luxuries, king by the Grace of God over all the fruits of the earth. When one has tasted it, he knows what the angels eat. It was not a southern watermelon that Eve took; we know it because she repented."

Charles Reagan Wilson
University of Mississippi

Ellen Ficklen, *Watermelon* (1984). ☆

YERBY, FRANK
||||||||||||||||||||||||||||||||||||||||
(b. 1916) Writer.

Frank Garvin Yerby, one of the most popular novelists to set tales in the Old South, was born in Augusta, Ga., on 5

September 1916. He completed degrees at Paine College (A.B., 1937) and Fisk University (M.A., 1938) and did graduate work at the University of Chicago. A black man, Yerby published several excellent short stories from 1944 to 1946 dealing with racial themes. Although he won a major award for his short fiction, Yerby's fame and fortune rest on his widely popular romance novels, the first of which was published in 1946 and sold over 2 million copies. Like many of his novels to follow, *The Foxes of Harrow* was set in the antebellum South and tapped public interest in the Old South that had been fostered by the phenomenal success of Margaret Mitchell's *Gone with the Wind* (1936).

Yerby's southern romances, including such titles as *A Woman Called Fancy* (1951), *Benton's Row* (1954), and *Griffin's Way* (1962), dominated popular fiction set in the Old South for nearly two decades. His works were meticulously researched and included a wealth of elaborate and surprisingly accurate period detail in such areas as costuming, architecture, southern society, and even slave life. One critic termed *Fair Oaks* (1957) a "primer in black history."

The novels were primarily romantic glimpses of the planter elite and were aimed at a predominantly white, female audience. This led many critics to condemn his work as potboiler fiction, and others have often charged that he ignored racial issues. Yerby once countered the latter charge by saying that the novelist does not have the right to "inflict on the public his private ideas on politics, religion or race." In most respects the charges were unfair, for Yerby managed to influence the ideas and values of far more readers through historical romance than could possibly have been reached by other forms of fiction. This point is demonstrated by

Yerby's own career, for he did attempt a few novels with racial themes. These included *The Old Gods Laugh* (1964) and *The Dahomian* (1971), both of which sold poorly in comparison to his plantation novels.

Yet Frank Yerby's impact was not in the area of popular and accurate history. His importance rests on his fostering of public interest in the antebellum South and his fiction's impact on extending the romantic ideal of the South as one great plantation. Besides Mitchell's *Gone with the Wind* and Kyle Onstott's *Mandingo* (1957), the novels of Frank Yerby did more to standardize the plantation fiction genre than did the works of any other author. Apart from his careful attention to historic detail, Yerby's major contribution to the fictional portrayal of the Old South was an entrance into the bedrooms of the planters. His incredibly successful fiction helped to solidify the popular impression of the antebellum South as a land of "moonlight and magnolias," of aristocratic lifestyles, of beautiful belles, and of dashing and handsome young gentlemen.

Christopher D. Geist
Bowling Green State University

Jack Temple Kirby, *Media-Made Dixie: The South in the American Imagination* (1978); Jack B. Moore, *Journal of Popular Culture* (Spring 1975); Frank Yerby, *Harper's* (October 1959). ☆

YOKNAPATAWPHA COUNTY
‖‖‖

"William Faulkner, Sole Owner & Proprietor," states the legend on the map, and no claim to title is any more indisputable, though the reader may wander within the realm identified there by the proprietor for as long as he or she is inclined—and without fear of trespass, for, through one of its paradoxes, Yoknapatawpha County belongs to everyone as well as to the author. It is the setting for all of Faulkner's major fiction and is itself a fictional creation.

Faulkner named his county after the Yoknapatawpha River, which was the old name of the Yocona River, an actual river that runs south of Oxford, Miss. Initially Faulkner used the current name, and it appears as such in *Flags in the Dust*. The *Flags* manuscript was not published until 1973, however, having first been rejected, then edited and published as *Sartoris* (1929). Thus, *Sartoris* was the first published novel in the Yoknapatawpha series, followed in the same year by *The Sound and the Fury*. Faulkner did not employ the old name Yoknapatawpha until *As I Lay Dying* (1930), by which time he had a good start on the chronicle that would ultimately include over a dozen novels and numerous short stories spanning the period from the late 1700s to the middle of the present century.

Faulkner's county is situated in northern Mississippi and consists of 2,400 square miles. It was settled by whites, some with slaves, in the early 1800s, following the Chickasaw Indian cessions. The county seat, Jefferson, originally a Chickasaw Agency trading post dating from the late 1700s, was founded in 1833 with the hasty erection of a log courthouse and named not after the former U.S. president but for a mail rider serving the area. Faulkner's comic rendering of this founding appears in *Requiem for a Nun* (1951), a dramatic work not otherwise known for levity. The families of some of the founders and early settlers figure throughout the entire Yoknapatawpha saga; others die out or disappear. Their genealogies are often elaborate and sometimes confusing. The trajectories of fortune in their lives—and the lives of characters who appear in Yoknapatawpha later—are as varied as those in our own, though more often than not in Faulkner's world the tracings of fortune follow a widely erratic course. They are families at all levels of southern society with names such as Beauchamp, Bundren, Compson, Sartoris, Snopes, and Varner; individuals named Luster, Dilsey, or Ikkemotubbe, the chief of the Chickasaws, whose river gave Faulkner a name for his world.

The two Chickasaw Indian words of which the word *Yoknapatawpha* is constituted mean "split land," though Faulkner said that the two words together mean "water flowing slow through the flatland." And because on one side of the paradox he is the sole owner, Yoknapatawpha means what he said.

In addition to the matter of proprietorship, there are other paradoxes, some specific to all literary creations: Jefferson, the geographic center and county seat of Yoknapatawpha County, Miss., is and is not Oxford, the center and county seat of Lafayette County, Miss., where Faulkner grew up and lived most of his life. He drew on the town and region as a primary source, as many writers draw on a particular place, and there are countless identifiable parallels, geographic and cultural; but in the accounting required with art, Yoknapatawpha exists unto itself.

Similarly, Yoknapatawpha exists both in and out of time. It is timeless in the way that the landscape and human motion arrested on Keats's Grecian urn are timeless, and in the way that Keats's ode itself—which Faulkner refers to in "The Bear," summoning the same idea—exists out of time.

Where temporality does obtain, in the recorded history of Yoknapatawpha, there are discrepancies. (Its sole historian had lapses of memory and changes of heart in the 37 or so years of its progress as a chronicle and admitted as much in his short preface to *The Mansion* [1959].) Yet—the paradox—there is no chronicle any more accurate or rich in information, if one regards the history of Yoknapatawpha as emblematic of the history of the South.

A fanciful way of accounting for these paradoxes would be to observe that Yoknapatawpha County is bordered both to the north and the south by water and is thus mystical (that is, if one accepts Walker Percy's notion that water is the mystical element). Further, these parallel borders—the Tallahatchie River to the north and the Yoknapatawpha River to the south—run east and west, and Faulkner's map (the one drawn for *Absalom, Absalom!* [1936]) shows that in those directions he left Yoknapatawpha County seemingly borderless. His Yoknapatawpha extends irresistibly toward horizons associated with beginnings and endings, the old and the new, the origins of the world's religions, the myths and archetypes that inform much of the drama of Yoknapatawpha. For the county does indeed exist in a borderless confluence of the mystical and the mythical, the synchronic, the spiritual, and the dramatic.

See also GEOGRAPHY: / Faulkner's Geography; LITERATURE: / Faulkner, William

James Seay
University of North Carolina
at Chapel Hill

Elizabeth M. Kerr, *Yoknapatawpha: Faulkner's "Little Postage Stamp of Native Soil"* (1969). ☆

POLITICS

NUMAN BARTLEY

University of Georgia

CONSULTANT

☆ ☆ ☆ ☆ ☆ ☆ ☆ ☆ ☆ ☆

*Overleaf: Broderick Crawford as Willie Stark
(far right) at campaign rally in a scene from
All the King's Men (1949)*

POLITICS AND IDEOLOGY

||||||||||||||||||||||||||||||||||||||||||||||||||||

During the 1970s southern political practices came to resemble more closely national norms. The election of a Deep South resident to the presidency in 1976 seemingly confirmed the region's newfound respectability. In earlier years the South's political image was a distinctive and largely negative one. Indeed, the region's long-established reputation as the home of demagogues, Dixiecrats, and disfranchisement contributed to making the region a subject of endless interest, scorn, and puzzlement. V. O. Key's classic study *Southern Politics in State and Nation*, which appeared in 1949, began with the statement: "The South may not be the nation's number one political problem, as some northerners assert, but politics is the South's number one problem." After devoting almost 700 pages to a masterful examination of southern political practices, Key chose to title the final chapter of the book "Is There a Way Out?" Key closely associated southern political problems with three relatively distinctive southern political institutions: the one-party system, disfranchisement, and the pervasive ethos of Jim Crow segregation.

These institutions were crucial to southern electoral politics, particularly during the first half of the 20th century, but more recent scholarship has suggested that southern political problems have been more deeply embedded in the region's social and economic fabric than the statement that "politics is the

South's number one problem" would imply. Social and economic developments quite early in southern history were to have long-lasting significance for southern politics. Most important was the creation of an economy based on plantation agriculture and slave labor. Following the perfection of the cotton gin in the late 18th century, the rapid westward expansion of cotton and caste laid the foundation for southern unity. Slavery and plantation agriculture, although profitable for the planters who held the slaves, were not so materially beneficial for southern society as a whole. The purchase of slaves absorbed an enormous amount of southern capital, and the general self-sufficiency of southern agriculture debased the domestic market and hampered economic development. As a result, the antebellum South achieved little in the way of a "modern" economic infrastructure while at the same time it enjoyed a great deal of individual affluence.

Under these conditions agrarian democracy flourished. Popular political participation shot upward during the 1830s, and voter turnout—in terms of the percentage of the eligible electorate that actually appeared at the polls—during the middle years of the 19th century was the highest it has ever been in southern history. Similarly, the South by the 1840s had developed a functioning two-party system. The relatively evenly balanced Whigs and Democrats competed vigorously for the favor of southern voters at all levels of government. It was the most thoroughly developed two-party system the South has ever had.

One of the explanations for such a vigorous assertion of democracy was that white southerners were in general agreement on substantive issues: land should be taken from Indians; agriculture should be promoted; slavery should be advanced; and the South should be defended from the meddling activities of antislavery advocates. A white male consensus on these points tended to promote political democracy and two-party competition.

Herrenvolk Democracy and Paternalism. Southern democracy was herrenvolk—that is, master race democracy with political citizenship limited to white males—and, significantly, its origins were herrenvolk rather than popular. It is of symbolic interest that in August 1619 the first representative assembly to meet in English America convened in Jamestown, Va., where in the same month a Dutch warship sold the first 20 Africans known to have arrived in America, thus providing an early linkage between liberty and slavery. Developments in the South reinforced this paradoxical and symbiotic relationship. Rather early in American history, land hunger fueled growing hostility toward Indians. The need for labor on southern plantations was met by the importation of slaves. Thus, Edmund S. Morgan, in his important study of slavery and freedom in Virginia, concluded: "By lumping Indians, mulattoes, and Negroes in a single pariah class, Virginians had paved the way for a similar lumping of small and large planters in a single master class." Southern democracy not only limited political participation to a master race but rested directly on the ex-

ploitation of other races. Indeed, William J. Cooper has observed in *Liberty and Slavery* (1983) that "before 1860, free, white southerners could not conceive of holding on to their own liberty except by keeping black southerners enslaved."

Labor exploitation in the Old South, at least in the direct sense, normally meant whites exploiting blacks rather than each other. Such an arrangement undermined class conflict, encouraged what W. J. Cash termed a "Proto-Dorian" bond between whites, and fostered an autonomous independence that in some ways was conducive to citizenship and republican ideals, as the career of Thomas Jefferson would suggest. But despite generating high voter turnout among white males, herrenvolk democracy had severe inherent limitations. Not only did it rest squarely on racism and exploitation, it also limited the legitimate range of debate. Southern freedom and democracy, even before slavery came under attack from the outside, had tendencies toward "the savage ideal," which Cash described as "that ideal whereunder dissent and variety are completely suppressed."

The paternalistic social values that grew from master-slave relationships further influenced the ideological context of southern politics. Historians continue to disagree over the extent to which the South was capitalist and the extent to which it was a premodern, prebourgeois, traditional society, but, whatever the ultimate resolution of the debate, southern social values were clearly different from those prevalent in the North. In the North Jacksonian democracy marked the coming of age of a laissez-faire society and an ideology of free labor individualism that appealed to independent artisans, farmers, and businessmen; in the South Jacksonian democracy did strengthen the herrenvolk civic concept of autonomous independence, but the region's forced labor system and the mutual dependence of masters and slaves also supported a patriarchal ideology. Southern thought tended to extol a paternal, organic, and hierarchical society, which contrasted with northern ideals of laissez-faire individualism, economic freedom, and legal equality. The southern paternal ethos projected, in the words of Eugene D. Genovese, "an aristocratic, antibourgeois spirit with values and morés emphasizing family and status, a strong code of honor, and aspirations to luxury, ease and accomplishment." Gunnar Myrdal, commenting on conservative southern political thought, pointed out in his epic, *An American Dilemma* (1944): "Slavery was only part of a greater social order which established an ideal division of labor and of responsibility in society between the sexes, the age groups, the social classes and the two races."

Herrenvolk democracy tempered by ideological paternalism produced for a brief period intense partisan competition. During the 1850s the two-party system collapsed under the strain of sectional strife. Following the Civil War and emancipation, the South again experimented with two-party politics. The Fourteenth and Fifteenth Amendments offered citizenship and suffrage to the newly freed blacks, and the black-oriented Radical Republicans in the South accomplished the remarkable feat of politically mobilizing the freedmen. Conservative whites reorganized under the Democratic banner. For varying periods of time, the southern states were battlegrounds for the contending Radical Republicans and conservative Democrats. Conservative whites organized the Ku Klux Klan and other terrorist groups, while the Republicans relied heavily upon federal forces for protection. The Democratic combination of terrorism and political rhetoric that appealed for herrenvolk unity proved successful and Republicanism rapidly declined. The last of the Republican governments in the South collapsed in 1877, when southern Democrats and northern Republicans engineered a historic compromise whereby the southern conservatives accepted northeastern capitalist policies nationally in exchange for federal nonintervention in southern social affairs.

New South Politics. Effectively, the southern leadership tacitly acquiesced to the South remaining economically a colony of the North. The Civil War and emancipation swept away the plantation prosperity that had marked the region's real economic problems. Bereft of capital, bound more closely to the North by postwar railroad construction, overwhelmed by the rapid growth of population and manufacturing above the Potomac, and hampered by northeastern oriented tariff, banking, and other policies, the South provided cotton, lumber products, minerals and other raw materials, and, to a lesser extent, markets for the more advanced northern economy. A fundamental requirement imposed by the South's colonial dependency was cheap labor, and the maintenance of a cheap labor force was an underlying factor in the politics of the New South.

Presiding over these developments were the Bourbon Democrats. By controlling the Democratic party machinery and by manipulating the race issue, the Bourbons were able to maintain themselves in office, and that fact ensured that state power would be exercised on behalf of the employing classes. But if the Bourbon system accomplished the rudimentary goals of those who were most likely to benefit from the South's colonial status, it was not particularly successful in providing political and social stability. The tensions and conflicts in southern society were severe. Civil War, emancipation, and Reconstruction left southern society deeply divided. The failure of plantation agriculture to restore prewar prosperity, the decline of the yeoman farmers, the breakdown of agricultural self-sufficiency, and the economic competition between black and white laborers produced further social stress and helped to explain the growth of lynching and other forms of social violence. The Populist movement of the 1890s grew out of this atmosphere and, indeed, brought to culmination a variety of long-simmering conflicts. So profound were the implications of the Populist radical critique of state and national policy that the conservative Bourbon Democrats responded with violence and with massive fraud in the counting and casting of ballots.

Unlike the antebellum era when the electorate was in general agreement on substantive policies, the New South was rent by social dissension. During the Reconstruction crisis, the conservative Democrats relied upon Ku Klux Klan terrorism to regain control of the southern states; during the post-Reconstruction era, they turned back independent insurgency by using their control of land, credit, and the law to influence the behavior of black voters; and during the Populist crisis they resorted to violence and fraud. Beyond that, they sought more institutionalized methods to ensure the social stability that ulti-

mately rested on white supremacy and cheap labor. The result was the establishment of those institutions so ably described by V. O. Key: disfranchisement, the one-party system, and Jim Crow segregation.

The disfranchisement of black people was such an obvious way to ensure political white supremacy and thereby to bolster the whole southern system of labor relationships that the surprising thing is that conservative white southern political elites did not do it sooner. The explanation for the delay seems to relate to the ability of the Bourbons to manipulate the black vote and to earlier fears that disfranchisement might prompt federal intervention. The Democratic conservatives also demonstrated the willingness to support, often quite openly, the disfranchisement of whites. The president of the Alabama disfranchising convention of 1901 explained: "The true philosophy of the movement was to establish restricted suffrage, and to place the power of government in the hands of the intelligent and virtuous." Although such views were compatible with ideological paternalism, disfranchisement reversed the trend toward the expansion of democracy that had been evident in the antebellum South and the Reconstruction period. The high voter turnout of the antebellum era extended into the postbellum period. Voter turnout remained high after the enfranchisement of blacks, though it did begin to drop off following the end of Reconstruction. Despite this decline, voter participation remained respectable—above 50 percent of the eligible electorate in the former Confederate states—until the disfranchisement movement.

The conservative Democrats' disfranchisement of whites was not at all illogical. After all, inexpensive white labor was as important as black labor, and it was doubtlessly easier to maintain if the electorate were limited to "the intelligent and virtuous." But beyond this, the removal of the lower levels of the white working class from the electorate suggests the extent to which white sharecroppers and mill workers had already been relegated to what J. Wayne Flynt has termed "the Southern poor white caste." Prior to the Civil War southern poor whites were a part of the overall population. In the New South, as Flynt says, "poor whites assumed many aspects of a caste system and were increasingly identifiable within the general population."

It is not entirely surprising that segregation, although having deep roots in southern history, assumed its particularly cruel Jim Crow form at approximately the same time as the disfranchisement movement. The motives for segregationist legislation were complex, but the Jim Crow system contributed substantially to social stability. It virtually guaranteed the continuing existence of cheap black labor, and it further divided the black caste from the poor white caste and encouraged each of them to direct hostility toward the other.

Segregation and disfranchisement not only served as formidable barriers to future Populist heresies but they also strengthened the Solid South. The one-party system discouraged the emergence of divisive issues at home while at the same time unifying southern political power nationally in defense of the region's peculiar social practices. During the first half of the 20th century, few southerners voted and those who did voted overwhelmingly Democratic. When in 1924 Republican Calvin Coo-

lidge received about 1,200 of South Carolina's approximately 50,000 presidential votes, Senator Coleman L. Blease exclaimed: "I do not know where he got them. I was astonished to know they were cast and shocked to know they were counted."

But if these reforms did place southern politics in the hands of "the intelligent and virtuous," there remains the question of just who "the intelligent and virtuous" were. Presumably they were not black southerners, who in the year 1910 made up more than one-third of the population of the former Confederate states. Thus, using 1910 figures, segregation placed 35 percent of the population and even more of the work force in an inferior caste. Not all blacks were poor, of course, but discrimination ensured that most would be. The "intelligent and virtuous" also presumably did not include most of the poor whites. It is difficult to estimate the size of that group or even to define it in statistical terms, but huge numbers of whites labored at occupations not much different from positions held by blacks, and, defined in that manner, a fair estimate would be that the poor white class was probably no smaller than was the black caste around 1910. Thus, the black and white underclass made up approximately two-thirds of the southern population.

During the first four decades of the 20th century, the active southern electorate encompassed between one-fourth and one-third of the adult population, although the figures varied significantly from state to state. The "intelligent and virtuous" made up approximately one-third of the population, and southern election returns indicated that approximately one-fourth of the citizens voted. These figures seem to be compatible because not all people would have necessarily paid their poll taxes and made their way through all the other pitfalls that protected the polls from the voters even though they were otherwise sufficiently white to vote in the white primaries and sufficiently literate to deal with literacy and understanding requirements. Thus, the bulk of southern voters were drawn from that third of southern society that was both whiter and more economically prosperous than the population as a whole; generally speaking, these "intelligent and virtuous" citizens included three more or less distinct social groups. One might be termed the plantation-oriented county-seat governing class; one could be called the uptown elites; and one was the white common folk.

Huey Long image over front steps of the state capitol at the inauguration of Louisiana Governor Richard Leche, Baton Rouge, 1936

The Governing Elite and the Common Folk. As the name implies, the county-seat governing class was the South's dominant political group. The Civil War and Reconstruction broke the national power of the planter class, but thereafter southern planters and their allies emerged victorious from the political wars of Reconstruction to become the most powerful social group in southern politics. Geographically concentrated in the region's lowland-plantation counties, the planter-merchant-banker-lawyer governing class set much of the tone for the politics of the region. They were the foremost defenders of the southern way of life, the most devoted proponents of Lost Cause mythology, and the most loyal adherents to paternal social values. They provided the basic hard-core support for Bourbon democracy, marshalled the conservative forces to turn back the Populist threat, and led the disfranchisement movement. V. O. Key was certainly correct when he stated, "The hard core of the political South— and the backbone of political unity—is made up of those counties and sections of the southern states in which Negroes constitute a substantial proportion of the population." At the crucial junctures in the politics of the New South, the plantation-county-seat governing class won the decisive engagements.

The greatest long-term potential threat to the power of the county-seat governing class was the uptown elite in the South's expanding cities. The term "uptown" denotes the leadership of the region's urban areas and suggests a Henry W. Grady New South style of politics. Although lacking the authority and political prestige of the county-seat governing class, uptown elites were the South's most affluent people and in some ways the most strategically placed. They normally controlled the region's larger and more influential newspapers, banks, and other sources of influence. In addition to being the foremost proponents of the New South creed, they were leaders in the drive for segregation. They of course suffered from the South's being for so long so overwhelmingly rural—in 1910 only 2 people of every 10 in the former Confederate states resided in a town of above 2,500 population. Furthermore, the widening economic disparity between the prospering cities and the poverty-ridden country contributed to an increasing rural hostility toward the cities, a fact that further limited uptown influence.

Normally uptown elites were the allies of the county-seat governing class. Not only did the two groups share class interest but southern urban prosperity was closely tied to the overall southern colonial economy. With a few exceptions, most notably Birmingham, southern cities served as the great distributing centers for the products that ultimately appeared on country-store shelves and as the centers for marketing and transporting southern cotton and raw materials to the North. Andre Gunder Frank has observed that Latin America "had a colonial class structure which inevitably gave its dominant bourgeoisie an economic self-interest in freely exporting raw materials and importing manufactured products." This applied equally to New South merchants and businessmen. The prosperity of the cities and towns was deeply enmeshed in existing economic arrangements. As a consequence uptown elites remained only a long-term potential threat to county-seat power in the Solid South.

The largest of the three social groups was the common folk: the farmers, skilled workers, tradesmen, and all the others in southern society who found themselves situated between the black and white underclasses and the county-seat and urban elites. Lacking the ideological and political unity of the county-seat governing class and the strategic and material advantages of uptown, "The Man at the Center" lacked organization and consistent direction. The middle did, however, play a major role in New South politics. The middle was the social base for the southern demagogues. The Baltimore journalist H. L. Mencken lamented on numerous occasions the tragic descent of southern politics from the wise and aristocratic leadership of southern statesmen in the early years of the Republic to the unprincipled buffoonery of the 20th century and always assigned the cause for this catastrophe to the rise of southern poor whites. Mencken's contention that demagoguery was a poor white phenomenon was essentially nonsense. Southern poor whites did not vote, and the great era of the southern demagogues coincided precisely with the period when disfranchisement was most effective.

The common folk were the social base for demagoguery and they were much courted at election time. Their attraction to the demagogues— who at least had redeeming value as spectator entertainment—suggests the extent to which they found the candidates of county seat and uptown inadequate. The demagogues were overwhelmingly antiurban in their politics if not necessarily their policies, a fact that indicates the extent to which the cities of the New South had become alienated from the countryside. To some degree, demagoguery was a politics of protest and insurgency, an antiestablishment thrust that whatever its inadequacies often gave ordinary whites more in the way of program and attention than they were apt to get otherwise. But most of all, demagoguery was a politics of frustration, resulting from the common folk's place in the social structure. The common white folk had the unenviable task of challenging those above while protecting themselves from those below, and any meaningful radical or semiradical assault on the power and pomp of those above would ultimately have involved those below, which incidentally was precisely what happened with Populism. The result was demagoguery, protest, and even on occasion moderate reform without the disruption of the existing social order.

The Conservative Solid South. The South was changing, but in important ways it was still a premodern society with an underdeveloped colonial economy. The unfolding of the region's peculiar and vexing history led to the creation of a politically conservative Solid South that patterned southern political behavior for two-thirds of a century. So enmeshed were its economic, social, and political institutions that the Solid South's longevity is understandable. So undemocratic and exploitive were its arrangements that the criticisms directed against them seem unobjectionable.

Modernizing forces ultimately eroded the economic and social order that underlay the politics of the Solid South. The Great Depression of the 1930s and World War II fundamentally redirected southern development, although several decades were required for the region's people to absorb such a change, and certainly that was true of politics. Franklin D. Roosevelt and the New Deal responded to the Depression with a programic liberalism that won the support of huge numbers of southerners. The Roosevelt Administration's *Report on Economic Conditions of the South* signaled a critical turning point in federal policy. Whereas national governmental policies had usually accepted and often buttressed the South's position as a co-

lonial appendage of the northern economy, the *Report* declared the South to be "the Nation's No. 1 economic problem—the Nation's problem, not merely the South's," thereby justifying the federal government's emerging role as an active sponsor of southern economic development. Although most agricultural historians are sharply critical of New Deal agricultural policies, which contributed so significantly to the depopulation of the southern countryside, the catastrophic condition of southern agriculture made any aid popular; and given the South's huge population of blacks and poor working-class whites, it is little wonder that New Deal liberalism won a very substantial following. Indeed, if public opinion polls are to be believed, the South was the most liberal area of the nation during the 1930s, and the Solid Democratic South became even more solidly Democratic.

But despite the mass appeal of New Deal liberalism in the South, the region's politics was far more conservative than its people. New Deal liberalism was, of course, politically ineffective because a huge percentage of the South's black and white working people were both unorganized and voteless. Beginning in the mid-1930s Solid South political elites increasingly turned away from the New Deal, allying instead with Republicans to form the conservative coalition in Congress. Thus, the area that opinion polls suggested was the nation's most liberal region produced the politicians who most successfully opposed the New Deal. Perhaps understandably, northern liberals chafed under such arrangements and persistently searched for ways to extend the liberal-labor-minority coalition into the South and thereby to transform southern politics.

The most formidable opponents of

such a strategy were the Old Guard southern Democrats, who, with their prestige as the defenders of the Southland and their seniority in Congress, remained the most powerful element in southern politics. In Congress, they allied with Republicans in an informal but effective anti-New Deal coalition. The emergence of this coalition protected southern influence in Congress, but it also laid the foundation for an escalating sectional conflict within the Democratic party. New Deal liberals sought to extend the New Deal coalition into the South. Southern conservative elites, while entrenched in Congress, fretted over liberal control of presidential politics and endeavored to restore their influence in national party affairs. This struggle between the northern liberal-labor-minority coalition and the once Solid Democratic South was a crucial factor in American politics from the mid-1930s until the mid-1960s. The

Leander Perez, Louisiana political leader, 1950s

conflict escalated when President Truman asked Congress to enact civil rights legislation in 1948 and when later in the year the Democratic national convention endorsed Truman's program.

Outraged southern conservatives responded with the formation of the Dixiecrats, and thereafter third-party movements in presidential politics were common. By depriving the national Democrats of southern electoral votes, southern conservatives hoped to force concessions from the party and to deadlock the electoral college, thereby creating an opportunity to negotiate another sectional compromise as their ideological ancestors had done to end Reconstruction in 1877.

Massive Resistance. The Supreme Court's *Brown* v. *Board of Education* desegregation decision in 1954 further inflamed the southern leadership. Old Guard conservatives launched a determined program of massive resistance to desegregation. If the southern states refused to obey the *Brown* decision, what could the court eventually do but reverse the decision? To accomplish this task, southern conservatives adopted the hoary theory of interposition and sought to interpose state power between the federal courts and southern citizens. In practice that resulted in an astonishing variety of segregationist laws that spewed forth from the malapportioned southern state legislatures.

Like the third party presidential movements, massive resistance began as an elite enterprise. The Old Guard conservative leadership, its ideological roots deeply anchored in Bourbon democracy, placed defense of the southern social system above such things as public education. They had been defending the southern way of life since the Compromise of 1877, and even in the 1950s the planter-merchant-banker-lawyer county-seat governing class that the southern conservatives represented remained a fundamental locus of political power.

During these years, the agenda for both the national liberals and the southern conservatives changed and, indeed, narrowed. Northern New Deal liberals had viewed southern problems within an economic context and had sought to expand political and industrial democracy. During the postwar era, northern liberals moved rather rapidly away from the perception of the South as "the Nation's No. 1 economic problem" to the position that the South was the nation's number one moral problem. Whereas New Deal liberals viewed southern social problems in class terms—as a conflict between haves and have nots—postwar northern liberals tended to see the South in terms of a morality play featuring evil whites and virtuous blacks. A northern liberal agenda, then, which had once defined southern problems in relatively broad terms with profoundly meaningful implications for both southern whites and blacks, became narrowed to race as a moral issue. Similarly, while the southern conservatives defended a paternal order that encouraged such southern virtues as concern for family, kinship, community, church, roots, and place, they, like the liberals, reduced a broad range of values to the one issue of race, a massive resistance to desegregation.

Although originally promoted by conservative elites, the resistance to desegregation did ultimately become a popular reaction. As a result of federal court decisions and other factors, voter turnout steadily increased in the South, and by the late 1950s, the growing restiveness of black southerners and the gradual spread of desegregation made the race issue more salient to southern voters. The group that responded most positively to conservative appeals was the southern white common folk, the people who had often supported demagoguery in the past but who had shown strong proclivities toward New Deal reformism during the 1930s and 1940s. Thus, that social group upon which liberals had based so much hope for the future of liberalism ended up in the camp of the conservatives. The race issue—and the success of both the northern liberals and the southern conservatives in confining the political debate to that issue—completed the rout of the southern political liberals, who found themselves identified with the politically unpopular side of the controversy. Indeed, when the aging and declining southern Old Guard conservatives proved unable to turn back the desegregationist tide, working whites promoted their own spokesmen, the foremost of whom was George Wallace.

The Old Guard conservatives defined the issue as race, branded white liberals as traitors, and propounded a scorched-earth policy of closing the schools. The massive resistance strategy received its test when the schools actually started closing. In the fall of 1958 the governor of Arkansas closed the high schools in Little Rock and the governor of Virginia closed schools in a number of Virginia communities. The schools eventually reopened desegregated, but the process was repeated throughout much of the South. In the state of Georgia the crisis came in 1961 when a federal court ordered the admission of two black students to the University of Georgia. The state legislature had displayed the extent of its wisdom by enacting the usual bevy of massive resistance laws that included measures requiring that any desegregating institution be closed, that state funds be denied, that any instructor that taught mixed black and white students be arrested for felony, that any law enforcement official who failed to arrest a teacher for teaching in a desegregated classroom be himself arrested for felony, and so on. But in Georgia, as elsewhere, state authorities, when faced with the actual consequences of closing down the public schools and state universities, ultimately relented.

Leading the political opposition to closing the schools was the educated and affluent white middle class in the South's rapidly expanding cities and suburbs. Throughout the South it was the urban-suburban middle class, the heirs of the uptown elite, that organized the "save our school" movements in defense of public education. Avoiding the race issue, these campaigns merely insisted that public schools were essential to the continuing economic growth of the region. By endeavoring to avoid the race issue, the urban-suburban middle-class position was perceived as moderate, and in a massive resistance atmosphere their candidates for public office attracted the support of the rapidly expanding black electorate. Thus, the least materially affluent people in the South—the blacks—became the allies of the most affluent people in the South—the white business-professional-metropolitan elites.

Industrialization and Civil Rights. The middle-class uptown moderates provided much of the impetus for the drive to attract new industry. There was little novel in the notion that the South should endeavor to attract outside industry, although, as an important ideo-

logical force, its origins were relatively recent. The urban boosterism of the 1920s gained sustained momentum after the Great Depression had exposed the bankruptcy of southern agriculture and the economic thrust generated by World War II had propelled the South in the direction of further rapid economic growth. In 1936 Mississippi created its Balance Agriculture with Industry program, and thereafter all the other southern states created industrial development commissions. In the post–World War II period southern state government competed vigorously with a variety of programs and policies designed to offer services, tax concessions, and public subsidization to national and international corporations that chose to expand into the South. The old-style southern plantations gradually disappeared as agriculture became capital intensive and mechanized, and the diversifying southern economy benefited from labor mobility more than from the coercive forms of labor control that had been such a central factor in the politics and ideology of the New South.

The economic growth ethos had wide appeal. It had been a favored liberal program in earlier years, although the liberals had sought industrialization with industrial democracy. It also appealed to Old Guard conservatives, who hoped to combine industrialization with segregation and paternal social values. While dominating the headlines with their frantic attempts to preserve the southern way of life, conservative governors and legislators also encouraged and funded industrial development programs, though generally taking less interest in them than did such moderate governors as Luther Hodges in North Carolina and Leroy Collins in Florida. Indeed, the economic growth ethos provided one of the inspirations for the black protest movement. The black sit-in movement, which began in 1960, was in the beginning the work of young, educated, upwardly mobile blacks who wanted an opportunity to participate in the increasingly flourishing southern marketplace. The success of the black freedom movement in capturing the imagination of much of the nation ultimately forced the federal government to override the Congressional Dixieland Band and to enact the 1964 and 1965 Civil Rights Acts, which, when combined with other developments of this period, dismantled the social and political system that had for so long regulated wide areas of southern life. The 1964 act included an equality of economic opportunity provision that came to be interpreted in terms of affirmative action, and Lyndon B. Johnson's Great Society program did include what cynics came to call the skirmish on poverty. These measures broadened enormously the opportunities for better educated, more highly skilled, upwardly mobile black people. Lower-class blacks, while perhaps gaining psychological and even some social benefits from desegregation, remained about where they had always been.

As a result, despite the successes of the civil rights campaign, important elements of the black freedom movement turned steadily leftward. The Student Nonviolent Coordinating Committee, formed in 1960 to coordinate the student sit-ins, became a cadre of professional organizers. Rejecting the race-as-a-moral-issue argument, the SNCC workers developed a radical agenda that fueled their conflict, not only with the conservatives, but with both the southern moderates and the national liberals. Unable to find white allies, they carried their peculiar, semirevolutionary blend of socioeconomic realism and pan-African cultural romanticism into the great metropolitan ghettoes of the nation in an effort to build black power bases from which to negotiate with the white power blocs.

Perhaps more significantly, Martin Luther King, Jr., and the Southern Christian Leadership Conference, which in the beginning stood squarely within the national liberal mainstream in depicting the race issue as a moral question, also moved to the left. Breaking with the Johnson Administration and with many southern moderates, King threw the resources of SCLC into a poor people's campaign that sought to restore a broadly based economic and social liberalism by uniting outgroups behind a demand for a massive Marshall Plan at home. King's assassination in the spring of 1968 was a mortal blow to whatever prospects the campaign may have had. These developments, combined with black rioting mainly in northern ghettoes, contributed to making the decade of the 1960s one of upheaval and conflict.

In the wake of these developments southern Old Guard conservatives declined decisively. It was the county-seat Old Guard who suffered most directly from the demographic and economic transformation of the region, who benefited least from such political reforms as legislative reapportionment and black suffrage, and who most obviously lost prestige when unable to deliver on their massive resistance promises. The southern white common folk also lost in the political battles of the 1960s. Moving beyond the declining appeal of the Old Guard leadership, the white working class rallied under the banners of George Wallace and such lesser lights as Lester Maddox of Georgia. But the Wallace brand of popular resistance was essentially a negative program that was unable to sustain its appeal, at least without its most able practitioner to head it. The Wallace movement was in decline by the early 1970s, and any prospect that the Alabama governor might revive it terminated with the attempted assassination, and permanent crippling, of Wallace at a Maryland campaign rally in 1972. At any rate, white workers remained alienated from a national liberalism that for so long had placed them in the role of the heavies in the moral crusade for black rights, and they found little to applaud in President Johnson's black-oriented Great Society. Black southerners did of course benefit from the upheavals of the 1960s, but the failure of SNCC, the death of King, and the breakup of the civil rights movement left them with few viable options except—like the white working class—to support the southern moderate claim that economic growth would solve southern social problems.

As all this suggests, the basic result of the great political conflicts of the post–World War II years was to transfer the locus of southern political power from plantation-oriented county-seat elites to corporation-oriented metropolitan elites. The Republican party, which was once anathema in the South, attracted increasing support from well-off suburbanites and from white southerners disenchanted with the national Democratic party's liberal racial policies. The southern state elections of the early 1970s swept into office a wave of New South moderates and thereby signaled the triumph of a new political order. Reapportionment, the end of disfranchisement, desegregation, and the decline of the one-party system destroyed the institutional foundations of the old political system. If voter turnout was still low in the South, it was substantial when compared to the recent southern past and it included a far greater range of citizens. The antebellum era and the modern age are the two periods in which southern citizens seem to have been most ideologically united and in which the South has had two-party politics and popular democracy.

The best known of the New South moderates was Jimmy Carter. Like other moderates, Carter welcomed black support and endeavored—especially symbolically—to recognize black aspirations. But most of all he championed continued economic expansion, rationalized governmental procedures, and looked to corporate elites for guidance. By the 1970s the economic growth ethos had come to dominate the formulation of southern state policy, and economic expansion had come to be seen as *the* panacea for southern public problems, in somewhat the same manner that slavery had once been seen as the key to antebellum development. Certainly, differences do exist in southern politics, but the range of debate has vastly narrowed. Whether state governmental policies that favor public aid for industrialists, oppose labor organization, support relatively low taxes and services, and tailor social policies to the needs of land developers and real estate brokers will benefit the region's people as a whole and will alleviate racial and other social problems remains an open question.

See also BLACK LIFE: Politics, Black; / Hancock, Gordon B.; Jackson, Jesse; Lynch, John Roy; EDUCATION: Politics of Education; HISTORY AND MANNERS articles; LAW: States' Rights Constitutionalism;

MYTHIC SOUTH: / Carter Era; RELIGION: / Hays, Brooks; SOCIAL CLASS: Politics and Social Class; / Bourbon/Redeemer South; VIOLENCE: Political Violence; WOMEN'S LIFE: Politics, Women in; / Carter, Rosalynn; Johnson, Lady Bird; Mitchell, Martha

Numan Bartley
University of Georgia

Numan Bartley, *The Creation of Modern Georgia* (1983), *The Rise of Massive Resistance: Race and Politics in the South during the 1950s* (1969), with Hugh Davis Graham, *Southern Politics and the Second Reconstruction* (1975); Jack Bass and Walter DeVries, *The Transformation of Southern Politics: Social Change and Political Consequences since 1945* (1976); Dwight B. Billings, *Planters and the Making of a "New South": Class, Politics, and Development in North Carolina, 1865–1900* (1979); Earl Black and Merle Black, *Politics and Society in the South* (1987); W. J. Cash, *The Mind of the South* (1941); James C. Cobb, *The Selling of the South: The Southern Crusade for Industrial Development, 1936–1980* (1982); William J. Cooper, Jr., *Liberty and Slavery: Southern Politics to 1860* (1983); Anthony P. Dunbar, *Against the Grain: Southern Radicals and Prophets, 1929–1959* (1981); J. Wayne Flynt, *Dixie's Forgotten People: The South's Poor Whites* (1979); George M. Fredrickson, *The Black Image in the White Mind: The Debate on Afro-American Character and Destiny, 1817–1914* (1971); Eugene D. Genovese, *The Political Economy of Slavery: Studies in the Economy and Society of the Slave South* (1965), *Roll, Jordan, Roll: The World the Slaves Made* (1974), *The World the Slaveholders Made: Two Essays in Interpretation* (1969); V. O. Key, Jr., *Southern Politics in State and Nation* (1949); Alexander P. Lamis, *The Two-Party South* (1984); Steven F. Lawson, *Black Ballots: Voting Rights in the South, 1944–1969* (1976); Donald R. Matthews and James W. Prothro, *Negroes and the New Southern Politics* (1966); Edmund S. Morgan, *American Slavery, American Freedom: The Ordeal of Colonial Virginia* (1975); Gunnar Myrdal, *An American Dilemma* (1944); Jonathan M. Wiener, *Social Origins of the New South: Alabama, 1860–1885* (1978); Bertram Wyatt-Brown, *Southern Honor: Ethics and Behavior in the Old South* (1982). ☆

Alienation, Political

||||||||||||||||||||||||||||||||||||||||||||||||||||

The idea of political alienation has, at least since the time of Marx, been a major concern of political theorists and analysts. When viewed as a subjective part of the political system, alienation is manifested in at least two different ways: distrust of the political system and apathy toward it, feeling that one can have little impact on political authorities or political outcomes.

Southerners have historically felt alienated from the national political system, especially since the Civil War. Secession, followed by Reconstruction and the Compromise of 1877, reinforced the region's sense of political impotence. In addition, the South suffered economically, consistently trailing the rest of the nation in mean income. Insurgent political movements from the late 19th century to the present, including Huey Long's "Every Man a King" program, the Dixiecrat movement, and the American Independent party, have traditionally appealed to alienated southern voters in their efforts to change the political system. Given such a history, regional differences in alienation might be expected at the individual level, even in recent years.

Nationally, trust in political authority has shown a major drop since the late 1950s, when it was first measured in a national survey by the University of Michigan Survey Research Center. For example, as late as 1964, 76 percent of the national sample said they could "trust the government in Washington to do what is right most of the time" or "always." By 1972 this percentage had dropped to 53 percent and by 1978 to 30 percent. Other questions tapping political trust showed a similar downward trend.

Because of the traditional racial divisions in the South, blacks and whites not surprisingly differed in their degree of political trust. Although aggregate South-non-South differences (defining the South as the states of the Confederacy minus Tennessee and the non-South as the rest of the 48 contiguous states) are small through the 1964–78 period, when election year samples are divided by race as well as by region a clearer picture of regional differences emerges. Whereas southern whites have often perceived themselves to be victims of federal intrusion, southern blacks have seen themselves as the beneficiaries of federal involvement. As a result of these different perspectives, blacks and whites show opposite effects of region on political trust. From 1964 to 1976 southern whites were less trusting on the Political Trust Index than northern whites in every year (the Political Trust Index is derived from a multiitem scale and ranges from 100, when all respondents in a group are trusting, to −100, when all respondents in a group are distrusting), while southern blacks were consistently more trusting of the federal government than nonsouthern blacks (see Figure 1). A second racial difference also shows up. Although regional differences in political trust have been diminishing among whites, there is no evidence of such a nationalization

of attitudes among blacks. In fact, the regional difference for blacks in 1978 is actually greater than the average over the entire 1964–78 period.

One basis for nationalization is of course immigration by nonsouthern whites. Southern migrants (defined here as those currently living in the South, but having spent their childhood outside of the South) were substantially more trusting than native-born southerners over the 1964–72 period. They were, on average, even more trusting than nonsouthern whites as a whole. Considering that they made up over 25 percent of the white southern sample in every year, their impact was substantial. In contrast, no complementary influx of black southern migrants occurred, so the southern black population remained regionally distinct.

In addition to region and race, trust is related to education. Even controlling for education, though, southern whites were significantly less trusting than nonsouthern whites (p<.05) in 1964; among southern whites, migration continued to have a significant effect (p<.05) in 1964, 1968, and 1972, with

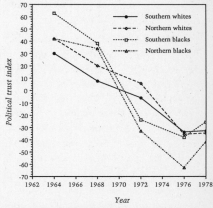

Figure 1. Political Trust by Region and Race

Source: University of Michigan Survey Research Center.

migrants being more trusting in all years. Strong regional effects for the earlier years, but not the later years, further attest to the nationalization of politics in the South (among whites) and the important role of migrants in that nationalization. For blacks, region's effect on political trust remains strong up to the present. Significant effects of region, controlling for education, existed in 1964, 1976, and 1978.

Although migration does account for a large part of the nationalization that occurred among whites through the mid-1970s, in both 1976 and 1978 the level of trust of native southern whites did not differ significantly from that of either nonsouthern whites or southern migrants. Perhaps this can be attributed to the presidency of a southerner, Jimmy Carter (the South showed an absolute gain in trust between 1976 and 1978 in distinction to the rest of the country), as well as to continued generational replacement. Neither migration to the South nor age replacement can, of course, explain the continued regional effect on political trust among blacks. Two factors present themselves, however. First, while there was little migration of blacks to the South in the last 30 years, a great deal of migration to the North has occurred. Whereas white migrants to the South are more trusting than either white southerners or white nonsoutherners, blacks who migrated from the South show levels of trust almost equal to those of native nonsouthern blacks, born and living outside the South, and substantially lower than current southern blacks. This is due mainly to the youthfulness of nonsouthern black migrants and the resulting ease of their assimilation and resocialization, compared with the generally older southern migrants.

A second reason for the continued

regional effect among blacks is the role of the federal government vis-á-vis state and local government in the South. The federal government remains a more important guarantor of black rights in the South than in the North. Whereas in 1976 southern blacks were 25 points higher on an index of trust toward federal government than non-southern blacks, they were at the same time less trusting of state government than were non-southern blacks. Every other regional racial group was at least 15 percent more likely to trust the state than the federal government to do what is right most or all of the time; southern blacks were only 1 percent more likely.

Looking at the difference in regional effects on political trust for the two races is a reminder that while the South has become part of a more homogenous nation, southerners have not completely transcended the influence of their past.

Ronald B. Rapoport
College of William and Mary

Joel Aberbach, *American Political Science Review* (March 1969); James Wright, *The Dissent of the Governed: Alienation and Democracy in America* (1976). ☆

Black Politics
||||||||||||||||||||||||||||||||||||||

See BLACK LIFE: Politics, Black

Congress
||||||||||||||||||||||||||||

Southern concern for protecting distinctive regional interests has often focused on Congress, and the South has sent some of its greatest talent to that institution. South Carolina Congressman and later Senator John C. Calhoun, for example, developed a major American political theory for protection of minority rights in Congress. He maneuvered for decades in Washington, in a losing battle, to protect slave plantation interests. The growing antebellum North-South conflict erupted into outright violence on the floor of Congress in 1856, when South Carolina Congressman Preston Brooks beat Massachusetts Senator Charles Sumner with his cane, as a stunned gallery watched.

Southerners in Congress have displayed a regional love of words through their oratory. John Randolph (1773–1833) of Roanoke, the eccentric Virginian of the early 19th century, was a brilliant extemporaneous speaker, quick witted and frequently acrimonious. Like many later southern congressmen, he defended states' rights. The modern comic image of the southern congressman as "Senator Claghorn"—a verbose, obfuscating, loud speaker—was a satirical distortion of real-life individuals who powerfully used words.

Southerners in Congress also developed unusual skills at procedural maneuvering. Henry Clay (1777–1852) regarded himself as more western than southern but this Kentucky congressman who served six terms as speaker of the House of Representatives represented a slave state and displayed a seemingly regional talent for mastering the way Congress operates. He put together the Missouri Compromise (1820) and the Compromise Tariff (1833) that ended the nullification crisis, and his ideas became the basis of the Compromise of 1850. Southerners who later rose to prominence as congressional leaders because of unusual legislative

skill included speakers of the House John Nance "Cactus Jack" Garner, Sam Rayburn, and William Bankhead, and Senate Majority Leader Lyndon Johnson. The filibuster became associated with southern congressional leaders in the mid-20th century, as James Eastland and John Stennis of Mississippi, Richard Russell of Georgia, Strom Thurmond of South Carolina, and others used it as a delaying tactic when Congress considered civil rights legislation.

The file of southern congressional notables would include those from a variety of political positions. Fire-eaters such as William Lowndes Yancey and Robert Barnwell Rhett were extremists in the defense of southern liberty, but Mississippi's Lucius Quintus Cincinnatus Lamar became a famed conciliator between the regions while serving in the House of Representatives (1873–77) and the Senate (1877–85) after the Civil War. Demagogues such as Cole Blease (South Carolina), Jeff Davis (Arkansas), Thomas "Tom-Tom" Heflin (Alabama), and Theodore Bilbo (Mississippi) first achieved notoriety at the state level but then transferred their harsh racial rhetoric to the halls of Congress. Maury Maverick (Texas), though, was a great defender of civil liberties and equality; Lister Hill and John Sparkman of Alabama were famed as racial moderates; and Albert Gore of Tennessee and Ralph Yarborough of Texas were downright liberal on the issue. Southern congressional leaders such as Thomas T. Connally of Texas, J. William Fulbright of Arkansas, and John Tower of Texas have played an active role in foreign affairs, some as "hawks," others as "doves," but most committed to internationalism rather than isolation.

Southern political families such as the Bankheads of Alabama and the Byrds of Virginia have sometimes seemed to claim a genealogical interest in Congress. John Hollis Bankhead, Sr. (1842–1920), for example, served in the House (1887–1907) and Senate (1907), while his sons John Hollis Bankhead, Jr. (1872–1946) and William Brockman Bankhead (1874–1940) played key roles in the Senate and the House in the 1930s.

Southern Democrats have traditionally dominated Congress in the 20th century. Their political longevity, their coalition with northern conservatives, and their ability to act in concert gave them a big advantage over other congressional factions. Southern one-party politics produced long careers in Congress for southern representatives and senators who, once secure as incumbents, rarely faced significant opposition. This factor, working in tandem with the legislature's seniority system, gave southerners the chairmanships of most major congressional committees. They strengthened that advantage in 1946 when many northern representatives and senators of equal seniority went down in defeat at the hands of Republicans. The southern Democrats parlayed their political windfall into a lasting advantage by renewing their cooperation with midwestern conservative Republicans in order to thwart subsequent legislative reform efforts until the Great Society of the 1960s. Congressional southerners acted as a unanimous power bloc, however, only in opposition to civil rights legislation. In the postwar era, civil rights became the keystone of southern congressional unity, as it came to control southern politics generally.

When President Harry Truman made civil rights an important part of his 1948 reelection campaign, he directly threatened customary southern racial relations. Congressional southerners were able to defeat Truman's legislative moves because of their unity of purpose exercised through control of all major committees. Occasionally, civil rights legislation and initiatives did manage to pass through the House of Representatives, where the southerners could be easily outvoted. All these efforts were halted in the Senate, however, where southern senators, led by Richard B. Russell of Georgia, prevented civil rights bills from coming to a vote by waging filibusters and exploiting the chamber's tradition of unlimited debate. This legislative stalemate continued through Truman's term and into the Eisenhower Administration until 1957 when the first civil rights bill since Reconstruction passed both houses. Nevertheless, that act and another approved in 1960 did little to change southern society, and both can be seen as tactical retreats by southern congressmen and senators, providing the illusion of progress while retaining the reality of white supremacy.

Meanwhile, other forces outside Congress were working to transform the South. The Supreme Court's 1954 *Brown* v. *Board of Education* desegregation decision and the 1957 use of presidential power to achieve integrated education in Little Rock, Ark., were beyond the reach of congressional southerners to stop or alter. In response to the Court, southern senators drafted, and southern House members signed, a 1956 "Declaration of Constitutional Principles," better known as the "Southern Manifesto." The document was little more than a condemnation of the *Brown* decision and a call for legal, peaceful resistance, using states' rights as a justification. Consequently, southerners in Congress were reaching the limits of their power by the early 1960s. With growing nationwide sentiment for a strong civil rights act, marshalled first by President John F. Kennedy and more effectively later by President Lyndon B. Johnson, reformers rammed through legislation in 1964 and 1965 that eventually transformed southern society and politics.

The civil rights acts and urbanization of southern society combined to transform the region's congressional politics. The subsequent decline of civil rights as a political issue encouraged a moderation of the South's political environment, which prompted the emergence of a wider spectrum of political concerns. The section's one-party political society began to weaken as the Republican party gained footholds in a number of states. The advent of ultraconservative southern Republicanism and the attrition of the Old Guard through death and retirement encouraged younger southern Democrats to shift from opposing their party leadership toward cooperation. These older southern Democrats softened their positions on race and other social issues to accommodate the rising numbers of black voters and a growing racial moderation by whites. Although neither a full-fledged two-party system nor a broad political spectrum emerged, the seeds for these vital parts of a political society were laid.

In Congress the South declined from its former position of dominance. As the southern Old Guard passed from positions of power, northerners took their places. The growing political diversity of the region further weakened the cohesiveness of the southerners in acting as a unit to support or oppose legislation. Finally, modifications in the seniority system diluted an important source of their legislative strength, since length of service no longer automatically

assured access to positions of power. The distinctive southern identity in Congress consequently declined.

David Potenziani
Memphis State University

Numan Bartley and Hugh Davis Graham, *Southern Politics and the Second Reconstruction* (1975); Jack Bass and Walter DeVries, *The Transformation of Southern Politics: Social Change and Political Consequence since 1945* (1976); James MacGregor Burns, *The Deadlock of Democracy: Four Party Politics in America* (1963); Neil MacNeil, *Forge of Democracy: The House of Representatives* (1963); Robert L. Peabody and Nelson W. Polsby, eds., *New Perspectives on the House of Representatives* (1969); Nelson W. Polsby, *Congress and the Presidency* (3d ed., 1976); Frank E. Smith, *Congressman from Mississippi* (1964). ☆

County Politics

||||||||||||||||||||||||||||||||||||||||

Few if any popular perceptions of southern politics are more deeply engrained than that of the courthouse "clique" or "ring." Film and fiction, scholarly tomes, and journalistic exposés have united in fostering an image of county governments dominated by self-serving officials closely aligned with business and agricultural wealth and exercising arbitrary, undemocratic control over local affairs. As with other generalizations about the South, this stereotype is more accurate for some eras than others, more applicable to some states and counties than to their neighbors. Nevertheless, a survey of the region's historical experience offers much support for this uncomplimentary appraisal of grassroots political conduct.

The beginnings of the courthouse cliques are readily discernible in the English origins of southern society. Acting for the crown, the king's counsellors appointed militia officers, sheriffs, and justices of the peace in the counties of the mother country during the 1500s and 1600s. The justices of the peace constituted the linchpins of the system. Functioning collectively as members of county courts, they administered governmental affairs in the shires and handled routine judicial matters as well.

These practices exerted an enduring influence. Unlike their dissenting Puritan contemporaries to the north, who fashioned a distinctive amalgam of Calvinist theocracy and town-meeting democracy, the dominant groups in the colonial South willingly adopted the oligarchic governmental forms of Tudor-Stuart England—as modified to accommodate provincial needs and circumstances. Developments in Virginia set the pattern for the region. There the royal governors selected county officials, including justices of the peace. In the Old Dominion—as in England— the justices directed local affairs, establishing tax rates, regulating businesses, overseeing road maintenance, and performing a multitude of other functions. Drawn from the ranks of the plantation gentry and enjoying lifetime tenure on the county courts, the justices soon established a marked degree of independence from gubernatorial control. Most notably, they began to assert the right to fill vacancies in their ranks, and royal governors generally acquiesced in this claim by confirming the justices' nominees (as well as their choices for

sheriffs and other county offices). Exercising peremptory control over local administration, members of the county courts also held considerable sway in elections to the House of Burgesses. Rule of, by, and for the planters thus became a fact of political life in Virginia and elsewhere in the region—in spite of sporadic protests by backwoods dissidents and other would-be reformers during the colonial and revolutionary periods.

Indeed, the South's oligarchic county courts escaped significant change until the first decades of the 19th century. By that time various abuses, including the appointment of excessive numbers of new justices and the consequent growth of court membership to unwieldy proportions (ranging upward to 90 men in some counties), demanded public attention. Professional lawyers led the assault by criticizing the planter-justices' lack of legal training, and charges of inefficiency, ineptitude, and corruption proliferated. More importantly, perhaps, democratic ideological currents of the Jacksonian era found obvious targets in the self-perpetuating county courts. This ferment produced dramatic results. Commencing in the new states of the Deep South cotton frontier and spreading throughout the region, legislative enactments and constitutional revisions transformed the tone and conduct of local politics. By the eve of the Civil War voters in most of the southern states could elect their sheriffs, coroners, overseers of the poor, school commissioners, and constables. Life-tenured justices of the peace had given way to county judges chosen by state legislatures or the electorate for limited, specified terms. Although planters still occupied many positions in local government, they could no longer ignore the interests and wishes of ordinary voters.

These democratic trends broadened and deepened during the turmoil of the Reconstruction era, only to experience a stunning reversal during the white supremacist "Redemption" of the 1870s and 1880s. Appalled by the preeminence of scalawags, carpetbaggers, and blacks during the brief heyday of Radical Republicanism, the resurgent planter Democrats and their New South commercial-industrial allies moved inexorably to eliminate or neutralize potentially disruptive influences. Reflecting this antiegalitarian bias, popular election of local officials was replaced by legislative or gubernatorial appointment in Florida, Louisiana, and North Carolina, while violence and ballot box fraud hampered voter participation elsewhere, especially in closely contested Black Belt areas. Entrenched county officeholders provided the organizational cement for long-term Democratic hegemony, and successive generations of Republicans, Populists, and Independents railed against the abuses (real or imagined) of courthouse cliques and rings. Oligarchic control was, once again, the fashion at the grassroots.

One-party rule persisted almost unchallenged through the first half of the 20th century, but county-level politics in the "Solid South" was characterized by considerable diversity. Courthouse cliques generally exerted greater influence in lowland plantation districts than in comparatively egalitarian mountain or piedmont areas. By the 1930s and 1940s, moreover, local officials in Louisiana, Tennessee, and Virginia tended to be closely aligned with dominant machine factions in their respective state Democratic parties, while county officeholders elsewhere in the region formed shifting, ephemeral alliances in state primary races. Courthouse politicos exerted particular influence in Georgia where a county-unit system (similar to the federal electoral college) determined the outcome of statewide primary contests. Exemplifying yet other variations, county seat political dominance in Alabama was typically enjoyed by probate judges; in Virginia, by circuit court judges; in Louisiana and Mississippi, by sheriffs with an abiding interest in the preservation of home rule over gambling and bootlegging in their jurisdictions.

Byzantine in its complexities, sometimes baroque in its manifestations, the courthouse regime constituted a bedrock reality of southern politics until the 1940s and 1950s. Even so, forces of change were omnipresent in the post–World War II years, eroding the authority and imperiling the permanence of the previously invincible cliques and rings. Urbanization, industrial growth, northern migration to the emerging Sunbelt, enhanced educational opportunities, and the advent of mass communications media were fashioning a more cosmopolitan social order, a South less attuned to one-party rule. In the aftermath of the New Deal, state and federal bureaucracies were on the rise and they created alternative centers of power and influence. Most important of all, the civil rights revolution exerted a pervasive impact on the South. Encouraged by federal legislative enactments and judicial decrees, millions of blacks reentered the political process, while the Supreme Court's "one-man, one-vote" rulings bolstered the representation of urban residents at the expense of the old-style crossroads elite. Beset by external antagonists and internal stresses, the cliques and rings

John McCrady, **Political Rally** *(1935)*

were in retreat throughout the region by the 1960s and 1970s. Nevertheless, historical experience suggests that it may be premature, as yet, to write their epitaph.

See also GEOGRAPHY: / Courthouse Square

James Tice Moore
Virginia Commonwealth University

Monroe Billington, *The Political South in the Twentieth Century* (1975); V. O. Key, Jr., *Southern Politics in State and Nation* (1949); Charles S. Sydnor, *Gentleman Freeholders: Political Practices in Washington's Virginia* (1952), *The Development of Southern Sectionalism, 1819–1848* (1948); C. Vann Woodward, *Origins of the New South, 1877–1913* (1951); Ralph A. Wooster, *The People in Power: Courthouse and Statehouse in the Lower South, 1850–1860* (1969), *Politicians, Planters, and Plain Folk: Courthouse and Statehouse in the Upper South, 1850–1860* (1975). ☆

Demagogues

||||||||||||||||||||||||||||||||

Political demagoguery is at least as old as the early Greek term (from *demos*, for people, and *agog*, for leader) for unscrupulous politicians who gain power by appealing to the electorate's emotions, passions, and prejudices. Throughout Western history, demagogues have symbolized the fear of privileged elites that expanding democracy inevitably degenerates into rabble-rousing. In America, no era or region has been free of demagogues, but the classic southern variety flourished with unusual vigor during the six decades between Reconstruction and World War II.

The term has been applied to successful southern politicians as diverse as Benjamin Tillman, Tom Watson, Jeff Davis, Coleman Blease, James K. Vardaman, Theodore Bilbo, Thomas Heflin, James and Marian Ferguson, W. Lee O'Daniel, Eugene Talmadge, and Huey Long. Their appeals to poor rural whites variously featured irresponsible campaign promises, flamboyant personal styles, violent rhetoric, appeals to racial and religious bigotry and antiintellectualism, and attacks upon the predatory corporate interests. Mississippi's Bilbo denounced from the stump a typical pantheon of enemies of the common people: "farmer murderers, poor-folks haters, shooters of widows and orphans, international well-poisoners, charity hospital destroyers, spitters on our heroic veterans, rich enemies of our public schools, private bankers, European debt cancellors, unemployment makers, Pacifists, Communists, munitions manufacturers, and skunks who steal Gideon Bibles." As for the disfranchised and vulnerable blacks, Blease would "wipe the inferior race from the face of the earth." To Vardaman the Negro was a "lazy, lying, lustful animal which no conceivable amount of training can transform into a tolerable citizen." Bilbo, who shot a black man on a Washington streetcar, called for solving the unemployment problem by shipping 12 million black southern citizens "back" to Africa. Not surprisingly, racial lynching flourished in such an atmosphere—Blease boasted that "whenever the constitution comes between me and the virtues of the white women of the South, I say to hell with the constitution."

These appeals understandably took root in an environment characterized by poverty, illiteracy, racism, Civil War and Populist defeat, agrarian decline, and a small-town and rural cultural barrenness that was only occasionally enlivened by revivals and political campaigns. Reinforcing this socioeconomic and cultural legacy was the South's one-party system and the direct (white) Democratic primary, which strengthened personality-centered stump politics at the expense of issue-focused debates, blurred policy continuities that linked incumbent regimes to policy outcomes, and invited the manipulation of faction-ridden legislatures by organized, well-funded lobbies against the collective interests of the "have-nots." As a result, victorious demagogues rarely implemented such promised and popularly mandated reforms as better schools, hospitals, roads, and pensions, and many of their regimes were riddled with corruption. Richard Hofstadter referred to this phenomenon as the "devolution of reform into reaction," whereby the highly educated Georgia Populist, Tom Watson, was transformed into the embittered baiter of Negroes, Jews, and Catholics, and the modest attempts at reform under the Tillman regime in South Carolina degenerated into the empty promises of Blease, who as governor even opposed compulsory education and child labor laws. As late as the mid-20th century, such common-folk champions as Governor Talmadge in Georgia and the Fergusons and O'Daniel in Texas would attack their state universities while corruption shaped their own administrations and swelled their pockets; as Talmadge explained, "Sure I stole, but I stole it for you." This in turn invited "good government" counterattacks by conservative elites who typically called for slashing both taxes and social services—which amounted, in the classic lament of Gerald W. Johnson, to a dismal choice between a "Live Demagogue or a Dead Gentleman."

The dominant stereotype of the southern demagogue masked considerable diversity and irony as well. These masters of the common tongue and taste generally enjoyed a superior education; champions of the downtrodden, they

Pappy Lee O'Daniel, Texas governor and country-western musician, c. 1940

typically lived and retired in material comfort. Although most Deep South demagogues were race-baiters, their Rim South equivalents, such as Jeff Davis of Arkansas and "Pappy" O'Daniel of Texas, generally were not. The most nationally spectacular embodiment of the triumphant demagogue, "Kingfish" Huey Long of Louisiana, staked his presidential bid against Roosevelt on the economic nostrum of "Share Our Wealth." But in Louisiana, Long not only refused to race-bait, he also refused to sell out, once elected, to the corporate interests he had attacked. After seizing near dictatorial control of Louisiana's government, Long taxed the extractive industries and delivered the roads, bridges, hospitals, schoolbooks, and utility regulation that his campaigns had promised.

Many political journalists of the 1930s viewed Long as a forerunner of American fascism, and thereby demonstrated their misunderstanding both of the mainstream American political

tradition and of its exaggerated southern variant. Contemporaries of Long watched Europe descend into a fascist nightmare, and with victory in World War II came an understandable surge of domestic social scientific interest in identifying the origin, structure, and location of America's equivalent fascist personality. University-based psychologists generated such test-battery inventories as the "f-scale" (for fascism) to identify the authoritarian personality, and sociologists employed the new tool of survey research to locate its distribution. But southerners proved to be no more inclined toward fascism than other Americans, primarily because America had no fascist tradition.

Southern demagoguery has always confused political analysts, because it tends to appeal simultaneously to the populist left and to the bigoted right. Neither tendency is alien to the American political tradition, but in the prostrate South from Reconstruction through the Great Depression, the bitterness of poverty and defeat was compounded by four warping political institutions—disfranchisement, the one-party system, malapportionment, and de jure Jim Crow—that whiplashed southern politics into a grotesque caricature of the American democratic ideal. Few contemporary observers understood that the pathological environment was temporary, and that its passing would reveal a deeper bedrock of regionally shared American political values.

World War II ushered in a belated surge of prosperity throughout the South, and with it slowly came the improved education and broadened political participation that would relegate the classic post-Reconstruction demagogues to history. Desegregation and the civil rights movement sparked a brief resurgence from the mid-1950s through the mid-1960s of the old demagogic strains, most notably in defiant governors Orville Faubus, Ross Barnett, George Wallace, and Lester Maddox. But the long and circular career of Alabama's Wallace testifies ironically not only to the depth of the South's racial tension, but also to the strength of its populistic tradition and to the liberating effect of a genuinely democratic franchise, of two-party competition, of public education, and ultimately of the South's long submerged but abiding commitment to the norms and goals of American democracy.

Hugh Davis Graham
University of Maryland
Baltimore County

William Anderson, *The Wild Man from Sugar Creek: The Political Career of Eugene Talmadge* (1975); Hugh Davis Graham, ed., *Huey Long* (1970); William F. Holmes, *The White Chief: James Kimble Vardaman* (1970); Gerald W. Johnson, *Virginia Quarterly Review* (January 1936); Albert Kirwan, *Revolt of the Rednecks: Mississippi Politics, 1876–1925* (1951); Reinhard Luthin, *American Demagogues: Twentieth Century* (1954); Daniel M. Robison, *Journal of Southern History* (August 1937); Francis Butler Simkins, *Pitchfork Ben Tillman: South Carolinian* (1944); T. Harry Williams, *Huey Long* (1969), *Journal of Southern History* (February 1960); C. Vann Woodward, *Tom Watson: Agrarian Rebel* (1938). ☆

Government Administration

||||||||||||||||||||||||||||||||||||||||

Government administration in the South has traditionally been considered less professional, less vigorous, less accountable, and more affected by personalized political influences than administration in other regions. To a considerable extent this distinctiveness can be attributed to southern governments' having typically had a much smaller revenue base on which to finance public programs. The administrative establishment had fewer employees per capita, salaries were lower, merit systems were less feasible, and professionalism and administrative effectiveness were less developed. However, much of what is distinctive about southern government administration is not a simple result of the traditionally low level of personal wealth in the South. The special character of partisan and interest-group politics also influences the quality and nature of administration. Consequently, southern government administration may continue to be somewhat distinctive even as the region catches up with the rest of the nation economically.

Perhaps the most important actor in southern government administration is the governor. There is something paradoxical about the way this office has been viewed by political and historical observers. V. O. Key, Jr., classified most southern states as "loose factional systems," because they were characterized by an "issueless politics" and an inability to "carry out sustained programs of action." The absence of a viable, well-defined system of party competition created a situation in which political power was not effectively tied to partisan forces. Thus, southern governors were not normally led to enforce party platforms or to follow party preferences in administrative appointments. Instead, southern governors have often had considerable *personal* control over government jobs, roads, purchasing, and local public improvements. In short, the southern governor was traditionally possessed of notorious personal power, making him highly unpredictable, and yet, in the absence of a cohesive party organization and effective party competition, weak in terms of policy effectiveness.

The institutional weakness of the southern governor is reflected in (1) a lack of exclusive responsibility for budget development (currently a shared responsibility in five southern states, but earlier a shared responsibility in all of them), (2) relatively restricted appointment powers, and (3) the inability, until recently, of governors in many southern states to succeed themselves. In addition to the weakness of the gubernatorial office, the formal administrative procedures of southern state agencies have not traditionally been subject to the kind of "judicialization" accomplished long ago on the federal level and in most other states. Administrative hearing and rule-making procedures were subject to fewer procedural requirements, raising questions about the thoroughness and accountability of administrative activity. Government administration, as a result of all these factors, has often been fragmented, personalized, and unprofessional when compared to administration in non-southern states.

The interest group situation in the South is rather ambiguous. Some researchers have concluded that organized groups are effectively unopposed by countervailing interests, suggesting that interest groups are more powerful in the South than elsewhere. Others, most notably Mancur Olson, Jr., argue that the historically brief period of stable industrialization in the South has prevented the development of groups devoted to collective action. Labor unions, for example, are less numerous and less powerful in the South than elsewhere. One can, therefore, construct and support arguments suggesting that the South is characterized by "strong" or "weak" interest groups, depending upon one's interpretations.

Actually, either view lends support to the idea that southern politics is *not* characterized by persistent, institutionalized conflict among well-established interest organizations to the same degree as are the politics of non-southern states. Government administration is more particularized, less "open," because interest groups do not accumulate broad interests any better than the fragmented one-party political machines. A professional, cohesive, merit-oriented bureaucracy is, in part, a response to the kind of effective, broad-based patterns of political influence that traditionally have not characterized the South. Ironically, such influences should be less developed both in states with weak interest groups *and* in those with organized interests not effectively opposed by others.

Much of what is distinctive about government administration in the South is rapidly disappearing. Southern governors are becoming more powerful. Well over half the states that have recently removed their prohibitions against a governor succeeding himself are southern states. According to a recent study on state party organization, "regional differences in organizational strength have declined . . . as the Republicans in the South developed modern party organizations and the Southern Democrats were forced to follow." As industrialization in the South completes its "catching up" process, the interest group climate should become like that in other states as well. Personality in southern politics and government is so well established a factor, though, it will likely endure for some time to come.

Marcus Ethridge
University of Wisconsin—Milwaukee

Virginia Gray, Herbert Jacob, and Kenneth Vines, eds., *Politics in the American States: A Comparative Analysis* (1983); V. O. Key, Jr., *Southern Politics in State and Nation* (1949); Sarah Morehouse, *State Politics, Parties, and Policy* (1981); Laurence W. Moreland, Tod A. Baker, and Robert P. Steed, eds., *Contemporary Southern Political Attitudes and Behavior: Studies and Essays* (1982); Ira Sharkansky, *The Maligned States: Policy Accomplishments, Problems, and Opportunities* (2d ed., 1978). ☆

Ideology, Political

Not too long ago scholars of southern politics invariably unearthed demagogues, one-party politics based on massive disfranchisement of blacks, malapportionment of representation, factionalism based on issueless friends-and-neighbors politics, a militant and defensive southern bloc in national politics, and, above all else, a politics dedicated to white supremacy. By the end of the 1970s these issues lay dead and the South had conformed to national political ideals. Southern political ideology, though conservative, particularly on social and Cold War issues, is no more conservative than that of the mountain states or even Orange County, Calif. But it has not always been that way.

American political ideology is celebrated in the catchwords of our everyday life—freedom, democracy, and equality. The political culture of the United States includes both the noble ideas of the founding documents, the Declaration of Independence and the Constitution (particularly the first 10 amendments), and the reality of conflict among citizens based on race, ethnicity, class, and region. The development of a distinctive southern political ideology was part of this broader culture. At times in open conflict with theoretical national sentiments, it was based on regional conflict with the North and eventually overrode the subcultures and bands of dissenters within the region.

A distinctive southern political ideology was elusive in the colonial South. The foundations of a system of belief different from that of the nation were there in the beginnings of the plantation system and large-scale black slavery, but the lack of any generalized American nationalism meant no southern regionalism existed either. The years from the Declaration of Independence (1776) to the Missouri controversy (1819–20) were a transitional period in the history of southern political ideology. The South participated fully in the creation of the American system of government and in the political ideals of the new nation. Its greatest leaders—Washington, Jefferson, and Madison—were from southern states, with Jefferson remaining the central figure of American political democracy. But sectionalism lurked everywhere, and the requisite compromises of the 1789 Constitution, particularly those concerning slavery and centralization versus state powers, reflected the South's emerging political differences. Nevertheless, the transitional years left no record of blatant assertion of southern difference or serious calls for a southern polity.

The Missouri controversy was a landmark in the growth of a southern political ideology. The debate gathered up all the bundles of an emerging sectionalism—the division of power between North and South, slavery, the pattern of the growing national economy, and more significantly, the meaning of American democracy and its values, however compromised they were by intergroup conflict. The debate impelled southerners to define their political views in relationship to the North and to articulate their separate political culture. By the 1830s and 1840s events such as the nullification crisis, the growth of antislavery movements, and the Mexican War overwhelmingly channeled sectional political differences into the single stream of the slavery question. In its defense of slavery the South slid into a political orthodoxy and social conservatism that adjusted the political and social reform movements of the first half of the 19th century to a southern standard. The South's greatest politician of this period, John C. Calhoun, defended southern political differences. Calhoun created a political ideology that attacked democratic values and accepted class- and race-stratified authoritarianism— an ideology that was more distinctive and more at variance with that of the Founding Fathers than any other major American political philosophy of the time.

Recent scholars have shown the importance of paternalism to southern ideology. Defenders of slavery believed that southern society was a hierarchical one, marked by accepted obligations and responsibilities on the part of everyone from the slave to the planter. Eugene D. Genovese has even argued that the personal relationships inherent in paternalism worked against "solidarity among the oppressed by linking them as individuals to their oppressors." The concept of personal honor became closely tied to paternalism as a guiding concept of the antebellum elite.

During the crucial years of the 1850s and 1860s the southern political ideal of orthodoxy and conservatism transformed itself into the radical concept of separate southern nationalism; only the massive defeat of the Confederacy killed the dream. The Old South's political ideals did not wither away in the bitterness of conflict and defeat. The modern political South was born in defeat, and the struggle of Reconstruction only confirmed its distinctive political ideology built around a tense amalgam of rugged, freewill individualism, states' rightsism, white supremacy, social conservatism, a paternalistic class division, and political loyalties to systems that protected these principles.

The values of a white, male-dominated democracy (herrenvolk democracy) and the master-race cultural views of southern planters persisted after the Civil War. The emerging capitalist entrepreneurs in the New South's commerce and industry seemed more captive to this political ideology than such figures elsewhere in the nation, and a distinctive form of conservative politics emerged. It favored a rural county elite ideology that was frankly class centered in the paternalistic ways of the plantation and the cotton mill. As Numan Bartley wrote: "The transfer of political leadership from plantation-oriented county-seat elites to business-oriented metropolitan elites was a long, complex and divisive process."

After Reconstruction, political change came slowly to the South. The ideology of orthodoxy and conservatism weathered the Populist challenge and the subsequent Progressive movement. Southern politicians overwhelmingly supported the Democratic party and used their power to protect all things southern. But the interwar years of the 1920s and 1930s created visible cracks in the foundation of the southern system, and widespread economic changes after the 1940s and 1950s remade southern politics. The civil rights revolution, the impact of a postwar American culture of television, shopping malls, big cities, and major league sports, and the national acceptance of southern music suggested that the Americanization of Dixie had occurred. The result was that southern political ideology began to look suspiciously American. As elsewhere, groups divided or came together by race, income level, lifestyle, occupation, place of residence, transient issues, and education. Southerners now gave ardent homage to all the value words of the American political tradition. By the 1980s journeys to the southern political land revealed fewer exotic, strange, or even different phenomena than earlier. National polling data suggested the South in the 1980s remained the nation's most conservative region on great and small economic and social questions, but its controlling ideologies found ready allies all over the country. At least in terms of political ideology, it no longer appeared to be the "nation within a nation" that V. O. Key described late in the 1940s.

See also HISTORY AND MANNERS: Jacksonian Democracy; SOCIAL CLASS: Politics and Social Class

James A. Hodges
The College of Wooster

Numan Bartley, *The Creation of Modern Georgia* (1983), *Reviews in American History* (December 1982), with Hugh Davis Graham, *Southern Politics and the Second Reconstruction* (1975); John Bass and Walter DeVries, *The Transformation of Southern Politics: Social Change and Political Consequences since 1945* (1976); Dwight B. Billings, *Planters and the Making of a "New South": Class, Politics, and Development in North Carolina, 1865–1900* (1979); W. J. Cash, *The Mind of the South* (1941); Eugene D. Genovese, *The Political Economy of Slavery: Studies in the Economy and Society of the Slave South* (1965); Dewey Grantham, *The Democratic South* (1963); V. O. Key, Jr., *Southern Politics in State and Nation* (1949); John McCardell, *The Idea of a Southern Nation: Southern Nationalists and Southern Nationalism, 1830–1860* (1979); John Shelton Reed, *The Enduring South: Subcultural Persistence in Mass Society* (1972); Jonathan M. Weiner, *Social Origins of the New South: Alabama, 1860–1885* (1978); Bertram Wyatt-Brown, *Southern Honor: Ethics and Behavior in the Old South* (1982). ☆

Legislatures, State

Though governors and senators have been famous as individuals, the office of state legislator has best embodied the stereotype of the southern politician. The white male lawyer cum country bumpkin who rants against Yankee capitalists, spouts racial slurs, and is careless toward public policy embodies the stereotype. Whatever the validity of that image in the past, it is far from accurate in the 1980s. Southern legislatures as institutions and legislators as members are in the midst of changes. Although some of these changes reduce regional differences, others underscore the distinctiveness of the South. Much of the change has come as a result of legislatures' gaining the power to counterbalance that of southern governors.

In recent decades similar developments in southern and non-southern legislatures have reduced regional differences. United States legislatures in the 1950s, for example, commonly met only in biennial sessions, with the proportion of southern legislatures especially high in this pattern (90 percent to 70 percent). By 1983 the proportion was identical (20 percent) in both the North and the South. The shift to annual sessions has been an important step toward active and informed participation in shaping state public policy.

Southern state legislatures still have more committees than do their northern counterparts, but the number of committees per legislature in both the North and the South has been reduced by over a third. In the process, the disparity between the two regions has lessened. Both changes—increase in frequency of sessions and reduction in the number of committees—were vigorously advanced in the 1960s and 1970s as essential reforms to increase the capacity of legislatures to act. Both trends have been as fully felt in the South as nationally.

Likewise, legislatures throughout the country are now quite similar in the availability of staff support for members and committees. A quarter of the legislatures in each region now provide professional assistance, and close to a majority of states provide only secretarial and other nonprofessional assistance. Another indication of interregional similarities among state legislatures is seen in their attempt to control federal funding. Both state governors and legislatures want control over the disposal of these funds. By the mid-

dle of 1982, about a quarter of the states, North and South, had left considerable discretion to their governors, but about 40 percent of the legislatures in each region were taking active steps both to monitor and to decide upon the allocation of such federal funds.

Regional differences, however, still persist. Southern legislatures, for example, on the average consider fewer bills per session but enact a larger number and a higher proportion of all bills introduced than do those outside the South. A higher proportion of southern states lack home rule for municipalities than in other regions, despite the fabled southern belief in localism, and thus a sizable number of bills must be processed to accommodate local requests.

Though the South has traditionally been the locale of strong, flamboyant governors, recent reforms have greatly strengthened the capacity of legislatures to act independently of the governor. The South has adopted, to a greater extent than elsewhere, provisions for "sunset" review of programs and administrative agencies. Over half the southern legislatures may review and terminate the full range of administrative agencies, whereas legislatures elsewhere are much more limited in the scope of their review. Southern state legislatures depend upon regular committees to conduct agency reviews, but legislatures elsewhere tend to rely more upon specialized review bodies.

Perhaps the greatest changes that have taken place in southern legislatures involve membership. Members in the past were almost exclusively white male rural Democrats. The narrowness of representation came not only from strong political ties to the Democratic party, but also from the selection of legislators from multimember districts that were malapportioned to favor rural areas. Judicial decisions on reapportionment combined with Department of Justice rulings under the Voting Rights Act of 1965 have required state legislatures throughout the country to shift to single-member districts drawn in accordance with the location of population. Thus, in keeping with national trends, southern legislatures are becoming more urban and suburban, and less rural, than previously. An integral part of these changes has been an increase in the election of blacks and to some extent Republicans to the legislatures.

By 1982 the number of black state legislators in the South was triple that of 1971, while blacks had increased by less than half in legislatures in the rest of the country. In 1971, of all black state legislators in the country, 24 percent sat in southern capitals; by 1982, that proportion had risen to almost 41 percent. The average southern state legislature in 1971 had two black members, but by 1982 the number had grown to six—compared to only three in other states. As a result, legislatures that once fostered Jim Crow laws now have the nation's largest numbers of black representatives.

In spite of the numerous changes cited, the most distinctive feature of southern legislatures remains the partisan dominance of the Democratic party. A southern legislature in the 1950s without a single Republican was not uncommon. In 1951, 7 of the 13 southern states had no Republican solons. In 1961 Democrats controlled on an average 95 percent of the seats in both the upper and lower chambers of southern legislatures. The Democratic dominance in the South during the 1950s and the 1960s was even more pronounced when compared to state leg-

islatures throughout the rest of the country where Democrats averaged only 40 percent of the seats. In 1981, across the 13 states used in this analysis (the 11 states of the Confederacy, plus Oklahoma and Kentucky), the Democrats averaged 80 percent of the House seats and 84 percent of the Senate positions. Though southern states have frequently elected Republicans as both governor and U.S. senators and have supported Republican presidential candidates, Republicanism has not trickled down into the essentially local-district elections of state legislatures.

Although some changes have occurred in this area, any sudden or drastic change in the partisan composition of state legislatures appears unlikely, largely because a substantial number of legislative districts are safe. Over 75 percent of the legislative elections in nine of the southern states were won by the comfortable margin of more than 60 percent of the votes. In two other states over half the elections were safe.

Notable differences exist among the southern state legislatures themselves. Variations within the South in partisanship, structure, and behavior persist in the 1980s. The strong South Carolina Legislature stands in contrast to the gubernatorial-dominated Louisiana Legislature. Still, southern state legislatures are a definable group in contrast with those in the rest of the nation. Having experienced dramatic changes and especially growing power since World War II, they remain distinctive institutions with their southern political outlook.

David M. Olsen
E. Lee Bernick
University of North Carolina
at Greensboro

Council of State Governments, *Book of States* (biennial eds., various years); Virginia Gray, Herbert Jacob, and Kenneth Vines, *Politics in the American States: A Comparative Analysis* (1983); Malcolm E. Jewell, *Legislative Representation in the Contemporary South* (1967), *Representation in State Legislatures* (1982); V. O. Key, Jr., *Southern Politics in State and Nation* (1949); Alan Rosenthal, *Legislative Life* (1981). ☆

National Politics

IIIIIIIIIIIIIIIIIIIIIIIIIIIIIIIIIIIIIIIIIIII

Alexis de Tocqueville, the oft-quoted French visitor to the young American Republic in the 1830s, observed in *Democracy in America* (1835), "Two branches may be distinguished in the great Anglo-American family, which have hitherto grown without entirely comingling; the one in the South, the other in the North." Politically, that was not entirely true at the time, but it would soon become so. The South had been an integral part of national life in its first half-century, providing talented leaders such as Jefferson, Madison, Jackson, and Marshall, and during the 1840s and early 1850s southern politics were intertwined with the nation's. Whigs and Democrats competed on similar levels in the South as elsewhere and the region's electorate participated at the same high rate as other Americans of that time.

The South's political goals were, of course, somewhat different from those of the rest of the country because of its economy. Madison had stressed in *Federalist* no. 10 how "the possession of different degrees and kinds of property" influences "the sentiments and views of the respective proprietors." This creates "a division of the society into different interests and parties" or factions. The slave economy, a rural and agricultural one, produced a faction of planter elites from the Black Belt areas—where the fertile topsoil was deep and dark—who fought from the constitutional period to Tocqueville's time for a certain agenda. In the Philadelphia Convention of 1787 this influential class shaped several provisions of the new Constitution to their ends, among them the infamous Three-Fifths Compromise, a 20-year protection against halting the importation of slaves, and a $10 tax limit on those brought in, plus a prohibition on direct taxes on personal wealth or income. In ensuing decades they engaged repeatedly in the titanic tariff struggles against the northern manufacturing interests who sought to protect themselves from foreign goods while the planters sought free trade.

Madison had explained in his seminal essay that the federal, republican form of government could effectively rule over an enormous territory through an array of formal checks and balances to fragment elite power and through divided constituencies to do likewise for mass sovereignty. An advantage of this system would be the "security afforded . . . in the greater obstacles to the concert and accomplishment of the majority." By the time of Tocqueville's visit, such protections were becoming increasingly important to the slaveholding elite for a host of reasons.

At the time of the passage of the Constitution the populations of North and South plus their economies and political balance were roughly equal, but that was changing as the nation began its second half-century. The economic advantages of the northern manufacturing and commercial interests grew steadily while the admission of new western states began to alter the political alignment, and by 1850 the North had grown to some 13.5 million, whereas the South grew to only 9.5 million. These and other adverse trends led John C. Calhoun to bemoan to southerners in the 1830s on the Senate floor that "we are here but a handful in the midst of an overwhelming majority." The eminent historian Richard Hofstadter wrote in *The American Political Tradition* of that critical era: "The Southern leaders reacted with the most intense and exaggerated anxiety to every fluctuation in the balance of sectional power. How to maintain this balance became the central concern." It would remain so for the next 150 years.

Thus, the southern planter elite embarked on a futile struggle to maintain a semifeudal, agrarian, and racially stratified society. This eventually made residents of the region the only Americans (until Vietnam) ever to lose a war and the sole ones ever to be governed by a conquering military occupation force. After the war the struggle resumed as the elite, Bourbons or Redeemers as they came to be called, reestablished the state Democratic parties, engineered the removal of the Reconstruction governments in the Compromise of 1877, and moved in the 1880s and 1890s to isolate Republicans to the upland areas that had opposed secession, to squelch the radical Populist uprising of small farmers, and to establish Jim Crow in the turn-of-the-century constitutions. Thus, the Solid South was built on one-party politics, racism, formal and informal disfranchisement of the masses, malapportionment in favor of Black Belt areas, and—perhaps most important of all—regional autonomy from national politics and, in particular, undesirable policies on racial matters.

The foremost scholar of Dixie politics, the late political scientist V. O. Key, Jr., said of this Solid South system in his brilliant study in 1949: "The coin of southern politics has two sides; on one is seen the relations of the South as a whole with the rest of the nation; on the other, the political battle within each state. And the two aspects are, like the faces of a coin, closely connected." He traced how the relatively small white minority of the Black Belt counties ruled Dixie through the unchallenged hegemony of the Democratic party. Democrats won, for example, 113 of 114 gubernatorial elections and 131 of 132 senatorial ones from 1919 to 1948. Also, with the single exception of 1928 when five rim states abandoned the wet, Catholic, urban New York Democrat Al Smith, Dixie gave all its electoral votes to the Democratic ticket in the 17 presidential elections from 1880 to 1944.

Such loyalty provided the region's elite enormous leverage in national politics, particularly in Congress, where the solid bloc of southern Democratic senators consistently controlled the Senate and the overwhelmingly Democratic southern congressional delegations likewise controlled the House. The seniority system adopted in 1910 for choosing chairpersons promoted the South's members into positions of great power, so that by the 1950s Dixie, with some one-fifth of the total population and number of states, commanded approximately 60 percent of the chairs. Because of their power and because of the practice of senatorial courtesy southern senators greatly influenced the federal judiciary, especially at the lower levels. And until 1936 the requirement that

Democratic presidential nominees acquire two-thirds of the delegate votes gave the South an effective veto over unacceptable candidates. The thoroughness with which regional autonomy was achieved through these and related devices is highlighted by the observation of W. J. Cash, a full century after Tocqueville, that the South "was not quite a nation within a nation, but the next thing to it."

The use of this power to resist nationalizing, industrializing, and egalitarian trends greatly retarded the economic, political, and social development of the region. In 1938 President Roosevelt assembled a major Conference on Economic Conditions in the South, stating that the "South presents right now the Nation's No. 1 economic problem." Key would write at mid-century, "The cold hard fact is that the South as a whole has developed no system or practice of political organization and leadership adequate to cope with its problems." Racially, the historic gulf between white and black southerners flared into violence often in the civil-rights years, during the Little Rock school crisis in 1958, the University of Mississippi riots in 1962, at Selma in 1965, and in many other locales as well.

The oligarchic, one-dimensional, closed, and inflexible Solid South system that served Black Belt elites so well was shattered in the 1950s and 1960s. These two decades were the watershed years between the politics begun so long ago by Calhoun and his generation and the emerging, as yet undefined politics of the current generation. Many developments in this era transformed the style and substance of southern politics, from the region's increased prosperity to the reemergence of a two-party system with

John Tower's election to the Senate from Texas in 1961 on the Republican ticket, victories of the Goldwater forces in 1964, Republican gains in the off-year congressional elections of 1966, and Nixon's wins in 1968 and 1972. The black protest movement was led by a native son, Dr. Martin Luther King, Jr., and the national Democratic party's push for civil rights resulted in the Civil Rights Act of 1964 and the Voting Rights Act of 1965. The seminal court case, *Brown* v. *Board of Education* (1954), ruled segregated schools in violation of the Fourteenth Amendment's "equal protection clause," and another case, *Baker* v. *Carr* (1962), began the process of fair apportionment.

The American nation embarked on its third century with over 4 million southern blacks registered to vote. There were 2,000 black officials in the region; its schools were more desegregated than the rest of the country's; it boasted a rapidly growing population, an expanding economy, and a developing two-party system. Now in the states of Mississippi, Louisiana, and Georgia, blacks constitute approximately 25 percent of the electorate, and they are a force to be reckoned with throughout the South. In a real sense the election of 1976 was, like that famous one a century earlier, one of redemption. Walker Percy summed up the change nicely in the late 1970s: "The South has entered the mainstream of American life for the first time in perhaps 150 years, that is, in a sense that has not been the case since the 1820s or '30s."

The South's role in contemporary national politics is much more akin to the pre-Calhoun, pre-Civil War era than to the century or more of political resistance and isolation that followed. National issues, from abortion to foreign affairs, educational reform, and budgetary matters, are as important in the South as elsewhere. Presidential elections are now vigorously contested throughout Dixie. In 1984, for example, South Carolina native Jesse Jackson made a credible race for the Democratic nomination, and the 13 March southern primaries in Alabama, Florida, and Georgia proved of crucial importance to him. Jackson's campaign and the primaries, dubbed "Super Tuesday" by the media, received extensive national attention.

Southern political leaders who exercise great national influence include Republican senator Jesse Helms (N.C.), former Senate majority leader Howard Baker (Tenn.), and the current assistant minority leader in the House, Trent Lott (Miss.). Democratic senators Sam Nunn (Ga.), Lloyd Bentson (Tex.), and John Stennis (Miss.) wield significant power on the other side of the aisle, and Jim Wright (Tex.) was Speaker of the House from 1987 until 1989. Governor Lamar Alexander of Tennessee, a Republican, assumed the chair of the National Governors' Conference in 1985, while Mayor Ernest Morial of New Orleans, a Democrat, became chairperson of the National Mayors' Conference the following year.

Because of the changing political scene plus population growth—which saw every southern state outstrip the national average of 11.4 percent in the 1970s, thereby giving the region eight additional congressional seats and electoral votes—and an economic performance better than the nation as a whole, some believe America is in the midst of a historic shift in power to the "Sunbelt," the South and West. If this proves true, then the South's role in national politics will be even more critical in the future.

See also BLACK LIFE: Politics, Black; HISTORY AND MANNERS articles; SOCIAL CLASS: Politics and Social Class; WOMEN'S LIFE: Politics, Women in

Jimmy Lea
University of Southern Mississippi

Numan Bartley and Hugh Davis Graham, *Southern Politics and the Second Reconstruction* (1975); Jack Bass and Walter DeVries, *The Transformation of Southern Politics: Social Change and Political Consequences since 1945* (1976); W. J. Cash, *The Mind of the South* (1941); William C. Havard, ed., *The Changing Politics of the South* (1972); V. O. Key, Jr., *Southern Politics in State and Nation* (1949); Alexander P. Lamis, *The Two-Party South* (1984); Donald R. Matthews and James W. Prothro, *Negroes and the New Southern Politics* (1966); T. Harry Williams, *Romance and Realism In Southern Politics* (1961). ☆

One-Party Politics

IIIIIIIIIIIIIIIIIIIIIIIIIIIIIIIIIIIIIIIIIIIIIII

The disfranchisement of practically all blacks and many white have-nots in the period between 1890 and 1910 decimated the Republican and Populist parties in the South and left the region with only a single important political party. In the era of classic one-party politics, roughly 1910–50, Democrats monopolized state offices and deterred serious opposition in general elections. The national political interests of white southerners were likewise managed exclusively by Democrats; the region regularly cast all of its electoral college votes for Democratic presidential candidates and sent virtually all Democrats to the House of Representatives and the Senate.

As a consequence of the decline in meaningful interparty competition, general elections in the region became empty rituals. Less than one-fifth of the eligible electorate voted in any four-year wave of gubernatorial general elections in the South from 1920 through 1951. Interest in electoral politics, meager as it was, shifted to the relatively new arena of Democratic nominating primaries, which were initially regarded as voluntary organizations open only to whites. In the Democratic primaries, turnout usually exceeded one-fifth of the eligible electorate but never included as many as three-tenths of the potential electorate in the 1920–51 era. One-party politics helped to "anesthetize" or "sterilize" between two-thirds and four-fifths of the region's white adults. As a consequence, politicians representing the interests of more affluent southerners usually triumphed over spokesmen for the region's have-nots.

Until fairly recently the campaigns that counted in the South were conducted as a politics of faction rather than a politics of party, as a struggle among groups of rival Democrats as opposed to a battle between Democrats and Republicans. It is useful to distinguish between *faction* (any subunit of a political party) and *factional system* (the pattern of competition among factions). Students of factional systems have typically followed V. O. Key's lead in identifying three varieties of intraparty competition based on the number of factions seeking a particular office and the distribution of the first primary vote among the factions: unifactionalism, where one faction wins a commanding majority of the vote; bifactionalism, where the vote is divided more or less evenly between two

Election posters along a Mississippi roadside, 1968

factions; and multifactionalism, where the vote is split, not necessarily evenly, among three or more factions.

By far the most common electoral situation in the 1920–49 era was multifactionalism, which appeared in 70 percent of the first gubernatorial primary elections. This outcome was hardly surprising. Because ambitious politicians were plentiful while opportunities to win the governorship were rare, multifactionalism would have been the natural mode of intraparty competition once the Democratic party's dominance in general elections had been established. The most plausible deterrent to multifactionalism is the candidacy of an incumbent governor, whose usual advantages in campaign fundraising, name and face recognition, patronage, and the like should discourage some challengers from running against him. Southern governors, however, were denied by law from succeeding themselves in states with four-year terms; though succession in states with two-year terms was constitutional, most governors limited their aspirations to two two-year terms. Accordingly, most gubernatorial primaries in the South were efforts to fill open seats, which simply reinforced the attractiveness of the governorship to many candidates.

The other patterns of factional cleavage appeared less frequently. Unifactionalism was present in approximately one-fifth of the gubernatorial contests and was the most common form of factional competition in only a single state (Virginia). Bifactional cleavage was even less likely to occur (13 percent of the elections). Tennessee and Georgia provided most of the examples of conflict between two groups of rival Democrats.

When the form of intraparty competition is related to the type of faction that usually won nomination, four central tendencies can be distinguished in intraparty politics in the southern states: bifactional primaries won by successful durable factions (Tennessee), unifactional primaries won by successful durable factions (Virginia), multifactional primaries won by successful durable factions (Louisiana, Mississippi, Alabama, North Carolina, and Georgia), and, as the most chaotic and disorganized of all systems, multifactional primaries won by moderately successful transient factions (Florida, Texas, South Carolina, and Arkansas).

In national presidential politics the Solid South actually ended during the mid-20th-century period covered by Key in *Southern Politics*. Not since 1944 have all 11 former Confederate states voted for the Democratic presidential nominee. The most recent approximation of regional solidarity for the Democrats occurred in 1976, when 10 southern states were carried by Jimmy Carter, but it was short lived and a poor imitation of the real thing. The disintegration of the Solid South has deprived the national Democrats of crucial electoral college votes and has required the Democrats to be disproportionately successful outside the South in order to win the presidency.

Southern congressional delegations remained overwhelmingly Democratic for a longer period. From the late 1930s until the late 1950s most non-southern Senate and House seats were held by Republicans, and only the Democrats' near-monopoly on southern Senate and House seats enabled the Democrats to control both houses of Congress. The weakness of the Democratic party outside the South permitted conservative southern Democrats to exert considerable influence on public policy and, in particular, to prevent passage of meaningful civil rights legislation. Once the white conservatives from the region lost the ability to control the agenda of race relations, the rationale for sending only Democrats to Congress from the South was weakened considerably.

Merle Black
University of North Carolina at Chapel Hill

Earl Black
University of South Carolina

Earl Black and Merle Black, Politics and Society in the South (1987), in *Contemporary Southern Political Attitudes and Behavior*, ed. Laurence W. Moreland, Tod A. Baker, and Robert P. Steed (1982); Bradley C. Canon, *American Journal of Political Science* (November 1978); Malcolm E. Jewell and David M. Olson, *American State Political Parties and Elections* (1978); V. O. Key, Jr., *Southern Politics in State and Nation* (1949); J. Morgan Kousser, *The Shaping of Southern Politics: Suffrage Restriction and the Establishment of the One-Party South, 1880–1910* (1974). ☆

Partisan Politics

||||||||||||||||||||||||||||||||||||||||

The dominance of a one-party political system in the South after the Civil War and into the mid-20th century belies the existence of earlier two-party systems in the South. Party systems before the Civil War were influenced by the same concerns of personality, ideology, and organization as elsewhere in the country.

The first partisan conflict in the southern United States emerged in the 1790s and led to the appearance of the Federalist party and the Democratic-Republican party. The Federalists in the South were strongest in South Carolina and, to a lesser degree, Virginia and North Carolina. It was a party of merchants, planters, lawyers, editors, speculators, and those, in general, who profited from the national financial politics of Alexander Hamilton in the George Washington Administration. The Federalists declined after 1800, though, as Thomas Jefferson's Democratic-Republicans gained control of the presidency and Congress in that year's elections. Jefferson's party was strong in the South and West from its beginnings and came to stand for local control of government, financial conservatism, and an ideology of individual freedom. The party gradually absorbed Federalist supporters and policies until the South—like the nation—had a virtual one-party system from 1816 to 1828.

After the election of Andrew Jackson as president in 1828, a new party system slowly appeared—the Democratic party of Jackson and the Whig party of Henry Clay and Daniel Webster. Recent studies suggest little philosophical or class difference between the groups, with the personality of Jackson and the organi-

zational techniques of the Democrats at first giving them dominance in the South as elsewhere.

The Reconstruction era after the Civil War witnessed the first partisan conflict between blacks and whites in southern history. Blacks identified with the Republican party—which had emerged as a northern, free-soil political group in the 1850s—while most southern whites moved into the Democratic party. The latter called itself the conservative Democratic party through most of the late 19th century to separate itself, to a degree, from the national Democrats and to attract pre-Civil War Whigs. From the end of Reconstruction in 1877 to the 1960s partisan politics in the South was, in most areas, conducted within a one-party framework.

The annals of American regional partisan change have rarely, if ever, witnessed such a dramatic transformation as occurred in the South from the 1960s to the 1980s. When the national Democratic party effectively advocated equal rights for blacks in the early 1960s, the rationale for the South's unique one-party system collapsed, blacks entered the political process with strong federal support, and the present top-heavy two-party system took hold throughout the 11 states of the former Confederacy.

The overriding purpose of the one-party system was to preserve white supremacy, the argument being that if whites divided their votes blacks would hold the balance of power. This reasoning was destroyed in the mid-1960s when national Democratic leaders "betrayed" the white South and pushed passage of the Civil Rights Act of 1964 and the Voting Rights Act of 1965. The partisan impact of these events was reinforced by the highly publicized opposition to the Civil Rights Act of

1964 by Republican presidential nominee Barry Goldwater. In November 1964 President Lyndon B. Johnson won a landslide Democratic victory nationwide, but Goldwater swept the Deep South, carrying Mississippi, always an extreme case, with 87.1 percent of the vote.

The national Democratic party's civil rights activism unleashed a torrent of Republican activity in the region. The fuel for this GOP spurt was white antagonism toward all things remotely connected with the national Democratic party integrationists. Figure 2 pinpoints the Republican leap forward to the mid-1960s. There was, however, another feature to the GOP's rise that was separable, if not always separated, from the race issue. With the collapse of the one-party system, the economic and philosophical divisions found in party politics outside the South—dating from the class-oriented New Deal realignment—had an opportunity to descend into the region's emerging partisan structure. Thus, in the forefront of the nascent southern GOP movement were well-to-do businessmen and professionals seeking to help along this process in order to give the region's economic conservatives a permanent home. And the southern Republican party made its most faithful converts among those attracted by the party's conservative position on economic-class issues.

Simultaneously, however, the race issue became enmeshed in the emerging class-based two-party system that seemed to be taking hold in the post-1964 period. Twisted into the situation was the logical compatibility of conservative economic-class Republicanism with the racial protest. The GOP, as the party philosophically opposed to an activist federal government in economic matters, gained adherents also from those who objected to federal intervention to end racial segregation in the states.

Steady Republican growth ended in the early 1970s when the race issue abated sufficiently to result in a mild resurgence on the part of the region's transformed Democratic party, which had gradually shed its segregationist leaders after blacks entered the electorate in large numbers. Figure 2 reflects this mid-1970s Democratic gain by showing a dip in Republican fortunes in those years. The resurgence was accomplished by clever white Democratic politicians who recognized that the post–civil rights era offered them the potential to put together an effective black-white alliance. This biracial coalition is composed of those traditionally Democratic white voters who returned to their party in the 1970s as the race issue eased *and* of southern blacks, who carried strong Democratic allegiance in gratitude for what the national party did for them during the 1960s. It became a mere matter of arithmetic in some states—especially in the Deep South—for the Republicans to realize that this black-white Democratic alliance arrayed against them was a powerful one indeed.

The irony present in the situation—namely, that the traditional party of segregation in the South should become the home of, and dependent on, black voters—did not escape Republican notice. One Georgia Republican party chairman ruefully bemoaned the existence of this diverse Democratic coalition that had demolished the once bright GOP potential in his state, complaining that there was "no tie-in" between the twin pillars of the Georgia Democracy—rural, small-town whites of south Geor-

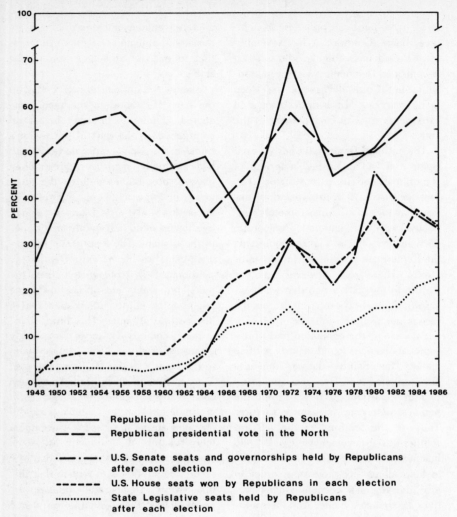

Figure 2. The Uneven Growth of the Republican Party in the South, 1948–1986

Source: Alexander P. Lamis, **The Two-Party South** *(1984).*

gia and blacks. "They're as far apart as night and day," he noted. And yet, "They're voting hand in hand, and . . . they're squeezing the lives out of us."

This disparate southern Democratic coalition contained serious tensions. Through the early 1980s the alliance held together—although the national victory of Ronald Reagan in 1980 gave the southern GOP a boost—primarily as the result of the canny maneuvers of white moderate leaders, who were its chief beneficiaries. These leaders walked a political tightrope that required Olympian balancing because racial distrust and class antagonisms constantly threatened to divide the coalition's contradictory elements. The alliance's future well-being could be threatened if left-leaning Democratic leaders supplant them and champion the economic interests of, as V. O. Key, Jr., said, "those who have less" of both races. In such an event, more and more white conservative Democrats could be expected to move to the Republican party, a development that would complete the penetration of national party cleavages into the region's once isolated partisan life. The flaring of racial antagonism in the South would also have the same effect of driving white Democrats into the arms of the GOP, although in this case the defecting whites would probably come equally from all economic groups.

See also BLACK LIFE: Politics, Black; WOMEN'S LIFE: Politics, Women in

Alexander P. Lamis
University of Mississippi

Lance Banning, *The Jeffersonian Persuasion: Evolution of a Party Ideology* (1978); Numan Bartley, *The Rise of Massive Resistance: Race and Politics in the South during the 1950s* (1969); Jack Bass and Walter DeVries, *The Transformation of Southern Politics: Social Change and Political Consequence since 1945* (1976); William J. Cooper, Jr., *Liberty and Slavery: Southern Politics to 1860* (1983); Alexander Heard, *A Two-Party South?* (1952); Richard Hofstadter, *The Idea of a Party System: The Rise of Legitimate Opposition in the United States, 1780–1840* (1969); V. O. Key, Jr., *Southern Politics in State and Nation* (1949); Alexander P. Lamis, *The Two-Party South* (1984); Richard P. McCormick, *The Second American Party System: Party Formation in the Jacksonian Era* (1966); C. Vann Woodward, *Origins of the New South, 1877–1913* (1951). ☆

Protest Movements

When Tom Watson, the one-time Georgia Populist, was asked the difference between his campaign and the one run by William Jennings Bryan, he replied, "Bryan had *no everlasting* and overshadowing *Negro Question* to hamper *and handicap his progress*: I HAD." Historians may quarrel about what makes the South different from the rest of the nation—a lost cause, secession, poverty, an agrarian tradition, race. But most would agree, along with Tom Watson, that the issue of race relations has dominated, hindered, and shaped protest movements in southern society.

The South emerged from the Civil War as a region committed politically to the Democratic party. The Democrats had supported both slavery and secession. Moreover, white southerners blamed the Republican party for Reconstruction, which allowed black folks to participate in the political process, an activity that implied racial equality. That was a concept the vast majority of southern whites repudiated. In addition, Reconstruction occurred simultaneously with the first postwar panic (1870–76); Republicans were thus identified with depression and agricultural poverty. By 1877 the "Solid South" stood solidly for the memory of the Confederacy and the Democratic party.

There were, however, cracks in the frame that held the Solid South together. Isolated areas with large black populations elected some Republicans to public offices. Within the Democratic party, both agrarian and conservative—sometimes called Bourbon or Redeemer—constituencies existed. The latter, committed to the New South, warned agrarians that to break with the Democracy would simply bring those black Republicans back into power, destroying both the white man's party and any chance for economic prosperity. Instead, Redeemers argued, the cost of government should be held down, white immigration into the region encouraged, crops diversified, and government stabilized, through the auspices of the Democratic party; eventually, they argued, such acts of austerity and change would bring new industries and prosperity to the New South.

Until 1885 or so, most farmers were willing to heed such pleas. The agrarians, however, always applied pressure to the uneasy alliance between the conservative haves and the farming have-nots. Consequently the Patrons of Husbandry, or the Grange, as it was more popularly called, enlisted 220,000 white southern farmers into its cause. The organization advocated crop diversification, economic cooperatives, and social and educational activities, but eschewed politics. Where possible, it sent representatives to Redeemer constitutional conventions. There Grangers took the lead in defeating poll tax provisions, passing laws that defined railroads as public carriers, and supporting any measure that held down the cost of government. The Patrons of Husbandry opposed both Republicans and third parties. Certainly the issue of race and politics inhibited Granger political protest, yet the organization's limited dissent from the New South orthodoxy was always watched with suspicion by the more conservative Redeemers.

The organization did train potential political protesters. Indeed, some contemporary observers maintained that the Greenback crusade attracted so many Grangers that the Patrons of Husbandry died. The Greenbackers, who wanted to issue legal tender notes to counteract agricultural depressions, organized third parties in Arkansas, Alabama, Texas, Kentucky, West Virginia, and Mississippi—all states with large Granger constituencies. These protest movements ran candidates for local offices in 1876 and for statewide offices in 1878 and 1880, when James B. Weaver was a presidential candidate. The party, although optimistic, ran well only in Texas, Oklahoma, and Kentucky. Tom Watson explained its failure: "The Democrats . . . wrote Greenback platforms, and then said to receding Greenbackers, 'Don't leave your old party; get your reforms inside the party; we white people of the South cannot afford to divide.' " Thus the policy of the Democratic party toward political dissenters in the Solid South was to co-opt, use racial issues to divide, and promise moderate reforms. To a large measure, that policy never changed, and never did it succeed as well as in its defeat of southern Populism.

Populism grew from a sizable number of agricultural societies that appeared as the Grange declined. Historians have designated the Farmers' Alliance, first organized in Lampasas, Tex., in 1875, as the oldest of these voluntary associations. After intermittent stops and starts, the organization began again in 1879 and claimed 50,000 members by 1885. That same period, however, produced organizations throughout the South, such as Reliefmen in Mississippi, Brothers of Freedom and Commonwealth Organizations in Louisiana, the Cross Timbers of Texas, the Arkansas Agricultural Wheel, and the Farmers' Union of Louisiana. In short, southern farmers awaited only a charismatic leader to unite them in an agrarian crusade.

Charles W. Macune of Texas was that

man. In 1886 he took over the Texas Farmers' Alliance. Within two years, he joined that organization with the Farmers' Union of Louisiana and the Agricultural Wheel of Arkansas, and the National Farmers' Alliance and Industrial Union, called the Southern Farmers' Alliance, was born. By 1890 the Southern Alliance claimed 3 million members, recruiting not only in all the southern states but in Kansas and the Dakotas as well. In addition, 1.3 million black people joined an affiliate known as the Colored Alliance. These organizations advocated free silver, improved public services, governmental control or regulation of public transportation, no convict leasing, repeal of the national bank act, fairer taxation laws, national and state election reforms, and the subtreasury plan. By 1890 no southern politician could ignore Alliance demands.

Ironically, Macune's organization spun off a political party more radical than most of its members. The key was the subtreasury plan. Macune proposed that subtreasuries be located throughout rural areas and that these government warehouses loan farmers, at 1 percent interest in legal tender notes, up to 80 percent of the value of staple crops. This plan attacked both banks and furnishing merchants and created a flexible currency. Orthodox Democratic politicians could not endorse this scheme, even when radical members of the Alliance demanded that local and state officeholders embrace the subtreasury, warning that failure to do so would mean that farmers would choose an opposition candidate. The result was a third-party movement that spread throughout the South during the depression years of the 1890s. The Populist party would divide and destroy the Alliance, but it became the major challenge on the left to Democratic hegemony in the Gilded Age.

Democratic politicians struck back in two ways. First, the party moved to the left. James S. Hogg of Texas, John B. Gordon of Georgia, James Z. George of Mississippi, Ben Tillman of South Carolina, and Zebulon Vance of North Carolina, for example, all argued that they supported Alliance platforms but opposed such radical measures as government ownership of railroads and the subtreasury. They in turn passed moderate reforms, such as commission regulation, and spoke for free silver. Their slight move to the left prevented a massive switch of dirt farmers from the Democratic to the Populist party.

The second maneuver was even more effective politically, longer lasting, and absolutely devastating to Populist hopes. The Democrats used racism to destroy the third party. Populists called for an alliance between poor blacks and whites. Their platforms denounced lynching and convict leasing and asked for guarantees of black suffrage. White Democrats charged that the unholy alliance of blacks and whites would corrupt southern morality and return the hated Republican party to power. Meanwhile, southern conservatives shamelessly bought and intimidated black voters and used the free machinery of the state to cheat or "count-out" from office many successful Populist candidates.

After the death of Leonidas Polk of North Carolina in June 1892, southern Populists lacked a popular presidential contender. James B. Weaver, the old Greenbacker from Iowa, won the nomination in 1892. Conservatives reclaimed much of what they had lost in 1890, and in no southern state did Weaver win 40 percent of the vote. The panic of 1893 refueled the Populist charge. Democrats defeated their greatest challenge in 1894 by seizing silver as an issue, exploiting racism, proposing moderate reform, and controlling party machinery. In 1896 silver forces controlled the Democratic convention and nominated William Jennings Bryan, who carried the South but not the nation, and Populists saw their victories of 1892 and 1894 melt away, as white, upland farmers returned to the Democratic party.

The Democrats, however, and their opponents needed to chain the unleashed racism. Conservatives and liberals alike argued that politics could not be purified until blacks were disfranchised. Consequently, southern politicians began with poll taxes and continued through Jim Crow laws, carving out a separate and unequal society. The poll tax legislation that disfranchised blacks did the same to most poor whites. Conservatives thus used the specter of Reconstruction to restrict the left in the South. They convinced small farmers to reject third parties and their own economic welfare by threatening "Negro domination," and they convinced the same group to disfranchise part of their own numbers and to remain in support of conservative politics to keep the black in a subordinate position. The left never overcame the myth of "Negro Domination."

Consequently, the two great events of 19th-century southern history, the Civil War and the agrarian revolts, left the Democratic party in control; political wars pitted one faction of that party against another. Occasionally the left would secede briefly and challenge the Democrats. Socialism claimed voting strength ranging from 20 percent of the electorate in Oklahoma to 32 percent in South Carolina in 1912. The xenophobia produced by World War I, however, ended the socialist crusade in the South

as elsewhere. Likewise, negrophobia, in particular the outcry in the region against Booker T. Washington's friendship with Teddy Roosevelt, eliminated any appeal that the National Progressive party might have had in the South. The first three decades or so of the 20th century thus saw the left organize the Farmers' Union, voluntary acreage associations, and economic cooperatives, and support such moderate reformers as Hoke Smith of Georgia and Braxton B. Comer of Alabama.

Conservatives retained control of the South until the New Deal. Franklin Roosevelt's policies galvanized southern politics because the region was so poor. Conservative Democrats came quickly to fear that the New Deal threatened their control of the southern economy with legislation like the Tennessee Valley Authority and the activities of the Department of Agriculture. They identified the Congress of Industrial Organizations, the Southern Tenant Farmers' Union, and the Farm Security Administration as political threats. Conservatives believed rightly that these federal and radical organizations sprang from the New Deal reform impulse.

Once more, conservatives turned to race to protect their economic interests. Many southern whites resented the New Deal's drive to win over urban voters, and its consequent appeal to northern blacks. Although certainly not color blind, the New Deal offered economic and social programs that included endorsement of a Fair Employment Practices Commission, antilynching legislation, and repeal of the poll tax; later came Harry Truman's Fair Deal, integration of the armed services, and civil rights legislation. The conservative wing of the Democratic party struck back. In 1944 corporation lawyers, well-to-do businessmen, representatives of industry, and Black Belt conservatives organized the Jeffersonian Democrats in Texas, Mississippi, and South Carolina. In 1948 others in the Deep South joined this group and ran South Carolina Governor Strom Thurmond for president on a Dixiecrat ticket. Dixiecrats carried only South Carolina, Alabama, Mississippi, and Louisiana, but battlelines were once more drawn and race was once more the central issue of southern politics.

As southern conservatives cooperated with the Republican party in the national Congress, supported Dwight D. Eisenhower in 1952 and 1956, and criticized the northern Democrats as being anti-South, the southern left endorsed and fought for the national Democratic party. Liberal southerners created such organizations as the Democrats of Texas, and endorsed such politicians as Senator Ralph Yarborough (Texas) or William Fulbright (Arkansas)—all activities designed to commit southern Democrats to the national party's goals. A major goal after 1954 was, increasingly, an integrated society, and the cause of the southern left became first and foremost integration. Conservatives' goals were to prevent it. Racism was used, as against Populism, as a barrier to any economic or social reform.

In the 1960 presidential race Richard Nixon formulated the "Southern Strategy," implying federal foot-dragging on integration in exchange for a conservative, Republican South. It was not successful in 1960, but in 1972 Nixon succeeded and the Solid South in some places is now more solidly Republican than Democratic.

The Republican party in the South is composed largely of whites. Partially this is in reaction to the civil rights movement of the 1960s, a crusade endorsed by the southern left. As SNCC, CORE, and the SCLC fought for equality, and Dr. Martin Luther King, Jr., Stokely Carmichael, and James Farmer advocated civil rights, their cause dominated all other liberal concerns. The national Democratic party endorsed these goals, and it won the support of southern blacks and other minorities. The 1960s witnessed triumphs for equality: the Civil Rights Act of 1964, the Voting Rights Act of 1965, the end of the poll tax, and an increase in black and brown voters. The left predicted that a political coalition of blacks, browns, feminists, poor whites, liberals, and progressives would seize the South and bring about a myriad of reforms. Then, in the late 1960s, the antiwar movement swept the country and hopes of a broad coalition collapsed, as southern whites rebelled against black power, the student movement, feminism, and reform.

George Wallace led a major southern protest movement in the late 1960s and early 1970s, drawing supporters from a white backlash against the black freedom movement and liberal reform activities in general. Wallace was the charismatic governor of Alabama who first came into office in 1962 vowing "segregation forever." Using populist rhetoric and appealing to rural and working-class voters, Wallace mounted a major third-party effort in 1968, carrying Alabama, Arkansas, Georgia, Louisiana, and Mississippi in the presidential campaign. After an assassin's bullet crippled Wallace in 1972, his influence on national politics waned, but he remained a force in Deep South politics until the late 1970s.

By 1984 the left in the South, as well as in the nation, was in disarray. De jure segregation, but not de facto, had ceased to exist. Civil rights no longer was the bellwether of reform. The left concentrated simply on defeating maneuvers of Republicans to roll back the New Deal, Fair Deal, Great Society, and Supreme Court mandates for civil rights. Most southern blacks were Democrats, and most southern whites were Republicans. Consequently, party battles, in the South as in the nation, revolved around a liberal Democratic versus a conservative Republican party rather than third parties or a Solid South.

See also BLACK LIFE: Freedom Movement, Black; Politics, Black; HISTORY AND MANNERS: Jacksonian Democracy; Jeffersonian Tradition; New Deal; Populism; Progressivism; LAW: Civil Rights Movement; SOCIAL CLASS: Communism; Marxist History; Politics and Social Class; Religion and Social Class; Socialism

Robert A. Calvert
Texas A&M University

Numan Bartley, *The Rise of Massive Resistance: Race and Politics in the South during the 1950s* (1960); Carl N. Degler, *The Other South: Southern Dissenters in the Nineteenth Century* (1982); Lawrence Goodwyn, *Democratic Promise: The Populist Moment in America* (1976); Dewey Grantham, *Southern Progressivism: The Reconciliation of Progress and Tradition* (1983); James R. Green, *Grass-roots Socialism: Radical Movements in the Southwest, 1895–1943* (1978); John B. Kirby, *Black Americans in the Roosevelt Era: Liberalism and Race* (1980); Robert C. McMath, *The Populist Vanguard: A History of the Southern Farmers' Alliance* (1975); Theodore Saloutos, *Farmer Movements in the South, 1865–1933* (1960); Harvard Sitkoff, *The Struggle for Black Equality, 1954–1980* (1981). ☆

Segregation, Defense of
||||||||||||||||||||||||||||||||||||||||||||||||||||||||

The 17 May 1954 Supreme Court decision in *Brown* v. *Board of Education* is frequently perceived as the start of both the Second Reconstruction and the white South's struggle to maintain the racial status quo. To be sure, the *Brown* decision had the type of crystallizing impact in the South that the Court's ruling a century earlier in *Dred Scott* v. *Sanford* had had in the North. Both decisions were followed by regional efforts to thwart the law of the land. Still, the perception that the Supreme Court in 1954 inaugurated a new era of federal involvement on behalf of the nation's black citizens is false. Moreover, southern resistance to federal attacks on segregation was ongoing.

During the decade prior to the *Brown* decision, for example, the Supreme Court had invalidated the white primary, ordered blacks admitted to all-white graduate and law schools, struck at racial segregation on interstate carriers, and barred states from enacting legislation designed to enforce racially restrictive property covenants. The President's Committee on Civil Rights was created by President Truman in 1946. Truman also ordered the desegregation of the armed forces.

Although all the aforementioned actions had not occurred prior to the 1948 National Democratic Convention, southern politicians clearly knew by that date the way the wind was blowing. Of special concern to white southerners was the report of the President's Committee on Civil Rights. *To Secure These Rights* (1947) contained 35 recommendations that touched upon virtually every facet of racial discrimination, including education, the armed forces, employment, and voting rights. When a majority of the delegates to the party's 1948 national convention adopted a strong civil rights platform, the entire Mississippi delegation and much of the Alabama delegation bolted the convention. A few days later segregationists from the South held a convention in Birmingham, where they created the States' Rights Democratic Party (Dixiecrats) and nominated Governor J. Strom Thurmond of South Carolina as their presidential candidate. The hope of the Dixiecrats was to secure enough electoral votes to prevent victory by either the Republicans or Democrats; the election would then be decided in the House of Representatives. In the House, according to the plan, the South would be able to negotiate a regional compromise that would protect the southern pattern of race relations. Although the States' Rights Democrats failed, they did focus attention on the "threat from Washington."

In many ways the Supreme Court decisions of the 1940s, the adoption of a civil rights platform by the Democrats in 1948, and the actions of President Truman were a prelude to the events that would follow the *Brown* decision. Indeed, the cumulative effect of the actions of all three branches of the national government was to abolish legal racial discrimination. Such a drastic change over a short time was, of course, resisted by many white southerners. The southern effort to resist change was based on an outdated philosophy and involved legal tactics, economic pressure, and violence.

Southern ideology had at its core the interrelated ideas of racial superiority and the natural order of things. According to the natural order argument, everything in nature had its proper place. In the words of a Florida jurist, "fish in the sea segregate in schools of their kind." The judge, as noted by Numan Bartley in *The Rise of Massive Resistance* (1969), used the example in an opinion that justified segregation. White southerners generally believed that the natural place for blacks was below that of whites. Quite simply, whites believed that blacks were inherently inferior.

The primary disseminators of literature that focused on the alleged inferiority of blacks were the Citizens' Councils of America (CCA) and the various state Citizens' Councils. These organizations had their beginning in Mississippi as part of the reaction to the *Brown* ruling. At first the Citizens' Councils concentrated on the school issue, but as the civil rights protest expanded, council members fought to maintain all forms of segregation. Unlike the Ku Klux Klan, the Citizens' Councils rejected the use of violence.

Convinced that the average white northerner held essentially the same racial beliefs as white southerners, the CCA embarked upon a propaganda campaign designed to demonstrate black inferiority. One tract cited in Neil R. McMillen's *Citizens' Council* (1971) lists the "eleven most essential differences between the two races." As was the case with racist literature of an earlier era, the CCA handbook contended that there were differences between the eyes, ears, hair, lips, noses, cheekbones, jaws, skulls, and voices of whites and blacks. Of special significance was an alleged difference in brain weight. *Racial Facts*, a publication of the Mississippi Council, asserted that the IQ of blacks was between 15 and 20 points below the average for whites.

Segregationists were especially prone to utilize the writings of Carleton Putnam and Carleton Coon. Putnam, a native of the North and a retired airline executive, was the author of *Race and Reason: A Yankee View* (1961). He first came to the attention of segregationists in 1958 through an open letter to President Eisenhower in which he defended segregation. In *Race and Reason* Putnam asserted that blacks were intellectually inferior and that the American public had been misled by a "pseudoscientific hoax" put forth by anthropologists who were advocates of "racial equipotentiality."

Coon, a former president of the American Association of Physical Anthropologists, was the author of *The Origin of Races* (1962). In this study Coon concluded that over 500,000 years ago one species of man, *homo erectus*, existed. According to Coon, *homo erectus* evolved into *homo sapiens* at different times and in different geographic locations. Five such evolutionary processes occurred. His research also led Coon to conclude that Caucasoids were about 500,000 years ahead of Negroids in terms of evolutionary development.

Segregationists, both those belonging to Citizens' Councils and those holding political office, frequently cited the writings of Coon and Putnam. Southerners were interested in the two men because of the belief that such individuals gave credibility to the segregationists' perspective. Credibility was essential to any campaign designed to convince northerners that the South should be allowed to continue its way of life.

From a political perspective southerners resorted to the compact theory of government in their effort to overturn the *Brown* decision and to protect regional values. Drawing upon the writings of Jefferson and Calhoun, southern theorists concluded that the *Brown* ruling was unconstitutional. According to this rationale, public education was constitutionally a function of the states and not the federal government. Therefore, the Supreme Court had exceeded its authority by amending the Constitution, rather than merely interpreting it. In the effort to nullify the Court's action, southern politicians proposed to utilize the tools of massive resistance and interposition.

Interposition, a doctrine adopted by eight southern states in 1956 and 1957, was designed to defeat court-ordered desegregation. Under the plan, the sovereignty of the state would be interposed between the federal courts and local school officials. Advocates of the doctrine were convinced that federal judges would not issue contempt of court citations and jail governors and other elected state officials who refused to obey desegregation orders. Critical to the success of the plan was regionwide noncompliance. Total or near-total opposition to desegregation would persuade northerners to abandon efforts to force the South to give up its way of life.

The campaign for massive resistance was encouraged by southerners serving in Congress. In 1956 all but 27 of the southerners in Congress signed a "Southern Manifesto" in which they urged the states to resist integration. Likewise, pressure was brought to bear upon newspaper editors to ensure that they not encourage compliance with the law. And in Orangeburg, S.C., economic pressure was applied to those black parents who had petitioned to have their children attend desegregated schools; the schools in Orangeburg remained segregated. Meanwhile, schools in portions of some states (Prince Edward County, Va., for example) were closed to prevent integration. Several states favored the idea of closing the public schools and providing tuition grants to students who would attend private segregated schools. Finally, in four states (Alabama, Mississippi, Florida, and Georgia) the doctrine of nullification was implemented as legal action was taken to declare the *Brown* decision to be null and void. In these four states, as well as others in the old Confederacy, over 450 new segregation measures were passed. The new laws protected segregation and made desegregation illegal.

With the coming of the sit-in movement and the freedom rides of the 1960s, violence began to characterize part of the resistance to change. In *SNCC: The New Abolitionists* (1964), Howard Zinn describes the violence that confronted civil rights workers. Among the more prominent acts of violence perpetrated upon civil rights workers were the fire-bombing of a bus carrying freedom riders at Anniston, Ala. (1961), the murders in Mississippi of Medgar Evers (1963) and of three civil rights fieldworkers—Andrew Goodman, James Chaney, and Michael Schwerner (1964), and the police violence of law enforcement officials in Birmingham, Ala. (1963). In Birmingham police used fire hoses and police dogs against demonstrators, many of whom were children. The use of force against civil rights activists was counterproductive. Each night citizens throughout the land who watched the evening news on television witnessed acts of violence being perpetrated upon fellow Americans. Northerners, as well as many white southerners, were shocked by the tactics of Birmingham officials. Equally disturbing to Americans was the bombing of Birmingham's Sixteenth Street Bap-

tist Church, an incident that killed four black children who were attending Sunday school. Without doubt the acts of violence destroyed any sympathy that southern propagandists had created in the North and stimulated the passage of the Civil Rights Act of 1964.

By the mid-1960s the civil rights movement had moved beyond the limits of the South and into the North's ghettoes. Here the frustrations associated with joblessness, poverty, and hopelessness led to the long hot summers of rioting, burning, and looting. As the nation's great cities burned, a white backlash against blacks became apparent. Governor George Wallace of Alabama exploited this backlash, as well as a growing working-class anger with student demonstrators, antiwar activists, and the nation's welfare system. Using a "law and order" argument that had strong racial overtones, Wallace emerged as a national political force. As the candidate of the American Independent party in 1968, he won 46 electoral votes and 13.5 percent of the popular vote.

In the final analysis, southern attempts to maintain legal segregation failed. Indeed, not one of the tactics employed brought eventual success. Americans rejected the outdated belief that blacks are inherently inferior. Interposition ultimately forced whites to decide that desegregated schools were far more preferable than no schools. Violence was counterproductive. And even a majority of the South's voters rejected the third party candidacies of Thurmond in 1948 and Wallace in 1968.

Just as there was no clearly defined beginning to the South's resistance to change, there is no clearly defined end. As legal segregation was abolished, patterns of de facto segregation emerged. Whites fled to the suburbs, argued in favor of neighborhood schools, and opposed court-ordered busing of students to achieve racially balanced schools. In the final analysis, the types of race-related problems that now exist in the South are essentially the same as those that exist elsewhere in the nation.

See also BLACK LIFE: Freedom Movement, Black; Race Relations; / Citizens' Councils; LAW: Civil Rights Movement; / *Brown* v. *Board of Education;* MYTHIC SOUTH: Racial Attitudes

William J. Brophy
Stephen F. Austin State University

Taxing and Spending

||||||||||||||||||||||||||||||||||||||||||||||||||||||

Southern state governments have long been distinguished by their relatively low levels of government spending and taxation, and by the often regressive nature of their tax systems. Three examples illustrate: (1) southern states spent an average of $1,657 per pupil for education in 1977–78, while the national average was $2,002; (2) the average southern state spent 0.11 percent of its total expenditures on land and water quality control while the national average was 0.31 percent; (3) the average southern state's Aid to Families with Dependent Children grant received an "adequacy score" of 8.09 percent while the national average was 13.58 percent.

Southern states generally obtain a greater share of their operating revenue from sales taxes than other states do, and their income-tax structures are often

less progressive. In fact, one of the few southern governmental innovations was the sales tax itself, pioneered by Mississippi in 1934. These tax patterns help to account for the widely held perception that the southern states are not normally as active, vigorous, or "forward-thinking" as the rest of the country.

Perhaps because governments are often evaluated on the basis of their taxing and spending policies, much research has been devoted to a systematic analysis of the causes and effects of the distinctive southern patterns of taxing and spending. An appreciation of the issues addressed in these studies is necessary to understand the extent to which southern cultural traditions and circumstances are related to the fiscal policies so readily observed.

The most frequently cited explanation for southern taxing and spending patterns is the traditional absence of effective party competition. V. O. Key, Jr., suggested that one-party states spend less on social programs than states with a competitive structure simply because a single dominant party does not have to advocate and implement responsive policies in order to win elections. This notion appeared to have considerable validity when it was advanced in the 1940s, because it was consistent with impressionistic and anecdotal accounts of one-party politics and because it was derived from a straightforward theory of parties and government. The degree of party competition and the level of government spending for various social programs were statistically associated when all states were compared, and this provided additional support for Key's argument.

Key's theory became widely accepted and provided a solid foundation for linking basic southern political characteristics to public policy choices. Certainly, the tradition of Democratic party dominance is a fundamental part of the southern political heritage, and it was not surprising that government expenditures reflected its influence. However, by the 1960s a different view was presented by scholars, particularly Thomas R. Dye. Low government spending and regressive taxation could be explained by economic variables. According to Dye, "when the effects of economic development are controlled . . . almost all of the association between party competition and policy disappears."

This finding, and the voluminous research that it spawned, was unsettling to many students of politics because it suggested that basic political factors, such as party competition, were not important in terms of public policy. It also directly challenged the notion that the special character of southern politics and culture was fundamentally important in explaining why southern governments behaved differently; Dye's research indicated that *any* poor, rural state would adopt the taxing and spending patterns associated with the South.

The most compelling responses to Dye's line of reasoning emphasized political culture. Daniel Elazar suggested that three political subcultures can be identified among the American states—moralistic, individualistic, and traditionalistic. The southern states generally are dominated by traditionalistic subcultures, according to Elazar, which means that their governments should be expected to "maintain traditional patterns" and to be generally conservative in public policy. Conversely, moralistic states, such as Minnesota, Oregon, and Wisconsin, use government to further a representative conception of the good of the "commonwealth." Individualistic states have both moralistic and traditionalistic traits.

In 1969 Ira Sharkansky performed a systematic comparison of the states Elazar identified as moralistic, traditionalistic, and individualistic to determine whether they actually were different in the ways Elazar predicted and, more importantly, to determine whether the differences were simply a result of differences in economic and industrial development. Sharkansky found that the cultural differences were still important after the effects of the economic variables were taken into account. Southern states, with traditionalistic cultures, spent less on certain social programs and had fewer public employees per capita than other states, even those with similar economic circumstances.

The regional norms thus identified have been persistent. Sharkansky reports that "during 1952–1974, per capita personal income in the old Confederacy went from 68 percent of the national average to 83 percent of the national average. Meanwhile, state expenditures per capita moved only slightly, from 87 percent to 88 percent of the national average."

The distinctive southern character identified by novelists, essayists, and journalists apparently has a real effect on the most tangible and concrete aspects of government—taxing and spending. Southerners are not as likely as their northern compatriots to turn to government for various social purposes or to redistribute income, even when their states become economically developed. Analysis of the more simplistic versions of V. O. Key, Jr.'s, ideas indicates, however, that the effect of southern culture on government policy is complicated, and that economic factors are critical in explaining much regional variety.

Marcus Ethridge
University of Wisconsin
at Milwaukee

Thomas R. Dye, *Politics, Economics, and the Public: Policy Outcome in the American States* (1966); Daniel Elazar, *American Federalism: A View from the States* (2d ed., 1972); Virginia Gray, Herbert Jacob, and Kenneth N. Vines, eds., *Politics in the American States: A Comparative Analysis* (1983); V. O. Key, Jr., *Southern Politics in State and Nation* (1949); Ira Sharkansky, *The Maligned States: Policy Accomplishments, Problems, and Opportunities* (2d ed., 1978). ☆

Voting
|||||||||||||||||||

"**A**mong the great democracies of the world," V. O. Key, Jr., noted in 1949, "the Southern states remain the chief considerable area in which an extremely small proportion of citizens vote." Yet the South has not always been the most backward, least democratic region in the Western world. Although other countries have, gradually or in sudden spurts, expanded the proportion of their citizens who enjoy and exercise the right to vote, the United States has followed a zig-zag, not a linear, path. Born comparatively free, America contracted as well as expanded its suffrage thereafter. In its patterns of voting participation, as in other facets of society, the South exaggerated national trends.

Suffrage theory of the colonial South, like that of the colonial North, mim-

icked Britain's. "The laws of England," the Virginia Legislature declared in 1655, "grant a voice in such election only to such as by their estates real or personal have interest enough to tie them to the endeavor of the public good." Accordingly, during most of the colonial period, only property holders could vote. Because of the much greater availability of land in the New World, however, freehold suffrage in practice enfranchised a much higher proportion of the free adult males in America than in the mother country. Substantial majorities, in Virginia as well as in Massachusetts, could and did vote. Property restrictions for officeholding, some class deference, and the common interest of large and small planters, in addition to the wider reputations and greater availability of time and money enjoyed by the economic elite, guaranteed men of standing a disproportionate share of the political posts. Yet their tenure existed only at the sufferance of their neighbors (social inferiors, but often political near equals), and they failed to pay at least rhetorical tribute to white male equality at their peril.

Two factors—legal restrictions on the suffrage and the degree of party competition—have chiefly determined voter turnout levels in the South, and, of these, the former has been much more important. As Figure 1 shows, the pattern of voter participation in the 11 ex-Confederate states was quite similar to that in the other states of the Union from 1840 through the 1880s. The massive divergence that Key noted opened up only after 1892, as southern states passed laws and standardized administrative practices that disfranchised large proportions of blacks and poorer whites. Designed to have a disproportionately adverse impact on the Republican and Populist parties, the restrictive laws virtually ended party competition in most of the South, thereby further discouraging people from voting. Even though literacy tests and other restraints on the suffrage were employed in the North as well as the South, the qualifications were not applied as severely above the Mason-Dixon line. Since 1940, as blacks gradually regained the vote and as Republicans contested more and more elections in the South, participation rates in the two sections have converged. By 1980 the difference in turnout was only 8 percent.

Although the 20th-century sectional gulf in Figure 1 is the most striking, other facets of the graph also deserve attention. In this as in many cases, the choice of the denominator presents a moral problem. Few free black males and no male slaves or women of any status were allowed to vote before 1860. Had black males, slave and emancipated, instead of only adult white males, been included in the antebellum denominators, southern turnout would have been only about two-thirds as high as northern in the antebellum period. Had women been counted, both lines would have shifted downward.

Following convention by calculating turnout on the basis of all males, regardless of race, in the denominator from 1868 to 1908, adding females in a few non-southern states in 1912 and 1916 and in all states thereafter, also hides two shifts that did *not* take place in the South. There were no overall voting declines as a result of the addition of freedmen and women to the voting polls. In 1860, 67 percent of the southern adult white males voted. In 1868, in the seven southern states that held elections, 70 percent of southern adult

males, black as well as white, turned out. When compared to the political behavior of the early- or mid-19th-century British or the late-20th-century American voter of lower social status, it seems amazing that such a large portion of the poverty-stricken, largely illiterate, recently slave population should have voted. Just as impressive, they overwhelmingly opposed the wishes of their former owners and then-current landlords. And whereas northern turnout dropped by more than 10 percent with the expansion of women's suffrage, southern women appear to have bounded off their pedestals to participate in politics in approximately the same—very low—proportion as the men.

Figure 4 lays to rest two other hoary notions. First, the left section of the graph shows that the high level of antebellum southern turnout was not merely a product of contests for the presidency or of Jacksonian democracy. Southern governors' races attracted large majorities of the adult white males long before battles for the White House did and continued to attract somewhat higher proportions of voters than presidential elections after the Old Hero retired. Second, although the Democratic primaries constituted the real elections in the first half of this century, the right portion of Figure 2 shows that turnout in those races barely exceeded that in southern presidential contests: only about one of three southern white adults generally managed to cast ballots. Competition unstructured by parties did not foster participation; blacks were not the only ones deterred by the post-Populist southern political system.

In 1938 Ralph Bunche estimated that but 4 percent of southern blacks could vote. Legal attacks on the white pri-

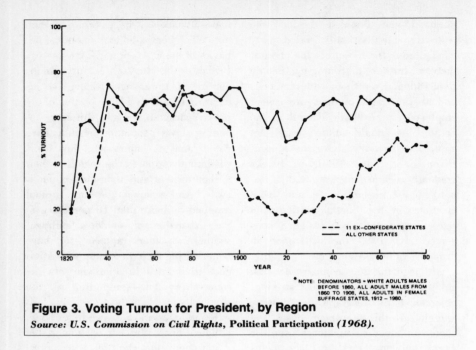

NOTE: DENOMINATORS = WHITE ADULTS MALES BEFORE 1860, ALL ADULT MALES FROM 1860 TO 1908, ALL ADULTS IN FEMALE SUFFRAGE STATES, 1912 – 1960.

Figure 3. Voting Turnout for President, by Region
Source: U.S. Commission on Civil Rights, Political Participation *(1968).*

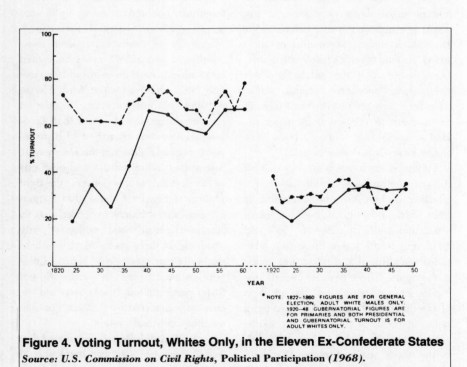

NOTE: 1822–1860 FIGURES ARE FOR GENERAL ELECTION, ADULT WHITE MALES ONLY. 1920–48 GUBERNATORIAL FIGURES ARE FOR PRIMARIES AND BOTH PRESIDENTIAL AND GUBERNATORIAL TURNOUT IS FOR ADULT WHITES ONLY.

Figure 4. Voting Turnout, Whites Only, in the Eleven Ex-Confederate States
Source: U.S. Commission on Civil Rights, Political Participation *(1968).*

mary, the poll tax, and other restrictive devices, culminating in the passage of the 1965 national Voting Rights Act, in addition to the return to the South of a Republican party that was almost the negative image of its Reconstruction-era predecessor, vastly increased political activity among all groups, whites as well as black and Latinos. The vote brought change, real and symbolic. Public services expanded and were opened more freely to all. Black and Spanish-surnamed southern mayors and congressmen became almost common. Former race baiters kissed black babies and black homecoming queens. Yet in many rural areas and small cities, harsh discrimination persisted; and electoral structures, such as at-large provisions, which had the intent and effect of diminishing minority political power, discouraged blacks and Latinos from voting and diluted the impact of their franchises when they did turn out. The struggle to guarantee equal political opportunity in the South continues.

J. Morgan Kousser
California Institute of Technology

See also BLACK LIFE: Politics, Black

Robert E. Brown and B. Katherine Brown, *Virginia, 1705–1786: Democracy or Aristocracy?* (1964); Ralph J. Bunche, *The Political Status of the Negro in the Age of* FDR (1973); V. O. Key, Jr., *Southern Politics in State and Nation* (1949); J. Morgan Kousser, *The Shaping of Southern Politics: Suffrage Restriction and the Establishment of the One-Party South, 1880–1910* (1974); Steven F. Lawson, *Black Ballots: Voting Rights in the South, 1944–1969* (1976); U.S. Commission on Civil Rights, *Political Participation* (1968), *The Voting Rights Act: Ten Years After* (1975), *The Voting Rights Act: Unfulfilled Goals* (1981); Chilton Williamson, *American Suffrage from Property to Democracy, 1760–1860* (1960). ☆

Women in Politics

See WOMEN'S LIFE: Politics, Women in

BAKER, HOWARD, JR.

(b. 1925) Politician.

Baker is the heir to a rich tradition of Republican politics. His family has lived in mountainous east Tennessee since the 1700s, and Baker still makes his home in the small town of Huntsville. Both his father and his stepmother served in the House of Representatives, and Baker's father-in-law, Republican Everett Dirksen of Illinois, was Senate minority leader in the 1950s and 1960s. Republicans have won every congressional election since 1858 in Baker's native second district. A World War II veteran, Baker returned from the war to earn a law degree at the University of Tennessee and began a lucrative practice with the law firm his grandfather had established in 1885. Banking, coal, and real estate investments made him a wealthy man.

Baker entered elective politics in 1964 as a candidate for the U.S. Senate. Defeated after a strong campaign, he ran again two years later and became the state's first popularly elected Republican senator. Baker's success heralded a Republican surge in Tennessee that enabled the party to capture the state's other Senate seat and the governor's mansion in 1970. Baker is a bridge between two important sources of Republican strength in the South. Through his family he is linked to the mountain Republicanism that has flourished in Tennessee since the Civil War, but he is also popular with educated, affluent, white business and professional people across the state who have built the southern Republican party into a significant force.

Baker first attracted national attention with his skillful performance as the ranking Republican on the Senate Watergate Committee in 1973. Three years later he won the post of minority leader and became majority leader when the Republicans took over the Senate after the 1980 elections. Ambitious for national office, Baker has frequently been considered for a vice-presidential nomination, but his bid for the White House in 1980 fizzled early in the campaign. The hallmark of Baker's Senate career was an emphasis on leadership through consensus. A centrist by instinct, his temperate rhetoric and charming manner made him highly effective in the clubby atmosphere of the Senate, although some conservative members of his own party were skeptical of his ideological leanings. He retired from the Senate in 1985 but returned to the national scene in 1987 as President Reagan's chief of staff. Proud to be called a professional politician, Baker typified the moderate stance long characteristic of Tennessee politics.

David D. Lee
Western Kentucky University

Jack Bass and Walter DeVries, *The Transformation of Southern Politics: Social Change and Political Consequence since 1945* (1976); Robert Corlew, *Tennessee: A Short History* (1981); Neal Peirce, *The Border South States: People, Politics and Power in the Five States of the Border South* (1975). ☆

BARNETT, ROSS
||||||||||||||||||||||||||||||||||||||||||||||
(1898–1988) Politician.

Ross Robert Barnett became a symbol of resistance to integration as governor of Mississippi because he precipitated a riot on the campus of the University of Mississippi against federal marshals attempting to register the first black in a "white" Mississippi educational institution. Born the last of a Civil War veteran's 10 children in the Standing Pine community of Leake County, Barnett struggled against poverty to educate himself. While a student of the county agricultural high school, he worked as a janitor and a barber. He continued those occupations and sold aluminum cookware in the summer during his years at Mississippi College. After graduation he taught school and coached in Pontotoc before attending law school at Vanderbilt and the University of Mississippi. Moving to Jackson in 1926, he opened an independent practice. In 1943 he was elected president of the state bar association and by 1951 was secure enough to attempt to fulfill his boyhood dream of becoming governor. Without political experience and never having held a public post, he launched his first campaign for the state's highest office. He lost badly in the primaries of 1951 and 1955. But in 1959 the Citizens' Council wanted an ardent segregationist as its candidate, and Barnett was a complete racist.

While other candidates temporized by calling blacks "niggras," Barnett openly said "nigger" and told audiences, "The Negro is different because God made him different to punish him." Aside from his racism, Barnett was known for his folksy humor, but not all of it was intentional. He once told the Beth-Israel Temple in Jackson that "there is nothing finer than a group of people meeting in true Christian fellowship." Asked what could be done about (the disputed Chinese islands of) Quemoy and Matsu, Barnett responded, "Well, I expect we could find a place for them in the Fish and Game Commission."

The first year of his administration was less than successful. His was "good old boy" style government, and he fought with the legislature for control of state agencies in order to provide the needed jobs. His primary contribution as governor was to promote industrial development through effective, prompt government service to industry, using his sales skills over promotional breakfasts with businessmen at the mansion.

When the federal courts ordered the University of Mississippi to admit James Meredith, a black man, Barnett defied the courts and was found in contempt. He answered Washington's demands with public assertions of state sovereignty while he secretly dealt with President John Kennedy and Attorney General Robert Kennedy. But the secret deal failed because Barnett could not resist playing to the public at an Ole Miss football game just prior to Meredith's enrollment. With over 40,000 people waving Confederate flags and singing "Go Mississippi" to the tune of his campaign song, Barnett said, "I love Mississippi. I love our people. I love our customs." His campaign publicist has written of the moment, "As he stood there, smiling, acknowledging the cheers of the multitude, he was more than just a governor of Mississippi. He was a symbol of the South, with the red blood of his Confederate soldier father running through his veins. He represented the traditions that emerged after Reconstruction, a way of life that white southerners had vowed to continue." After some of the cheering crowd returned to Oxford to riot against federal authority, Barnett surrendered to overwhelming military force.

Despite his surrender, Barnett was enormously popular at the end of his term, a symbol of defeated but unbowed resistance to integration. Political observers predicted that he would dominate state politics for years, but he chose not to run for the U.S. Senate immediately, and as the story of his secret dealings with the Kennedys leaked out, his popularity waned. Another segregationist defeated him in the next gubernatorial primary, and Barnett was reduced quickly to a dated relic of a discredited philosophy. He appeared regularly at the Neshoba County Fair to entertain with stories and songs but had no more role in politics.

Dennis J. Mitchell
Jackson State University

Erie Johnson, *I Rolled with Ross: A Political Portrait* (1980); Robert Sherrill, *Gothic Politics in the Deep South* (1968). ☆

BILBO, THEODORE

(1877–1947) Politician.

Theodore Gilmore Bilbo was born at Juniper Grove in Pearl River County, Miss., on 13 October 1877. He attended public school in Pearl River County and took courses but never earned a degree at Peabody College, Vanderbilt University, and the University of Michigan. He first entered politics in 1903 but was defeated for county clerk by a one-armed Confederate veteran. Displaying a sense of humor that would be a part of his political style, Bilbo confided to friends that he "started to vote for him myself."

Bilbo's 40-year political career was punctuated by victories and defeats. He served as state senator from 1908 to 1912. He became famous statewide for his involvement in "The Secret Causes" of 1910, during which he accepted a bribe in order to gain evidence that James K. Vardaman's opponents were bribing legislators. A vote to expel him from the state senate fell one vote short of the two-thirds necessary. In 1911 he was elected lieutenant governor and thereby became the presiding officer of the senate. Although implicated in a conflict-of-interest scandal while lieutenant governor, Bilbo was elected governor in 1915. His first administration was tainted by charges of sexual improprieties, and he lost a bid for the U.S. Congress in 1918. In 1922 he postponed a bid for a U.S. Senate seat because he was jailed by a federal judge for refusing to honor a summons to testify in the seduction and breach-of-promise suit filed against Governor Lee Russell by a former secretary. Instead, Bilbo announced his candidacy for governor in 1923 but was defeated. In 1927 he ran again and won.

During his second administration, 1928–32, Bilbo became deeply involved in the governance of higher education. After the legislature refused to restructure the governing boards and relocate the University of Mississippi from Oxford to Jackson, Governor Bilbo, as chairman of the three existing governing boards, ordered extensive personnel changes at most of the state's colleges, but especially at the state university, the agricultural college, and the women's college. Bilbo's intrusion into personnel matters was neither new nor unusual. The state's institutions of higher learning had long been subject to the fury of factional politics. It was the epic sweep of his purge and his disdain for the Southern Association of Colleges and its accrediting standards that prompted several accrediting agencies to censure or withdraw their accreditation from the Mississippi institutions of higher learning.

After Governor Bilbo's second term expired, he organized a campaign for the U.S. Senate. In 1934 he was elected, then reelected in 1940 and 1946. Early in his senatorial career he was an ardent New Dealer, but as relief and recovery gradually gave way to reform his ardor waned. He did, however, strongly endorse President Franklin D. Roosevelt's war policies.

In 1946 Senator Bilbo was confronted by two very serious challenges to his seat. First, a Senate investigating committee had prepared conflict of interest charges against him and planned to challenge his right to be sworn in for his third term. Secondly, a group of black Mississippians had filed suit seeking to overturn his reelection in 1946 on the grounds that large numbers of blacks had been systematically denied the right to vote in the Democratic primary.

However, before either of those two challenges could be resolved, Senator Bilbo, whose health had been declining rapidly during the past several months, was admitted to Ochsner's Clinic in New Orleans. He died on 21 August 1947.

David Sansing
University of Mississippi

Theodore Bilbo, Manuscripts, University of Southern Mississippi; A. W. Green, *The Man Bilbo* (1963); Chester M. Morgan, *Redneck Liberal: Theodore G. Bilbo and the New Deal* (1985). ✫

BYRD MACHINE

The Byrd machine of Virginia (1922–65) was an expression of the unique cultural and political heritage of the Old Dominion, which cherished elitist and traditional values. Created by Harry Flood Byrd, Sr., and other members of the state Democratic party during the 1920s, the machine took advantage of restrictive electoral regulations that made it possible for a small percentage of conservative rural and small town white voters to control elective offices. Byrd served successively as state party chairman, governor, and U.S. senator (1933–65). At his retirement in 1965, Byrd arranged to have his Senate seat passed to his son, Harry Flood Byrd, Jr.

During the 1930s Byrd joined other southern Democratic and Republican conservatives to oppose the more liberal politics of the New Deal administration of Franklin D. Roosevelt. However, as urban areas in northern and southeastern Virginia developed after World War II the control of the machine was gradually eroded. The machine's last stand was to organize a "massive resistance" campaign to oppose court-ordered integration of public schools after 1954. By the time Byrd retired from the Senate in 1965, the machine was ill-defined and many of its former loyalists had defected to the growing ranks of the southern Republican party.

Raymond H. Pulley
Appalachian State University

Harry Flood Byrd, Sr., Papers, University of Virginia; Raymond H. Pulley, *Old Virginia Restored: An Interpretation of the Progressive Impulse, 1870–1930* (1968); Francis M. Wilhoit, *The Politics of Massive Resistance* (1973); J. Harvey Wilkinson III, *Harry Byrd and the Changing Face of Virginia Politics, 1945–1966* (1968). ☆

CALHOUN, JOHN C.

(1782–1850) Politician and political philosopher.

Born of Scotch-Irish ancestry in the South Carolina upcountry in the wake of the American Revolution, John Caldwell Calhoun traveled north for his education. He graduated from Yale and read law with Federalist Judge Tapping Reeve in Litchfield, Conn. Calhoun returned home, practiced law, won a seat in the legislature, and then represented South Carolina in the U.S. Congress from 1811 to 1817. A devout nationalist during this phase of his career, Calhoun was a War Hawk and an avid supporter of the War of 1812. He voted for a protective tariff in 1816 and introduced the bill chartering the Second Bank of the United States in 1817. He served as secretary of war in James Monroe's Cabinet and in 1824 won election as vice president of the United States.

Calhoun was elected vice president again in 1828 and entered the administration of Andrew Jackson as heir apparent to the presidency. Within four years, however, Calhoun and Jackson were bitter enemies; Calhoun had resigned his office, and he had become an ardent sectionalist. Calhoun's *South Carolina Exposition and Protest* was the philosophical underpinning of the nullification movement in South Carolina. During the nullification crisis and after, Calhoun devoted his energies and considerable talents to the minority interests of the South. As South Carolina senator and during a brief term as John Tyler's secretary of state (1844–45), Calhoun was the South's political champion and spokesman.

In a sense Calhoun's career in public life embodied southern political behavior. A nationalist during the Virginia

Dynasty, he became a sectionalist when he came to believe that nationalism conflicted with southern interests. To his death in 1850 Calhoun fought the South's political battles with considerable skill. His greatest significance, however, lay in his capacity for political thought and analysis. His prime concern was for minority interests in American democracy. He believed the Union to be a compact; southern states had entered the compact when they ratified the Constitution, and they were free to dissolve the compact and leave the Union if they so chose. However, Calhoun revered the Union and attempted to discover some moderate constitutional course that would preserve both southern interests and the Union, that would offer the minority South some alternatives to submission and secession. He never resolved the dilemma, but in the process of defining and articulating the southern political stance, Calhoun became a constructive critic of American democracy and perhaps the foremost American political thinker of the 19th century.

Emory Thomas
University of Georgia

Gerald M. Capers, *John C. Calhoun, Opportunist: A Reappraisal* (1960); Margaret L. Coit, *John C. Calhoun: American Portrait* (1950); Richard N. Current, *John C. Calhoun* (1963); Charles M. Wiltse, *John C. Calhoun, Nullifier, 1829–1839* (1949). ☆

CARTER, JIMMY

(b. 1924) Politician.

"I am a Southerner and an American," Jimmy Carter wrote in his campaign autobiography, *Why Not the Best?* It would be difficult to quarrel with either assertion. Born and reared in the heart of the southwest Georgia Black Belt, James Earl "Jimmy" Carter could trace both his American and southern ancestry back to the early 17th century when the first Carters arrived in Virginia. By the decade of the 1780s ancestors of the future president had made their way to Georgia, eventually settling in Sumter County where Jimmy Carter was born and raised.

The son of a moderately wealthy landowner and businessman, Carter, like many of the other progeny of upper-middle-class southerners, aspired to a military career. After completing his elementary and secondary education in Plains and matriculating for a year at Georgia Southwestern College in nearby Americus, he enrolled in the naval ROTC program at the Georgia Institute of Technology prior to securing an appointment to the U.S. Naval Academy in Annapolis. There the young cadet did well, finishing in the upper 10 percent of his 1946 graduating class. Thereafter, he entered the submarine service after completing his required two years of surface duty.

The young naval officer's promising military career ended in 1953, however, when he returned to Plains to manage the family's business affairs after the death of his father. Within a few years of his return, he was deeply involved in a variety of community affairs and soon was campaigning for the state senate seat once held by his father. After two terms in the Georgia General Assembly, Carter ran unsuccessfully for the Democratic gubernatorial nomination in 1966 before succeeding in the same quest four years later.

On the first day of his governorship, Carter attracted national attention by dramatically proclaiming that the time for racial discrimination in Georgia had ended. During the next four years Carter promoted a moderately liberal, business-progressive reform program, which included state government reorganization, judicial reform, consumer protection, welfare reform, tax reform, and environmental concerns. Following through on earlier commitments, he also appointed numerous black Georgians and women to important positions in state government. Unable to succeed himself in the governorship, Carter in 1974 began laying the groundwork for a successful run for the presidency of the United States. His 1976 campaign focused national attention on changes in the South in the previous decade. Carter played a crucial role within the South in strengthening, at least temporarily, a black-white coalition in the Democratic party. He won black support and also appealed to the white rural South. For the first time since 1964, Democratic politicians across the South enthusiastically supported their party's presidential nominee.

Once installed in the presidential office, Carter, with less success, sought to push the same type of reforms that he had sponsored during his governorship. Domestic economic programs and international crises contributed to Carter's presidential woes, however, and in 1980 he was repudiated by the same voters, many of them southerners, who had supported him four years earlier. Several weeks later he was back in Plains, from which he had launched his meteoric rise to national prominence a few years earlier.

An unorthodox politician in many ways, Carter nevertheless was clearly a product of the southern culture into which he was born and in which he was raised. An inherited sense of noblesse oblige, which he shared with numerous others in the southern elite, combined in Carter with religious convictions (he was a "born again" Baptist) and a sense of history to produce a code of social ethics that permitted him to transcend the race issue that had been the burden of so many other white southerners. In so doing, symbolically at least, Carter's rise to the presidency represented the ultimate reunification of the South with the rest of the nation.

See also MYTHIC SOUTH: / Carter Era

Gary M. Fink
Georgia State University

Gary M. Fink, *Prelude to the Presidency: The Political Character and Legislative Leadership Style of Governor Jimmy Carter* (1980); David Kucharsky, *The Man from Plains: The Mind and Spirit of Jimmy Carter* (1975); William L. Miller, *Yankee from Georgia: The Emergence of Jimmy Carter* (1978). ☆

CRUMP, E. H.
(1874–1954) Politician.

Born and raised in Holly Springs, Miss., Edward Hull Crump moved to Memphis as a young man. His business efforts prospered, especially his insurance firm, and Crump eventually built a sizable personal fortune. Politically active almost from his arrival in Memphis, Crump was elected mayor in 1909, 1911, and 1915, but his refusal to enforce Tennessee's prohibition law prompted the state to initiate legal proceedings, which resulted in his resignation in 1916. Despite the setback, Crump continued to build a political machine that, by the mid-1920s, utterly dominated the large Shelby County vote. In 1932 the Crump-backed candidate for governor won election, and for the next 16 years the Memphis boss and his organization influenced the outcome of most major statewide races. Finally, in 1948, insurgents led by Estes Kefauver and Gordon Browning defeated the Crump choices for senator and governor in the Democratic primary. His power across Tennessee substantially weakened, Crump still controlled Memphis politics until his death in 1954.

A self-described progressive, Crump stressed efficient government and improved public services, policies that generally kept him in good stead with respectable Memphis business leaders, as did his bitter opposition to unions. At the same time, however, the Crump machine was closely linked to the Bluff City's seamy vice trade, a prime source of money and votes for organization candidates. The Crump machine also included the local black community, tied to the boss by his special blend of patronage and coercion. Consequently, Memphis was one of the few places in the South that tolerated black voting during the segregation era. W. C. Handy celebrated Crump in his "Memphis Blues" (1912), a catchy tune that the mayor then used to gain black and white votes. "Mister Crump don't 'low no easy riders here," it said. Crump delighted in conducting well-publicized charity drives to benefit various causes, but he dealt harshly with potential opponents. City bureaucrats and policemen harassed his critics, while curious reporters and persistent labor organizers occasionally encountered strong-arm tactics. Although many Crump policies and practices were generally typical of machine politics in other parts of the country, Crump himself struck the pose of the paternalistic southern gentleman. Dapper and flamboyant, he was an unusually visible political boss who often castigated his enemies in splashy newspaper advertisements. A uniquely skillful politician, Crump wielded more power outside his own city than any other urban boss in the South.

See also URBANIZATION: / Memphis

David D. Lee
Western Kentucky University

William Miller, *Mr. Crump of Memphis* (1964); *Memphis during the Progressive Era, 1900–1917* (1957); David Tucker, *Memphis since Crump: Bossism, Blacks, and Civic Reformers, 1948–1968* (1980). ☆

E. H. Crump, Mayor of Memphis, Tennessee, c. 1940

DIXIECRATS

In 1948 several southern Democrats rejected the liberal leadership of their national party and pursued an independent course. At issue was President Harry Truman's proposal on civil rights that advocated an antilynching law, a permanent fair employment practices commission, desegregation of the armed forces, and elimination of the poll tax. After a special committee of the Southern Governors' Conference unsuccessfully sought concessions on civil rights from the Democratic National Committee, many southerners, fearing the destruction of their regional traditions, considered a revolt against the national party. Under the guidance of Fielding Wright of Mississippi, Frank Dixon of Alabama, Strom Thurmond of South Carolina, and Leander Perez of Louisiana, disgruntled southerners launched a grass-roots organization in the region.

When the South failed to prevent the nomination of Truman at the Democratic national convention in Philadelphia and suffered reversals on civil rights, the rights of states to control tidelands' oil reserves, and the two-thirds rule, several delegates bolted. Six thousand southerners, mainly from Mississippi and Alabama, met later in Birmingham. Influenced by Charles Wallace Collins's *Whither Solid South?* (1947) and seeking to force the presidential election into the House of Representatives, these states rights' supporters "recommended" a separate ticket of Thurmond and Wright. Although race was clearly their key concern, the States' Rights Democrats included, in addition to white supremacists, antiunion industrialist oilmen and constitutional conservatives who abhorred civil rights and communism. Branded "Dixiecrats" by Bill Weisner of the Charlotte *News*, the dissident southerners advanced no positive programs, sought primarily to save the South from the clutches of political

modernism, and reflected a historical consciousness that romanticized their regional past and social heritage.

Although States' Rights Democrats generally opposed the creation of a separate southern party, they seized control of the party machinery in Alabama, Mississippi, Louisiana, and South Carolina. Thurmond carried these four states, where he appeared on the ballot as the Democratic nominee and received 1.2 million votes, but Truman triumphed in the remainder of the South and won the election. Throughout the controversy, most prominent southern leaders stayed within the Democratic party. After the election, the Dixiecrat movement evaporated. The South's vocal dissent in 1948, however, forecast the sectional unrest of the following decades, weakened the region's loyalty to the Democratic party, and prepared the way for future political realignment.

Edward F. Haas
Louisiana State Museum
Tulane University

Richard C. Etheridge, "Mississippi's Role in the Dixiecrat Movement" (Ph.D. dissertation, Mississippi State University, 1971); Robert A. Garson, *The Democratic Party and the Politics of Sectionalism, 1941–1948* (1974); Gary C. Ness, "The States' Rights Democratic Movement of 1948" (Ph.D. dissertation, Duke University, 1972). ☆

FAUBUS, ORVAL
(b. 1910) Politician.

Six-term governor of Arkansas (1955–67), Orval Eugene Faubus gained notoriety around the world in 1957 for his defiance of the federal government in preventing the integration of Little Rock Central High School. Faubus quickly became one of the powerful symbols of southern resistance to desegregation, embodying in his person—and especially in his rhetoric—much that was of value to the South. Of humble origins, Faubus communicated effectively his distaste for the city and for the "Cadillac brigade" that wielded power there. He was a strong individualist who spoke the language of the states' rights advocates and the opponents of big government. Faubus earned the admiration of many southerners (and others) for standing up to the powerful forces that threatened the traditional values of his region. An ambivalent leader who vacillated in his own mind between liberalism and conservatism, Faubus reflected the southern tension between the forces of continuity and change. His folksy manner, his defiant tone, his regard for the common man, and his orientation toward the past all exemplified a southern cultural style, and all contributed to making Orval Faubus a kind of hillbilly hero.

Born in 1910 in the tiny Ozark Mountain community of Combs, Ark., Orval Eugene Faubus was reared in an environment of poverty and political radicalism (his father was a follower of the Socialist, Eugene V. Debs). After three years of military service the young schoolteacher and newspaperman came to the attention of another GI reformer, the liberal Governor Sid McMath, and landed a job on the Arkansas Highway Commission. In 1954 Faubus ran against an incumbent governor and won in one of the most scurrilous elections in Arkansas history. His opponent labeled him a Communist because of his early association with the Commonwealth College. Faubus's first term was uneventful, and he ran successfully for a second term against an arch-segrega-

tionist, whom he characterized as a "purveyor of hate." Hardly a model of political conservatism, Orval Faubus approached 1957 with a solid reputation as a moderate.

As Orval Faubus would say years later, 1957 overshadowed everything. His defiant stand against the forces of change and racial justice earned him momentary fame, six terms as governor, and tremendous power in his own state, but eventually it left him a captive of his image as a racist and an opportunist.

Elizabeth Jacoway
University of Arkansas at
Little Rock

Orval Eugene Faubus, *Down from the Hills* (1980); Willard B. Gatewood, Jr., and Timothy Donovan, eds., *The Governors of Arkansas: Essays in Political Biography* (1981). ☆

FELTON, REBECCA
(1835–1930) Politician and writer.

Rebecca Ann Latimer Felton was a strong-willed, outspoken individual who defied the tradition that women should not become involved in politics. She played an active role in the career of her husband, Dr. William H. Felton, an early leader of Georgia's Independent Democrat party. She managed his campaigns, helped draft bills, advised him on legislative strategy, and responded to his critics with innumerable letters to newspapers. She was perfectly capable of vehemently attacking male opponents, but when they responded she condemned them for criticizing a woman. The extent of her role in her husband's career is illustrated by the comment of one of Dr. Felton's opponents that he had been defeated "by the political she of Georgia" and by a newspaper headline that read "Mrs. Felton and Husband Returned."

Felton supported the temperance movement, worked to abolish the convict lease system, and defended state-supported schools against attacks by denominational colleges. She campaigned for vocational training for poor white girls and agitated for admission of women to state universities. She wrote three books and was a columnist for the rural editions of the Atlanta *Journal*. In her columns she defended working conditions in southern cotton mills and criticized child labor laws, Jews, Catholics, and the theory of evolution. Early in the 1900s she became active in the women's suffrage movement, arguing that giving women the vote was necessary to keep power out of the hands of aliens and blacks. Her attacks on blacks were especially virulent. When the Wilming-

ton, N.C., race riot broke out after she had defended lynching, she responded to criticism of her views by advocating that 1,000 blacks be lynched every week if necessary to prevent rapes. When Georgia's U.S. senator died in office, Felton was appointed to complete his term. She served for one day before resigning in favor of the senator-elect.

Rebecca Latimer Felton defies any simple categorization. Although she shared the conservative economic views and intense racial prejudice of many of her southern contemporaries, her feminism set her apart. Unlike many southern women who were involved in the temperance and suffrage movements, she did not move on to work for improved race relations. A rural woman, she enjoyed her role as one of the two lady managers from Georgia at the World's Columbian Exposition in Chicago. Her dogged determination, energy, and outspoken nature resulted in an unusually active public life and made her a force to be reckoned with in her native state.

Jane Walker Herndon
Dekalb Community College

Rebecca Felton, *Country Life in Georgia in the Days of My Youth* (1919); *My Memoirs of Georgia Politics* (1911); John E. Talmadge, *Rebecca Latimer Felton: Nine Stormy Decades* (1960). ☆

Rebecca Latimer Felton, Georgia politician and writer, c. 1920s

FOLSOM, JIM
(b. 1908) Politician.

James Elisha "Big Jim" Folsom won the Alabama governorship in 1946 and 1954. He introduced classic southern populist campaign techniques to the state, using country music, powerful symbols, and humorous parables to appeal directly to the voters. Folsom used campaigns as a platform from which to educate the electorate about the need to fight for their rights against the "Big Mules," meaning the elite. He spoke of the evils of racial discrimination, the need for reapportionment on a one-person, one-vote basis, women's rights, improved education, and better roads.

His forthright and principled campaign speeches were followed by vigorous but mainly unsuccessful attempts as governor to transform rhetoric into reality. His opponents were entrenched in a gerrymandered legislature controlled by Black Belt and Jefferson County (Birmingham) politicians. His efforts were also inhibited by the image, and often the reality, of corruption that surrounded his administrations and by a drinking problem that sapped his strength and ruined his judgment.

Folsom was born in 1908 in Coffee County, Ala., in the southeastern corner of the state known as the Wiregrass. The Wiregrass had a small-farm economic base, low concentrations of blacks, and a strong populist political tradition. Folsom's many populist-oriented challenges to the state's political elite and his racial moderation had clear origins in his Coffee County upbringing.

His political beliefs were strongly influenced by three people. His father, Joshua Folsom, held many county elective offices and introduced him to courthouse politics. Folsom's uncle, John Dunnavant, a Populist party activist, was a brilliant storyteller who spoke glowingly of Grandfather Dunnavant's freeing of his slaves and of his opposition to the Civil War. Folsom's first father-in-law, Probate Judge J. A. Carnley, was another active and articulate populist advocate, but one who stayed within the Democratic party.

Folsom was not a pure populist. His political views were also influenced by the Great Depression. He received an especially clear perspective on the suffering of that period in his position as Civil Works Administration director in north Alabama's Marshall County. From then on he favored large-scale government assistance programs.

Moving to north Alabama in the later 1930s, Folsom went to a region of the state with a political culture similar to that of the Wiregrass. His election victories united these two very similar regions against the state's Black Belt. In 1962 Folsom was defeated in a reelection bid by George Wallace, who used race-baiting rhetoric to win.

> Carl Grafton
> Anne Permaloff
> Auburn University at Montgomery

Carl Grafton and Anne Permaloff, *Big Mules and Branchheads: James E. Folsom and Political Power in Alabama* (1985). ☆

HELMS, JESSE
(b. 1921) Politician.

Jesse Alexander Helms, Jr., was born 18 October 1921 in the Piedmont North Carolina community of Monroe, the son of the town's police and fire chief. Following a Tom Sawyer childhood, a summer at a tiny Baptist college, and a year at Wake Forest, Helms dropped out of college to become a sports reporter with the Raleigh *News and Observer*. During World War II he served with the naval reserve. After the war he was briefly city editor with the *Raleigh Times*, then worked as a reporter with a Roanoke Rapids radio station before returning to Raleigh as news director at WRAL radio station.

While with WRAL, Helms became involved in the successful 1950 Democratic senatorial runoff primary campaign of Raleigh lawyer Willis Smith against Frank Porter Graham, the respected former president of the University of North Carolina, who had been appointed to the Senate in 1949. The Smith-Graham campaign was one of the dirtiest in North Carolina history. Smith literature depicted Graham as a Communist sympathizer and integrationist, exhorting "White People Wake Up!" and warning of "Negroes working beside you, your wife and daughter in your mills and factories," should Graham be elected. In later years, critics claimed that Helms had played a significant role in the Smith campaign—a charge Helms has consistently denied.

Whatever his role in the campaign, Helms became Smith's administrative assistant and served until the senator's death in 1953. Following a brief stint as aide to Smith's successor, Helms returned again to Raleigh and became executive director of the North Carolina Bankers' Association and editor of its conservative monthly bulletin. From 1957 to 1961 he also served on the Raleigh city council.

In 1960 Helms became an executive, editorialist, and minor stockholder with WRAL radio and television stations. Over a 12-year period, he delivered some 2,700 five-minute commentaries over WRAL and the Tobacco Radio Network, a hookup of some 70 rural stations, railing against growing federal power, school desegregation, welfare fraud and waste, and racial "agitators." His *Viewpoint* editorials made Helms a familiar and popular figure in thousands of North Carolina homes. In 1970 he changed his party registration to Republican and in 1972 became the first Republican elected to the Senate from North Carolina since 1894. With the slogan "Elect Jesse Helms—He's One of Us," he won 54 percent of the vote against moderate Durham Congressman Nick Galifianakis, the son of Greek immigrant parents.

During his first term, Helms was little more than a Senate curiosity, opposing abortion and sex education and defending school prayer, curbs on the federal courts, capital punishment, defense spending, and U.S. support for the white minority government of South Africa, but rarely exerting meaningful influence. At the same time, however, his outspoken sympathy for "pro-family" and other religiopolitical causes of the radical right began to attract a national following. Moreover, his Congressional Club, organized initially to retire a 1972 campaign debt, became an extremely successful political action committee, providing funds and technical assistance for a variety of conservative causes and candidates. The club spent over $7 million on Helms's 1978 reelection, outspending his opponent 30 to 1, and over $4 million on Ronald Reagan's 1980 presidential campaign.

The election of President Reagan and a Republican Senate majority in 1980, combined with the conservative national mood the 1980 election results seemed to reflect, gave Helms's movement respectability and the senator considerable national influence. By 1983, however, his position had seriously eroded. Relations with the Reagan Administration—its policies and personalities entirely too moderate for Helms's tastes—had become strained at best. In the Senate, colleagues unsympathetic to his intransigence on "pro-family" issues and opposition to food stamps had countered with attacks on tobacco and other price-support programs important to North Carolina's agricultural economy. At home, every 1982 congressional candidate sponsored by the Congressional Club lost, with that organization's exorbitant spending and negative campaign strategy perhaps the major election issue.

In 1984, however, Helms won reelection over Governor James B. Hunt in the most expensive congressional campaign yet waged. Helms's campaign strategy was reminiscent of that employed so successfully against Frank Graham a quarter-century earlier. Hunt was condemned for supporting a national holiday honoring Martin Luther King, Jr., and depicted as a tax-happy racial and political liberal, the candidate of "the bloc vote," "gays, porno kings, union bosses, and crooks." Campaign leaflets featured photographs of Hunt with Jesse Jackson and Helms with President Reagan, noting the "stark contrast." The ploy worked. Aided by Reagan's lengthy North Carolina coattails, a $15 million campaign chest, and Hunt's liberal image, the senator won 52 percent of the total vote, 63 percent of whites, but less than one percent of the black electorate.

Tinsley E. Yarbrough
East Carolina University

Wayne Greenhaw, *Elephants in the Cottonfields: Ronald Reagan and the New Republican South* (1982); Bill Peterson, *Washington Post National Weekly Edition* (3 December 1984); Peter Ross Range, *New York Times Magazine* (8 February 1981). ☆

HULL, CORDELL
(1871–1955) Diplomat.

It is a long way from the Tennessee mountains to the State Department corridors, and there was little in Cordell Hull's Overton County roots that prepared him to be the leading diplomat in Franklin Roosevelt's foreign-policy entourage. In fact, in his memoirs Hull mentioned two experiences that prepared him for world affairs; both were outside Tennessee. One was a year and a half of college in Ohio, where he was able to meet people with different habits and ideas; the other was his Spanish-American War service in Cuba where he became aware of the wider world in which the United States would have to exist.

Hull had broad-ranging experience at the state, national, and international levels. A graduate of the law program at Cumberland University, he practiced law briefly before serving two terms in the state legislature. After serving in the Spanish-American War, Hull was a circuit court judge for four years and then was elected to the U.S. House of Representatives, serving from 1907 to 1930 (except for 1921–23). Among his many legislative accomplishments was the proposal of a graduated income tax measure in 1913. In 1930 Hull was elected to the U.S. Senate and served until his appointment as secretary of state.

During his 11 years as secretary of state (1933–44), Hull showed his Tennessee roots. Contemporaries dwelled upon such superficial points as his penchant for telling stories about his days in Tennessee, the colorful profanity that dotted his private conversations when he was angered, and his quiet, almost taciturn demeanor. Like other staunch southern Democrats of his day, Hull worked diligently for a program to lower tariffs. But Secretary of State Hull's views on trade were not those of the local politician who had to protect his constituents. He took a loftier view that a free-trading world would progress while an autarchic world order where nations conquered and hoarded markets and resources would lead to economic stagnation. As secretary of state, Hull engineered the Reciprocal Trade Agreements Act, worked especially to improve Latin American relations, helped shape the Good Neighbor policy, supported strengthening of America's military preparedness, and proposed an international diplomatic organization. Called by President Truman the "Father of the United Nations," Hull received the Nobel Peace Prize in 1945.

If Hull's worldview went beyond the parochial views of most of his fellow Tennesseans, he brought to the Department of State a faith in absoluteness drawn from his early years in the Cumberland Mountains, where certainty mattered above all. To the men of his region during the Civil War, Hull recalled, it made little difference whether you fought in the Confederate or Union armies as long as you fought. His father personified the certainty of right and wrong when he tracked down and publicly killed a man who had informed on him during the war, an act for which his father was neither prosecuted nor chastised.

Even as a law-and-order judge riding circuit in Tennessee, Hull showed he had absorbed this black-white view of life. There were good people and bad people, and it was as simple as that. Similarly, during World War II Secretary Hull saw Nazi Germany and Imperial Japan in this black-white view.

Jonathan G. Utley
University of Tennessee

Harold B. Hinton, *Cordell Hull: A Biography* (1942); Cordell Hull, *The Memoirs of Cordell Hull*, 2 vols. (1948); J. W. Pratt, *American Secretaries of State*, vols. 12, 13 (1964). ☆

JACKSON, ANDREW

(1767–1845) Politician.

Born near the border of North and South Carolina—the exact spot is in dispute—Andrew Jackson moved to frontier Tennessee in 1788 at the age of 19, an early pioneer in a significant migration pattern that eventually redrew the boundaries of "the South." Tennessee at the time, and throughout Jackson's life, was more western than southern. Although he developed substantial landholdings near Nashville, held slaves, and lived the life of a gentleman planter at "The Hermitage," Jackson as late as the 1840s considered himself a westerner and a nationalist, never a southerner, and he was so perceived by his contemporaries.

Nonetheless Jackson's career was rife with consequences for the South. His defeat of the British at New Orleans and of the Seminoles in Florida nailed down southern borders once and for all. He moved carefully on the issue of expansion into Texas while in office, but his passionate interest in the area eventually resulted in extension of the southern frontier westward.

The Democratic party that he led to the presidency and institutionalized around Jacksonian issues represented an alliance of "Southern Planters and Plain Republicans of the North," as Martin Van Buren put it; it was rooted in the "Old Republican" ideology of Thomas Jefferson and coupled with a strong overlay of western pragmatism. Committed to the Union and to strict construction of the Constitution, the party served for decades as a shield for southern slaveowners against the rising anti-

Andrew Jackson, frontier hero and U.S. president, date unknown

slavery clamor. Paradoxically, it also embodied and promoted the democratic impulse whose egalitarian values and reform tendencies were ultimately subversive of the southern slavery system.

Although Jackson's Scotch-Irish parents had only recently emigrated at the time of his birth, his formative years in the upcountry Carolinas doubtless contributed to his fierce combativeness, his attraction to the law and the militia, his love of horses and horseracing, and his patrician style. It was as frontier lawyer and politician, militia leader and military hero, that he rose to fame, an ardent unionist and an instinctive democrat.

Richard H. Brown
Newberry Library
Chicago, Illinois

James Curtis, *Andrew Jackson and the Search for Vindication* (1976); Burke Davis, *Old Hickory: A Life of Andrew Jackson*

(1977); Robert V. Remini, *The Revolutionary Age of Andrew Jackson* (1976). ☆

JOHNSON, LYNDON B.

(1908–1973) Politician.

Convinced that a southerner could not be elected to the presidency in his lifetime, Lyndon Baines Johnson sought to minimize his southern credentials. Describing himself as an American, a westerner, a Texan, and, only lastly, a southerner, he attempted to divorce himself from the region and its conservative racial and social image. As a southerner, a congressional leader with a mixed civil rights record, and the successor to a slain president whose reform image loomed larger in death than in life, Lyndon B. Johnson sensed a special need to convince the nation that he too was dedicated to the cause of equality and a decent standard of living for all Americans. Pursuing this goal during the five years of his presidency (1963–69), he pushed through the Congress the most significant civil rights legislation since Reconstruction—the legislation outlawing discrimination in education, public accommodations, voting, employment, and housing. Armed with authority to cut off federal funds to segregated public schools, his administration integrated the schools at a pace that repeated court decisions had largely failed to effect. And his 1965 voting rights legislation produced a 50 percent increase in southern black voter registration by 1966—an increase that facilitated the election of black officeholders (387 in Mississippi alone by mid-1980) and ultimately moderated the region's racial politics.

The administration's War on Poverty attempted to cope, moreover, with the plight of the poor in the South and the rest of the nation. For children, Johnson created the federal school breakfast, Head Start, day care, and foster grandparent programs; for the elderly, Medicare and special housing; for the unemployed, the Job Corps; for the myriad problems confronting the poor, VISTA and the Community Action Program. Nor were such programs intended only for economic relief. They also provided a political base for minorities, especially in the South. Many VISTA volunteers, for example, became heavily involved in southern politics; and the Community Action Program through which federal poverty funds were channeled to largely private, minority-related agencies was designed in part to bypass the traditional federal, state, and local power structures.

While president, Lyndon Johnson was never able to convince most civil rights leaders and social activists of his commitment to reform. For them, as for his critics of the right, he was simply a calculating politician posturing for liberal and minority votes. More critically, urban riots, rising inflation, the growing national preoccupation with Vietnam, the merging of the civil rights movement with the antiwar effort, and the increasingly radical character of the two movements largely derailed Johnson's social programs and dampened public enthusiasm for further civil rights reform. Ironically, too, though he was a creature of the Solid Democratic South, his administration probably did more to drive white southerners into the ranks of the GOP than all the efforts of Republican presidents and presidential aspirants. Whatever its direction, however, his impact on southern politics was to be truly profound. In later years, moreover, liberals would develop a more sympathetic image of his presidency and its role in social reform. That image

moved former SNCC leader and caustic Johnson critic Julian Bond to describe the former president in 1972 as "an activist, human-hearted man [who] had his hands on the levers of power and a vision beyond the next election. He was there when we and the Nation needed him, and, oh my God, do I wish he was there now."

Tinsley E. Yarbrough
East Carolina University

Robert A. Divine, ed., *Exploring the Johnson Years* (1981); Eric Goldman, *The Tragedy of Lyndon Johnson* (1968); Doris Kearns, *Lyndon Johnson and the American Dream* (1976). ☆

KEFAUVER, ESTES
(1903–1963) Politician.

Carey Estes Kefauver, U.S. senator from Tennessee for 14 years and Democratic vice-presidential nominee in 1956, is credited with having influenced incorporation of more direct popular appeal in presidential campaign methods, as contrasted with traditional reliance on local political organizations. Less tangible but probably more important was his possible influence on elimination of the customary stance and image of the southern senator.

Before Kefauver's consistently controversial career in the U.S. Senate, the image of the verbose gentleman with flowing hair and tie—like his first Tennessee Senate colleague, K. D. McKellar—was not universally applicable to southern politicians, but it was associated with a solid bloc of Dixie legislators whose votes on certain issues, especially civil rights legislation, were predictable. Kefauver's refusal to conform to that image never lessened his popularity, and his stances probably undermined the assumption that southern senators and congressmen are distinct from—and often opposed to—the mainstream.

Kefauver's almost unheard-of challenge to an incumbent administration of his own party in plunging into the 1952 presidential race against the will of then-President Harry Truman also marked the beginning of the end of the once-traditional axiom that "no southerner can ever become president." He did not make it himself, but two southerners, Lyndon B. Johnson and Jimmy Carter, attained the office after his death. An unacceptable liberal to southern colleagues yet not liberal enough for northern Democratic leaders, Kefauver won successes both in the Senate and on the campaign trail almost exclusively through his ability to appeal directly to the voters, not only in his own state but nationwide.

A Yale graduate who left a successful Chattanooga law practice for a decade in the House of Representatives, Kefauver reached the U.S. Senate in 1948 through a successful challenge to the statewide political hegemony of Memphis's E. H. Crump. He was boosted into the 1952 presidential picture by his televised investigation of organized crime, and his soft voice and unavoidable handshake gave him name recognition second only to that of Dwight D. Eisenhower, according to a Gallup poll. After his second failure, in 1956, to win the Democratic presidential nomination, Kefauver spent the rest of his career leading a series of Senate investigations, the most notable into antitrust violations and prescription drugs.

Charles L. Fontenay
Nashville, Tennessee

Charles L. Fontenay, *Estes Kefauver: A Biography* (1980); Richard Harris, *The Real Voice* (1964); William Howard Moore, *The Kefauver Committee and the Politics of Crime, 1950–1952* (1974). ☆

LONG, HUEY
(1893–1935) Politician.

Governor of Louisiana, U.S. senator, and popular leader during the Great Depression, Huey Pierce Long emerged from the relatively poor hill country of northern Louisiana to transform forever the politics of his state. After eight years as a member of the Public Service Commission, he was elected governor in 1928 as the champion of the common people against the Old Guard, the oil interests, and the planter elite. Although his opponents often decried his radicalism, Long was in many respects a rather conventional progressive reformer. He oversaw a massive public works program, an improvement of state educational and health facilities, and a modest reform of the tax codes. But if Long was relatively moderate in his legislative aims, he was decidedly immoderate in the means he adopted to attain them. In his eight years as leader of Louisiana—four as governor and four as U.S. senator, from which position he continued to control the state through carefully chosen surrogates—he created a political machine without precedent in American history. By skillful use of both his wide popularity and his official powers, he won total mastery of the state legislature; from there, he proceeded to transform state government —through a series of constitutional amendments and other devices—to concentrate virtually all power in his own hands.

After entering the Senate in 1932,

Long quickly rose to national prominence as well—first as a supporter and then as a foe of Franklin Roosevelt, but always as an advocate of redistribution of wealth. As leader of his own national political organization—the Share Our Wealth Society—he mobilized a following that alarmed even the president himself. At the peak of his power, positioning himself for a national campaign in 1936, Long was assassinated in September 1935 by a Baton Rouge physician, whose motives remain unknown.

Long was both a classic example of and a radical departure from the southern demagogue. Like others, he rose to power on the basis of explicit, if crudely expressed, class grievances. Like others, he drew from the traditions of populism, defending the sanctity of local communities against the encroachments of powerful interests. But unlike most southern demagogues, Long translated his popular appeal into lasting and far-reaching political power; he compiled a record of substantive accomplishment; and he achieved and maintained authority without exploiting the issue of race. No southern politician of his era, moreover, could match Long's popular appeal outside the region. Long's career exposed in the starkest possible form both the dangers and the opportunities of effective populist appeals to the discontented and dispossessed. He used his popularity to accumulate great and menacing power, but at the same time he turned the gaze of troubled Louisianians (and many others as well) away from the cultural, religious, and racial issues that had dampened economic progress and social reform in the past, and elevated to prominence basic questions of power and wealth. After Huey Long, Louisiana's conservative oligarchy would never rest entirely comfortable again.

Alan Brinkley
Harvard University

Alan Brinkley, *Voices of Protest: Huey Long, Father Coughlin and the Great Depression* (1982); Huey P. Long, *Every Man a King* (1933), *My First Days in the White House* (1935); Allan P. Sindler, *Huey Long's Louisiana* (1956); T. Harry Williams, *Huey Long* (1969). ☆

MADDOX, LESTER

(b. 1915) Politician.

In January 1967, with the South in the midst of dramatic change initiated by the civil rights movement, Lester Garfield Maddox was elected governor of Georgia. For a decade prior to his election, he had made himself a symbol of white resistance to integration. Each Saturday in the Atlanta newspapers he advertised his fried chicken restaurant, the Pickrick, and purchased space for a political column that attacked liberals as enemies of America, God, individual freedom, and states' rights. His particular brand of right-wing thinking combined religious fundamentalism with racism and classical laissez-faire doctrines. The combination proved to be appealing to many Georgians who shared aspects of his background.

Maddox was born in Atlanta in 1915, one of seven children of parents who had left rural Georgia to seek better employment opportunities in Atlanta. His father worked in a small steel factory and found it difficult to support his family during the Depression. Lester dropped out of high school, married at an early age, and worked at a variety of jobs before starting a small restaurant that he and his wife turned into a highly successful enterprise. Active in the Baptist church and several fraternal orders, Maddox began in the 1950s to challenge the racial moderation that characterized Atlanta's political leadership. In 1964 he attracted national attention when he refused to obey the recently passed Civil Rights Act by denying service to blacks at his restaurant. Brandishing a pistol and distributing ax handles to his supporters, he forcibly turned away blacks from his door. When the federal courts ordered him to end discrimination, he sold the restaurant to friends rather than operate it on an integrated basis.

Maddox's highly visible defiance of federal authority served as a springboard for his pursuit of the governorship in 1966. With little financial support and no assistance from established political leaders, he launched his campaign in rural areas of central and southern Georgia. On fence posts and pine trees he nailed signs announcing, "This Is Maddox Country," and on election day his claims were supported. In the Democratic primary he toppled a former governor, Ellis Arnall, whose moderate stance on racial issues and longstanding opposition to the Talmadge forces in Georgia politics proved to be handicaps. In the general election Maddox was opposed by Republican Howard "Bo" Callaway, a millionaire segregationist who had recently left the Democratic party. Neither man received a majority in the election because 7 percent of the electorate, blacks and white liberals, wrote in the name of Ellis Arnall. The Georgia Legislature convened in January to decide between the two leading candidates; the outcome was not in question as rural Democrats who dominated the proceedings cast their votes for the intrepid Atlanta gadfly, Lester G. Maddox.

As governor, Maddox did not effect any significant changes in the state's institutions. He did not close the public schools nor use the powers of his office to challenge federal authority. White Georgians continued the slow process of adjusting to the end of segregation while their governor delivered regular verbal assaults on those who had brought about the change. In 1968 Maddox made an abortive two week campaign for the presidential nomination of the Democratic party; afterwards he supported the independent candidacy of George Wallace. When he completed his term as governor and could not succeed himself, he handily won election as lieutenant governor. But in 1974 the voters rejected his bid for the governor's office in favor of a moderate, George Busbee. The majority no longer wanted the state to be led by an extremist defender of the old order of segregation.

James C. Lanier
Rhodes College

Numan Bartley, *From Thurmond to Wallace: Political Tendencies in Georgia, 1948–1968* (1970); Marshall Frady, *Southerners: A Journalist's Odyssey* (1980); Lester Maddox, *Speaking Out: The Autobiography of Lester Garfield Maddox* (1975). ☆

PEPPER, CLAUDE
(1900–1989) Politician.

The oldest of four children, Claude Denson Pepper was born on the family farm near Dudleyville, Ala. "Full grown" before he had ever traveled on a paved road, when he accompanied his debate team to Chapel Hill, N.C., as a college freshman, it was the farthest north he had ever been. A southerner, a Baptist, and a lifelong unwavering Democrat, a New Deal liberal who in a 1950 smear campaign was branded a "leader of radicals" and "advocate of treason," Pepper has nevertheless been hailed as a representative American, "the nearest thing this country has to a national congressman."

Pepper's wide ambition and indomitability surfaced early. A school teacher for a time in Dothan, Ala., then a steel mill worker, he continued to hold down a part-time job while attending the University of Alabama. He graduated Phi Beta Kappa in 1921 and, after receiving a law degree from Harvard in 1924, taught for a year at the University of Arkansas before setting up practice in Perry, Fla. In 1929 he was elected to the Florida House of Representatives but was defeated two years later and resumed his law practice, this time in Tallahassee.

After an unsuccessful bid for the U.S. Senate in 1934 (lost by only 4,000 votes), Pepper filed for a vacancy two years later and was nominated by his party, unopposed. Committed to Roosevelt's economic programs for the good of the South and the nation, Pepper gained the president's support for election to his first six-year term in 1938. He consistently risked antagonizing both big business and social conservative interests in Florida by opposing racism and by favoring minimum wage laws, national health insurance, old age pensions, and federal aid to education.

Pepper was reelected in 1944 but his postwar record that included such things as encouraging rapprochement with the Soviet Union, early backing of Dwight Eisenhower against Truman, opposition to union-regulating Taft-Hartley legislation, and support for anti-poll tax laws led his enemies to close ranks in 1950. Florida boss Edward W. Ball, assisted with funds gleaned nationally, groomed Representative George A. Smathers to run against Pepper in what has been called "the most elaborate crusade for political annihilation ever conducted in Southern politics." Coupled with slanderous slogans and speeches, a pamphlet, *The Red Record of Senator Claude Pepper*, circulated throughout Florida. On election night, when Pepper had lost by 67,000 votes, people passing his house shouted obscenities and applauded his defeat.

With law offices in Tallahassee, Washington, and Miami, Pepper again returned to a successful private practice, but was discontented out of office. In 1962 he ran for and won a House seat newly created for the Miami congressional district. He has been consistently reelected since.

With nearly four decades of congressional service spanning nine presidential administrations behind him, Pepper was confident that he was "doing more good now" than if he had managed to stay in the Senate. He remained responsive to a diverse constituency that included Haitian refugees, blacks, Hispanics, and many white retirees. He introduced legislation to support housing projects and cancer research, crime prevention programs, and economic aid to South Americans. Undaunted by administration pressure to cut social programs, Pepper continued to pursue his maverick policy in an era of conservatism. As chair of the House Select Committee on Aging, he became a particularly staunch defender of government responsibility for the elderly: "I refuse to believe that a country as rich and powerful as ours can't afford to guarantee the basic comfort and security of its older citizens. I know we can do it," he added, characteristically, "and I intend to be long and loud about it."

Elizabeth M. Makowski
University of Mississippi

John Egerton, *New York Times Magazine* (29 November 1981); Lawrence F. Kennedy, compiler, *Biographical Directory of the American Congress 1774–1971* (1971); Robert Sherrill, *Gothic Politics in the Deep South* (1968); *Time* (25 April 1983). ☆

RADICAL REPUBLICANS

Radical Republicans was a frequently used but often imprecisely defined term applying to one faction of the Republican party in the South after the Civil War. In 1867, at the outset of the congressional program of Reconstruction, the nature of southern Radicalism was reasonably clear: Radicals favored guaranteed equal rights for the freedmen, the establishment of public schools, and fairly sweeping disfranchisement of former Confederates. In some states the Radicals insisted that schools be nonsegregated and that public accommodations be open to both races. The Radicals' opponents, the moderate Republicans, would extend political and civil equality, but nothing more, to the freedmen and hoped to attract part of the native white electorate with a program of economic development. Political alignments and party factionalism make generalization somewhat difficult, but on the whole northern-born white people who came to the South after 1861 (the carpetbaggers), along with the freedmen, were most likely to belong to the Radical faction. However, the majority of the native white Republicans (or scalawags), many with Whig loyalties from the antebellum years, were moderates. Also, as a general rule, the larger the black voting majority in a given district, the greater was the likelihood that Radical candidates—either carpetbaggers or blacks—would be elected.

Southern Radicalism owed much to northern influence, through the power of the carpetbaggers in the party hierarchy and in its commitment both to racial justice and, on occasion, to the social equality of the races. In the 1870s, after some Republican governments had fallen to the Conservatives (or Democrats) and those remaining were under assault, southern Radicals looked to their northern counterparts to intervene once more in southern affairs and salvage their political power, if not the broader goals of Reconstruction. Further intervention, however, was an impossibility after 1872. Finally, the fluidity of political alignments and the serious divisions between moderate and Radical Republicans that weakened the federal government's commitment to Reconstruction also plagued and weakened the southern parties. Radical Republicanism was an artificial development in the South, introduced by outsiders, and, despite its name, it proved to be less than truly radical in its dedication to the freedmen.

Radical strength varied in the southern states, but it was best embodied in the administrations of Adelbert Ames in Mississippi (1874–76), William P. Kellogg in Louisiana (1873–77), and Edmund J. Davis in Texas (1870–74). On the other hand, Radicalism was fairly weak in Florida, North Carolina, and Georgia, where nearly all prominent Republicans were scalawags, and was almost nonexistent in Virginia. In most states, however, Republican parties were divided and greatly weakened by factional and ideological struggles and found it difficult to combat the increasingly strong challenges from Conservatives. White southerners came to equate Radicalism with Republicanism, thereby rejecting the party of the freedmen, drawing a clear color line in politics, driving most whites into the Democratic party, and helping to create a solidly Democratic South, which lasted until the 20th century.

John M. Matthews
Georgia State University

Warren A. Ellem, *Journal of Southern History* (May 1972); Richard L. Hume, *Journal of American History* (September 1977). ☆

RAYBURN, SAM
||||||||||||||||||||||||||||||||||||||||||
(1882–1961) Politician.

Rayburn, congressman from a rural northeast Texas district from 1913 until his death in 1961, was one of the most powerful congressmen in the 20th century. Born in Roane County, Tenn., on 6 January 1882, the son of a Confederate soldier, he moved to Fannin County, Tex., at the age of five. He was educated in country schools and attended Mayo College in Commerce, Tex. After a brief stint as a schoolteacher, Rayburn was elected to the Texas House of Representatives in 1906. In 1911 he was elected speaker of the Texas House, and during reapportionment in that year he carved a congressional district that was to elect and reelect him for 25 terms.

In his early years Rayburn was a fol-

lower of the charismatic Texas senator Joseph Weldon Bailey. With Bailey's fall from power, Rayburn's ambitions for higher statewide office were thwarted. He became a lieutenant of the influential Texas congressman John Nance Garner and in 1932 directed Garner's campaign for the presidency. Rayburn was heavily involved in the negotiations that led to the Roosevelt-Garner ticket.

After Roosevelt's election Rayburn became a workhorse of the New Deal through his role as chairman of the Interstate and Foreign Commerce Committee. His southern populist leanings led him to support most of Roosevelt's economic policies, and his committee handled such legislation as the Truth-in-Securities Act (1933), the Securities Exchange Act (1934), the Federal Communications Act (1934), the Public Utility Holding Company Act (1935), and the Rural Electrification Act (1936).

In 1937 he was elected majority leader of the House of Representatives, and in 1940, upon the death of William Bankhead of Alabama, he was elected speaker. With the exception of the four years that the Republicans controlled the House, Rayburn was speaker from 1940 to 1961. During those years his primary goal was to serve as a bridge in the House between the southern and northern wings of the Democratic party.

He worked closely with southern committee chairmen, presidents, and his protegé in the Senate, Lyndon B. Johnson, to build the coalitions necessary for national policymaking. Rayburn was a strong supporter of defense preparedness, prolabor legislation, public power, and farm programs. Although a segregationist, he supported the 1957 Civil Rights Act and counseled moderation in the reaction to *Brown* v. *Board of Education*.

Though a national leader, he maintained a strong tie to his district and to the rural South. He died of cancer of the pancreas on 16 November 1961, in Bonham, Tex.

Anthony Champagne
University of Texas at Dallas

Anthony Champagne, *Congressman Sam Rayburn* (1984); C. Dwight Dorough, *Mr. Sam* (1962); H. G. Dulaney, Edward Hake Phillips, and MacPhelan Reese, eds., *Speak, Mr. Speaker* (1978); Alfred Steinberg, *Sam Rayburn: A Biography* (1975). ☆

RUSSELL, RICHARD B.

(1897–1971) Politician.

Richard Brevard Russell, a dominant force in the U.S. Senate for almost four decades, was born in Winder, Ga., on 2 November 1897. After earning a law degree at the University of Georgia in 1918, he began practicing law in his hometown.

The son of a state legislator who became the chief justice of the Georgia Supreme Court, Russell began his public career in 1921 when he won election to the Georgia House of Representatives. By the time he was 30 he was the speaker of that assembly, and in 1931 he became Georgia's youngest chief executive. His two years as governor are remembered for the reorganization which reduced the number of agencies and departments.

When the incumbent U.S. senator died in 1932, Russell won the special election to replace him. From 1933 until his death on 21 January 1971, he served on the Appropriations Committee, rising through the seniority system to be its chairman during his last two years. Of perhaps greater note was his service on the Naval Affairs Committee and, after the 1947 Legislative Reorganization Act, on the Armed Services Committee, which he chaired for 16 years prior to 1969. From this base Russell developed his reputation as a leading Senate expert on national defense. Although an advocate of a strong military, he opposed the commitment of American troops to Southeast Asia. Nonetheless, once his advice was rejected, he staunchly supported the military action.

The other major feature of Russell's career—the second longest in Senate history—was his leadership of the southern wing of the Democratic party. He was a master of the chamber's rules, which he used to thwart liberal policy initiatives. He was the chief strategist in southern efforts to defeat, or at least weaken, civil rights bills. Although Russell became a leader of the bipartisan Conservative Coalition, he began his career as a New Deal Democrat. Once the economic crisis receded, Russell, like many southern members of Congress, backed away from additional welfare proposals and government regulations.

In 1948 and 1952 Russell's name was placed in nomination for the presidency at the Democratic National Convention. Considered a gifted political leader, Russell was ambitious for the presidency and frustrated by never gaining it. He and many political commentators blamed this failure on his being southern; his opposition to civil rights legislation did, in fact, effectively limit his national appeal. Russell was instrumental in promoting the career of Lyndon B. Johnson, much of whose presidency Russell came to oppose.

Charles S. Bullock III
University of Georgia

Harry Conn, *New Republic* (12 May 1952); Harold H. Martin, *Saturday Evening Post* (2 June 1951); *New Republic* (6 February 1971); *Time* (1 February 1971). ☆

SECESSION
||||||||||||||||||||||||||||||

The politics of secession consisted of the separate actions of individual southern states in late 1860 and early 1861 and did not represent a unified South acting as a concerted whole. Secession was triggered in November 1860 by the election of Lincoln to the presidency, at the head of a sectionalized Republican party that was publicly committed to prohibiting the expansion of slavery into the federal territories and pledged—though recognizing slavery in the states where it already existed—to the ultimate extinction of slavery. Secession itself occurred in two distinct waves; in each it generally received its strongest support from those areas with the heaviest concentrations of slaves.

After a series of hastily called, highly localized, and often closely contested elections, delegates chosen on a countywide basis attended state conventions convened to decide the question of secession. Seven states had left the Union by 1 February 1861. This first wave—South Carolina, Mississippi, Florida, Alabama, Georgia, Louisiana, and Texas—comprised the original Confederate States of America, the provisional constitution for which was adopted in Montgomery, Ala., on 7 February 1861.

In the meantime Unionist sentiment remained dominant in the states of the Upper South. Here the proportion of slaves to the total population was but half that of the Lower South (25 as opposed to 50 percent), fears of slave uprisings were less intense, economic and cultural ties with the free states were deeper, and the prosecessionist wing of the Democratic party did not control local politics. Secession was temporarily halted. Nonetheless, virtually all political factions in the Upper South conceded the legal right of secession and agreed that any effort to coerce a seceded state back into the Union should be resisted.

Lincoln was inaugurated in early March, and any lingering opportunity for reunion floundered over the issue of the expansion of slavery. The second wave of secession was unleashed when Fort Sumter fell to the Confederacy in April and Lincoln called for state militia to put down what the North believed was a rebellion. Four additional slave states from the Upper South—Arkansas, North Carolina, Virginia, and Tennessee—joined the Confederacy rather than bear arms against fellow southern whites.

The secessionists had appealed successfully to values of individual autonomy, freedom from arbitrary power, and political self-determination. Embedded within America's 19th-century political culture and most often applied to whites only, these values could be used either for or against the Union and either to attack or defend slavery. The politics of secession ensured that this debate would be settled only by a civil war.

William L. Barney
University of North Carolina
at Chapel Hill

David M. Potter, *The Impending Crisis, 1848–1861*, ed. Don E. Fehrenbacher (1976); Ralph A. Wooster, *The Secession Conventions of the South* (1962). ☆

SMITH, FRANK
||||||||||||||||||||||||||||||||||
(b. 1918) Politician.

Smith represented white southerners who rejected segregation during the 1950s and 1960s. Despite being born (21 February 1918) and reared in the Mississippi Delta where segregation of the races was the unquestioned social system, Smith developed "liberal" social and political attitudes. Educated at Sunflower Junior College and the University of Mississippi, Smith went to war in 1942 as a private and returned a captain, a veteran of General Patton's Third Army. He came back to the Delta, to Greenwood, to help establish the liberal *Morning Star* and entered the state senate in 1947. Leaving the newspaper, he worked in John Stennis's Senate campaign and went to Washington as Stennis's assistant.

In 1950 Smith ran for the Delta's congressional seat and defeated a states' rights candidate. Smith established himself through constituent service and good congressional relationships as a strong representative. Keeping his belief in racial integration secret, he worked to mitigate the effects of segregation. In Congress, he also worked for free-trade and consumer-protection laws such as the act requiring content labeling on clothing. Although he obscured his liberalism as much as possible from Delta voters, voting analysis exposed his record, and following the *Brown* decision in 1954 his "moderation" became more evident as Mississippi withdrew from national politics. Smith's adherence to the national Democratic party's platforms and his backing of John F. Kennedy alienated many supporters. In 1962 the segregationists redistricted Smith into a race that he would not win.

Smith's defeat coincided with the integration crisis at the University of Mississippi. Because Smith publicly condemned the state's segregationist government, he was effectively exiled from the state by a power structure that saw him as a traitor. Kennedy appointed Smith to the TVA board of directors; from that office Smith wrote an autobiography to explain his development into a liberal and advocated integration and voting rights for blacks. During Smith's years at TVA (1962–72) he wrote increasingly about environmental issues. Through his books and his position he worked for intelligent management of natural resources, doing battle with both industry and preservationists.

He continued to work toward leading Mississippi and the South into the American mainstream socially and politically. During his exile from Mississippi, Smith discreetly encouraged a moderate group within the Mississippi Democratic party and worked for cooperation with newly enfranchised black voters. Leaving TVA Smith ran for Congress in a new district of central Mississippi. Defeated and denied appointive positions in Mississippi, he turned to academic posts in Illinois and Virginia. In the first, he dealt with a plan for environmental education, and in the second, he examined southern politics.

Although Smith published a book of essays outlining his philosophy entitled *Look Away from Dixie*, he did not look away. Instead, he ended his years of public service as special assistant to Governor William Winter of Mississippi (1980–84). In a sense his life's work was realized because metaphorically Mississippi had rejoined the Union.

Smith's personal correspondence is filled with letters from Mississippians praising his defiance of the segregationist power structure and lamenting their forced silence. Smith clearly was spokesman for southern white integrationists and moderates offended by the excesses of the segregationists. He was important as a symbol for whites because he was undeniably a Mississippian. Other integrationists were dismissed as outsiders who did not understand, but Frank Smith was one of their own and an integrationist. Retired from politics, Smith now runs a bookstore in Jackson.

Dennis J. Mitchell
Jackson State University

Frank Smith, *Congressman from Mississippi* (1964), *Look Away from Dixie* (1965), *The Politics of Conservation* (1966), *The Yazoo River* (1954). ☆

SOUTHERN GOVERNORS' ASSOCIATION

In 1932 President Franklin D. Roosevelt summoned governors from several southeastern states to the Little White House in Warm Springs, Ga., to urge that they establish a regional organization to assist in the development of the South. Within a few weeks the governors of Virginia, Kentucky, North Carolina, South Carolina, Georgia, Florida, Tennessee, Alabama, Mississippi, and Louisiana announced the formation of what was originally called the Southeastern Governors' Association.

Their primary concerns were the economic gap between the South and the rest of the country, how to bring industry to what was at that time a rural economy, and how to raise the overall and individual incomes of the region and its cit-

izens. The first resolution adopted by the conference was directed at changing the territorial freight rate system, which was used to determine costs for transporting goods by rail. Appealing to the courts and to Congress, the governors' efforts were finally successful in ending a system that had forced southerners to pay discriminatory charges.

An equally important result of the early meetings of the governors was the genesis of a permanent organization designed to bring closer cooperation among governors of the southern states, and between these states collectively and the federal government. In the late 1930s a committee for a Balanced Prosperity Program became the forerunner of innumerable committees, task forces, and ad hoc groups, which the governors empowered to attend to the specific details of regional growth and cooperation.

Permanent organizations were set up beginning in the 1940s to address areas of highest priority and ongoing interest to the South. In 1948 the governors formed the Southern Regional Education Board, the oldest interstate compact for higher education and a pioneer in regional planning and action. In 1961 the governors established the Southern Interstate Nuclear Board to encourage proper development of nuclear energy in attaining a balanced, thriving economy in the South. In 1978 the name of the agency was changed to the Southern States Energy Board, reflecting its expanded role in the development of all energy sources and its concern for broad environmental issues. In 1971 the governors launched the Southern Growth Policies Board to give full attention to the problems of economic disparity and unplanned growth. It was authorized to keep a current Statement of Regional Objectives, including recommended approaches to problems and projects deemed to be of regional significance.

In 1982 the Southern Governors' Association voted to move the organization's base of operations to Washington, D.C. Today, the association has 19 member governors, representing the 10 original members plus Arkansas, Delaware, Maryland, Missouri, Oklahoma, Puerto Rico, Texas, the Virgin Islands, and West Virginia. It is the largest and oldest of the regional governors' organizations. Transportation and economic development continue to be important concerns as well as issues ranging from energy and human resources to education and government management.

See also INDUSTRY: / Southern Growth Policies Board

John W. Wilson, Jr.
Southern Governors' Association

Southern Governors' Association, *Annual Report 1984–1985* (1985). ☆

SOUTHERN STRATEGY

In his political dictionary journalist and ex-Nixon aide William Safire defines "Southern Strategy" as "an attack phrase attributing racist or at least political motives toward any position taken on desegregation or busing that would be well received by most Southern whites." William Rusher of the conservative *National Review* has claimed that the term was invented by liberal opponents of Senator Barry Goldwater to suggest that the 1964 Republican presidential candidate was in league with southern bigots, while the senator himself once contended that a journalist

actually coined the term in the 1950s to describe Republican efforts to make congressional gains in the Southwest— efforts in no way related to the race issue. Harry S. Dent, former aide to both President Nixon and South Carolina Democrat-Dixiecrat-Republican Senator Strom Thurmond, has traced its origins to John F. Kennedy's 1960 presidential campaign, specifically to Kennedy's selection of Texas Senator Lyndon B. Johnson as a running mate, the candidate's promise to protect the southern textile industry from low-cost imports, and his sympathy call to jailed civil rights leader Martin Luther King, Jr.

Each of these contentions contains some truth. Southern Strategy also encompasses, however, the rhetoric, tactics, and government policies employed by post–World War II Republican presidents and presidential aspirants to lure the southern voter from the traditional Democratic fold. In marshaling southern support Dwight D. Eisenhower did little more than advocate state control of (largely southern) offshore oil deposits and appoint a number of Eisenhower Democrats to patronage positions. Even so, he was able to capitalize on the southern discontent with the Democratic party, which the Dixiecrat movement of 1948 had reflected, and make impressive gains in the South—gains only partially and temporarily deflected by Ike appointee Earl Warren's authorship of the historic 1954 *Brown* decision. The Goldwater movement nudged even more southerners into the GOP ranks in 1964—a disaster year for the Republicans in every other part of the nation but a banner year in the South.

What the Goldwater movement had begun, Richard M. Nixon and Ronald W. Reagan developed and refined. In an effort to woo southerners away, first from Reagan, then from George C. Wallace's third-party candidacy, Nixon complained often and vehemently during the 1968 presidential campaign about court-ordered busing and criminal-coddling judges. As president, moreover, he opposed busing, promoted a federal project to upgrade (segregated) urban ghetto schools, and ordered an IRS tax exemption for segregated private schools that promised—but did not necessarily deliver—an open admissions policy. He also vowed to appoint a "strict constructionist" southerner to the Supreme Court; the liberal Republican Ripon Society, among others, attacked his appointments of social-economic conservatives to the federal bench in the South—including one nominee who, when asked his position regarding segregation, replied, "That's a difficult question to respond to without being put on the spot." During the 1980 presidential campaign, Ronald Reagan promised to get able-bodied "bucks" off the welfare rolls and won every southern state but President Carter's native Georgia. As president, he too opposed busing, slashed federal welfare budgets, promoted massive increases in defense spending, sought to resurrect the Nixon policy of tax exemptions for segregated private schools, and pushed for a constitutional amendment to restore public school devotional programs—all positions dear to the hearts of conservative southerners. Much in the Nixon-Reagan programs and rhetoric was a response to a perceived national conservative trend. This national conservative strategy had its origins, however, in a Southern Strategy.

Tinsley E. Yarbrough
East Carolina University

Harry S. Dent, *The Prodigal South Returns to Power* (1978); Reg Murphy and Hal Gulliver, *The Southern Strategy* (1971). ☆

TALMADGE, EUGENE

(1884–1946) Politician.

Born in Forsyth, Monroe County, Ga., the son of Thomas and Carrie Talmadge and father of U.S. Senator Herman Talmadge, Eugene Talmadge served several terms as governor of Georgia during the period of ferment in which he dominated Georgia politics (1926–46). He was known for his fiery political style that evoked fanatical loyalty from thousands of agrarian supporters who responded to his appeals in celebration and defense of rural Georgia's embattled culture and lifestyle.

As his political style evolved from populistic agrarianism to virulent racism, Talmadge gained notoriety as the stereotype of a southern demagogue, a "Cracker buffoon," a "redneck racist." At the peak of his popularity, Talmadge drew crowds of 20,000 to 30,000 for campaign rallies in small towns throughout Georgia. Country folk from everywhere in the state came to stand in the hot Georgia sun and eat barbecue, sneak a swig or two of corn liquor, listen to "Fiddlin' John" Carson's country music, and take in "Farmer Gene's" political road show. With the appropriate southern drawl and proper quotations from the Scriptures, Talmadge conjured up vivid images of a blessed but embattled rural lifestyle, condemned the farmers' enemies as if he were a country preacher railing against Satan, and promised "he-man" action in the farmers' interests against the minions of such alien forces as "mastadon trusts" and Wall Street.

Eugene Talmadge (seated) on the Georgia campaign trail, 1936

Talmadge's rural political style represented in many ways a significant agrarian response to the vast changes associated with the emergence of modern America. In a process begun in the late 19th century, the older America of autonomous rural communities was breaking down before the new centralized bureaucratic order, which served "the regulative hierarchical needs of urban-industrial life." "Farmer Gene's" response was similar to the earlier efforts of the Southern Farmers' Alliance and the Populist party led in Georgia by Thomas Watson.

Both Talmadge and Watson made cultural appeals to Georgia farmers at times when their rural lifestyle seemed seriously threatened by circumstances largely beyond their control. In many ways Talmadge's style reflected his support of southern agrarian culture. This can be said about his appeals to his fellow Georgians' fundamentalist religious beliefs, to their habits of "macho"

individualism and personal violence, and to their localistic lifestyle centering on long-term attachments to specific places and specific people. Moreover, many of his actions seemed to be designed to preserve Georgia's rural culture in the face of powerful assaults from the outside world, including his attacks on the New Deal federal government. Talmadge always based his defense of rural Georgia on traditional Democratic party principles: the "classical" economic doctrines of Adam Smith and the political doctrines of Thomas Jefferson and the Jacksonian Democrats. When "Farmer Gene" burst upon the Georgia political scene, the Bourbon Democratic establishment supported the New South creed, which celebrated the union in the South of the American pastoral and industrial images described by Leo Marx in *The Machine in the Garden*. Talmadge's political style rejected the Bourbons' ideological synthesis and constructed a sacred mysticism out of the elements of southern rural culture. Earlier, "Farmer Gene's" Populist precursors had called for variation in the traditional principles of the Democratic party when they proposed legislation and other actions requiring significant government power to bring the party's outlook into line with changing realities. Once this effort failed, however, their defense of the rural lifestyle and of the traditional Democratic principles turned into something akin to an irrational emotional response to attacks on a sacred mysticism.

At the zenith of his career, Talmadge was bold enough to muster his agrarian forces against President Franklin D. Roosevelt, but something went awry and "Farmer Gene's" rural political style failed to hold enough supporters firmly to his banner to carry him through the fight. Under normal circumstances his style offered great promise of success. It focused on the cultural issues (tied to rural Georgians' "personally structured value systems"), which, along with purely local concerns, usually dominated American politics before the New Deal. After such a serious crisis as the Great Depression allowed economic issues to capture the voters' attention, however, Talmadge's rural and political style declined in effectiveness from its peak of the mid-1930s. In his later campaigns, "Farmer Gene" focused on the race issue as he tried to find another cultural issue that could earn him votes in rural Georgia.

Karl Rodabaugh
East Carolina University

William Anderson, *The Wild Man from Sugar Creek: The Political Career of Eugene Talmadge* (1975); Sarah Lemmon, "The Public Career of Eugene Talmadge, 1926–1936" (Ph.D. dissertation, University of North Carolina, Chapel Hill, 1952); Karl Rodabaugh, *Southern Studies* (Spring 1982). ☆

THURMOND, STROM
(b. 1902) Politician.

Born in Edgefield, S.C., on 5 December 1902 of a prominent political family, Strom Thurmond has been active in politics for more than half a century. Personifying the conservative nature of the region, Thurmond is an ageless institution reminiscent of W. J. Cash's metaphorical South, "a tree with many age rings . . . bent and twisted by all the winds of the years, but with roots in the Old South."

The formative influences on Thurmond began with his father and were enhanced by the deep political and historical forces of his native Edgefield. William Watts Ball, editor of the Charleston *News and Courier*, once observed that Edgefield "had more dashing, brilliant, romantic figures, statesmen, orators, soldiers, adventurers, and daredevils than any [other] county of South Carolina." This rural county has produced 10 governors, half as many lieutenant governors, and a number of U.S. senators. Additionally, Edgefield harbors a deep strain of violence, which originated in the 18th century and has been rather proudly maintained into the 20th. There is also in the area a core of evangelical fundamentalism, which has emerged in Thurmond's personality and value system.

The blood feuds of the 19th century and the *code duello* that characterized much of the South have approached a cultural norm in South Carolina. In

1856 Congressman Preston Brooks of Edgefield caned Massachusetts Senator Charles Sumner into insensibility because of a Sumner speech regarded as slanderous by Brooks. Strom's father "had to kill a man" as a result of a political feud. Senator Benjamin Ryan Tillman, also from Edgefield, and a close personal friend of Thurmond's father, initiated a fist fight on the Senate floor with a colleague. A less spectacular example of the Edgefield tradition occurred when Strom Thurmond twice pinned Senator Ralph Yarborough outside a committee room in order to prevent a quorum.

Thurmond made his national reputation as a presidential candidate in 1948, leading a dissident band of segregationists in their defection from the national Democratic party. Thurmond and his Dixiecrats were manifestations of the stress inherent in the New Deal coalition bequeathed to Harry Truman. Thurmond's secession in 1948 was reminiscent of pre-Civil War tensions when regional candidates bolted the Democ-

Strom Thurmond, Dixiecrat leader and Republican U.S. senator, 1980s

racy to close ranks behind defenders of southern values and their peculiar institutions. Not since the days of John C. Calhoun had the South seen such a popular symbolic leader as Thurmond. Indeed, Thurmond as a neo-Calhounite added a fascinating historical dimension as the South faced its "Second Reconstruction."

By a kind of historic osmosis Thurmond absorbed the ethos of familial and regional values. The development of his personal value system mirrored his social environment. Thurmond's conceptual interaction with the world around him has been essentially fundamentalist. As a literalist he sees things in absolute terms. A Manichaean by nature, Thurmond has a vision of events dominated, as Robert Sherrill put it, by "metaphysical absolutes" where there is "one Eden, one Hell, one Heaven, one Right, one Wrong, and one Strom." The most revealing account of Thurmond's political fundamentalism, vision of history, and analysis of contemporary political events is his book, *The Faith We Have Not Kept*, published in 1966.

To some, Strom Thurmond is nothing more than a segregationist with a penchant for young women. However, deeper analysis shows Thurmond to possess a prism-like quality through which national issues are refracted, making him a symbolic figure of a South in transition. After the Voting Rights Act of 1965 and the increase of black voters in South Carolina, Thurmond ended his overtly segregationist rhetoric and began seeking black votes. The South of 1948 is light years from the South of today, and the evolution of Thurmond and the South stand as twin testaments to a man and a region that have achieved some accommodation with their history.

The appeal of Strom Thurmond is best

captured by the reply of a mill worker, when asked why he was voting for Thurmond: "Strom stands up for what he believes in, even when he's wrong." In sum, Thurmond remains the quintessential southern politician: enduring yet resilient, simple but canny, militaristic yet biblical, and always the candidate.

James G. Banks
Cuyahoga Community College

James G. Banks, "Strom Thurmond and the Revolt Against Modernity" (Ph.D. dissertation, Kent State University, 1970); Jack Bass and Walter DeVries, *The Transformation of Southern Politics: Social Change and Political Consequences since 1945* (1976). ☆

WALLACE, GEORGE
(b. 1919) Politician.

George Corley Wallace entered Alabama politics in 1946 when he was elected to the state legislature. Six years later be became a state circuit judge. In 1958 he ran for governor, and when he lost the contest to a blatant racist, Wallace vowed that he was "not goin' to be out-niggahed again." Keeping his promise, he was elected governor in 1962 on a racist platform. In his inaugural address he shouted, "Segregation now! Segregation tomorrow! Segregation forever!" While governor, Wallace criticized the passage of the Civil Rights Act of 1964 and the Voting Rights Act of 1965, unsuccessfully tried to prevent the racial desegregation of the University of Alabama, and had to contend with a voting rights march on the state capitol organized by Martin Luther King, Jr. Wallace entered the national political scene in 1964 when he ran for the Democratic presidential nomination, although he withdrew from that contest before the convention.

When he could not succeed himself as governor, he successfully ran his wife Lurleen for the office in 1966. Two years later Wallace ran for the presidency as the candidate of the American Independent party. He appealed to the latent racism of voters all over the country when he orated for law and order in a racially troubled society and against federal interference in local schools, the liberal Supreme Court, and federal restrictions in regard to racial considerations and the sale of private homes. While his 46 electoral votes came from the South, approximately one-half of his 10 million popular votes were cast by supporters living outside that region.

In 1970, after his wife had died of cancer while in office, Wallace ran for the gubernatorial post again, barely defeating the lieutenant governor who had completed Lurleen Wallace's term. In 1972 Wallace coveted the Democratic nomination for president, billing himself as a national, not a regional, candidate, and as best representing the people's attitudes on the major issues of the day. In the primary contests Wallace

George Wallace campaign button

called for law and order and opposed busing to achieve racial integration in the schools. Wallace won, or showed great voting strength, not only in the South but also in states such as Wisconsin, Pennsylvania, Indiana, Michigan, and Maryland. His campaign was abruptly sidetracked when he was shot. Paralyzed from the waist down, he was thereafter confined to a wheelchair. The would-be assassin had ended not only Wallace's campaign but also his growing national political power.

In 1974 Wallace won the Alabama governorship for an unprecedented third term. In 1976 he made another race for the presidency, but when his campaign had no appeal in the southern primaries his national plans collapsed, and he devoted himself to being governor. As in the past, Wallace worked for increased expenditures for education and highways, but also, as in the past, his accomplishments were overshadowed by his stance on civil rights for blacks.

Wallace once again ran for governor in 1982 and won. His campaign was especially noteworthy because he reversed his previous arch-segregationist position and appealed for—and got—black support, an indication of the dramatic racial and political changes in Alabama in the quarter-century of Wallace's career. Citing health problems, Wallace announced on 2 April 1986 that he would not seek a fifth term as governor, thus terminating his active political career. Wallace is perhaps the most influential political figure in Alabama in the 20th century.

Monroe Billington
New Mexico State University

Numan Bartley and Hugh Davis Graham, *Southern Politics and the Second Reconstruc-*

tion (1975); Monroe Billington, *The Political South in the Twentieth Century* (1975); Marshall Frady, *Wallace* (1968); Lance Morrow, *Time* (14 April 1986); Robert Sherrill, *Gothic Politics in the Deep South* (1968). ☆

WATSON, TOM
||||||||||||||||||||||||||||||||||||||||
(1856–1922) Politician.

Thomas Edward Watson spent most of his life in the village of Thomson, Ga. As a young man he taught in country schools, later becoming a highly successful lawyer who practiced in small towns. He succeeded in part because he knew country people well and spoke in a colorful, rural idiom. For Watson the ideal society embraced the life he had known as a young boy, when his grandfather had owned a valuable plantation. After the Civil War his family lost that estate and sank into poverty. Although Watson became a wealthy lawyer, he knew that many southern farmers—plagued by falling cotton prices and increasing tenancy—faced hard times. He did not believe that the New South creed, with its call for industrialization and urbanization, would help them. Instead, Watson championed the ideal of a South that consisted largely of prosperous farmers.

With the rise of the Farmers' Alliance in the 1880s, Watson hoped that its programs could help country people. In 1890 he won a seat in Congress as an Alliance candidate, and during his one term he introduced a resolution that eventually resulted in free delivery of rural mail. In 1891 Watson joined the People's party and became a leading spokesman for southern Populism, a movement of landowning farmers and tenants who wanted to improve rural life by making reforms in the prevailing economic system. To achieve that, Watson called on blacks and whites to join forces in working for economic reforms. He did not advocate social equality between the races, but his attempt to win black votes caused white Democrats to denounce him and his fellow Populists as threats to white supremacy. During the congressional elections of 1892 and 1894, the Democrats resorted to massive frauds to insure Watson's defeat. In the face of that harsh treatment, Watson remained loyal to the People's party; in 1896 he served as its vice presidential candidate.

Following his defeat in that election, Watson retired to private life, where he devoted himself to practicing law, writing history, and editing several magazines. Between 1900 and 1920 he continued to use his influence with former Populists to determine the outcome of Georgia elections, and near the end of his life he served for two years in the U.S. Senate. After 1900 he no longer demonstrated the idealism that he had displayed as a Populist leader in the 1890s. Instead of encouraging blacks and whites to work together for common political objectives, he advocated the disfranchisement of blacks. He also became a leading proponent of anti-Catholicism and anti-Semitism. When he died in 1922, the newly revived Ku Klux Klan held him in high esteem.

William F. Holmes
University of Georgia

Charles Crowe, *Journal of Negro History* (April 1970); Robert Saunders, *Georgia Historical Quarterly* (Fall 1970); Thomas E. Watson Papers, Southern Historical Collection, University of North Carolina, Chapel Hill; C. Vann Woodward, *Tom Watson: Agrarian Rebel* (1938). ☆

YOUNG, ANDREW

(b. 1932) Minister, civil rights worker, politician, and diplomat.

Andrew Jackson Young, Jr., was born 12 March 1932 in New Orleans to the middle-class household of Andrew Jackson Young, Sr., a dentist, and Daisy Fuller Young. He attended Dillard University (1947–48) and Howard University, where he received his B.S. degree in biology (1951). After leaving Howard, Young attended Hartford Theological Seminary, where he received a degree in divinity (1955). He was ordained by the Congregational church before returning south to pastor churches in Georgia (Beachton and Thomasville) until 1957. That year, unfulfilled with his small-town ministry, he became executive director of the National Council of Churches' New York-based Department of Youth Programs. In that capacity he hosted the nationally televised, youth-oriented series *Look Up and Live*.

Then, captivated by the burgeoning southern civil rights movement, Young returned south again as head of the United Church of Christ's (UCC) voter registration program headquartered in Alabama. While working with the UCC, Young joined the staff of the Southern Christian Leadership Conference (SCLC) in 1961 at the request of its president, Martin Luther King, Jr. Young acquired the reputation of being a moderating force within King's spirited inner circle. While other King lieutenants played firebrand roles during the initial stages of campaigns in such cities as Birmingham and Selma, Young came in later as SCLC's negotiator in meetings with segregationists. Young served as SCLC's executive director and its executive vice president, and he drafted versions of the

1964 and 1965 Civil Rights Acts. He left SCLC in 1970 to make the transition from protest politics to electoral politics.

Young's initial campaign for Georgia's Fifth Congressional District seat was unsuccessful, but he won in 1972. He and Barbara Jordan, who was elected to the House of Representatives from Texas in the same year, thus became the first southern blacks since 1898 to win congressional elections. Young was reelected in 1974 and 1976. During his tenure as congressman, Young opposed the Holt Amendment, which sought to prohibit federal withholding as a means to compel school desegregation. He actively supported the extension of the Voting Rights Act of 1965, citing the increase in black registration (29 percent in 1964 to 56 percent in 1972) in states affected by this law. He also favored the subsequent broadening of the act to include language minorities, and he served on the committees for Banking and Currency and for Rules.

Young was one of the first nationally known black leaders to support Jimmy Carter's 1976 bid to become the first

Andrew Young, civil rights activist and mayor of Atlanta, Georgia, 1980s

modern president from the Deep South. Young, as Carter's major advisor, allayed the suspicions of many black leaders and voters about Carter and his southern background. Young came to Carter's defense, nullifying criticism of the former Georgia governor, when he made a campaign blunder by stating his support for the "ethnic purity" of white neighborhoods. When some 90 percent of the more than 6 million black voters cast their ballots for Carter, providing him with his slim margin of victory over Gerald Ford, Young's active support was seen as pivotal by many. In fact, Carter stated that Young was the only person to whom he owed a political debt.

Carter appointed Young U.S. ambassador to the United Nations. In this position, Young was able to create a viable dialogue between the U.S. government and the Third World after a period of intense alienation during the Nixon-Ford years. In particular, relations between Africa and the United States bettered as a result of Young's efforts to do away with apartheid. His negotiations contributed to the coming of majority rule to Zimbabwe in 1980. Young's time in the United Nations was marked by a bluntness unusual to diplomacy. His statements that Britain had institutionalized racism and that Cuban troops were a stabilizing force in Angola, among others, created much controversy. Young resigned his post in 1979 when an uproar occurred after he met with a Palestine Liberation Organization representative, counter to official U.S. government policy. He came back to Atlanta and was elected its mayor in 1981.

Expressing the conviction that foreign and domestic policies of the Reagan Administration were "clear failures," Young's mayoral career has been characterized by continued support for Atlanta's affirmative action programs ("good business" as well as the law) and attempts to link the gateway city economically with the "new frontier" markets of Latin America, Africa, and the Middle East.

Vincent D. Fort
Morehouse College

Robert H. Brisbane, *Black Activism* (1974); James Gaskins, *Andrew Young: Man with a Mission* (1979); *New York Times* (3 January 1982); Howell Raines, *My Soul Is Rested: Movement Days in the Deep South Remembered* (1977); Eddie Stone, *Andrew Young: Biography of a Realist* (1980). ☆

RECREATION

JOHN SHELTON REED

University of North Carolina

CONSULTANT

☆ ☆ ☆ ☆ ☆ ☆ ☆ ☆ ☆ ☆

*Overleaf: Cajun children fishing, Schriever,
Louisiana, 1940*

LEISURE

||||||||||||||||||||||||||||||||||||||||

C. Vann Woodward begins his *American Counterpoint* with a lengthy treatment of southern leisure. He points out that like so many other myths about the South, this one tends to be "Janus-faced," to present contrary aspects that change depending on the observer's point of view. For some, southern leisure has been a gracious thing, involving careful attention to nonpecuniary values and activities in a world mad with materialistic frenzy. Others, looking at the reverse side, see the unattractive countenance, the Lazy South, the "Sahara of the Bozart," with all its blemishes—"idleness, indolence, slothfulness, languor, lethargy, and dissipation."

Leisure / Laziness Myth. These two contrary aspects notwithstanding, the leisure/laziness myth has consistently involved two distinct cultural subjects—work and nonwork—and has represented the typical southerner as less interested in the former than most Americans and more interested in the latter. The myth's Janus-faced quality becomes clear only when values have been assigned to work and to leisure. Some northern observers and proponents of the "new Industrial South" have focused on the South's distaste for work, viewing it as a destructive anachronism that needed to be reformed, and dismissed the various claims about the virtues of free time. But apologists for the South have tended to emphasize the value of leisure as a time for human culture, spiritual reflection, contemplation, friends, family, nature—those things that make life worth the effort—and at the same time to criticize the American preoccupation with busy work, mindless growth, and the resultant spiritual and cultural exhaustion.

This myth, then, has generated two kinds of statements, those about facts and those about values. As such, it may be analyzed on two levels. On the one hand, one may attempt to determine the extent to which the myth is true—the extent to which southern attitudes and behavior correspond to the stereotype. The social scientist, for example, may test southern mass attitudes and behavior and speculate about their causes. On the other hand, the myth may be accepted on its own terms, as an expression of values and as a part of the larger cultural dialogue or "counterpoint" that has existed between the South and the rest of the country. In this regard historians and literary critics may investigate the opinions of articulate and influential writers concerning work and leisure in order to show how at its highest reaches culture emerges in dialogue about questions of values, about what should or might be, rather than about what already exists.

The cultural debate surrounding the leisure/laziness myth goes back a long way. During the mid-18th century southerners such as John Hammond portrayed their region as a land of tropical abundance where tranquility and leisure were the rule. Such idyllic descriptions, echoed by men such as Robert Beverley and William Byrd II, were mainly designed to counter a bad European press and attract settlers. But still these early allurement accounts sounded one major mythic value that by the Civil War was completely developed—that work should be a means to an end, that it should be a way to earn a livelihood and to free oneself from time to time for more important things.

During the antebellum period southern spokesmen expanded, developed, and defended the leisure myth. According to people such as Virginia's Governor Henry Wise, leisure was indispensable for the natural aristocrat, providing the opportunity for learning and public service, freeing him from the servile arts and drudgery for the liberal arts and the creation of new culture, a culture that would benefit all classes. The second part of the myth included an indictment of northern money grubbing, business, and harsh treatment of workers. The North had made money its god, work an end in itself, and had forgotten about human, nonpecuniary needs and the importance of leisure.

But even as the myth developed, critics from both the North and South recognized that the ideal did not match the reality, that the lack of work was more a problem than an opportunity. They pointed out that free time in the South was more the occasion for drunkenness, idleness, and dissipation than for learning, culture, and service. It was work and the discipline of work that held a people together, not the freedom of leisure. It was in the marketplace, not the saloon, that culture grew.

This sort of dialogue, involving a blend of voices, some enthusiastic, others ironic or even cynical, smoldered

after the Civil War, especially in the works of southern writers such as Sidney Lanier. It was later rekindled and flared briefly in the 20th century as a response to rapid industrial changes.

Agrarians and the New South. As did many of their contemporaries and the majority of historians who have written about the period, the Twelve Agrarians of *I'll Take My Stand* believed that American industry and business had taken a new direction in the 1920s— had shifted attention from production to consumption. According to the Agrarians, "It [was] an inevitable consequence of industrial process that production [outran] the rate of natural consumption." This overrun had resulted in chronic overproduction and unemployment. But instead of dealing with these consequences of success in a humane fashion, American business had "romanticized" industry and work and developed a "new gospel of consumption." Promoting "the incessant extension of industrialism," the multiplication of luxuries, and the cultivation of fantastic and even lethal desires for them, this new gospel "never proposed a specific goal; it initiated the infinite series"—a squirrel-cage existence where growth was for growth's sake, work purposeless and never ending, and consumption artificial and manipulated.

The Agrarians proposed a traditionally southern alternative to this mindless "progress." Instead of work that was brutal, harried, and meaningless, they offered "a form of labor that [was] pursued with intelligence and leisure"— that was more natural and task oriented, connected to the soil and to a stable social order. Instead of free time that was lost to consumption, satiety, and aimlessness, they suggested a leisure in the "culture of the soil" where art and religion flourished; "a free and disinterested approach to existence" was possible; the amenities of life such as manners, conversation, sympathy, family life, and romantic love were carried on; and the enjoyment of life could be spontaneous. To the Agrarians, leisure should be an integral part of life. It should be a part of work, with a social and economic place. It should not, like industrial free time, alienate more than it brings people together.

Walter Hines Page agreed that leisureliness was a hallmark of regional identity. But unlike the Agrarians, he welcomed industry to the New South because, in addition to its material blessings, it would offer "the inestimable boon of leisure." For Page, leisure was an industrial product as important as consumer goods because it could be used to redeem parts of southern culture even as the traditional forms of work were being lost.

But spokesmen for the New South have generally dismissed these dreams. People such as Henry W. Grady and Richard Edmunds welcomed industry with none of Page's hopes for leisure and saw the South's casual approach to work as a curable weakness. Grady saw the South falling "in love with its work"; Edmunds observed that his compatriots had learned that "time is money." New southern businessmen have been as busy as their northern friends promoting goods and services designed for the "leisure market." City leaders court industry, boasting that the work ethic is stronger in their region than elsewhere. Following the national trend, southerners as a group have lost interest in increased leisure and have remained content with 40 hours' work a week for over 40 years—this after a 20-year period of rapid reduction in the hours of labor.

Even southern historians, while not so much welcoming the Puritan work ethic, have joined in the general condemnation of leisure. W. J. Cash saw the old southern assumptions about leisure—"that the first end of life is living itself"—woefully out of date, a way of degeneration and "incompatible with success." David Bertelson saw leisure as the traditional myth, but laziness as the traditional reality. According to Bertelson, laziness worked against a sense of community because it fragmented southerners and encouraged a preoccupation with self instead of the community.

The discussion has largely ended. Even though a few echoes are heard from time to time, southern life and leisure are no longer seriously proposed as alternatives to industrialism nor is increasing free time offered as a way for the South to accommodate modernism and retain its identity. The lively exchanges about what was more meaningless, work in the industrial squirrel-cage or free time in a disintegrating culture, are mostly forgotten. Yet the perception in its simplest form—that southerners prefer leisure more and work less—remains.

In magazine articles, in newspaper Sunday supplements, and even in advertisements, the region's lazy-leisurely reputation continues to be spread, even internationally. Occasionally a journalist will editorialize and condemn or praise the lazy, leisurely South. But usually, these portrayals are not serious business. Rather they tend to be amusing reports about a charming, regional peculiarity. Public attitudes tend to conform to these popular reports. John Shelton Reed and others have demon-

Watching the bathers at Gulfport, Mississippi, postcard, early 20th century

strated that college students North and South still hold on to this regional stereotype. Apparently, the old dialogue produced a vivid enough image in the public awareness to survive its passing.

But another possibility remains—that the myth is true, and the dialogue, too, about both a reality and an ideal. Those who engaged in the dialogue often thought of themselves as reporters as well as leaders and spokesmen. Even the Agrarians, calling their region back to tradition, made claims about historical truth and existing culture. The extent to which myth matches reality has been approached empirically with some interesting results.

Distinctive Southern Behavior. Statistical evidence for the first three decades of this century indicates that southerners did prefer leisure more and work for wages less than other Americans. For example, in 1920 a typical northern worker making the same hourly wage as his southern brother worked longer hours. If he got a raise he would work even longer hours while the typical southerner would take more time off at higher income levels. But this regional difference disappeared by the 1940s and the South, like the rest of the nation, became content with the 40-hour week.

When investigators study attitudes about work directly, instead of opinions about stereotypes, they have so far failed to find regional variations. There is simply not enough evidence to support or contradict the belief that southerners value work more or less than other Americans. Nor is there much in the way of systematic evidence about southern attitudes toward leisure.

But indications can be found that southerners are distinctive when it comes to leisure behavior. The evidence comes from a variety of sources and it is remarkably consistent. By and large, southerners simply do less in their leisure time than other Americans—or at least less of most things that social scientists and market researchers are interested in.

The U.S. Department of Labor's 1972

survey of consumer expenditures shows that southerners spend a smaller percentage of their income on "recreational goods and services" than other Americans—from the lowest to the highest income classification. Research undertaken by private marketing firms also shows that southerners engage in less "commercially relevant behavior" in their leisure than others. In general, these studies have found that the South is not as good a market as its population would suggest and that it is a particularly bad market for recreational products.

Other studies show lower levels of magazine and newspaper circulation, miles driven per year (a stand-in for billboard advertising), television watching and radio listening, memberships in hobby and special interest groups, voting and political activity in general, and what the National Endowment for the Humanities (NEH) called the fine or beaux arts (with the exceptions found by the 1973 Louis Harris Poll of singing in a choir, listening to religious music, and listening to country and western music).

These regional differences are not enormous. Region makes less difference than education does, for instance. But regional differences are about the same size as differences between black and white—about the same size, that is, of some other "cultural" or "ethnic" differences in the United States.

One may reasonably ask at this point what do southerners do when they are not consuming, watching television, reading the newspaper or magazines, or participating in clubs? A Harris Poll in 1978 found a number of these things that were included in the NEH study, mentioned above. According to this poll, southerners spend more time fixing things around the house, helping others,

having a good time with friends and relatives, resting after work, getting away from problems, taking naps, and "just doing nothing."

One good way to summarize these findings is to point out that the South has a pattern of leisure that is more "time intensive" and less "goods intensive." Southerners are more likely to choose activities that take more time but less money than other late 20th-century Americans. From all indications the modern South is still holding on to vestiges of a preindustrial folk culture in its leisure. Considering that he wrote over 50 years ago about a South he feared was vanishing, John Crowe Ransom's observations in *I'll Take My Stand* that the arts of the South are the "social arts of dress, conversation, manners, the table, the hunt, politics, oratory, the pulpit, the arts of living and not the arts of escape . . . ; community arts in which every class of society could participate after its kind," are remarkably accurate today.

Since the myth, if not the proven reality, has been around so long, there is certainly no shortage of explanations for the lazy-leisurely South. H. L. Mencken's view, echoed more recently by the Kentucky-born gonzo journalist, Dr. Hunter Thompson, was that white southerners are genetically disposed to idleness and vicious habits. The South Carolina poet Josephine Pinckney, on the other hand, argued that these are innate black traits, somehow spread to whites by contagion. Southerners' favorite explanation—or excuse—has probably been the weather. In its old version, favored by Robert Beverley and William Byrd II, this argument has it that it is too easy to get by where food grows almost by itself and nobody needs many clothes. A version more applicable to the urban, industrial South says that it is just too hot to do much of anything. Another popular theory points to the effects of slavery, producing laziness in slaves and slaveholders alike, and also leading nonslaveholders to believe that exertion was for slaves and beneath their dignity. Still another recalls the earlier, fanciful notion that the South's supposed Cavalier heritage produced individuals fleeing Puritan constraints while pursuing a hedonistic, "long-haired" lifestyle in the southern climes.

C. Vann Woodward, on the other hand, saw a distinctive skepticism emerging in the South after the Civil War about the American dream of endless progress, industrial work, and human perfectibility in general. Resulting from the regional experience of defeat, failure, sin, poverty, and guilt, this skepticism has produced a people less caught up in the fervid rush of modern life and more content with the leisurely enjoyment of the simple present. Finally, the old myth and debate about the defects and virtues of work and leisure may have percolated down through the South, so that the culture comes to resemble what its mythmakers imagined. George B. Tindall has shown how southern myths have a definite way of influencing regional realities. For the lazy-leisurely South, it may be a case of nature imitating art.

Whatever their origins, southern attitudes toward work and leisure are part of the regional culture. Like other cultural traits, these are not things that individuals work out for themselves. *They are learned* from those around us while we are growing up and from each other after we are grown. A large part of any culture is made up of shared views of what is appropriate; success in any culture depends on learning what those views are and, ordinarily, on coming to share them. One is not born knowing what to do with leisure time, nor do individuals make it up as they go along. People learn how to pass the time appropriately. Those who share the same culture—a regional culture, for instance—have learned more or less similar lessons.

See also ART AND ARCHITECTURE: Resort Architecture; BLACK LIFE: Sports, Black; FOLKLIFE: Storytelling; HISTORY AND MANNERS: Manners; INDUSTRY: Industrialization and Change; LANGUAGE: Conversation; LITERATURE: Agrarianism in Literature; MYTHIC SOUTH: New South Myth; / Agrarians, Vanderbilt

John Shelton Reed
University of North Carolina
at Chapel Hill

Benjamin K. Hunnicutt
University of Iowa

David Bertelson, *The Lazy South* (1967); H. C. Brearley, *American Scholar* (Winter 1949); W. J. Cash, *The Mind of the South* (1941); Norval Glenn and Charles Weaver, *Texas Business Review* (November–December 1982); Fred C. Hobson, *Alabama Heritage* (Summer 1986); Lewis Killian, *White Southerners* (1970); Forrest McDonald and Grady McWhiney, *American Historical Review* (December 1980); Peter Marsden et al., *Social Forces* (June 1982); H. L. Mencken, *Prejudices, Second Series* (1920); Josephine Pinckney, in *Culture in the South*, ed. W. T. Couch (1934); John Shelton Reed, *The Enduring South: Subcultural Persistence in Mass Society* (1974), *North Carolina Historical Review* (April 1983); *One South: An Ethnic Approach to Regional Culture* (1982), *Southerners: The Social Psychology of Sectionalism* (1983); Joe Gray Taylor, *Eating, Drinking, and Visiting in the South: An In-*

formal History (1982); George B. Tindall, *The Ethnic Southerners* (1976); Twelve Southerners, *I'll Take My Stand: The South and the Agrarian Tradition* (1930); Rupert B. Vance, *Human Geography of the South: A Study in Regional Resources and Human Adequacy* (1935); C. Vann Woodward, *American Counterpoint: Slavery and Racism in the North-South Dialogue* (1964), *The Burden of Southern History* (1960). ☆

Baseball

||||||||||||||||||||||

Throughout baseball history only four former Confederate cities have enjoyed major league baseball status. Richmond was in the American Association for part of a single season in 1884, and the current Houston organization began play in 1962. The move that really counted in southern terms was the move of the Milwaukee Braves to Atlanta in 1966. When the expansion Washington Senators became the Texas Rangers in 1972, the picture was completed.

Exclusion from the big leagues for so long did not mean the South had been divorced from baseball. Far from it. The region had produced many major leaguers, including some of the greatest and most colorful, such as Ty Cobb. The South contributed some of the most influential broadcasters the game has had, including Jay "Dizzy" Dean and Pee Wee Reese, who worked television's game of the week in the 1950s and early 1960s, and radio's Mel Allen and Red Barber. Major southern cities such as Memphis, Nashville, Birmingham, Louisville, and Little Rock have long supported minor league teams and industrial leagues, and southern college teams have dominated competition. The South manufactured the great majority of the game's bats, including the Louisville Slugger, and since 1886 it has been the site of spring training camps.

What then explains the absence of major league membership for so long? The overpowering heat and humidity of the South was one consideration, especially in an age preceding night games, air-conditioning, and summer-weight uniforms. Connie Mack and Clark Griffith, two of the most influential major league owners in the first half of the 20th century, insisted that the weather in St. Louis, Cincinnati, and Washington sapped the strength of players on their teams even before mid-season. Mack stated that those teams "must be 25 percent better than any other in order to win a pennant." Players spoke of soaking their feet, baseball spikes and all, in pails of ice water, then sloshing into the steamy fields in those cities. They bemoaned the nights of fitful sleep in roasting hotel rooms, and recalled soaking their bedsheets in tub water, then wrapping themselves in them for relief. Thoughts of playing in locations farther south were not broadly entertained.

Another basic problem was travel. The population centers of the South that might have supported major league play were too far removed from the long established northern teams. Perhaps even more important, they were separated by great distances from each other. Not until 1958 and the age of convenient and extensive airline travel did the majors open up the West Coast, which was far from populous. In this respect, the South was not far behind.

Until the 1960s southern culture was exported to the nation's baseball fans in the personalities of regional sons who made major league rosters. Often what this meant was little more than an image of Snuffy Smith in the dugout. A short biographical sketch of Mississippian Guy "Joe" Bush appeared in a 1932 issue of the baseball bible, *The Sporting News*, for example. Its opening sentence was: "No lazy bones in the body of this Cub pitcher, his Southern birth notwithstanding." An earlier generation had grown up with the illiteracy of "Shoeless" Joe Jackson, a South Carolinian who had been so frightened of the big cities of the North that he fled from his first train ride en route to the major leagues. He had needed an adult babysitter to ensure his later arrival in Philadelphia. Fans would shout from the grandstands, asking him to spell "cat." It was good storytelling and reinforced a powerful stereotype America had of its southern citizens.

Jackson's contemporary, Ty Cobb, epitomized the violent southerner. All big league teams had their sons of the South. They made good copy for baseball writers, many of whom were noted for their cynicism and expertise with one-line putdowns. To be sure, all players from the South were not reported in comic or glaring fashion, but more than enough were. Especially demeaning were instances of players' statements being spelled in dialect. Georgian Luke Appling, a Hall of Fame shortstop who played in the majors for two decades, sometimes referred to in print as a cracker, was repeatedly quoted as saying such words as "jes" (for just), "shucks," "gonna," " 'spect," "cain't," "reckon," "uster" (for used to), and "nuthin." "Leg" somehow even became "laig" in Appling's mouth, as reported by the *New York Times*. Fellow Georgian Cecil Travis, another longtime American Leaguer, was once referred to as a "Geawgian."

Yet, a pair of broadcasters from the Deep South—Mel Allen and Red Barber—brought their homespun qualities to New York, the biggest baseball market in the world, and became the most respected of their profession. Both men, extremely fair and balanced in their reportage, represented baseball at its ideal, sportsmanlike best. In doing so their colloquialisms gained undenied respect. Barber's talk about tearing up the pea patch swept Brooklyn. His "catbird seat" was shared by millions of Dodger fans. Nevertheless, the players remained the focus.

Baseball in the South involved nearly every hamlet in the region, though decades went by before the sport was played on a par with the rest of the nation. The game's early history in Dixie featured men from north of the Mason-Dixon line taking leadership. Indeed, quite a few of these early baseball "teachers" carried the label of "carpetbagger." Returning Confederate veterans, many of whom had learned the game from Union soldiers, had preceded them and created a taste for the sport among the white citizenry. Exslaves had learned in the same way and played their own brand of ball on their side of the tracks. Not until Reconstruction ended, however, did baseball expand and improve.

The game, as had already happened elsewhere in the nation, became dominated by community teams, with sponsorship often supplied by businessmen. Jewish merchants, in particular, funded teams in New Orleans, Macon, Atlanta, Augusta, Mobile, Houston, and Birmingham. In the mid-1880s the original Southern League was instituted, and organized professional baseball finally set up shop in the region. Atlanta *Constitution* editor Henry W. Grady, in the forefront in promoting a modern, industrial New South, was key to the establishment of the Atlanta franchise in that league. The team was an obvious example of boosterism.

The Southern League unfortunately led a miserable existence, needing frequent reorganization efforts to prevent its demise. Team rosters had very few players from the South, as locals were not yet talented enough to get contracts with even second-rate minor league clubs. The players who had the contracts performed so poorly that it was believed their ineptness was typical of "northerners sick in the heat."

By the 20th century the sport was extremely significant in southern culture. Wherever there was a mill or mine, that company fielded a team. Competition in the many industrial leagues that developed was fierce, promoting a notable improvement on the ball diamond. Workers who detested the long days and dangerous conditions of their underpaid employment nonetheless were exuberant when their company team was victorious, especially if a championship was at stake. Community spirit was present, at least on game days. Management recognized this and did their utmost to keep their best players and to add the best from other teams. A winning ball club meant a stable work force. Who would want to leave a mill with a title team to take a job with a competitor that fielded losing nines?

Improved skills drew notice from the major league cities to the north. Community and regional pride was enhanced more than ever as increasing numbers of homegrown players advanced to the "bigs." Ty Cobb roared out of Georgia, Joe Jackson came up from South Carolina, Tris Speaker from Texas, Clyde Milan from Tennessee, and the march

was on. Throughout the 20th century the lineups of major league clubs have been dotted with such nicknames as "Dixie," "Reb," "Tex," and "Catfish." The South became and remained a chief stomping ground for big league scouts.

Only since the late 1940s, however, when organized baseball was finally desegregated, has that scouting included blacks. Yet black players in the South had been competing on their own fields since the late 1880s. Most of the black semipro players who toured the United States decades later were from the South. Not surprisingly, their struggle was frequently marred by racist insults, even when their playing ability was held to be superior to that of whites.

Even as late as 1953 a Jackson, Miss., team in the Cotton States League refused to play against their Hot Springs opponent because the Arkansas squad was going to use a black pitcher. To compound the situation, the league's officers forfeited the game to Jackson. Hot Springs, to their way of thinking, had no right to expect Jackson to play against a black. Their ruling was overturned by the commissioner of minor league baseball, who made it clear that blacks could not be refused the right to play. In 1955, however, a Pine Bluff, Ark., team in the same Cotton States League signed three blacks to contracts and then released them a few days later, citing the pressure placed on them by other league teams.

The South by the mid-20th century had enthusiastically supported numerous minor league teams, 43 cities in North Carolina alone actually fielding professional teams in seven separate leagues in 1949. Over the years the South had seen play in leagues with names like Texas, Piedmont, Southern, Longhorn, South Atlantic, and Appalachian. Their own sons had graduated to the majors by the many hundreds, often stereotyped in scapegoat images associated with the South. When racism was involved, the term *southerner* assumed an extra burden. In recent years, black and white southerners, such as Dennis "Oil Can" Boyd (Miss.), Ron Guidry (La.), Nolan Ryan (Tex.), and Dwight Gooden (Fla.) have been among the game's best players.

A single major league team declared itself to be "America's Team" in the 1980s. This bold stroke fit nicely into the apparent "southernizing" of the United States. The Atlanta Braves, the only major league baseball franchise ever based in the Deep South, claimed *national* sovereignty because of its owner's extensive television cable system. Fans in all corners of the nation watched the Braves on WTBS-TV and, familiar with that team's personnel because of its frequent television exposure, became supporters of Ted Turner's organization. The Braves, in essence sole baseball representatives of the South, are owned by a white man, utilize the American Indian as their symbol, and had a black, Hank Aaron, as the best player in their history. If anything tells the story of change in America, and particularly in the South, that is it.

See also MEDIA: / Turner, Ted

John E. DiMeglio
Mankato State University

Charles C. Alexander, *Ty Cobb: Baseball's Fierce Immortal* (1984); Alfred Duckett, *I Never Had It Made* (1972); Harvey Frommer, *Rickey and Robinson* (1982); Donald Gropman, *Say It Ain't So, Joe!: The Story of Shoeless Joe Jackson* (1979); John D. McCallum, *The Tiger Wore Spikes: An Informal Biography of Ty Cobb* (1956); Daniel Okrent and Harris Lewine, ed., *The Ultimate Baseball Book* (1979); Lawrence S. Ritter, *The Glory of Their Times: The Story of the Early Days of Baseball Told by Men Who Played It* (1974). ☆

Basketball
|||||||||||||||||||||||||||||

"**B**asketball is a city game," writes Pete Axthelm in his 1970 book, *The City Game.* "Its battlegrounds are strips of asphalt between tattered wire fences or crumbling buildings; its rhythms grow from the uneven thump of a ball against hard surfaces. . . . Basketball belongs to the cities." Indeed, basketball does belong to the cities. However, the classification of basketball as a "city game" overlooks the tradition of basketball in the South, where the game is played in both urban and rural areas, and where it has for years flourished as a rural game. Basketball courts of all descriptions and designs blanket the South. Salvaged stop signs or sheets of metal or wood often make functional backboards for young players who attach a suitable rim, as their desire to play basketball overrules any prescribed notion of a conventional goal or court.

Shortly after the invention of basketball by James A. Naismith in 1891, southerners began to experiment with the game. As early as the 1920s, high school boys throughout the South played on organized school teams and generally on outdoor courts. The indoor gym was a later addition to the southern game, and it was not uncommon at first for a Mississippi team to dress in spiffy uniforms, patterned after the indoor teams, and play on outdoor courts in subfreezing weather. School systems and towns dedicated to the game could perhaps afford the fancy uniforms, but it would be many years before they could afford the big gymnasium. For high schools and colleges in the South, neither of which had as large a budget as their northern counterparts, the cost of football was often prohibitive. Basketball, on the other hand, required a smaller investment and by the 1950s was earning large revenues for colleges such as Kentucky, North Carolina State, and Western Kentucky. In 1946, North Carolina State "imported" Everett Case, a coach from basketball-rich Indiana; by 1950 the school's annual attendance had reached 230,000, the largest in the country. Part of the increased attendance was the result of increasing postwar college enrollment. College athletic facilities could not hold the crowds, and at a University of North Carolina–North Carolina State game the problem reached crisis proportion. A large crowd of followers, frustrated after being denied admission, tore down the doors of the gym, poured in, and stood around the perimeter of the court. The game eventually was canceled as fans continually spilled onto the court. A similar problem caused cancellation of a game between North Carolina State and Duke in 1948.

Even before World War II, college basketball in North Carolina was very popular. Beginning in 1933, Raleigh hosted the Southern Conference Tournament with Chamber of Commerce support. In 1947 the tournament was shifted to Duke University's 9,000-seat gym, still in use today and a vivid symbol of the richness of basketball tradition in the South. With the catalyst of a $100,000 donation from the Charles Babcock family, the North Carolina Legislature appropriated money for Reynolds Coliseum at North Carolina State, finished in 1951. Not surprisingly, smoking was always permitted in the facility, and R. J. Reynolds tobacco supporters bragged about the ventilation system capable of providing "a complete change of air every 15 minutes." With the new coliseum, North Carolina State dubbed itself the "basketball capital of the South."

North Carolina was also home to a very competitive and successful group of women's basketball teams, led by Hanes Hosiery of Winston-Salem, N.C., the dominant force in the Southern Textile League. Writing about women's basketball in the South in a 1979 issue of *Southern Exposure*, Elva Bishop and Katherine Fulton assert that "high caliber women's basketball wasn't born in the South in the 1970s; it merely got its second wind." Indeed, such teams as Hanes Hosiery and Nashville Business College were very high caliber. By 1947, in large part because of the dominance of Hanes, newspapers in Winston-Salem were hailing the city as the "new women's cage capital." Up until 1947, Hanes had limited competition in the Southern Textile League, made up of company teams formed to induce corporate pride and competition in workers. The dominance of Hanes in that league led the team to compete nationally through the Amateur Athletic Union's (AAU) national playoff. Though Hanes did not win the 1948 tournament, it did reach the quarterfinals where six out of the eight teams were from North Carolina, Georgia, and Tennessee. In 1951 Hanes won the AAU National Championship, defeating the Flying Queens of Wayland College, Tex., 50–34.

North Carolina State and Raleigh may have boasted that, with the completion of Reynolds Coliseum, they were the basketball capital of the South, but one school and one state could lay more legitimate claim to such a title. If there is one team and one region of the South that is most noted for its basketball it is Kentucky. Much of that fame, ironically, is because of a basketball sage from Kansas. Adolph Rupp, who coached the Kentucky Wildcats from 1930 to 1971, came to Kentucky from Kansas where he played under Phog Allen. After 28 seasons at Kentucky, Rupp won his 772nd game, passing the record previously held by Allen, his former coach and teacher. Rupp was to southern basketball what Bear Bryant was to football, though Rupp's longer tenure made him more dominant in his sport. A gruff, determined man, Rupp had the image of a country farm boy turned basketball genius. He became known as a Kentucky gentleman, one who loved his cattle and his bourbon. Dubbed "the Baron," Rupp was a strict father to all of his players. Like other teams in the Southeastern Conference (SEC), Kentucky resisted recruiting black players until the late 1960s, and Rupp's paternal callousness made him seem all the more reluctant to integrate his team. Shy he was not, and in a 1929 interview he claimed he took the job at Kentucky on the advice of a gas station attendant, "because I'm the best damn coach in the country." Such remarks were not uncommon from "the Baron," whose superstitious attachment to wearing brown suits led many to refer to him simply as "the man in the brown suit." In his final years at Kentucky, with his program suffering from lesser talent and from Rupp's genuine fatigue and poor health, he made a modest proposal to

the press, again reinforcing his well-earned agrarian image: "The legislature should pass a law that at 3 o'clock every afternoon any basketball coach who is 70 years old gets a shot of bourbon. These damned bouncing, bouncing, bouncing basketballs are putting me to sleep."

Not far from Rupp's Lexington is Bowling Green, Ky., home of the Western Kentucky University Hilltoppers and another coach who embodied southern basketball style and tradition. Edgar Allen Diddle, known as Eddie Diddle, began as the coach of all sports at Western in 1922. A basketball pioneer from outdoor court days, Diddle was a native of Gradyville, in Adair County, where he had played and coached. The son of a lumberman, farmer, and livestock trader, Diddle brought a rural wit and savvy to basketball. Always preferring man-to-man defense, Diddle often said his teams "just play by ear." "Attack is our stock in trade," Diddle once said. "And there are three ways to attack: down one side of the floor, down the middle and down the other side. And you don't even need a play if you get a half-step start on the opposing team." His "half-step" approach bred a very successful fast-break style of basketball at WKU, an approach that after 42 seasons at WKU had won him 759 games.

Fast-break basketball was the backbone of both the Diddle and Rupp games. The success of both of these coaches and schools led many other programs in the South to emulate the "run-and-gun" style of basketball, but not until the mid-1970s could any school approach the success and dominance of Kentucky.

Jim Crow was a member of nearly every major college basketball team in the South, but nowhere was he more visible than in the Southeastern Conference. Perry Wallace of Nashville became the first black player to start for an SEC team when he took the floor for Vanderbilt in 1967. Thinking back on those days he once remarked, "I heard a lot of racial jokes. At Ole Miss they waved the rebel flag. They yelled a lot of things I'd as soon forget." The rebel flag still waves at SEC basketball contests, particularly when the Universities of Mississippi or Georgia play, as a vivid reminder of the history of racial inequality in the South.

By the early 1970s all SEC schools were successfully recruiting black players, but in the mid-1960s many episodes clearly reflected the racial conflict and change on the basketball floor. The strangest of these tales concerns an all-white Mississippi State team that won the SEC in 1963. As champions of the all-white SEC, State was slated to play Loyola University, which started four black players. Mississippi politicians, particularly Governor Ross Barnett, who six months previously had attempted to block James Meredith's entrance to the University of Mississippi, endeavored to make the Bulldogs of State stay home. A Jackson *Clarion-Ledger* editorial said segregationists felt that "if Mississippi State University plays against a Negro outside the state, what would be greatly different in bringing integrated teams into the state? And why not recruit a Negro of special basketball ability to play on the Mississippi State team? This is the road we seem to be traveling." Barnett and his fellow segregationists said "no" to the trip, but white fans, students, and the Mississippi State president let their basketball pride override racial prejudice, claiming loudly that State should make the trip to Ann Arbor, Mich., to play Loyola. Barnett's next

tactic, a court injunction prohibiting the team from traveling, was deflected with the help of a local sheriff, also a State basketball rooter. Legend has it that the Oktibbeha County sheriff failed to serve the injunction and turned his back long enough for the players to board a Southern Airlines plane in Starkville for the trip to the National Collegiate Athletic Association (NCAA) tournament. They went on to lose a close, hard-fought game to Loyola, eventual NCAA Champions.

As collegiate teams in the South have become integrated in the last two decades, southern schools have "imported" coaches and players from across the country, and the game in the South has lost much of the regional identity it once had. Such college teams as Kentucky and North Carolina, once dominant, are now just two of a large pack of schools that consistently field excellent teams and battle for a trip to the finals of the NCAA tournament. The Atlantic Coast Conference (ACC) and the SEC, the South's two major conferences, are two of the most powerful conferences in the country in the 1980s. Players and coaches on the various SEC and ACC teams, however, hail from all parts of America. The South has recently seen a trend to hire very able coaches with roots in urban areas of the Northeast. Bobby Cremins of Georgia Tech and Jim Valvano of North Carolina State are two examples of the new brash "yankee" coach who recruits as easily on the playgrounds of Brooklyn and Atlanta as he does in rural North Carolina or Georgia. Dean Smith of the University of North Carolina, the "dean" of southern coaches and a product of Kansas, is the current basketball sage of the region. UNC recently completed a new coliseum, named after Smith, that was built just large enough to surpass the capacity of Rupp Arena in Lexington, Ky. While players and coaches battle for victory on the court, the alumni and university officials try to "beat" each other by building the biggest coliseum. The "Dean Dome" is currently the South's basketball showpiece.

The days of Diddle and Rupp have certainly passed, and with them passed an important era of southern basketball. No longer does a coach, with a serious tone, explain that his team, like the Saturday night dance fiddler from western Kentucky, "plays by ear." But throughout the South, especially in Kentucky and North Carolina, the sounds of a basketball, whether dribbled on a steep hillside or a packed-dirt court in the low country, are music to the ears of many. Basketball goals and courts of every description fill the landscape of the South's cities, towns, and rural communities. Television commentator Joe Dean, broadcasting the SEC game of the week, echoes the feelings of many southern fans, players, and coaches. As a Tennessee forward pushes a soft 20-foot jump shot through the net, Joe Dean typically calls out with excitement: "String music from Tuscaloosa, Alabama."

Tom Rankin
Southern Arts Federation

Pete Axthelm, *The City Game* (1970); Elva Bishop and Katherine Fulton, *Southern Exposure* (No. 2, 1979); Bill Finger, *Southern Exposure* (No. 2, 1979); *Newsweek* (6 January 1947); *Newsweek* (12 February 1968); Harry T. Paxton, *Saturday Evening Post* (10 March 1951); Fred Russell, *Saturday Evening Post* (19 January 1957); *Time* (12 January 1959). ☆

Boxing
||||||||||||||||||

Modern boxing grew out of the fairs and gambling rooms of early 18th-century England. A bloody and violent sport that placed a premium on courage and a low price on human life, it also reinforced the class structure of England. Poor men fought and sometimes died for the entertainment of wealthy patrons, who risked only the money they bet. By the Regency period, boxing had achieved remarkable popularity. It excited the imaginations of Lord Byron, William Hazlitt, and Dr. Samuel Johnson, and it received the patronage of members of the royal family.

Wealthy southerners who traveled to England learned the intricacies of boxing. Lovers of English sports and pastimes, and especially of the English class system, planters sometimes staged impromptu matches between slaves, although there were probably fewer of these matches than once believed. In addition, throughout the 19th century the South provided a moral climate conducive to the growth of boxing.

In part, this moral climate was the result of southern attitudes toward leisure. Even before the Revolution, a leisure ethos was apparent in the South. Whereas northerners emphasized the moral importance of work and criticized sport, southerners viewed the enjoyment of leisure as an important aspect of a gentleman's life. Consumption and hospitality, pride and defense of one's honor, were apt to gain more social approval than the pursuit of money and respectability.

The first important American boxer was a southerner. On 18 December

1810 in a field 25 miles from London, Tom Molineaux, an ex-slave from the South, battled English champion Tom Cribb for title of the world's best fighter. Molineaux was backed by another American black, Bill Richmond, who had fought a few matches himself but spent most of his time running a pub. The fight was close and controversial, but in the end Cribb won. Molineaux stayed in England, engaged in several more important contests, and died young and penniless after a serious bout with dissipation.

Molineaux's career stirred little American interest. Organized boxing was practiced seldom in the South until the 1830s. By that time the sport faced troubles in England. Fixed fights, ring deaths, and Victorian piety and moral earnestness all hurt boxing in England. In 1836 English champion James "Deaf" Burke left the Old Country for America, or, as he referred to it, "Yankeeshire." Searching for an area in which to hold a prize fight, he looked toward the South. In 1837 he fought Sam O'Rourke in New Orleans. The most important result of the fight was to show that New Orleans would tolerate a sport that was barred in most other parts of the country. Even during the opening tense days of the Civil War, patrons of the prize ring were not too busy to journey to Kenner, La., to watch Mike McCool take "the conceit out of big Tom Jennings."

By the time of the Civil War, a pattern in American boxing had emerged. Although promoters staged a number of championship fights in the South, few southerners became important boxers. Most boxing champions came from the cities of the North, and a high percentage of these were immigrants (or sons of immigrants) from England and Ire-

land. Nevertheless, wealthy southerners enjoyed watching boxing matches and often took lessons in "the manly science of self-defense" at exclusive men's clubs in southern cities.

The "golden age" of southern boxing occurred in the 1880s and early 1890s. On 7 February 1882 John L. Sullivan defeated Paddy Ryan for the American championship in a bout staged in Mississippi. Sullivan soon attracted a large national following, and boxing momentarily came out of the shadows and saloons into the sun of public acclaim. In this dash for quasi-respectability for boxing, New Orleans led the way. The height of 19th-century American boxing occurred during a remarkable three-day period in September 1892. On consecutive days, New Orleans's Olympic Club staged three world championship fights. In the final of the matches, James J. Corbett defeated Sullivan. The triple event was a great critical and financial success.

After 1892 New Orleans declined as the boxing center of the nation. The focus of the ring followed the hands of gamblers, first to the West, then to New York and Chicago, and most recently to Las Vegas and Atlantic City. In the 20th century the South produced some leading fighters and even a few great champions, but the South was never again the center of boxing.

The South produced two of the 20th-century's greatest boxers—Joe Louis and Muhammad Ali. Louis (1914–81) was born to sharecropping parents on a farm near Lafayette, Ala. The young Louis moved with his mother and stepfather to Detroit, where he became active in amateur boxing and had his first professional fight in 1934. The "Brown Bomber" went on to be a legendary heavyweight champion from 1937 to

1949. He was a symbol of the triumph of the underdog, a popular Depression-era figure for many Americans, but his greatest significance was as a symbol for black Americans. He was a soft-spoken, clean-living, God-fearing man, and southern blacks looked on him as one of their greatest heroes.

Muhammad Ali (Cassius Clay) was the preeminent boxer of the 1960s and 1970s. Born 18 January 1942 in Louisville, Ky., to a close-knit, working-class family, Ali won a 1960 Olympic gold medal in boxing, and after 19 victorious professional bouts he defeated Sonny Liston for the heavyweight championship in 1963. Ali became a controversial champion. His refusal to enter the armed services resulted in the World Boxing Association stripping him of his championship. He later became the only person to regain the heavyweight crown twice. A black Muslim in religion, Ali became one of the best known and most admired Americans in the Third World. He was a colorful champion with his quick wit, graceful style, and dominating personality. He was an appropriate figure in the turbulent 1960s and became a major cultural symbol for the black pride uniting blacks in the South of his birth, in the nation, and in the world.

Randy Roberts
South West Texas State
University

Elliot Gorn, "The Manly Art: Bare-Knuckle Fighting and the Rise of American Sports" (Ph.D. dissertation, Yale University, 1983); Randy Roberts, *Papa Jack: Jack Johnson and the Era of White Hopes* (1983); Dale A. Somers, *The Rise of Sports in New Orleans 1850–1900* (1972). ☆

Cheerleading and Twirling

Cheerleading and twirling are found in a variety of forms in the South, ranging from children's informal playground routines to highly formalized and choreographed performances at high school, college, and professional sports and musical entertainment activities. There are rewards for participants in competitions, including trophies, travel, scholarships, prize money, and prestige. Southern cultural spirit and identity are revitalized through these activities.

Formalized cheerleading seems to have originated in eastern and midwestern colleges at the turn of the century. It quickly spread to high schools and colleges nationwide, taking a particularly strong hold in the South. Cheerleading began as a student extracurricular leadership activity tied to athletics and performed by two to five males to inspire school or class loyalties and good citizenship in the student body.

After World War I more women studied at coed institutions and chose to participate in extracurricular events. By the end of World War II cheerleading had become predominantly a female activity. Squads of 5 to 18 girls were selected on the basis of physical or social characteristics, performance skills, and popularity. The entertainment aspect of cheerleading has grown to rival its original focus on school leadership and has broadened the range of performances.

In the last 15 years male cheerleaders have become more prominent—now representing about 40 percent in the college ranks. The popularity of gymnastics, which grew from the influence of the Olympics, has made cheerleading a true athletic activity and attracted better male and female athletes. Two cheerleading groups—the Dallas-based National Cheerleading Association (NCA) and the Universal Cheerleading Association (UCA)—promote, supply, and generally address the administrative needs of southern cheerleaders. The NCA, for example, trains over 150,000 high-school and college students annually in 350 clinics and workshops. It markets cheerleader goods of all sorts—uniforms, megaphones, and pompons. The modern pompon was invented by a southerner, Lawrence "Herkie" Herkimer, a former Southern Methodist University cheerleader, who applied colored streamers to batons. The NCA, which Herkimer founded, sells crepe, plastic, and metallic pompons. The NCA and the UCA both stage annual nationally televised cheerleading championships.

In 1972 the Dallas Cowboys broke a long tradition of using high school cheerleaders for their games and began the first professional cheerleading squad consisting of seven scantily clad professional dancers. The pattern was soon followed by such National Football League cities as Houston, Atlanta, Washington, D.C., and others in an effort to capitalize on the potent entertainment value of a successful blend of sex with sports. Their style is an extension of the cheerleading and pompon girl traditions, and it has stimulated a revitalization of amateur cheerleading.

Formalized baton twirling also began as a male activity in the early 20th century, but during the 1930s it evolved into performances by groups of beautiful women dressed in skimpy costumes and using smaller, lighter batons than their male counterparts had carried. Best known as an activity for a marching corps in association with marching bands in halftime shows and parades,

baton twirling also features solo and team performances in entertainment and competitive settings. Although batons are the most popular of twirled objects, flags, sabres, and flaming batons are among the specialty items used by experienced twirlers.

The dream of becoming a professional cheerleader or a baton-twirling Miss America has inspired many southern girls. By the age of three or four, some girls have begun to publicly perform as mascots with groups of older, more skilled performers as well as with girls their own age. While many girls eventually take private lessons to strengthen their physical coordination skills and to master specific techniques, most begin to learn necessary skills by watching friends or siblings and then attempting to execute various maneuvers in the backyard or on the playground. In many urban and suburban neighborhoods, it is common to find girls gathering to play and practice their skills on a daily basis. They bring these street skills to school and recreation center squads and attend camps and workshops where their skills mature and are refined. Terry Southern in "Twirling at Ole Miss" (1962) discusses the Dixie National Baton Twirling Institute, one of the largest twirling clinics, which is held annually at the University of Mississippi.

Cheerleading and twirling combine African and European cultural elements. Robert Farris Thompson argues for the African source of "the main baton-twirling pose, with left hand on hip," and he believes that cheerleading, in general, was mainly derived from southern black influences. *Time* magazine noted (11 December 1939) that "some of the most versatile cheerleaders" were "at Southern colleges (notably Alabama and Tennessee)." Swiss flag-twirling was another influence, and

European-style precision marching provided the context for twirling at football halftimes.

Whatever the origins, Afro-American culture, particularly in the South, has developed these activities into extraordinary art forms drawing on performance principles based in the aesthetics of black American traditional and urban cultures. Syncopation, black dance styles, and soul music have changed the rhythmic character and style of movement for both cheerleading and baton twirling, injecting a new rhythmic energy for black and white performance styles.

Phyllis M. May
University of Indiana

Phyllis M. May, " 'Uhn! Ain't It Funky Now?' Folkloric and Ethnomusicological Perspectives on Afro-American Cheerleading Performance as Play and Display" (Ph.D. dissertation, Indiana University, forthcoming); Fred Miller et al., *The Complete Book of Baton Twirling* (1978); Randy L. Neil, *The Official Cheerleaders Handbook* (1979); Terry Southern, *Esquire* (February 1963); Robert Farris Thompson and Joseph Cornet, *The Four Movements of the Sun: Kongo Art in Two Worlds* (1981). ☆

Cock Fighting
||||||||||||||||||||||||||||||||||||||

See VIOLENCE: Cockfighting

Fairs
||||||||||||||||

"**S**tep right up! You won't believe your eyes!" Such cries of midway carnies

Child eating cotton candy at the annual Cotton Carnival, Memphis, Tennessee, 1940

have rung out in the South at state, county, and local fairs, accompanying animal and homemaking exhibitions and a variety of competitions. Southern fairs—like all fairs—have roots in primitive festivities that focused on religious celebrations and bartering. In the Middle Ages fairs were well-established trade mechanisms, evolving by the 1800s toward the grand-scale educational and commercial expositions known as world's fairs. Evolving also in the 1800s in the United States were the agricultural fairs, with their prizes and competitive displays, which most strongly shaped the nature and growth of fairs in the South.

Merging agricultural society exhibitions and traveling carnivals, southern fairs began as mechanisms for promotion of agricultural societies. Planters' clubs were formed in the 18th century for discussion of agricultural problems and stimulation of farm improvements.

In 1810 Elkanah Watson organized in Massachusetts the nation's first agricultural fair, and the tradition of annual fairs spread quickly in the eastern seaboard states and more slowly into the South. During the 1840s and 1850s fairs in the livestock states of Kentucky, Tennessee, and Missouri prospered, and by the late 1850s to 1860s most of the southern states boasted annual state fairs. So popular and successful were the fairs that many of the sponsoring agricultural societies— increasingly organized on a statewide basis—purchased permanent fairgrounds and equipment. Georgia's fair in Macon in 1831 stands out as one of the earliest in the Deep South, where fairs were apparently fewer in number than in such states as Virginia and the Carolinas. In most southern states the legislatures readily supported the agricultural societies and fair associations through allocation of state funds; both the societies and fairs promoted commerce and the planters' interests. Businesses and private individuals also offered support.

Fairs have always lured crowds with the exotic, the new, the exciting. Southern farmers and planters in the early to mid-1800s perused the newly imported Cashmere goats and Berkshire hogs in the exhibition stalls, while their children gawked at the two-headed snakes and miniature horses in the sideshows. Fairs served as important mechanisms for transmission of knowledge about improved breeds of domestic animals and innovations in farm machinery. Not only did farmers learn of improvements through local and state fairs; southerners garnered international recognition at the world's fair level, as did one Tennessee livestock baron with his blue-ribbon Saxony sheep at the London World's Fair in 1851.

The South has hosted its share of large expositions. Eight regional expositions, planned mainly to promote cotton and other southern products, had been held in the South by 1907. The Atlanta World's Fair and Great International Exposition in 1881 attracted some 225,000 persons and received considerable financial backing from northerners. In 1883 Louisville's Southern Exposition drew 375,000 people and trumpeted its 15 acres of exhibit floor space. The federal government earmarked approximately $1,300,000 in loans and contributions for the New Orleans World's Industrial and Cotton Centennial Exposition (1884–86), which highlighted the South's industrial prospects. Other successful expositions followed. Despite the economic panic and depression in 1893, Atlanta launched the Cotton States and International Exposition and attracted over 1,200,000 attendees. South American and European countries as well as a variety of states contributed buildings and displays. Booker T. Washington played a prominent role in the exposition's efforts to promote racial reconciliation.

More recently, San Antonio, Tex., dazzled the world in 1968 with HemisFair, an international exposition celebrating the city's 250th anniversary. With a theme of "The Confluence of Civilizations in the Americas," this world's fair contained on its 92.6 acres, among other things, a 622-foot-high observation tower, a multimillion-dollar pavilion, a mile-long lagoon, and a mini-monorail train. Twenty-two countries and 19 private corporations participated as exhibitors, and Texas's colorful, multiethnic heritage was the focus of several key exhibits. Knoxville, Tenn., served as the South's next world's fair host in 1982. Congruent with the theme

"Energy Turns the World," the Sunsphere, a 266-foot-high tower topped by a restaurant and observation decks, punctuated the skyline and rivaled the six-story, cantilevered, prism-like U.S. Pavilion for attention. In addition to major exhibitions by corporations and foreign nations (most notably the People's Republic of China), the fair featured a variety of shows and displays heralding the culture of the state and the region: a Tennessee music revue, the Stokely Folk Life Festival with southern Appalachian musicians and craftspersons, and a two-barge exhibit on the history of the Tennessee Valley Authority.

Just two years later New Orleans hosted the Louisiana World Exhibition, whose theme was "The World of Rivers: Fresh Water as a Source of Life." The 84-acre site contained a 2,300-foot collage, the Wonder Wall, plus a maze of streams and other water conduits. Displays ranged from an exhibit of Vatican art treasures to a full-scale oil rig. Local flavor on a large scale appeared in the form of jazz and Cajun musical performances, twice-a-day Mardi Gras parades, boat parades on the Mississippi River, and the Louisiana/Gulf South Folklife Festival. Both the Knoxville and New Orleans fairs suffered from disappointingly low attendance and major financial problems, coloring the prospects for the 1992 Miami World's Fair.

To most southerners, though, the character of the fair is embodied in the sights, sounds, and smells of the state, county, or local fair. Usually held in September or October, each state fair is held in one of the larger cities, such as Birmingham, Ala., or Raleigh, N.C. Especially in years past, the location allowed for many rural children's first trip to a big city and for many young city dwellers' first contacts with farm animals. Showmanship, competition, recreation, education, social exchange— all have been inextricably entwined in the history of southern fairs. Exhibitions of prize livestock and displays of award-winning jams and pies stand a room or a building away from school children's science fair entries and artwork. Government agencies' demonstrations show the newest developments in space technology or flood control, and private enterprises promote their wares and distribute literature. Just yards away beckons the other world of the fair— the midway.

Once providing entertainment in the form of horse races, state and county fairs became dependent upon the traveling carnivals that proliferated after the Chicago World's Columbian Exposition in 1893. Within a short time many fairgoers felt that the midway carnival was the heart of a fair. The heyday of the carnival business was in the 1920s, and freak shows were common sideshow entertainment in the 1930s and 1940s. Images of the midways in the 1920s to the 1940s converge with those of today's midways: gaudily and scantily clad women doing a striptease to blaring, bawdy music; carnies shouting "test your skill and win the prize" from booth after booth lined with cheap trinkets and brightly colored stuffed animals; monkeys racing on tiny motorcycles; a tattooed man turning to display a body covered with lines and pictures; children laughing and screaming as they meander through the house of mirrors; teenagers boasting of five turns on the scariest amusement ride; grownups clamoring to lift baubles out of a bin using a toy earth mover. Eudora Welty celebrates these worlds through her photographs of country fairs and in her short story "The Petrified Man."

The excitement of being free of usual social constraints for a few evenings continues to have appeal—if not full approval from the community. Church and civic groups have long protested the lewd shows and gambling practices in carnivals. During the last several decades northern states cracked down both through legislation and enforcement on gambling and other illegal enterprises at fair carnivals, but southern states were somewhat slower to act and have had the reputation for having local authorities more willing to take bribes to overlook illegalities. For this and other reasons certain images are frequently associated with southern fairs: the "rube," or country bumpkin who gets fleeced, and the hotheaded brawler infuriated by losses in rigged carnival games. Although tighter policing now prevails, a certain amount of rigging persists and is considered by some to be part of the risqué character of the fair. The midway dazzle increasingly accompanies performances of musical stars, often country singers, and special events such as car races or tractor pulls.

County fairs often try to emulate the offerings of the state fairs. At county fairs, however, more local color is evident in the activities, the foods, and the participants. Alongside common fair foods such as hotdogs, cotton candy, and popcorn, fairgoers often find special treats, such as hickory-smoked barbecue, peanut brittle, and fried pork rinds. Many county fairs host a local beauty pageant and competitive activities for local youth, often members of 4-H clubs. The Neshoba County Fair in Philadelphia, Miss., is an unusual but excellent example of down-home southern atmosphere at the county level.

About 12,000 people descend on Philadelphia and pack into cabins built for the fair and passed down through generations. The 70,000-plus additional daytime fairgoers hear local and state politicians engaged in old-time stump speaking. Horse races, parties, contests, and a carnival midway offer excitement; but a different revelry marks the night-long songfests, prayer and memorial services, and the hours of play and visiting for scattered family members drawn together for the annual event. Although many county fairs lack the permanent structuring of the Neshoba County Fair and more closely mimic the state fairs, most boast distinctive local touches.

Outstanding among smaller southern fairs are various Native American celebrations, such as the Cherokee Fall Festival at Scottsboro, Ala., and the Choctaw Indian Fair in Philadelphia, Miss. Traditional Native American dances, crafts, games, and foods highlight the festivities. Growing in popularity at the local level are festivals with many features of fairs. Various festivals celebrate the European heritage of area residents, as with the Scottish Festival and Highland Games at Stone Mountain, Ga; the Mexican Heritage Fiesta in Port Arthur, Tex.; and the British Faire in Mobile, Ala. Native products are the focus of countless festivals; for example, the Seafood Festival in Cedar Key, Fla.; the Tobacco Festival in Bloomfield and the Wool Festival in Falmouth, Ky.; the Brushy Mountain Apple Festival in North Wilkesboro, N.C.; the Pumpkin Festival in Pumpkintown, S.C.; and the Sorghum Festival in Springville, Ala. Of note, too, are the festivals and contests centered on southern pastimes, such as the Athens, Ala., Tennessee Valley Oldtime Fiddler's

Contest; the Raleigh, N.C., National Tobacco Spitting Contest; the Yellville, Ark., National Wild Turkey Calling Contest and Turkey Trot; the Buford, Ga., Masters Invitational Clogging Hoedown; and the Jonesborough, Tenn., National Storytelling Festival. Fairs, carnivals, and festivals thrive at all levels in the South, and most actively promote the unique heritage and character of the region.

Sharon A. Sharp
University of Mississippi

Theodore M. Dembroski, *Journal of Popular Culture* (Winter 1973); John Ezell, *The South since 1865* (1978); Lewis C. Gray, *History of Agriculture in the Southern United States to 1860*, 2 vols. (1933); Melton A. McLaurin, *North Carolina Historical Review* (Summer 1982); Wayne C. Neely, *The Agricultural Fair* (1935); *Newsweek* (5 November 1984); Carolyn B. Patterson, *National Geographic* (June 1980); *Southern Living* (May 1982); Don B. Wilmeth, *Variety Entertainment and Outdoor Amusements: A Reference Guide* (1982); Pat Zajac, *Southern Living* (May 1984). ☆

Festivals

|||||||||||||||||||||||||

The southern festival of today is the direct descendant of the camp meeting and political barbecue, the Saturday night dance and Sunday's "all-day meeting and dinner-on-the-ground." Those were the gatherings that gave southerners the chance to lay aside the plow and pick up the fiddle. Although some fairs and festivals date to those times, most arose in the decades after World War II, when southerners were more edu-

cated, better traveled, and one generation removed from the cotton field. The festivals southerners initiated then, and attend today, reflect either that new urbane sophistication or the heritage of the rural past.

Each June in South Carolina, two celebrations, only 80 miles apart in distance but a world apart in content, demonstrate that tradition. While thousands gather in Charleston for Spoleto Festival with its outpouring of fine arts, thousands of others fill the streets of tiny Hampton for the town's watermelon festival, now more than 40 years old. From late May through June, Spoleto Festival, held in Charleston since 1977, may offer a playwright's world premiere, a New York choreographer's newest creation, an orchestra's concert of classical music. Celebrants in Hampton, meanwhile, are listening to gospel music and dancing to country bands, picking among the goods of an arts and crafts fair, watching a parade led by a beauty queen, and, most of all, feasting on the traditional southern delicacy. It is not unlikely that some in Charleston, after getting their fill of Balanchine and Bach, hop in their car and gorge on watermelon a weekend or so later in Hampton. If many southerners hunger for fine arts today, just as many yearn for the tidbits of their inheritance.

Southern festivals provide both. The themes of most small-town festivals center around some aspect of their heritage or livelihood. Even in many urban festivals focusing on the fine arts there are southern features. Spoleto Festival often includes such Dixie-nurtured music forms as jazz and blues, country, and soul and gospel. So does Memphis in May, a monthlong celebration that combines its regional customs of music and food (barbecue) with the cultural characteristics of a different country each year. Heritage Weekends in Louisville, Ky., feature the arts, crafts, food, costumes, and music of Old World ethnic groups that settled in the city.

Southern customs, traditions, and products are most often extolled in the small-town festival. If there is a vegetable that ripens in fall, a plant that blooms in spring, an animal that grazes in pastures, or a food served on local tables, some community has found a way to praise it. Gilmer, Tex., honors the yam; Dothan, Ala., the peanut; Tonitown, Ark., the grape. Towns and cities from Palestine, Tex., to Norfolk, Va., celebrate the arrival of spring in azalea and dogwood festivals. Food festivals often combine cookery with contests. At the Oyster Festival in Leonardtown, Md., the champion of the oyster-shucking contest goes on to international competition. Crawfish races highlight the biannual salute to the local crustacean in Breaux Bridge, La.

Some small-town festivals have helped to preserve a slice of the southern past. In mule festivals, towns like Columbia, Tenn.; Benson, N.C.; and Calvary, Ga., trot out the legendary but endangered species that plowed farms, scraped out roads, and built river levees. At these gatherings, younger generations hear for the first time words that once sprinkled southern conversation; jack and jenny, hames and singletree, or what it means to "bust the middles" or "lay by a crop."

Although the themes of small-town festivals vary widely, they differ little in form and function. Salley, S.C., may be the only town that honors chitterlings, but its Chitlin' Strut, held one November day malodorous from the aroma of five tons of frying chitterlings, incorporates most all the earmarks of a small-town festival. Along with a lunch of chitlins, gobbled with gusto or tossed away after one nibble, celebrants pick among the tacky and tasteful offerings of the ubiquitous arts and crafts display, listen to country music, and watch a parade led by Miss Chitlin' Strut. Some don t-shirts that may read "I got the guts to strut" or "Chitlin Fever—Catch it!," then enter the chitlin' strut contest. The freestyle choreography many create is often determined by the amount of whiskey surreptitiously spiking their soft drinks.

Although most festivals are used for boosterism or fund-raising, they nevertheless offer townspeople a chance to gather and renew acquaintances, a byproduct of gatherings since the first southerners gathered in a pioneer forest clearing to help a neighbor raise a new barn.

To renew family and friendship ties is still the main reason residents and former residents of Neshoba County, Miss., have assembled faithfully each year since 1889 in the laying-by time of late July. At the Neshoba County Fair near Philadelphia, families live for a week, many in rude cabins their ancestors built. There is harness racing, a carnival midway, and lots of "visiting around," preaching, and political speech-making at the open-air Founders Pavilion, with its sawdust floor and wooden benches. In recent years the pavilion has provided the last hurrah for old-time southern politicians. As late as 1979 former Mississippi Governor Ross Barnett brought the house down with his stump-speaking, gallus-snapping, out-seg-your-opponent brand of rhetoric from a bygone era.

Fairgoers today arrive by Chevrolet instead of mule and wagon, but transportation is about the only ingredient of the fair that has changed since its 19th-century beginning. Certainly, the weather is the same, as afternoon rainstorms turn red dirt to mud, and the white heat of midday sun forces fairgoers to the shade of porches. "If you can't take the heat, mud, and dirt, you oughta stay home," says one fairgoer. But at Neshoba County Fair, as in most southern festivals, few stay at home. Festivals offer them a chance to lay aside their work—the pocket calculator now, if no longer the plow; to renew friendships with acquaintances; and, in most cases, to pay homage to a slice of southern life that may be long past. With their festivals, southern towns and cities insure that old times there will not be forgotten.

See also MUSIC: Music Festivals

Gary D. Ford
Southern Living

Alice M. Geffen and Carole Berglie, *Southern Exposure* (January–February 1986); Jane M. Hatch, *The American Book of Days* (3d ed., 1978); *Southern Living* (monthly calendar of festivals); Beverly J. Stoeltje, in *Handbook of American Folklore*, ed. Richard M. Dorson (1983); Paul Wasserman and Esther Herman, eds., *Festivals Sourcebook: A Reference Guide to Fairs, Festivals, and Celebrations* (1977); David E. Whisnant, *All That Is Native and Fine: The Politics of Culture in an American Region* (1983); William Wiggins, in *Discovering Afro-America*, ed. Roger D. Abrahams and John F. Szwed (1975), *Prospects*, vol. 5 (1979). ☆

Fishing

||||||||||||||||||||

More than one-half of the contiguous U.S. coastline is in the South. Within these limits are the most prolific estuarine complexes in the nation—the Chesapeake Bay, Pamlico Sound, and the Gulf of Mexico. The rich waters of the Gulf Stream pass closest to land in the South, and the barrier islands that shelter the mainland South from the ocean are rich breeding grounds for fish. The rivers draining the southern highlands offer fishing of a different kind. There are few natural lakes in the South, but hydroelectric, flood-control, and irrigation impoundments have created a unique inland fishery.

Fishing thus offers an integral form of recreation and livelihood in this region. Its popularity is part of the legacy of agrarian small-farm existence where every farm needed and often constructed a reliable water source. Fishing followed as a matter of course. Pond fishing today is one of the great pleasures of the region.

Fishing is a predominantly masculine activity, passed along from one generation to the next. It fulfills a need to provide; it is a private challenge—success or failure is the individual's alone; and, most important, failure can quickly be attributed to outside circumstances, beyond the individual's control. Fishing can be relatively inexpensive, but the more you fish, the more likely you are to spend to fish.

According to U.S. Commerce Department annual statistics, the South is one of the most important fisheries in the nation. In 1980–81 Louisiana led the nation in thousands of pounds of live catch, followed by Alaska, California, Virginia, North Carolina, Mississippi, and Massachusetts. The South and Gulf states ranked highest in millions of pounds of fish, netting 2,243 million pounds of all commercial-fishing species taken (the North Atlantic region, which includes Virginia, ranked second with 1,528 million pounds). During 1978–81 four of the top five fishing ports were in Louisiana or Mississippi.

Each regional fishery of the South has a cultural heritage comprised of unique boat styles developed for local waters. The character of these fisheries is based on the available harvest of the offshore waters as well as distinctive cuisine and social customs. Several regions have unique products: Chesapeake Bay blue crab; Lynnhaven oyster of Virginia; Bon Secour oyster of the Gulf; red snapper from Florida; and Georgia and Louisiana shrimp. (President William Howard Taft consumed seven dozen Lynnhaven Oysters at one sitting.)

Through their culture and cuisine, the Cajuns of Louisiana, the Low Country people of South Carolina and Georgia, the watermen of the Chesapeake, and the downeasters of North Carolina have maintained and reinforced a clear identity. These individual groups are clannish and sustain tradition from one generation to the next. They are not open societies—the vehement opposition to Mexican and Vietnamese immigrants and to religious cult-related fishermen by traditional groups bears witness to their strong emotions and fears of economic and social change. Outsiders are warily watched, seldom welcomed, and even when accepted as "fellow fishermen" still remain outsiders.

Sea Grant Research in North Carolina reveals a very precise social network, which distributes fishing information in one typical small coastal North Carolina village. Information and innovation become legitimate only when certain accepted and admired fishermen advocate or legitimize them. This would seem to indicate a traditional subculture, rigidly set in its ways.

Nevertheless, commercial fishing is being forced to change because of circumstances beyond the control of fishermen. Fuel prices, declining and polluted fisheries, and the substantial cost of a vessel (to $250,000) have altered regional patterns. Fishermen have shifted from local water, seasonal fishing to open water, year-round fishing. It is simply not possible to make fishing pay on a local basis unless a monopoly exists, such as legal rights to rich oyster grounds. Fishermen must follow the catch to make ends meet, and this reality, along with foreign competition, is gradually altering the traditional commercial fishing industry.

Southerners are serious about fishing for fun, and no other region works so hard to have a good time at recreational fishing. The numbers are staggering— 450,000 fishing licenses were sold in North Carolina in 1981–82, representing almost 8 percent of the population. Only freshwater fishermen must be licensed, so the actual numbers of fishermen may well top a million individuals.

Across the South, fishermen sustain a fishing publication, *B.A.S.S.* (the magazine of the Bass Anglers' Sportsman's Society) and regional editions of *Field and Stream* and *Sports Afield*. There is a professional fishing circuit, saltwater fishing rodeos, tournaments, invitational fish-offs, derbies, and contests with substantial prizes. North Carolina State University offers a sportfishing short course, and every southern city of any size has an outdoor commercial show, highlighting the latest in outdoor gear and equipment, which includes fishing necessities.

State wildlife agencies actively work to develop the fisheries resource through the construction of fishing attractors, artificial reefs, boat ramps, and docking facilities—all of this funded by licens-

Fishermen with their haul, Bay St. Louis, Mississippi, early 20th century

ing revenue. Good fishing has a constituency in the South: public works projects as noncontroversial as the Blue Ridge Parkway have been sidetracked because of potential fishing stream pollution by the completion of the roadway as originally proposed.

The two major categories of southern recreational fishing are saltwater and freshwater—everything else is derivative. Within these categories are curious subcategories, many of which are identified by either the technique they use, or the species of fish they pursue.

The three most popular means of catching saltwater game fish are by boat, private or rental; pier fishing; or surf casting. The U.S. Commerce Department statistics confirm that the greatest number of saltwater fish landed are caught within three miles of beachfront, the distance corresponding most frequently to pier fishing, surf casting, and both private and charter (or rental) boating.

Sixty percent of the South's population lives within two hours' driving time of saltwater, so it is not surprising that saltwater fishing is extremely popular. Saltwater fishermen are willing to catch anything and do not simply pursue one species of gamefish to the exclusion of others. They spend extravagant sums of money to achieve their goals. A properly equipped surf fisherman can spend as much as $17,000 for a recreational vehicle that will negotiate the sandy stretches of barrier islands such as the Outer Banks of North Carolina and Padre Island in Texas. In addition to the vehicle cost, there are substantial expenses for tackle and clothing. A serious surf fisherman can justify all of the expense, for only with such equipment can he or she achieve the mobility needed to properly fish the beaches. The expense may make this sport seem an improbable one, but it is commonplace. In 1977 more than 100,000 people drove the sands of Cape Hatteras National Seashore, and the number has increased steadily since.

There is a definite camaraderie among surf fishermen as opposed to private boat owners who fish open and sound waters. A community is created by a shared experience of testy weather conditions and successful fishing "runs." Many fishermen return to the same beaches year after year—indeed, so established are the routines that an element of superstition seems to govern the planning of annual surf-fishing trips.

On the Outer Banks of North Carolina, the surf-fishing mecca in the South if not the nation, motel owners have booked the same rooms to the same fishing parties for many years—often because of the success of a past trip. In 1984, a world record Red Drum, the prized surf gamefish, weighing 94 pounds was landed near Avon, N.C. This catch alone will doubtlessly bring fishermen to the Outer Banks in droves, and there again will be another season of Hatteras Island sunrises, silhouetting shoulder-to-shoulder anglers, and vehicles bristling with poles and as chockfull of equipment as any tackle shop. They will want to better the record of the unfortunate angler who, if he had waited a week later to land his drum, would have pocketed $50,000 during the annual Red Drum Tourney.

Freshwater fishermen tend to pursue one game fish more than others. The fish may be either native or naturalized trout, hybrid and striped bass, crappie, bream and other sunfish, catfish, or the king of all freshwater game fish, the large-mouth bass. The method may be flyrod, spinning tackle, ultralight spinning tackle, bait casting, or cork or bobber fishing with natural bait.

There seems to be a correlation between the economic and social stature of fishermen, the game fish they pursue, and the method they prefer to use. At the bottom of the economic scale, the preferred fishing is catfish/bream by cork or bobber fishing/bait casting, bass/spinner fishing is the choice of blue-collar families, bass flyrod fishing of white-collar workers, and artificial fly fishing for native trout is the preserve of upper-income professionals.

This observation is grounded in economic realities. The expense required for bream and catfish fishing is substantially lower than that for trout fishing. Bream and catfish may be caught from the edge of a lake—a boat is not required; bass fishermen need a boat to fish large impoundments, and trout fishermen must have the means and time to travel and stay in the remote highlands where trout are found.

The large-mouth bass is a southern institution. The fish is widely distributed, easily caught, and a dependable fighter. Bass is also good to eat. Its following is fanatical, almost cultic in devotion. The large-mouth bass may have been placed in the waters of the South so that fishermen have a preordained reason for idleness and spending money.

Bass is frequently used as a verb— "bassin." This is not the same as fishing, but refers to the pursuit of the large-mouth bass with the fire of a crusade. "To bass" is to spend money—on a bass boat with a swivel chair and an outboard motor that could power an aircraft carrier, on a trolling motor, on a fish finder, temperature gauge, fishing maps, boat trailer, docking fees, a suitcase full of tackle, membership in the Bass Anglers' Sportsman's Society (and subscription to their magazine), on beer, on a "gimme cap," but never on suntan lotion. Bass fishermen are always sunburned to the "gimme cap" line.

Magazine articles are devoted to fishing the remote corners of one lake for bass, professional bass fishermen cast for prizes up to $50,000, and substantial multimillion-dollar industries produce equipment for bass fishing. No other fish has such a following in the South, and no other group of fishermen spends so much money as do the Bassers. Indeed, the name is almost synonymous with fishing.

Although smaller in numbers, trout fishermen are equally devoted to their fish. Trout are confined to the pure running water streams and rivers of the mountains and to a few mountain impoundments. This restricted range places the fish out of reach of much of the region's population, but does not diminish its popularity. In 1981 40,000 trout licenses were sold in North Carolina, a state with extensive trout waters.

Trout are wary fish, caught by stalking, rather than fishing. Much of the appeal of trout fishing is in the enjoyment of the fish's environment, and so, to a greater degree than perhaps other game fish, there is an "aesthetic" to trout fishing. The value of catching the fish is often surpassed by the quest for it. This is not a hard and fast rule. For every trout fisherman arduously using an artificially tied fly at the end of a $500 rod, there is a mountain native working the stream with canned corn or worms. Trout fishermen write most often about one single issue: the threatened destruction of a prime trout stream. Indeed, so fragile are the southern waters supporting trout, and so limited is the number of fishable miles, it could very well be the South's most tenuous outdoor recreation.

One further aspect of recreational fishing should be noted—the active stocking of created fisheries funded by wildlife revenues. Money from the sale of licenses has gone to provide a number of "unnatural" prime fishing opportunities, such as inland striped bass fishing on lakes such as the Santee-Cooper in South Carolina. Normally an ocean species, striped bass have adapted very nicely to the all-freshwater habitat of certain reservoirs. This has resulted in a superb inland recreational fishery of an endangered native ocean species. In addition, extensive artificial hybridization has developed cross-specific game fish, which are more readily adapted to the growth conditions of inland impoundments.

Inland fishing is enormously popular in the South. This is a region where the first bream on a worm-baited hook marks a rite of passage in its own way and means passing the love of angling from one generation to the next.

Glenn Morris
Durham, North Carolina

Havilah Babcock, *My Health Is Better in November: Thirty-five Stories of Hunting and Fishing in the South* (1985); William Elliot, *Carolina Sports by Land and Water* (1846); Patrick Mullen, *Southern Exposure* (Summer–Fall 1977); Louis D. Rubin, Jr., *Southern Living* (March 1983); Frank Sargeant, *Outdoor Life* (March 1981); Southeastern Association of Fish and Wildlife Agencies, *Proceedings of Annual Conference* (annual); *Southern Exposure* (May–June 1982); U.S. National Oceanic and Atmospheric Administration, *Fishery Statistics* (annual); Dianne Young, *Southern Living* (July 1983). ☆

Football

More than any other sport, football seems to reflect cultural characteristics of the South. It has a long and noteworthy place in the history of the region. Not long after the inaugural Princeton-Rutgers game of 1869, Washington and Lee played Virginia Military Institute in the first official football game in the South. The year was 1877, and by 1895 John Heisman had instituted the innovation of using offensive guards as blockers for running backs at Auburn University. The infamous, outlawed formation referred to as the "flying wedge" was used by Vanderbilt University as early as 1892 in a game against North Carolina. Southern football's contribution to modern-day football continued with the advent of the forward pass as an offensive weapon in 1906. As early as 1914 Clyde Littlefield of the University of Texas was heralded as one of the best passers in the country. The well-known "Heisman Shift" was introduced by John Heisman at Georgia Tech, and from 1915 to 1917 his Georgia Tech teams were undefeated. Beginning in the 1920s General Bob Neyland introduced the "single-wing" formation at the University of Tennessee with great success. The contributions of these early southern teams, coaches, and players to football were critical for establishing the game as it is played today.

Modern football in the South is characterized by a subcultural passion unrivaled in other regions of the United States. This affinity for the game of football is reflected in the popularity of the sport at the high school, college, and, most recently, professional levels of play. Because the South was predominantly a rural area throughout the first half of the 20th century, community identity with high school teams fostered intense competition. Increased industrial and urban development over the last 50 years has changed the demog

raphy of the South; however, high school football remains the most popular Friday night activity in such football-oriented states as Alabama, Florida, Georgia, Louisiana, Mississippi, Tennessee, and Texas.

The regional and community interest in high school football in the South provided a rich pool of talent for the development of this sport at the intercollegiate level. As early as 1921, when tiny Centre College of Danville, Ky., upset a powerful team from Harvard, 6–0, southern teams have been competitors for national titles. A review of the Associated Press National Polls, which began in 1936, reveals the following southern college teams claiming the national title: Texas Christian University (1938); Texas A&M University (1939); Tennessee (1951); Maryland (1953); Auburn (1957); Louisiana State University (1958); Alabama (1961, 1964, 1965, 1978, 1979); Texas (1963, 1969); Georgia (1980); Clemson (1981); and Miami of Florida (1983). In addition, in terms of overall winning percentages, 6 southern teams are ranked in the top 25 all-time winners: Alabama (.732), Texas (.729), Tennessee (.680), Louisiana State (.639), Georgia (.630), and Auburn (.602). These and numerous other outstanding southern football teams have provided many great individual stars.

Eleven southern players have received the Heisman trophy, given to the outstanding college football player in the United States for each year of competition. Southern football players who have achieved such distinction are Davey O'Brien (TCU, 1938), Frank Sinkwich (Georgia, 1942), Doak Walker (SMU, 1948), John David Crow (Texas A&M, 1957), Billy Cannon (LSU, 1959), Steve Spurrier (Florida, 1966),

Davey O'Brien, the South's first Heisman trophy winner, 1940s

Pat Sullivan (Auburn, 1966), Earl Campbell (Texas, 1977), George Rogers (South Carolina, 1980), Herschel Walker (Georgia, 1982), and Bo Jackson (Auburn, 1985).

The South has provided college football with some of the most outstanding coaches in the history of the sport. In 1899 Herman Suter coached the famous "iron men" of the University of the South. In a six-day period Suter's Sewanee Tigers defeated Texas, Texas A&M, Houston, Tulane, Louisiana State, and Mississippi. The national attention generated by Coach Suter at Sewanee was continued through Daniel E. McGugin's coaching achievements at Vanderbilt. Coach McGugin's influence on southern football was profound. In his 30-year career at Vanderbilt, McGugin's teams won 13 titles and 196 games. Following McGugin's accomplishments, John Heisman, the person

for whom the Heisman trophy was named, succeeded McGugin as the outstanding coach in the Deep South. Heisman's Georgia Tech teams won four straight national titles from 1915 to 1918. His 1916 Georgia Tech team set the record for most points in a game when they defeated Cumberland University 222–0.

Many other coaches in the South made outstanding contributions to the game of football in the early 1900s. Dana X. Bible, in 12 seasons at Texas A&M, won five Southwest Conference titles and posted a winning percentage of over .77 (1917–28). Frank Bridges of Baylor, who has been characterized as "one of the most original and inventive football coaches who ever lived," experimented with innovative formations during the early 1920s. Wallace Wade's records at Alabama and Duke were outstanding during the late 1920s and early 1930s. However, with the emergence of General Robert Reese Neyland as head coach of the University of Tennessee, one of the first coaching legends of the South emerged. Coach Bob Neyland won 173 games, and his coaching career at Tennessee spanned from 1925 to the modern era of big time football. Coach Neyland's teams were known for outstanding defensive play, and several of his former players—most notably, Bowden Wyatt (Tennessee) and Bobby Dodd (Georgia Tech)—became outstanding college coaches.

Formed in 1953, the Atlantic Coast Conference (ACC) provided football in the South with one of its most colorful and witty coaches in Frank Howard. Coach Howard's Clemson Tigers consistently gained national attention with appearances in the Orange, Sugar, Cotton, and Bluebonnet bowl games. Howard's teams won a total of 165 games, providing the ACC with a team that consistently gained national recognition. The Southwest Conference provided modern football with two coaches who built and maintained football dynasties at Arkansas and Texas. The names of Frank Broyles and Darryl Royal echo legendary achievements on the gridiron from 1959 to the early 1970s. Broyles's teams recorded 74 Southwest Conference victories during his tenure at Arkansas, while Royal's Texas teams won 80 conference games. During the 14-year span in which Broyles and Royal coached in the Southwest Conference, only one other conference team (SMU, 1966) placed in the top 10 of the final national collegiate rankings. The coaching success of Frank Broyles and Darryl Royal consistently focused national attention on the Southwest Conference.

The most legendary southern collegiate football coach, however, was Paul William "Bear" Bryant. Coach Bryant not only established himself as the winningest coach in the history of collegiate football, but he also became a charismatic symbol of success to football fans throughout the world. Bear Bryant's coaching career and incredible record as a major-college coach of 323 victories, 85 losses, and 17 ties spanned 38 years and four southern universities—Maryland, Kentucky, Texas A&M, and Alabama. A true modern hero in the South, Bear Bryant's influence on football in this region and throughout the United States will remain as long as the game is played. The continuing achievements of numerous former players of Coach Bryant in professional football, as well as in collegiate coaching, reflect not only his coaching genius, but also his personal charisma.

There have been many other outstanding football coaches in the South.

Ralph Sasse (Mississippi State), Wallace Butts (Georgia), John Vaught (Mississippi), Ralph "Shug" Jordan (Auburn), and Paul Dietzel (Louisiana State) all had winning records and teams in the Southeastern Conference. Among southern teams that were not affiliated with major conferences, Pie Vann (Southern Mississippi), A. C. "Scrappy" Moore (University of Chattanooga), and Bill Peterson (Florida State) had outstanding winning records. Eddie Robinson of Grambling became another coaching legend by achieving more career victories than Bear Bryant. Coach Robinson has been a consistent winner for 44 years at the predominantly black college located in north Louisiana. Both Coach Robinson (324 wins) and Jake Gaither (Florida A&M) have not only had many championship teams, but they also have coached numerous players who have achieved outstanding professional careers.

Professional football arrived in the South in 1960. Both the Dallas Cowboys and the Houston Oilers franchises played their first National Football League (NFL) schedule that year. Six years later, professional teams in Atlanta and Miami were established. The New Orleans Saints franchise had its first season in 1967, and the Tampa Bay Buccaneers (1976) was the last NFL team to be located in a southern city. These six NFL teams have been very competitive in professional football. The Dallas Cowboys have played in five Super Bowl games, winning twice, as have the Miami Dolphins. Tom Landry was, until 1989, the only coach for the Dallas Cowboys since their beginnings in 1960. Coach Landry recorded 250 wins, 162 losses, and 6 ties in his 29 years as the head coach of the Cowboys. Often referred to as "America's team," the Cowboys gained wide television coverage in the southern region during the first six years of their franchise. Today they are still one of the most popular teams in the National Football League.

Coach Don Shula of the Miami Dolphins has posted the third highest winning percentage of all coaches in the National Football League (.716). Only the legendary Vince Lombardi (.740) and John Madden (.731) have better winning percentages than Shula. Coach Shula's ultimate achievement as Miami's head coach came in 1972 when the Dolphins compiled the first unbeaten and untied record (17–0) in the league's history. Shula was also the youngest coach to compile 100 victories in the National Football League, and if one included his record while at Baltimore, his six Super Bowl appearances as head coach remain an NFL all-time record.

Many observers claim football has taken on almost religious significance for southerners. As writer Willie Morris has written in *Terrains of the Heart* (1981), "It is no doubt a cliché, yet true, that Southern football is a religion, emanating directly from its bedeviled landscape and the burden of its past." Michael Novak in *The Joy of Sports* (1976) explores the religious implications of southern football. In the Deep South football is "a statewide religion" that celebrates each state and the region itself. The region's dominant evangelical churches "cherish emotion, inspiration, charismatic speaking in tongues, the surges of personal conversion and sudden seizure," and the football of the South reflects such traits. Southern sports are rugged, but football in the region is best described as "fleet, explosive, difficult to contain." Football in the Midwest is closest to that in the South, both driven by a "passional religion," but midwestern sport grows out of its people and their religious style. The churches of the Midwest, says Novak, "are filled by far more orderly and sober folk" than those of the South,

Texas Stadium, home of the NFL Dallas Cowboys, constructed in 1970s, Arlington Texas

and midwestern football is appropriately "hard, orderly, cleanly executed, disciplined, tight."

John Egerton in *The Americanization of Dixie* (1974) suggests that football, "the religion of the masses," is celebrated in the South "with all the ritual and pageantry and spectacle of a High Church ceremony." There is patriotism, militarism, prayer, music, conspicuous consumption, politics, sex, white supremacy, and sport. He believes that southern football has become, though, more a ritual of an American civil religion than of a purely southern faith.

The South as a region has a heritage of great teams, coaches, and fans. It is within such a context that one can claim that football is a very real and vibrant component of the culture of the modern South. Football in the South remains an important source for a variety of social activities. A typical fall weekend includes numerous community activities that are associated with high school, college, and professional football. Friday evening football games involve "pep rallies," band performances, and drill teams. Saturday afternoons and evenings witness tailgate parties, pregame socials, and postgame parties, while on Sunday afternoons professional teams throughout the region draw large crowds, as well as national television coverage.

At the end of the season, the South hosts most of the nation's bowl games, including the All American Bowl (Birmingham), the Bluebonnet Bowl (Houston), the Blue-Gray All-Star Football Classic (Montgomery), the Cotton Bowl (Dallas), the Florida Citrus Bowl (Orlando), the Gator Bowl (Jacksonville), the Independence Bowl (Shreveport), the Liberty Bowl (Memphis), the Orange Bowl (Miami), the Peach Bowl (Atlanta),

the Senior Bowl (Mobile), the Sugar Bowl (New Orleans), and the Sun Bowl (El Paso). New Orleans and Miami have been the most frequent sites for pro football's Super Bowl every January.

J. Steven Picou
Duane Gill
Texas A&M University

The Birmingham News, *Remembering Bear* (1983); Clyde Bolton, *Unforgettable Days in Southern Football* (1974); Allison Danzig, *The History of American Football* (1983); D. Stanley Eitzen and George H. Sage, *Sociology of American Sport* (1978); Wilbur Evans and H. B. McElroy, *The Twelfth Man: A Story of Texas A&M Football* (1974); Lawrence Goodwyn, *Southern Exposure* (Fall 1974); Marty Mule, *Sugar Bowl: The First Fifty Years* (1983); Alexander M. Weyand, *The Saga of American Football* (1955); Geoff Winningham and Al Reinert, *Rites of Fall: High School Football in Texas* (1979). ☆

Gambling

||||||||||||||||||||||||||

Wagering on games of chance has been a recurrent feature of southern social life from the colonial era to modern times. In the 1700s, for example, it offered clues as to social status in the early South. When colonial planters gathered, especially in Virginia, they typically played cards and backgammon or rolled the dice. Wealthy tobacco growers, living in a society with fewer restraints than Puritan New England, were willing to risk much of their wealth on anything involving chance. George Washington kept a list of his gains and losses at gaming and typically preferred large stakes. Above all, southerners bet on horse racing. After 1730 quarter-horse racing was popular, and then at mid-century English thoroughbreds were introduced into the colonies. Races were held in conjunction with fairs, which also brought occasions for gambling. Historian Timothy Breen has argued that gambling on horse racing identified one as a member of the gentry. Honor was gained through victory over one's peers, and this was a safety valve for planters, nurturing structured competition within the group without endangering its hegemony.

The inhabitants of the Old South, proclaimed a foreign visitor, "are universally addicted to gambling." Betting during the antebellum period in the Northeast was "about as common as in England," reported an Englishman, but in the South it was far more prevalent. New Orleans was a major center of gambling, but even rural southerners bet on cards, dice, dominoes, billiards, lotteries, cockfights, horse races, and many other activities. Southerners were such inveterate gamblers, claimed one eyewitness, that many "lost in a night their all."

Professional gamblers frequented riverboats and bars; some got rich and a few got lynched—five in 1835 in Vicksburg alone. But many gamblers considered themselves respectable members of southern society. A Yankee, induced to share his bed at a crowded tavern by the assurance of a landlord that his bedfellow was a gentleman, grew concerned when his heavily armed roommate placed a bowie knife and a pistol by the bedside and a pistol under his pillow. "I shuddered," admitted the Yankee, "having never slept with pistols," but he raised no objection until his bedfellow announced that he was a "gambler *by profession*." Horrified, the Yankee

leapt from bed and exclaimed: "The landlord assured me that you were a gentleman, sir, but had he told me of your profession, I would not have consented to share my bed." The gambler, who failed to understand such squeamishness, "entered into an elaborate argument to prove that his profession was as honest and honorable as that of the physician."

New Englanders, in keeping with their Puritan heritage, were much less tolerant of gamblers and gambling than were southerners, who were as fond of wagers and risks as their Scottish, Irish, and Welsh ancestors. Expressing his objection to horse racing, a Yankee wrote from South Carolina: "Curiosity induced me to go once, which will satisfy me for life." President Timothy Dwight of Yale College boasted: "In New England horse racing is almost and cockfighting absolutely unknown." Both activities enjoyed widespread popularity in the Old South, where spectators frequently gathered at cockpits and racetracks and wagered large sums. Whole seasons were devoted to racing, which so appealed to southerners, noted an observer, that "they have race-paths near each town and in many parts of the country." If gambling was not quite a universal pastime, it had far more adherents, among planters and plain folk alike, in the Old South than in the Old North.

After the Civil War, organized, big-time gaming was rationalized in some southern states as a way to generate money for depleted treasuries or worthwhile charities in hard times. Legal lotteries had existed earlier in some areas, and these were revived. Civic and charitable groups were formed to raise money through lotteries for orphans, widows, crippled Confederate veterans, museums, libraries, schools, and various artistic activities.

The Louisiana Lottery, the largest in the South, was chartered in 1868 in New Orleans, with a 25-year charter. It held daily drawings, with prizes up to $5,000, plus monthly drawings and a six-month drawing, which awarded a grand prize of $600,000. A popular referendum in the 1890s turned down the proposed renewal of the lottery's franchise, but southerners continued, illegally at times, to take part in lotteries of various sorts. New Orleans remained a gambling center, with its activities tied in with boxing promotion and, especially, red-light district prostitution.

Southerners continued in the postbellum era to gamble on horse racing at tracks in places such as New Orleans, Memphis, Nashville, Montgomery, and Little Rock. They won and lost at fairs, carnivals, and circuses, as professional gamblers descended on communities where these shows appeared. Neither could they resist wagering on cockfighting, dogfighting, and other sporting events.

By the 1880s, however, a rising moral consciousness among the South's religious people led to restrictions on gambling. New laws were passed outlawing horse racing, which earlier had been *the* sport of the southern gentleman. Large-scale gambling activities, and particularly wagering on horse racing, came to be concentrated in resort areas such as Hot Springs, Ark., and in coastal towns such as Galveston, Tex., and Miami, Fla., as well as continuing in New Orleans. Though sometimes hidden, gambling continued in other regions of the South. Even where illegal, gambling houses were still found.

Gambling has been celebrated in southern culture from Mark Twain's por-

Georgia gentlemen playing cards and smoking, 1918

trayal of the riverboat gambler on the Mississippi to country music singer Kenny Rogers's 1970s hit song and film, "The Gambler." The early Mississippi country singer, Jimmie Rodgers, who knew the world of small-town gambling as a traveling railroad worker and later as a musical performer, sang such songs as "Gambling Bar Room Blues," "Those Gambler's Blues," and "Gambling Polka Dot Blues."

The image of the sharp-dressed, successful gambler has been a recurrent one in southern black literature and music, especially in the blues. Lack of economic security and low social status surely encouraged poor blacks to risk gambling as a way to temporary economic betterment. Stuck in oppressive jobs or in the boredom of unemployment, many of the southern poor, black and white, found excitement and thrills in the risk taking of gambling. Blues performers sang the "Poker Woman Blues," "Gambler's Blues," "Dying Crap Shooter's Blues," and "Gambling Man." Card games such as Georgia skin and coon-can are associated with black gamblers, as well as "skin-ball" and shooting craps (the popularity of the latter in the South shown by southerners calling it by such names as Memphis dominoes or Mississippi marbles).

Grady McWhiney
Texas Christian University

Herbert Asbury, *Sucker's Progress: An Informal History of Gambling in America from the Colonies to Canfield* (1938); Timothy H. Breen, *William and Mary Quarterly* (April 1977); George Devol, *Forty Years a Gambler on the Mississippi* (1887); John M. Findlay, *People of Chance: Gambling in American Society from Jamestown to Las Vegas* (1985); Paul Oliver, *Blues Fell This Morning: The Meaning of the Blues* (1960). ☆

Golf
||||||||||||

William Faulkner's *The Sound and the Fury* (1929) begins with the idiot Benjy Compson and his young black companion retrieving golf balls. Faulkner himself frequently played golf in the 1920s at the nine-hole University of Mississippi golf course and even acted as chairman of a tournament committee. Faulkner regarded himself as a sportsman, and his interest in golf reflected the South's changing sports scene in the early 20th century. Golf has not traditionally been regarded as a sport particularly associated with the South, yet the region has produced great athletes in that field, and since World War II it has increasingly become a part of the life of middle-class southerners.

The popularity of golf in the United States reflects the British influence on American sport. Golf came to this country from Scotland, with the first organized play here in New York, where country clubs were organized in the 1880s. The U.S. Golf Association appeared in 1894 to provide institutional direction, but at the turn of the century few golf courses had appeared in the South, except for Florida. Before 1900 golf had an elitist air to it and was mainly a pursuit of the leisured classes. Chicago and other cities of the Middle West led in building public courses in the early 20th century, but the appearance of amateur championship golf tournaments and celebrity golfers in the 1920s, along with the prosperity and consumerism of the people of that decade, helped to popularize golf. The South lagged in these developments, although Georgia and Texas were leaders; Georgia Institute of Technology, for example, from the 1920s on fielded successful intercollegiate golf teams, while Texas produced a number of prominent professional golfers.

The country club appeared in many southern communities in the 1920s, although its widespread popularity in the region was a post–World War II phenomenon. Country clubs were organized for social activities, such as dancing, dining, card playing, and drinking, in addition to athletics. Members joined in order to meet influential people and to promote their business interests. The young in small towns especially had a new focus for combining athletic activities and courting. Golf was a social sport well designed to these ends. Unlike urban athletic clubs, country clubs were for both men and women, and golf proved early to be popular among both sexes.

The South has produced some of the most prominent amateur and professional golfers. In a recent survey of the

70 greatest players of all time, 16 were from the South, including 7 from Texas. Prominent golfers have included Jimmy Demaret, Ben Hogan, John Byron Nelson, and Lee Trevino, all from Texas, Cary Middlecoff from Tennessee, and Betsy Rawls from South Carolina. Robert Tyre Jones, Jr., from Atlanta, is generally recognized as the game's greatest performer. The media of the 1920s and 1930s nurtured his image as the modern southern gentleman and helped make him a nationally popular hero. Sammy Snead of Hot Springs, Va., cultivated an image, according to *Golf* magazine, as "a hillbilly type who always had a vast storehouse of pungent jokes." "Slammin' Sammy," who won over 100 tournaments, claimed he had his earnings buried in tin cans back in the hills of home. Mildred "Babe" Didrikson Zaharias, from Port Arthur, Tex., is referred to in virtually all surveys as the greatest American woman athlete. She excelled in every sport she attempted, was a star of the 1932 Olympic Games, and dominated women's golf in the 1930s. Figures from the Professional Golf Association in 1967 showed that southerners have continued to play a prominent role in the game. Of the top 100 money winners for the previous year, 35 were southern natives, with 15 of them coming from Texas.

The South's interest in golf can also be seen in its premier courses. The Augusta National Country Club in Georgia, the Pinehurst Country Club in North Carolina, the Seminole Golf Club in Palm Beach, Fla., the Dunes Golf and Beach Club in South Carolina, and the Ocean Course at Sea Pines Plantation in Hilton Head, S.C., are among the South's nationally recognized courses. The Atlantic shore of the Southeast has been referred to as "The Golf Coast of America." Florida and South Carolina are particularly well known for the number and quality of resorts built around golfing for the region's, and indeed the nation's, vacationing elite. Almost half of the professional tournaments in the United States take place on southern courses.

The Masters Tournament at the Augusta National Country Club is one of the game's four most significant professional championships (along with those of the U.S. Open, the British Open, and the Professional Golfers' Association). Georgian Robert Tyre "Bobby" Jones, Jr., retired in 1930 from competitive golf, then conceived the idea of creating the Augusta course. Wall Street banker Clifford Roberts became his development partner and Scotland's Alistair Mackenzie was the designer of the course. Its site was 365 acres of rolling Georgia pinelands, which had for 100 years been a nursery. A Belgian baron named Prosper Jules Alphonse Berckmans moved to Augusta in 1857 and established the first nursery in the South. He disseminated hundreds of species of flowers, shrubs, and trees; in his catalogue of items in 1861 were 1,300 varieties of pears, 900 of apples, 300 of grapes, and over 100 each of azaleas and camellias. This natural background has made the Augusta course famed for its beauty, with long lines of magnolias, brilliant colors from azaleas, redbuds, and white dogwoods, and a chorus of sounds from the mockingbirds and cardinals. The architecture at Augusta adds to the stereotypical southern ambience. People sip mint juleps at café tables under huge magnolia trees on the front lawn of the sedate, Georgian-styled clubhouse, which could be from the *Gone with the Wind* set. Despite the southern setting, the

Augusta Country Club is a national institution. When the club was organized, only 30 members from Augusta itself were allowed. Most members have always been from outside Georgia, including many outside the South.

As Associated Press sportswriter Will Grimsley has noted, the Masters Tournament "has been called autocratic, arrogant, snobbish, and racist." At the same time it has been lauded as the best organized, most relaxed, and most pleasant of the professional tournaments. As Florida golfing great Gene Sarazen says, "It's the only tournament with class." Tournament directors carefully regulate the players and spectators, prohibiting cans, tents, and the sale of junk food and programs. CBS television has been televising the tournament since 1956, but even television trucks must be covered in green for camouflage. The key word at the Masters is "tradition," a word not unknown in the South. This emphasis led to conflict in the 1960s, however, when strong press criticism was directed at the tournament directors for never having invited a black to compete. A rule was soon adopted so that any winner of a Professional Golfers' Association tournament could compete, and Lee Elder, winner of the 1974 Monsanto Open, became the first black to receive a bid from Augusta, playing in 1975 without incident.

Charles Reagan Wilson
University of Mississippi

John R. Betts, *America's Sporting Heritage, 1850–1950* (1974); Frank DeFord, *Sports Illustrated* (7 April 1986); John M. Ross, ed., *Golf Magazine's Encyclopedia of Golf* (1979); *Southern Living* (August 1967); Dawson Taylor, *The Masters: An Illustrated History* (1973). ☆

Horses

The distinctive role of horses in the South began in the antebellum era. The plantation economy created sufficient wealth to permit the development of a gentry class and to permit the breeding of horses for pleasure and sport. This resulted in three native American breeds, all developed in significant part in the South: the American Quarter Horse, the American Saddlebred Horse, and the Tennessee Walking Horse.

Prior to the Civil War, the Old South was the center of thoroughbred breeding and racing. Williamsburg, Va., and Charleston, S.C., each claims to be the first community of established racing in America. Virginia was the early center for thoroughbred breeding. Andrew Jackson established an important center for racing at Nashville, Tenn., and for a long time this area was second only to Virginia in thoroughbred breeding. Kentucky became the dominant breeding area in the early 19th century and is still so, although thoroughbreds are

Kentucky Derby, Churchill Downs, Louisville, Kentucky, 1931

bred in other parts of the South, most notably Florida, Virginia, and Maryland.

Horse racing ceased during the Civil War. It came back strongly after the war, but without the dominance of the Old South. Racetracks were widespread and many were disreputable. The establishment of the Jockey Club with legislative, judicial, and executive functions in 1894 commenced the process of cleaning up racing. Racing, nevertheless, declined in the period immediately preceding World War I, probably because of its bad reputation and moral objections of the public to betting. A slow and steady renaissance was led by men of integrity and substance. Since World War I flat racing has steadily increased in popularity and acceptability and is now the largest spectator sport in the United States. The most significant southern tracks operate in Florida, Maryland, Kentucky, Arkansas, and Louisiana. Other states in the South either have, or are about to adopt, active racing programs.

The classic three-year-old thoroughbred races (the Triple Crown) were all instituted in the decade following the Civil War, one in the North and two in border states: the Belmont Stakes (New York), in 1867; the Preakness Stake (Maryland), in 1873; and the best-known horse race in America, the Kentucky Derby, in 1875. These races are regularly contested by southern-bred horses.

Fox hunting (riding to hounds), a natural for the plantation class, developed in the colonies as it was developing in Great Britain and became the principal sport of the planter class prior to the Civil War. (The first pack of hounds was probably imported to southern Maryland in 1650 by Robert Brooks.)

The destruction of the South in the Civil War almost destroyed fox hunting. After the war, the sport was revived and is now very active, with Virginia and Maryland generally considered to be its center. However, almost every state in the South boasts at least one recognized hunt, and the Deep South has produced one of the outstanding fox hunters of all time. Benjamin H. Hardaway III, Master of Foxhounds and Huntsman of the Midland Fox Hounds, Midland, Ga., is a keen student of fox hunting and a worthy successor to Peter Beckford, an early pioneer of modern fox hunting. The world famous Midland Fox Hounds, developed entirely by Hardaway, are deer proof, big mouthed, and aggressive, and will effectively drive a fox. The Midland Hounds hunt continuously in Georgia and Alabama and regularly in Pennsylvania, Maryland, and Virginia.

Hunting is a direct ancestor of steeple chasing. The introduction of jumping horses in the hunt field led to races across the countryside from one landmark to another, usually the steeples of village churches. Early American jump racing was much like the British counterpart. The sport developed in the South where the vast majority of the races are still held.

The horse, necessary for a civilized existence and important for recreation, was an indispensable partner in war. Aside from the mundane, but essential, matter of supply, the horse provided the mobility needed for intelligence gathering and communication, and in battle, the horse made the difference.

Mounted infantrymen who rode to battle and fought on foot appeared in frontier conflicts of the prerevolutionary period. These frontiersmen penetrated deep into enemy territory and appeared where least expected. Horse soldiers flourished in the Revolutionary War, especially in the South where irregular cavalry contributed significantly to the American war effort. Cavalry was a primary factor in the South's early successes in the Civil War and permitted it to last as long as it did. The Confederacy had a brilliant array of cavalry chieftains. Two of the best known of these gifted horse soldiers were the almost invincible Nathan Bedford Forrest and the colorful and dashing James Ewell Brown "Jeb" Stuart.

Today, the cavalry is gone and mules no longer plod the cotton rows or pull the freight and cotton wagons. Churchyards and town squares are not filled with wagons, buggies, and saddle horses. Human existence, with a high level of material comfort, can be maintained without a horse. Nonetheless, the bugle call to the post and the hunting horn are still heard. The Walking Horse and the American Saddlebred Horse are not necessary for plantation management, but throughout the South ringmasters at Horse Shows are heard to say, "Let your horses walk on" or "Let your horses rack on."

Racing and the breeding of race horses are large industries. Horse shows range from small one-breed shows to the week-long or more events in large urban centers such as Dallas, Houston, Atlanta, New Orleans, Memphis, and Louisville. Lengthy affairs are devoted to selecting the best of a breed, such as the Walking Horse Celebration in Shelbyville, Tenn., and its counterpart for the American Saddlebred in Louisville, Ky., where annually the champion of the breed is chosen. Many of the contestants at the annual Quarter Horse World Congress in Ohio come from the South. The return of draft horses and mules has led to shows devoted entirely to these animals.

Although a product of the West, the rodeo has become one of the most popular of the horse sports or shows in the South. The roots of rodeo are in the work of the 19th-century cowboys of the West. Ranch life was demanding and tough. Cattle herds were brought in each spring from winter pasture and tended until the autumn trail drives. Each cowboy required a string of horses, and no one could afford the time to train them. Therefore, green and sometimes freshly caught wild horses were roped and ridden. At the end of annual trail drives, when the cowboys gathered in the railroad towns, conversations, particularly with the aid of liquor, soon turned to boasts of prowess with lariat and horse. Impromptu riding and roping contests resulted. Thus, the rodeo was born. Two of the five standard rodeo events, calf roping and saddle bronc riding, grew out of practical cowboy work. The three remaining events, bareback bronc riding, bull riding, and steer wrestling, rose from bragging.

The subject of horses in the South cannot be left without a reference to polo. Polo, a stick-and-ball game that originated in the Orient over 2,000 years ago, was introduced into the United States in 1876 and reached its golden age during the 1920s and 1930s. Once considered the province of the very rich in areas outside the South, it is now played by many people throughout the region on courses ranging from cow pastures to the well-appointed clubs of the wealthy.

Not to be overlooked is the just plain horse of dubious pedigree and faulted conformation found on farms and in backyards. An experienced horse fancier would pass him by, but he can turn a child into a gallant knight, a wild West marshall, or a reincarnation of Jeb Stuart or Nathan Bedford Forest. Perhaps his real value exceeds that of the blooded horses of the race tracks and show rings.

Frank Hampton McFadden
Pike Road, Alabama

Robert Denhardt, *The Horse of the Americas* (1975); J. Frank Dobie, ed., *Mustangs and Cow Horses* (1940); Kent Hollingsworth, *The Kentucky Thoroughbred* (1976); Robert W. Howard, *The Horse in America* (1965); Kitty Slater, *The Hunt Country of America* (1973). ☆

Hunting
||||||||||||||||||||

During the South's colonial and antebellum periods, wildlife was abundant and its pursuit provided settlers a diversion from their ordinary work routines as well as supplements to their sometimes meager stocks of food. Settlers also hunted to control the numbers of larger mammals in their vicinity, for their crops were vulnerable to grazing by deer and their free-roaming livestock fell prey to wolves.

Wealthy planters sought to emulate European aristocrats with their privileges and refinements. In some areas, the pursuit of certain wild game became identified with the prerogatives of power and status. For influential, wealthy individuals, hunting was an important social activity. The hunt, the chase, and the shoot are described in the hunting narratives of the antebellum period. Although purported to be factual accounts, these hunting narratives are actually standardized accounts whose recurrent themes provide insights into the ideol-

ogy of wealthy planters and the ways in which they sought to distinguish themselves.

Many planters believed that hunting enabled them to understand nature and man's place in the world. Southern hunters loved nature for its supposed order and stability, which their own organized social life based on a hierarchical arrangement of people and contingent upon the judicial applicaton of force could only approximate. For these planters, hunting was a socially sanctioned expression of force, and its violence was necessary to participate in the natural world and to appreciate its indestructible order. Southern planters contrasted their modes of hunting with others on the basis of presumed motive and purpose. If most whites and blacks in the South hunted out of necessity, planters insisted they participated for sport and amusement. Although other classes pursued wild animals for meat and for tangible trophies, planters saw the process itself as the most important part of the chase. For them, the end was unimportant and inconsequential. Hunting conventions (sportsmanship) became prerequisites for membership in polite society and provided its participants the opportunity to learn the important lessons of self-discipline and control.

Plantation-style hunting was not for everyone. Outside restricted circles of gentility, most men hunted wildlife for food and for profit. Most subsisted on the land and sold skins and game meat whenever they found buyers.

After the Civil War the processes of urbanization and industrialization gradually concentrated many people in towns and cities. Leisure and wealth for increasing numbers in the cities made a return to nature and the land attractive. These ventures became possible for those owning or leasing large tracts of land, for in the rural areas city hunters came into increasing conflict with rural landowners, market hunters, and game dealers over the declining stocks of wild game. State trespass and federal game laws, with effective enforcement, became the solution to these conflicts and seemed the most democratic way to handle access for those aspiring to hunt. By 1910 most southern states had joined the rest of the nation in enacting trespass and game laws and providing cadres of enforcement officers. With these legal structures in place, market hunting and the sale of wild animals became illegal. State legislatures empowered wildlife agencies to monitor the populations of species now defined by law as game and to determine the ways and means by which these species were to be hunted. Restrictions in the variety of huntable species and the formalization of some hunting norms were the outcome of legal processes begun by urbanites. These statutes and regulations provide the ground rules and boundaries indicating what, where, when, and how species are hunted today. Hunting now is largely for sport and recreation. Nonetheless, a few people continue to hunt for food and to poach.

From organized groups in the cities have come most initiatives affecting field sports—the antihunting leagues, for example, as well as hunting and conservation organizations such as Ducks Unlimited, the National Turkey Federation, and the National Wildlife Federation, to name a few. Each organization publishes its own journal, solicits contributions, and maintains lobbies that seek to influence legislation favorable to their causes. From these journals today hunters glean the latest tips and techniques for tracking their game, learn about the big ones that escaped, and read about current fads in men's games.

Modernization has influenced some types of hunting more than others. Most affected is hunting for which dogs are specially bred and trained. Centered on particular breeds of dogs, a number of national organizations keep breeding records and sponsor an annual series of field trials. The trading, purchase, and breeding of hounds is big business in many rural areas of the South where the various field trials are hosted. The influences of technology and the changing patterns of landownership are apparent in the organization of hunt clubs as well. Hunt clubs began in colonial days when neighbors joined together for game drives. Then their organization was informal, often spontaneous, with no fees or formal membership. Later, when the large estates were divided or sold, individuals joined to lease land for their game and to afford the costs of maintaining the dogs throughout the year. Formal hunt clubs began about 1900. These clubs had a paid and limited membership and set times for hunting. Agribusiness with its mechanized operations on large tracts of land reduced game habitat on the better lands while most of the marginal lands, previously occupied and tilled by tenants, reverted to pine plantations and scrub. With the secondary growth, deer returned to these marginal lands, which now featured a hunt club with its headquarters in a refurbished tenant's shack.

Today precision firearms largely replace the muskets of former times, although a few purists prefer to stalk their deer with primitive weapons such as bows and arrows. Four-wheel-drive vehicles have superseded horses and wagons, dirt roads the foot trails, and CB radios and loudspeakers the hunter's horn. Yet the informal, intimate rituals between close associates and the traditions of time and place continue to make the hunt club a seasonal feature of southern life.

Southern distinctiveness in hunting stems from a peculiar combination of traits found in the region. The myth of a plantation lifestyle continues to inform the traditions of those who can afford them and to influence many others. The reality persists in the hunting plantations, many purchased and maintained by northern wealth in the 20th century, for quail and deer, and in the colorful pageantries of the exclusive hunt clubs located throughout the region. Extensive landownership, wealth, power, and leisure sustain these plantations and clubs, luring many to join or to observe their seasonal rituals. Still others read about them or participate in regional or national field trials for fox, quail, and coon, species associated with plantation life.

Most hunting in the rural South lacks the pretentiousness of the plantation tradition, yet its contours continue to show the gender, racial, and socioeconomic

Hunters standing over prey, location unknown, c. 1900

stratification of the region. Over two-thirds of southern hunters come from small towns or live in rural areas. Most are whites and Indians. Youngsters are taught to hunt by their fathers or close relatives. Guns are often heirlooms passed between generations. Blacks are underrepresented and, in contrast to the other races, they learn to hunt later in life, if at all, and their socialization is more often by peer groups than by their fathers. Hunters tend to be less well educated, make under $15,000 annual income, and are generally under 40 years of age. The expressed motivation for hunting varies, but it is normally for sport rather than for food. However, most game taken is eaten. Hunting continues as a masculine domain with a few inroads by women among either the poor or the wealthy. Because hunting is a masculine activity, game meat falls to the men to clean, to cook, and to serve on special occasions such as for Sunday dinners or at reunions.

Socialization as a hunter begins at an early age, with fathers or within an intimate circle of friends. In these close groups, young boys learn about conceptions of masculinity and their identity with the community, together with skills useful in their transition to manhood. Their maturation and accomplishments are celebrated in coming of age rituals aptly described by William Faulkner in *Go Down, Moses*. For most boys, initial kills are of small game such as squirrels and rabbits, which make relatively easy targets. Youngsters generally pursue a variety of mammals and birds as their time allows, but as they mature, they tend to specialize in one or a few species depending upon their associations with other men, their jobs, and costs of maintaining trained dogs. Men who hunt together are influential in other areas of community social and political life as well. Increasingly, family and work commitments are major disruptions to these male hunting fraternities. Jobs outside of the local community may disrupt these networks temporarily, but some men return religiously for the fall hunting season.

The types of game pursued reflect stratification along socioeconomic and racial lines. Ownership of extensive tracts and trained dogs are the prerequisites for the most prestigious types of game such as quail, deer, fox, and turkey. Access to these species remains difficult for many, although they may be hunted on public lands. Dove shoots, which generally open the fall hunting season, are social occasions. They are generally open to most people because the shoot requires guns positioned in as many places as possible around a recently harvested field to keep the birds flying. (In many northern states, doves are classified as song birds and not hunted.) Blacks and the rural poor generally hunt squirrels, rabbits, racoons, and possums, species normally avoided by others.

As a region, the South still retains an edge over other areas in numbers of households containing a hunter. According to Gallup polls taken in 1959, slightly over half of southern white households contained a hunter compared to one-third for the rest of the nation. By 1965 these percentages had dropped, but the South still led other regions. White southerners have led the nation in ownership of guns and revolvers. Gallup polls for 1960 showed about two-thirds of white southern households possessing firearms, whereas less than half of those in the non-South did so. In 1968 these polls showed 52 percent for the South and 27 percent elsewhere.

See also VIOLENCE: Guns

Stuart A. Marks
University of Florida

Dickson D. Bruce. Jr., *Violence and Culture in the Antebellum South* (1979); Hennig Cohen and William B. Dillingham, eds., *Humor of the Old Southwest* (2d ed., 1975); William Elliot, *Carolina Sports by Land and Water* (1859); William Faulkner, "The Bear," in *Go Down, Moses* (1942); H. Gibson, "Deer Hunting Clubs in Concordia Parish: The Role of Male Sodalities in the Maintenance of Social Values" (M.A. thesis, Louisiana State University, 1976); C. Gondes, ed., *Hunting in the Old South* (1967); Clifton Paisley, *From Cotton to Quail: An Agricultural Chronicle of Leon County, Florida, 1860–1967* (1968); Robert Ruark, *The Old Man and the Boy* (1957); Louis D. Rubin, Jr., *William Elliot Shoots a Bear: Essays on the Southern Literary Imagination* (1976); Francis Utley, Lynn Bloom, and Arthur F. Kinney, eds., *Bear, Man, and God: Seven Approaches to William Faulkner's "The Bear"* (1964). ☆

Mardi Gras
||||||||||||||||||||||||||||||

The celebration of Mardi Gras along the central Gulf Coast portions of Louisiana, Mississippi, and Alabama marks the region's historical and cultural difference from the rest of the South. Mardi Gras ("Fat Tuesday"), or Carnival ("fleshly excess"), is celebrated with costumed float parades, neighborhood marches, informal parties, and formal balls in New Orleans, Biloxi, and Mobile among other Gulf Coast cities. In contrast, a rural Louisiana Cajun and black Creole *courir de Mardi Gras* or Mardi Gras run is carried out by horseback-mounted revelers in over a dozen French-speaking communities of southwest Louisiana.

Mardi Gras is historically associated with French and Spanish populations along the Gulf Coast. However, many ethnic groups now join in the traditional festive occasion, which falls in February or March prior to Ash Wednesday and 40 days before Easter. It has been speculated that the Mediterranean-Latin roots of Mardi Gras are to be found in the pre-Roman rites of spring and later Roman festival or ritual occasions such as Baccanalia, Lupercalia and Saturnalia. Over time such occasions became part of the Catholic liturgical calendar. Thus, the Gulf Coast Carnival season officially begins on January 6, the Epiphany and Feast of Kings. On this date in New Orleans "King Cakes"— with a plastic miniature baby inside each and adorned in Mardi Gras colors of gold, purple, and green—are consumed in celebration. The season may be as short as three and a half weeks or as long as two months, depending upon the date of Easter. The culmination of Carnival is Mardi Gras day or Shrove Tuesday (referring to a time to be "shriven of one's sins"). The festive eating, dancing, and drinking associated with Mardi Gras are followed by the relative austerity and penitence of the Lenten period.

Just as Roman Catholicism absorbed earlier pre-Roman Carnival elements, so too the worldwide variations on Carnival now reflect regional cultural diversity. Thus, Gulf Coast Carnival, like Carnival in related societies of the Caribbean and Latin America, represents a syncretism of French/Spanish, Native American, and African/Afro-Caribbean performance styles and structures. That the earliest European settlers of the Gulf

Coast celebrated Mardi Gras is verified by the explorer D'Iberville's naming of Mardi Gras Bayou along the Mississippi in southern Louisiana. Informal parades and festive masquerades are reported to have occurred in major centers like Mobile and New Orleans throughout the early 19th century; and by midcentury (1857 in New Orleans) officially sanctioned parades began.

The early public parades in New Orleans and Mobile were founded by the Anglo and Creole (French/Spanish) elites of both cities. In New Orleans, such "krewes" as Comus, Momus, Proteus, and Rex have continued from the 19th century into the present. Some krewes still utilize smaller antique floats depicting mythological scenes crafted in *papier-mâché*. These floats were originally drawn by mules, which were eventually replaced by tractors in the 1950s. The artwork found on newer floats is made of plastic.

Today as many as 60 different krewes parade in the roughly two-week period prior to and including Mardi Gras day. Some, such as Arabi and Argus, are quite recent and represent suburban neighborhoods. All parades throw doubloons (introduced in the early 1960s) and other plastic trinkets to the crowds that line such primary parade routes as St. Charles Avenue and Canal Street. The varied krewes both reflect and invert the social structure of New Orleans on a day when the upper classes play at being kings, fools, and mythological beings. Suburban middle classes may likewise assert their right to be royalty for a day. Elite old-line krewes maintain an aura of secrecy about the selection of their royalty and invitation to their balls and affiliated social events. The newer krewes such as Bacchus, on the other hand, charge admission to their open gatherings in the Superdome and elsewhere at the end of parades.

The Zulu parade of New Orleans's black middle class and elite community, founded in 1909 as a reaction to white stereotypes of blacks as "savages," is a Carnival activity rivaled only by the Rex Parade on Mardi Gras day. Zulu members dress in grass skirts and "wooley wigs," put on blackface, and throw rubber spears and decorated coconuts to the delighted crowds. Working-class blacks, particularly those of Creole (French/Spanish) ancestry, also invoke white stereotypes of "wildness" by masquerading pridefully in stylized Plains Indians costumes.

The black "Mardi Gras Indians" are hierarchical groups of men with titles such as Big Chief, Spyboy, Wildman, and Li'l Chief who dress in elaborate bead and feather costumes weighing up to 100 pounds. After months of time and money invested in sewing costumes and practice sessions at local bars, a dozen or more "tribes" appear early on Mardi Gras day to sing, dance, and parade through back street neighborhoods. Some of these black Indians, with "tribe" names such as "Creole Wild West," "White Cloud Hunters," "Yellow Pocahontas," and "Wild Tchoupitoulas," do in fact have partial Native American ancestry and speak in mythological fashion about Indian spirits and customs. Their performance style, however, is essentially Afro-Caribbean, as expressed in competitive dance and song and the call-and-response chants that mark their foot parades. These chants are often based on a secret code language consisting of a group leader's call and responses such as "Hey pocky way" and "Ja ca mo feen non nay." They also use standard tunes such as "Li'l Liza Jane" and "Shoo Fly" to improvise

tales of their daring and exploits as they "go to town" on Mardi Gras day.

While the Mardi Gras Indians and the Zulu parade utilize Mardi Gras to make statements about group pride through inverted stereotypes of Indian and African tribes, many blacks also work at the service of whites on Carnival, thereby reflecting the postcolonial social structure of New Orleans. Some, for example, lead horses for major white parades such as Rex and Momus. Others dress in pointed white hoods and cloaks and carry torches called "flambeaux" that light the way for night parades of old elite krewes such as Comus.

Although smaller in scale and less widely known than New Orleans Carnival, Mardi Gras in Mobile has been celebrated in various ways since the beginning of the 19th century. The Cowbellions, an early parading group using cowbells and other noisemakers, formed in the 1830s and later ordered their costumes from Paris. During the Civil War Mobile's public Mardi Gras ceased. It was revived in 1866 by a veteran named Joe Cain, who dressed that year as a mock Chickasaw Indian chief called "Slacabamorinico" and drove through the then-occupied city in a decorated wagon. On Sunday before the Mobile Carnival Joe Cain is now commemorated with a jazz funeral procession. Various other Mobile krewes such as the Comic Cowboys and the Infant Mystics date to the 19th century. The Order of Myths, the oldest krewe (1867), was modeled after the early Cowbellions. The symbol of the Order of Myths, which is the last krewe to parade on Mardi Gras, is Folly chasing Death around a broken neoclassical column and flailing him with a golden pig bladder. Although this imagery symbolizes a general Mardi Gras theme of mirth's triumph over gloom, some suggest that the broken column originally alluded to the broken dreams of the Confederacy.

The large float parades in the Mardi Gras celebrations of Mobile and New Orleans represent Mediterranean and Caribbean traditions. In contrast, the Cajun and black Creole *courir de Mardi Gras* of rural southwest Louisiana reflects country French traditions brought by Acadians of Nova Scotia who came to Louisiana in the latter part of the 18th century. In a manner not unlike Christmas mumming in Europe and the West Indies, a band of masked male revelers goes from house to house on the open prairie land of southwest Louisiana. The men, on horses or flatbed trucks, dress as clowns, thieves, women, and devils. Some wear the traditional pointed *capuchon* hats with bells and streamers. The group is led by a *capitaine* who may wear an elegant silk costume in the

Cajun Mardi Gras celebrant, Church Point, Louisiana, 1978

Cajun bands or simple work clothes in some black Creole Mardi Gras bands. The Mardi Gras bands come as quasi-vigilantes and clowns in search of *charité* in the form of live chickens, rice, spices, grease, sausages, and other ingredients for a gumbo supper. The *capitaine*, standing apart from the group as a keeper of the law, tries to prevent the men from getting too disorderly or drunk and sees that they carry out their agreed-upon rounds for the day. At each visited farmstead the *capitaine* or a flagman will visit ahead of the band to see if the household will receive the Mardi Gras. There is usually an affirmative response to the courtly request, *"Voulez-vous recevoir cette band des Mardi Gras?"* ("Do you want to receive the Mardi Gras band?"), whereupon the clowns are waved on to charge the house on horseback. After dismounting and dancing together (which men do only on Mardi Gras), a competitive chase is often held for a live chicken. (This chase is usually preceded by a song of request to the man or lady of the house.) The chicken chase involves a designated bird, or one tossed into the air, and is a hilarious spectacle as men in costume pursue elusive birds through the muddy rice fields of early spring, leaping fences and crossing pig styes. After a chicken is caught, it is killed and put with other spoils in a sack, which is sent back to town where the cooking begins at midday. As the Mardi Gras runners depart a house, they sing a word of thanks and invite the householders to the dance and communal supper to be held in town or at a rural club late in the night.

The Mardi Gras song is especially significant because it is sung in a minor modal style reminiscent of Medieval French folk music, generally not found in Cajun music today. The song also contains a description of the Mardi Gras band's activities. Sung in French, the song is usually performed by musicians who ride in a sound truck. The translated song is as follows:

THE MARDI GRAS DANCE

The Mardi Gras riders come from
  everywhere
All around, around the hub.
They pass once a year
To ask for charity
Even if it's a potato.
A potato and some cracklins.
The Mardi Gras riders are on a long
  voyage
All around, around the hub.
They pass once a year
To ask for charity
Even if it's a skinny chicken
And three or four corn cobs.
Captain, captain, wave your flag.
Let's go to the other neighbor's place
To ask for charity.
You all come meet us.
You all come meet us.
Yes, at the gumbo tonight.

By the end of the afternoon the band heads back toward "the hub" or their starting point in rice- and soybean-growing and cattleraising towns like Mamou, Church Point, L'Anse Maigre, and Swords. The riders on horseback may enter at a gallop. Those who are sober enough entertain waiting crowds with stunts and various acts of bravado. The gumbo from the day's catch is served to the riders and the general public followed by a large dance ending at midnight and the beginning of the Lenten season.

The parallel black Creole Mardi Gras bands are often located near the Cajun towns in tiny rural settlements established in the 19th century by manumitted slaves and other people of color. The black Creole Mardi Gras celebrations are usually smaller (10–20 men), more intimate, and more traditional than today's Cajun *courirs*. The cowboy style of Cajun Mardi Gras has not taken hold in the black Creole community. For example, the black bands take great care not to trample house gardens or urinate in public while pursuing the fowl. Elders are helped down from their flatbed trucks by younger men, and the bands present themselves more as polite beggars than as vigilantes. The older Creoles especially take great stock in such details and are critical of young men who do not behave or sing properly. The Creole Mardi Gras song is similar to that of the Cajuns but is often performed in a call-response manner showing Afro-Caribbean influences. The usual response line to the leader's song is *"Ouais mon/bon cher camarade"* ("Yes my/good dear friend").

While old traditions and Carnival groups continue, in recent years new Mardi Gras events and locales have emerged to meet new social concerns and issues. For example, in New Orleans gay krewes and their French Quarter costume contests have become highly visible. In New Orleans and Baton Rouge the Krewe of Clones and the Spanishtown Mardi Gras, respectively, have become avant-garde satires on Carnival itself and on Louisiana topics such as politics and pollution. Suburban Mardi Gras celebrations have sprung up with children included and excessive drunkenness or sexual suggestiveness excluded. Adjacent Anglo-American regions have also started Mardi Gras celebrations. Monroe, La., for example, held its first parade in 1985, and the celebration was criticized by local fundamentalist preachers as "devil worship."

Films such as *Always for Pleasure* (Les Blank, director, Flower Films, 1978) and *Fat Tuesday* (Armand Ruhlman, director, Goofy Gator productions, 1981) offer rich visual documentation of Mardi Gras. Whatever locale and shape Mardi Gras takes in the Gulf Coast region, it will continue to reflect the historical and contemporary cultural traditions of its celebrants.

See also BLACK LIFE: / Mardi Gras Indians; ETHNIC LIFE: Caribbean Influence; / Cajuns and Creoles; Creole; URBANIZATION: / Mobile; New Orleans

Nicholas R. Spitzer
Smithsonian Institution

Always for Pleasure (Les Blank, producer, Flower Films, El Cerrito, Calif., 1978); Erwin Craighead, in *Mobile: Fact and Tradition* (1930); Munro Edmunson, *Caribbean Quarterly* (No. 3, 1956); Arthur La Cour and Stuart Landry, *New Orleans Masquerade: Chronicles of Carnival* (1952); Rosary H. O'Brien, "The New Orleans Carnival Organizations: Theatre of Prestige" (Ph.D. dissertation, University of California at Berkeley, 1973); Harry Oster and Revon Reed, *Louisiana Folklore Miscellany* (No. 1, 1960); Phyllis H. Rabbe, "Status and Its Impact: New Orleans Carnival, The Social Upper Class and Upper Class Power" (Ph.D. dissertation, Pennsylvania State University, 1973); Michael P. Smith, *Spirit World: Pattern in the Expressive Folk Culture of Afro-American New Orleans* (1984); Nicholas R. Spitzer, "Zydeco and Mardi Gras: Creole Identity and Performance Genres in Rural French Louisiana" (Ph.D. dissertation, University of Texas, 1986); Robert Tallant, *Mardi Gras* (1949); Calvin Trillin, *New Yorker* (20 June 1964); Perry Young, *The Mystick Krewe: Chronicles of Comus and His Kin* (1931). ☆

Pets

||||||||||

Keeping domestic animals as pets and as companions is a widespread, almost ubiquitous, pattern in human societies. Pets are of several types: (1) the pet animal kept for pleasure or amusement predominantly, but with no utilitarian function; (2) the food animal, hand- and/or house-raised, which enjoys pet status during some or all of its lifetime; and (3) the companion animal, fulfilling multiple overlapping roles, ranging from comrade to such other roles as work assistant, recreational partner, or surrogate family or household member, any of which meets the key elements described above. In addition, tamed wild animals are sometimes kept as pets.

Earliest evidence of pet or companion animals in the South comes from an A.D. 1100 site in North Carolina. The special pet or companion status of a dog is inferred from a burial site, where careful arrangement of remains indicates a close relationship between the animal and a person or the community. Both pets and companion animals have persisted within southern culture, as have careful burials and memorials for companion animals. Franklin County, Ala., has an elaborate coon dog graveyard, complete with a monument said to have cost $5,000.

Southern pet-keeping practices must be viewed within the larger context of general attitudes toward animals more characteristic of southern culture than of other regions: southerners are more likely to express concern for the practical and material value of animals or their habitat. They are less likely to express concern about the right and wrong treatment of animals or to strongly oppose exploitation or cruelty toward animals. On the other hand, while expressing indifference or incredulity toward the idea of "loving" animals, many southerners form strong affectional attachments to individual animals. This feeling is best expressed in the rural South through the ambivalent relationship between a man and his hound. Other southerners report no such ambivalence in their relationships with their pets and companion animals, readily expressing strong and enduring attachment to them and mourning their loss, whether these companions are household residents or working companions.

The importance of the animal as working companion is reflected in the emergence of several regional dog breeds. The breeds usually derive from stock registered by national breeding registries, but offspring are no longer registered with national bodies. They are identified with the region and local area and are a source of great community pride. Examples are the multiple varieties of coonhounds (many locally recognized as separate pure breeds, with strong local sanctions against breeding back to nonregional stock), the Boykin Spaniel (a variety of Field Spaniel, developed as a hunting spaniel but also suitable as a household companion), and the Catahoula Leopard Dog (a stock dog prized for working ability and companionship, developed from several breeds of stock dogs). Few of these are known or seen outside the South. Small mixed-breed dogs are still routinely referred to as "feist" or "fice" and within local areas may be so similar to one another in appearance and ancestry as to be recognized as the "feist" of a particular area. William Faulkner celebrated the bravery of a "fice" in "The Bear."

The species of pets and companion animals in the South do not differ notably from those in other regions of the United States, especially in urban areas. Dogs are most common, with a greater proportion of the regional purebred and mixed breeds than found in other regions. Some patterns of the dog-human relationship do differ. Individuals and household members develop strong attachments to individual dogs and, while treating them with affection, evaluate them on the basis of their working ability. Once unable to work, however, they still retain a special status within the household. Because their primary function is that of working animal, the special status within the household does not necessarily mean the animal resides inside. This is true for many pets and companion animals in southern culture: The key elements of companion animal status are frequently fulfilled without inside residence for the animal. This remains true when people migrate or obtain animals of other species or breeds. When the need for an animal to assist with work is no longer present, many southerners select an animal solely for companionship purposes. Special status is earned on the basis of satisfaction with fulfillment of companionship function. Country musicians sing sentimental songs of dogs, such as "Old Shep." Writer Willie Morris wrote of the companionship and death of his dog Pete in *The Courting of Marcus Dupree* (1984).

Cats are kept as pets less frequently than in other areas. Most cats kept as pets or companions live in urban areas. In rural areas of the South many barn cats are kept to control rodent populations, with attachments to the territory on which they live and hunt, rather than to people. Breeding cats for companionship functions has occurred only recently. The recentcy of this is not peculiar to the South, however. Although selective breeding of the dog has occurred for over 2,000 years, selective breeding of cats in most areas of the world has occurred only within the last 100 years.

As in other areas, horses have risen in popularity as companion animals. Previously kept primarily as performance animals by members of the upper and upper middle classes, they are increasingly acquired for companionship and pleasure riding by members of the middle class. Frequently, a strong mutual attachment develops between horse and owner, and the horse spends an entire lifetime with a single owner, rather than being regularly sold and replaced as are many performance animals.

Southerners also keep their share of "pocket pets": guinea pigs, rats, mice, rabbits, gerbils, ferrets, birds, amphibians, and fish. Patterns of keeping these species do not differ notably from other regions of the United States; they are more popular in urban areas.

Boy with dog, Vicksburg, Mississippi, 1972

Another common practice in the South persists even among those who express a utilitarian attitude toward animals: hand raising food animals and selecting an occasional food animal to be kept as a pet. In the past this practice has involved very few animals but has included hogs, dairy and beef cattle, sheep, and poultry. As southern animal agriculture shifts from small operations to large agribusiness, the practice persists, but the types of animals change: goats have become increasingly popular, as have pigs. Both provide food and animal by-products. Both species are also social animals, a fact that increases the probability of becoming a successful companion.

The practices of raising orphaned and keeping tamed wild animals as if they were pets are far more common in the South than in other regions. In many southern towns and rural areas, these are long-standing customs, often considered as much a part of southern culture as nurturing regional breeds or lines of dogs. In the past most of the tamed wild animals have been small and native to the South—raccoons, skunks, possums, squirrels, and birds. They frequently fulfilled some marginal companionship function. Recently, however, there has been a marked increase in the keeping of exotic or endangered animals, including cougars, wolves, buffaloes, wolf-hybrids, parrotlike birds, monkeys, and large snakes. The latter species are kept largely for amusement or as status symbols rather than for utility or companionship. Such practices are currently being actively discouraged in many southern communities as lawsuits against owners of animals that kill or injure people are successfully prosecuted, as the incidence of rabies among wild animals increases, as zoonotic diseases are transmitted from animals to people, and as existing laws that prohibit keeping such animals are more strictly enforced. Efforts to discourage keeping wild animals as pets are usually met with strong resistance and are viewed as attempts of outsiders to interfere with southern rights.

Patterns of keeping companion animals in the South are similar to those in other areas of the United States in many ways. Dogs are still the most popular companion animals, with cats, birds, and other small domestic animals becoming more popular, especially as urbanization increases. But the South has several notable differences from patterns in other regions. Companion animals in the rural South are more likely to be employed actively in some work-assistant role, and they are more frequently kept for herding, hunting, or controlling pests, while enjoying special status within the household or farmstead.

Ownership patterns also differ. The use of the companion animal in its work function is frequently shared by various members in the community; however, the primary figure for attachment, loyalty, affection, and care is an individual rather than a group. Other animals are kept primarily as household companions or working companions during most of the year and employed in communal work-recreational functions (such as raccoon or bird hunting) at intervals throughout the year. In addition, in the South, human companions to companion animals are less likely to be legal owners of the animals than in other regions.

Residence patterns of companions and pets differ from other regions. In the South, many animals are sheltered outside the house. In other regions most are housed in the same structure as their owners. Types of pet animals vary. More wild animals are kept as pets, as are more farm animals. Regional breeds are more highly valued, and animals are more likely to be evaluated on performance of their companionship function than on their status as pure or mixed breed.

Margaret Sery Young
University of North Carolina
at Chapel Hill

David S. Favre and Murray Loring, *Animal Law* (1983); James W. Jordan, *Appalachian Journal* (Spring 1975); Stephen R. Kellert, *Transactions of the 45th North American Wildlife and Natural Resources Conference* (1980); Margaret Sery Young, *Veterinary Clinics of North America: Small Animal Practice* (March 1985). ☆

Resorts

||||||||||||||||||||

The color photographs in brochures publicizing southern resorts portray romantic luxury in magnificent scenic settings. Handsome couples frolic in the wash of surf, ride bicycles along moss-draped live-oak-lined paths, play golf on green-barbered fairways. They dine by candlelight and enjoy a leisurely breakfast on the terrace of their room, overlooking a sweep of mountains or an expanse of sea. The point of such literature, of course, is to coax the reader to make reservations for a few days in paradise.

Essentially, resorts are rooms with a view, a combination of lodging and nature where the natural beauty of the outdoors, like room service, is offered as an amenity. Resorts are the rich relatives of the poor-cousin interstate motel, inhabiting their own little world on barrier islands and mainland coast, beside lakes and warm springs, in the mountain valleys and in the folds of piedmont. Their guests are mostly middle and upper-class couples and families who escape home and work for a weekend, a week, even a season to find rest and recreation.

Lodging in most resorts may include both hotel-type rooms for rent and individually owned units, such as condominiums. Through lease agreements, owners permit the resort to rent the property to other guests most of the year. Increasingly popular are timeshare vacation units. In this arrangement, the guest buys a space of time, say a week in June, and the vacation home is theirs for that period each year.

The first southern resorts appeared as early as the late 18th and early 19th centuries and were built around the waters of warm springs. The Greenbrier in White Sulphur Springs, W. Va., and The Homestead in Hot Springs, Va., trace their origins to those times. Early lodging conditions were often no better than the common ordinary (tavern) of that day.

A minister from Charleston in 1838 described White Sulphur Springs as "decidedly the meanest, most nasty place in point of filth, dust, and every other bad quality." Yet, despite the fleas in his bed and the grunting hogs outside his window, the minister paid his money to rub shoulders with the elite of the South and the nation. Southern resorts drew the rich and famous. One of the last photographs of Robert E. Lee, sitting among his Confederate general comrades, was taken at White Sulphur Springs in 1869.

Although southerners used health as an excuse to spend a season at a resort, the purpose of their visit was also pleasure. The resort season glittered with balls, sumptuous meals, music, and gambling. In the late 19th century northerners were also checking into southern resorts and resort towns, not only to bathe in springs, but also to drink the mineral waters. Travel guidebooks, such as *Health Resorts in the South*, published in 1893, were a mixture of boosterism and scholarly treatise, praising the towns and resorts and listing the medical benefits of each locale's water and climate.

Many towns were considered beneficial for specific ailments. Consumptives often headed for mountain towns such as Asheville, N.C. Grove Park Inn, still in operation there today, was built in 1886 by a St. Louis businessman who first came to the area seeking relief from his bronchial ailments.

Railroad transportation provided easier access to resorts and encouraged the building of new ones. In the early 20th century northerners rode the rails further down the southern coastline as these resorts opened. At Jekyll Island, Ga., it is said that one-sixth of the world's wealth gathered each winter on this barrier island. In Florida, Henry Morrison Flagler, the Standard Oil Company magnate, welcomed wintering northerners to a string of coastal resorts he built along his railroad from Jacksonville to Miami.

In the decades after World War II, when the upper class preferred jet travel to Europe, many old resort hotels fell into disrepair. Others, however, survived as oases of grandeur in the neon desert of the chain motel. Such properties as The Breakers in Palm Beach, Fla., The Greenbrier, The Homestead, and Grand Hotel in Point Clear, Ala., constantly upgraded facilities and kept service standards high. They continued

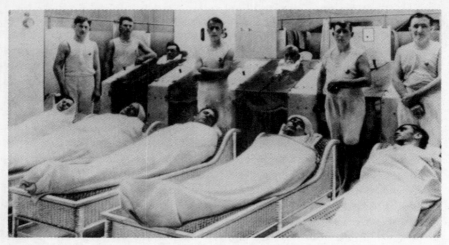

Men's bathing department, Buckstaff Bath House, Hot Springs, Ark., postcard, c. 1900

to pamper guests with afternoon tea, chamber music, and carriage rides. Ladies and gentlemen dressed for meals prepared by European chefs and served in elegant dining rooms.

Where the upper class goes, the middle class will scrimp and save and surely follow. They, too, took their overseas vacations, but they also trekked to old resorts and to newer ones that began to arise around the early 1960s. These stretch along beaches and huddle in mountain valleys, offering units with kitchens for guests. Property was also sold to families who bought or built vacation or retirement homes.

As stepchildren to the grand old hotels, these nouveau riche resorts attempt to buy instant tradition and class. Many hire European chefs to prepare continental cuisine, and offer afternoon tea. They pay handsome sums to top golf course designers to lay out their 18 holes, and hire professional golfers and tennis stars, who represent the resort as "touring pro." These stars drop by for cameo appearances to teach clinics and play exhibition matches. At these new resorts, vacationers may still rub elbows with the rich and famous.

Nearly all offer golf and tennis, water sports, bicycling, and shopping. But despite the similarities, each resort attempts to produce a distinctive ambience. On Greers Ferry Lake, in the foothills of the Arkansas Ozarks, two resorts stretch along opposite shorelines. One, Fairfield Bay, moves with a snappy urbane flair, with rooms as plush as city hotel suites and with entertainment in its nightclub. Red Apple Inn, on the other hand, is flavored with a warm, winesap scent, and is as comfortable as worn tweeds. Its rooms are filled with European antiques, fireplaces, and fresh apples. Guests are expected to dress for dinner, which is served with a view of the sunset over the lake.

To build resorts with views from rooms unencumbered by signs of civilization, developers often shouldered into empty pockets of pristine wilderness. Many were gentle invaders. They attached strict building codes to blend vacation structures with natural surroundings, stilted boardwalks above sacred dunes, and left portions of their property in its natural state. On South Carolina's Hilton Head Island, for example, at least 75 percent of Sea Pines Plantation remains in forest and marshland.

One resort in Pine Mountain, Ga., was built specifically as a caretaker of its land. In the early 1950s Cason Calloway, a retired textile magnate, nursed 2,500 acres of eroded cotton fields into a paradise, Callaway Gardens, which is run by a nonprofit foundation for horticultural and environmental research and preservation. In greenhouses and formal gardens, along woodland paths, or bordering an inn, cottage, condominium, tennis court, or golf course, Callaway Gardens blushes with floral color each season.

Traffic sometimes backs up three miles from Pine Mountain as motorists come in spring to see some 700 varieties of azaleas in bloom. The garden's horticulture and education staffs conduct research in plant life and the local environment and pass that knowledge on to guests in nature walks and seminars. At Callaway Gardens the resort is a backdrop to the land and the flowers that grow upon it.

The land itself is a resort's most important asset, groomed and cared for as meticulously as its rooms and restaurants. Guests come for a resort's outdoor features, first for health and later for recreation. Nature—a woodland path, a sunset-kissed curl of golden beach—comprises the main ingredients visitors need "to get away from it all." Visitors still trek to resorts for their health, if not necessarily for the body, at least for peace of mind and of the soul.

See also ART AND ARCHITECTURE: Resort Architecture

Gary D. Ford
Southern Living

"Callaway Gardens: A Place for Everyone" (information pamphlet published by Callaway Gardens); George H. Chapin, *Health Resorts of the South* (1893); Marshall Fishwick, *Springlore in Virginia* (1978); Jeffrey Limerick, Nancy Ferguson, and Richard Oliver, *America's Grand Resort Hotels* (1979); Donald E. Lundberg, *The Tourist Business* (1974); *Southern Living* (September 1979, August 1982, February 1984). ☆

Restaurants
|||||||||||||||||||||||||||||||||||

From the colonial period through Reconstruction, southerners did not care for commercial hospitality. Except in the large cities such as New Orleans, restaurants were unheard of. The word, derived from the French, was not in general use until late in the 18th century, and the word "hotel" was not used until the 19th century. Even in the larger cities, most eating places were operated in conjunction with lodging.

When southerners traveled, they frequently stopped with friends or relations. Roadside taverns and inns were intended primarily for convivial drinking rather than eating. Food that was supplied was meager and unappetizing; some of it, travelers discovered, was tainted or spoiled. However, some of the inns were run by widows or private families wishing to supplement their incomes, and in such establishments, the traveler fared better.

The food on the eastern seacoast tended to be better and more appetizing than that found elsewhere. As the traveler moved westward through the frontier areas, the quality of the food deteriorated rapidly. Too, those states farther north tended to serve better fare than those farther south. In Mississippi and Louisiana (other than New Orleans), food was frequently so bad that it had to be chased down with whiskey. Contemporary reports indicate that the worst accommodations of all were in Arkansas and Texas because of their frontier status. Available food was generally wild game, chicken, or pork served with locally grown vegetables, fruits, and berries when they were in season.

Spas and resorts, which later became popular in the South, did little to improve commercial dining. Food and accommodations at such hotels as Gray Sulfur Springs, Red Sulfur Springs, and White Sulfur left much to be desired. The dining rooms were frequently out of most food, and the straw-stuffed mattresses were hard and uneven. The Englishman J. S. Buckingham commented with some amazement in his study *The Slave States of America* that most Americans accepted bad accommodations and worse food without complaint.

As the southerner traveled to cities such as Mobile, Charleston, and New Orleans, his chances of finding good food served well in commercial settings improved. Buckingham, for example, ate in the dining room of the Saint Charles Hotel in New Orleans, which accommodated some 500 guests—300 men at one table and 200 women at another. Many immigrants brought with them the more sophisticated knowledge of cuisine from Europe. The Creole and French influences in New Orleans cuisine are still strongly felt.

One area of interest regarding commercial hospitality of the time was the river steamer. Here southerners could find food that frequently equalled the quality of that served in the cities. On one such steamer the cabin passengers dined first, followed by the ship's officers, white deck passengers, white waiters, black passengers, and black waiters, in sequence. Steamers seemed to offer more beef and less pork and, when they departed from New Orleans, frequently served seafood, especially shellfish.

The manners and eating habits of southerners of the time left much to be desired. They frequently averaged 10 minutes to eat a meal and left the table while they were still chewing. The knife seemed to be the main utensil they used while eating, and coffee was as frequently sipped from the saucer as from the cup.

The old frontier ways of commercial dining in the South began to change by the middle of the 19th century. More attention was paid not only to the preparation and service of food but also to the environment in which it was served. The Saint Cloud Hotel in Nashville in 1866 had, for example, separate tables for diners, clean and well-appointed surroundings, and, above all, good and appetizing food. The great restaurants continued to appear in the cities, and their reputations spread throughout the area.

In the 20th century urbanization has been perhaps the most notable change in southern life affecting foodways. As late as 1920 only nine southern cities had populations of over 100,000 people; in 1980 there were that many or more with populations over a million. Many of the poorest southerners have migrated to cities in the North and West, and this change has affected their eating habits. Modern conveniences, such as electric refrigeration, have also affected the eating habits of southerners. Mass production of meats such as chicken has forced quality down but increased availability. Fast-food shops have changed the eating patterns of many southerners, although Colonel Sanders's Kentucky Fried Chicken represents the marketing of traditional southern fare. Increasing urbanization has also resulted in more sophisticated tastes for southerners, many of whom now eat out more often than they did in the past.

Family-style buffet restaurants are more popular in the South than elsewhere, according to restaurant trade journals, and five major cafeteria chains —Luby's, based in San Antonio, Morrison's in Mobile, Wyatt's in Dallas, Piccadilly in Baton Rouge, and Furr's, which began in Texas but is now owned by K Mart of Troy, Mich.—provide what has become a distinctive southern form of dining. The *New York Times* reported on 18 August 1985 that while cafeterias had virtually died out in the North, they were steadily expanding in the South. They are, according to the *Times*, "as Southern in spirit as the drawl, wilting heat, and country cooking," the latter of which is the basis of the cafeteria cuisine served to a generally over-40, suburban clientele.

Great restaurants from the past continue to exist and are found primarily in New Orleans—a city that, because of its distinctive European tradition, remains *sui generis* within the region. Antoine's, founded in 1840 and reputed to be the oldest continuously operated restaurant in North America, serves its famous oysters Rockefeller (an original), soufflé potatoes, steak, and seafood dishes in both its public front and its plush private dining rooms in the rear. Galatoire's, also in the French Quarter and also one of New Orleans's oldest restaurants, retains its staunch democratic tradition—no reservations, at any time, for anyone—requiring its hopeful patrons to queue up to sample an original Creole shrimp remoulade, oysters Bienville, or trout Marguery. The city is also home to less historic but no less grand establishments such as the famed Le Ruth's and Paul Prudhomme's Cajun miracle, K-Paul's Louisiana Kitchen.

Outside the Crescent City the South continues to gain national recognition. The Inn at Little Washington, the Trellis in Virginia, Hudson's in South Carolina, and La Residence in North Carolina were listed in *Food and Wine*'s recent "honor roll" of the nation's most promising culinary finds. Southern connoisseurs can now indulge their taste for creme amandine and truffled foie gras in elegant surroundings. They can also visit Doe's Eat Place, a Greenville, Miss., cinderblock shack featuring succulent steaks and sensational tamales prepared with steak suet rather than lard. It is one of a handful of aggressively unpretentious restaurants that have become regional landmarks.

See also GEOGRAPHY: Foodways, Geography of; HISTORY AND MANNERS: Cookbooks; Foodways; INDUSTRY: / Sanders, Colonel Harlan; MYTHIC SOUTH: / Hospitality

Curtis C. Whittington
McNeese State University

John Egerton, *Southern Food: At Home, on the Road, in History* (1987); *Food and Wine* (May 1983); Jane Stern and Michael Stern, *Goodfood: The Adventurous Eater's Guide to Restaurants Serving America's Best Regional Specialties* (1983), *Roadfood* (rev. ed., 1980); Joe Gray Taylor, *Eating, Drinking, and Visiting in the South: An Informal History* (1982); *Washington Post* (26 January 1975). ☆

Roadhouses

||||||||||||||||||||||||||||||||

Southern roadhouses, which are usually called "juke joints" and "honky-tonks," had their origins in the antebellum "groggeries," or taverns, that were found throughout the South. In these establishments, groggery keepers dispensed questionable liquors to local customers and travelers. Consisting of little more than a room for drinking and a room for gambling, these groggeries were the haunts of white farmers, who exchanged their hard-earned cash for "bust-head" whiskey, and black slaves, who traded produce for "red-eye" rum.

Following the Civil War the integrated camaraderie of the antebellum groggeries gave way to racial segregation. In much of the New South, whites claimed the roadside taverns as their own, leaving the newly freed blacks to find their own recreational sites. In response, some rural blacks opened their homes to the public, selling homemade liquors to friends and strangers alike. To entertain their customers, the owners of such houses employed local musicians, who played "jump-ups" and blues for dancing couples and gambling men. Offering entertainment as well as refreshments, these black-owned houses were invariably known as "jukes" or "juke-joints."

"Juke" is the common pronunciation of "joog," a word meaning disorderly, which is found among Gullah-Geechee blacks of coastal South Carolina and Georgia. "Joog," in turn, may ultimately derive from "dzugu," a Bambara African word meaning wicked. The term *juke* is applied to black roadhouses throughout the South, but it can also refer to white taverns, especially in Florida and Georgia. It is not uncommon in those states to hear whites speak of "going jukin" after work.

Most southern whites, however, refer to their roadhouses as "honky-tonks." The etymology of this curious word is unknown; but "honky-tonk" first appeared in print in 1894, when a correspondent for the *Daily Ardmoreite* (Ardmore, Okla.) wrote the following: "The honk-a-tonk last night was well attended by ball-heads, bachelors, and leading citizens." Whatever its origins, the term *honky-tonk* was applied to the roadside taverns that dotted the outskirts of oil boom towns in Oklahoma and Texas. The "honky-tonks" contained little more than a bar, a dance floor, and a tiny stage for the musicians (in some instances shielded by chicken wire to protect the performers from flying objects when the fights broke out). Amid these small but noisy honky-tonk crowds, musicians amplified their guitars and Dobros, overcoming the sounds of shuffling dancers and gambling men to play their mournful ballads about drinking, divorce, and downfall.

Honky-tonks remained a phenomenon associated primarily with the Southwest until 1935, when the Texas-born musician Al Dexter recorded his popular "Honky-Tonk Blues." Within a few years white roadhouses throughout the South were known as "honky-tonks" or "honkies." In the Southwest, it was not uncommon for whites to attend black jukes and for blacks to visit white honky-tonks. But in the Southeast the racial barriers proved more rigid. Although intermingling was not unknown there, black jukes and white honky-tonks remained segregated by custom. Even today southeastern jukes and honky-tonks are segregated at a time when racial integration in public places has become commonplace.

"Honky-tonks" and "juke joints" continue to provide rural southerners with music, recreation, and, all too often, violence. The commercial success of middle-of-the-road country music has given "honky-tonks" a heretofore undreamed of commercial popularity, but even in the midst of commercial boom the rural "honky" survives. The urban migration of blacks has likewise taken its toll on the southern "jukes," but they too remain a part of the southern rural landscape.

See also MUSIC: Blues; Country Music; Honky-Tonk Music

John S. Otto and
Augustus M. Burns
University of Florida

Daniel R. Hundley, *Social Relations in Our Southern States*, ed. William J. Cooper, Jr. (1979); Bill C. Malone, *Country Music U.S.A.: A Fifty-year History* (1968); Mitford M. Mathews, *Americanisms: A Dictionary of Selected Americanisms on Historical Principles* (1966); Paul Oliver, liner notes to "Juke Joint Blues," Blues Classics 23, *Savannah Syncopators: African Retentions in the Blues* (1970); John S. Otto and Augustus M. Burns, *John Edwards Memorial Foundation Quarterly* (Spring 1974); Nick Tosches, *Country: The Biggest Music in America* (1977). ☆

Sports

||||||||||||||||

During the antebellum period southern sports were distinctive, important parts of the regional culture. With its relative lack of Puritan influence, generous climate, and less work-regulated population, the South tended to play more than other regions. The list of southern sports is long and shows the influence not only of the English sporting tradition, but also influences of Spanish, French, African, and Indian cultures. Southerners before and just after the Civil War amused themselves by riding, hunting, fishing, cockfighting, ninepins, fencing, fives, bowls, billiards, dancing, quoits, boxing, wrestling, animal baiting, cricket, *raquette* (an Indian lacrosse game), pedestrian races, target-shooting matches, medieval-like ring tournaments, bandy, boat races, fistfights, gander pulling, and horseshoes.

Historians have interpreted popular southern sports as reflecting regional values and characteristics—blood sports and militaristic games show the violent penchant, and Sunday prohibitions and sanctions against gambling on games of chance show the South's religious sensibilities. Sports have also embodied the old southern caste system: the leisured planter classes engaging in genteel and mannered pursuits (horse racing, fencing, elaborate hunts), the plain folk amusing themselves in more earthy fashions (cockfighting, wrestling), and slaves finding the rare occasion for their own games (races, hunting, fistfights, fishing, work matches).

During the 20th century southern sports became ever more like the rest of the nation's. Sports were a major influence on the homogenization of American culture as the big three, football, basketball, and baseball, came to dominate, overwhelmingly, interest in games. There was little regional variation to be found in these mass sports, in their rules, styles of play, coaching and organization, and the passion and pride generated in those who watch them. They had their own structure and even their own histories that have become increasingly exact and unchanging in form, allowing few alterations from sources outside the game. An innovator such as Dean Smith might still initiate the Tarheel "four corners" offense in basketball, but such a change has nothing to do with North Carolina culture—it has to do with the rules and logic of the game. Similarly, erudite discussions of Atlantic Coast Conference vs. Big Ten Conference sports and referee styles notwithstanding, the way these games are played is remarkably the same nationwide. It is possible to see differing ethnic playing styles in black ghetto and white suburban "pickup" basketball, but such stylistic variations have yet to be documented in the South. Organization of sports is also uniform and largely hierarchical, founded in the schools, colleges, and professional teams. Indigenous local teams exist, but do so at the margins of southern sports life.

Certainly local, state, and even regional pride is excited when a winning team comes along, and especially when a winning tradition is established in an Alabama and a folk hero is found in a Bear Bryant. But this is hardly limited to the South. Such emotions are as readily generated in Michigan, Nebraska, and even Boston.

The similarity of watching sports, nationwide, is also striking. A Hawkeye fan in Iowa watches the same kind of game on television or in the stadium, drinks roughly the same kind of beverage, is as limited in his movements and actions—shouting, booing, eating, and arguing the finer points—as the LSU Tiger booster. The art of being a fan, like the skill of the player, has to do with the game itself, not the culture outside the stadium.

Similarly, the hardy, nonprofessional adult who participates in sports at least once a year generally plays one of a handful of regional sports that remain

popular. An April 1980 Gallup poll showed that southerners play exactly the same top 20 games as the rest of the nation.

Nevertheless, in the midst of the homogenization of American sports, a few slightly significant regional differences remain. It would be claiming too much to speak of a southern sports culture; rather, these differences point to a faint but apparently resilient tradition existing on the margin of mass, popular sport—vestigial, ethnic-like traces within the dominant culture.

In the first place, the South has been slower than the rest of the nation to embrace popular sports. Though southerners play the same popular sports as everyone else, fewer of them are involved and for shorter periods of time. Southerners are much less involved in bowling, hiking, exercise in a gym, and jogging; only a bit less active in golf, tennis, baseball, volleyball, frisbee, swimming, bicycling, and camping; and about average in fishing, basketball, softball, touch football, and boating. The only sport that they do more of is hunting. They also lead the way in inactivity—about one-third of all southerners participate in no sport, even once a year, a condition that is three or four percentage points above the average.

Southern sports thus follow the general pattern of southern leisure—southerners simply do less. The regional interest in blood sports, and hence in the ownership of sports firearms (well above the average), may have something to do with what many writers have seen as this region's penchant for violence or violent attitudes; on the other hand, it may just be a rural phenomenon.

Racial barriers, although hardly limited to the South, have been a feature of sports history. The South has been slow in lowering these barriers and has done so in gradual, painful ways—taking care to regulate the racial composition of teams and the assignment of positions such as the quarterback and coaches. Most of these restrictions have been removed, and it is no longer uncommon to see all-black southern teams, black quarterbacks, and black superstars. Black coaches are still the exception, but this is true nationwide.

Southern sports, it is sometimes claimed, have even led the way in racial progress, opening up opportunities for blacks and increasing racial respect and understanding. Herschel Walker's return to his Georgia hometown as a hero, for example, represented a breakthrough in the general recognition of grace and ability that transcends color; Marcus Dupree, born in Neshoba County, Miss., the same month in 1964 as the murder there of three civil rights activists, later became a symbol for ra-

Child with kite, location unknown, 1930s

cial reconciliation in the community. However, it might also be argued that southerners since the antebellum era have pitted "their" blacks against one another in fistfights and wrestling matches, taking proprietary pride in their champions, a pride similar to that attached to bantam roosters and pit bulldogs. If this alternative interpretation of racial "progress" in sports is true, then there has been little progress indeed, and the South still distinguishes itself as a place apart through its own kind of sports racism.

A few regional sports exist in the South. Cockfighting and pit bulldog fighting may still be found in some of the backwaters of the bayou country and rural areas of Georgia and South Carolina. Traditional kinds of hunting with special rituals, equipment, manners and styles still exist for raccoon, quail, fox, dove, boar, deer, and even possum. Southerners have also played with technology in unusual ways. Stock car racing and drag racing seem to have originated in the South and remain more popular there. Tom Wolfe attributes much significance to stock car racing, seeing in events like the Charlotte 500 a blending of old and new that produces a distinctive hero—a Junior Johnson, part good-old-boy, whiskey runner, hell-bent-for-leather adventurer, and cavalier.

But perhaps the most curious regional "sports" have been of very recent origin. In a self-conscious and deliberate way, city fathers and clubs have set about making games or pastimes out of regional peculiarities. Today, the region is full of hollering, cow chip tossing, chili making, watermelon seed and tobacco juice spitting contests; armadillo, turtle, frog, and steamboat "races"; azalea, rose, rhododendron, and magnolia judgings; fiddlers' conventions and bluegrass music competitions; and Civil War battle reenactments. Participants often feel special attachment to their southernness. Whereas the games and sports of the Old South have faded, the "game of the South" flourishes.

Play and games, according to Johan Huizinga and others, keep alive and conserve cultural forms that have lost their usefulness, or which for some reason are no longer taken seriously. Cultural conservation seems especially developed in the South. Some of this region's once distinctive ways of living—agricultural skills, abilities with animals, physical strength, conversational abilities—have been undermined by the modernization and Americanization of the region. Self-conscious southerners have tended to "enframe" some of these things, to keep them alive long after they have lost their original economic or social function. This setting apart and playing with a fading culture is common among other American ethnic groups. Throughout the nation one finds Scandinavian festivals, Bohemian reunions, German Octoberfests, Scottish highland games, Irish parades, all celebrating old cultures.

One might suggest that even renewed scholarly interest in southern history and sociology has traces of play and the sportive. Certainly the amateur southern archaeologist with his metal detector, prowling old battlefields, and the family genealogist, haunting state archives, would admit to some playful, intrinsic motivations. Those who are paid to uncover the "real South" might also admit from time to time that it is, after all, fun; to be southern as well as to write about the South is no longer as serious or as much work as it used to be, and has become in some ways "mere" sport.

See also BLACK LIFE: Sports, Black; GEOGRAPHY: Sports, Geography of; VIOLENCE: Cockfighting

Benjamin K. Hunnicutt
University of Iowa

Dickson D. Bruce, Jr., *Southern Folklore Quarterly*, vol. 41 (1977); S. L. Del Sesto, *Southern Folklore Quarterly* (March 1975); Fred Hobson, *Alabama Heritage* (Summer 1986); John Shelton Reed, *The Enduring South: Subcultural Persistence in Mass Society* (1972); John F. Rooney, *American Demographics* (September 1986), *Geography of American Sport* (1974), *Geographical Review* (October 1969); Dale A. Somers, *Rise of Sports in New Orleans, 1850–1900* (1972); *Southern Exposure* (Fall 1979); Donald Spivey, *Sport in America: New Historical Perspectives* (1985). ☆

Stock Car Racing

||||||||||||||||||||||||||||||||||||||||||||

Stock car racing is a form of racing with automobiles that resemble standard production passenger cars. Stock car racing has become especially popular in the South where in its most developed forms it takes place in specialized amphitheaters using expensive, powerful, and carefully made machinery.

Automobiles were initially more plentiful in the industrialized parts of the nation, so much early automobile racing was done in the North and Midwest. Informal races were soon moved from the streets onto existing horse racing "tracks," which were surfaced with dirt. Starting around the turn of the century, the brick-surfaced oval track at Indianapolis, Ind., served as a new focus for racing activity.

It took longer for the automobile to reach rural areas, and not until the 1930s did stock car racing as it is known today become popular in the rural Midwest and South. Mass-produced automobiles gave working-class rural southerners more personal mobility than had been provided by horses. Farmers used cars for speedier delivery of their crops to more distant markets. In some cases, they distilled crops into liquor and transported the liquor to market as part of a long-standing family business. Liquor was a compact means of transporting crops and provided a greater return. This trade was opposed by governmental authorities, because most home-liquor makers ("moonshiners") did not pay taxes on their sales. In their efforts to outdistance law officers, some of the liquor runners skillfully modified their cars for greater power and higher speeds. The drivers of these vehicles also participated in informal races between themselves and others interested in automobiles. Liquor runners, although a small minority of those who entered early races, were among the most famous and proficient drivers and race organizers. Some of them became legends.

With the greater affluence and hence

Alabama International Motor Speedway, Talladega, Alabama, late 1970s

more widespread automobile ownership that followed World War II, racing became more popular than before, especially in the South. However, the rules under which the racing was conducted and the administration of the tracks were often uncertain. A concerted effort to standardize the rules and the administration of racing resulted in the formation in 1947 of the National Association for Stock Car Auto Racing, Inc. (NASCAR). NASCAR has become the largest and best known of such sanctioning organizations in the United States, with wide media coverage of its activities.

Virtually ignored by the national media, the first major paved amphitheater ("superspeedway") built in the South especially for auto racing opened in 1950 in Darlington, S.C. As a result of its success, tracks opened in other parts of the South. At present, stock car races are held from New England to California, although most of the big speedways are in the South. The Carolina Piedmont has the largest concentration of tracks, major races, driver home bases, and driver folk heroes. The heartland goes from central Virginia down to Talledega, Ala.

During the 1950s and 1960s auto makers noticed that successes of a make of car in the races led to increased sales. The auto companies and other sponsors poured money into the sport as a form of advertising. Support for racing has also come from other large corporations. For instance, a cigarette company sponsors several major race series. Individual racers and racing machines also are sponsored by small businesses and individuals.

Throughout its history, stock car racing has been identified with rural white southern males. Blacks and women, although occasional participants, have never made it to the top. Racing has become an accepted way (along with others, including singing and athletics) for a rural white male to achieve fame, money, and the trappings of success. Successful participants in the sport, such as Richard Petty, Junior Johnson, and Cale Yarborough, keep aspects of their southern heritage while they develop an ability to work with big business. Many of the best racers have, along with driving skill and a mechanical genius, a razor-sharp business acumen. They base their racing activities in their hometowns and maintain close family ties. Their "pit crews" tend to be drawn from the local population. They build closeness to their fans through personal appearances and project a "good old boy" image by expressing an interest in such male activities as hunting, fishing, and, of course, tinkering with automobiles. They are folk heroes with which the average southern male can identify. Stock car racing, with its noise, dirt, powerful cars, and consumption of alcoholic beverages, has become a symbol of the southern way of living.

Stock car racing combines a fascination with technology and a spirit of competition. It has become identified with the South, where it has served both as a sport and as a way for participants to leave rural poverty. At first glance, the cars appear to be like those available to the average person. However, the cars are in fact highly specialized technical accomplishments. The cost of the machinery keeps it from being a widely popular participant sport. As a result, there is mass popular support for a relatively small number of athletes. The drivers epitomize the successful southern male who has managed to retain his

"down-home" manner. The average southern male can identify with the races, both because he drives a car that looks like theirs and because he shares their identification with things southern. At present, many of the prominent drivers are in their 40s, an age by which athletes in many other sports have retired. A few younger drivers are beginning to gain recognition in Winston Cup racing, often through their successes in local competition. Winston Cup racing is the most publicized form of stock car racing.

There are different kinds of racing, varying with the scale of the effort and the technical details of the cars. Categories often are based on the age of the cars and their construction, especially their power plants and wheelbase lengths. Rules also vary with the track where the races are run.

There is a continuum of size and complexity in racing tracks. At the amateur level are small tracks (usually oval in shape and 1/4 to 1/2 mile long), which draw spectators and participants from immediately surrounding areas. In these races, older passenger cars are modified for increased safety and speed. As in other sports, there are many participants in local level, dirt track races, which require less money and effort.

At the professional end of the scale are Winston Cup (formerly called Grand National) races on larger speedways. Contestants come from all over the nation. Media reporters jockey for position to interview the winning drivers. At this level, vehicles are usually constructed by specialty builders solely for racing and have little relation to production cars beyond outward appearance.

At all levels of racing, each vehicle has one or more mechanics who build and maintain the vehicle. The "pit crew" services the car during races by refueling, replacing tires, cleaning the windshield, giving the driver refreshments, etc.

Sponsors are individuals or businesses who provide money to support the racing effort. Their names are painted on the sides of the cars (along with each car's number) so that the fans will be encouraged to buy their products. Some drivers have consistently used particular makes of automobiles, endorsing the manufacturer. Fans are fiercely partisan toward particular drivers. Many fans wear clothing and other items imprinted with the car number and name of their driver and belong to fan clubs boosting their favorite.

Track officials work to ensure that the race goes smoothly. There are often also officials from the organization ("sanctioning body") that writes the racing rules. Although NASCAR is the best known of these organizations, smaller, local sanctioning bodies organize most racing events. These bodies write rules to promote safety and competition.

"Technical inspections" of cars are made to ensure that cars conform to the rules. Nevertheless, clever racers try to interpret the rules to their advantage. The emphasis on technical sophistication in the preparation of the vehicles is one of the excitements of the sport, and fans and racers alike are constantly alert to innovations that increase the cars' speeds.

Each driver is involved with several kinds of competition simultaneously. Competition for winning the race by being the first to complete the required number of laps around the track is the most visible. Winning is a combination of driver skill and chance. Winning is also dependent on the speed and efficiency of the pit crew and the ability of the machinery to last up to 500 laps at speeds up to 200 miles an hour. Behind the scenes, drivers compete for the best sponsors and mechanics.

Before the race, drivers compete in trials designed to see which car can go fastest around the track. The faster a car runs in the trials, the closer it is placed to the front of the pack of 30 to 40 starting cars. The fastest car gets the most advantageous position (the "pole" position) at the front. Drivers compete over a season to accumulate the most "points" from various accomplishments, such as the position of their car in comparison to the winner's at the end of each race, the number of races entered, and the number of laps completed.

See also HISTORY AND MANNERS: Automobile; / Moonshine and Moonshining

David M. Johnson
North Carolina Agricultural
and Technical State University

Patrick Bedard, *Car & Driver* (June 1982); Jerry Bledsoe, *The World's Number One, Flat-Out, All-Time Great, Stock Car Racing Book* (1975); *Handbook of American Popular Culture*, vol. 1, ed. M. Thomas Inge (1979); Jim Hunter, *Official 1982 NASCAR Record Book and Press Guide* (1982); Bill Libby with Richard Petty, *"King Richard:" The Richard Petty Story* (1977); Bob Nagy, *Motor Trend* (June 1981); Richard Pillsbury, *Journal of Geography* (1974); Don Sherman, *Car & Driver* (June 1982); *Southern MotoRacing* (biweekly newspaper about stock car racing, Winston-Salem, N.C.); Sylvia Wilkinson, in *American South: Portrait of a Culture*, ed. Louis D. Rubin, Jr., (1980); Tom Wolfe, *Esquire* (March 1965). ☆

Tennis

||||||||||||||||||

Lawn tennis in the South shares much of the same general history as golf. Lawn tennis originated in the United States in New York in the 1870s and soon spread through the Northeast, Middle West, and the Pacific Coast. A few southern cities such as New Orleans promoted the sport, but it was not a popular one until well into the 20th century. It lost many of its aristocratic trappings in the 1920s and became a middle-class game. Tennis celebrities such as Big Bill Tilden and Suzanne Lenglen became popular in the South as well as elsewhere. In the South the game was a country club sport, but the 1930s saw an increase in the building of public courts along with community golf courses.

Tennis did not lose its country club image until the 1950s and 1960s. The game became more popular in those years with the emergence of appealing young stars, television coverage of major tournaments, large money payoffs to tournament winners, and the establishment of an open system of competition between amateurs and professionals. Major tournaments are now held in the South. In 1970 Texas millionaire Lamar Hunt financed World Championship Tennis, which sent professional players on tours around the world.

Tennis can now be found as an activity at southern resorts and it can be played on public courts in cities and small towns throughout the region. The South, however, has produced surprisingly few of the game's great players. Chris Evert from Florida is one of those, and Althea Gibson from North Carolina and Arthur Ashe from Virginia were prominent southern black tennis stars.

Tennis has not drawn the attention of many southern writers, but Rita Mae Brown's *Sudden Death* (1983) and Barry Hannah's *Tennis Handsome* (1985) have tennis players as the central characters.

Charles Reagan Wilson
University of Mississippi

Will Grimsley, *Tennis: Its History, People and Events* (1971); United States Lawn Tennis Association, *Official Encyclopedia of Tennis* (1972). ☆

Theme Parks

||||||||||||||||||||||||||||||||

Amusement parks, closely related to carnivals, have been an important part of American culture since the beginning of the 20th century. Vacationing families visited the thrilling rides, shows, and concessions of such parks as those at Coney Island in Brooklyn, N.Y., where the concept of the modern amusement park largely was developed. The popularity of amusement parks declined significantly after World War II, and theme parks came to dominate the outdoor amusement business. Disneyland in Anaheim, Calif., has served as a model for the contemporary theme park from its opening in 1954.

Since the Walt Disney cartoon characters came to the South with Disneyworld in Orlando, Fla., in 1971, southerners have brought their own unique heritage and traditions to theme-park entertainment. Southern theme parks offer the region's history, music, food, religion, art, and humor to attract both southern and non-southern families. Although some people might argue

that the picture of southern culture offered in the theme-park setting is often
an idealized and stereotypical view of
life in the South, millions of visitors
flock to the parks every summer, attracted not by their authenticity but by
the simple, family entertainment they
offer.

The prototype of southern-oriented
theme parks is Opryland, U.S.A., in
Nashville, which opened in the summer
of 1972. Opryland capitalized on Nashville's reputation as the center of the
country music industry and on the rise
in popularity of the music in the 1970s.
Since its opening, the park has continuously broadened its image and now
bills itself as "the home of American
music." Opryland offers a variety of
music, including rock and roll from the
1950s and contemporary tunes, music
of the American West (from such musicals as *Annie Get Your Gun*), Dixieland
jazz, and folk music. Much of the music
is country and western, but it is not the
rough sound found in the honky-tonks
around Nashville. Many of the music
shows at the park, like those at other
modern theme parks, are staged in elaborate, air-conditioned theaters and
resemble Broadway productions in costuming, music, and choreography. In
addition to live musical entertainment,
Opryland offers rides, food, shops,
games, art, and crafts—all with a southern flavor and often a country or musical
theme.

The food at the park, in keeping with
the southern image, includes fried
chicken, iced tea, and ham and biscuits
in establishments such as "The Country
Kitchen." Vendors on the sidewalks sell
ice cream bars in the shapes of musical
instruments. Numerous shops offer tourists a wide assortment of music memorabilia, replicas of frontier clothing and

implements, craft items such as handmade dulcimers and carved wooden figures, and various products bearing the
Confederate flag. Consistent with Opryland's theme are rides called "The
Tennessee Waltz," "Grizzly River Ram-
page," the "Old Mill Scream," and the
"Wabash Cannon Ball." Opryland has
even incorporated a carnival midway
into its offerings, complete with contest
booths and prizes commonly found at
county fairs. Opryland is particularly
proud of its setting—120 acres of trees
and man-made lakes. Approximately 25
percent of the complex, including a
roller coaster called the "Timber Top-
per," is in native woods transplanted
when the park was built. Today, the
Opryland theme park is one part of the
Opryland, U.S.A., complex, which has
grown to include the Grand Ole Opry,
the Opryland Hotel and Convention
Center, and the General Jackson showboat. Opryland's success has inspired
other parks (such as Libertyland in
Memphis, Tenn.), once simple amusement parks and without clearly defined
themes, to incorporate more elaborate
shows and music into their offerings.

Since Opryland's success, country
music culture has provided the theme
for other southern parks such as Dollywood, country music star Dolly Parton's
400-acre park outside Pigeon Forge,
Tenn. The park's inspiration is Parton's
childhood, which she spent in the
Smoky Mountain foothills where the
park is located, and her career in music
and films. Parton was involved in the
planning of the park, which includes a
replica of the house in which she was
born and an outdoor concert stage that
is a copy of the porch where she and
her family used to sing together. Like
Opryland, Dollywood tries to keep the
theme consistent throughout the park.

A restaurant called Aunt Granny's Dixie Fixin's serves biscuits and gravy, and cider is served at Apple Jack's Mill. Smoky Mountain heritage is featured in exhibits of quilting and dulcimer making.

Other country music celebrities have become the focus of southern theme parks, such as Conway Twitty, who lives and works inside an entertainment complex called Twitty City. Twitty City, located just outside Nashville, contains the memorabilia of Twitty and several other country music stars and includes a concession-entertainment pavilion and an audio-visual show that tells Twitty's life story. Open year-round, Twitty City draws hundreds of visitors during the Christmas season, when the park is decorated with 250,000 lights and adds 40 special exhibits, including a life-size nativity scene. Other country music stars who have parks associated with their names include Loretta Lynn (Loretta Lynn's Dude Ranch in Hurricane Mills, Tenn.) and George Jones (George Jones Country Music Park outside Colmesneil, Tex.).

A similar regional theme is portrayed at Arkansas's Dogpatch U.S.A., a park based on the characters from Al Capp's *Li'l Abner* comic strip. The events at Dogpatch feature the hillbilly characters, and the attractions (such as canoe rides) supposedly reflect their lifestyle. The park also highlights the Ozark Mountain culture, offering such exhibits as an authentic gristmill, one of the largest wooden water wheels in the world, and shops specializing in the area's many arts and crafts. The region's natural beauty is also spotlighted here; the park is particularly proud of its huge waterfall and spring-fed lakes.

The newest development in the southern outdoor amusement business is the religious theme park. The biggest of these is Heritage USA, a resort in Fort Mill, S.C., opened in 1977 by Pentecostal television evangelists Jim and Tammy Faye Bakker. The park, which has been called a "spiritual Disneyland," is part of a complex covering 2,300 acres and encompassing time-sharing vacation homes, rental apartments, condominiums, campsites, the five-story Heritage Grand Hotel, a halfway house for ex-convicts, and a home for unwed mothers. Heritage USA offers the world's largest wave pool and a 52-foot water slide, evangelist Billy Graham's childhood home, a Passion play staged in Heritage's own 3,000-seat amphitheater, tours of the Christian broadcasting studio on the grounds, amusement rides such as "Jonah in the Belly of the Whale," and shopping at Main Street, USA—designed in turn-of-the-century style with cobblestone streets and quaint storefronts. In 1985 Heritage USA attracted almost 5 million visitors, making it third only to Disneyland and Disney World in attendance. The park has cultivated an image as the preserver of old-time values and old-time southern religion, sometimes calling itself the modern equivalent of camp meetings or Christian campgrounds. Although Heritage USA is by far the largest, other southern theme parks, such as The Living Waters in Johnson City, Tex., also offer biblical messages.

Other theme parks in the South use state histories as the basis for their entertainment, such as Six Flags over Texas in Arlington and Six Flags over Georgia in Atlanta. Busch Gardens (The Dark Continent) in Tampa, Fla., displays the exotic environment of Africa, and Busch Gardens (The Old Country) in Williamsburg, Va., highlights the history and culture of Europe. Both

Busch parks feature elaborate animal and plant exhibits and are owned and operated by Anheuser-Busch Co.

Karen M. McDearman
University of Mississippi

Jackson *Clarion-Ledger* (31 August 1986); *Southern Living* (June 1981); Jeff Ulmer, *Amusement Parks of America: A Comprehensive Guide* (1980). ☆

Tourism

||||||||||||||||||||||||

Tourist. The word evokes images of Hawaiian shirts and Bermuda shorts, Instamatic cameras and sun-reddened skin, a clay-streaked station wagon, laden with luggage and sacks of Florida oranges. Those millions of wayfarers who hurdle along interstates to bake on sunny beaches and see Rock City pump some $60 billion into the southern economy each year.

That figure alone suggests that traveling in the South is more than a now-and-again whim. Tourism has become as much a part of life for Americans as work in the week and church on Sunday. The modern burst of tourism began in the late 1940s. Veterans, who could not be kept down on the farm after they had seen the world during the war, earned their two weeks of vacation and hit the highways for recreation, relaxation, and entertainment. Nearly every family now marks days off its calendar for a vacation, even two or three a year. Despite oil shortages and the recessions of the 1970s and early 1980s, Americans winced at gasoline prices, dipped into savings, and pointed their cars and campers South.

A century and more before, the purpose of most travels in the South was for health. By the late 1700s travelers eased into hot springs baths to soak their muscles. Modern-day resorts such as The Greenbrier in West Virginia and The Homestead in Virginia trace their origins to those times and still offer bathing facilities.

For more than a century Carolinians who lived along the coast traveled to save their lives. Spring through fall, or "frost to frost," they fled the malarial, soggy low country for the spice of mountain air. Hendersonville, N.C., is still called "Little Charleston in the Mountains," and many of the summer cottages, dating back to the mid-1800s and handed down through the generations, still stand.

In the decades after the Civil War, northerners invaded the South again, but this time as tourists in a campaign for their health. The mineral waters of southern springs and the salubrious southern climate were touted for their curative benefits. Physicians prescribed winter vacations in towns like Thomasville, Ga., which once boasted 15 hotels, 25 boardinghouses, and 50 winter cottages.

From the late 19th century to the mid-20th, pleasure travel evolved from a privilege of a wealthy few to an affordable luxury for the average family. A growing economy was partly the reason, but so also was the increasing ease of transportation—from carriages on dirt roads to railroads to family cars on interstates.

Of all southern states, Florida best symbolizes the rise of tourism. To see Florida in the mid-1800s, when much of the state was still wilderness, travelers had to go by boat. Honeymooners took romantic excursions along the Suwannee River, the St. John's, and the Oklawaha to Silver Springs. Often the land alongside was scented with orange blossoms in spring, and, at night, the light from burning pine knots played on the overhang of cypress and Spanish moss. By the 1890s railroads were skimming the shoreline of both coasts; Henry Flagler linked Jacksonville to the squat settlement of Miami, building alongside his railroad such palatial hotels as the Ponce de Leon in St. Augustine and The Breakers in Palm Beach.

Down Flagler's railroad came the very rich. But along the increasing miles of paved highways came the families of average means, who, in the flush times of the 1920s, could afford pleasure travel. They fashioned homemade campers on Model-T's, ate store-bought food from tin cans, and camped beside the roads. These "tin-can tourists," as Floridians called them, pioneered the major mode of travel of two decades later—the family car. In the exuberance of release from the Depression, and with a car in every garage, Americans joyously flooded the highways of the South.

With war boom babies in the back seat, they traveled to the beach in summer and the mountains in the fall. Quiet seaside villages like Myrtle Beach, S.C., and mountain towns like Gatlinburg, Tenn., grew into garish neon playgrounds. The family spent nights in tourist courts, stopped at roadside souvenir stands, visited alligator farms, toured Mammoth Cave, walked Civil War battlefields, and yes, saw Rock City. Later, such "attractions" as theme parks offered rides and Broadway-type entertainment in a milk-and-cookies family atmosphere.

Quickly, tourism became an industry with a manufacturing mentality to mass produce. Entrepreneurs like Kemmons Wilson of Memphis, founder of Holiday Inns, stamped one motel after another from the same mold. Fast-food franchises arched their signs above highways. Many of those motels and packaged food restaurants rose at exits of interstates that tie doorsteps to destinations, bypass towns, and hold the countryside at arm's length. Now, in driving 800 interstate miles, travelers may sleep in the same room every night, eat the same hamburger for every meal, and never see a town.

Why and to where do tourists today go on vacation? One large segment of the population indicates that three main factors, excluding cost, determine vacation destinations. Readers of *Southern Living* magazine, certainly the epitome of the middle-class southerner, say they travel primarily for scenery. And to most, scenery means mountains and seashore. Second, they go where they will find good restaurants and lodging: to resort condominiums on barrier islands and to quiet country inns in the mountains. And third, they choose routes and destinations to see historical sites. Even on pleasure trips to fish, swim, play golf and tennis, shop, hike, and canoe, southerners will stop a time or two to pay homage to the past.

Tourists who walk the narrow streets of Charleston pour some $460 million annually into the local economy. About 1 million visitors each year walk the battlefield at Vicksburg, Miss., and stroll through the re-created city of Colonial Williamsburg in Virginia. Through travel, southerners continue to learn about life of a century or two ago. In the 1930s garden club ladies in Natchez introduced a new genre of travel when they opened a few antebellum homes each spring to visitors. The name of such tours—pilgrimage—is appropriate for southerners' reverence of the past.

Many historic homes are open for lodging as well as tours, so guests may dream they dwelt in marble halls. At preserved villages like Old Salem in Winston-Salem, N.C., visitors watch costumed docents work at the crafts and cookery of two centuries ago. The Mississippi Museum of Agriculture and Forestry in Jackson moved an entire 100-year-old farm to its premises, where southerners hear words that have almost vanished from the daily vocabulary: singletree, laying-by time, bust the middles. Workers at the farm even plant a tiny patch of cotton and let the visitor try his or her hand at picking.

The flow of tourists' money helps maintain these historic sites, which, in turn, provide the tie that binds the generations and the times of the South. Recently, at Powers Crossroads Arts and Crafts Fair, spread across the old cotton fields of a plantation near Newnan, Ga., a man from Atlanta and his small son strolled up to the mule-powered cane press.

"Look, daddy, a horse," the boy shouted excitedly.

"Mule, son," the father replied.

See also ART AND ARCHITECTURE: Resort Architecture; ETHNIC LIFE: Caribbean Influence; GEOGRAPHY: Roadside; HISTORY AND MANNERS: / Pilgrimage; INDUSTRY: / Flagler, Henry

Gary D. Ford
Southern Living

Ruth Camblos and Virginia Winger, *Shopping Round the Mountains* (1973); Charleston Trident Chamber of Commerce, *Tourism Profile, 1982–83*; John A. Jakle, *The Tourist: Travel in Twentieth-Century North America* (1985); Jeffrey Limerick, Nancy Ferguson, and Richard Oliver, *America's Grand Resort Hotels* (1979); Edward A. Mueller, *Steamboating on the St. John's, 1830–1885* (1980); *Southern Living* (December 1983, April 1984); *Travel Survey of Southern Living Subscribers* (1984). ☆

Tourism, Automobile

||||||||||||||||||||||||||||||||||||||||||||||||||||||

Except for an occasional group of bicyclists who toured the Shenandoah Valley, most 19th-century Americans had only a secondhand knowledge of the South. By the mid-1920s, however, widespread automobile ownership, hard-surfaced roads, and the magnetic attraction of Florida brought droves of tourists into the South from every state in the Union.

Around the turn of the century, automobile manufacturers began to test their fledgling machines in races on the broad, firm beaches of Ormond-Daytona Beach, Fla. These contests, held during the winter months, attracted great attention to the Florida east coast, and in subsequent years more and more northerners entertained the notion of driving—instead of shipping—their automobiles to Florida.

After a group of tourists on a reliability run in 1909 carefully negotiated their way from New York to Atlanta over a route named the "National Highway," the American Automobile Association for the first time mapped a route for motorists wishing to brave a trip into the South. Although it fell short of detailing specific routes and distances, volume three of the AAA's 1910 *Automobile Blue Book* gave adventuresome tourists enough incentive to attempt the trip. As more drivers traveled south and reported their experiences to the AAA and as routing information in popular motoring journals like *American Motorists*, *Motor Travel*, and *Motor Life* improved, the uncertainty of driving a motor vehicle into the unchartered South waned.

With more motorists on the road, southerners began to realize the importance of tourism to local profits. Enterprising boosters of many southern towns went to great lengths to accommodate visiting tourists. In 1910 the first interstate highway association in the South, the Capital Highway Association, was formed. Its purpose was to promote tourism and a route that would link the national capital with the state capitals of Virginia, North Carolina, South Carolina, and Georgia. Leonard Tufts, who was in the initial stages of developing Pinehurst, N.C., as a resort, served as the first president of this organization. Tufts realized the tremendous potential that tourism had for the South.

Floridians were among the first southerners to actively recruit tourists. In 1919 Tampa opened DeSoto Park, located on the banks of the Hillsborough River, to motorists who had come south for the winter. Soon autocamps sprang up throughout Florida and in other southern states along main routes to Florida recommended by the Automobile Club of America. The 1918 *Automobile Blue Book* contained accurate and detailed running information for over 24,000 miles of roads in Virginia, Tennessee, Georgia, North Carolina, South Carolina, Alabama, Mississippi, and Florida.

The motorists who traveled these hazardous routes were a new breed of tourists. They were doctors, lawyers, bankers, dairymen, farmers, building contractors, and retired businessmen who had leisure time to travel. Unlike their 19th-century predecessors, these men and women resisted the comforts of hotel accommodations by carrying everything they needed with them. Tents, suitcases, and mattresses were strapped to running boards, and other necessities like canned goods and cooking utensils were packed wherever they would fit. At night these so-called tin-can tourists pulled into autocamps where they extended their tents over part of their cars, greeted other travelers, fixed supper, and went to bed. For less rustic motorists, it was not difficult to find a tourist home that provided bed, board, and a bath for a nominal fee.

The number of tourists coming into the South increased sharply following World War I. During the winter of 1920–21 so many took advantage of Tampa's free accommodations in DeSoto Park that by the following spring city officials were forced to close the park to out-of-state visitors. That same year the tourist bureau of one of the most active automobile clubs in the South, the Chattanooga Automobile Club, answered approximately 8,000 inquiries from tourists requesting route information. During the winter of 1924–25, however, the volume reached its pre-Depression high. Efforts by southerners to improve their roads, together with federal aid to road construction, bettered travel conditions and led the AAA to recommend as "fascinating" an automobile trip into the South. That advice was well heeded, for in November of 1924, 16,833 automobiles crossed the St. Johns River bridge leading into Jacksonville, Fla. Every state in the United States was represented, and 90 cars came from as far away as Canada.

One writer called this mass migration to Florida a national "pneumatic hegira" and sublimely pronounced its implication to be as far reaching as "the descent of the Goths on Rome, the Mongols on China, the Dutch on South Africa, or the Mormon trek from Illinois to Utah." Another observer, cited in the March 1925 issue of the *Hollywood Magazine*, captured the phenomenon in poetry:

It squeaked and groaned; 'twas rusty, worn;
Its fenders bent, its curtains torn,
Its windshield cracked, its wheels not mates
Caked with mud of seven states,
Headed South.

Nevertheless, the great influx of motorists gave southerners added incentive to upgrade their roads, and for the first time since the Civil War large numbers of ordinary men and women from the North and South met one another. The cultural isolation of southerners began to end as they came in contact with new ideas, new products, and new ways of doing things. Many southerners saw themselves in a new light and began to sell their region as a place of recreation and relaxation. Tourism became a mainstay of the South's economy, encouraging national companies to seek new markets in southern states. In the view of historian Thomas D. Clark, the migration of tourists to the South amounted to nothing short of a "Yankee invasion that ever disturbed southern complacency. The established way of life in the South was shaken to its very foundation."

See also AGRICULTURE: Good Roads Movement; HISTORY AND MANNERS: Automobile

Howard Preston
Spartanburg, South Carolina

American Automobile Association, *The Official 1910 Automobile Blue Book*, vol. 3 (1910); *American Motorist* (1910–1924); Warren J. Belasco, *Americans on the Road: From Autocamps to Motel, 1910–1945* (1979); *Dixie Highway* (1915–1925); James J. Fink, *America Adopts the Automobile, 1895–1910* (1970), *The Car Culture* (1975); David Gary, *Collier's Weekly* (11 February 1911); Elon Jessup, *The Outlook* (25 May 1921); *Southern Good Roads* (1910–1920). ☆

Traveling Shows

A visit from a traveling show was a major event in the life of the southern small town in the late 19th and early 20th centuries. Colorfully decorated wagons and, later, trucks drove slowly through towns, with jugglers and acrobats drawing children and their parents out of their homes and into a happy procession of people anticipating fun at the show grounds. The coming of traveling shows signaled an unusual period of gaiety, when normal moral restrictions might be loosened and humdrum daily life enlivened. Most of these shows flourished from the end of the Civil War to World War I. After World War I grass-roots show business in the South continued to be dynamic, providing the training and experiences for many performers and businessmen in entertainment industries such as country music, jazz, the blues, and gospel. In addition to the circuses, carnivals, Wild West shows, and minstrels that had earlier become staples, there were tent shows, burlesque houses, magicians, freak shows, vaudeville bills, aerial daredevils, water circuses, and medicine shows.

The American circus, with its animal and clown shows, had antecedents in antiquity, but the real beginnings of the modern circus were in England in the mid-1700s. Animal trainers, acrobats, jugglers, and itinerant actors traveled through the American colonies, but the first recorded appearance of the circus in America was in 1791. Early circuses were city shows, and the predominantly rural South had less exposure than the North to circuses in the antebellum era, although circuses did appear along the lower Mississippi River in the 1820s. The basic pattern of the circus was established by the 1850s—circus parades, to draw crowds, exhibitions under canvas walls or tents, trained animals, clowns, acrobats and aerialists, jugglers, ventriloquists, and freak shows. Multiple rings were introduced in the 1870s. The golden age of the circus was from 1870 to 1914. Phineas T. Barnum, George F. Bailey, W. C. Coup, and the Ringling brothers were leading circus entrepreneurs. In 1918 a merger brought the appearance of the Ringling Brothers and Barnum and Bailey Combined Shows. As circus audiences became larger in the early 20th century, the circus shows became more elaborate. The Wild West show became part of the event, and stages and rings were added, more dangerous animal acts were encouraged, and money was poured into acts, costumes, and pageants.

Circus owners adapted to the South by advertising their shows as classical and biblical, because they featured chariot races and religious depictions. The most popular circuses touring the South were John Robinson's Circus and Menagerie, W. C. Coup's Monster Shows, and the Grand New Orleans Menagerie and Circus (which had a Mademoiselle Eugene marching ahead of lions and tigers down southern streets to stir interest). In the 1890s almost 40 groups annually toured the region, from April to December, some of them touring only the South. Southerners turned out in large numbers for the circus, with rural people coming into town ahead of the circus in order to camp in or under wagons, watch the circus set up, and view the circus parade and opening ceremonies. Excursion trains brought thousands of people to the cities where the largest circuses were held. The appeal of the circus was universal, but the poor and children were its most fervent enthusiasts. Blacks and whites sat on opposite sides of the same tent. Gamblers and pickpockets frequently accompanied the circus, taking advantage of the rural folk coming out for the show, and the circus always seemed to bring out drinking and fighting. Community and religious leaders objected to them.

Only a dozen or so circuses continue to tour the nation today, but attendance at these is still large. Florida has served as the winter quarters for the Ringling Brothers circus, and Florida State University has become a prominent circus center because of the amateur productions on campus.

The carnival was another traveling show, closely related to the circus. "Pleasure gardens," modelled on London's Vauxhall and Ranelagh, were forerunners of carnivals, appearing in North America near the time of the American Revolution, offering the chance for visitors to stroll, eat, and drink. By the turn of the 20th century, trolley parks had emerged in eastern cities offering more exciting amusements. The beginnings of the American carnival are usually dated from the 1893 World's Columbian Exposition in Chicago, which included outdoor rides, fun houses, and games of chance. Coney Island opened the same year, but even before this, in the 1880s, the traditional state fairs had begun to set aside special areas for outdoor amusements.

Carnivals traveled the South, with their heydey between the world wars. Elaborate shows came to bigger cities, but smaller affairs hit the region's more typical small towns. They included set features: machine rides such as the Ferris wheel, roller coaster, and tunnel of love; the midway featuring food (such as popcorn, cotton candy, corn dogs, and caramel candy), shooting arcades, and gypsy fortune tellers; the freak shows (featuring the Fat Lady, Tattooed Man, or midgets); and the girlie shows with risqué strippers. Gamblers, hustlers, and pickpockets of all sorts frequently accompanied the traveling carnival, as well as the circus. Harry Crews's article "Carny," which appeared in *Blood and Grits* (1979), portrays life on the road for carnival workers in the South; he discusses the distinctive vocabulary of "carny talk" and the social hierarchy among the carnival workers. Those who set up shows rank at the bottom of this society; the hustlers who run the working games rank higher; the "patch man," who exists to patch over conflicts that emerge within the carnival community and between it and the outside world, ranks still higher. Crews stresses that the farther south the carnival went, the rougher the shows were; a strip show that was relatively tame in Pennsylvania could be gross in Georgia.

The medicine show was a popular aspect of southern entertainment after the Civil War. During the fall, especially, when southern farmers had whatever money they would have during the year to spend, traveling salesmen of cheap patent medicines would appear. Few of these were of much value, as they were typically filled with alcohol or were strong purgatives that usually caused more illness than they cured. To attract attention, medicine salesmen would employ singers, such as the bluesman Sonny Terry or country singer Jimmie Rodgers (who sometimes worked in blackface), to put on a "medicine show" that would draw people together, creating an audience for the salesman to hawk his goods. In normally quiet southern towns and rural areas, this entertainment, no matter how poor in quality, was worth listening to, and people willingly came out to hear it. Performers would pass out Congo oil, liniments, or similar remedies designed to cure whatever ailed anyone with money in hand. Colorful pitchmen with names such as Joe "Fine Arts" Hanks, the Canadian Kid, Doc Zip Hibler, Mad Cody Fleming, Widow Rollins, and Population Charlie were hustlers who went back and forth between medicine shows, carnivals, tent shows, and other forms of grass-roots show business.

The road company theater was another example of the traveling show in the South. Before the Civil War, permanent theaters had existed in southern cities such as Charleston, New Orleans, and Richmond, many of them presenting road show spectaculars featuring exciting stage activities, musical performances, Shakespeare and other dramatic fare, and melodrama. After the war, this continued, with new auditoriums and opera houses appearing. In Atlanta, the 400-seat Davis Hall was built in 1865 as an essential part of the rebuilding of the city. Dallas erected its first opera house in 1872. The new theaters and opera houses were elaborately decorated with balustraded verandas, crimson velvet wall hangings, glass chandeliers, and several tiers of seats for those of different social classes. Blacks and prostitutes were generally restricted to the highest galleries.

In 1869–70 the Wilmington, N.C., theater presented 50 evenings of entertainment, including Shakespearean plays, magicians, and Italian opera. Established theaters in cities presented the best American and European performers and plays, but in smaller places the offerings were less ambitious. The average theatergoer seemed to prefer the extravagant and sentimental, but originality was valued little until after World War I. Italian touring companies performed *Rigoletto*, *Il Trovatore*, and *Mignon* among others; Shakespeare continued to be a favorite; and less uplifting shows, especially melodramas with such titles as *Ten Nights in a Bar Room* and *The Drunkard*, and spectacles with mechanical thrills, as in the chariot race in *Ben Hur* and the railroad crossing the stage in *Under the Gas Lights*, were also popular. Stock companies presenting these programs typically were in a town for a week or so, offering different shows daily. By the 1880s a new star system emerged, leading to shows centered around a celebrity performer giving a single show. Broadway shows from New York—which was the source for many of these performances throughout the period—also went on the road in the early 20th century.

A special aspect of the touring theater was the tent show. The first theater company to tour under canvas was an Illinois group in 1855, and the tent show continued to be mainly a midwestern and southern phenomenon even after permanent theaters proliferated in towns. Rural and small-town audiences seemed especially fond of these shows and continued to support them well into the 20th century. The average tent could hold almost 1,500 people. The tent show presented family-oriented dramatic performances, with three-act plays and specialty entertainers. They were clean shows, avoiding the kind of suggestive material in carnivals and vaudeville. After the movies became popular, the tent shows boasted of offering "a decent alternative to epics, orgies, sex, and horror." Traveling "rep" groups, with such names as Harley Sadler's Own, the Ted North Players, and Swain's Dramatic Show, played a town for three days to a week, offering repertoires of six to nine plays a season. Usually presenting comedies, they also tried to include at least one serious play, sometimes an adaption of a popular novel such as *The Virginian*, *The Trail of the Lonesome Pines*, or *The Shepherd of the Hills*.

The tent shows brought vaudeville to the South. It was not urban entertainment, as in the North, but rather performances designed to appeal to small-town folk. They offered popular singers such as Jimmie Rodgers, who served his apprenticeship in the 1920s in the traveling shows. Black blues singers also performed in this context, as did novelty bands such as Happy Cook's Kentucky Buddies. Impresarios such as W. T. Swain, known as Colonel Swain or "Old Double Eyes" to some who had done business with him, worked the South. Described by Nolan Porterfield as "sort of a cross between P. T. Barnum, William Randolph Hearst, and a snake-oil salesman," Swain typically wore a black suit, set off by a white bow tie and his silver gray hair. For four decades he was a major figure in the traveling theater of the mid-South and Southwest. Colonel

Tom Parker, who eventually struck paydirt as manager of Elvis Presley, was another typical tent show manager.

Almost 400 tent-show companies traveled the nation in 1925, mostly in the Midwest and South, visiting 16,000 communities and entertaining 76,800,000 people. The Great Depression hit the shows hard, and eventually the competition from radio and television led to their decline. In the 1950s, 30 companies still toured under canvas, but by 1968 only 3 remained.

The tent road show contributed a popular character to show business lore and to regional imagery—Toby. He was the country bumpkin, a humorous figure who appeared in these shows around 1910. One manager, Fred Wilson, built the character into his shows and others copied him, until rural and small-town audiences knew him and looked forward to the character's appearance. A rustic, seemingly backward man, Toby would outwit and confuse the city slickers who tried to take advantage of him. Awkward, bumptious, but shrewd and full of common sense, Toby embodied the southern rural self-imagery of the Arkansas traveler. The character was adapted to different regions—in the Midwest, he was simply a rural hayseed; in the South, a hillbilly from the mountains; in Texas, he was a cowboy. By 1916 some 200 actors traveled specializing in Toby, and always appearing the same—redhaired, freckled, with blacked out tooth and farm clothes.

See also FOLKLIFE: / Arkansas traveler; LITERATURE; Theater, Contemporary; Theater, Early; MUSIC: Minstrelsy; / Rodgers, Jimmie; SCIENCE AND MEDICINE: Self-Dosage

Charles Reagan Wilson
University of Mississippi

George L. Chindahl, *History of the Circus in America* (1959); Joseph Csida and June Bundy Csida, *American Entertainment: A Unique History of Popular Show Business* (1978); John E. DiMeglio, *Vaudeville U.S.A.* (1973); Neil Harris, *Humbug: The Art of P. T. Barnum* (1973); Joe McKennon, *A Pictorial History of the American Carnival* (1972); Brooks McNamara, *Step Right Up: An Illustrated History of the American Medicine Show* (1976); Russel Nye, *The Unembarrassed Muse: The Popular Arts in America* (1970); Nolan Porterfield, *Jimmie Rodgers: The Life and Times of America's Blue Yodeler* (1979); William L. Slout, *Theatre in a Tent: The Development of Provincial Entertainment* (1972); Marcello Truzzi, *Journal of Popular Culture* (Winter 1972); Don B. Wilmeth, *American and English Popular Entertainment: A Guide to Information Sources* (1980), in *Concise Histories of American Popular Culture*, ed. M. Thomas Inge (1982). ☆

Wrestling

||||||||||||||||||||||||

William Faulkner wrote that Thomas Sutpen, the Old South planter who is the central character of *Absalom, Absalom!*, would watch an evening of slave wrestling. At the end of "the spectacle," he would enter the ring, "perhaps as a matter of sheer deadly forethought toward the retention of supremacy, domination." He and a slave would soon be "naked to the waist and gouging at one another's eyes."

Physical grappling is an old tradition for southern men. In the colonial era well-off gentry planters presided over and sometimes joined in sports such as wrestling, which served as a communal bonding experience between social classes. One of the rituals in frontier areas of the antebellum South, which spawned real-life Thomas Sutpens, was the gouging match. It was a brutal sport where each man tried to pry his opponent's eyes out of their sockets using a thumb for leverage. Brutal though they were, wrestling and eye gouging were not surprising pastimes for men in a society where violence was common. Indians, animals, outlaws, and nature were threats to life; physical labor was long and grueling. Gouging matches tested a man's strength, dexterity, and ferocity. In *Life on the Mississippi* Mark Twain told of an appropriate product of this world, a self-styled Arkansas wrestling champion called "Sudden Death and General Desolation."

Twain's character would have been at home in the contemporary South. Although college football packs southern stadiums, stock car racing is a regional phenomenon, and baseball remains popular, the sport that draws most southerners today is professional wrestling. The National Wrestling Alliance regularly publishes statistics claiming that professional wrestling has a greater paid attendance than college or professional football, basketball, or baseball. The wrestling season, of course, is 52 weeks long, and matches are promoted in countless towns and cities so small other sports would never give them a second thought. An estimated 60 percent of the national attendance is in the South. In 1984 a record 43,000 fans turned out at Texas Stadium in Dallas for a match.

In arenas like that in Dothan, Ala., the setting, wrestlers, and fans are probably typical. The Dothan arena is a drab, barn-like building with a dirt floor and concrete seats, but its center contains a red, white, and blue wrestling ring brilliantly lighted by rows of television lights. Since the 1930s farmers and other Dothan area folk have been

coming here for Friday night entertainment. Part athletic competition and part soap opera, professional wrestling is the only sport many of these fans know, and they are intensely loyal and enthusiastic. In the wrestling ring good and evil are distinct, and the fans pour into the arena to cheer the good guys and to jeer and curse the bad ones.

Wrestling promoters say their patrons are predominantly working class, with the average wrestling crowd made up of the kind of people whose pickups in the parking lot wear bumper stickers with messages such as "I Fight Poverty, I Work."

The price of an average wrestling ticket is $4, and the annual paid gate for the industry is estimated at between $100 million and $150 million. Whether sport or entertainment, professional wrestling is big business. It is also a closed business, in many ways a family business. At one time, promoters in almost every city in north Alabama and Tennessee were related by blood or marriage, and many of the wrestlers and promoters active today got into the business through their families or in-laws.

The most frequently asked question by outsiders is whether professional wrestling is *only* entertainment. Are these guys athletes or entertainers? A fair answer is that they are both, that most of them have the skills, stamina, and strength for legitimate wrestling. But the wrestlers say that the fans, especially in the South, want to see "catch as catch can" competition, replete with exaggerated falls, wild punches, and frenzied action.

"A wrestling fan is not like a football fan," says Ox Baker, a well-known wrestler from Texas. "They are more vicious, more sadistic. They want to see the bad guys out there ranting and raving. They won't come to see anything else. You can have the NCAA finals in college wrestling and you can't even get a crowd; it won't even make the papers in most places. People want action and we're professionals, we're geared to it, so we give it to them. But then there's blood out there, it's real blood. I've had teeth knocked out, my knees are boogered up, my wrist has been broken." (Even fans have been known to get into the action, and wrestlers have been stabbed, punched, and beaten over the head by canes wielded by grandfathers.)

Baker acknowledges that there are limits to the slugging wrestlers can do to one another night after night. "We do have agreement among ourselves. Wrestlers know they have to restrain themselves." Wrestlers say this means not that matches are prearranged and rehearsed, but that to fit the schedule and to please the crowd the wrestling may be mixed with soap opera. "Say we're on TV and it's an hour program. Now I can beat my opponent in 45 seconds," says Baker. "But the promoter may tell me, 'Ox, I need seven minutes.' So I'll entertain the people for seven minutes before I put the man down."

Wrestlers also have an incentive to win consistently and to build up a reputation because their earnings depend on it. A wrestler can do preliminary bouts every night and he may earn as much as $40,000 a year if he is willing to travel enough. But a main event wrestler like Ox Baker will earn $300–$700 for 15 minutes of work in Dothan, Ala.; before a bigger crowd his evening's pay may run as high as $2,000.

There are about 3,000 professional wrestlers in the United States, and only a handful of new performers break in each year. Those who do usually make it with some kind of gimmick to attract either the adoration or the hatred of the fans. It does not matter which, because

both sell at the box office. Southern wrestlers sometimes adapt regional imagery for their personas. "Haystack" Calhoun was 600 "pounds of fury" from Dixie, and Hillbilly Jim sometimes still appears on wrestling talk shows while his "Granny" plucks a newly killed chicken in the background. Since the Jimmy Carter era of the late 1970s, the Good Old Boy has been one of the most successful wrestling types. Typically, he takes a physical pounding because he will not engage in dishonorable tactics.

A good promoter instinctively knows what will sell and when to introduce something new. The Dothan promoter, for example, found a pair of strapping black twins. Because they were black, they went over well in heavily black south Alabama, and because they were polite and had "good guy" images (partly because they were matched against known "bad guys") they proved popular with white fans as well.

Keeping the fans excited week after week, however, takes effort. This responsibility belongs partly to the promoter and partly to a "matchmaker," who is employed by the individual or group sponsoring matches in a region. The matchmaker's job is to decide which pairings of wrestlers, because of reputation or chemistry, are likely to please and excite the crowd.

Because the same dozen or so wrestlers compete against each other week after week around the circuit, the pairings have to be adjusted to maintain interest. Once the matchmaker gives the assignment to the wrestlers, they must build up as much interest as possible before the match and then make the match itself as exciting as possible.

The prematch buildup is boosted with television shows taped and shown in each of the cities on the circuit a couple of days in advance of the live wrestling. The promoters pay for the television time, and the show includes some wrestling and a generous amount of interview time in which the wrestlers describe what they are going to do to their next opponents.

The matchmaker will also bring in big-name outside wrestlers like Ox Baker to increase attendance. Baker is well-known around the country partly because of his size and strength—6'5", 318 pounds—and partly because of his legendary heart punch, with which, the promos say, he has killed two wrestlers.

Those in the business who know the facts about Baker's "victims" confide that the story is myth, but the "bad" image nevertheless lives on. Psychologists and sociologists periodically publish treatises on the symbolism and ritual significance of football, but professional wrestling is really the morality play of modern sports. If the good guy wins his match, that is simple justice, and if he loses, that is life.

Baker probably could not change his image if he wanted to because it is so well set in the minds of his fans. Mellonee Kapner is 67 and has been an institution at the Dothan arena for two decades. She gives Ox Baker hell from the minute he enters the arena. She gets up from her ringside seat and walks right up next to the ropes, calling Baker profane names—names she would never utter outside this arena—until he leans over the ropes and shakes his giant fist at her. The sight is almost comical: the huge man towering over the little white-haired woman. Later, Mrs. Kapner is telling some other people what she thinks of Ox Baker: "You know, he's killed two men," she says solemnly.

Randall Williams
Southern Changes

Elliott Gorn, "The Manly Art: Bare-Knuckle Prize Fighting and the Rise of American Sports" (Ph.D. dissertation, Yale University, 1983); John Gutowski, *Keystone Folklore* (1972); Gerald W. Morton and George M. O'Brien, *Wrestling to Rasslin': Ancient Sport to American Ritual* (1986); *Newsweek* (11 March 1985); Randall Williams, *Southern Exposure* (Fall 1979); Mark F. Workman, *Folklore Forum* (1977). ☆

AARON, HANK
||||||||||||||||||||||||||||||||||||||||||
(b. 1934) Baseball player.

Mobile, Ala., has produced several great baseball players, including Willie McCovey, Amos Otis, and Satchel Paige. Perhaps the greatest of them all is Henry Louis "Hank" Aaron. Born 5 February 1934 in Toulminville, a black community in Mobile, he began playing amateur baseball while in high school at the Josephine Allen Institute. Playing first with the Pritchett Athletics, Aaron later played on weekends with a local semiprofessional team, the Mobile Black Bears. An exhibition game between the Bears and the Indianapolis Clowns of the Negro American League proved to be Aaron's breakthrough into professional baseball.

The Clowns were impressed with the young player's performance and offered him $200 a month to join the team. Aaron accepted, playing with the Clowns in 1952 and compiling a .467 batting average with his cross-handed swing. Team owner Syd Pollock attracted attention from the Boston Braves when he ended a letter with the postscript "We've got an eighteen-year-old shortstop batting cleanup for us." On 12 June 1952 the Braves purchased Aaron from the Clowns for $10,000 and sent him to play in the Class C Northern League at Eau Claire, Wis. After being named "Rookie of the Year" there, he was sent to Jacksonville, Fla., where he played second base for the Braves' Class A South Atlantic team. During the off-season he trained in Puerto Rico to play in the outfield and in 1954 won a starting job with the Braves (who had moved to Milwaukee) when outfielder Bobby Thompson was injured during spring training.

No longer a cross-handed hitter, Aaron became best known for his hitting ability and power. In 1956 he won the National League batting championship with a .328 average. Bypassing such stars as Stan Musial and Red Schoendienst, the league gave its Most Valuable Player award to Aaron the following year, the same year he clinched the league pennant for the Braves with an 11th-inning home run against the St. Louis Cardinals. A Milwaukee real estate firm supposedly accepted that home run ball from Aaron as a $1,000 down payment on a home.

When the Braves moved to Atlanta in 1966, Aaron hit 44 home runs and signed a $100,000-a-year contract with the team. In 1972 he signed a contract for $200,000 a year, the largest player salary in baseball history at the time.

During his major league career Aaron steadily approached the record number of home runs set by Babe Ruth, who hit 714. In Cincinnati on 4 April 1974 Aaron hit his 714th home run. Braves officials wanted him to hit his record-breaking home run in Atlanta, so they decided that he would not play in the remaining games in Cincinnati. When Baseball Commissioner Bowie Kuhn objected and threatened to penalize the team, Aaron was put back in the lineup, but he returned to Atlanta without another hit.

The game in Atlanta on 8 April 1974 between the Braves and the Los Angeles Dodgers was sold out and nationally televised. A *New York Times* writer said that "to many Atlantans, it was like the city's festive premier of 'Gone with the Wind' during the 1930s when Babe Ruth was still the hero of the New York Yankees and the titan of professional sports." That evening, Aaron hit his 715th home run, this one on a fastball thrown by pitcher Al Downing.

With a total of 755 home runs and numerous other major league records, "Hammerin' Hank" or the "Hammer," as Aaron was called, retired in 1976, after playing his final years with the Milwaukee Brewers. He was elected to the Baseball Hall of Fame in 1982 and currently serves as vice president and director of player development with the Atlanta Braves.

Jessica Foy
Cooperstown Graduate Programs
Cooperstown, New York

Marjorie Dent Candee, ed., *Current Biography* (1958); *New York Times* (9 April 1974); Edna Rust and Art Rust, Jr., *Art Rust's Illustrated History of the Black Athlete* (1985); Charles Van Doren, ed., *Webster's American Biographies* (1979). ☆

BRYANT, BEAR

(1913–1983) Football coach.

Born 11 September 1913 to a sharecropping family in Moro Bottom, Ark., Paul "Bear" Bryant became the most successful college football coach in history. The youngest of 11 children of Wilson Monroe and Ida Kilgore Bryant, Paul Bryant was born on a farm and sold farm goods to help his invalid father and his mother. At age 12 he earned his nickname by fighting a bear at the Lyric Theater in Fordyce, Ark. He played football for the Fordyce High School

Red Bugs and received a football scholarship to the University of Alabama, where he played end.

Bryant was an assistant coach at the University of Alabama and at Vanderbilt University, then served two years in the U.S. Navy during World War II. He was head coach at Maryland, Kentucky, Texas A&M, and Alabama. After coaching his last game in the Liberty Bowl in Memphis, Tenn., in December of 1982, Bryant had a record 323 victories. He died in January 1983, and his funeral was one of the largest in southern history, with an estimated 500,000 people turning out to see the funeral procession from Tuscaloosa to the Birmingham burial site.

Bryant was one of the modern South's preeminent mythic figures. A product of the rural poverty so typical of the South in his youth, Bryant rose to national success. The Bear Bryant story is a rags to riches American tale, told in the southern vernacular. In his origins, Bryant symbolized the poor sharecropping South, but he became a middle-class hero to well-off southerners who made football a part of their lifestyles.

Sportswriters created a legend about Bryant with their stories of his toughness, generosity, compassion, shrewdness, and democratic egalitarianism. "Generations from now they will speak in hushed tones about the backwoodsy man from Fordyce whom the city slickers couldn't beat," wrote Memphis sportswriter Al Dunning when Bryant died. The *New Yorker* magazine referred to him as an "actual genius." Observers compared him with Douglas MacArthur, John Wayne, and, most frequently, George Patton.

Although he was a national figure, southerners felt a special claim on Bryant. He was most admired in the

Paul "Bear" Bryant, University of Alabama football coach, 1970s

South because he was a winning leader. For a people whose heroes sometimes symbolized lost causes, Bryant was a change. The Bryant legend was not just one of power and victory. Observers stressed his character and class, his concern for making athletes decent people. In his early career there were recruiting scandals and stories of his meanness, but these were forgotten when sportswriters began his apotheosis in the 1970s. The Bryant legend embodied aspects of earlier regional mythology—the New South hope of education transforming the region; the fighting South, with football as Celtic sublimation; and the Jeffersonian agrarian dream with Bryant as wise rural rustic. The Bryant legend is part of the Sports South myth, which views sports as central to the modern southern identity. Bryant was one of the first Deep South coaches to recruit black athletes. He embodies the hope for a biracial

South, in which southern blacks and whites, working together, will achieve great things off the football field as well as on it.

Charles Reagan Wilson
University of Mississippi

The Birmingham News, *Remembering Bear* (1983); James Peterson and Bill Cromartie, *Bear Bryant: Countdown to Glory* (1984); Charles Reagan Wilson, *South Atlantic Quarterly* (Summer 1987). ☆

COBB, TY
||||||||||||||||||||||||||||
(1886–1961). Baseball player.

Tyrus Raymond "Ty" Cobb, arguably the greatest of all professional baseball players and the first nationally known southern player, was born on 19 December 1886 in Banks County, Ga. His father was William Herchel Cobb, an itinerant schoolmaster who, after moving his family to Royston in Franklin County, Ga., served as state senator, county school superintendent, and editor of the local newspaper. His mother, Amanda Chitwood Cobb, was the daughter of a prominent Banks County landowner.

Tyrus Cobb showed early signs of being an intelligent, hard-driving youngster, impatient with his own and others' shortcomings. Skinny but fast and well coordinated, he starred on the town baseball team and acquired a burning ambition to pursue the game professionally. That ambition clashed with the wishes of his equally strong-willed father, who intended his elder son to be a lawyer, physician, or career military man. Finally Tyrus won W. H. Cobb's permission to try out with the Augusta team in the South Atlantic League. Although he was a failure at Augusta in 1904, Cobb came back the next year to lead the league in hitting and thus gained the attention of major league scouts. The 18-year-old Cobb was about to join the Detroit Tigers in the American League when he learned that his father had been shot to death by his mother, who claimed she had mistaken him for a prowler.

Arriving in Detroit late in August 1905, "Ty" Cobb (as sportswriters soon dubbed him) finished that season with the Tigers. The next spring, while his mother was tried and acquitted on a charge of voluntary manslaughter, young Cobb struggled to gain a regular place on the Detroit ball club. It was, he said long afterward, "the most miserable and humiliating experience I've ever been through." Cobb was subjected to the customary harassments and petty cruelties that rookies usually had to endure in that day. But as a sensitive, troubled young man, a proud southerner among ballplayers who were mainly Irish-American northerners, Cobb reacted strongly against such treatment and ended up a friendless loner on the Detroit team. The death of his father and his painful early experiences with his teammates largely account for why he became, as he later described himself, "a snarling wildcat," driven to prove himself to everybody, including himself, season after season and game after game.

Prove himself he did. In 1907 Cobb won the American League batting title, in the course of leading the Tigers to the first of three straight league championships. For 11 of the next 12 years he outhit everyone else in the American League and frequently led as well in runs scored and bases stolen. Unquestionably the top star of baseball's "dead-ball" era, Cobb remained an outstanding player after the advent of the "lively ball" in 1920 and the emergence of the power-oriented style of baseball heralded by Babe Ruth's home run exploits. From 1921 through 1926 Cobb managed the Detroit team and continued to play the outfield; his final two years as a baseball player were with Connie Mack's Philadelphia Athletics. He retired with an astonishing lifetime batting average of .367 and some 42 other records.

Already a millionaire by the time he hung up his uniform, Cobb ultimately built his personal fortune to $10 million. A man who had quarreled and brawled with teammates, umpires, opposing players, spectators, and many people off the field, Cobb continued to be a hard man to get along with in his long years of retirement. In 1947 his marriage of 39 years to Charlie Marion Lombard Cobb, an Augusta native, ended in divorce, and nine years later a second marriage, to Frances Fairburn Cass Cobb of Buffalo, N.Y., came to a similar end. Moreover, he became estranged from his surviving three children. By the time of his own death from cancer on 17 July 1961, in Atlanta, few people remained whom Cobb could call his friends. His renown in baseball, however, remains undiminished.

Charles C. Alexander
Ohio University

Charles C. Alexander, *Ty Cobb: Baseball's Fierce Immortal* (1984); Ty Cobb, with Al Stump, *My Life in Baseball: The True Record* (1961); John D. McCallum, *The Tiger Wore Spikes: An Informal Biography of Ty Cobb* (1956); Lawrence S. Ritter, *The Glory of Their Times: The Story of the Early Days of Baseball Told by Men Who Played It* (1974). ☆

COLONIAL WILLIAMSBURG

Something more ubiquitously American than uniquely southern permeates the air about Colonial Williamsburg. What appears to epitomize southern genteel traditions is more a slice of general Americana—a replica of history as all Americans might wish it had been—than a monument to the Tidewater aristocracy that bred generations of influential southerners.

The real Williamsburg, founded in 1699, appeared less tidy and behaved less decorously than today's bewigged guides would have the tourists believe. About 2,000 people lived permanently in what served Virginia more as a political and cultural mecca than as a trading center. At least half those residents were black, slaves who served the wishes of the other half. The pace of life shuffled along leisurely except during the "Publick Times"—generally held once each season during the 1700s, but daily fare for the interpretive 1900s—when either the provincial courts or legislatures held sessions. Williamsburg surged and ebbed to its own social tides through the colonial period, until 1781 when the capital was moved upriver to Richmond. Then, except for the frenzy of the Peninsula campaign in 1862, it declined into dormant insignificance.

Revival came at the hands of the local rector, W. A. R. Goodwin, who convinced John D. Rockefeller, Jr., to bequeath part of the family fortune to fund a restoration project. Work began in 1926, and by the 1930s buildings were being opened to the public. Rockefeller spent over $80 million in 40 years as 600 postcolonial structures were demolished, more than 80 existing period buildings restored, and replicas recon-

Governor's Palace, built in 1705 and restored in the 1930s to its mid-18th century appearance, Williamsburg, Virginia

structed over excavated foundations. His success spawned other restoration projects across the South, notably those in Salem and Savannah. Yet Williamsburg has persisted as the most popular "preserved" area. By the 1960s more than 15 million visitors had crowded the 130-acre site, and a second phase of restoration and reinterpretation was instituted to meet demand. Popularity peaked during the American Revolution Bicentennial.

A cultural commitment is explicit in the purpose behind Colonial Williamsburg—to interpret American history in light of acknowledged national values. John D. Rockefeller, III, son of the restorer, said: "Colonial Williamsburg must help make history—not simply serve as a reminder of history." As such, there is more to the pristine atmosphere than a mere commercialization of a past regional graciousness. The guided tours stress less the lifestyles of the gentry than the values of liberty they came to

hold. Journalist Bill Moyers has argued that in a place where "people lived routinely and seldom easily," more modern Americans, from all regions, find cultural significance from a presentation "too tidy to be real," but too encompassing to be missed.

Gary Freeze
University of North Carolina
at Chapel Hill

Taylor B. Lewis, *Window on Williamsburg* (1966); James H. Soltow, *The Economic Role of Williamsburg* (1965). ☆

DEAN, DIZZY
||||||||||||||||||||||||||||||||||||
(1911–1974) Baseball player.

Jay Hanna "Dizzy" Dean, who was born in Lucas, Ark., in 1911, toiled in cotton fields all over the South as the son of a poor migratory farmer. Dean never advanced past the second grade. Enlistment in the army during the Great

Dizzy Dean, Arkansas-born baseball player and sportscaster, 1930s

Depression gave him comparative stability and a nickname that lasted—"Dizzy."

Dean's return to civilian life brought him a contract in the far-reaching St. Louis Cardinals farm system and a quick advancement to the parent club. It was his first step en route to an eventual place in baseball's Hall of Fame. Dean's fastball became a feared weapon for the Cardinals. Many hitters knew what it was to be knocked down by a loud and proud Dean. A high-and-tight Dean fastball was described very accurately by the opposition as "high neck in."

The boldness of the flame-throwing Dean gained just as much attention as his pitching. His first employer, Branch Rickey, quickly learned this when he confronted Dean, telling the young pitcher he was quite a braggart. Dean's reply, quoted in dialect, was an unblinking " 'Tain't braggin' if you kin really do it!" The combination of excellent pitching and colorful personality made Dean one of the sport's greatest gate attractions and, in turn, one of its wealthiest ballplayers. Yet, his eccentricities drove many crazy. In one game, troubled by an umpire's call and what he believed to be poor backing by his own team, he decided to lob the ball to opposing hitters.

One of many high points in Dean's career was the 1934 World Series. After winning the first game, he was put on a shortwave hookup to Antarctica to talk with famed explorer Admiral Richard E. Byrd. "Howdy, Dick Byrd," shouted Dean. In the fourth game of the Series, in a pinch-running role, he was flattened by an infielder's throw and carried off on a stretcher. He reported later, "They X-rayed my head and found nothing." The statement was used to full advantage by the press. Then, in the seventh and final game, he shut out the Detroit Tigers.

A broken toe, the result of a line drive during an all-star game, reduced Dean's efficiency considerably and led to an earlier retirement than desired. Dean had learned well, however, how to take advantage of his uniqueness and was soon entertaining people from the radio booth, doing play-by-play broadcasts. The hillbilly image was played to the hilt—and very profitably. A Dizzy Dean broadcast introduced such terms as *slud*, *swang*, *press-peration*, *airs* (errors), and *spart* (spirit), as well as players called Scorn (Skowron), Bearer (Berra), Mannul (Mantle), and Richison (Richardson), always intermingled with a very liberal sprinkling of "ain't." When his cornpone English brought protests from teachers, among others, Dean candidly assessed, "A lot of people who ain't saying ain't, ain't eating." If he had a favorite word, though, it was "I."

Wealthy and retired, Dean moved "down home" to the Ozarks to live out his life. He is buried in Wiggins, Miss., and the Dizzy Dean Museum displays his memorabilia in Jackson, Miss.

John E. DiMeglio
Mankato State University

Curt Smith, *America's Dizzy Dean* (1978). ☆

DISNEY WORLD

Walt Disney World, near Orlando, Fla., is a vacation resort complex that ranks as one of the South's most popular holiday spots and draws non-southerners to the region as well. It includes an amusement park ("The Magic Kingdom"), hotels, campgrounds, golf courses, shopping centers, and the EPCOT Center (Experimental Prototype Community of Tomorrow). This complex, which opened in 1971, is on 27,400 acres of land and is run like a municipality, providing many of its own services. It represents the fruition of Walt Disney's ideas, which were first expressed in the opening of "Disneyland," near Anaheim, Calif., in 1955.

Disneyland pioneered as the prototype "theme park," but later parks, such as "Six Flags over Georgia" (Atlanta), "Six Flags over Texas" (Dallas), "Opryland" (Nashville), and even "Dollywood" (Pigeon Forge, Tenn.), which all borrowed heavily from Disney, focused on aspects of the past or present southern experience. Both Disneyland in California and Disney World in Florida originated ideas that relate to city planning and architecture, such as the extensive use of mass transit and the design of spaces to entertain people.

The "Magic Kingdom," Disney World's amusement park, covers 100 acres with activities—ranging from exhibits and rides to services such as restaurants—oriented around particular conceptual or historic themes. These themes come from Disney's perceptions of popular ideas about the American experience, and include small-town Midwest America about 1900 in "Main Street USA," American history in "Frontierland," the importance of technology in "Tomorrowland," and literary and mythic figures and themes in "Fantasyland." Despite their location in the South, few of these popularizations embodied in Disney World relate directly to the region. Most of the rides, shows, and performances are given by extremely sophisticated, computer controlled ("audio-animatronics") robots, appropriate perhaps to the high-technology South of Florida. These robots ensure identical presentations for each audience. Numerous forms of mass transit, ranging from a monorail to horse-drawn wagons, move visitors around the park and allow easy access to other parts of the resort. The park has many other architectural and city planning features that make the experience pleasant for visitors as well as serving as models for what humanized technology can do.

Disney's graphics, architecture, and technology blend to create a "magic" aura where visitors can suspend their disbelief and enjoy themselves. The rides, robots, and attractions allow them to return for a moment to their own childhoods and to relive the mythic origins of the nation. The parks, with their own versions of American history, folklore, and technology, serve as a unifying experience for the millions of Americans who have visited them. The parks provide a shared cultural experience, a common interpretation of history (albeit somewhat fantasized), and an attractive vision of the future that will result in greater cultural sameness among southerners as well as among other groups of Americans.

David M. Johnson
North Carolina Agricultural
and Technical State University

Margaret J. King, ed., *Journal of Popular Culture* (Summer 1981); Walt Disney Productions, *The Story of Walt Disney World* (1973). ☆

GILLEY'S

Gilley's, in Pasadena, Tex., was founded by Sherwood Cryer as "Shelly's." Its success, like its present name, dates from 1971, when Cryer went into partnership with Mickey Gilley, a country music singer and piano player once probably best known as Jerry Lee Lewis's cousin. Billed at one time as "the World's Largest Saloon" (it could accommodate 4,500 customers), it eventually offered, besides the traditional drinking and dancing, such challenging entertainments as a punching-bag machine and "El Toro," a mechanical bull for customers to ride. Dancing at the club was to music supplied by Gilley, by the house band (the Bayou City Beats), or by visiting country music entertainers, and it included group dances like the cotton-eyed Joe (punctuated with rhythmic chants of "Bull-*shit!*") and the schottische.

Despite these attractions, Gilley's was little known outside the Houston area, except in country music circles, before 1978, when *Esquire* published an article by Aaron Latham on the club and some of its patrons. Latham's article was accompanied by a photographic feature on designer Ralph Lauren's new line, "embracing the rugged natural look of the American cowboy." When the movie *Urban Cowboy*, starring John Travolta, was actually filmed in Gilley's, scores of more or less frankly imitative establishments sprang up across the country. These "cowboy" bars sometimes replaced discos that had been inspired by Travolta's performance in "Saturday Night Fever" and catered to much the same clientele, even more urban and less plausibly cowboy than the young oil workers Latham had chronicled. The most bravura of these new establishments was also in Texas, a Fort Worth club called "Billy Bob's" that offered live bull-riding in place of Gilley's machine-simulated version. (Rumors that a patron had been stomped and gored did not hurt at all.) Billy Bob's was even larger than Gilley's, and on one occasion Merle Haggard treated all 5,095 customers to drinks.

The era of "Texas chic" soon faded, but not before Gilley's had become a major tourist attraction with its own magazine, its own brand of beer, and complete line of souvenirs. Mickey Gilley himself had become a major country music singer with a number of hits to his credit, including "Don't the Girls All Get Prettier at Closing Time"—a traditional number at the club.

Southerners themselves have often collaborated in—and occasionally profited from—the marketing of the South. But the story of Gilley's may reflect a new development in the nation's old, on-again/off-again love affair with the South. Gilley's represents, and *Esquire* and Hollywood marketed, a blue-collar South, populated by the same good old boys (and girls) whom the mass media had generally portrayed a decade earlier (in such movies as *Easy Rider* and *Deliverance*, for instance) as vicious rednecks. The increasing national respectability of their music, the popularity of Burt Reynolds and the *Dukes of Hazzard*, and, not least, the "Urban Cowboy" phenomenon—all attest to a metamorphosis that was one of the stranger aspects of a strange decade.

John Shelton Reed
University of North Carolina
at Chapel Hill

Bob Claypool, *Saturday Night at Gilley's* (1980); Aaron Latham, *Esquire* (September 1978). ☆

HILTON HEAD
|||||||||||||||||||||||||||||||||||

As a forested refuge for nomadic Indian tribes, as the site for 17th-century Spanish and French fortifications, and as the location of antebellum Sea Island cotton plantations, Hilton Head has lured people through its climate and its geographical diversity.

Now one of the South's most famous resort areas, Hilton Head had historic significance in the 19th century. On 7 November 1861, 17 Union warships blocked South Carolina's Port Royal Sound, capturing the Confederate stronghold of Fort Walker on the island. The Port Royal anchorage remained the principal base of federal naval operations for the duration of the war, and Hilton Head's Port Royal Plantation, quartering some 30,000 troops, was transformed into a boomtown, complete with hotels and a theater. Along with other southern sea islands, Hilton Head became the focus for a social and agrarian experiment, in which large plantations and town property were claimed by the Treasury Department and redistributed to freedmen.

Called a "dress rehearsal for Reconstruction," the Port Royal experiment influenced the formation of federal policy concerning the status of emancipated slaves. Its schools, military training, and wage labor programs acted as a proving ground for freedmen and provided experience for postwar Reconstruction leaders such as General O. O. Howard, head of the Freedman's Bureau, and Congressman Robert Smalls.

After the war, prosperous northern investors were attracted to the sound. Huge tracts of land, and sometimes whole islands, were purchased for use as hunting preserves and winter havens. The largest of South Carolina's barrier islands—12 miles long and covering about 42 square miles—Hilton Head escaped sole proprietorship and became instead a popular contribution of resort and residential development.

Gulf breezes keep temperatures on the island at a semitropical 60° to 80° range year-round. The ocean and networks of freshwater lagoons, meadows, forest area, and marshland support some 260 varieties of birds, as well as bream, bass, and blue marlin. Sea oats and palmetto share the landscape with magnolia, pine, and live oak.

Hilton Head offers its more than 700,000 annual visitors recreational diversity. There are 6 marinas, 17 golf courses, and over 200 tennis courts on the island. Accommodations range from hotel rooms to oceanfront villas with names like Bayberry Dune and Xanadu. Abounding in secluded white sand beaches and quiet nature trails, yet only hours from the urbane charm of Charleston, Hilton Head represents a fusion of society and serenity that has a characteristically southern flavor.

Elizabeth M. Makowski
University of Mississippi

Guion Griffis Johnson, *A Social History of the Sea Islands* (1930); Willie Lee Rose, *Rehearsal for Reconstruction: The Port Royal Experiment* (1964); *Southern Living* (April 1982); David D. Wallace, *South Carolina: A Short History, 1520–1948.* ☆

JOHNSON, JUNIOR
|||||||||||||||||||||||||||||||||||||||||||||||||||
(b. 1931?) Sports car driver.

Robert Glenn "Junior" Johnson is the most famous resident of Ingle Hollow in Wilkes County, N.C. Neighbors used to admire him for his adeptness at outwitting and outmaneuvering tax agents on moonshine runs. Now they and fans throughout the South and the nation revere him for his accomplishments as a stock car driver.

Johnson's father operated a still in

Wilkes County, one of the most productive moonshine regions in the country. The size of his profit often depended on whether or not Junior could deliver the product to customers in nearby cities and towns without getting caught, so Junior learned to drive fast and skillfully, often evading would-be captors by implementing his "bootleg turn," a technique that evolved into the "power slide" he later used as a stock car driver to maintain and accelerate speed coming out of turns on the racetrack. In 1955 agents caught him, not on a delivery, but standing in front of the still. He served just over 10 months in a Chillicothe, Ohio, prison.

At the time of his arrest, Johnson was already well on his way to becoming a successful stock car driver. He had won championships in the Sportsman and Modified classifications and, in 1955, captured the first of his seven Grand National victories. Ten years later he retired as a driver, having won the Daytona 500 and 49 other races. He was one of the sport's most popular figures.

Since 1965 Johnson has been hiring drivers for his cars and, with employees like Bobby Allison, Cale Yarborough, and most recently, Darrell Waltrip, his success has continued. Recognized as a master mechanic, Johnson has been a consultant to General Motors, but he still operates from his home in Ingle Hollow, where he and his staff build parts, make repairs, and work constantly to keep the team's cars among the fastest on the track.

Success has not separated Johnson from his heritage in the rural South. He is a prototypical good old boy who likes coon hunting and chicken farming. He even helped found the Holly Farms Chicken company in North Wilkesboro, N.C. Writer Tom Wolfe called him the "Last American Hero," and Johnson's neighbors would probably agree. His bootlegging days may be well past, but somewhere in Ingle Hollow, he still has his old moonshining car safely stored away.

Jessica Foy
Cooperstown Graduate Programs
Cooperstown, New York

Larry Griffin, *Car & Driver* (April 1982); Charles Leerhsen, *Newsweek* (16 November 1981); Tom Wolfe, *Esquire* (March 1965). ☆

JONES, BOBBY

(1902–1971) Golfer.

Born on 17 March 1902 in Atlanta, Ga., Robert Tyre "Bobby" Jones, Jr., was a child prodigy at golf, studying under Stewart Maiden, a Scottish pro who worked at Atlanta's East Lake course. Jones played in the 1916 U.S. Amateur Tournament when he was only 14 years old. He went on to win 13 major championships, climaxed in 1930 by capturing in a single season the "Grand Slam of Golf," which was then the championships of the British Amateur, the British Open, the U.S. Open, and the U.S. Amateur. New York City treated him to an enormous ticker tape parade that year, appropriate to one who had become a national hero. Later, he received a similar outpouring of affection from his hometown in Atlanta. At the height of his fame, at age 28, Jones announced his retirement. He returned to his law practice and business endeavors in Atlanta, starting a long involvement with the A. G. Spalding Company, making a series of instructional film shorts for Warner Brothers studios, and conceiving and assisting in the design of the Augusta National Golf Course in Augusta, Ga., home of the Masters Tournament.

Jones's career reflected the rise of spectator sports in the South and the nation during the 1920s. Although golf was not as popular in the South as in the Northeast and on the West Coast, Jones nonetheless consciously worked to increase its popularity in his home region. He conceived the idea of the Augusta course, because "my native Southland, especially my own neighborhood, had very few, if any, golf courses of championship quality." He regarded it "as an opportunity to make a contribution to golf in my own section of the country."

Jones was frequently referred to as the embodiment of the southern gentleman. Journalist and commentator Alistair Cooke wrote that Jones was "a gentleman, a combination of goodness and grace, an unwavering courtesy, self-deprecation, and consideration for other people." Graceful in his athletic performance, poised at all times, modest in his success, and self-consciously "southern" in his attitudes, Jones symbolized a transitional figure—the traditional regional image of the gentleman in a new 20th-century mass culture context. Through the press and radio in the 1920s, the exploits of "The Emperor Jones" were publicized, and he thereby helped popularize golf with southerners and others who had once dismissed it as an effete game for the wealthy.

Charles Reagan Wilson
University of Mississippi

John R. Betts, *America's Sporting Heritage, 1850–1950* (1974); Robert Tyre Jones, Jr., *Golf Is My Game* (1959). ✩

KENTUCKY DERBY

The Kentucky Derby, America's premier race classic for three-year-old thoroughbreds, showcases some of the South's most established traditions: honorable sporting competition, high fashion, and the love of pageantry. This mile-and-a-quarter test has been run at Churchill Downs in Louisville, Ky., since May 1875. The race originally was proposed as a match between Kentucky's and Tennessee's best three-year-old horses. However, its founder, Colonel M. Lewis Clark of Louisville, after visiting the racecourses of Europe, changed the inaugural to a derby patterned after England's one-and-a-half-mile Epsom Derby.

The names and traditions associated with the Kentucky Derby are a tapestry of American racing history. There was Matt Winn (1861–1949), the colorful track president who had seen every Derby and whose flair for showmanship transformed the race into a national and world event. There was Isaac Murphy (1871–96), the legendary black jockey with three winning rides. And Colonel E. R. "Bet-a-Million" Bradley, whose four winners—Behave Yourself (1921), Bubbling Over (1926), Burgoo King (1934), and Brokers Tip (1933)—like all his horses, began their names with the letter "B." The year 1919 produced Sir Barton, the first Triple Crown winner, and 1941, Whirlaway, the chestnut speedster with the flying tail. Then, too, there was "R-r-r-racing fans, this is Clem McCarthy" calling the race on national radio (1928–50); Citation (1948), one of eight horses to carry the devil's red silks of Calumet Stables to victory; and, finally, Penny Tweedy's wonder horse,

Secretariat, the race record holder (1.59⅖, 1973).

Mint juleps, roses, steamboat and balloon races, parades, and southern fashion on display constitute the Kentucky Derby for many. For the thousands that jam into the track infield on Derby Day it is picnic coolers, beer, and lighthearted revelry. Still for others, it is parties, out-of-town guests, good food, and a television or radio tuned to the race.

Run on the first Saturday in May, the Derby is an American tradition, an unofficial holiday that focuses on the spectacle of finely conditioned animals competing in the ultimate two minute test. For the winner, there is racing immortality, a purse in excess of $100,000, and the chance to win America's racing Triple Crown. For the audience, there is an opportunity to enjoy the traditions and to savor a flavoring of timeless culture. When the familiar strains of "My Old Kentucky Home" are sung as the horses are led onto the track, everyone becomes both a Kentuckian and a southerner. In this sense, the Kentucky Derby is more than a race; it is, instead, an expression of national heritage.

James C. Claypool
Northern Kentucky University

Peter Chew, *The Kentucky Derby, the First 100 Years* (1974); Annie Harrison, *The Kentucky Derby: Its Traditions and Triumphs* (1980). ☆

LOUISIANA STATE LOTTERY COMPANY

The Louisiana State Lottery Company had its genesis in 1866 when the legislature, controlled by Confederate veterans, passed an act permitting lottery vending in the state. Two years later a Republican-dominated legislature assisted by Charles T. Howard, a skilled lobbyist, pushed through a bill chartering the Louisiana State Lottery Company. The 25-year charter gave the company a monopoly on the sale of lottery tickets and exempted the organization from state taxes, except for an annual license fee of $40,000. Its capital stock was set at $1 million with 10,000 shares valued at $100 each. Operations began on 31 December 1868.

By the time the Republican government fell in 1877 the company was a lucrative and politically powerful enterprise. Anxious to maintain its privileges and to foil opposition from Louisiana's Redeemers, lotterymen in 1879 allied themselves with the reactionary Bourbon faction of the Democratic party, wrote a new state constitution that ousted unfriendly state officials, installed lottery supporters in key government positions, and gave legal sanction to lotteries until 1 January 1895.

With opposition temporarily stayed, lotterymen improved the image of the organization by undertaking philanthropic endeavors and enshrining their enterprise in the sacrosanct shroud of the Lost Cause. Two ex-Confederate generals, P. G. T. Beauregard and Jubal Early, presided over drawings, thereby ensuring honesty. Yet, with 47 percent of its gross receipts retained as profit, there was little need for chicanery. Conservative estimates of profits accrued in the 1880s range from $8 million to $14 million annually, and by 1890 the company reportedly took in from $20 million to $30 million.

At the peak of its economic and political power, opposition to the company increased locally and nationally. From 1890 to 1892 debates over the renewal of the company's charter raged throughout the state, split both major parties, divided the Populists, and submerged all other issues. The antilottery forces won the battle in Louisiana, but the U.S. Congress, taking direct aim at the Louisiana Lottery, delivered the fatal blow by passing a bill denying the use of the mails to lotteries. Since 90 percent of the Louisiana Lottery's proceeds came from states other then Louisiana, this legislation dried up profits and closed down operations in the state in December 1893. In January diehard lotterymen transferred the company to Honduras, and for some years they sponsored illegal activities in the United States. Federal law enforcement authorities checked these operations, and the company collapsed in 1907.

Carolyn DeLatte
McNeese State University

Berthold C. Alwes, *Louisiana Historical Quarterly* (October 1944); Henry C. Dethloff, *Louisiana History* (Spring 1965); William I. Hair, *Bourbonism and Agrarian Protest: Louisiana Politics, 1877–1900* (1969). ☆

MANNING, ARCHIE
‖‖
(b. 1949) Football player.

Archie Manning was representative of many southern football players who have become heroes in the modern South. They are often identified with a particular university or state, but some are well known throughout the region. Traditional southern military imagery and evangelical religious fervor are applied to them. A few such as Manning tran-

scend the region and become national celebrities, symbolic of their native region. Manning was particularly significant of the few football heroes who played in the South at both the college and professional ranks.

Elisha Archie Manning III was born 19 March 1949 to a Baptist family in the Delta town of Drew, Miss. Young Manning was given a tiny helmet and uniform as soon as he could walk and often slept with a football cradled in his arms. Recruited out of high school by only a few area colleges, Manning accepted a scholarship to play quarterback at the University of Mississippi.

Manning, with his red hair, freckles, and a prominent nose, became known as college football's Huckleberry Finn. The 6′ 3½″ player could spot receivers over charging linemen, and with his 10.2 seconds' speed in the 100-yard dash he was fast enough to elude the rush. Manning started at quarterback his sophomore year and led his team to a 7-3-1 record.

The next season, 1969, a year of Vietnam protests, Woodstock, and the moon landing, Archie Manning became a folk hero. Mississippi played Alabama in the third game of the season. It was the first nationally televised nighttime broadcast of a college game. Manning and Alabama's Scott Hunter put on a brilliant display of passing as Alabama won the game 33–32. Manning's effort set a Southeastern Conference record for total offense that still stands—540 yards, including 33 completions out of 52 pass attempts. Sportswriters referred to "Super" Manning as "Archie Fever" continued to grow. After the University of Mississippi defeated unbeaten and second-ranked Tennessee 38–0, "The Ballad of Archie Who," written by a postal clerk in Magnolia, Miss., hit the airwaves, and the song quickly sold 35,000 copies.

By his senior year, the quiet boy from Drew with the rifle arm had become a national hero. *Sports Illustrated* called the phenomenon "one of the wildest displays of adulation ever accorded any athlete anywhere, anytime." In 1970 Manning was on the cover of *Sports Illustrated* and *College Football* magazines. Then he broke his left arm in the homecoming game, ruining his chances for the Heisman trophy.

Manning was the second player chosen in the 1971 National Football League draft, going to the lowly New Orleans Saints. His 14-year professional career included two Pro Bowl appearances and selection as the league's most valuable player. Manning never played on a winning team as a professional, but he said "no matter how bad we got beat, in the eyes of Mississippians it was never my fault." He retired in 1985, after brief stays with the Houston Oilers and Minnesota Vikings. Manning lives in New Orleans, where he is a stockbroker and sports announcer for Saints games.

Tom Rieland
University of Mississippi

Pat Putnam, *Sports Illustrated* (24 November 1969); William F. Reed, *Sports Illustrated* (14 September and 12 October 1970). ☆

PAIGE, SATCHEL
|||||||||||||||||||||||||||||||||||||||||||||
(1906–1982) Baseball player.

LeRoy "Satchel" Paige was born in Mobile, Ala., on 7 July 1906. As a youngster he was a porter at the railroad station, where he was given the nickname "Satchel" because he built a device that enabled him to carry many more bags than normal. He was in trouble early in life and spent over five years at the Industrial School for Negro Children at Mount Meig, Ala.

As a teenager he attracted attention for his baseball pitching, and he began playing professionally in 1924 for the Mobile Tigers, a black semipro club. By 1928 he had risen to the highest level of black baseball, playing with the Birmingham Black Barons of the Negro National League. He achieved his greatest fame in the Negro Leagues pitching for the Pittsburgh Crawfords during the 1930s and the Kansas City Monarchs during the 1940s, but he pitched for as many as 250 independent ballclubs, usually on a one-game exhibition basis.

His fastball was virtually impossible to hit, and his reputation spread well beyond the world of black baseball, aided by his enormous showmanship and inexhaustible energy. In exhibition games he was frequently advertised as "guaranteed to strike out the first six men," and he was known to call in the outfield or instruct his infielders to sit down.

His reputation was enhanced by a series of historic encounters with white major league players that followed the major league World Series. These games, during the era of segregation, enabled black and white ballplayers to assess each other's skills. Dizzy Dean called Paige the greatest pitcher of his era, and major league testimony to Paige's ability is abundant. Paige's many victories over white major leaguers gave him a symbolic importance to blacks during segregation, and black baseball fans everywhere followed Paige's exploits through the highly developed sports pages of the national black newspapers.

Shortly after the integration of baseball by Jackie Robinson, Paige became the first black pitcher in the American League, with the Cleveland Indians in 1948. He pitched for Cleveland in 1948 and 1949, with the St. Louis Browns in 1951–53, and briefly with the Kansas City Athletics in 1965, all of which helped qualify him for a major league pension.

Paige was the ultimate barnstorming baseball player, pitching virtually every day. His talent was extraordinary, and his success was coupled with a flamboyant, comic style that augmented his reputation. Paige's career illustrated the typical Negro League history of southern roots and northern achievement. In 1971 Paige was elected to the Baseball Hall of Fame, the first Negro Leaguer admitted under a new admissions policy. Paige died in 1982 in Kansas City, Mo.

See also BLACK LIFE: / Negro Baseball Leagues

Donn Rogosin
WSWP-TV
Beckley, West Virginia

Donn Rogosin, *Invisible Men: Life in Baseball's Negro Leagues* (1983); Edna Rust and Art Rust, Jr., *Art Rust's Illustrated History of the Black Athlete* (1985). ☆

PETTY, RICHARD
(b. 1937) Sports car driver.

Among modern southern sports legends, few have had as sustained and dedicated a following as Richard Petty, often dubbed "King of the Road" in stock car racing. Petty's dominance of the asphalt ovals in the South has created a following that adores him as much for his traditional lifestyle as for his driving exploits.

His racing record has been impressive. In his first 25 seasons (1958–83), Petty won 198 races, far more than any of his competitors. His earnings exceeded $4.5 million. Although slow to gain prominence—he went winless his first two seasons—Petty dominated the tracks from the early 1960s to the mid-1970s. His peak performances came from 1967 through 1971, when the familiar Petty blue Plymouth was driven into victory lane in 40 percent of the 233 races he entered. Over the course of his career, Petty has won the prestigious Daytona 500 seven times, received seven Winston Cups for the best seasonal performance among drivers, and finished among the first 10 drivers in 70 percent of the 900 races he has entered.

Yet more than simple performance explains the hold of the Petty legend on so many southerners. Intensely personal and familial traits exist in stock car racing. Fans become attached to a particular driver and espouse his cause as if he were kin. Petty's career style has been both an extension of, and a reaction to, such traits. He frequently spends hours after races signing autographs. He has been known, when eliminated early in competition, to use public restrooms to change his clothes. When a movie was made about his life, Petty himself played the lead role. Such closeness to his fans has bred deep loyalties. Through the years those who become Petty fans remain Petty fans.

The depth of such attachments can be best explained by the common origins Petty shares with most of his fans. His background, like theirs, is deeply rooted in the rural South. Petty grew up in the Uwharrie hills of Randolph County, N.C. He has remained there, and, until the late stages of his career, used mostly family members and neighbors to man his pit crew. Racing has been a hereditary trait among the Pettys. Richard succeeded his father Lee and now has a son of his own, Kyle, on the tracks. Much like traditional rural skills such as weaving and smithing, racing is passed along through generations.

Petty fans remain loyal because the racer has remained just like them, even though he achieved uncommon financial success. The Pettys have lived "like folks" even though they have a five-car garage. The Pettys reinforce the ambitions of their fans, who through stock car racing strive to hold on to the identities of their impoverished, rural past as they seek the urbane riches of the Sunbelt. A symbol of this dichotomy is the new Petty brick house, built near the old frame cottage where he grew up. On the dining room wall of the new house is a printed mural of an Old South plantation scene.

Gary Freeze
University of North Carolina
at Chapel Hill

Bill Libby with Richard Petty, *"King Richard": The Richard Petty Story* (1977). ☆

ROBINSON, EDDIE

(b. 1919) Football coach.

Eddie Robinson was born 12 February 1919 in Jackson, La., to sharecropper parents. At age eight he moved with his parents to Baton Rouge, where, according to Robinson, he watched a high school football team practice and de- cided he wanted to be a coach. Robinson played football at McKinley High School in Baton Rouge and at Leland College. After graduating in 1940, he worked during the day at a Baton Rouge feed mill and at night on an ice truck. In 1941 Grambling hired Robinson as head football coach, and he began his legendary career.

Robinson's success in developing the football program at Grambling was phenomenal. When he first arrived on campus, Robinson assumed chores assigned to support staffs at larger schools, such as mowing the playing field, taping ankles, and even writing game stories for the newspapers. With the support of the Grambling administration, Robinson built the fledgling program into one of the most respected collegiate programs in the country. More than 200 of Robinson's Grambling players have gone on to play on professional teams, a record that testifies to Robinson's success as a coach. Robinson's coaching style has changed little during his years at Grambling. His teams have been characterized by the wing-T formation on offense and a pro-style 4–3 on defense.

During the fall 1985 season, Robinson won his 324th game, surpassing the record previously held by Paul (Bear) Bryant of Alabama. Although some observers charge that Robinson's record meant less than Bryant's because most of his victories came against Division I-AA-caliber teams, others point out that Robinson has had to overcome difficulties Bryant never faced at Alabama, such as low recruitment and operating budgets, and racial discrimination. Robinson remains humble about his victories and characteristically tries to divert attention from the inevitable comparisons between himself and Bryant. "I could win 1,000 games and never replace the Bear," Robinson said about his 324th win.

Karen M. McDearman
University of Mississippi

Paul Hemphill, *Southern Magazine* (December 1986); Rick Reilly, *Sports Illustrated* (14 October 1985); William C. Rhoden, *New York Times* (16 September 1985). ☆

ST. CECILIA BALL

A private, exclusive subscription ball, the St. Cecilia is an outgrowth of the oldest musical society in the United States. One of a variety of social, charitable, cultural, and educational organizations in antebellum Charleston, the St. Cecilia Society was founded in 1762. Gentlemen amateurs came together "to indulge a common taste and to pass an agreeable hour" and organized two concerts each month for members, featuring talented musicians from within the city and elsewhere in the nation.

By 1773, when visiting Bostonian Josiah Quincy decreed its first violinist "incomparably better" than any other he had ever heard, the society had a membership of 120 and a professional orchestra comparable in size to European ensembles of the period. Though carefully managed by its officers—the peerage of Charleston—difficulties in obtaining musicians and the increased popularity of dancing led to a gradual change in emphasis. After 1822 subscription balls entirely replaced the concerts.

There were three St. Cecilias during the winter "gay" season: one in January and two in February, the latter cautiously arranged to avoid interfering with Lent. The balls were held on Thursdays (St. Cecilia's day) in St. Andrew's Hall, Broad Street, and, after that hall was destroyed in the fire of 1861, in the Hibernian. Invitations were hand delivered to members; and new membership in the society was strictly limited, typically, to the sons or grandsons of current members. When a man was elected, the names of the ladies of his household were added to "the list." Their names were removed only upon death or departure from the city, "change of fortune affecting them not at all."

When invited as guests, visiting strangers were expected to follow the traditons of the ball, designed to insure "the greatest decorum." Young ladies always arrived and returned home with chaperons who, during the course of the ball, sat on a slightly raised platform surrounding the dance floor. Men engaged girls for dances by signing a card. Before each dance, the orchestra signalled ladies to return to their chaperons to await the next partner.

At midnight the president of the society led the march to supper with the newest bride in the group on his arm. Replete with fine food and wine, silver and monogrammed Irish linen, the elegant suppers were capped by a "scramble of the men for a sugar figure placed on the top of a huge fancy structure of spun sugar," which each tried to secure as a souvenir for his partner.

Still held yearly, the St. Cecilia balls have changed little since the 1800s. In an effort to preserve social distinctions and traditions without, in the words of a former society president, "stirring up jealousies and animosities which seriously impair the goodwill normally existing between members and nonmembers," secrecy continues to surround both rules for admission and customs of the ball, leading outsiders to view the affairs with a mix of awe and incredulity. "It is remarkable," wrote one early 20th-century journalist, "that such exclusive and elective balls, bound by such rigid rules, and so opposed to new members, should exist so long in the whirling change of American life."

Elizabeth M. Makowski
University of Mississippi

Ainslee's Magazine (October 1905); Frederick P. Bowes, *The Culture of Early Charleston* (1942); John J. Hindman, "Concert Life in Ante Bellum Charleston" (Ph.D. dissertation, University of North Carolina, Chapel Hill, 1971); Mrs. St. Julien Ravenel, *Charleston: The Place and the People* (1907). ☆

SHOWBOATS

Beginning in the 1830s and reaching a peak from 1870 to 1910, showboats steamed the waterways of the Atlantic Coast and the Mississippi River Valley, bringing spectacular entertainment to people in communities along the way. Some showboats were little more than flatboats with primitive structures on top, but the most elaborate were floating palaces, which had fancy decor and comfortable quarters. Among the most famous showboats were Edwin Price's *Water Queen*, William Chapman's *Floating Theatre*, Norman Thom's *Princess*, Spaulding and Rogers's *Floating Circus Palace*, John McNair's *New Era*, and Augustus French's *New Sensation*. Loud calliopes and brightly colored flags announced the coming of the showboats, and a parade and free concert would be held if the community was big enough. The showboats presented family fare,

including musical performances, sentimental melodramas, minstrel routines, acrobatics, fiddlers' contests, humorous speeches, and magic shows. Thousands of people in isolated river towns and on plantations turned out enthusiastically, and uncritically, to see the shows.

In the 20th century showboats declined because of competition from other forms of mass culture, especially the movies. In the early 1900s, though, even more elaborate showboats than before were built, such as the *Cotton Blossom*, the *Goldenrod*, and the *Sunny South*. They were large, sometimes seating almost 1,000 people, and they began specializing in dramatic performances and stage plays from the New York theater. This did not reverse the decline, though, as the number of showboats on the Mississippi fell from 22 in 1910 to 4 in 1938.

Showboats have become so identified with southern entertainment history that contemporary southerners have shown a renewed interest in them. In 1948 Vicksburg, Miss., for example, purchased the *Sprague*, a huge towboat built in 1901, and converted it into a showboat of sorts. Metro-Goldwyn-Mayer studios used it in 1950 for the musical film *Show Boat*. It then housed a river museum in Vicksburg and served

Moonlight on Old Man River, *Mississippi River, Greenville, Miss., postcard, c. 1900*

as the stage for a Gay Nineties melodrama, *Gold in the Hills.*

The *Delta Queen* is the most famous paddle-wheel steamer still cruising the Mississippi. The 285-foot-long, 58-foot-wide steamer regularly makes the trip from Cincinnati to New Orleans as well as numerous shorter trips. Its sister ship, the *Mississippi Queen*, is a larger, more modern vessel. Those on their cruises are entertained with presentations of shows such as *The Mississippi Gambler* and Mark Twain's *Huckleberry Finn* and *Tom Sawyer.* The sound of the calliope playing "My Old Kentucky Home," "Are You from Dixie?," or " 'Way Down Yonder in New Orleans" still summons people to river towns to greet the boat as it steams into port. Amusement parks such as Nashville's Opryland use steamboats (the *Andrew Jackson*) as stages for musical entertainment, and museums such as Memphis's Mud Island use riverboat replicas—all evoking memories of an earlier southern form of amusement.

Charles Reagan Wilson
University of Mississippi

Philip Graham, *Georgia Review* (Summer 1958), *Showboats: The History of an American Institution* (1951). ☆

SPOLETO FESTIVAL, U.S.A.

Spoleto Festival U.S.A. is the American equivalent to Gian Carlo Menotti's Festival of Two Worlds, staged annually since 1957 in the Umbrian town of Spoleto, Italy.

With a long tradition of support for theater companies and music societies, such as the venerable St. Cecilia, and

unique architectural beauty paralleling its Italian counterpart, Charleston, S.C., was selected in 1977 as the site for this interdisciplinary arts festival. For two-and-one-half weeks each spring, from the end of May to the first week in June, as many as 12 events a day highlight both traditional and experimental forms in the visual arts, music, theater, and dance. Offerings range from Bellini's *La Sonnambula*, Rachmaninoff concerts, and medieval liturgical drama to performances by the Spoleto Express Breakdancers. Pianist Misha Dichter, Dizzy Gillespie (a native South Carolinian), Dance Theatre of Harlem, and members of such distinguished ensembles as the Saint Paul Chamber Orchestra and the Pittsburgh Symphony have appeared on Spoleto stages.

Piccolo Spoleto ("Little Spoleto") supplements these paid-admission events. Emphasizing local and regional talent and children's activities, Piccolo Spoleto holds performances in community centers, schools, and churches throughout Charleston.

Education is an important part of Spoleto. Each year over 800 young musicians from conservatories and universities across the nation are auditioned by music director Christian Baeda. Finalists (106 in 1984) are chosen to join the Festival Orchestra and to perform in Italy at the close of the Charleston program. Opportunities to work with international talents extend to administrators and technicians as well, because in addition to performance, apprentice programs cover most aspects of arts management and production.

More than a showcase for the arts, Spoleto Festival U.S.A. links the established polished performer with the innovative, young artist and European cultural traditions with those of the South.

Elizabeth M. Makowski
University of Mississippi

John Ardoin, *Opera News* (October 1983); Andrew Porter, *New Yorker* (15 July 1985); Harold Rosenthal, *New Grove Dictionary of Music and Musicians*, vol. 18, ed. Stanley Sadie (1980); *Southern Living* (May 1980). ☆

TOURNAMENTS

Usually called lancing tournaments in South Carolina and Georgia and ring tournaments elsewhere, these displays of equestrian skill represent survivals in the South of ancient medieval tourneys. Traditionally held on holidays, particularly Independence Day, and sometimes at agricultural fairs in antebellum times, in the New South tournaments lost most of their quality as spectacle and remained largely an entertainment at planter-class family outings. Extant today in their natural form only in much-simplified versions and in a few localities, they have become essentially folk practices, occasionally retaining some hint of their original pageantry.

Originating in France in the mid-11th century, medieval tournaments—exhibitions of military prowess by horsemen in mock battles—were introduced by the Norman Conquest into England, where they flourished for over 300 years. Though the introduction of gunpowder and small arms in the 14th and 15th centuries made knightly skills obsolete in warfare, the popularity of tournaments as spectacle continued through the first half of the 16th century. But after the death of Henry VIII the necessity to economize put such costly

shows out of fashion in England, and in 1559 the killing of the French king, Henry II, in a tournament accident blighted the practice everywhere.

Royal tournaments disappeared altogether, but local noblemen in England continued the practice, on a much reduced scale, as private entertainment. In the course of the 17th century the tradition was transplanted to England's American colonies. While in 18th-century England tournaments died out, in the colonies, particularly in the South, they survived.

Still intact in the South at the opening of the 19th century, the tournament tradition got a new lease on life from the Romantic movement and the Gothic revival. Tournaments were incorporated into the southern ideal of chivalry and achieved phenomenal popularity in the Old South. Five thousand people attended an 1856 tournament in Fredericksburg, Va., for example, and 6,000 were at one in Jackson, Miss., in 1859.

Typically, mounted tournament contestants, often military cadets and officers, styled themselves knights—the Knight of the Old Dominion or the Knight of the Black Prince. Each carried a pointed "lance," a long wooden dowel or, in less polished versions, a small pole from which the bark had been carefully stripped. Contestants in turn "ran the rings," charging down a course of 100 or so yards, along which a series of three or more rings, in diameters diminishing from about three inches to half an inch, were hung on wire hooks suspended from bars fixed to the tops of posts lining the course. After finishing the course, each contestant rode before the judges who counted the rings he had collected on his lance and calculated his time. The winner became the tournament king and crowned a queen.

Tournaments in the New South often

lost their medieval trappings and became associated with hunts, particularly with fox hunts. Hence they were often played out in traditional red, white, and black hunting clothes. Very few tournaments in that form remain today, having lost virtually all elements of pageantry.

Jerah Johnson
University of New Orleans

Esther J.Crooks and Ruth W. Crooks, *The Ring Tournament in the United States* (1936); John Hope Franklin, *The Militant South, 1800–1861* (1956). ☆

WALKER, HERSCHEL

(b. 1962) Football player.

In 1980 Herschel Walker began a three-year football career at the University of Georgia during which he established himself as the Deep South's first universally acclaimed black collegiate superstar. Having set numerous high-school records in the tiny south Georgia town of Wrightsville, Walker led his team to one national and three Southeastern Conference Championships, claiming for himself not only statistical records and the Heisman trophy, but a unique place in the hearts of his region's white football fanatics.

Despite the often unpleasant experiences of his black predecessors in southern collegiate athletics, most white football fans refused to let several centuries of racial paranoia come between them and an athlete who could run like Herschel Walker. Walker received some racist hate mail, but even his controversial early departure from the University of Georgia for a lucrative contract with the New Jersey Generals of the United States Football League and

his challenge of the white South's ultimate racial taboo—dating and marrying a white woman—did little to damage his overall popularity in Georgia and throughout the region. He joined the National Football League Dallas Cowboys in 1986.

Southern whites developed an affection for Walker because of both his physical prowess and the unassuming grace with which he wore their adulation. (Jack Armstrong, the "All-American boy," was a smart-mouthed street punk by comparison.) Walker's conservatism and reticence brought criticism from some black militants and white activists who felt that black athletic heroes should speak out on racial issues. Walker refused to become a social reformer, however, steering clear of civil rights demonstrations in his native Wrightsville and thwarting the efforts of the most determined interviewers to lead him into controversial areas.

Mature and intelligent, Walker realized it was in his best interest to watch what he said and did. He remained, despite his fame, a country boy, profoundly influenced by two determined, God-fearing parents. Walker's mother and father instilled in their children courtesy and humility familiar in the rural and small-town South. The key to Herschel Walker's identity and appeal was his down-to-earth southern upbringing. That upbringing, however, included no color-coded parental instructions to stay in his "place." No one, black or white, doubted that Walker knew what he could do, and his interracial courtship and marriage indicated that he had no qualms about violating southern social norms that he did not accept.

It is difficult to determine whether Herschel Walker parted the waters of racism in the South, or simply walked

Herschel Walker, football great for the University of Georgia and the Dallas Cowboys, 1980s

expertly across them. His miracle was primarily a personal one. A decade after Georgia's "Redcoat" marching band had dropped "Dixie" from its title as well as its repertoire, many of the same fans who had lost their hearts to Herschel continued to demand that the band resume playing the song that black southerners saw as the anthem of slavery, segregation, and the Ku Klux Klan. Across the football-mad South, racial epithets still reached the ears of black players and fans, and many whites still objected to starting lineups that were predominantly black. Such evidence suggested that the level of acceptance that Walker achieved would remain exceptional until another uniquely "All-American on-and-off-the-field" black superhero came along to again strike white fans color-blind.

James C. Cobb
University of Mississippi

Sue Burchard, *Herschel Walker* (1984); Pat Conroy, *Southern Living* (September 1983); Terry Todd, *Sports Illustrated* (4 October 1982). ☆

INDEX OF CONTRIBUTORS

Index

||||||||||||||||||||

Boldfaced page numbers refer to main articles.

Italicized page numbers refer to illustrations.

Aaron, Hank, **704–5**
Abingdon, Va., 60
Absalom, Absalom! (Faulkner), 40, 82, 701–2
Accordions, 276, 277, 317, 349
Actors and actresses, **124–28,** 293–96
Actors Theater, 62
Acuff, Roy, 287, *350,* **350–51**
Adventures of Huckleberry Finn, The (Clemens), 6, 32–33, 74, 75
African influences: literature, 30; spirituals, 338–39
Agee (film), 141
Agee, James, 9, 17, **68–69,** *69,* 141; on *Birth of a Nation,* 211–12; on poor whites, 517; Renoir and, 228; travel writing, 67
Agrarianism: ideas associated with, 13; in literature, **13–15;** politics and, 14, 572–73
Agrarians, Nashville. *See* Agrarians, Vanderbilt
Agrarians, Vanderbilt, 14, **497–98;** mythic aspects, 443; New Criticism and, 38–39; Southern Literary Renaissance and, 9–10; on work and leisure, 626–27, 629. *See also I'll Take My Stand; specific writers*
Agricultural protest movements, 572–73
Agriculture, fairs and, 642–43
Alabama: actors and actresses, 126; county politics, 551; Folsom and, 595–96; newspapers, 167; secession, 609; television stations, 176; Wallace and, 617–18
Alabama Departure (film), 142
Alamo, *462*
Albany, Ga., 129
Ali, Muhammad, 640
Alienation, political, **544–46,** *545*
All-day singing, **351–52**
Allen, James Lane, 56
Allen, Mel, 632
Alley Theater, 61
Alliance Theater, 62
Allman Brothers Band, 297, 329–30
All My Babies (film), 138–39
All the King's Men (film), 135, *530*
All the King's Men (Warren), 110, 461

Alsop, George, 3
Altman, Robert, 135, **185–86**
Amazing Rhythm Aces (musical group), 330
American Hunger (Wright), 41–42
American Independent party, 617
Amusement parks, 690
Andrews, Dana, 127
Andy Griffith Show, The (TV show), 181, *186,* **186–87**
Anglo-Saxon South, **498–99**
Animals and animal life: fish, 651–52; horses, **662–65,** 675; hunting and, 665–66, 668; pets, **673–76,** *675*
Anniston, Ala., 62
Appalachia and Appalachians: bluegrass music, 266; culture, **446–48;** literature, **15–19;** myth of Appalachia, **499–501;** whites, poor, 516–17
Appalshop arts and education center, **187–88**
Arkansas: desegregation, 540; Faubus and, 593–94; newspapers, 167; secession, 609; television stations, 176
Armstrong, Louis, 258, *352,* **352–54**
Arnow, Harriette Simpson, 16, 17
Arp, Bill, 35
Ashes in the Wind (Woodiwiss), 49
Asheville, N.C., 113–14, 677
Assertiveness training, 460
Atlanta, Ga.: baseball, 631, 632–33, 634, 705; radio stations, 175; theater, 62, 699; Young, Andrew, and, 620–21
Atlanta Braves, 634, 705
Atlanta *Constitution,* 167, **188–89,** 220
Atlanta *Journal,* 169
At the Moon's Inn (Lytle), 93
Augusta, Ga., 62
Augusta National Country Club, 661–62, 715
Austin, Tex., 176, 263
Autobiography, **19–22**
Autobiography of Miss Jane Pittman, The (film), 178
Automobiles: stock car racing, 685, **686–89,** *687;* tourism and, **695–97**
Autry, Gene, 261, 286, **354–55**

Baby Doll (film), 137, *137,* 214, 243
"Backwoods" tales, 48

731

Picture Credits
||||||||||||||||||||||||||||||||||||||||||

263 Ray Funk Collection, Fairbanks, Alaska
269 Country Music Foundation, Library and Media Center, Nashville, Tennessee
274 Diane Allmen, photographer, Living Blues Archival Collection, University of Mississippi Blues Archive, Oxford
280 Ann Rayburn Paper Americana Collection, Archives and Special Collections, University of Mississippi Library, Oxford
284 Country Music Foundation, Library and Media Center, Nashville, Tennessee
290 Woodward Iron Company Collection, Special Collections, University of Alabama Library, Tuscaloosa
311 Copyright © William P. Gottlieb, Hogan Jazz Archive, Tulane University, New Orleans, Louisiana
320 Brazos Films/Arhoolie Records, El Cerrito, California
334 William Ferris Collection, Archives and Special Collections, University of Mississippi Library, Oxford
338 William Ferris Collection, Archives and Special Collections, University of Mississippi Library, Oxford
350 Country Music Foundation, Library and Media Center, Nashville, Tennessee
352 Hogan Jazz Archive, Tulane University, New Orleans, Louisiana
356 Robert Winans, photographer, Gettysburg college, Gettysburg, Pennsylvania
361 Skylite Records photograph, Cheryl Thurber Collection, Memphis, Tennessee
363 Solid Smoke Records photograph, Living Blues Archival Collection, University of Mississippi Blues Archive, Oxford
366 Hogan Jazz Archive, Tulane University, New Orleans, Louisiana
371 Country Music Foundation Library and Media Center, Nashville, Tennessee
373 Ray Funk Collection, Fairbanks, Alaska
376 Amy Van Singel, photographer, Living Blues Archival Collection, University of Mississippi Blues Archive, Oxford
379 William Ferris Collection, Archives and Special Collections, University of Mississippi Library, Oxford
385 Country Music Foundation, Library and Media Center, Nashville, Tennessee
389 Michael Stachnik, photographer, Living Blues Archival Collection, University of Mississippi Blues Archive, Oxford
391 William Ferris Collection, Archives and Special Collections, University of Mississippi Library, Oxford

397 William Ferris Collection, Archives and Special Collections, University of Mississippi Library, Oxford
405 Ray Flerlage, photographer, Living Blues Archival Collection, University of Mississippi Blues Archive, Oxford
406 Hogan Jazz Archive, Tulane University, New Orleans, Louisnana
408 Columbia Records, New York, New York
414 Graceland, Inc., Memphis, Tennessee
417 16th Avenue Records, Nashville, Tennessee
421 Jimmie Rodgers Museum, Meridian, Mississippi
434 Country Music Foundation, Library and Media Center, Nashville, Tennessee

Mythic South

439 Ann Rayburn Paper Americana Collection, Archives and Special Collections, University of Mississippi Library, Oxford
462 Texas Tourist Development Agency, Austin
469 Doris Ulmann, Southern Historical Collection, University of North Carolina, Chapel Hill
481 Brown and Williamson Tobacco Company Archives, Louisville, Kentucky
494 Southern Historical Collection, University of North Carolina, Chapel Hill
509 Eudora Welty, Mississippi Department of Archives and History, Jackson
510 Everhard Collection, Amon Carter Museum, Fort Worth, Texas
524 William Ferris Collection, Archives and Special Collections, University of Mississippi Library, Oxford

Politics

529 Film Stills Archives, Museum of Modern Art, New York, New York
536 Louisiana State Library, Baton Rouge
539 Louisiana State Library, Baton Rouge
552 Mr. and Mrs. Jack M. McLarty, Jackson, Mississippi
554 Courtesy of Archives Division—Texas State Library, Austin
566 William Ferris Collection, Archives and Special Collections, University of Mississippi Library, Oxford
592 Tennessee State Library and Archives, Nashville

595 No photographer given, Library of Congress (LC-USZ-62-20175), Washington, D.C.

600 Tennessee State Library and Archives, Nashville

614 Georgia Department of Archives and History, Atlanta

616 Senate Office, Strom Thurmond, Washington, D.C.

617 Charles Reagan Wilson Collection, University of Mississippi, Oxford

620 Mayor's Office, Atlanta, Georgia

Recreation

623 Marion Post Wolcott, Library of Congress (LC-USF-54259-D), Washington, D.C.

628 Ann Rayburn Paper Americana Collection, Archives and Special Collections, University of Mississippi Library, Oxford

642 Marion Post Wolcott, Library of Congress (LC-USF-33-30905-M3), Washington, D.C.

650 Ann Rayburn Paper Americana Collection, Archives and Special Collections, University of Mississippi Library, Oxford

654 National Football League Hall of Fame, Canton, Ohio

656 Dallas Cowboys, Dallas, Texas

659 Georgia Department of Archives and History, Atlanta

662 Photographic Archives, University of Louisville (Kentucky)

667 Ann Rayburn Paper Americana Collection, Archives and Special Collections, University of Mississippi Library, Oxford

671 Philip Gould, photographer, Lafayette, Louisiana

675 William Ferris Collection, Archives and Special Collections, University of Mississippi Library, Oxford

678 Ann Rayburn Paper Americana Collection, Archives and Special Collections, University of Mississippi Library, Oxford

685 Eudora Welty, Mississippi Department of Archives and History, Jackson

687 Alabama International Motor Speedway, Talladega

706 Sports Information Office, University of Alabama, Tuscaloosa

709 Edward R. Hollen, Library of Congress (LCUSW-3-24585C), Washington, D.C.

709 National Baseball Library, Cooperstown, New York

722 Ann Rayburn Paper Americana Collection, Archives and Special Collections, University of Mississippi Library, Oxford

726 Dallas Cowboys, Dallas, Texas